Collins

# Collins
# French
## Dictionary

**HarperCollins Publishers**
Westerhill Road
Bishopbriggs
Glasgow
G64 2QT
Great Britain

Fifth Edition 2007

Previously published as
Collins Express French Dictionary
© HarperCollins Publishers 2006

Reprint 10 9 8 7 6 5 4

© William Collins Sons & Co. Ltd 1990
© HarperCollins Publishers 1995, 1998,
2001, 2006
© Collins Bartholomew Ltd 2005

ISBN 978-0-00-720889-0

www.collins.co.uk

A catalogue record for this book is
available from the British Library

HarperCollins Publishers,
10 East 53rd Street,
New York, NY 10022

COLLINS FRENCH POCKET DICTIONARY.
Fifth US Edition 2008

ISBN 978-0-06-143862-2

www.harpercollins.com

HarperCollins books may be purchased
for educational, business, or sales
promotional use. For information, please
write to: Special Markets Department,
HarperCollins Publishers,
10 East 53rd Street,
New York, NY 10022

Typeset by Thomas Callan
'French in focus' supplement typeset by
Wordcraft, Glasgow
Verb supplement typeset by
Davidson Pre-Press, Glasgow

Printed in Italy by
Rotolito Lombarda S.p.A.

**Acknowledgements**
We would like to thank those authors and
publishers who kindly gave permission
for copyright material to be used in the
Collins Word Web. We would also like to
thank Times Newspapers Ltd for
providing valuable data.

MANAGING EDITOR
Michela Clari

CONTRIBUTORS
Maree Airlie
Jean-François Allain
Gaëlle Amiot-Cadey
Cécile Aubinière-Robb
Sabine Citron
Wendy Lee
Catherine Love
Rose Rociola

SERIES EDITOR
Lorna Knight

BASED ON THE FIRST EDITION BY
Pierre-Henri Cousin
Renée Birks
Elizabeth Campbell
Hélène Lewis
Claude Nimmo
Philippe Patry
Lorna Knight

# TABLE DES MATIÈRES   CONTENTS

William Collins' dream of knowledge for all began with the publication of his first book in 1819. A self-educated mill worker, he not only enriched millions of lives, but also founded a flourishing publishing house. Today, staying true to this spirit, Collins books are packed with inspiration, innovation, and practical expertise. They place you at the centre of a world of possibility and give you exactly what you need to explore it.

Language is the key to this exploration, and at the heart of Collins Dictionaries is language as it is really used. New words, phrases, and meanings spring up every day, and all of them are captured and analysed by the Collins Word Web. Constantly updated, and with over 2.5 billion entries, this living language resource is unique to our dictionaries.

Words are tools for life. And a Collins Dictionary makes them work for you.

**Collins. Do more**

# INTRODUCTION

Nous sommes très heureux que vous ayez choisi ce dictionnaire et espérons que vous aimerez l'utiliser et que vous en tirerez profit au lycée, à la maison, en vacances ou au travail.

Cette introduction a pour but de vous donner quelques conseils sur la façon d'utiliser au mieux votre dictionnaire, en vous référant non seulement à son importante nomenclature mais aussi aux informations contenues dans chaque entrée. Ceci vous aidera à lire et à comprendre, mais aussi à communiquer et à vous exprimer en anglais contemporain.

Au début du dictionnaire, vous trouverez la liste des abréviations utilisées dans le texte et celle de la transcription des sons par des symboles phonétiques. Vous y trouverez également la liste des verbes irréguliers en anglais, suivis d'une section finale sur les nombres et sur les expressions de temps.

## COMMENT UTILISER VOTRE DICTIONNAIRE

Ce dictionnaire offre une richesse d'informations et utilise diverses formes et tailles de caractères, symboles, abréviations, parenthèses et crochets. Les conventions et symboles utilisés sont expliqués dans les sections qui suivent.

## ENTRÉES

Les mots que vous cherchez dans le dictionnaire - les entrées - sont classés par ordre alphabétique. Ils sont imprimés en couleur pour pouvoir être repérés rapidement. Les entrées figurant en haut de page indiquent le premier (sur la page de gauche) et le dernier mot (sur la page de droite) des deux pages en question.

Des informations sur l'usage ou sur la forme de certaines entrées sont données entre parenthèses, après la transcription phonétique. Ces indications apparaissent sous forme abrégée et en italiques (par ex. *(fam)*, *(Comm)*).

Pour plus de facilité, les mots de la même famille sont regroupés sous la même entrée (**ronger, rongeur; accept, acceptance**) et apparaissent également en couleur.

Les expressions courantes dans lesquelles apparaît l'entrée sont indiquées par des caractères romains gras différents (par exemple **retard** : [...] **avoir du ~**).

### TRANSCRIPTION PHONÉTIQUE
La transcription phonétique de chaque entrée (indiquant sa prononciation) est indiquée entre crochets immédiatement après l'entrée (par ex. **fumer** [fyme]; **knee** [niː]). La liste des symboles phonétiques figure page xiii.

### TRADUCTIONS
Les traductions des entrées apparaissent en caractères ordinaires ; lorsque plusieurs sens ou usages coexistent, ces traductions sont séparées par un point-virgule. Vous trouverez des synonymes de l'entrée en italiques entre parenthèses avant les traductions (par ex. **poser** *(installer : moquette, carrelage)*) ou des mots qui fournissent le contexte dans lequel l'entrée est susceptible d'être utilisée (par ex. **poser** *(question)*).

## MOTS-CLÉS

Une importance particulière est accordée à certains mots français et anglais qui sont considérés comme des « mots-clés » dans chacune des langues. Cela peut être dû à leur utilisation très fréquente ou au fait qu'ils ont divers types d'usage (par ex. vouloir, plus; get, that). L'utilisation de triangles et de chiffres aide à distinguer différentes catégories grammaticales et différents sens. D'autres renseignements utiles apparaissent en italiques et entre parenthèses dans la langue de l'utilisateur.

## DONNÉES GRAMMATICALES

Les catégories grammaticales sont données sous forme abrégée et en italiques après la transcription phonétique (par ex. *vt, adv, conj*). Les genres des noms français sont indiqués de la manière suivante : *nm* pour un nom masculin et *nf* pour un nom féminin. Le féminin et le pluriel irréguliers de certains noms sont également indiqués (par ex. directeur, -trice ; cheval, -aux).

Le masculin et le féminin des adjectifs sont indiqués lorsque ces deux formes sont différentes (par ex. noir, e). Lorsque l'adjectif a un féminin ou un pluriel irrégulier, ces formes sont clairement indiquées (par ex. net, nette). Les pluriels irréguliers des noms, et les formes irrégulières des verbes anglais sont indiqués entre parenthèses, avant la catégorie grammaticale (par ex. man [...] (*pl* **men**) *n* ; give (*pt* **gave**; *pp* **~n**) *vt*).

# INTRODUCTION

We are delighted that you have decided to buy this dictionary and hope you will enjoy and benefit from using it at school, at home, on holiday or at work.

This introduction gives you a few tips on how to get the most out of your dictionary – not simply from its comprehensive wordlist but also from the information provided in each entry. This will help you to read and understand modern French, as well as communicate and express yourself in the language. This dictionary begins by listing the abbreviations used in the text and illustrating the sounds shown by the phonetic symbols. You will also find French verb tables, followed by a final section on numbers and time expressions.

## USING YOUR DICTIONARY

A wealth of information is presented in the dictionary, using various typefaces, sizes of type, symbols, abbreviations and brackets. The various conventions and symbols used are explained in the following sections.

## HEADWORDS

The words you look up in a dictionary – 'headwords' – are listed alphabetically. They are printed in **colour** for rapid identification. The headwords appearing at the top of each page indicate the first (if it appears on a left-hand page) and last word (if it appears on a right-hand page) dealt with on the page in question.

Information about the usage or form of certain headwords is given in brackets after the phonetic spelling. This usually appears in abbreviated form and in italics (e.g. (*fam*), (*Comm*)).

Where appropriate, words related to headwords are grouped in the same entry (**ronger, rongeur; accept, acceptance**) and are also in colour. Common expressions in which the headword appears are shown in a bold roman type (e.g. **retard:** [...] **avoir du ~**).

## PHONETIC SPELLINGS
The phonetic spelling of each headword (indicating its pronunciation) is given in square brackets immediately after the headword (e.g. **fumer** [fyme]; **knee** [ni:]). A list of these symbols is given on page xiii.

## TRANSLATIONS
Headword translations are given in ordinary type and, where more than one meaning or usage exists, these are separated by a semi-colon. You will often find other words in brackets before the translations. These offer suggested contexts in which the headword might appear (e.g. **rough** (*voice*), [...] (*weather*)) or provide synonyms (e.g. **rough** (*violent*)). The gender of the translation also appears in italics immediately following the key element of the translation.

## KEY WORDS
Special status is given to certain French and English words which are considered as 'key' words in each language. They may, for example, occur very frequently or have several types of usage (e.g. **vouloir, plus; get, that**). A combination of triangles and numbers helps you to distinguish different parts of speech and different meanings. Further helpful information is provided in brackets and italics.

Parts of speech are given in abbreviated form in italics after the phonetic spellings of headwords (e.g. *vt, adv, conj*). Genders of French nouns are indicated as follows: *nm* for a masculine and *nf* for a feminine noun. Feminine and irregular plural forms of nouns are also shown (directeur, -trice; cheval, -aux).

Adjectives are given in both masculine and feminine forms where these forms are different (e.g. noir, e). Clear information is provided where adjectives have an irregular feminine or plural form (e.g. net, nette).

| | | |
|---|---|---|
| abréviation | *ab(b)r* | abbreviation |
| adjectif, locution adjectivale | *adj* | adjective, adjectival phrase |
| administration | *Admin* | administration |
| adverbe, locution adverbiale | *adv* | adverb, adverbial phrase |
| agriculture | *Agr* | agriculture |
| anatomie | *Anat* | anatomy |
| architecture | *Archit* | architecture |
| article défini | *art déf* | definite article |
| article indéfini | *art indéf* | indefinite article |
| automobile | *Aut(o)* | the motor car and motoring |
| aviation, voyages aériens | *Aviat* | flying, air travel |
| biologie | *Bio(l)* | biology |
| botanique | *Bot* | botany |
| anglais britannique | *BRIT* | British English |
| chimie | *Chem* | chemistry |
| commerce, finance, banque | *Comm* | commerce, finance, banking |
| informatique | *Comput* | computing |
| conjonction | *conj* | conjunction |
| construction | *Constr* | building |
| nom utilisé comme adjectif | *cpd* | compound element |
| cuisine | *Culin* | cookery |
| article défini | *def art* | definite article |
| déterminant: article; adjectif démonstratif ou indéfini *etc* | *dét* | determiner: article, demonstrative *etc* |
| économie | *Écon, Econ* | economics |
| électricité, électronique | *Élec, Elec* | electricity, electronics |
| en particulier | *esp* | especially |
| exclamation, interjection | *excl* | exclamation, interjection |
| féminin | *f* | feminine |
| langue familière (! emploi vulgaire) | *fam(!)* | colloquial usage (! particularly offensive) |
| emploi figuré | *fig* | figurative use |
| (verbe anglais) dont la particule est inséparable | *fus* | (phrasal verb) where the particle is inseparable |
| généralement | *gén, gen* | generally |
| géographie, géologie | *Géo, Geo* | geography, geology |
| géométrie | *Géom, Geom* | geometry |
| langue familière (! emploi vulgaire) | *inf(!)* | colloquial usage (! particularly offensive) |
| infinitif | *infin* | infinitive |
| informatique | *Inform* | computing |
| invariable | *inv* | invariable |
| irrégulier | *irreg* | irregular |
| domaine juridique | *Jur* | law |

| | | |
|---|---|---|
| grammaire, linguistique | Ling | grammar, linguistics |
| masculin | m | masculine |
| mathématiques, algèbre | Math | mathematics, calculus |
| médecine | Méd, Med | medical term, medicine |
| masculin ou féminin | m/f | masculine or feminine |
| domaine militaire, armée | Mil | military matters |
| musique | Mus | music |
| nom | n | noun |
| navigation, nautisme | Navig, Naut | sailing, navigation |
| nom ou adjectif numéral | num | numeral noun or adjective |
| | o.s. | oneself |
| péjoratif | péj, pej | derogatory, pejorative |
| photographie | Phot(o) | photography |
| physiologie | Physiol | physiology |
| pluriel | pl | plural |
| politique | Pol | politics |
| participe passé | pp | past participle |
| préposition | prép, prep | preposition |
| pronom | pron | pronoun |
| psychologie, psychiatrie | Psych | psychology, psychiatry |
| temps du passé | pt | past tense |
| quelque chose | qch | |
| quelqu'un | qn | |
| religion, domaine ecclésiastique | Rel | religion |
| | sb | somebody |
| enseignement, système scolaire et universitaire | Scol | schooling, schools and universities |
| singulier | sg | singular |
| | sth | something |
| subjonctif | sub | subjunctive |
| sujet (grammatical) | su(b)j | (grammatical) subject |
| superlatif | superl | superlative |
| techniques, technologie | Tech | technical term, technology |
| télécommunications | Tél, Tel | telecommunications |
| télévision | TV | television |
| typographie | Typ(o) | typography, printing |
| anglais des USA | US | American English |
| verbe (auxiliaire) | vb (aux) | (auxiliary) verb |
| verbe intransitif | vi | intransitive verb |
| verbe transitif | vt | transitive verb |
| zoologie | Zool | zoology |
| marque déposée | ® | registered trademark |
| indique une équivalence culturelle | ≈ | introduces a cultural equivalent |

# TRANSCRIPTION PHONÉTIQUE

## CONSONNES · CONSONANTS

NB. **p, b, t, d, k, g** sont suivis d'une aspiration en anglais.

NB. **p, b, t, d, k, g** are not aspirated in French.

| Français | | Anglais |
|---|---|---|
| poupée | p | puppy |
| bombe | b | baby |
| tente thermal | t | tent |
| dinde | d | daddy |
| coq qui képi | k | cork kiss chord |
| gage bague | g | gag guess |
| sale ce nation | s | so rice kiss |
| zéro rose | z | cousin buzz |
| tache chat | ʃ | sheep sugar |
| gilet juge | ʒ | pleasure beige |
| | tʃ | church |
| | dʒ | judge general |
| fer phare | f | farm raffle |
| verveine | v | very revel |
| | θ | thin maths |
| | ð | that other |
| lent salle | l | little ball |
| rare rentrer | ʀ | |
| | r | rat rare |
| maman femme | m | mummy comb |
| non bonne | n | no ran |
| agneau vigne | ɲ | |
| | ŋ | singing bank |
| | h | hat rehearse |
| yeux paille pied | j | yet |
| nouer oui | w | wall wail |
| huile lui | ɥ | |
| | x | loch |

## DIVERS · MISCELLANEOUS

| | | |
|---|---|---|
| pour l'anglais: le r final se prononce en liaison devant une voyelle | r | in English transcription: final r can be pronounced before a vowel |
| pour l'anglais: précède la syllabe accentuée | ' | in French wordlist: no liaison before aspirate h |

En règle générale, la prononciation est donnée entre crochets après chaque entrée. Toutefois, du côté anglais-français et dans le cas des expressions composées de deux ou plusieurs mots non réunis par un trait d'union et faisant l'objet d'une entrée séparée, la prononciation doit être cherchée sous chacun des mots constitutifs de l'expression en question.

# PHONETIC TRANCRIPTION

| VOYELLES | | VOWELS |
| --- | --- | --- |

NB. La mise en équivalence de certains sons n'indique qu'une ressemblance approximative.

NB. The pairing of some vowel sounds only indicates approximate equivalence.

| | | |
| --- | --- | --- |
| ici vie lyrique | i i: | heel bead |
| | ɪ | hit pity |
| jouer été | e | |
| lait jouet merci | ɛ | set tent |
| plat amour | a æ | bat apple |
| bas pâte | ɑ ɑ: | after car calm |
| | ʌ | fun cousin |
| le premier | ə | over above |
| beurre peur | œ | |
| peu deux | ø ə: | urgent fern work |
| or homme | ɔ | wash pot |
| mot eau gauche | o ɔ: | born cork |
| genou roue | u | full hook |
| | u: | boom shoe |
| rue urne | y | |

| DIPHTONGUES | | DIPHTHONGS |
| --- | --- | --- |
| | ɪə | beer tier |
| | ɛə | tear fair there |
| | eɪ | date plaice day |
| | aɪ | life buy cry |
| | au | owl foul now |
| | əu | low no |
| | ɔɪ | boil boy oily |
| | uə | poor tour |

| NASALES | | NASAL VOWELS |
| --- | --- | --- |
| matin plein | ɛ̃ | |
| brun | œ̃ | |
| sang an dans | ɑ̃ | |
| non pont | ɔ̃ | |

In general, we give the pronunciation of each entry in square brackets after the word in question. However, on the English-French side, where the entry is composed of two or more unhyphenated words, each of which is given elsewhere in this dictionary, you will find the pronunciation of each word in its alphabetical position.

# FRENCH VERB TABLES

1 Present participle 2 Past participle 3 Present 4 Imperfect 5 Future
6 Conditional 7 Present subjunctive

acquérir 1 acquérant 2 acquis
   3 acquiers, acquérons,
   acquièrent 4 acquérais
   5 acquerrai 7 acquière
ALLER 1 allant 2 allé 3 vais, vas, va,
   allons, allez, vont 4 allais 5 irai
   6 irais 7 aille
asseoir 1 asseyant 2 assis 3 assieds,
   asseyons, asseyez, asseyent
   4 asseyais 5 assiérai 7 asseye
atteindre 1 atteignant 2 atteint
   3 atteins, atteignons
   4 atteignais 7 atteigne
AVOIR 1 ayant 2 eu 3 ai, as, a,
   avons, avez, ont 4 avais 5 aurai
   6 aurais 7 aie, aies, ait, ayons,
   ayez, aient
battre 1 battant 2 battu 3 bats, bat,
   battons 4 battais 7 batte
boire 1 buvant 2 bu 3 bois, buvons,
   boivent 4 buvais 7 boive
bouillir 1 bouillant 2 bouilli 3 bous,
   bouillons 4 bouillais 7 bouille
conclure 1 concluant 2 conclu
   3 conclus, concluons
   4 concluais 7 conclue
conduire 1 conduisant 2 conduit
   3 conduis, conduisons
   4 conduisais 7 conduise
connaître 1 connaissant 2 connu
   3 connais, connaît, connaissons
   4 connaissais 7 connaisse
coudre 1 cousant 2 cousu 3 couds,
   cousons, cousez, cousent
   4 cousais 7 couse
courir 1 courant 2 couru 3 cours,
   courons 4 courais 5 courrai
   7 coure
couvrir 1 couvrant 2 couvert
   3 couvre, couvrons 4 couvrais
   7 couvre

craindre 1 craignant 2 craint
   3 crains, craignons 4 craignais
   7 craigne
croire 1 croyant 2 cru 3 crois,
   croyons, croient 4 croyais
   7 croie
croître 1 croissant 2 crû, crue, crus,
   crues 3 croîs, croissons
   4 croissais 7 croisse
cueillir 1 cueillant 2 cueilli
   3 cueille, cueillons 4 cueillais
   5 cueillerai 7 cueille
devoir 1 devant 2 dû, due, dus,
   dues 3 dois, devons, doivent
   4 devais 5 devrai 7 doive
dire 1 disant 2 dit 3 dis, disons,
   dites, disent 4 disais 7 dise
dormir 1 dormant 2 dormi 3 dors,
   dormons 4 dormais 7 dorme
écrire 1 écrivant 2 écrit 3 écris,
   écrivons 4 écrivais 7 écrive
ÊTRE 1 étant 2 été 3 suis, es, est,
   sommes, êtes, sont 4 étais
   5 serai 6 serais 7 sois, sois, soit,
   soyons, soyez, soient
FAIRE 1 faisant 2 fait 3 fais, fais,
   fait, faisons, faites, font
   4 faisais 5 ferai 6 ferais 7 fasse
falloir 2 fallu 3 faut 4 fallait
   5 faudra 7 faille
FINIR 1 finissant 2 fini 3 finis,
   finis, finit, finissons, finissez,
   finissent 4 finissais 5 finirai
   6 finirais 7 finisse
fuir 1 fuyant 2 fui 3 fuis, fuyons,
   fuient 4 fuyais 7 fuie
joindre 1 joignant 2 joint 3 joins,
   joignons 4 joignais 7 joigne
lire 1 lisant 2 lu 3 lis, lisons 4 lisais
   7 lise
luire 1 luisant 2 lui 3 luis, luisons

4 luisais 7 luise

maudire 1 maudissant 2 maudit
3 maudis, maudissons
4 maudissait 7 maudisse

mentir 1 mentant 2 menti 3 mens,
mentons 4 mentais 7 mente

mettre 1 mettant 2 mis 3 mets,
mettons 4 mettais 7 mette

mourir 1 mourant 2 mort 3 meurs,
mourons, meurent 4 mourais
5 mourrai 7 meure

naître 1 naissant 2 né 3 nais, naît,
naissons 4 naissais 7 naisse

offrir 1 offrant 2 offert 3 offre,
offrons 4 offrais 7 offre

PARLER 1 parlant 2 parlé 3 parle,
parles, parle, parlons, parlez,
parlent 4 parlais, parlais,
parlait, parlions, parliez,
parlaient 5 parlerai, parleras,
parlera, parlerons, parlerez,
parleront 6 parlerais, parlerais,
parlerait, parlerions, parleriez,
parleraient 7 parle, parles,
parle, parlions, parliez, parlent
impératif parle! parlons! parlez!

partir 1 partant 2 parti 3 pars,
partons 4 partais 7 parte

plaire 1 plaisant 2 plu 3 plais, plaît,
plaisons 4 plaisais 7 plaise

pleuvoir 1 pleuvant 2 plu 3 pleut,
pleuvent 4 pleuvait 5 pleuvra
7 pleuve

pourvoir 1 pourvoyant 2 pourvu
3 pourvois, pourvoyons,
pourvoient 4 pourvoyais
7 pourvoie

pouvoir 1 pouvant 2 pu 3 peux,
peut, pouvons, peuvent 4
pouvais 5 pourrai 7 puisse

prendre 1 prenant 2 pris 3 prends,
prenons, prennent 4 prenais
7 prenne

prévoir like voir 5 prévoirai

RECEVOIR 1 recevant 2 reçu
3 reçois, reçois, reçoit, recevons,
recevez, rerçoivent 4 recevais

5 recevrai 6 recevrais 7 reçoive

RENDRE 1 rendant 2 rendu
3 rends, rends, rend, rendons,
rendez, rendent 4 rendais
5 rendrai 6 rendrais 7 rende

résoudre 1 résolvant 2 résolu
3 résous, résout, résolvons
4 résolvais 7 résolve

rire 1 riant 2 ri 3 ris, rions 4 riais
7 rie

savoir 1 sachant 2 su 3 sais,
savons, savent 4 savais 5 saurai
7 sache impératif sache! sachons!
sachez!

servir 1 servant 2 servi 3 sers,
servons 4 servais 7 serve

sortir 1 sortant 2 sorti 3 sors,
sortons 4 sortais 7 sorte

souffrir 1 souffrant 2 souffert
3 souffre, souffrons 4 souffrais
7 souffre

suffire 1 suffisant 2 suffi 3 suffis,
suffisons 4 suffisais 7 suffise

suivre 1 suivant 2 suivi 3 suis,
suivons 4 suivais 7 suive

taire 1 taisant 2 tu 3 tais, taisons
4 taisais 7 taise

tenir 1 tenant 2 tenu 3 tiens,
tenons, tiennent 4 tenais
5 tiendrai 7 tienne

vaincre 1 vainquant 2 vaincu
3 vaincs, vainc, vainquons
4 vainquais 7 vainque

valoir 1 valant 2 valu 3 vaux, vaut,
valons 4 valais 5 vaudrai 7 vaille

venir 1 venant 2 venu 3 viens,
venons, viennent 4 venais
5 viendrai 7 vienne

vivre 1 vivant 2 vécu 3 vis, vivons
4 vivais 7 vive

voir 1 voyant 2 vu 3 vois, voyons,
voient 4 voyais 5 verrai 7 voie

vouloir 1 voulant 2 voulu 3 veux,
veut, voulons, veulent 4 voulais
5 voudrai 7 veuille; impératif
veuillez!

## VERBES IRRÉGULIERS ANGLAIS

| PRÉSENT | PASSÉ | PARTICIPE | PRÉSENT | PASSÉ | PARTICIPE |
|---------|-------|-----------|---------|-------|-----------|
| arise | arose | arisen | fight | fought | fought |
| awake | awoke | awoken | find | found | found |
| be | was, were | been | flee | fled | fled |
| (am, is, | | | fling | flung | flung |
| are; being) | | | fly | flew | flown |
| bear | bore | born(e) | forbid | forbad(e) | forbidden |
| beat | beat | beaten | forecast | forecast | forecast |
| become | became | become | forget | forgot | forgotten |
| begin | began | begun | forgive | forgave | forgiven |
| bend | bent | bent | forsake | forsook | forsaken |
| bet | bet, | bet, | freeze | froze | frozen |
| | betted | betted | get | got | got, |
| bid (*at auction,* | bid | bid | | | (US) gotten |
| cards) | | | give | gave | given |
| bid (*say*) | bade | bidden | go (goes) | went | gone |
| bind | bound | bound | grind | ground | ground |
| bite | bit | bitten | grow | grew | grown |
| bleed | bled | bled | hang | hung | hung |
| blow | blew | blown | hang (*execute*) | hanged | hanged |
| break | broke | broken | have | had | had |
| breed | bred | bred | hear | heard | heard |
| bring | brought | brought | hide | hid | hidden |
| build | built | built | hit | hit | hit |
| burn | burnt, | burnt, | hold | held | held |
| | burned | burned | hurt | hurt | hurt |
| burst | burst | burst | keep | kept | kept |
| buy | bought | bought | kneel | knelt, | knelt, |
| can | could | (*been able*) | | kneeled | kneeled |
| cast | cast | cast | know | knew | known |
| catch | caught | caught | lay | laid | laid |
| choose | chose | chosen | lead | led | led |
| cling | clung | clung | lean | leant, | leant, |
| come | came | come | | leaned | leaned |
| cost | cost | cost | leap | leapt, | leapt, |
| cost (*work | costed | costed | | leaped | leaped |
| out price of*) | | | learn | learnt, | learnt, |
| creep | crept | crept | | learned | learned |
| cut | cut | cut | leave | left | left |
| deal | dealt | dealt | lend | lent | lent |
| dig | dug | dug | let | let | let |
| do (*does*) | did | done | lie (*lying*) | lay | lain |
| draw | drew | drawn | light | lit, | lit, |
| dream | dreamed, | dreamed, | | lighted | lighted |
| | dreamt | dreamt | lose | lost | lost |
| drink | drank | drunk | make | made | made |
| drive | drove | driven | may | might | – |
| dwell | dwelt | dwelt | mean | meant | meant |
| eat | ate | eaten | meet | met | met |
| fall | fell | fallen | mistake | mistook | mistaken |
| feed | fed | fed | mow | mowed | mown, |
| feel | felt | felt | | | mowed |

xvii

| PRÉSENT | PASSÉ | PARTICIPE | PRÉSENT | PASSÉ | PARTICIPE |
|---------|-------|-----------|---------|-------|-----------|
| must | (had to) | (had to) | spend | spent | spent |
| pay | paid | paid | spill | spilt, | spilt, |
| put | put | put | | spilled | spilled |
| quit | quit, | quit, | spin | spun | spun |
| | quitted | quitted | spit | spat | spat |
| read | read | read | spoil | spoiled, | spoiled, |
| rid | rid | rid | | spoilt | spoilt |
| ride | rode | ridden | spread | spread | spread |
| ring | rang | rung | spring | sprang | sprung |
| rise | rose | risen | stand | stood | stood |
| run | ran | run | steal | stole | stolen |
| saw | sawed | sawed, | stick | stuck | stuck |
| | | sawn | sting | stung | stung |
| say | said | said | stink | stank | stunk |
| see | saw | seen | stride | strode | stridden |
| seek | sought | sought | strike | struck | struck |
| sell | sold | sold | strive | strove | striven |
| send | sent | sent | swear | swore | sworn |
| set | set | set | sweep | swept | swept |
| sew | sewed | sewn | swell | swelled | swollen, |
| shake | shook | shaken | | | swelled |
| shear | sheared | shorn, | swim | swam | swum |
| | | sheared | swing | swung | swung |
| shed | shed | shed | take | took | taken |
| shine | shone | shone | teach | taught | taught |
| shoot | shot | shot | tear | tore | torn |
| show | showed | shown | tell | told | told |
| shrink | shrank | shrunk | think | thought | thought |
| shut | shut | shut | throw | threw | thrown |
| sing | sang | sung | thrust | thrust | thrust |
| sink | sank | sunk | tread | trod | trodden |
| sit | sat | sat | wake | woke, | woken, |
| slay | slew | slain | | waked | waked |
| sleep | slept | slept | wear | wore | worn |
| slide | slid | slid | weave | wove | woven |
| sling | slung | slung | weave (wind) | weaved | weaved |
| slit | slit | slit | wed | wedded, | wedded, |
| smell | smelt, | smelt, | | wed | wed |
| | smelled | smelled | weep | wept | wept |
| sow | sowed | sown, | win | won | won |
| | | sowed | wind | wound | wound |
| speak | spoke | spoken | wring | wrung | wrung |
| speed | sped, | sped, | write | wrote | written |
| | speeded | speeded | | | |
| spell | spelt, | spelt, | | | |
| | spelled | spelled | | | |

| LES NOMBRES | | NUMBERS |
|---|---|---|
| un (une) | 1 | one |
| deux | 2 | two |
| trois | 3 | three |
| quatre | 4 | four |
| cinq | 5 | five |
| six | 6 | six |
| sept | 7 | seven |
| huit | 8 | eight |
| neuf | 9 | nine |
| dix | 10 | ten |
| onze | 11 | eleven |
| douze | 12 | twelve |
| treize | 13 | thirteen |
| quatorze | 14 | fourteen |
| quinze | 15 | fifteen |
| seize | 16 | sixteen |
| dix-sept | 17 | seventeen |
| dix-huit | 18 | eighteen |
| dix-neuf | 19 | nineteen |
| vingt | 20 | twenty |
| vingt et un (une) | 21 | twenty-one |
| vingt-deux | 22 | twenty-two |
| trente | 30 | thirty |
| quarante | 40 | forty |
| cinquante | 50 | fifty |
| soixante | 60 | sixty |
| soixante-dix | 70 | seventy |
| soixante-et-onze | 71 | seventy-one |
| soixante-douze | 72 | seventy |
| quatre-vingts | 80 | eighty |
| quatre-vingt-un (-une) | 81 | eighty-one |
| quatre-vingt-dix | 90 | ninety |
| cent | 100 | a hundred, one hundred |
| cent un (une) | 101 | a hundred and one |
| deux cents | 200 | two hundred |
| deux cent un (une) | 201 | two hundred and one |
| quatre cents | 400 | four hundred |
| mille | 1000 | a thousand |
| cinq mille | 5000 | five thousand |
| un million | 1000000 | a million |

## LES NOMBRES

premier (première), 1<sup>er</sup> (1<sup>ère</sup>)
deuxième, 2<sup>e</sup> or 2<sup>ème</sup>
troisième, 3<sup>e</sup> or 3<sup>ème</sup>
quatrième, 4<sup>e</sup> or 4<sup>ème</sup>
cinquième, 5<sup>e</sup> or 5<sup>ème</sup>
sixième, 6<sup>e</sup> or 6<sup>ème</sup>
septième
huitième
neuvième
dixième
onzième
douzième
treizième
quartorzième
quinzième
seizième
dix-septième
dix-huitième
dix-neuvième
vingtième
vingt-et-unième
vingt-deuxième
trentième
centième
cent-unième
millième

## NUMBERS

first, 1st
second, 2nd
third, 3rd
fourth, 4th
fifth, 5th
sixth, 6th
seventh
eighth
ninth
tenth
eleventh
twelfth
thirteenth
fourteenth
fifteenth
sixteenth
seventeenth
eighteenth
nineteenth
twentieth
twenty-first
twenty-second
thirtieth
hundredth
hundred-and-first
thousandth

## LES FRACTIONS ETC

un demi
un tiers
un quart
un cinquième
zéro virgule cinq, 0,5
trois virgule quatre, 3,4
dix pour cent
cent pour cent

## FRACTIONS ETC

a half
a third
a quarter
a fifth
(nought) point five, 0.5
three point four, 3.4
ten per cent
a hundred per cent

## EXEMPLES

elle habite au septième (étage)
il habite au sept
au chapitre/à la page sept
il est arrivé (le) septième

## EXAMPLES

she lives on the 7th floor
he lives at number 7
chapter/page 7
he came in 7th

## L'HEURE

*quelle heure est-il?*

*il est ...*

minuit
une heure (du matin)

une heure cinq
une heure dix
une heure et quart

une heure vingt-cinq

une heure et demie, une heure trente
deux heures moins vingt-cinq, une
    heure trente-cinq
deux heures moins vingt, une heure
    quarante
deux heures moins le quart, une heure
    quarante-cinq
deux heures moins dix, une heure
    cinquante
midi

deux heures (de l'après-midi),
    quatorze heures
sept heures (du soir), dix-sept heures

*à quelle heure?*

à minuit
à sept heures

dans vingt minutes
il y a un quart d'heure

## THE TIME

*what time is it?*

*it's ou it is ...*

midnight, twelve p.m.
one o'clock (in the
    morning), one (a.m.)
five past one
ten past one
a quarter past one,
    one fifteen
twenty-five past one,
    one twenty-five
half-past one, one thirty
twenty-five to two,
    one thirty-five
twenty to two, one forty

a quarter to two,
    one forty-five
ten to two, one fifty

twelve o'clock, midday,
    noon
two o'clock (in the
    afternoon), two (p.m.)
seven o'clock (in the
    evening), seven (p.m.)

*(at) what time?*

at midnight
at seven o'clock

in twenty minutes
fifteen minutes ago

**a** [a] *vb voir* **avoir**

○ **MOT-CLÉ**

**à** [a] (*à + le* = **au**, *à + les* = **aux**) *prép*
**1** (*endroit, situation*) at, in; **être à Paris/au Portugal** to be in Paris/Portugal; **être à la maison/à l'école** to be at home/at school; **à la campagne** in the country; **c'est à 10 km/à 20 minutes (d'ici)** it's 10 km/20 minutes away
**2** (*direction*) to; **aller à Paris/au Portugal** to go to Paris/Portugal; **aller à la maison/à l'école** to go home/to school; **à la campagne** to the country
**3** (*temps*): **à 3 heures/minuit** at 3 o'clock/midnight; **au printemps/mois de juin** in the spring/the month of June; **à Noël/Pâques** at Christmas/Easter; **à demain/lundi!** see you tomorrow/on Monday!
**4** (*attribution, appartenance*) to; **le livre est à Paul/à lui/à nous** this book is Paul's/his/ours; **un ami à moi** a friend of mine; **donner qch à qn** to give sth to sb
**5** (*moyen*) with; **se chauffer au gaz** to have gas heating; **à bicyclette** on a *ou* by bicycle; **à pied** on foot; **à la main/machine** by hand/machine
**6** (*provenance*) from; **boire à la bouteille** to drink from the bottle
**7** (*caractérisation, manière*): **l'homme aux yeux bleus** the man with the blue eyes; **à leur grande surprise** much to their surprise; **à ce qu'il prétend** according to him, from what he says; **à la russe** the Russian way; **à nous deux nous n'avons pas su le faire** we couldn't do it, even between the two of us
**8** (*but, destination*): **tasse à café** coffee cup; **maison à vendre** house for sale; **je n'ai rien à lire** I don't have anything to read; **à bien réfléchir ...** thinking about it ..., on reflection ...
**9** (*rapport, évaluation, distribution*): **100 km/unités à l'heure** 100 km/units per *ou* an hour; **payé au mois/à l'heure** paid monthly/by the hour; **cinq à six** five to six; **ils sont arrivés à quatre** four of them arrived

**abaisser** [abese] *vt* to lower, bring down; (*manette*) to pull down; **s'abaisser** *vi* to go down; (*fig*) to demean o.s.
**abandon** [abãdɔ̃] *nm* abandoning; giving up; withdrawal; **être à l'~** to be in a state of neglect; **laisser à l'~** to abandon
**abandonner** [abãdɔne] *vt* (*personne*) to abandon; (*projet, activité*) to abandon, give up; (*Sport*) to retire *ou* withdraw from; (*céder*) to surrender; **s'~ à** (*paresse, plaisirs*) to give o.s. up to
**abat-jour** [abaʒuʀ] *nm inv* lampshade
**abats** [aba] *nmpl* (*de bœuf, porc*) offal *sg*; (*de volaille*) giblets
**abattement** [abatmã] *nm*: **abattement fiscal** ≈ tax allowance
**abattoir** [abatwaʀ] *nm*

slaughterhouse

**abattre** [abatʀ] vt (arbre) to cut down, fell; (mur, maison) to pull down; (avion, personne) to shoot down; (animal) to shoot, kill; (fig) to wear out, tire out; to demoralize; **s'abattre** vi to crash down; **ne pas se laisser ~** to keep one's spirits up, not to let things get one down; **s'~ sur** to beat down on; (fig) to rain down on; **~ du travail** ou **de la besogne** to get through a lot of work

**abbaye** [abei] nf abbey

**abbé** [abe] nm priest; (d'une abbaye) abbot

**abcès** [apsɛ] nm abscess

**abdiquer** [abdike] vi to abdicate

**abdominaux** [abdɔmino] nmpl: **faire des ~** to do sit-ups

**abeille** [abɛj] nf bee

**aberrant, e** [abeʀɑ̃, ɑ̃t] adj absurd

**aberration** [abeʀasjɔ̃] nf aberration

**abîme** [abim] nm abyss, gulf

**abîmer** [abime] vt to spoil, damage; **s'abîmer** vi to get spoilt ou damaged

**aboiement** [abwamɑ̃] nm bark, barking

**abolir** [abɔliʀ] vt to abolish

**abominable** [abɔminabl] adj abominable

**abondance** [abɔ̃dɑ̃s] nf abundance

**abondant, e** [abɔ̃dɑ̃, ɑ̃t] adj plentiful, abundant, copious; **abonder** vi to abound, be plentiful; **abonder dans le sens de qn** to concur with sb

**abonné, e** [abɔne] nm/f subscriber; season ticket holder

**abonnement** [abɔnmɑ̃] nm subscription; (transports, concerts) season ticket

**abonner** [abɔne] vt: **s'~ à** to subscribe to, take out a subscription to

**abord** [abɔʀ] nm: **au premier ~** at first sight, initially; **abords** nmpl (environs) surroundings; **d'~** first

**abordable** [abɔʀdabl] adj (prix) reasonable; (personne) approachable

**aborder** [abɔʀde] vi to land ▷ vt (sujet, difficulté) to tackle; (personne) to approach; (rivage etc) to reach

**aboutir** [abutiʀ] vi (négociations etc) to succeed; **~ à** to end up at; **n'~ à rien** to come to nothing

**aboyer** [abwaje] vi to bark

**abréger** [abʀeʒe] vt to shorten

**abreuver** [abʀœve]: **s'abreuver** vi to drink; **abreuvoir** nm watering place

**abréviation** [abʀevjasjɔ̃] nf abbreviation

**abri** [abʀi] nm shelter; **être à l'~** to be under cover; **se mettre à l'~** to shelter; **à l'~ de** (vent, soleil) sheltered from; (danger) safe from

**abricot** [abʀiko] nm apricot

**abriter** [abʀite] vt to shelter; **s'abriter** vt to shelter, take cover

**abrupt, e** [abʀypt] adj sheer, steep; (ton) abrupt

**abruti, e** [abʀyti] adj stunned, dazed ▷ nm/f (fam) idiot, moron; **~ de travail** overworked

**absence** [apsɑ̃s] nf absence; (Méd) blackout; **avoir des ~s** to have mental blanks

**absent, e** [apsɑ̃, ɑ̃t] adj absent ▷ nm/f absentee; **absenter**: **s'absenter** vi to take time off work; (sortir) to leave, go out

**absolu, e** [apsɔly] adj absolute; **absolument** adv absolutely

**absorbant, e** [apsɔʀbɑ̃, ɑ̃t] adj absorbent

**absorber** [apsɔʀbe] vt to absorb; (gén Méd: manger, boire) to take

**abstenir** [apstəniʀ] vb: **s'~ de qch/de faire** to refrain from sth/from doing

**abstrait, e** [apstʀɛ, ɛt] adj abstract

**absurde** [apsyʀd] adj absurd

**abus** [aby] nm abuse; **~ de confiance** breach of trust; **il y a de l'~!** (fam) that's a bit much!; **abuser** vi to go too far, overstep the mark; **abuser de** (duper) to take advantage of; **s'abuser** vi (se méprendre) to be mistaken; **abusif, -ive** adj exorbitant; (punition) excessive

**académie** [akademi] nf academy; (Scol: circonscription) ≈ regional education authority

○ **ACADÉMIE FRANÇAISE**
○
○ The **Académie française** was
○ founded by Cardinal Richelieu in
○ 1635, during the reign of Louis XIII. It
○ is made up of forty elected scholars
○ and writers who are known as 'les
○ Quarante' or 'les Immortels'. One
○ of the **Académie**'s functions is to
○ keep an eye on the development
○ of the French language, and its
○ recommendations are frequently
○ the subject of lively public debate. It
○ has produced several editions of its
○ famous dictionary and also awards
○ various literary prizes.

**acajou** [akaʒu] *nm* mahogany
**acariâtre** [akaʀjɑtʀ] *adj* cantankerous
**accablant, e** [akɑblɑ̃, ɑ̃t] *adj* (*chaleur*)
oppressive; (*témoignage, preuve*)
overwhelming
**accabler** [akɑble] *vt* to overwhelm,
overcome; **~ qn d'injures** to heap *ou*
shower abuse on sb; **~ qn de travail** to
overwork sb
**accalmie** [akalmi] *nf* lull
**accaparer** [akapaʀe] *vt* to
monopolize; (*suj: travail etc*) to take up
(all) the time *ou* attention of
**accéder** [aksede]: **~ à** *vt* (*lieu*) to reach;
(*accorder: requête*) to grant, accede to
**accélérateur** [akseleʀatœʀ] *nm*
accelerator
**accélérer** [akseleʀe] *vt* to speed up ▷ *vi*
to accelerate
**accent** [aksɑ̃] *nm* accent; (*Phonétique,
fig*) stress; **mettre l'~ sur** (*fig*) to stress;
**~ aigu/grave/circonflexe** acute/
grave/circumflex accent; **accentuer**
*vt* (*Ling*) to accent; (*fig*) to accentuate,
emphasize; **s'accentuer** *vi* to become
more marked *ou* pronounced
**acceptation** [akseptasjɔ̃] *nf*
acceptance
**accepter** [aksepte] *vt* to accept; **~ de**

**faire** to agree to do; **acceptez-vous
les cartes de crédit?** do you take
credit cards?
**accès** [akse] *nm* (*à un lieu*) access; (*Méd:
de toux*) fit; (: *de fièvre*) bout; **d'~ facile**
easily accessible; **facile d'~** easy to
get to; **accès de colère** fit of anger;
**accessible** *adj* accessible; (*livre, sujet*):
**accessible à qn** within the reach of sb
**accessoire** [akseswaʀ] *adj* secondary;
incidental ▷ *nm* accessory; (*Théâtre*)
prop
**accident** [aksidɑ̃] *nm* accident; **par
~** by chance; **j'ai eu un ~** I've had an
accident; **accident de la route** road
accident; **accidenté, e** *adj* damaged;
injured; (*relief, terrain*) uneven; hilly;
**accidentel, le** *adj* accidental
**acclamer** [aklame] *vt* to cheer,
acclaim
**acclimater** [aklimate]: **s'acclimater**
*vi* (*personne*) to adapt (o.s.)
**accolade** [akɔlad] *nf* (*amicale*)
embrace; (*signe*) brace
**accommoder** [akɔmɔde] *vt* (*Culin*)
to prepare; **s'accommoder de** *vt* to
put up with; (*se contenter de*) to make
do with
**accompagnateur, -trice**
[akɔ̃paɲatœʀ, tʀis] *nm/f* (*Mus*)
accompanist; (*de voyage: guide*) guide;
(*de voyage organisé*) courier
**accompagner** [akɔ̃paɲe] *vt* to
accompany, be *ou* go *ou* come with;
(*Mus*) to accompany
**accompli, e** [akɔ̃pli] *adj*
accomplished; *voir aussi* **fait**
**accomplir** [akɔ̃pliʀ] *vt* (*tâche, projet*) to
carry out; (*souhait*) to fulfil; **s'accomplir**
*vi* to be fulfilled
**accord** [akɔʀ] *nm* agreement; (*entre des
styles, tons etc*) harmony; (*Mus*) chord;
**d'~!** OK!; **se mettre d'~** to come to an
agreement; **être d'~ (pour faire qch)**
to agree (to do) sth
**accordéon** [akɔʀdeɔ̃] *nm* (*Mus*)
accordion
**accorder** [akɔʀde] *vt* (*faveur, délai*) to

grant; (*harmoniser*) to match; (*Mus*) to tune; (*valeur, importance*) attach

**accoster** [akɔste] *vt* (*Navig*) to draw alongside ▷ *vi* to berth

**accouchement** [akuʃmɑ̃] *nm* delivery, (child)birth; labour

**accoucher** [akuʃe] *vi* to give birth, have a baby; **~ d'un garçon** to give birth to a boy

**accouder** [akude]: **s'accouder** *vi*: **s'~ à/contre/sur** to rest one's elbows on/ against/on; **accoudoir** *nm* armrest

**accoupler** [akuple] *vt* to couple; (*pour la reproduction*) to mate; **s'accoupler** *vt* to mate

**accourir** [akuRiR] *vi* to rush *ou* run up

**accoutumance** [akutymɑ̃s] *nf* (*gén*) adaptation; (*Méd*) addiction

**accoutumé, e** [akutyme] *adj* (*habituel*) customary, usual

**accoutumer** [akutyme] *vt*: **s'~ à** to get accustomed *ou* used to

**accroc** [akRo] *nm* (*déchirure*) tear; (*fig*) hitch, snag

**accrochage** [akRoʃaʒ] *nm* (*Auto*) collision; (*dispute*) clash, brush

**accrocher** [akRoʃe] *vt* (*fig*) to catch, attract; **s'accrocher** (*se disputer*) to have a clash *ou* brush; **~ qch à** (*suspendre*) to hang sth (up) on; (*attacher: remorque*) to hitch sth (up) to; **~ qch (à)** (*déchirer*) to catch sth (on); **il a accroché ma voiture** he bumped into my car; **s'~ à** (*rester pris à*) to catch on; (*agripper, fig*) to hang on *ou* cling to

**accroissement** [akRwasmɑ̃] *nm* increase

**accroître** [akRwatR]: **s'accroître** *vi* to increase

**accroupir** [akRupiR]: **s'accroupir** *vi* to squat, crouch (down)

**accru, e** [akRy] *pp de* **accroître**

**accueil** [akœj] *nm* welcome; **comité d'~** reception committee; **accueillir** *vt* to welcome; (*aller chercher*) to meet, collect

**accumuler** [akymyle] *vt* to accumulate, amass; **s'accumuler** *vi* to accumulate; to pile up

**accusation** [akyzasjɔ̃] *nf* (*gén*) accusation; (*Jur*) charge; (*partie*): **l'~** the prosecution

**accusé, e** [akyze] *nm/f* accused; defendant; **accusé de réception** acknowledgement of receipt

**accuser** [akyze] *vt* to accuse; (*fig*) to emphasize, bring out; to show; **~ qn de** to accuse sb of; (*Jur*) to charge sb with; **~ réception de** to acknowledge receipt of

**acéré, e** [aseRe] *adj* sharp

**acharné, e** [aʃaRne] *adj* (*efforts*) relentless; (*lutte, adversaire*) fierce, bitter

**acharner** [aʃaRne] *vb*: **s'~ contre** to set o.s. against; (*suj: malchance*) to dog; **s'~ à faire** to try doggedly to do; (*persister*) to persist in doing; **s'~ sur qn** to hound sb

**achat** [aʃa] *nm* purchase; **faire des ~s** to do some shopping; **faire l'~ de qch** to purchase sth

**acheter** [aʃ(ə)te] *vt* to buy, purchase; (*soudoyer*) to buy; **~ qch à** (*marchand*) to buy *ou* purchase sth from; (*ami etc: offrir*) to buy sth for; **où est-ce que je peux ~ des cartes postales?** where can I buy (some) postcards?; **acheteur, -euse** *nm/f* buyer; shopper; (*Comm*) buyer

**achever** [aʃ(ə)ve] *vt* to complete, finish; (*blessé*) to finish off; **s'achever** *vi* to end

**acide** [asid] *adj* sour, sharp; (*Chimie*) acid(ic) ▷ *nm* (*Chimie*) acid; **acidulé, e** *adj* slightly acid; **bonbons acidulés** acid drops

**acier** [asje] *nm* steel; **aciérie** *nf* steelworks *sg*

**acné** [akne] *nf* acne

**acompte** [akɔ̃t] *nm* deposit

**à-côté** [akote] *nm* side-issue; (*argent*) extra

**à-coup** [aku] *nm*: **par ~s** by fits and starts

**acoustique** [akustik] *nf* (*d'une salle*) acoustics *pl*

**acquéreur** [akeRœR] nm buyer, purchaser

**acquérir** [akeRiR] vt to acquire

**acquis, e** [aki, iz] pp de **acquérir** ▷ nm (accumulated) experience; **son aide nous est ~e** we can count on her help

**acquitter** [akite] vt (Jur) to acquit; (facture) to pay, settle; **s'acquitter de** vt (devoir) to discharge; (promesse) to fulfil

**âcre** [ɑkʀ] adj acrid, pungent

**acrobate** [akʀɔbat] nm/f acrobat; **acrobatie** nf acrobatics sg

**acte** [akt] nm act, action; (Théâtre) act; **prendre ~ de** to note, take note of; **faire ~ de candidature** to apply; **faire ~ de présence** to put in an appearance; **acte de naissance** birth certificate

**acteur** [aktœʀ] nm actor

**actif, -ive** [aktif, iv] adj active ▷ nm (Comm) assets pl; (fig): **avoir à son ~ to** have to one's credit; **population active** working population

**action** [aksjɔ̃] nf (gén) action; (Comm) share; **une bonne ~** a good deed; **actionnaire** nm/f shareholder; **actionner** vt (mécanisme) to activate; (machine) to operate

**activer** [aktive] vt to speed up; **s'activer** vi to bustle about; to hurry up

**activité** [aktivite] nf activity; **en ~** (volcan) active; (fonctionnaire) in active life

**actrice** [aktʀis] nf actress

**actualité** [aktɥalite] nf (d'un problème) topicality; (événements): **l'~** current events; **actualités** nfpl (Cinéma, TV) the news; **d'~** topical

**actuel, le** [aktɥɛl] adj (présent) present; (d'actualité) topical; **à l'heure ~le** at the present time; **actuellement** adv at present, at the present time

> Attention à ne pas traduire *actuellement* par *actually*.

**acuponcture** [akypɔ̃ktyʀ] nf acupuncture

**adaptateur** [adaptatœʀ] nm (Élec) adapter

**adapter** [adapte] vt to adapt; **s'adapter (à)** (suj: personne) to adapt (to); **~ qch à** (approprier) to adapt sth to; (fit); **~ qch sur/dans/à** (fixer) to fit sth on/into/to

**addition** [adisjɔ̃] nf addition; (au café) bill; **l'~, s'il vous plaît** could I have the bill, please?; **additionner** vt to add (up)

**adepte** [adɛpt] nm/f follower

**adéquat, e** [adekwa(t), at] adj appropriate, suitable

**adhérent, e** [adeRɑ̃, ɑ̃t] nm/f member

**adhérer** [adeʀe] vt: **~ à** vt (coller) to adhere ou stick to; (se rallier à) to join; **adhésif, -ive** adj adhesive, sticky; **ruban adhésif** sticky ou adhesive tape

**adieu, x** [adjø] excl goodbye ▷ nm farewell

**adjectif** [adʒɛktif] nm adjective

**adjoint, e** [adʒwɛ̃, wɛ̃t] nm/f assistant; **adjoint au maire** deputy mayor; **directeur adjoint** assistant manager

**admettre** [admɛtʀ] vt (laisser entrer) to admit; (candidat: Scol) to pass; (tolérer) to allow, accept; (reconnaître) to admit, acknowledge

**administrateur, -trice** [administʀatœʀ, tʀis] nm/f (Comm) director; (Admin) administrator

**administration** [administʀasjɔ̃] nf administration; **l'A~** ≈ the Civil Service

**administrer** [administʀe] vt (firme) to manage, run; (biens, remède, sacrement etc) to administer

**admirable** [admiʀabl] adj admirable, wonderful

**admirateur, -trice** [admiʀatœʀ, tʀis] nm/f admirer

**admiration** [admiʀasjɔ̃] nf admiration

**admirer** [admiʀe] vt to admire

**admis, e** [admi, iz] pp de **admettre**

**admissible** [admisibl] adj (candidat) eligible; (comportement) admissible, acceptable

**ADN** sigle m (= acide désoxyribonucléique) DNA

**adolescence** [adɔlesɑ̃s] *nf*
adolescence

**adolescent, e** [adɔlesɑ̃, ɑ̃t] *nm/f*
adolescent, teenager

**adopter** [adɔpte] *vt* to adopt; **adoptif,
-ive** *adj* (*parents*) adoptive; (*fils, patrie*)
adopted

**adorable** [adɔrabl] *adj* delightful,
adorable

**adorer** [adɔre] *vt* to adore; (*Rel*) to
worship

**adosser** [adose] *vt*: **~ qch à** *ou* **contre** to
stand sth against; **s'adosser à/contre**
to lean with one's back against

**adoucir** [adusir] *vt* (*goût, température*)
to make milder; (*avec du sucre*) to
sweeten; (*peau, voix*) to soften;
(*caractère*) to mellow

**adresse** [adrɛs] *nf* (*domicile*)
address; (*dextérité*) skill, dexterity; **~
électronique** email address

**adresser** [adrɛse] *vt* (*lettre: expédier*)
to send; (: *écrire l'adresse sur*) to address;
(*injure, compliments*) to address;
**s'adresser à** (*parler à*) to speak to,
address; (*s'informer auprès de*) to go and
see; (: *bureau*) to inquire at; (*suj: livre,
conseil*) to be aimed at; **~ la parole à** to
speak to, address

**adroit, e** [adrwa, wat] *adj* skilful,
skilled

**ADSL** *sigle m* (= *asymmetrical digital
subscriber line*) ADSL, broadband

**adulte** [adylt] *nm/f* adult, grown-up
▷ *adj* (*chien, arbre*) fully-grown, mature;
(*attitude*) adult, grown-up

**adverbe** [advɛrb] *nm* adverb

**adversaire** [advɛrsɛr] *nm/f* (*Sport,
gén*) opponent, adversary

**aération** [aerasjɔ̃] *nf* airing; (*circulation
de l'air*) ventilation

**aérer** [aere] *vt* to air; (*fig*) to lighten

**aérien, ne** [aerjɛ̃, jɛn] *adj* (*Aviat*) air
*cpd*, aerial; (*câble, métro*) overhead; (*fig*)
light; **compagnie ~ne** airline

**aéro...** [aero] *préfixe*: **aérobic** *nm*
aerobics *sg*; **aérogare** *nf* airport
(*buildings*); (*en ville*) air terminal;

**aéroglisseur** *nm* hovercraft;
**aérophagie** *nf* (*Méd*) wind, aerophagia
(*Méd*); **aéroport** *nm* airport; **aérosol**
*nm* aerosol

**affaiblir** [afeblir]: **s'affaiblir** *vi* to
weaken

**affaire** [afɛr] *nf* (*problème, question*)
matter; (*criminelle, judiciaire*) case;
(*scandaleuse etc*) affair; (*entreprise*)
business; (*marché, transaction*) deal;
business *no pl*; (*occasion intéressante*)
bargain; **affaires** *nfpl* (*intérêts publics
et privés*) affairs; (*activité commerciale*)
business *sg*; (*effets personnels*) things,
belongings; **ce sont mes ~s** (*cela me
concerne*) that's my business; **occupe-
toi de tes ~s!** mind your own business!;
**ça fera l'~** that will do (nicely); **se tirer
d'~** to sort it *ou* things out for o.s.; **avoir
~ à** (*être en contact*) to be dealing with;
**les A~s étrangères** Foreign Affairs;
**affairer: s'affairer** *vi* to busy o.s.,
bustle about

**affamé, e** [afame] *adj* starving

**affecter** [afɛkte] *vt* to affect; **~ qch
à** to allocate *ou* allot sth to; **~ qn à** to
appoint sb to; (*diplomate*) to post sb to

**affectif, -ive** [afɛktif, iv] *adj*
emotional

**affection** [afɛksjɔ̃] *nf* affection; (*mal*)
ailment; **affectionner** *vt* to be fond of;
**affectueux, -euse** *adj* affectionate

**affichage** [afiʃaʒ] *nm* billposting;
(*électronique*) display; **"~ interdit"** "stick
no bills"; **affichage à cristaux liquides**
liquid crystal display, LCD

**affiche** [afiʃ] *nf* poster; (*officielle*) notice;
(*Théâtre*) bill; **être à l'~** to be on

**afficher** [afiʃe] *vt* (*affiche*) to put up;
(*réunion*) to put up a notice about;
(*électroniquement*) to display; (*fig*) to
exhibit, display; **"défense d'~"** "no bill
posters"; **s'afficher** *vr* (*péj*) to flaunt
o.s.; (*électroniquement*) to be displayed

**affilée** [afile]: **d'~** *adv* at a stretch

**affirmatif, -ive** [afirmatif, iv] *adj*
affirmative

**affirmer** [afirme] *vt* to assert

**affligé, e** [aflize] adj distressed, grieved; **~ de** (maladie, tare) afflicted with

**affliger** [aflize] vt (peiner) to distress, grieve

**affluence** [aflyɑ̃s] nf crowds pl; **heures d'~** rush hours; **jours d'~** busiest days

**affluent** [aflyɑ̃] nm tributary

**affolement** [afɔlmɑ̃] nm panic

**affoler** [afɔle] vt to throw into a panic; **s'affoler** vi to panic

**affranchir** [afrɑ̃ʃir] vt (à la machine) to put a stamp ou stamps on; (à la machine) to frank (BRIT), meter (US); (fig) to free, liberate; **affranchissement** nm postage

**affreux, -euse** [afrø, øz] adj dreadful, awful

**affront** [afrɔ̃] nm affront; **affrontement** nm clash, confrontation

**affronter** [afrɔ̃te] vt to confront, face

**affût** [afy] nm: **à l'~ (de)** (gibier) lying in wait (for); (fig) on the look-out (for)

**Afghanistan** [afganistɑ̃] nm: **l'~** Afghanistan

**afin** [afɛ̃] nm: **~ que** conj so that, in order that; **~ de faire** in order to do, so as to do

**africain, e** [afrikɛ̃, ɛn] adj African ▷ nm/f: **A~, e** African

**Afrique** [afrik] nf: **l'~** Africa; **l'Afrique du Nord/Sud** North/South Africa

**agacer** [agase] vt to irritate

**âge** [ɑʒ] nm age; **quel ~ as-tu?** how old are you?; **prendre de l'~** to be getting on (in years); **le troisième ~** (période) retirement; (personnes âgées) senior citizens; **âgé, e** adj old, elderly; **âgé de 10 ans** 10 years old

**agence** [aʒɑ̃s] nf agency, office; (succursale) branch; **agence de voyages** travel agency; **agence immobilière** estate (BRIT) ou real estate (US) agent's (office)

**agenda** [aʒɛ̃da] nm diary; **~ électronique** PDA

Attention à ne pas traduire **agenda** par le mot anglais **agenda**.

**agenouiller** [aʒ(ə)nuje]: **s'agenouiller** vi to kneel (down)

**agent, e** [aʒɑ̃, ɑ̃t] nm/f (aussi: **~(e) de police**) policeman(policewoman); (Admin) official, officer; **agent immobilier** estate agent (BRIT), realtor (US)

**agglomération** [aglɔmerasjɔ̃] nf town; built-up area; **l'~ parisienne** the urban area of Paris

**aggraver** [agrave]: **s'aggraver** vi to worsen

**agile** [aʒil] adj agile, nimble

**agir** [aʒir] vi to act; **il s'agit de** (ça traite de); (il est important de) it's about; it's a matter ou question of; **il s'agit de faire** we (ou you etc) must do; **de quoi s'agit-il?** what is it about?

**agitation** [aʒitasjɔ̃] nf (hustle and) bustle; (trouble) agitation, excitement; (politique) unrest, agitation

**agité, e** [aʒite] adj fidgety, restless; (troublé) agitated, perturbed; (mer) rough

**agiter** [aʒite] vt (bouteille, chiffon) to shake; (bras, mains) to wave; (préoccuper, exciter) to perturb

**agneau, x** [aɲo] nm lamb

**agonie** [agɔni] nf mortal agony, death pangs pl; (fig) death throes pl

**agrafe** [agraf] nf (de vêtement) hook, fastener; (de bureau) staple; **agrafer** vt to fasten; to staple; **agrafeuse** nf stapler

**agrandir** [agrɑ̃dir] vt to enlarge; **s'agrandir** vi (ville, famille) to grow, expand; (trou, écart) to get bigger; **agrandissement** nm (Photo) enlargement

**agréable** [agreabl] adj pleasant, nice

**agréé, e** [agree] adj: **concessionnaire ~** registered dealer

**agréer** [agree] vt (requête) to accept; **~ à** to please, suit; **veuillez ~, Monsieur/Madame, mes salutations distinguées** (personne nommée) yours sincerely; (personne non nommée) yours faithfully

**agrégation** [agʀegasjɔ̃] *nf* highest teaching diploma in France; **agrégé, e** *nm/f* holder of the *agrégation*

**agrément** [agʀemɑ̃] *nm* (*accord*) consent, approval; (*attraits*) charm, attractiveness; (*plaisir*) pleasure

**agresser** [agʀese] *vt* to attack; **agresseur** *nm* aggressor, attacker; (*Pol, Mil*) aggressor; **agressif, -ive** *adj* aggressive

**agricole** [agʀikɔl] *adj* agricultural; **agriculteur** *nm* farmer; **agriculture** *nf* agriculture, farming

**agripper** [agʀipe] *vt* to grab, clutch; **s'agripper à** to cling (on) to, clutch, grip

**agro-alimentaire** [agʀoalimɑ̃tɛʀ] *nm* farm-produce industry

**agrumes** [agʀym] *nmpl* citrus fruit(s)

**aguets** [agɛ] *nmpl*: **être aux ~** to be on the look out

**ai** [ɛ] *vb voir* **avoir**

**aide** [ɛd] *nm/f* assistant; carer ▷ *nf* assistance, help; (*secours financier*) aid; **à l'~ de** (*avec*) with the help ou aid of; **appeler (qn) à l'~** to call for help (from sb); **à l'~!** help!; **aide judiciaire** legal aid; **aide ménagère** ≈ home help (BRIT) ou helper (US); **aide-mémoire** *nm inv* memoranda pages *pl*; (*key facts*) handbook; **aide-soignant, e** *nm/f* auxiliary nurse

**aider** [ede] *vt* to help; **~ à qch** to help (towards) sth; **~ qn à faire qch** to help sb to do sth; **pouvez-vous m'~?** can you help me?; **s'aider de** (*se servir de*) to use, make use of

**aïe** [aj] *excl* ouch!

**aie** *etc* [ɛ] *vb voir* **avoir**

**aigle** [ɛgl] *nm* eagle

**aigre** [ɛgʀ] *adj* sour, sharp; (*fig*) sharp, cutting; **aigre-doux, -ce** *adj* (*sauce*) sweet and sour; **aigreur** *nf* sourness, sharpness; **aigreurs d'estomac** heartburn *sg*

**aigu, ë** [egy] *adj* (*objet, douleur*) sharp; (*son, voix*) high-pitched, shrill; (*note*) high(-pitched)

**aiguille** [egɥij] *nf* needle; (*de montre*) hand; **aiguille à tricoter** knitting needle

**aiguiser** [egize] *vt* to sharpen; (*fig*) to stimulate; (*: sens*) to excite

**ail** [aj] *nm* garlic

**aile** [ɛl] *nf* wing; **aileron** *nm* (*de requin*) fin; **ailier** *nm* winger

**aille** *etc* [aj] *vb voir* **aller**

**ailleurs** [ajœʀ] *adv* elsewhere, somewhere else; **partout/nulle part ~** everywhere/nowhere else; **d'~** (*du reste*) moreover, besides; **par ~** (*d'autre part*) moreover, furthermore

**aimable** [ɛmabl] *adj* kind, nice

**aimant** [ɛmɑ̃] *nm* magnet

**aimer** [eme] *vt* to love; (*d'amitié, affection, par goût*) to like; (*souhait*): **j'aimerais …** I would like …; **j'aime faire du ski** I like skiing; **je t'aime** I love you; **bien ~ qn/qch** to like sb/sth; **j'aime mieux Paul (que Pierre)** I prefer Paul (to Pierre); **j'aimerais mieux faire** I'd much rather do

**aine** [ɛn] *nf* groin

**aîné, e** [ene] *adj* elder, older; (*le plus âgé*) eldest, oldest ▷ *nm/f* oldest child ou one, oldest boy ou son/girl ou daughter

**ainsi** [ɛ̃si] *adv* (*de cette façon*) like this, in this way, thus; (*ce faisant*) thus ▷ *conj* thus; so; **~ que** (*comme*) (just) as; (*et aussi*) as well as; **pour ~ dire** so to speak; **et ~ de suite** and so on

**air** [ɛʀ] *nm* air; (*mélodie*) tune; (*expression*) look, air; **prendre l'~** to get some (fresh) air; **avoir l'~** (*sembler*) to look, appear; **il a l'~ triste/malade** he looks sad/ill; **avoir l'~ de** to look like; **il a l'~ de dormir** he looks as if he's sleeping; **en l'~** (*promesses*) empty

**airbag** [ɛʀbag] *nm* airbag

**aisance** [ɛzɑ̃s] *nf* ease; (*richesse*) affluence

**aise** [ɛz] *nf* comfort; **être à l'~** ou **à son ~** to be comfortable; (*pas embarrassé*) to be at ease; (*financièrement*) to be comfortably off; **se mettre à l'~** to make o.s. comfortable; **être mal à l'~**

to be uncomfortable; (*gêné*) to be ill at ease; **en faire à son ~** to do as one likes; **aisé, e** *adj* easy; (*assez riche*) well-to-do, well-off

**aisselle** [ɛsɛl] *nf* armpit

**ait** [ɛ] *vb voir* **avoir**

**ajonc** [aʒɔ̃] *nm* gorse *no pl*

**ajourner** [aʒuʀne] *vt* (*réunion*) to adjourn; (*décision*) to defer, postpone

**ajouter** [aʒute] *vt* to add

**alarme** [alaʀm] *nf* alarm; **donner l'~** to give *ou* raise the alarm; **alarmer** *vt* to alarm; **s'alarmer** *vi* to become alarmed

**Albanie** [albani] *nf*: **l'~** Albania

**album** [albɔm] *nm* album

**alcool** [alkɔl] *nm*: **l'~** alcohol; **un ~** a spirit, a brandy; **bière sans ~** non-alcoholic *ou* alcohol-free beer; **alcool à brûler** methylated spirits (*BRIT*), wood alcohol (*US*); **alcool à 90°** surgical spirit; **alcoolique** *adj, nm/f* alcoholic; **alcoolisé, e** *adj* alcoholic; **une boisson non alcoolisée** a soft drink; **alcoolisme** *nm* alcoholism; **alco(o)test®** *nm* Breathalyser®; (*test*) breath-test

**aléatoire** [aleatwaʀ] *adj* uncertain; (*Inform*) random

**alentour** [alɑ̃tuʀ] *adv* around, round about; **alentours** *nmpl* (*environs*) surroundings; **aux ~s de** in the vicinity *ou* neighbourhood of, round about; (*temps*) round about

**alerte** [alɛʀt] *adj* agile, nimble; brisk, lively ▷ *nf* alert; warning; **alerte à la bombe** bomb scare; **alerter** *vt* to alert

**algèbre** [alʒɛbʀ] *nf* algebra

**Alger** [alʒe] *n* Algiers

**Algérie** [alʒeʀi] *nf*: **l'~** Algeria; **algérien, ne** *adj* Algerian ▷ *nm/f*: **Algérien, ne** Algerian

**algue** [alg] *nf* (*gén*) seaweed *no pl*; (*Bot*) alga

**alibi** [alibi] *nm* alibi

**aligner** [aliɲe] *vt* to align, line up; (*idées, chiffres*) to string together; (*adapter*): **~ qch sur** to bring sth into

alignment with; **s'aligner** (*soldats etc*) to line up; **s'~ sur** (*Pol*) to align o.s. on

**aliment** [alimɑ̃] *nm* food; **alimentation** *nf* (*commerce*) food trade; (*magasin*) grocery store; (*régime*) diet; (*en eau etc, de moteur*) supplying; (*Inform*) feed; **alimenter** *vt* to feed; (*Tech*): **alimenter (en)** to supply (with); to feed (with); (*fig*) to sustain, keep going

**allaiter** [alete] *vt* to (breast-)feed, nurse; (*suj: animal*) to suckle

**allécher** [aleʃe] *vt*: **~ qn** to make sb's mouth water; to tempt *ou* entice sb

**allée** [ale] *nf* (*de jardin*) path; (*en ville*) avenue, drive; **~s et venues** comings and goings

**allégé, e** [aleʒe] *adj* (*yaourt etc*) low-fat

**alléger** [aleʒe] *vt* (*voiture*) to make lighter; (*chargement*) to lighten; (*souffrance*) to alleviate, soothe

**Allemagne** [almaɲ] *nf*: **l'~** Germany; **allemand, e** *adj* German ▷ *nm/f*: **Allemand, e** German ▷ *nm* (*Ling*) German

**aller** [ale] *nm* (*trajet*) outward journey; (*billet: aussi*: **~ simple**) single (*BRIT*) *ou* one-way (*US*) ticket; **~ (et) retour** return (ticket) (*BRIT*), round-trip ticket (*US*) ▷ *vi* (*gén*) to go; **~ à** (*convenir*) to suit; (*suj: forme, pointure etc*) to fit; **~ (bien) avec** (*couleurs, style etc*) to go (well) with; **je vais y ~/me fâcher** I'm going to go/to get angry; **~ chercher qn** to go and get *ou* fetch (*BRIT*) sb; **~ voir** to go and see, go to see; **allez!** come on!; **allons!** come now!; **comment allez-vous?** how are you?; **comment ça va?** how are you?; (*affaires etc*) how are things?; **il va bien/mal** he's well/not well, he's fine/ill; **ça va bien/mal** (*affaires etc*) it's going well/not going well; **~ mieux** to be better; **s'en ~** (*partir*) to be off, go, leave; (*disparaître*) to go away

**allergie** [alɛʀʒi] *nf* allergy

**allergique** [alɛʀʒik] *adj*: **~ à** allergic to; **je suis ~ à la pénicilline** I'm allergic to penicillin

**alliance** [aljɑ̃s] nf (Mil, Pol) alliance; (bague) wedding ring

**allier** [alje] vt (Pol, gén) to ally; (fig) to combine; **s'allier** to become allies; to combine

**allô** [alo] excl hullo, hallo

**allocation** [alɔkasjɔ̃] nf allowance; **allocation (de) chômage** unemployment benefit; **allocations familiales** ≈ child benefit

**allonger** [alɔ̃ʒe] vt to lengthen, make longer; (étendre: bras, jambe) to stretch (out); **s'allonger** vi to get longer; (se coucher) to lie down, stretch out; **~ le pas** to hasten one's step(s)

**allumage** [alymaʒ] nm (Auto) ignition

**allume-cigare** [alymsigaʀ] nm inv cigar lighter

**allumer** [alyme] vt (lampe, phare, radio) to put ou switch on; (pièce) to put ou switch the light(s) on in; (feu) to light; **s'allumer** vi (lumière, lampe) to come ou go on; **je n'arrive pas à ~ le chauffage** I can't turn the heating on

**allumette** [alymɛt] nf match

**allure** [alyʀ] nf (vitesse) speed, pace; (démarche) walk; (aspect, air) look; **avoir de l'~** to have style; **à toute ~** at top speed

**allusion** [a(l)lyzjɔ̃] nf allusion; (sous-entendu) hint; **faire ~ à** to allude ou refer to; to hint at

**MOT-CLÉ**

**alors** [alɔʀ] adv 1 (à ce moment-là) then, at that time; **il habitait alors à Paris** he lived in Paris at that time 2 (par conséquent) then; **tu as fini? alors je m'en vais** have you finished? I'm going then; **et alors?** so what? ▷ conj: **alors que** 1 (au moment où) when, as; **il est arrivé alors que je partais** he arrived as I was leaving 2 (tandis que) whereas, while; **alors que son frère travaillait dur, lui se reposait** while his brother was

working hard, HE would rest 3 (bien que) even though; **il a été puni alors qu'il n'a rien fait** he was punished, even though he had done nothing

**alourdir** [aluʀdiʀ] vt to weigh down, make heavy

**Alpes** [alp] nfpl: **les ~** the Alps

**alphabet** [alfabɛ] nm alphabet; (livre) ABC (book)

**alpinisme** [alpinism] nm mountaineering, climbing

**Alsace** [alzas] nf Alsace; **alsacien, ne** adj Alsatian ▷ nm/f: **Alsacien, ne** Alsatian

**altermondialisme** [altɛʀmɔ̃djalism] nm anti-globalism; **altermondialiste** adj, nm/f anti-globalist

**alternatif, -ive** [altɛʀnatif, iv] adj alternating; **alternative** nf (choix) alternative; **alterner** vi to alternate

**altitude** [altityd] nf altitude, height

**alto** [alto] nm (instrument) viola

**aluminium** [alyminjɔm] nm aluminium (BRIT), aluminum (US)

**amabilité** [amabilite] nf kindness

**amaigrissant, e** [amegʀisɑ̃, ɑ̃t] adj (régime) slimming

**amande** [amɑ̃d] nf (de l'amandier) almond; **amandier** nm almond (tree)

**amant** [amɑ̃] nm lover

**amas** [amɑ] nm heap, pile; **amasser** vt to amass

**amateur** [amatœʀ] nm amateur; **en ~** (péj) amateurishly; **amateur de musique/sport** music/sport lover

**ambassade** [ɑ̃basad] nf embassy; **l'~ de France** the French Embassy; **ambassadeur, -drice** nm/f ambassador(-dress)

**ambiance** [ɑ̃bjɑ̃s] nf atmosphere; **il y a de l'~** there's a great atmosphere

**ambigu, ë** [ɑ̃bigy] adj ambiguous

**ambitieux, -euse** [ɑ̃bisjø, jøz] adj ambitious

**ambition** [ɑ̃bisjɔ̃] nf ambition

**ambulance** [ɑ̃bylɑ̃s] nf ambulance;

**appelez une ~!** call an ambulance!;
**ambulancier, -ière** nm/f ambulance
man(-woman) (BRIT), paramedic (US)
**âme** [ɑm] nf soul; **âme sœur** kindred
spirit
**amélioration** [ameljɔʀasjɔ̃] nf
improvement
**améliorer** [ameljɔʀe] vt to improve;
**s'améliorer** vi to improve, get better
**aménager** [amenaʒe] vt (agencer,
transformer) to fit out; to lay out;
(: quartier, territoire) to develop;
(installer) to fix up, put in; **ferme
aménagée** converted farmhouse
**amende** [amɑ̃d] nf fine; **faire ~
honorable** to make amends
**amener** [am(ə)ne] vt to bring; (causer)
to bring about; **s'amener** vi to show
up (fam), turn up; **~ qn à faire qch** to
lead sb to do sth
**amer, amère** [amɛʀ] adj bitter
**américain, e** [ameʀikɛ̃, ɛn] adj
American ▷ nm/f: **A~, e** American
**Amérique** [ameʀik] nf: **l'~** America;
**Amérique centrale/latine** Central/
Latin America; **l'Amérique du Nord/
Sud** North/South America
**amertume** [amɛʀtym] nf bitterness
**ameublement** [amœbləmɑ̃] nm
furnishing; (meubles) furniture
**ami, e** [ami] nm/f friend; (amant/
maîtresse) boyfriend/girlfriend ▷ adj:
**pays/groupe ~** friendly country/
group; **petit ~/petite ~e** boyfriend/
girlfriend
**amiable** [amjabl]: **à l'~** adv (Jur) out of
court; (gén) amicably
**amiante** [amjɑ̃t] nm asbestos
**amical, e, -aux** [amikal, o] adj
friendly; **amicalement** adv in a
friendly way; (dans une lettre) (with)
best wishes
**amincir** [amɛ̃siʀ] vt: **~ qn** to make sb
thinner ou slimmer; (suj: vêtement) to
make sb look slimmer
**amincissant, e** [amɛ̃sisɑ̃, ɑ̃t] adj:
**régime ~** (slimming) diet; **crème ~e**
slimming cream

**amiral, -aux** [amiʀal, o] nm admiral
**amitié** [amitje] nf friendship; **prendre
en ~** to befriend; **faire ou présenter
ses ~s à qn** to send sb one's best
wishes; **"~s"** (dans une lettre) "(with)
best wishes"
**amonceler** [amɔ̃s(ə)le] vt to pile ou
heap up; **s'amonceler** vi to pile ou
heap up; (fig) to accumulate
**amont** [amɔ̃]: **en ~** adv upstream
**amorce** [amɔʀs] nf (sur un hameçon)
bait; (explosif) cap; primer; priming; (fig:
début) beginning(s), start
**amortir** [amɔʀtiʀ] vt (atténuer: choc)
to absorb, cushion; (bruit, douleur) to
deaden; (Comm: dette) to pay off; **~ un
achat** to make a purchase pay for itself;
**amortisseur** nm shock absorber
**amour** [amuʀ] nm love; **faire l'~** to
make love; **amoureux, -euse** adj
(regard, tempérament) amorous; (vie,
problèmes) love cpd; (personne): **être
amoureux (de qn)** to be in love (with
sb); **tomber amoureux (de qn)** to
fall in love (with sb) ▷ nmpl courting
couple(s); **amour-propre** nm self-
esteem, pride
**ampère** [ɑ̃pɛʀ] nm amp(ere)
**amphithéâtre** [ɑ̃fiteɑtʀ] nm
amphitheatre; (d'université) lecture hall
ou theatre
**ample** [ɑ̃pl] adj (vêtement) roomy,
ample; (gestes, mouvement) broad;
(ressources) ample; **amplement** adv:
**c'est amplement suffisant** that's
more than enough; **ampleur** nf (de
dégâts, problème) extent
**amplificateur** [ɑ̃plifikatœʀ] nm
amplifier
**amplifier** [ɑ̃plifje] vt (fig) to expand,
increase
**ampoule** [ɑ̃pul] nf (électrique) bulb;
(de médicament) phial; (aux mains, pieds)
blister
**amusant, e** [amyzɑ̃, ɑ̃t] adj
(divertissant, spirituel) entertaining,
amusing; (comique) funny, amusing
**amuse-gueule** [amyzɡœl] nm inv

appetizer, snack

**amusement** [amyzmã] *nm* (*divertissement*) amusement; (*jeu etc*) pastime, diversion

**amuser** [amyze] *vt* (*divertir*) to entertain, amuse; (*égayer, faire rire*) to amuse; **s'amuser** *vi* (*jouer*) to play; (*se divertir*) to enjoy o.s., have fun; (*fig*) to mess around

**amygdale** [amidal] *nf* tonsil

**an** [ã] *nm* year; **avoir quinze ans** to be fifteen (years old); **le jour de l'an, le premier de l'an, le nouvel an** New Year's Day

**analphabète** [analfabɛt] *nm/f* illiterate

**analyse** [analiz] *nf* analysis; (*Méd*) test; **analyser** *vt* to analyse; to test

**ananas** [anana(s)] *nm* pineapple

**anatomie** [anatɔmi] *nf* anatomy

**ancêtre** [ãsɛtʀ] *nm/f* ancestor

**anchois** [ãʃwa] *nm* anchovy

**ancien, ne** [ãsjɛ̃, jɛn] *adj* old; (*de jadis, de l'antiquité*) ancient; (*précédent, ex-*) former, old; (*par l'expérience*) senior ▷ *nm/f* (*dans une tribu*) elder; **ancienneté** *nf* (*Admin*) (length of) service; (*privilèges obtenus*) seniority

**ancre** [ãkʀ] *nf* anchor; **jeter/lever l'~** to cast/weigh anchor; **ancrer** *vt* (*Constr: câble etc*) to anchor; (*fig*) to fix firmly

**Andorre** [ãdɔʀ] *nf* Andorra

**andouille** [ãduj] *nf* (*Culin*) sausage made of chitterlings; (*fam*) clot, nit

**âne** [ɑn] *nm* donkey, ass; (*péj*) dunce

**anéantir** [aneãtiʀ] *vt* to annihilate, wipe out; (*fig*) to obliterate, destroy

**anémie** [anemi] *nf* anaemia; **anémique** *adj* anaemic

**anesthésie** [anɛstezi] *nf* anaesthesia; **faire une ~ locale/générale à qn** to give sb a local/general anaesthetic

**ange** [ãʒ] *nm* angel; **être aux ~s** to be over the moon

**angine** [ãʒin] *nf* throat infection; **angine de poitrine** angina

**anglais, e** [ãglɛ, ɛz] *adj* English ▷ *nm/f*: **A~, e** Englishman(-woman) ▷ *nm*

(*Ling*) English; **les A~** the English; **filer à l'~e** to take French leave

**angle** [ãgl] *nm* angle; (*coin*) corner; **angle droit** right angle

**Angleterre** [ãglətɛʀ] *nf*: **l'~** England

**anglo...** [ãglo] *préfixe* Anglo-, anglo(-); **anglophone** *adj* English-speaking

**angoisse** [ãgwas] *nf* anguish, distress; **angoissé, e** *adj* (*personne*) distressed

**anguille** [ãgij] *nf* eel

**animal, e, -aux** [animal, o] *adj, nm* animal

**animateur, -trice** [animatœʀ, tʀis] *nm/f* (*de télévision*) host; (*de groupe*) leader, organizer

**animation** [animasjɔ̃] *nf* (*voir animé*) busyness; liveliness; (*Cinéma: technique*) animation

**animé, e** [anime] *adj* (*lieu*) busy, lively; (*conversation, réunion*) lively, animated

**animer** [anime] *vt* (*ville, soirée*) to liven up; (*mener*) to lead

**anis** [ani(s)] *nm* (*Culin*) aniseed; (*Bot*) anise

**ankyloser** [ãkiloze]: **s'ankyloser** *vi* to get stiff

**anneau, x** [ano] *nm* (*de rideau, bague*) ring; (*de chaîne*) link

**année** [ane] *nf* year

**annexe** [anɛks] *adj* (*problème*) related; (*document*) appended; (*salle*) adjoining ▷ *nf* (*bâtiment*) annex(e); (*jointe à une lettre*) enclosure

**anniversaire** [anivɛʀsɛʀ] *nm* birthday; (*d'un événement, bâtiment*) anniversary

**annonce** [anɔ̃s] *nf* announcement; (*signe, indice*) sign; (*aussi*: **~ publicitaire**) advertisement; **les petites ~s** the classified advertisements, the small ads

**annoncer** [anɔ̃se] *vt* to announce; (*être le signe de*) to herald; **s'~ bien/difficile** to look promising/difficult

**annuaire** [anɥɛʀ] *nm* yearbook, annual; **annuaire téléphonique** (telephone) directory, phone book

**annuel, le** [anɥɛl] *adj* annual, yearly

**annulation** [anylasjɔ̃] nf cancellation

**annuler** [anyle] vt (rendez-vous, voyage) to cancel, call off; (jugement) to quash (BRIT), repeal (US); (Math, Physique) to cancel out; **je voudrais ~ ma réservation** I'd like to cancel my reservation

**anonymat** [anɔnima] nm anonymity; **garder l'~** to remain anonymous

**anonyme** [anɔnim] adj anonymous; (fig) impersonal

**anorak** [anɔrak] nm anorak

**anorexie** [anɔrɛksi] nf anorexia

**anormal, e, -aux** [anɔrmal, o] adj abnormal

**ANPE** sigle f (= Agence nationale pour l'emploi) national employment agency

**antarctique** [ɑ̃tarktik] adj Antarctic ▷ nm: **l'A~** the Antarctic

**antenne** [ɑ̃tɛn] nf (de radio) aerial; (d'insecte) antenna, feeler; (poste avancé) outpost; (petite succursale) sub-branch; **passer à l'~** to go on the air; **antenne parabolique** satellite dish

**antérieur, e** [ɑ̃terjœr] adj (d'avant) previous, earlier; (de devant) front

**anti...** [ɑ̃ti] préfixe anti...; **antialcoolique** adj anti-alcohol; **antibiotique** nm antibiotic; **antibrouillard** adj: **phare antibrouillard** fog lamp (BRIT) ou light (US)

**anticipation** [ɑ̃tisipasjɔ̃] nf: **livre/ film d'~** science fiction book/film

**anticipé, e** [ɑ̃tisipe] adj: **avec mes remerciements ~s** thanking you in advance ou anticipation

**anticiper** [ɑ̃tisipe] vt (événement, coup) to anticipate, foresee

**anti...**: **anticorps** nm antibody; **antidote** nm antidote; **antigel** nm antifreeze; **antihistaminique** nm antihistamine

**antillais, e** [ɑ̃tijɛ, ɛz] adj West Indian, Caribbean ▷ nm/f: **A~, e** West Indian, Caribbean

**Antilles** [ɑ̃tij] nfpl: **les ~** the West Indies; **les Grandes/Petites ~** the Greater/Lesser Antilles

**antilope** [ɑ̃tilɔp] nf antelope

**anti...**: **antimite(s)** adj, nm: **(produit) antimite(s)** mothproofer; moth repellent; **antimondialisation** nf anti-globalization; **antipathique** adj unpleasant, disagreeable; **antipelliculaire** adj anti-dandruff

**antiquaire** [ɑ̃tikɛr] nm/f antique dealer

**antique** [ɑ̃tik] adj antique; (très vieux) ancient, antiquated; **antiquité** nf (objet) antique; **l'Antiquité** Antiquity; **magasin d'antiquités** antique shop

**anti...**: **antirabique** adj rabies cpd; **antirouille** adj inv anti-rust cpd; **antisémite** adj anti-Semitic; **antiseptique** adj, nm antiseptic

**antivirus** [ɑ̃tivirys] nm (Inform) antivirus; **antivol** adj, nm: **(dispositif) antivol** anti-theft device

**anxieux, -euse** [ɑ̃ksjø, jøz] adj anxious, worried

**AOC** sigle f (= appellation d'origine contrôlée) label guaranteeing the quality of wine

**août** [u(t)] nm August

**apaiser** [apeze] vt (colère, douleur) to soothe; (personne) to calm (down), pacify; **s'apaiser** vi (tempête, bruit) to die down, subside; (personne) to calm down

**apercevoir** [apɛrsəvwar] vt to see; **s'apercevoir de** vt to notice; **s'~ que** to notice that

**aperçu** [apɛrsy] nm (vue d'ensemble) general survey

**apéritif** [aperitif] nm (boisson) aperitif; (réunion) drinks pl

**à-peu-près** [apøprɛ] (péj) nm inv vague approximation

**apeuré, e** [apœre] adj frightened, scared

**aphte** [aft] nm mouth ulcer

**apitoyer** [apitwaje] vt to move to pity; **s'apitoyer (sur)** to feel pity (for)

**aplatir** [aplatir] vt to flatten; **s'aplatir** vi to become flatter; (écrasé) to be flattened

**aplomb** [aplɔ̃] nm (équilibre) balance, equilibrium; (fig) self-assurance; nerve; **d'~** steady

**apostrophe** [apɔstʀɔf] nf (signe) apostrophe

**apparaître** [apaʀɛtʀ] vi to appear

**appareil** [apaʀɛj] nm (outil, machine) piece of apparatus, device; (électrique, ménager) appliance; (avion) (aero)plane, aircraft inv; (téléphonique) phone; (dentier) brace (BRIT), braces (US); **"qui est à l'~?"** "who's speaking?"; **dans le plus simple ~** in one's birthday suit; **appareil(-photo)** camera; **appareiller** vi (Navig) to cast off, get under way ▷ vt (assortir) to match up

**apparemment** [apaʀamɑ̃] adv apparently

**apparence** [apaʀɑ̃s] nf appearance; **en ~** apparently

**apparent, e** [apaʀɑ̃, ɑ̃t] adj visible; (évident) obvious; (superficiel) apparent

**apparenté, e** [apaʀɑ̃te] adj: **~ à** related to; (fig) similar to

**apparition** [apaʀisjɔ̃] nf appearance; (surnaturelle) apparition

**appartement** [apaʀtəmɑ̃] nm flat (BRIT), apartment (US)

**appartenir** [apaʀtəniʀ]: **~ à** vt to belong to; **il lui appartient de** it is his duty to

**apparu, e** [apaʀy] pp de **apparaître**

**appât** [apɑ] nm (Pêche) bait; (fig) lure, bait

**appel** [apɛl] nm call; (nominal) roll call; (: Scol) register; (Mil: recrutement) call-up; **faire ~ à** (invoquer) to appeal to; (avoir recours à) to call on; (nécessiter) to call for, require; **faire** ou **interjeter ~** (Jur) to appeal; **faire l'~** to call the roll; (Scol) to call the register; **sans ~** (fig) final, irrevocable; **faire un ~ de phares** to flash one's headlights; **appel d'offres** (Comm) invitation to tender; **appel (téléphonique)** (tele)phone call

**appelé** [ap(ə)le] nm (Mil) conscript

**appeler** [ap(ə)le] vt to call; (faire venir: médecin etc) to call, send for; **s'appeler** vi: **elle s'appelle Gabrielle** her name is Gabrielle, she's called Gabrielle; **comment vous appelez-vous?** what's your name?; **comment ça s'appelle?** what is it called?; **être appelé à** (fig) to be destined to

**appendicite** [apɑ̃disit] nf appendicitis

**appesantir** [apəzɑ̃tiʀ]: **s'appesantir** vi to grow heavier; **s'~ sur** (fig) to dwell on

**appétissant, e** [apetisɑ̃, ɑ̃t] adj appetizing, mouth-watering

**appétit** [apeti] nm appetite; **bon ~!** enjoy your meal!

**applaudir** [aplodiʀ] vt to applaud ▷ vi to applaud, clap; **applaudissements** nmpl applause sg, clapping sg

**application** [aplikasjɔ̃] nf application

**appliquer** [aplike] vt to apply; (loi) to enforce; **s'appliquer** vi (élève etc) to apply o.s.; **s'~ à** to apply to

**appoint** [apwɛ̃] nm (extra) contribution ou help; **avoir/faire l'~** to have/give the right change ou money; **chauffage d'~** extra heating

**apporter** [apɔʀte] vt to bring

**appréciable** [apʀesjabl] adj appreciable

**apprécier** [apʀesje] vt to appreciate; (évaluer) to estimate, assess

**appréhender** [apʀeɑ̃de] vt (craindre) to dread; (arrêter) to apprehend

**apprendre** [apʀɑ̃dʀ] vt to learn; (événement, résultats) to learn of, hear of; **~ qch à qn** (informer) to tell sb (of) sth; (enseigner) to teach sb sth; **~ à faire qch** to learn to do sth; **~ à qn à faire qch** to teach sb to do sth; **apprenti, e** nm/f apprentice; **apprentissage** nm learning; (Comm, Scol: période) apprenticeship

**apprêter** [apʀete] vt: **s'~ à faire qch** to get ready to do sth

**appris, e** [apʀi, iz] pp de **apprendre**

**apprivoiser** [apʀivwaze] vt to tame

**approbation** [apʀɔbasjɔ̃] nf approval

**approcher** [apʁɔʃe] vi to approach, come near ▷ vt to approach; (rapprocher): **~ qch (de qch)** to bring ou put sth near (to sth); **s'approcher de** to approach, go ou come near to; **~ de** (lieu, but) to draw near to; (quantité, moment) to approach

**approfondir** [apʁɔfɔ̃diʁ] vt to deepen; (question) to go further into

**approprié, e** [apʁɔpʁije] adj: **~ (à)** appropriate (to), suited to

**approprier** [apʁɔpʁije]: **s'approprier** vt to appropriate, take over; **s'~ en** to stock up with

**approuver** [apʁuve] vt to agree with; (trouver louable) to approve of

**approvisionner** [apʁɔvizjɔne] vt to supply; (compte bancaire) to pay funds into; **s'approvisionner en** to stock up with

**approximatif, -ive** [apʁɔksimatif, iv] adj approximate, rough; (termes) vague

**appt** abr = **appartement**

**appui** [apɥi] nm support; **prendre ~ sur** to lean on; (objet) to rest on; **l'~ de la fenêtre** the windowsill, the window ledge

**appuyer** [apɥije] vt (poser): **~ qch sur/contre** to lean ou rest sth on/against; (soutenir: personne, demande) to support, back (up) ▷ vi: **~ sur** (bouton) to press, push; (mot, détail) to stress, emphasize; **~ sur le frein** to brake, to apply the brakes; **s'appuyer sur** to lean on; (fig: compter sur) to rely on

**après** [apʁɛ] prép after ▷ adv afterwards; **2 heures ~** 2 hours later; **~ qu'il est ou soit parti** after he left; **~ avoir fait** after having done; **d'~** (selon) according to; **~ coup** after the event, afterwards; **~ tout** (au fond) after all; **et (puis) ~?** so what?; **après-demain** adv the day after tomorrow; **après-midi** nm ou nf inv afternoon; **après-rasage** nm inv aftershave; **après-shampooing** nm inv conditioner; **après-ski** nm inv snow boot

**après-soleil** [apʁɛsɔlɛj] adj inv after-sun cpd ▷ nm after-sun cream ou lotion

**apte** [apt] adj capable; **~ à qch/faire qch** capable of sth/doing sth; **~ (au service)** (Mil) fit (for service)

**aquarelle** [akwaʁɛl] nf watercolour

**aquarium** [akwaʁjɔm] nm aquarium

**arabe** [aʁab] adj Arabic; (désert, cheval) Arabian; (nation, peuple) Arab ▷ nm/f: **A~** Arab ▷ nm (Ling) Arabic

**Arabie** [aʁabi] nf: **l'~ (Saoudite)** Saudi Arabia

**arachide** [aʁaʃid] nf (plante) groundnut (plant); (graine) peanut, groundnut

**araignée** [aʁeɲe] nf spider

**arbitraire** [aʁbitʁɛʁ] adj arbitrary

**arbitre** [aʁbitʁ] nm (Sport) referee; (: Tennis, Cricket) umpire; (fig) arbiter, judge; (Jur) arbitrator; **arbitrer** vt to referee; to umpire; to arbitrate

**arbre** [aʁbʁ] nm tree; (Tech) shaft

**arbuste** [aʁbyst] nm small shrub

**arc** [aʁk] nm (arme) bow; (Géom) arc; (Archit) arch; **en ~ de cercle** semi-circular

**arcade** [aʁkad] nf arch(way); **arcades** nfpl (série) arcade sg, arches

**arc-en-ciel** [aʁkɑ̃sjɛl] nm rainbow

**arche** [aʁʃ] nf arch; **arche de Noé** Noah's Ark

**archéologie** [aʁkeɔlɔʒi] nf arch(a)eology; **archéologue** nm/f arch(a)eologist

**archet** [aʁʃɛ] nm bow

**archipel** [aʁʃipɛl] nm archipelago

**architecte** [aʁʃitɛkt] nm architect

**architecture** [aʁʃitɛktyʁ] nf architecture

**archives** [aʁʃiv] nfpl (collection) archives

**arctique** [aʁktik] adj Arctic ▷ nm: **l'A~** the Arctic

**ardent, e** [aʁdɑ̃, ɑ̃t] adj (soleil) blazing; (amour) ardent, passionate; (prière) fervent

**ardoise** [aʁdwaz] nf slate

**ardu, e** [aʁdy] adj (travail) arduous; (problème) difficult

**arène** [aʀɛn] nf arena; **arènes** nfpl
(amphithéâtre) bull-ring sg

**arête** [aʀɛt] nf (de poisson) bone; (d'une
montagne) ridge

**argent** [aʀʒɑ̃] nm (métal) silver;
(monnaie) money; **argent de poche**
pocket money; **argent liquide** ready
money, (ready) cash; **argenterie** nf
silverware

**argentin, e** [aʀʒɑ̃tɛ̃, in] adj
Argentinian ▷ nm/f: **A~, e** Argentinian

**Argentine** [aʀʒɑ̃tin] nf: **l'~** Argentina

**argentique** [aʀʒɑ̃tik] adj (appareil-
photo) film cpd

**argile** [aʀʒil] nf clay

**argot** [aʀɡo] nm slang; **argotique** adj
slang cpd; (très familier) slangy

**argument** [aʀɡymɑ̃] nm argument

**argumenter** [aʀɡymɑ̃te] vi to argue

**aride** [aʀid] adj arid

**aristocratie** [aʀistɔkʀasi] nf
aristocracy; **aristocratique** adj
aristocratic

**arithmétique** [aʀitmetik] adj
arithmetic(al) ▷ nf arithmetic

**arme** [aʀm] nf weapon; **armes** nfpl
(armement) weapons, arms; (blason)
(coat of) arms; **~s de destruction
massive** weapons of mass destruction;
**arme à feu** firearm

**armée** [aʀme] nf army; **armée de l'air**
Air Force; **armée de terre** Army

**armer** [aʀme] vt to arm; (arme à feu) to
cock; (appareil-photo) to wind on; **~ qch
de** to reinforce sth with; **s'armer de** to
arm o.s. with

**armistice** [aʀmistis] nm armistice;
**l'A~** ≈ Remembrance (BRIT) ou Veterans
(US) Day

**armoire** [aʀmwaʀ] nf (tall) cupboard;
(penderie) wardrobe (BRIT), closet (US)

**armure** [aʀmyʀ] nf armour no pl, suit
of armour; **armurier** nm gunsmith

**arnaque** [aʀnak] (fam) nf swindling;
**c'est de l'~** it's a rip-off; **arnaquer** (fam)
vt to swindle

**arobase** [aʀɔbaz] nf (symbole) at
symbol; **"paul ~ société point fr"** "paul

at société dot fr"

**aromates** [aʀɔmat] nmpl seasoning
sg, herbs (and spices)

**aromathérapie** [aʀɔmateʀapi] nf
aromatherapy

**aromatisé, e** [aʀɔmatize] adj
flavoured

**arôme** [aʀom] nm aroma

**arracher** [aʀaʃe] vt to pull out; (page
etc) to tear off, tear out; (légumes,
herbe) to pull up; (bras etc) to tear off;
**s'arracher** vt (article recherché) to fight
over; **~ qch à qn** to snatch sth from sb;
(fig) to wring sth out of sb

**arrangement** [aʀɑ̃ʒmɑ̃] nm
agreement, arrangement

**arranger** [aʀɑ̃ʒe] vt (gén) to arrange;
(réparer) to fix, put right; (régler:
différend) to settle, sort out; (convenir
à) to suit, be convenient for; **cela
m'arrange** that suits me (fine);
**s'arranger** vi (se mettre d'accord) to
come to an agreement; **je vais m'~** I'll
manage; **ça va s'~** it'll sort itself out

**arrestation** [aʀɛstasjɔ̃] nf arrest

**arrêt** [aʀɛ] nm stopping; (de bus etc)
stop; (Jur) judgment, decision; **à l'~**
stationary; **tomber en ~ devant**
to stop short in front of; **sans ~**
(sans interruption) non-stop; (très
fréquemment) continually; **arrêt de
travail** stoppage (of work)

**arrêter** [aʀete] vt to stop; (chauffage
etc) to turn off, switch off; (fixer: date
etc) to appoint, decide on; (criminel,
suspect) to arrest; **s'arrêter** vi to stop;
**~ de faire** to stop doing; **arrêtez-vous
ici/au coin, s'il vous plaît** could you
stop here/at the corner, please?

**arrhes** [aʀ] nfpl deposit sg

**arrière** [aʀjɛʀ] nm back; (Sport) fullback
▷ adj inv: **siège/roue ~** back ou rear
seat/wheel; **à l'~** behind, at the back;
**en ~** behind; (regarder) back, behind;
(tomber, aller) backwards; **arrière-goût**
nm aftertaste; **arrière-grand-mère**
nf great-grandmother; **arrière-
grand-père** nm great-grandfather;

**arrière-pays** nm inv hinterland;
**arrière-pensée** nf ulterior motive;
mental reservation; **arrière-plan** nm
background; **à l'arrière-plan** in the
background; **arrière-saison** nf late
autumn
**arrimer** [aʀime] vt to secure;
(cargaison) to stow
**arrivage** [aʀivaʒ] nm consignment
**arrivée** [aʀive] nf arrival; (ligne d'arrivée)
finish
**arriver** [aʀive] vi to arrive; (survenir)
to happen, occur; **il arrive à Paris à
8h** he gets to ou arrives in Paris at 8; **à
quelle heure arrive le train de Lyon?**
what time does the train from Lyons
get in?; **~ à** (atteindre) to reach; **~ à faire
qch** to succeed in doing sth; **en ~ à**
(finir par) to come to; **il arrive que** it
happens that; **il lui arrive de faire** he
sometimes does
**arrobase** [aʀɔbaz] nf (Inform) @,
'at' sign
**arrogance** [aʀɔgɑ̃s] nf arrogance
**arrogant, e** [aʀɔgɑ̃, ɑ̃t] adj arrogant
**arrondissement** [aʀɔ̃dismɑ̃] nm
(Admin) ≈ district
**arroser** [aʀoze] vt to water; (victoire) to
celebrate (over a drink); (Culin) to baste;
**arrosoir** nm watering can
**arsenal, -aux** [aʀsənal, o] nm (Navig)
naval dockyard; (Mil) arsenal; (fig) gear,
paraphernalia
**art** [aʀ] nm art
**artère** [aʀtɛʀ] nf (Anat) artery; (rue)
main road
**arthrite** [aʀtʀit] nf arthritis
**artichaut** [aʀtiʃo] nm artichoke
**article** [aʀtikl] nm article; (Comm)
item, article; **à l'~ de la mort** at the
point of death
**articulation** [aʀtikylasjɔ̃] nf
articulation; (Anat) joint
**articuler** [aʀtikyle] vt to articulate
**artificiel, le** [aʀtifisjɛl] adj artificial
**artisan** [aʀtizɑ̃] nm artisan, (self-
employed) craftsman; **artisanal, e,
-aux** adj of ou made by craftsmen; (péj)

cottage industry cpd; **de fabrication
artisanale** home-made; **artisanat** nm
arts and crafts pl
**artiste** [aʀtist] nm/f artist; (de variétés)
entertainer; (musicien etc) performer;
**artistique** adj artistic
**as¹** [a] vb voir **avoir**
**as²** [ɑs] nm ace
**ascenseur** [asɑ̃sœʀ] nm lift (BRIT),
elevator (US)
**ascension** [asɑ̃sjɔ̃] nf ascent;
(de montagne) climb; **l'A~** (Rel) the
Ascension

● **ASCENSION**
●
● The **fête de l'Ascension** is a public
● holiday in France. It always falls on
● a Thursday, usually in May. Many
● French people take the following
● Friday off work too and enjoy a long
● weekend.

**asiatique** [azjatik] adj Asiatic, Asian
▷ nm/f: **A~** Asian
**Asie** [azi] nf: **l'~** Asia
**asile** [azil] nm (refuge) refuge,
sanctuary; (Pol): **droit d'~** (political)
asylum
**aspect** [aspɛ] nm appearance, look;
(fig) aspect, side; **à l'~ de** at the sight of
**asperge** [aspɛʀʒ] nf asparagus no pl
**asperger** [aspɛʀʒe] vt to spray, sprinkle
**asphalte** [asfalt] nm asphalt
**asphyxier** [asfiksje] vt to suffocate,
asphyxiate; (fig) to stifle
**aspirateur** [aspiʀatœʀ] nm vacuum
cleaner; **passer l'~** to vacuum
**aspirer** [aspiʀe] vt (air) to inhale;
(liquide) to suck (up); (suj: appareil) to
suck up; **~ à** to aspire to
**aspirine** [aspiʀin] nf aspirin
**assagir** [asaʒiʀ]: **s'assagir** vi to
quieten down, settle down
**assaisonnement** [asɛzɔnmɑ̃] nm
seasoning
**assaisonner** [asɛzɔne] vt to season
**assassin** [asasɛ̃] nm murderer;

assassin; **assassiner** vt to murder; (esp Pol) to assassinate

**assaut** [aso] nm assault, attack; **prendre d'~** to storm, assault; **donner l'~ à** to attack

**assécher** [aseʃe] vt to drain

**assemblage** [asɑ̃blaʒ] nm (action) assembling; (de couleurs, choses) collection

**assemblée** [asɑ̃ble] nf (réunion) meeting; (assistance) gathering; (Pol) assembly; **l'A~ nationale** the National Assembly (the lower house of the French Parliament)

**assembler** [asɑ̃ble] vt (joindre, monter) to assemble, put together; (amasser) to gather (together), collect (together); **s'assembler** vi to gather

**asseoir** [aswar] vt (malade, bébé) to sit up; (personne debout) to sit down; (autorité, réputation) to establish; **s'asseoir** vi to sit (o.s.) down

**assez** [ase] adv (suffisamment) enough, sufficiently; (passablement) rather, quite, fairly; **~ de pain/livres** enough ou sufficient bread/books; **vous en avez ~?** have you got enough?; **j'en ai ~!** I've had enough!

**assidu, e** [asidy] adj (appliqué) assiduous, painstaking; (ponctuel) regular

**assied** etc [asje] vb voir **asseoir**

**assiérai** etc [asjere] vb voir **asseoir**

**assiette** [asjet] nf plate; (contenu) plate(ful); **il n'est pas dans son ~** he's not feeling quite himself; **assiette à dessert** dessert plate; **assiette anglaise** assorted cold meats; **assiette creuse** (soup) dish, soup plate; **assiette plate** (dinner) plate

**assimiler** [asimile] vt to assimilate, absorb; (comparer): **~ qch/qn à** to liken ou compare sth/sb to; **s'assimiler** vr (s'intégrer) to be assimilated, assimilate

**assis, e** [asi, iz] pp de **asseoir** ▷ adj sitting (down), seated

**assistance** [asistɑ̃s] nf (public) audience; (aide) assistance; **enfant de**

**l'A~ publique** child in care

**assistant, e** [asistɑ̃, ɑ̃t] nm/f assistant; (d'université) probationary lecturer; **assistant(e) social(e)** social worker

**assisté, e** [asiste] adj (Auto) power assisted; **~ par ordinateur** computer-assisted; **direction ~e** power steering

**assister** [asiste] vt (aider) to assist; **~ à** (scène, événement) to witness; (conférence, séminaire) to attend, be at; (spectacle, match) to be at, see

**association** [asɔsjasjɔ̃] nf association

**associé, e** [asɔsje] nm/f associate; (Comm) partner

**associer** [asɔsje] vt to associate; **s'associer** vi to join together; **s'~ à qn pour faire** to join (forces) with sb to do; **s'~ à** (couleurs, qualités) to be combined with; (opinions, joie de qn) to share in; **~ qn à** (profits) to give sb a share of; (affaire) to make sb a partner in; (joie, triomphe) to include sb in; **~ qch à** (allier à) to combine sth with

**assoiffé, e** [aswafe] adj thirsty

**assommer** [asɔme] vt (étourdir, abrutir) to knock out, stun

**Assomption** [asɔ̃psjɔ̃] nf: **l'~** the Assumption

**ASSOMPTION**

- The **fête de l'Assomption**, more
- commonly known as **'le 15 août'**
- is a national holiday in France.
- Traditionally, large numbers of
- holidaymakers leave home on 15
- August, frequently causing chaos
- on the roads.

**assorti, e** [asɔrti] adj matched, matching; (varié) assorted; **~ à** matching; **assortiment** nm assortment, selection

**assortir** [asɔrtir] vt to match; **~ qch à** to match sth with; **~ qch de** to accompany sth with

**assouplir** [asuplir] vt to make supple;

(*fig*) to relax; **assouplissant** *nm* (fabric) softener

**assumer** [asyme] *vt* (*fonction, emploi*) to assume, take on

**assurance** [asyʀɑ̃s] *nf* (*certitude*) assurance; (*confiance en soi*) (self-)confidence; (*contrat*) insurance (policy); (*secteur commercial*) insurance; **assurance au tiers** third-party insurance; **assurance maladie** health insurance; **assurance tous risques** (*Auto*) comprehensive insurance; **assurances sociales** ≈ National Insurance (*BRIT*), ≈ Social Security (*US*); **assurance-vie** *nf* life assurance *ou* insurance

**assuré, e** [asyʀe] *adj* (*certain: réussite, échec*) certain, sure; (*air*) assured; (*pas*) steady ▷ *nm/f* insured (person); **assurément** *adv* assuredly, most certainly

**assurer** [asyʀe] *vt* (*Finance*) to insure; (*victoire etc*) to ensure; (*frontières, pouvoir*) to make secure; (*service*) to provide, operate; **s'assurer (contre)** (*Comm*) to insure o.s. (against); **s'~ de/ que** (*vérifier*) to make sure of/that; **s'~ (de)** (*aide de qn*) to secure; **~ à qn que** to assure sb that; **~ qn de** to assure sb of

**asthmatique** [asmatik] *adj, nm/f* asthmatic

**asthme** [asm] *nm* asthma

**asticot** [astiko] *nm* maggot

**astre** [astʀ] *nm* star

**astrologie** [astʀɔlɔʒi] *nf* astrology

**astronaute** [astʀonot] *nm/f* astronaut

**astronomie** [astʀɔnɔmi] *nf* astronomy

**astuce** [astys] *nf* shrewdness, astuteness; (*truc*) trick, clever way; **astucieux, -euse** *adj* clever

**atelier** [atəlje] *nm* workshop; (*de peintre*) studio

**athée** [ate] *adj* atheistic ▷ *nm/f* atheist

**Athènes** [atɛn] *n* Athens

**athlète** [atlɛt] *nm/f* (*Sport*) athlete; **athlétisme** *nm* athletics *sg*

**atlantique** [atlɑ̃tik] *adj* Atlantic ▷ *nm*: **l'(océan) A~** the Atlantic (Ocean)

**atlas** [atlɑs] *nm* atlas

**atmosphère** [atmosfɛʀ] *nf* atmosphere

**atome** [atom] *nm* atom; **atomique** *adj* atomic, nuclear

**atomiseur** [atɔmizœʀ] *nm* atomizer

**atout** [atu] *nm* trump; (*fig*) asset

**atroce** [atʀɔs] *adj* atrocious

**attachant, e** [ataʃɑ̃, ɑ̃t] *adj* engaging, lovable, likeable

**attache** [ataʃ] *nf* clip, fastener; (*fig*) tie

**attacher** [ataʃe] *vt* to tie up; (*étiquette*) to attach, tie on; (*ceinture*) to fasten ▷ *vi* (*poêle, riz*) to stick; **s'attacher à** (*par affection*) to become attached to; **~ qch à** to tie ou attach sth to

**attaque** [atak] *nf* attack; (*cérébrale*) stroke; (*d'épilepsie*) fit

**attaquer** [atake] *vt* to attack ▷ *vi* to attack; **s'attaquer à** *vt* (*personne*) to attack; (*problème*) to tackle; **~ qn en justice** to bring an action against sb, sue sb

**attarder** [ataʀde]: **s'attarder** *vi* to linger

**atteindre** [atɛ̃dʀ] *vt* to reach; (*blesser*) to hit; (*émouvoir*) to affect; **atteint, e** *adj* (*Méd*): **être atteint de** to be suffering from; **atteinte** *nf*: **hors d'atteinte** out of reach; **porter atteinte à** to strike a blow at

**attendant** [atɑ̃dɑ̃] *adv*: **en ~** meanwhile, in the meantime

**attendre** [atɑ̃dʀ] *vt* (*gén*) to wait for; (*être destiné ou réservé à*) to await, be in store for ▷ *vi* to wait; **s'attendre à (ce que)** to expect (that); **attendez-moi, s'il vous plaît** wait for me, please; **~ un enfant** to be expecting a baby; **~ de faire/d'être** to wait until one does/is; **attendez qu'il vienne** wait until he comes; **~ qch de** to expect sth of

> Attention à ne pas traduire *attendre* par to *attend*.

**attendrir** [atɑ̃dʀiʀ] *vt* to move (to pity); (*viande*) to tenderize

**attendu, e** [atɑ̃dy] *adj* (*visiteur*) expected; (*événement*) long-awaited; **~ que** considering that, since

**attentat** [atɑ̃ta] *nm* assassination attempt; **attentat à la pudeur** indecent assault *no pl*; **attentat suicide** suicide bombing

**attente** [atɑ̃t] *nf* wait; (*espérance*) expectation

**attenter** [atɑ̃te]: **~ à** *vt* (*liberté*) to violate; **~ à la vie de qn** to make an attempt on sb's life

**attentif, -ive** [atɑ̃tif, iv] *adj* (*auditeur*) attentive; (*examen*) careful; **~ à** careful to

**attention** [atɑ̃sjɔ̃] *nf* attention; (*prévenance*) attention, thoughtfulness *no pl*; **à l'~ de** for the attention of; **faire ~ (à)** to be careful (of); **faire ~ (à ce) que** to be *ou* make sure that; **~!** careful!, watch out!; **~ à la voiture!** watch out for that car!; **attentionné, e** *adj* thoughtful, considerate

**atténuer** [atenɥe] *vt* (*douleur*) to alleviate, ease; (*couleurs*) to soften; **s'atténuer** *vi* to ease; (*violence etc*) to abate

**atterrir** [ateʀiʀ] *vi* to land; **atterrissage** *nm* landing

**attestation** [atɛstasjɔ̃] *nf* certificate

**attirant, e** [atirɑ̃, ɑ̃t] *adj* attractive, appealing

**attirer** [atiʀe] *vt* to attract; (*appâter*) to lure, entice; **~ qn dans un coin/vers soi** to draw sb into a corner/towards one; **~ l'attention de qn** to attract sb's attention; **~ l'attention de qn sur** to draw sb's attention to; **s'~ des ennuis** to bring trouble upon o.s., get into trouble

**attitude** [atityd] *nf* attitude; (*position du corps*) bearing

**attraction** [atʀaksjɔ̃] *nf* (*gén*) attraction; (*de cabaret, cirque*) number

**attrait** [atʀɛ] *nm* appeal, attraction

**attraper** [atʀape] *vt* (*gén*) to catch; (*habitude, amende*) to get, pick up; (*fam: duper*) to con; **se faire ~** (*fam*) to be told off

**attrayant, e** [atʀejɑ̃, ɑ̃t] *adj* attractive

**attribuer** [atʀibɥe] *vt* (*prix*) to award; (*rôle, tâche*) to allocate, assign; (*imputer*): **~ qch à** to attribute sth to; **s'attribuer** *vt* (*s'approprier*) to claim for o.s.

**attrister** [atʀiste] *vt* to sadden

**attroupement** [atʀupmɑ̃] *nm* crowd

**attrouper** [atʀupe]: **s'attrouper** *vi* to gather

**au** [o] *prép +dét* = **à +le**

**aubaine** [obɛn] *nf* godsend

**aube** [ob] *nf* dawn, daybreak; **à l'~** at dawn *ou* daybreak

**aubépine** [obepin] *nf* hawthorn

**auberge** [obɛʀʒ] *nf* inn; **auberge de jeunesse** youth hostel

**aubergine** [obɛʀʒin] *nf* aubergine

**aucun, e** [okœ̃, yn] *dét* no, *tournure négative +*any; (*positif*) any ▷ *pron* none, *tournure négative +*any; any(one); **sans ~ doute** without any doubt; **plus qu'~ autre** more than any other; **il le fera mieux qu'~ de nous** he'll do it better than any of us; **~ des deux** neither of the two; **~ d'entre eux** none of them

**audace** [odas] *nf* daring, boldness; (*péj*) audacity; **audacieux, -euse** *adj* daring, bold

**au-delà** [od(ə)la] *adv* beyond ▷ *nm*: **l'~** the hereafter; **~ de** beyond

**au-dessous** [odsu] *adv* underneath; below; **~ de** under(neath), below; (*limite, somme etc*) below, under; (*dignité, condition*) below

**au-dessus** [odsy] *adv* above; **~ de** above

**au-devant** [od(ə)vɑ̃]: **~ de** *prép*: **aller ~ de** (*personne, danger*) to go (out) and meet; (*souhaits de qn*) to anticipate

**audience** [odjɑ̃s] *nf* audience; (*Jur: séance*) hearing

**audiovisuel, le** [odjovizɥɛl] *adj* audiovisual

**audition** [odisjɔ̃] *nf* (*ouïe, écoute*)

hearing; (*Jur: de témoins*) examination; (*Mus, Théâtre: épreuve*) audition

**auditoire** [oditwar] *nm* audience

**augmentation** [ɔgmãtasjɔ̃] *nf* increase; **augmentation (de salaire)** rise (in salary) (BRIT), (pay) raise (US)

**augmenter** [ɔgmãte] *vt* (*gén*) to increase; (*salaire, prix*) to increase, raise, put up; (*employé*) to increase the salary of ▷ *vi* to increase

**augure** [ogyr] *nm*: **de bon/mauvais ~** of good/ill omen

**aujourd'hui** [oʒurdɥi] *adv* today

**aumône** [omon] *nf inv* alms *sg*; **aumônier** *nm* chaplain

**auparavant** [oparavã] *adv* before(hand)

**auprès** [oprε]: **~ de** *prép* next to, close to; (*recourir, s'adresser*) to; (*en comparaison de*) compared with

**auquel** [okεl] *prép +pron* = **à +lequel**

**aurai** *etc* [ore] *vb voir* **avoir**

**aurons** *etc* [orɔ̃] *vb voir* **avoir**

**aurore** [ˋr] *nf* dawn, daybreak

**ausculter** [ɔskylte] *vt* to sound (the chest of)

**aussi** [osi] *adv* (*également*) also, too; (*de comparaison*) as ▷ *conj* therefore, consequently; **~ fort que** as strong as; **moi ~** me too

**aussitôt** [osito] *adv* straight away, immediately; **~ que** as soon as

**austère** [ostεr] *adj* austere

**austral, e** [ostral] *adj* southern

**Australie** [ostrali] *nf*: **l'~** Australia; **australien, ne** *adj* Australian ▷ *nm/f*: **Australien, ne** Australian

**autant** [otã] *adv* (*intensité*) so much; **je ne savais pas que tu la détestais ~** I didn't know you hated her so much; (*comparatif*): **~ (que)** as much (as); (*nombre*) as many (as); **~ (de)** so much (*ou* many); as much (*ou* many); **~ partir** we (*ou* you *etc*) may as well leave; **~ dire que ...** one might as well say that ...; **pour ~** for all that; **d'~ plus/mieux (que)** all the more/the better (since)

**autel** [otεl] *nm* altar

**auteur** [otœr] *nm* author

**authentique** [otãtik] *adj* authentic, genuine

**auto** [oto] *nf* car

**auto...**: **autobiographie** *nf* autobiography; **autobronzant** *nm* self-tanning cream (*or* lotion *etc*); **autobus** *nm* bus; **autocar** *nm* coach

**autochtone** [ɔtɔktɔn] *nm/f* native

**auto...**: **autocollant, e** *adj* self-adhesive; (*enveloppe*) self-seal ▷ *nm* sticker; **autocuiseur** *nm* pressure cooker; **autodéfense** *nf* self-defence; **autodidacte** *nm/f* self-taught person; **auto-école** *nf* driving school; **autographe** *nm* autograph

**automate** [ɔtɔmat] *nm* (*machine*) (automatic) machine

**automatique** [ɔtɔmatik] *adj* automatic ▷ *nm*: **l'~** direct dialling

**automne** [ɔtɔn] *nm* autumn (BRIT), fall (US)

**automobile** [ɔtɔmɔbil] *adj* motor *cpd*, car *cpd* ▷ *nf* (motor) car; **automobiliste** *nm/f* motorist

**autonome** [ɔtɔnɔm] *adj* autonomous; **autonomie** *nf* autonomy; (*Pol*) self-government, autonomy

**autopsie** [ɔtɔpsi] *nf* post-mortem (examination), autopsy

**autoradio** [otoradjo] *nm* car radio

**autorisation** [ɔtɔrizasjɔ̃] *nf* permission, authorization; (*papiers*) permit

**autorisé, e** [ɔtɔrize] *adj* (*opinion, sources*) authoritative

**autoriser** [ɔtɔrize] *vt* to give permission for, authorize; (*fig*) to allow (of)

**autoritaire** [ɔtɔritεr] *adj* authoritarian

**autorité** [ɔtɔrite] *nf* authority; **faire ~** to be authoritative; **les ~s** the authorities

**autoroute** [otorut] *nf* motorway (BRIT), highway (US); **~ de**

**l'information** (*Inform*) information superhighway

● AUTOROUTE
○

○ Motorways in France, indicated
● by blue road signs with the letter A
● followed by a number, are toll roads.
● The speed limit is 130 km/h (110 km/
● h when it is raining). At the tollgate,
● the lanes marked 'réservé' and with
● an orange 't' are reserved for people
● who subscribe to 'télépéage', an
● electronic payment system.

**auto-stop** [otostɔp] *nm*: **faire de l'~** to hitch-hike; **prendre qn en ~** to give sb a lift; **auto-stoppeur, -euse** *nm/f* hitch-hiker

**autour** [otuʀ] *adv* around; **~ de** around; **tout ~** all around

○ MOT-CLÉ

**autre** [otʀ] *adj* **1** (*différent*) other, different; **je préférerais un autre verre** I'd prefer another *ou* a different glass
**2** (*supplémentaire*) other; **je voudrais un autre verre d'eau** I'd like another glass of water
**3**: **autre chose** something else; **autre part** somewhere else; **d'autre part** on the other hand
▷ *pron*: **un autre** another (one); **nous/vous autres** us/you; **d'autres** others; **l'autre** the other (one); **les autres** the others; (*autrui*) others; **l'un et l'autre** both of them; **se détester l'un l'autre/les uns les autres** to hate each other *ou* one another; **d'une semaine à l'autre** from one week to the next; (*incessamment*) any week now; **entre autres** (*personnes*) among others; (*choses*) among other things

**autrefois** [otʀəfwa] *adv* in the past
**autrement** [otʀəmɑ̃] *adv* differently; (*d'une manière différente*) in another way; (*sinon*) otherwise; **~ dit** in other words
**Autriche** [otʀiʃ] *nf*: **l'~** Austria; **autrichien, ne** *adj* Austrian ▷ *nm/f*: **Autrichien, ne** Austrian
**autruche** [otʀyʃ] *nf* ostrich
**aux** [o] *prép* +*dét* = **à +les**
**auxiliaire** [oksiljɛʀ] *adj, nm/f* auxiliary
**auxquelles** [okɛl] *prép* +*pron* = **à +lesquelles**
**auxquels** [okɛl] *prép* +*pron* = **à +lesquels**
**avalanche** [avalɑ̃ʃ] *nf* avalanche
**avaler** [avale] *vt* to swallow
**avance** [avɑ̃s] *nf* (*de troupes etc*) advance; progress; (*d'argent*) advance; (*sur un concurrent*) lead; **avances** *nfpl* (*amoureuses*) advances; **(être) en ~** (to be) early; (*sur un programme*) (to be) ahead of schedule; **à l'~, d'~** in advance
**avancé, e** [avɑ̃se] *adj* advanced; (*travail*) well on, well under way
**avancement** [avɑ̃smɑ̃] *nm* (*professionnel*) promotion
**avancer** [avɑ̃se] *vi* to move forward, advance; (*projet, travail*) to make progress; (*montre, réveil*) to be fast; to gain ▷ *vt* to move forward, advance; (*argent*) to advance; (*montre, pendule*) to put forward; **s'avancer** *vi* to move forward, advance; (*fig*) to commit o.s.
**avant** [avɑ̃] *prép, adv* before ▷ *adj inv*: **siège/roue ~** front seat/wheel ▷ *nm* (*d'un véhicule, bâtiment*) front; (*Sport: joueur*) forward; **~ qu'il (ne) parte** before he goes *ou* leaves; **~ de partir** before leaving; **~ tout** (*surtout*) above all; **à l'~** (*dans un véhicule*) in (the) front; **en ~** (*se pencher, tomber*) forward(s); **partir en ~** to go on ahead; **en ~ de** in front of
**avantage** [avɑ̃taʒ] *nm* advantage; **avantages sociaux** fringe benefits; **avantager** *vt* (*favoriser*) to favour; (*embellir*) to flatter; **avantageux, -euse** *adj* (*prix*) attractive
**avant...**: **avant-bras** *nm inv* forearm; **avant-coureur** *adj inv*: **signe avant-**

**coureur** advance indication *ou* sign; **avant-dernier, -ière** *adj, nm/f* next to last, last but one; **avant-goût** *nm* foretaste; **avant-hier** *adv* the day before yesterday; **avant-première** *nf (de film)* preview; **avant-veille** *nf*: **l'avant-veille** two days before

**avare** [avaʀ] *adj* miserly, avaricious ▷ *nm/f* miser; **~ de** *(compliments etc)* sparing of

**avec** [avɛk] *prép* with; *(à l'égard de)* to(wards), with; **et ~ ça?** *(dans magasin)* anything else?

**avenir** [avniʀ] *nm* future; **à l'~** in future; **politicien/métier d'~** politician/job with prospects *ou* a future

**aventure** [avɑ̃tyʀ] *nf* adventure; *(amoureuse)* affair; **aventureux, -euse** *adj* adventurous, venturesome; *(projet)* risky, chancy

**avenue** [avny] *nf* avenue

**avérer** [aveʀe]: **s'avérer** *vb +attrib* to prove (to be)

**averse** [avɛʀs] *nf* shower

**averti, e** [avɛʀti] *adj* (well-)informed

**avertir** [avɛʀtiʀ] *vt*: **~ qn (de qch/que)** to warn sb (of sth/that); *(renseigner)* to inform sb (of sth/that); **avertissement** *nm* warning; **avertisseur** *nm* horn, siren

**aveu, x** [avø] *nm* confession

**aveugle** [avœgl] *adj* blind ▷ *nm/f* blind man/woman

**aviation** [avjasjɔ̃] *nf* aviation; *(sport)* flying; *(Mil)* air force

**avide** [avid] *adj* eager; *(péj)* greedy, grasping

**avion** [avjɔ̃] *nm* (aero)plane *(BRIT)*, (air)plane *(US)*; **aller (quelque part) en ~** to go (somewhere) by plane, fly (somewhere); **par ~** by airmail; **avion à réaction** jet (plane)

**aviron** [aviʀɔ̃] *nm* oar; *(sport)*: **l'~** rowing

**avis** [avi] *nm* opinion; *(notification)* notice; **à mon ~** in my opinion; **changer d'~** to change one's mind;

jusqu'à nouvel ~ until further notice

**aviser** [avize] *vt (informer)*: **~ qn de/que** to advise *ou* inform sb of/that ▷ *vi* to think about things, assess the situation; **nous ~ons sur place** we'll work something out once we're there; **s'~ de qch/que** to become suddenly aware of sth/that; **s'~ de faire** to take it into one's head to do

**avocat, e** [avɔka, at] *nm/f (Jur)* barrister *(BRIT)*, lawyer ▷ *nm (Culin)* avocado (pear); **~ de la défense** counsel for the defence; **avocat général** assistant public prosecutor

**avoine** [avwan] *nf* oats *pl*

**MOT-CLÉ**

**avoir** [avwaʀ] *nm* assets *pl*, resources *pl*; *(Comm)* credit
▷ *vt* **1** *(posséder)* to have; **elle a 2 enfants/une belle maison** she has (got) 2 children/a lovely house; **il a les yeux bleus** he has (got) blue eyes; **vous avez du sel?** do you have any salt?; **avoir du courage/de la patience** to be brave/patient

**2** *(âge, dimensions)* to be; **il a 3 ans** he is 3 (years old); **le mur a 3 mètres de haut** the wall is 3 metres high; *voir aussi* **faim; peur** *etc*

**3** *(fam: duper)* to do, have; **on vous a eu!** *(dupé)* you've been done *ou* had!; *(fait une plaisanterie)* we *ou* they had you there

**4**: **en avoir après** *ou* **contre qn** to have a grudge against sb; **en avoir assez** to be fed up; **j'en ai pour une demi-heure** it'll take me half an hour

**5** *(obtenir, attraper)* to get; **j'ai réussi à avoir mon train** I managed to get *ou* catch my train; **j'ai réussi à avoir le renseignement qu'il me fallait** I managed to get (hold of) the information I needed

**6** *(éprouver)*: **avoir de la peine** to be *ou* feel sad

▷ *vb aux* **1** to have; **avoir mangé/dormi**

to have eaten/slept
**2** (*avoir +à +infinitif*): **avoir à faire qch**
to have to do sth; **vous n'avez qu'à lui
demander** you only have to ask him
▷ *vb impers* **1**: **il y a** (+ *singulier*) there is; (+
*pluriel*) there are; **il y avait du café/des
gâteaux** there was coffee/there were
cakes; **qu'y-a-t-il?, qu'est-ce qu'il y a?**
what's the matter?, what is it?; **il doit
y avoir une explication** there must be
an explanation; **il n'y a qu'à ...** we (*ou*
you *etc*) will just have to ...; **il ne peut y
en avoir qu'un** there can only be one
**2** (*temporel*): **il y a 10 ans** 10 years ago;
**il y a 10 ans/longtemps que je le sais**
I've known it for 10 years/a long time; **il
y a 10 ans qu'il est arrivé** it's 10 years
since he arrived

**avortement** [avɔʀtəmɑ̃] *nm* abortion
**avouer** [avwe] *vt* (*crime, défaut*) to
confess (to); **~ avoir fait/que** to admit
*ou* confess to having done/that
**avril** [avʀil] *nm* April
**axe** [aks] *nm* axis; (*de roue etc*) axle;
(*fig*) main line; **axe routier** main road,
trunk road (ʙʀɪᴛ), highway (ᴜs)
**ayons** *etc* [ɛjɔ̃] *vb voir* **avoir**

**bâbord** [babɔʀ] *nm*: **à ~** to port, on the
port side
**baby-foot** [babifut] *nm* table football
**bac** [bak] *abr m* = **baccalauréat** ▷ *nm*
(*récipient*) tub
**baccalauréat** [bakalɔʀea] *nm* high
school diploma
**bâcler** [bakle] *vt* to botch (up)
**baffe** [baf] (*fam*) *nf* slap, clout
**bafouiller** [bafuje] *vi, vt* to stammer
**bagage** [bagaʒ] *nm* piece of luggage;
(*connaissances*) background,
knowledge; **nos ~s ne sont pas arrivés**
our luggage hasn't arrived; **bagage à
main** piece of hand-luggage
**bagarre** [bagaʀ] *nf* fight, brawl;
**bagarrer: se bagarrer** *vi* to have a
fight *ou* scuffle, fight
**bagnole** [baɲɔl] (*fam*) *nf* car
**bague** [bag] *nf* ring; **bague de
fiançailles** engagement ring
**baguette** [bagɛt] *nf* stick; (*cuisine
chinoise*) chopstick; (*de chef d'orchestre*)
baton; (*pain*) stick of (French) bread;

**baguette magique** magic wand
**baie** [bɛ] *nf* (*Géo*) bay; (*fruit*) berry; **baie
(vitrée)** picture window
**baignade** [bɛɲad] *nf* bathing; **"~
interdite"** "no bathing"
**baigner** [beɲe] *vt* (*bébé*) to bath;
**se baigner** *vi* to have a swim, go
swimming *ou* bathing; **baignoire** *nf*
bath(tub)
**bail** [baj, bo] (*pl* **baux**) *nm* lease
**bâiller** [baje] *vi* to yawn; (*être ouvert*)
to gape
**bain** [bɛ̃] *nm* bath; **prendre un ~** to
have a bath; **se mettre dans le ~** (*fig*)
to get into it *ou* things; **bain de bouche**
mouthwash; **bain moussant** bubble
bath; **bain de soleil: prendre un bain
de soleil** to sunbathe; **bain-marie** *nm*:
**faire chauffer au bain-marie** (*boîte
etc*) to immerse in boiling water
**baiser** [beze] *nm* kiss ▷ *vt* (*main, front*)
to kiss; (*fam!*) to screw (!)
**baisse** [bɛs] *nf* fall, drop; **être en ~** to be
falling, be declining
**baisser** [bese] *vt* to lower; (*radio,
chauffage*) to turn down ▷ *vi* to fall,
drop, go down; (*vue, santé*) to fail,
dwindle; **se baisser** *vi* to bend down
**bal** [bal] *nm* dance; (*grande soirée*) ball;
**bal costumé** fancy-dress ball
**balade** [balad] (*fam*) *nf* (*à pied*) walk,
stroll; (*en voiture*) drive; **balader** (*fam*):
**se balader** *vi* to go for a walk *ou* stroll;
to go for a drive; **baladeur** *nm* personal
stereo, Walkman®
**balai** [balɛ] *nm* broom, brush
**balance** [balɑ̃s] *nf* scales *pl*; (*signe*):
**la B~** Libra; **balance commerciale**
balance of trade
**balancer** [balɑ̃se] *vt* to swing; (*fam:
lancer*) to fling, chuck; (: *jeter*) to chuck
out; **se balancer** *vi* to swing, rock; **se ~
de** (*fam*) not to care about; **balançoire**
*nf* swing; (*sur pivot*) seesaw
**balayer** [baleje] *vt* (*feuilles etc*) to
sweep up, brush up; (*pièce*) to sweep;
(*objections*) to sweep aside; (*suj:
radar*) to scan; **balayeur, -euse** *nm/f*

roadsweeper
**balbutier** [balbysje] *vi*, *vt* to stammer
**balcon** [balkɔ̃] *nm* balcony; (*Théâtre*)
dress circle; **avez-vous une chambre
avec ~?** do you have a room with a
balcony?
**Bâle** [bɑl] *n* Basle, Basel
**Baléares** [baleaʀ] *nfpl*: **les ~** the
Balearic Islands, the Balearics
**baleine** [balɛn] *nf* whale
**balise** [baliz] *nf* (*Navig*) beacon;
(marker) buoy; (*Aviat*) runway light,
beacon; (*Auto, Ski*) sign, marker; **baliser**
*vt* to mark out (with lights *etc*)
**balle** [bal] *nf* (*de fusil*) bullet; (*de sport*)
ball; (*fam: franc*) franc
**ballerine** [bal(ə)ʀin] *nf* (*danseuse*)
ballet dancer; (*chaussure*) ballet shoe
**ballet** [balɛ] *nm* ballet
**ballon** [balɔ̃] *nm* (*de sport*) ball; (*jouet,
Aviat*) balloon; **ballon de football**
football
**balnéaire** [balneɛʀ] *adj* seaside *cpd*;
**station ~** seaside resort
**balustrade** [balystʀad] *nf* railings
*pl*, handrail
**bambin** [bɑ̃bɛ̃] *nm* little child
**bambou** [bɑ̃bu] *nm* bamboo
**banal, e** [banal] *adj* banal,
commonplace; (*péj*) trite; **banalité**
*nf* banality
**banane** [banan] *nf* banana; (*sac*) waist-
bag, bum-bag
**banc** [bɑ̃] *nm* seat, bench; (*de poissons*)
shoal; **banc d'essai** (*fig*) testing ground
**bancaire** [bɑ̃kɛʀ] *adj* banking; (*chèque,
carte*) bank *cpd*
**bancal, e** [bɑ̃kal] *adj* wobbly
**bandage** [bɑ̃daʒ] *nm* bandage
**bande** [bɑ̃d] *nf* (*de tissu etc*) strip; (*Méd*)
bandage; (*motif*) stripe; (*magnétique etc*)
tape; (*groupe*) band; (: *péj*) bunch; **faire ~
à part** to keep to o.s.; **bande dessinée**
comic strip; **bande sonore** sound track
**bande-annonce** [bɑ̃dɑnɔ̃s] *nf* trailer
**bandeau, x** [bɑ̃do] *nm* headband; (*sur
les yeux*) blindfold
**bander** [bɑ̃de] *vt* (*blessure*) to bandage;

**~ les yeux à qn** to blindfold sb
**bandit** [bãdi] *nm* bandit
**bandoulière** [bãduljɛʀ] *nf:* **en ~** (slung *ou* worn) across the shoulder
**Bangladesh** [bãɡladɛʃ] *nm:* **le ~** Bangladesh
**banlieue** [bãljø] *nf* suburbs *pl;* **lignes/ quartiers de ~** suburban lines/areas; **trains de ~** commuter trains
**bannir** [baniʀ] *vt* to banish
**banque** [bãk] *nf* bank; *(activités)* banking; **banque de données** data bank
**banquet** [bãkɛ] *nm* dinner; *(d'apparat)* banquet
**banquette** [bãkɛt] *nf* seat
**banquier** [bãkje] *nm* banker
**banquise** [bãkiz] *nf* ice field
**baptême** [batɛm] *nm* christening; baptism; **baptême de l'air** first flight
**baptiser** [batize] *vt* to baptize, christen
**bar** [baʀ] *nm* bar
**baraque** [baʀak] *nf* shed; *(fam)* house; *(dans une fête foraine)* stall, booth; **baraqué, e** *(fam) adj* well-built, hefty
**barbare** [baʀbaʀ] *adj* barbaric
**barbe** [baʀb] *nf* beard; **la ~!** *(fam)* damn it!; **quelle ~!** *(fam)* what a drag *ou* bore!; **à la ~ de qn** under sb's nose; **barbe à papa** candy-floss *(BRIT),* cotton candy *(US)*
**barbelé** [baʀbəle] *adj, nm:* **(fil de fer) ~** barbed wire *no pl*
**barbiturique** [baʀbityʀik] *nm* barbiturate
**barbouiller** [baʀbuje] *vt* to daub; **avoir l'estomac barbouillé** to feel queasy
**barbu, e** [baʀby] *adj* bearded
**barder** [baʀde] *(fam) vi:* **ça va ~** sparks will fly, things are going to get hot
**barème** [baʀɛm] *nm (Scol)* scale; *(table de référence)* table
**baril** [baʀi(l)] *nm* barrel; *(poudre)* keg
**bariolé, e** [baʀjɔle] *adj* gaudily-coloured
**baromètre** [baʀɔmɛtʀ] *nm* barometer

**baron, ne** [baʀɔ̃] *nm/f* baron(ess)
**baroque** [baʀɔk] *adj (Art)* baroque; *(fig)* weird
**barque** [baʀk] *nf* small boat
**barquette** [baʀkɛt] *nf (pour repas)* tray; *(pour fruits)* punnet
**barrage** [baʀaʒ] *nm* dam; *(sur route)* roadblock, barricade
**barre** [baʀ] *nf* bar; *(Navig)* helm; *(écrite)* line, stroke
**barreau, x** [baʀo] *nm* bar; *(Jur):* **le ~** the Bar
**barrer** [baʀe] *vt (route etc)* to block; *(mot)* to cross out; *(chèque)* to cross *(BRIT); (Navig)* to steer; **se barrer** *(fam)* ▷ *vi* to clear off
**barrette** [baʀɛt] *nf (pour cheveux)* (hair) slide *(BRIT) ou* clip *(US)*
**barricader** [baʀikade]: **se barricader** *vi* to barricade o.s.
**barrière** [baʀjɛʀ] *nf* fence; *(obstacle)* barrier; *(porte)* gate
**barrique** [baʀik] *nf* barrel, cask
**bar-tabac** [baʀtaba] *nm* bar *(which sells tobacco and stamps)*
**bas, basse** [bɑ, bɑs] *adj* low ▷ *nm* bottom, lower part; *(vêtement)* stocking ▷ *adv* low; *(parler)* softly; **au ~ mot** at the lowest estimate; **en ~** down below; *(d'une liste, d'un mur etc)* at/to the bottom; *(dans une maison)* downstairs; **en ~ de** at the bottom of; **un enfant en ~ âge** a young child; **à ~ ...!** down with ...!
**bas-côté** [bakote] *nm (de route)* verge *(BRIT),* shoulder *(US)*
**basculer** [baskyle] *vi* to fall over, topple (over); *(benne)* to tip up ▷ *vt (contenu)* to tip out; *(benne)* to tip up
**base** [bɑz] *nf* base; *(Pol)* rank and file; *(fondement, principe)* basis; **de ~** basic; **à ~ de café** *etc* coffee *etc* -based; **base de données** database; **baser** *vt* to base; **se baser sur** *vt (preuves)* to base one's argument on
**bas-fond** [bɑfɔ̃] *nm (Navig)* shallow; **bas-fonds** *nmpl (fig)* dregs
**basilic** [bazilik] *nm (Culin)* basil

**basket** [baskɛt] nm trainer (BRIT), sneaker (US); (aussi: **~-ball**) basketball

**basque** [bask] adj Basque ▷ nm/f: **B~** Basque; **le Pays Basque** the Basque Country

**basse** [bas] adj voir **bas** ▷ nf (Mus) bass; **basse-cour** nf farmyard

**bassin** [basɛ̃] nm (pièce d'eau) pond, pool; (de fontaine;: Géo) basin; (Anat) pelvis; (portuaire) dock

**bassine** [basin] nf (ustensile) basin; (contenu) bowl(ful)

**basson** [basɔ̃] nm bassoon

**bat** [ba] vb voir **battre**

**bataille** [bataj] nf (Mil) battle; (rixe) fight; **elle avait les cheveux en ~** her hair was a mess

**bateau, x** [bato] nm boat, ship; **bateau-mouche** nm passenger pleasure boat (on the Seine)

**bâti, e** [bati] adj: **bien ~** well-built; **terrain ~** piece of land that has been built on

**bâtiment** [batimɑ̃] nm building; (Navig) ship, vessel; (industrie) building trade

**bâtir** [batir] vt to build

**bâtisse** [batis] nf building

**bâton** [batɔ̃] nm stick; **parler à ~s rompus** to chat about this and that

**bats** [ba] vb voir **battre**

**battement** [batmɑ̃] nm (de cœur) beat; (intervalle) interval; **10 minutes de ~** 10 minutes to spare

**batterie** [batri] nf (Mil, Élec) battery; (Mus) drums pl, drum kit; **batterie de cuisine** pots and pans pl, kitchen utensils pl

**batteur** [batœr] nm (Mus) drummer; (appareil) whisk

**battre** [batr] vt to beat; (blé) to thresh; (passer au peigne fin) to scour; (cartes) to shuffle ▷ vi (cœur) to beat; (volets etc) to bang, rattle; **se battre** vi to fight; **~ la mesure** to beat time; **~ son plein** to be at its height, be going full swing; **~ des mains** to clap one's hands

**baume** [bom] nm balm

**bavard, e** [bavar, ard] adj (very) talkative; gossipy; **bavarder** vi to chatter; (commérer) to gossip; (divulguer un secret) to blab

**baver** [bave] vi to dribble; (chien) to slobber; **en ~** (fam) to have a hard time (of it)

**bavoir** [bavwar] nm bib

**bavure** [bavyr] nf smudge; (fig) hitch; (policière etc) blunder

**bazar** [bazar] nm general store; (fam) jumble; **bazarder** (fam) vt to chuck out

**BCBG** sigle adj (= bon chic bon genre) preppy, smart and trendy

**BD** sigle f = **bande dessinée**

**bd** abr = **boulevard**

**béant, e** [beɑ̃, ɑ̃t] adj gaping

**beau, bel, belle** [bo, bɛl] (mpl **~x**) adj beautiful, lovely; (homme) handsome; (femme) beautiful ▷ adv: **il fait ~** the weather's fine ▷ nm: **faire le ~** (chien) to sit up and beg; **un ~ jour** one (fine) day; **de plus belle** more than ever, even more; **on a ~ essayer** however hard we try; **bel et bien** well and truly; **le plus ~ c'est que ...** the best of it is that ...

MOT-CLÉ

**beaucoup** [boku] adv **1** a lot; **il boit beaucoup** he drinks a lot; **il ne boit pas beaucoup** he doesn't drink much ou a lot

**2** (suivi de plus, trop etc) much, a lot; **il est beaucoup plus grand** he is much ou a lot taller; **c'est beaucoup plus cher** it's a lot ou much more expensive; **il a beaucoup plus de temps que moi** he has much ou a lot more time than me; **il y a beaucoup plus de touristes ici** there are a lot ou many more tourists here; **beaucoup trop vite** much too fast; **il fume beaucoup trop** he smokes far too much

**3**: **beaucoup de** (nombre) many, a lot of; (quantité) a lot of; **beaucoup d'étudiants/de touristes** a lot of ou many students/tourists; **beaucoup**

**de courage** a lot of courage; **il n'a pas beaucoup d'argent** he hasn't got much *ou* at lot of money
**4: de beaucoup** by far

**beau...: beau-fils** *nm* son-in-law; *(remariage)* stepson; **beau-frère** *nm* brother-in-law; **beau-père** *nm* father-in-law; *(remariage)* stepfather
**beauté** [bote] *nf* beauty; **de toute ~** beautiful; **finir qch en ~** to complete sth brilliantly
**beaux-arts** [bozar] *nmpl* fine arts
**beaux-parents** [boparã] *nmpl* wife's/husband's family, in-laws
**bébé** [bebe] *nm* baby
**bec** [bɛk] *nm* beak, bill; *(de théière)* spout; *(de casserole)* lip; *(fam)* mouth; **bec de gaz** (street) gaslamp
**bêche** [bɛʃ] *nf* spade; **bêcher** *vt* to dig
**bedaine** [bədɛn] *nf* paunch
**bedonnant, e** [bədɔnã, ãt] *adj* potbellied
**bée** [be] *adj:* **bouche ~** gaping
**bégayer** [begeje] *vt, vi* to stammer
**beige** [bɛʒ] *adj* beige
**beignet** [bɛɲɛ] *nm* fritter
**bel** [bɛl] *adj voir* **beau**
**bêler** [bele] *vi* to bleat
**belette** [bəlɛt] *nf* weasel
**belge** [bɛlʒ] *adj* Belgian ▷ *nm/f:* **B~** Belgian
**Belgique** [bɛlʒik] *nf:* **la ~** Belgium
**bélier** [belje] *nm* ram; *(signe):* **le B~** Aries
**belle** [bɛl] *adj voir* **beau** ▷ *nf (Sport):* **la ~** the decider; **belle-fille** *nf* daughter-in-law; *(remariage)* stepdaughter; **belle-mère** *nf* mother-in-law; stepmother; **belle-sœur** *nf* sister-in-law
**belvédère** [bɛlvedɛr] *nm* panoramic viewpoint *(or small building there)*
**bémol** [bemɔl] *nm (Mus)* flat
**bénédiction** [benediksjɔ̃] *nf* blessing
**bénéfice** [benefis] *nm (Comm)* profit; *(avantage)* benefit; **bénéficier: bénéficier de** *vt* to enjoy; *(situation)* to benefit by *ou* from; **bénéfique** *adj* beneficial

**Benelux** [benelyks] *nm:* **le ~** Benelux, the Benelux countries
**bénévole** [benevɔl] *adj* voluntary, unpaid
**bénin, -igne** [benɛ̃, iɲ] *adj* minor, mild; *(tumeur)* benign
**bénir** [benir] *vt* to bless; **bénit, e** *adj* consecrated; **eau bénite** holy water
**benne** [bɛn] *nf* skip; *(de téléphérique)* (cable) car; **benne à ordures** *(amovible)* skip
**béquille** [bekij] *nf* crutch; *(de bicyclette)* stand
**berceau, x** [bɛrso] *nm* cradle, crib
**bercer** [bɛrse] *vt* to rock, cradle; *(suj: musique etc)* to lull; **~ qn de** *(promesses etc)* to delude sb with; **berceuse** *nf* lullaby
**béret** [berɛ] *nm (aussi:* **~ basque)** beret
**berge** [bɛrʒ] *nf* bank
**berger, -ère** [bɛrʒe, ɛr] *nm/f* shepherd(-ess); **berger allemand** alsatian *(brit)*, German shepherd
**Berlin** [bɛrlɛ̃] *n* Berlin
**Bermudes** [bɛrmyd] *nfpl:* **les (îles) ~** Bermuda
**Berne** [bɛrn(ə)] *n* Bern
**berner** [bɛrne] *vt* to fool
**besogne** [bəzɔɲ] *nf* work *no pl,* job
**besoin** [bəzwɛ̃] *nm* need; **avoir ~ de qch/faire qch** to need sth/to do sth; **au ~** if need be; **le ~** *(pauvreté)* need, want; **être dans le ~** to be in need *ou* want; **faire ses ~s** to relieve o.s.
**bestiole** [bɛstjɔl] *nf* (tiny) creature
**bétail** [betaj] *nm* livestock, cattle *pl*
**bête** [bɛt] *nf* animal; *(bestiole)* insect, creature ▷ *adj* stupid, silly; **il cherche la petite ~** he's being pernickety *ou* over fussy; **bête noire** pet hate; **bête sauvage** wild beast *ou* animal
**bêtise** [betiz] *nf* stupidity; *(action)* stupid thing (to say *ou* do)
**béton** [betɔ̃] *nm* concrete; **(en) ~** *(alibi, argument)* cast iron; **béton armé** reinforced concrete
**betterave** [bɛtrav] *nf* beetroot *(brit),* beet *(us);* **betterave sucrière**

sugar beet

**Beur** [bœʀ] *nm/f* person of North African origin living in France

**beurre** [bœʀ] *nm* butter; **beurrer** *vt* to butter; **beurrier** *nm* butter dish

**biais** [bjɛ] *nm* (*moyen*) device, expedient; (*aspect*) angle; **en ~, de ~** (*obliquement*) at an angle; **par le ~ de** by means of

**bibelot** [biblo] *nm* trinket, curio

**biberon** [bibʀɔ̃] *nm* (feeding) bottle; **nourrir au ~** to bottle-feed

**bible** [bibl] *nf* bible

**biblio...** [bibl] *préfixe*: **bibliobus** *nm* mobile library van; **bibliothécaire** *nm/f* librarian; **bibliothèque** *nf* library; (*meuble*) bookcase

**bic®** [bik] *nm* Biro®

**bicarbonate** [bikaʀbɔnat] *nm*: **~ (de soude)** bicarbonate of soda

**biceps** [bisɛps] *nm* biceps

**biche** [biʃ] *nf* doe

**bicolore** [bikɔlɔʀ] *adj* two-coloured

**bicoque** [bikɔk] (*péj*) *nf* shack

**bicyclette** [bisiklɛt] *nf* bicycle

**bidet** [bidɛ] *nm* bidet

**bidon** [bidɔ̃] *nm* can ▷ *adj inv* (*fam*) phoney

**bidonville** [bidɔ̃vil] *nm* shanty town

**bidule** [bidyl] (*fam*) *nm* thingumajig

**O** MOT-CLÉ

**bien** [bjɛ̃] *nm* 1 (*avantage, profit*): **faire du bien à qn** to do sb good; **dire du bien de** to speak well of; **c'est pour son bien** it's for his own good

2 (*possession, patrimoine*) possession, property; **son bien le plus précieux** his most treasured possession; **avoir du bien** to have property; **biens (de consommation** *etc***)** (consumer *etc*) goods

3 (*moral*): **le bien** good; **distinguer le bien du mal** to tell good from evil ▷ *adv* 1 (*de façon satisfaisante*) well; **elle travaille/mange bien** she works/eats well; **croyant bien faire, je/il ...** thinking I/he was doing the right thing, I/he ...; **tiens-toi bien!** (*assieds-toi correctement*) sit up straight!; (*debout*) stand up straight!; (*sois sage*) behave yourself!; (*prépare-toi*) wait for it!; **c'est bien fait!** it serves him (*ou* her *etc*) right!

2 (*valeur intensive*) quite; **bien jeune** quite young; **bien assez** quite enough; **bien mieux** (very) much better; **j'espère bien y aller** I do hope to go; **je veux bien le faire** (*concession*) I'm quite willing to do it; **il faut bien le faire** it has to be done; **Paul est bien venu, n'est-ce pas?** Paul did come, didn't he?; **où peut-il bien être passé?** where can he have got to?

3 (*beaucoup*): **bien du temps/des gens** quite a time/a number of people

4 (*au moins*) at least; **cela fait bien deux ans que je ne l'ai pas vu** I haven't seen him for at least *ou* a good two years ▷ *adj inv* 1 (*en bonne forme, à l'aise*): **je me sens bien** I feel fine; **je ne me sens pas bien** I don't feel well; **on est bien dans ce fauteuil** this chair is very comfortable

2 (*joli, beau*) good-looking; **tu es bien dans cette robe** you look good in that dress

3 (*satisfaisant*) good; **elle est bien, cette maison/secrétaire** it's a good house/she's a good secretary; **c'est bien?** is that *ou* it O.K.?; **c'est très bien (comme ça)** it's fine (like that)

4 (*moralement*) right; (: *personne*) good, nice; (*respectable*) respectable; **ce n'est pas bien de ...** it's not right to ...; **elle est bien, cette femme** she's a nice woman, she's a good sort; **des gens bien** respectable people

5 (*en bons termes*): **être bien avec qn** to be on good terms with sb ▷ *préfixe*: **bien-aimé, e** *adj, nm/f* beloved; **bien-être** *nm* well-being; **bienfaisance** *nf* charity; **bienfait** *nm* act of generosity, benefaction; (*de la science etc*) benefit; **bienfaiteur, -trice**

*nm/f* benefactor/benefactress; **bien-fondé** *nm* soundness; **bien que** *conj* (al)though; **bien sûr** *adv* certainly

**bientôt** [bjɛ̃to] *adv* soon; **à ~** see you soon

**bienveillant, e** [bjɛ̃vɛjɑ̃, ɑ̃t] *adj* kindly

**bienvenu, e** [bjɛ̃vny] *adj* welcome; **bienvenue** *nf*: **souhaiter la bienvenue à** to welcome; **bienvenue à** welcome to

**bière** [bjɛʀ] *nf* (*boisson*) beer; (*cercueil*) bier; **bière blonde** lager; **bière brune** brown ale (BRIT), dark beer (US); **bière (à la) pression** draught beer

**bifteck** [biftɛk] *nm* steak

**bigorneau, x** [bigɔʀno] *nm* winkle

**bigoudi** [bigudi] *nm* curler

**bijou, x** [biʒu] *nm* jewel; **bijouterie** *nf* jeweller's (shop); **bijoutier, -ière** *nm/f* jeweller

**bikini** [bikini] *nm* bikini

**bilan** [bilɑ̃] *nm* (*fig*) (net) outcome; (: *de victimes*) toll; (*Comm*) balance sheet(s); **un ~ de santé** a (medical) checkup; **faire le ~ de** to assess, review; **déposer son ~** to file a bankruptcy statement

**bile** [bil] *nf* bile; **se faire de la ~** (*fam*) to worry o.s. sick

**bilieux, -euse** [biljø, øz] *adj* bilious; (*fig: colérique*) testy

**bilingue** [bilɛ̃g] *adj* bilingual

**billard** [bijaʀ] *nm* (*jeu*) billiards *sg*; (*table*) billiard table

**bille** [bij] *nf* (*gén*) ball; (*du jeu de billes*) marble

**billet** [bijɛ] *nm* (*aussi:* **~ de banque**) (bank)note; (*de cinéma, de bus etc*) ticket; (*courte lettre*) note; **billet électronique** e-ticket; **billetterie** *nf* ticket office; (*distributeur*) ticket machine; (*Banque*) cash dispenser

**billion** [biljɔ̃] *nm* billion (BRIT), trillion (US)

**bimensuel, le** [bimɑ̃sɥɛl] *adj* bimonthly

**bio** [bjo] *adj inv* organic

**bio...** [bjo] *préfixe* bio...; **biochimie**

*nf* biochemistry; **biographie** *nf* biography; **biologie** *nf* biology; **biologique** *adj* biological; (*produits, aliments*) organic; **biométrie** *nf* biometrics; **biotechnologie** *nf* biotechnology; **bioterrorisme** *nm* bioterrorism

**Birmanie** [biʀmani] *nf* Burma

**bis** [bis] *adv*: **12 ~** 12a *ou* A ▷ *excl*, *nm* encore

**biscotte** [biskɔt] *nf* toasted bread (*sold in packets*)

**biscuit** [biskɥi] *nm* biscuit (BRIT), cookie (US)

**bise** [biz] *nf* (*fam: baiser*) kiss; (*vent*) North wind; **grosses ~s (de)** (*sur lettre*) love and kisses (from)

**bisexuel, le** [bisɛksɥɛl] *adj* bisexual

**bisou** [bizu] (*fam*) *nm* kiss

**bissextile** [bisɛkstil] *adj*: **année ~** leap year

**bistro(t)** [bistʀo] *nm* bistro, café

**bitume** [bitym] *nm* asphalt

**bizarre** [bizaʀ] *adj* strange, odd

**blague** [blag] *nf* (*propos*) joke; (*farce*) trick; **sans ~!** no kidding!; **blaguer** *vi* to joke

**blaireau, x** [blɛʀo] *nm* (*Zool*) badger; (*brosse*) shaving brush

**blâme** [blɑm] *nm* blame; (*sanction*) reprimand; **blâmer** *vt* to blame

**blanc, blanche** [blɑ̃, blɑ̃ʃ] *adj* white; (*non imprimé*) blank ▷ *nm/f* white, white man(-woman) ▷ *nm* (*couleur*) white; (*espace non écrit*) blank; (*aussi:* **~ d'œuf**) (egg-)white; (*aussi:* **~ de poulet**) breast, white meat; (*aussi:* **vin ~**) white wine; **~ cassé** off-white; **chèque en ~** blank cheque; **à ~** (*chauffer*) white-hot; (*tirer, charger*) with blanks; **blanche** *nf* (*Mus*) minim (BRIT), half-note (US); **blancheur** *nf* whiteness

**blanchir** [blɑ̃ʃiʀ] *vt* (*gén*) to whiten; (*linge*) to launder; (*Culin*) to blanch; (*fig: disculper*) to clear ▷ *vi* (*cheveux*) to go white; **blanchisserie** *nf* laundry

**blason** [blazɔ̃] *nm* coat of arms

**blasphème** [blasfɛm] *nm* blasphemy

**blazer** [blazɛʀ] *nm* blazer
**blé** [ble] *nm* wheat; **blé noir** buckwheat
**bled** [blɛd] (*péj*) *nm* hole
**blême** [blɛm] *adj* pale
**blessé, e** [blese] *adj* injured ▷ *nm/f*
injured person, casualty
**blesser** [blese] *vt* to injure;
(*délibérément*) to wound; (*offenser*) to
hurt; **se blesser** to injure o.s.; **se ~
au pied** to injure one's foot; **blessure**
*nf* (*accidentelle*) injury; (*intentionnelle*)
wound
**bleu, e** [blø] *adj* blue; (*bifteck*) very rare
▷ *nm* (*couleur*) blue; (*contusion*) bruise;
(*vêtement: aussi: ~s*) overalls *pl*; (*fromage*)
blue cheese; **bleu marine** navy blue;
**bleuet** *nm* cornflower
**bloc** [blɔk] *nm* (*de pierre etc*) block; (*de
papier à lettres*) pad; (*ensemble*) group,
block; **serré à ~** tightened right down;
**en ~** as a whole; **bloc opératoire**
operating *ou* theatre block; **blocage**
*nm* (*des prix*) freezing; (*Psych*) hang-up;
**bloc-notes** *nm* note pad
**blog, blogue** [blɔg] *nm* blog; **bloguer**
*vi* to blog
**blond, e** [blɔ̃, blɔ̃d] *adj* fair, blond;
(*sable, blés*) golden
**bloquer** [blɔke] *vt* (*passage*) to block;
(*pièce mobile*) to jam; (*crédits, compte*)
to freeze
**blottir** [blɔtiʀ]: **se blottir** *vi* to
huddle up
**blouse** [bluz] *nf* overall
**blouson** [bluzɔ̃] *nm* blouson jacket;
**blouson noir** (*fig*) ≈ rocker
**bluff** [blœf] *nm* bluff
**bobine** [bɔbin] *nf* reel; (*Élec*) coil
**bobo** [bɔbo] *abr m/f* = *bourgeois bohème*
(*fam*) boho
**bocal, -aux** [bɔkal, o] *nm* jar
**bock** [bɔk] *nm* glass of beer
**bœuf** [bœf] *nm* ox; (*Culin*) beef
**bof** [bɔf] (*fam*) *excl* don't care!; (*pas
terrible*) nothing special
**bohémien, ne** [bɔemjɛ̃, -ɛn] *nm/f*
gipsy
**boire** [bwaʀ] *vt* to drink; (*s'imprégner
de*) to soak up; **~ un coup** (*fam*) to have
a drink
**bois** [bwɑ] *nm* wood; **de ~, en ~**
wooden; **boisé, e** *adj* woody, wooded
**boisson** [bwasɔ̃] *nf* drink
**boîte** [bwat] *nf* box; (*fam: entreprise*)
firm; **aliments en ~** canned *ou* tinned
(*BRIT*) foods; **boîte à gants** glove
compartment; **boîte à ordures**
dustbin (*BRIT*), trashcan (*US*); **boîte aux
lettres** letter box; **boîte d'allumettes**
box of matches; (*vide*) matchbox; **boîte
de conserves** can *ou* tin (*BRIT*) of food;
**boîte (de nuit)** night club; **boîte de
vitesses** gear box; **boîte postale** PO
Box; **boîte vocale** (*Tél*) voice mail
**boiter** [bwate] *vi* to limp; (*fig:
raisonnement*) to be shaky
**boîtier** [bwatje] *nm* case
**boive** *etc* [bwav] *vb voir* **boire**
**bol** [bɔl] *nm* bowl; **un ~ d'air** a breath of
fresh air; **j'en ai ras le ~** (*fam*) I'm fed up
with this; **avoir du ~** (*fam*) to be lucky
**bombarder** [bɔ̃baʀde] *vt* to bomb;
**~ qn de** (*cailloux, lettres*) to bombard
sb with
**bombe** [bɔ̃b] *nf* bomb; (*atomiseur*)
(aerosol) spray

**MOT-CLÉ**

**bon, bonne** [bɔ̃, bɔn] *adj* 1 (*agréable,
satisfaisant*) good; **un bon repas/
restaurant** a good meal/restaurant;
**être bon en maths** to be good at
maths (*BRIT*) *ou* math (*US*)
2 (*charitable*): **être bon (envers)** to be
good (to)
3 (*correct*) right; **le bon numéro/
moment** the right number/moment
4 (*souhaits*): **bon anniversaire!** happy
birthday!; **bon voyage!** have a good
trip!; **bonne chance!** good luck!; **bonne
année!** happy New Year!; **bonne nuit!**
good night!
5 (*approprié, apte*): **bon à/pour** fit
to/for; **à quoi bon?** what's the use?
6: **bon enfant** *adj inv* accommodating,

easy-going; **bonne femme** (*péj*) woman; **de bonne heure** early; **bon marché** *adj inv, adv* cheap; **bon mot** witticism; **bon sens** common sense; **bon vivant** jovial chap; **bonnes œuvres** charitable works, charities ▷ *nm* **1** (*billet*) voucher; (*aussi*: **bon cadeau**) gift voucher; **bon d'essence** petrol coupon; **bon du Trésor** Treasury bond

**2**: **avoir du bon** to have its good points; **pour de bon** for good ▷ *adv*: **il fait bon** it's *ou* the weather is fine; **sentir bon** to smell good; **tenir bon** to stand firm ▷ *excl* good!; **ah bon?** really?; **bon, je reste** right then, I'll stay; *voir aussi* **bonne**

**bonbon** [bɔ̃bɔ̃] *nm* (boiled) sweet
**bond** [bɔ̃] *nm* leap; **faire un ~** to leap in the air
**bondé, e** [bɔ̃de] *adj* packed (full)
**bondir** [bɔ̃diʀ] *vi* to leap
**bonheur** [bɔnœʀ] *nm* happiness; **porter ~ (à qn)** to bring (sb) luck; **au petit ~** haphazardly; **par ~** fortunately
**bonhomme** [bɔnɔm] (*pl* **bonshommes**) *nm* fellow; **bonhomme de neige** snowman
**bonjour** [bɔ̃ʒuʀ] *excl, nm* hello; (*selon l'heure*) good morning/afternoon; **c'est simple comme ~!** it's easy as pie!
**bonne** [bɔn] *adj voir* **bon** ▷ *nf* (*domestique*) maid
**bonnet** [bɔnɛ] *nm* hat; (*de soutien-gorge*) cup; **bonnet de bain** bathing cap
**bonsoir** [bɔ̃swaʀ] *excl* good evening
**bonté** [bɔte] *nf* kindness *no pl*
**bonus** [bɔnys] *nm* no-claims bonus; (*de DVD*) extras *pl*
**bord** [bɔʀ] *nm* (*de table, verre, falaise*) edge; (*de rivière, lac*) bank; (*de route*) side; **(monter) à ~** (to go) on board; **jeter par-dessus ~** to throw overboard; **le commandant de/les hommes du ~** the ship's master/crew; **au ~ de la mer** at the seaside; **au ~ de la route** at the

roadside; **être au ~ des larmes** to be on the verge of tears
**bordeaux** [bɔʀdo] *nm* Bordeaux (wine) ▷ *adj inv* maroon
**bordel** [bɔʀdɛl] *nm* brothel; (*fam!*) bloody mess (!)
**border** [bɔʀde] *vt* (*être le long de*) to line; (*qn dans son lit*) to tuck up; (*garnir*): **~ qch de** to edge sth with
**bordure** [bɔʀdyʀ] *nf* border; **en ~ de** on the edge of
**borne** [bɔʀn] *nf* boundary stone; (*aussi*: **~ kilométrique**) kilometre-marker, ≈ milestone; **bornes** *nfpl* (*fig*) limits; **dépasser les ~s** to go too far
**borné, e** [bɔʀne] *adj* (*personne*) narrow-minded
**borner** [bɔʀne] *vt*: **se ~ à faire** (*se contenter de*) to content o.s. with doing; (*se limiter à*) to limit o.s. to doing
**bosniaque** [bɔsnjak] *adj* Bosnian ▷ *nm/f*: **B~** Bosnian
**Bosnie-Herzégovine** [bɔsniɛʀzegɔvin] *nf* Bosnia-Herzegovina
**bosquet** [bɔskɛ] *nm* grove
**bosse** [bɔs] *nf* (*de terrain etc*) bump; (*enflure etc*) lump; (*du bossu, du chameau*) hump; **avoir la ~ des maths** *etc* (*fam*) to have a gift for maths *etc*; **il a roulé sa ~** (*fam*) he's been around
**bosser** [bɔse] (*fam*) *vi* (*travailler*) to work; (*travailler dur*) to slave (away)
**bossu, e** [bɔsy] *nm/f* hunchback
**botanique** [bɔtanik] *nf* botany ▷ *adj* botanic(al)
**botte** [bɔt] *nf* (*soulier*) (high) boot; (*gerbe*): **~ de paille** bundle of straw; **botte de radis/d'asperges** bunch of radishes/asparagus; **bottes de caoutchouc** wellington boots
**bottin** [bɔtɛ̃] *nm* directory
**bottine** [bɔtin] *nf* ankle boot
**bouc** [buk] *nm* goat; (*barbe*) goatee; **bouc émissaire** scapegoat
**boucan** [bukɑ̃] (*fam*) *nm* din, racket
**bouche** [buʃ] *nf* mouth; **faire du ~ à ~ à qn** to give sb the kiss of life *ou* mouth-

to-mouth resuscitation (BRIT); **rester ~ bée** to stand open-mouthed; **bouche d'égout** manhole; **bouche d'incendie** fire hydrant; **bouche de métro** métro entrance

**bouché, e** [buʃe] adj (flacon etc) stoppered; (temps, ciel) overcast; (péj fam: personne) thick (fam); **c'est un secteur ~** there's no future in that area; **avoir le nez ~** to have a blocked(-up) nose; **l'évier est ~** the sink's blocked

**bouchée** [buʃe] nf mouthful; **bouchées à la reine** chicken vol-au-vents

**boucher, -ère** [buʃe] nm/f butcher ▷ vt (trou) to fill up; (obstruer) to block (up); **se boucher** vi (tuyau etc) to block up, get blocked up; **j'ai le nez bouché** my nose is blocked; **se ~ le nez** to hold one's nose; **boucherie** nf butcher's (shop); (fig) slaughter

**bouchon** [buʃɔ̃] nm stopper; (de tube) top; (en liège) cork; (fig: embouteillage) holdup; (Pêche) float

**boucle** [bukl] nf (forme, figure) loop; (objet) buckle; **boucle (de cheveux)** curl; **boucle d'oreille** earring

**bouclé, e** [bukle] adj (cheveux) curly

**boucler** [bukle] vt (fermer: ceinture etc) to fasten; (terminer) to finish off; (fam: enfermer) to shut away; (quartier) to seal off ▷ vi to curl

**bouder** [bude] vi to sulk ▷ vt to stay away from

**boudin** [budɛ̃] nm: **~ (noir)** black pudding; **boudin blanc** white pudding

**boue** [bu] nf mud

**bouée** [bwe] nf buoy; **bouée (de sauvetage)** lifebuoy

**boueux, -euse** [bwø, øz] adj muddy

**bouffe** [buf] (fam) nf grub (fam), food

**bouffée** [bufe] nf (de cigarette) puff; **une ~ d'air pur** a breath of fresh air; **bouffée de chaleur** hot flush (BRIT) ou flash (US)

**bouffer** [bufe] (fam) vi to eat

**bouffi, e** [bufi] adj swollen

**bouger** [buʒe] vi to move; (dent etc) to be loose; (s'activer) to get moving ▷ vt

to move; **les prix/les couleurs n'ont pas bougé** prices/colours haven't changed

**bougie** [buʒi] nf candle; (Auto) spark(ing) plug

**bouillabaisse** [bujabɛs] nf type of fish soup

**bouillant, e** [bujɑ̃, ɑ̃t] adj (qui bout) boiling; (très chaud) boiling (hot)

**bouillie** [buji] nf (de bébé) cereal; **en ~** (fig) crushed

**bouillir** [bujiʀ] vi, vt to boil; **~ d'impatience** to seethe with impatience

**bouilloire** [bujwaʀ] nf kettle

**bouillon** [bujɔ̃] nm (Culin) stock no pl; **bouillonner** vi to bubble; (fig: idées) to bubble up

**bouillotte** [bujɔt] nf hot-water bottle

**boulanger, -ère** [bulɑ̃ʒe, ɛʀ] nm/f baker; **boulangerie** nf bakery

**boule** [bul] nf (gén) ball; (de pétanque) bowl; **boule de neige** snowball

**boulette** [bulɛt] nf (de viande) meatball

**boulevard** [bulvaʀ] nm boulevard

**bouleversement** [bulvɛʀsəmɑ̃] nm upheaval

**bouleverser** [bulvɛʀse] vt (émouvoir) to overwhelm; (causer du chagrin) to distress; (pays, vie) to disrupt; (papiers, objets) to turn upside down

**boulimie** [bulimi] nf bulimia

**boulimique** [bulimik] adj bulimic

**boulon** [bulɔ̃] nm bolt

**boulot, te** [bulo, ɔt] adj plump, tubby ▷ nm (fam: travail) work

**boum** [bum] nm bang ▷ nf (fam) party

**bouquet** [bukɛ] nm (de fleurs) bunch (of flowers), bouquet; (de persil etc) bunch; **c'est le ~!** (fam) that takes the biscuit!

**bouquin** [bukɛ̃] (fam) nm book; **bouquiner** (fam) vi to read

**bourdon** [buʀdɔ̃] nm bumblebee

**bourg** [buʀ] nm small market town

**bourgeois, e** [buʀʒwa, waz] (péj) adj ≈ (upper) middle class; **bourgeoisie** nf ≈ upper middle classes pl

**bourgeon** [buʀʒɔ̃] nm bud

**Bourgogne** [buʀɡɔɲ] *nf*: **la ~** Burgundy ▷ *nm*: **bourgogne** burgundy (wine)

**bourguignon, ne** [buʀɡiɲɔ̃, ɔn] *adj* of *ou* from Burgundy, Burgundian

**bourrasque** [buʀask] *nf* squall

**bourratif, -ive** [buʀatif, iv] *(fam) adj* filling, stodgy *(pej)*

**bourré, e** [buʀe] *adj (fam: ivre)* plastered, tanked up *(BRIT)*; *(rempli)*: **~ de** crammed full of

**bourrer** [buʀe] *vt (pipe)* to fill; *(poêle)* to pack; *(valise)* to cram (full)

**bourru, e** [buʀy] *adj* surly, gruff

**bourse** [buʀs] *nf (subvention)* grant; *(porte-monnaie)* purse; **la B~** the Stock Exchange

**bous** [bu] *vb voir* **bouillir**

**bousculade** [buskylad] *nf (hâte)* rush; *(cohue)* crush; **bousculer** *vt (heurter)* to knock into; *(fig)* to push, rush

**boussole** [busɔl] *nf* compass

**bout** [bu] *vb voir* **bouillir** ▷ *nm* bit; *(d'un bâton etc)* tip; *(d'une ficelle, table, rue, période)* end; **au ~ de** at the end of, after; **pousser qn à ~** to push sb to the limit; **venir à ~ de** to manage to finish; **à ~ portant** (at) point-blank (range)

**bouteille** [butɛj] *nf* bottle; *(de gaz butane)* cylinder

**boutique** [butik] *nf* shop

**bouton** [butɔ̃] *nm* button; *(sur la peau)* spot; *(Bot)* bud; **boutonner** *vt* to button up; **boutonnière** *nf* buttonhole; **bouton-pression** *nm* press stud

**bovin, e** [bɔvɛ̃, in] *adj* bovine; **bovins** *nmpl* cattle *pl*

**bowling** [buliŋ] *nm* (tenpin) bowling; *(salle)* bowling alley

**boxe** [bɔks] *nf* boxing

**BP** *abr* = **boîte postale**

**bracelet** [bʀaslɛ] *nm* bracelet

**braconnier** [bʀakɔnje] *nm* poacher

**brader** [bʀade] *vt* to sell off; **braderie** *nf* cut-price shop/stall

**braguette** [bʀaɡɛt] *nf* fly *ou* flies *pl (BRIT)*, zipper *(US)*

**braise** [bʀɛz] *nf* embers *pl*

**brancard** [bʀɑ̃kaʀ] *nm (civière)* stretcher; **brancardier** *nm* stretcher-bearer

**branche** [bʀɑ̃ʃ] *nf* branch

**branché, e** [bʀɑ̃ʃe] *(fam) adj* trendy

**brancher** [bʀɑ̃ʃe] *vt* to connect (up); *(en mettant la prise)* to plug in

**brandir** [bʀɑ̃diʀ] *vt* to brandish

**braquer** [bʀake] *vi (Auto)* to turn (the wheel) ▷ *vt (revolver etc)*: **~ qch sur** to aim sth at, point sth at; *(mettre en colère)*: **~ qn** to put sb's back up

**bras** [bʀa] *nm* arm; **~ dessus, ~ dessous** arm in arm; **se retrouver avec qch sur les ~** *(fam)* to be landed with sth; **bras droit** *(fig)* right hand man

**brassard** [bʀasaʀ] *nm* armband

**brasse** [bʀas] *nf (nage)* breast-stroke; **brasse papillon** butterfly (stroke)

**brassée** [bʀase] *nf* armful

**brasser** [bʀase] *vt* to mix; **~ l'argent/ les affaires** to handle a lot of money/business

**brasserie** [bʀasʀi] *nf (restaurant)* café-restaurant; *(usine)* brewery

**brave** [bʀav] *adj (courageux)* brave; *(bon, gentil)* good, kind

**braver** [bʀave] *vt* to defy

**bravo** [bʀavo] *excl* bravo ▷ *nm* cheer

**bravoure** [bʀavuʀ] *nf* bravery

**break** [bʀɛk] *nm (Auto)* estate car

**brebis** [bʀəbi] *nf* ewe; **brebis galeuse** black sheep

**bredouiller** [bʀəduje] *vi, vt* to mumble, stammer

**bref, brève** [bʀɛf, ɛv] *adj* short, brief ▷ *adv* in short; **d'un ton ~** sharply, curtly; **en ~** in short, in brief

**Brésil** [bʀezil] *nm* Brazil

**Bretagne** [bʀətaɲ] *nf* Brittany

**bretelle** [bʀətɛl] *nf (de vêtement, de sac)* strap; *(d'autoroute)* slip road *(BRIT)*, entrance/exit ramp *(US)*; **bretelles** *nfpl (pour pantalon)* braces *(BRIT)*, suspenders *(US)*

**breton, ne** [bʀətɔ̃, ɔn] *adj* Breton ▷ *nm/f*: **B~, ne** Breton

**brève** [bʀɛv] *adj voir* **bref**

**brevet** [bʀəvɛ] *nm* diploma, certificate; **brevet des collèges** *exam taken at the age of 15*; **brevet (d'invention)** patent; **breveté, e** *adj* patented

**bricolage** [bʀikɔlaʒ] *nm*: **le ~** do-it-yourself

**bricoler** [bʀikɔle] *vi* (*petits travaux*) to do DIY jobs; (*passe-temps*) to potter about ▷ *vt* (*réparer*) to fix up; **bricoleur, -euse** *nm/f* handyman(-woman), DIY enthusiast

**bridge** [bʀidʒ] *nm* (*Cartes*) bridge

**brièvement** [bʀijɛvmɑ̃] *adv* briefly

**brigade** [bʀigad] *nf* (*Police*) squad; (*Mil*) brigade; **brigadier** *nm* sergeant

**brillamment** [bʀijamɑ̃] *adv* brilliantly

**brillant, e** [bʀijɑ̃, ɑ̃t] *adj* (*remarquable*) bright; (*luisant*) shiny, shining

**briller** [bʀije] *vi* to shine

**brin** [bʀɛ̃] *nm* (*de laine, ficelle etc*) strand; (*fig*): **un ~ de** a bit of

**brindille** [bʀɛ̃dij] *nf* twig

**brioche** [bʀijɔʃ] *nf* brioche (bun); (*fam: ventre*) paunch

**brique** [bʀik] *nf* brick; (*de lait*) carton

**briquet** [bʀikɛ] *nm* (*cigarette*) lighter

**brise** [bʀiz] *nf* breeze

**briser** [bʀize] *vt* to break; **se briser** *vi* to break

**britannique** [bʀitanik] *adj* British ▷ *nm/f*: **B~** British person, Briton; **les B~s** the British

**brocante** [bʀɔkɑ̃t] *nf* junk, second-hand goods *pl*; **brocanteur, -euse** *nm/f* junkshop owner; junk dealer

**broche** [bʀɔʃ] *nf* brooch; (*Culin*) spit; (*Méd*) pin; **à la ~** spit-roasted

**broché, e** [bʀɔʃe] *adj* (*livre*) paper-backed

**brochet** [bʀɔʃɛ] *nm* pike *inv*

**brochette** [bʀɔʃɛt] *nf* (*ustensile*) skewer; (*plat*) kebab

**brochure** [bʀɔʃyʀ] *nf* pamphlet, brochure, booklet

**broder** [bʀɔde] *vt* to embroider ▷ *vi*: **~ (sur les faits** *ou* **une histoire)** to embroider the facts; **broderie** *nf* embroidery

**bronches** [bʀɔ̃ʃ] *nfpl* bronchial tubes; **bronchite** *nf* bronchitis

**bronze** [bʀɔ̃z] *nm* bronze

**bronzer** [bʀɔ̃ze] *vi* to get a tan; **se bronzer** to sunbathe

**brosse** [bʀɔs] *nf* brush; **coiffé en ~** with a crewcut; **brosse à cheveux** hairbrush; **brosse à dents** toothbrush; **brosse à habits** clothesbrush; **brosser** *vt* (*nettoyer*) to brush; (*fig: tableau etc*) to paint; **se brosser les dents** to brush one's teeth

**brouette** [bʀuɛt] *nf* wheelbarrow

**brouillard** [bʀujaʀ] *nm* fog

**brouiller** [bʀuje] *vt* (*œufs, message*) to scramble; (*idées*) to mix up; (*rendre trouble*) to cloud; (*désunir: amis*) to set at odds; **se brouiller** *vi* (*vue*) to cloud over; (*gens*) **se ~ (avec)** to fall out (with)

**brouillon, ne** [bʀujɔ̃, ɔn] *adj* (*sans soin*) untidy; (*qui manque d'organisation*) disorganized ▷ *nm* draft; **(papier) ~** rough paper

**broussailles** [bʀusaj] *nfpl* undergrowth *sg*; **broussailleux, -euse** *adj* bushy

**brousse** [bʀus] *nf*: **la ~** the bush

**brouter** [bʀute] *vi* to graze

**brugnon** [bʀyɲɔ̃] *nm* (*Bot*) nectarine

**bruiner** [bʀɥine] *vb impers*: **il bruine** it's drizzling, there's a drizzle

**bruit** [bʀɥi] *nm*: **un ~** a noise, a sound; (*fig: rumeur*) a rumour; **le ~** noise; **sans ~** without a sound, noiselessly; **bruit de fond** background noise

**brûlant, e** [bʀylɑ̃, ɑ̃t] *adj* burning; (*liquide*) boiling (hot)

**brûlé, e** [bʀyle] *adj* (*fig: démasqué*) blown ▷ *nm*: **odeur de ~** smell of burning

**brûler** [bʀyle] *vt* to burn; (*suj: eau bouillante*) to scald; (*consommer: électricité, essence*) to use; (*feu rouge, signal*) to go through ▷ *vi* to burn; (*jeu*): **tu brûles!** you're getting hot!; **se brûler** to burn o.s.; (*s'ébouillanter*) to scald o.s.

**brûlure** [bʀylyʀ] *nf* (*lésion*) burn; **brûlures d'estomac** heartburn *sg*

**brume** [bʀym] nf mist

**brun, e** [bʀœ̃, bʀyn] adj (gén, bière) brown; (cheveux, tabac) dark; **elle est ~e** she's got dark hair

**brunch** [bʀœntʃ] nm brunch

**brushing** [bʀœʃiŋ] nm blow-dry

**brusque** [bʀysk] adj abrupt

**brut, e** [bʀyt] adj (minerai, soie) raw; (diamant) rough; (Comm) gross; **(pétrole) ~** crude (oil)

**brutal, e, -aux** [bʀytal, o] adj brutal

**Bruxelles** [bʀysɛl] n Brussels

**bruyamment** [bʀyjamɑ̃] adv noisily

**bruyant, e** [bʀyjɑ̃, ɑ̃t] adj noisy

**bruyère** [bʀyjɛʀ] nf heather

**BTS** sigle m (= brevet de technicien supérieur) vocational training certificate taken at the end of a higher education course

**bu, e** [by] pp de **boire**

**buccal, e, -aux** [bykal, o] adj: **par voie ~e** orally

**bûche** [byʃ] nf log; **prendre une ~** (fig) to come a cropper; **bûche de Noël** Yule log

**bûcher** [byʃe] nm (funéraire) pyre; (supplice) stake ▷ vi (fam) to swot (BRIT), slave (away) ▷ vt (fam) to swot up (BRIT), slave away at

**budget** [bydʒɛ] nm budget

**buée** [bɥe] nf (sur une vitre) mist

**buffet** [byfɛ] nm (meuble) sideboard; (de réception) buffet; **buffet (de gare)** (station) buffet, snack bar

**buis** [bɥi] nm box tree; (bois) box(wood)

**buisson** [bɥisɔ̃] nm bush

**bulbe** [bylb] nm (Bot, Anat) bulb

**Bulgarie** [bylgaʀi] nf Bulgaria

**bulle** [byl] nf bubble

**bulletin** [byltɛ̃] nm (communiqué, journal) bulletin; (Scol) report; **bulletin d'informations** news bulletin; **bulletin (de vote)** ballot paper; **bulletin météorologique** weather report

**bureau, x** [byʀo] nm (meuble) desk; (pièce, service) office; **bureau de change** (foreign) exchange office

ou bureau; **bureau de poste** post office; **bureau de tabac** tobacconist's (shop); **bureaucratie** [byʀokʀasi] nf bureaucracy

**bus¹** [by] vb voir **boire**

**bus²** [bys] nm bus; **à quelle heure part le ~?** what time does the bus leave?

**buste** [byst] nm (torse) chest; (seins) bust

**but¹** [by] vb voir **boire**

**but²** [by(t)] nm (cible) target; (fig) goal, aim; (Football etc) goal; **de ~ en blanc** point-blank; **avoir pour ~ de faire** to aim to do; **dans le ~ de** with the intention of

**butane** [bytan] nm (camping) butane; (usage domestique) Calor gas®

**butiner** [bytine] vi (abeilles) to gather nectar

**buvais** etc [byvɛ] vb voir **boire**

**buvard** [byvaʀ] nm blotter

**buvette** [byvɛt] nf bar

# C

**c'** [s] dét voir **ce**

**ça** [sa] pron (pour désigner) this; (: plus loin) that; (: comme sujet indéfini) it; **ça m'étonne que ...** it surprises me that ...; **comment ça va?** how are you?; **ça va?** (d'accord?) O.K.?, all right?; **où ça?** where's that?; **pourquoi ça?** why's that?; **qui ça?** who's that?; **ça alors!** well really!; **ça fait 10 ans (que)** it's 10 years (since); **c'est ça** that's right; **ça y est** that's it

**cabane** [kaban] nf hut, cabin

**cabaret** [kabaʀɛ] nm night club

**cabillaud** [kabijo] nm cod inv

**cabine** [kabin] nf (de bateau) cabin; (de piscine etc) cubicle; (de camion, train) cab; (d'avion) cockpit; **cabine d'essayage** fitting room; **cabine (téléphonique)** call ou (tele)phone box

**cabinet** [kabinɛ] nm (petite pièce) closet; (de médecin) surgery (BRIT), office (US); (de notaire etc) office; (: clientèle) practice; (Pol) Cabinet; **cabinets** nmpl (w.-c.) toilet sg; **cabinet de toilette** toilet

**câble** [kabl] nm cable; **le ~** (TV) cable television, cablevision (US)

**cacahuète** [kakaɥɛt] nf peanut

**cacao** [kakao] nm cocoa

**cache** [kaʃ] nm mask, card (for masking)

**cache-cache** [kaʃkaʃ] nm: **jouer à ~** to play hide-and-seek

**cachemire** [kaʃmiʀ] nm cashmere

**cacher** [kaʃe] vt to hide, conceal; **se cacher** vi (volontairement) to hide; (être caché) to be hidden ou concealed; **~ qch à qn** to hide ou conceal sth from sb

**cachet** [kaʃɛ] nm (comprimé) tablet; (de la poste) postmark; (rétribution) fee; (fig) style, character

**cachette** [kaʃɛt] nf hiding place; **en ~** on the sly, secretly

**cactus** [kaktys] nm cactus

**cadavre** [kadavʀ] nm corpse, (dead) body

**caddie®** [kadi] nm (supermarket) trolley (BRIT), (grocery) cart (US)

**cadeau, x** [kado] nm present, gift; **faire un ~ à qn** to give sb a present ou gift; **faire ~ de qch à qn** to make a present of sth to sb, give sb sth as a present

**cadenas** [kadna] nm padlock

**cadet, te** [kadɛ, ɛt] adj younger; (le plus jeune) youngest ▷ nm/f youngest child ou one

**cadran** [kadʀɑ̃] nm dial; **cadran solaire** sundial

**cadre** [kadʀ] nm frame; (environnement) surroundings pl ▷ nm/f (Admin) managerial employee, executive; **dans le ~ de** (fig) within the framework ou context of

**cafard** [kafaʀ] nm cockroach; **avoir le ~** (fam) to be down in the dumps

**café** [kafe] nm coffee; (bistro) café ▷ adj inv coffee(-coloured); **café au lait** white coffee; **café noir** black coffee; **café tabac** tobacconist's or newsagent's serving coffee and spirits; **cafetière** nf (pot) coffee-pot

**cage** [kaʒ] nf cage; **cage (d'escalier)** stairwell; **cage thoracique** rib cage

**cageot** [kaʒo] nm crate

**cagoule** [kagul] nf (passe-montagne) balaclava

**cahier** [kaje] nm notebook; **cahier de brouillon** jotter (BRIT), rough notebook; **cahier d'exercices** exercise book

**caille** [kaj] nf quail

**caillou, x** [kaju] nm (little) stone; **caillouteux, -euse** adj (route) stony

**Caire** [kɛʀ] nm: **le ~** Cairo

**caisse** [kɛs] nf box; (tiroir où l'on met la recette) till; (où l'on paye) cash desk (BRIT), check-out; (de banque) cashier's desk; **caisse d'épargne** savings bank; **caisse de retraite** pension fund; **caisse enregistreuse** cash register; **caissier, -ière** nm/f cashier

**cake** [kɛk] nm fruit cake

**calandre** [kalɑ̃dʀ] nf radiator grill

**calcaire** [kalkɛʀ] nm limestone ▷ adj (eau) hard; (Géo) limestone cpd

**calcul** [kalkyl] nm calculation; **le ~** (Scol) arithmetic; **calcul (biliaire)** (gall)stone; **calculatrice** nf calculator; **calculer** vt to calculate, work out; **calculette** nf pocket calculator

**cale** [kal] nf (de bateau) hold; (en bois) wedge

**calé, e** [kale] (fam) adj clever, bright

**caleçon** [kalsɔ̃] nm (d'homme) boxer shorts; (de femme) leggings

**calendrier** [kalɑ̃dʀije] nm calendar; (fig) timetable

**calepin** [kalpɛ̃] nm notebook

**caler** [kale] vt to wedge ▷ vi (moteur, véhicule) to stall

**calibre** [kalibʀ] nm calibre

**câlin, e** [kɑlɛ̃, in] adj cuddly, cuddlesome; (regard, voix) tender

**calmant** [kalmɑ̃] nm tranquillizer, sedative; (pour la douleur) painkiller

**calme** [kalm] adj calm, quiet ▷ nm calm(ness), quietness; **sans perdre son ~** without losing one's cool (inf) ou composure; **calmer** vt to calm (down);

(douleur, inquiétude) to ease, soothe; **se calmer** vi to calm down

**calorie** [kalɔʀi] nf calorie

**camarade** [kamaʀad] nm/f friend, pal; (Pol) comrade

**Cambodge** [kɑ̃bɔdʒ] nm: **le ~** Cambodia

**cambriolage** [kɑ̃bʀijɔlaʒ] nm burglary; **cambrioler** vt to burgle (BRIT), burglarize (US); **cambrioleur, -euse** nm/f burglar

**camelote** [kamlɔt] (fam) nf rubbish, trash, junk

**caméra** [kameʀa] nf (Cinéma, TV) camera; (d'amateur) cine-camera

**Cameroun** [kamʀun] nm: **le ~** Cameroon

**caméscope®** [kameskɔp] nm camcorder®

**camion** [kamjɔ̃] nm lorry (BRIT), truck; **camion de dépannage** breakdown (BRIT) ou tow (US) truck; **camionnette** nf (small) van; **camionneur** nm (chauffeur) lorry (BRIT) ou truck driver; (entrepreneur) haulage contractor (BRIT), trucker (US)

**camomille** [kamɔmij] nf camomile; (boisson) camomile tea

**camp** [kɑ̃] nm camp; (fig) side

**campagnard, e** [kɑ̃paɲaʀ, aʀd] adj country cpd

**campagne** [kɑ̃paɲ] nf country, countryside; (Mil, Pol, Comm) campaign; **à la ~** in the country

**camper** [kɑ̃pe] vi to camp ▷ vt to sketch; **se ~ devant** to plant o.s. in front of; **campeur, -euse** nm/f camper

**camping** [kɑ̃piŋ] nm camping; **faire du ~** to go camping; **(terrain de) camping** campsite, camping site; **camping-car** nm camper, motorhome (US); **camping-gaz®** nm inv camp(ing) stove

**Canada** [kanada] nm: **le ~** Canada; **canadien, ne** adj Canadian ▷ nm/f: **Canadien, ne** Canadian; **canadienne** nf (veste) fur-lined jacket

**canal, -aux** [kanal, o] nm canal;

(naturel, TV) channel; **canalisation** nf (tuyau) pipe

**canapé** [kanape] nm settee, sofa

**canard** [kanaʀ] nm duck; (fam: journal) rag

**cancer** [kɑ̃sɛʀ] nm cancer; (signe): **le C~** Cancer

**cancre** [kɑ̃kʀ] nm dunce

**candidat, e** [kɑ̃dida, at] nm/f candidate; (à un poste) applicant, candidate; **candidature** nf (Pol) candidature; (à poste) application; **poser sa candidature à un poste** to apply for a job

**cane** [kan] nf (female) duck

**canette** [kanɛt] nf (de bière) (flip-top) bottle

**canevas** [kanva] nm (Couture) canvas

**caniche** [kaniʃ] nm poodle

**canicule** [kanikyl] nf scorching heat

**canif** [kanif] nm penknife, pocket knife

**canne** [kan] nf (walking) stick; **canne à pêche** fishing rod; **canne à sucre** sugar cane

**cannelle** [kanɛl] nf cinnamon

**canoë** [kanɔe] nm canoe; (sport) canoeing; **canoë (kayak)** kayak

**canot** [kano] nm ding(h)y; **canot de sauvetage** lifeboat; **canot pneumatique** inflatable ding(h)y

**cantatrice** [kɑ̃tatʀis] nf (opera) singer

**cantine** [kɑ̃tin] nf canteen

**canton** [kɑ̃tɔ̃] nm district consisting of several communes; (en Suisse) canton

**caoutchouc** [kautʃu] nm rubber; **caoutchouc mousse** foam rubber

**cap** [kap] nm (Géo) cape; (promontoire) headland; (fig: tournant) watershed; (Navig): **changer de ~** to change course; **mettre le ~ sur** to head ou steer for

**CAP** sigle m (= Certificat d'aptitude professionnelle) vocational training certificate taken at secondary school

**capable** [kapabl] adj able, capable; **~ de qch/faire** capable of sth/doing

**capacité** [kapasite] nf (compétence) ability; (Jur, contenance) capacity

**cape** [kap] nf cape, cloak; **rire sous ~** to laugh up one's sleeve

**CAPES** [kapɛs] sigle m (= Certificat d'aptitude pédagogique à l'enseignement secondaire) teaching diploma

**capitaine** [kapitɛn] nm captain

**capital, e, -aux** [kapital, o] adj (œuvre) major; (question, rôle) fundamental ▷ nm capital; (fig) stock; **d'une importance ~e** of capital importance; **capitaux** nmpl (fonds) capital sg; **capital (social)** authorized capital; **capitale** nf (ville) capital; (lettre) capital (letter); **capitalisme** nm capitalism; **capitaliste** adj, nm/f capitalist

**caporal, -aux** [kapɔʀal, o] nm lance corporal

**capot** [kapo] nm (Auto) bonnet (BRIT), hood (US)

**câpre** [kɑpʀ] nf caper

**caprice** [kapʀis] nm whim, caprice; **faire des ~s** to make a fuss; **capricieux, -euse** adj (fantasque) capricious, whimsical; (enfant) awkward

**Capricorne** [kapʀikɔʀn] nm: **le ~** Capricorn

**capsule** [kapsyl] nf (de bouteille) cap; (Bot etc, spatiale) capsule

**capter** [kapte] vt (ondes radio) to pick up; (fig) to win, capture

**captivant, e** [kaptivɑ̃, ɑ̃t] adj captivating

**capturer** [kaptyʀe] vt to capture

**capuche** [kapyʃ] nf hood

**capuchon** [kapyʃɔ̃] nm hood; (de stylo) cap, top

**car** [kaʀ] nm coach ▷ conj because, for

**carabine** [kaʀabin] nf rifle

**caractère** [kaʀaktɛʀ] nm (gén) character; **avoir bon/mauvais ~** to be good-/ill-natured; **en ~s gras** in bold type; **en petits ~s** in small print; **~s d'imprimerie** (block) capitals

**caractériser** [kaʀakteʀize] vt to be characteristic of; **se ~ par** to be characterized ou distinguished by

**caractéristique** [kaʀakteʀistik] adj,

*nf* characteristic

**carafe** [kaʁaf] *nf* (*pour eau, vin ordinaire*) carafe

**caraïbe** [kaʁaib] *adj* Caribbean ▷ *n*: **les C~s** the Caribbean (Islands)

**carambolage** [kaʁɑ̃bɔlaʒ] *nm* multiple crash, pileup

**caramel** [kaʁamɛl] *nm* (*bonbon*) caramel, toffee; (*substance*) caramel

**caravane** [kaʁavan] *nf* caravan; **caravaning** *nm* caravanning

**carbone** [kaʁbɔn] *nm* carbon; (*double*) carbon (copy)

**carbonique** [kaʁbɔnik] *adj*: **gaz ~** carbon dioxide; **neige ~** dry ice

**carbonisé, e** [kaʁbɔnize] *adj* charred

**carburant** [kaʁbyʁɑ̃] *nm* (motor) fuel

**carburateur** [kaʁbyʁatœʁ] *nm* carburettor

**cardiaque** [kaʁdjak] *adj* cardiac, heart *cpd* ▷ *nm/f* heart patient; **être ~** to have heart trouble

**cardigan** [kaʁdigɑ̃] *nm* cardigan

**cardiologue** [kaʁdjɔlɔg] *nm/f* cardiologist, heart specialist

**carême** [kaʁɛm] *nm*: **le C~** Lent

**carence** [kaʁɑ̃s] *nf* (*manque*) deficiency

**caresse** [kaʁɛs] *nf* caress

**caresser** [kaʁese] *vt* to caress; (*animal*) to stroke

**cargaison** [kaʁgɛzɔ̃] *nf* cargo, freight

**cargo** [kaʁgo] *nm* cargo boat, freighter

**caricature** [kaʁikatyʁ] *nf* caricature

**carie** [kaʁi] *nf*: **la ~ (dentaire)** tooth decay; **une ~** a bad tooth

**carnaval** [kaʁnaval] *nm* carnival

**carnet** [kaʁnɛ] *nm* (*calepin*) notebook; (*de tickets, timbres etc*) book; **carnet de chèques** cheque book

**carotte** [kaʁɔt] *nf* carrot

**carré, e** [kaʁe] *adj* square; (*fig: franc*) straightforward ▷ *nm* (*Math*) square; **mètre/kilomètre ~** square metre/ kilometre

**carreau, x** [kaʁo] *nm* (*par terre*) (floor) tile; (*au mur*) (wall) tile; (*de fenêtre*) (window) pane; (*motif*) check, square; (*Cartes: couleur*) diamonds *pl*; **tissu à ~x**

checked fabric

**carrefour** [kaʁfuʁ] *nm* crossroads *sg*

**carrelage** [kaʁlaʒ] *nm* (*sol*) (tiled) floor

**carrelet** [kaʁlɛ] *nm* (*poisson*) plaice

**carrément** [kaʁemɑ̃] *adv* (*franchement*) straight out, bluntly; (*sans hésiter*) straight; (*intensif*) completely; **c'est ~ impossible** it's completely impossible

**carrière** [kaʁjɛʁ] *nf* (*métier*) career; (*de roches*) quarry; **militaire de ~** professional soldier

**carrosserie** [kaʁɔsʁi] *nf* body, coachwork *no pl*

**carrure** [kaʁyʁ] *nf* build; (*fig*) stature, calibre

**cartable** [kaʁtabl] *nm* satchel, (school)bag

**carte** [kaʁt] *nf* (*de géographie*) map; (*marine, du ciel*) chart; (*d'abonnement, à jouer*) card; (*au restaurant*) menu; (*aussi:* **~ de visite**) (visiting) card; **pouvez-vous me l'indiquer sur la ~?** can you show me (it) on the map?; **à la ~** (*au restaurant*) à la carte; **est-ce qu'on peut voir la ~?** can we see the menu?; **donner ~ blanche à qn** to give sb a free rein; **carte bancaire** cash card; **Carte Bleue®** debit card; **carte à puce** smart card; **carte de crédit** credit card; **carte de fidélité** loyalty card; **carte d'identité** identity card; **carte de séjour** residence permit; **carte grise** (*Auto*) ≈ (car) registration book, logbook; **carte memoire** (*d'appareil-photo numérique*) memory card; **carte postale** postcard; **carte routière** road map

**carter** [kaʁtɛʁ] *nm* sump

**carton** [kaʁtɔ̃] *nm* (*matériau*) cardboard; (*boîte*) (cardboard) box; **faire un ~** (*fam*) to score a hit; **carton (à dessin)** portfolio

**cartouche** [kaʁtuʃ] *nf* cartridge; (*de cigarettes*) carton

**cas** [kɑ] *nm* case; **ne faire aucun ~ de** to take no notice of; **en aucun ~** on no account; **au ~ où** in case; **en ~ de** in case of, in the event of; **en ~ de besoin**

if need be; **en tout ~** in any case, at any rate

**cascade** [kaskad] *nf* waterfall, cascade

**case** [kɑz] *nf* (*hutte*) hut; (*compartiment*) compartment; (*sur un formulaire, de mots croisés etc*) box

**caser** [kɑze] (*fam*) *vt* (*placer*) to put (away); (*loger*) to put up; **se caser** *vi* (*se marier*) to settle down; (*trouver un emploi*) to find a (steady) job

**caserne** [kazɛʀn] *nf* barracks *pl*

**casier** [kazje] *nm* (*pour courrier*) pigeonhole; (*compartiment*) compartment; (*à clef*) locker; **casier judiciaire** police record

**casino** [kazino] *nm* casino

**casque** [kask] *nm* helmet; (*chez le coiffeur*) (hair-)drier; (*pour audition*) (head-)phones *pl*, headset

**casquette** [kaskɛt] *nf* cap

**casse...**: **casse-croûte** *nm inv* snack; **casse-noix** *nm inv* nutcrackers *pl*; **casse-pieds** (*fam*) *adj inv*: **il est casse-pieds** he's a pain in the neck

**casser** [kɑse] *vt* to break; (*Jur*) to quash; **se casser** *vi* to break; **~ les pieds à qn** (*fam: irriter*) to get on sb's nerves; **se ~ la tête** (*fam*) to go to a lot of trouble

**casserole** [kasʀɔl] *nf* saucepan

**casse-tête** [kɑstɛt] *nm inv* (*difficultés*) headache (*fig*)

**cassette** [kasɛt] *nf* (*bande magnétique*) cassette; (*coffret*) casket

**cassis** [kasis] *nm* blackcurrant

**cassoulet** [kasulɛ] *nm* bean and sausage hot-pot

**catalogue** [katalɔg] *nm* catalogue

**catalytique** [katalitik] *adj*: **pot ~** catalytic convertor

**catastrophe** [katastʀɔf] *nf* catastrophe, disaster

**catéchisme** [kateʃism] *nm* catechism

**catégorie** [kategɔʀi] *nf* category; **catégorique** *adj* categorical

**cathédrale** [katedʀal] *nf* cathedral

**catholique** [katɔlik] *adj, nm/f* (Roman) Catholic; **pas très ~** a bit shady *ou* fishy

**cauchemar** [koʃmaʀ] *nm* nightmare

**cause** [koz] *nf* cause; (*Jur*) lawsuit, case; **à ~ de** because of, owing to; **pour ~ de** on account of; **(et) pour ~** and for (a very) good reason; **être en ~** (*intérêts*) to be at stake; **remettre en ~** to challenge; **causer** *vt* to cause ▷ *vi* to chat, talk

**caution** [kosjɔ̃] *nf* guarantee, security; (*Jur*) bail (bond); (*fig*) backing, support; **libéré sous ~** released on bail

**cavalier, -ière** [kavalje, jɛʀ] *adj* (*désinvolte*) offhand ▷ *nm/f* rider; (*au bal*) partner ▷ *nm* (*Échecs*) knight

**cave** [kav] *nf* cellar

**CD** *sigle m* (= *compact disc*) CD

**CD-ROM** [sederɔm] *sigle m* CD-ROM

---

**MOT-CLÉ**

**ce, cette** [sə, sɛt] (*devant nm* **cet** + *voyelle ou h aspiré; pl* **ces**) *dét* (*proximité*) this; these *pl*; (*non-proximité*) that; those *pl*; **cette maison(-ci/là)** this/that house; **cette nuit** (*qui vient*) tonight; (*passée*) last night
▷ *pron* 1: **c'est** it's *ou* it is; **c'est un peintre** he's *ou* he is a painter; **ce sont des peintres** they're *ou* they are painters; **c'est le facteur** *etc* (*à la porte*) it's the postman; **c'est toi qui lui a parlé** it was you who spoke to him; **qui est-ce?** who is it?; (*en désignant*) who is he/she?; **qu'est-ce?** what is it?
2: **ce qui, ce que**: **ce qui me plaît, c'est sa franchise** what I like about him *ou* her is his *ou* her frankness; **il est bête, ce qui me chagrine** he's stupid, which saddens me; **tout ce qui bouge** everything *ou* that *ou* which moves; **tout ce que je sais** all I know; **ce dont j'ai parlé** what I talked about; **ce que c'est grand!** it's so big!; *voir aussi* **-ci**; **est-ce que; n'est-ce pas; c'est-à-dire**

---

**ceci** [səsi] *pron* this

**céder** [sede] *vt* (*donner*) to give up ▷ *vi* (*chaise, barrage*) to give way; (*personne*) to give in; **~ à** to yield to, give in to

**CEDEX** [sedɛks] sigle m (= courrier d'entreprise à distribution exceptionnelle) postal service for bulk users

**cédille** [sedij] nf cedilla

**ceinture** [sɛ̃tyʀ] nf belt; (taille) waist; **ceinture de sécurité** safety ou seat belt

**cela** [s(ə)la] pron that; (comme sujet indéfini) it; **~ m'étonne que ...** it surprises me that ...; **quand/où ~?** when/where (was that)?

**célèbre** [selɛbʀ] adj famous; **célébrer** vt to celebrate

**céleri** [sɛlʀi] nm: **~(-rave)** celeriac; **céleri en branche** celery

**célibataire** [selibatɛʀ] adj single, unmarried ▷ nm bachelor ▷ nf unmarried woman

**celle, celles** [sɛl] pron voir **celui**

**cellule** [selyl] nf (gén) cell; **~ souche** stem cell

**cellulite** [selylit] nf cellulite

⬤ **MOT-CLÉ**

**celui, celle** [səlɥi, sɛl] (mpl **ceux**, fpl **celles**) pron 1: **celui-ci/là, celle-ci/là** this one/that one; **ceux-ci, celles-ci** these (ones); **ceux-là, celles-là** those (ones)

2: **celui qui bouge** the one which ou that moves; (personne) the one who moves; **celui que je vois** the one (which ou that) I see; (personne) the one (whom) I see; **celui dont je parle** the one I'm talking about; **celui de mon frère** my brother's; **celui du salon/du dessous** the one in (ou from) the lounge/below

3 (valeur indéfinie): **celui qui veut** whoever wants

**cendre** [sɑ̃dʀ] nf ash; **cendres** nfpl (d'un défunt) ashes; **sous la ~** (Culin) in (the) embers; **cendrier** nm ashtray

**censé, e** [sɑ̃se] adj: **être ~ faire** to be supposed to do

**censeur** [sɑ̃sœʀ] nm (Scol) deputy-head

(BRIT), vice-principal (US)

**censure** [sɑ̃syʀ] nf censorship; **censurer** vt (Cinéma, Presse) to censor; (Pol) to censure

**cent** [sɑ̃] num a hundred, one hundred ▷ nm (US, Canada etc) cent; (partie de l'euro) cent; **centaine** nf: **une centaine (de)** about a hundred, a hundred or so; **des centaines (de)** hundreds (of); **centenaire** adj hundred-year-old ▷ nm (anniversaire) centenary; (monnaie) cent; **centième** num hundredth; **centigrade** nm centigrade; **centilitre** nm centilitre; **centime** nm centime; **centime d'euro** nm euro cent; **centimètre** nm centimetre; (ruban) tape measure, measuring tape

**central, e, -aux** [sɑ̃tʀal, o] adj central ▷ nm: **~ (téléphonique)** (telephone) exchange; **centrale** nf power station; **centrale électrique/nucléaire** power/nuclear power station

**centre** [sɑ̃tʀ] nm centre; **centre commercial/sportif/culturel** shopping/sports/arts centre; **centre d'appels** call centre; **centre-ville** town centre, downtown (area) (US)

**cèpe** [sɛp] nm (edible) boletus

**cependant** [s(ə)pɑ̃dɑ̃] adv however

**céramique** [seʀamik] nf ceramics sg

**cercle** [sɛʀkl] nm circle; **cercle vicieux** vicious circle

**cercueil** [sɛʀkœj] nm coffin

**céréale** [seʀeal] nf cereal

**cérémonie** [seʀemɔni] nf ceremony; **sans ~** (inviter, manger) informally

**cerf** [sɛʀ] nm stag

**cerf-volant** [sɛʀvɔlɑ̃] nm kite

**cerise** [s(ə)ʀiz] nf cherry; **cerisier** nm cherry (tree)

**cerner** [sɛʀne] vt (Mil etc) to surround; (fig: problème) to delimit, define

**certain, e** [sɛʀtɛ̃, ɛn] adj certain ▷ dét certain; **d'un ~ âge** past one's prime, not so young; **un ~ temps** (quite) some time; **un ~ Georges** someone called Georges; **~s** pron some; **certainement** adv (probablement) most probably ou

likely; (*bien sûr*) certainly, of course
**certes** [sɛʀt] *adv* (*sans doute*)
admittedly; (*bien sûr*) of course
**certificat** [sɛʀtifika] *nm* certificate
**certifier** [sɛʀtifje] *vt*: **~ qch à qn**
to assure sb of sth; **copie certifiée**
**conforme** certified copy of the original
**certitude** [sɛʀtityd] *nf* certainty
**cerveau, x** [sɛʀvo] *nm* brain
**cervelas** [sɛʀvəla] *nm* saveloy
**cervelle** [sɛʀvɛl] *nf* (*Anat*) brain; (*Culin*)
brains
**ces** [se] *dét voir* **ce**
**CES** *sigle m* (= *collège d'enseignement*
*secondaire*) ≈ (junior) secondary school
(BRIT)
**cesse** [sɛs]: **sans ~** *adv* (*tout le temps*)
continually, constantly; (*sans*
*interruption*) continuously; **il n'a eu de**
**~ que** he did not rest until; **cesser** *vt*
to stop ▷ *vi* to stop, cease; **cesser de**
**faire** to stop doing; **cessez-le-feu** *nm*
*inv* ceasefire
**c'est-à-dire** [sɛtadiʀ] *adv* that is (to say)
**cet, cette** [sɛt] *dét voir* **ce**
**ceux** [sø] *pron voir* **celui**
**chacun, e** [ʃakœ̃, yn] *pron* each;
(*indéfini*) everyone, everybody
**chagrin** [ʃagʀɛ̃] *nm* grief, sorrow; **avoir**
**du ~** to be grieved
**chahut** [ʃay] *nm* uproar; **chahuter** *vt*
to rag, bait ▷ *vi* to make an uproar
**chaîne** [ʃɛn] *nf* chain; (*Radio, TV:*
*stations*) channel; **travail à la ~**
production line work; **réactions**
**en ~** chain reaction *sg*; **chaîne de**
**montagnes** mountain range; **chaîne**
**(hi-fi)** hi-fi system
**chair** [ʃɛʀ] *nf* flesh; **avoir la ~ de poule**
to have goosepimples *ou* gooseflesh;
**bien en ~** plump, well-padded; **en**
**~ et en os** in the flesh; **~ à saucisse**
sausage meat
**chaise** [ʃɛz] *nf* chair; **chaise longue**
deckchair
**châle** [ʃal] *nm* shawl
**chaleur** [ʃalœʀ] *nf* heat; (*fig: accueil*)
warmth; **chaleureux, -euse** *adj* warm

**chamailler** [ʃamaje]: **se chamailler** *vi*
to squabble, bicker
**chambre** [ʃɑ̃bʀ] *nf* bedroom; (*Pol,*
*Comm*) chamber; **faire ~ à part** to sleep
in separate rooms; **je voudrais une ~**
**pour deux personnes** I'd like a double
room; **chambre à air** (*de pneu*) (inner)
tube; **chambre à coucher** bedroom;
**chambre à un lit/à deux lits** (*à*
*l'hôtel*) single-/twin-bedded room;
**chambre d'amis** spare *ou* guest room;
**chambre d'hôte** ≈ bed and breakfast;
**chambre meublée** bedsit(ter) (BRIT),
furnished room; **chambre noire** (*Photo*)
darkroom
**chameau, x** [ʃamo] *nm* camel
**chamois** [ʃamwa] *nm* chamois
**champ** [ʃɑ̃] *nm* field; **champ de bataille**
battlefield; **champ de courses**
racecourse
**champagne** [ʃɑ̃paɲ] *nm* champagne
**champignon** [ʃɑ̃piɲɔ̃] *nm* mushroom;
(*terme générique*) fungus; **champignon**
**de Paris** *ou* **de couche** button
mushroom
**champion, ne** [ʃɑ̃pjɔ̃, jɔn] *adj,*
*nm/f* champion; **championnat** *nm*
championship
**chance** [ʃɑ̃s] *nf*: **la ~** luck; **chances** *nfpl*
(*probabilités*) chances; **avoir de la ~** to
be lucky; **il a des ~s de réussir** he's got
a good chance of passing; **bonne ~!**
good luck!
**change** [ʃɑ̃ʒ] *nm* (*devises*) exchange
**changement** [ʃɑ̃ʒmɑ̃] *nm* change;
**changement de vitesses** gears *pl*
**changer** [ʃɑ̃ʒe] *vt* (*modifier*) to change,
alter; (*remplacer, Comm*) to change ▷ *vi*
to change, alter; **se changer** *vi* to
change (o.s.); **~ de** (*remplacer: adresse,*
*nom, voiture etc*) to change one's;
(*échanger: place, train etc*) to change;
**~ d'avis** to change one's mind; **~ de**
**vitesse** to change gear; **il faut ~ à Lyon**
you *ou* we *etc* have to change in Lyons;
**où est-ce que je peux ~ de l'argent?**
where can I change some money?
**chanson** [ʃɑ̃sɔ̃] *nf* song

**chant** [ʃɑ̃] nm song; (art vocal) singing; (d'église) hymn

**chantage** [ʃɑ̃taʒ] nm blackmail; **faire du ~** to use blackmail

**chanter** [ʃɑ̃te] vt, vi to sing; **si cela lui chante** (fam) if he feels like it; **chanteur, -euse** nm/f singer

**chantier** [ʃɑ̃tje] nm (building) site; (sur une route) roadworks pl; **mettre en ~** to put in hand; **chantier naval** shipyard

**chantilly** [ʃɑ̃tiji] nf voir **crème**

**chantonner** [ʃɑ̃tɔne] vi, vt to sing to oneself, hum

**chapeau, x** [ʃapo] nm hat; **~!** well done!

**chapelle** [ʃapɛl] nf chapel

**chapitre** [ʃapitʀ] nm chapter

**chaque** [ʃak] dét each, every; (indéfini) every

**char** [ʃaʀ] nm (Mil): **~ (d'assaut)** tank; **~ à voile** sand yacht

**charbon** [ʃaʀbɔ̃] nm coal; **charbon de bois** charcoal

**charcuterie** [ʃaʀkytʀi] nf (magasin) pork butcher's shop and delicatessen; (produits) cooked pork meats pl; **charcutier, -ière** nm/f pork butcher

**chardon** [ʃaʀdɔ̃] nm thistle

**charge** [ʃaʀʒ] nf (fardeau) load, burden; (Élec, Mil, Jur) charge; (rôle, mission) responsibility; **charges** nfpl (du loyer) service charges; **à la ~ de** (dépendant de) dependent upon; (aux frais de) chargeable to; **prendre en ~** to take charge of; (suj: véhicule) to take on; (dépenses) to take care of; **charges sociales** social security contributions

**chargement** [ʃaʀʒəmɑ̃] nm (objets) load

**charger** [ʃaʀʒe] vt (voiture, fusil, caméra) to load; (batterie) to charge ▷ vi (Mil etc) to charge; **se ~ de** to see to, take care of

**chariot** [ʃaʀjo] nm trolley; (charrette) waggon

**charité** [ʃaʀite] nf charity; **faire la ~ à** to give (something) to

**charmant, e** [ʃaʀmɑ̃, ɑ̃t] adj charming

**charme** [ʃaʀm] nm charm; **charmer** vt to charm

**charpente** [ʃaʀpɑ̃t] nf frame(work); **charpentier** nm carpenter

**charrette** [ʃaʀɛt] nf cart

**charter** [ʃaʀtɛʀ] nm (vol) charter flight

**chasse** [ʃas] nf hunting; (au fusil) shooting; (poursuite) chase; (aussi: **~ d'eau**) flush; **prendre en ~** to give chase to; **tirer la ~ (d'eau)** to flush the toilet, pull the chain; **~ à courre** hunting; **chasse-neige** nm inv snowplough (BRIT), snowplow (US); **chasser** vt to hunt; (expulser) to chase away ou out, drive away ou out; **chasseur, -euse** nm/f hunter ▷ nm (avion) fighter

**chat[1]** [ʃa] nm cat

**chat[2]** [tʃat] nm (Internet) chat room

**châtaigne** [ʃatɛɲ] nf chestnut

**châtain** [ʃatɛ̃] adj inv (cheveux) chestnut (brown); (personne) chestnut-haired

**château, x** [ʃɑto] nm (forteresse) castle; (résidence royale) palace; (manoir) mansion; **château d'eau** water tower; **château fort** stronghold, fortified castle

**châtiment** [ʃatimɑ̃] nm punishment

**chaton** [ʃatɔ̃] nm (Zool) kitten

**chatouiller** [ʃatuje] vt to tickle; **chatouilleux, -euse** adj ticklish

**chatte** [ʃat] nf (she-)cat

**chatter** [tʃate] vi (Internet) to chat

**chaud, e** [ʃo, ʃod] adj (gén) warm; (très chaud) hot; **il fait ~** it's warm; it's hot; **avoir ~** to be warm; to be hot; **ça me tient ~** it keeps me warm; **rester au ~** to stay in the warm

**chaudière** [ʃodjɛʀ] nf boiler

**chauffage** [ʃofaʒ] nm heating; **chauffage central** central heating

**chauffe-eau** [ʃofo] nm inv water-heater

**chauffer** [ʃofe] vt to heat ▷ vi to heat up, warm up; (trop chauffer: moteur) to overheat; **se chauffer** vi (au soleil) to warm o.s.

**chauffeur** [ʃofœʀ] nm driver; (privé) chauffeur

**chaumière** [ʃomjɛʀ] nf (thatched) cottage

**chaussée** [ʃose] nf road(way)

**chausser** [ʃose] vt (bottes, skis) to put on; (enfant) to put shoes on; **~ du 38/42** to take size 38/42

**chaussette** [ʃosɛt] nf sock

**chausson** [ʃosɔ̃] nm slipper; (de bébé) bootee; **chausson (aux pommes)** (apple) turnover

**chaussure** [ʃosyʀ] nf shoe; **chaussures basses** flat shoes; **chaussures montantes** ankle boots; **chaussures de ski** ski boots

**chauve** [ʃov] adj bald; **chauve-souris** nf bat

**chauvin, e** [ʃovɛ̃, in] adj chauvinistic

**chaux** [ʃo] nf lime; **blanchi à la ~** whitewashed

**chef** [ʃɛf] nm head, leader; (de cuisine) chef; **commandant en ~** commander-in-chief; **chef d'accusation** charge; **chef d'entreprise** company head; **chef d'État** head of state; **chef de famille** head of the family; **chef de file** (de parti etc) leader; **chef de gare** station master; **chef d'orchestre** conductor; **chef-d'œuvre** nm masterpiece; **chef-lieu** nm county town

**chemin** [ʃ(ə)mɛ̃] nm path; (itinéraire, direction, trajet) way; **en ~** on the way; **chemin de fer** railway (BRIT), railroad (US)

**cheminée** [ʃ(ə)mine] nf chimney; (à l'intérieur) chimney piece, fireplace; (de bateau) funnel

**chemise** [ʃ(ə)miz] nf shirt; (dossier) folder; **chemise de nuit** nightdress

**chemisier** [ʃ(ə)mizje] nm blouse

**chêne** [ʃɛn] nm oak (tree); (bois) oak

**chenil** [ʃ(ə)nil] nm kennels pl

**chenille** [ʃ(ə)nij] nf (Zool) caterpillar

**chèque** [ʃɛk] nm cheque (BRIT), check (US); **est-ce que je peux payer par ~?** can I pay by cheque?; **chèque sans provision** bad cheque; **chèque de voyage** traveller's cheque; **chéquier** [ʃekje] nm cheque book

**cher, -ère** [ʃɛʀ] adj (aimé) dear; (coûteux) expensive, dear ▷ adv: **ça coûte ~** it's expensive

**chercher** [ʃɛʀʃe] vt to look for; (gloire etc) to seek; **aller ~** to go for, go and fetch; **~ à faire** to try to do; **chercheur, -euse** nm/f researcher, research worker

**chéri, e** [ʃeʀi] adj beloved, dear; **(mon) ~** darling

**cheval, -aux** [ʃ(ə)val, o] nm horse; (Auto): **~ (vapeur)** horsepower no pl; **faire du ~** to ride; **à ~** on horseback; **à ~ sur** astride; (fig) overlapping; **cheval de course** racehorse

**chevalier** [ʃ(ə)valje] nm knight

**chevalière** [ʃ(ə)valjɛʀ] nf signet ring

**chevaux** [ʃəvo] nmpl de **cheval**

**chevet** [ʃ(ə)vɛ] nm: **au ~ de qn** at sb's bedside; **lampe de chevet** bedside lamp

**cheveu, x** [ʃ(ə)vø] nm hair; **cheveux** nmpl (chevelure) hair sg; **avoir les ~x courts** to have short hair

**cheville** [ʃ(ə)vij] nf (Anat) ankle; (de bois) peg; (pour une vis) plug

**chèvre** [ʃɛvʀ] nf (she-)goat

**chèvrefeuille** [ʃɛvʀəfœj] nm honeysuckle

**chevreuil** [ʃəvʀœj] nm roe deer inv; (Culin) venison

О **MOT-CLÉ**

**chez** [ʃe] prép **1** (à la demeure de) at; (: direction) to; **chez qn** at/to sb's house ou place; **je suis chez moi** I'm at home; **je rentre chez moi** I'm going home; **allons chez Nathalie** let's go to Nathalie's

**2** (+profession) at; (: direction) to; **chez le boulanger/dentiste** at ou to the baker's/dentist's

**3** (dans le caractère, l'œuvre de) in; **chez ce poète** in this poet's work; **c'est ce que je préfère chez lui** that's what I like best about him

**chic** [ʃik] adj inv chic, smart; (fam:

*généreux*) nice, decent ▷ *nm* stylishness; **~ (alors)!** (*fam*) great!; **avoir le ~ de** to have the knack of

**chicorée** [ʃikɔʀe] *nf* (*café*) chicory; (*salade*) endive

**chien** [ʃjɛ̃] *nm* dog; **chien d'aveugle** guide dog; **chien de garde** guard dog

**chienne** [ʃjɛn] *nf* dog, bitch

**chiffon** [ʃifɔ̃] *nm* (piece of) rag; **chiffonner** *vt* to crumple; (*fam: tracasser*) to concern

**chiffre** [ʃifʀ] *nm* (*représentant un nombre*) figure, numeral; (*montant, total*) total, sum; **en ~s ronds** in round figures; **chiffre d'affaires** turnover; **chiffrer** *vt* (*dépense*) to put a figure to, assess; (*message*) to (en)code, cipher; **se chiffrer à** to add up to, amount to

**chignon** [ʃiɲɔ̃] *nm* chignon, bun

**Chili** [ʃili] *nm*: **le ~** Chile; **chilien, ne** *adj* Chilean ▷ *nm/f*: **Chilien, ne** Chilean

**chimie** [ʃimi] *nf* chemistry; **chimiothérapie** [ʃimjɔteʀapi] *nf* chemotherapy; **chimique** *adj* chemical; **produits chimiques** chemicals

**chimpanzé** [ʃɛ̃pɑ̃ze] *nm* chimpanzee

**Chine** [ʃin] *nf*: **la ~** China; **chinois, e** *adj* Chinese ▷ *nm/f*: **Chinois, e** Chinese ▷ *nm* (*Ling*) Chinese

**chiot** [ʃjo] *nm* pup(py)

**chips** [ʃips] *nfpl* crisps (*BRIT*), (potato) chips (*US*)

**chirurgie** [ʃiʀyʀʒi] *nf* surgery; **chirurgie esthétique** plastic surgery; **chirurgien, ne** *nm/f* surgeon

**chlore** [klɔʀ] *nm* chlorine

**choc** [ʃɔk] *nm* (*heurt*) impact, shock; (*collision*) crash; (*moral*) shock; (*affrontement*) clash

**chocolat** [ʃɔkɔla] *nm* chocolate; **chocolat au lait** milk chocolate

**chœur** [kœʀ] *nm* (*chorale*) choir; (*Opéra, Théâtre*) chorus; **en ~** in chorus

**choisir** [ʃwaziʀ] *vt* to choose, select

**choix** [ʃwa] *nm* choice, selection; **avoir le ~** to have the choice; **premier ~** (*Comm*) class one; **de ~** choice, selected;

**au ~** as you wish

**chômage** [ʃomaʒ] *nm* unemployment; **mettre au ~** to make redundant, put out of work; **être au ~** to be unemployed *ou* out of work; **chômeur, -euse** *nm/f* unemployed person

**choquer** [ʃɔke] *vt* (*offenser*) to shock; (*deuil*) to shake

**chorale** [kɔʀal] *nf* choir

**chose** [ʃoz] *nf* thing; **c'est peu de ~** it's nothing (really)

**chou, x** [ʃu] *nm* cabbage; **mon petit ~** (my) sweetheart; **chou à la crème** choux bun; **chou de Bruxelles** Brussels sprout; **choucroute** *nf* sauerkraut

**chouette** [ʃwɛt] *nf* owl ▷ *adj* (*fam*) great, smashing

**chou-fleur** [ʃuflœʀ] *nm* cauliflower

**chrétien, ne** [kʀetjɛ̃, jɛn] *adj, nm/f* Christian

**Christ** [kʀist] *nm*: **le ~** Christ; **christianisme** *nm* Christianity

**chronique** [kʀɔnik] *adj* chronic ▷ *nf* (*de journal*) column, page; (*historique*) chronicle; (*Radio, TV*): **la ~ sportive** the sports review

**chronologique** [kʀɔnɔlɔʒik] *adj* chronological

**chronomètre** [kʀɔnɔmɛtʀ] *nm* stopwatch; **chronométrer** *vt* to time

**chrysanthème** [kʀizɑ̃tɛm] *nm* chrysanthemum

---

● **CHRYSANTHÈME**
●
● Chrysanthemums are strongly
● associated with funerals in France,
● and therefore should not be given
● as gifts.

---

**chuchotement** [ʃyʃɔtmɑ̃] *nm* whisper

**chuchoter** [ʃyʃɔte] *vt, vi* to whisper

**chut** [ʃyt] *excl* sh!

**chute** [ʃyt] *nf* fall; (*déchet*) scrap; **faire une ~ (de 10 m)** to fall (10 m); **chute (d'eau)** waterfall; **chute libre** free fall; **chutes de pluie/neige** rainfall/snowfall

**Chypre** [ʃipʀ] *nm/f* Cyprus

**-ci** [si] *adv voir* **par** ▷ *dét*: **ce garçon~** this boy; **ces femmes~** these women

**cible** [sibl] *nf* target

**ciboulette** [sibulɛt] *nf* (small) chive

**cicatrice** [sikatʀis] *nf* scar; **cicatriser** *vt* to heal

**ci-contre** [sikɔ̃tʀ] *adv* opposite

**ci-dessous** [sidəsu] *adv* below

**ci-dessus** [sidəsy] *adv* above

**cidre** [sidʀ] *nm* cider

**Cie** *abr* (= *compagnie*) Co.

**ciel** [sjɛl] *nm* sky; (*Rel*) heaven

**cieux** [sjø] *nmpl de* **ciel**

**cigale** [sigal] *nf* cicada

**cigare** [sigaʀ] *nm* cigar

**cigarette** [sigaʀɛt] *nf* cigarette

**ci-inclus, e** [siɛ̃kly, yz] *adj, adv* enclosed

**ci-joint, e** [siʒwɛ̃, ɛ̃t] *adj, adv* enclosed

**cil** [sil] *nm* (eye)lash

**cime** [sim] *nf* top; (*montagne*) peak

**ciment** [simɑ̃] *nm* cement

**cimetière** [simtjɛʀ] *nm* cemetery; (*d'église*) churchyard

**cinéaste** [sineast] *nm/f* film-maker

**cinéma** [sinema] *nm* cinema

**cinq** [sɛ̃k] *num* five; **cinquantaine** *nf*: **une cinquantaine (de)** about fifty; **avoir la cinquantaine** (*âge*) to be around fifty; **cinquante** *num* fifty; **cinquantenaire** *adj, nm/f* fifty-year-old; **cinquième** *num* fifth ▷ *nf* (*Scol*) year 8 (*BRIT*), seventh grade (*US*)

**cintre** [sɛ̃tʀ] *nm* coat-hanger

**cintré, e** [sɛ̃tʀe] *adj* (*chemise*) fitted

**cirage** [siʀaʒ] *nm* (shoe) polish

**circulaire** [siʀkylɛʀ] *adj, nf* circular

**circulation** [siʀkylasjɔ̃] *nf* circulation; (*Auto*): **la ~** (the) traffic

**circuler** [siʀkyle] *vi* (*sang, devises*) to circulate; (*véhicules*) to drive (along); (*passants*) to walk along; (*train, bus*) to run; **faire ~** (*nouvelle*) to spread (about), circulate; (*badauds*) to move on

**cire** [siʀ] *nf* wax; **ciré** *nm* oilskin; **cirer** *vt* to wax, polish

**cirque** [siʀk] *nm* circus; (*fig*) chaos, bedlam; **quel ~!** what a carry-on!

**ciseau, x** [sizo] *nm*: **~ (à bois)** chisel; **ciseaux** *nmpl* (*paire de ciseaux*) (pair of) scissors

**citadin, e** [sitadɛ̃, in] *nm/f* city dweller

**citation** [sitasjɔ̃] *nf* (*d'auteur*) quotation; (*Jur*) summons *sg*

**cité** [site] *nf* town; (*plus grande*) city; **cité universitaire** students' residences *pl*

**citer** [site] *vt* (*un auteur*) to quote (from); (*nommer*) to name; (*Jur*) to summon

**citoyen, ne** [sitwajɛ̃, jɛn] *nm/f* citizen

**citron** [sitʀɔ̃] *nm* lemon; **citron pressé** (fresh) lemon juice; **citron vert** lime; **citronnade** *nf* still lemonade

**citrouille** [sitʀuj] *nf* pumpkin

**civet** [sive] *nm*: **~ de lapin** rabbit stew

**civière** [sivjɛʀ] *nf* stretcher

**civil, e** [sivil] *adj* (*mariage, poli*) civil; (*non militaire*) civilian; **en ~** in civilian clothes; **dans le ~** in civilian life

**civilisation** [sivilizasjɔ̃] *nf* civilization

**clair, e** [klɛʀ] *adj* light; (*pièce*) light, bright; (*eau, son, fig*) clear ▷ *adv*: **voir ~** to see clearly; **tirer qch au ~** to clear sth up, clarify sth; **mettre au ~** (*notes etc*) to tidy up ▷ *nm*: **~ de lune** moonlight; **clairement** *adv* clearly

**clairière** [klɛʀjɛʀ] *nf* clearing

**clandestin, e** [klɑ̃dɛstɛ̃, in] *adj* clandestine, secret; (*mouvement*) underground; (*travailleur, immigration*) illegal; **passager ~** stowaway

**claque** [klak] *nf* (*gifle*) slap; **claquer** *vi* (*porte*) to bang, slam; (*fam: mourir*) to snuff it ▷ *vt* (*porte*) to slam, bang; (*doigts*) to snap; (*fam: dépenser*) to blow; **il claquait des dents** his teeth were chattering; **être claqué** (*fam*) to be dead tired; **se claquer un muscle** to pull ou strain a muscle; **claquettes** nfpl tap-dancing sg; (chaussures) flip-flops

**clarinette** [klaʀinɛt] nf clarinet

**classe** [klas] nf class; (Scol: local) class(room); (: leçon, élèves) class; **aller en ~** to go to school; **classement** nm (rang: Scol) place; (: Sport) placing; (liste: Scol) class list (in order of merit); (: Sport) placings pl

**classer** [klase] vt (idées, livres) to classify; (papiers) to file; (candidat, concurrent) to grade; (Jur: affaire) to close; **se ~ premier/dernier** to come first/last; (Sport) to finish first/last; **classeur** nm (cahier) file

**classique** [klasik] adj classical; (sobre: coupe etc) classic(al); (habituel) standard, classic

**clavecin** [klav(ə)sɛ̃] nm harpsichord

**clavicule** [klavikyl] nf collarbone

**clavier** [klavje] nm keyboard

**clé** [kle] nf key; (Mus) clef; (de mécanicien) spanner (BRIT), wrench (US); **prix ~s en main** (d'une voiture) on-the-road price; **clé de contact** ignition key; **clé USB** USB key

**clef** [kle] nf = **clé**

**clergé** [klɛʀʒe] nm clergy

**cliché** [kliʃe] nm (fig) cliché; (négatif) negative; (photo) print

**client, e** [klijɑ̃, klijɑ̃t] nm/f (acheteur) customer, client; (d'hôtel) guest, patron; (du docteur) patient; (de l'avocat) client; **clientèle** nf (du magasin) customers pl, clientèle; (du docteur, de l'avocat) practice

**cligner** [kliɲe] vi: **~ des yeux** to blink (one's eyes); **~ de l'œil** to wink; **clignotant** nm (Auto) indicator; **clignoter** vi (étoiles etc) to twinkle; (lumière) to flicker

**climat** [klima] nm climate

**climatisation** [klimatizasjɔ̃] nf air conditioning; **climatisé, e** adj air-conditioned

**clin d'œil** [klɛ̃dœj] nm wink; **en un clin d'œil** in a flash

**clinique** [klinik] nf private hospital

**clip** [klip] nm (boucle d'oreille) clip-on; **(vidéo) ~** (pop) video

**cliquer** [klike] vt to click; **~ sur** to click on

**clochard, e** [klɔʃaʀ, aʀd] nm/f tramp

**cloche** [klɔʃ] nf (d'église) bell; (fam) clot; **clocher** nm church tower; (en pointe) steeple ▷ vi (fam) to be ou go wrong; **de clocher** (péj) parochial

**cloison** [klwazɔ̃] nf partition (wall)

**clonage** [klɔnaʒ] nm cloning

**cloner** [klone] vt to clone

**cloque** [klɔk] nf blister

**clore** [klɔʀ] vt to close

**clôture** [klotyʀ] nf closure; (barrière) enclosure

**clou** [klu] nm nail; **clous** nmpl (passage clouté) pedestrian crossing; **pneus à ~s** studded tyres; **le ~ du spectacle** the highlight of the show; **clou de girofle** clove

**clown** [klun] nm clown

**club** [klœb] nm club

**CNRS** sigle m (= Centre nationale de la recherche scientifique) ≈ SERC (BRIT), ≈ NSF (US)

**coaguler** [kɔagyle] vt, vi (aussi: **se ~**: sang) to coagulate

**cobaye** [kɔbaj] nm guinea-pig

**coca** [kɔka] nm Coke®

**cocaïne** [kɔkain] nf cocaine

**coccinelle** [kɔksinɛl] nf ladybird (BRIT), ladybug (US)

**cocher** [kɔʃe] vt to tick off

**cochon, ne** [kɔʃɔ̃, ɔn] nm pig ▷ adj (fam) dirty, smutty; **cochon d'Inde** guinea pig; **cochonnerie** (fam) nf (saleté) filth; (marchandise) rubbish, trash

**cocktail** [kɔktɛl] nm cocktail; (réception) cocktail party

**cocorico** [kɔkɔriko] excl, nm cock-a-doodle-do

**cocotte** [kɔkɔt] nf (en fonte) casserole; **ma ~** (fam) sweetie (pie); **cocotte (minute)®** pressure cooker

**code** [kɔd] nm code ▷ adj: **phares ~s** dipped lights; **se mettre en ~(s)** to dip one's (head)lights; **code à barres** bar code; **code civil** Common Law; **code de la route** highway code; **code pénal** penal code; **code postal** (numéro) post (BRIT) ou zip (US) code

**cœur** [kœʀ] nm heart; (Cartes: couleur) hearts pl; (: carte) heart; **avoir bon ~** to be kind-hearted; **avoir mal au ~** to feel sick; **par ~** by heart; **de bon ~** willingly; **cela lui tient à ~** that's (very) close to his heart

**coffre** [kɔfʀ] nm (meuble) chest; (d'auto) boot (BRIT), trunk (US); **coffre-fort** nm safe; **coffret** nm casket

**cognac** [kɔɲak] nm brandy, cognac

**cogner** [kɔɲe] vi to knock; **se ~ contre** to knock ou bump into; **se ~ la tête** to bang one's head

**cohérent, e** [kɔeʀɑ̃, ɑ̃t] adj coherent, consistent

**coiffé, e** [kwafe] adj: **bien/mal ~** with tidy/untidy hair; **~ d'un chapeau** wearing a hat

**coiffer** [kwafe] vt (fig: surmonter) to cover, top; **se coiffer** vi to do one's hair; **~ qn** to do sb's hair; **coiffeur, -euse** nm/f hairdresser; **coiffeuse** nf (table) dressing table; **coiffure** nf (cheveux) hairstyle, hairdo; (art): **la coiffure** hairdressing

**coin** [kwɛ̃] nm corner; (pour coincer) wedge; **l'épicerie du ~** the local grocer; **dans le ~** (aux alentours) in the area, around about; (habiter) locally; **je ne suis pas du ~** I'm not from here; **au ~ du feu** by the fireside; **regard en ~** sideways glance

**coincé, e** [kwɛ̃se] adj stuck, jammed; (fig: inhibé) inhibited, hung up (fam)

**coïncidence** [kɔɛ̃sidɑ̃s] nf coincidence

**coing** [kwɛ̃] nm quince

**col** [kɔl] nm (de chemise) collar; (encolure, cou) neck; (de montagne) pass; **col de l'utérus** cervix; **col roulé** polo-neck

**colère** [kɔlɛʀ] nf anger; **une ~** a fit of anger; **(se mettre) en ~ (contre qn)** (to get) angry (with sb); **coléreux, -euse, colérique** adj quick-tempered, irascible

**colin** [kɔlɛ̃] nm hake

**colique** [kɔlik] nf diarrhoea

**colis** [kɔli] nm parcel

**collaborer** [kɔ(l)labɔʀe] vi to collaborate; **~ à** to collaborate on; (revue) to contribute to

**collant, e** [kɔlɑ̃, ɑ̃t] adj sticky; (robe etc) clinging, skintight; (péj) clinging ▷ nm (bas) tights pl; (de danseur) leotard

**colle** [kɔl] nf glue; (à papiers peints) (wallpaper) paste; (fam: devinette) teaser, riddle; (Scol: fam) detention

**collecte** [kɔlɛkt] nf collection; **collectif, -ive** adj collective; (visite, billet) group cpd

**collection** [kɔlɛksjɔ̃] nf collection; (Édition) series; **collectionner** vt to collect; **collectionneur, -euse** nm/f collector

**collectivité** [kɔlɛktivite] nf group; **collectivités locales** (Admin) local authorities

**collège** [kɔlɛʒ] nm (école) (secondary) school; (assemblée) body; **collégien** nm schoolboy

**collègue** [kɔ(l)lɛg] nm/f colleague

**coller** [kɔle] vt (papier, timbre) to stick (on); (affiche) to stick up; (enveloppe) to stick down; (morceaux) to stick ou glue together; (Comput) to paste; (fam: mettre, fourrer) to stick, shove; (Scol: fam) to keep in ▷ vi (être collant) to be sticky; (adhérer) to stick; **~ à** to stick to; **être collé à un examen** (fam) to fail an exam

**collier** [kɔlje] nm (bijou) necklace; (de chien, Tech) collar

**colline** [kɔlin] nf hill

**collision** [kɔlizjɔ̃] nf collision, crash; **entrer en ~ (avec)** to collide (with)

**collyre** [kɔliʀ] nm eye drops

**colombe** [kɔlɔ̃b] nf dove

**Colombie** [kɔlɔ̃bi] nf: **la ~** Colombia

**colonie** [kɔlɔni] nf colony; **colonie (de vacances)** holiday camp (for children)

**colonne** [kɔlɔn] nf column; **se mettre en ~ par deux** to get into twos;

**colonne (vertébrale)** spine, spinal column

**colorant** [kɔlɔrɑ̃] *nm* colouring

**colorer** [kɔlɔre] *vt* to colour

**colorier** [kɔlɔrje] *vt* to colour (in)

**coloris** [kɔlɔri] *nm* colour, shade

**colza** [kɔlza] *nm* rape(seed)

**coma** [kɔma] *nm* coma; **être dans le ~** to be in a coma

**combat** [kɔ̃ba] *nm* fight, fighting *no pl*; **combat de boxe** boxing match; **combattant** *nm*: **ancien combattant** war veteran; **combattre** *vt* to fight; (*épidémie, ignorance*) to combat, fight against

**combien** [kɔ̃bjɛ̃] *adv* (*quantité*) how much; (*nombre*) how many; **~ de** (*quantité*) how much; (*nombre*) how many; **~ de temps** how long; **~ ça coûte/pèse?** how much does it cost/weigh?; **on est le ~ aujourd'hui?** (*fam*) what's the date today?

**combinaison** [kɔ̃binɛzɔ̃] *nf* combination; (*astuce*) scheme; (*de femme*) slip; (*de plongée*) wetsuit; (*bleu de travail*) boiler suit (BRIT), coveralls *pl* (US)

**combiné** [kɔ̃bine] *nm* (*aussi: ~ téléphonique*) receiver

**comble** [kɔ̃bl] *adj* (*salle*) packed (full) ▷ *nm* (*du bonheur, plaisir*) height; **combles** *nmpl* (*Constr*) attic *sg*, loft *sg*; **c'est le ~!** that beats everything!

**combler** [kɔ̃ble] *vt* (*trou*) to fill in; (*besoin, lacune*) to fill; (*déficit*) to make good; (*satisfaire*) to fulfil

**comédie** [kɔmedi] *nf* comedy; (*fig*) playacting *no pl*; **faire la ~** (*fam*) to make a fuss; **comédie musicale** musical; **comédien, ne** *nm/f* actor(-tress)

**comestible** [kɔmɛstibl] *adj* edible

**comique** [kɔmik] *adj* (*drôle*) comical; (*Théâtre*) comic ▷ *nm* (*artiste*) comic, comedian

**commandant** [kɔmɑ̃dɑ̃] *nm* (*gén*) commander, commandant; (*Navig, Aviat*) captain

**commande** [kɔmɑ̃d] *nf* (*Comm*) order; **commandes** *nfpl* (*Aviat etc*) controls; **sur ~** to order; **commander** *vt* (*Comm*) to order; (*diriger, ordonner*) to command; **commander à qn de faire** to command *ou* order sb to do; **je peux commander, s'il vous plaît?** can I order, please?

 **MOT-CLÉ**

**comme** [kɔm] *prép* 1 (*comparaison*) like; **tout comme son père** just like his father; **fort comme un bœuf** as strong as an ox; **joli comme tout** ever so pretty

2 (*manière*) like; **faites-le comme ça** do it like this, do it this way; **comme ci, comme ça** so-so, middling; **comme il faut** (*correctement*) properly

3 (*en tant que*) as a; **donner comme prix** to give as a prize; **travailler comme secrétaire** to work as a secretary

▷ *conj* 1 (*ainsi que*) as; **elle écrit comme elle parle** she writes as she talks; **comme si** as if

2 (*au moment où, alors que*) as; **il est parti comme j'arrivais** he left as I arrived

3 (*parce que, puisque*) as; **comme il était en retard, il ...** as he was late, he ...

▷ *adv*: **comme il est fort/c'est bon!** he's so strong/it's so good!

**commencement** [kɔmɑ̃smɑ̃] *nm* beginning, start

**commencer** [kɔmɑ̃se] *vt, vi* to begin, start; **~ à** *ou* **de faire** to begin *ou* start doing

**comment** [kɔmɑ̃] *adv* how; **~?** (*que dites-vous*) pardon?; **et ~!** and how!

**commentaire** [kɔmɑ̃tɛr] *nm* (*remarque*) comment, remark; (*exposé*) commentary

**commerçant, e** [kɔmɛrsɑ̃, ɑ̃t] *nm/f* shopkeeper, trader

**commerce** [kɔmɛrs] *nm* (*activité*) trade, commerce; (*boutique*) business; **~ électronique** e-commerce; **~**

**équitable** fair trade; **commercial, e, -aux** adj commercial, trading; (*péj*) commercial; **les commerciaux** the sales people; **commercialiser** vt to market

**commissaire** [kɔmisɛʀ] nm (*de police*) ≈ (police) superintendent; **commissaire aux comptes** (*Admin*) auditor; **commissariat** nm police station

**commission** [kɔmisjɔ̃] nf (*comité, pourcentage*) commission; (*message*) message; (*course*) errand; **commissions** nfpl (*achats*) shopping sg

**commode** [kɔmɔd] adj (*pratique*) convenient, handy; (*facile*) easy; (*personne*): **pas ~** awkward (to deal with) ▷ nf chest of drawers

**commun, e** [kɔmœ̃, yn] adj common; (*pièce*) communal, shared; (*effort*) joint; **ça sort du ~** it's out of the ordinary; **le ~ des mortels** the common run of people; **en ~** (*faire*) jointly; **mettre en ~** to pool, share; **communs** nmpl (*bâtiments*) outbuildings; **d'un ~ accord** by mutual agreement

**communauté** [kɔmynote] nf community

**commune** [kɔmyn] nf (*Admin*) commune, ≈ district; (*: urbaine*) ≈ borough

**communication** [kɔmynikasjɔ̃] nf communication

**communier** [kɔmynje] vi (*Rel*) to receive communion

**communion** [kɔmynjɔ̃] nf communion

**communiquer** [kɔmynike] vt (*nouvelle, dossier*) to pass on, convey; (*peur etc*) to communicate ▷ vi to communicate; **se communiquer à** (*se propager*) to spread to

**communisme** [kɔmynism] nm communism; **communiste** adj, nm/f communist

**commutateur** [kɔmytatœʀ] nm (*Élec*) (change-over) switch, commutator

**compact, e** [kɔ̃pakt] adj (*dense*) dense; (*appareil*) compact

**compagne** [kɔ̃paɲ] nf companion

**compagnie** [kɔ̃paɲi] nf (*firme, Mil*) company; **tenir ~ à qn** to keep sb company; **fausser ~ à qn** to give sb the slip, slip ou sneak away from sb; **compagnie aérienne** airline (company)

**compagnon** [kɔ̃paɲɔ̃] nm companion

**comparable** [kɔ̃paʀabl] adj: **~ (à)** comparable (to)

**comparaison** [kɔ̃paʀɛzɔ̃] nf comparison

**comparer** [kɔ̃paʀe] vt to compare; **~ qch/qn à** ou **et** (*pour choisir*) to compare sth/sb with ou and; (*pour établir une similitude*) to compare sth/sb to

**compartiment** [kɔ̃paʀtimɑ̃] nm compartment; **un ~ non-fumeurs** a non-smoking compartment (*BRIT*) ou car (*US*)

**compas** [kɔ̃pɑ] nm (*Géom*) (pair of) compasses pl; (*Navig*) compass

**compatible** [kɔ̃patibl] adj compatible

**compatriote** [kɔ̃patʀijɔt] nm/f compatriot

**compensation** [kɔ̃pɑ̃sasjɔ̃] nf compensation

**compenser** [kɔ̃pɑ̃se] vt to compensate for, make up for

**compétence** [kɔ̃petɑ̃s] nf competence

**compétent, e** [kɔ̃petɑ̃, ɑ̃t] adj (*apte*) competent, capable

**compétition** [kɔ̃petisjɔ̃] nf (*gén*) competition; (*Sport: épreuve*) event; **la ~ automobile** motor racing

**complément** [kɔ̃plemɑ̃] nm complement; (*reste*) remainder; **complément d'information** (*Admin*) supplementary ou further information; **complémentaire** adj complementary; (*additionnel*) supplementary

**complet, -ète** [kɔ̃plɛ, ɛt] adj complete; (*plein: hôtel etc*) full ▷ nm (*aussi*: **~-veston**) suit; **pain complet** wholemeal bread; **complètement** adv completely; **compléter** vt (*porter à la quantité voulue*) to complete;

(augmenter: connaissances, études) to complement, supplement; (: garde-robe) to add to

**complexe** [kɔ̃plɛks] adj, nm complex; **complexe hospitalier/industriel** hospital/industrial complex; **complexé, e** adj mixed-up, hung-up

**complication** [kɔ̃plikasjɔ̃] nf complexity, intricacy; (difficulté, ennui) complication; **complications** nfpl (Méd) complications

**complice** [kɔ̃plis] nm accomplice

**compliment** [kɔ̃plimɑ̃] nm (louange) compliment; **compliments** nmpl (félicitations) congratulations

**compliqué, e** [kɔ̃plike] adj complicated, complex; (personne) complicated

**comportement** [kɔ̃pɔrtəmɑ̃] nm behaviour

**comporter** [kɔ̃pɔrte] vt (consister en) to consist of, comprise; (inclure) to have; **se comporter** vi to behave

**composer** [kɔ̃poze] vt (musique, texte) to compose; (mélange, équipe) to make up; (numéro) to dial; (constituer) to make up, form ▷ vi (transiger) to come to terms; **se composer de** to be composed of, be made up of; **compositeur, -trice** nm/f (Mus) composer; **composition** nf composition; (Scol) test

**composter** [kɔ̃pɔste] vt (billet) to punch

● **COMPOSTER**
●
● In France you have to punch your
● ticket on the platform to validate it
● before getting onto the train.

**compote** [kɔ̃pɔt] nf stewed fruit no pl; **compote de pommes** stewed apples

**compréhensible** [kɔ̃preɑ̃sibl] adj comprehensible; (attitude) understandable

**compréhensif, -ive** [kɔ̃preɑ̃sif, iv] adj understanding

▌ Attention à ne pas traduire **compréhensif** par **comprehensive**.

**comprendre** [kɔ̃prɑ̃dr] vt to understand; (se composer de) to comprise, consist of

**compresse** [kɔ̃prɛs] nf compress

**comprimé** [kɔ̃prime] nm tablet

**compris, e** [kɔ̃pri, iz] pp de **comprendre** ▷ adj (inclus) included; ~ **entre** (situé) contained between; **l'électricité ~e/non ~e, y/non ~ l'électricité** including/excluding electricity; **100 euros tout ~** 100 euros all inclusive ou all-in

**comptabilité** [kɔ̃tabilite] nf (activité) accounting, accountancy; (comptes) accounts pl, books pl; (service) accounts office

**comptable** [kɔ̃tabl] nm/f accountant

**comptant** [kɔ̃tɑ̃] adv: **payer ~** to pay cash; **acheter ~** to buy for cash

**compte** [kɔ̃t] nm count; (total, montant) count, (right) number; (bancaire, facture) account; **comptes** nmpl (Finance) accounts, books; (fig) explanation sg; **en fin de ~** all things considered; **s'en tirer à bon ~** to get off lightly; **pour le ~ de** on behalf of; **pour son propre ~** for one's own benefit; **régler un ~** (s'acquitter de qch) to settle an account; (se venger) to get one's own back; **rendre des ~s à qn** (fig) to be answerable to sb; **tenir ~ de** to take account of; **travailler à son ~** to work for oneself; **rendre ~ (à qn) de qch** to give (sb) an account of sth; voir aussi **rendre**; **compte à rebours** countdown; **compte courant** current account; **compte rendu** account, report; (de film, livre) review; **compte-gouttes** nm inv dropper

**compter** [kɔ̃te] vt to count; (facturer) to charge for; (avoir à son actif, comporter) to have; (prévoir) to allow, reckon; (penser, espérer): ~ **réussir** to expect to succeed ▷ vi to count; (être économe) to economize; (figurer): ~ **parmi** to be ou rank among; ~ **sur** to count (up)on;

**~ avec qch/qn** to reckon with *ou* take account of sth/sb; **sans ~ que** besides which

**compteur** [kɔ̃tœʀ] *nm* meter; **compteur de vitesse** speedometer

**comptine** [kɔ̃tin] *nf* nursery rhyme

**comptoir** [kɔ̃twaʀ] *nm* (*de magasin*) counter; (*bar*) bar

**con, ne** [kɔ̃, kɔn] (*fam!*) *adj* damned *ou* bloody (BRIT) stupid (!)

**concentrer** [kɔ̃sãtʀe] *vt* to concentrate; **se concentrer** *vi* to concentrate

**concerner** [kɔ̃sɛʀne] *vt* to concern; **en ce qui me concerne** as far as I am concerned

**concert** [kɔ̃sɛʀ] *nm* concert; **de ~** (*décider*) unanimously

**concessionnaire** [kɔ̃sesjɔnɛʀ] *nm/f* agent, dealer

**concevoir** [kɔ̃s(ə)vwaʀ] *vt* (*idée, projet*) to conceive (of); (*comprendre*) to understand; (*enfant*) to conceive; **bien/ mal conçu** well-/badly-designed

**concierge** [kɔ̃sjɛʀʒ] *nm/f* caretaker

**concis, e** [kɔ̃si, iz] *adj* concise

**conclure** [kɔ̃klyʀ] *vt* to conclude; **conclusion** *nf* conclusion

**conçois** *etc* [kɔ̃swa] *vb voir* **concevoir**

**concombre** [kɔ̃kɔ̃bʀ] *nm* cucumber

**concours** [kɔ̃kuʀ] *nm* competition; (*Scol*) competitive examination; (*assistance*) aid, help; **concours de circonstances** combination of circumstances; **concours hippique** horse show

**concret, -ète** [kɔ̃kʀɛ, ɛt] *adj* concrete

**conçu, e** [kɔ̃sy] *pp de* **concevoir**

**concubinage** [kɔ̃kybinaʒ] *nm* (*Jur*) cohabitation

**concurrence** [kɔ̃kyʀãs] *nf* competition; **faire ~ à** to be in competition with; **jusqu'à ~ de** up to

**concurrent, e** [kɔ̃kyʀã, ãt] *nm/f* (*Sport, Écon etc*) competitor; (*Scol*) candidate

**condamner** [kɔ̃dane] *vt* (*blâmer*) to condemn; (*Jur*) to sentence; (*porte,*

*ouverture*) to fill in, block up; **~ qn à 2 ans de prison** to sentence sb to 2 years' imprisonment

**condensation** [kɔ̃dãsasjɔ̃] *nf* condensation

**condition** [kɔ̃disjɔ̃] *nf* condition; **conditions** *nfpl* (*tarif, prix*) terms; (*circonstances*) conditions; **sans ~s** unconditionally; **à ~ de** *ou* **que** provided that; **conditionnel, le** *nm* conditional (tense)

**conditionnement** [kɔ̃disjɔnmã] *nm* (*emballage*) packaging

**condoléances** [kɔ̃dɔleãs] *nfpl* condolences

**conducteur, -trice** [kɔ̃dyktœʀ, tʀis] *nm/f* driver ▷ *nm* (*Élec etc*) conductor

**conduire** [kɔ̃dɥiʀ] *vt* to drive; (*délégation, troupeau*) to lead; **se conduire** *vi* to behave; **~ à** to lead to; **~ qn quelque part** to take sb somewhere; to drive sb somewhere

**conduite** [kɔ̃dɥit] *nf* (*comportement*) behaviour; (*d'eau, de gaz*) pipe; **sous la ~ de** led by

**confection** [kɔ̃fɛksjɔ̃] *nf* (*fabrication*) making; (*Couture*) **la ~** the clothing industry

**conférence** [kɔ̃feʀãs] *nf* conference; (*exposé*) lecture; **conférence de presse** press conference

**confesser** [kɔ̃fese] *vt* to confess; **confession** *nf* confession; (*culte: catholique etc*) denomination

**confetti** [kɔ̃feti] *nm* confetti *no pl*

**confiance** [kɔ̃fjãs] *nf* (*en l'honnêteté de qn*) confidence, trust; (*en la valeur de qch*) faith; **avoir ~ en** to have confidence *ou* faith in, trust; **faire ~ à qn** to trust sb; **mettre qn en ~** to win sb's trust; **confiance en soi** self-confidence

**confiant, e** [kɔ̃fjã, jãt] *adj* confident; trusting

**confidence** [kɔ̃fidãs] *nf* confidence; **confidentiel, le** *adj* confidential

**confier** [kɔ̃fje] *vt*: **~ à qn** (*objet, travail*) to entrust to sb; (*secret, pensée*) to confide to sb; **se ~ à qn** to confide in sb

**confirmation** [kɔ̃firmasjɔ̃] *nf* confirmation

**confirmer** [kɔ̃firme] *vt* to confirm

**confiserie** [kɔ̃fizri] *nf* (*magasin*) confectioner's *ou* sweet shop; **confiseries** *nfpl* (*bonbons*) confectionery *sg*

**confisquer** [kɔ̃fiske] *vt* to confiscate

**confit, e** [kɔ̃fi, it] *adj*: **fruits ~s** crystallized fruits; **confit d'oie** *nm* conserve of goose

**confiture** [kɔ̃fityr] *nf* jam

**conflit** [kɔ̃fli] *nm* conflict

**confondre** [kɔ̃fɔ̃dr] *vt* (*jumeaux, faits*) to confuse, mix up; (*témoin, menteur*) to confound; **se confondre** *vi* to merge; **se ~ en excuses** to apologize profusely

**conforme** [kɔ̃fɔrm] *adj*: **~ à** (*loi, règle*) in accordance with; **conformément** *adv*: **conformément à** in accordance with; **conformer** *vt*: **se conformer à** to conform to

**confort** [kɔ̃fɔr] *nm* comfort; **tout ~** (*Comm*) with all modern conveniences; **confortable** *adj* comfortable

**confronter** [kɔ̃frɔ̃te] *vt* to confront

**confus, e** [kɔ̃fy, yz] *adj* (*vague*) confused; (*embarrassé*) embarrassed; **confusion** *nf* (*voir confus*) confusion; embarrassment; (*voir confondre*) confusion, mixing up

**congé** [kɔ̃ʒe] *nm* (*vacances*) holiday; **en ~** on holiday; **semaine/jour de ~** week/day off; **prendre ~ de qn** to take one's leave of sb; **donner son ~ à** to give in one's notice to; **congé de maladie** sick leave; **congé de maternité** maternity leave; **congés payés** paid holiday

**congédier** [kɔ̃ʒedje] *vt* to dismiss

**congélateur** [kɔ̃ʒelatœr] *nm* freezer

**congeler** [kɔ̃ʒ(ə)le] *vt* to freeze; **les produits congelés** frozen foods

**congestion** [kɔ̃ʒɛstjɔ̃] *nf* congestion

**Congo** [kɔ̃o] *nm*: **le ~** Congo, the Democratic Republic of the Congo

**congrès** [kɔ̃grɛ] *nm* congress

**conifère** [kɔnifɛr] *nm* conifer

**conjoint, e** [kɔ̃ʒwɛ̃, wɛ̃t] *adj* joint ▷ *nm/f* spouse

**conjonctivite** [kɔ̃ʒɔ̃ktivit] *nf* conjunctivitis

**conjoncture** [kɔ̃ʒɔ̃ktyr] *nf* circumstances *pl*; **la ~ actuelle** the present (economic) situation

**conjugaison** [kɔ̃ʒygɛzɔ̃] *nf* (*Ling*) conjugation

**connaissance** [kɔnɛsɑ̃s] *nf* (*savoir*) knowledge *no pl*; (*personne connue*) acquaintance; **être sans ~** to be unconscious; **perdre/reprendre ~** to lose/regain consciousness; **à ma/sa ~** to (the best of) my/his knowledge; **faire la ~ de qn** to meet sb

**connaisseur, -euse** [kɔnɛsœr, øz] *nm/f* connoisseur

**connaître** [kɔnɛtr] *vt* to know; (*éprouver*) to experience; (*avoir: succès*) to have, enjoy; **~ de nom/vue** to know by name/sight; **ils se sont connus à Genève** they (first) met in Geneva; **s'y ~ en qch** to know a lot about sth

**connecter** [kɔnɛkte] *vt* to connect; **se ~ à Internet** to log onto the Internet

**connerie** [kɔnri] (*fam!*) *nf* stupid thing (to do/say)

**connexion** [kɔnɛksjɔ̃] *nf* connection

**connu, e** [kɔny] *adj* (*célèbre*) well-known

**conquérir** [kɔ̃kerir] *vt* to conquer; **conquête** *nf* conquest

**consacrer** [kɔ̃sakre] *vt* (*employer*) to devote, dedicate; (*Rel*) to consecrate; **se ~ à qch** to dedicate *ou* devote o.s. to sth

**conscience** [kɔ̃sjɑ̃s] *nf* conscience; **avoir/prendre ~ de** to be/become aware of; **perdre ~** to lose consciousness; **avoir bonne/mauvaise ~** to have a clear/guilty conscience; **consciencieux, -euse** *adj* conscientious; **conscient, e** *adj* conscious

**consécutif, -ive** [kɔ̃sekytif, iv] *adj* consecutive; **~ à** following sth

**conseil** [kɔ̃sɛj] *nm* (*avis*) piece of advice; (*assemblée*) council; **des ~s**

advice; **prendre ~ (auprès de qn)** to take advice (from sb); **conseil d'administration** board (of directors); **conseil des ministres** ≈ the Cabinet; **conseil municipal** town council

**conseiller, -ère** [kɔ̃seje, ɛʀ] nm/f adviser ▷ vt (personne) to advise; (méthode, action) to recommend, advise; **~ à qn de** to advise sb to; **pouvez-vous me ~ un bon restaurant?** can you suggest a good restaurant?

**consentement** [kɔ̃sɑ̃tmɑ̃] nm consent

**consentir** [kɔ̃sɑ̃tiʀ] vt to agree, consent

**conséquence** [kɔ̃sekɑ̃s] nf consequence; **en ~** (donc) consequently; (de façon appropriée) accordingly; **conséquent, e** adj logical, rational; (fam: important) substantial; **par conséquent** consequently

**conservateur, -trice** [kɔ̃sɛʀvatœʀ, tʀis] nm/f (Pol) conservative; (de musée) curator ▷ nm (pour aliments) preservative

**conservatoire** [kɔ̃sɛʀvatwaʀ] nm academy

**conserve** [kɔ̃sɛʀv] nf (gén pl) canned ou tinned (BRIT) food; **en ~** canned, tinned (BRIT)

**conserver** [kɔ̃sɛʀve] vt (faculté) to retain, keep; (amis, livres) to keep; (préserver, Culin) to preserve

**considérable** [kɔ̃sideʀabl] adj considerable, significant, extensive

**considération** [kɔ̃sideʀasjɔ̃] nf consideration; (estime) esteem

**considérer** [kɔ̃sideʀe] vt to consider; **~ qch comme** to regard sth as

**consigne** [kɔ̃siɲ] nf (de gare) left luggage (office) (BRIT), checkroom (US); (ordre, instruction) instructions pl; **consigne automatique** left-luggage locker

**consister** [kɔ̃siste] vi: **~ en/à faire** to consist of/in doing

**consoler** [kɔ̃sɔle] vt to console

**consommateur, -trice** [kɔ̃sɔmatœʀ, tʀis] nm/f (Écon) consumer; (dans un café) customer

**consommation** [kɔ̃sɔmasjɔ̃] nf (boisson) drink; (Écon) consumption; **de ~** (biens, sociétés) consumer cpd

**consommer** [kɔ̃sɔme] vt (suj: personne) to eat ou drink, consume; (: voiture, machine) to use, consume; (mariage) to consummate ▷ vi (dans un café) to (have a) drink

**consonne** [kɔ̃sɔn] nf consonant

**constamment** [kɔ̃stamɑ̃] adv constantly

**constant, e** [kɔ̃stɑ̃, ɑ̃t] adj constant; (personne) steadfast

**constat** [kɔ̃sta] nm (de police, d'accident) report; **~ (à l')amiable** jointly-agreed statement for insurance purposes; **~ d'échec** acknowledgement of failure

**constatation** [kɔ̃statasjɔ̃] nf (observation) (observed) fact, observation

**constater** [kɔ̃state] vt (remarquer) to note; (Admin, Jur: attester) to certify

**consterner** [kɔ̃stɛʀne] vt to dismay

**constipé, e** [kɔ̃stipe] adj constipated

**constitué, e** [kɔ̃stitɥe] adj: **~ de** made up ou composed of

**constituer** [kɔ̃stitɥe] vt (équipe) to set up; (dossier, collection) to put together; (suj: éléments: composer) to make up, constitute; (représenter, être) to constitute; **se ~ prisonnier** to give o.s. up

**constructeur, -trice** [kɔ̃stʀyktœʀ, tʀis] nm/f manufacturer, builder

**constructif, -ive** [kɔ̃stʀyktif, iv] adj constructive

**construction** [kɔ̃stʀyksjɔ̃] nf construction, building

**construire** [kɔ̃stʀɥiʀ] vt to build, construct

**consul** [kɔ̃syl] nm consul; **consulat** nm consulate

**consultant** [kɔ̃syltɑ̃] adj, nm consultant

**consultation** [kɔ̃syltasjɔ̃] nf consultation; **heures de ~** (Méd) surgery (BRIT) ou office (US) hours

**consulter** [kɔsylte] vt to consult ▷ vi (médecin) to hold surgery (BRIT), be in (the office) (US)

**contact** [kɔtakt] nm contact; **au ~ de** (air, peau) on contact with; (gens) through contact with; **mettre/ couper le ~** (Auto) to switch on/off the ignition; **entrer en** ou **prendre ~ avec** to get in touch ou contact with; **contacter** vt to contact, get in touch with

**contagieux, -euse** [kɔtaʒjø, jøz] adj infectious; (par le contact) contagious

**contaminer** [kɔtamine] vt to contaminate

**conte** [kɔt] nm tale; **conte de fées** fairy tale

**contempler** [kɔtɑple] vt to contemplate, gaze at

**contemporain, e** [kɔtɑpɔrɛ, ɛn] adj, nm/f contemporary

**contenir** [kɔt(ə)nir] vt to contain; (avoir une capacité de) to hold

**content, e** [kɔtɑ, ɑt] adj pleased, glad; **~ de** pleased with; **contenter** vt to satisfy, please; **se contenter de** to content o.s. with

**contenu** [kɔt(ə)ny] nm (d'un récipient) contents pl; (d'un texte) content

**conter** [kɔte] vt to recount, relate

**conteste** [kɔtɛst]: **sans ~** adv unquestionably, indisputably; **contester** vt to question ▷ vi (Pol, gén) rebel (against established authority)

**contexte** [kɔtɛkst] nm context

**continent** [kɔtinɑ] nm continent

**continu, e** [kɔtiny] adj continuous; **faire la journée ~e** to work without taking a full lunch break; **(courant) continu** direct current, DC

**continuel, le** [kɔtinɥɛl] adj (qui se répète) constant, continual; (continu) continuous

**continuer** [kɔtinɥe] vt (travail, voyage etc) to continue (with), carry on (with), go on (with); (prolonger: alignement, rue) to continue ▷ vi (vie, bruit) to continue,

go on; **~ à** ou **de faire** to go on ou continue doing

**contourner** [kɔturne] vt to go round; (difficulté) to get round

**contraceptif, -ive** [kɔtrasɛptif, iv] adj, nm contraceptive; **contraception** nf contraception

**contracté, e** [kɔtrakte] adj tense

**contracter** [kɔtrakte] vt (muscle etc) to tense, contract; (maladie, dette) to contract; (assurance) to take out; **se contracter** vi (muscles) to contract

**contractuel, le** [kɔtraktɥɛl] nm/f (agent) traffic warden

**contradiction** [kɔtradiksjɔ] nf contradiction; **contradictoire** adj contradictory, conflicting

**contraignant, e** [kɔtrɛɲɑ, ɑt] adj restricting

**contraindre** [kɔtrɛdr] vt: **~ qn à faire** to compel sb to do; **contrainte** nf constraint

**contraire** [kɔtrɛr] adj, nm opposite; **~ à** contrary to; **au ~** on the contrary

**contrarier** [kɔtrarje] vt (personne: irriter) to annoy; (fig: projets) to thwart, frustrate; **contrariété** nf annoyance

**contraste** [kɔtrast] nm contrast

**contrat** [kɔtra] nm contract

**contravention** [kɔtravɑsjɔ] nf parking ticket

**contre** [kɔtr] prép against; (en échange) (in exchange) for; **par ~** on the other hand

**contrebande** [kɔtrəbɑd] nf (trafic) contraband, smuggling; (marchandise) contraband, smuggled goods pl; **faire la ~ de** to smuggle

**contrebas** [kɔtrəbɑ]: **en ~** adv (down) below

**contrebasse** [kɔtrəbas] nf (double) bass

**contre...**: **contrecoup** nm repercussions pl; **contredire** vt (personne) to contradict; (faits) to refute

**contrefaçon** [kɔtrəfasɔ] nf forgery

**contre...**: **contre-indication** (pl **contre-indications**) nf (Méd) contraindication; **"contre-indication en cas d'eczéma"** "should not be used by people with eczema"; **contre-indiqué, e** adj (Méd) contraindicated; (déconseillé) unadvisable, ill-advised

**contremaître** [kɔ̃trəmɛtr] nm foreman

**contre-plaqué** [kɔ̃trəplake] nm plywood

**contresens** [kɔ̃trəsɑ̃s] nm (erreur) misinterpretation; (de traduction) mistranslation; **à ~** the wrong way

**contretemps** [kɔ̃trətɑ̃] nm hitch; **à ~** (fig) at an inopportune moment

**contribuer** [kɔ̃tribɥe]: **~ à** vt to contribute towards; **contribution** nf contribution; **mettre à contribution** to call upon; **contributions directes/indirectes** direct/indirect taxation

**contrôle** [kɔ̃trol] nm checking no pl, check; (des prix) monitoring, control; (test) test, examination; **perdre le ~ de** (véhicule) to lose control of; **contrôle continu** (Scol) continuous assessment; **contrôle d'identité** identity check

**contrôler** [kɔ̃trole] vt (vérifier) to check; (surveiller: opérations) to supervise; (: prix) to monitor, control; (maîtriser, Comm: firme) to control; **contrôleur, -euse** nm/f (de train) (ticket) inspector; (de bus) (bus) conductor(-tress)

**controversé, e** [kɔ̃trɔvɛrse] adj (personnage, question) controversial

**contusion** [kɔ̃tyzjɔ̃] nf bruise, contusion

**convaincre** [kɔ̃vɛ̃kr] vt: **~ qn (de qch)** to convince sb (of sth); **~ qn (de faire)** to persuade sb (to do)

**convalescence** [kɔ̃valesɑ̃s] nf convalescence

**convenable** [kɔ̃vnabl] adj suitable; (assez bon, respectable) decent

**convenir** [kɔ̃vnir] vi to be suitable; **~ à** to suit; **~ de** (bien-fondé de qch) to admit (to), acknowledge; (date, somme etc) to agree upon; **~ que** (admettre) to admit that; **~ de faire** to agree to do

**convention** [kɔ̃vɑ̃sjɔ̃] nf convention; **conventions** nfpl (convenances) convention sg; **convention collective** (Écon) collective agreement; **conventionné, e** adj (Admin) applying charges laid down by the state

**convenu, e** [kɔ̃vny] pp de **convenir** ▷ adj agreed

**conversation** [kɔ̃vɛrsasjɔ̃] nf conversation

**convertir** [kɔ̃vɛrtir] vt: **~ qn (à)** to convert sb (to); **se convertir (à)** to be converted (to); **~ qch en** to convert sth into

**conviction** [kɔ̃viksjɔ̃] nf conviction

**convienne** etc [kɔ̃vjɛn] vb voir **convenir**

**convivial, e, -aux** [kɔ̃vivjal, jo] adj (Inform) user-friendly

**convocation** [kɔ̃vɔkasjɔ̃] nf (document) notification to attend; (: Jur) summons sg

**convoquer** [kɔ̃vɔke] vt (assemblée) to convene; (subordonné) to summon; (candidat) to ask to attend

**coopération** [kɔɔperasjɔ̃] nf cooperation; (Admin): **la C~** ≈ Voluntary Service Overseas (brit), ≈ Peace Corps (us)

**coopérer** [kɔɔpere] vi: **~ (à)** to co-operate (in)

**coordonné, e** [kɔɔrdɔne] adj coordinated; **coordonnées** nfpl (adresse etc) address and telephone number

**coordonner** [kɔɔrdɔne] vt to coordinate

**copain** [kɔpɛ̃] (fam) nm mate, pal; (petit ami) boyfriend

**copie** [kɔpi] nf copy; (Scol) script, paper; **copier** vt, vi to copy; **copier coller** (Comput) copy and paste; **copier sur** to copy from; **copieur** nm (photo)copier

**copieux, -euse** [kɔpjø, jøz] adj copious

**copine** [kɔpin] (fam) nf mate, pal; (petite amie) girlfriend

**coq** [kɔk] nm cock, rooster

**coque** [kɔk] nf (de noix, mollusque) shell; (de bateau) hull; **à la ~** (Culin) (soft-)boiled

**coquelicot** [kɔkliko] nm poppy

**coqueluche** [kɔklyʃ] nf whooping-cough

**coquet, te** [kɔkɛ, ɛt] adj appearance-conscious; (logement) smart, charming

**coquetier** [kɔk(ə)tje] nm egg-cup

**coquillage** [kɔkijaʒ] nm (mollusque) shellfish inv; (coquille) shell

**coquille** [kɔkij] nf shell; (Typo) misprint; **coquille St Jacques** scallop

**coquin, e** [kɔkɛ̃, in] adj mischievous, roguish; (polisson) naughty

**cor** [kɔr] nm (Mus) horn; (Méd): **~ (au pied)** corn

**corail, -aux** [kɔraj, o] nm coral no pl

**Coran** [kɔrɑ̃] nm: **le ~** the Koran

**corbeau, x** [kɔrbo] nm crow

**corbeille** [kɔrbɛj] nf basket; **corbeille à papier** waste paper basket ou bin

**corde** [kɔrd] nf rope; (de violon, raquette) string; **usé jusqu'à la ~** threadbare; **corde à linge** washing ou clothes line; **corde à sauter** skipping rope; **cordes vocales** vocal cords; **cordée** nf (d'alpinistes) rope, roped party

**cordialement** [kɔrdjalmɑ̃] adv (formule épistolaire) (kind) regards

**cordon** [kɔrdɔ̃] nm cord, string; **cordon de police** police cordon; **cordon ombilical** umbilical cord

**cordonnerie** [kɔrdɔnri] nf shoe repairer's (shop); **cordonnier** nm shoe repairer

**Corée** [kɔre] nf: **la ~ du Sud/du Nord** South/North Korea

**coriace** [kɔrjas] adj tough

**corne** [kɔrn] nf horn; (de cerf) antler

**cornée** [kɔrne] nf cornea

**corneille** [kɔrnɛj] nf crow

**cornemuse** [kɔrnəmyz] nf bagpipes pl

**cornet** [kɔrnɛ] nm (paper) cone; (de glace) cornet, cone

**corniche** [kɔrniʃ] nf (route) coast road

**cornichon** [kɔrniʃɔ̃] nm gherkin

**Cornouailles** [kɔrnwaj] nf Cornwall

**corporel, le** [kɔrpɔrɛl] adj bodily; (punition) corporal

**corps** [kɔr] nm body; **à ~ perdu** headlong; **prendre ~** to take shape; **corps électoral** the electorate; **corps enseignant** the teaching profession

**correct, e** [kɔrɛkt] adj correct; (fam: acceptable: salaire, hôtel) reasonable, decent; **correcteur, -trice** nm/f (Scol) examiner; **correction** nf (voir corriger) correction; (voir correct) correctness; (coups) thrashing

**correspondance** [kɔrɛspɔ̃dɑ̃s] nf correspondence; (de train, d'avion) connection; **cours par ~** correspondence course; **vente par ~** mail-order business

**correspondant, e** [kɔrɛspɔ̃dɑ̃, ɑ̃t] nm/f correspondent; (Tél) person phoning (ou being phoned)

**correspondre** [kɔrɛspɔ̃dr] vi to correspond, tally; **~ à** to correspond to; **~ avec qn** to correspond with sb

**corrida** [kɔrida] nf bullfight

**corridor** [kɔridɔr] nm corridor

**corrigé** [kɔriʒe] nm (Scol: d'exercice) correct version

**corriger** [kɔriʒe] vt (devoir) to correct; (punir) to thrash; **~ qn de** (défaut) to cure sb of

**corrompre** [kɔrɔ̃pr] vt to corrupt; (acheter: témoin etc) to bribe

**corruption** [kɔrypsjɔ̃] nf corruption; (de témoins) bribery

**corse** [kɔrs] adj, nm/f Corsican ▷ nf: **la C~** Corsica

**corsé, e** [kɔrse] adj (café) full-flavoured; (sauce) spicy; (problème) tough

**cortège** [kɔrtɛʒ] nm procession

**cortisone** [kɔrtizɔn] nf cortisone

**corvée** [kɔrve] nf chore, drudgery no pl

**cosmétique** [kɔsmetik] nm beauty care product

**cosmopolite** [kɔsmɔpɔlit] adj cosmopolitan

**costaud, e** [kɔsto, od] (fam) adj strong, sturdy

**costume** [kɔstym] *nm* (*d'homme*) suit; (*de théâtre*) costume; **costumé, e** *adj* dressed up; **bal costumé** fancy dress ball

**cote** [kɔt] *nf* (*en Bourse*) quotation; **cote d'alerte** danger *ou* flood level; **cote de popularité** (popularity) rating

**côte** [kot] *nf* (*rivage*) coast(line); (*pente*) hill; (*Anat*) rib; (*d'un tricot, tissu*) rib, ribbing *no pl*; **~ à ~** side by side; **la Côte (d'Azur)** the (French) Riviera

**côté** [kote] *nm* (*gén*) side; (*direction*) way, direction; **de chaque ~ (de)** on each side (of); **de tous les ~s** from all directions; **de quel ~ est-il parti?** which way did he go?; **de ce/de l'autre ~** this/the other way; **du ~ de** (*provenance*) from; (*direction*) towards; (*proximité*) nearby; **de ~** (*regarder*) sideways; **mettre qch de ~** to put sth aside; **mettre de l'argent de ~** to save some money; **à ~** (right) nearby; (*voisins*) next door; **à ~ de** beside, next to; (*en comparaison*) compared to; **être aux ~s de** to be by the side of

**Côte d'Ivoire** [kotdivwaʀ] *nf*: **la Côte d'Ivoire** Côte d'Ivoire, the Ivory Coast

**côtelette** [kotlɛt] *nf* chop

**côtier, -ière** [kotje, jɛʀ] *adj* coastal

**cotisation** [kɔtizasjɔ̃] *nf* subscription, dues *pl*; (*pour une pension*) contributions *pl*

**cotiser** [kɔtize] *vi*: **~ (à)** to pay contributions (to); **se cotiser** *vi* to club together

**coton** [kɔtɔ̃] *nm* cotton; **coton hydrophile** cotton wool (BRIT), absorbent cotton (US); **Coton-tige®** *nm* cotton bud

**cou** [ku] *nm* neck

**couchant** [kuʃɑ̃] *adj*: **soleil ~** setting sun

**couche** [kuʃ] *nf* layer; (*de peinture, vernis*) coat; (*de bébé*) nappy (BRIT), diaper (US); **couches sociales** social levels *ou* strata

**couché, e** [kuʃe] *adj* lying down; (*au lit*) in bed

**coucher** [kuʃe] *vt* (*personne*) to put to bed; (: *loger*) to put up; (*objet*) to lay on its side ▷ *vi* to sleep; **~ avec qn** to sleep with sb; **se coucher** *vi* (*pour dormir*) to go to bed; (*pour se reposer*) to lie down; (*soleil*) to set; **coucher de soleil** sunset

**couchette** [kuʃɛt] *nf* couchette; (*pour voyageur, sur bateau*) berth

**coucou** [kuku] *nm* cuckoo

**coude** [kud] *nm* (*Anat*) elbow; (*de tuyau, de la route*) bend; **~ à ~** shoulder to shoulder, side by side

**coudre** [kudʀ] *vt* (*bouton*) to sew on ▷ *vi* to sew

**couette** [kwɛt] *nf* duvet, quilt; **couettes** *nfpl* (*cheveux*) bunches

**couffin** [kufɛ̃] *nm* Moses basket

**couler** [kule] *vi* to flow, run; (*fuir: stylo, récipient*) to leak; (*nez*) to run; (*sombrer: bateau*) to sink ▷ *vt* (*cloche, sculpture*) to cast; (*bateau*) to sink; (*faire échouer: personne*) to bring down

**couleur** [kulœʀ] *nf* colour (BRIT), color (US); (*Cartes*) suit; **film/télévision en ~s** colo(u)r film/television; **de ~** (*homme, femme: vieilli*) colo(u)red

**couleuvre** [kulœvʀ] *nf* grass snake

**coulisses** [kulis] *nfpl* (*Théâtre*) wings; (*fig*): **dans les ~** behind the scenes

**couloir** [kulwaʀ] *nm* corridor, passage; (*d'avion*) aisle; (*de bus*) gangway; **~ aérien/de navigation** air/shipping lane

**coup** [ku] *nm* (*heurt, choc*) knock; (*affectif*) blow, shock; (*agressif*) blow; (*avec arme à feu*) shot; (*de l'horloge*) stroke; (*tennis, golf*) stroke; (*boxe*) blow; (*fam: fois*) time; **donner un ~ de balai** to give the floor a sweep; **boire un ~** (*fam*) to have a drink; **être dans le ~** (*impliqué*) to be in on it; (*à la page*) to be hip *ou* trendy; **du ~ ...** as a result; **d'un seul ~** (*subitement*) suddenly; (*à la fois*) at one go; **du premier ~** first time; **du même ~** at the same time; **à tous les ~s** (*fam*) every time; **tenir le ~** to hold out; **après ~** afterwards; **à ~ sûr** definitely, without fail; **~ sur ~** in

quick succession; **sur le ~** outright;
**sous le ~ de** (*surprise etc*) under the
influence of; **coup de chance** stroke
of luck; **coup de coude** nudge (with
the elbow); **coup de couteau** stab (of
a knife); **coup d'envoi** kick-off; **coup
d'essai** first attempt; **coup d'État**
coup; **coup de feu** shot; **coup de filet**
(*Police*) haul; **coup de foudre** (*fig*) love
at first sight; **coup de frein** (sharp)
braking *no pl*; **coup de grâce** coup
de grâce, death blow; **coup de main**:
**donner un coup de main à qn** to give
sb a (helping) hand; **coup d'œil** glance;
**coup de pied** kick; **coup de poing**
punch; **coup de soleil** sunburn *no pl*;
**coup de sonnette** ring of the bell;
**coup de téléphone** phone call; **coup
de tête** (*fig*) (sudden) impulse; **coup de
théâtre** (*fig*) dramatic turn of events;
**coup de tonnerre** clap of thunder;
**coup de vent** gust of wind; **en coup
de vent** (*rapidement*) in a tearing hurry;
**coup franc** free kick

**coupable** [kupabl] *adj* guilty ▷ *nm/f*
(*gén*) culprit; (*Jur*) guilty party

**coupe** [kup] *nf* (*verre*) goblet; (*à
fruits*) dish; (*Sport*) cup; (*de cheveux, de
vêtement*) cut; (*graphique, plan*) (cross)
section

**couper** [kupe] *vt* to cut; (*retrancher*)
to cut (out); (*route, courant*) to cut off;
(*appétit*) to take away; (*vin à table*) to
dilute ▷ *vi* to cut; (*prendre un raccourci*)
to take a short-cut; **se couper** *vi* (*se
blesser*) to cut o.s.; **~ la parole à qn** to
cut sb short; **nous avons été coupés**
we've been cut off

**couple** [kupl] *nm* couple

**couplet** [kuplɛ] *nm* verse

**coupole** [kupɔl] *nf* dome

**coupon** [kupɔ̃] *nm* (*ticket*) coupon;
(*reste de tissu*) remnant

**coupure** [kupyʀ] *nf* cut; (*billet de
banque*) note; (*de journal*) cutting;
**coupure de courant** power cut

**cour** [kuʀ] *nf* (*de ferme, jardin*)
(court)yard; (*d'immeuble*) back yard; (*Jur,*

*royale*) court; **faire la ~ à qn** to court sb;
**cour d'assises** court of assizes; **cour
de récréation** playground

**courage** [kuʀaʒ] *nm* courage,
bravery; **courageux, -euse** *adj* brave,
courageous

**couramment** [kuʀamɑ̃] *adv*
commonly; (*parler*) fluently

**courant, e** [kuʀɑ̃, ɑ̃t] *adj* (*fréquent*)
common; (*Comm, gén: normal*) standard;
(*en cours*) current ▷ *nm* current; (*fig*)
movement; (*: d'opinion*) trend; **être
au ~ (de)** (*fait, nouvelle*) to know
(about); **mettre qn au ~ (de)** to tell sb
(about); (*nouveau travail etc*) to teach
sb the basics (of); **se tenir au ~ (de)**
(*techniques etc*) to keep o.s. up-to-date
(on); **dans le ~ de** (*pendant*) in the
course of; **le 10 ~** (*Comm*) the 10th
inst.; **courant d'air** draught; **courant
électrique** (electric) current, power

**courbature** [kuʀbatyʀ] *nf* ache

**courbe** [kuʀb] *adj* curved ▷ *nf* curve

**coureur, -euse** [kuʀœʀ, øz]
*nm/f* (*Sport*) runner (*ou* driver); (*péj*)
womanizer; manhunter

**courge** [kuʀʒ] *nf* (*Culin*) marrow;
**courgette** *nf* courgette (*BRIT*),
zucchini (*US*)

**courir** [kuʀiʀ] *vi* to run; (*Sport:
épreuve*) to compete in; (*risque*) to run;
(*danger*) to face; **~ les magasins** to go
round the shops; **le bruit court que** the
rumour is going round that

**couronne** [kuʀɔn] *nf* crown; (*de fleurs*)
wreath, circlet

**courons** *etc* [kuʀɔ̃] *vb voir* **courir**

**courriel** [kuʀjɛl] *nm* e-mail

**courrier** [kuʀje] *nm* mail, post; (*lettres
à écrire*) letters *pl*; **est-ce que j'ai du ~?**
are there any letters for me?; **courrier
électronique** e-mail

▌ Attention à ne pas traduire **courrier**
par le mot anglais **courier**.

**courroie** [kuʀwa] *nf* strap; (*Tech*) belt

**courons** *etc* [kuʀɔ̃] *vb voir* **courir**

**cours** [kuʀ] *nm* (*leçon*) class;
(*: particulier*) lesson; (*série de leçons,*

*cheminement*) course; (*écoulement*) flow; (*Comm: de devises*) rate; (: *de denrées*) price; **donner libre ~ à** to give free expression to; **avoir ~** (*Scol*) to have a class *ou* lecture; **en ~** (*année*) current; (*travaux*) in progress; **en ~ de route** on the way; **au ~ de** in the course of, during; **le ~ de change** the exchange rate; **cours d'eau** waterway; **cours du soir** night school

**course** [kuʀs] *nf* running; (*Sport: épreuve*) race; (*d'un taxi*) journey, trip; (*commission*) errand; **courses** *nfpl* (*achats*) shopping *sg*; **faire des ~s** to do some shopping

**court, e** [kuʀ, kuʀt(ə)] *adj* short ▷ *adv* short ▷ *nm:* **~ (de tennis)** (tennis) court; **à ~ de** short of; **prendre qn de ~** to catch sb unawares; **court-circuit** *nm* short-circuit

**courtoisie** [kuʀtwazi] *nf* courtesy

**couru, e** [kuʀy] *pp de* **courir**

**cousais** *etc* [kuze] *vb voir* **coudre**

**couscous** [kuskus] *nm* couscous

**cousin, e** [kuzɛ̃, in] *nm/f* cousin

**coussin** [kusɛ̃] *nm* cushion

**cousu, e** [kuzy] *pp de* **coudre**

**coût** [ku] *nm* cost; **le ~ de la vie** the cost of living

**couteau, x** [kuto] *nm* knife

**coûter** [kute] *vt, vi* to cost; **combien ça coûte?** how much is it?, what does it cost?; **ça coûte trop cher** it's too expensive; **coûte que coûte** at all costs; **coûteux, -euse** *adj* costly, expensive

**coutume** [kutym] *nf* custom

**couture** [kutyʀ] *nf* sewing; (*profession*) dressmaking; (*points*) seam; **couturier** *nm* fashion designer; **couturière** *nf* dressmaker

**couvent** [kuvɑ̃] *nm* (*de sœurs*) convent; (*de frères*) monastery

**couver** [kuve] *vt* to hatch; (*maladie*) to be coming down with ▷ *vi* (*feu*) to smoulder; (*révolte*) to be brewing

**couvercle** [kuvɛʀkl] *nm* lid; (*de bombe aérosol etc, qui se visse*) cap, top

**couvert, e** [kuvɛʀ, ɛʀt] *pp de* **couvrir** ▷ *adj* (*ciel*) overcast ▷ *nm* place setting; (*place à table*) place; **couverts** *nmpl* (*ustensiles*) cutlery *sg*; **~ de** covered with *ou* in; **mettre le ~** to lay the table

**couverture** [kuvɛʀtyʀ] *nf* blanket; (*de livre, assurance, fig*) cover; (*presse*) coverage

**couvre-lit** [kuvʀəli] *nm* bedspread

**couvrir** [kuvʀiʀ] *vt* to cover; **se couvrir** *vi* (*s'habiller*) to cover up; (*se coiffer*) to put on one's hat; (*ciel*) to cloud over

**cow-boy** [kɔbɔj] *nm* cowboy

**crabe** [kʀab] *nm* crab

**cracher** [kʀaʃe] *vi, vt* to spit

**crachin** [kʀaʃɛ̃] *nm* drizzle

**craie** [kʀɛ] *nf* chalk

**craindre** [kʀɛ̃dʀ] *vt* to fear, be afraid of; (*être sensible à: chaleur, froid*) to be easily damaged by

**crainte** [kʀɛ̃t] *nf* fear; **de ~ de/que** for fear of/that; **craintif, -ive** *adj* timid

**crampe** [kʀɑ̃p] *nf* cramp; **j'ai une ~ à la jambe** I've got cramp in my leg

**cramponner** [kʀɑ̃pɔne] *vb:* **se ~ (à)** to hang *ou* cling on (to)

**cran** [kʀɑ̃] *nm* (*entaille*) notch; (*de courroie*) hole; (*fam: courage*) guts *pl*

**crâne** [kʀɑn] *nm* skull

**crapaud** [kʀapo] *nm* toad

**craquement** [kʀakmɑ̃] *nm* crack, snap; (*du plancher*) creak, creaking *no pl*

**craquer** [kʀake] *vi* (*bois, plancher*) to creak; (*fil, branche*) to snap; (*couture*) to come apart; (*fig: accusé*) to break down; (: *fam*) to crack up ▷ *vt* (*allumette*) to strike; **j'ai craqué** (*fam*) I couldn't resist it

**crasse** [kʀas] *nf* grime, filth; **crasseux, -euse** *adj* grimy, filthy

**cravache** [kʀavaʃ] *nf* (*riding*) crop

**cravate** [kʀavat] *nf* tie

**crawl** [kʀol] *nm* crawl; **dos ~é** backstroke

**crayon** [kʀɛjɔ̃] *nm* pencil; **crayon à bille** ball-point pen; **crayon de couleur** crayon, colouring pencil; **crayon-feutre** (*pl* **crayons-feutres**) *nm* felt(-tip) pen

**création** [kreasjɔ̃] *nf* creation

**crèche** [krɛʃ] *nf* (*de Noël*) crib; (*garderie*) crèche, day nursery

**crédit** [kredi] *nm* (*gén*) credit; **crédits** *nmpl* (*fonds*) funds; **payer/acheter à ~** to pay/buy on credit *ou* on easy terms; **faire ~ à qn** to give sb credit; **créditer** *vt*: **créditer un compte (de)** to credit an account (with)

**créer** [kree] *vt* to create

**crémaillère** [kremajɛr] *nf*: **pendre la ~** to have a house-warming party

**crème** [krɛm] *nf* cream; (*entremets*) cream dessert ▷ *adj inv* cream(-coloured); **un (café) ~** ≈ a white coffee; **crème anglaise** (egg) custard; **crème Chantilly** whipped cream; **crème à raser** shaving cream; **crème solaire** suntan lotion

**créneau, x** [kreno] *nm* (*de fortification*) crenel(le); (*dans marché*) gap, niche; (*Auto*): **faire un ~** to reverse into a parking space (*between two cars alongside the kerb*)

**crêpe** [krɛp] *nf* (*galette*) pancake ▷ *nm* (*tissu*) crêpe; **crêperie** *nf* pancake shop *ou* restaurant

**crépuscule** [krepyskyl] *nm* twilight, dusk

**cresson** [kresɔ̃] *nm* watercress

**creuser** [krøze] *vt* (*trou, tunnel*) to dig; (*sol*) to dig a hole in; (*fig*) to go (deeply) into; **ça creuse** that gives you a real appetite; **se ~ la cervelle** (*fam*) to rack one's brains

**creux, -euse** [krø, krøz] *adj* hollow ▷ *nm* hollow; **heures creuses** slack periods; (*électricité, téléphone*) off-peak periods; **avoir un ~** (*fam*) to be hungry

**crevaison** [krəvɛzɔ̃] *nf* puncture

**crevé, e** [krəve] (*fam*) *adj* (*fatigué*) shattered (*BRIT*), exhausted

**crever** [krəve] *vt* (*ballon*) to burst ▷ *vi* (*pneu*) to burst; (*automobiliste*) to have a puncture (*BRIT*) *ou* a flat (tire) (*US*); (*fam*) to die

**crevette** [krəvɛt] *nf*: **~ (rose)** prawn;

**crevette grise** shrimp

**cri** [kri] *nm* cry, shout; (*d'animal: spécifique*) cry, call; **c'est le dernier ~** (*fig*) it's the latest fashion

**criard, e** [krijar, krijard] *adj* (*couleur*) garish, loud; (*voix*) yelling

**cric** [krik] *nm* (*Auto*) jack

**crier** [krije] *vi* (*pour appeler*) to shout, cry (out); (*de douleur etc*) to scream, yell ▷ *vt* (*injure*) to shout (out), yell (out)

**crime** [krim] *nm* crime; (*meurtre*) murder; **criminel, le** *nm/f* criminal; (*assassin*) murderer

**crin** [krɛ̃] *nm* (*de cheval*) hair *no pl*

**crinière** [krinjɛr] *nf* mane

**crique** [krik] *nf* creek, inlet

**criquet** [krikɛ] *nm* grasshopper

**crise** [kriz] *nf* crisis; (*Méd*) attack; (*: d'épilepsie*) fit; **piquer une ~ de nerfs** to go hysterical; **crise cardiaque** heart attack; **crise de foie: avoir une crise de foie** to have really bad indigestion

**cristal, -aux** [kristal, o] *nm* crystal

**critère** [kritɛr] *nm* criterion

**critiquable** [kritikabl] *adj* open to criticism

**critique** [kritik] *adj* critical ▷ *nm/f* (*de théâtre, musique*) critic ▷ *nf* criticism; (*Théâtre etc: article*) review

**critiquer** [kritike] *vt* (*dénigrer*) to criticize; (*évaluer*) to assess, examine (critically)

**croate** [krɔat] *adj* Croatian ▷ *nm/f*: **C~** Croat, Croatian

**Croatie** [krɔasi] *nf*: **la ~** Croatia

**crochet** [krɔʃɛ] *nm* hook; (*détour*) detour; (*Tricot: aiguille*) crochet hook; (*: technique*) crochet; **vivre aux ~s de qn** to live *ou* sponge off sb

**crocodile** [krɔkɔdil] *nm* crocodile

**croire** [krwar] *vt* to believe; **se ~ fort** to think one is strong; **~ que** to believe *ou* think that; **~ à, ~ en** to believe in

**croisade** [krwazad] *nf* crusade

**croisement** [krwazmɑ̃] *nm* (*carrefour*) crossroads *sg*; (*Bio*) crossing; (*: résultat*) crossbreed

**croiser** [krwaze] *vt* (*personne, voiture*)

to pass; (*route*) to cross, cut across; (*Bio*) to cross; **se croiser** *vi* (*personnes, véhicules*) to pass each other; (*routes, lettres*) to cross; (*regards*) to meet; **~ les jambes/bras** to cross one's legs/fold one's arms

**croisière** [kʀwazjɛʀ] *nf* cruise

**croissance** [kʀwasɑ̃s] *nf* growth

**croissant** [kʀwasɑ̃] *nm* (*à manger*) croissant; (*motif*) crescent

**croître** [kʀwatʀ] *vi* to grow

**croix** [kʀwa] *nf* cross; **la Croix Rouge** the Red Cross

**croque-monsieur** [kʀɔkməsjø] *nm inv* toasted ham and cheese sandwich

**croquer** [kʀɔke] *vt* (*manger*) to crunch; (: *fruit*) to munch; (*dessiner*) to sketch; **chocolat à croquer** plain dessert chocolate

**croquis** [kʀɔki] *nm* sketch

**crotte** [kʀɔt] *nf* droppings *pl*; **crottin** *nm* dung, manure; (*fromage*) (small round) cheese (*made of goat's milk*)

**croustillant, e** [kʀustijɑ̃, ɑ̃t] *adj* crisp

**croûte** [kʀut] *nf* crust; (*du fromage*) rind; (*Méd*) scab; **en ~** (*Culin*) in pastry

**croûton** [kʀutɔ̃] *nm* (*Culin*) crouton; (*bout du pain*) crust, heel

**croyant, e** [kʀwajɑ̃, ɑ̃t] *nm/f* believer

**CRS** *sigle fpl* (= Compagnies républicaines de sécurité) state security police force ▷ *sigle m* member of the CRS

**cru, e** [kʀy] *pp de* **croire** ▷ *adj* (*non cuit*) raw; (*lumière, couleur*) harsh; (*paroles*) crude ▷ *nm* (*vignoble*) vineyard; (*vin*) wine; **un grand ~** a great vintage; **jambon ~** Parma ham

**crû** [kʀy] *pp de* **croître**

**cruauté** [kʀyote] *nf* cruelty

**cruche** [kʀyʃ] *nf* pitcher, jug

**crucifix** [kʀysifi] *nm* crucifix

**crudités** [kʀydite] *nfpl* (*Culin*) selection of raw vegetables

**crue** [kʀy] *nf* (*inondation*) flood

**cruel, le** [kʀyɛl] *adj* cruel

**crus** *etc* [kʀy] *vb voir* **croire**; **croître**

**crûs** *etc* [kʀy] *vb voir* **croître**

**crustacés** [kʀystase] *nmpl* shellfish

**Cuba** [kyba] *nf* Cuba; **cubain, e** *adj* Cuban ▷ *nm/f*: **Cubain, e** Cuban

**cube** [kyb] *nm* cube; (*jouet*) brick; **mètre ~** cubic metre; **2 au ~** 2 cubed

**cueillette** [kœjɛt] *nf* picking; (*quantité*) crop, harvest

**cueillir** [kœjiʀ] *vt* (*fruits, fleurs*) to pick, gather; (*fig*) to catch

**cuiller** [kɥijɛʀ], **cuillère** [kɥijɛʀ] *nf* spoon; **cuiller à café** coffee spoon; (*Culin*) ≈ teaspoonful; **cuiller à soupe** soup-spoon; (*Culin*) ≈ tablespoonful; **cuillerée** *nf* spoonful

**cuir** [kɥiʀ] *nm* leather; **cuir chevelu** scalp

**cuire** [kɥiʀ] *vt* (*aliments*) to cook; (*au four*) to bake ▷ *vi* to cook; **bien cuit** (*viande*) well done; **trop cuit** overdone

**cuisine** [kɥizin] *nf* (*pièce*) kitchen; (*art culinaire*) cookery, cooking; (*nourriture*) cooking, food; **faire la ~** to cook; **cuisiné, e** *adj*: **plat cuisiné** ready-made meal *ou* dish; **cuisiner** *vt* to cook; (*fam*) to grill ▷ *vi* to cook; **cuisinier, -ière** *nm/f* cook; **cuisinière** *nf* (*poêle*) cooker

**cuisse** [kɥis] *nf* thigh; (*Culin*) leg

**cuisson** [kɥisɔ̃] *nf* cooking

**cuit, e** [kɥi, kɥit] *pp de* **cuire**

**cuivre** [kɥivʀ] *nm* copper; **les cuivres** (*Mus*) the brass

**cul** [ky] (*fam!*) *nm* arse (!)

**culminant, e** [kylminɑ̃, ɑ̃t] *adj*: **point ~** highest point

**culot** [kylo] (*fam*) *nm* (*effronterie*) cheek

**culotte** [kylɔt] *nf* (*de femme*) knickers *pl* (*BRIT*), panties *pl*

**culte** [kylt] *nm* (*religion*) religion; (*hommage, vénération*) worship; (*protestant*) service

**cultivateur, -trice** [kyltivatœʀ, tʀis] *nm/f* farmer

**cultivé, e** [kyltive] *adj* (*personne*) cultured, cultivated

**cultiver** [kyltive] *vt* to cultivate; (*légumes*) to grow, cultivate

**culture** [kyltyʀ] *nf* cultivation; (*connaissances etc*) culture; **les ~s**

**intensives** intensive farming; **culture physique** physical training; **culturel, le** *adj* cultural

**cumin** [kymɛ̃] *nm* cumin

**cure** [kyʀ] *nf* (*Méd*) course of treatment; **cure d'amaigrissement** slimming (*BRIT*) *ou* weight-loss (*US*) course; **cure de repos** rest cure

**curé** [kyʀe] *nm* parish priest

**cure-dent** [kyʀdɑ̃] *nm* toothpick

**curieux, -euse** [kyʀjø, jøz] *adj* (*indiscret*) curious, inquisitive; (*étrange*) strange, curious ▷ *nmpl* (*badauds*) onlookers; **curiosité** *nf* curiosity; (*site*) unusual feature

**curriculum vitae** [kyʀikylɔmvite] *nm inv* curriculum vitae

**cutané, e** [kytane] *adj* skin

**cuve** [kyv] *nf* vat; (*à mazout etc*) tank

**cuvée** [kyve] *nf* vintage

**cuvette** [kyvɛt] *nf* (*récipient*) bowl, basin; (*Géo*) basin

**CV** *sigle m* (*Auto*) = **cheval vapeur**; (*Comm*) = **curriculum vitae**

**cybercafé** [sibɛʀkafe] *nm* Internet café

**cyberespace** [sibɛʀɛspas] *nm* cyberspace

**cybernaute** [sibɛʀnot] *nm/f* Internet user

**cyclable** [siklabl] *adj*: **piste ~** cycle track

**cycle** [sikl] *nm* cycle; **cyclisme** *nm* cycling; **cycliste** *nm/f* cyclist ▷ *adj* cycle *cpd*; **coureur cycliste** racing cyclist

**cyclomoteur** [siklomɔtœʀ] *nm* moped

**cyclone** [siklon] *nm* hurricane

**cygne** [siɲ] *nm* swan

**cylindre** [silɛ̃dʀ] *nm* cylinder; **cylindrée** *nf* (*Auto*) (cubic) capacity; **une (voiture de) grosse cylindrée** a big-engined car

**cymbale** [sɛ̃bal] *nf* cymbal

**cynique** [sinik] *adj* cynical

**cystite** [sistit] *nf* cystitis

**d'** [d] *prép voir* **de**

**dactylo** [daktilo] *nf* (*aussi*: **~graphe**) typist; (*aussi*: **~graphie**) typing

**dada** [dada] *nm* hobby-horse

**daim** [dɛ̃] *nm* (fallow) deer *inv*; (*cuir suédé*) suede

**daltonien, ne** [daltɔnjɛ̃, jɛn] *adj* colour-blind

**dame** [dam] *nf* lady; (*Cartes, Échecs*) queen; **dames** *nfpl* (*jeu*) draughts *sg* (*BRIT*), checkers *sg* (*US*)

**Danemark** [danmaʀk] *nm* Denmark

**danger** [dɑ̃ʒe] *nm* danger; **être en ~** (*personne*) to be in danger; **mettre en ~** (*personne*) to put in danger; (*projet, carrière*) to jeopardize; **dangereux, -euse** *adj* dangerous

**danois, e** [danwa, waz] *adj* Danish ▷ *nm/f*: **D~, e** Dane ▷ *nm* (*Ling*) Danish

○ MOT-CLÉ

**dans** [dɑ̃] *prép* **1** (*position*) in; (*à l'intérieur de*) inside; **c'est dans le tiroir/le salon**

it's in the drawer/lounge; **dans la boîte** in *ou* inside the box; **je l'ai lu dans le journal** I read it in the newspaper; **marcher dans la ville** to walk about the town

**2** (*direction*) into; **elle a couru dans le salon** she ran into the lounge; **monter dans une voiture/le bus** to get into a car/on to the bus

**3** (*provenance*) out of, from; **je l'ai pris dans le tiroir/salon** I took it out of *ou* from the drawer/lounge; **boire dans un verre** to drink out of *ou* from a glass

**4** (*temps*): **dans 2 mois** in 2 months, in 2 months' time

**5** (*approximation*) about; **dans les 20 euros** about 20 euros

**danse** [dɑ̃s] *nf*: **la ~** dancing; **une ~** a dance; **la ~ classique** ballet; **danser** *vi, vt* to dance; **danseur, -euse** *nm/f* ballet dancer; (*au bal etc*) dancer; (: *cavalier*) partner

**date** [dat] *nf* date; **de longue ~** longstanding; **date de naissance** date of birth; **date limite** deadline; **dater** *vt, vi* to date; **dater de** to date from; **à dater de** (as) from

**datte** [dat] *nf* date

**dauphin** [dofɛ̃] *nm* (*Zool*) dolphin

**davantage** [davɑ̃taʒ] *adv* more; (*plus longtemps*) longer; **~ de** more

**MOT-CLÉ**

**de, d'** [də] (*de +le = du, de +les = des*) *prép*

**1** (*appartenance*) of; **le toit de la maison** the roof of the house; **la voiture d'Ann/de mes parents** Ann's/my parents' car

**2** (*provenance*) from; **il vient de Londres** he comes from London; **elle est sortie du cinéma** she came out of the cinema

**3** (*caractérisation, mesure*): **un mur de brique/bureau d'acajou** a brick wall/mahogany desk; **un billet de 50 euros** a 50 euro note; **une pièce de 2 m de large** *ou* **large de 2 m** a room 2m wide,

a 2m-wide room; **un bébé de 10 mois** a 10-month-old baby; **12 mois de crédit/travail** 12 months' credit/work; **être payé 20 euros de l'heure** to be paid 20 euros an *ou* per hour; **augmenter de 10 euros** to increase by 10 euros; **de 14 à 18** from 14 to 18

**4** (*moyen*) with; **je l'ai fait de mes propres mains** I did it with my own two hands

**5** (*cause*): **mourir de faim** to die of hunger; **rouge de colère** red with fury

**6** (*devant infinitif*) to; **il m'a dit de rester** he told me to stay

▷ *dét* **1** (*phrases affirmatives*) some (*souvent omis*); **du vin, de l'eau, des pommes** (some) wine, (some) water, (some) apples; **des enfants sont venus** some children came; **pendant des mois** for months

**2** (*phrases interrogatives et négatives*) any; **a-t-il du vin?** has he got any wine?; **il n'a pas de pommes/d'enfants** he hasn't (got) any apples/children, he has no apples/children

**dé** [de] *nm* (*à jouer*) die *ou* dice; (*aussi*: **dé à coudre**) thimble

**déballer** [debale] *vt* to unpack

**débarcadère** [debaʀkadɛʀ] *nm* wharf

**débardeur** [debaʀdœʀ] *nm* (*maillot*) tank top

**débarquer** [debaʀke] *vt* to unload, land ▷ *vi* to disembark; (*fig: fam*) to turn up

**débarras** [debaʀɑ] *nm* (*pièce*) lumber room; (*placard*) junk cupboard; **bon ~!** good riddance!; **débarrasser** *vt* to clear; **se débarrasser de** *vt* to get rid of; **débarrasser qn de** (*vêtements, paquets*) to relieve sb of; **débarrasser (la table)** to clear the table

**débat** [deba] *nm* discussion, debate; **débattre** *vt* to discuss, debate; **se débattre** *vi* to struggle

**débit** [debi] *nm* (*d'un liquide, fleuve*) flow; (*d'un magasin*) turnover (of goods); (*élocution*) delivery; (*bancaire*) debit; **débit de boissons** drinking establishment; **débit de tabac** tobacconist's

**déblayer** [debleje] vt to clear

**débloquer** [debloke] vt (prix, crédits) to free

**déboîter** [debwate] vt (Auto) to pull out; **se ~ le genou** etc to dislocate one's knee etc

**débordé, e** [deborde] adj: **être ~ (de)** (travail, demandes) to be snowed under (with)

**déborder** [deborde] vi to overflow; (lait etc) to boil over; **~ (de) qch** (dépasser) to extend beyond sth; **~ de** (joie, zèle) to be brimming over with ou bursting with

**débouché** [debuʃe] nm (pour vendre) outlet; (perspective d'emploi) opening

**déboucher** [debuʃe] vt (évier, tuyau etc) to unblock; (bouteille) to uncork ▷ vi: **~ de** to emerge from; **~ sur** (études) to lead on to

**debout** [d(ə)bu] adv: **être ~** (personne) to be standing, stand; (: levé, éveillé) to be up; **se mettre ~** to stand up; **se tenir ~** to stand; **~!** stand up!; (du lit) get up!; **cette histoire ne tient pas ~** this story doesn't hold water

**déboutonner** [debutone] vt to undo, unbutton

**débraillé, e** [debraje] adj slovenly, untidy

**débrancher** [debrɑ̃ʃe] vt to disconnect; (appareil électrique) to unplug

**débrayage** [debrɛjaʒ] nm (Auto) clutch; **débrayer** vi (Auto) to declutch; (cesser le travail) to stop work

**débris** [debri] nmpl fragments; **des ~ de verre** bits of glass

**débrouillard, e** [debrujar, ard] (fam) adj smart, resourceful

**débrouiller** [debruje] vt to disentangle, untangle; **se débrouiller** vi to manage; **débrouillez-vous** you'll have to sort things out yourself

**début** [deby] nm beginning, start; **débuts** nmpl (de carrière) début sg; **~**

**juin** in early June; **débutant, e** nm/f beginner, novice; **débuter** vi to begin, start; (faire ses débuts) to start out

**décaféiné, e** [dekafeine] adj decaffeinated

**décalage** [dekalaʒ] nm gap; **décalage horaire** time difference

**décaler** [dekale] vt to shift

**décapotable** [dekapotabl] adj convertible

**décapsuleur** [dekapsylœr] nm bottle-opener

**décédé, e** [desede] adj deceased

**décéder** [desede] vi to die

**décembre** [desɑ̃br] nm December

**décennie** [deseni] nf decade

**décent, e** [desɑ̃, ɑ̃t] adj decent

**déception** [desɛpsjɔ̃] nf disappointment

**décès** [desɛ] nm death

**décevoir** [des(ə)vwar] vt to disappoint

**décharge** [deʃarʒ] nf (dépôt d'ordures) rubbish tip ou dump; (électrique) electrical discharge; **décharger** vt (marchandise, véhicule) to unload; (tirer) to discharge; **décharger qn de** (responsabilité) to relieve sb of, release sb from

**déchausser** [deʃose] vt (skis) to take off; **se déchausser** vi to take off one's shoes; (dent) to come ou work loose

**déchet** [deʃɛ] nm (reste) scrap; **déchets** nmpl (ordures) refuse sg, rubbish sg; **~s nucléaires** nuclear waste

**déchiffrer** [deʃifre] vt to decipher

**déchirant, e** [deʃirɑ̃, ɑ̃t] adj heartrending

**déchirement** [deʃirmɑ̃] nm (chagrin) wrench, heartbreak; (gén pl: conflit) rift, split

**déchirer** [deʃire] vt to tear; (en morceaux) to tear up; (arracher) to tear out; (fig: conflit) to tear (apart); **se déchirer** vi to tear, rip; **se ~ un muscle** to tear a muscle

**déchirure** [deʃiryr] nf (accroc) tear, rip; **déchirure musculaire** torn muscle

**décidé, e** [deside] *adj* (*personne, air*) determined; **c'est ~** it's decided; **décidément** *adv* really

**décider** [deside] *vt*: **~ qch** to decide on sth; **~ de faire/que** to decide to do/that; **~ qn (à faire qch)** to persuade sb (to do sth); **se décider (à faire)** to decide (to do), make up one's mind (to do); **se ~ pour** to decide on *ou* in favour of

**décimal, e, -aux** [desimal, o] *adj* decimal

**décimètre** [desimetʀ] *nm* decimetre

**décisif, -ive** [desizif, iv] *adj* decisive

**décision** [desizjɔ̃] *nf* decision

**déclaration** [deklaʀasjɔ̃] *nf* declaration; (*discours: Pol etc*) statement; **déclaration d'impôts** *ou* **de revenus** ≈ tax return; **déclaration de vol**: **faire une déclaration de vol** to report a theft

**déclarer** [deklaʀe] *vt* to declare; (*décès, naissance*) to register; **se déclarer** *vi* (*feu*) to break out

**déclencher** [deklɑ̃ʃe] *vt* (*mécanisme etc*) to release; (*sonnerie*) to set off; (*attaque, grève*) to launch; (*provoquer*) to trigger off; **se déclencher** *vi* (*sonnerie*) to go off

**décliner** [dekline] *vi* to decline ▷ *vt* (*invitation*) to decline; (*nom, adresse*) to state

**décoiffer** [dekwafe] *vt*: **~ qn** to mess up sb's hair; **je suis toute décoiffée** my hair is in a real mess

**déçois** *etc* [deswa] *vb voir* **décevoir**

**décollage** [dekɔlaʒ] *nm* (*Aviat*) takeoff

**décoller** [dekɔle] *vt* to unstick ▷ *vi* (*avion*) to take off; **se décoller** *vi* to come unstuck

**décolleté, e** [dekɔlte] *adj* low-cut ▷ *nm* low neck(line); (*plongeant*) cleavage

**décolorer** [dekɔlɔʀe]: **se décolorer** *vi* to fade; **se faire ~ les cheveux** to have one's hair bleached

**décommander** [dekɔmɑ̃de] *vt* to cancel; **se décommander** *vi* to cry off

**déconcerter** [dekɔ̃sɛʀte] *vt* to disconcert, confound

**décongeler** [dekɔ̃ʒ(ə)le] *vt* to thaw

**déconner** [dekɔne] (*fam*) *vi* to talk rubbish

**déconseiller** [dekɔ̃seje] *vt*: **~ qch (à qn)** to advise (sb) against sth; **c'est déconseillé** it's not recommended

**décontracté, e** [dekɔ̃tʀakte] *adj* relaxed, laid-back (*fam*)

**décontracter** [dekɔ̃tʀakte]: **se décontracter** *vi* to relax

**décor** [dekɔʀ] *nm* décor; (*paysage*) scenery; **décorateur** *nm* (interior) decorator; **décoration** *nf* decoration; **décorer** *vt* to decorate

**décortiquer** [dekɔʀtike] *vt* to shell; (*fig: texte*) to dissect

**découdre** [dekudʀ]: **se découdre** *vi* to come unstitched

**découper** [dekupe] *vt* (*papier, tissu etc*) to cut up; (*viande*) to carve; (*article*) to cut out

**décourager** [dekuʀaʒe] *vt* to discourage; **se décourager** *vi* to lose heart, become discouraged

**décousu, e** [dekuzy] *adj* unstitched; (*fig*) disjointed, disconnected

**découvert, e** [dekuvɛʀ, ɛʀt] *adj* (*tête*) bare, uncovered; (*lieu*) open, exposed ▷ *nm* (*bancaire*) overdraft; **découverte** *nf* discovery; **faire la découverte de** to discover

**découvrir** [dekuvʀiʀ] *vt* to discover; (*enlever ce qui couvre*) to uncover; (*dévoiler*) to reveal; **se découvrir** *vi* (*chapeau*) to take off one's hat; (*vêtement*) to take something off; (*ciel*) to clear

**décrire** [dekʀiʀ] *vt* to describe

**décrocher** [dekʀɔʃe] *vt* (*détacher*) to take down; (*téléphone*) to take off the hook; (: *pour répondre*) to lift the receiver; (*fam: contrat etc*) to get, land ▷ *vi* (*fam: abandonner*) to drop out; (: *cesser d'écouter*) to switch off

**déçu, e** [desy] *pp de* **décevoir**

**dédaigner** [dedeɲe] *vt* to despise, scorn; (*négliger*) to disregard, spurn;

**dédaigneux, -euse** adj scornful, disdainful; **dédain** nm scorn, disdain

**dedans** [dədɑ̃] adv inside; (pas en plein air) indoors, inside ▷ nm inside; **au ~** inside

**dédicacer** [dedikase] vt: **~ (à qn)** to sign (for sb), autograph (for sb)

**dédier** [dedje] vt: **~ à** to dedicate to

**dédommagement** [dedɔmaʒmɑ̃] nm compensation

**dédommager** [dedɔmaʒe] vt: **~ qn (de)** to compensate sb (for)

**dédouaner** [dedwane] vt to clear through customs

**déduire** [dedɥiʀ] vt: **~ qch (de)** (ôter) to deduct sth (from); (conclure) to deduce ou infer sth (from)

**défaillance** [defajɑ̃s] nf (syncope) blackout; (fatigue) (sudden) weakness no pl; (technique) fault, failure; **défaillance cardiaque** heart failure

**défaire** [defɛʀ] vt (installation) to take down, dismantle; **se défaire** vi to come undone; **se ~ de** to get rid of

**défait, e** [defɛ, ɛt] adj (visage) haggard, ravaged; **défaite** nf defeat

**défaut** [defo] nm (moral) fault, failing, defect; (tissus) fault, flaw; (manque, carence): **~ de** shortage of; **prendre qn en ~** to catch sb out; **faire ~** (manquer) to be lacking; **à ~ de** for lack ou want of

**défavorable** [defavɔʀabl] adj unfavourable (BRIT), unfavorable (US)

**défavoriser** [defavɔʀize] vt to put at a disadvantage

**défectueux, -euse** [defɛktɥø, øz] adj faulty, defective

**défendre** [defɑ̃dʀ] vt to defend; (interdire) to forbid; **se défendre** vi to defend o.s.; **~ à qn qch/de faire** to forbid sb sth/to do; **il se défend** (fam: se débrouille) he can hold his own; **se ~ de/contre** (se protéger) to protect o.s. from/against; **se ~ de** (se garder de) to refrain from

**défense** [defɑ̃s] nf defence; (d'éléphant etc) tusk; **ministre de la ~** Minister of Defence (BRIT), Defence Secretary (US);

**"~ de fumer"** "no smoking"

**défi** [defi] nm challenge; **lancer un ~ à qn** to challenge sb; **sur un ton de ~** defiantly

**déficit** [defisit] nm (Comm) deficit

**défier** [defje] vt (provoquer) to challenge; (mort, autorité) to defy; **~ qn de faire qch** to challenge ou defy sb to do sth

**défigurer** [defigyʀe] vt to disfigure

**défilé** [defile] nm (Géo) (narrow) gorge ou pass; (soldats) parade; (manifestants) procession, march

**défiler** [defile] vi (troupes) to march past; (sportifs) to parade; (manifestants) to march; (visiteurs) to pour, stream; **faire ~ un document** (Comput) to scroll a document; **se défiler** vi: **il s'est défilé** (fam) he wriggled out of it

**définir** [definiʀ] vt to define

**définitif, -ive** [definitif, iv] adj (final) final, definitive; (pour longtemps) permanent, definitive; (refus) definite; **définitive** nf: **en définitive** eventually; (somme toute) in fact; **définitivement** adv (partir, s'installer) for good

**déformer** [defɔʀme] vt to put out of shape; (pensée, fait) to distort; **se déformer** vi to lose its shape

**défouler** [defule]: **se défouler** vi to unwind, let off steam

**défunt, e** [defœ̃, œ̃t] adj (mort) late before n ▷ nm/f deceased

**dégagé, e** [degaʒe] adj (route, ciel) clear; **sur un ton ~** casually

**dégager** [degaʒe] vt (exhaler) to give off; (délivrer) to free, extricate; (désencombrer) to clear; (isoler: idée, aspect) to bring out; **~ qn de** (engagement, parole etc) to release ou free sb from; **se dégager** vi (passage, ciel) to clear

**dégâts** [dega] nmpl damage sg; **faire des ~** to cause damage

**dégel** [deʒɛl] nm thaw; **dégeler** vt to thaw (out)

**dégivrer** [deʒivʀe] vt (frigo) to defrost; (vitres) to de-ice

**dégonflé, e** [degɔ̃fle] adj (pneu) flat
**dégonfler** [degɔ̃fle] vt (pneu, ballon) to let down, deflate; **se dégonfler** vi (fam) to chicken out
**dégouliner** [deguline] vi to trickle, drip
**dégourdi, e** [degurdi] adj smart, resourceful
**dégourdir** [degurdir] vt: **se ~ les jambes** to stretch one's legs (fig)
**dégoût** [degu] nm disgust, distaste; **dégoûtant, e** adj disgusting; **dégoûté, e** adj disgusted; **dégoûté de** sick of; **dégoûter** vt to disgust; **dégoûter qn de qch** to put sb off sth
**dégrader** [degrade] vt (Mil: officier) to degrade; (abîmer) to damage, deface; **se dégrader** vi (relations, situation) to deteriorate
**degré** [dəgre] nm degree
**dégressif, -ive** [degresif, iv] adj on a decreasing scale
**dégringoler** [degrɛ̃gɔle] vi to tumble (down)
**déguisement** [degizmɑ̃] nm (pour s'amuser) fancy dress
**déguiser** [degize]: **se déguiser (en)** vi (se costumer) to dress up (as); (pour tromper) to disguise o.s. (as)
**dégustation** [degystasjɔ̃] nf (de fromages etc) sampling; **~ de vins** wine-tasting session
**déguster** [degyste] vt (vins) to taste; (fromages etc) to sample; (savourer) to enjoy, savour
**dehors** [dəɔr] adv outside; (en plein air) outdoors ▷ nm outside ▷ nmpl (apparences) appearances; **mettre ou jeter ~** (expulser) to throw out; **au ~** outside; **au ~ de** outside; **en ~ de** (hormis) apart from
**déjà** [deʒa] adv already; (auparavant) before, already
**déjeuner** [deʒœne] vi to (have) lunch; (le matin) to have breakfast ▷ nm lunch
**delà** [dəla] adv: **en ~ (de), au ~ (de)** beyond
**délacer** [delase] vt (chaussures) to undo

**délai** [dele] nm (attente) waiting period; (sursis) extension (of time); (temps accordé) time limit; **sans ~** without delay; **dans les ~s** within the time limit
**délaisser** [delese] vt to abandon, desert
**délasser** [delase] vt to relax; **se délasser** vi to relax
**délavé, e** [delave] adj faded
**délayer** [deleje] vt (Culin) to mix (with water etc); (peinture) to thin down
**delco(r)** [dɛlko] nm (Auto) distributor
**délégué, e** [delege] nm/f representative
**déléguer** [delege] vt to delegate
**délibéré, e** [delibere] adj (conscient) deliberate
**délicat, e** [delika, at] adj delicate; (plein de tact) tactful; (attention) thoughtful; **délicatement** adv delicately; (avec douceur) gently
**délice** [delis] nm delight
**délicieux, -euse** [delisjø, jøz] adj (au goût) delicious; (sensation) delightful
**délimiter** [delimite] vt (terrain) to delimit, demarcate
**délinquant, e** [delɛ̃kɑ̃, -ɑ̃t] adj, nm/f delinquent
**délirer** [delire] vi to be delirious; **tu délires!** (fam) you're crazy!
**délit** [deli] nm (criminal) offence
**délivrer** [delivre] vt (prisonnier) to (set) free, release; (passeport) to issue
**deltaplane(r)** [dɛltaplan] nm hang-glider
**déluge** [delyʒ] nm (pluie) downpour; (biblique) Flood
**demain** [d(ə)mɛ̃] adv tomorrow; **~ matin/soir** tomorrow morning/evening
**demande** [d(ə)mɑ̃d] nf (requête) request; (revendication) demand; (d'emploi) application; (Écon): **la ~** demand; **"~s d'emploi"** (annonces) "situations wanted"
**demandé, e** [d(ə)mɑ̃de] adj (article etc): **très ~** (very) much in demand
**demander** [d(ə)mɑ̃de] vt to ask for;

(*chemin, heure etc*) to ask; (*nécessiter*) to require, demand; **~ qch à qn** to ask sb for sth; **~ un service à qn** to ask sb a favour; **~ à qn de faire qch** to ask sb to do sth; **je ne demande pas mieux que de ...** I'll be only too pleased to ...; **se ~ si/pourquoi** *etc* to wonder whether/why *etc*; **demandeur, -euse** *nm/f*: **demandeur d'emploi** job-seeker; **demandeur d'asile** asylum-seeker

**démangeaison** [demãʒɛzɔ̃] *nf* itching; **avoir des ~s** to be itching

**démanger** [demãʒe] *vi* to itch

**démaquillant** [demakijã] *nm* make-up remover

**démaquiller** [demakije] *vt*: **se démaquiller** to remove one's make-up

**démarche** [demaʀʃ] *nf* (*allure*) gait, walk; (*intervention*) step; (*fig: intellectuelle*) thought processes *pl*; **faire les ~s nécessaires (pour obtenir qch)** to take the necessary steps (to obtain sth)

**démarrage** [demaʀaʒ] *nm* start

**démarrer** [demaʀe] *vi* (*conducteur*) to start (up); (*véhicule*) to move off; (*travaux*) to get moving; **démarreur** *nm* (*Auto*) starter

**démêlant** [demɛlã] *nm* conditioner

**démêler** [demele] *vt* to untangle; **démêlés** *nmpl* problems

**déménagement** [demenaʒmã] *nm* move; **camion de déménagement** removal van

**déménager** [demenaʒe] *vt* (*meubles*) to (re)move ▷ *vi* to move (house); **déménageur** *nm* removal man

**démerder** [demɛʀde] (*fam*): **se démerder** *vi* to sort things out for o.s.

**démettre** [demɛtʀ] *vt*: **~ qn de** (*fonction, poste*) to dismiss sb from; **se ~ l'épaule** *etc* to dislocate one's shoulder *etc*

**demeurer** [d(ə)mœʀe] *vi* (*habiter*) to live; (*rester*) to remain

**demi, e** [dəmi] *adj* half ▷ *nm* (*bière*) ≈ half-pint (0,25 litres) ▷ *préfixe*: **~...** half-, semi..., demi-; **trois heures/bouteilles et ~es** three and a half hours/bottles, three hours/bottles and a half; **il est 2 heures et ~e/midi et ~** it's half past 2/half past 12; **à ~** half-; **à la ~e** (*heure*) on the half-hour; **demi-douzaine** *nf* half-dozen, half a dozen; **demi-finale** *nf* semifinal; **demi-frère** *nm* half-brother; **demi-heure** *nf* half-hour, half an hour; **demi-journée** *nf* half-day, half a day; **demi-litre** *nm* half-litre, half a litre; **demi-livre** *nf* half-pound, half a pound; **demi-pension** *nf* (*à l'hôtel*) half-board; **demi-pensionnaire** *nm/f*: **être demi-pensionnaire** to take school lunches

**démis, e** [demi, iz] *adj* (*épaule etc*) dislocated

**demi-sœur** [dəmisœʀ] *nf* half-sister

**démission** [demisjɔ̃] *nf* resignation; **donner sa ~** to give *ou* hand in one's notice; **démissionner** *vi* to resign

**demi-tarif** [dəmitaʀif] *nm* half-price; **voyager à ~** to travel half-fare

**demi-tour** [dəmituʀ] *nm* about-turn; **faire ~** to turn (and go) back

**démocratie** [demɔkʀasi] *nf* democracy; **démocratique** *adj* democratic

**démodé, e** [demɔde] *adj* old-fashioned

**demoiselle** [d(ə)mwazɛl] *nf* (*jeune fille*) young lady; (*célibataire*) single lady, maiden lady; **demoiselle d'honneur** bridesmaid

**démolir** [demɔliʀ] *vt* to demolish

**démon** [demɔ̃] *nm* (*enfant turbulent*) devil, demon; **le D~** the Devil

**démonstration** [demɔ̃stʀasjɔ̃] *nf* demonstration

**démonter** [demɔ̃te] *vt* (*machine etc*) to take down, dismantle; **se démonter** (*meuble*) to be dismantled, be taken to pieces; (*personne*) to lose countenance

**démontrer** [demɔ̃tʀe] *vt* to demonstrate

**démouler** [demule] *vt* to turn out

**démuni, e** [demyni] *adj* (*sans argent*) impoverished; **~ de** without

**dénicher** [deniʃe] (*fam*) *vt* (*objet*) to

unearth; (*restaurant etc*) to discover

**dénier** [denje] *vt* to deny

**dénivellation** [denivelasjɔ̃] *nf* (*pente*) slope

**dénombrer** [denɔ̃bʀe] *vt* to count

**dénomination** [denɔminasjɔ̃] *nf* designation, appellation

**dénoncer** [denɔ̃se] *vt* to denounce; **se dénoncer** to give o.s. up, come forward

**dénouement** [denumɑ̃] *nm* outcome

**dénouer** [denwe] *vt* to unknot, undo

**denrée** [dɑ̃ʀe] *nf*: **denrées alimentaires** foodstuffs

**dense** [dɑ̃s] *adj* dense; **densité** *nf* density

**dent** [dɑ̃] *nf* tooth; **dent de lait/de sagesse** milk/wisdom tooth; **dentaire** *adj* dental; **cabinet dentaire** dental surgery (BRIT), dentist's office (US)

**dentelle** [dɑ̃tɛl] *nf* lace *no pl*

**dentier** [dɑ̃tje] *nm* denture

**dentifrice** [dɑ̃tifʀis] *nm* toothpaste

**dentiste** [dɑ̃tist] *nm/f* dentist

**dentition** [dɑ̃tisjɔ̃] *nf* teeth

**dénué, e** [denɥe] *adj*: **~ de** devoid of

**déodorant** [deɔdɔʀɑ̃] *nm* deodorant

**déontologie** [deɔ̃tɔlɔʒi] *nf* code of practice

**dépannage** [depanaʒ] *nm*: **service de ~** (*Auto*) breakdown service

**dépanner** [depane] *vt* (*voiture, télévision*) to fix, repair; (*fig*) to bail out, help out; **dépanneuse** *nf* breakdown lorry (BRIT), tow truck (US)

**dépareillé, e** [depaʀeje] *adj* (*collection, service*) incomplete; (*objet*) odd

**départ** [depaʀ] *nm* departure; (*Sport*) start; **au ~** at the start; **la veille de son ~** the day before he leaves/left

**département** [depaʀtəmɑ̃] *nm* department

● **DÉPARTEMENT**
●
● France is divided into 96
● administrative units called
● **départements**. These local
● government divisions are headed

● by a state-appointed 'préfet',
● and administered by an elected
● 'Conseil général'. **Départements**
● are usually named after prominent
● geographical features such as rivers
● or mountain ranges.

**dépassé, e** [depase] *adj* superseded, outmoded; **il est complètement ~** he's completely out of his depth, he can't cope

**dépasser** [depase] *vt* (*véhicule, concurrent*) to overtake; (*endroit*) to pass, go past; (*somme, limite*) to exceed; (*fig: en beauté etc*) to surpass, outshine ▷ *vi* (*jupon etc*) to show; **se dépasser** to excel o.s.

**dépaysé, e** [depeize] *adj* disoriented

**dépaysement** [depeizmɑ̃] *nm* (*changement*) change of scenery

**dépêcher** [depeʃe]: **se dépêcher** *vi* to hurry

**dépendance** [depɑ̃dɑ̃s] *nf* dependence; (*bâtiment*) outbuilding

**dépendre** [depɑ̃dʀ]: **~ de** *vt* to depend on; (*financièrement etc*) to be dependent on; **ça dépend** it depends

**dépens** [depɑ̃] *nmpl*: **aux ~ de** at the expense of

**dépense** [depɑ̃s] *nf* spending *no pl*, expense, expenditure *no pl*; **dépenser** *vt* to spend; (*énergie*) to expend, use up; **se dépenser** *vi* to exert o.s.

**dépeupler** [depœple]: **se dépeupler** *vi* to become depopulated

**dépilatoire** [depilatwaʀ] *adj*: **crème ~** hair-removing *ou* depilatory cream

**dépister** [depiste] *vt* to detect; (*voleur*) to track down

**dépit** [depi] *nm* vexation, frustration; **en ~ de** in spite of; **en ~ du bon sens** contrary to all good sense; **dépité, e** *adj* vexed, frustrated

**déplacé, e** [deplase] *adj* (*propos*) out of place, uncalled-for

**déplacement** [deplasmɑ̃] *nm* (*voyage*) trip, travelling *no pl*; **en ~** away

**déplacer** [deplase] *vt* (*table, voiture*) to

move, shift; **se déplacer** vi to move;
(voyager) to travel; **se ~ une vertèbre**
to slip a disc
**déplaire** [deplɛʀ] vt: **ça me déplaît** I
don't like this, I dislike this; **se déplaire**
vi to be unhappy; **déplaisant, e** adj
disagreeable
**dépliant** [deplijɑ̃] nm leaflet
**déplier** [deplije] vt to unfold
**déposer** [depoze] vt (gén: mettre,
poser) to lay ou put down; (à la banque,
à la consigne) to deposit; (passager) to
drop (off), set down; (roi) to depose;
(plainte) to lodge; (marque) to register;
**se déposer** vi to settle; **dépositaire**
nm/f (Comm) agent; **déposition** nf
statement
**dépôt** [depo] nm (à la banque, sédiment)
deposit; (entrepôt) warehouse, store
**dépourvu, e** [depuʀvy] adj: **~ de**
lacking in, without; **prendre qn au ~** to
catch sb unprepared
**dépression** [depʀesjɔ̃] nf depression;
**dépression (nerveuse)** (nervous)
breakdown
**déprimant, e** [depʀimɑ̃, ɑ̃t] adj
depressing
**déprimer** [depʀime] vi to be/get
depressed

○ **MOT-CLÉ**

**depuis** [dəpɥi] prép 1 (point de départ
dans le temps) since; **il habite Paris
depuis 1983/l'an dernier** he has been
living in Paris since 1983/last year;
**depuis quand?** since when?; **depuis
quand le connaissez-vous?** how long
have you known him?
2 (temps écoulé) for; **il habite Paris
depuis 5 ans** he has been living in Paris
for 5 years; **je le connais depuis 3 ans**
I've known him for 3 years
3 (lieu): **il a plu depuis Metz** it's been
raining since Metz; **elle a téléphoné
depuis Valence** she rang from Valence
4 (quantité, rang) from; **depuis les plus
petits jusqu'aux plus grands** from the

youngest to the oldest
▷ adv (temps) since (then); **je ne lui
ai pas parlé depuis** I haven't spoken
to him since (then); **depuis que** conj
(ever) since; **depuis qu'il m'a dit ça**
(ever) since he said that to me

**député, e** [depyte] nm/f (Pol)
≈ Member of Parliament (BRIT),
≈ Member of Congress (US)
**dérangement** [deʀɑ̃ʒmɑ̃] nm (gêne)
trouble; (gastrique etc) disorder; **en ~**
(téléphone, machine) out of order
**déranger** [deʀɑ̃ʒe] vt (personne) to
trouble, bother; (projets) to disrupt,
upset; (objets, vêtements) to disarrange;
**se déranger** vi: **surtout ne vous
dérangez pas pour moi** please don't
put yourself out on my account; **est-ce
que cela vous dérange si ...?** do you
mind if ...?
**déraper** [deʀape] vi (voiture) to skid;
(personne, semelles) to slip
**dérégler** [deʀegle] vt (mécanisme) to
put out of order; (estomac) to upset
**dérisoire** [deʀizwaʀ] adj derisory
**dérive** [deʀiv] nf: **aller à la ~** (Navig,
fig) to drift
**dérivé, e** [deʀive] nm (Tech) by-product
**dermatologue** [dɛʀmatɔlɔg] nm/f
dermatologist
**dernier, -ière** [dɛʀnje, jɛʀ] adj last; (le
plus récent) latest, last; **lundi/le mois ~**
last Monday/month; **c'est le ~ cri** it's
the very latest thing; **en ~** last; **ce ~** the
latter; **dernièrement** adv recently
**dérogation** [deʀɔgasjɔ̃] nf (special)
dispensation
**dérouiller** [deʀuje] vt: **se ~ les jambes**
to stretch one's legs (fig)
**déroulement** [deʀulmɑ̃] nm (d'une
opération etc) progress
**dérouler** [deʀule] vt (ficelle) to unwind;
**se dérouler** vi (avoir lieu) to take
place; (se passer) to go (off); **tout s'est
déroulé comme prévu** everything
went as planned
**dérouter** [deʀute] vt (avion, train) to

reroute, divert; (*étonner*) to disconcert, throw (out)

**derrière** [dɛRjɛR] *adv, prép* behind ▷ *nm* (*d'une maison*) back; (*postérieur*) behind, bottom; **les pattes de ~** the back *ou* hind legs; **par ~** from behind; (*fig*) behind one's back

**des** [de] *dét voir* **de** ▷ *prép* +*dét* = **de** +**les**

**dès** [dɛ] *prép* from; **~ que** as soon as; **~ son retour** as soon as he was (*ou* is) back

**désaccord** [dezakɔR] *nm* disagreement

**désagréable** [dezagReabl] *adj* unpleasant

**désagrément** [dezagRemɑ̃] *nm* annoyance, trouble *no pl*

**désaltérer** [dezaltere] *vt*: **se désaltérer** to quench one's thirst

**désapprobateur, -trice** [dezapRɔbatœR, tRis] *adj* disapproving

**désapprouver** [dezapRuve] *vt* to disapprove of

**désarmant, e** [dezaRmɑ̃, ɑ̃t] *adj* disarming

**désastre** [dezastR] *nm* disaster; **désastreux, -euse** *adj* disastrous

**désavantage** [dezavɑ̃taʒ] *nm* disadvantage; **désavantager** *vt* to put at a disadvantage

**descendre** [desɑ̃dR] *vt* (*escalier, montagne*) to go (*ou* come) down; (*valise, paquet*) to take *ou* get down; (*étagère etc*) to lower; (*fam: abattre*) to shoot down ▷ *vi* to go (*ou* come) down; (*passager: s'arrêter*) to get out, alight; **~ à pied/en voiture** to walk/drive down; **~ de** (*famille*) to be descended from; **~ du train** to get out of *ou* get off the train; **~ de cheval** to dismount; **~ d'un arbre** to climb down from a tree; **~ à l'hôtel** to stay at a hotel

**descente** [desɑ̃t] *nf* descent, going down; (*chemin*) way down; (*Ski*) downhill (race); **au milieu de la ~** halfway down; **descente de lit** bedside rug; **descente (de police)** (police) raid

**description** [dɛskRipsjɔ̃] *nf* description

**déséquilibre** [dezekilibR] *nm* (*position*): **en ~** unsteady; (*fig: des forces, du budget*) imbalance

**désert, e** [dezɛR, ɛRt] *adj* deserted ▷ *nm* desert; **désertique** *adj* desert *cpd*

**désespéré, e** [dezɛspere] *adj* desperate

**désespérer** [dezɛspere] *vi*: **~ (de)** to despair (of); **désespoir** *nm* despair; **en désespoir de cause** in desperation

**déshabiller** [dezabije] *vt* to undress; **se déshabiller** *vi* to undress (o.s.)

**déshydraté, e** [dezidRate] *adj* dehydrated

**désigner** [dezine] *vt* (*montrer*) to point out, indicate; (*dénommer*) to denote; (*candidat etc*) to name

**désinfectant, e** [dezɛ̃fɛktɑ̃, ɑ̃t] *adj, nm* disinfectant

**désinfecter** [dezɛ̃fɛkte] *vt* to disinfect

**désintéressé, e** [dezɛ̃terese] *adj* disinterested, unselfish

**désintéresser** [dezɛ̃terese] *vt*: **se ~ (de)** to lose interest (in)

**désintoxication** [dezɛ̃tɔksikasjɔ̃] *nf*: **faire une cure de ~** to undergo treatment for alcoholism (*ou* drug addiction)

**désinvolte** [dezɛ̃vɔlt] *adj* casual, off-hand

**désir** [deziR] *nm* wish; (*sensuel*) desire; **désirer** *vt* to want, wish for; (*sexuellement*) to desire; **je désire ...** (*formule de politesse*) I would like ...

**désister** [deziste]: **se désister** *vi* to stand down, withdraw

**désobéir** [dezɔbeiR] *vi*: **~ (à qn/qch)** to disobey (sb/sth); **désobéissant, e** *adj* disobedient

**désodorisant** [dezɔdɔRizɑ̃] *nm* air freshener, deodorizer

**désolé, e** [dezɔle] *adj* (*paysage*) desolate; **je suis ~** I'm sorry

**désordonné, e** [dezɔRdɔne] *adj* untidy

**désordre** [dezɔRdR] *nm* disorder(liness), untidiness; (*anarchie*)

disorder; **en ~** in a mess, untidy
**désormais** [dezɔrmɛ] *adv* from now on
**desquelles** [dekɛl] *prép +pron* = **de +lesquelles**
**desquels** [dekɛl] *prép +pron* = **de +lesquels**
**dessécher** [deseʃe]: **se dessécher** *vi* to dry out
**desserrer** [desere] *vt* to loosen; (*frein*) to release
**dessert** [desɛr] *nm* dessert, pudding
**desservir** [desɛrvir] *vt* (*ville, quartier*) to serve; (*débarrasser*): **~ (la table)** to clear the table
**dessin** [desɛ̃] *nm* (*œuvre, art*) drawing; (*motif*) pattern, design; **dessin animé** cartoon (film); **dessin humoristique** cartoon; **dessinateur, -trice** *nm/f* drawer; (*de bandes dessinées*) cartoonist; (*industriel*) draughtsman(-woman) (BRIT), draftsman(-woman) (US); **dessiner** *vt* to draw; (*concevoir*) to design; **se dessiner** *vi* (*forme*) to be outlined; (*fig: solution*) to emerge
**dessous** [d(ə)su] *adv* underneath, beneath ▷ *nm* underside ▷ *nmpl* (*sous-vêtements*) underwear *sg*; **en ~, par ~** underneath; **au-~ (de)** below; (*peu digne de*) beneath; **avoir le ~** to get the worst of it; **les voisins du ~** the downstairs neighbours; **dessous-de-plat** *nm inv* tablemat
**dessus** [d(ə)sy] *adv* on top; (*collé, écrit*) on it ▷ *nm* top; **en ~** above; **par ~** *adv* over it ▷ *prép* over; **au-~ (de)** above; **les voisins de ~** the upstairs neighbours; **avoir le ~** to get the upper hand; **sens ~ dessous** upside down; **dessus-de-lit** *nm inv* bedspread
**destin** [dɛstɛ̃] *nm* fate; (*avenir*) destiny
**destinataire** [dɛstinatɛr] *nm/f* (*Postes*) addressee; (*d'un colis*) consignee
**destination** [dɛstinasjɔ̃] *nf* (*lieu*) destination; (*usage*) purpose; **à ~ de** bound for, travelling to
**destiner** [dɛstine] *vt*: **~ qch à qn**

(*envisager de donner*) to intend sb to have sth; (*adresser*) to intend sth for sb; **être destiné à** (*usage*) to be meant for; **se ~ à l'enseignement** to intend to become a teacher
**détachant** [detaʃɑ̃] *nm* stain remover
**détacher** [detaʃe] *vt* (*enlever*) to detach, remove; (*délier*) to untie; (*Admin*): **~ qn (auprès de** *ou* **à)** to post sb (to); **se détacher** *vi* (*se séparer*) to come off; (*: page*) to come out; (*se défaire*) to come undone; **se ~ sur** to stand out against; **se ~ de** (*se désintéresser*) to grow away from
**détail** [detaj] *nm* detail; (*Comm*): **le ~** retail; **en ~** in detail; **au ~** (*Comm*) retail; **détaillant** *nm* retailer; **détaillé, e** *adj* (*plan, explications*) detailed; (*facture*) itemized; **détailler** *vt* (*expliquer*) to explain in detail
**détecter** [detɛkte] *vt* to detect
**détective** [detɛktiv] *nm*: **détective (privé)** private detective
**déteindre** [detɛ̃dr] *vi* (*au lavage*) to run, lose its colour; **~ sur** (*vêtement*) to run into; (*fig*) to rub off on
**détendre** [detɑ̃dr] *vt* (*corps, esprit*) to relax; **se détendre** *vi* (*ressort*) to lose its tension; (*personne*) to relax
**détenir** [det(ə)nir] *vt* (*record, pouvoir, secret*) to hold; (*prisonnier*) to detain, hold
**détente** [detɑ̃t] *nf* relaxation
**détention** [detɑ̃sjɔ̃] *nf* (*d'armes*) possession; (*captivité*) detention; **détention préventive** custody
**détenu, e** [det(ə)ny] *nm/f* prisoner
**détergent** [detɛrʒɑ̃] *nm* detergent
**détériorer** [deterjɔre] *vt* to damage; **se détériorer** *vi* to deteriorate
**déterminé, e** [detɛrmine] *adj* (*résolu*) determined; (*précis*) specific, definite
**déterminer** [detɛrmine] *vt* (*fixer*) to determine; **~ qn à faire qch** to decide sb to do sth; **se ~ à faire qch** to make up one's mind to do sth
**détester** [detɛste] *vt* to hate, detest
**détour** [detur] *nm* detour; (*tournant*)

bend, curve; **ça vaut le ~** it's worth the trip; **sans ~** (fig) plainly

**détourné, e** [deturne] adj (moyen) roundabout

**détourner** [deturne] vt to divert; (par la force) to hijack; (yeux, tête) to turn away; (de l'argent) to embezzle; **se détourner** vi to turn away

**détraquer** [detrake] vt to put out of order; (estomac) to upset; **se détraquer** vi (machine) to go wrong

**détriment** [detrimã] nm: **au ~ de** to the detriment of

**détroit** [detrwa] nm strait

**détruire** [detrɥir] vt to destroy

**dette** [dɛt] nf debt

**DEUG** sigle m (= diplôme d'études universitaires générales) diploma taken after 2 years at university

**deuil** [dœj] nm (perte) bereavement; (période) mourning; **être en ~** to be in mourning

**deux** [dø] num two; **tous les ~** both; **ses ~ mains** both his hands, his two hands; **~ fois** twice; **deuxième** num second; **deuxièmement** adv secondly; **deux-pièces** nm inv (tailleur) two-piece suit; (de bain) two-piece (swimsuit); (appartement) two-roomed flat (BRIT) ou apartment (US); **deux-points** nm inv colon sg; **deux-roues** nm inv two-wheeled vehicle

**devais** [dəvɛ] vb voir **devoir**

**dévaluation** [devalɥasjõ] nf devaluation

**devancer** [d(ə)vãse] vt (coureur, rival) to get ahead of; (arriver) to arrive before; (prévenir: questions, désirs) to anticipate

**devant** [d(ə)vã] adv in front; (à distance: en avant) ahead ▷ prép in front of; (en avant) ahead of; (avec mouvement: passer) past; (en présence de) before, in front of; (étant donné) in view of ▷ nm front; **prendre les ~s** to make the first move; **les pattes de ~** the front legs, the forelegs; **par ~** (boutonner) at the front; (entrer) the front way; **aller au-~ de**

**qn** to go out to meet sb; **aller au-~ de** (désirs de qn) to anticipate

**devanture** [d(ə)vãtyr] nf (étalage) display; (vitrine) (shop) window

**développement** [devɛl(ə)ɔpmã] nm development; **pays en voie de ~** developing countries

**développer** [devɛl(ə)ɔpe] vt to develop; **se développer** vi to develop

**devenir** [dəv(ə)nir] vb +attrib to become; **que sont-ils devenus?** what has become of them?

**devez** [dəve] vb voir **devoir**

**déviation** [devjasjõ] nf (Auto) diversion (BRIT), detour (US)

**devienne** etc [dəvjɛn] vb voir **devenir**

**deviner** [d(ə)vine] vt to guess; (apercevoir) to distinguish; **devinette** nf riddle

**devis** [d(ə)vi] nm estimate, quotation

**devise** [dəviz] nf (formule) motto, watchword; **devises** nfpl (argent) currency sg

**dévisser** [devise] vt to unscrew, undo; **se dévisser** vi to come unscrewed

**devoir** [d(ə)vwar] nm duty; (Scol) homework no pl; (: en classe) exercise ▷ vt (argent, respect): **~ qch (à qn)** to owe (sb) sth; (+infin: obligation): **il doit le faire** he has to do it, he must do it; (: intention): **le nouveau centre commercial doit ouvrir en mai** the new shopping centre is due to open in May; (: probabilité): **il doit être tard** it must be late; (: fatalité): **cela devait arriver** it was bound to happen; **combien est-ce que je vous dois?** how much do I owe you?

**dévorer** [devɔre] vt to devour

**dévoué, e** [devwe] adj devoted

**dévouer** [devwe]: **se dévouer** vi (se sacrifier): **se ~ (pour)** to sacrifice o.s. (for); (se consacrer): **se ~ à** to devote ou dedicate o.s. to

**devrai** [dəvre] vb voir **devoir**

**dézipper** [dezipe] vt to unzip

**diabète** [djabɛt] nm diabetes sg; **diabétique** nm/f diabetic

**diable** [djabl] nm devil

**diabolo** [djabɔlo] nm (boisson) lemonade with fruit cordial

**diagnostic** [djagnɔstik] nm diagnosis sg; **diagnostiquer** vt to diagnose

**diagonal, e, -aux** [djagonal, o] adj diagonal; **diagonale** nf diagonal; **en diagonale** diagonally

**diagramme** [djagram] nm chart, graph

**dialecte** [djalɛkt] nm dialect

**dialogue** [djalɔg] nm dialogue

**diamant** [djamã] nm diamond

**diamètre** [djamɛtr] nm diameter

**diapositive** [djapozitiv] nf transparency, slide

**diarrhée** [djare] nf diarrhoea

**dictateur** [diktatœr] nm dictator; **dictature** nf dictatorship

**dictée** [dikte] nf dictation

**dicter** [dikte] vt to dictate

**dictionnaire** [diksjɔnɛr] nm dictionary

**dièse** [djɛz] nm sharp

**diesel** [djezɛl] nm diesel ▷ adj inv diesel

**diète** [djɛt] nf (jeûne) starvation diet; (régime) diet; **diététique** adj: **magasin diététique** health food shop (BRIT) ou store (US)

**dieu, x** [djø] nm god; **D~** God; **mon D~!** good heavens!

**différemment** [diferamã] adv differently

**différence** [diferãs] nf difference; **à la ~ de** unlike; **différencier** vt to differentiate

**différent, e** [diferã, ãt] adj (dissemblable) different; **~ de** different from; (divers) different, various

**différer** [difere] vt to postpone, put off ▷ vi: **~ (de)** to differ (from)

**difficile** [difisil] adj difficult; (exigeant) hard to please; **difficilement** adv with difficulty

**difficulté** [difikylte] nf difficulty; **en ~** (bateau, alpiniste) in difficulties

**diffuser** [difyze] vt (chaleur) to diffuse; (émission, musique) to broadcast; (nouvelle) to circulate; (Comm) to distribute

**digérer** [dizere] vt to digest; (fam: accepter) to stomach, put up with; **digestif** nm (after-dinner) liqueur; **digestion** nf digestion

**digne** [diɲ] adj dignified; **~ de** worthy of; **~ de foi** trustworthy; **dignité** nf dignity

**digue** [dig] nf dike, dyke

**dilemme** [dilɛm] nm dilemma

**diligence** [dilizãs] nf stagecoach

**diluer** [dilɥe] vt to dilute

**dimanche** [dimãʃ] nm Sunday

**dimension** [dimãsjɔ̃] nf (grandeur) size; (dimensions) dimensions

**diminuer** [diminɥe] vt to reduce, decrease; (ardeur etc) to lessen; (dénigrer) to belittle ▷ vi to decrease, diminish; **diminutif** nm (surnom) pet name

**dinde** [dɛ̃d] nf turkey

**dindon** [dɛ̃dɔ̃] nm turkey

**dîner** [dine] nm dinner ▷ vi to have dinner

**dingue** [dɛ̃g] (fam) adj crazy

**dinosaure** [dinozɔr] nm dinosaur

**diplomate** [diplɔmat] adj diplomatic ▷ nm diplomat; (fig) diplomatist; **diplomatie** nf diplomacy

**diplôme** [diplom] nm diploma; **avoir des ~s** to have qualifications; **diplômé, e** adj qualified

**dire** [dir] nm: **au ~ de** according to ▷ vt to say; (secret, mensonge, heure) to tell; **~ qch à qn** to tell sb sth; **~ à qn qu'il fasse** ou **de faire** to tell sb to do; **on dit que** they say that; **ceci** ou **cela dit** that being said; **si cela lui dit** (plaire) if he fancies it; **que dites-vous de** (penser) what do you think of; **on dirait que** it looks (ou sounds etc) as if; **dis/dites (donc)!** I say!; **se ~ (à soi-même)** to say to o.s.; **se ~ malade** (se prétendre) to claim one is ill; **ça ne se dit pas** (impoli) you shouldn't say that; (pas en usage) you don't say that

**direct, e** [dirɛkt] adj direct ▷ nm (TV):

**en ~** live; **directement** adv directly
**directeur, -trice** [diʀɛktœʀ, tʀis] nm/f (d'entreprise) director; (de service) manager(-eress); (d'école) head(teacher) (BRIT), principal (US)
**direction** [diʀɛksjɔ̃] nf (sens) direction; (d'entreprise) management; (Auto) steering; **"toutes ~s"** "all routes"
**dirent** [diʀ] vb voir **dire**
**dirigeant, e** [diʀiʒɑ̃, ɑ̃t] adj (classe) ruling ▷ nm/f (d'un parti etc) leader
**diriger** [diʀiʒe] vt (entreprise) to manage, run; (véhicule) to steer; (orchestre) to conduct; (recherches, travaux) to supervise; **~ sur** (arme) to point ou level ou aim at; **~ son regard sur** to look in the direction of; **se diriger** vi (s'orienter) to find one's way; **se ~ vers** ou **sur** to make ou head for
**dis** [di] vb voir **dire**
**discerner** [disɛʀne] vt to discern, make out
**discipline** [disiplin] nf discipline; **discipliner** vt to discipline
**discontinu, e** [diskɔ̃tiny] adj intermittent
**discontinuer** [diskɔ̃tinɥe] vi: **sans ~** without stopping, without a break
**discothèque** [diskɔtɛk] nf (boîte de nuit) disco(thèque)
**discours** [diskuʀ] nm speech
**discret, -ète** [diskʀɛ, ɛt] adj discreet; (parfum, maquillage) unobtrusive; **discrétion** nf discretion; **à discrétion** as much as one wants
**discrimination** [diskʀiminasjɔ̃] nf discrimination; **sans ~** indiscriminately
**discussion** [diskysjɔ̃] nf discussion
**discutable** [diskytabl] adj debatable
**discuter** [diskyte] vt (débattre) to discuss; (contester) to question, dispute ▷ vi to talk; (protester) to argue; **~ de** to discuss
**dise** [diz] vb voir **dire**
**disjoncteur** [disʒɔ̃ktœʀ] nm (Élec) circuit breaker
**disloquer** [dislɔke]: **se disloquer** vi

(parti, empire) to break up; (meuble) to come apart; (épaule) to be dislocated
**disons** [dizɔ̃] vb voir **dire**
**disparaître** [dispaʀɛtʀ] vi to disappear; (se perdre: traditions etc) to die out; **faire ~** (tache) to remove; (douleur) to get rid of
**disparition** [dispaʀisjɔ̃] nf disappearance; **espèce en voie de ~** endangered species
**disparu, e** [dispaʀy] nm/f missing person ▷ adj: **être porté ~** to be reported missing
**dispensaire** [dispɑ̃sɛʀ] nm community clinic
**dispenser** [dispɑ̃se] vt: **~ qn de** to exempt sb from
**disperser** [dispɛʀse] vt to scatter; **se disperser** vi to break up
**disponible** [disponibl(ə)] adj available
**disposé, e** [dispoze] adj: **bien/mal ~** (humeur) in a good/bad mood; **~ à** (prêt à) willing ou prepared to
**disposer** [dispoze] vt to arrange ▷ vi: **vous pouvez ~** you may leave; **~ de** to have (at one's disposal); **se ~ à faire** to prepare to do, be about to do
**dispositif** [dispozitif] nm device; (fig) system, plan of action
**disposition** [dispozisjɔ̃] nf (arrangement) arrangement, layout; (humeur) mood; **prendre ses ~s** to make arrangements; **avoir des ~s pour la musique** etc to have a special aptitude for music etc; **à la ~ de qn** at sb's disposal; **je suis à votre ~** I am at your service
**disproportionné, e** [dispʀɔpɔʀsjɔne] adj disproportionate, out of all proportion
**dispute** [dispyt] nf quarrel, argument; **disputer** vt (match) to play; (combat) to fight; **se disputer** vi to quarrel
**disqualifier** [diskalifje] vt to disqualify
**disque** [disk] nm (Mus) record; (forme, pièce) disc; (Sport) discus; **disque compact** compact disc; **disque dur**

hard disk; **disquette** nf floppy disk, diskette

**dissertation** [disɛʀtasjɔ̃] nf (Scol) essay

**dissimuler** [disimyle] vt to conceal

**dissipé, e** [disipe] adj (élève) undisciplined, unruly

**dissolvant** [disɔlvɑ̃] nm nail polish remover

**dissuader** [disɥade] vt: **~ qn de faire** to dissuade sb from doing

**distance** [distɑ̃s] nf distance; (fig: écart) gap; **à ~** at ou from a distance; **distancer** vt to outdistance

**distant, e** [distɑ̃, ɑ̃t] adj (réservé) distant; **~ de** (lieu) far away from

**distillerie** [distilʀi] nf distillery

**distinct, e** [distɛ̃(kt), ɛ̃kt] adj distinct; **distinctement** adv distinctly, clearly; **distinctif, -ive** adj distinctive

**distingué, e** [distɛ̃ge] adj distinguished

**distinguer** [distɛ̃ge] vt to distinguish; **se ~ de** to be distinguished by

**distraction** [distʀaksjɔ̃] nf (inattention) absent-mindedness; (passe-temps) distraction, entertainment

**distraire** [distʀɛʀ] vt (divertir) to entertain, divert; (déranger) to distract; **se distraire** vi to amuse ou enjoy o.s.; **distrait, e** adj absent-minded

**distrayant, e** [distʀɛjɑ̃, ɑ̃t] adj entertaining

**distribuer** [distʀibɥe] vt to distribute, hand out; (Cartes) to deal (out); (courrier) to deliver; **distributeur** nm (Comm) distributor; **distributeur (automatique)** (vending) machine; **distributeur de billets** (cash) dispenser

**dit, e** [di, dit] pp de **dire** ▷ adj (fixé): **le jour ~** the arranged day; (surnommé): **X, ~ Pierrot** X, known as Pierrot

**dites** [dit] vb voir **dire**

**divan** [divɑ̃] nm divan

**divers, e** [divɛʀ, ɛʀs] adj (varié) diverse, varied; (différent) different, various; **~es**

**personnes** various ou several people

**diversité** [divɛʀsite] nf (variété) diversity

**divertir** [divɛʀtiʀ]: **se divertir** vi to amuse ou enjoy o.s.; **divertissement** nm distraction, entertainment

**diviser** [divize] vt to divide; **division** nf division

**divorce** [divɔʀs] nm divorce; **divorcé, e** nm/f divorcee; **divorcer** vi to get a divorce, get divorced; **divorcer de** ou **d'avec qn** to divorce sb

**divulguer** [divylge] vt to disclose

**dix** [dis] num ten; **dix-huit** num eighteen; **dix-huitième** num eighteenth; **dixième** num tenth; **dix-neuf** num nineteen; **dix-neuvième** num nineteenth; **dix-sept** num seventeen; **dix-septième** num seventeenth

**dizaine** [dizɛn] nf: **une ~ (de)** about ten, ten or so

**do** [do] nm (note) C; (en chantant la gamme) do(h)

**docile** [dɔsil] adj docile

**dock** [dɔk] nm dock; **docker** nm docker

**docteur** [dɔktœʀ] nm doctor; **doctorat** nm doctorate

**doctrine** [dɔktʀin] nf doctrine

**document** [dɔkymɑ̃] nm document; **documentaire** adj, nm documentary; **documentation** nf documentation, literature; **documenter** vt: **se documenter (sur)** to gather information (on)

**dodo** [dodo] nm (langage enfantin): **aller faire ~** to go to beddy-byes

**dogue** [dɔg] nm mastiff

**doigt** [dwa] nm finger; **à deux ~s de** within an inch of; **un ~ de lait/whiskey** a drop of milk/whisky; **doigt de pied** toe

**doit** etc [dwa] vb voir **devoir**

**dollar** [dɔlaʀ] nm dollar

**domaine** [dɔmɛn] nm estate, property; (fig) domain, field

**domestique** [dɔmɛstik] adj domestic ▷ nm/f servant, domestic

**domicile** [dɔmisil] *nm* home, place of residence; **à ~** at home; **livrer à ~** to deliver; **domicilié, e** *adj*: **"domicilié à ..."** "address ..."

**dominant, e** [dɔminã, ãt] *adj* (*opinion*) predominant

**dominer** [dɔmine] *vt* to dominate; (*sujet*) to master; (*surpasser*) to outclass, surpass; (*surplomber*) to tower above, dominate ▷ *vi* to be in the dominant position; **se dominer** *vi* to control o.s.

**domino** [dɔmino] *nm* domino; **dominos** *nmpl* (*jeu*) dominoes *sg*

**dommage** [dɔmaʒ] *nm*: **~s** (*dégâts*) damage *no pl*; **c'est ~!** what a shame!; **c'est ~ que** it's a shame ou pity that

**dompter** [dɔ̃(p)te] *vt* to tame; **dompteur, -euse** *nm/f* trainer

**DOM-ROM** [dɔmʀɔm] *sigle m* (= *départements et régions d'outre-mer*) French overseas departments and regions

**don** [dɔ̃] *nm* gift; (*charité*) donation; **avoir des ~s pour** to have a gift ou talent for; **elle a le ~ de m'énerver** she's got a knack of getting on my nerves

**donc** [dɔ̃k] *conj* therefore, so; (*après une digression*) so, then

**donné, e** [dɔne] *adj* (*convenu: lieu, heure*) given; (*pas cher: fam*): **c'est ~** it's a gift; **étant ~ que ...** given that ...; **données** *nfpl* data

**donner** [dɔne] *vt* to give; (*vieux habits etc*) to give away; (*spectacle*) to put on; **~ qch à qn** to give sb sth, give sth to sb; **~ sur** (*suj: fenêtre, chambre*) to look (out) onto; **ça donne soif/faim** it makes you (feel) thirsty/hungry; **se ~ à fond** to give one's all; **se ~ du mal** to take (great) trouble; **s'en ~ à cœur joie** (*fam*) to have a great time

**MOT-CLÉ**

**dont** [dɔ̃] *pron relatif* **1** (*appartenance: objets*) whose, of which; (*appartenance: êtres animés*) whose; **la maison dont le toit est rouge** the house the roof of which is red, the house whose roof is red; **l'homme dont je connais la sœur** the man whose sister I know

**2** (*parmi lesquel(le)s*): **2 livres, dont l'un est ...** 2 books, one of which is ...; **il y avait plusieurs personnes, dont Gabrielle** there were several people, among them Gabrielle; **10 blessés, dont 2 grièvement** 10 injured, 2 of them seriously

**3** (*complément d'adjectif, de verbe*): **le fils dont il est si fier** the son he's so proud of; **le pays dont il est originaire** the country he's from; **la façon dont il l'a fait** the way he did it; **ce dont je parle** what I'm talking about

**dopage** [dɔpaʒ] *nm* (*Sport*) drug use; (*de cheval*) doping

**doré, e** [dɔʀe] *adj* golden; (*avec dorure*) gilt, gilded

**dorénavant** [dɔʀenavã] *adv* henceforth

**dorer** [dɔʀe] *vt* to gild; (*faire*) **~** (*Culin*) to brown

**dorloter** [dɔʀlɔte] *vt* to pamper

**dormir** [dɔʀmiʀ] *vi* to sleep; (*être endormi*) to be asleep

**dortoir** [dɔʀtwaʀ] *nm* dormitory

**dos** [do] *nm* back; (*de livre*) spine; **"voir au ~"** "see over"; **de ~** from the back

**dosage** [dozaʒ] *nm* mixture

**dose** [doz] *nf* dose; **doser** *vt* to measure out; **il faut savoir doser ses efforts** you have to be able to pace yourself

**dossier** [dosje] *nm* (*documents*) file; (*de chaise*) back; (*Presse*) feature; (*Comput*) folder; **un ~ scolaire** a school report

**douane** [dwan] *nf* customs *pl*; **douanier, -ière** *adj* customs *cpd* ▷ *nm* customs officer

**double** [dubl] *adj, adv* double ▷ *nm* (2 *fois plus*): **le ~ (de)** twice as much (ou many) (as); (*autre exemplaire*) duplicate, copy; (*sosie*) double; (*Tennis*) doubles *sg*; **en ~ (exemplaire)** in duplicate; **faire ~ emploi** to be redundant; **double-cliquer** *vi* (*Inform*) to double-click

**doubler** [duble] *vt* (*multiplier par 2*) to double; (*vêtement*) to line; (*dépasser*) to overtake, pass; (*film*) to dub; (*acteur*) to stand in for ▷ *vi* to double

**doublure** [dublyʀ] *nf* lining; (*Cinéma*) stand-in

**douce** [dus] *adj voir* **doux**; **douceâtre** *adj* sickly sweet; **doucement** *adv* gently; (*lentement*) slowly; **douceur** *nf* softness; (*de quelqu'un*) gentleness; (*de climat*) mildness

**douche** [duʃ] *nf* shower; **prendre une ~** to have *ou* take a shower; **doucher: se doucher** *vi* to have *ou* take a shower

**doué, e** [dwe] *adj* gifted, talented; **être ~ pour** to have a gift for

**douille** [duj] *nf* (*Élec*) socket

**douillet, te** [dujɛ, ɛt] *adj* cosy; (*péj: à la douleur*) soft

**douleur** [dulœʀ] *nf* pain; (*chagrin*) grief, distress; **douloureux, -euse** *adj* painful

**doute** [dut] *nm* doubt; **sans ~** no doubt; (*probablement*) probably; **sans aucun ~** without a doubt; **douter** *vt* to doubt; **douter de** (*sincérité de qn*) to have (one's) doubts about; (*réussite*) to be doubtful of; **douter que** to doubt if *ou* whether; **se douter de qch/que** to suspect sth/that; **je m'en doutais** I suspected as much; **douteux, -euse** *adj* (*incertain*) doubtful; (*péj*) dubious-looking

**Douvres** [duvʀ] *n* Dover

**doux, douce** [du, dus] *adj* soft; (*sucré*) sweet; (*peu fort: moutarde, climat*) mild; (*pas brusque*) gentle

**douzaine** [duzɛn] *nf* (12) dozen; (*environ 12*): **une ~ (de)** a dozen or so

**douze** [duz] *num* twelve; **douzième** *num* twelfth

**dragée** [dʀaʒe] *nf* sugared almond

**draguer** [dʀage] *vt* (*rivière*) to dredge; (*fam*) to try to pick up

**dramatique** [dʀamatik] *adj* dramatic; (*tragique*) tragic ▷ *nf* (*TV*) (television) drama

**drame** [dʀam] *nm* drama

**drap** [dʀa] *nm* (*de lit*) sheet; (*tissu*) woollen fabric

**drapeau, x** [dʀapo] *nm* flag

**drap-housse** [dʀaus] *nm* fitted sheet

**dresser** [dʀese] *vt* (*mettre vertical, monter*) to put up, erect; (*liste*) to draw up; (*animal*) to train; **se dresser** *vi* (*obstacle*) to stand; (*personne*) to draw o.s. up; **~ qn contre qn** to set sb against sb; **~ l'oreille** to prick up one's ears

**drogue** [dʀɔg] *nf* drug; **la ~** drugs *pl*; **drogué, e** *nm/f* drug addict; **droguer** *vt* (*victime*) to drug; **se droguer** *vi* (*aux stupéfiants*) to take drugs; (*péj: de médicaments*) to dose o.s. up; **droguerie** *nf* hardware shop; **droguiste** *nm* keeper/owner of a hardware shop

**droit, e** [dʀwa, dʀwat] *adj* (*non courbe*) straight; (*vertical*) upright, straight; (*fig: loyal*) upright, straight(forward); (*opposé à gauche*) right, right-hand ▷ *adv* straight ▷ *nm* (*prérogative*) right; (*taxe*) duty, tax; (: *d'inscription*) fee; (*Jur*): **le ~** law; **avoir le ~ de** to be allowed to; **avoir ~ à** to be entitled to; **être dans son ~** to be within one's rights; **à ~e** on the right; (*direction*) (to the) right; **droits d'auteur** royalties; **droits d'inscription** enrolment fee; **droite** *nf* (*Pol*): **la droite** the right (wing); **droitier, -ière** *adj* right-handed

**drôle** [dʀol] *adj* funny; **une ~ d'idée** a funny idea

**dromadaire** [dʀɔmadɛʀ] *nm* dromedary

**du** [dy] *dét voir* **de** ▷ *prép* +*dét* = **de + le**

**dû, due** [dy] *vb voir* **devoir** ▷ *adj* (*somme*) owing, owed; (*causé par*): **dû à** due to ▷ *nm* due

**dune** [dyn] *nf* dune

**duplex** [dypleks] *nm* (*appartement*) split-level apartment, duplex

**duquel** [dykel] *prép* +*pron* = **de +lequel**

**dur, e** [dyʀ] *adj* (*pierre, siège, travail, problème*) hard; (*voix, climat*) harsh; (*sévère*) hard, harsh; (*cruel*) hard(-hearted); (*porte, col*) stiff; (*viande*) tough ▷ *adv* hard ▷ *nm* (*fam*:

**meneur**) tough nut; **~ d'oreille** hard of hearing

**durant** [dyrɑ̃] *prép* (*au cours de*) during; (*pendant*) for; **des mois ~** for months

**durcir** [dyrsir] *vt, vi* to harden; **se durcir** *vi* to harden

**durée** [dyre] *nf* length; (*d'une pile etc*) life; **de courte ~** (*séjour*) short

**durement** [dyrmɑ̃] *adv* harshly

**durer** [dyre] *vi* to last

**dureté** [dyrte] *nf* hardness; harshness; stiffness; toughness

**durit(r)** [dyrit] *nf* (car radiator) hose

**duvet** [dyvɛ] *nm* down; (*sac de couchage*) down-filled sleeping bag

**DVD** *sigle m* (= *digital versatile disc*) DVD

**dynamique** [dinamik] *adj* dynamic; **dynamisme** *nm* dynamism

**dynamo** [dinamo] *nf* dynamo

**dyslexie** [dislɛksi] *nf* dyslexia, word-blindness

**eau, x** [o] *nf* water; **eaux** *nfpl* (*Méd*) waters; **prendre l'~** to leak, let in water; **tomber à l'~** (*fig*) to fall through; **eau de Cologne** eau de Cologne; **eau courante** running water; **eau de javel** bleach; **eau de toilette** toilet water; **eau douce** fresh water; **eau gazeuse** sparkling (mineral) water; **eau minérale** mineral water; **eau plate** still water; **eau salée** salt water; **eau-de-vie** *nf* brandy

**ébène** [ebɛn] *nf* ebony; **ébéniste** *nm* cabinetmaker

**éblouir** [ebluir] *vt* to dazzle

**éboueur** [ebwœr] *nm* dustman (BRIT), garbageman (US)

**ébouillanter** [ebujɑ̃te] *vt* to scald; (*Culin*) to blanch

**éboulement** [ebulmɑ̃] *nm* rock fall

**ébranler** [ebrɑ̃le] *vt* to shake; (*affaiblir*) to weaken; **s'ébranler** *vi* (*partir*) to move off

**ébullition** [ebylisjɔ̃] *nf* boiling point; **en ~** boiling

**écaille** [ekɑj] nf (de poisson) scale; (matière) tortoiseshell; **écailler** vt (poisson) to scale; **s'écailler** vi to flake ou peel (off)

**écart** [ekaʁ] nm gap; **à l'~** out of the way; **à l'~ de** away from; **faire un ~** (voiture) to swerve

**écarté, e** [ekaʁte] adj (lieu) out-of-the-way, remote; (ouvert): **les jambes ~es** legs apart; **les bras ~s** arms outstretched

**écarter** [ekaʁte] vt (séparer) to move apart, separate; (éloigner) to push back, move away; (ouvrir: bras, jambes) to spread, open; (: rideau) to draw (back); (éliminer: candidat, possibilité) to dismiss; **s'écarter** vi to part; (s'éloigner) to move away; **s'~ de** to wander from

**échafaudage** [eʃafodaʒ] nm scaffolding

**échalote** [eʃalɔt] nf shallot

**échange** [eʃɑ̃ʒ] nm exchange; **en ~ de** in exchange ou return for; **échanger** vt: **échanger qch (contre)** to exchange sth (for)

**échantillon** [eʃɑ̃tijɔ̃] nm sample

**échapper** [eʃape]: **à** vt (gardien) to escape (from); (punition, péril) to escape; **s'échapper** vi to escape; **~ à qn** (détail, sens) to escape sb; (objet qu'on tient) to slip out of sb's hands; **laisser ~** (cri etc) to let out; **l'~ belle** to have a narrow escape

**écharde** [eʃaʁd] nf splinter (of wood)

**écharpe** [eʃaʁp] nf scarf; **avoir le bras en ~** to have one's arm in a sling

**échauffer** [eʃofe] vt (moteur) to overheat; **s'échauffer** vi (Sport) to warm up; (dans la discussion) to become heated

**échéance** [eʃeɑ̃s] nf (d'un paiement: date) settlement date; (fig) deadline; **à brève ~** in the short term; **à longue ~** in the long run

**échéant** [eʃeɑ̃]: **le cas ~** adv if the case arises

**échec** [eʃɛk] nm failure; (Échecs): **~ et mat/au roi** checkmate/check; **échecs** nmpl (jeu) chess sg; **tenir en ~** to hold in check

**échelle** [eʃɛl] nf ladder; (fig, d'une carte) scale

**échelon** [eʃ(ə)lɔ̃] nm (d'échelle) rung; (Admin) grade; **échelonner** vt to space out

**échiquier** [eʃikje] nm chessboard

**écho** [eko] nm echo; **échographie** nf: **passer une échographie** to have a scan

**échouer** [eʃwe] vi to fail; **s'échouer** vi to run aground

**éclabousser** [eklabuse] vt to splash

**éclair** [eklɛʁ] nm (d'orage) flash of lightning, lightning no pl; (gâteau) éclair

**éclairage** [eklɛʁaʒ] nm lighting

**éclaircie** [eklɛʁsi] nf bright interval

**éclaircir** [eklɛʁsiʁ] vt to lighten; (fig: mystère) to clear up; (: point) to clarify; **s'éclaircir** vi (ciel) to clear; **s'~ la voix** to clear one's throat; **éclaircissement** nm (sur un point) clarification

**éclairer** [eklɛʁe] vt (lieu) to light (up); (personne: avec une lampe etc) to light the way for; (fig: problème) to shed light on ▷ vi: **~ mal/bien** to give a poor/good light; **s'~ à la bougie** to use candlelight

**éclat** [ekla] nm (de bombe, de verre) fragment; (du soleil, d'une couleur etc) brightness, brilliance; (d'une cérémonie) splendour; (scandale): **faire un ~** to cause a commotion; **éclats de voix** shouts; **éclat de rire** roar of laughter

**éclatant, e** [eklatɑ̃, ɑ̃t] adj brilliant

**éclater** [eklate] vi (pneu) to burst; (bombe) to explode; (guerre) to break out; (groupe, parti) to break up; **~ en sanglots/de rire** to burst out sobbing/laughing

**écluse** [eklyz] nf lock

**écœurant, e** [ekœrɑ̃, ɑ̃t] adj (gâteau etc) sickly; (fig) sickening

**écœurer** [ekœre] vt: **~ qn** (nourriture) to make sb feel sick; (conduite, personne) to disgust sb

**école** [ekɔl] nf school; **aller à l'~** to go

to school; **école maternelle** nursery school; **école primaire** primary (*BRIT*) *ou* grade (*US*) school; **école secondaire** secondary (*BRIT*) *ou* high (*US*) school; **écolier, -ière** *nm/f* schoolboy(-girl)

**écologie** [ekɔlɔʒi] *nf* ecology; **écologique** *adj* environment-friendly; **écologiste** *nm/f* ecologist

**économe** [ekɔnɔm] *adj* thrifty ▷ *nm/f* (*de lycée etc*) bursar (*BRIT*), treasurer (*US*)

**économie** [ekɔnɔmi] *nf* economy; (*gain: d'argent, de temps etc*) saving; (*science*) economics *sg*; **économies** *nfpl* (*pécule*) savings; **économique** *adj* (*avantageux*) economical; (*Écon*) economic; **économiser** *vt, vi* to save

**écorce** [ekɔʀs] *nf* bark; (*de fruit*) peel

**écorcher** [ekɔʀʃe] *vt*: **s'~ le genou/la main** to graze one's knee/one's hand; **écorchure** *nf* graze

**écossais, e** [ekɔsɛ, ɛz] *adj* Scottish ▷ *nm/f*: **É~, e** Scot

**Écosse** [ekɔs] *nf*: **l'~** Scotland

**écouter** [ekute] *vt* to listen to; **s'écouter** (*malade*) to be a bit of a hypochondriac; **si je m'écoutais** if I followed my instincts; **écouteur** *nm* (*Tél*) receiver; **écouteurs** *nmpl* (*casque*) headphones *pl*, headset

**écran** [ekʀɑ̃] *nm* screen; **petit ~** television; **~ total** sunblock

**écrasant, e** [ekʀazɑ̃, ɑ̃t] *adj* overwhelming

**écraser** [ekʀaze] *vt* to crush; (*piéton*) to run over; **s'écraser** *vi* to crash; **s'~ contre** to crash into

**écrémé, e** [ekʀeme] *adj* (*lait*) skimmed

**écrevisse** [ekʀəvis] *nf* crayfish *inv*

**écrire** [ekʀiʀ] *vt* to write; **s'écrire** to write to each other; **ça s'écrit comment?** how is it spelt?; **écrit** *nm* (*examen*) written paper; **par écrit** in writing

**écriteau, x** [ekʀito] *nm* notice, sign

**écriture** [ekʀityʀ] *nf* writing; **écritures** *nfpl* (*Comm*) accounts, books; **l'É~ (sainte), les É~s** the Scriptures

**écrivain** [ekʀivɛ̃] *nm* writer

**écrou** [ekʀu] *nm* nut

**écrouler** [ekʀule]: **s'écrouler** *vi* to collapse

**écru, e** [ekʀy] *adj* (*couleur*) off-white, écru

**écume** [ekym] *nf* foam

**écureuil** [ekyʀœj] *nm* squirrel

**écurie** [ekyʀi] *nf* stable

**eczéma** [ɛgzema] *nm* eczema

**EDF** *sigle f* (= *Électricité de France*) *national electricity company*

**Édimbourg** [edɛ̃buʀ] *n* Edinburgh

**éditer** [edite] *vt* (*publier*) to publish; (*annoter*) to edit; **éditeur, -trice** *nm/f* publisher; **édition** *nf* edition; (*industrie du livre*) publishing

**édredon** [edʀədɔ̃] *nm* eiderdown

**éducateur, -trice** [edykatœʀ, tʀis] *nm/f* teacher; (*en école spécialisée*) instructor

**éducatif, -ive** [edykatif, iv] *adj* educational

**éducation** [edykasjɔ̃] *nf* education; (*familiale*) upbringing; (*manières*) (good) manners *pl*; **éducation physique** physical education

**éduquer** [edyke] *vt* to educate; (*élever*) to bring up

**effacer** [efase] *vt* to erase, rub out; **s'effacer** *vi* (*inscription etc*) to wear off; (*pour laisser passer*) to step aside

**effarant, e** [efaʀɑ̃, ɑ̃t] *adj* alarming

**effectif, -ive** [efɛktif, iv] *adj* real ▷ *nm* (*Scol*) (pupil) numbers *pl*; (*entreprise*) staff, workforce; **effectivement** *adv* (*réellement*) actually, really; (*en effet*) indeed

**effectuer** [efɛktɥe] *vt* (*opération*) to carry out; (*trajet*) to make

**effervescent, e** [efɛʀvesɑ̃, ɑ̃t] *adj* effervescent

**effet** [efɛ] *nm* effect; (*impression*) impression; **effets** *nmpl* (*vêtements etc*) things; **faire ~** (*médicament*) to take effect; **faire de l'~** (*impressionner*) to make an impression; **faire bon/ mauvais ~ sur qn** to make a good/bad impression on sb; **en ~** indeed; **effet de**

serre greenhouse effect

**efficace** [efikas] adj (personne) efficient; (action, médicament) effective; **efficacité** nf efficiency; effectiveness

**effondrer** [efɔ̃dʀe]: **s'effondrer** vi to collapse

**efforcer** [efɔʀse]: **s'efforcer de** vt: **s'~ de faire** to try hard to do

**effort** [efɔʀ] nm effort

**effrayant, e** [efʀejɑ̃, ɑ̃t] adj frightening

**effrayer** [efʀeje] vt to frighten, scare; **s'~ (de)** to be frightened ou scared (by)

**effréné, e** [efʀene] adj wild

**effronté, e** [efʀɔ̃te] adj cheeky

**effroyable** [efʀwajabl] adj horrifying, appalling

**égal, e, -aux** [egal, o] adj equal; (constant: vitesse) steady ▷ nm/f equal; **être ~** (prix, nombre) to be equal to; **ça lui est ~** it's all the same to him, he doesn't mind; **sans ~** matchless, unequalled; **d'~ à ~** as equals; **également** adv equally; (aussi) too, as well; **égaler** vt to equal; **égaliser** vt (sol, salaires) to level (out); (chances) to equalize ▷ vi (Sport) to equalize; **égalité** nf equality; **être à égalité** to be level

**égard** [egaʀ] nm: **~s** mpl consideration sg; **à cet ~** in this respect; **par ~ pour** out of consideration for; **à l'~ de** towards

**égarer** [egaʀe] vt to mislay; **s'égarer** vi to get lost, lose one's way; (objet) to go astray

**églefin** [egləfɛ̃] nm haddock

**église** [egliz] nf church; **aller à l'~** to go to church

**égoïsme** [egɔism] nm selfishness; **égoïste** adj selfish

**égout** [egu] nm sewer

**égoutter** [egute] vi to drip; **s'égoutter** vi to drip; **égouttoir** nm draining board; (mobile) draining rack

**égratignure** [egʀatiɲyʀ] nf scratch

**Égypte** [eʒipt] nf: **l'~** Egypt; **égyptien, ne** adj Egyptian ▷ nm/f:

**Égyptien, ne** Egyptian

**eh** [e] excl hey!; **eh bien!** well!

**élaborer** [elabɔʀe] vt to elaborate; (projet, stratégie) to work out; (rapport) to draft

**élan** [elɑ̃] nm (Zool) elk, moose; (Sport) run up; (fig: de tendresse etc) surge; **prendre de l'~** to gather speed

**élancer** [elɑ̃se]: **s'élancer** vi to dash, hurl o.s.

**élargir** [elaʀʒiʀ] vt to widen; **s'élargir** vi to widen; (vêtement) to stretch

**élastique** [elastik] adj elastic ▷ nm (de bureau) rubber band; (pour la couture) elastic no pl

**élection** [elɛksjɔ̃] nf election

**électricien, ne** [elɛktʀisjɛ̃, jɛn] nm/f electrician

**électricité** [elɛktʀisite] nf electricity; **allumer/éteindre l'~** to put on/off the light

**électrique** [elɛktʀik] adj electric(al)

**électrocuter** [elɛktʀɔkyte] vt to electrocute

**électroménager** [elɛktʀomenaʒe] adj, nm: **appareils ~s, l'~** domestic (electrical) appliances

**électronique** [elɛktʀonik] adj electronic ▷ nf electronics sg

**élégance** [elegɑ̃s] nf elegance

**élégant, e** [elegɑ̃, ɑ̃t] adj elegant

**élément** [elemɑ̃] nm element; (pièce) component, part; **élémentaire** adj elementary

**éléphant** [elefɑ̃] nm elephant

**élevage** [el(ə)vaʒ] nm breeding; (de bovins) cattle rearing; **truite d'~** farmed trout

**élevé, e** [el(ə)ve] adj high; **bien/mal ~** well-/ill-mannered

**élève** [elɛv] nm/f pupil

**élever** [el(ə)ve] vt (enfant) to bring up, raise; (animaux) to breed; (hausser: taux, niveau) to raise; (édifier: monument) to put up, erect; **s'élever** vi (avion) to go up; (niveau, température) to rise; **s'~ à** (suj: frais, dégâts) to amount to, add up to; **s'~ contre qch** to rise up against

sth; **~ la voix** to raise one's voice;
**éleveur, -euse** nm/f breeder

**éliminatoire** [eliminatwaʀ] nf
(Sport) heat

**éliminer** [elimine] vt to eliminate

**élire** [eliʀ] vt to elect

**elle** [ɛl] pron (sujet) she; (: chose) it;
(complément) her; it; **~s** (sujet) they;
(complément) them; **~-même** herself;
itself; **~s-mêmes** themselves; voir
aussi **il**

**éloigné, e** [elwaɲe] adj distant, far-off;
(parent) distant

**éloigner** [elwaɲe] vt (échéance) to put
off, postpone; (: soupçons, danger) to
ward off; (objet): **~ qch (de)** to move
ou take sth away (from); (personne):
**~ qn (de)** to take sb away ou remove
sb (from); **s'éloigner (de)** (personne)
to go away (from); (véhicule) to move
away (from); (affectivement) to grow
away (from)

**élu, e** [ely] pp de **élire** ▷ nm/f (Pol)
elected representative

**Élysée** [elize] nm: **(le palais de) l'~**
the Élysée Palace (the French president's
residence)

**émail, -aux** [emaj, o] nm enamel

**e-mail** [imɛl] nm e-mail; **envoyer qch
par ~** to e-mail sth

**émanciper** [emãsipe]: **s'émanciper**
vi (fig) to become emancipated ou
liberated

**emballage** [ãbalaʒ] nm (papier)
wrapping; (boîte) packaging

**emballer** [ãbale] vt to wrap (up); (dans
un carton) to pack (up); (fig: fam) to thrill
(to bits); **s'emballer** vi (moteur) to race;
(cheval) to bolt; (fig: personne) to get
carried away

**embarcadère** [ãbaʀkadeʀ] nm
wharf, pier

**embarquement** [ãbaʀkəmã] nm (de
passagers) boarding; (de marchandises)
loading

**embarquer** [ãbaʀke] vt (personne) to
embark; (marchandise) to load; (fam)
to cart off ▷ vi (passager) to board;

**s'embarquer** vi to board; **s'~ dans**
(affaire, aventure) to embark upon

**embarras** [ãbaʀa] nm (gêne)
embarrassment; **mettre qn dans
l'~** to put sb in an awkward position;
**vous n'avez que l'~ du choix** the only
problem is choosing

**embarrassant, e** [ãbaʀasã, ãt] adj
embarrassing

**embarrasser** [ãbaʀase] vt (encombrer)
to clutter (up); (gêner) to hinder,
hamper; **~ qn** to put sb in an awkward
position; **s'~ de** to burden o.s. with

**embaucher** [ãboʃe] vt to take on, hire

**embêter** [ãbete] vt to bother;
**s'embêter** vi (s'ennuyer) to be bored

**emblée** [ãble]: **d'~** adv straightaway

**embouchure** [ãbuʃyʀ] nf (Géo) mouth

**embourber** [ãbuʀbe]: **s'embourber** vi
to get stuck in the mud

**embouteillage** [ãbutejaʒ] nm
traffic jam

**embranchement** [ãbʀãʃmã] nm
(routier) junction

**embrasser** [ãbʀase] vt to kiss; (sujet,
période) to embrace, encompass

**embrayage** [ãbʀejaʒ] nm clutch

**embrouiller** [ãbʀuje] vt to muddle up;
(fils) to tangle (up); **s'embrouiller** vi
(personne) to get in a muddle

**embruns** [ãbʀœ̃] nmpl sea spray sg

**embué, e** [ãbɥe] adj misted up

**émeraude** [em(ə)ʀod] nf emerald

**émerger** [emɛʀʒe] vi to emerge; (faire
saillie, aussi fig) to stand out

**émeri** [em(ə)ʀi] nm: **toile** ou **papier ~**
emery paper

**émerveiller** [emɛʀveje] vt to fill with
wonder; **s'émerveiller de** to marvel at

**émettre** [emɛtʀ] vt (son, lumière) to
give out, emit; (message etc: Radio) to
transmit; (billet, timbre, emprunt) to
issue; (hypothèse, avis) to voice, put
forward ▷ vi to broadcast

**émeus** etc [emø] vb voir **émouvoir**

**émeute** [emøt] nf riot

**émigrer** [emigʀe] vi to emigrate

**émincer** [emɛ̃se] vt to cut into thin

slices

**émission** [emisjɔ̃] *nf* (*Radio, TV*) programme, broadcast; (*d'un message*) transmission; (*de timbre*) issue

**emmêler** [ɑ̃mele] *vt* to tangle (up); (*fig*) to muddle up; **s'emmêler** *vi* to get in a tangle

**emménager** [ɑ̃menaʒe] *vi* to move in; **~ dans** to move into

**emmener** [ɑ̃m(ə)ne] *vt* to take (with one); (*comme otage, capture*) to take away; **~ qn au cinéma** to take sb to the cinema

**emmerder** [ɑ̃mɛʀde] *vt* (*fam!*) to bug, bother; **s'emmerder** *vi* to be bored stiff

**émoticone** [emɔticɔn] *nm* smiley

**émotif, -ive** [emɔtif, iv] *adj* emotional

**émotion** [emosjɔ̃] *nf* emotion

**émouvoir** [emuvwaʀ] *vt* to move; **s'émouvoir** *vi* to be moved; (*s'indigner*) to be roused

**empaqueter** [ɑ̃pakte] *vt* to parcel up

**emparer** [ɑ̃paʀe]: **s'emparer de** *vt* (*objet*) to seize, grab; (*comme otage, MIL*) to seize; (*suj: peur etc*) to take hold of

**empêchement** [ɑ̃pɛʃmɑ̃] *nm* (unexpected) obstacle, hitch

**empêcher** [ɑ̃peʃe] *vt* to prevent; **~ qn de faire** to prevent ou stop sb (from) doing; **il n'empêche que** nevertheless; **il n'a pas pu s'~ de rire** he couldn't help laughing

**empereur** [ɑ̃pʀœʀ] *nm* emperor

**empiffrer** [ɑ̃pifʀe]: **s'~** (*fam*) *vi* to stuff o.s.

**empiler** [ɑ̃pile] *vt* to pile (up)

**empire** [ɑ̃piʀ] *nm* empire; (*fig*) influence

**empirer** [ɑ̃piʀe] *vi* to worsen, deteriorate

**emplacement** [ɑ̃plasmɑ̃] *nm* site

**emploi** [ɑ̃plwa] *nm* (*utilisation*) use; (*Comm, Écon*) employment; (*poste*) job, situation; **mode d'~** directions for use; **emploi du temps** timetable, schedule

**employé, e** [ɑ̃plwaje] *nm/f* employee; **employé de bureau** office employee ou clerk

**employer** [ɑ̃plwaje] *vt* to use; (*ouvrier, main-d'œuvre*) to employ; **s'~ à faire** to apply ou devote o.s. to doing; **employeur, -euse** *nm/f* employer

**empoigner** [ɑ̃pwaɲe] *vt* to grab

**empoisonner** [ɑ̃pwazɔne] *vt* to poison; (*empester: air, pièce*) to stink out; (*fam*): **~ qn** to drive sb mad

**emporter** [ɑ̃pɔʀte] *vt* to take (with one); (*en dérobant ou enlevant, emmener: blessés, voyageurs*) to take away; (*entraîner*) to carry away; **s'emporter** *vi* (*de colère*) to lose one's temper; **l'~ (sur)** to get the upper hand (of); **plats à ~** take-away meals

**empreinte** [ɑ̃pʀɛ̃t] *nf*: **~ (de pas)** footprint; **empreintes (digitales)** fingerprints

**empressé, e** [ɑ̃pʀese] *adj* attentive

**empresser** [ɑ̃pʀese]: **s'empresser** *vi*: **s'~ auprès de qn** to surround sb with attentions; **s'~ de faire** (*se hâter*) to hasten to do

**emprisonner** [ɑ̃pʀizɔne] *vt* to imprison

**emprunt** [ɑ̃pʀœ̃] *nm* loan

**emprunter** [ɑ̃pʀœ̃te] *vt* to borrow; (*itinéraire*) to take, follow

**ému, e** [emy] *pp de* **émouvoir** ▷ *adj* (*gratitude*) touched; (*compassion*) moved

⬤ **MOT-CLÉ**

**en** [ɑ̃] *prép* **1** (*endroit, pays*) in; (*direction*) to; **habiter en France/ville** to live in France/town; **aller en France/ville** to go to France/town

**2** (*moment, temps*) in; **en été/juin** in summer/June; **en 3 jours** in 3 days

**3** (*moyen*) by; **en avion/taxi** by plane/taxi

**4** (*composition*) made of; **c'est en verre** it's (made of) glass; **un collier en argent** a silver necklace

**5** (*description, état*): **une femme (habillée) en rouge** a woman (dressed) in red; **peindre qch en rouge** to paint sth red; **en T/étoile** T/star-shaped; **en**

**chemise/chaussettes** in one's shirt-sleeves/socks; **en soldat** as a soldier; **cassé en plusieurs morceaux** broken into several pieces; **en réparation** being repaired, under repair; **en vacances** on holiday; **en deuil** in mourning; **le même en plus grand** the same but ou only bigger
6 (*avec gérondif*) while, on, by; **en dormant** while sleeping, as one sleeps; **en sortant** on going out, as he *etc* went out; **sortir en courant** to run out
7 (*comme*) as; **je te parle en ami** I'm talking to you as a friend
▷ *pron* 1 (*indéfini*): **j'en ai/veux** I have/want some; **en as-tu?** have you got any?; **je n'en veux pas** I don't want any; **j'en ai 2** I've got 2; **combien y en a-t-il?** how many (of them) are there?; **j'en ai assez** I've got enough (of it ou them); (*j'en ai marre*) I've had enough
2 (*provenance*) from there; **j'en viens** I've come from there
3 (*cause*): **il en est malade/perd le sommeil** he is ill/can't sleep because of it
4 (*complément de nom, d'adjectif, de verbe*): **j'en connais les dangers** I know its ou the dangers; **j'en suis fier** I am proud of it ou him ou her ou them; **j'en ai besoin** I need it ou them

**encadrer** [ākadʀe] *vt* (*tableau, image*) to frame; (*fig: entourer*) to surround; (*personnel, soldats etc*) to train
**encaisser** [ākese] *vt* (*chèque*) to cash; (*argent*) to collect; (*fam: coup, défaite*) to take
**en-cas** [āka] *nm* snack
**enceinte** [āsɛ̃t] *adj f*: **~ (de 6 mois)** (6 months) pregnant ▷ *nf* (*mur*) wall; (*espace*) enclosure; **enceinte (acoustique)** (loud)speaker
**encens** [āsā] *nm* incense
**enchaîner** [āʃene] *vt* to chain up; (*mouvements, séquences*) to link (together) ▷ *vi* to carry on
**enchanté, e** [āʃāte] *adj* (*ravi*)

delighted; (*magique*) enchanted; **~ (de faire votre connaissance)** pleased to meet you
**enchère** [āʃɛʀ] *nf* bid; **mettre/vendre aux ~s** to put up for (sale by)/sell by auction
**enclencher** [āklāʃe] *vt* (*mécanisme*) to engage; **s'enclencher** *vi* to engage
**encombrant, e** [ākɔ̃brā, āt] *adj* cumbersome, bulky
**encombrement** [ākɔ̃brəmā] *nm*: **être pris dans un ~** to be stuck in a traffic jam
**encombrer** [ākɔ̃bre] *vt* to clutter (up); (*gêner*) to hamper; **s'~ de** (*bagages etc*) to load ou burden o.s. with

 **MOT-CLÉ**

**encore** [ākɔʀ] *adv* 1 (*continuation*) still; **il y travaille encore** he's still working on it; **pas encore** not yet
2 (*de nouveau*) again; **j'irai encore demain** I'll go again tomorrow; **encore une fois** (once) again; **(et puis) quoi encore?** what next?
3 (*en plus*) more; **encore un peu de viande?** a little more meat?; **encore deux jours** two more days
4 (*intensif*) even, still; **encore plus fort/mieux** even louder/better, louder/better still
5 (*restriction*) even so ou then, only; **encore pourrais-je le faire si ...** even so, I might be able to do it if ...; **si encore** if only

**encourager** [ākuraʒe] *vt* to encourage; **~ qn à faire qch** to encourage sb to do sth
**encourir** [ākurir] *vt* to incur
**encre** [ākr] *nf* ink; **encre de Chine** Indian ink
**encyclopédie** [āsiklɔpedi] *nf* encyclopaedia
**endetter** [ādete]: **s'endetter** *vi* to get into debt
**endive** [ādiv] *nf* chicory *no pl*

**endormi, e** [ɑ̃dɔrmi] adj asleep

**endormir** [ɑ̃dɔrmir] vt to put to sleep; (suj: chaleur etc) to send to sleep; (Méd: dent, nerf) to anaesthetize; (fig: soupçons) to allay; **s'endormir** vi to fall asleep, go to sleep

**endroit** [ɑ̃drwa] nm place; (opposé à l'envers) right side; **à l'~** (vêtement) the right way out; (objet posé) the right way round

**endurance** [ɑ̃dyrɑ̃s] nf endurance

**endurant, e** [ɑ̃dyrɑ̃, ɑ̃t] adj tough, hardy

**endurcir** [ɑ̃dyrsir] : **s'endurcir** vi (physiquement) to become tougher; (moralement) to become hardened

**endurer** [ɑ̃dyre] vt to endure, bear

**énergétique** [enɛrʒetik] adj (aliment) energy-giving

**énergie** [enɛrʒi] nf (Physique) energy; (Tech) power; (morale) vigour, spirit; **énergique** adj energetic, vigorous; (mesures) drastic, stringent

**énervant, e** [enɛrvɑ̃, ɑ̃t] adj irritating, annoying

**énerver** [enɛrve] vt to irritate, annoy; **s'énerver** vi to get excited, get worked up

**enfance** [ɑ̃fɑ̃s] nf childhood

**enfant** [ɑ̃fɑ̃] nm/f child; **enfantin, e** adj (puéril) childlike; (langage, jeu etc) children's cpd

**enfer** [ɑ̃fɛr] nm hell

**enfermer** [ɑ̃fɛrme] vt to shut up; (à clef, interner) to lock up; **s'enfermer** to shut o.s. away

**enfiler** [ɑ̃file] vt (vêtement) to slip on, slip into; (perles) to string; (aiguille) to thread

**enfin** [ɑ̃fɛ̃] adv at last; (en énumérant) lastly; (toutefois) still; (pour conclure) in a word; (somme toute) after all

**enflammer** [ɑ̃flame] : **s'enflammer** vi to catch fire; (Méd) to become inflamed

**enflé, e** [ɑ̃fle] adj swollen

**enfler** [ɑ̃fle] vi to swell (up)

**enfoncer** [ɑ̃fɔ̃se] vt (clou) to drive in; (faire pénétrer) : **~ qch dans** to push (ou drive) sth into; (forcer: porte) to break open; **s'enfoncer** vi to sink; **s'~ dans** to sink into; (forêt, ville) to disappear into

**enfouir** [ɑ̃fwir] vt (dans le sol) to bury; (dans un tiroir etc) to tuck away

**enfuir** [ɑ̃fɥir] : **s'enfuir** vi to run away ou off

**engagement** [ɑ̃gaʒmɑ̃] nm commitment; **sans ~** without obligation

**engager** [ɑ̃gaʒe] vt (embaucher) to take on; (: artiste) to engage; (commencer) to start; (lier) to bind, commit; (impliquer) to involve; (investir) to invest, lay out; (inciter) to urge; (introduire: clé) to insert; **s'engager** vi (promettre) to commit o.s.; (Mil) to enlist; (débuter: conversation etc) to start (up); **s'~ à faire** to undertake to do; **s'~ dans** (rue, passage) to turn into; (fig: affaire, discussion) to enter into, embark on

**engelures** [ɑ̃ʒlyr] nfpl chilblains

**engin** [ɑ̃ʒɛ̃] nm machine; (outil) instrument; (Auto) vehicle; (Aviat) aircraft inv

> Attention à ne pas traduire **engin** par le mot anglais **engine**.

**engloutir** [ɑ̃glutir] vt to swallow up

**engouement** [ɑ̃gumɑ̃] nm (sudden) passion

**engouffrer** [ɑ̃gufre] vt to swallow up, devour; **s'engouffrer dans** to rush into

**engourdir** [ɑ̃gurdir] vt to numb; (fig) to dull, blunt; **s'engourdir** vi to go numb

**engrais** [ɑ̃grɛ] nm manure; **engrais chimique** chemical fertilizer

**engraisser** [ɑ̃grese] vt to fatten (up)

**engrenage** [ɑ̃grənaʒ] nm gears pl, gearing; (fig) chain

**engueuler** [ɑ̃gœle] (fam) vt to bawl at

**enhardir** [ɑ̃ardir] : **s'enhardir** vi to grow bolder

**énigme** [enigm] nf riddle

**enivrer** [ɑ̃nivre] vt: **s'~** to get drunk

**enjamber** [ɑ̃ʒɑ̃be] vt to stride over

**enjeu, x** [ɑ̃ʒø] nm stakes pl

**enjoué, e** [ɑ̃ʒwe] adj playful

**enlaidir** [ɑ̃lediʀ] vt to make ugly ▷ vi to become ugly

**enlèvement** [ɑ̃lɛvmɑ̃] nm (rapt) abduction, kidnapping

**enlever** [ɑ̃l(ə)ve] vt (ôter: gén) to remove; (: vêtement, lunettes) to take off; (emporter: ordures etc) to take away; (kidnapper) to abduct, kidnap; (obtenir: prix, contrat) to win; (prendre): ~ **qch à qn** to take sth (away) from sb

**enliser** [ɑ̃lize]: **s'enliser** vi to sink, get stuck

**enneigé, e** [ɑ̃neʒe] adj (route, maison) snowed-up; (paysage) snowy

**ennemi, e** [ɛnmi] adj hostile; (Mil) enemy cpd ▷ nm/f enemy

**ennui** [ɑ̃nɥi] nm (lassitude) boredom; (difficulté) trouble no pl; **avoir des ~s** to have problems; **ennuyer** vt to bother; (lasser) to bore; **s'ennuyer** vi to be bored; **si cela ne vous ennuie pas** if it's no trouble (to you); **ennuyeux, -euse** adj boring, tedious; (embêtant) annoying

**énorme** [enɔʀm] adj enormous, huge; **énormément** adv enormously; **énormément de neige/gens** an enormous amount of snow/number of people

**enquête** [ɑ̃kɛt] nf (de journaliste, de police) investigation; (judiciaire, administrative) inquiry; (sondage d'opinion) survey; **enquêter** vi: **enquêter (sur)** to investigate

**enragé, e** [ɑ̃ʀaʒe] adj (Méd) rabid, with rabies; (fig) fanatical

**enrageant, e** [ɑ̃ʀaʒɑ̃, ɑ̃t] adj infuriating

**enrager** [ɑ̃ʀaʒe] vi to be in a rage

**enregistrement** [ɑ̃ʀ(ə)ʒistʀəmɑ̃] nm recording; **enregistrement des bagages** baggage check-in

**enregistrer** [ɑ̃ʀ(ə)ʒistʀe] vt (Mus etc) to record; (fig: mémoriser) to make a mental note of; (bagages: à l'aéroport) to check in

**enrhumer** [ɑ̃ʀyme] vt: **s'~, être enrhumé** to catch a cold

**enrichir** [ɑ̃ʀiʃiʀ] vt to make rich(er); (fig) to enrich; **s'enrichir** vi to get rich(er)

**enrouer** [ɑ̃ʀwe]: **s'enrouer** vi to go hoarse

**enrouler** [ɑ̃ʀule] vt (fil, corde) to wind (up); **s'~ (autour de qch)** to wind (around sth)

**enseignant, e** [ɑ̃sɛɲɑ̃, ɑ̃t] nm/f teacher

**enseignement** [ɑ̃sɛɲ(ə)mɑ̃] nm teaching; (Admin) education

**enseigner** [ɑ̃seɲe] vt, vi to teach; **~ qch à qn** to teach sb sth

**ensemble** [ɑ̃sɑ̃bl] adv together ▷ nm (groupement) set; (vêtements) outfit; (totalité): **l'~ du/de la** the whole ou entire; (unité, harmonie) unity; **impression/idée d'~** overall ou general impression/idea; **dans l'~** (en gros) on the whole

**ensoleillé, e** [ɑ̃sɔleje] adj sunny

**ensuite** [ɑ̃sɥit] adv then, next; (plus tard) afterwards, later

**entamer** [ɑ̃tame] vt (pain, bouteille) to start; (hostilités, pourparlers) to open

**entasser** [ɑ̃tase] vt (empiler) to pile up, heap up; **s'entasser** vi (s'amonceler) to pile up; **s'~ dans** (personnes) to cram into

**entendre** [ɑ̃tɑ̃dʀ] vt to hear; (comprendre) to understand; (vouloir dire) to mean; **s'entendre** vi (sympathiser) to get on; (se mettre d'accord) to agree; **j'ai entendu dire que** I've heard (it said) that; **~ parler de** to hear of

**entendu, e** [ɑ̃tɑ̃dy] adj (réglé) agreed; (au courant: air) knowing; **(c'est) ~** all right, agreed; **bien ~** of course

**entente** [ɑ̃tɑ̃t] nf understanding; (accord, traité) agreement; **à double ~** (sens) with a double meaning

**enterrement** [ɑ̃tɛʀmɑ̃] nm (cérémonie) funeral, burial

**enterrer** [ɑ̃teʀe] vt to bury

**entêtant, e** [ɑ̃tɛtɑ̃, ɑ̃t] adj heady

**en-tête** [ɑ̃tɛt] nm heading; **papier à ~** headed notepaper

**entêté, e** [ɑ̃tete] *adj* stubborn

**entêter** [ɑ̃tete]: **s'entêter** *vi*: **s'~ (à faire)** to persist (in doing)

**enthousiasme** [ɑ̃tuzjasm] *nm* enthusiasm; **enthousiasmer** *vt* to fill with enthusiasm; **s'enthousiasmer (pour qch)** to get enthusiastic (about sth); **enthousiaste** *adj* enthusiastic

**entier, -ère** [ɑ̃tje, jɛʀ] *adj* whole; (*total: satisfaction etc*) complete; (*fig: caractère*) unbending ▷ *nm* (*Math*) whole; **en ~** totally; **lait ~** full-cream milk; **entièrement** *adv* entirely, wholly

**entonnoir** [ɑ̃tɔnwaʀ] *nm* funnel

**entorse** [ɑ̃tɔʀs] *nf* (*Méd*) sprain; (*fig*): **~ au règlement** infringement of the rule

**entourage** [ɑ̃tuʀaʒ] *nm* circle; (*famille*) circle of family/friends; (*ce qui enclôt*) surround

**entourer** [ɑ̃tuʀe] *vt* to surround; (*apporter son soutien à*) to rally round; **~ de** to surround with; **s'~ de** to surround o.s. with

**entracte** [ɑ̃tʀakt] *nm* interval

**entraide** [ɑ̃tʀɛd] *nf* mutual aid

**entrain** [ɑ̃tʀɛ̃] *nm* spirit; **avec/sans ~** spiritedly/half-heartedly

**entraînement** [ɑ̃tʀɛnmɑ̃] *nm* training

**entraîner** [ɑ̃tʀene] *vt* (*charrier*) to carry *ou* drag along; (*Tech*) to drive; (*emmener: personne*) to take (off); (*influencer*) to lead; (*Sport*) to train; (*impliquer*) to entail; **s'entraîner** *vi* (*Sport*) to train; **s'~ à qch/à faire** to train o.s. for sth/to do; **~ qn à faire** (*inciter*) to lead sb to do; **entraîneur, -euse** *nm/f* (*Sport*) coach, trainer ▷ *nm* (*Hippisme*) trainer

**entre** [ɑ̃tʀ] *prép* between; (*parmi*) among(st); **l'un d'~ eux/nous** one of them/us; **ils se battent ~ eux** they are fighting among(st) themselves; **~ autres (choses)** among other things; **entrecôte** *nf* entrecôte *ou* rib steak

**entrée** [ɑ̃tʀe] *nf* entrance; (*accès: au cinéma etc*) admission; (*billet*) (admission) ticket; (*Culin*) first course

**entre...: entrefilet** *nm* paragraph (*short article*); **entremets** *nm* (cream) dessert

**entrepôt** [ɑ̃tʀəpo] *nm* warehouse

**entreprendre** [ɑ̃tʀəpʀɑ̃dʀ] *vt* (*se lancer dans*) to undertake; (*commencer*) to begin *ou* start (upon)

**entrepreneur, -euse** [ɑ̃tʀəpʀənœʀ, øz] *nm/f*: **entrepreneur (en bâtiment)** (building) contractor

**entreprise** [ɑ̃tʀəpʀiz] *nf* (*société*) firm, concern; (*action*) undertaking, venture

**entrer** [ɑ̃tʀe] *vi* to go (*ou* come) in, enter ▷ *vt* (*Inform*) to enter, input; **(faire) ~ qch dans** to get sth into; **~ dans** (*gén*) to enter; (*pièce*) to go (*ou* come) into, enter; (*club*) to join; (*heurter*) to run into; **~ à l'hôpital** to go into hospital; **faire ~** (*visiteur*) to show in

**entre-temps** [ɑ̃tʀətɑ̃] *adv* meanwhile

**entretenir** [ɑ̃tʀət(ə)niʀ] *vt* to maintain; (*famille, maîtresse*) to support, keep; **~ qn (de)** to speak to sb (about)

**entretien** [ɑ̃tʀətjɛ̃] *nm* maintenance; (*discussion*) discussion, talk; (*pour un emploi*) interview

**entrevoir** [ɑ̃tʀəvwaʀ] *vt* (*à peine*) to make out; (*brièvement*) to catch a glimpse of

**entrevue** [ɑ̃tʀəvy] *nf* (*audience*) interview

**entrouvert, e** [ɑ̃tʀuvɛʀ, ɛʀt] *adj* half-open

**énumérer** [enymeʀe] *vt* to list

**envahir** [ɑ̃vaiʀ] *vt* to invade; (*suj: inquiétude, peur*) to come over; **envahissant, e** (*péj*) *adj* (*personne*) intrusive

**enveloppe** [ɑ̃v(ə)lɔp] *nf* (*de lettre*) envelope; (*crédits*) budget; **envelopper** *vt* to wrap; (*fig*) to envelop, shroud

**enverrai** *etc* [ɑ̃veʀe] *vb voir* **envoyer**

**envers** [ɑ̃vɛʀ] *prép* towards, to ▷ *nm* other side; (*d'une étoffe*) wrong side; **à l'~** (*verticalement*) upside down; (*pull*) back to front; (*chaussettes*) inside out

**envie** [ɑ̃vi] *nf* (*sentiment*) envy; (*souhait*) desire, wish; **avoir ~ de (faire)** to feel like (doing); (*plus fort*) to want (to do); **avoir ~ que** to wish that; **cette glace me fait ~** I fancy some of that ice cream; **envier** vt to envy; **envieux, -euse** adj envious

**environ** [ãvirɔ̃] adv: **~ 3 h/2 km** (around) about 3 o'clock/2 km; voir aussi **environs**

**environnant, e** [ãvirɔnã, ãt] adj surrounding

**environnement** [ãvirɔnmã] nm environment

**environs** [ãvirɔ̃] nmpl surroundings; **aux ~ de** (round) about

**envisager** [ãvizaʒe] vt to contemplate, envisage; **~ de faire** to consider doing

**envoler** [ãvɔle]: **s'envoler** vi (oiseau) to fly away ou off; (avion) to take off; (papier, feuille) to blow away; (fig) to vanish (into thin air)

**envoyé, e** [ãvwaje] nm/f (Pol) envoy; (Presse) correspondent; **envoyé spécial** special correspondent

**envoyer** [ãvwaje] vt to send; (lancer) to hurl, throw; **~ chercher** to send for; **~ promener qn** (fam) to send sb packing

**épagneul, e** [epaɲœl] nm/f spaniel

**épais, se** [epɛ, ɛs] adj thick; **épaisseur** nf thickness

**épanouir** [epanwir]: **s'épanouir** vi (fleur) to bloom, open out; (visage) to light up; (personne) to blossom

**épargne** [eparɲ] nf saving

**épargner** [eparɲe] vt to save; (ne pas tuer ou endommager) to spare ▷ vi to save; **~ qch à qn** to spare sb sth

**éparpiller** [eparpije] vt to scatter; **s'éparpiller** vi to scatter; (fig) to dissipate one's efforts

**épatant, e** [epatã, ãt] (fam) adj super

**épater** [epate] (fam) vt (étonner) to amaze; (impressionner) to impress

**épaule** [epol] nf shoulder

**épave** [epav] nf wreck

**épée** [epe] nf sword

**épeler** [ep(ə)le] vt to spell

**éperon** [eprɔ̃] nm spur

**épervier** [epɛrvje] nm sparrowhawk

**épi** [epi] nm (de blé, d'orge) ear; (de maïs) cob

**épice** [epis] nf spice

**épicé, e** [epise] adj spicy

**épicer** [epise] vt to spice

**épicerie** [episri] nf grocer's shop; (denrées) groceries pl; **épicerie fine** delicatessen; **épicier, -ière** nm/f grocer

**épidémie** [epidemi] nf epidemic

**épiderme** [epidɛrm] nm skin

**épier** [epje] vt to spy on, watch closely

**épilepsie** [epilɛpsi] nf epilepsy

**épiler** [epile] vt (jambes) to remove the hair from; (sourcils) to pluck

**épinards** [epinar] nmpl spinach sg

**épine** [epin] nf thorn, prickle; (d'oursin etc) spine

**épingle** [epɛ̃gl] nf pin; **épingle de nourrice** ou **de sûreté** safety pin

**épisode** [epizɔd] nm episode; **film/roman à ~s** serial; **épisodique** adj occasional

**épluche-légumes** [eplyʃlegym] nm inv (potato) peeler

**éplucher** [eplyʃe] vt (fruit, légumes) to peel; (fig) to go over with a fine-tooth comb; **épluchures** nfpl peelings

**éponge** [epɔ̃ʒ] nf sponge; **éponger** vt (liquide) to mop up; (surface) to sponge; (fig: déficit) to soak up

**époque** [epɔk] nf (de l'histoire) age, era; (de l'année, la vie) time; **d'~** (meuble) period cpd

**épouse** [epuz] nf wife; **épouser** vt to marry

**épousseter** [epuste] vt to dust

**épouvantable** [epuvãtabl] adj appalling, dreadful

**épouvantail** [epuvãtaj] nm scarecrow

**épouvante** [epuvãt] nf terror; **film d'~** horror film; **épouvanter** vt to terrify

**époux** [epu] nm husband ▷ nmpl (married) couple

**épreuve** [eprœv] nf (d'examen) test; (malheur, difficulté) trial, ordeal; (Photo) print; (Typo) proof; (Sport) event; **à toute ~** unfailing; **mettre à l'~** to put to the test

**éprouver** [epruve] vt (tester) to

test; (marquer, faire souffrir) to afflict, distress; (ressentir) to experience

**épuisé, e** [epчize] adj exhausted; (livre) out of print; **épuisement** nm exhaustion

**épuiser** [epчize] vt (fatiguer) to exhaust, wear ou tire out; (stock, sujet) to exhaust; **s'épuiser** vi to wear ou tire o.s. out, exhaust o.s.

**épuisette** [epчizet] nf shrimping net

**équateur** [ekwatœr] nm equator; **(la république de) l'É~** Ecuador

**équation** [ekwasjɔ̃] nf equation

**équerre** [ekɛr] nf (à dessin) (set) square

**équilibre** [ekilibr] nm balance; **garder/perdre l'~** to keep/lose one's balance; **être en ~** to be balanced; **équilibré, e** adj well-balanced; **équilibrer** vt to balance

**équipage** [ekipaʒ] nm crew

**équipe** [ekip] nf team; **travailler en ~** to work as a team

**équipé, e** [ekipe] adj: **bien/mal ~** well-/poorly-equipped

**équipement** [ekipmɑ̃] nm equipment

**équiper** [ekipe] vt to equip; **~ qn/qch de** to equip sb/sth with

**équipier, -ière** [ekipje, jɛr] nm/f team member

**équitation** [ekitasjɔ̃] nf (horse-)riding; **faire de l'~** to go riding

**équivalent, e** [ekivalɑ̃, ɑ̃t] adj, nm equivalent

**équivaloir** [ekivalwar]: **~ à** vt to be equivalent to

**érable** [erabl] nm maple

**érafler** [erafle] vt to scratch; **éraflure** nf scratch

**ère** [ɛr] nf era; **en l'an 1050 de notre ~** in the year 1050 A.D.

**érection** [erɛksjɔ̃] nf erection

**éroder** [erɔde] vt to erode

**érotique** [erɔtik] adj erotic

**errer** [ere] vi to wander

**erreur** [erœr] nf mistake, error; **faire ~** to be mistaken; **par ~** by mistake

**éruption** [erypsjɔ̃] nf eruption; (Méd) rash

**es** [ɛ] vb voir **être**

**ès** [ɛs] prép: **licencié ès lettres/sciences** ≈ Bachelor of Arts/Science

**ESB** sigle f (= encéphalopathie spongiforme bovine) BSE

**escabeau, x** [eskabo] nm (tabouret) stool; (échelle) stepladder

**escalade** [eskalad] nf climbing no pl; (Pol etc) escalation; **escalader** vt to climb

**escale** [eskal] nf (Navig: durée) call; (endroit) port of call; (Aviat) stop(over); **faire ~ à** (Navig) to put in at; (Aviat) to stop over at; **vol sans ~** nonstop flight

**escalier** [eskalje] nm stairs pl; **dans l'~** ou **les ~s** on the stairs; **escalier mécanique** ou **roulant** escalator

**escapade** [eskapad] nf: **faire une ~** to go on a jaunt; (s'enfuir) to run away ou off

**escargot** [eskargo] nm snail

**escarpé, e** [eskarpe] adj steep

**esclavage** [esklavaʒ] nm slavery

**esclave** [esklav] nm/f slave

**escompte** [eskɔ̃t] nm discount

**escrime** [eskrim] nf fencing

**escroc** [eskro] nm swindler, conman; **escroquer** vt: **escroquer qch (à qn)** to swindle sth (out of sb); **escroquerie** nf swindle

**espace** [espas] nm space; **espacer** vt to space out; **s'espacer** vi (visites etc) to become less frequent

**espadon** [espadɔ̃] nm swordfish inv

**espadrille** [espadrij] nf rope-soled sandal

**Espagne** [espaɲ] nf: **l'~** Spain; **espagnol, e** adj Spanish ▷ nm/f: **Espagnol, e** Spaniard ▷ nm (Ling) Spanish

**espèce** [espɛs] nf (Bio, Bot, Zool) species inv; (gén: sorte) sort, kind, type; (péj): **~ de maladroit/de brute!** you clumsy oaf/you brute!; **espèces** nfpl (Comm) cash sg; **payer en ~** to pay (in) cash

**espérance** [esperɑ̃s] nf hope; **espérance de vie** life expectancy

**espérer** [espere] vt to hope for;

**j'espère (bien)** I hope so; **~ que/faire** to hope that/to do

**espiègle** [ɛspjɛgl] *adj* mischievous

**espion, ne** [ɛspjɔ̃, jɔn] *nm/f* spy; **espionnage** *nm* espionage, spying; **espionner** *vt* to spy (up)on

**espoir** [ɛspwaʀ] *nm* hope; **dans l'~ de/que** in the hope of/that; **reprendre ~** not to lose hope

**esprit** [ɛspʀi] *nm* (*intellect*) mind; (*humour*) wit; (*mentalité, d'une loi etc, fantôme etc*) spirit; **faire de l'~** to try to be witty; **reprendre ses ~s** to come to; **perdre l'~** to lose one's mind

**esquimau, de, -x** [ɛskimo, od] *adj* Eskimo ▷ *nm/f*: **E~, de** Eskimo ▷ *nm*: **E~®** ice lolly (BRIT), popsicle (US)

**essai** [esɛ] *nm* (*tentative*) attempt, try; (*de produit*) testing; (*Rugby*) try; (*Littérature*) essay; **à l'~** on a trial basis; **mettre à l'~** to put to the test

**essaim** [esɛ̃] *nm* swarm

**essayer** [eseje] *vt* to try; (*vêtement, chaussures*) to try (on); (*méthode, voiture*) to try (out) ▷ *vi* to try; **~ de faire** to try *ou* attempt to do

**essence** [esɑ̃s] *nf* (*de voiture*) petrol (BRIT), gas(oline) (US); (*extrait de plante*) essence; (*espèce: d'arbre*) species *inv*

**essentiel, le** [esɑ̃sjɛl] *adj* essential; **c'est l'~** (*ce qui importe*) that's the main thing; **l'~ de** the main part of

**essieu, x** [esjø] *nm* axle

**essor** [esɔʀ] *nm* (*de l'économie etc*) rapid expansion

**essorer** [esɔʀe] *vt* (*en tordant*) to wring (out); (*par la force centrifuge*) to spin-dry; **essoreuse** *nf* spin-dryer

**essouffler** [esufle]: **s'essouffler** *vi* to get out of breath

**essuie-glace** [esɥiglas] *nm inv* windscreen (BRIT) *ou* windshield (US) wiper

**essuyer** [esɥije] *vt* to wipe; (*fig: échec*) to suffer; **s'essuyer** *vi* (*après le bain*) to dry o.s.; **~ la vaisselle** to dry up

**est¹** [ɛ] *vb voir* **être**

**est²** [ɛst] *nm* east ▷ *adj inv* east; (*région*) east(ern); **à l'~** in the east; (*direction*) to the east, east(wards); **à l'~ de** (to the) east of

**est-ce que** [ɛskə] *adv*: **~ c'est cher/ c'était bon?** is it expensive/was it good?; **quand est-ce qu'il part?** when does he leave?, when is he leaving?; *voir aussi* **que**

**esthéticienne** [ɛstetisjɛn] *nf* beautician

**esthétique** [ɛstetik] *adj* attractive

**estimation** [ɛstimasjɔ̃] *nf* valuation; (*chiffre*) estimate

**estime** [ɛstim] *nf* esteem, regard; **estimer** *vt* (*respecter*) to esteem; (*expertiser: bijou etc*) to value; (*évaluer: coût etc*) to assess, estimate; (*penser*): **estimer que/être** to consider that/o.s. to be

**estival, e, -aux** [ɛstival, o] *adj* summer *cpd*

**estivant, e** [ɛstivɑ̃, ɑ̃t] *nm/f* (summer) holiday-maker

**estomac** [ɛstɔma] *nm* stomach

**estragon** [ɛstʀagɔ̃] *nm* tarragon

**estuaire** [ɛstɥɛʀ] *nm* estuary

**et** [e] *conj* and; **et lui?** what about him?; **et alors!** so what!

**étable** [etabl] *nf* cowshed

**établi** [etabli] *nm* (work)bench

**établir** [etabliʀ] *vt* (*papiers d'identité, facture*) to make out; (*liste, programme*) to draw up; (*entreprise*) to set up; (*réputation, usage, fait, culpabilité*) to establish; **s'établir** *vi* to be established; **s'~ (à son compte)** to set up in business; **s'~ à/près de** to settle in/near

**établissement** [etablismɑ̃] *nm* (*entreprise, institution*) establishment; **établissement scolaire** school, educational establishment

**étage** [etaʒ] *nm* (*d'immeuble*) storey, floor; **à l'~** upstairs; **au 2ème ~** on the 2nd (BRIT) *ou* 3rd (US) floor; **c'est à quel ~?** what floor is it on?

**étagère** [etaʒɛʀ] *nf* (*rayon*) shelf; (*meuble*) shelves *pl*

**étai** [etɛ] nm stay, prop

**étain** [etɛ̃] nm pewter no pl

**étais** etc [etɛ] vb voir **être**

**étaler** [etale] vt (carte, nappe) to spread (out); (peinture) to spread; (échelonner: paiements, vacances) to spread, stagger; (marchandises) to display; (connaissances) to parade; **s'étaler** vi (liquide) to spread out; (fam) to fall flat on one's face; **s'~ sur** (suj: paiements etc) to be spread out over

**étalon** [etalɔ̃] nm (cheval) stallion

**étanche** [etɑ̃ʃ] adj (récipient) watertight; (montre, vêtement) waterproof

**étang** [etɑ̃] nm pond

**étant** [etɑ̃] vb voir **être**; **donné**

**étape** [etap] nf stage; (lieu d'arrivée) stopping place; (: Cyclisme) staging point

**état** [eta] nm (Pol, condition) state; **en mauvais ~** in poor condition; **en ~ (de marche)** in (working) order; **remettre en ~** to repair; **hors d'~** out of order; **être en ~/hors d'~ de faire** to be in a/in no fit state to do; **être dans tous ses ~s** to be in a state; **faire ~ de** (alléguer) to put forward; **l'É~** the State; **état civil** civil status; **état des lieux** inventory of fixtures; **États-Unis** nmpl: **les États-Unis** the United States

**etc.** [ɛtseteʀa] adv etc

**et c(a)etera** [ɛtseteʀa] adv et cetera, and so on

**été** [ete] pp de **être** ▷ nm summer

**éteindre** [etɛ̃dʀ] vt (lampe, lumière, radio) to turn ou switch off; (cigarette, feu) to put out, extinguish; **s'éteindre** vi (feu, lumière) to go out; (mourir) to pass away; **éteint, e** adj (fig) lacklustre, dull; (volcan) extinct

**étendre** [etɑ̃dʀ] vt (pâte, liquide) to spread; (carte etc) to spread out; (linge) to hang up; (bras, jambes) to stretch out; (fig: agrandir) to extend; **s'étendre** vi (augmenter, se propager) to spread; (terrain, forêt etc) to stretch; (s'allonger) to stretch out; (se coucher) to lie down;

(fig: expliquer) to elaborate

**étendu, e** [etɑ̃dy] adj extensive

**éternel, le** [etɛʀnɛl] adj eternal

**éternité** [etɛʀnite] nf eternity; **ça a duré une ~** it lasted for ages

**éternuement** [etɛʀnymɑ̃] nm sneeze

**éternuer** [etɛʀnɥe] vi to sneeze

**êtes** [ɛt(z)] vb voir **être**

**Éthiopie** [etjɔpi] nf: **l'~** Ethiopia

**étiez** [etje] vb voir **être**

**étinceler** [etɛ̃s(ə)le] vi to sparkle

**étincelle** [etɛ̃sɛl] nf spark

**étiquette** [etikɛt] nf label; (protocole): **l'~** etiquette

**étirer** [etiʀe] : **s'étirer** vi (personne) to stretch; (convoi, route): **s'~ sur** to stretch out over

**étoile** [etwal] nf star; **à la belle ~** in the open; **étoile de mer** starfish; **étoile filante** shooting star; **étoilé, e** adj starry

**étonnant, e** [etɔnɑ̃, ɑ̃t] adj amazing

**étonnement** [etɔnmɑ̃] nm surprise, amazement

**étonner** [etɔne] vt to surprise, amaze; **s'étonner que/de** to be amazed that/at; **cela m'~ait (que)** (j'en doute) I'd be very surprised (if)

**étouffer** [etufe] vt to suffocate; (bruit) to muffle; (scandale) to hush up ▷ vi to suffocate; **s'étouffer** vi (en mangeant etc) to choke; **on étouffe** it's stifling

**étourderie** [etuʀdəʀi] nf (caractère) absent-mindedness no pl; (faute) thoughtless blunder

**étourdi, e** [etuʀdi] adj (distrait) scatterbrained, heedless

**étourdir** [etuʀdiʀ] vt (assommer) to stun, daze; (griser) to make dizzy ou giddy; **étourdissement** nm dizzy spell

**étrange** [etʀɑ̃ʒ] adj strange

**étranger, -ère** [etʀɑ̃ʒe, ɛʀ] adj foreign; (pas de la famille, non familier) strange ▷ nm/f foreigner; stranger ▷ nm: **à l'~** abroad

**étrangler** [etʀɑ̃gle] vt to strangle; **s'étrangler** vi (en mangeant etc) to choke

○ **MOT-CLÉ**

**être** [εtʀ] nm being; **être humain** human being
▷ vb +attrib **1** (état, description) to be; **il est instituteur** he is ou he's a teacher; **vous êtes grand/intelligent/fatigué** you are ou you're tall/clever/tired
**2** (+à: appartenir) to be; **le livre est à Paul** the book is Paul's ou belongs to Paul; **c'est à moi/eux** it is ou it's mine/theirs
**3** (+de: provenance): **il est de Paris** he is from Paris; (: appartenance): **il est des nôtres** he is one of us
**4** (date): **nous sommes le 10 janvier** it's the 10th of January (today)
▷ vi to be; **je ne serai pas ici demain** I won't be here tomorrow
▷ vb aux **1** you to have; to be; **être arrivé/allé** to have arrived/gone; **il est parti** he has left, he has gone
**2** (forme passive) to be; **être fait par** to be made by; **il a été promu** he has been promoted
**3** (+à: obligation): **c'est à réparer** it needs repairing; **c'est à essayer** it should be tried; **il est à espérer que ...** it is ou it's to be hoped that ...
▷ vb impers **1**: **il est** +adjectif it is +adjective; **il est impossible de le faire** it's impossible to do it
**2** (heure, date): **il est 10 heures** it is ou it's 10 o'clock
**3** (emphatique): **c'est moi** it's me; **c'est à lui de le faire** it's up to him to do it

**étrennes** [etʀεn] nfpl Christmas box sg
**étrier** [etʀije] nm stirrup
**étroit, e** [etʀwa, wat] adj narrow; (vêtement) tight; (fig: liens, collaboration) close; **à l'~** cramped; **~ d'esprit** narrow-minded
**étude** [etyd] nf studying; (ouvrage, rapport) study; (Scol: salle de travail) study room; **études** nfpl (Scol) studies; **être à l'~** (projet etc) to be under consideration; **faire des ~s (de droit/**

médecine) to study (law/medicine)
**étudiant, e** [etydjɑ̃, jɑ̃t] nm/f student
**étudier** [etydje] vt, vi to study
**étui** [etɥi] nm case
**eu, eue** [y] pp de **avoir**
**euh** [ø] excl er
**euro** [øʀo] nm euro
**Europe** [øʀɔp] nf: **l'~** Europe; **européen, ne** adj European ▷ nm/f: **Européen, ne** European
**eus** etc [y] vb voir **avoir**
**eux** [ø] pron (sujet) they; (objet) them
**évacuer** [evakɥe] vt to evacuate
**évader** [evade]: **s'évader** vi to escape
**évaluer** [evalɥe] vt (expertiser) to appraise, evaluate; (juger approximativement) to estimate
**évangile** [evɑ̃ʒil] nm gospel; **É~** Gospel
**évanouir** [evanwiʀ]: **s'évanouir** vi to faint; (disparaître) to vanish, disappear; **évanouissement** nm (syncope) fainting fit
**évaporer** [evapɔʀe]: **s'évaporer** vi to evaporate
**évasion** [evazjɔ̃] nf escape
**éveillé, e** [eveje] adj awake; (vif) alert, sharp; **éveiller** vt to (a)waken; (soupçons etc) to arouse; **s'éveiller** vi to (a)waken; (fig) to be aroused
**événement** [evenmɑ̃] nm event
**éventail** [evɑ̃taj] nm fan; (choix) range
**éventualité** [evɑ̃tɥalite] nf eventuality; possibility; **dans l'~ de** in the event of
**éventuel, le** [evɑ̃tɥεl] adj possible
▌ Attention à ne pas traduire **éventuel** par eventual.
**éventuellement** adv possibly
▌ Attention à ne pas traduire **éventuellement** par eventually.
**évêque** [evεk] nm bishop
**évidemment** [evidamɑ̃] adv (bien sûr) of course; (certainement) obviously
**évidence** [evidɑ̃s] nf obviousness; (fait) obvious fact; **de toute ~** quite obviously ou evidently; **être en ~** to be clearly visible; **mettre en ~** (fait) to highlight; **évident, e** adj obvious,

evident; **ce n'est pas évident!** (*fam*) it's not that easy!

**évier** [evje] *nm* (kitchen) sink

**éviter** [evite] *vt* to avoid; **~ de faire** to avoid doing; **~ qch à qn** to spare sb sth

**évoluer** [evolɥe] *vi* (*enfant, maladie*) to develop; (*situation, moralement*) to evolve, develop; (*aller et venir*) to move about; **évolution** *nf* development, evolution

**évoquer** [evɔke] *vt* to call to mind, evoke; (*mentionner*) to mention

**ex-** [ɛks] *préfixe* ex-; **son ~mari** her ex-husband; **son ~femme** his ex-wife

**exact, e** [ɛgza(kt), ɛgzakt] *adj* exact; (*correct*) correct; (*ponctuel*) punctual; **l'heure ~** the right *ou* exact time; **exactement** *adv* exactly

**ex aequo** [ɛgzeko] *adj* equally placed; **arriver ~** to finish neck and neck

**exagéré, e** [ɛgzaʒere] *adj* (*prix etc*) excessive

**exagérer** [ɛgzaʒere] *vt* to exaggerate ▷ *vi* to exaggerate; (*abuser*) to go too far

**examen** [ɛgzamɛ̃] *nm* examination; (*Scol*) exam, examination; **à l'~** under consideration; **examen médical** (medical) examination; (*analyse*) test

**examinateur, -trice** [ɛgzaminatœʀ, tʀis] *nm/f* examiner

**examiner** [ɛgzamine] *vt* to examine

**exaspérant, e** [ɛgzaspeʀɑ̃, ɑ̃t] *adj* exasperating

**exaspérer** [ɛgzaspeʀe] *vt* to exasperate

**exaucer** [ɛgzose] *vt* (*vœu*) to grant

**excéder** [ɛksede] *vt* (*dépasser*) to exceed; (*agacer*) to exasperate

**excellent, e** [ɛkselɑ̃, ɑ̃t] *adj* excellent

**excentrique** [ɛksɑ̃tʀik] *adj* eccentric

**excepté, e** [ɛksɛpte] *adj, prép*: **les élèves ~s, ~ les élèves** except for the pupils

**exception** [ɛksɛpsjɔ̃] *nf* exception; **à l'~ de** except for, with the exception of; **d'~** (*mesure, loi*) special, exceptional; **exceptionnel, le** *adj* exceptional; **exceptionnellement** *adv* exceptionally

**excès** [ɛksɛ] *nm* surplus ▷ *nmpl* excesses; **faire des ~** to overindulge; **excès de vitesse** speeding *no pl*; **excessif, -ive** *adj* excessive

**excitant, e** [ɛksitɑ̃, ɑ̃t] *adj* exciting ▷ *nm* stimulant; **excitation** *nf* (*état*) excitement

**exciter** [ɛksite] *vt* to excite; (*suj: café etc*) to stimulate; **s'exciter** *vi* to get excited

**exclamer** [ɛksklame]: **s'exclamer** *vi* to exclaim

**exclure** [ɛksklyʀ] *vt* (*faire sortir*) to expel; (*ne pas compter*) to exclude, leave out; (*rendre impossible*) to exclude, rule out; **il est exclu que** it's out of the question that ...; **il n'est pas exclu que ...** it's not impossible that ...; **exclusif, -ive** *adj* exclusive; **exclusion** *nf* exclusion; **à l'exclusion de** with the exclusion *ou* exception of; **exclusivité** *nf* (*Comm*) exclusive rights *pl*; **film passant en exclusivité à** film showing only at

**excursion** [ɛkskyʀsjɔ̃] *nf* (*en autocar*) excursion, trip; (*à pied*) walk, hike

**excuse** [ɛkskyz] *nf* excuse; **excuses** *nfpl* (*regret*) apology *sg*, apologies; **excuser** *vt* to excuse; **s'excuser (de)** to apologize (for); **excusez-moi** I'm sorry; (*pour attirer l'attention*) excuse me

**exécuter** [ɛgzekyte] *vt* (*tuer*) to execute; (*tâche etc*) to execute, carry out; (*Mus: jouer*) to perform, execute; **s'exécuter** *vi* to comply

**exemplaire** [ɛgzɑ̃plɛʀ] *nm* copy

**exemple** [ɛgzɑ̃pl] *nm* example; **par ~** for instance, for example; **donner l'~** to set an example

**exercer** [ɛgzɛʀse] *vt* (*pratiquer*) to exercise, practise; (*influence, contrôle*) to exert; (*former*) to exercise, train; **s'exercer** *vi* (*sportif, musicien*) to practise

**exercice** [ɛgzɛʀsis] *nm* exercise

**exhiber** [ɛgzibe] *vt* (*montrer: papiers, certificat*) to present, produce; (*péj*) to

display, flaunt; **s'exhiber** vi to parade;
(suj: exhibitionniste) to expose o.s;
**exhibitionniste** nm/f flasher
**exigeant, e** [ɛgziʒɑ̃, ɑ̃t] adj
demanding; (péj) hard to please
**exiger** [ɛgziʒe] vt to demand, require
**exil** [ɛgzil] nm exile; **exiler** vt to exile;
**s'exiler** vi to go into exile
**existence** [ɛgzistɑ̃s] nf existence
**exister** [ɛgziste] vi to exist; **il existe
un/des** there is a/are (some)
**exorbitant, e** [ɛgzɔʀbitɑ̃, ɑ̃t] adj
exorbitant
**exotique** [ɛgzɔtik] adj exotic; **yaourt
aux fruits ~s** tropical fruit yoghurt
**expédier** [ɛkspedje] vt (lettre, paquet)
to send; (troupes) to dispatch; (fam:
travail etc) to dispose of, dispatch;
**expéditeur, -trice** nm/f sender;
**expédition** nf sending; (scientifique,
sportive, Mil) expedition
**expérience** [ɛkspeʀjɑ̃s] nf (de la vie)
experience; (scientifique) experiment
**expérimenté, e** [ɛkspeʀimɑ̃te] adj
experienced
**expérimenter** [ɛkspeʀimɑ̃te] vt to
test out, experiment with
**expert, e** [ɛkspeʀ, ɛʀt] adj, nm expert;
**~ en objets d'art** art appraiser;
**expert-comptable** nm ≈ chartered
accountant (BRIT), ≈ certified public
accountant (US)
**expirer** [ɛkspiʀe] vi (prendre fin, mourir)
to expire; (respirer) to breathe out
**explication** [ɛksplikasjɔ̃] nf
explanation; (discussion) discussion;
(dispute) argument
**explicite** [ɛksplisit] adj explicit
**expliquer** [ɛksplike] vt to explain;
**s'expliquer** to explain (o.s.); **s'~ avec
qn** (discuter) to explain o.s. to sb; **son
erreur s'explique** one can understand
his mistake
**exploit** [ɛksplwa] nm exploit, feat;
**exploitant, e** nm/f; **exploitant
(agricole)** farmer; **exploitation** nf
exploitation; (d'une entreprise) running;
**exploitation agricole** farming

concern; **exploiter** vt (personne, don)
to exploit; (entreprise, ferme) to run,
operate; (mine) to work, work
**explorer** [ɛksplɔʀe] vt to explore
**exploser** [ɛksploze] vi to explode, blow
up; (engin explosif) to go off; (personne: de
colère) to flare up; **explosif, -ive** adj, nm
explosive; **explosion** nf explosion; (de
joie, colère) outburst
**exportateur, -trice** [ɛkspɔʀtatœʀ,
tʀis] adj export cpd, exporting ▷ nm
exporter
**exportation** [ɛkspɔʀtasjɔ̃] nf (action)
exportation; (produit) export
**exporter** [ɛkspɔʀte] vt to export
**exposant** [ɛkspozɑ̃] nm exhibitor
**exposé, e** [ɛkspoze] nm talk ▷ adj: **~ au
sud** facing south
**exposer** [ɛkspoze] vt (marchandise)
to display; (peinture) to exhibit, show;
(parler de) to explain, set out; (mettre
en danger, orienter, Photo) to expose;
**s'~ à** (soleil, danger) to expose o.s.
to; **exposition** nf (manifestation)
exhibition; (Photo) exposure
**exprès¹** [ɛkspʀɛ] adv (délibérément) on
purpose; (spécialement) specially; **faire ~
de faire qch** to do sth on purpose
**exprès², -esse** [ɛkspʀɛs] adj inv (lettre,
colis) express
**express** [ɛkspʀɛs] adj, nm: **(café) ~**
espresso (coffee); **(train) ~** fast train
**expressif, -ive** [ɛkspʀesif, iv] adj
expressive
**expression** [ɛkspʀesjɔ̃] nf expression
**exprimer** [ɛkspʀime] vt (sentiment,
idée) to express; (jus, liquide) to press
out; **s'exprimer** vi (personne) to
express o.s
**expulser** [ɛkspylse] vt to expel;
(locataire) to evict; (Sport) to send off
**exquis, e** [ɛkski, iz] adj exquisite
**extasier** [ɛkstazje]: **s'extasier sur** vt
to go into raptures over
**exténuer** [ɛkstenɥe] vt to exhaust
**extérieur, e** [ɛksteʀjœʀ] adj (porte,
mur etc) outer, outside; (au dehors:
escalier, w.-c.) outside; (commerce)

foreign; (*influences*) external; (*apparent: calme, gaieté etc*) surface cpd ▷ nm (*d'une maison, d'un récipient etc*) outside, exterior; (*apparence*) exterior; **à l'~** outside; (*à l'étranger*) abroad

**externat** [ɛkstɛʀna] nm day school

**externe** [ɛkstɛʀn] adj external, outer ▷ nm/f (*Méd*) non-resident medical student (BRIT), extern (US); (*Scol*) day pupil

**extincteur** [ɛkstɛ̃ktœʀ] nm (fire) extinguisher

**extinction** [ɛkstɛ̃ksjɔ̃] nf: **extinction de voix** loss of voice

**extra** [ɛkstʀa] adj inv first-rate; (*fam*) fantastic ▷ nm inv extra help

**extraire** [ɛkstʀɛʀ] vt to extract; **~ qch de** to extract sth from; **extrait** nm extract; **extrait de naissance** birth certificate

**extraordinaire** [ɛkstʀaɔʀdinɛʀ] adj extraordinary; (*Pol: mesures etc*) special

**extravagant, e** [ɛkstʀavagɑ̃, ɑ̃t] adj extravagant

**extraverti, e** [ɛkstʀavɛʀti] adj extrovert

**extrême** [ɛkstʀɛm] adj, nm extreme; **d'un ~ à l'autre** from one extreme to another; **extrêmement** adv extremely; **Extrême-Orient** nm Far East

**extrémité** [ɛkstʀemite] nf end; (*situation*) straits pl, plight; (*geste désespéré*) extreme action; **extrémités** nfpl (*pieds et mains*) extremities

**exubérant, e** [ɛgzybeʀɑ̃, ɑ̃t] adj exuberant

**F** abr = **franc**; (*appartement*): **un F2/F3** a one-/two-bedroom flat (BRIT) ou apartment (US)

**fa** [fa] nm inv (*Mus*) F; (*en chantant la gamme*) fa

**fabricant, e** [fabʀikɑ̃, ɑ̃t] nm/f manufacturer

**fabrication** [fabʀikasjɔ̃] nf manufacture

**fabrique** [fabʀik] nf factory; **fabriquer** vt to make; (*industriellement*) to manufacture; (*fig*): **qu'est-ce qu'il fabrique?** (*fam*) what is he doing?

**fac** [fak] (*fam*) abr f (*Scol*) = **faculté**

**façade** [fasad] nf front, façade

**face** [fas] nf face; (*fig: aspect*) side ▷ adj: **le côté ~** heads; **en ~ de** opposite; (*fig*) in front of; **de ~** (*voir*) face on; **~ à** facing; (*fig*) faced with, in the face of; **faire ~ à** to face; **~ à ~** adv facing each other ▷ nm inv encounter

**fâché, e** [faʃe] adj angry; (*désolé*) sorry

**fâcher** [faʃe] vt to anger; **se fâcher (contre qn)** vi to get angry (with sb);

**se ~ avec** (se brouiller) to fall out with
**facile** [fasil] adj easy; (caractère) easy-going; **facilement** adv easily; **facilité** nf easiness; (disposition, don) aptitude; **facilités** (possibilités) facilities; (Comm) terms; **faciliter** vt to make easier
**façon** [fasɔ̃] nf (manière) way; (d'une robe etc) making-up, cut; **façons** nfpl (péj) fuss sg; **de ~ à/à ce que** so as to/that; **de toute ~** anyway, in any case; **sans ~** (accepter) without fuss; **non merci, sans ~** no thanks, honestly
**facteur, -trice** [faktœʀ] nm/f postman(-woman) (BRIT), mailman(-woman) (US) ▷ nm (Math, fig: élément) factor
**facture** [faktyʀ] nf (à payer: gén) bill; (Comm) invoice
**facultatif, -ive** [fakyltatif, iv] adj optional
**faculté** [fakylte] nf (intellectuelle, d'université) faculty; (pouvoir, possibilité) power
**fade** [fad] adj insipid
**faible** [fɛbl] adj weak; (voix, lumière, vent) faint; (rendement, revenu) low ▷ nm (pour quelqu'un) weakness, soft spot; **faiblesse** nf weakness; **faiblir** vi to weaken; (lumière) to dim; (vent) to drop
**faïence** [fajɑ̃s] nf earthenware no pl
**faillir** [fajiʀ] vi: **j'ai failli tomber** I almost ou very nearly fell
**faillite** [fajit] nf bankruptcy; **faire ~** to go bankrupt
**faim** [fɛ̃] nf hunger; **avoir ~** to be hungry; **rester sur sa ~** (aussi fig) to be left wanting more
**fainéant, e** [fɛneɑ̃, ɑ̃t] nm/f idler, loafer

⭕ **MOT-CLÉ**

**faire** [fɛʀ] vt 1 (fabriquer, être l'auteur de) to make; **faire du vin/une offre/un film** to make wine/an offer/a film; **faire du bruit** to make a noise
2 (effectuer: travail, opération) to do; **que faites-vous?** (quel métier etc) what do

you do?; (quelle activité: au moment de la question) what are you doing?; **faire la lessive** to do the washing
3 (études) to do; (sport, musique) to play; **faire du droit/du français** to do law/French; **faire du rugby/piano** to play rugby/the piano
4 (simuler): **faire le malade/l'innocent** to act the invalid/the innocent
5 (transformer, avoir un effet sur): **faire de qn un frustré/avocat** to make sb frustrated/a lawyer; **ça ne me fait rien** (m'est égal) I don't care ou mind; (me laisse froid) it has no effect on me; **ça ne fait rien** it doesn't matter; **faire que** (impliquer) to mean that
6 (calculs, prix, mesures): **2 et 2 font 4** 2 and 2 are ou make 4; **ça fait 10 m/15 euros** it's 10 m/15 euros; **je vous le fais 10 euros** I'll let you have it for 10 euros; **je fais du 40** I take a size 40
7 (distance): **faire du 50 (à l'heure)** to do 50 (km an hour); **nous avons fait 1000 km en 2 jours** we did ou covered 1000 km in 2 days; **faire l'Europe** to tour ou do Europe; **faire les magasins** to go shopping
8: **qu'a-t-il fait de sa valise?** what has he done with his case?
9: **ne faire que: il ne fait que critiquer** (sans cesse) all he (ever) does is criticize; (seulement) he's only criticizing
10 (dire) to say; **"vraiment?" fit-il** "really?" he said
11 (maladie) to have; **faire du diabète** to have diabetes sg
▷ vi 1 (agir, s'y prendre) to act, do; **il faut faire vite** we (ou you etc) must act quickly; **comment a-t-il fait pour?** how did he manage to?; **faites comme chez vous** make yourself at home
2 (paraître) to look; **faire vieux/démodé** to look old/old-fashioned; **ça fait bien** it looks good
▷ vb substitut to do; **ne le casse pas comme je l'ai fait** don't break it as I did; **je peux le voir? — faites!** can I see

it? — please do!

▷ vb impers 1: **il fait beau** etc the weather is fine etc; voir aussi **jour**; **froid** etc

2 (temps écoulé, durée): **ça fait 2 ans qu'il est parti** it's 2 years since he left; **ça fait 2 ans qu'il y est** he's been there for 2 years

▷ vb semi-aux 1: **faire** (+infinitif: action directe) to make; **faire tomber/bouger qch** to make sth fall/move; **faire démarrer un moteur/chauffer de l'eau** to start up an engine/heat some water; **cela fait dormir** it makes you sleep; **faire travailler les enfants** to make the children work ou get the children to work; **il m'a fait traverser la rue** he helped me to cross the street

2 (indirectement, par un intermédiaire): **faire réparer qch** to get ou have sth repaired; **faire punir les enfants** to have the children punished

**se faire** vi 1 (être convenable): **cela se fait beaucoup/ne se fait pas** it's done a lot/not done

2: **se faire** +nom ou pron: **se faire une jupe** to make o.s. a skirt; **se faire des amis** to make friends; **se faire du souci** to worry; **il ne s'en fait pas** he doesn't worry

3: **se faire** +adj (devenir): **se faire vieux** to be getting old; **se faire beau** to do o.s. up

4: **se faire à** (s'habituer) to get used to; **je n'arrive pas à me faire à la nourriture/au climat** I can't get used to the food/climate

5: **se faire** +infinitif: **se faire examiner la vue/opérer** to have one's eyes tested/have an operation; **se faire couper les cheveux** to get one's hair cut; **il va se faire tuer/punir** he's going to get himself killed/get punished; **il s'est fait aider** he got somebody to help him; **il s'est fait aider par Simon** he got Simon to help him; **se faire faire un vêtement** to get a garment made for o.s.

6 (impersonnel): **comment se fait-il/faisait-il que?** how is it/was it that?

**faire-part** [fɛʀpaʀ] nm inv announcement (of birth, marriage etc)

**faisan, e** [fəzɑ̃, an] nm/f pheasant

**faisons** [fəzɔ̃] vb voir **faire**

**fait, e** [fɛ, fɛt] adj (mûr: fromage, melon) ripe ▷ nm (événement) event, occurrence; (réalité, donnée) fact; **être au ~ (de)** to be informed (of); **au ~** (à propos) by the way; **en venir au ~** to get to the point; **du ~ de ceci/qu'il a menti** because of ou on account of this/his having lied; **de ce ~** for this reason; **en ~** in fact; **prendre qn sur le ~** to catch sb in the act; **c'est bien ~ pour lui** (ou eux etc) it serves him (ou them etc) right; **fait divers** news item

**faites** [fɛt] vb voir **faire**

**falaise** [falɛz] nf cliff

**falloir** [falwaʀ] vb impers: **il faut qu'il parte/a fallu qu'il parte** (obligation) he has to ou must leave/had to leave; **il a fallu le faire** it had to be done; **il faudrait qu'elle rentre** she should come ou go back, she ought to come ou go back; **il faut faire attention** you have to be careful; **il me faudrait 100 euros** I would need 100 euros; **il vous faut tourner à gauche après l'église** you have to turn left past the church; **nous avons ce qu'il (nous) faut** we have what we need; **il ne fallait pas** you shouldn't have (done); **comme il faut** (personne) proper; (agir) properly; **s'en falloir** vr: **il s'en est fallu de 100 euros/5 minutes** we/they etc were 100 euros short/5 minutes late (ou early); **il s'en faut de beaucoup qu'il soit** he is far from being; **il s'en est fallu de peu que cela n'arrive** it very nearly happened

**famé, e** [fame] adj: **mal ~** disreputable, of ill repute

**fameux, -euse** [famø, øz] adj (illustre) famous; (bon: repas, plat etc) first-rate, first-class; (valeur intensive) real, downright

**familial, e, -aux** [familjal, jo] *adj*
family *cpd*

**familiarité** [familjaʀite] *nf* familiarity

**familier, -ère** [familje, jɛʀ] *adj*
(*connu*) familiar; (*atmosphère*) informal,
friendly; (*Ling*) informal, colloquial
▷ *nm* regular (visitor)

**famille** [famij] *nf* family; **il a de la ~ à
Paris** he has relatives in Paris

**famine** [famin] *nf* famine

**fanatique** [fanatik] *adj* fanatical
▷ *nm/f* fanatic

**faner** [fane]: **se faner** *vi* to fade

**fanfare** [fɑ̃faʀ] *nf* (*orchestre*) brass
band; (*musique*) fanfare

**fantaisie** [fɑ̃tezi] *nf* (*spontanéité*) fancy,
imagination; (*caprice*) whim ▷ *adj*:
**bijou ~** costume jewellery

**fantasme** [fɑ̃tasm] *nm* fantasy

**fantastique** [fɑ̃tastik] *adj* fantastic

**fantôme** [fɑ̃tom] *nm* ghost, phantom

**faon** [fɑ̃] *nm* fawn

**FAQ** *sigle f* (= *foire aux questions*) FAQ

**farce** [faʀs] *nf* (*viande*) stuffing; (*blague*)
(practical) joke; (*Théâtre*) farce; **farcir** *vt*
(*viande*) to stuff

**farder** [faʀde]: **se farder** *vi* to make
(o.s.) up

**farine** [faʀin] *nf* flour

**farouche** [faʀuʃ] *adj* (*timide*) shy, timid

**fart** [faʀt] *nm* (ski) wax

**fascination** [fasinasjɔ̃] *nf* fascination

**fasciner** [fasine] *vt* to fascinate

**fascisme** [faʃism] *nm* fascism

**fasse** *etc* [fas] *vb voir* **faire**

**fastidieux, -euse** [fastidjø, jøz] *adj*
tedious, tiresome

**fatal, e** [fatal] *adj* fatal; (*inévitable*)
inevitable; **fatalité** *nf* (*destin*) fate;
(*coïncidence*) fateful coincidence

**fatidique** [fatidik] *adj* fateful

**fatigant, e** [fatigɑ̃, ɑ̃t] *adj* tiring;
(*agaçant*) tiresome

**fatigue** [fatig] *nf* tiredness, fatigue;
**fatigué, e** *adj* tired; **fatiguer** *vt* to tire,
make tired; (*fig: agacer*) to annoy ▷ *vi*
(*moteur*) to labour, strain; **se fatiguer**
to get tired

**fauché, e** [foʃe] (*fam*) *adj* broke

**faucher** [foʃe] *vt* (*herbe*) to cut; (*champs,
blés*) to reap; (*fig: véhicule*) to mow
down; (*fam: voler*) to pinch

**faucon** [fokɔ̃] *nm* falcon, hawk

**faudra** [fodʀa] *vb voir* **falloir**

**faufiler** [fofile] *vi*: **se ~
dans** to edge one's way into; **se ~
parmi/entre** to thread one's way
among/between

**faune** [fon] *nf* (*Zool*) wildlife, fauna

**fausse** [fos] *adj voir* **faux; faussement**
*adv* (*accuser*) wrongly, wrongfully;
(*croire*) falsely

**fausser** [fose] *vt* (*objet*) to bend, buckle;
(*fig*) to distort; **~ compagnie à qn** to
give sb the slip

**faut** [fo] *vb voir* **falloir**

**faute** [fot] *nf* (*erreur*) mistake, error;
(*mauvaise action*) misdemeanour;
(*Football etc*) offence; (*Tennis*) fault;
**c'est de sa/ma ~** it's his *ou* her/my
fault; **être en ~** to be in the wrong; **~ de**
(*temps, argent*) for *ou* through lack of;
**sans ~** without fail; **faute de frappe**
typing error; **faute professionnelle**
professional misconduct *no pl*

**fauteuil** [fotœj] *nm* armchair;
(*au théâtre*) seat; **fauteuil roulant**
wheelchair

**fautif, -ive** [fotif, iv] *adj* (*responsable*)
at fault, in the wrong; (*incorrect*)
incorrect, inaccurate; **il se sentait ~**
he felt guilty

**fauve** [fov] *nm* wildcat ▷ *adj* (*couleur*)
fawn

**faux¹** [fo] *nf* scythe

**faux², fausse** [fo, fos] *adj* (*inexact*)
wrong; (*voix*) out of tune; (*billet*) fake,
forged; (*sournois, postiche*) false ▷ *adv*
(*Mus*) out of tune ▷ *nm* (*copie*) fake,
forgery; **faire ~ bond à qn** to let sb
down; **faire un ~ pas** to trip; (*fig*) to
make a faux pas; **fausse alerte** false
alarm; **fausse couche** miscarriage;
**faux frais** *nmpl* extras, incidental
expenses; **faux mouvement** awkward

movement; **fausse note** wrong note; **faux témoignage** (délit) perjury; **faux-filet** nm sirloin

**faveur** [favœR] nf favour; **traitement de ~** preferential treatment; **en ~ de** in favour of

**favorable** [favoRabl] adj favourable

**favori, te** [favoRi, it] adj, nm/f favourite

**favoriser** [favoRize] vt to favour

**fax** [faks] nm fax

**fécond, e** [fekɔ̃, ɔ̃d] adj fertile; **féconder** vt to fertilize

**féculent** [fekylɑ̃] nm starchy food

**fédéral, e, -aux** [fedeRal, o] adj federal

**fée** [fe] nf fairy

**feignant, e** [fɛɲɑ̃, ɑ̃t] nm/f = **fainéant, e**

**feindre** [fɛ̃dR] vt to feign; **~ de faire** to pretend to do

**fêler** [fele] vt to crack; **se fêler** to crack

**félicitations** [felisitasjɔ̃] nfpl congratulations

**féliciter** [felisite] vt: **~ qn (de)** to congratulate sb (on)

**félin, e** [felɛ̃, in] nm (big) cat

**femelle** [fəmɛl] adj, nf female

**féminin, e** [feminɛ̃, in] adj feminine; (sexe) female; (équipe, vêtements etc) women's ▷ nm (Ling) feminine; **féministe** adj feminist

**femme** [fam] nf woman; (épouse) wife; **femme au foyer** housewife; **femme de chambre** chambermaid; **femme de ménage** cleaning lady

**fémur** [femyR] nm femur, thighbone

**fendre** [fɑ̃dR] vt (couper en deux) to split; (fissurer) to crack; (traverser: foule, air) to cleave through; **se fendre** vi to crack

**fenêtre** [f(ə)nɛtR] nf window

**fenouil** [fənuj] nm fennel

**fente** [fɑ̃t] nf (fissure) crack; (de boîte à lettres etc) slit

**fer** [fɛR] nm iron; **fer à cheval** horseshoe; **fer à friser** curling tongs pl; **fer (à repasser)** iron; **fer forgé** wrought iron

**ferai** etc [fəRe] vb voir **faire**

**fer-blanc** [fɛRblɑ̃] nm tin(plate)

**férié, e** [feRje] adj: **jour ~** public holiday

**ferions** etc [fəRjɔ̃] vb voir **faire**

**ferme** [fɛRm] adj firm ▷ adv (travailler etc) hard ▷ nf (exploitation) farm; (maison) farmhouse

**fermé, e** [fɛRme] adj closed, shut; (gaz, eau etc) off; (fig: milieu) exclusive

**fermenter** [fɛRmɑ̃te] vi to ferment

**fermer** [fɛRme] vt to close, shut; (cesser l'exploitation de) to close down, shut down; (eau, électricité, robinet) to turn off; (aéroport, route) to close ▷ vi to close, shut; (magasin: définitivement) to close down, shut down; **à clef** to lock; **se fermer** vi to close, shut

**fermeté** [fɛRməte] nf firmness

**fermeture** [fɛRmətyR] nf closing; (dispositif) catch; **heures de ~** closing times; **fermeture éclair®** ou **à glissière** zip (fastener) (BRIT), zipper (US)

**fermier** [fɛRmje] nm farmer

**féroce** [feRos] adj ferocious, fierce

**ferons** etc [fəRɔ̃] vb voir **faire**

**ferrer** [feRe] vt (cheval) to shoe

**ferroviaire** [feRovjɛR] adj rail(way) cpd (BRIT), rail(road) cpd (US)

**ferry(-boat)** [feRe(-bot)] nm ferry

**fertile** [fɛRtil] adj fertile; **~ en incidents** eventful, packed with incidents

**fervent, e** [fɛRvɑ̃, ɑ̃t] adj fervent

**fesse** [fɛs] nf buttock; **fessée** nf spanking

**festin** [festɛ̃] nm feast

**festival** [festival] nm festival

**festivités** [festivite] nfpl festivities

**fêtard, e** [fɛtaR, aRd] (fam) nm/f high liver, merry-maker

**fête** [fɛt] nf (religieuse) feast; (publique) holiday; (réception) party; (kermesse) fête, fair; (du nom) feast day, name day; **faire la ~** to live it up; **faire ~ à qn** to give sb a warm welcome; **les ~s (de fin d'année)** the festive season; **la salle des ~s** the village hall; **la ~ des Mères/**

**Pères** Mother's/Father's Day; **fête foraine** (fun) fair; **fêter** vt to celebrate; (personne) to have a celebration for

**feu, x** [fø] nm (gén) fire; (signal lumineux) light; (de cuisinière) ring; **feux** nmpl (Auto) (traffic) lights; **au ~!** (incendie) fire!; **à ~ doux/vif** over a slow/brisk heat; **à petit ~** (Culin) over a gentle heat; (fig) slowly; **faire ~** to fire; **ne pas faire long ~** not to last long; **prendre ~** to catch fire; **mettre le ~ à** to set fire to; **faire du ~** to make a fire; **avez-vous du ~?** (pour cigarette) have you (got) a light?; **feu arrière** rear light; **feu d'artifice** (spectacle) fireworks pl; **feu de joie** bonfire; **feu orange/rouge/vert** amber (BRIT) ou yellow (US)/red/green light; **feux de brouillard** fog lights ou lamps; **feux de croisement** dipped (BRIT) ou dimmed (US) headlights; **feux de position** sidelights; **feux de route** headlights

**feuillage** [fœjaʒ] nm foliage, leaves pl

**feuille** [fœj] nf (d'arbre) leaf; (de papier) sheet; **feuille de calcul** spreadsheet; **feuille d'impôts** tax form; **feuille de maladie** medical expenses claim form; **feuille de paie** pay slip

**feuillet** [fœjɛ] nm leaf

**feuilleté, e** [fœjte] adj: **pâte ~** flaky pastry

**feuilleter** [fœjte] vt (livre) to leaf through

**feuilleton** [fœjtɔ̃] nm serial

**feutre** [føtr] nm felt; (chapeau) felt hat; (aussi: **stylo-~**) felt-tip pen; **feutré, e** adj (atmosphère) muffled

**fève** [fɛv] nf broad bean

**février** [fevrije] nm February

**fiable** [fjabl] adj reliable

**fiançailles** [fjɑ̃saj] nfpl engagement sg

**fiancé, e** [fjɑ̃se] nm/f fiancé(e) ▷ adj: **être ~ (à)** to be engaged (to)

**fiancer** [fjɑ̃se]: **se fiancer (avec)** vi to become engaged (to)

**fibre** [fibr] nf fibre; **fibre de verre** fibreglass, glass fibre

**ficeler** [fis(ə)le] vt to tie up

**ficelle** [fisɛl] nf string no pl; (morceau) piece ou length of string

**fiche** [fiʃ] nf (pour fichier) (index) card; (formulaire) form; (Élec) plug; **fiche de paye** pay slip

**ficher** [fiʃe] vt (dans un fichier) to file; (Police) to put on file; (fam: faire) to do; (: donner) to give; (: mettre) to stick ou shove; **fiche-(moi) le camp!** (fam) clear off!; **fiche-moi la paix!** (fam) leave me alone!; **se ficher de** (fam: rire de) to make fun of; (être indifférent à) not to care about

**fichier** [fiʃje] nm file; **~ joint** (Comput) attachment

**fichu, e** [fiʃy] pp de **ficher (fam)** ▷ adj (fam: fini, inutilisable) bust, done for; (: intensif) wretched, darned ▷ nm (foulard) (head)scarf; **mal ~** (fam) feeling lousy

**fictif, -ive** [fiktif, iv] adj fictitious

**fiction** [fiksjɔ̃] nf fiction; (fait imaginé) invention

**fidèle** [fidɛl] adj faithful ▷ nm/f (Rel): **les ~s** (à l'église) the congregation sg; **fidélité** nf (d'un conjoint) fidelity, faithfulness; (d'un ami, client) loyalty

**fier¹** [fje]: **se fier à** vt to trust

**fier², fière** [fjɛr] adj proud; **~ de** proud of; **fierté** nf pride

**fièvre** [fjɛvr] nf fever; **avoir de la ~/39 de ~** to have a high temperature/a temperature of 39˚C; **fiévreux, -euse** adj feverish

**figer** [fiʒe]: **se figer** vi (huile) to congeal; (personne) to freeze

**fignoler** [fiɲɔle] (fam) vt to polish up

**figue** [fig] nf fig; **figuier** nm fig tree

**figurant, e** [figyrɑ̃, ɑ̃t] nm/f (Théâtre) walk-on; (Cinéma) extra

**figure** [figyr] nf (visage) face; (forme, personnage) figure; (illustration) picture, diagram

**figuré, e** [figyre] adj (sens) figurative

**figurer** [figyre] vi to appear ▷ vt to represent; **se figurer que** to imagine that

**fil** [fil] nm (brin, fig: d'une histoire) thread;

(*électrique*) wire; (*d'un couteau*) edge; **au ~ des années** with the passing of the years; **au ~ de l'eau** with the stream *ou* current; **coup de ~** (*fam*) phone call; **donner/recevoir un coup de ~** to make/get *ou* receive a phone call; **fil de fer** wire; **fil de fer barbelé** barbed wire

**file** [fil] *nf* line; (*Auto*) lane; **en ~ indienne** in single file; **à la ~** (*d'affilée*) in succession; **file (d'attente)** queue (BRIT), line (US)

**filer** [file] *vt* (*tissu, toile*) to spin; (*prendre en filature*) to shadow, tail; (*fam: donner*): **~ qch à qn** to slip sb sth ▷ *vi* (*bas*) to run; (*aller vite*) to fly past; (*fam: partir*) to make *ou* be off; **~ doux** to toe the line

**filet** [filε] *nm* net; (*Culin*) fillet; (*d'eau, de sang*) trickle; **filet (à provisions)** string bag

**filiale** [filjal] *nf* (*Comm*) subsidiary

**filière** [filjεR] *nf* (*carrière*) path; **suivre la ~** (*dans sa carrière*) to work one's way up (through the hierarchy)

**fille** [fij] *nf* girl; (*opposé à fils*) daughter; **vieille ~** old maid; **fillette** *nf* (little) girl

**filleul, e** [fijœl] *nm/f* godchild, godson/daughter

**film** [film] *nm* (*pour photo*) (roll of) film; (*œuvre*) film, picture, movie

**fils** [fis] *nm* son; **fils à papa** daddy's boy

**filtre** [filtR] *nm* filter; **filtrer** *vt* to filter; (*fig: candidats, visiteurs*) to screen

**fin¹** [fɛ̃] *nf* end; **fins** *nfpl* (*but*) ends; **prendre ~** to come to an end; **mettre ~ à** to put an end to; **à la ~** in the end, eventually; **en ~ de compte** in the end; **sans ~** endless; **~ juin** at the end of June; **fin prêt** quite ready

**fin², e** [fɛ̃, fin] *adj* (*papier, couche, fil*) thin; (*cheveux, visage*) fine; (*taille*) neat, slim; (*esprit, remarque*) subtle ▷ *adv* (*couper*) finely; **fines herbes** mixed herbs; **avoir la vue/l'ouïe fine** to have keen eyesight/hearing; **repas/vin fin** gourmet meal/fine wine

**final, e** [final, o] *adj* final ▷ *nm* (*Mus*) finale; **finale** *nf* final; **quarts de finale** quarter finals; **finalement** *adv* finally,

in the end; (*après tout*) after all

**finance** [finɑ̃s]: **finances** *nfpl* (*situation*) finances; (*activités*) finance *sg*; **moyennant ~** for a fee; **financer** *vt* to finance; **financier, -ière** *adj* financial

**finesse** [finεs] *nf* thinness; (*raffinement*) fineness; (*subtilité*) subtlety

**fini, e** [fini] *adj* finished; (*Math*) finite ▷ *nm* (*d'un objet manufacturé*) finish

**finir** [finiR] *vt* to finish ▷ *vi* to finish, end; **~ par faire** to end up *ou* finish up doing; **~ de faire** to finish doing; (*cesser*) to stop doing; **il finit par m'agacer** he's beginning to get on my nerves; **en ~ avec** to be *ou* have done with; **il va mal ~** he will come to a bad end

**finition** [finisjɔ̃] *nf* (*résultat*) finish

**finlandais, e** [fɛ̃lɑ̃dɛ, εz] *adj* Finnish ▷ *nm/f*: **F~, e** Finn

**Finlande** [fɛ̃lɑ̃d] *nf*: **la ~** Finland

**finnois, e** [finwa, waz] *adj* Finnish ▷ *nm* (*Ling*) Finnish

**fioul** [fjul] *nm* fuel oil

**firme** [firm] *nf* firm

**fis** [fi] *vb voir* **faire**

**fisc** [fisk] *nm* tax authorities *pl*; **fiscal, e, -aux** *adj* tax *cpd*, fiscal; **fiscalité** *nf* tax system

**fissure** [fisyR] *nf* crack; **fissurer** *vt* to crack; **se fissurer** *vi* to crack

**fit** [fi] *vb voir* **faire**

**fixation** [fiksasjɔ̃] *nf* (*attache*) fastening; (*Psych*) fixation

**fixe** [fiks] *adj* fixed; (*emploi*) steady, regular ▷ *nm* (*salaire*) basic salary; (*téléphone*) landline; **à heure ~** at a set time; **menu à prix ~** set menu

**fixé, e** [fikse] *adj*: **être ~ (sur)** (*savoir à quoi s'en tenir*) to have made up one's mind (about)

**fixer** [fikse] *vt* (*attacher*): **~ qch (à/sur)** to fix *ou* fasten sth (to/onto); (*déterminer*) to fix, set; (*regarder*) to stare at; **se fixer** *vi* (*s'établir*) to settle down; **se ~ sur** (*suj: attention*) to focus on

**flacon** [flakɔ̃] *nm* bottle

**flageolet** [flaʒɔlɛ] nm (Culin) dwarf kidney bean

**flagrant, e** [flagʀɑ̃, ɑ̃t] adj flagrant, blatant; **en ~ délit** in the act

**flair** [flɛʀ] nm sense of smell; (fig) intuition; **flairer** vt (humer) to sniff (at); (détecter) to scent

**flamand, e** [flamɑ̃, ɑ̃d] adj Flemish ▷ nm (Ling) Flemish ▷ nm/f: **F~, e** Fleming

**flamant** [flamɑ̃] nm flamingo

**flambant, e** [flɑ̃bɑ̃, ɑ̃t] adv: **~ neuf** brand new

**flambé, e** [flɑ̃be] adj (Culin) flambé

**flambée** [flɑ̃be] nf blaze; (fig: des prix) explosion

**flamber** [flɑ̃be] vi to blaze (up)

**flamboyer** [flɑ̃bwaje] vi to blaze (up)

**flamme** [flam] nf flame; (fig) fire, fervour; **en ~s** on fire, ablaze

**flan** [flɑ̃] nm (Culin) custard tart ou pie

**flanc** [flɑ̃] nm side; (Mil) flank

**flancher** [flɑ̃ʃe] (fam) vi to fail, pack up

**flanelle** [flanɛl] nf flannel

**flâner** [flɑne] vi to stroll

**flanquer** [flɑ̃ke] vt to flank; (fam: mettre) to chuck, shove; (: jeter): **~ par terre/à la porte** to fling to the ground/chuck out

**flaque** [flak] nf (d'eau) puddle; (d'huile, de sang etc) pool

**flash** [flaʃ] (pl **~es**) nm (Photo) flash; **flash d'information** newsflash

**flatter** [flate] vt to flatter; **se ~ de qch** to pride o.s. on sth; **flatteur, -euse** adj flattering

**flèche** [flɛʃ] nf arrow; (de clocher) spire; **monter en ~** (fig) to soar, rocket; **partir en ~** to be off like a shot; **fléchette** nf dart

**flétrir** [fletʀiʀ]: **se flétrir** vi to wither

**fleur** [flœʀ] nf flower; (d'un arbre) blossom; **en ~** (arbre) in blossom; **à ~s** flowery

**fleuri, e** [flœʀi] adj (jardin) in flower ou bloom; (tissu, papier) flowery

**fleurir** [flœʀiʀ] vi (rose) to flower; (arbre) to blossom; (fig) to flourish ▷ vt (tombe) to put flowers on; (chambre) to decorate with flowers

**fleuriste** [flœʀist] nm/f florist

**fleuve** [flœv] nm river

**flexible** [flɛksibl] adj flexible

**flic** [flik] (fam: péj) nm cop

**flipper** [flipœʀ] nm pinball (machine)

**flirter** [flœʀte] vi to flirt

**flocon** [flɔkɔ̃] nm flake

**flore** [flɔʀ] nf flora

**florissant, e** [flɔʀisɑ̃, ɑ̃t] adj (économie) flourishing

**flot** [flo] nm flood, stream; **flots** nmpl (de la mer) waves; **être à ~** (Navig) to be afloat; **entrer à ~s** to stream ou pour in

**flottant, e** [flɔtɑ̃, ɑ̃t] adj (vêtement) loose

**flotte** [flɔt] nf (Navig) fleet; (fam: eau) water; (: pluie) rain

**flotter** [flɔte] vi to float; (nuage, odeur) to drift; (drapeau) to fly; (vêtements) to hang loose; (fam: pleuvoir) to rain; **faire ~** to float; **flotteur** nm float

**flou, e** [flu] adj fuzzy, blurred; (fig) woolly, vague

**fluide** [flɥid] adj fluid; (circulation etc) flowing freely ▷ nm fluid

**fluor** [flyɔʀ] nm: **dentifrice au ~** fluoride toothpaste

**fluorescent, e** [flyɔʀesɑ̃, ɑ̃t] adj fluorescent

**flûte** [flyt] nf flute; (verre) flute (glass); (pain) (thin) French stick; **~!** drat it!; **flûte traversière/à bec** flute/recorder

**flux** [fly] nm incoming tide; (écoulement) flow; **le ~ et le reflux** the ebb and flow

**foc** [fɔk] nm jib

**foi** [fwa] nf faith; **digne de ~** reliable; **être de bonne/mauvaise ~** to be sincere/insincere; **ma ~ ...** well ...

**foie** [fwa] nm liver; **crise de ~** stomach upset

**foin** [fwɛ̃] nm hay; **faire du ~** (fig: fam) to kick up a row

**foire** [fwaʀ] nf fair; (fête foraine) (fun) fair; **faire la ~** (fig: fam) to whoop it up; **~ aux questions** (Internet) FAQs; **foire (exposition)** trade fair

**fois** [fwa] *nf* time; **une/deux ~** once/twice; **2 ~ 2** 2 times 2; **une ~** (*passé*) once; (*futur*) sometime; **une ~ pour toutes** once and for all; **une ~ que** once; **des ~** (*parfois*) sometimes; **à la ~** (*ensemble*) at once

**fol** [fɔl] *adj voir* **fou**

**folie** [fɔli] *nf* (*d'une décision, d'un acte*) madness, folly; (*état*) madness, insanity; **la ~ des grandeurs** delusions of grandeur; **faire des ~s** (*en dépenses*) to be extravagant

**folklorique** [fɔlklɔRik] *adj* folk *cpd*; (*fam*) weird

**folle** [fɔl] *adj, nf voir* **fou**; **follement** *adv* (*très*) madly, wildly

**foncé, e** [fɔ̃se] *adj* dark

**foncer** [fɔ̃se] *vi* to go darker; (*fam: aller vite*) to tear *ou* belt along; **~ sur** to charge at

**fonction** [fɔ̃ksjɔ̃] *nf* function; (*emploi, poste*) post, position; **fonctions** *nfpl* (*professionnelles*) duties; **voiture de ~** company car; **en ~ de** (*par rapport à*) according to; **faire ~ de** to serve as; **la ~ publique** the state *ou* civil (BRIT) service; **fonctionnaire** *nm/f* state employee, local authority employee; (*dans l'administration*) ≈ civil servant; **fonctionner** *vi* to work, function

**fond** [fɔ̃] *nm* (*d'un récipient, trou*) bottom; (*d'une salle, scène*) back; (*d'un tableau, décor*) background; (*opposé à la forme*) content; (*Sport*): **le ~** long distance (running); **au ~ de** at the bottom of; at the back of; **à ~** (*connaître, soutenir*) thoroughly; (*appuyer, visser*) right down *ou* home; **à ~ (de train)** (*fam*) full tilt; **dans le ~, au ~** (*en somme*) basically, really; **de ~ en comble** from top to bottom; **fond de teint** foundation (cream); *voir aussi* **fonds**

**fondamental, e, -aux** [fɔ̃damɑ̃tal, o] *adj* fundamental

**fondant, e** [fɔ̃dɑ̃, ɑ̃t] *adj* (*neige*) melting; (*poire*) that melts in the mouth

**fondation** [fɔ̃dasjɔ̃] *nf* founding; (*établissement*) foundation; **fondations** *nfpl* (*d'une maison*) foundations

**fondé, e** [fɔ̃de] *adj* (*accusation etc*) well-founded; **être ~ à** to have grounds for *ou* good reason to

**fondement** [fɔ̃dmɑ̃] *nm*: **sans ~** (*rumeur etc*) groundless, unfounded

**fonder** [fɔ̃de] *vt* to found; (*fig*) to base; **se fonder sur** (*suj: personne*) to base o.s. on

**fonderie** [fɔ̃dRi] *nf* smelting works *sg*

**fondre** [fɔ̃dR] *vt* (*aussi:* **faire ~**) to melt; (*dans l'eau*) to dissolve; (*fig: mélanger*) to merge, blend ▷ *vi* (*à la chaleur*) to melt; (*dans l'eau*) to dissolve; (*fig*) to melt away; (*se précipiter*): **~ sur** to swoop down on; **~ en larmes** to burst into tears

**fonds** [fɔ̃] *nm* (*Comm*): **~ (de commerce)** business ▷ *nmpl* (*argent*) funds

**fondu, e** [fɔ̃dy] *adj* (*beurre, neige*) melted; (*métal*) molten; **fondue** *nf* (*Culin*) fondue

**font** [fɔ̃] *vb voir* **faire**

**fontaine** [fɔ̃tɛn] *nf* fountain; (*source*) spring

**fonte** [fɔ̃t] *nf* melting; (*métal*) cast iron; **la ~ des neiges** the (spring) thaw

**foot** [fut] (*fam*) *nm* football

**football** [futbol] *nm* football, soccer; **footballeur** *nm* footballer

**footing** [futiŋ] *nm* jogging; **faire du ~** to go jogging

**forain, e** [fɔRɛ̃, ɛn] *adj* fairground *cpd* ▷ *nm* (*marchand*) stallholder; (*acteur*) fairground entertainer

**forçat** [fɔRsa] *nm* convict

**force** [fɔRs] *nf* strength; (*Physique, Mécanique*) force; **forces** *nfpl* (*physiques*) strength *sg*; (*Mil*) forces; **à ~ d'insister** by dint of insisting; as he (*ou* I etc) kept on insisting; **de ~** forcibly, by force; **dans la ~ de l'âge** in the prime of life; **les forces de l'ordre** the police *no pl*

**forcé, e** [fɔRse] *adj* forced; **c'est ~** (*fam*) it's inevitable; **forcément** *adv* inevitably; **pas forcément** not necessarily

**forcer** [fɔʀse] vt to force; (voix) to strain
▷ vi (Sport) to overtax o.s.; **~ la dose**
(fam) to overdo it; **se ~ (à faire)** to force
o.s. (to do)

**forestier, -ère** [fɔʀɛstje, jɛʀ] adj
forest cpd

**forêt** [fɔʀɛ] nf forest

**forfait** [fɔʀfɛ] nm (Comm) all-in deal
ou price; **déclarer ~** to withdraw;
**forfaitaire** adj inclusive

**forge** [fɔʀʒ] nf forge, smithy; **forgeron**
nm (black)smith

**formaliser** [fɔʀmalize]: **se formaliser**
vi: **se ~ (de)** to take offence (at)

**formalité** [fɔʀmalite] nf formality;
**simple ~** mere formality

**format** [fɔʀma] nm size; **formater** vt
(disque) to format

**formation** [fɔʀmasjɔ̃] nf
(développement) forming; (apprentissage)
training; **formation permanente** ou
**continue** continuing education

**forme** [fɔʀm] nf (gén) form; (d'un objet)
shape, form; **formes** nfpl (bonnes
manières) proprieties; (d'une femme)
figure sg; **en ~ de poire** pear-shaped,
in the shape of a pear; **être en ~** (Sport
etc) to be on form; **en bonne et due ~**
in due form

**formel, le** [fɔʀmɛl] adj (catégorique)
definite, positive; **formellement** adv
(absolument) positively; **formellement
interdit** strictly forbidden

**former** [fɔʀme] vt to form; (éduquer) to
train; **se former** vi to form

**formidable** [fɔʀmidabl] adj
tremendous

**formulaire** [fɔʀmylɛʀ] nm form

**formule** [fɔʀmyl] nf (gén) formula;
(expression) phrase; **formule de
politesse** polite phrase; (en fin de lettre)
letter ending

**fort, e** [fɔʀ, fɔʀt] adj strong; (intensité,
rendement) high, great; (corpulent)
stout; (doué) good, able ▷ adv (serrer,
frapper) hard; (parler) loud(ly); (beaucoup)
greatly, very much; (très) very ▷ nm
(édifice) fort; (point fort) strong point,

forte; **forte tête** rebel; **forteresse** nf
stronghold

**fortifiant** [fɔʀtifjɑ̃] nm tonic

**fortune** [fɔʀtyn] nf fortune; **faire ~** to
make one's fortune; **de ~** makeshift;
**fortuné, e** adj wealthy

**forum** [fɔʀɔm] nm forum; **~ de discussion**
(Internet) message board

**fosse** [fos] nf (grand trou) pit; (tombe)
grave

**fossé** [fose] nm ditch; (fig) gulf, gap

**fossette** [fosɛt] nf dimple

**fossile** [fosil] nm fossil

**fou (fol), folle** [fu, fɔl] adj mad;
(déréglé etc) wild, erratic; (fam: extrême,
très grand) terrific, tremendous ▷ nm/f
madman(-woman) ▷ nm (du roi) jester;
**être fou de** to be mad ou crazy about;
**avoir le fou rire** to have the giggles

**foudre** [fudʀ] nf: **la ~** lightning

**foudroyant, e** [fudʀwajɑ̃, ɑ̃t]
adj (progrès) lightning cpd; (succès)
stunning; (maladie, poison) violent

**fouet** [fwɛ] nm whip; (Culin) whisk; **de
plein ~** (se heurter) head on; **fouetter** vt
to whip; (crème) to whisk

**fougère** [fuʒɛʀ] nf fern

**fougue** [fug] nf ardour, spirit;
**fougueux, -euse** adj fiery

**fouille** [fuj] nf search; **fouilles** nfpl
(archéologiques) excavations; **fouiller**
vt to search; (creuser) to dig ▷ vi to
rummage; **fouillis** nm jumble, muddle

**foulard** [fulaʀ] nm scarf

**foule** [ful] nf crowd; **la ~** crowds pl; **une
~ de** masses of

**foulée** [fule] nf stride

**fouler** [fule] vt to press; (sol) to tread
upon; **se ~ la cheville** to sprain one's
ankle; **ne pas se ~** not to overexert
o.s.; **il ne se foule pas** he doesn't put
himself out; **foulure** nf sprain

**four** [fuʀ] nm oven; (de potier) kiln;
(Théâtre: échec) flop

**fourche** [fuʀʃ] nf pitchfork

**fourchette** [fuʀʃɛt] nf fork; (Statistique)
bracket, margin

**fourgon** [fuʀgɔ̃] nm van; (Rail)

wag(g)on; **fourgonnette** nf (small) van

**fourmi** [furmi] nf ant; **avoir des ~s dans les jambes/mains** to have pins and needles in one's legs/hands; **fourmilière** nf ant-hill; **fourmiller** vi to swarm

**fourneau, x** [furno] nm stove

**fourni, e** [furni] adj (barbe, cheveux) thick; (magasin): **bien ~ (en)** well stocked with

**fournir** [furnir] vt to supply; (preuve, exemple) to provide, supply; (effort) to put in; **~ qch à qn** to supply sth to sb, supply ou provide sb with sth; **fournisseur, -euse** nm/f supplier; **fournisseur d'accès à Internet** (Internet) service provider, ISP; **fourniture** nf supply(ing); **fournitures scolaires** school stationery

**fourrage** [furaʒ] nm fodder

**fourré, e** [fure] adj (bonbon etc) filled; (manteau etc) fur-lined ▷ nm thicket

**fourrer** [fure] (fam) vt to stick, shove; **se fourrer dans/sous** to get into/under

**fourrière** [furjɛr] nf pound

**fourrure** [furyr] nf fur; (sur l'animal) coat

**foutre** [futr] (fam!) vt = **ficher**; **foutu, e** (fam!) adj = **fichu, e**

**foyer** [fwaje] nm (maison) home; (famille) family; (de cheminée) hearth; (de jeunes etc) (social) club; (résidence) hostel; (salon) foyer; **lunettes à double ~** bi-focals

**fracassant, e** [frakasɑ̃, ɑ̃t] adj (succès) thundering

**fraction** [fraksjɔ̃] nf fraction

**fracture** [fraktyr] nf fracture; **fracture du crâne** fractured skull; **fracturer** vt (coffre, serrure) to break open; (os, membre) to fracture; **se fracturer le crâne** to fracture one's skull

**fragile** [fraʒil] adj fragile, delicate; (fig) frail; **fragilité** nf fragility

**fragment** [fragmɑ̃] nm (d'un objet)

fragment, piece

**fraîche** [frɛʃ] adj voir **frais**; **fraîcheur** nf coolness; (d'un aliment) freshness; **fraîchir** vi to get cooler; (vent) to freshen

**frais, fraîche** [frɛ, frɛʃ] adj fresh; (froid) cool ▷ adv (récemment) newly, fresh(ly) ▷ nm: **mettre au ~** to put in a cool place ▷ nmpl (gén) expenses; (Comm) costs; **il fait ~** it's cool; **servir ~** serve chilled; **prendre le ~** to take a breath of cool air; **faire des ~** to go to a lot of expense; **frais de scolarité** school fees (BRIT), tuition (US); **frais généraux** overheads

**fraise** [frɛz] nf strawberry; **fraise des bois** wild strawberry

**framboise** [frɑ̃bwaz] nf raspberry

**franc, franche** [frɑ̃, frɑ̃ʃ] adj (personne) frank, straightforward; (visage) open; (net: refus) clear; (: coupure) clean; (intensif) downright ▷ nm franc

**français, e** [frɑ̃sɛ, ɛz] adj French ▷ nm/f: **F~, e** Frenchman(-woman) ▷ nm (Ling) French

**France** [frɑ̃s] nf: **la ~** France; **~ 2, ~ 3** public-sector television channels

● **FRANCE TÉLÉVISION**
●
● **France 2** and **France 3** are public-
● sector television channels. France
● 2 is a national general interest and
● entertainment channel; France
● 3 provides regional news and
● information as well as programmes
● for the national network.

**franche** [frɑ̃ʃ] adj voir **franc**; **franchement** adv frankly; (nettement) definitely; (tout à fait: mauvais etc) downright

**franchir** [frɑ̃ʃir] vt (obstacle) to clear, get over; (seuil, ligne, rivière) to cross; (distance) to cover

**franchise** [frɑ̃ʃiz] nf frankness; (douanière) exemption; (Assurances) excess

**franc-maçon** [fʀɑ̃masɔ̃] nm
freemason

**franco** [fʀɑ̃ko] adv (Comm): **~ (de port)**
postage paid

**francophone** [fʀɑ̃kɔfɔn] adj French-speaking

**franc-parler** [fʀɑ̃paʀle] nm inv
outspokenness; **avoir son ~** to speak
one's mind

**frange** [fʀɑ̃ʒ] nf fringe

**frangipane** [fʀɑ̃ʒipan] nf almond
paste

**frappant, e** [fʀapɑ̃, ɑ̃t] adj striking

**frappé, e** [fʀape] adj iced

**frapper** [fʀape] vt to hit, strike;
(étonner) to strike; **~ dans ses mains** to
clap one's hands; **frappé de stupeur**
dumbfounded

**fraternel, le** [fʀatɛʀnɛl] adj brotherly,
fraternal; **fraternité** nf brotherhood

**fraude** [fʀod] nf fraud; (Scol) cheating;
**passer qch en ~** to smuggle sth in (ou
out); **fraude fiscale** tax evasion

**frayeur** [fʀɛjœʀ] nf fright

**fredonner** [fʀədɔne] vt to hum

**freezer** [fʀizœʀ] nm freezing
compartment

**frein** [fʀɛ̃] nm brake; **mettre un ~
à** (fig) to curb, check; **frein à main**
handbrake; **freiner** vi to brake ▷ vt
(progrès etc) to check

**frêle** [fʀɛl] adj frail, fragile

**frelon** [fʀəlɔ̃] nm hornet

**frémir** [fʀemiʀ] vi (de peur, d'horreur) to
shudder; (de colère) to shake; (feuillage)
to quiver

**frêne** [fʀɛn] nm ash

**fréquemment** [fʀekamɑ̃] adv
frequently

**fréquent, e** [fʀekɑ̃, ɑ̃t] adj frequent

**fréquentation** [fʀekɑ̃tasjɔ̃] nf
frequenting; **fréquentations** nfpl
(relations) company sg; **avoir de
mauvaises ~s** to be in with the wrong
crowd, keep bad company

**fréquenté, e** [fʀekɑ̃te] adj: **très ~**
(very) busy; **mal ~** patronized by
disreputable elements

**fréquenter** [fʀekɑ̃te] vt (lieu)
to frequent; (personne) to see; **se
fréquenter** to see each other

**frère** [fʀɛʀ] nm brother

**fresque** [fʀɛsk] nf (Art) fresco

**fret** [fʀɛ(t)] nm freight

**friand, e** [fʀijɑ̃, fʀijɑ̃d] adj: **~ de** very
fond of ▷ nm: **~ au fromage** cheese puff

**friandise** [fʀijɑ̃diz] nf sweet

**fric** [fʀik] (fam) nm cash, bread

**friche** [fʀiʃ]: **en ~** adj, adv (lying) fallow

**friction** [fʀiksjɔ̃] nf (massage) rub, rub-
down; (Tech, fig) friction

**frigidaire®** [fʀiʒidɛʀ] nm refrigerator

**frigo** [fʀigo] (fam) nm fridge

**frigorifique** [fʀigɔʀifik] adj
refrigerating

**frileux, -euse** [fʀilø, øz] adj sensitive
to (the) cold

**frimer** [fʀime] (fam) vi to show off

**fringale** [fʀɛ̃gal] (fam) nf: **avoir la ~** to
be ravenous

**fringues** [fʀɛ̃g] (fam) nfpl clothes

**fripé, e** [fʀipe] adj crumpled

**frire** [fʀiʀ] vt, vi: **faire ~** to fry

**frisé, e** [fʀize] adj (cheveux) curly;
(personne) curly-haired

**frisson** [fʀisɔ̃] nm (de froid) shiver; (de
peur) shudder; **frissonner** vi (de fièvre,
froid) to shiver; (d'horreur) to shudder

**frit, e** [fʀi, fʀit] pp de **frire**; **frite** nf:
**(pommes) frites** chips (BRIT), French
fries; **friteuse** nf chip pan; **friteuse
électrique** deep fat fryer; **friture** nf
(huile) (deep) fat; (plat): **friture (de
poissons)** fried fish

**froid, e** [fʀwa, fʀwad] adj, nm cold; **il
fait ~** it's cold; **avoir/prendre ~** to be/
catch cold; **être en ~ avec** to be on bad
terms with; **froidement** adv (accueillir)
coldly; (décider) coolly

**froisser** [fʀwase] vt to crumple (up),
crease; (fig) to hurt, offend; **se froisser**
vi to crumple, crease; (personne) to
take offence; **se ~ un muscle** to strain
a muscle

**frôler** [fʀole] vt to brush against; (suj:
projectile) to skim past; (fig) to come

very close to

**fromage** [fʀɔmaʒ] *nm* cheese;
**fromage blanc** soft white cheese

**froment** [fʀɔmã] *nm* wheat

**froncer** [fʀɔ̃se] *vt* to gather; **~ les
sourcils** to frown

**front** [fʀɔ̃] *nm* forehead, brow; *(Mil)*
front; **de ~** *(se heurter)* head-on;
*(rouler)* together *(i.e. 2 or 3 abreast)*;
*(simultanément)* at once; **faire ~ à** to
face up to

**frontalier, -ère** [fʀɔ̃talje, jɛʀ] *adj*
border *cpd*, frontier *cpd*; **(travailleurs)
~s** people who commute across the border

**frontière** [fʀɔ̃tjɛʀ] *nf* frontier, border

**frotter** [fʀɔte] *vi* to rub, scrape ▷ *vt* to
rub; *(pommes de terre, plancher)* to scrub;
**~ une allumette** to strike a match

**fruit** [fʀɥi] *nm* fruit *gen no pl*; **fruits
de mer** seafood(s); **fruits secs** dried
fruit *sg*; **fruité, e** *adj* fruity; **fruitier,
-ère** *adj*: **arbre fruitier** fruit tree

**frustrer** [fʀystʀe] *vt* to frustrate

**fuel(-oil)** [fjul(ɔjl)] *nm* fuel oil;
*(domestique)* heating oil

**fugace** [fygas] *adj* fleeting

**fugitif, -ive** [fyʒitif, iv] *adj* *(fugace)*
fleeting ▷ *nm/f* fugitive

**fugue** [fyg] *nf*: **faire une ~** to run away,
abscond

**fuir** [fɥiʀ] *vt* to flee from; *(éviter)* to shun
▷ *vi* to run away; *(gaz, robinet)* to leak

**fuite** [fɥit] *nf* flight; *(écoulement,
divulgation)* leak; **être en ~** to be on the
run; **mettre en ~** to put to flight

**fulgurant, e** [fylgyʀã, ãt] *adj*
lightning *cpd*, dazzling

**fumé, e** [fyme] *adj* *(Culin)* smoked;
*(verre)* tinted; **fumée** *nf* smoke

**fumer** [fyme] *vi* to smoke; *(soupe)* to
steam ▷ *vt* to smoke

**fûmes** [fym] *vb voir* **être**

**fumeur, -euse** [fymœʀ, øz] *nm/f*
smoker

**fumier** [fymje] *nm* manure

**funérailles** [fyneʀɑj] *nfpl* funeral *sg*

**fur** [fyʀ]: **au ~ et à mesure** *adv* as one
goes along; **au ~ et à mesure que** as

**furet** [fyʀɛ] *nm* ferret

**fureter** [fyʀ(ə)te] *(péj)* *vi* to nose about

**fureur** [fyʀœʀ] *nf* fury; **être en ~** to be
infuriated; **faire ~** to be all the rage

**furie** [fyʀi] *nf* fury; *(femme)* shrew,
vixen; **en ~** *(mer)* raging; **furieux, -euse**
*adj* furious

**furoncle** [fyʀɔ̃kl] *nm* boil

**furtif, -ive** [fyʀtif, iv] *adj* furtive

**fus** [fy] *vb voir* **être**

**fusain** [fyzɛ̃] *nm* *(Art)* charcoal

**fuseau, x** [fyzo] *nm* *(pour filer)* spindle;
*(pantalon)* (ski) pants; **fuseau horaire**
time zone

**fusée** [fyze] *nf* rocket

**fusible** [fyzibl] *nm* *(Élec: fil)* fuse wire;
*(: fiche)* fuse

**fusil** [fyzi] *nm* *(de guerre, à canon rayé)*
rifle, gun; *(de chasse, à canon lisse)*
shotgun, gun; **fusillade** *nf* gunfire
*no pl*, shooting *no pl*; **fusiller** *vt* to
shoot; **fusiller qn du regard** to look
daggers at sb

**fusionner** [fyzjɔne] *vi* to merge

**fût** [fy] *vb voir* **être** ▷ *nm* *(tonneau)*
barrel, cask

**futé, e** [fyte] *adj* crafty; **Bison ~®** *TV
and radio traffic monitoring service*

**futile** [fytil] *adj* futile; frivolous

**futur, e** [fytyʀ] *adj, nm* future

**fuyard, e** [fɥijaʀ, aʀd] *nm/f* runaway

# g

**Gabon** [gabɔ̃] *nm*: **le ~** Gabon
**gâcher** [gɑʃe] *vt* (*gâter*) to spoil;
(*gaspiller*) to waste; **gâchis** *nm*
waste *no pl*
**gaffe** [gaf] *nf* blunder; **faire ~** (*fam*) to
be careful
**gage** [gaʒ] *nm* (*dans un jeu*) forfeit; (*fig:
de fidélité, d'amour*) token; **gages** *nmpl*
(*salaire*) wages; **mettre en ~** to pawn
**gagnant, e** [gaɲɑ̃, ɑ̃t] *adj*: **billet/
numéro ~** winning ticket/number
▷ *nm/f* winner
**gagne-pain** [gaɲpɛ̃] *nm inv* job
**gagner** [gaɲe] *vt* to win; (*somme
d'argent, revenu*) to earn; (*aller vers,
atteindre*) to reach; (*envahir: sommeil,
peur*) to overcome; (: *mal*) to spread to
▷ *vi* to win; (*fig*) to gain; **~ du temps/de
la place** to gain time/save space; **~ sa
vie** to earn one's living
**gai, e** [ge] *adj* cheerful; (*un peu ivre*)
merry; **gaiement** *adv* cheerfully;
**gaieté** *nf* cheerfulness; **de gaieté de
cœur** with a light heart

**gain** [gɛ̃] *nm* (*revenu*) earnings *pl*;
(*bénéfice: gén pl*) profits *pl*
**gala** [gala] *nm* official reception; **de ~**
(*soirée etc*) gala
**galant, e** [galɑ̃, ɑ̃t] *adj* (*courtois*)
courteous, gentlemanly; (*entreprenant*)
flirtatious, gallant; (*scène, rendez-vous*)
romantic
**galerie** [galʀi] *nf* gallery; (*Théâtre*)
circle; (*de voiture*) roof rack; (*fig:
spectateurs*) audience; **galerie de
peinture** (private) art gallery; **galerie
marchande** shopping arcade
**galet** [galɛ] *nm* pebble
**galette** [galɛt] *nf* flat cake; **galette des
Rois** *cake eaten on Twelfth Night*

- **GALETTE DES ROIS**
-
- A **galette des Rois** is a cake eaten on
- Twelfth Night containing a figurine.
- The person who finds it is the king
- (or queen) and gets a paper crown.
- They then choose someone else to be
- their queen (or king).

**galipette** [galipɛt] *nf* somersault
**Galles** [gal] *nfpl*: **le pays de ~** Wales;
**gallois, e** *adj* Welsh ▷ *nm/f*: **Gallois, e**
Welshman(-woman) ▷ *nm* (*Ling*) Welsh
**galon** [galɔ̃] *nm* (*Mil*) stripe; (*décoratif*)
piece of braid
**galop** [galo] *nm* gallop; **galoper** *vi*
to gallop
**gambader** [gɑ̃bade] *vi* (*animal, enfant*)
to leap about
**gamin, e** [gamɛ̃, in] *nm/f* kid ▷ *adj*
childish
**gamme** [gam] *nf* (*Mus*) scale; (*fig*) range
**gang** [gɑ̃g] *nm* (*de criminels*) gang
**gant** [gɑ̃] *nm* glove; **gant de toilette**
face flannel (BRIT), face cloth
**garage** [gaʀaʒ] *nm* garage; **garagiste**
*nm/f* garage owner; (*employé*) garage
mechanic
**garantie** [gaʀɑ̃ti] *nf* guarantee; **(bon
de) ~** guarantee *ou* warranty slip
**garantir** [gaʀɑ̃tiʀ] *vt* to guarantee; **~ à**

**qn que** to assure sb that
**garçon** [gaʀsɔ̃] nm boy; (*célibataire*):
**vieux ~** bachelor; **garçon (de café)**
(*serveur*) waiter; **garçon de courses**
messenger
**garde** [gaʀd(ə)] nm (*de prisonnier*)
guard; (*de domaine etc*) warden; (*soldat,
sentinelle*) guardsman ▷ nf (*soldats*)
guard; **de ~** on duty; **monter la ~** to
stand guard; **mettre en ~** to warn;
**prendre ~ (à)** to be careful (of); **garde
champêtre** nm rural policeman; **garde
du corps** nm bodyguard; **garde à vue**
nf (*Jur*) ≈ police custody; **garde-boue**
nm inv mudguard; **garde-chasse** nm
gamekeeper
**garder** [gaʀde] vt (*conserver*) to keep;
(*surveiller: enfants*) to look after;
(: *immeuble, lieu, prisonnier*) to guard;
**se garder** vi (*aliment: se conserver*) to
keep; **se ~ de faire** to be careful not
to do; **~ le lit/la chambre** to stay in
bed/indoors; **pêche/chasse gardée**
private fishing/hunting (ground)
**garderie** [gaʀdəʀi] nf day nursery,
crèche
**garde-robe** [gaʀdəʀɔb] nf wardrobe
**gardien, ne** [gaʀdjɛ̃, jɛn] nm/f
(*garde*) guard; (*de prison*) warder; (*de
domaine, réserve*) warden; (*de musée etc*)
attendant; (*de phare, cimetière*) keeper;
(*d'immeuble*) caretaker; (*fig*) guardian;
**gardien de but** goalkeeper; **gardien
de la paix** policeman; **gardien de nuit**
night watchman
**gare¹** [gaʀ] nf station; **gare routière**
bus station
**gare²** [gaʀ] excl: **~ à …!** mind …!; **~ à toi!**
watch out!
**garer** [gaʀe] vt to park; **se garer** vi
to park
**garni, e** [gaʀni] adj (*plat*) served with
vegetables (*and chips or rice etc*)
**garniture** [gaʀnityʀ] nf (*Culin*)
vegetables pl; **garniture de frein**
brake lining
**gars** [gɑ] (*fam*) nm guy
**Gascogne** [gaskɔɲ] nf Gascony; **le**

**golfe de ~** the Bay of Biscay
**gas-oil** [gazɔjl] nm diesel (oil)
**gaspiller** [gaspije] vt to waste
**gastronome** [gastʀɔnɔm]
nm/f gourmet; **gastronomique** adj
gastronomic
**gâteau, x** [gɑto] nm cake; **gâteau
sec** biscuit
**gâter** [gɑte] vt to spoil; **se gâter** vi
(*dent, fruit*) to go bad; (*temps, situation*)
to change for the worse
**gâteux, -euse** [gɑtø, øz] adj senile
**gauche** [goʃ] adj left, left-hand;
(*maladroit*) awkward, clumsy ▷ nf (*Pol*)
left (wing); **le bras ~** the left arm; **le
côté ~** the left-hand side; **à ~** on the
left; (*direction*) (to the) left; **gaucher,
-ère** adj left-handed; **gauchiste** nm/f
leftist
**gaufre** [gofʀ] nf waffle
**gaufrette** [gofʀɛt] nf wafer
**gaulois, e** [golwa, waz] adj Gallic
▷ nm/f: **G~, e** Gaul
**gaz** [gaz] nm inv gas; **ça sent le ~** I can
smell gas, there's a smell of gas
**gaze** [gaz] nf gauze
**gazette** [gazɛt] nf news sheet
**gazeux, -euse** [gazø, øz] adj (*boisson*)
fizzy; (*eau*) sparkling
**gazoduc** [gazodyk] nm gas pipeline
**gazon** [gazɔ̃] nm (*herbe*) grass; (*pelouse*)
lawn
**geai** [ʒɛ] nm jay
**géant, e** [ʒeɑ̃, ɑ̃t] adj gigantic; (*Comm*)
giant-size ▷ nm/f giant
**geindre** [ʒɛ̃dʀ] vi to groan, moan
**gel** [ʒɛl] nm frost
**gélatine** [ʒelatin] nf gelatine
**gelée** [ʒ(ə)le] nf jelly; (*gel*) frost
**geler** [ʒ(ə)le] vt, vi to freeze; **il gèle** it's
freezing
**gélule** [ʒelyl] nf (*Méd*) capsule
**Gémeaux** [ʒemo] nmpl: **les ~** Gemini
**gémir** [ʒemiʀ] vi to groan, moan
**gênant, e** [ʒɛnɑ̃, ɑ̃t] adj (*irritant*)
annoying; (*embarrassant*) embarrassing
**gencive** [ʒɑ̃siv] nf gum
**gendarme** [ʒɑ̃daʀm] nm gendarme;

**gendarmerie** nf military police force in countryside and small towns; their police station or barracks

**gendre** [ʒɑ̃dʀ] nm son-in-law

**gêné, e** [ʒene] adj embarrassed

**gêner** [ʒene] vt (incommoder) to bother; (encombrer) to be in the way; (embarrasser): **~ qn** to make sb feel ill-at-ease; **se gêner** to put o.s. out; **ne vous gênez pas!** don't mind me!

**général, e, -aux** [ʒeneʀal, o] adj, nm general; **en ~** usually, in general; **généralement** adv generally; **généraliser** vt, vi to generalize; **se généraliser** vi to become widespread; **généraliste** nm/f general practitioner, G.P.

**génération** [ʒeneʀasjɔ̃] nf generation

**généreux, -euse** [ʒeneʀø, øz] adj generous

**générique** [ʒeneʀik] nm (Cinéma) credits pl

**générosité** [ʒeneʀozite] nf generosity

**genêt** [ʒ(ə)nɛ] nm broom no pl (shrub)

**génétique** [ʒenetik] adj genetic

**Genève** [ʒ(ə)nɛv] n Geneva

**génial, e, -aux** [ʒenjal, jo] adj of genius; (fam: formidable) fantastic, brilliant

**génie** [ʒeni] nm genius; (Mil): **le ~** the Engineers pl; **génie civil** civil engineering

**genièvre** [ʒənjɛvʀ] nm juniper

**génisse** [ʒenis] nf heifer

**génital, e, -aux** [ʒenital, o] adj genital; **les parties ~es** the genitals

**génoise** [ʒenwaz] nf sponge cake

**genou, x** [ʒ(ə)nu] nm knee; **à ~x** on one's knees; **se mettre à ~x** to kneel down

**genre** [ʒɑ̃ʀ] nm kind, type, sort; (Ling) gender; **avoir bon ~** to look a nice sort; **avoir mauvais ~** to be coarse-looking; **ce n'est pas son ~** it's not like him

**gens** [ʒɑ̃] nmpl (f in some phrases) people pl

**gentil, le** [ʒɑ̃ti, ij] adj kind; (enfant: sage) good; (endroit etc) nice;

**gentillesse** nf kindness; **gentiment** adv kindly

**géographie** [ʒeɔgʀafi] nf geography

**géologie** [ʒeɔlɔʒi] nf geology

**géomètre** [ʒeɔmɛtʀ] nm/f (arpenteur) (land) surveyor

**géométrie** [ʒeɔmetʀi] nf geometry; **géométrique** adj geometric

**géranium** [ʒeʀanjɔm] nm geranium

**gérant, e** [ʒeʀɑ̃, ɑ̃t] nm/f manager(-eress); **gérant d'immeuble** (managing) agent

**gerbe** [ʒɛʀb] nf (de fleurs) spray; (de blé) sheaf

**gercé, e** [ʒɛʀse] adj chapped

**gerçure** [ʒɛʀsyʀ] nf crack

**gérer** [ʒeʀe] vt to manage

**germain, e** [ʒɛʀmɛ̃, ɛn] adj: **cousin ~** first cousin

**germe** [ʒɛʀm] nm germ; **germer** vi to sprout; (semence) to germinate

**geste** [ʒɛst] nm gesture

**gestion** [ʒɛstjɔ̃] nf management

**Ghana** [gana] nm: **le ~** Ghana

**gibier** [ʒibje] nm (animaux) game

**gicler** [ʒikle] vi to spurt, squirt

**gifle** [ʒifl] nf slap (in the face); **gifler** vt to slap (in the face)

**gigantesque** [ʒigɑ̃tɛsk] adj gigantic

**gigot** [ʒigo] nm leg (of mutton ou lamb)

**gigoter** [ʒigɔte] vi to wriggle (about)

**gilet** [ʒilɛ] nm waistcoat; (pull) cardigan; **gilet de sauvetage** life jacket

**gin** [dʒin] nm gin; **~-tonic** gin and tonic

**gingembre** [ʒɛ̃ʒɑ̃bʀ] nm ginger

**girafe** [ʒiʀaf] nf giraffe

**giratoire** [ʒiʀatwaʀ] adj: **sens ~** roundabout

**girofle** [ʒiʀɔfl] nf: **clou de ~** clove

**girouette** [ʒiʀwɛt] nf weather vane ou cock

**gitan, e** [ʒitɑ̃, an] nm/f gipsy

**gîte** [ʒit] nm (maison) home; (abri) shelter; **gîte (rural)** (country) holiday cottage (BRIT), gîte (self-catering accommodation in the country)

**givre** [ʒivʀ] nm (hoar) frost; **givré, e** adj

covered in frost; (*fam: fou*) nuts; **orange givrée** orange sorbet (*served in peel*)

**glace** [glas] *nf* ice; (*crème glacée*) ice cream; (*miroir*) mirror; (*de voiture*) window

**glacé, e** [glase] *adj* (*mains, vent, pluie*) freezing; (*lac*) frozen; (*boisson*) iced

**glacer** [glase] *vt* to freeze; (*gâteau*) to ice; (*fig*): **~ qn** (*intimider*) to chill sb; (*paralyser*) to make sb's blood run cold

**glacial, e** [glasjal, jo] *adj* icy

**glacier** [glasje] *nm* (*Géo*) glacier; (*marchand*) ice-cream maker

**glacière** [glasjɛʀ] *nf* icebox

**glaçon** [glasɔ̃] *nm* icicle; (*pour boisson*) ice cube

**glaïeul** [glajœl] *nm* gladiolus

**glaise** [glɛz] *nf* clay

**gland** [glɑ̃] *nm* acorn; (*décoration*) tassel

**glande** [glɑ̃d] *nf* gland

**glissade** [glisad] *nf* (*par jeu*) slide; (*chute*) slip; **faire des ~s sur la glace** to slide on the ice

**glissant, e** [glisɑ̃, ɑ̃t] *adj* slippery

**glissement** [glismɑ̃] *nm*: **glissement de terrain** landslide

**glisser** [glise] *vi* (*avancer*) to glide *ou* slide along; (*coulisser, tomber*) to slide; (*déraper*) to slip; (*être glissant*) to be slippery ▷ *vt* to slip; **se glisser dans/ entre** to slip into/between

**global, e, -aux** [glɔbal, o] *adj* overall

**globe** [glɔb] *nm* globe

**globule** [glɔbyl] *nm* (*du sang*): **~ blanc/ rouge** white/red corpuscle

**gloire** [glwaʀ] *nf* glory

**glousser** [gluse] *vi* to cluck; (*rire*) to chuckle

**glouton, ne** [glutɔ̃, ɔn] *adj* gluttonous

**gluant, e** [glyɑ̃, ɑ̃t] *adj* sticky, gummy

**glucose** [glykoz] *nm* glucose

**glycine** [glisin] *nf* wisteria

**GO** *sigle* (= *grandes ondes*) LW

**goal** [gol] *nm* goalkeeper

**gobelet** [gɔblɛ] *nm* (*en étain, verre, argent*) tumbler; (*d'enfant, de pique-nique*) beaker; (*à dés*) cup

**goéland** [gɔelɑ̃] *nm* (sea)gull

**goélette** [gɔelɛt] *nf* schooner

**goinfre** [gwɛ̃fʀ] *nm* glutton

**golf** [gɔlf] *nm* golf; (*terrain*) golf course; **golf miniature** crazy (BRIT) *ou* miniature golf

**golfe** [gɔlf] *nm* gulf; (*petit*) bay

**gomme** [gɔm] *nf* (*à effacer*) rubber (BRIT), eraser; **gommer** *vt* to rub out (BRIT), erase

**gonflé, e** [gɔ̃fle] *adj* swollen; **il est ~** (*fam: courageux*) he's got some nerve; (*impertinent*) he's got a nerve

**gonfler** [gɔ̃fle] *vt* (*pneu, ballon: en soufflant*) to blow up; (: *avec une pompe*) to pump up; (*nombre, importance*) to inflate ▷ *vi* to swell (up); (*Culin: pâte*) to rise

**gonzesse** [gɔ̃zɛs] (*fam*) *nf* chick, bird (BRIT)

**gorge** [gɔʀʒ] *nf* (*Anat*) throat; (*vallée*) gorge; **gorgée** *nf* (*petite*) sip; (*grande*) gulp

**gorille** [gɔʀij] *nm* gorilla; (*fam*) bodyguard

**gosse** [gɔs] (*fam*) *nm/f* kid

**goudron** [gudʀɔ̃] *nm* tar; **goudronner** *vt* to tar(mac) (BRIT), asphalt (US)

**gouffre** [gufʀ] *nm* abyss, gulf

**goulot** [gulo] *nm* neck; **boire au ~** to drink from the bottle

**goulu, e** [guly] *adj* greedy

**gourde** [guʀd] *nf* (*récipient*) flask; (*fam*) (clumsy) clot *ou* oaf ▷ *adj* oafish

**gourdin** [guʀdɛ̃] *nm* club, bludgeon

**gourmand, e** [guʀmɑ̃, ɑ̃d] *adj* greedy; **gourmandise** *nf* greed; (*bonbon*) sweet

**gousse** [gus] *nf*: **gousse d'ail** clove of garlic

**goût** [gu] *nm* taste; **avoir bon ~** to taste good; **de bon ~** tasteful; **de mauvais ~** tasteless; **prendre ~ à** to develop a taste *ou* a liking for

**goûter** [gute] *vt* (*essayer*) to taste; (*apprécier*) to enjoy ▷ *vi* to have (afternoon) tea ▷ *nm* (afternoon) tea; **je peux ~?** can I have a taste?

**goutte** [gut] *nf* drop; (*Méd*) gout; (*alcool*) brandy; **tomber ~ à ~** to drip;

une **~ de whisky** a drop of whisky; **goutte-à-goutte** nm (Méd) drip
**gouttière** [gutjɛʀ] nf gutter
**gouvernail** [guvɛʀnaj] nm rudder; (barre) helm, tiller
**gouvernement** [guvɛʀnəmã] nm government
**gouverner** [guvɛʀne] vt to govern
**grâce** [gʀɑs] nf (charme, Rel) grace; (faveur) favour; (Jur) pardon; **faire ~ à qn de qch** to spare sb sth; **demander ~** to beg for mercy; **~ à** thanks to; **gracieux, -euse** adj graceful
**grade** [gʀad] nm rank; **monter en ~** to be promoted
**gradin** [gʀadɛ̃] nm tier; step; **gradins** nmpl (de stade) terracing sg
**gradué, e** [gʀadɥe] adj: **verre ~** measuring jug
**graduel, le** [gʀadɥɛl] adj gradual
**graduer** [gʀadɥe] vt (effort etc) to increase gradually; (règle, verre) to graduate
**graffiti** [gʀafiti] nmpl graffiti
**grain** [gʀɛ̃] nm (gén) grain; (Navig) squall; **grain de beauté** beauty spot; **grain de café** coffee bean; **grain de poivre** peppercorn
**graine** [gʀɛn] nf seed
**graissage** [gʀɛsaʒ] nm lubrication, greasing
**graisse** [gʀɛs] nf fat; (lubrifiant) grease; **graisser** vt to lubricate, grease; (tacher) to make greasy; **graisseux, -euse** adj greasy
**grammaire** [gʀa(m)mɛʀ] nf grammar
**gramme** [gʀam] nm gramme
**grand, e** [gʀɑ̃, gʀɑ̃d] adj (haut) tall; (gros, vaste, large) big, large; (long) long; (plus âgé) big; (adulte) grown-up; (important, brillant) great ▷ adv: **~ ouvert** wide open; **au ~ air** in the open (air); **les grands blessés** the severely injured; **grand ensemble** housing scheme; **grand magasin** department store; **grande personne** grown-up; **grande surface** hypermarket; **grandes écoles** prestigious schools at university

level; **grandes lignes** (Rail) main lines; **grandes vacances** summer holidays (BRIT) ou vacation (US); **grand-chose** nm/f inv: **pas grand-chose** not much; **Grande-Bretagne** nf (Great) Britain; **grandeur** nf (dimension) size; **grandeur nature** life-size; **grandiose** adj imposing; **grandir** vi to grow ▷ vt: **grandir qn** (suj: vêtement, chaussure) to make sb look taller; **grand-mère** nf grandmother; **grand-peine: à grand-peine** adv with difficulty; **grand-père** nm grandfather; **grands-parents** nmpl grandparents
**grange** [gʀɑ̃ʒ] nf barn
**granit** [gʀanit] nm granite
**graphique** [gʀafik] adj graphic ▷ nm graph
**grappe** [gʀap] nf cluster; **grappe de raisin** bunch of grapes
**gras, se** [gʀɑ, gʀɑs] adj (viande, soupe) fatty; (personne) fat; (surface, main) greasy; (plaisanterie) coarse; (Typo) bold ▷ nm (Culin) fat; **faire la ~se matinée** to have a lie-in (BRIT), sleep late (US); **grassement** adv: **grassement payé** handsomely paid
**gratifiant, e** [gʀatifjã, jãt] adj gratifying, rewarding
**gratin** [gʀatɛ̃] nm (plat) cheese-topped dish; (croûte) cheese topping; (fam: élite) upper crust; **gratiné, e** adj (Culin) au gratin
**gratis** [gʀatis] adv free
**gratitude** [gʀatityd] nf gratitude
**gratte-ciel** [gʀatsjɛl] nm inv skyscraper
**gratter** [gʀate] vt (avec un outil) to scrape; (enlever: avec un outil) to scrape off; (: avec un ongle) to scratch; (enlever avec un ongle) to scratch off ▷ vi (irriter) to be scratchy; (démanger) to itch; **se gratter** to scratch (o.s.)
**gratuit, e** [gʀatɥi, ɥit] adj (entrée, billet) free; (fig) gratuitous
**grave** [gʀav] adj (maladie, accident) serious, bad; (sujet, problème) serious, grave; (air) grave, solemn; (voix, son)

deep, low-pitched; **gravement** *adv* seriously; (*parler, regarder*) gravely

**graver** [gʀave] *vt* (*plaque, nom*) to engrave; (*CD, DVD*) to burn

**graveur** [gʀavœʀ] *nm* engraver; **graveur de CD/DVD** CD/DVD writer

**gravier** [gʀavje] *nm* gravel *no pl*; **gravillons** *nmpl* loose chippings *ou* gravel *sg*

**gravir** [gʀaviʀ] *vt* to climb (up)

**gravité** [gʀavite] *nf* (*de maladie, d'accident*) seriousness; (*de sujet, problème*) gravity

**graviter** [gʀavite] *vi* to revolve

**gravure** [gʀavyʀ] *nf* engraving; (*reproduction*) print

**gré** [gʀe] *nm*: **à son ~** to one's liking; **de bon ~** willingly; **contre le ~ de qn** against sb's will; **de son (plein) ~** of one's own free will; **bon ~ mal ~** like it or not; **de ~ ou de force** whether one likes it or not; **savoir ~ à qn de qch** to be grateful to sb for sth

**grec, grecque** [gʀɛk] *adj* Greek; (*classique: vase etc*) Grecian ▷ *nm/f*: **G~, Grecque** Greek ▷ *nm* (*Ling*) Greek

**Grèce** [gʀɛs] *nf*: **la ~** Greece

**greffe** [gʀɛf] *nf* (*Bot, Méd: de tissu*) graft; (*Méd: d'organe*) transplant; **greffer** *vt* (*Bot, Méd: tissu*) to graft; (*Méd: organe*) to transplant

**grêle** [gʀɛl] *adj* (very) thin ▷ *nf* hail; **grêler** *vb impers*: **il grêle** it's hailing; **grêlon** *nm* hailstone

**grelot** [gʀəlo] *nm* little bell

**grelotter** [gʀəlɔte] *vi* to shiver

**grenade** [gʀənad] *nf* (*explosive*) grenade; (*Bot*) pomegranate; **grenadine** *nf* grenadine

**grenier** [gʀənje] *nm* attic; (*de ferme*) loft

**grenouille** [gʀənuj] *nf* frog

**grès** [gʀɛ] *nm* sandstone; (*poterie*) stoneware

**grève** [gʀɛv] *nf* (*d'ouvriers*) strike; (*plage*) shore; **se mettre en/faire ~** to go on/ be on strike; **grève de la faim** hunger strike; **grève sauvage** wildcat strike

**gréviste** [gʀevist] *nm/f* striker

**grièvement** [gʀijɛvmɑ̃] *adv* seriously

**griffe** [gʀif] *nf* claw; (*de couturier*) label; **griffer** *vt* to scratch

**grignoter** [gʀiɲɔte] *vt* (*personne*) to nibble at; (*souris*) to gnaw at ▷ *vi* to nibble

**gril** [gʀil] *nm* steak *ou* grill pan; **faire cuire au ~** to grill; **grillade** *nf* (*viande etc*) grill

**grillage** [gʀijaʒ] *nm* (*treillis*) wire netting; (*clôture*) wire fencing

**grille** [gʀij] *nf* (*clôture*) wire fence; (*portail*) (metal) gate; (*d'égout*) (metal) grate; (*fig*) grid

**grille-pain** [gʀijpɛ̃] *nm inv* toaster

**griller** [gʀije] *vt* (*pain*) to toast; (*viande*) to grill; (*fig: ampoule etc*) to blow; **faire ~** to toast; to grill; (*châtaignes*) to roast; **~ un feu rouge** to jump the lights

**grillon** [gʀijɔ̃] *nm* cricket

**grimace** [gʀimas] *nf* grimace; (*pour faire rire*): **faire des ~s** to pull *ou* make faces

**grimper** [gʀɛ̃pe] *vi, vt* to climb

**grincer** [gʀɛ̃se] *vi* (*objet métallique*) to grate; (*plancher, porte*) to creak; **~ des dents** to grind one's teeth

**grincheux, -euse** [gʀɛ̃ʃø, øz] *adj* grumpy

**grippe** [gʀip] *nf* flu, influenza; **grippe aviaire** bird flu; **grippé, e** *adj*: **être grippé** to have flu

**gris, e** [gʀi, gʀiz] *adj* grey; (*ivre*) tipsy

**grisaille** [gʀizaj] *nf* greyness, dullness

**griser** [gʀize] *vt* to intoxicate

**grive** [gʀiv] *nf* thrush

**Groenland** [gʀɔɛnlɑ̃d] *nm* Greenland

**grogner** [gʀɔɲe] *vi* to growl; (*fig*) to grumble; **grognon, ne** *adj* grumpy

**grommeler** [gʀɔm(ə)le] *vi* to mutter to o.s.

**gronder** [gʀɔ̃de] *vi* to rumble; (*fig: révolte*) to be brewing ▷ *vt* to scold; **se faire ~** to get a telling-off

**gros, se** [gʀo, gʀos] *adj* big, large; (*obèse*) fat; (*travaux, dégâts*) extensive; (*épais*) thick; (*rhume, averse*) heavy ▷ *adv*: **risquer/gagner ~** to risk/win a lot ▷ nm/f fat man/woman ▷ nm (Comm): **le ~** the wholesale business; **le ~ de** the bulk of; **prix de gros** wholesale price; **par ~ temps/grosse mer** in rough weather/heavy seas; **en ~** roughly; (Comm) wholesale; **gros lot** jackpot; **gros mot** swearword; **gros plan** (Photo) close-up; **gros sel** cooking salt; **gros titre** headline; **grosse caisse** big drum

**groseille** [ɡʁozɛj] nf: **~ (rouge/ blanche)** red/white currant; **groseille à maquereau** gooseberry

**grosse** [ɡʁos] adj voir **gros**; **grossesse** nf pregnancy; **grosseur** nf size; (tumeur) lump

**grossier, -ière** [ɡʁosje, jɛʁ] adj coarse; (insolent) rude; (dessin) rough; (travail) roughly done; (imitation, instrument) crude; (évident: erreur) gross; **grossièrement** adv (sommairement) roughly; (vulgairement) coarsely; **grossièreté** nf rudeness; (mot): **dire des grossièretés** to use coarse language

**grossir** [ɡʁosiʁ] vi (personne) to put on weight ▷ vt (exagérer) to exaggerate; (au microscope) to magnify; (suj: vêtement): **~ qn** to make sb look fatter

**grossiste** [ɡʁosist] nm/f wholesaler

**grotesque** [ɡʁotɛsk] adj (extravagant) grotesque; (ridicule) ludicrous

**grotte** [ɡʁot] nf cave

**groupe** [ɡʁup] nm group; **groupe de parole** support group; **groupe sanguin** blood group; **groupe scolaire** school complex; **grouper** vt to group; **se grouper** vi to gather

**grue** [ɡʁy] nf crane

**GSM** [ʒeɛsɛm] nm, adj GSM

**guenon** [ɡənɔ̃] nf female monkey

**guépard** [ɡepaʁ] nm cheetah

**guêpe** [ɡɛp] nf wasp

**guère** [ɡɛʁ] adv (avec adjectif, adverbe): **ne ... ~** hardly; (avec verbe: pas beaucoup): **ne ... ~** tournure négative +much; (pas souvent) hardly ever; (pas longtemps) tournure négative +(very) long; **il n'y a**

**~ que/de** there's hardly anybody (ou anything) but/hardly any; **ce n'est ~ difficile** it's hardly difficult; **nous n'avons ~ de temps** we have hardly any time

**guérilla** [ɡeʁija] nf guerrilla warfare

**guérillero** [ɡeʁijeʁo] nm guerrilla

**guérir** [ɡeʁiʁ] vt (personne, maladie) to cure; (membre, plaie) to heal ▷ vi (malade, maladie) to be cured; (blessure) to heal; **guérison** nf (de maladie) curing; (de membre, plaie) healing; (de malade) recovery; **guérisseur, -euse** nm/f healer

**guerre** [ɡɛʁ] nf war; **en ~** at war; **faire la ~ à** to wage war against; **guerre civile/mondiale** civil/world war; **guerrier, -ière** adj warlike ▷ nm/f warrior

**guet** [ɡɛ] nm: **faire le ~** to be on the watch ou look-out; **guet-apens** [ɡetapɑ̃] nm ambush; **guetter** vt (épier) to watch (intently); (attendre) to watch (out) for; (hostilement) to be lying in wait for

**gueule** [ɡœl] nf (d'animal) mouth; (fam: figure) face; (: bouche) mouth; **ta ~!** (fam) shut up!; **avoir la ~ de bois** (fam) to have a hangover, be hung over; **gueuler** (fam) vi to bawl

**gui** [ɡi] nm mistletoe

**guichet** [ɡiʃɛ] nm (de bureau, banque) counter; **les ~s** (à la gare, au théâtre) the ticket office sg

**guide** [ɡid] nm (personne) guide; (livre) guide (book) ▷ nf (éclaireuse) girl guide; **guider** vt to guide

**guidon** [ɡidɔ̃] nm handlebars pl

**guignol** [ɡiɲɔl] nm ≈ Punch and Judy show; (fig) clown

**guillemets** [ɡijmɛ] nmpl: **entre ~** in inverted commas

**guindé, e** [ɡɛ̃de] adj (personne, air) stiff, starchy; (style) stilted

**Guinée** [ɡine] nf Guinea

**guirlande** [ɡiʁlɑ̃d] nf (fleurs) garland; **guirlande de Noël** tinsel garland

**guise** [ɡiz] nf: **à votre ~** as you wish ou

please; **en ~ de** by way of

**guitare** [gitaʀ] *nf* guitar

**Guyane** [gɥijan] *nf*: **la ~ (française)**
French Guiana

**gym** [ʒim] *nf* (*exercices*) gym; **gymnase**
*nm* (nasium); **gymnaste** *nm/f*
gymnast; **gymnastique** *nf* gymnastics
*sg*; (*au réveil etc*) keep-fit exercises *pl*

**gynécologie** [ʒinekɔlɔʒi] *nf*
gynaecology; **gynécologique** *adj*
gynaecological; **gynécologue** *nm/f*
gynaecologist

**habile** [abil] *adj* skilful; (*malin*) clever;
**habileté** [abilte] *nf* skill, skilfulness;
cleverness

**habillé, e** [abije] *adj* dressed; (*chic*)
dressy

**habiller** [abije] *vt* to dress; (*fournir en
vêtements*) to clothe; (*couvrir*) to cover;
**s'habiller** *vi* to dress (o.s.); (*se déguiser,
mettre des vêtements chic*) to dress up

**habit** [abi] *nm* outfit; **habits** *nmpl*
(*vêtements*) clothes; **habit (de soirée)**
evening dress; (*pour homme*) tails *pl*

**habitant, e** [abitɑ̃, ɑ̃t] *nm/f*
inhabitant; (*d'une maison*) occupant;
**loger chez l'~** to stay with the locals

**habitation** [abitasjɔ̃] *nf* house;
**habitations à loyer modéré** (block of)
council flats

**habiter** [abite] *vt* to live in ▷ *vi*: **~
à/dans** to live in; **où habitez-vous?**
where do you live?

**habitude** [abityd] *nf* habit; **avoir l'~ de
qch** to be used to sth; **avoir l'~ de faire**
to be in the habit of doing; (*expérience*)

to be used to doing; **d'~** usually;
**comme d'~** as usual

**habitué, e** [abitye] nm/f (de maison)
regular visitor; (de café) regular
(customer)

**habituel, le** [abituɛl] adj usual

**habituer** [abitue] vt: **~ qn à** to get sb
used to; **s'habituer à** to get used to

**'hache** ['aʃ] nf axe

**'hacher** ['aʃe] vt (viande) to mince;
(persil) to chop; **'hachis** nm mince no pl;
**hachis Parmentier** ≈ shepherd's pie

**'haie** ['ɛ] nf hedge; (Sport) hurdle

**'haillons** ['ɑjɔ̃] nmpl rags

**'haine** ['ɛn] nf hatred

**'haïr** ['aiʀ] vt to detest, hate

**'hâlé, e** ['ɑle] adj (sun)tanned,
sunburnt

**haleine** [alɛn] nf breath; **hors d'~** out
of breath; **tenir en ~** (attention) to hold
spellbound; (incertitude) to keep in
suspense; **de longue ~** long-term

**'haleter** ['alte] vt to pant

**'hall** ['ol] nm hall

**'halle** ['al] nf (covered) market; **halles**
nfpl (d'une grande ville) central food
market sg

**hallucination** [alysinasjɔ̃] nf
hallucination

**'halte** ['alt] nf stop, break; (endroit)
stopping place ▷ excl stop!; **faire halte**
to stop

**haltère** [altɛʀ] nm dumbbell, barbell;
**haltères** nmpl: **(poids et) ~s** (activité)
weightlifting sg; **haltérophilie** nf
weightlifting

**'hamac** ['amak] nm hammock

**'hameau, x** ['amo] nm hamlet

**hameçon** [amsɔ̃] nm (fish) hook

**'hanche** ['ɑ̃ʃ] nf hip

**'handball** ['ɑ̃dbal] nm handball

**'handicapé, e** ['ɑ̃dikape] adj disabled,
handicapped ▷ nm/f handicapped
person; **handicapé mental/physique**
mentally/physically handicapped
person; **'handicapé moteur** person
with a movement disorder

**'hangar** ['ɑ̃gaʀ] nm shed; (Aviat) hangar

**'hanneton** ['antɔ̃] nm cockchafer

**'hanter** ['ɑ̃te] vt to haunt

**'hantise** ['ɑ̃tiz] nf obsessive fear

**'harceler** ['aʀsəle] vt to harass;
**harceler qn de questions** to plague sb
with questions

**'hardi, e** ['aʀdi] adj bold, daring

**'hareng** ['aʀɑ̃] nm herring; **hareng
saur** kipper, smoked herring

**'hargne** ['aʀɲ] nf aggressiveness;
**'hargneux, -euse** adj aggressive

**'haricot** ['aʀiko] nm bean; **'haricot
blanc** haricot bean; **'haricot vert**
green bean; **'haricot rouge** kidney
bean

**harmonica** [aʀmɔnika] nm mouth
organ

**harmonie** [aʀmɔni] nf harmony;
**harmonieux, -euse** adj harmonious;
(couleurs, couple) well-matched

**'harpe** ['aʀp] nf harp

**'hasard** ['azaʀ] nm: **le hasard** chance,
fate; **un hasard** a coincidence; **au
hasard** (aller) aimlessly; (choisir) at
random; **par hasard** by chance; **à tout
hasard** (en cas de besoin) just in case; (en
espérant trouver ce qu'on cherche) on the
off chance (BRIT)

**'hâte** ['ɑt] nf haste; **à la hâte** hurriedly,
hastily; **en hâte** posthaste, with
all possible speed; **avoir hâte de** to
be eager ou anxious to; **'hâter** vt to
hasten; **se hâter** vi to hurry; **'hâtif,
-ive** adj (travail) hurried; (décision,
jugement) hasty

**'hausse** ['os] nf rise, increase; **être en
hausse** to be going up; **'hausser** vt to
raise; **hausser les épaules** to shrug
(one's shoulders)

**'haut, e** ['o, 'ot] adj high; (grand) tall
▷ adv high ▷ nm top (part); **de 3 m
de haut** 3 m high, 3 m in height; **des
hauts et des bas** ups and downs; **en
haut lieu** in high places; **à haute voix,
(tout) haut** aloud, out loud; **du haut
de** from the top of; **de haut en bas**
from top to bottom; **plus haut** higher
up, further up; (dans un texte) above;

(*parler*) louder; **en haut** (*être/aller*) at/to the top; (*dans une maison*) upstairs; **en haut de** at the top of; **'haut débit** broadband

**'hautain, e** ['otɛ̃, ɛn] *adj* haughty

**'hautbois** ['obwa] *nm* oboe

**'hauteur** ['otœʀ] *nf* height; **à la hauteur de** (*accident*) near; (*fig: tâche, situation*) equal to; **à la hauteur** (*fig*) up to it

**'haut-parleur** *nm* (loud)speaker

**Hawaï** [awai] *n*: **les îles ~** Hawaii

**'Haye** ['ɛ] *n*: **la Haye** the Hague

**hebdomadaire** [ɛbdɔmadɛʀ] *adj, nm* weekly

**hébergement** [ebɛʀʒəmã] *nm* accommodation

**héberger** [ebɛʀʒe] *vt* (*touristes*) to accommodate, lodge; (*amis*) to put up; (*réfugiés*) to take in

**hébergeur** [ebɛʀʒœʀ] *nm* (*Internet*) host

**hébreu, x** [ebʀø] *adj m, nm* Hebrew

**Hébrides** [ebʀid] *nf*: **les ~** the Hebrides

**hectare** [ɛktaʀ] *nm* hectare

**'hein** ['ɛ̃] *excl* eh?

**'hélas** ['elas] *excl* alas! ▷ *adv* unfortunately

**'héler** ['ele] *vt* to hail

**hélice** [elis] *nf* propeller

**hélicoptère** [elikɔptɛʀ] *nm* helicopter

**helvétique** [ɛlvetik] *adj* Swiss

**hématome** [ematom] *nm* nasty bruise

**hémisphère** [emisfɛʀ] *nm*: **l'~ nord/sud** the northern/southern hemisphere

**hémorragie** [emɔʀaʒi] *nf* bleeding *no pl*, haemorrhage

**hémorroïdes** [em`id] *nfpl* piles, haemorrhoids

**'hennir** ['eniʀ] *vi* to neigh, whinny

**hépatite** [epatit] *nf* hepatitis

**herbe** [ɛʀb] *nf* grass; (*Culin, Méd*) herb; **~s de Provence** mixed herbs; **en ~** unripe; (*fig*) budding; **herbicide** *nm* weed-killer; **herboriste** *nm/f* herbalist

**héréditaire** [eʀeditɛʀ] *adj* hereditary

**'hérisson** ['eʀisɔ̃] *nm* hedgehog

**héritage** [eʀitaʒ] *nm* inheritance; (*coutumes, système*) heritage, legacy

**hériter** [eʀite] *vi*: **~ de qch (de qn)** to inherit sth (from sb); **héritier, -ière** *nm/f* heir(-ess)

**hermétique** [ɛʀmetik] *adj* airtight; watertight; (*fig: obscur*) abstruse; (*: impénétrable*) impenetrable

**hermine** [ɛʀmin] *nf* ermine

**'hernie** ['ɛʀni] *nf* hernia

**héroïne** [eʀɔin] *nf* heroine; (*drogue*) heroin

**héroïque** [eʀɔik] *adj* heroic

**'héron** ['eʀɔ̃] *nm* heron

**'héros** ['eʀo] *nm* hero

**hésitant, e** [ezitã, ãt] *adj* hesitant

**hésitation** [ezitasjɔ̃] *nf* hesitation

**hésiter** [ezite] *vi*: **~ (à faire)** to hesitate (to do)

**hétérosexuel, le** [eteʀɔsɛkɥɛl] *adj* heterosexual

**'hêtre** ['ɛtʀ] *nm* beech

**heure** [œʀ] *nf* hour; (*Scol*) period; (*moment*) time; **c'est l'~** it's time; **quelle ~ est-il?** what time is it?; **2 ~s (du matin)** 2 o'clock (in the morning); **être à l'~** to be on time; (*montre*) to be right; **mettre à l'~** to set right; **à une ~ avancée (de la nuit)** at a late hour (of the night); **de bonne ~** early; **à toute ~** at any time; **24 ~s sur 24** round the clock, 24 hours a day; **à l'~ qu'il est** at this time (of day); by now; **sur l'~** at once; **à quelle ~ ouvre le musée/magasin?** what time does the museum/shop open?; **heures de bureau** office hours; **heure de pointe** rush hour; (*téléphone*) peak period; **heures supplémentaires** overtime *sg*

**heureusement** [œʀøzmã] *adv* (*par bonheur*) fortunately, luckily

**heureux, -euse** [œʀø, øz] *adj* happy; (*chanceux*) lucky, fortunate

**'heurt** ['œʀ] *nm* (*choc*) collision; (*conflit*) clash

**'heurter** ['œʀte] *vt* (*mur*) to strike, hit; (*personne*) to collide with

**hexagone** [ɛgzagɔn] *nm* hexagon; **l'H~** (*la France*) France (*because of its shape*)

**hiberner** [ibɛʀne] *vi* to hibernate

**'hibou, x** ['ibu] *nm* owl

**'hideux, -euse** ['idø, øz] *adj* hideous

**hier** [jɛʀ] *adv* yesterday; **~ matin/midi** yesterday morning/lunchtime; **~ soir** last night, yesterday evening; **toute la journée d'~** all day yesterday; **toute la matinée d'~** all yesterday morning

**'hiérarchie** ['jeʀaʀʃi] *nf* hierarchy

**hindou, e** [ɛ̃du] *adj* Hindu ▷ *nm/f*: **H~, e** Hindu

**hippique** [ipik] *adj* equestrian, horse *cpd*; **un club ~** a riding centre; **un concours ~** a horse show; **hippisme** *nm* (horse)riding

**hippodrome** [ipɔdʀom] *nm* racecourse

**hippopotame** [ipɔpɔtam] *nm* hippopotamus

**hirondelle** [iʀɔ̃dɛl] *nf* swallow

**'hisser** ['ise] *vt* to hoist, haul up

**histoire** [istwaʀ] *nf* (*science, événements*) history; (*anecdote, récit, mensonge*) story; (*affaire*) business *no pl*; **histoires** *nfpl* (*chichis*) fuss *no pl*; (*ennuis*) trouble *sg*; **historique** *adj* historical; (*important*) historic ▷ *nm*: **faire l'historique de** to give the background to

**'hit-parade** ['itpaʀad] *nm*: **le hit-parade** the charts

**hiver** [ivɛʀ] *nm* winter; **hivernal, e, -aux** *adj* winter *cpd*; (*glacial*) wintry; **hiverner** *vi* to winter

**HLM** *nm ou f* (= *habitation à loyer modéré*) council flat; **des ~** council housing

**'hobby** ['ɔbi] *nm* hobby

**'hocher** ['ɔʃe] *vt*: **hocher la tête** to nod; (*signe négatif ou dubitatif*) to shake one's head

**'hockey** ['ɔkɛ] *nm*: **hockey (sur glace/gazon)** (ice/field) hockey

**'hold-up** ['ɔldœp] *nm inv* hold-up

**'hollandais, e** ['ɔlɑ̃dɛ, ɛz] *adj* Dutch ▷ *nm* (*Ling*) Dutch ▷ *nm/f*: **Hollandais, e** Dutchman(-woman)

**'Hollande** ['ɔlɑ̃d] *nf*: **la Hollande** Holland

**'homard** ['ɔmaʀ] *nm* lobster

**homéopathique** [ɔmeɔpatik] *adj* homoeopathic

**homicide** [ɔmisid] *nm* murder; **homicide involontaire** manslaughter

**hommage** [ɔmaʒ] *nm* tribute; **rendre ~ à** to pay tribute to

**homme** [ɔm] *nm* man; **homme d'affaires** businessman; **homme d'État** statesman; **homme de main** hired man; **homme de paille** stooge; **l'homme de la rue** the man on the street

**homo...**: **homogène** *adj* homogeneous; **homologue** *nm/f* counterpart; **homologué, e** *adj* (*Sport*) ratified; (*tarif*) authorized; **homonyme** *nm* (*Ling*) homonym; (*d'une personne*) namesake; **homosexuel, le** *adj* homosexual

**'Hong Kong** ['ɔ̃gkɔ̃g] *n* Hong Kong

**'Hongrie** ['ɔ̃gʀi] *nf*: **la Hongrie** Hungary; **'hongrois, e** *adj* Hungarian ▷ *nm/f*: **Hongrois, e** Hungarian ▷ *nm* (*Ling*) Hungarian

**honnête** [ɔnɛt] *adj* (*intègre*) honest; (*juste, satisfaisant*) fair; **honnêtement** *adv* honestly; **honnêteté** *nf* honesty

**honneur** [ɔnœʀ] *nm* honour; (*mérite*) credit; **en l'~ de** in honour of; (*événement*) on the occasion of; **faire ~ à** (*engagements*) to honour; (*famille*) to be a credit to; (*fig: repas etc*) to do justice to

**honorable** [ɔnɔʀabl] *adj* worthy, honourable; (*suffisant*) decent

**honoraire** [ɔnɔʀɛʀ] *adj* honorary; **professeur ~** professor emeritus; **honoraires** *nmpl* fees

**honorer** [ɔnɔʀe] *vt* to honour; (*estimer*) to hold in high regard; (*faire honneur à*) to do credit to

**'honte** ['ɔ̃t] *nf* shame; **avoir honte de** to be ashamed of; **faire honte à qn** to make sb (feel) ashamed; **'honteux, -euse** *adj* ashamed; (*conduite, acte*) shameful, disgraceful

**hôpital, -aux** [ɔpital, o] *nm* hospital; **où est l'~ le plus proche?** where is the nearest hospital?

**'hoquet** ['ɔkɛ] *nm*: **avoir le hoquet** to have (the) hiccoughs

**horaire** [ɔRɛR] *adj* hourly ▷ *nm* timetable, schedule; **horaires** *nmpl* (*d'employé*) hours; **horaire souple** flexitime

**horizon** [ɔRizɔ̃] *nm* horizon

**horizontal, e, -aux** [ɔRizɔ̃tal, o] *adj* horizontal

**horloge** [ɔRlɔʒ] *nf* clock; **l'~ parlante** the speaking clock; **horloger, -ère** *nm/f* watchmaker; clockmaker

**'hormis** ['ɔRmi] *prép* save

**horoscope** [`skɔp] *nm* horoscope

**horreur** [ɔRœR] *nf* horror; **quelle ~!** how awful!; **avoir ~ de** to loathe *ou* detest; **horrible** *adj* horrible; **horrifier** *vt* to horrify

**'hors** ['ɔR] *prép*: **hors de** out of; **hors pair** outstanding; **hors de propos** inopportune; **être hors de soi** to be beside o.s.; **'hors d'usage** out of service; **'hors-bord** *nm inv* speedboat (*with outboard motor*); **'hors-d'œuvre** *nm inv* hors d'œuvre; **'hors-la-loi** *nm inv* outlaw; **'hors-service** *adj inv* out of order; **'hors-taxe** *adj* (*boutique, articles*) duty-free

**hortensia** [ɔRtɑ̃sja] *nm* hydrangea

**hospice** [ɔspis] *nm* (*de vieillards*) home

**hospitalier, -ière** [ɔspitalje, jɛR] *adj* (*accueillant*) hospitable; (*Méd: service, centre*) hospital *cpd*

**hospitaliser** [ɔspitalize] *vt* to take/send to hospital, hospitalize

**hospitalité** [ɔspitalite] *nf* hospitality

**hostie** [ɔsti] *nf* host (*Rel*)

**hostile** [ɔstil] *adj* hostile; **hostilité** *nf* hostility

**hôte** [ot] *nm* (*maître de maison*) host; (*invité*) guest

**hôtel** [otɛl] *nm* hotel; **aller à l'~** to stay in a hotel; **hôtel de ville** town hall; **hôtel (particulier)** (private) mansion; **hôtellerie** *nf* hotel business

● **HÔTELS**
●
● There are six categories of hotel
● in France, from zero ('non classé')
● to four stars and luxury four stars
● ('quatre étoiles luxe'). Prices include
● VAT but not breakfast. In some
● towns, guests pay a small additional
● tourist tax, the 'taxe de séjour'.

**hôtesse** [otɛs] *nf* hostess; **hôtesse (de l'air)** stewardess, air hostess (BRIT)

**'houblon** ['ublɔ̃] *nm* (*Bot*) hop; (*pour la bière*) hops *pl*

**'houille** ['uj] *nf* coal; **'houille blanche** hydroelectric power

**'houle** ['ul] *nf* swell; **'houleux, -euse** *adj* stormy

**'hourra** ['uRa] *excl* hurrah!

**'housse** ['us] *nf* cover

**'houx** ['u] *nm* holly

**'hublot** ['yblo] *nm* porthole

**'huche** ['yʃ] *nf*: **huche à pain** bread bin

**'huer** ['ɥe] *vt* to boo

**huile** [ɥil] *nf* oil

**huissier** [ɥisje] *nm* usher; (*Jur*) ≈ bailiff

**'huit** ['ɥi(t)] *num* eight; **samedi en huit** a week on Saturday; **dans huit jours** in a week; **'huitaine** *nf*: **une huitaine (de jours)** a week or so; **'huitième** *num* eighth

**huître** [ɥitR] *nf* oyster

**humain, e** [ymɛ̃, ɛn] *adj* human; (*compatissant*) humane ▷ *nm* human (being); **humanitaire** *adj* humanitarian; **humanité** *nf* humanity

**humble** [œ̃bl] *adj* humble

**'humer** ['yme] *vt* (*plat*) to smell; (*parfum*) to inhale

**humeur** [ymœR] *nf* mood; **de bonne/mauvaise ~** in a good/bad mood

**humide** [ymid] *adj* damp; (*main, yeux*) moist; (*climat, chaleur*) humid; (*saison, route*) wet

**humilier** [ymilje] *vt* to humiliate

**humilité** [ymilite] *nf* humility, humbleness

**humoristique** [ymɔRistik] *adj*

humorous

**humour** [ymuʀ] nm humour; **avoir de l'~** to have a sense of humour; **humour noir** black humour

**'huppé, e** ['ype] (fam) adj posh

**'hurlement** ['yʀləmɑ̃] nm howling no pl, howl, yelling no pl, yell

**'hurler** ['yʀle] vi to howl, yell

**'hutte** ['yt] nf hut

**hydratant, e** [idʀatɑ̃, ɑ̃t] adj (crème) moisturizing

**hydraulique** [idʀolik] adj hydraulic

**hydravion** [idʀavjɔ̃] nm seaplane

**hydrogène** [idʀɔʒɛn] nm hydrogen

**hydroglisseur** [idʀɔglisœʀ] nm hydroplane

**hyène** [jɛn] nf hyena

**hygiène** [iʒjɛn] nf hygiene

**hygiénique** [iʒenik] adj hygienic

**hymne** [imn] nm hymn

**hyperlien** [ipɛʀljɛ̃] nm hyperlink

**hypermarché** [ipɛʀmaʀʃe] nm hypermarket

**hypermétrope** [ipɛʀmetʀɔp] adj long-sighted

**hypertension** [ipɛʀtɑ̃sjɔ̃] nf high blood pressure

**hypnose** [ipnoz] nf hypnosis; **hypnotiser** vt to hypnotize

**hypocrisie** [ipɔkʀizi] nf hypocrisy; **hypocrite** adj hypocritical

**hypothèque** [ipɔtɛk] nf mortgage

**hypothèse** [ipɔtɛz] nf hypothesis

**hystérique** [isteʀik] adj hysterical

**iceberg** [ajsbɛʀg] nm iceberg

**ici** [isi] adv here; **jusqu'~** as far as this; (temps) so far; **d'~ demain** by tomorrow; **d'~ là** by then, in the meantime; **d'~ peu** before long

**icône** [ikon] nf icon

**idéal, e, -aux** [ideal, o] adj ideal ▷ nm ideal; **idéaliste** adj idealistic ▷ nm/f idealist

**idée** [ide] nf idea; **avoir dans l'~ que** to have an idea that; **se faire des ~s** to imagine things, get ideas into one's head; **avoir des ~s noires** to have black ou dark thoughts; **idées reçues** received wisdom sg

**identifier** [idɑ̃tifje] vt to identify; **s'identifier** vi: **s'~ avec** ou **à qn/qch** (héros etc) to identify with sb/sth

**identique** [idɑ̃tik] adj: **~ (à)** identical (to)

**identité** [idɑ̃tite] nf identity

**idiot, e** [idjo, idjɔt] adj idiotic ▷ nm/f idiot

**idole** [idɔl] nf idol

**if** [if] *nm* yew

**ignoble** [iɲɔbl] *adj* vile

**ignorant, e** [iɲɔʀɑ̃, ɑ̃t] *adj* ignorant; **~ de** ignorant of, not aware of

**ignorer** [iɲɔʀe] *vt* not to know; (*personne*) to ignore

**il** [il] *pron* he; (*animal, chose, en tournure impersonnelle*) it; **il fait froid** it's cold; **Pierre est-il arrivé?** has Pierre arrived?; **il a gagné** he won; *voir* **avoir**

**île** [il] *nf* island; **l'Île Maurice** Mauritius; **les îles anglo-normandes** the Channel Islands; **les îles britanniques** the British Isles

**illégal, e, -aux** [i(l)legal, o] *adj* illegal

**illimité, e** [i(l)limite] *adj* unlimited

**illisible** [i(l)lizibl] *adj* illegible; (*roman*) unreadable

**illogique** [i(l)lɔʒik] *adj* illogical

**illuminer** [i(l)lymine] *vt* to light up; (*monument, rue: pour une fête*) to illuminate; (: *au moyen de projecteurs*) to floodlight

**illusion** [i(l)lyzjɔ̃] *nf* illusion; **se faire des ~s** to delude o.s.; **faire ~** to delude *ou* fool people

**illustration** [i(l)lystʀasjɔ̃] *nf* illustration

**illustré, e** [i(l)lystʀe] *adj* illustrated ▷ *nm* comic

**illustrer** [i(l)lystʀe] *vt* to illustrate; **s'illustrer** to become famous, win fame

**ils** [il] *pron* they

**image** [imaʒ] *nf* (*gén*) picture; (*métaphore*) image; **image de marque** brand image; (*fig*) public image; **imagé, e** *adj* (*texte*) full of imagery; (*langage*) colourful

**imaginaire** [imaʒinɛʀ] *adj* imaginary

**imagination** [imaʒinasjɔ̃] *nf* imagination; **avoir de l'~** to be imaginative

**imaginer** [imaʒine] *vt* to imagine; (*inventer: expédient*) to devise, think up; **s'imaginer** *vt* (*se figurer: scène etc*) to imagine, picture; **s'~ que** to imagine that

**imbécile** [ɛ̃besil] *adj* idiotic ▷ *nm/f* idiot

**imbu, e** [ɛ̃by] *adj*: **~ de** full of

**imitateur, -trice** [imitatœʀ, tʀis] *nm/f* (*gén*) imitator; (*Music-Hall*) impersonator

**imitation** [imitasjɔ̃] *nf* imitation; (*de personnalité*) impersonation

**imiter** [imite] *vt* to imitate; (*contrefaire*) to forge; (*ressembler à*) to look like

**immangeable** [ɛ̃mɑ̃ʒabl] *adj* inedible

**immatriculation** [imatʀikylasjɔ̃] *nf* registration

- **IMMATRICULATION**
-
- The last two numbers on vehicle
- licence plates show which
- 'département' of France the vehicle
- is registered in. For example, a car
- registered in Paris has the number 75
- on its licence plates.

**immatriculer** [imatʀikyle] *vt* to register; **faire/se faire ~** to register

**immédiat, e** [imedja, jat] *adj* immediate ▷ *nm*: **dans l'~** for the time being; **immédiatement** *adv* immediately

**immense** [i(m)mɑ̃s] *adj* immense

**immerger** [imɛʀʒe] *vt* to immerse, submerge

**immeuble** [imœbl] *nm* building; (*à usage d'habitation*) block of flats

**immigration** [imigʀasjɔ̃] *nf* immigration

**immigré, e** [imigʀe] *nm/f* immigrant

**imminent, e** [iminɑ̃, ɑ̃t] *adj* imminent

**immobile** [i(m)mɔbil] *adj* still, motionless

**immobilier, -ière** [imɔbilje, jɛʀ] *adj* property *cpd* ▷ *nm*: **l'~** the property business

**immobiliser** [imɔbilize] *vt* (*gén*) to immobilize; (*circulation, véhicule, affaires*) to bring to a standstill; **s'immobiliser** (*personne*) to stand still; (*machine, véhicule*) to come to a halt

**immoral, e, -aux** [i(m)mɔʀal, o] *adj* immoral

**immortel, le** [imɔʀtɛl] *adj* immortal

**immunisé, e** [im(m)ynize] *adj*: **~ contre** immune to

**immunité** [imynite] *nf* immunity

**impact** [ɛ̃pakt] *nm* impact

**impair, e** [ɛ̃pɛʀ] *adj* odd ▷ *nm* faux pas, blunder

**impardonnable** [ɛ̃paʀdɔnabl] *adj* unpardonable, unforgivable

**imparfait, e** [ɛ̃paʀfɛ, ɛt] *adj* imperfect

**impartial, e, -aux** [ɛ̃paʀsjal, jo] *adj* impartial, unbiased

**impasse** [ɛ̃pas] *nf* dead end, cul-de-sac; *(fig)* deadlock

**impassible** [ɛ̃pasibl] *adj* impassive

**impatience** [ɛ̃pasjɑ̃s] *nf* impatience

**impatient, e** [ɛ̃pasjɑ̃, jɑ̃t] *adj* impatient; **impatienter: s'impatienter** *vi* to get impatient

**impeccable** [ɛ̃pekabl] *adj* *(parfait)* perfect; *(propre)* impeccable; *(fam)* smashing

**impensable** [ɛ̃pɑ̃sabl] *adj* *(événement hypothétique)* unthinkable; *(événement qui a eu lieu)* unbelievable

**impératif, -ive** [ɛ̃peʀatif, iv] *adj* imperative ▷ *nm* *(Ling)* imperative; **impératifs** *nmpl* *(exigences: d'une fonction, d'une charge)* requirements; *(: de la mode)* demands

**impératrice** [ɛ̃peʀatʀis] *nf* empress

**imperceptible** [ɛ̃pɛʀsɛptibl] *adj* imperceptible

**impérial, e, -aux** [ɛ̃peʀjal, jo] *adj* imperial

**impérieux, -euse** [ɛ̃peʀjø, jøz] *adj* *(caractère, ton)* imperious; *(obligation, besoin)* pressing, urgent

**impérissable** [ɛ̃peʀisabl] *adj* undying

**imperméable** [ɛ̃pɛʀmeabl] *adj* waterproof; *(fig)*: **~ à** impervious to ▷ *nm* raincoat

**impertinent, e** [ɛ̃pɛʀtinɑ̃, ɑ̃t] *adj* impertinent

**impitoyable** [ɛ̃pitwajabl] *adj* pitiless, merciless

**implanter** [ɛ̃plɑ̃te]: **s'implanter** *vi* to be set up

**impliquer** [ɛ̃plike] *vt* to imply; **~ qn (dans)** to implicate sb (in)

**impoli, e** [ɛ̃pɔli] *adj* impolite, rude

**impopulaire** [ɛ̃pɔpylɛʀ] *adj* unpopular

**importance** [ɛ̃pɔʀtɑ̃s] *nf* importance; *(de somme)* size; *(de retard, dégâts)* extent; **sans ~** unimportant

**important, e** [ɛ̃pɔʀtɑ̃, ɑ̃t] *adj* important; *(en quantité: somme, retard)* considerable, sizeable; *(: dégâts)* extensive; *(péj: airs, ton)* self-important ▷ *nm*: **l'~** the important thing

**importateur, -trice** [ɛ̃pɔʀtatœʀ, tʀis] *nm/f* importer

**importation** [ɛ̃pɔʀtasjɔ̃] *nf* importation; *(produit)* import

**importer** [ɛ̃pɔʀte] *vt* to import; *(maladies, plantes)* to introduce ▷ *vi* *(être important)* to matter; **il importe qu'il fasse** it is important that he should do; **peu m'importe** *(je n'ai pas de préférence)* I don't mind; *(je m'en moque)* I don't care; **peu importe (que)** it doesn't matter (if); *voir aussi* **n'importe**

**importun, e** [ɛ̃pɔʀtœ̃, yn] *adj* irksome, importunate; *(arrivée, visite)* inopportune, ill-timed ▷ *nm* intruder; **importuner** *vt* to bother

**imposant, e** [ɛ̃pozɑ̃, ɑ̃t] *adj* imposing

**imposer** [ɛ̃poze] *vt* *(taxer)* to tax; **s'imposer** *(être nécessaire)* to be imperative; **~ qch à qn** to impose sth on sb; **en ~ à** to impress; **s'~ comme** to emerge as; **s'~ par** to win recognition through

**impossible** [ɛ̃pɔsibl] *adj* impossible; **il m'est ~ de le faire** it is impossible for me to do it, I can't possibly do it; **faire l'~** to do one's utmost

**imposteur** [ɛ̃pɔstœʀ] *nm* impostor

**impôt** [ɛ̃po] *nm* tax; **impôt foncier** land tax; **impôt sur le chiffre d'affaires** corporation (BRIT) *ou* corporate (US) tax; **impôt sur le revenu** income tax; **impôts locaux** rates, local taxes (US),

≈ council tax (BRIT)

**impotent, e** [ɛ̃pɔtɑ̃, ɑ̃t] *adj* disabled

**impraticable** [ɛ̃pratikabl] *adj* (*projet*) impracticable, unworkable; (*piste*) impassable

**imprécis, e** [ɛ̃presi, iz] *adj* imprecise

**imprégner** [ɛ̃preɲe] *vt* (*tissu*) to impregnate; (*lieu*, *air*) to fill; **s'imprégner de** (*fig*) to absorb

**imprenable** [ɛ̃prənabl] *adj* (*forteresse*) impregnable; **vue ~** unimpeded outlook

**impression** [ɛ̃presjɔ̃] *nf* impression; (*d'un ouvrage*, *tissu*) printing; **faire bonne/mauvaise ~** to make a good/bad impression; **impressionnant, e** *adj* (*imposant*) impressive; (*bouleversant*) upsetting; **impressionner** *vt* (*frapper*) to impress; (*bouleverser*) to upset

**imprévisible** [ɛ̃previzibl] *adj* unforeseeable

**imprévu, e** [ɛ̃prevy] *adj* unforeseen, unexpected ▷ *nm* (*incident*) unexpected incident; **des vacances pleines d'~** holidays full of surprises; **en cas d'~** if anything unexpected happens; **sauf ~** unless anything unexpected crops up

**imprimante** [ɛ̃primɑ̃t] *nf* printer; **imprimante (à) laser** laser printer

**imprimé** [ɛ̃prime] *nm* (*formulaire*) printed form; (*Postes*) printed matter *no pl*; (*tissu*) printed fabric; **~ à fleur** floral print

**imprimer** [ɛ̃prime] *vt* to print; (*publier*) to publish; **imprimerie** *nf* printing; (*établissement*) printing works *sg*; **imprimeur** *nm* printer

**impropre** [ɛ̃prɔpr] *adj* inappropriate; **~ à** unfit for

**improviser** [ɛ̃prɔvize] *vt*, *vi* to improvise

**improviste** [ɛ̃prɔvist]: **à l'~** *adv* unexpectedly, without warning

**imprudence** [ɛ̃prydɑ̃s] *nf* (*d'une personne*, *d'une action*) carelessness *no pl*; (*d'une remarque*) imprudence *no pl*; **commettre une ~** to do something foolish

**imprudent, e** [ɛ̃prydɑ̃, ɑ̃t] *adj* (*conducteur*, *geste*, *action*) careless; (*remarque*) unwise, imprudent; (*projet*) foolhardy

**impuissant, e** [ɛ̃pɥisɑ̃, ɑ̃t] *adj* helpless; (*sans effet*) ineffectual; (*sexuellement*) impotent

**impulsif, -ive** [ɛ̃pylsif, iv] *adj* impulsive

**impulsion** [ɛ̃pylsjɔ̃] *nf* (*Élec*, *instinct*) impulse; (*élan*, *influence*) impetus

**inabordable** [inabɔrdabl] *adj* (*cher*) prohibitive

**inacceptable** [inakseptabl] *adj* unacceptable

**inaccessible** [inaksesibl] *adj* inaccessible; **~ à** impervious to

**inachevé, e** [inaʃ(ə)ve] *adj* unfinished

**inactif, -ive** [inaktif, iv] *adj* inactive; (*remède*) ineffective; (*Bourse: marché*) slack

**inadapté, e** [inadapte] *adj* (*gén*): **~ à** not adapted to, unsuited to; (*Psych*) maladjusted

**inadéquat, e** [inadekwa(t), kwat] *adj* inadequate

**inadmissible** [inadmisibl] *adj* inadmissible

**inadvertance** [inadvɛrtɑ̃s]: **par ~** *adv* inadvertently

**inanimé, e** [inanime] *adj* (*matière*) inanimate; (*évanoui*) unconscious; (*sans vie*) lifeless

**inanition** [inanisjɔ̃] *nf*: **tomber d'~** to faint with hunger (and exhaustion)

**inaperçu, e** [inapɛrsy] *adj*: **passer ~** to go unnoticed

**inapte** [inapt] *adj*: **~ à** incapable of; (*Mil*) unfit for

**inattendu, e** [inatɑ̃dy] *adj* unexpected

**inattentif, -ive** [inatɑ̃tif, iv] *adj* inattentive; **~ à** (*dangers*, *détails*) heedless of; **inattention** *nf* lack of attention; **une faute** *ou* **une erreur d'inattention** a careless mistake

**inaugurer** [inogyre] *vt* (*monument*) to unveil; (*exposition*, *usine*) to open; (*fig*) to inaugurate

**inavouable** [inavwabl] *adj* shameful; (*bénéfices*) undisclosable

**incalculable** [ɛ̃kalkylabl] *adj* incalculable

**incapable** [ɛ̃kapabl] *adj* incapable; **~ de faire** incapable of doing; (*empêché*) unable to do

**incapacité** [ɛ̃kapasite] *nf* (*incompétence*) incapability; (*impossibilité*) incapacity; **dans l'~ de faire** unable to do

**incarcérer** [ɛ̃karsere] *vt* to incarcerate, imprison

**incassable** [ɛ̃kasabl] *adj* unbreakable

**incendie** [ɛ̃sãdi] *nm* fire; **incendie criminel** arson *no pl*; **incendie de forêt** forest fire; **incendier** *vt* (*mettre le feu à*) to set fire to, set alight; (*brûler complètement*) to burn down

**incertain, e** [ɛ̃sɛrtɛ̃, ɛn] *adj* uncertain; (*temps*) unsettled; (*imprécis: contours*) indistinct, blurred; **incertitude** *nf* uncertainty

**incessamment** [ɛ̃sesamã] *adv* very shortly

**incident** [ɛ̃sidã] *nm* incident; **incident de parcours** minor hitch *ou* setback; **incident technique** technical difficulties *pl*

**incinérer** [ɛ̃sinere] *vt* (*ordures*) to incinerate; (*mort*) to cremate

**incisive** [ɛ̃siziv] *nf* incisor

**inciter** [ɛ̃site] *vt*: **~ qn à (faire) qch** to encourage sb to do sth; (*à la révolte etc*) to incite sb to do sth

**incivilité** [ɛ̃sivilite] *nf* (*grossièreté*) incivility; **incivilités** *nfpl* antisocial behaviour *sg*

**inclinable** [ɛ̃klinabl] *adj*: **siège à dossier ~** reclining seat

**inclination** [ɛ̃klinasjɔ̃] *nf* (*penchant*) inclination

**incliner** [ɛ̃kline] *vt* (*pencher*) to tilt ▷ *vi*: **~ à qch/à faire** to incline towards sth/doing; **s'incliner** *vr* (*se pencher*) to bow; **s'~ devant** (*par respect*) to pay one's respects

**inclure** [ɛ̃klyr] *vt* to include; (*joindre à un envoi*) to enclose

**inclus, e** [ɛ̃kly, -yz] *pp de* **inclure** ▷ *adj* included; (*joint à un envoi*) enclosed ▷ *adv*: **est-ce que le service est ~?** is service included?; **jusqu'au 10 mars ~** until 10th March inclusive

**incognito** [ɛ̃kɔɲito] *adv* incognito ▷ *nm*: **garder l'~** to remain incognito

**incohérent, e** [ɛ̃kɔerã, ãt] *adj* (*comportement*) inconsistent; (*geste, langage, texte*) incoherent

**incollable** [ɛ̃kɔlabl] *adj* (*riz*) non-stick; **il est ~** (*fam*) he's got all the answers

**incolore** [ɛ̃kɔlɔr] *adj* colourless

**incommoder** [ɛ̃kɔmɔde] *vt* (*chaleur, odeur*): **~ qn** to bother sb

**incomparable** [ɛ̃kɔparabl] *adj* incomparable

**incompatible** [ɛ̃kɔpatibl] *adj* incompatible

**incompétent, e** [ɛ̃kɔpetã, ãt] *adj* incompetent

**incomplet, -ète** [ɛ̃kɔplɛ, ɛt] *adj* incomplete

**incompréhensible** [ɛ̃kɔpreãsibl] *adj* incomprehensible

**incompris, e** [ɛ̃kɔpri, iz] *adj* misunderstood

**inconcevable** [ɛ̃kɔs(ə)vabl] *adj* inconceivable

**inconfortable** [ɛ̃kɔfɔrtabl(ə)] *adj* uncomfortable

**incongru, e** [ɛ̃kɔgry] *adj* unseemly

**inconnu, e** [ɛ̃kɔny] *adj* unknown ▷ *nm/f* stranger ▷ *nm*: **l'~** the unknown; **inconnue** *nf* unknown factor

**inconsciemment** [ɛ̃kɔsjamã] *adv* unconsciously

**inconscient, e** [ɛ̃kɔsjã, jãt] *adj* unconscious; (*irréfléchi*) thoughtless, reckless; (*sentiment*) subconscious ▷ *nm* (*Psych*): **l'~** the unconscious; **~ de** unaware of

**inconsidéré, e** [ɛ̃kɔsidere] *adj* ill-considered

**inconsistant, e** [ɛ̃kɔsistã, ãt] *adj* (*fig*) flimsy, weak

**inconsolable** [ɛ̃kɔ̃sɔlabl] *adj*
inconsolable

**incontestable** [ɛ̃kɔ̃tɛstabl] *adj*
indisputable

**incontinent, e** [ɛ̃kɔ̃tinɑ̃, ɑ̃t] *adj*
incontinent

**incontournable** [ɛ̃kɔ̃tuʀnabl] *adj*
unavoidable

**incontrôlable** [ɛ̃kɔ̃tʀolabl]
*adj* unverifiable; *(irrépressible)*
uncontrollable

**inconvénient** [ɛ̃kɔ̃venjɑ̃] *nm*
disadvantage, drawback; **si vous n'y
voyez pas d'~** if you have no objections

**incorporer** [ɛ̃kɔʀpɔʀe] *vt*: **~ (à)** to
mix in (with); **~ (dans)** *(paragraphe
etc)* to incorporate (in); *(Mil: appeler)*
to recruit (into); **il a très bien su s'~
à notre groupe** he was very easily
incorporated into our group

**incorrect, e** [ɛ̃kɔʀɛkt] *adj (impropre,
inconvenant)* improper; *(défectueux)*
faulty; *(inexact)* incorrect; *(impoli)*
impolite; *(déloyal)* underhand

**incorrigible** [ɛ̃kɔʀiʒibl] *adj*
incorrigible

**incrédule** [ɛ̃kʀedyl] *adj* incredulous;
*(Rel)* unbelieving

**incroyable** [ɛ̃kʀwajabl] *adj* incredible

**incruster** [ɛ̃kʀyste] *vt (Art)* to inlay;
**s'incruster** *vi (invité)* to take root

**inculpé, e** [ɛ̃kylpe] *nm/f* accused

**inculper** [ɛ̃kylpe] *vt*: **~ (de)** to charge
(with)

**inculquer** [ɛ̃kylke] *vt*: **~ qch à** to
inculcate sth in *ou* instil sth into

**Inde** [ɛ̃d] *nf*: **l'~** India

**indécent, e** [ɛ̃desɑ̃, ɑ̃t] *adj* indecent

**indécis, e** [ɛ̃desi, iz] *adj (par nature)*
indecisive; *(temporairement)* undecided

**indéfendable** [ɛ̃defɑ̃dabl] *adj*
indefensible

**indéfini, e** [ɛ̃defini] *adj (imprécis,
incertain)* undefined; *(illimité, Ling)*
indefinite; **indéfiniment** *adv*
indefinitely; **indéfinissable** *adj*
indefinable

**indélébile** [ɛ̃delebil] *adj* indelible

**indélicat, e** [ɛ̃delika, at] *adj* tactless

**indemne** [ɛ̃dɛmn] *adj* unharmed;
**indemniser** *vt*: **indemniser qn (de)** to
compensate sb (for)

**indemnité** [ɛ̃dɛmnite] *nf*
*(dédommagement)* compensation *no pl*;
*(allocation)* allowance; **indemnité de
licenciement** redundancy payment

**indépendamment** [ɛ̃depɑ̃damɑ̃]
*adv* independently; **~ de** *(abstraction
faite de)* irrespective of; *(en plus de)* over
and above

**indépendance** [ɛ̃depɑ̃dɑ̃s] *nf*
independence

**indépendant, e** [ɛ̃depɑ̃dɑ̃, ɑ̃t] *adj*
independent; **~ de** independent of;
**travailleur ~** self-employed worker

**indescriptible** [ɛ̃dɛskʀiptibl] *adj*
indescribable

**indésirable** [ɛ̃deziʀabl] *adj*
undesirable

**indestructible** [ɛ̃dɛstʀyktibl] *adj*
indestructible

**indéterminé, e** [ɛ̃detɛʀmine] *adj*
*(date, cause, nature)* unspecified; *(forme,
longueur, quantité)* indeterminate

**index** [ɛ̃dɛks] *nm (doigt)* index finger;
*(d'un livre etc)* index; **mettre à l'~** to
blacklist

**indicateur** [ɛ̃dikatœʀ] *nm (Police)*
informer; *(Tech)* gauge, indicator ▷ *adj*:
**panneau ~** signpost; **indicateur des
chemins de fer** railway timetable;
**indicateur de rues** street directory

**indicatif, -ive** [ɛ̃dikatif, iv] *adj*: **à titre
~** for (your) information ▷ *nm (Ling)*
indicative; *(Radio)* theme *ou* signature
tune; *(Tél)* dialling code (BRIT), area
code (US); **quel est l'~ de ...** what's the
code for ...?

**indication** [ɛ̃dikasjɔ̃] *nf* indication;
*(renseignement)* information *no
pl*; **indications** *nfpl (directives)*
instructions

**indice** [ɛ̃dis] *nm (marque, signe)*
indication, sign; *(Police: lors d'une
enquête)* clue; *(Jur: présomption)* piece
of evidence; *(Science, Écon, Tech)* index;

**~ de protection** (sun protection) factor
**indicible** [ɛ̃disibl] *adj* inexpressible
**indien, ne** [ɛ̃djɛ̃, jɛn] *adj* Indian
▷ *nm/f*: **I~, ne** Indian
**indifféremment** [ɛ̃diferamɑ̃] *adv*
(*sans distinction*) equally (well)
**indifférence** [ɛ̃diferɑ̃s] *nf* indifference
**indifférent, e** [ɛ̃diferɑ̃, ɑ̃t] *adj* (*peu
intéressé*) indifferent; **ça m'est ~** it
doesn't matter to me; **elle m'est ~e**
I am indifferent to her
**indigène** [ɛ̃diʒɛn] *adj* native,
indigenous; (*des gens du pays*) local
▷ *nm/f* native
**indigeste** [ɛ̃diʒɛst] *adj* indigestible
**indigestion** [ɛ̃diʒɛstjɔ̃] *nf* indigestion
*no pl*; **avoir une ~** to have indigestion
**indigne** [ɛ̃diɲ] *adj* unworthy
**indigner** [ɛ̃diɲe] *vt*: **s'~ de qch** to get
annoyed about sth; **s'~ contre qn** to
get annoyed with sb
**indiqué, e** [ɛ̃dike] *adj* (*date, lieu*)
agreed; (*traitement*) appropriate;
(*conseillé*) advisable
**indiquer** [ɛ̃dike] *vt* (*suj: pendule, aiguille*)
to show; (: *étiquette, panneau*) to show,
indicate; (*renseigner sur*) to point out,
tell; (*déterminer: date, lieu*) to give, state;
(*signaler, dénoter*) to indicate, point
to; **~ qch/qn à qn** (*montrer du doigt*) to
point sth/sb out to sb; (*faire connaître:
médecin, restaurant*) to tell sb of sth/sb;
**pourriez-vous m'~ les toilettes/
l'heure?** could you direct me to the
toilets/tell me the time?
**indiscipliné, e** [ɛ̃disipline] *adj*
undisciplined
**indiscret, -ète** [ɛ̃diskʀɛ, ɛt] *adj*
indiscreet
**indiscutable** [ɛ̃diskytabl] *adj*
indisputable
**indispensable** [ɛ̃dispɑ̃sabl] *adj*
indispensable, essential
**indisposé, e** [ɛ̃dispoze] *adj* indisposed
**indistinct, e** [ɛ̃distɛ̃(kt), ɛ̃kt] *adj*
indistinct; **indistinctement** *adv* (*voir,
prononcer*) indistinctly; (*sans distinction*)
indiscriminately

**individu** [ɛ̃dividy] *nm* individual;
**individuel, le** *adj* (*gén*) individual;
(*responsabilité, propriété, liberté*)
personal; **chambre individuelle** single
room; **maison individuelle** detached
house
**indolore** [ɛ̃dɔlɔʀ] *adj* painless
**Indonésie** [ɛ̃dɔnezi] *nf* Indonesia
**indu, e** [ɛ̃dy] *adj*: **à une heure ~e** at
some ungodly hour
**indulgent, e** [ɛ̃dylʒɑ̃, ɑ̃t] *adj* (*parent,
regard*) indulgent; (*juge, examinateur*)
lenient
**industrialisé, e** [ɛ̃dystʀijalize] *adj*
industrialized
**industrie** [ɛ̃dystʀi] *nf* industry;
**industriel, le** *adj* industrial ▷ *nm*
industrialist
**inébranlable** [inebʀɑ̃labl] *adj* (*masse,
colonne*) solid; (*personne, certitude, foi*)
unshakeable
**inédit, e** [inedi, it] *adj* (*correspondance,
livre*) hitherto unpublished; (*spectacle,
moyen*) novel, original; (*film*) unreleased
**inefficace** [inefikas] *adj* (*remède,
moyen*) ineffective; (*machine, employé*)
inefficient
**inégal, e, -aux** [inegal, o] *adj*
unequal; (*irrégulier*) uneven; **inégalable**
*adj* matchless; **inégalé, e** *adj* (*record*)
unequalled; (*beauté*) unrivalled;
**inégalité** *nf* inequality
**inépuisable** [inepɥizabl] *adj*
inexhaustible
**inerte** [inɛʀt] *adj* (*immobile*) lifeless;
(*sans réaction*) passive
**inespéré, e** [inɛspere] *adj*
unexpected, unhoped-for
**inestimable** [inɛstimabl] *adj*
priceless; (*fig: bienfait*) invaluable
**inévitable** [inevitabl] *adj*
unavoidable; (*fatal, habituel*) inevitable
**inexact, e** [inɛgza(kt), akt] *adj*
inaccurate
**inexcusable** [inɛkskyzabl] *adj*
unforgivable
**inexplicable** [inɛksplikabl] *adj*
inexplicable

**in extremis** [inɛkstʀemis] *adv* at the
last minute ▷ *adj* last-minute
**infaillible** [ɛ̃fajibl] *adj* infallible
**infarctus** [ɛ̃faʀktys] *nm*: **~ (du
myocarde)** coronary (thrombosis)
**infatigable** [ɛ̃fatigabl] *adj* tireless
**infect, e** [ɛ̃fɛkt] *adj* revolting;
(*personne*) obnoxious; (*temps*) foul
**infecter** [ɛ̃fɛkte] *vt* (*atmosphère, eau*)
to contaminate; (*Méd*) to infect;
**s'infecter** to become infected *ou*
septic; **infection** *nf* infection;
(*puanteur*) stench
**inférieur, e** [ɛ̃feʀjœʀ] *adj* lower; (*en
qualité, intelligence*) inferior; **~ à** (*somme,
quantité*) less *ou* smaller than; (*moins bon
que*) inferior to
**infernal, e, -aux** [ɛ̃fɛʀnal, o] *adj*
(*insupportable: chaleur, rythme*) infernal;
(*: enfant*) horrid; (*satanique, effrayant*)
diabolical
**infidèle** [ɛ̃fidɛl] *adj* unfaithful
**infiltrer** [ɛ̃filtʀe]: **s'infiltrer** *vr*: **s'~
dans** to get into; (*liquide*) to seep
through; (*fig: groupe, ennemi*) to
infiltrate
**infime** [ɛ̃fim] *adj* minute, tiny
**infini, e** [ɛ̃fini] *adj* infinite ▷ *nm*
infinity; **à l'~** endlessly; **infiniment** *adv*
infinitely; **infinité** *nf*: **une infinité de**
an infinite number of
**infinitif** [ɛ̃finitif] *nm* infinitive
**infirme** [ɛ̃fiʀm] *adj* disabled ▷ *nm/f*
disabled person
**infirmerie** [ɛ̃fiʀməʀi] *nf* medical room
**infirmier, -ière** [ɛ̃fiʀmje] *nm/f* nurse;
**infirmière chef** sister
**infirmité** [ɛ̃fiʀmite] *nf* disability
**inflammable** [ɛ̃flamabl] *adj*
(in)flammable
**inflation** [ɛ̃flasjɔ̃] *nf* inflation
**influençable** [ɛ̃flyɑ̃sabl] *adj* easily
influenced
**influence** [ɛ̃flyɑ̃s] *nf* influence;
**influencer** *vt* to influence; **influent, e**
*adj* influential
**informaticien, ne** [ɛ̃fɔʀmatisjɛ̃, jɛn]
*nm/f* computer scientist

**information** [ɛ̃fɔʀmasjɔ̃] *nf*
(*renseignement*) piece of information;
(*Presse, TV: nouvelle*) item of
news; (*diffusion de renseignements,
Inform*) information; (*Jur*) inquiry,
investigation; **informations** *nfpl* (*TV*)
news *sg*
**informatique** [ɛ̃fɔʀmatik] *nf*
(*technique*) data processing; (*science*)
computer science ▷ *adj* computer *cpd*;
**informatiser** *vt* to computerize
**informer** [ɛ̃fɔʀme] *vt*: **~ qn (de)** to
inform sb (of); **s'informer** *vr*: **s'~
(de/si)** to inquire *ou* find out (about/
whether); **s'~ sur** to inform o.s. about
**infos** [ɛ̃fo] *nfpl*: **les ~** the news *sg*
**infraction** [ɛ̃fʀaksjɔ̃] *nf* offence; **~ à**
violation *ou* breach of; **être en ~** to be
in breach of the law
**infranchissable** [ɛ̃fʀɑ̃ʃisabl] *adj*
impassable; (*fig*) insuperable
**infrarouge** [ɛ̃fʀaʀuʒ] *adj* infrared
**infrastructure** [ɛ̃fʀastʀyktyʀ] *nf*
(*Aviat, Mil*) ground installations *pl*;
(*Écon: touristique etc*) infrastructure
**infuser** [ɛ̃fyze] *vt, vi* (*thé*) to brew;
(*tisane*) to infuse; **infusion** *nf* (*tisane*)
herb tea
**ingénier** [ɛ̃ʒenje]: **s'ingénier** *vi*: **s'~ à
faire** to strive to do
**ingénierie** [ɛ̃ʒeniʀi] *nf* engineering
**ingénieur** [ɛ̃ʒenjœʀ] *nm* engineer;
**ingénieur du son** sound engineer
**ingénieux, -euse** [ɛ̃ʒenjø, jøz] *adj*
ingenious, clever
**ingrat, e** [ɛ̃gʀa, at] *adj* (*personne*)
ungrateful; (*travail, sujet*) thankless;
(*visage*) unprepossessing
**ingrédient** [ɛ̃gʀedjɑ̃] *nm* ingredient
**inhabité, e** [inabite] *adj* uninhabited
**inhabituel, le** [inabituɛl] *adj* unusual
**inhibition** [inibisjɔ̃] *nf* inhibition
**inhumain, e** [inymɛ̃, ɛn] *adj* inhuman
**inimaginable** [inimaʒinabl] *adj*
unimaginable
**ininterrompu, e** [inɛ̃teʀɔ̃py] *adj*
(*file, série*) unbroken; (*flot, vacarme*)
uninterrupted, non-stop; (*effort*)

unremitting, continuous; (suite, ligne) unbroken

**initial, e, -aux** [inisjal, jo] adj initial; **initiales** nfpl (d'un nom, sigle etc) initials

**initiation** [inisjasjɔ̃] nf: **~ à** introduction to

**initiative** [inisjativ] nf initiative

**initier** [inisje] vt: **~ qn à** to initiate sb into; (faire découvrir: art, jeu) to introduce sb to

**injecter** [ɛ̃ʒɛkte] vt to inject; **injection** nf injection; **à injection** (Auto) fuel injection cpd

**injure** [ɛ̃ʒyʀ] nf insult, abuse no pl; **injurier** vt to insult, abuse; **injurieux, -euse** adj abusive, insulting

**injuste** [ɛ̃ʒyst] adj unjust, unfair; **injustice** nf injustice

**inlassable** [ɛ̃lɑsabl] adj tireless

**inné, e** [i(n)ne] adj innate, inborn

**innocent, e** [inɔsɑ̃, ɑ̃t] adj innocent; **innocenter** vt to clear, prove innocent

**innombrable** [i(n)nɔ̃bʀabl] adj innumerable

**innover** [inɔve] vi to break new ground

**inoccupé, e** [inɔkype] adj unoccupied

**inodore** [inɔdɔʀ] adj (gaz) odourless; (fleur) scentless

**inoffensif, -ive** [inɔfɑ̃sif, iv] adj harmless, innocuous

**inondation** [inɔ̃dasjɔ̃] nf flood

**inonder** [inɔ̃de] vt to flood; **~ de** to flood with

**inopportun, e** [inɔpɔʀtœ̃, yn] adj ill-timed, untimely

**inoubliable** [inublijabl] adj unforgettable

**inouï, e** [inwi] adj unheard-of, extraordinary

**inox** [inɔks] nm stainless steel

**inquiet, -ète** [ɛ̃kjɛ, ɛ̃kjɛt] adj anxious; **inquiétant, e** adj worrying, disturbing; **inquiéter** vt to worry; **s'inquiéter** to worry; **s'inquiéter de** to worry about; (s'enquérir de) to inquire about; **inquiétude** nf anxiety

**insaisissable** [ɛ̃sezisabl] adj (fugitif, ennemi) elusive; (différence, nuance) imperceptible

**insalubre** [ɛ̃salybʀ] adj insalubrious

**insatisfait, e** [ɛ̃satisfɛ, ɛt] adj (non comblé) unsatisfied; (mécontent) dissatisfied

**inscription** [ɛ̃skʀipsjɔ̃] nf inscription; (immatriculation) enrolment

**inscrire** [ɛ̃skʀiʀ] vt (marquer: sur son calepin etc) to note ou write down; (: sur un mur, une affiche etc) to write; (: dans la pierre, le métal) to inscribe; (mettre: sur une liste, un budget etc) to put down; **s'inscrire** (pour une excursion etc) to put one's name down; **s'~ (à)** (club, parti) to join; (université) to register ou enrol (at); (examen, concours) to register (for); **~ qn à** (club, parti) to enrol sb at

**insecte** [ɛ̃sɛkt] nm insect; **insecticide** nm insecticide

**insensé, e** [ɛ̃sɑ̃se] adj mad

**insensible** [ɛ̃sɑ̃sibl] adj (nerf, membre) numb; (dur, indifférent) insensitive

**inséparable** [ɛ̃sepaʀabl] adj inseparable ▷ nm: **~s** (oiseaux) lovebirds

**insigne** [ɛ̃siɲ] nm (d'un parti, club) badge; (d'une fonction) insignia ▷ adj distinguished

**insignifiant, e** [ɛ̃siɲifjɑ̃, jɑ̃t] adj insignificant; trivial

**insinuer** [ɛ̃sinɥe] vt to insinuate; **s'insinuer dans** (fig) to worm one's way into

**insipide** [ɛ̃sipid] adj insipid

**insister** [ɛ̃siste] vi to insist; (continuer à sonner) to keep on trying; **~ sur** (détail, sujet) to lay stress on

**insolation** [ɛ̃sɔlasjɔ̃] nf (Méd) sunstroke no pl

**insolent, e** [ɛ̃sɔlɑ̃, ɑ̃t] adj insolent

**insolite** [ɛ̃sɔlit] adj strange, unusual

**insomnie** [ɛ̃sɔmni] nf insomnia no pl; **avoir des ~s** to sleep badly, not be able to sleep

**insouciant, e** [ɛ̃susjɑ̃, jɑ̃t] adj carefree; **~ du danger** heedless of (the) danger

**insoupçonnable** [ɛ̃supsɔnabl] adj unsuspected; (personne) above suspicion

**insoupçonné, e** [ɛ̃supsɔne] *adj*
unsuspected

**insoutenable** [ɛ̃sut(ə)nabl] *adj*
(*argument*) untenable; (*chaleur*)
unbearable

**inspecter** [ɛ̃spɛkte] *vt* to inspect;
**inspecteur, -trice** *nm/f* inspector;
**inspecteur d'Académie** (regional)
director of education; **inspecteur
des finances** = tax inspector (BRIT),
≈ Internal Revenue Service agent
(US); **inspecteur (de police)** (police)
inspector; **inspection** *nf* inspection

**inspirer** [ɛ̃spire] *vt* (*gén*) to inspire ▷ *vi*
(*aspirer*) to breathe in; **s'inspirer** *vr*: **s'~
de** to be inspired by

**instable** [ɛ̃stabl] *adj* unstable; (*meuble,
équilibre*) unsteady; (*temps*) unsettled

**installation** [ɛ̃stalasjɔ̃] *nf* (*mise en
place*) installation; **installations** *nfpl*
(*de sport, dans un camping*) facilities;
**l'installation électrique** wiring

**installer** [ɛ̃stale] *vt* (*loger, placer*) to put;
(*meuble, gaz, électricité*) to put in; (*rideau,
étagère, tente*) to put up; (*appartement*)
to fit out; **s'installer** (*s'établir: artisan,
dentiste etc*) to set o.s. up; (*se loger*) to
settle; (*emménager*) to settle in; (*sur
un siège, à un emplacement*) to settle
(down); (*fig: maladie, grève*) to take a
firm hold

**instance** [ɛ̃stɑ̃s] *nf* (Admin: *autorité*)
authority; **affaire en ~** matter pending;
**être en ~ de divorce** to be awaiting
a divorce

**instant** [ɛ̃stɑ̃] *nm* moment, instant;
**dans un ~** in a moment; **à l'~** this
instant; **je l'ai vu à l'~** I've just this
minute seen him, I saw him a moment
ago; **pour l'~** for the moment, for the
time being

**instantané, e** [ɛ̃stɑ̃tane] *adj* (*lait, café*)
instant; (*explosion, mort*) instantaneous
▷ *nm* snapshot

**instar** [ɛ̃staʀ]: **à l'~ de** *prép* following
the example of, like

**instaurer** [ɛ̃stɔʀe] *vt* to institute;

(*couvre-feu*) to impose; **s'instaurer** *vr*
(*paix*) to be established; (*doute*) to set in

**instinct** [ɛ̃stɛ̃] *nm* instinct;
**instinctivement** *adv* instinctively

**instituer** [ɛ̃stitɥe] *vt* to establish

**institut** [ɛ̃stity] *nm* institute; **institut
de beauté** beauty salon; **Institut
universitaire de technologie**
≈ polytechnic

**instituteur, -trice** [ɛ̃stitytœʀ, tʀis]
*nm/f* (primary school) teacher

**institution** [ɛ̃stitysjɔ̃] *nf* institution;
(*collège*) private school; **institutions**
*nfpl* (*structures politiques et sociales*)
institutions

**instructif, -ive** [ɛ̃stʀyktif, iv] *adj*
instructive

**instruction** [ɛ̃stʀyksjɔ̃] *nf*
(*enseignement, savoir*) education;
(Jur) (preliminary) investigation and
hearing; **instructions** *nfpl* (*ordres, mode
d'emploi*) instructions; **instruction
civique** civics *sg*

**instruire** [ɛ̃stʀɥiʀ] *vt* (*élèves*) to teach;
(*recrues*) to train; (Jur: *affaire*) to conduct
the investigation for; **s'instruire** to
educate o.s.; **instruit, e** *adj* educated

**instrument** [ɛ̃stʀymɑ̃] *nm*
instrument; **instrument à cordes/à
vent** stringed/wind instrument;
**instrument de mesure** measuring
instrument; **instrument de musique**
musical instrument; **instrument de
travail** (working) tool

**insu** [ɛ̃sy] *nm*: **à l'~ de qn** without sb
knowing (it)

**insuffisant, e** [ɛ̃syfizɑ̃, ɑ̃t] *adj* (*en
quantité*) insufficient; (*en qualité*)
inadequate; (*sur une copie*) poor

**insulaire** [ɛ̃sylɛʀ] *adj* island *cpd*;
(*attitude*) insular

**insuline** [ɛ̃sylin] *nf* insulin

**insulte** [ɛ̃sylt] *nf* insult; **insulter** *vt*
to insult

**insupportable** [ɛ̃sypɔʀtabl] *adj*
unbearable

**insurmontable** [ɛ̃syʀmɔ̃tabl] *adj*
(*difficulté*) insuperable; (*aversion*)

unconquerable

**intact, e** [ɛ̃takt] *adj* intact

**intarissable** [ɛ̃taʀisabl] *adj* inexhaustible

**intégral, e, -aux** [ɛ̃tegʀal, o] *adj* complete; **texte ~** unabridged version; **bronzage ~** all-over suntan; **intégralement** *adv* in full; **intégralité** *nf* whole; **dans son intégralité** in full; **intégrant, e** *adj*: **faire partie intégrante de** to be an integral part of

**intègre** [ɛ̃tegʀ] *adj* upright

**intégrer** [ɛ̃tegʀe]: **s'intégrer** *vr*: **s'~ à** *ou* **dans qch** to become integrated into sth; **bien s'~** to fit in

**intégrisme** [ɛ̃tegʀism] *nm* fundamentalism

**intellectuel, le** [ɛ̃telɛktɥel] *adj* intellectual ▷ *nm/f* intellectual; (*péj*) highbrow

**intelligence** [ɛ̃teliʒɑ̃s] *nf* intelligence; (*compréhension*): **l'~ de** the understanding of; (*complicité*): **regard d'~** glance of complicity; (*accord*): **vivre en bonne ~ avec qn** to be on good terms with sb

**intelligent, e** [ɛ̃teliʒɑ̃, ɑ̃t] *adj* intelligent

**intelligible** [ɛ̃teliʒibl] *adj* intelligible

**intempéries** [ɛ̃tɑ̃peʀi] *nfpl* bad weather *sg*

**intenable** [ɛ̃t(ə)nabl] *adj* (*chaleur*) unbearable

**intendant, e** [ɛ̃tɑ̃dɑ̃] *nm/f* (*Mil*) quartermaster; (*Scol*) bursar

**intense** [ɛ̃tɑ̃s] *adj* intense; **intensif, -ive** [ɛ̃tɑ̃s] *adj* intensive; **un cours intensif** a crash course

**intenter** [ɛ̃tɑ̃te] *vt*: **~ un procès contre** *ou* **à** to start proceedings against

**intention** [ɛ̃tɑ̃sjɔ̃] *nf* intention; (*Jur*) intent; **avoir l'~ de faire** to intend to do; **à l'~ de** for; (*renseignement*) for the benefit of; (*film, ouvrage*) aimed at; **à cette ~** with this aim in view; **intentionné, e** *adj*: **bien intentionné** well-meaning *ou* -intentioned; **mal intentionné** ill-intentioned

**interactif, -ive** [ɛ̃teʀaktif, iv] *adj* (*Comput*) interactive

**intercepter** [ɛ̃teʀsɛpte] *vt* to intercept; (*lumière, chaleur*) to cut off

**interchangeable** [ɛ̃teʀʃɑ̃ʒabl] *adj* interchangeable

**interdiction** [ɛ̃teʀdiksjɔ̃] *nf* ban; **interdiction de fumer** no smoking

**interdire** [ɛ̃teʀdiʀ] *vt* to forbid; (*Admin*) to ban, prohibit; (: *journal, livre*) to ban; **~ à qn de faire** to forbid sb to do; (*suj: empêchement*) to prevent sb from doing

**interdit, e** [ɛ̃teʀdi, it] *pp de* **interdire** ▷ *adj* (*stupéfait*) taken aback; **film ~ aux moins de 18/12 ans** ≈ 18-/12A-rated film; **"stationnement ~"** "no parking"

**intéressant, e** [ɛ̃teʀesɑ̃, ɑ̃t] *adj* interesting; (*avantageux*) attractive

**intéressé, e** [ɛ̃teʀese] *adj* (*parties*) involved, concerned; (*amitié, motifs*) self-interested

**intéresser** [ɛ̃teʀese] *vt* (*captiver*) to interest; (*toucher*) to be of interest to; (*Admin: concerner*) to affect, concern; **s'intéresser** *vr*: **s'~ à** to be interested in

**intérêt** [ɛ̃teʀe] *nm* interest; (*égoïsme*) self-interest; **tu as ~ à accepter** it's in your interest to accept; **tu as ~ à te dépêcher** you'd better hurry

**intérieur, e** [ɛ̃teʀjœʀ] *adj* (*mur, escalier, poche*) inside; (*commerce, politique*) domestic; (*cour, calme, vie*) inner; (*navigation*) inland ▷ *nm*: **l'~** (*d'une maison, d'un récipient etc*) the inside; (*d'un pays, aussi: décor, mobilier*) the interior; **à l'~ (de)** inside; **ministère de l'I~e** ≈ Home Office (BRIT), ≈ Department of the Interior (US); **intérieurement** *adv* inwardly

**intérim** [ɛ̃teʀim] *nm* interim period; **faire de l'~** to temp; **assurer l'~ (de)** to deputize (for); **par ~** interim

**intérimaire** [ɛ̃teʀimeʀ] *adj* (*directeur, ministre*) acting; (*secrétaire, personnel*) temporary ▷ *nm/f* (*secrétaire*) temporary secretary, temp (BRIT)

**interlocuteur, -trice** [ɛ̃teʀlɔkytœʀ, tʀis] *nm/f* speaker; **son ~** the person he was speaking to

**intermédiaire** [ɛ̃tɛʀmedjɛʀ] *adj* intermediate; (*solution*) temporary ▷ *nm/f* intermediary; (*Comm*) middleman; **sans ~** directly; **par l'~ de** through

**interminable** [ɛ̃tɛʀminabl] *adj* endless

**intermittence** [ɛ̃tɛʀmitɑ̃s] *nf*: **par ~** sporadically, intermittently

**internat** [ɛ̃tɛʀna] *nm* boarding school

**international, e, -aux** [ɛ̃tɛʀnasjɔnal, o] *adj, nm/f* international

**internaute** [ɛ̃tɛʀnot] *nm/f* Internet user

**interne** [ɛ̃tɛʀn] *adj* internal ▷ *nm/f* (*Scol*) boarder; (*Méd*) houseman

**Internet** [ɛ̃tɛʀnɛt] *nm*: **l'~** the Internet

**interpeller** [ɛ̃tɛʀpǝle] *vt* (*appeler*) to call out to; (*apostropher*) to shout at; (*Police, Pol*) to question; (*concerner*) to concern

**interphone** [ɛ̃tɛʀfɔn] *nm* intercom; (*d'immeuble*) entry phone

**interposer** [ɛ̃tɛʀpoze] *vt*: **s'interposer** to intervene; **par personnes interposées** through a third party

**interprète** [ɛ̃tɛʀpʀɛt] *nm/f* interpreter; (*porte-parole*) spokesperson; **pourriez-vous nous servir d' ~?** could you act as our interpreter?

**interpréter** [ɛ̃tɛʀpʀete] *vt* to interpret; (*jouer*) to play; (*chanter*) to sing

**interrogatif, -ive** [ɛ̃tɛʀɔgatif, iv] *adj* (*Ling*) interrogative

**interrogation** [ɛ̃tɛʀɔgasjɔ̃] *nf* question; (*action*) questioning; **~ écrite/orale** (*Scol*) written/oral test

**interrogatoire** [ɛ̃tɛʀɔgatwaʀ] *nm* (*Police*) questioning *no pl*; (*Jur, aussi fig*) cross-examination

**interroger** [ɛ̃tɛʀɔʒe] *vt* to question; (*Inform*) to consult; (*Scol*) to test

**interrompre** [ɛ̃tɛʀɔ̃pʀ] *vt* (*gén*) to interrupt; (*négociations*) to break off;

(*match*) to stop; **s'interrompre** to break off; **interrupteur** *nm* switch; **interruption** *nf* interruption; (*pause*) break; **sans interruption** without stopping; **interruption (volontaire) de grossesse** termination (of pregnancy)

**intersection** [ɛ̃tɛʀsɛksjɔ̃] *nf* intersection

**intervalle** [ɛ̃tɛʀval] *nm* (*espace*) space; (*de temps*) interval; **dans l'~** in the meantime; **à deux jours d'~** two days apart

**intervenir** [ɛ̃tɛʀvǝniʀ] *vi* (*gén*) to intervene; **~ auprès de qn** to intervene with sb; **intervention** *nf* intervention; (*discours*) speech; **intervention chirurgicale** (*Méd*) (surgical) operation

**interview** [ɛ̃tɛʀvju] *nf* interview

**intestin** [ɛ̃tɛstɛ̃] *nm* intestine

**intime** [ɛ̃tim] *adj* intimate; (*vie*) private; (*conviction*) inmost; (*dîner, cérémonie*) quiet ▷ *nm/f* close friend; **un journal ~** a diary

**intimider** [ɛ̃timide] *vt* to intimidate

**intimité** [ɛ̃timite] *nf*: **dans l'~** in private; (*sans formalités*) with only a few friends, quietly

**intolérable** [ɛ̃tɔleʀabl] *adj* intolerable

**intox** [ɛ̃tɔks] (*fam*) *nf* brainwashing

**intoxication** [ɛ̃tɔksikasjɔ̃] *nf*: **intoxication alimentaire** food poisoning

**intoxiquer** [ɛ̃tɔksike] *vt* to poison; (*fig*) to brainwash

**intraitable** [ɛ̃tʀɛtabl] *adj* inflexible, uncompromising

**intransigeant, e** [ɛ̃tʀɑ̃ziʒɑ̃, ɑ̃t] *adj* intransigent

**intrépide** [ɛ̃tʀepid] *adj* dauntless

**intrigue** [ɛ̃tʀig] *nf* (*scénario*) plot; **intriguer** *vt* to puzzle, intrigue

**introduction** [ɛ̃tʀɔdyksjɔ̃] *nf* introduction

**introduire** [ɛ̃tʀɔdɥiʀ] *vt* to introduce; (*visiteur*) to show in; (*aiguille, clef*) **~ qch dans** to insert *ou* introduce sth into; **s'introduire** *vr* (*techniques, usages*) to be introduced; **s'~ (dans)** to get in(to); (*dans un groupe*) to get o.s. accepted (into)

**introuvable** [ɛ̃tʀuvabl] *adj* which cannot be found; (*Comm*) unobtainable

**intrus, e** [ɛ̃tʀy, yz] *nm/f* intruder

**intuition** [ɛ̃tɥisjɔ̃] *nf* intuition

**inusable** [inyzabl] *adj* hard-wearing

**inutile** [inytil] *adj* useless; (*superflu*) unnecessary; **inutilement** *adv* unnecessarily; **inutilisable** *adj* unusable

**invalide** [ɛ̃valid] *adj* disabled ▷ *nm:* **~ de guerre** disabled ex-serviceman

**invariable** [ɛ̃vaʀjabl] *adj* invariable

**invasion** [ɛ̃vazjɔ̃] *nf* invasion

**inventaire** [ɛ̃vɑ̃tɛʀ] *nm* inventory; (*Comm: liste*) stocklist; (: *opération*) stocktaking *no pl*

**inventer** [ɛ̃vɑ̃te] *vt* to invent; (*subterfuge*) to devise, invent; (*histoire, excuse*) to make up, invent; **inventeur** *nm* inventor; **inventif, -ive** *adj* inventive; **invention** *nf* invention

**inverse** [ɛ̃vɛʀs] *adj* opposite ▷ *nm:* **l'~** the opposite; **dans l'ordre ~** in the reverse order; **en sens ~** in (*ou* from) the opposite direction; **dans le sens ~ des aiguilles d'une montre** anticlockwise; **tu t'es trompé, c'est l'~** you've got it wrong, it's the other way round; **inversement** *adv* conversely; **inverser** *vt* to invert, reverse; (*Élec*) to reverse

**investir** [ɛ̃vɛstiʀ] *vt* to invest; **~ qn de** (*d'une fonction, d'un pouvoir*) to vest *ou* invest sb with; **s'investir** *vr:* **s'~ dans** (*Psych*) to put a lot into; **investissement** *nm* investment

**invisible** [ɛ̃vizibl] *adj* invisible

**invitation** [ɛ̃vitasjɔ̃] *nf* invitation

**invité, e** [ɛ̃vite] *nm/f* guest

**inviter** [ɛ̃vite] *vt* to invite; **~ qn à faire qch** to invite sb to do sth

**invivable** [ɛ̃vivabl] *adj* unbearable

**involontaire** [ɛ̃vɔlɔ̃tɛʀ] *adj* (*mouvement*) involuntary; (*insulte*) unintentional; (*complice*) unwitting

**invoquer** [ɛ̃vɔke] *vt* (*Dieu, muse*) to call upon, invoke; (*prétexte*) to put forward (as an excuse); (*loi, texte*) to refer to

**invraisemblable** [ɛ̃vʀɛsɑ̃blabl] *adj* (*fait, nouvelle*) unlikely, improbable; (*insolence, habit*) incredible

**iode** [jɔd] *nm* iodine

**irai** *etc* [iʀe] *vb voir* **aller**

**Irak** [iʀak] *nm* Iraq; **irakien, ne** *adj* Iraqi ▷ *nm/f:* **Irakien, ne** Iraqi

**Iran** [iʀɑ̃] *nm* Iran; **iranien, ne** *adj* Iranian ▷ *nm/f:* **Iranien, ne** Iranian

**irions** *etc* [iʀjɔ̃] *vb voir* **aller**

**iris** [iʀis] *nm* iris

**irlandais, e** [iʀlɑ̃dɛ, ɛz] *adj* Irish ▷ *nm/f:* **I~, e** Irishman(-woman)

**Irlande** [iʀlɑ̃d] *nf* Ireland; **la République d'~** the Irish Republic; **la mer d'~** the Irish Sea; **Irlande du Nord** Northern Ireland

**ironie** [iʀɔni] *nf* irony; **ironique** *adj* ironical; **ironiser** *vi* to be ironical

**irons** *etc* [iʀɔ̃] *vb voir* **aller**

**irradier** [iʀadje] *vt* to irradiate

**irraisonné, e** [iʀɛzɔne] *adj* irrational

**irrationnel, le** [iʀasjɔnɛl] *adj* irrational

**irréalisable** [iʀealizabl] *adj* unrealizable; (*projet*) impracticable

**irrécupérable** [iʀekypeʀabl] *adj* beyond repair; (*personne*) beyond redemption

**irréel, le** [iʀeɛl] *adj* unreal

**irréfléchi, e** [iʀefleʃi] *adj* thoughtless

**irrégularité** [iʀegylaʀite] *nf* irregularity; (*de travail, d'effort, de qualité*) unevenness *no pl*

**irrégulier, -ière** [iʀegylje, jɛʀ] *adj* irregular; (*travail, effort, qualité*) uneven; (*élève, athlète*) erratic

**irrémédiable** [iʀemedjabl] *adj* irreparable

**irremplaçable** [iʀɑ̃plasabl] *adj* irreplaceable

**irréparable** [iʀepaʀabl] *adj* (*objet*) beyond repair; (*dommage etc*) irreparable

**irréprochable** [iʀepʀɔʃabl] *adj* irreproachable, beyond reproach;

(*tenue*) impeccable

**irrésistible** [iʀezistibl] *adj* irresistible; (*besoin, désir, preuve, logique*) compelling; (*amusant*) hilarious

**irrésolu, e** [iʀezɔly] *adj* (*personne*) irresolute; (*problème*) unresolved

**irrespectueux, -euse** [iʀɛspɛktɥø, øz] *adj* disrespectful

**irresponsable** [iʀɛspɔ̃sabl] *adj* irresponsible

**irriguer** [iʀige] *vt* to irrigate

**irritable** [iʀitabl] *adj* irritable

**irriter** [iʀite] *vt* to irritate

**irruption** [iʀypsjɔ̃] *nf*: **faire ~ (chez qn)** to burst in (on sb)

**Islam** [islam] *nm*: **l'~** Islam; **islamique** *adj* Islamic; **islamophobie** *nf* Islamophobia

**Islande** [islɑ̃d] *nf* Iceland

**isolant, e** [izɔlɑ̃, ɑ̃t] *adj* insulating; (*insonorisant*) soundproofing

**isolation** [izɔlasjɔ̃] *nf* insulation; **~ acoustique** soundproofing

**isolé, e** [izɔle] *adj* isolated; (*contre le froid*) insulated

**isoler** [izɔle] *vt* to isolate; (*prisonnier*) to put in solitary confinement; (*ville*) to cut off, isolate; (*contre le froid*) to insulate; **s'isoler** *vi* to isolate o.s.

**Israël** [isʀaɛl] *nm* Israel; **israélien, ne** *adj* Israeli ▷ *nm/f*: **Israélien, ne** Israeli; **israélite** *adj* Jewish ▷ *nm/f*: **Israélite** Jew (Jewess)

**issu, e** [isy] *adj*: **~ de** (*né de*) descended from; (*résultant de*) stemming from; **issue** *nf* (*ouverture, sortie*) exit; (*solution*) way out, solution; (*dénouement*) outcome; **à l'issue de** at the conclusion *ou* close of; **voie sans issue** dead end; **issue de secours** emergency exit

**Italie** [itali] *nf* Italy; **italien, ne** *adj* Italian ▷ *nm/f*: **Italien, ne** Italian ▷ *nm* (*Ling*) Italian

**italique** [italik] *nm*: **en ~** in italics

**itinéraire** [itineʀɛʀ] *nm* itinerary, route; **itinéraire bis** alternative route

**IUT** *sigle m* = **Institut universitaire de technologie**

**IVG** *sigle f* (= *interruption volontaire de grossesse*) abortion

**ivoire** [ivwaʀ] *nm* ivory

**ivre** [ivʀ] *adj* drunk; **~ de** (*colère, bonheur*) wild with; **ivrogne** *nm/f* drunkard

**j**

**j'** [ʒ] pron voir **je**

**jacinthe** [ʒasɛ̃t] nf hyacinth

**jadis** [ʒadis] adv long ago

**jaillir** [ʒajiʀ] vi (liquide) to spurt out; (cris, réponses) to burst forth

**jais** [ʒɛ] nm jet; **(d'un noir) de ~** jet-black

**jalousie** [ʒaluzi] nf jealousy; (store) slatted blind

**jaloux, -ouse** [ʒalu, uz] adj jealous; **être ~ de** to be jealous of

**jamaïquain, e** [ʒamaikɛ̃, -ɛn] adj Jamaican ▷ nm/f: **J~, e** Jamaican

**Jamaïque** [ʒamaik] nf: **la ~** Jamaica

**jamais** [ʒamɛ] adv never; (sans négation) ever; **ne ... ~** never; **je ne suis ~ allé en Espagne** I've never been to Spain; **si ... vous passez dans la région, venez nous voir** if you happen to be/if you're ever in this area, come and see us; **à ~** for ever

**jambe** [ʒɑ̃b] nf leg

**jambon** [ʒɑ̃bɔ̃] nm ham

**jante** [ʒɑ̃t] nf (wheel) rim

**janvier** [ʒɑ̃vje] nm January

**Japon** [ʒapɔ̃] nm Japan; **japonais, e** adj Japanese ▷ nm/f: **Japonais, e** Japanese ▷ nm (Ling) Japanese

**jardin** [ʒaʀdɛ̃] nm garden; **jardin d'enfants** nursery school; **jardinage** nm gardening; **jardiner** vi to do some gardening; **jardinier, -ière** nm/f gardener; **jardinière** nf planter; (de fenêtre) window box; **jardinière de légumes** (Culin) mixed vegetables

**jargon** [ʒaʀgɔ̃] nm (baragouin) gibberish; (langue professionnelle) jargon

**jarret** [ʒaʀɛ] nm back of knee; (Culin) knuckle, shin

**jauge** [ʒoʒ] nf (instrument) gauge; **jauge (de niveau) d'huile** (Auto) dipstick

**jaune** [ʒon] adj, nm yellow ▷ adv (fam): **rire ~** to laugh on the other side of one's face; **jaune d'œuf** (egg) yolk; **jaunir** vi, vt to turn yellow; **jaunisse** nf jaundice

**Javel** [ʒavɛl] nf voir **eau**

**javelot** [ʒavlo] nm javelin

**je, j'** [ʒə] pron I

**jean** [dʒin] nm jeans pl

**Jésus-Christ** [ʒezykʀi(st)] n Jesus Christ; **600 avant/après ~ ou J.-C.** 600 B.C./A.D.

**jet** [ʒɛ] nm (lancer: action) throwing no pl; (: résultat) throw; (jaillissement: d'eaux) jet; (: de sang) spurt; **jet d'eau** spray

**jetable** [ʒ(ə)tabl] adj disposable

**jetée** [ʒəte] nf jetty; (grande) pier

**jeter** [ʒ(ə)te] vt (gén) to throw; (se défaire de) to throw away ou out; **~ qch à qn** to throw sth to sb; (de façon agressive) to throw sth at sb; **~ un coup d'œil (à)** to take a look (at); **~ un sort à qn** to cast a spell on sb; **se ~ sur qn** to rush at sb; **se ~ dans** (suj: fleuve) to flow into

**jeton** [ʒ(ə)tɔ̃] nm (au jeu) counter

**jette** etc [ʒɛt] vb voir **jeter**

**jeu, x** [ʒø] nm (divertissement, Tech: d'une pièce) play; (Tennis: partie, Football etc: façon de jouer) game; (Théâtre etc) acting; (série d'objets, jouet) set; (Cartes) hand; (au casino): **le ~** gambling; **remettre en ~** (Football) to throw in; **être en ~** (fig) to be at stake; **entrer/mettre en ~** (fig) to come/bring into play; **jeu de cartes** pack of cards; **jeu d'échecs** chess set; **jeu de hasard** game of chance; **jeu de mots** pun; **jeu de société** board game; **jeu télévisé** television quiz; **jeu vidéo** video game

**jeudi** [ʒødi] nm Thursday

**jeun** [ʒœ̃]: **à ~** adv on an empty stomach; **être à ~** to have eaten nothing; **rester à ~** not to eat anything

**jeune** [ʒœn] adj young; **jeunes** nmpl: **les ~s** young people; **jeune fille** girl; **jeune homme** young man; **jeunes gens** young people

**jeûne** [ʒøn] nm fast

**jeunesse** [ʒœnɛs] nf youth; (aspect) youthfulness

**joaillier, -ière** [ʒɔaje, -jɛR] nm/f jeweller

**jogging** [dʒɔgiŋ] nm jogging; (survêtement) tracksuit; **faire du ~** to go jogging

**joie** [ʒwa] nf joy

**joindre** [ʒwɛ̃dR] vt to join; (à une lettre): **~ qch à** to enclose sth with; (contacter) to contact, get in touch with; **se ~ à qn** to join sb; **se ~ à qch** to join in sth

**joint, e** [ʒwɛ̃, ɛ̃t] adj: **pièce ~e** (de lettre) enclosure; (de mail) attachment ▷ nm joint; (ligne) join; **joint de culasse** cylinder head gasket

**joli, e** [ʒɔli] adj pretty, attractive; **une ~e somme/situation** a tidy sum/a nice little job; **c'est du ~!** (ironique) that's very nice!; **c'est bien ~, mais ...** that's all very well but ...

**jonc** [ʒɔ̃] nm (bul)rush

**jonction** [ʒɔ̃ksjɔ̃] nf junction

**jongleur, -euse** [ʒɔ̃glœR, øz] nm/f juggler

**jonquille** [ʒɔ̃kij] nf daffodil

**Jordanie** [ʒɔRdani] nf: **la ~** Jordan

**joue** [ʒu] nf cheek

**jouer** [ʒwe] vt to play; (somme d'argent, réputation) to stake, wager; (simuler: sentiment) to affect, feign ▷ vi to play; (Théâtre, Cinéma) to act; (au casino) to

gamble; (bois, porte: se voiler) to warp; (clef, pièce: avoir du jeu) to be loose; **~ sur** (miser) to gamble on; **~ de** (Mus) to play; **~ à** (jeu, sport, roulette) to play; **~ un tour à qn** to play a trick on sb; **~ serré** to play a close game; **~ la comédie** to put on an act; **à toi/nous de ~** it's your/our go ou turn; **bien joué!** well done!; **on joue Hamlet au théâtre X** Hamlet is on at the X theatre

**jouet** [ʒwɛ] nm toy; **être le ~ de** (illusion etc) to be the victim of

**joueur, -euse** [ʒwœR, øz] nm/f player; **être beau/mauvais ~** to be a good/bad loser

**jouir** [ʒwiR] vi (sexe: fam) to come ▷ vt: **~ de** to enjoy

**jour** [ʒuR] nm day; (opposé à la nuit) day, daytime; (clarté) daylight; (fig: aspect) light; (ouverture) gap; **de ~** (crème, service) day cpd; **travailler de ~** to work during the day; **voyager de ~** to travel by day; **au ~ le ~** from day to day; **de nos ~s** these days; **du ~ au lendemain** overnight; **il fait ~** it's daylight; **au grand ~** (fig) in the open; **mettre au ~** to disclose; **mettre à ~** to update; **donner le ~ à** to give birth to; **voir le ~** to be born; **le ~ J** D-day; **jour férié** public holiday; **jour ouvrable** working day

**journal, -aux** [ʒuRnal, o] nm (news)paper; (spécialisé) journal; (intime) diary; **journal de bord** log; **journal parlé/télévisé** radio/ television news sg

**journalier, -ière** [ʒuRnalje, jɛR] adj daily; (banal) everyday

**journalisme** [ʒuRnalism] nm journalism; **journaliste** nm/f journalist

**journée** [ʒuRne] nf day; **faire la ~ continue** to work over lunch

**joyau, x** [ʒwajo] nm gem, jewel

**joyeux, -euse** [ʒwajø, øz] adj joyful, merry; **~ Noël!** merry Christmas!; **~ anniversaire!** happy birthday!

**jubiler** [ʒybile] vi to be jubilant, exult

**judas** [ʒyda] nm (trou) spy-hole

**judiciaire** [ʒydisjɛʀ] *adj* judicial
**judicieux, -euse** [ʒydisjø, jøz] *adj* judicious
**judo** [ʒydo] *nm* judo
**juge** [ʒyʒ] *nm* judge; **juge d'instruction** examining (*BRIT*) *ou* committing (*US*) magistrate; **juge de paix** justice of the peace
**jugé** [ʒyʒe] : **au ~** *adv* by guesswork
**jugement** [ʒyʒmɑ̃] *nm* judgment; (*Jur: au pénal*) sentence; (: *au civil*) decision
**juger** [ʒyʒe] *vt* to judge; (*estimer*) to consider; **~ qn/qch satisfaisant** to consider sb/sth (to be) satisfactory; **~ bon de faire** to see fit to do
**juif, -ive** [ʒɥif, ʒɥiv] *adj* Jewish ▷ *nm/f*: **J~, ive** Jew (Jewess)
**juillet** [ʒɥijɛ] *nm* July

● **14 JUILLET**
●
● **Le 14 juillet** is a national holiday
● in France and commemorates the
● storming of the Bastille during the
● French Revolution. Throughout
● the country there are celebrations,
● which feature parades, music,
● dancing and firework displays. In
● Paris a military parade along the
● Champs-Élysées is attended by the
● President.

**juin** [ʒɥɛ̃] *nm* June
**jumeau, -elle, x** [ʒymo, ɛl] *adj, nm/f* twin
**jumeler** [ʒym(ə)le] *vt* to twin
**jumelle** [ʒymɛl] *adj, nf voir* **jumeau**; **jumelles** *nfpl* (*appareil*) binoculars
**jument** [ʒymɑ̃] *nf* mare
**jungle** [ʒœ̃gl] *nf* jungle
**jupe** [ʒyp] *nf* skirt
**jupon** [ʒypɔ̃] *nm* waist slip
**juré, e** [ʒyʀe] *nm/f* juror ▷ *adj*: **ennemi ~** sworn enemy
**jurer** [ʒyʀe] *vt* (*obéissance etc*) to swear, vow ▷ *vi* (*dire des jurons*) to swear, curse; (*dissoner*): **~ (avec)** to clash (with); **~ de faire/que** to swear to do/that; **~ de**

**qch** (*s'en porter garant*) to swear to sth
**juridique** [ʒyʀidik] *adj* legal
**juron** [ʒyʀɔ̃] *nm* curse, swearword
**jury** [ʒyʀi] *nm* jury; (*Art, Sport*) panel of judges; (*Scol*) board of examiners
**jus** [ʒy] *nm* juice; (*de viande*) gravy, (meat) juice; **jus de fruit** fruit juice
**jusque** [ʒysk]: **jusqu'à** *prép* (*endroit*) as far as, (up) to; (*moment*) until, till; (*limite*) up to; **~ sur/dans** up to; (*y compris*) even on/in; **jusqu'à ce que** until; **jusqu'à présent** *ou* **maintenant** so far; **jusqu'où?** how far?
**justaucorps** [ʒystokɔʀ] *nm* leotard
**juste** [ʒyst] *adj* (*équitable*) just, fair; (*légitime*) just; (*exact*) right; (*pertinent*) apt; (*étroit*) tight; (*insuffisant*) on the short side ▷ *adv* rightly, correctly; (*chanter*) in tune; (*exactement, seulement*) just; **~ assez/au-dessus** just enough/above; **au ~** exactly; **le ~ milieu** the happy medium; **c'était ~** it was a close thing; **pouvoir tout ~ faire** to be only just able to do; **justement** *adv* justly; (*précisément*) just, precisely; **justesse** *nf* (*précision*) accuracy; (*d'une remarque*) aptness; (*d'une opinion*) soundness; **de justesse** only just
**justice** [ʒystis] *nf* (*équité*) fairness, justice; (*Admin*) justice; **rendre ~ à qn** to do sb justice
**justificatif, -ive** [ʒystifikatif, iv] *adj* (*document*) supporting; **pièce justificative** written proof
**justifier** [ʒystifje] *vt* to justify; **~ de** to prove
**juteux, -euse** [ʒytø, øz] *adj* juicy
**juvénile** [ʒyvenil] *adj* youthful

**kiwi** [kiwi] *nm* kiwi
**klaxon** [klaksɔn] *nm* horn; **klaxonner**
  *vi, vt* to hoot (*BRIT*), honk (*US*)
**km** *abr* = **kilomètre**
**km/h** *abr* (= *kilomètres/heure*) ≈ mph
**K.-O.** (*fam*) *adj inv* shattered, knackered
**Kosovo** [kɔsɔvo] *nm* Kosovo
**Koweit, Kuweit** [kɔwɛt] *nm:* **le ~**
  Kuwait
**k-way®** [kawɛ] *nm* (lightweight nylon)
  cagoule
**kyste** [kist] *nm* cyst

**K** [ka] *nm* (*Inform*) K
**kaki** [kaki] *adj inv* khaki
**kangourou** [kãguʀu] *nm* kangaroo
**karaté** [kaʀate] *nm* karate
**kascher** [kaʃɛʀ] *adj* kosher
**kayak** [kajak] *nm* canoe, kayak; **faire**
  **du ~** to go canoeing
**képi** [kepi] *nm* kepi
**kermesse** [kɛʀmɛs] *nf* fair; (*fête de*
  *charité*) bazaar, (charity) fête
**kidnapper** [kidnape] *vt* to kidnap
**kilo** [kilo] *nm* = **kilogramme**
**kilo...:** **kilogramme** *nm* kilogramme;
  **kilométrage** *nm* number of kilometres
  travelled, ≈ mileage; **kilomètre** *nm*
  kilometre; **kilométrique** *adj* (*distance*)
  in kilometres
**kinésithérapeute** [kineziteʀapøt]
  *nm/f* physiotherapist
**kiosque** [kjɔsk] *nm* kiosk, stall
**kir** [kiʀ] *nm* kir (*white wine with*
  *blackcurrant liqueur*)
**kit** [kit] *nm* kit; **~ piéton** *ou* **mains libres**
  hands-free kit; **en ~** in kit form

*remarque*) to let slip, come out with ▷ *vi*
(*freins*) to fail; **~ les amarres** (*Navig*) to
cast off (the moorings); **~ prise** to let go

**lacrymogène** [lakʀimɔʒɛn] *adj*: **gaz
~** teargas

**lacune** [lakyn] *nf* gap

**là-dedans** [ladədɑ̃] *adv* inside (there),
in it; (*fig*) in that

**là-dessous** [ladsu] *adv* underneath,
under there; (*fig*) behind that

**là-dessus** [ladsy] *adv* on there; (*fig*:
*sur ces mots*) at that point; (: *à ce sujet*)
about that

**lagune** [lagyn] *nf* lagoon

**là-haut** [lao] *adv* up there

**laid, e** [lɛ, lɛd] *adj* ugly; **laideur** *nf*
ugliness *no pl*

**lainage** [lɛnaʒ] *nm* (*vêtement*) woollen
garment; (*étoffe*) woollen material

**laine** [lɛn] *nf* wool

**laïque** [laik] *adj* lay, civil; (*Scol*) state *cpd*
▷ *nm/f* layman(-woman)

**laisse** [lɛs] *nf* (*de chien*) lead, leash; **tenir
en ~** to keep on a lead *ou* leash

**laisser** [lese] *vt* to leave ▷ *vb aux*: **~ qn
faire** to let sb do; **se ~ aller** to let o.s.
go; **laisse-toi faire** let me (*ou* him *etc*)
do it; **laisser-aller** *nm* carelessness,
slovenliness; **laissez-passer** *nm
inv* pass

**lait** [lɛ] *nm* milk; **frère/sœur de ~** foster
brother/sister; **lait concentré/
condensé** condensed/evaporated
milk; **lait écrémé/entier** skimmed/
full-cream (*BRIT*) *ou* whole milk; **laitage**
*nm* dairy product; **laiterie** *nf* dairy;
**laitier, -ière** *adj* dairy *cpd* ▷ *nm/f*
milkman (dairywoman)

**laiton** [lɛtɔ̃] *nm* brass

**laitue** [lety] *nf* lettuce

**lambeau, x** [lɑ̃bo] *nm* scrap; **en ~x** in
tatters, tattered

**lame** [lam] *nf* blade; (*vague*) wave;
(*lamelle*) strip; **lame de fond** ground
swell *no pl*; **lame de rasoir** razor blade;
**lamelle** *nf* thin strip *ou* blade

**lamentable** [lamɑ̃tabl] *adj* appalling

**lamenter** [lamɑ̃te] *vb*: **se ~ (sur)** to

**l'** [l] *art déf voir* **le**

**la** [la] *art déf voir* **le** ▷ *nm* (*Mus*) A; (*en
chantant la gamme*) la

**là** [la] *adv* there; (*ici*) here; (*dans le temps*)
then; **elle n'est pas là** she isn't here;
**c'est là que** this is where; **là où** where;
**de là** (*fig*) hence; **par là** (*fig*) by that; *voir
aussi* **-ci**; **ce**; **celui**; **là-bas** *adv* there

**laboratoire** [labɔʀatwaʀ] *nm*
laboratory; **laboratoire de langues**
language laboratory

**laborieux, -euse** [labɔʀjø, jøz] *adj*
(*tâche*) laborious

**labourer** *vt* to plough

**labyrinthe** [labiʀɛ̃t] *nm* labyrinth,
maze

**lac** [lak] *nm* lake

**lacet** [lasɛ] *nm* (*de chaussure*) lace; (*de
route*) sharp bend; (*piège*) snare

**lâche** [lɑʃ] *adj* (*poltron*) cowardly;
(*desserré*) loose, slack ▷ *nm/f* coward

**lâcher** [lɑʃe] *vt* to let go of; (*ce qui tombe,
abandonner*) to drop; (*oiseau, animal:
libérer*) to release, set free; (*fig: mot,*

moan (over)

**lampadaire** [lɑ̃padɛʀ] nm (de salon) standard lamp; (dans la rue) street lamp

**lampe** [lɑ̃p] nf lamp; (Tech) valve; **lampe à bronzer** sun lamp; **lampe à pétrole** oil lamp; **lampe de poche** torch (BRIT), flashlight (US); **lampe halogène** halogen lamp

**lance** [lɑ̃s] nf spear; **lance d'incendie** fire hose

**lancée** [lɑ̃se] nf: **être/continuer sur sa ~** to be under way/keep going

**lancement** [lɑ̃smɑ̃] nm launching

**lance-pierres** [lɑ̃spjɛʀ] nm inv catapult

**lancer** [lɑ̃se] nm (Sport) throwing no pl, throw ▷ vt to throw; (émettre, projeter) to throw out, send out; (produit, fusée, bateau, artiste) to launch; (injure) to hurl, fling; **se lancer** vi (prendre de l'élan) to build up speed; (se précipiter): **se ~ sur** ou **contre** to rush at; **se ~ dans** (discussion) to launch into; (aventure) to embark on; **~ qch à qn** to throw sth to sb; (de façon agressive) to throw sth at sb; **~ un cri** ou **un appel** to shout ou call out; **lancer du poids** putting the shot

**landau** [lɑ̃do] nm pram (BRIT), baby carriage (US)

**lande** [lɑ̃d] nf moor

**langage** [lɑ̃gaʒ] nm language

**langouste** [lɑ̃gust] nf crayfish inv; **langoustine** nf Dublin Bay prawn

**langue** [lɑ̃g] nf (Anat, Culin) tongue; (Ling) language; **tirer la ~ (à)** to stick out one's tongue (at); **de ~ française** French-speaking; **quelles ~s parlez-vous?** what languages do you speak?; **langue maternelle** native language, mother tongue; **langues vivantes** modern languages

**langueur** [lɑ̃gœʀ] nf languidness

**languir** [lɑ̃giʀ] vi to languish; (conversation) to flag; **faire ~ qn** to keep sb waiting

**lanière** [lanjɛʀ] nf (de fouet) lash; (de sac, bretelle) strap

**lanterne** [lɑ̃tɛʀn] nf (portable) lantern;

(électrique) light, lamp; (de voiture) (side)light

**laper** [lape] vt to lap up

**lapidaire** [lapidɛʀ] adj (fig) terse

**lapin** [lapɛ̃] nm rabbit; (peau) rabbitskin; (fourrure) cony; **poser un ~ à qn** (fam) to stand sb up

**Laponie** [laponi] nf Lapland

**laps** [laps] nm: **~ de temps** space of time, time no pl

**laque** [lak] nf (vernis) lacquer; (pour cheveux) hair spray

**laquelle** [lakɛl] pron voir **lequel**

**larcin** [laʀsɛ̃] nm theft

**lard** [laʀ] nm (bacon) (streaky) bacon; (graisse) fat

**lardon** [laʀdɔ̃] nm: **~s** chopped bacon

**large** [laʀʒ] adj wide, broad; (fig) generous ▷ adv: **calculer/voir ~** to allow extra/think big ▷ nm (largeur): **5 m de ~** 5 m wide ou in width; (mer): **le ~** the open sea; **au ~ de** off; **large d'esprit** broad-minded; **largement** adv widely; (de loin) greatly; (au moins) easily; (généreusement) generously; **c'est largement suffisant** that's ample; **largesse** nf generosity; **largesses** nfpl (dons) liberalities; **largeur** nf (qu'on mesure) width; (impression visuelle) wideness, width; (d'esprit) broadness

**larguer** [laʀge] vt to drop; **~ les amarres** to cast off (the moorings)

**larme** [laʀm] nf tear; (fam: goutte) drop; **en ~s** in tears; **larmoyer** vi (yeux) to water; (se plaindre) to whimper

**larvé, e** [laʀve] adj (fig) latent

**laryngite** [laʀɛ̃ʒit] nf laryngitis

**las, lasse** [lɑ, lɑs] adj weary

**laser** [lazɛʀ] nm: **(rayon) ~** laser (beam); **chaîne** ou **platine ~** laser disc (player); **disque ~** laser disc

**lasse** [lɑs] adj voir **las**

**lasser** [lɑse] vt to weary, tire; **se lasser de** vt to grow weary ou tired of

**latéral, e, -aux** [lateʀal, o] adj side cpd, lateral

**latin, e** [latɛ̃, in] adj Latin ▷ nm/f: **L~, e** Latin ▷ nm (Ling) Latin

**latitude** [latityd] *nf* latitude
**lauréat, e** [lɔʀea, at] *nm/f* winner
**laurier** [lɔʀje] *nm* (*Bot*) laurel; **feuille de ~** (*Culin*) bay leaf
**lavable** [lavabl] *adj* washable
**lavabo** [lavabo] *nm* washbasin; **lavabos** *nmpl* (*toilettes*) toilet *sg*
**lavage** [lavaʒ] *nm* washing *no pl*, wash; **lavage de cerveau** brainwashing *no pl*
**lavande** [lavɑ̃d] *nf* lavender
**lave** [lav] *nf* lava *no pl*
**lave-linge** [lavlɛ̃ʒ] *nm inv* washing machine
**laver** [lave] *vt* to wash; (*tache*) to wash off; **se laver** *vi* to have a wash, wash; **se ~ les mains/dents** to wash one's hands/clean one's teeth; **~ la vaisselle/le linge** to wash the dishes/clothes; **~ qn de** (*accusation*) to clear sb of; **laverie** *nf*: **laverie (automatique)** launderette; **lavette** *nf* dish cloth; (*fam*) drip; **laveur, -euse** *nm/f* cleaner; **lave-vaisselle** *nm inv* dishwasher; **lavoir** *nm* wash house; (*évier*) sink
**laxatif, -ive** [laksatif, iv] *adj, nm* laxative
**layette** [lɛjɛt] *nf* baby clothes

⊙ **MOT-CLÉ**

**le** [lə], **la, l'** (*pl* **les**) *art déf* **1** the; **le livre/la pomme/l'arbre** the book/the apple/the tree; **les étudiants** the students
**2** (*noms abstraits*): **le courage/l'amour/la jeunesse** courage/love/youth
**3** (*indiquant la possession*): **se casser la jambe** *etc* to break one's leg *etc*; **levez la main** put your hand up; **avoir les yeux gris/le nez rouge** to have grey eyes/a red nose
**4** (*temps*): **le matin/soir** in the morning/evening; mornings/evenings; **le jeudi** *etc* (*d'habitude*) on Thursdays *etc*; (*ce jeudi-là etc*) on (the) Thursday
**5** (*distribution, évaluation*) a, an; **10**

**euros le mètre/kilo** 10 euros a *ou* per metre/kilo; **le tiers/quart de** a third/quarter of
▷ *pron* **1** (*personne: mâle*) him; (: *femelle*) her; (: *pluriel*) them; **je le/la/les vois** I can see him/her/them
**2** (*animal, chose: singulier*) it; (: *pluriel*) them; **je le** (*ou* **la**) **vois** I can see it; **je les vois** I can see them
**3** (*remplaçant une phrase*): **je ne le savais pas** I didn't know (about it); **il était riche et ne l'est plus** he was once rich but no longer is

**lécher** [leʃe] *vt* to lick; (*laper: lait, eau*) to lick *ou* lap up; **se ~ les doigts/lèvres** to lick one's fingers/lips; **lèche-vitrines** *nm*: **faire du lèche-vitrines** to go window-shopping
**leçon** [l(ə)sɔ̃] *nf* lesson; **faire la ~ à** (*fig*) to give a lecture to; **leçons de conduite** driving lessons; **leçons particulières** private lessons *ou* tuition *sg* (*BRIT*)
**lecteur, -trice** [lɛktœʀ, tʀis] *nm/f* reader; (*d'université*) foreign language assistant ▷ *nm* (*Tech*): **~ de cassettes/CD/DVD** cassette/CD/DVD player; **lecteur de disquette(s)** disk drive; **lecteur MP3** MP3 player
**lecture** [lɛktyʀ] *nf* reading
┃ Attention à ne pas traduire *lecture* par le mot anglais *lecture*.
**ledit** [lədi], **ladite** (*mpl* **lesdits**, *fpl* **lesdites**) *dét* the aforesaid
**légal, e, -aux** [legal, o] *adj* legal; **légaliser** *vt* to legalize; **légalité** *nf* law
**légendaire** [leʒɑ̃dɛʀ] *adj* legendary
**légende** [leʒɑ̃d] *nf* (*mythe*) legend; (*de carte, plan*) key; (*de dessin*) caption
**léger, -ère** [leʒe, ɛʀ] *adj* light; (*bruit, retard*) slight; (*personne: superficiel*) thoughtless; (: *volage*) free and easy; **à la légère** (*parler, agir*) rashly, thoughtlessly; **légèrement** *adv* (*s'habiller, bouger*) lightly; (*un peu*) slightly; **manger légèrement** to eat a light meal; **légèreté** *nf* lightness; (*d'une remarque*) flippancy

**législatif, -ive** [leʒislatif, iv] adj
legislative; **législatives** nfpl general
election sg
**légitime** [leʒitim] adj (Jur) lawful,
legitimate; (fig) rightful, legitimate; **en
état de ~ défense** in self-defence
**legs** [lɛg] nm legacy
**léguer** [lege] vt: **~ qch à qn** (Jur) to
bequeath sth to sb
**légume** [legym] nm vegetable;
**légumes secs** pulses; **légumes verts**
green vegetables, greens
**lendemain** [lɑ̃dmɛ̃] nm: **le ~** the next
ou following day; **le ~ matin/soir** the
next ou following morning/evening; **le
~ de** the day after
**lent, e** [lɑ̃, lɑ̃t] adj slow; **lentement** adv
slowly; **lenteur** nf slowness no pl
**lentille** [lɑ̃tij] nf (Optique) lens sg;
(Culin) lentil; **lentilles de contact**
contact lenses
**léopard** [leɔpaʀ] nm leopard
**lèpre** [lɛpʀ] nf leprosy

**MOT-CLÉ**

**lequel, laquelle** [ləkɛl, lakɛl] (mpl
**lesquels**, fpl **lesquelles**) (à + lequel =
**auquel**, de + lequel = **duquel** etc) pron
1 (interrogatif) which, which one; **lequel
des deux?** which one?
2 (relatif: personne: sujet) who; (: objet,
après préposition) whom; (: chose) which
▷ adj: **auquel cas** in which case

**les** [le] dét voir **le**
**lesbienne** [lɛsbjɛn] nf lesbian
**léser** [leze] vt to wrong
**lésiner** [lezine] vi: **ne pas ~ sur les
moyens** (pour mariage etc) to push the
boat out
**lésion** [lezjɔ̃] nf lesion, damage no pl
**lessive** [lesiv] nf (poudre) washing
powder; (linge) washing no pl, wash;
**lessiver** vt to wash; (fam: fatiguer) to
tire out, exhaust
**lest** [lɛst] nm ballast
**leste** [lɛst] adj sprightly, nimble

**lettre** [lɛtʀ] nf letter; **lettres** nfpl
(littérature) literature sg; (Scol) arts
(subjects); **en toutes ~s**
in full; **lettre piégée** letter bomb
**leucémie** [løsemi] nf leukaemia

**MOT-CLÉ**

**leur** [lœʀ] adj possessif their; **leur
maison** their house; **leurs amis** their
friends
▷ pron 1 (objet indirect) (to) them; **je leur
ai dit la vérité** I told them the truth;
**je le leur ai donné** I gave it to them, I
gave them it
2 (possessif): **le(la) leur, les leurs** theirs

**levain** [ləvɛ̃] nm leaven
**levé, e** [ləve] adj: **être ~** to be up; **levée**
nf (Postes) collection
**lever** [l(ə)ve] vt (vitre, bras etc) to raise;
(soulever de terre, supprimer: interdiction,
siège) to lift; (impôts, armée) to levy ▷ vi
to rise ▷ nm: **au ~** on getting up; **se
lever** vi to get up; (soleil) to rise; (jour)
to break; (brouillard) to lift; **ça va se ~**
(temps) it's going to clear up; **lever de
soleil** sunrise; **lever du jour** daybreak
**levier** [ləvje] nm lever
**lèvre** [lɛvʀ] nf lip
**lévrier** [levʀije] nm greyhound
**levure** [l(ə)vyʀ] nf yeast; **levure
chimique** baking powder
**lexique** [lɛksik] nm vocabulary;
(glossaire) lexicon
**lézard** [lezaʀ] nm lizard
**lézarde** [lezaʀd] nf crack
**liaison** [ljɛzɔ̃] nf (rapport) connection;
(transport) link; (amoureuse) affair;
(Phonétique) liaison; **entrer/être en ~
avec** to get/be in contact with
**liane** [ljan] nf creeper
**liasse** [ljas] nf wad, bundle
**Liban** [libɑ̃] nm: **le ~** (the) Lebanon
**libeller** [libele] vt (chèque, mandat): **~
(au nom de)** to make out (to); (lettre)
to word
**libellule** [libelyl] nf dragonfly

**libéral, e, -aux** [libeʀal, o] *adj,
nm/f* liberal; **profession ~e** (liberal)
profession
**libérer** [libeʀe] *vt* (*délivrer*) to free,
liberate; (*relâcher: prisonnier*) to
discharge, release; (: *d'inhibitions*) to
liberate; (*gaz*) to release; **se libérer** *vi*
(*de rendez-vous*) to get out of previous
engagements
**liberté** [libeʀte] *nf* freedom; (*loisir*) free
time; **libertés** *nfpl* (*privautés*) liberties;
**mettre/être en ~** to set/be free; **en ~
provisoire/surveillée/conditionnelle**
on bail/probation/parole
**libraire** [libʀɛʀ] *nm/f* bookseller
**librairie** [libʀɛʀi] *nf* bookshop

Attention à ne pas traduire *librairie*
par *library*.

**libre** [libʀ] *adj* free; (*route, voie*) clear;
(*place, salle*) free; (*ligne*) not engaged;
(*Scol*) non-state; **~ de qch/de faire** free
from sth/to do; **la place est ~?** is this
seat free?; **libre arbitre** free will; **libre-
échange** *nm* free trade; **libre-service**
*nm* self-service store
**Libye** [libi] *nf:* **la ~** Libya
**licence** [lisɑ̃s] *nf* (*permis*) permit;
(*diplôme*) degree; (*liberté*) liberty;
**licencié, e** *nm/f* (*Scol*): **licencié
ès lettres/en droit** ≈ Bachelor of
Arts/Law
**licenciement** [lisɑ̃simɑ̃] *nm*
redundancy
**licencier** [lisɑ̃sje] *vt* (*débaucher*) to
make redundant, lay off; (*renvoyer*)
to dismiss
**licite** [lisit] *adj* lawful
**lie** [li] *nf* dregs *pl*, sediment
**lié, e** [lje] *adj:* **très ~ avec** very friendly
with *ou* close to
**Liechtenstein** [liʃtɛnʃtain] *nm:* **le ~**
Liechtenstein
**liège** [ljɛʒ] *nm* cork
**lien** [ljɛ̃] *nm* (*corde, fig: affectif*) bond;
(*rapport*) link, connection; **lien de
parenté** family tie; **lien hypertexte**
hyperlink
**lier** [lje] *vt* (*attacher*) to tie up; (*joindre*)

to link up; (*fig: unir, engager*) to bind;
**~ conversation (avec)** to strike up a
conversation (with); **~ connaissance
avec** to get to know
**lierre** [ljɛʀ] *nm* ivy
**lieu, x** [ljø] *nm* place; **lieux** *nmpl*
(*locaux*) premises; (*endroit: d'un accident
etc*) scene *sg*; **en ~ sûr** in a safe place; **en
premier ~** in the first place; **en dernier
~** lastly; **avoir ~** to take place; **tenir ~
de** to serve as; **donner ~ à** to give rise
to; **au ~ de** instead of; **arriver/être sur
les ~x** to arrive at/be on the scene; **lieu
commun** cliché; **lieu-dit** (*pl* **lieux-dits**)
*nm* locality
**lieutenant** [ljøt(ə)nɑ̃] *nm* lieutenant
**lièvre** [ljɛvʀ] *nm* hare
**ligament** [ligamɑ̃] *nm* ligament
**ligne** [liɲ] *nf* (*gén*) line; (*Transports:
liaison*) service; (: *trajet*) route;
(*silhouette*) figure; **garder la ~** to keep
one's figure; **entrer en ~ de compte** to
come into it; **en ~** (*Inform*) online; **~ fixe**
(*Tél*) land line (phone)
**lignée** [liɲe] *nf* line, lineage
**ligoter** [ligɔte] *vt* to tie up
**ligue** [lig] *nf* league
**lilas** [lila] *nm* lilac
**limace** [limas] *nf* slug
**limande** [limɑ̃d] *nf* dab
**lime** [lim] *nf* file; **lime à ongles** nail file;
**limer** *vt* to file
**limitation** [limitasjɔ̃] *nf:* **limitation
de vitesse** speed limit
**limite** [limit] *nf* (*de terrain*) boundary;
(*partie ou point extrême*) limit; **à la ~** (*au
pire*) if the worst comes (*ou* came) to the
worst; **vitesse/charge ~** maximum
speed/load; **cas ~** borderline
case; **date ~** deadline; **date ~ de
vente/consommation** sell-by/best-
before date; **limiter** *vt* (*restreindre*) to
limit, restrict; (*délimiter*) to border;
**limitrophe** *adj* border *cpd*
**limoger** [limɔʒe] *vt* to dismiss
**limon** [limɔ̃] *nm* silt
**limonade** [limɔnad] *nf* lemonade
**lin** [lɛ̃] *nm* (*tissu*) linen

**linceul** [lɛ̃sœl] nm shroud

**linge** [lɛ̃ʒ] nm (serviettes etc) linen; (lessive) washing; (aussi: ~ **de corps**) underwear; **lingerie** nf lingerie, underwear

**lingot** [lɛ̃go] nm ingot

**linguistique** [lɛ̃ɡµistik] adj linguistic ▷ nf linguistics sg

**lion, ne** [ljɔ̃, ljɔn] nm/f lion (lioness); (signe): **le L~** Leo; **lionceau, x** nm lion cub

**liqueur** [likœʀ] nf liqueur

**liquidation** [likidasjɔ̃] nf (vente) sale

**liquide** [likid] adj liquid ▷ nm liquid; (Comm): **en ~** in ready money ou cash; **je n'ai pas de ~** I haven't got any cash; **liquider** vt to liquidate; (Comm: articles) to clear, sell off

**lire** [liʀ] nf (monnaie) lira ▷ vt, vi to read

**lis** [lis] nm = **lys**

**Lisbonne** [lizbɔn] n Lisbon

**lisible** [lizibl] adj legible

**lisière** [lizjɛʀ] nf (de forêt) edge

**lisons** [lizɔ̃] vb voir **lire**

**lisse** [lis] adj smooth

**liste** [list] nf list; **faire la ~ de** to list; **liste de mariage** wedding (present) list; **liste électorale** electoral roll; **listing** nm (Inform) printout

**lit** [li] nm bed; **petit ~, ~ à une place** single bed; **grand ~, ~ à deux places** double bed; **faire son ~** to make one's bed; **aller/se mettre au ~** to go to/get into bed; **lit de camp** campbed; **lit d'enfant** cot (BRIT), crib (US)

**literie** [litʀi] nf bedding, bedclothes pl

**litige** [litiʒ] nm dispute

**litre** [litʀ] nm litre

**littéraire** [liteʀɛʀ] adj literary ▷ nm/f arts student; **elle est très ~** she's very literary

**littéral, e, -aux** [liteʀal, o] adj literal

**littérature** [liteʀatyʀ] nf literature

**littoral, -aux** [litɔʀal, o] nm coast

**livide** [livid] adj livid, pallid

**livraison** [livʀɛzɔ̃] nf delivery

**livre** [livʀ] nm book ▷ nf (monnaie) pound; (poids) half a kilo, ≈ pound; **livre de poche** paperback

**livré, e** [livʀe] adj: **~ à soi-même** left to o.s. ou one's own devices

**livrer** [livʀe] vt (Comm) to deliver; (otage, coupable) to hand over; (secret, information) to give away; **se livrer à** (se confier) to confide in; (se rendre, s'abandonner) to give o.s. up to; (faire: pratiques, actes) to indulge in; (enquête) to carry out

**livret** [livʀɛ] nm booklet; (d'opéra) libretto; **livret de caisse d'épargne** (savings) bank-book; **livret de famille** (official) family record book; **livret scolaire** (school) report book

**livreur, -euse** [livʀœʀ, øz] nm/f delivery boy ou man/girl ou woman

**local, e, -aux** [lɔkal] adj local ▷ nm (salle) premises pl; voir aussi **locaux**; **localité** nf locality

**locataire** [lɔkatɛʀ] nm/f tenant; (de chambre) lodger

**location** [lɔkasjɔ̃] nf (par le locataire, le loueur) renting; (par le propriétaire) renting out, letting; (Théâtre) booking office; **"~ de voitures"** "car rental"; **habiter en ~** to live in rented accommodation; **prendre une ~ (pour les vacances)** to rent a house etc (for the holidays)

> Attention à ne pas traduire location par le mot anglais location.

**locomotive** [lɔkɔmɔtiv] nf locomotive, engine

**locution** [lɔkysjɔ̃] nf phrase

**loge** [lɔʒ] nf (Théâtre: d'artiste) dressing room; (: de spectateurs) box; (de concierge, franc-maçon) lodge

**logement** [lɔʒmɑ̃] nm accommodation no pl (BRIT), accommodations pl (US); (appartement) flat (BRIT), apartment (US); (Pol, Admin): **le ~** housing no pl

**loger** [lɔʒe] vt to accommodate ▷ vi to live; **être logé, nourri** to have board and lodging; **se loger** vr: **trouver à se ~** to find somewhere to live; **se ~ dans** (suj: balle, flèche) to lodge itself in;

**logeur, -euse** *nm/f* landlord(-lady)
**logiciel** [lɔʒisjɛl] *nm* software
**logique** [lɔʒik] *adj* logical ▷ *nf* logic
**logo** [lɔgo] *nm* logo
**loi** [lwa] *nf* law; **faire la ~** to lay down the law
**loin** [lwɛ̃] *adv* far; (*dans le temps: futur*) a long way off; (: *passé*) a long time ago; **plus ~** further; **~ de** far from; **c'est ~ d'ici?** is it far from here?; **au ~** far off; **de ~** from a distance; (*fig: de beaucoup*) by far
**lointain, e** [lwɛ̃tɛ̃, ɛn] *adj* faraway, distant; (*dans le futur, passé*) distant; (*cause, parent*) remote, distant ▷ *nm*: **dans le ~** in the distance
**loir** [lwaʀ] *nm* dormouse
**Loire** [lwaʀ] *nf*: **la ~** the (River) Loire
**loisir** [lwaziʀ] *nm*: **heures de ~** spare time; **loisirs** *nmpl* (*temps libre*) leisure *sg*; (*activités*) leisure activities; **avoir le ~ de faire** to have the time *ou* opportunity to do; **à ~** at leisure
**londonien, ne** [lɔ̃dɔnjɛ̃, jɛn] *adj* London *cpd*, of London ▷ *nm/f*: **L~, ne** Londoner
**Londres** [lɔ̃dʀ] *n* London
**long, longue** [lɔ̃, lɔ̃g] *adj* long ▷ *adv*: **en savoir ~** to know a great deal ▷ *nm*: **de 3 m de ~** 3 m long, 3 m in length; **ne pas faire ~ feu** not to last long; **(tout) le ~ de** (all) along; **tout au ~ de** (*année, vie*) throughout; **de ~ en large** (*marcher*) to and fro, up and down; *voir aussi* **longue**
**longer** [lɔ̃ʒe] *vt* to go (*ou* walk *ou* drive) along(side); (*suj: mur, route*) to border
**longiligne** [lɔ̃ʒiliɲ] *adj* long-limbed
**longitude** [lɔ̃ʒityd] *nf* longitude
**longtemps** [lɔ̃tɑ̃] *adv* (for) a long time, (for) long; **avant ~** before long; **pour** *ou* **pendant ~** for a long time; **mettre ~ à faire** to take a long time to do; **il en a pour ~?** will he be long?
**longue** [lɔ̃g] *adj voir* **long** ▷ *nf*: **à la ~** in the end; **longuement** *adv* (*longtemps*) for a long time; (*en détail*) at length
**longueur** [lɔ̃gœʀ] *nf* length;

**longueurs** *nfpl* (*fig: d'un film etc*) tedious parts; **en ~** lengthwise; **tirer en ~** to drag on; **à ~ de journée** all day long
**loquet** [lɔkɛ] *nm* latch
**lorgner** [lɔʀɲe] *vt* to eye; (*fig*) to have one's eye on
**lors** [lɔʀ]: **~ de** *prép* at the time of; during
**lorsque** [lɔʀsk] *conj* when, as
**losange** [lɔzɑ̃ʒ] *nm* diamond
**lot** [lo] *nm* (*part*) share; (*de loterie*) prize; (*fig: destin*) fate, lot; (*Comm, Inform*) batch; **le gros ~** the jackpot
**loterie** [lɔtʀi] *nf* lottery
**lotion** [losjɔ̃] *nf* lotion; **lotion après rasage** aftershave (lotion)
**lotissement** [lɔtismɑ̃] *nm* housing development; (*parcelle*) plot, lot
**loto** [lɔto] *nm* lotto
**lotte** [lɔt] *nf* monkfish
**louanges** [lwɑ̃ʒ] *nfpl* praise *sg*
**loubard** [lubaʀ] (*fam*) *nm* lout
**louche** [luʃ] *adj* shady, fishy, dubious ▷ *nf* ladle; **loucher** *vi* to squint
**louer** [lwe] *vt* (*maison: suj: propriétaire*) to let, rent (out); (: *locataire*) to rent; (*voiture etc: entreprise*) to hire out (BRIT), rent (out); (: *locataire*) to hire, rent; (*réserver*) to book; (*faire l'éloge de*) to praise; **"à ~"** "to let" (BRIT), "for rent" (US); **je voudrais ~ une voiture** I'd like to hire (BRIT) *ou* rent (US) a car
**loup** [lu] *nm* wolf; **jeune ~** young go-getter
**loupe** [lup] *nf* magnifying glass; **à la ~** in minute detail
**louper** [lupe] (*fam*) *vt* (*manquer*) to miss; (*examen*) to flunk
**lourd, e** [luʀ, luʀd] *adj, adv* heavy; **c'est trop ~** it's too heavy; **~ de** (*conséquences, menaces*) charged with; **il fait ~** the weather is close, it's sultry; **lourdaud, e** (*péj*) *adj* clumsy; **lourdement** *adv* heavily
**loutre** [lutʀ] *nf* otter
**louveteau, x** [luv(ə)to] *nm* wolf-cub; (*scout*) cub (scout)
**louvoyer** [luvwaje] *vi* (*fig*) to hedge,

evade the issue

**loyal, e, -aux** [lwajal, o] *adj* (*fidèle*) loyal, faithful; (*fair-play*) fair; **loyauté** *nf* loyalty, faithfulness; fairness

**loyer** [lwaje] *nm* rent

**lu, e** [ly] *pp de* **lire**

**lubie** [lybi] *nf* whim, craze

**lubrifiant** [lybrifjɑ̃] *nm* lubricant

**lubrifier** [lybrifje] *vt* to lubricate

**lubrique** [lybrik] *adj* lecherous

**lucarne** [lykarn] *nf* skylight

**lucide** [lysid] *adj* lucid; (*accidenté*) conscious

**lucratif, -ive** [lykratif, iv] *adj* lucrative, profitable; **à but non ~** non profit-making

**lueur** [lɥœr] *nf* (*pâle*) (faint) light; (*chatoyante*) glimmer *no pl*; (*fig*) glimmer; gleam

**luge** [lyʒ] *nf* sledge (BRIT), sled (US)

**lugubre** [lygybr] *adj* gloomy, dismal

◯ **MOT-CLÉ**

**lui** [lɥi] *pron* **1** (*objet indirect: mâle*) (to) him; (: *femelle*) (to) her; (: *chose, animal*) (to) it; **je lui ai parlé** I have spoken to him (*ou* to her); **il lui a offert un cadeau** he gave him (*ou* her) a present **2** (*après préposition, comparatif: personne*) him; (: *chose, animal*) it; **elle est contente de lui** she is pleased with him; **je la connais mieux que lui** I know her better than he does; I know her better than him; **ce livre est à lui** this book is his, this is his book; **c'est à lui de jouer** it's his turn *ou* go **3** (*sujet, forme emphatique*) he; **il est à Paris** HE is in Paris; **c'est lui qui l'a fait** HE did it **4** (*objet, forme emphatique*) him; **c'est lui que j'attends** I'm waiting for HIM **5**: **lui-même** himself; itself

**luire** [lɥir] *vi* to shine; (*en rougeoyant*) to glow

**lumière** [lymjɛr] *nf* light; **mettre en ~** (*fig*) to highlight; **lumière du jour** daylight

**luminaire** [lyminɛr] *nm* lamp, light

**lumineux, -euse** [lyminø, øz] *adj* luminous; (*éclairé*) illuminated; (*ciel, couleur*) bright; (*rayon*) of light, light *cpd*; (*fig: regard*) radiant

**lunatique** [lynatik] *adj* whimsical, temperamental

**lundi** [lœ̃di] *nm* Monday; **on est ~** it's Monday; **le(s) ~(s)** on Mondays; **"à ~"** "see you on Monday"; **lundi de Pâques** Easter Monday

**lune** [lyn] *nf* moon; **lune de miel** honeymoon

**lunette** [lynɛt] *nf*: **~s** *nfpl* glasses, spectacles; (*protectrices*) goggles; **lunette arrière** (*Auto*) rear window; **lunettes de soleil** sunglasses; **lunettes noires** dark glasses

**lustre** [lystr] *nm* (*de plafond*) chandelier; (*fig: éclat*) lustre; **lustrer** *vt* to shine

**luth** [lyt] *nm* lute

**lutin** [lytɛ̃] *nm* imp, goblin

**lutte** [lyt] *nf* (*conflit*) struggle; (*sport*) wrestling; **lutter** *vi* to fight, struggle

**luxe** [lyks] *nm* luxury; **de ~** luxury *cpd*

**Luxembourg** [lyksɑ̃bur] *nm*: **le ~** Luxembourg

**luxer** [lykse] *vt*: **se ~ l'épaule** to dislocate one's shoulder

**luxueux, -euse** [lyksɥø, øz] *adj* luxurious

**lycée** [lise] *nm* ≈ secondary school; **lycéen, ne** *nm/f* secondary school pupil

**Lyon** [ljɔ̃] *n* Lyons

**lyophilisé, e** [ljɔfilize] *adj* (*café*) freeze-dried

**lyrique** [lirik] *adj* lyrical; (*Opéra*) lyric; **artiste ~** opera singer

**lys** [lis] *nm* lily

# m

**M** *abr* = **Monsieur**

**m'** [m] *pron voir* **me**

**ma** [ma] *adj voir* **mon**

**macaron** [makaʀɔ̃] *nm* (*gâteau*) macaroon; (*insigne*) (round) badge

**macaronis** [makaʀɔni] *nmpl* macaroni *sg*; **~ au fromage** *ou* **en gratin** macaroni cheese (*BRIT*), macaroni and cheese (*US*)

**macédoine** [masedwan] *nf*: **~ de fruits** fruit salad; **~ de légumes** mixed vegetables; **la M~** Macedonia

**macérer** [maseʀe] *vi*, *vt* to macerate; (*dans du vinaigre*) to pickle

**mâcher** [maʃe] *vt* to chew; **ne pas ~ ses mots** not to mince one's words

**machin** [maʃɛ̃] (*fam*) *nm* thing(umajig); (*personne*): **M~(e)** *nm(f)* what's-his(*ou* her)-name

**machinal, e, -aux** [maʃinal, o] *adj* mechanical, automatic

**machination** [maʃinasjɔ̃] *nf* frame-up

**machine** [maʃin] *nf* machine; (*locomotive*) engine; **machine à laver/**
coudre washing/sewing machine; **machine à sous** fruit machine

**mâchoire** [maʃwaʀ] *nf* jaw

**mâchonner** [maʃɔne] *vt* to chew (at)

**maçon** [masɔ̃] *nm* builder; (*poseur de briques*) bricklayer; **maçonnerie** *nf* (*murs*) brickwork; (*pierres*) masonry, stonework

**Madagascar** [madagaskaʀ] *nf* Madagascar

**Madame** [madam] (*pl* **Mesdames**) *nf*: **~ Dupont** Mrs Dupont; **occupez-vous de ~/Monsieur/Mademoiselle** please serve this lady/gentleman/(young) lady; **bonjour ~/Monsieur/Mademoiselle** good morning; (*ton déférent*) good morning Madam/Sir/Madam; (*le nom est connu*) good morning Mrs/Mr/Miss X; **~/Monsieur/Mademoiselle!** (*pour appeler*) Madam/Sir/Miss!; **~/Monsieur/Mademoiselle** (*sur lettre*) Dear Madam/Sir/Madam; **chère ~/ cher Monsieur/chère Mademoiselle** Dear Mrs/Mr/Miss X; **Mesdames** Ladies; **mesdames, mesdemoiselles, messieurs** ladies and gentlemen

**madeleine** [madlɛn] *nf* madeleine, *small sponge cake*

**Mademoiselle** [madmwazɛl] (*pl* **Mesdemoiselles**) *nf* Miss; *voir aussi* **Madame**

**madère** [madɛʀ] *nm* Madeira (wine)

**Madrid** [madʀid] *n* Madrid

**magasin** [magazɛ̃] *nm* (*boutique*) shop; (*entrepôt*) warehouse; **en ~** (*Comm*) in stock

- **MAGASINS**
-
- French shops are usually open from
- 9am to noon and from 2pm to 7pm.
- Most shops are closed on Sunday
- and some do not open on Monday. In
- bigger towns and shopping centres,
- most shops are open throughout
- the day.

**magazine** [magazin] *nm* magazine

**Maghreb** [magʀɛb] nm: **le ~** North Africa; **maghrébin, e** adj North African ▷ nm/f: **Maghrébin, e** North African

**magicien, ne** [maʒisjɛ̃, jɛn] nm/f magician

**magie** [maʒi] nf magic; **magique** adj magic; (enchanteur) magical

**magistral, e, -aux** [maʒistʀal, o] adj (œuvre, adresse) masterly; (ton) authoritative; **cours ~** lecture

**magistrat** [maʒistʀa] nm magistrate

**magistrature** [maʒistʀatyʀ] nf magistracy

**magnétique** [maɲetik] adj magnetic

**magnétophone** [maɲetɔfɔn] nm tape recorder; **magnétophone à cassettes** cassette recorder

**magnétoscope** [maɲetɔskɔp] nm video-tape recorder

**magnifique** [maɲifik] adj magnificent

**magret** [magʀɛ] nm: **~ de canard** duck steaklet

**mai** [mɛ] nm May

● **MAI**
●
●
● **Le premier mai** is a public holiday
● in France and commemorates the
● trades union demonstrations in the
● United States in 1886 when workers
● demanded the right to an eight-hour
● working day. Sprigs of lily of the
● valley are traditionally exchanged.
● **Le 8 mai** is also a public holiday and
● commemorates the surrender of
● the German army to Eisenhower
● on 7 May, 1945. It is marked by
● parades of ex-servicemen and ex-
● servicewomen in most towns.

**maigre** [mɛgʀ] adj (very) thin, skinny; (viande) lean; (fromage) low-fat; (végétation) thin, sparse; (fig) poor, meagre, skimpy; **jours ~s** days of abstinence, fish days; **maigreur** nf thinness; **maigrir** vi to get thinner, lose weight; **maigrir de 2 kilos** to lose 2 kilos

**mail** [mɛl] nm e-mail

**maille** [maj] nf stitch; **maille à l'endroit/l'envers** plain/purl stitch

**maillet** [majɛ] nm mallet

**maillon** [majɔ̃] nm link

**maillot** [majo] nm (aussi: **~ de corps**) vest; (de sportif) jersey; **maillot de bain** swimming ou bathing (BRIT) costume, swimsuit; (d'homme) (swimming ou bathing (BRIT)) trunks pl

**main** [mɛ̃] nf hand; **à la ~** (tenir, avoir) in one's hand; (faire, tricoter etc) by hand; **se donner la ~** to hold hands; **donner** ou **tendre la ~ à qn** to hold out one's hand to sb; **se serrer la ~** to shake hands; **serrer la ~ à qn** to shake hands with sb; **sous la ~** to ou at hand; **haut les ~s!** hands up!; **attaque à ~ armée** armed attack; **à remettre en ~s propres** to be delivered personally; **mettre la dernière ~ à** to put the finishing touches to; **se faire/perdre la ~** to get one's hand in/lose one's touch; **avoir qch bien en ~** to have (got) the hang of sth; **main-d'œuvre** nf manpower, labour; **mainmise** nf (fig): **mainmise sur** complete hold on; **mains libres** adj inv (téléphone, kit) hands-free

**maint, e** [mɛ̃, mɛ̃t] adj many a; **~s** many; **à ~es reprises** time and (time) again

**maintenant** [mɛ̃t(ə)nɑ̃] adv now; (actuellement) nowadays

**maintenir** [mɛ̃t(ə)niʀ] vt (retenir, soutenir) to support; (contenir: foule etc) to hold back; (conserver, affirmer) to maintain; **se maintenir** vi (prix) to keep steady; (amélioration) to persist

**maintien** [mɛ̃tjɛ̃] nm (sauvegarde) maintenance; (attitude) bearing

**maire** [mɛʀ] nm mayor; **mairie** nf (bâtiment) town hall; (administration) town council

**mais** [mɛ] conj but; **~ non!** of course not!; **~ enfin** but after all; (indignation) look here!

**maïs** [mais] nm maize (BRIT), corn (US)

**maison** [mɛzɔ̃] nf house; (chez-soi)

home; (*Comm*) firm ▷ *adj inv* (*Culin*) home-made; (*fig*) in-house, own; **à la ~** at home; (*direction*) home; **maison de repos** convalescent home; **maison de retraite** old people's home; **maison close** *ou* **de passe** brothel; **maison de santé** mental home; **maison des jeunes** ≈ youth club; **maison mère** parent company

**maître, -esse** [mɛtʁ, mɛtʁɛs] *nm/f* master (mistress); (*Scol*) teacher, schoolmaster(-mistress) ▷ *nm* (*peintre etc*) master; (*titre*): **M~** Maître, *term of address gen for a barrister* ▷ *adj* (*principal, essentiel*) main; **être ~ de** (*soi, situation*) to be in control of; **une ~sse femme** a managing woman; **maître chanteur** blackmailer; **maître d'école** schoolmaster; **maître d'hôtel** (*domestique*) butler; (*d'hôtel*) head waiter; **maître nageur** lifeguard; **maîtresse** *nf* (*amante*) mistress; **maîtresse (d'école)** teacher, (school)mistress; **maîtresse de maison** hostess; (*ménagère*) housewife

**maîtrise** [metʁiz] *nf* (*aussi*: **~ de soi**) self-control, self-possession; (*habileté*) skill, mastery; (*suprématie*) mastery, command; (*diplôme*) ≈ master's degree; **maîtriser** *vt* (*cheval, incendie*) to (bring under) control; (*sujet*) to master; (*émotion*) to control, master; **se maîtriser** to control o.s.

**majestueux, -euse** [maʒɛstɥø, øz] *adj* majestic

**majeur, e** [maʒœʁ] *adj* (*important*) major; (*Jur*) of age ▷ *nm* (*doigt*) middle finger; **en ~e partie** for the most part; **la ~e partie de** most of

**majorer** [maʒɔʁe] *vt* to increase

**majoritaire** [maʒɔʁitɛʁ] *adj* majority *cpd*

**majorité** [maʒɔʁite] *nf* (*gén*) majority; (*parti*) party in power; **en ~** mainly; **avoir la ~** to have the majority

**majuscule** [maʒyskyl] *adj, nf*: **(lettre) ~** capital (letter)

**mal** [mal, mo] (*pl* **maux**) *nm* (*opposé*

*au bien*) evil; (*tort, dommage*) harm; (*douleur physique*) pain, ache; (*maladie*) illness, sickness *no pl* ▷ *adv* badly ▷ *adj* bad, wrong; **être ~** to be uncomfortable; **être ~ avec qn** to be on bad terms with sb; **il a ~ compris** he misunderstood; **se sentir** *ou* **se trouver ~** to feel ill *ou* unwell; **dire/penser du ~ de** to speak/think ill of; **ne voir aucun ~ à** to see no harm in, see nothing wrong in; **faire ~ à qn** to hurt sb; **se faire ~** to hurt o.s.; **avoir du ~ à faire qch** to have trouble doing sth; **se donner du ~ pour faire qch** to go to a lot of trouble to do sth; **ça fait ~** it hurts; **j'ai ~ au dos** my back hurts; **avoir ~ à la tête/à la gorge/aux dents** to have a headache/a sore throat/toothache; **avoir le ~ du pays** to be homesick; *voir aussi* **cœur**; **maux**; **mal de mer** seasickness; **mal en point** in a bad state

**malade** [malad] *adj* ill, sick; (*poitrine, jambe*) bad; (*plante*) diseased ▷ *nm/f* invalid, sick person; (*à l'hôpital etc*) patient; **tomber ~** to fall ill; **être ~ du cœur** to have heart trouble *ou* a bad heart; **malade mental** mentally ill person; **maladie** *nf* (*spécifique*) disease, illness; (*mauvaise santé*) illness, sickness; **maladif, -ive** *adj* sickly; (*curiosité, besoin*) pathological

**maladresse** [maladʁɛs] *nf* clumsiness *no pl*; (*gaffe*) blunder

**maladroit, e** [maladʁwa, wat] *adj* clumsy

**malaise** [malɛz] *nm* (*Méd*) feeling of faintness; (*fig*) uneasiness, malaise; **avoir un ~** to feel faint

**Malaisie** [malɛzi] *nf*: **la ~** Malaysia

**malaria** [malaʁja] *nf* malaria

**malaxer** [malakse] *vt* (*pétrir*) to knead; (*mélanger*) to mix

**malbouffe** [malbuf] (*fam*) *nf*: **la ~** junk food

**malchance** [malʃɑ̃s] *nf* misfortune, ill luck *no pl*; **par ~** unfortunately; **malchanceux, -euse** *adj* unlucky

**mâle** [mɑl] *adj (aussi Élec, Tech)* male; (*viril: voix, traits*) manly ▷ *nm* male

**malédiction** [malediksjɔ̃] *nf* curse

**mal...: malentendant, e** *nm/f:* **les malentendants** the hard of hearing; **malentendu** *nm* misunderstanding; **il y a eu un malentendu** there's been a misunderstanding; **malfaçon** *nf* fault; **malfaisant, e** *adj* evil, harmful; **malfaiteur** *nm* lawbreaker, criminal; (*voleur*) burglar, thief; **malfamé, e** *adj* disreputable

**malgache** [malgaʃ] *adj* Madagascan, Malagasy ▷ *nm/f:* **M~** Madagascan, Malagasy ▷ *nm (Ling)* Malagasy

**malgré** [malgre] *prép* in spite of, despite; **~ tout** all the same

**malheur** [malœR] *nm (situation)* adversity, misfortune; (*événement*) misfortune; (: *très grave*) disaster, tragedy; **faire un ~** to be a smash hit; **malheureusement** *adv* unfortunately; **malheureux, -euse** *adj* (*triste*) unhappy, miserable; (*infortuné, regrettable*) unfortunate; (*malchanceux*) unlucky; (*insignifiant*) wretched ▷ *nm/f* poor soul

**malhonnête** [malɔnɛt] *adj* dishonest; **malhonnêteté** *nf* dishonesty

**malice** [malis] *nf* mischievousness; (*méchanceté*) **par ~** out of malice ou spite; **sans ~** guileless; **malicieux, -euse** *adj* mischievous

▌ Attention à ne pas traduire *malicieux* par *malicious*.

**malin, -igne** [malɛ̃, maliɲ] *adj (futé: f gén: aussi:* **maline**) smart, shrewd; (*Méd*) malignant

**malingre** [malɛ̃gR] *adj* puny

**malle** [mal] *nf* trunk; **mallette** *nf* (*small*) suitcase; (*porte-documents*) attaché case

**malmener** [malməne] *vt* to manhandle; (*fig*) to give a rough handling to

**malodorant, e** [malɔdɔRɑ̃, ɑ̃t] *adj* foul- *ou* ill-smelling

**malpoli, e** [malpɔli] *adj* impolite

**malsain, e** [malsɛ̃, ɛn] *adj* unhealthy

**malt** [malt] *nm* malt

**Malte** [malt] *nf* Malta

**maltraiter** [maltRete] *vt* to manhandle, ill-treat

**malveillance** [malvɛjɑ̃s] *nf* (*animosité*) ill will; (*intention de nuire*) malevolence

**malversation** [malvɛRsasjɔ̃] *nf* embezzlement

**maman** [mamɑ̃] *nf* mum(my), mother

**mamelle** [mamɛl] *nf* teat

**mamelon** [mam(ə)lɔ̃] *nm (Anat)* nipple

**mamie** [mami] (*fam*) *nf* granny

**mammifère** [mamifɛR] *nm* mammal

**mammouth** [mamut] *nm* mammoth

**manche** [mɑ̃ʃ] *nf (de vêtement)* sleeve; (*d'un jeu, tournoi*) round; (*Géo*): **la M~** the Channel ▷ *nm (d'outil, casserole)* handle; (*de pelle, pioche etc*) shaft; **à ~s courtes/longues** short-/long-sleeved; **manche à balai** broomstick; (*Inform, Aviat*) joystick *m inv*

**manchette** [mɑ̃ʃɛt] *nf (de chemise)* cuff; (*coup*) forearm blow; (*titre*) headline

**manchot** [mɑ̃ʃo] *nm* one-armed man; armless man; (*Zool*) penguin

**mandarine** [mɑ̃daRin] *nf* mandarin (orange), tangerine

**mandat** [mɑ̃da] *nm (postal)* postal *ou* money order; (*d'un député etc*) mandate; (*procuration*) power of attorney, proxy; (*Police*) warrant; **mandat d'arrêt** warrant for arrest; **mandat de perquisition** search warrant; **mandataire** *nm/f* (*représentant*) representative; (*Jur*) proxy

**manège** [manɛʒ] *nm* riding school; (*à la foire*) roundabout, merry-go-round; (*fig*) game, ploy

**manette** [manɛt] *nf* lever, tap; **manette de jeu** joystick

**mangeable** [mɑ̃ʒabl] *adj* edible, eatable

**mangeoire** [mɑ̃ʒwaR] *nf* trough, manger

**manger** [mɑ̃ʒe] *vt* to eat; (*ronger: suj: rouille etc*) to eat into *ou* away ▷ *vi* to eat; **donner à ~ à** (*enfant*) to feed; **est-**

**ce qu'on peut ~ quelque chose?** can we have something to eat?

**mangue** [mɑ̃g] nf mango

**maniable** [manjabl] adj (outil) handy; (voiture, voilier) easy to handle

**maniaque** [manjak] adj finicky, fussy ▷ nm/f (méticuleux) fusspot; (fou) maniac

**manie** [mani] nf (tic) odd habit; (obsession) mania; **avoir la ~ de** to be obsessive about

**manier** [manje] vt to handle

**manière** [manjɛʀ] nf (façon) way, manner; **manières** nfpl (attitude) manners; (chichis) fuss sg; **de ~ à** so as to; **de cette ~** in this way ou manner; **d'une certaine ~** in a way; **de toute ~** in any case; **d'une ~ générale** generally speaking, as a general rule

**maniéré, e** [manjeʀe] adj affected

**manifestant, e** [manifɛstɑ̃, ɑ̃t] nm/f demonstrator

**manifestation** [manifɛstasjɔ̃] nf (de joie, mécontentement) expression, demonstration; (symptôme) outward sign; (culturelle etc) event; (Pol) demonstration

**manifeste** [manifɛst] adj obvious, evident ▷ nm manifesto; **manifester** vt (volonté, intentions) to show, indicate; (joie, peur) to express, show ▷ vi to demonstrate; **se manifester** vi (émotion) to show ou express itself; (difficultés) to arise; (symptômes) to appear

**manigancer** [manigɑ̃se] vt to plot

**manipulation** [manipylasjɔ̃] nf handling; (Pol, génétique) manipulation

**manipuler** [manipyle] vt to handle; (fig) to manipulate

**manivelle** [manivɛl] nf crank

**mannequin** [mankɛ̃] nm (Couture) dummy; (Mode) model

**manœuvre** [manœvʀ] nf (gén) manoeuvre (BRIT), maneuver (US) ▷ nm labourer; **manœuvrer** vt to manoeuvre (BRIT), maneuver (US); (levier, machine) to operate ▷ vi to

manoeuvre

**manoir** [manwaʀ] nm manor ou country house

**manque** [mɑ̃k] nm (insuffisance): **~ de** lack of; (vide) emptiness, gap; (Méd) withdrawal; **être en état de ~** to suffer withdrawal symptoms

**manqué, e** [mɑ̃ke] adj failed; **garçon ~** tomboy

**manquer** [mɑ̃ke] vi (faire défaut) to be lacking; (être absent) to be missing; (échouer) to fail ▷ vt to miss ▷ vb impers: **il (nous) manque encore 10 euros** we are still 10 euros short; **il manque des pages (au livre)** there are some pages missing (from the book); **il/cela me manque** I miss him/this; **~ à** (règles etc) to be in breach of, fail to observe; **~ de** to lack; **je ne ~ai pas de lui dire** I'll be sure to tell him; **il a manqué (de) se tuer** he very nearly got killed

**mansarde** [mɑ̃saʀd] nf attic; **mansardé, e** adj: **chambre mansardée** attic room

**manteau, x** [mɑ̃to] nm coat

**manucure** [manykyʀ] nf manicurist

**manuel, le** [manɥɛl] adj manual ▷ nm (ouvrage) manual, handbook

**manufacture** [manyfaktyʀ] nf factory; **manufacturé, e** adj manufactured

**manuscrit, e** [manyskʀi, it] adj handwritten ▷ nm manuscript

**manutention** [manytɑ̃sjɔ̃] nf (Comm) handling

**mappemonde** [mapmɔ̃d] nf (plane) map of the world; (sphère) globe

**maquereau, x** [makʀo] nm (Zool) mackerel inv; (fam) pimp

**maquette** [makɛt] nf (à échelle réduite) (scale) model; (d'une page illustrée) paste-up

**maquillage** [makijaʒ] nm making up; (crème etc) make-up

**maquiller** [makije] vt (personne, visage) to make up; (truquer: passeport, statistique) to fake; (: voiture volée) to do over (respray vb); **se maquiller** vi to make up (one's face)

**maquis** [maki] *nm* (*Géo*) scrub; (*Mil*) maquis, underground fighting *no pl*

**maraîcher, -ère** [maʀeʃe, ɛʀ] *adj*: **cultures maraîchères** market gardening *sg* ▷ *nm/f* market gardener

**marais** [maʀɛ] *nm* marsh, swamp

**marasme** [maʀasm] *nm* stagnation, slump

**marathon** [maʀatɔ̃] *nm* marathon

**marbre** [maʀbʀ] *nm* marble

**marc** [maʀ] *nm* (*de raisin, pommes*) marc

**marchand, e** [maʀʃɑ̃, ɑ̃d] *nm/f* shopkeeper, tradesman(-woman); (*au marché*) stallholder; (*de vins, charbon*) merchant ▷ *adj*: **prix/valeur ~(e)** market price/value; **marchand de fruits** fruiterer (*BRIT*), fruit seller (*US*); **marchand de journaux** newsagent; **marchand de légumes** greengrocer (*BRIT*), produce dealer (*US*); **marchand de poissons** fishmonger (*BRIT*), fish seller (*US*); **marchander** *vi* to bargain, haggle; **marchandise** *nf* goods *pl*, merchandise *no pl*

**marche** [maʀʃ] *nf* (*d'escalier*) step; (*activité*) walking; (*promenade, trajet, allure*) walk; (*démarche*) walk, gait; (*Mil etc, Mus*) march; (*fonctionnement*) running; (*des événements*) course; **dans le sens de la ~** (*Rail*) facing the engine; **en ~** (*monter etc*) while the vehicle is moving *ou* in motion; **mettre en ~** to start; **se mettre en ~** (*personne*) to get moving; (*machine*) to start; **être en état de ~** to be in working order; **marche à suivre** (correct) procedure; **marche arrière** reverse (gear); **faire marche arrière** to reverse; (*fig*) to backtrack, back-pedal

**marché** [maʀʃe] *nm* market; (*transaction*) bargain, deal; **faire du ~ noir** to buy and sell on the black market; **marché aux puces** flea market

**marcher** [maʀʃe] *vi* to walk; (*Mil*) to march; (*aller: voiture, train, affaires*) to go; (*prospérer*) to go well; (*fonctionner*) to

work, run; (*fam: consentir*) to go along, agree; (: *croire naïvement*) to be taken in; **faire ~ qn** (*taquiner*) to pull sb's leg; (*tromper*) to lead sb up the garden path; **comment est-ce que ça marche?** how does this work?; **marcheur, -euse** *nm/f* walker

**mardi** [maʀdi] *nm* Tuesday; **Mardi gras** Shrove Tuesday

**mare** [maʀ] *nf* pond; (*flaque*) pool

**marécage** [maʀekaʒ] *nm* marsh, swamp; **marécageux, -euse** *adj* marshy

**maréchal, -aux** [maʀeʃal, o] *nm* marshal

**marée** [maʀe] *nf* tide; (*poissons*) fresh (sea) fish; **marée haute/basse** high/low tide; **marée noire** oil slick

**marelle** [maʀɛl] *nf*: **(jouer à) la ~** (to play) hopscotch

**margarine** [maʀgaʀin] *nf* margarine

**marge** [maʀʒ] *nf* margin; **en ~ de** (*fig*) on the fringe of; **marge bénéficiaire** profit margin

**marginal, e, -aux** [maʀʒinal, o] *nm/f* (*original*) eccentric; (*déshérité*) dropout

**marguerite** [maʀgəʀit] *nf* marguerite, (oxeye) daisy; (*d'imprimante*) daisy-wheel

**mari** [maʀi] *nm* husband

**mariage** [maʀjaʒ] *nm* marriage; (*noce*) wedding; **mariage civil/religieux** registry office (*BRIT*) *ou* civil wedding/church wedding

**marié, e** [maʀje] *adj* married ▷ *nm* (bride)groom; **les ~s** the bride and groom; **les (jeunes) ~s** the newly-weds

**marier** [maʀje] *vt* to marry; (*fig*) to blend; **se ~ (avec)** to marry, get married to

**marin, e** [maʀɛ̃, in] *adj* sea *cpd*, marine ▷ *nm* sailor

**marine** [maʀin] *adj voir* **marin** ▷ *adj inv* navy (blue) ▷ *nm* (*Mil*) marine ▷ *nf* navy; **marine marchande** merchant navy

**mariner** [maʀine] *vt*: **faire ~** to marinade

**marionnette** [maʀjɔnɛt] *nf* puppet

**maritalement** [maʀitalmɑ̃] *adv*:
**vivre ~** to live as husband and wife

**maritime** [maʀitim] *adj* sea *cpd*,
maritime

**mark** [maʀk] *nm* mark

**marmelade** [maʀməlad] *nf* stewed
fruit, compote; **marmelade d'oranges**
marmalade

**marmite** [maʀmit] *nf* (cooking-)pot

**marmonner** [maʀmɔne] *vt, vi* to
mumble, mutter

**marmotter** [maʀmɔte] *vt* to mumble

**Maroc** [maʀɔk] *nm*: **le ~** Morocco;
**marocain, e** [maʀɔkɛ̃, ɛn] *adj*
Moroccan ▷ *nm/f*: **Marocain, e**
Moroccan

**maroquinerie** [maʀɔkinʀi] *nf*
(*articles*) fine leather goods *pl*; (*boutique*)
shop selling fine leather goods

**marquant, e** [maʀkɑ̃, ɑ̃t] *adj*
outstanding

**marque** [maʀk] *nf* mark; (*Comm: de
nourriture*) brand; (: *de voiture, produits
manufacturés*) make; (*de disques*) label;
**de ~** (*produits*) high-class; (*visiteur
etc*) distinguished, well-known; **une
grande ~ de vin** a well-known brand of
wine; **marque de fabrique** trademark;
**marque déposée** registered
trademark

**marquer** [maʀke] *vt* to mark; (*inscrire*)
to write down; (*bétail*) to brand; (*Sport:
but etc*) to score; (: *joueur*) to mark;
(*accentuer: taille etc*) to emphasize;
(*manifester: refus, intérêt*) to show
▷ *vi* (*événement*) to stand out, be
outstanding; (*Sport*) to score; **~ les
points** to keep the score

**marqueterie** [maʀkɛtʀi] *nf* inlaid
work, marquetry

**marquis** [maʀki] *nm* marquis,
marquess

**marraine** [maʀɛn] *nf* godmother

**marrant, e** [maʀɑ̃, ɑ̃t] (*fam*) *adj* funny

**marre** [maʀ] (*fam*) *adv*: **en avoir ~ de** to
be fed up with

**marrer** [maʀe]: **se ~** (*fam*) *vi* to have a

(good) laugh

**marron** [maʀɔ̃] *nm* (*fruit*) chestnut
▷ *adj inv* brown; **marrons glacés**
candied chestnuts; **marronnier** *nm*
chestnut (tree)

**mars** [maʀs] *nm* March

**Marseille** [maʀsɛj] *n* Marseilles

**marteau, x** [maʀto] *nm* hammer; **être
~** (*fam*) to be nuts; **marteau-piqueur**
*nm* pneumatic drill

**marteler** [maʀtəle] *vt* to hammer

**martien, ne** [maʀsjɛ̃, jɛn] *adj*
Martian, of *ou* from Mars

**martyr, e** [maʀtiʀ] *nm/f* martyr ▷ *adj*:
**enfants ~s** battered children; **martyre**
*nm* martyrdom; (*fig: sens affaibli*) agony,
torture; **martyriser** *vt* (*Rel*) to martyr;
(*fig*) to bully; (*enfant*) to batter, beat

**marxiste** [maʀksist] *adj, nm/f* Marxist

**mascara** [maskaʀa] *nm* mascara

**masculin, e** [maskylɛ̃, in] *adj*
masculine; (*sexe, population*) male;
(*équipe, vêtements*) men's; (*viril*) manly
▷ *nm* masculine

**masochiste** [mazɔʃist] *adj*
masochistic

**masque** [mask] *nm* mask; **masque de
beauté** face pack *ou* mask; **masque
de plongée** diving mask; **masquer** *vt*
(*cacher: paysage, porte*) to hide, conceal;
(*dissimuler: vérité, projet*) to mask,
obscure

**massacre** [masakʀ] *nm* massacre,
slaughter; **massacrer** *vt* to massacre,
slaughter; (*fam: texte etc*) to murder

**massage** [masaʒ] *nm* massage

**masse** [mas] *nf* mass; (*Élec*) earth;
(*maillet*) sledgehammer; (*péj*): **la ~** the
masses *pl*; **une ~ de** (*fam*) masses *ou*
loads of; **en ~** *adv* (*acheter*) in bulk;
(*en foule*) en masse ▷ *adj* (*exécutions,
production*) mass *cpd*

**masser** [mase] *vt* (*assembler: gens*) to
gather; (*pétrir*) to massage; **se masser**
*vi* (*foule*) to gather; **masseur, -euse**
*nm/f* masseur(-euse)

**massif, -ive** [masif, iv] *adj* (*porte*)
solid, massive; (*visage*) heavy, large;

(*bois, or*) solid; (*dose*) massive; (*déportations etc*) mass *cpd* ▷ *nm* (*montagneux*) massif; (*de fleurs*) clump, bank; **le M~ Central** the Massif Central

**massue** [masy] *nf* club, bludgeon

**mastic** [mastik] *nm* (*pour vitres*) putty; (*pour fentes*) filler

**mastiquer** [mastike] *vt* (*aliment*) to chew, masticate

**mat, e** [mat] *adj* (*couleur, métal*) mat(t); (*bruit, son*) dull ▷ *adj inv* (*Échecs*): **être ~** to be checkmate

**mât** [mɑ] *nm* (*Navig*) mast; (*poteau*) pole, post

**match** [matʃ] *nm* match; **faire ~ nul** to draw; **match aller** first leg; **match retour** second leg, return match

**matelas** [mat(ə)lɑ] *nm* mattress; **matelas pneumatique** air bed *ou* mattress

**matelot** [mat(ə)lo] *nm* sailor, seaman

**mater** [mate] *vt* (*personne*) to bring to heel, subdue; (*révolte*) to put down

**matérialiser** [materjalize]: **se matérialiser** *vi* to materialize

**matérialiste** [materjalist] *adj* materialistic

**matériau** [materjo] *nm* material; **matériaux** *nmpl* material(s)

**matériel, le** [materjɛl] *adj* material ▷ *nm* equipment *no pl*; (*de camping etc*) gear *no pl*; (*Inform*) hardware

**maternel, le** [matɛrnɛl] *adj* (*amour, geste*) motherly, maternal; (*grand-père, oncle*) maternal; **maternelle** *nf* (*aussi*: **école maternelle**) (state) nursery school

**maternité** [matɛrnite] *nf* (*établissement*) maternity hospital; (*état de mère*) motherhood, maternity; (*grossesse*) pregnancy; **congé de ~** maternity leave

**mathématique** [matematik] *adj* mathematical; **mathématiques** *nfpl* (*science*) mathematics *sg*

**maths** [mat] (*fam*) *nfpl* maths

**matière** [matjɛr] *nf* matter; (*Comm, Tech*) material, matter *no pl*; (*fig: d'un*

livre etc) subject matter, material; (*Scol*) subject; **en ~ de** as regards; **matières grasses** fat content *sg*; **matières premières** raw materials

**Matignon** [matiɲɔ̃] *nm*: (**l'hôtel**) **~** the French Prime Minister's residence

**matin** [matɛ̃] *nm, adv* morning; **le ~** (*pendant le matin*) in the morning; **demain/hier/dimanche ~** tomorrow/yesterday/Sunday morning; **tous les ~s** every morning; **une heure du ~** one o'clock in the morning; **du ~ au soir** from morning till night; **de bon** *ou* **grand ~** early in the morning; **matinal, e, -aux** *adj* (*toilette, gymnastique*) morning *cpd*; **être matinal** (*personne*) to be up early; to be an early riser; **matinée** *nf* morning; (*spectacle*) matinée

**matou** [matu] *nm* tom(cat)

**matraque** [matrak] *nf* (*de policier*) truncheon (BRIT), billy (US)

**matricule** [matrikyl] *nm* (*Mil*) regimental number; (*Admin*) reference number

**matrimonial, e, -aux** [matrimɔnjal, jo] *adj* marital, marriage *cpd*

**maudit, e** [modi, -it] (*fam*) *adj* (*satané*) blasted, confounded

**maugréer** [mogree] *vi* to grumble

**maussade** [mosad] *adj* sullen; (*temps*) gloomy

**mauvais, e** [mɔvɛ, ɛz] *adj* bad; (*faux*): **le ~ numéro/moment** the wrong number/moment; (*méchant, malveillant*) malicious, spiteful ▷ *adv*: **il fait ~** the weather is bad; **sentir ~** to have a nasty smell, smell nasty; **la mer est ~e** the sea is rough; **mauvais joueur** bad loser; **mauvaise herbe** weed; **mauvaise langue** gossip, scandalmonger (BRIT); **mauvaise plaisanterie** nasty trick

**mauve** [mov] *adj* mauve

**maux** [mo] *nmpl de* **mal**

**maximum** [maksimɔm] *adj, nm* maximum; **au ~** (*le plus possible*) as much as one can; (*tout au plus*) at the (very) most *ou* maximum; **faire le ~** to do one's level best

**mayonnaise** [majɔnɛz] *nf* mayonnaise

**mazout** [mazut] *nm* (fuel) oil

**me, m'** [m(ə)] *pron* (*direct: téléphoner, attendre etc*) me; (*indirect: parler, donner etc*) (to) me; (*réfléchi*) myself

**mec** [mɛk] (*fam*) *nm* bloke, guy

**mécanicien, ne** [mekanisjɛ̃, jɛn] *nm/f* mechanic; (*Rail*) (train *ou* engine) driver; **pouvez-vous nous envoyer un ~?** can you send a mechanic?

**mécanique** [mekanik] *adj* mechanical ▷ *nf* (*science*) mechanics *sg*; (*mécanisme*) mechanism; **ennui ~** engine trouble *no pl*

**mécanisme** [mekanism] *nm* mechanism

**méchamment** [meʃamã] *adv* nastily, maliciously, spitefully

**méchanceté** [meʃãste] *nf* nastiness, maliciousness; **dire des ~s à qn** to say spiteful things to sb

**méchant, e** [meʃã, ãt] *adj* nasty, malicious, spiteful; (*enfant: pas sage*) naughty; (*animal*) vicious

**mèche** [mɛʃ] *nf* (*de cheveux*) lock; (*de lampe, bougie*) wick; (*d'un explosif*) fuse; **se faire faire des ~s** to have highlights put in one's hair; **de ~ avec** in league with

**méchoui** [meʃwi] *nm* barbecue of a whole roast sheep

**méconnaissable** [mekɔnɛsabl] *adj* unrecognizable

**méconnaître** [mekɔnɛtʀ] *vt* (*ignorer*) to be unaware of; (*mésestimer*) to misjudge

**mécontent, e** [mekɔ̃tã, ãt] *adj*: **~ (de)** discontented *ou* dissatisfied *ou* displeased (with); (*contrarié*) annoyed (at); **mécontentement** *nm* dissatisfaction, discontent, displeasure; (*irritation*) annoyance

**Mecque** [mɛk] *nf*: **la ~** Mecca

**médaille** [medaj] *nf* medal

**médaillon** [medajɔ̃] *nm* (*bijou*) locket

**médecin** [med(ə)sɛ̃] *nm* doctor

**médecine** [med(ə)sin] *nf* medicine

**média** [medja] *nmpl*: **les ~** the media; **médiatique** *adj* media *cpd*

**médical, e, -aux** [medikal, o] *adj* medical; **passer une visite ~e** to have a medical

**médicament** [medikamã] *nm* medicine, drug

**médiéval, e, -aux** [medjeval, o] *adj* medieval

**médiocre** [medjɔkʀ] *adj* mediocre, poor

**méditer** [medite] *vi* to meditate

**Méditerranée** [mediteʀane] *nf*: **la (mer) ~** the Mediterranean (Sea); **méditerranéen, ne** *adj* Mediterranean ▷ *nm/f*: **Méditerranéen, ne** native *ou* inhabitant of a Mediterranean country

**méduse** [medyz] *nf* jellyfish

**méfait** [mefɛ] *nm* (*faute*) misdemeanour, wrongdoing; **méfaits** *nmpl* (*ravages*) ravages, damage *sg*

**méfiance** [mefjãs] *nf* mistrust, distrust

**méfiant, e** [mefjã, jãt] *adj* mistrust, distrustful

**méfier** [mefje]: **se méfier** *vi* to be wary; to be careful; **se ~ de** to mistrust, distrust, be wary of

**mégaoctet** [megaɔktɛ] *nm* megabyte

**mégarde** [megaʀd] *nf*: **par ~** (*accidentellement*) accidentally; (*par erreur*) by mistake

**mégère** [meʒɛʀ] *nf* shrew

**mégot** [mego] (*fam*) *nm* cigarette end

**meilleur, e** [mɛjœʀ] *adj, adv* better ▷ *nm*: **le ~** the best; **le ~ des deux** the better of the two; **il fait ~ qu'hier** it's better weather than yesterday; **meilleur marché** (*inv*) cheaper

**mél** [mɛl] *nm* e-mail

**mélancolie** [melãkɔli] *nf* melancholy, gloom; **mélancolique** *adj* melancholic, melancholy

**mélange** [melãʒ] *nm* mixture;

**mélanger** vt to mix; (vins, couleurs) to blend; (mettre en désordre) to mix up, muddle (up)

**mêlée** [mele] nf mêlée, scramble; (Rugby) scrum(mage)

**mêler** [mele] vt (unir) to mix; (embrouiller) to muddle (up), mix up; **se mêler** vi to mix, mingle; **se ~ à** (personne: se joindre) to join; (: s'associer à) to mix with; **se ~ de** (suj: personne) to meddle with, interfere in; **mêle-toi de ce qui te regarde** ou **de tes affaires!** mind your own business!

**mélodie** [melodi] nf melody; **mélodieux, -euse** adj melodious

**melon** [m(ə)lɔ̃] nm (Bot) (honeydew) melon; (aussi: **chapeau ~**) bowler (hat)

**membre** [mɑ̃bʀ] nm (Anat) limb; (personne, pays, élément) member ▷ adj member cpd

**mémé** [meme] (fam) nf granny

O **MOT-CLÉ**

**même** [mɛm] adj **1** (avant le nom) same; **en même temps** at the same time; **ils ont les mêmes goûts** they have the same ou similar tastes

**2** (après le nom: renforcement): **il est la loyauté même** he is loyalty itself; **ce sont ses paroles mêmes** they are his very words

▷ pron: **le(la) même** the same one

▷ adv **1** (renforcement): **il n'a même pas pleuré** he didn't even cry; **même lui l'a dit** even HE said it; **ici même** at this very place; **même si** even if

**2**: **à même**: **à même la bouteille** straight from the bottle; **à même la peau** next to the skin; **être à même de faire** to be in a position to do, be able to do

**3**: **de même**: **faire de même** to do likewise; **lui de même** so does (ou did ou is) he; **de même que** just as; **il en va de même pour** the same goes for

**mémoire** [memwaʀ] nf memory ▷ nm (Scol) dissertation, paper; **mémoires** nmpl (souvenirs) memoirs; **à la ~ de** to the ou in memory of; **de ~** from memory; **mémoire morte** read-only memory, ROM; **mémoire vive** random access memory, RAM

**mémorable** [memɔʀabl] adj memorable, unforgettable

**menace** [mənas] nf threat; **menacer** vt to threaten

**ménage** [menaʒ] nm (travail) housework; (couple) (married) couple; (famille, Admin) household; **faire le ~** to do the housework; **ménagement** nm care and attention; **ménager, -ère** adj household cpd, domestic ▷ vt (traiter: personne) to handle with tact; (utiliser) to use sparingly; (prendre soin de) to take (great) care of, look after; (organiser) to arrange; **ménagère** nf housewife

**mendiant, e** [mɑ̃djɑ̃, jɑ̃t] nm/f beggar

**mendier** [mɑ̃dje] vi to beg ▷ vt to beg (for)

**mener** [m(ə)ne] vt to lead; (enquête) to conduct; (affaires) to manage ▷ vi: **~ à/dans** (emmener) to take to/into; **~ qch à bien** to see sth through (to a successful conclusion), complete sth successfully

**meneur, -euse** [mənœʀ, øz] nm/f leader; (péj) agitator

**méningite** [menɛ̃ʒit] nf meningitis no pl

**ménopause** [menopoz] nf menopause

**menottes** [mənɔt] nfpl handcuffs

**mensonge** [mɑ̃sɔ̃ʒ] nm lie; (action) lying no pl; **mensonger, -ère** adj false

**mensualité** [mɑ̃sɥalite] nf (traite) monthly payment

**mensuel, le** [mɑ̃sɥɛl] adj monthly

**mensurations** [mɑ̃syʀasjɔ̃] nfpl measurements

**mental, e, -aux** [mɑ̃tal, o] adj mental; **mentalité** nf mentality

**menteur, -euse** [mɑ̃tœʀ, øz] nm/f liar

**menthe** [mɑ̃t] nf mint

**mention** [mɑ̃sjɔ̃] nf (annotation) note,

comment; (*Scol*) grade; **~ bien** ≈ grade B, ≈ good pass; (*Université*) ≈ upper 2nd class pass (*BRIT*), ≈ pass with (high) honors (*US*); (*Admin*): **"rayer les ~s inutiles"** "delete as appropriate";
**mentionner** *vt* to mention

**mentir** [mãtiʀ] *vi* to lie

**menton** [mãtɔ̃] *nm* chin

**menu, e** [məny] *adj* (*personne*) slim, slight; (*frais, difficulté*) minor ▷ *adv* (*couper, hacher*) very fine ▷ *nm* menu; **~ touristique/gastronomique** economy/gourmet's menu

**menuiserie** [mənɥizʀi] *nf* (*métier*) joinery, carpentry; (*passe-temps*) woodwork; **menuisier** *nm* joiner, carpenter

**méprendre** [mepʀãdʀ]: **se méprendre** *vi*: **se ~ sur** to be mistaken (about)

**mépris** [mepʀi] *nm* (*dédain*) contempt, scorn; **au ~ de** regardless of, in defiance of; **méprisable** *adj* contemptible, despicable; **méprisant, e** *adj* scornful; **méprise** *nf* mistake, error; **mépriser** *vt* to scorn, despise; (*gloire, danger*) to scorn, spurn

**mer** [mɛʀ] *nf* sea; (*marée*) tide; **en ~** at sea; **en haute** *ou* **pleine ~** off shore, on the open sea; **la ~ du Nord/Rouge/ Noire/Morte** the North/Red/Black/ Dead Sea

**mercenaire** [mɛʀsənɛʀ] *nm* mercenary, hired soldier

**mercerie** [mɛʀsəʀi] *nf* (*boutique*) haberdasher's shop (*BRIT*), notions store (*US*)

**merci** [mɛʀsi] *excl* thank you ▷ *nf*: **à la ~ de qn/qch** at sb's mercy/the mercy of sth; **~ beaucoup** thank you very much; **~ de** thank you for; **sans ~** merciless(ly)

**mercredi** [mɛʀkʀədi] *nm* Wednesday; **~ des Cendres** Ash Wednesday; *voir aussi* **lundi**

**mercure** [mɛʀkyʀ] *nm* mercury

**merde** [mɛʀd] (*fam!*) *nf* shit (!) ▷ *excl* (bloody) hell (!)

**mère** [mɛʀ] *nf* mother; **mère célibataire** single parent, unmarried

mother; **mère de famille** housewife, mother

**merguez** [mɛʀgɛz] *nf* merguez sausage (*type of spicy sausage from N Africa*)

**méridional, e, -aux** [meʀidjɔnal, o] *adj* southern ▷ *nm/f* Southerner

**meringue** [məʀɛ̃g] *nf* meringue

**mérite** [meʀit] *nm* merit; **avoir du ~ (à faire qch)** to deserve credit (for doing sth); **mériter** *vt* to deserve

**merle** [mɛʀl] *nm* blackbird

**merveille** [mɛʀvɛj] *nf* marvel, wonder; **faire ~** to work wonders; **à ~** perfectly, wonderfully; **merveilleux, -euse** *adj* marvellous, wonderful

**mes** [me] *adj voir* **mon**

**mésange** [mezɑ̃ʒ] *nf* tit(mouse)

**mésaventure** [mezavɑ̃tyʀ] *nf* misadventure, misfortune

**Mesdames** [medam] *nfpl de* **Madame**

**Mesdemoiselles** [medmwazɛl] *nfpl de* **Mademoiselle**

**mesquin, e** [mɛskɛ̃, in] *adj* mean, petty; **mesquinerie** *nf* meanness; (*procédé*) mean trick

**message** [mesaʒ] *nm* message; **est-ce que je peux laisser un ~?** can I leave a message?; **~ SMS** text message; **messager, -ère** *nm/f* messenger; **messagerie** *nf* (*Internet*): **messagerie électronique** e-mail; **messagerie vocale** (*service*) voice mail; **messagerie instantanée** instant messenger

**messe** [mɛs] *nf* mass; **aller à la ~** to go to mass

**Messieurs** [mesjø] *nmpl de* **Monsieur**

**mesure** [m(ə)zyʀ] *nf* (*évaluation, dimension*) measurement; (*récipient*) measure; (*Mus: cadence*) time, tempo; (*: division*) bar; (*retenue*) moderation; (*disposition*) measure, step; **sur ~** (*costume*) made-to-measure; **dans la ~ où** insofar as, inasmuch as; **à ~ que** as; **être en ~ de** to be in a position to; **dans une certaine ~** to a certain extent

**mesurer** [məzyʀe] *vt* to measure; (*juger*) to weigh up, assess; (*modérer: ses*

*paroles etc*) to moderate
**métal, -aux** [metal, o] *nm* metal;
 **métallique** *adj* metallic
**météo** [meteo] *nf* (*bulletin*) weather
 report
**météorologie** [mete`lɔʒi] *nf*
 meteorology
**méthode** [metɔd] *nf* method; (*livre,
 ouvrage*) manual, tutor
**méticuleux, -euse** [metikylø, øz] *adj*
 meticulous
**métier** [metje] *nm* (*profession: gén*)
 job; (*: manuel*) trade; (*artisanal*) craft;
 (*technique, expérience*) (acquired) skill *ou*
 technique; (*aussi*: **~ à tisser**) (weaving)
 loom
**métis, se** [metis] *adj, nm/f* half-caste,
 half-breed
**métrage** [metraʒ] *nm*: **long/moyen/
 court ~** full-length/medium-length/
 short film
**mètre** [mɛtr] *nm* metre; (*règle*) (metre)
 rule; (*ruban*) tape measure; **métrique**
 *adj* metric
**métro** [metro] *nm* underground (*BRIT*),
 subway
**métropole** [metrɔpɔl] *nf* (*capitale*)
 metropolis; (*pays*) home country
**mets** [mɛ] *nm* dish
**metteur** [metœr] *nm*: **~ en scène**
 (*Théâtre*) producer; (*Cinéma*) director

O **MOT-CLÉ**

**mettre** [mɛtr] *vt* **1** (*placer*) to put;
 **mettre en bouteille/en sac** to bottle/
 put in bags *ou* sacks
 **2** (*vêtements: revêtir*) to put on; (*: porter*)
 to wear; **mets ton gilet** put your
 cardigan on; **je ne mets plus mon
 manteau** I no longer wear my coat
 **3** (*faire fonctionner: chauffage, électricité*)
 to put on; (*: réveil, minuteur*) to set;
 (*installer: gaz, eau*) to put in, lay on;
 **mettre en marche** to start up
 **4** (*consacrer*): **mettre du temps à faire
 qch** to take time to do sth *ou* over sth
 **5** (*noter, écrire*): to say, put (down);

**qu'est-ce qu'il a mis sur la carte?**
 what did he say *ou* write on the card?;
 **mettez au pluriel ...** put ... into the
 plural
 **6** (*supposer*): **mettons que ...** let's
 suppose *ou* say that ...
 **7**: **y mettre du sien** to pull one's weight
**se mettre** *vi* **1** (*se placer*): **vous pouvez
 vous mettre là** you can sit (*ou* stand)
 there; **où ça se met?** where does it
 go?; **se mettre au lit** to get into bed;
 **se mettre au piano** to sit down at the
 piano; **se mettre de l'encre sur les
 doigts** to get ink on one's fingers
 **2** (*s'habiller*): **se mettre en maillot de
 bain** to get into *ou* put on a swimsuit;
 **n'avoir rien à se mettre** to have
 nothing to wear
 **3**: **se mettre à** to begin, start; **se
 mettre à faire** to begin *ou* start doing
 *ou* to do; **se mettre au piano** to start
 learning the piano; **se mettre au
 régime** to go on a diet; **se mettre
 au travail/à l'étude** to get down to
 work/one's studies

**meuble** [mœbl] *nm* piece of furniture;
 **des ~s** furniture; **meublé** *nm* furnished
 flatlet (*BRIT*) *ou* room; **meubler** *vt* to
 furnish
**meuf** [mœf] *nf* (*fam*) woman
**meugler** [møgle] *vi* to low, moo
**meule** [møl] *nf* (*de foin, blé*) stack; (*de
 fromage*) round; (*à broyer*) millstone
**meunier** [mønje] *nm* miller
**meurs** *etc* [mœr] *vb voir* **mourir**
**meurtre** [mœrtr] *nm* murder;
 **meurtrier, -ière** *adj* (*arme etc*) deadly;
 (*fureur, instincts*) murderous ▷ *nm/f*
 murderer(-eress)
**meurtrir** [mœrtrir] *vt* to bruise; (*fig*)
 to wound
**meus** *etc* [mœ] *vb voir* **mouvoir**
**meute** [møt] *nf* pack
**mexicain, e** [mɛksikɛ̃, ɛn] *adj*
 Mexican ▷ *nm/f*: **M~, e** Mexican
**Mexico** [mɛksiko] *n* Mexico City
**Mexique** [mɛksik] *nm*: **le ~** Mexico

**mi** [mi] *nm* (*Mus*) E; (*en chantant la gamme*) mi ▷ *préfixe*: **mi...** half(-); mid-; **à la mi-janvier** in mid-January; **à mi-jambes/corps** (up *ou* down) to the knees/waist; **à mi-hauteur** halfway up

**miauler** [mjole] *vi* to mew

**miche** [miʃ] *nf* round *ou* cob loaf

**mi-chemin** [miʃmɛ̃]: **à ~** *adv* halfway, midway

**mi-clos, e** [miklo, kloz] *adj* half-closed

**micro** [mikʁo] *nm* mike, microphone; (*Inform*) micro

**microbe** [mikʁɔb] *nm* germ, microbe

**micro...**: **micro-onde** *nf*: **four à micro-ondes** microwave oven; **micro-ordinateur** *nm* microcomputer; **microscope** *nm* microscope; **microscopique** *adj* microscopic

**midi** [midi] *nm* midday, noon; (*moment du déjeuner*) lunchtime; (*sud*) south; **à ~** at 12 (o'clock) *ou* midday *ou* noon; **le M~** the South (of France), the Midi

**mie** [mi] *nf* crumb (of the loaf)

**miel** [mjɛl] *nm* honey; **mielleux, -euse** *adj* (*personne*) unctuous, syrupy

**mien, ne** [mjɛ̃, mjɛn] *pron*: **le(la) ~(ne), les ~(ne)s** mine; **les ~s** my family

**miette** [mjɛt] *nf* (*de pain, gâteau*) crumb; (*fig: de la conversation etc*) scrap; **en ~s** in pieces *ou* bits

**⊙ MOT-CLÉ**

**mieux** [mjø] *adv* **1** (*d'une meilleure façon*): **mieux (que)** better (than); **elle travaille/mange mieux** she works/eats better; **aimer mieux** to prefer; **elle va mieux** she is better; **de mieux en mieux** better and better

**2** (*de la meilleure façon*) best; **ce que je connais le mieux** what I know best; **les livres les mieux faits** the best-made books

▷ *adj* **1** (*plus à l'aise, en meilleure forme*) better; **se sentir mieux** to feel better

**2** (*plus satisfaisant*) better; **c'est mieux ainsi** it's better like this; **c'est le mieux**

**des deux** it's the better of the two; **le(la) mieux, les mieux** the best; **demandez-lui, c'est le mieux** ask him, it's the best thing

**3** (*plus joli*) better-looking; **il est mieux que son frère** (*plus beau*) he's better-looking than his brother; (*plus gentil*) he's nicer than his brother; **il est mieux sans moustache** he looks better without a moustache

**4**: **au mieux** at best; **au mieux avec** on the best of terms with; **pour le mieux** for the best

▷ *nm* **1** (*progrès*) improvement

**2**: **de mon/ton mieux** as best I/you can (*ou* could); **faire de son mieux** to do one's best

**mignon, ne** [miɲɔ̃, ɔn] *adj* sweet, cute

**migraine** [migʁɛn] *nf* headache; (*Méd*) migraine

**mijoter** [miʒɔte] *vt* to simmer; (*préparer avec soin*) to cook lovingly; (*fam: tramer*) to plot, cook up ▷ *vi* to simmer

**milieu, x** [miljø] *nm* (*centre*) middle; (*Bio, Géo*) environment; (*entourage social*) milieu; (*provenance*) background; (*pègre*): **le ~** the underworld; **au ~ de** in the middle of; **au beau** *ou* **en plein ~ (de)** right in the middle (of); **un juste ~** a happy medium

**militaire** [militɛʁ] *adj* military, army *cpd* ▷ *nm* serviceman

**militant, e** [militɑ̃, ɑ̃t] *adj, nm/f* militant

**militer** [milite] *vi* to be a militant

**mille** [mil] *num* a *ou* one thousand ▷ *nm* (*mesure*): **~ (marin)** nautical mile; **mettre dans le ~** (*fig*) to be bang on target; **millefeuille** *nm* cream *ou* vanilla slice; **millénaire** *nm* millennium ▷ *adj* thousand-year-old; (*fig*) ancient; **mille-pattes** *nm inv* centipede

**millet** [mijɛ] *nm* millet

**milliard** [miljaʁ] *nm* milliard, thousand million (*BRIT*), billion (*US*); **milliardaire** *nm/f* multimillionaire

(BRIT), billionaire (US)

**millier** [milje] nm thousand; **un ~ (de)** a thousand or so, about a thousand; **par ~s** in (their) thousands, by the thousand

**milligramme** [miligram] nm milligramme

**millimètre** [milimɛtʀ] nm millimetre

**million** [miljɔ̃] nm million; **deux ~s de** two million; **millionnaire** nm/f millionaire

**mime** [mim] nm/f (acteur) mime(r) ▷ nm (art) mime, miming; **mimer** vt to mime; (singer) to mimic, take off

**minable** [minabl] adj (décrépit) shabby(-looking); (médiocre) pathetic

**mince** [mɛ̃s] adj thin; (personne, taille) slim, slender; (fig: profit, connaissances) slight, small, weak ▷ excl: **~ alors!** drat it!, darn it! (US); **minceur** nf thinness; (d'une personne) slimness, slenderness; **mincir** vi to get slimmer

**mine** [min] nf (physionomie) expression, look; (allure) exterior, appearance; (de crayon) lead; (gisement, explosif, fig: source) mine; **avoir bonne ~** (personne) to look well; (ironique) to look an utter idiot; **avoir mauvaise ~** to look unwell ou poorly; **faire ~ de faire** to make a pretence of doing; **~ de rien** although you wouldn't think so

**miner** [mine] vt (saper) to undermine, erode; (Mil) to mine

**minerai** [minʀɛ] nm ore

**minéral, e, -aux** [mineral, o] adj, nm mineral

**minéralogique** [mineralɔʒik] adj: **plaque ~** number (BRIT) ou license (US) plate; **numéro ~** registration (BRIT) ou license (US) number

**minet, te** [minɛ, ɛt] nm/f (chat) pussy-cat; (péj) young trendy

**mineur, e** [minœʀ] adj minor ▷ nm/f (Jur) minor, person under age ▷ nm (travailleur) miner

**miniature** [minjatyʀ] adj, nf miniature

**minibus** [minibys] nm minibus

**minier, -ière** [minje, jɛʀ] adj mining

**mini-jupe** [miniʒyp] nf mini-skirt

**minime** [minim] adj minor, minimal

**minimessage** [minimesaʒ] nm text message

**minimiser** [minimize] vt to minimize; (fig) to play down

**minimum** [minimɔm] adj, nm minimum; **au ~** (au moins) at the very least

**ministère** [ministɛʀ] nm (aussi Rel) ministry; (cabinet) government

**ministre** [ministʀ] nm (aussi Rel) minister; **ministre d'État** senior minister ou secretary

**Minitel®** [minitɛl] nm videotext terminal and service

---

○ **MINITEL®**
○
○ **Minitel®** is a public information
○ system provided by France-Télécom
○ to telephone subscribers since
○ the early 80s. Among the services
○ available are a computerized
○ telephone directory and information
○ on travel timetables, stock-market
○ news and situations vacant.
○ Subscribers pay for their time on
○ screen as part of their phone bill.
○ Although this information is now
○ also available on the Internet, the
○ special Minitel® screens, terminals
○ and keyboards are still very much a
○ part of French daily life.

---

**minoritaire** [minɔʀitɛʀ] adj minority

**minorité** [minɔʀite] nf minority; **être en ~** to be in the ou a minority

**minuit** [minɥi] nm midnight

**minuscule** [minyskyl] adj minute, tiny ▷ nf: **(lettre) ~** small letter

**minute** [minyt] nf minute; **à la ~** (just) this instant; (faire) there and then; **minuter** vt to time; **minuterie** nf time switch

**minutieux, -euse** [minysjø, jøz] adj (personne) meticulous; (travail)

minutely detailed
**mirabelle** [miʀabɛl] nf (cherry) plum
**miracle** [miʀɑkl] nm miracle
**mirage** [miʀaʒ] nm mirage
**mire** [miʀ] nf: **point de ~** (fig) focal point
**miroir** [miʀwaʀ] nm mirror
**miroiter** [miʀwate] vi to sparkle, shimmer; **faire ~ qch à qn** to paint sth in glowing colours for sb, dangle sth in front of sb's eyes
**mis, e** [mi, miz] pp de **mettre** ▷ adj: **bien ~** well-dressed
**mise** [miz] nf (argent: au jeu) stake; (tenue) clothing, attire; **être de ~** to be acceptable ou in season; **mise à jour** updating; **mise au point** (fig) clarification; **mise de fonds** capital outlay; **mise en plis** set; **mise en scène** production
**miser** [mize] vt (enjeu) to stake, bet; **~ sur** (cheval, numéro) to bet on; (fig) to bank ou count on
**misérable** [mizeʀabl] adj (lamentable, malheureux) pitiful, wretched; (pauvre) poverty-stricken; (insignifiant, mesquin) miserable ▷ nm/f wretch
**misère** [mizɛʀ] nf (extreme) poverty, destitution; **misères** nfpl (malheurs) woes, miseries; (ennuis) little troubles; **salaire de ~** starvation wage
**missile** [misil] nm missile
**mission** [misjɔ̃] nf mission; **partir en ~** (Admin, Pol) to go on an assignment; **missionnaire** nm/f missionary
**mité, e** [mite] adj moth-eaten
**mi-temps** [mitɑ̃] nf inv (Sport: période) half; (: pause) half-time; **à ~** part-time
**miteux, -euse** [mitø, øz] adj (lieu) seedy
**mitigé, e** [mitiʒe] adj: **sentiments ~s** mixed feelings
**mitoyen, ne** [mitwajɛ̃, jɛn] adj (mur) common, party cpd; **maisons ~nes** semi-detached houses; (plus de deux) terraced (BRIT) ou row (US) houses
**mitrailler** [mitʀaje] vt to machine-gun; (fig) to pelt, bombard; (: photographier) to take shot after shot of; **mitraillette** nf submachine gun; **mitrailleuse** nf machine gun
**mi-voix** [mivwa]: **à ~** adv in a low ou hushed voice
**mixage** [miksaʒ] nm (Cinéma) (sound) mixing
**mixer** [miksœʀ] nm (food) mixer
**mixte** [mikst] adj (gén) mixed; (Scol) mixed, coeducational; **cuisinière ~** combined gas and electric cooker (BRIT) ou stove (US)
**mixture** [mikstyʀ] nf mixture; (fig) concoction
**Mlle** (pl **~s**) abr = **Mademoiselle**
**MM** abr = **Messieurs**
**Mme** (pl **~s**) abr = **Madame**
**mobile** [mɔbil] adj mobile; (pièce de machine) moving ▷ nm (motif) motive; (œuvre d'art) mobile; **(téléphone) ~** mobile (phone)
**mobilier, -ière** [mɔbilje, jɛʀ] nm furniture
**mobiliser** [mɔbilize] vt to mobilize
**mocassin** [mɔkasɛ̃] nm moccasin
**moche** [mɔʃ] (fam) adj (laid) ugly; (mauvais) rotten
**modalité** [mɔdalite] nf form, mode
**mode** [mɔd] nf fashion ▷ nm (manière) form, mode; (Ling) mood; (Mus, Inform) mode; **à la ~** fashionable, in fashion; **mode d'emploi** directions pl (for use); **mode de paiement** method of payment; **mode de vie** lifestyle
**modèle** [mɔdɛl] adj, nm model; (qui pose: de peintre) sitter; **modèle déposé** registered design; **modèle réduit** small-scale model; **modeler** vt to model
**modem** [mɔdɛm] nm modem
**modéré, e** [mɔdeʀe] adj, nm/f moderate
**modérer** [mɔdeʀe] vt to moderate; **se modérer** vi to restrain o.s.
**moderne** [mɔdɛʀn] adj modern ▷ nm (style) modern style; (meubles) modern furniture; **moderniser** vt to modernize
**modeste** [mɔdɛst] adj modest;

**modestie** nf modesty
**modifier** [mɔdifje] vt to modify, alter;
**se modifier** vi to alter
**modique** [mɔdik] adj modest
**module** [mɔdyl] nm module
**moelle** [mwal] nf marrow
**moelleux, -euse** [mwalø, øz] adj soft;
(gâteau) light and moist
**mœurs** [mœʀ] nfpl (conduite) morals;
(manières) manners; (pratiques sociales,
mode de vie) habits
**moi** [mwa] pron me; (emphatique): ~,
**je ...** for my part, I ..., I myself ...; **c'est
~ qui l'ai fait** I did it, it was me who
did it; **apporte-le-~** bring it to me; **à ~**
mine; (dans un jeu) my turn; **moi-même**
pron myself; (emphatique) I myself
**moindre** [mwɛ̃dʀ] adj lesser; lower;
**le(la) ~, les ~s** the least, the slightest;
**merci — c'est la ~ des choses!** thank
you — it's a pleasure!
**moine** [mwan] nm monk, friar
**moineau, x** [mwano] nm sparrow

**MOT-CLÉ**

**moins** [mwɛ̃] adv **1** (comparatif):
**moins (que)** less (than); **moins grand
que** less tall than, not as tall as; **il a
3 ans de moins que moi** he's 3 years
younger than me; **moins je travaille,
mieux je me porte** the less I work, the
better I feel
**2** (superlatif): **le moins** (the) least;
**c'est ce que j'aime le moins** it's what I like
(the) least; **le(la) moins doué(e)** the
least gifted; **au moins, du moins** at
least; **pour le moins** at the very least
**3**: **moins de** (quantité) less (than);
(nombre) fewer (than); **moins de
sable/d'eau** less sand/water; **moins
de livres/gens** fewer books/people;
**moins de 2 ans** less than 2 years;
**moins de midi** not yet midday
**4**: **de moins, en moins**: **100 euros/3
jours de moins** 100 euros/3 days less;
**3 livres en moins** 3 books fewer; **de
l'argent en moins**

less money; **le soleil en moins** but for
the sun, minus the sun; **de moins en
moins** less and less
**5**: **à moins de, à moins que** unless;
**à moins de faire** unless we do (ou he
does etc); **à moins que tu ne fasses**
unless you do; **à moins d'un accident**
barring any accident
▷ prép: **4 moins 2** 4 minus 2; **il est
moins 5** it's 5 to; **il fait moins 5** it's 5
(degrees) below (freezing), it's minus 5

**mois** [mwa] nm month
**moisi** [mwazi] nm mould, mildew;
**odeur de ~** musty smell; **moisir** vi to
go mouldy; **moisissure** nf mould no pl
**moisson** [mwasɔ̃] nf harvest;
**moissonner** vt to harvest, reap;
**moissonneuse** nf (machine) harvester
**moite** [mwat] adj sweaty, sticky
**moitié** [mwatje] nf half; **la ~** half; **la
~ de** half (of); **la ~ du temps** half the
time; **à la ~ de** halfway through; **à ~**
(avant le verbe) half; (avant l'adjectif)
half-; **à ~ prix** (at) half-price
**molaire** [mɔlɛʀ] nf molar
**molester** [mɔlɛste] vt to manhandle,
maul (about)
**molle** [mɔl] adj voir **mou**; **mollement**
adv (péj: travailler) sluggishly; (protester)
feebly
**mollet** [mɔlɛ] nm calf ▷ adj m: **œuf ~**
soft-boiled egg
**molletonné, e** [mɔltɔne] adj
fleece-lined
**mollir** [mɔliʀ] vi (fléchir) to relent;
(substance) to go soft
**mollusque** [mɔlysk] nm mollusc
**môme** [mom] (fam) nm/f (enfant) brat
**moment** [mɔmɑ̃] nm moment; **ce
n'est pas le ~** this is not the (right)
time; **au même ~** at the same time;
(instant) at the same moment; **pour un
bon ~** for a good while; **pour le ~** for the
moment, for the time being; **au ~ de**
at the time of; **à tout ~** at any time ou
(peut arriver etc) at any time; **au ~ où** just as;
(constamment) constantly, continually;

**en ce ~** at the moment; at present; **sur le ~** at the time; **par ~s** now and then, at times; **d'un ~ à l'autre** any time (now); **du ~ où** ou **que** seeing that, since; **momentané, e** adj temporary, momentary; **momentanément** adv (court instant) for a short while

**momie** [mɔmi] nf mummy

**mon, ma** [mɔ̃, ma] (pl **mes**) adj my

**Monaco** [mɔnako] nm Monaco

**monarchie** [mɔnaʀʃi] nf monarchy

**monastère** [mɔnastɛʀ] nm monastery

**mondain, e** [mɔ̃dɛ̃, ɛn] adj (vie) society cpd

**monde** [mɔ̃d] nm world; (haute société): **le ~** (high) society; **il y a du ~** (beaucoup de gens) there are a lot of people; (quelques personnes) there are some people; **beaucoup/peu de ~** many/few people; **mettre au ~** to bring into the world; **pas le moins du ~** not in the least; **mondial, e, -aux** adj (population) world cpd; (influence) world-wide; **mondialement** adv throughout the world; **mondialisation** nf globalization

**monégasque** [mɔnegask] adj Monegasque, of ou from Monaco ▷ nm/f: **M~** Monegasque, person from ou inhabitant of Monaco

**monétaire** [mɔnetɛʀ] adj monetary

**moniteur, -trice** [mɔnitœʀ, tʀis] nm/f (Sport) instructor(-tress); (de colonie de vacances) supervisor ▷ nm (écran) monitor

**monnaie** [mɔnɛ] nf (Écon, gén: moyen d'échange) currency; (petites pièces): **avoir de la ~** to have (some) change; **une pièce de ~** a coin; **faire de la ~** to get (some) change; **avoir/faire la ~ de 20 euros** to have change of/get change for 20 euros; **rendre à qn la ~ (sur 20 euros)** to give sb the change (out of ou from 20 euros); **gardez la ~** keep the change; **désolé, je n'ai pas de ~** sorry, I don't have any change; **avez-vous de la ~?** do you have any change?

**monologue** [mɔnɔlɔg] nm monologue, soliloquy; **monologuer** vi to soliloquize

**monopole** [mɔnɔpɔl] nm monopoly

**monotone** [mɔnɔtɔn] adj monotonous

**Monsieur** [məsjø] (pl **Messieurs**) titre Mr ▷ nm (homme quelconque): **un/le monsieur** a/the gentleman; **~, ...** (en tête de lettre) Dear Sir, ...; voir aussi **Madame**

**monstre** [mɔ̃stʀ] nm monster ▷ adj (fam: colossal) monstrous; **un travail ~** a fantastic amount of work; **monstrueux, -euse** adj monstrous

**mont** [mɔ̃] nm: **par ~s et par vaux** up hill and down dale; **le Mont Blanc** Mont Blanc

**montage** [mɔ̃taʒ] nm (assemblage: d'appareil) assembly; (Photo) photomontage; (Cinéma) editing

**montagnard, e** [mɔ̃taɲaʀ, aʀd] adj mountain cpd ▷ nm/f mountain-dweller

**montagne** [mɔ̃taɲ] nf (cime) mountain; (région): **la ~** the mountains pl; **montagnes russes** big dipper sg, switchback sg; **montagneux, -euse** adj mountainous; (basse montagne) hilly

**montant, e** [mɔ̃tɑ̃, ɑ̃t] adj rising; **pull à col ~** high-necked jumper ▷ nm (somme, total) (sum) total, (total) amount; (de fenêtre) upright; (de lit) post

**monte-charge** [mɔ̃tʃaʀʒ] nm inv goods lift, hoist

**montée** [mɔ̃te] nf (des prix, hostilités) rise; (escalade) climb; (côte) hill; **au milieu de la ~** halfway up

**monter** [mɔ̃te] vt (escalier, côte) to go (ou come) up; (valise, paquet) to take (ou bring) up; (étagère) to raise; (tente, échafaudage) to put up; (machine) to assemble; (Cinéma) to edit; (Théâtre) to put on, stage; (société etc) to set up ▷ vi to go (ou come) up; (prix, niveau, température) to go up, rise; (passager) to get on; **~ à cheval** (faire du cheval) to ride (a horse); **~ sur** to climb up onto; **~**

**sur** *ou* **à un arbre/une échelle** to climb (up) a tree/ladder; **se monter à** (*frais etc*) to add up to, come to

**montgolfière** [mɔ̃gɔlfjɛʀ] *nf* hot-air balloon

**montre** [mɔ̃tʀ] *nf* watch; **contre la ~** (*Sport*) against the clock

**Montréal** [mɔ̃real] *n* Montreal

**montrer** [mɔ̃tʀe] *vt* to show; **~ qch à qn** to show sb sth; **pouvez-vous me ~ où c'est?** can you show me where it is?

**monture** [mɔ̃tyʀ] *nf* (*cheval*) mount; (*de lunettes*) frame; (*d'une bague*) setting

**monument** [mɔnymɑ̃] *nm* monument; **monument aux morts** war memorial

**moquer** [mɔke]: **se moquer de** *vt* to make fun of, laugh at; (*fam: se désintéresser de*) not to care about; (*tromper*): **se ~ de qn** to take sb for a ride

**moquette** [mɔkɛt] *nf* fitted carpet

**moqueur, -euse** [mɔkœʀ, øz] *adj* mocking

**moral, e, -aux** [mɔʀal, o] *adj* moral ▷ *nm* morale; **avoir le ~** (*fam*) to be in good spirits; **avoir le ~ à zéro** (*fam*) to be really down; **morale** *nf* (*mœurs*) morals *pl*; (*valeurs*) moral standards *pl*, morality; (*d'une fable etc*) moral; **faire la morale à** to lecture, preach at; **moralité** *nf* morality; (*de fable*) moral

**morceau, x** [mɔʀso] *nm* piece, bit; (*d'une œuvre*) passage, extract; (*Mus*) piece; (*Culin: de viande*) cut; (*de sucre*) lump; **mettre en ~x** to pull to pieces *ou* bits; **manger un ~** to have a bite (to eat)

**morceler** [mɔʀsəle] *vt* to break up, divide up

**mordant, e** [mɔʀdɑ̃, ɑ̃t] *adj* (*ton, remarque*) scathing, cutting; (*ironie, froid*) biting ▷ *nm* (*style*) bite, punch

**mordiller** [mɔʀdije] *vt* to nibble at, chew at

**mordre** [mɔʀdʀ] *vt* to bite ▷ *vi* (*poisson*) to bite; **~ sur** (*fig*) to go over into, overlap into; **~ à l'hameçon** to bite, rise to the bait

**mordu, e** [mɔʀdy] (*fam*) *nm/f* enthusiast; **un ~ de jazz** a jazz fanatic

**morfondre** [mɔʀfɔ̃dʀ]: **se morfondre** *vi* to mope

**morgue** [mɔʀg] *nf* (*arrogance*) haughtiness; (*lieu: de la police*) morgue; (: *à l'hôpital*) mortuary

**morne** [mɔʀn] *adj* dismal, dreary

**morose** [mɔʀoz] *adj* sullen, morose

**mors** [mɔʀ] *nm* bit

**morse** [mɔʀs] *nm* (*Zool*) walrus; (*Tél*) Morse (code)

**morsure** [mɔʀsyʀ] *nf* bite

**mort¹** [mɔʀ] *nf* death

**mort², e** [mɔʀ, mɔʀt] *pp de* **mourir** ▷ *adj* dead ▷ *nm/f* (*défunt*) dead man *ou* woman; (*victime*): **il y a eu plusieurs ~s** several people were killed, there were several killed; **~ de peur/fatigue** frightened to death/dead tired

**mortalité** [mɔʀtalite] *nf* mortality, death rate

**mortel, le** [mɔʀtɛl] *adj* (*poison etc*) deadly, lethal; (*accident, blessure*) fatal; (*silence, ennemi*) deadly; (*péché*) mortal; (*fam: ennuyeux*) deadly boring

**mort-né, e** [mɔʀne] *adj* (*enfant*) stillborn

**mortuaire** [mɔʀtɥeʀ] *adj*: **avis ~** death announcement

**morue** [mɔʀy] *nf* (*Zool*) cod *inv*

**mosaïque** [mɔzaik] *nf* mosaic

**Moscou** [mɔsku] *n* Moscow

**mosquée** [mɔske] *nf* mosque

**mot** [mo] *nm* word; (*message*) line, note; **~ à ~** word for word; **mot de passe** password; **mots croisés** crossword (puzzle) *sg*

**motard** [mɔtaʀ] *nm* biker; (*policier*) motorcycle cop

**motel** [mɔtɛl] *nm* motel

**moteur, -trice** [mɔtœʀ, tʀis] *adj* (*Anat, Physiol*) motor; (*Tech*) driving; (*Auto*): **à 4 roues motrices** 4-wheel drive ▷ *nm* engine, motor; **à ~** power-driven, motor *cpd*; **moteur de recherche** search engine

**motif** [mɔtif] *nm* (*cause*) motive;

(*décoratif*) design, pattern, motif; **sans ~** groundless

**motivation** [mɔtivasjɔ̃] *nf* motivation

**motiver** [mɔtive] *vt* to motivate; (*justifier*) to justify, account for

**moto** [mɔto] *nf* (motor)bike; **motocycliste** *nm/f* motorcyclist

**motorisé, e** [mɔtɔʀize] *adj* (*personne*) having transport *ou* a car

**motrice** [mɔtʀis] *adj voir* **moteur**

**motte** [mɔt] *nf:* **~ de terre** lump of earth, clod (of earth); **motte de beurre** lump of butter

**mou (mol), molle** [mu, mɔl] *adj* soft; (*personne*) lethargic; (*protestations*) weak ▷ *nm:* **avoir du mou** to be slack

**mouche** [muʃ] *nf* fly

**moucher** [muʃe]: **se moucher** *vi* to blow one's nose

**moucheron** [muʃʀɔ̃] *nm* midge

**mouchoir** [muʃwaʀ] *nm* handkerchief, hanky; **mouchoir en papier** tissue, paper hanky

**moudre** [mudʀ] *vt* to grind

**moue** [mu] *nf* pout; **faire la ~** to pout; (*fig*) to pull a face

**mouette** [mwɛt] *nf* (sea)gull

**moufle** [mufl] *nf* (*gant*) mitt(en)

**mouillé, e** [muje] *adj* wet

**mouiller** [muje] *vt* (*humecter*) to wet, moisten; (*tremper*): **~ qn/qch** to make sb/sth wet ▷ *vi* (*Navig*) to lie *ou* be at anchor; **se mouiller** to get wet; (*fam: prendre des risques*) to commit o.s.

**moulant, e** [mulɑ̃, ɑ̃t] *adj* figure-hugging

**moule** [mul] *nf* mussel ▷ *nm* (*Culin*) mould; **moule à gâteaux** *nm* cake tin (BRIT) *ou* pan (US)

**mouler** [mule] *vt* (*suj: vêtement*) to hug, fit closely round

**moulin** [mulɛ̃] *nm* mill; **moulin à café** coffee mill; **moulin à eau** watermill; **moulin à légumes** (vegetable) shredder; **moulin à paroles** (*fig*) chatterbox; **moulin à poivre** pepper mill; **moulin à vent** windmill

**moulinet** [mulinɛ] *nm* (*de canne à pêche*) reel; (*mouvement*): **faire des ~s avec qch** to whirl sth around

**moulinette®** [mulinɛt] *nf* (vegetable) shredder

**moulu, e** [muly] *pp de* **moudre**

**mourant, e** [muʀɑ̃, ɑ̃t] *adj* dying

**mourir** [muʀiʀ] *vi* to die; (*civilisation*) to die out; **~ de froid/faim** to die of exposure/hunger; **~ de faim/d'ennui** (*fig*) to be starving/be bored to death; **~ d'envie de faire** to be dying to do

**mousse** [mus] *nf* (Bot) moss; (*de savon*) lather; (*écume: sur eau, bière*) froth, foam; (Culin) mousse ▷ *nm* (Navig) ship's boy; **mousse à raser** shaving foam

**mousseline** [muslin] *nf* muslin; **pommes ~** mashed potatoes

**mousser** [muse] *vi* (*bière, détergent*) to foam; (*savon*) to lather; **mousseux, -euse** *adj* frothy ▷ *nm:* **(vin) mousseux** sparkling wine

**mousson** [musɔ̃] *nf* monsoon

**moustache** [mustaʃ] *nf* moustache; **moustaches** *nfpl* (*du chat*) whiskers *pl*; **moustachu, e** *adj* with a moustache

**moustiquaire** [mustikɛʀ] *nf* mosquito net

**moustique** [mustik] *nm* mosquito

**moutarde** [mutaʀd] *nf* mustard

**mouton** [mutɔ̃] *nm* sheep *inv*; (*peau*) sheepskin; (Culin) mutton

**mouvement** [muvmɑ̃] *nm* movement; (*fig: impulsion*) gesture; **avoir un bon ~** to make a nice gesture; **en ~** in motion; on the move; **mouvementé, e** *adj* (*vie, poursuite*) eventful; (*réunion*) turbulent

**mouvoir** [muvwaʀ]: **se mouvoir** *vi* to move

**moyen, ne** [mwajɛ̃, jɛn] *adj* average; (*tailles, prix*) medium; (*de grandeur moyenne*) medium-sized ▷ *nm* (*façon*) means *sg*, way; **moyens** *nmpl* (*capacités*) means; **très ~** (*résultats*) pretty poor; **je n'en ai pas les ~s** I can't afford it; **au ~ de** by means of; **par tous les ~s** by every possible means, every possible way; **par ses propres ~s** all by oneself; **moyen âge** Middle Ages pl; **moyen de transport** means of transport

**moyennant** [mwajenɑ̃] *prép (somme)* for; *(service, conditions)* in return for; *(travail, effort)* with

**moyenne** [mwajɛn] *nf* average; *(Math)* mean; *(Scol)* pass mark; **en ~** on (an) average; **moyenne d'âge** average age

**Moyen-Orient** [mwajɛnɔʀjɑ̃] *nm:* **le ~** the Middle East

**moyeu, x** [mwajø] *nm* hub

**MST** *sigle f (= maladie sexuellement transmissible)* STD

**mû, mue** [my] *pp de* **mouvoir**

**muer** [mɥe] *vi (oiseau, mammifère)* to moult; *(serpent)* to slough; *(jeune garçon):* **il mue** his voice is breaking

**muet, te** [mɥɛ, mɥɛt] *adj* dumb; *(fig):* **~ d'admiration** *etc* speechless with admiration *etc; (Cinéma)* silent ▷ *nm/f* mute

**mufle** [myfl] *nm* muzzle; *(fam: goujat)* boor

**mugir** [myʒiʀ] *vi (taureau)* to bellow; *(vache)* to low; *(fig)* to howl

**muguet** [mygɛ] *nm* lily of the valley

**mule** [myl] *nf (Zool)* (she-)mule

**mulet** [mylɛ] *nm (Zool)* (he-)mule

**multinationale** [myltinasjɔnal] *nf* multinational

**multiple** [myltipl] *adj* multiple, numerous; *(varié)* many, manifold; **multiplication** *nf* multiplication; **multiplier** *vt* to multiply; **se multiplier** *vi* to multiply

**municipal, e, -aux** [mynisipal, o] *adj (élections, stade)* municipal; *(conseil)* town *cpd;* **piscine/bibliothèque ~e** public swimming pool/library; **municipalité** *nf (ville)* municipality; *(conseil)* town council

**munir** [myniʀ] *vt:* **~ qch de** to equip sth with; **se ~ de** to arm o.s. with

**munitions** [mynisjɔ̃] *nfpl* ammunition *sg*

**mur** [myʀ] *nm* wall; **mur du son** sound barrier

**mûr, e** [myʀ] *adj* ripe; *(personne)* mature

**muraille** [myʀaj] *nf* (high) wall

**mural, e, -aux** [myʀal, o] *adj* wall *cpd;* *(art)* mural

**mûre** [myʀ] *nf* blackberry

**muret** [myʀɛ] *nm* low wall

**mûrir** [myʀiʀ] *vi (fruit, blé)* to ripen; *(abcès)* to come to a head; *(fig: idée, personne)* to mature ▷ *vt (projet)* to nurture; *(personne)* to (make) mature

**murmure** [myʀmyʀ] *nm* murmur; **murmurer** *vi* to murmur

**muscade** [myskad] *nf (aussi:* **noix (de) ~)** nutmeg

**muscat** [myska] *nm (raisins)* muscat grape; *(vin)* muscatel (wine)

**muscle** [myskl] *nm* muscle; **musclé, e** *adj* muscular; *(fig)* strong-arm

**museau, x** [myzo] *nm* muzzle; *(Culin)* brawn

**musée** [myze] *nm* museum; *(de peinture)* art gallery

**museler** [myz(ə)le] *vt* to muzzle; **muselière** *nf* muzzle

**musette** [myzɛt] *nf (sac)* lunchbag

**musical, e, -aux** [myzikal, o] *adj* musical

**music-hall** [myzikol] *nm (salle)* variety theatre; *(genre)* variety

**musicien, ne** [myzisjɛ̃, jɛn] *adj* musical ▷ *nm/f* musician

**musique** [myzik] *nf* music

● **FÊTE DE LA MUSIQUE**
●
● The **Fête de la Musique** is a music
● festival which takes place every year
● on 21 June. Throughout France, local
● musicians perform free of charge in
● parks, streets and squares.

**musulman, e** [myzylmɑ̃, an] *adj, nm/f* Moslem, Muslim

**mutation** [mytasjɔ̃] *nf (Admin)* transfer

**muter** [myte] *vt* to transfer, move

**mutilé, e** [mytile] *nm/f* disabled

person (*through loss of limbs*)
**mutiler** [mytile] *vt* to mutilate, maim
**mutin, e** [mytɛ̃, in] *adj* (*air, ton*) mischievous, impish ▷ *nm/f* (*Mil, Navig*) mutineer; **mutinerie** *nf* mutiny
**mutisme** [mytism] *nm* silence
**mutuel, le** [mytɥɛl] *adj* mutual; **mutuelle** *nf* voluntary insurance premiums for back-up health cover
**myope** [mjɔp] *adj* short-sighted
**myosotis** [mjɔzɔtis] *nm* forget-me-not
**myrtille** [miʀtij] *nf* bilberry
**mystère** [mistɛʀ] *nm* mystery; **mystérieux, -euse** *adj* mysterious
**mystifier** [mistifje] *vt* to fool
**mythe** [mit] *nm* myth
**mythologie** [mitɔlɔʒi] *nf* mythology

**n'** [n] *adv voir* **ne**
**nacre** [nakʀ] *nf* mother of pearl
**nage** [naʒ] *nf* swimming; (*manière*) style of swimming, stroke; **traverser/ s'éloigner à la ~** to swim across/away; **en ~** bathed in sweat; **nageoire** *nf* fin; **nager** *vi* to swim; **nageur, -euse** *nm/f* swimmer
**naïf, -ïve** [naif, naiv] *adj* naïve
**nain, e** [nɛ̃, nɛn] *nm/f* dwarf
**naissance** [nɛsɑ̃s] *nf* birth; **donner ~ à** to give birth to; (*fig*) to give rise to; **lieu de ~** place of birth
**naître** [nɛtʀ] *vi* to be born; (*fig*): **~ de** to arise from, be born out of; **il est né en 1960** he was born in 1960; **faire ~** (*fig*) to give rise to, arouse
**naïveté** [naivte] *nf* naïvety
**nana** [nana] (*fam*) *nf* (*fille*) chick, bird (BRIT)
**nappe** [nap] *nf* tablecloth; (*de pétrole, gaz*) layer; **napperon** *nm* table-mat
**naquit** *etc* [naki] *vb voir* **naître**
**narguer** [naʀge] *vt* to taunt

**narine** [naʀin] *nf* nostril

**natal, e** [natal] *adj* native; **natalité**
*nf* birth rate

**natation** [natasjɔ̃] *nf* swimming

**natif, -ive** [natif, iv] *adj* native

**nation** [nasjɔ̃] *nf* nation;
**national, e, -aux** *adj* national;
**nationale** *nf*: **(route) nationale**
≈ A road (BRIT); ≈ state highway (US);
**nationaliser** *vt* to nationalize;
**nationalisme** *nm* nationalism;
**nationalité** *nf* nationality

**natte** [nat] *nf* (*cheveux*) plait; (*tapis*)
mat

**naturaliser** [natyʀalize] *vt* to
naturalize

**nature** [natyʀ] *nf* nature ▷ *adj, adv*
(*Culin*) plain, without seasoning or
sweetening; (*café, thé*) black, without
sugar; (*yaourt*) natural; **payer en ~**
to pay in kind; **nature morte** still
life; **naturel, le** *adj* (*gén, aussi enfant*)
natural ▷ *nm* (*absence d'affectation*)
naturalness; (*caractère*) disposition,
nature; **naturellement** *adv* naturally;
(*bien sûr*) of course

**naufrage** [nofʀaʒ] *nm* (ship)wreck;
**faire ~** to be shipwrecked

**nausée** [noze] *nf* nausea; **avoir la ~**
to feel sick

**nautique** [notik] *adj* nautical, water
*cpd*; **sports ~s** water sports

**naval, e** [naval] *adj* naval; (*industrie*)
shipbuilding

**navet** [navɛ] *nm* turnip; (*péj: film*)
rubbishy film

**navette** [navɛt] *nf* shuttle; **faire la
~ (entre)** to go to and fro *ou* shuttle
(between)

**navigateur** [navigatœʀ] *nm* (*Navig*)
seafarer; (*Inform*) browser

**navigation** [navigasjɔ̃] *nf* navigation,
sailing

**naviguer** [navige] *vi* to navigate, sail;
**~ sur Internet** to browse the Internet

**navire** [naviʀ] *nm* ship

**navrer** [navʀe] *vt* to upset, distress; **je
suis navré** I'm so sorry

**ne, n'** [n(ə)] *adv voir* **pas**; **plus**; **jamais**
*etc*; (*sans valeur négative: non traduit*):
**c'est plus loin que je ne le croyais** it's
further than I thought

**né, e** [ne] *pp* (*voir* naître): **né en 1960**
born in 1960; **née Scott** née Scott

**néanmoins** [neɑ̃mwɛ̃] *adv*
nevertheless

**néant** [neɑ̃] *nm* nothingness; **réduire à
~** to bring to nought; (*espoir*) to dash

**nécessaire** [neseseʀ] *adj* necessary
▷ *nm* necessary; (*sac*) kit; **je vais faire
le ~** I'll see to it; **nécessaire de couture**
sewing kit; **nécessaire de toilette**
toilet bag; **nécessité** *nf* necessity;
**nécessiter** *vt* to require

**nectar** [nɛktaʀ] *nm* nectar

**néerlandais, e** [neeʀlɑ̃dɛ, ɛz] *adj*
Dutch

**nef** [nɛf] *nf* (*d'église*) nave

**néfaste** [nefast] *adj* (*nuisible*) harmful;
(*funeste*) ill-fated

**négatif, -ive** [negatif, iv] *adj* negative
▷ *nm* (*Photo*) negative

**négligé, e** [negliʒe] *adj* (*en désordre*)
slovenly ▷ *nm* (*tenue*) negligee

**négligeable** [negliʒabl] *adj* negligible

**négligent, e** [negliʒɑ̃, ɑ̃t] *adj* careless,
negligent

**négliger** [negliʒe] *vt* (*tenue*) to be
careless about; (*avis, précautions*) to
disregard; (*épouse, jardin*) to neglect; **~
de faire** to fail to do, not bother to do

**négociant, e** [negosjɑ̃, jɑ̃t] *nm/f*
merchant

**négociation** [negosjasjɔ̃] *nf*
negotiation

**négocier** [negosje] *vi, vt* to negotiate

**nègre** [nɛgʀ] (*péj*) *nm* (*écrivain*) ghost
(writer)

**neige** [nɛʒ] *nf* snow; **neiger** *vi* to snow

**nénuphar** [nenyfaʀ] *nm* water-lily

**néon** [neɔ̃] *nm* neon

**néo-zélandais, e** [neozelɑ̃dɛ, ɛz]
*adj* New Zealand *cpd* ▷ *nm/f*: **Néo-
Zélandais, e** New Zealander

**Népal** [nepal] *nm*: **le ~** Nepal

**nerf** [nɛʀ] *nm* nerve; **être sur les ~s**

to be all keyed up; **nerveux, -euse** adj nervous; (*irritable*) touchy, nervy; (*voiture*) nippy, responsive; **nervosité** nf excitability, tenseness; (*irritabilité passagère*) irritability, nerviness

**n'est-ce pas?** [nɛspɑ] adv isn't it?, won't you? *etc, selon le verbe qui précède*

**Net** [nɛt] nm (*Internet*): **le ~** the Net

**net, nette** [nɛt] adj (*sans équivoque, distinct*) clear; (*évident: amélioration, différence*) marked, distinct; (*propre*) neat, clean; (*Comm: prix, salaire*) net ▷ adv (*refuser*) flatly ▷ nm: **mettre au ~** to copy out; **s'arrêter ~** to stop dead; **nettement** adv clearly, distinctly; (*incontestablement*) decidedly; **netteté** nf clearness

**nettoyage** [netwajaʒ] nm cleaning; **nettoyage à sec** dry cleaning

**nettoyer** [netwaje] vt to clean

**neuf¹** [nœf] num nine

**neuf², neuve** [nœf, nœv] adj new; **remettre à ~** to do up (as good as new), refurbish; **quoi de ~?** what's new?

**neutre** [nøtʁ] adj neutral; (*Ling*) neuter

**neuve** [nœv] adj voir **neuf²**

**neuvième** [nœvjɛm] num ninth

**neveu, x** [n(ə)vø] nm nephew

**New York** [njujɔʁk] n New York

**nez** [ne] nm nose; **~ à ~ avec** face to face with; **avoir du ~** to have flair

**ni** [ni] conj: **ni ... ni** neither ... nor; **je n'aime ni les lentilles ni les épinards** I like neither lentils nor spinach; **il n'a dit ni oui ni non** he didn't say either yes or no; **elles ne sont venues ni l'une ni l'autre** neither of them came; **il n'a rien vu ni entendu** he didn't see or hear anything

**niche** [niʃ] nf (*du chien*) kennel; (*de mur*) recess, niche; **nicher** vi to nest

**nid** [ni] nm nest; **nid de poule** pothole

**nièce** [njɛs] nf niece

**nier** [nje] vt to deny

**Nil** [nil] nm: **le ~** the Nile

**n'importe** [nɛ̃pɔʁt] adv: **n'importe qui/quoi/où** anybody/anything/anywhere; **n'importe quand** any time;

**n'importe quel/quelle** any; **n'importe lequel/laquelle** any (one); **n'importe comment** (*sans soin*) carelessly

**niveau, x** [nivo] nm level; (*des élèves, études*) standard; **niveau de vie** standard of living

**niveler** [niv(ə)le] vt to level

**noble** [nɔbl] adj noble; **noblesse** nf nobility; (*d'une action etc*) nobleness

**noce** [nɔs] nf wedding; (*gens*) wedding party (*ou* guests *pl*); **faire la ~** (*fam*) to go on a binge; **noces d'argent/d'or/de diamant** silver/golden/diamond wedding (anniversary)

**nocif, -ive** [nɔsif, iv] adj harmful

**nocturne** [nɔktyʁn] adj nocturnal ▷ nf late-night opening

**Noël** [nɔɛl] nm Christmas

**nœud** [nø] nm knot; (*ruban*) bow; **nœud papillon** bow tie

**noir, e** [nwaʁ] adj black; (*obscur, sombre*) dark ▷ nm/f black man/woman ▷ nm: **dans le ~** in the dark; **travail au ~** moonlighting; **travailler au ~** to work on the side; **noircir** vt, vi to blacken; **noire** nf (*Mus*) crotchet (*BRIT*), quarter note (*US*)

**noisette** [nwazɛt] nf hazelnut

**noix** [nwa] nf walnut; (*Culin*): **une ~ de beurre** a knob of butter; **à la ~** (*fam*) worthless; **noix de cajou** cashew nut; **noix de coco** coconut; **noix muscade** nutmeg

**nom** [nɔ̃] nm name; (*Ling*) noun; **nom de famille** surname; **nom de jeune fille** maiden name

**nomade** [nɔmad] nm/f nomad

**nombre** [nɔ̃bʁ] nm number; **venir en ~** to come in large numbers; **depuis ~ d'années** for many years; **au ~ de mes amis** among my friends; **nombreux, -euse** adj many, numerous; (*avec nom sg: foule etc*) large; **peu nombreux** few; **de nombreux cas** many cases

**nombril** [nɔ̃bʁi(l)] nm navel

**nommer** [nɔme] vt to name; (*élire*) to appoint, nominate; **se nommer**; **il se**

**nomme Pascal** his name's Pascal, he's called Pascal

**non** [nɔ̃] *adv* (*réponse*) no; (*avec loin, sans, seulement*) not; **~ (pas) que** not that; **moi ~ plus** neither do I, I don't either; **c'est bon ~?** (*exprimant le doute*) it's good, isn't it?; **je pense que ~** I don't think so

**non alcoolisé, e** [nɔ̃alkɔlize] *adj* non alcoholic

**nonchalant, e** [nɔ̃ʃalɑ̃, ɑ̃t] *adj* nonchalant

**non-fumeur, -euse** [nɔ̃fymœʀ, øz] *nm/f* non-smoker

**non-sens** [nɔ̃sɑ̃s] *nm* absurdity

**nord** [nɔʀ] *nm* North ▷ *adj* northern; north; **au ~** (*situation*) in the north; (*direction*) to the north; **au ~ de** (to the) north of; **nord-africain, e** *adj* North-African ▷ *nm/f*: **Nord-Africain, e** North African; **nord-est** *nm* North-East; **nord-ouest** *nm* North-West

**normal, e, -aux** [nɔʀmal, o] *adj* normal; **c'est tout à fait ~** it's perfectly natural; **vous trouvez ça ~?** does it seem right to you?; **normale** *nf*: **la normale** the norm, the average; **normalement** *adv* (*en général*) normally

**normand, e** [nɔʀmɑ̃, ɑ̃d] *adj* of Normandy ▷ *nm/f*: **N~, e** (*de Normandie*) Norman

**Normandie** [nɔʀmɑ̃di] *nf* Normandy

**norme** [nɔʀm] *nf* norm; (*Tech*) standard

**Norvège** [nɔʀvɛʒ] *nf* Norway; **norvégien, ne** *adj* Norwegian ▷ *nm/f*: **Norvégien, ne** Norwegian ▷ *nm* (*Ling*) Norwegian

**nos** [no] *adj voir* **notre**

**nostalgie** [nɔstalʒi] *nf* nostalgia; **nostalgique** *adj* nostalgic

**notable** [nɔtabl] *adj* (*fait*) notable, noteworthy; (*marqué*) noticeable, marked ▷ *nm* prominent citizen

**notaire** [nɔtɛʀ] *nm* solicitor

**notamment** [nɔtamɑ̃] *adv* in particular, among others

**note** [nɔt] *nf* (*écrite, Mus*) note; (*Scol*) mark (BRIT), grade; (*facture*) bill; **note de service** memorandum

**noter** [nɔte] *vt* (*écrire*) to write down; (*remarquer*) to note, notice; (*devoir*) to mark, grade

**notice** [nɔtis] *nf* summary, short article; (*brochure*) leaflet, instruction book

**notifier** [nɔtifje] *vt*: **~ qch à qn** to notify sb of sth, notify sth to sb

**notion** [nɔsjɔ̃] *nf* notion, idea

**notoire** [nɔtwaʀ] *adj* widely known; (*en mal*) notorious

**notre** [nɔtʀ] *adj* our

**nôtre** [notʀ] *pron*: **le ~, la ~, les ~s** ours ▷ *adj* ours; **les ~s** ours; (*alliés etc*) our own people; **soyez des ~s** join us

**nouer** [nwe] *vt* to tie, knot; (*fig: alliance etc*) to strike up

**noueux, -euse** [nwø, øz] *adj* gnarled

**nourrice** [nuʀis] *nf* (*gardienne*) child-minder

**nourrir** [nuʀiʀ] *vt* to feed; (*fig: espoir*) to harbour, nurse; **nourrissant, e** *adj* nourishing, nutritious; **nourrisson** *nm* (*unweaned*) infant; **nourriture** *nf* food

**nous** [nu] *pron* (*sujet*) we; (*objet*) us; **nous-mêmes** *pron* ourselves

**nouveau (nouvel), -elle, x** [nuvo, nuvɛl] *adj* new ▷ *nm*: **y a-t-il du nouveau?** is there anything new on this? ▷ *nm/f* new pupil (*ou* employee); **de nouveau, à nouveau** again; **nouveau venu, nouvelle venue** newcomer; **nouveaux mariés** newly-weds; **nouveau-né, e** *nm/f* newborn baby; **nouveauté** *nf* novelty; (*objet*) new thing *ou* article

**nouvel** [nuvɛl] *adj voir* **nouveau**; **Nouvel An** New Year

**nouvelle** [nuvɛl] *adj voir* **nouveau** ▷ *nf* (*piece of*) news *sg*; (*Littérature*) short story; **les ~s** (*Presse, TV*) the news; **je suis sans ~s de lui** I haven't heard from him; **Nouvelle-Calédonie** *nf* New Caledonia; **Nouvelle-Zélande** *nf* New Zealand

**novembre** [nɔvɑ̃bʀ] *nm* November

○ **NOVEMBRE**
○
○ **Le 11 novembre** is a public holiday in
○ France commemorating the signing
○ of the armistice, near Compiègne, at
○ the end of World War I.

**noyade** [nwajad] *nf* drowning *no pl*
**noyau, x** [nwajo] *nm* (*de fruit*) stone;
(*Bio, Physique*) nucleus; (*fig: centre*) core
**noyer** [nwaje] *nm* walnut (tree); (*bois*)
walnut ▷ *vt* to drown; (*moteur*) to flood;
**se noyer** *vi* to be drowned, drown;
(*suicide*) to drown o.s.
**nu, e** [ny] *adj* naked; (*membres*) naked,
bare; (*pieds, mains, chambre, fil électrique*)
bare ▷ *nm* (*Art*) nude; **tout nu** stark
naked; **se mettre nu** to strip
**nuage** [nɥaʒ] *nm* cloud; **nuageux,**
**-euse** *adj* cloudy
**nuance** [nɥɑ̃s] *nf* (*de couleur, sens*)
shade; **il y a une ~ (entre)** there's a
slight difference (between); **nuancer**
*vt* (*opinion*) to bring some reservations
*ou* qualifications to
**nucléaire** [nykleɛʀ] *adj* nuclear ▷ *nm*:
**le ~** nuclear energy
**nudiste** [nydist] *nm/f* nudist
**nuée** [nɥe] *nf*: **une ~ de** a cloud *ou* host
*ou* swarm of
**nuire** [nɥiʀ] *vi* to be harmful; **~ à** to
harm, do damage to; **nuisible** *adj*
harmful; **animal nuisible** pest
**nuit** [nɥi] *nf* night; **il fait ~** it's dark;
**cette ~** (*hier*) last night; (*aujourd'hui*)
tonight; **de ~** (*vol, service*) night *cpd*;
**nuit blanche** sleepless night
**nul, nulle** [nyl] *adj* (*aucun*) no; (*minime*)
nil, non-existent; (*non valable*) null; (*péj*):
**être ~ (en)** to be useless *ou* hopeless
(at) ▷ *pron* none, no one; **match** *ou*
**résultat ~** draw; **~le part** nowhere;
**nullement** *adv* by no means
**numérique** [nymeʀik] *adj* numerical;
(*affichage, son, télévision*) digital
**numéro** [nymeʀo] *nm* number;

(*spectacle*) act, turn; (*Presse*) issue,
number; **numéro de téléphone**
(tele)phone number; **numéro vert**
≈ freefone® number (*BRIT*), ≈ toll-free
number (*US*); **numéroter** *vt* to number
**nuque** [nyk] *nf* nape of the neck
**nu-tête** [nytɛt] *adj inv, adv* bareheaded
**nutritif, -ive** [nytʀitif, iv] *adj* (*besoins,*
*valeur*) nutritional; (*nourrissant*)
nutritious
**nylon** [nilɔ̃] *nm* nylon

**oasis** [ɔazis] *nf* oasis
**obéir** [ɔbeiʀ] *vi* to obey; **~ à** to obey;
**obéissance** *nf* obedience;
**obéissant, e** *adj* obedient
**obèse** [ɔbɛz] *adj* obese; **obésité** *nf*
obesity
**objecter** [ɔbʒɛkte] *vt*: **~ que** to object
that; **objecteur** *nm*: **objecteur de
conscience** conscientious objector
**objectif, -ive** [ɔbʒɛktif, iv] *adj*
objective ▷ *nm* objective; (*Photo*) lens
*sg*, objective
**objection** [ɔbʒɛksjɔ̃] *nf* objection
**objectivité** [ɔbʒɛktivite] *nf* objectivity
**objet** [ɔbʒɛ] *nm* object; (*d'une discussion,
recherche*) subject; **être** *ou* **faire l'~
de** (*discussion*) to be the subject of;
(*soins*) to be given *ou* shown; **sans ~**
purposeless; (*craintes*) groundless;
**(bureau des) ~s trouvés** lost property
*sg* (BRIT), lost-and-found *sg* (US); **objet
d'art** objet d'art; **objets de valeur**
valuables; **objets personnels** personal
items

**obligation** [ɔbligasjɔ̃] *nf* obligation;
(*Comm*) bond, debenture; **obligatoire**
*adj* compulsory, obligatory;
**obligatoirement** *adv* necessarily;
(*fam: sans aucun doute*) inevitably
**obliger** [ɔbliʒe] *vt* (*contraindre*): **~ qn à
faire** to force *ou* oblige sb to do; **je suis
bien obligé (de le faire)** I have to (do it)
**oblique** [ɔblik] *adj* oblique; **en ~**
diagonally
**oblitérer** [ɔblitere] *vt* (*timbre-poste*)
to cancel
**obnubiler** [ɔbnybile] *vt* to obsess
**obscène** [ɔpsɛn] *adj* obscene
**obscur, e** [ɔpskyʀ] *adj* dark; (*méconnu*)
obscure; **obscurcir** *vt* to darken; (*fig*)
to obscure; **s'obscurcir** *vi* to grow
dark; **obscurité** *nf* darkness; **dans
l'obscurité** in the dark, in darkness
**obsédé, e** [ɔpsede] *nm/f*: **un ~ de jazz** a
jazz fanatic; **obsédé sexuel** sex maniac
**obséder** [ɔpsede] *vt* to obsess, haunt
**obsèques** [ɔpsɛk] *nfpl* funeral *sg*
**observateur, -trice** [ɔpsɛʀvatœʀ,
tʀis] *adj* observant, perceptive ▷ *nm/f*
observer
**observation** [ɔpsɛʀvasjɔ̃] *nf*
observation; (*d'un règlement etc*)
observance; (*reproche*) reproof; **être en
~** (*Méd*) to be under observation
**observatoire** [ɔpsɛʀvatwaʀ] *nm*
observatory
**observer** [ɔpsɛʀve] *vt* (*regarder*) to
observe, watch; (*scientifiquement; aussi
règlement etc*) to observe; (*surveiller*) to
watch; (*remarquer*) to observe, notice;
**faire ~ qch à qn** (*dire*) to point out
sth to sb
**obsession** [ɔpsesjɔ̃] *nf* obsession
**obstacle** [ɔpstakl] *nm* obstacle;
(*Équitation*) jump, hurdle; **faire ~ à**
(*projet*) to hinder, put obstacles in
the path of
**obstiné, e** [ɔpstine] *adj* obstinate
**obstiner** [ɔpstine]: **s'obstiner** *vi* to
insist, dig one's heels in; **s'~ à faire** to
persist (obstinately) in doing
**obstruer** [ɔpstʀye] *vt* to block,

obstruct

**obtenir** [ɔptəniʀ] vt to obtain, get; (résultat) to achieve, obtain; **~ de pouvoir faire** to obtain permission to do

**obturateur** [ɔptyʀatœʀ] nm (Photo) shutter

**obus** [ɔby] nm shell

**occasion** [ɔkazjõ] nf (aubaine, possibilité) opportunity; (circonstance) occasion; (Comm: article non neuf) secondhand buy; (: acquisition avantageuse) bargain; **à plusieurs ~s** on several occasions; **à l'~** sometimes, on occasions; **d'~** secondhand; **occasionnel, le** adj (non régulier) occasional

**occasionner** [ɔkazjɔne] vt to cause

**occident** [ɔksidã] nm: **l'O~** the West; **occidental, e, -aux** adj western; (Pol) Western ▷ nm/f Westerner

**occupation** [ɔkypasjõ] nf occupation

**occupé, e** [ɔkype] adj (personne) busy; (place, sièges) taken; (toilettes) engaged; (Mil, Pol) occupied; **la ligne est ~e** the line's engaged (BRIT) ou busy (US)

**occuper** [ɔkype] vt to occupy; (poste) to hold; **s'occuper de** (être responsable de) to be in charge of; (se charger de: affaire) to take charge of, deal with; (: clients etc) to attend to; **s'~ (à qch)** to occupy o.s. ou keep o.s. busy (with sth)

**occurrence** [ɔkyʀãs] nf: **en l'~** in this case

**océan** [ɔseã] nm ocean

**octet** [ɔktɛ] nm byte

**octobre** [ɔktɔbʀ] nm October

**oculiste** [ɔkylist] nm/f eye specialist

**odeur** [ɔdœʀ] nf smell

**odieux, -euse** [ɔdjø, jøz] adj hateful

**odorant, e** [ɔdɔʀã, ãt] adj sweet-smelling, fragrant

**odorat** [ɔdɔʀa] nm (sense of) smell

**œil** [œj] (pl **yeux**) nm eye; **avoir un ~ au beurre noir** ou **poché** to have a black eye; **à l'~** (fam) for free; **à l'~ nu** with the naked eye; **ouvrir l'~** (fig) to keep one's eyes open ou an eye out; **fermer**

**les yeux (sur)** (fig) to turn a blind eye (to); **les yeux fermés** (aussi fig) with one's eyes shut

**œillères** [œjɛʀ] nfpl blinkers (BRIT), blinders (US)

**œillet** [œjɛ] nm (Bot) carnation

**œuf** [œf, pl ø] nm; **œuf à la coque** boiled egg; **œuf au plat** fried egg; **œuf dur** hard-boiled egg; **œuf de Pâques** Easter egg; **œufs brouillés** scrambled eggs

**œuvre** [œvʀ] nf (tâche) task, undertaking; (livre, tableau etc) work; (ensemble de la production artistique) works pl ▷ nm (Constr): **le gros ~** the shell; **mettre en ~** (moyens) to make use of; **œuvre de bienfaisance** charity; **œuvre d'art** work of art

**offense** [ɔfãs] nf insult; **offenser** vt to offend, hurt; **s'offenser de qch** to take offence (BRIT) ou offense (US) at sth

**offert, e** [ɔfɛʀ, ɛʀt] pp de **offrir**

**office** [ɔfis] nm (agence) bureau, agency; (Rel) service ▷ nm ou nf (pièce) pantry; **faire ~ de** to act as; **d'~** automatically; **office du tourisme** tourist bureau

**officiel, le** [ɔfisjɛl] adj, nm/f official

**officier** [ɔfisje] nm officer

**officieux, -euse** [ɔfisjø, jøz] adj unofficial

**offrande** [ɔfʀãd] nf offering

**offre** [ɔfʀ] nf offer; (aux enchères) bid; (Admin: soumission) tender; (Écon): **l'~ et la demande** supply and demand; **"~s d'emploi"** "situations vacant"; **offre d'emploi** job advertised; **offre publique d'achat** takeover bid

**offrir** [ɔfʀiʀ] vt: **~ (à qn)** to offer (to sb); (faire cadeau de) to give (to sb); **s'offrir** vt (vacances, voiture) to treat o.s. to; **~ (à qn) de faire qch** to offer to do sth (for sb); **~ à boire à qn** (chez soi) to offer sb a drink; **je vous offre un verre** I'll buy you a drink

**OGM** sigle m (= organisme génétiquement modifié) GMO

**oie** [wa] nf (Zool) goose

**oignon** [ɔɲõ] nm onion; (de tulipe

*etc*) bulb

**oiseau, x** [wazo] *nm* bird; **oiseau de proie** bird of prey

**oisif, -ive** [wazif, iv] *adj* idle

**oléoduc** [ɔleɔdyk] *nm* (oil) pipeline

**olive** [ɔliv] *nf* (Bot) olive; **olivier** *nm* olive (tree)

**OLP** *sigle f* (= Organisation de libération de la Palestine) PLO

**olympique** [ɔlɛ̃pik] *adj* Olympic

**ombragé, e** [ɔ̃bʀaʒe] *adj* shaded, shady

**ombre** [ɔ̃bʀ] *nf* (espace non ensoleillé) shade; (ombre portée, tache) shadow; **à l'~** in the shade; **dans l'~** (fig) in the dark; **ombre à paupières** eyeshadow

**omelette** [ɔmlɛt] *nf* omelette; **omelette norvégienne** baked Alaska

**omettre** [ɔmɛtʀ] *vt* to omit, leave out

**omoplate** [ɔmɔplat] *nf* shoulder blade

**MOT-CLÉ**

**on** [ɔ̃] *pron* **1** (indéterminé) you, one; **on peut le faire ainsi** you ou one can do it like this, it can be done like this

**2** (quelqu'un): **on les a attaqués** they were attacked; **on vous demande au téléphone** there's a phone call for you, you're wanted on the phone

**3** (nous) we; **on va y aller demain** we're going tomorrow

**4** (les gens) they; **autrefois, on croyait ...** they used to believe ...

**5**: **on ne peut plus** *adv*: **on ne peut plus stupide** as stupid as can be

**oncle** [ɔ̃kl] *nm* uncle

**onctueux, -euse** [ɔ̃ktɥø, øz] *adj* creamy, smooth

**onde** [ɔ̃d] *nf* wave; **~s courtes/ moyennes** short/medium wave *sg*; **grandes ~s** long wave *sg*

**ondée** [ɔ̃de] *nf* shower

**on-dit** [ɔ̃di] *nm inv* rumour

**onduler** [ɔ̃dyle] *vi* to undulate; (cheveux) to wave

**onéreux, -euse** [ɔneʀø, øz] *adj* costly

**ongle** [ɔ̃gl] *nm* nail

**ont** [ɔ̃] *vb voir* **avoir**

**ONU** *sigle f* (= Organisation des Nations Unies) UN

**onze** ['ɔ̃z] *num* eleven; **onzième** *num* eleventh

**OPA** *sigle f* = **offre publique d'achat**

**opaque** [ɔpak] *adj* opaque

**opéra** [ɔpeʀa] *nm* opera; (édifice) opera house

**opérateur, -trice** [ɔpeʀatœʀ, tʀis] *nm/f* operator; **opérateur (de prise de vues)** cameraman

**opération** [ɔpeʀasjɔ̃] *nf* operation; (Comm) dealing

**opératoire** [ɔpeʀatwaʀ] *adj* (choc etc) post-operative

**opérer** [ɔpeʀe] *vt* (personne) to operate on; (faire, exécuter) to carry out, make ▷ *vi* (remède: faire effet) to act, work; (Méd) to operate; **s'opérer** *vi* (avoir lieu) to occur, take place; **se faire ~** to have an operation

**opérette** [ɔpeʀɛt] *nf* operetta, light opera

**opinion** [ɔpinjɔ̃] *nf* opinion; **l'opinion (publique)** public opinion

**opportun, e** [ɔpɔʀtœ̃, yn] *adj* timely, opportune; **opportuniste** *nm/f* opportunist

**opposant, e** [ɔpozɑ̃, ɑ̃t] *nm/f* opponent

**opposé, e** [ɔpoze] *adj* (direction) opposite; (faction) opposing; (opinions, intérêts) conflicting; (contre): **~ à** opposed to, against ▷ *nm*: **l'~** the other ou opposite side (ou direction); (contraire) the opposite; **à l'~** (fig) on the other hand; **à l'~ de** (fig) contrary to, unlike

**opposer** [ɔpoze] *vt* (personnes, équipes) to oppose; (couleurs) to contrast; **s'opposer** *vi* (équipes) to confront each other; (opinions) to conflict; (couleurs, styles) to contrast; **s'~ à** (interdire) to oppose; **~ qch à** (comme obstacle, défense) to set sth against; (comme objection) to put sth forward against

**opposition** [ɔpozisjɔ̃] nf opposition; **par ~ à** as opposed to; **entrer en ~ avec** to come into conflict with; **faire ~ à un chèque** to stop a cheque

**oppressant, e** [ɔpresɑ̃, ɑ̃t] adj oppressive

**oppresser** [ɔprese] vt to oppress; **oppression** nf oppression

**opprimer** [ɔprime] vt to oppress

**opter** [ɔpte] vi: **~ pour** to opt for

**opticien, ne** [ɔptisjɛ̃, jɛn] nm/f optician

**optimisme** [ɔptimism] nm optimism; **optimiste** nm/f optimist ▷ adj optimistic

**option** [ɔpsjɔ̃] nf option; **matière à ~** (Scol) optional subject

**optique** [ɔptik] adj (nerf) optic; (verres) optical ▷ nf (fig: manière de voir) perspective

**or** [ɔr] nm gold ▷ conj now, but; **en or** (objet) gold cpd; **une affaire en or** a real bargain; **il croyait gagner or il a perdu** he was sure he would win and yet he lost

**orage** [ɔraʒ] nm (thunder)storm; **orageux, -euse** adj stormy

**oral, e, -aux** [ɔral, o] adj, nm oral; **par voie ~e** (Méd) orally

**orange** [ɔrɑ̃ʒ] nf orange ▷ adj inv orange; **orangé, e** adj orangey, orange-coloured; **orangeade** nf orangeade; **oranger** nm orange tree

**orateur** [ɔratœr] nm speaker

**orbite** [ɔrbit] nf (Anat) (eye-)socket; (Physique) orbit

**Orcades** [ɔrkad] nfpl: **les ~** the Orkneys, the Orkney Islands

**orchestre** [ɔrkɛstr] nm orchestra; (de jazz) band; (places) stalls pl (BRIT), orchestra (US)

**orchidée** [ɔrkide] nf orchid

**ordinaire** [ɔrdinɛr] adj ordinary; (qualité) standard; (péj: commun) common ▷ nm ordinary; (menus) everyday fare ▷ nf (essence) ≈ two-star (petrol) (BRIT), ≈ regular gas (US); **d'~** usually, normally; **comme à l'~** as usual

**ordinateur** [ɔrdinatœr] nm computer; **ordinateur individuel** ou **personnel** personal computer; **ordinateur portable** laptop (computer)

**ordonnance** [ɔrdɔnɑ̃s] nf (Méd) prescription; (Mil) orderly, batman (BRIT); **pouvez-vous me faire une ~?** can you write me a prescription?

**ordonné, e** [ɔrdɔne] adj tidy, orderly

**ordonner** [ɔrdɔne] vt (agencer) to organize, arrange; (donner un ordre): **~ à qn de faire** to order sb to do; (Rel) to ordain; (Méd) to prescribe

**ordre** [ɔrdr] nm order; (propreté et soin) orderliness, tidiness; (nature): **d'~ pratique** of a practical nature; **ordres** nmpl (Rel) holy orders; **mettre en ~** to tidy (up), put in order; **par ~ alphabétique/d'importance** in alphabetical order/in order of importance; **à l'~ de qn** payable to sb; **être aux ~s de qn/sous les ~s de qn** to be at sb's disposal/under sb's command; **jusqu'à nouvel ~** until further notice; **de premier ~** first-rate; **ordre du jour** (d'une réunion) agenda; **à l'ordre du jour** (fig) topical; **ordre publique** law and order

**ordure** [ɔrdyr] nf filth no pl; **ordures** nfpl (balayures, déchets) rubbish sg, refuse sg; **ordures ménagères** household refuse

**oreille** [ɔrɛj] nf ear; **avoir de l'~** to have a good ear (for music)

**oreiller** [ɔreje] nm pillow

**oreillons** [ɔrejɔ̃] nmpl mumps sg

**ores** [ɔr]: **d'~ et déjà** adv already

**orfèvrerie** [ɔrfɛvrəri] nf goldsmith's (ou silversmith's) trade; (ouvrage) gold (ou silver) plate

**organe** [ɔrgan] nm organ; (porte-parole) representative, mouthpiece

**organigramme** [ɔrganigram] nm (tableau hiérarchique) organization chart; (schéma) flow chart

**organique** [ɔrganik] adj organic

**organisateur, -trice** [ɔrganizatœr,

tris] nm/f organizer

**organisation** [ɔʀɡanizasjɔ̃] nf organization; **Organisation des Nations Unies** United Nations (Organization)

**organiser** [ɔʀɡanize] vt to organize; (mettre sur pied: service etc) to set up; **s'organiser** to get organized

**organisme** [ɔʀɡanism] nm (Bio) organism; (corps, Admin) body

**organiste** [ɔʀɡanist] nm/f organist

**orgasme** [ɔʀɡasm] nm orgasm, climax

**orge** [ɔʀʒ] nf barley

**orgue** [ɔʀɡ] nm organ

**orgueil** [ɔʀɡœj] nm pride; **orgueilleux, -euse** adj proud

**oriental, e, -aux** [ɔʀjɑ̃tal, -o] adj (langue, produit) oriental; (frontière) eastern

**orientation** [ɔʀjɑ̃tasjɔ̃] nf (de recherches) orientation; (d'une maison etc) aspect; (d'un journal) leanings pl; **avoir le sens de l'~** to have a (good) sense of direction; **orientation professionnelle** careers advisory service

**orienté, e** [ɔʀjɑ̃te] adj (fig: article, journal) slanted; **bien/mal ~** (appartement) well/badly positioned; **~ au sud** facing south, with a southern aspect

**orienter** [ɔʀjɑ̃te] vt (tourner: antenne) to direct, turn; (personne, recherches) to direct; (fig: élève) to orientate; **s'orienter** (se repérer) to find one's bearings; **s'~ vers** (fig) to turn towards

**origan** [ɔʀiɡɑ̃] nm oregano

**originaire** [ɔʀiʒinɛʀ] adj: **être ~ de** to be a native of

**original, e, -aux** [ɔʀiʒinal, o] adj original; (bizarre) eccentric ▷ nm/f eccentric ▷ nm (document etc, Art) original

**origine** [ɔʀiʒin] nf origin; **origines** nfpl (d'une personne) origins; **d'~** (pays) of origin; **d'~ suédoise** of Swedish origin; (pneus etc) original; **à l'~** originally; **originel, le** adj original

**orme** [ɔʀm] nm elm

**ornement** [ɔʀnəmɑ̃] nm ornament

**orner** [ɔʀne] vt to decorate, adorn

**ornière** [ɔʀnjɛʀ] nf rut

**orphelin, e** [ɔʀfəlɛ̃, in] adj orphan(ed) ▷ nm/f orphan; **orphelin de mère/de père** motherless/fatherless; **orphelinat** nm orphanage

**orteil** [ɔʀtɛj] nm toe; **gros ~** big toe

**orthographe** [ɔʀtɔɡʀaf] nf spelling

**ortie** [ɔʀti] nf (stinging) nettle

**os** [ɔs] nm bone; **os à moelle** marrowbone

**osciller** [ɔsile] vi (au vent etc) to rock; (fig): **~ entre** to waver ou fluctuate between

**osé, e** [oze] adj daring, bold

**oseille** [ozɛj] nf sorrel

**oser** [oze] vi, vt to dare; **~ faire** to dare (to) do

**osier** [ozje] nm willow; **d'~, en ~** wicker(work)

**osseux, -euse** [ɔsø, øz] adj bony; (tissu, maladie, greffe) bone cpd

**otage** [ɔtaʒ] nm hostage; **prendre qn comme ~** to take sb hostage

**OTAN** sigle f (= Organisation du traité de l'Atlantique Nord) NATO

**otarie** [ɔtaʀi] nf sea-lion

**ôter** [ote] vt to remove; (soustraire) to take away; **~ qch à qn** to take sth (away) from sb; **~ qch de** to remove sth from

**otite** [ɔtit] nf ear infection

**ou** [u] conj or; **ou ... ou** either ... or; **ou bien** or (else)

○ **MOT-CLÉ**

**où** [u] pron relatif 1 (position, situation) where, that (souvent omis); **la chambre où il était** the room (that) he was in, the room where he was; **la ville où je l'ai rencontré** the town where I met him; **la pièce d'où il est sorti** the room he came out of; **le village d'où je viens** the village I come from; **les villes par où il est passé** the towns he

went through
**2** (*temps, état*) that (*souvent omis*); **le jour où il est parti** the day (that) he left; **au prix où c'est** at the price it is ▷ *adv* **1** (*interrogation*) where; **où est-il/va-t-il?** where is he/is he going?; **par où?** which way?; **d'où vient que …?** how come …?
**2** (*position*) where; **je sais où il est** I know where he is; **où que l'on aille** wherever you go

**ouate** ['wat] *nf* cotton wool (BRIT), cotton (US)

**oubli** [ubli] *nm* (*acte*): **l'~ de** forgetting; (*trou de mémoire*) lapse of memory; (*négligence*) omission, oversight; **tomber dans l'~** to sink into oblivion

**oublier** [ublije] *vt* to forget; (*laisser quelque part: chapeau etc*) to leave behind; (*ne pas voir: erreurs etc*) to miss; **j'ai oublié ma clé/mon passeport** I've forgotten my key/passport

**ouest** [wɛst] *nm* west ▷ *adj inv* west; (*région*) western; **à l'~** in the west; (*direction*) (to the) west, westwards; **à l'~ de** (to the) west of

**ouf** ['uf] *excl* phew!

**oui** ['wi] *adv* yes

**ouï-dire** ['widir]: **par ~** *adv* by hearsay

**ouïe** [wi] *nf* hearing; **ouïes** *nfpl* (*de poisson*) gills

**ouragan** [uʀagɑ̃] *nm* hurricane

**ourlet** [uʀlɛ] *nm* hem

**ours** [uʀs] *nm* bear; **ours blanc/brun** polar/brown bear; **ours (en peluche)** teddy (bear)

**oursin** [uʀsɛ̃] *nm* sea urchin

**ourson** [uʀsɔ̃] *nm* (bear-)cub

**ouste** [ust] *excl* hop it!

**outil** [uti] *nm* tool; **outiller** *vt* to equip

**outrage** [utʀaʒ] *nm* insult; **outrage à la pudeur** indecent conduct *no pl*

**outrance** [utʀɑ̃s]: **à ~** *adv* excessively, to excess

**outre** [utʀ] *prép* besides ▷ *adv*: **passer ~ à** to disregard, take no notice of; **en ~** besides, moreover; **~ mesure** to excess;

(*manger, boire*) immoderately; **outre-Atlantique** *adv* across the Atlantic; **outre-mer** *adv* overseas

**ouvert, e** [uvɛʀ, ɛʀt] *pp de* **ouvrir** ▷ *adj* open; (*robinet, gaz etc*) on; **ouvertement** *adv* openly; **ouverture** *nf* opening; (*Mus*) overture; **heures d'ouverture** (*Comm*) opening hours; **ouverture d'esprit** open-mindedness

**ouvrable** [uvʀabl] *adj*: **jour ~** working day, weekday

**ouvrage** [uvʀaʒ] *nm* (*tâche, de tricot etc*) work *no pl*; (*texte, livre*) work

**ouvre-boîte(s)** [uvʀəbwat] *nm inv* tin (BRIT) *ou* can opener

**ouvre-bouteille(s)** [uvʀəbutɛj] *nm inv* bottle-opener

**ouvreuse** [uvʀøz] *nf* usherette

**ouvrier, -ière** [uvʀije, ijɛʀ] *nm/f* worker ▷ *adj* working-class; (*conflit*) industrial; (*mouvement*) labour *cpd*; **classe ouvrière** working class

**ouvrir** [uvʀiʀ] *vt* (*gén*) to open; (*brèche, passage, Méd: abcès*) to open up; (*commencer l'exploitation de, créer*) to open (up); (*eau, électricité, chauffage, robinet*) to turn on ▷ *vi* to open; to open up; **s'ouvrir** *vi* to open; **s'~ à qn** to open one's heart to sb; **est-ce ouvert au public?** is it open to the public?; **quand est-ce que le musée est ouvert?** when is the museum open?; **à quelle heure ouvrez-vous?** what time do you open?; **~ l'appétit à qn** to whet sb's appetite

**ovaire** [ovɛʀ] *nm* ovary

**ovale** [oval] *adj* oval

**OVNI** [ovni] *sigle m* (= *objet volant non identifié*) UFO

**oxyder** [okside]: **s'oxyder** *vi* to become oxidized

**oxygène** [oksiʒɛn] *nm* oxygen

**oxygéné, e** [oksiʒene] *adj*: **eau ~e** hydrogen peroxide

**ozone** [ozon] *nf* ozone; **la couche d'~** the ozone layer

**P**

brown/wholemeal (BRIT) ou wholewheat (US) bread; **pain d'épice** ≈ gingerbread; **pain de mie** sandwich loaf; **pain grillé** toast

**pair, e** [pɛʀ] adj (nombre) even ▷ nm peer; **aller de ~** to go hand in hand ou together; **jeune fille au ~** au pair; **paire** nf pair

**paisible** [pezibl] adj peaceful, quiet

**paix** [pɛ] nf peace; **faire/avoir la ~** to make/have peace; **fiche-lui la ~!** (fam) leave him alone!

**Pakistan** [pakistɑ̃] nm: **le ~** Pakistan

**palais** [palɛ] nm palace; (Anat) palate

**pâle** [pɑl] adj pale; **bleu ~** pale blue

**Palestine** [palɛstin] nf: **la ~** Palestine

**palette** [palɛt] nf (de peintre) palette; (produits) range

**pâleur** [pɑlœʀ] nf paleness

**palier** [palje] nm (d'escalier) landing; (fig) level, plateau; **par ~s** in stages

**pâlir** [pɑliʀ] vi to turn ou go pale; (couleur) to fade

**pallier** [palje] vt to offset, make up for

**palme** [palm] nf (de plongeur) flipper; **palmé, e** adj (pattes) webbed

**palmier** [palmje] nm palm tree; (gâteau) heart-shaped biscuit made of flaky pastry

**pâlot, te** [pɑlo, ɔt] adj pale, peaky

**palourde** [paluʀd] nf clam

**palper** [palpe] vt to feel, finger

**palpitant, e** [palpitɑ̃, ɑ̃t] adj thrilling

**palpiter** [palpite] vi (cœur, pouls) to beat; (: plus fort) to pound, throb

**paludisme** [palydism] nm malaria

**pamphlet** [pɑ̃flɛ] nm lampoon, satirical tract

**pamplemousse** [pɑ̃pləmus] nm grapefruit

**pan** [pɑ̃] nm section, piece ▷ excl bang!

**panache** [panaʃ] nm plume; (fig) spirit, panache

**panaché, e** [panaʃe] adj: **glace ~e** mixed-flavour ice cream ▷ nm (bière) shandy

**pancarte** [pɑ̃kaʀt] nf sign, notice

**pancréas** [pɑ̃kʀeas] nm pancreas

**pacifique** [pasifik] adj peaceful ▷ nm: **le P~, l'océan P~** the Pacific (Ocean)

**pack** [pak] nm pack

**pacotille** [pakɔtij] nf cheap junk

**PACS** sigle m (= pacte civil de solidarité) contract of civil partnership; **pacser: se pacser** vi to sign a contract of civil partnership

**pacte** [pakt] nm pact, treaty

**pagaille** [pagaj] nf mess, shambles sg

**page** [paʒ] nf page ▷ nm page (boy); **à la ~** (fig) up-to-date; **page d'accueil** (Inform) home page; **page Web** (Inform) web page

**paiement** [pɛmɑ̃] nm payment

**païen, ne** [pajɛ̃, pajɛn] adj, nm/f pagan, heathen

**paillasson** [pajasɔ̃] nm doormat

**paille** [paj] nf straw

**pain** [pɛ̃] nm (substance) bread; (unité) loaf (of bread); (morceau): **~ de savon** etc bar of soap etc; **pain au chocolat** chocolate-filled pastry; **pain aux raisins** currant bun; **pain bis/complet**

**pané, e** [pane] *adj* fried in breadcrumbs

**panier** [panje] *nm* basket; **mettre au ~** to chuck away; **panier à provisions** shopping basket; **panier-repas** *nm* packed lunch

**panique** [panik] *nf, adj* panic; **paniquer** *vi* to panic

**panne** [pan] *nf* breakdown; **être/ tomber en ~** to have broken down/ break down; **être en ~ d'essence** *ou* **sèche** to have run out of petrol (BRIT) *ou* gas (US); **ma voiture est en ~** my car has broken down; **panne d'électricité** *ou* **de courant** power cut ou failure

**panneau, x** [pano] *nm* (*écriteau*) sign, notice; **panneau d'affichage** notice board; **panneau de signalisation** roadsign; **panneau indicateur** signpost

**panoplie** [panɔpli] *nf* (*jouet*) outfit; (*fig*) array

**panorama** [panɔrama] *nm* panorama

**panse** [pɑ̃s] *nf* paunch

**pansement** [pɑ̃smɑ̃] *nm* dressing, bandage; **pansement adhésif** sticking plaster

**pantacourt** [pɑ̃takur] *nm* three-quarter length trousers *pl*

**pantalon** [pɑ̃talɔ̃] *nm* trousers *pl*, pair of trousers; **pantalon de ski** ski pants *pl*

**panthère** [pɑ̃tɛr] *nf* panther

**pantin** [pɑ̃tɛ̃] *nm* puppet

**pantoufle** [pɑ̃tufl] *nf* slipper

**paon** [pɑ̃] *nm* peacock

**papa** [papa] *nm* dad(dy)

**pape** [pap] *nm* pope

**paperasse** [papras] (*péj*) *nf* bumf *no pl*, papers *pl*; **paperasserie** (*péj*) *nf* paperwork *no pl*; (*tracasserie*) red tape *no pl*

**papeterie** [papetri] *nf* (*magasin*) stationer's (shop)

**papi** *nm* (*fam*) granddad

**papier** [papje] *nm* paper; (*article*) article; **papiers** *nmpl* (*aussi*: **~s d'identité**) (identity) papers; **papier à lettres** writing paper, notepaper;

**papier (d')aluminium** aluminium (BRIT) *ou* aluminum (US) foil, tinfoil; **papier calque** tracing paper; **papier de verre** sandpaper; **papier hygiénique** *ou* **(de) toilette** toilet paper; **papier journal** newspaper; **papier peint** wallpaper

**papillon** [papijɔ̃] *nm* butterfly; (*fam: contravention*) (parking) ticket; **papillon de nuit** moth

**papillote** [papijɔt] *nf*: **en ~** cooked in tinfoil

**papoter** [papɔte] *vi* to chatter

**paquebot** [pak(ə)bo] *nm* liner

**pâquerette** [pakrɛt] *nf* daisy

**Pâques** [pak] *nm, nfpl* Easter

---

- **PÂQUES**
-
- In France, Easter eggs are said to
- be brought by the Easter bells or
- **cloches de Pâques** which fly from
- Rome and drop them in people's
- gardens.

---

**paquet** [pakɛ] *nm* packet; (*colis*) parcel; (*fig: tas*): **~ pile** *ou* heap of; **un ~ de cigarettes, s'il vous plaît** a packet of cigarettes, please; **paquet-cadeau** *nm*: **pouvez-vous me faire un paquet-cadeau, s'il vous plaît?** can you gift-wrap it for me, please?

**par** [par] *prép* by; **finir** *etc* **~** to end *etc* with; **~ amour** out of love; **passer ~ Lyon/la côte** to go via *ou* through Lyons/along the coast; **~ la fenêtre** (*jeter, regarder*) out of the window; **3 ~ jour/personne** 3 a *ou* per day/person; **2 ~ 2** in twos; **~ ici** this way; (*dans le coin*) round here; **~-ci, ~-là** here and there; **~ temps de pluie** in wet weather

**parabolique** [parabɔlik] *adj*: **antenne ~** parabolic *ou* dish aerial

**parachute** [paraʃyt] *nm* parachute; **parachutiste** *nm/f* parachutist; (*Mil*) paratrooper

**parade** [parad] *nf* (*spectacle, défilé*) parade; (*Escrime, Boxe*) parry

**paradis** [paradi] nm heaven, paradise

**paradoxe** [paradɔks] nm paradox

**paraffine** [parafin] nf paraffin

**parages** [paraʒ] nmpl: **dans les ~ (de)** in the area ou vicinity (of)

**paragraphe** [paragraf] nm paragraph

**paraître** [paretr] vb +attrib to seem, look, appear ▷ vi to appear; (être visible) to show; (Presse, Édition) to be published, come out, appear ▷ vb impers: **il paraît que** it seems ou appears that, they say that

**parallèle** [paralɛl] adj parallel; (non officiel) unofficial ▷ nm (comparaison): **faire un ~ entre** to draw a parallel between ▷ nf parallel (line)

**paralyser** [paralize] vt to paralyse

**paramédical, e, -aux** [paramedikal, o] adj: **personnel ~** paramedics pl, paramedical workers pl

**paraphrase** [parafraz] nf paraphrase

**parapluie** [paraplʋi] nm umbrella

**parasite** [parazit] nm parasite; **parasites** nmpl (Tél) interference sg

**parasol** [parasɔl] nm parasol, sunshade

**paratonnerre** [paratɔnɛr] nm lightning conductor

**parc** [park] nm (public) park, gardens pl; (de château etc) grounds pl; (d'enfant) playpen; **parc à thème** theme park; **parc d'attractions** amusement park; **parc de stationnement** car park

**parcelle** [parsɛl] nf fragment, scrap; (de terrain) plot, parcel

**parce que** [parsk(ə)] conj because

**parchemin** [parʃəmɛ̃] nm parchment

**parc(o)mètre** [parkmɛtr] nm parking meter

**parcourir** [parkurir] vt (trajet, distance) to cover; (article, livre) to skim ou glance through; (lieu) to go all over, travel up and down; (suj: frisson) to run through

**parcours** [parkur] nm (trajet) journey; (itinéraire) route

**par-dessous** [pard(ə)su] prép, adv under(neath)

**pardessus** [pardəsy] nm overcoat

**par-dessus** [pard(ə)sy] prép over (the top of) ▷ adv over (the top); **~ le marché** on top of all that; **~ tout** above all; **en avoir ~ la tête** to have had enough

**par-devant** [pard(ə)vã] adv (passer) round the front

**pardon** [pardɔ̃] nm forgiveness no pl ▷ excl sorry!; (pour interpeller etc) excuse me!; **demander ~ à qn (de)** to apologize to sb (for); **je vous demande ~** I'm sorry; (pour interpeller) excuse me; **pardonner** vt to forgive; **pardonner qch à qn** to forgive sb for sth

**pare...**: **pare-brise** nm inv windscreen (BRIT), windshield (US); **pare-chocs** nm inv bumper; **pare-feu** nm inv (de foyer) fireguard; (Inform) firewall

**pareil, le** [parɛj] adj (identique) the same, alike; (similaire) similar; (tel): **un courage/livre ~** such courage/a book, courage/a book like this; **de ~s livres** such books; **faire ~** to do the same (thing); **~ à** the same as; (similaire) similar to; **sans ~** unparalleled, unequalled

**parent, e** [parã, ãt] nm/f: **un(e) ~(e)** a relative ou relation; **parents** nmpl (père et mère) parents; **parenté** nf (lien) relationship

**parenthèse** [parãtɛz] nf (ponctuation) bracket, parenthesis; (digression) parenthesis, digression; **entre ~s** in brackets; (fig) incidentally

**paresse** [parɛs] nf laziness; **paresseux, -euse** adj lazy

**parfait, e** [parfɛ, ɛt] adj perfect ▷ nm (Ling) perfect (tense); **parfaitement** adv perfectly ▷ excl (most) certainly

**parfois** [parfwa] adv sometimes

**parfum** [parfœ̃] nm (produit) perfume, scent; (odeur: de fleur) scent, fragrance; (goût) flavour; **quels ~s avez-vous?** what flavours do you have?; **parfumé, e** adj (fleur, fruit) fragrant; (femme) perfumed; **parfumé au café** coffee-flavoured; **parfumer** vt (suj: odeur, bouquet) to perfume; (crème, gâteau) to flavour; (crème, gâteau) perfumes pl; (boutique) perfume shop

**pari** [paʀi] nm bet; **parier** vt to bet

**Paris** [paʀi] n Paris; **parisien, ne** adj Parisian; (Géo, Admin) Paris cpd ▷ nm/f: **Parisien, ne** Parisian

**parité** [paʀite] nf (Pol): **~ hommes-femmes** balanced representation of men and women

**parjure** [paʀʒyʀ] nm perjury

**parking** [paʀkiŋ] nm (lieu) car park

Attention à ne pas traduire **parking** par le mot anglais **parking**.

**parlant, e** [paʀlɑ̃, ɑ̃t] adj (regard) eloquent; (Cinéma) talking

**parlement** [paʀləmɑ̃] nm parliament; **parlementaire** adj parliamentary ▷ nm/f member of parliament

**parler** [paʀle] vi to speak, talk; (avouer) to talk; **~ (à qn) de** to talk ou speak (to sb) about; **~ le/en français** to speak French/in French; **~ affaires** to talk business; **sans ~ de** (fig) not to mention, to say nothing of; **tu parles!** (fam: bien sûr) you bet!; **parlez-vous français?** do you speak French?; **je ne parle pas anglais** I don't speak English; **est-ce que je peux ~ à ...?** can I speak to ...?

**parloir** [paʀlwaʀ] nm (de prison, d'hôpital) visiting room

**parmi** [paʀmi] prép among(st)

**paroi** [paʀwa] nf wall; (cloison) partition

**paroisse** [paʀwas] nf parish

**parole** [paʀɔl] nf (faculté): **la ~** speech; (mot, promesse) word; **paroles** nfpl (Mus) words, lyrics; **tenir ~** to keep one's word; **prendre la ~** to speak; **demander la ~** to ask for permission to speak; **je te crois sur ~** I'll take your word for it

**parquet** [paʀkɛ] nm (parquet) floor; (Jur): **le ~** the Public Prosecutor's department

**parrain** [paʀɛ̃] nm godfather;

**parrainer** vt (suj: entreprise) to sponsor

**pars** [paʀ] vb voir **partir**

**parsemer** [paʀsəme] vt (suj: feuilles, papiers) to be scattered over; **~ qch de** to scatter sth with

**part** [paʀ] nf (qui revient à qn) share; (fraction, partie) part; **à ~** adv (séparément) separately; (de côté) aside ▷ prép apart from, except for; **prendre ~ à** (débat etc) to take part in; (soucis, douleur de qn) to share in; **faire ~ de qch à qn** to announce sth to sb, inform sb of sth; **pour ma ~** as for me, as far as I'm concerned; **à ~ entière** full; **de la ~ de** (au nom de) on behalf of; (donné par) from; **de toute(s) ~(s)** from all sides ou quarters; **de ~ et d'autre** on both sides, on either side; **d'une ~ ... d'autre ~** on the one hand ... on the other hand; **d'autre ~** (de plus) moreover; **faire la ~ des choses** to make allowances

**partage** [paʀtaʒ] nm (fractionnement) dividing up; (répartition) sharing (out) no pl, share-out

**partager** [paʀtaʒe] vt to share; (distribuer, répartir) to share (out); (morceler, diviser) to divide (up); **se partager** vt (héritage etc) to share between themselves (ou ourselves)

**partenaire** [paʀtənɛʀ] nm/f partner

**parterre** [paʀtɛʀ] nm (de fleurs) (flower) bed; (Théâtre) stalls pl

**parti** [paʀti] nm (Pol) party; (décision) course of action; (personne à marier) match; **tirer ~ de** to take advantage of, turn to good account; **prendre ~ (pour/contre)** to take sides ou a stand (for/against); **parti pris** bias

**partial, e, -aux** [paʀsjal, jo] adj biased, partial

**participant, e** [paʀtisipɑ̃, ɑ̃t] nm/f participant; (à un concours) entrant

**participation** [paʀtisipasjɔ̃] nf participation; (financière) contribution

**participer** [paʀtisipe]: **~ à** vt (course, réunion) to take part in; (frais etc) to contribute to; (chagrin, succès de qn) to share (in)

**particularité** [partikylarite] nf
(distinctive) characteristic

**particulier, -ière** [partikylje, jɛR]
adj (spécifique) particular; (spécial)
special, particular; (personnel, privé)
private; (étrange) peculiar, odd ▷ nm
(individu: Admin) private individual; **~ à**
peculiar to; **en ~** (surtout) in particular,
particularly; (en privé) in private;
**particulièrement** adv particularly

**partie** [parti] nf (gén) part; (Jur etc:
protagonistes) party; (de cartes, tennis etc)
game; **une ~ de pêche** a fishing party
ou trip; **en ~** partly, in part; **faire ~ de**
(suj: chose) to be part of; **prendre qn à ~**
to take sb to task; **en grande ~** largely,
in the main; **partie civile** (Jur) party
claiming damages in a criminal case

**partiel, le** [parsjɛl] adj partial ▷ nm
(Scol) class exam

**partir** [partiR] vi (gén) to go; (quitter)
to go, leave; (tache) to go, come out; **~
de** (lieu: quitter) to leave; (: commencer
à) to start from; **~ pour/à** (lieu, pays
etc) to leave for/go off to; **à ~ de** from;
**le train/le bus part à quelle heure?**
what time does the train/bus leave?

**partisan, e** [partizã, an] nm/f
partisan ▷ adj: **être ~ de qch/de faire**
to be in favour of sth/doing

**partition** [partisjɔ̃] nf (Mus) score

**partout** [partu] adv everywhere; **~
où il allait** everywhere ou wherever
he went

**paru** [pary] pp de **paraître**

**parution** [parysjɔ̃] nf publication

**parvenir** [parvəniR]: **~ à** vt (atteindre)
to reach; (réussir): **~ à faire** to manage
to do, succeed in doing; **faire ~ qch à
qn** to have sth sent to sb

**pas¹** [pɑ] nm (enjambée, Danse) step;
(allure, mesure) pace; (bruit) (foot)step;
(trace) footprint; **~ à ~** step by step;
**au ~** at walking pace; **marcher à
grands ~** to stride along; **à ~ de loup**
stealthily; **faire les cent ~** to pace up
and down; **faire le premier ~** to make
the first move; **sur le ~ de la porte** on

the doorstep

**MOT-CLÉ**

**pas²** [pɑ] adv **1** (en corrélation avec
ne, non etc) not; **il ne pleure pas**
(habituellement) he does not ou doesn't
cry; (maintenant) he's not ou isn't crying;
**il n'a pas pleuré/ne pleurera pas** he
did not ou didn't/will not ou won't cry;
**ils n'ont pas de voiture/d'enfants**
they don't have ou haven't got a car/any
children; **il m'a dit de ne pas le faire**
he told me not to do it; **non pas que ...**
not that ...
**2** (employé sans ne etc): **pas moi** not
me, I don't (ou can't etc); **elle travaille,
(mais) lui pas** ou **pas lui** she works but
he doesn't ou does not; **une pomme
pas mûre** an unripe apple; **pas du
tout** not at all; **pas de sucre, merci**
no sugar, thanks; **ceci est à vous ou
pas?** is this yours or not?, is this yours
or isn't it?
**3**: **pas mal** (joli: personne, maison) not
bad; **pas mal fait** not badly done ou
made; **comment ça va? — pas mal**
how are things? — not bad; **pas mal de**
quite a lot of

**passage** [pasaʒ] nm (fait de passer)
voir **passer**; (lieu, prix de la traversée,
extrait) passage; (chemin) way; **de ~**
(touristes) passing through; **passage à
niveau** level crossing; **passage clouté**
pedestrian crossing; **passage interdit**
no entry; **passage souterrain** subway
(BRIT), underpass

**passager, -ère** [pasaʒe, ɛR] adj
passing ▷ nm/f passenger

**passant, e** [pasã, ãt] adj (rue, endroit)
busy ▷ nm/f passer-by; **en ~** in passing

**passe** [pas] nf (Sport, Navig) pass; **être
en ~ de faire** to be on the way to doing;
**être dans une mauvaise ~** to be going
through a rough patch

**passé, e** [pase] adj (révolu) past; (dernier:
semaine etc) last; (couleur) faded ▷ prép

after ▷ *nm* past; (*Ling*) past (tense); **~ de mode** out of fashion; **passé composé** perfect (tense); **passé simple** past historic (tense)

**passe-partout** [pɑspaʀtu] *nm inv* master *ou* skeleton key ▷ *adj inv* all-purpose

**passeport** [pɑspɔʀ] *nm* passport

**passer** [pɑse] *vi* (*aller*) to go; (*voiture, piétons: défiler*) to pass (by), go by; (*facteur, laitier etc*) to come, call; (*pour rendre visite*) to call *ou* drop in; (*film, émission*) to be on; (*temps, jours*) to pass, go by; (*couleur*) to fade; (*mode*) to die out; (*douleur*) to pass, go away; (*Scol*) **~ dans la classe supérieure** to go up to the next class ▷ *vt* (*frontière, rivière etc*) to cross; (*douane*) to go through; (*examen*) to sit, take; (*visite médicale etc*) to have; (*journée, temps*) to spend; (*enfiler: vêtement*) to slip on; (*film, pièce*) to show, put on; (*disque*) to play, put on; (*commande*) to place; (*marché, accord*) to agree on; **se passer** *vi* (*avoir lieu: scène, action*) to take place; (*se dérouler: entretien etc*) to go; (*s'écouler: semaine etc*) to pass, go by; (*arriver*) **que s'est-il passé?** what happened?; **~ qch à qn** (*sel etc*) to pass sth to sb; (*prêter*) to lend sb sth; (*lettre, message*) to pass sth on to sb; (*tolérer*) to let sb get away with sth; **~ par** to go through; **~ avant qch/qn** (*fig*) to come before sth/sb; **~ un coup de fil à qn** (*fam*) to give sb a ring; **laisser ~** (*air, lumière, personne*) to let through; (*occasion*) to let slip, miss; (*erreur*) to overlook; **~ à la radio/télévision** to be on the radio/on television; **~ à table** to sit down to eat; **~ au salon** to go into the sitting-room; **~ son tour** to miss one's turn; **~ la seconde** (*Auto*) to change into second; **~ le balai/l'aspirateur** to sweep up/hoover; **je vous passe M. Dupont** (*je vous mets en communication avec lui*) I'm putting you through to Mr Dupont; (*je lui passe l'appareil*) here is Mr Dupont, I'll hand you over to Mr Dupont; **se ~ de** to go *ou* do without

**passerelle** [pɑsʀɛl] *nf* footbridge; (*de navire, avion*) gangway

**passe-temps** [pɑstɑ̃] *nm inv* pastime

**passif, -ive** [pasif, iv] *adj* passive

**passion** [pasjɔ̃] *nf* passion; **passionnant, e** *adj* fascinating; **passionné, e** *adj* (*personne*) passionate; (*récit*) impassioned; **être passionné de** to have a passion for; **passionner** *vt* (*personne*) to fascinate, grip

**passoire** [paswaʀ] *nf* sieve; (*à légumes*) colander; (*à thé*) strainer

**pastèque** [pastɛk] *nf* watermelon

**pasteur** [pastœʀ] *nm* (*protestant*) minister, pastor

**pastille** [pastij] *nf* (*à sucer*) lozenge, pastille

**patate** [patat] *nf* (*fam: pomme de terre*) spud; **patate douce** sweet potato

**patauger** [patoʒe] *vi* to splash about

**pâte** [pɑt] *nf* (*à tarte*) pastry; (*à pain*) dough; (*à frire*) batter; **pâtes** *nfpl* (*macaroni etc*) pasta *sg*; **pâte à modeler** modelling clay, Plasticine® (BRIT); **pâte brisée** shortcrust pastry; **pâte d'amandes** almond paste, marzipan; **pâte de fruits** crystallized fruit *no pl*; **pâte feuilletée** puff *ou* flaky pastry

**pâté** [pɑte] *nm* (*charcuterie*) pâté; (*tache*) ink blot; **pâté de maisons** block (of houses); **pâté (de sable)** sandpie; **pâté en croûte** ≈ pork pie

**pâtée** [pɑte] *nf* mash, feed

**patente** [patɑ̃t] *nf* (*Comm*) trading licence

**paternel, le** [patɛʀnɛl] *adj* (*amour, soins*) fatherly; (*ligne, autorité*) paternal

**pâteux, -euse** [pɑtø, øz] *adj* pasty; (*langue*) coated

**pathétique** [patetik] *adj* moving

**patience** [pasjɑ̃s] *nf* patience

**patient, e** [pasjɑ̃, jɑ̃t] *adj, nm/f* patient; **patienter** *vi* to wait

**patin** [patɛ̃] *nm* skate; (*sport*) skating; **patins (à glace)** (ice) skates; **patins à roulettes** roller skates

**patinage** [patinaʒ] *nm* skating

**patiner**[patine] vi to skate; (roue, voiture) to spin; **se patiner** vi (meuble, cuir) to acquire a sheen; **patineur, -euse** nm/f skater; **patinoire** nf skating rink, (ice) rink

**pâtir**[patiʀ]: **~ de** vt to suffer because of

**pâtisserie**[patisʀi] nf (boutique) cake shop; (gâteau) cake, pastry; (à la maison) pastry- ou cake-making, baking; **pâtissier, -ière** nm/f pastrycook

**patois**[patwa] nm dialect, patois

**patrie**[patʀi] nf homeland

**patrimoine**[patʀimwan] nm (culture) heritage

- **JOURNÉES DU PATRIMOINE**
- 
- Once a year, important public
- buildings are open to the public for
- a weekend. During these **Journées**
- **du Patrimoine**, there are guided
- visits and talks based on a particular
- theme.

**patriotique**[patʀijɔtik] adj patriotic

**patron, ne**[patʀɔ̃, ɔn] nm/f boss; (Rel) patron saint ▷ nm (Couture) pattern; **patronat** nm employers pl; **patronner** vt to sponsor, support

**patrouille**[patʀuj] nf patrol

**patte**[pat] nf (jambe) leg; (pied: de chien, chat) paw; (: d'oiseau) foot

**pâturage**[patyʀaʒ] nm pasture

**paume**[pom] nf palm

**paumé, e**[pome] (fam) nm/f drop-out

**paupière**[popjɛʀ] nf eyelid

**pause**[poz] nf (arrêt) break; (en parlant, Mus) pause

**pauvre**[povʀ] adj poor; **les pauvres** nmpl the poor; **pauvreté** nf (état) poverty

**pavé, e**[pave] adj (cour) paved; (chaussée) cobbled ▷ nm (bloc) paving stone; cobblestone

**pavillon**[pavijɔ̃] nm (de banlieue) small (detached) house; pavilion; (drapeau) flag

**payant, e**[pɛjɑ̃, ɑ̃t] adj (spectateurs etc) paying; (fig: entreprise) profitable; (effort) which pays off; **c'est ~** you have to pay, there is a charge

**paye**[pɛj] nf pay, wages pl

**payer**[peje] vt (créancier, employé, loyer) to pay; (achat, réparations, fig: faute) to pay for ▷ vi (métier) to be well-paid; (tactique etc) to pay off; **il me l'a fait ~ 10 euros** he charged me 10 euros for it; **~ qch à qn** to buy sth for sb, buy sb sth; **se ~ la tête de qn** (fam) to take the mickey out of sb; **est-ce que je peux ~ par carte de crédit?** can I pay by credit card?

**pays**[pei] nm country; (région) region; **du ~** local

**paysage**[peizaʒ] nm landscape

**paysan, ne**[peizɑ̃, an] nm/f farmer; (péj) peasant ▷ adj (agricole) farming; (rural) country

**Pays-Bas**[peiba] nmpl: **les ~** the Netherlands

**PC** nm (Inform) PC

**PDA** sigle m (= personal digital assistant) PDA

**PDG** sigle m = **président directeur général**

**péage**[peaʒ] nm toll; (endroit) tollgate

**peau, x**[po] nf skin; **gants de ~** fine leather gloves; **être bien/mal dans sa ~** to be quite at ease/ill-at-ease; **peau de chamois** (chiffon) chamois leather, shammy

**pêche**[pɛʃ] nf (fruit) peach; (sport, activité) fishing; (poissons pêchés) catch; **pêche à la ligne** (en rivière) angling

**péché**[peʃe] nm sin

**pécher**[peʃe] vi (Rel) to sin

**pêcher**[peʃe] nm peach tree ▷ vi to go fishing ▷ vt (attraper) to catch; (être pêcheur de) to fish for

**pécheur, -eresse**[peʃœʀ, peʃʀɛs] nm/f sinner

**pêcheur**[peʃœʀ] nm fisherman; (à la ligne) angler

**pédagogie**[pedagɔʒi] nf educational methods pl, pedagogy; **pédagogique**

*adj* educational

**pédale** [pedal] *nf* pedal

**pédalo** [pedalo] *nm* pedal-boat

**pédant, e** [pedã, ãt] (*péj*) *adj* pedantic

**pédestre** [pedɛstʀ] *adj*: **randonnée ~** ramble; **sentier ~** pedestrian footpath

**pédiatre** [pedjatʀ] *nm/f* paediatrician, child specialist

**pédicure** [pedikyʀ] *nm/f* chiropodist

**pègre** [pɛgʀ] *nf* underworld

**peigne** [pɛɲ] *nm* comb; **peigner** *vt* to comb (the hair of); **se peigner** *vi* to comb one's hair; **peignoir** *nm* dressing gown; **peignoir de bain** bathrobe

**peindre** [pɛ̃dʀ] *vt* to paint; (*fig*) to portray, depict

**peine** [pɛn] *nf* (*affliction*) sorrow, sadness *no pl*; (*mal, effort*) trouble *no pl*, effort; (*difficulté*) difficulty; (*Jur*) sentence; **avoir de la ~** to be sad; **faire de la ~ à qn** to distress *ou* upset sb; **prendre la ~ de faire** to go to the trouble of doing; **se donner de la ~** to make an effort; **ce n'est pas la ~ de faire** there's no point in doing, it's not worth doing; **à ~** scarcely, barely; **à ~ ... que** hardly ... than, no sooner ... than; **peine capitale** capital punishment; **peine de mort** death sentence *ou* penalty; **peiner** *vi* (*personne*) to work hard; (*moteur, voiture*) to labour ▷ *vt* to grieve, sadden

**peintre** [pɛ̃tʀ] *nm* painter; **peintre en bâtiment** painter (and decorator)

**peinture** [pɛ̃tyʀ] *nf* painting; (*matière*) paint; (*surfaces peintes: aussi:* **~s**) paintwork; **"~ fraîche"** "wet paint"

**péjoratif, -ive** [peʒɔʀatif, iv] *adj* pejorative, derogatory

**Pékin** [pekɛ̃] *n* Beijing

**pêle-mêle** [pɛlmɛl] *adv* higgledy-piggledy

**peler** [pəle] *vt, vi* to peel

**pèlerin** [pɛlʀɛ̃] *nm* pilgrim

**pèlerinage** [pɛlʀinaʒ] *nm* pilgrimage

**pelle** [pɛl] *nf* shovel; (*d'enfant, de terrassier*) spade

**pellicule** [pelikyl] *nf* film; **pellicules**

*nfpl* (*Méd*) dandruff *sg*; **je voudrais une ~ de 36 poses** I'd like a 36-exposure film

**pelote** [p(ə)lɔt] *nf* (*de fil, laine*) ball; **pelote basque** pelota

**peloton** [p(ə)lɔtɔ̃] *nm* group, squad; (*Cyclisme*) pack

**pelotonner** [p(ə)lɔtɔne]: **se pelotonner** *vi* to curl (o.s.) up

**pelouse** [p(ə)luz] *nf* lawn

**peluche** [p(ə)lyʃ] *nf*: (**animal en**) **~** fluffy animal, soft toy; **chien/lapin en ~** fluffy dog/rabbit

**pelure** [p(ə)lyʀ] *nf* peeling, peel *no pl*

**pénal, e, -aux** [penal, o] *adj* penal; **pénalité** *nf* penalty

**penchant** [pɑ̃ʃɑ̃] *nm* (*tendance*) tendency, propensity; (*faible*) liking, fondness

**pencher** [pɑ̃ʃe] *vi* to tilt, lean over ▷ *vt* to tilt; **se pencher** *vi* to lean over; (*se baisser*) to bend down; **se ~ sur** (*fig: problème*) to look into; **~ pour** to be inclined to favour

**pendant** [pɑ̃dɑ̃] *prép* (*au cours de*) during; (*indique la durée*) for; **~ que** while

**pendentif** [pɑ̃dɑ̃tif] *nm* pendant

**penderie** [pɑ̃dʀi] *nf* wardrobe

**pendre** [pɑ̃dʀ] *vt, vi* to hang; **se ~** (*se suicider*) to hang o.s.; **~ qch à** (*mur*) to hang sth (up) on; (*plafond*) to hang sth (up) from

**pendule** [pɑ̃dyl] *nf* clock ▷ *nm* pendulum

**pénétrer** [penetʀe] *vi, vt* to penetrate; **~ dans** to enter

**pénible** [penibl] *adj* (*travail*) hard; (*sujet*) painful; (*personne*) tiresome; **péniblement** *adv* with difficulty

**péniche** [peniʃ] *nf* barge

**pénicilline** [penisilin] *nf* penicillin

**péninsule** [penɛ̃syl] *nf* peninsula

**pénis** [penis] *nm* penis

**pénitence** [penitɑ̃s] *nf* (*peine*) penance; (*repentir*) penitence; **pénitencier** *nm* penitentiary

**pénombre** [penɔ̃bʀ] *nf* (*faible clarté*) half-light; (*obscurité*) darkness

**pensée** [pɑ̃se] *nf* thought; (*démarche,*

*doctrine)* thinking *no pl; (fleur)* pansy; **en ~** in one's mind

**penser** [pɑ̃se] *vi, vt* to think; **~ à** *(ami, vacances)* to think of *ou* about; *(réfléchir à: problème, offre)* to think about *ou* over; *(prévoir)* to think of; **faire ~ à** to remind one of; **~ faire qch** to be thinking of doing sth, intend to do sth; **pensif, -ive** *adj* pensive, thoughtful

**pension** [pɑ̃sjɔ̃] *nf (allocation)* pension; *(prix du logement)* board and lodgings, bed and board; *(école)* boarding school; **pension alimentaire** *(de divorcée)* maintenance allowance, alimony; **pension complète** full board; **pension de famille** boarding house, guesthouse; **pensionnaire** *nm/f (Scol)* boarder; **pensionnat** *nm* boarding school

**pente** [pɑ̃t] *nf* slope; **en ~** sloping

**Pentecôte** [pɑ̃tkot] *nf*: **la ~** Whitsun (BRIT), Pentecost

**pénurie** [penyʀi] *nf* shortage

**pépé** [pepe] *(fam) nm* grandad

**pépin** [pepɛ̃] *nm (Bot: graine)* pip; *(ennui)* snag, hitch

**pépinière** [pepinjɛʀ] *nf* nursery

**perçant, e** [pɛʀsɑ̃, ɑ̃t] *adj (cri)* piercing, shrill; *(regard)* piercing

**percepteur, -trice** [pɛʀsɛptœʀ, tʀis] *nm/f* tax collector

**perception** [pɛʀsɛpsjɔ̃] *nf* perception; *(bureau)* tax office

**percer** [pɛʀse] *vt* to pierce; *(ouverture etc)* to make; *(mystère, énigme)* to penetrate ▷ *vi* to break through; **perceuse** *nf* drill

**percevoir** [pɛʀsəvwaʀ] *vt (distinguer)* to perceive, detect; *(taxe, impôt)* to collect; *(revenu, indemnité)* to receive

**perche** [pɛʀʃ] *nf (bâton)* pole

**percher** [pɛʀʃe] *vt, vi* to perch; **se percher** *vi* to perch; **perchoir** *nm* perch

**perçois** *etc* [pɛʀswa] *vb voir* **percevoir**

**perçu, e** [pɛʀsy] *pp de* **percevoir**

**percussion** [pɛʀkysjɔ̃] *nf* percussion

**percuter** [pɛʀkyte] *vt* to strike; *(suj:*

*véhicule)* to crash into

**perdant, e** [pɛʀdɑ̃, ɑ̃t] *nm/f* loser

**perdre** [pɛʀdʀ] *vt* to lose; *(gaspiller: temps, argent)* to waste; *(personne: moralement etc)* to ruin ▷ *vi* to lose; *(sur une vente etc)* to lose out; **se perdre** *vi (s'égarer)* to get lost, lose one's way; *(denrées)* to go to waste; **j'ai perdu mon portefeuille/passeport** I've lost my wallet/passport; **je me suis perdu** *(et je le suis encore)* I'm lost; *(et je ne le suis plus)* I got lost

**perdrix** [pɛʀdʀi] *nf* partridge

**perdu, e** [pɛʀdy] *pp de* **perdre** ▷ *adj (isolé)* out-of-the-way; *(Comm: emballage)* non-returnable; *(malade)*: **il est ~** there's no hope left for him; **à vos moments ~s** in your spare time

**père** [pɛʀ] *nm* father; **père de famille** father; **le père Noël** Father Christmas

**perfection** [pɛʀfɛksjɔ̃] *nf* perfection; **à la ~** to perfection; **perfectionné, e** *adj* sophisticated; **perfectionner** *vt* to improve, perfect; **se perfectionner en anglais** to improve one's English

**perforer** [pɛʀfɔʀe] *vt (poinçonner)* to punch

**performant, e** [pɛʀfɔʀmɑ̃, ɑ̃t] *adj*: **très ~** high-performance *cpd*

**perfusion** [pɛʀfyzjɔ̃] *nf*: **faire une ~ à qn** to put sb on a drip

**péril** [peʀil] *nm* peril

**périmé, e** [peʀime] *adj (Admin)* out-of-date, expired

**périmètre** [peʀimɛtʀ] *nm* perimeter

**période** [peʀjɔd] *nf* period; **périodique** *adj* periodic ▷ *nm* periodical; **garniture** *ou* **serviette périodique** sanitary towel (BRIT) *ou* napkin (US)

**périphérique** [peʀifeʀik] *adj (quartiers)* outlying ▷ *nm (Auto)*: **boulevard ~** ring road (BRIT), beltway (US)

**périr** [peʀiʀ] *vi* to die, perish

**périssable** [peʀisabl] *adj* perishable

**perle** [pɛʀl] *nf* pearl; *(de plastique, métal, sueur)* bead

**permanence** [pɛʀmanɑ̃s] *nf*

permanence; (*local*) (*duty*) office; **assurer une ~** (*service public, bureaux*) to operate *ou* maintain a basic service; **être de ~** to be on call *ou* duty; **en ~** continuously

**permanent, e** [pɛʀmanɑ̃, ɑ̃t] *adj* permanent; (*spectacle*) continuous; **permanente** *nf* perm

**perméable** [pɛʀmeabl] *adj* (*terrain*) permeable; **~ à** (*fig*) receptive *ou* open to

**permettre** [pɛʀmɛtʀ] *vt* to allow, permit; **~ à qn de faire/qch** to allow sb to do/sth; **se ~ de faire** to take the liberty of doing

**permis** [pɛʀmi] *nm* permit, licence; **permis de conduire** driving licence (BRIT), driver's license (US); **permis de construire** planning permission (BRIT), building permit (US); **permis de séjour** residence permit; **permis de travail** work permit

**permission** [pɛʀmisjɔ̃] *nf* permission; (*Mil*) leave; **avoir la ~ de faire** to have permission to do; **en ~** on leave

**Pérou** [peʀu] *nm* Peru

**perpétuel, le** [pɛʀpetɥɛl] *adj* perpetual; **perpétuité** *nf*: **à perpétuité** for life; **être condamné à perpétuité** to receive a life sentence

**perplexe** [pɛʀplɛks] *adj* perplexed, puzzled

**perquisitionner** [pɛʀkizisjɔne] *vi* to carry out a search

**perron** [peʀɔ̃] *nm* steps *pl* (*leading to entrance*)

**perroquet** [peʀɔkɛ] *nm* parrot

**perruche** [peʀyʃ] *nf* budgerigar (BRIT), budgie (BRIT), parakeet (US)

**perruque** [peʀyk] *nf* wig

**persécuter** [pɛʀsekyte] *vt* to persecute

**persévérer** [pɛʀsevere] *vi* to persevere

**persil** [pɛʀsi] *nm* parsley

**Persique** [pɛʀsik] *adj*: **le golfe ~** the (Persian) Gulf

**persistant, e** [pɛʀsistɑ̃, ɑ̃t] *adj* persistent

**persister** [pɛʀsiste] *vi* to persist; **~ à faire qch** to persist in doing sth

**personnage** [pɛʀsɔnaʒ] *nm* (*individu*) character, individual; (*célébrité*) important person; (*de roman, film*) character; (*Peinture*) figure

**personnalité** [pɛʀsɔnalite] *nf* personality; (*personnage*) prominent figure

**personne** [pɛʀsɔn] *nf* person ▷ *pron* nobody, no one; (*avec négation en anglais*) anybody, anyone; **personne âgée** elderly person; **personnel, le** *adj* personal; (*égoïste*) selfish ▷ *nm* staff, personnel; **personnellement** *adv* personally

**perspective** [pɛʀspɛktiv] *nf* (*Art*) perspective; (*vue*) view; (*point de vue*) viewpoint, angle; (*chose envisagée*) prospect; **en ~** in prospect

**perspicace** [pɛʀspikas] *adj* clear-sighted, gifted with (*ou* showing) insight; **perspicacité** *nf* clear-sightedness

**persuader** [pɛʀsɥade] *vt*: **~ qn (de faire)** to persuade sb (to do); **persuasif, -ive** *adj* persuasive

**perte** [pɛʀt] *nf* loss; (*de temps*) waste; (*fig: morale*) ruin; **à ~ de vue** as far as the eye can (*ou* could) see; **pertes blanches** (vaginal) discharge *sg*

**pertinent, e** [pɛʀtinɑ̃, ɑ̃t] *adj* apt, relevant

**perturbation** [pɛʀtyʀbasjɔ̃] *nf*: **perturbation (atmosphérique)** atmospheric disturbance

**perturber** [pɛʀtyʀbe] *vt* to disrupt; (*Psych*) to perturb, disturb

**pervers, e** [pɛʀvɛʀ, ɛʀs] *adj* perverted

**pervertir** [pɛʀvɛʀtiʀ] *vt* to pervert

**pesant, e** [pəzɑ̃, ɑ̃t] *adj* heavy; (*fig: présence*) burdensome

**pèse-personne** [pɛzpɛʀsɔn] *nm* (bathroom) scales *pl*

**peser** [pəze] *vt* to weigh ▷ *vi* to weigh; (*fig: avoir de l'importance*) to carry weight; **~ lourd** to be heavy

**pessimiste** [pesimist] *adj* pessimistic

▷ nm/f pessimist
**peste** [pɛst] nf plague
**pétale** [petal] nm petal
**pétanque** [petɑ̃k] nf type of bowls

● **PÉTANQUE**
●
● **Pétanque** is a version of the game
● of 'boules', played on a variety of
● hard surfaces. Standing with their
● feet together, players throw steel
● bowls at a wooden jack. **Pétanque**
● originated in the South of France
● and is still very much associated
● with that area.

**pétard** [petaʀ] nm banger (BRIT),
firecracker
**péter** [pete] vi (fam: casser) to bust;
(fam!) to fart (!)
**pétillant, e** [petijɑ̃, ɑ̃t] adj (eau etc)
sparkling
**pétiller** [petije] vi (feu) to crackle;
(champagne) to bubble; (yeux) to sparkle
**petit, e** [p(ə)ti, it] adj small; (avec
nuance affective) little; (voyage) short,
little; (bruit etc) faint, slight ▷ nm/f
(petit enfant) little boy/girl, child; **petits**
nmpl (d'un animal) young no pl; **faire des
~s** to have kittens (ou puppies etc); **la
classe des ~s** the infant class; **les tout-
~s** the little ones, the tiny tots (fam); **~ à
~** bit by bit, gradually; **petit(e) ami(e)**
boyfriend/girlfriend; **petit déjeuner**
breakfast; **le petit déjeuner est à
quelle heure?** what time is breakfast?;
**petit four** petit four; **petit pain** (bread)
roll; **les petites annonces** the small
ads; **petits pois** (garden) peas; **petite-
fille** nf granddaughter; **petit-fils** nm
grandson
**pétition** [petisjɔ̃] nf petition
**petits-enfants** [pətizɑ̃fɑ̃] nmpl
grandchildren
**pétrin** [petʀɛ̃] nm (fig): **dans le ~** (fam)
in a jam ou fix
**pétrir** [petʀiʀ] vt to knead
**pétrole** [petʀɔl] nm oil; (pour lampe,
réchaud etc) paraffin (oil); **pétrolier,
-ière** nm oil tanker

> Attention à ne pas traduire **pétrole**
par le mot anglais **petrol**.

**○ MOT-CLÉ**

**peu** [pø] adv **1** (modifiant verbe, adjectif,
adverbe): **il boit peu** he doesn't drink
(very) much; **il est peu bavard** he's
not very talkative; **peu avant/après**
shortly before/afterwards
**2** (modifiant nom): **peu de: peu de
gens/d'arbres** few ou not (very) many
people/trees; **il a peu d'espoir** he
hasn't (got) much hope, he has little
hope; **pour peu de temps** for (only) a
short while
**3**: **peu à peu** little by little; **à peu près**
just about, more or less; **à peu près
10 kg/10 euros** approximately 10
kg/10 euros
▷ nm **1**: **le peu de gens qui** the few
people who; **le peu de sable qui** what
little sand, the little sand which
**2**: **un peu** a little; **un petit peu** a little
bit; **un peu d'espoir** a little hope;
**elle est un peu bavarde** she's quite
ou rather talkative; **un peu plus de**
slightly more than; **un peu moins de**
slightly less than; (avec pluriel) slightly
fewer than
▷ pron: **peu le savent** few know (it); **de
peu** (only) just

**peuple** [pœpl] nm people; **peupler** vt
(pays, région) to populate; (étang) to
stock; (suj: hommes, poissons) to inhabit
**peuplier** [pøplije] nm poplar (tree)
**peur** [pœʀ] nf fear; **avoir ~ (de/de
faire/que)** to be frightened ou afraid
(of/of doing/that); **faire ~ à** to
frighten; **de ~ de/que** for fear of/that;
**peureux, -euse** adj fearful, timorous
**peut** [pø] vb voir **pouvoir**
**peut-être** [pøtɛtʀ] adv perhaps,
maybe; **~ que** perhaps, maybe; **~ bien
qu'il fera/est** he may well do/be

**phare** [faʀ] nm (en mer) lighthouse; (de véhicule) headlight

**pharmacie** [faʀmasi] nf (magasin) chemist's (BRIT), pharmacy; (de salle de bain) medicine cabinet; **pharmacien, ne** nm/f pharmacist, chemist (BRIT)

**phénomène** [fenɔmɛn] nm phenomenon

**philosophe** [filɔzɔf] nm/f philosopher ▷ adj philosophical

**philosophie** [filɔzɔfi] nf philosophy

**phobie** [fɔbi] nf phobia

**phoque** [fɔk] nm seal

**phosphorescent, e** [fɔsfɔʀesɑ̃, ɑ̃t] adj luminous

**photo** [foto] nf photo(graph); **prendre en ~** to take a photo of; **pourriez-vous nous prendre en ~, s'il vous plaît?** would you take a picture of us, please?; **faire de la ~** to take photos; **photo d'identité** passport photograph; **photocopie** nf photocopy; **photocopier** vt to photocopy; **photocopieuse** nf photocopier; **photographe** nm/f photographer; **photographie** nf (technique) photography; (cliché) photograph; **photographier** vt to photograph

**phrase** [fʀɑz] nf sentence

**physicien, ne** [fizisjɛ̃, jɛn] nm/f physicist

**physique** [fizik] adj physical ▷ nm physique ▷ nf physics sg; **au ~** physically; **physiquement** adv physically

**pianiste** [pjanist] nm/f pianist

**piano** [pjano] nm piano; **pianoter** vi to tinkle away (at the piano)

**pic** [pik] nm (instrument) pick(axe); (montagne) peak; (Zool) woodpecker; **à ~** vertically; (fig: tomber, arriver) just at the right time

**pichet** [piʃɛ] nm jug

**picorer** [pikɔʀe] vt to peck

**pie** [pi] nf magpie

**pièce** [pjɛs] nf (d'un logement) room; (Théâtre) play; (de machine) part; (de monnaie) coin; (document) document; (fragment, de collection) piece; **dix euros ~** ten euros each; **vendre à la ~** to sell separately; **travailler à la ~** to do piecework; **un maillot une ~** a one-piece swimsuit; **un deux-~s cuisine** a two-room(ed) flat (BRIT) ou apartment (US) with kitchen; **pièce à conviction** exhibit; **pièce d'eau** ornamental lake ou pond; **pièce de rechange** spare (part); **pièce d'identité: avez-vous une pièce d'identité?** have you got any (means of) identification?; **pièce jointe** (Comput) attachment; **pièce montée** tiered cake; **pièces détachées** spares, (spare) parts; **pièces justificatives** supporting documents

**pied** [pje] nm foot; (de table) leg; (de lampe) base; **~s nus** ou **nu-~s** barefoot; **à ~** on foot; **au ~ de la lettre** literally; **avoir ~** to be able to touch the bottom, not to be out of one's depth; **avoir le ~ marin** to be a good sailor; **sur ~** (debout, rétabli) up and about; **mettre sur ~** (entreprise) to set up; **c'est le ~** (fam) it's brilliant; **mettre les ~s dans le plat** (fam) to put one's foot in it; **il se débrouille comme un ~** (fam) he's completely useless; **pied-noir** nm Algerian-born Frenchman

**piège** [pjɛʒ] nm trap; **prendre au ~** to trap; **piéger** vt (avec une bombe) to booby-trap; **lettre/voiture piégée** letter-/car-bomb

**piercing** [pjɛʀsiŋ] nm body piercing

**pierre** [pjɛʀ] nf stone; **pierre tombale** tombstone; **pierreries** nfpl gems, precious stones

**piétiner** [pjetine] vi (trépigner) to stamp (one's foot); (fig) to be at a standstill ▷ vt to trample on

**piéton, ne** [pjetɔ̃, ɔn] nm/f pedestrian; **piétonnier, -ière** adj: **rue** ou **zone piétonnière** pedestrian precinct

**pieu, x** [pjø] nm post; (pointu) stake

**pieuvre** [pjœvʀ] nf octopus

**pieux, -euse** [pjø, pjøz] adj pious

**pigeon** [piʒɔ̃] nm pigeon

**piger** [piʒe] (fam) vi, vt to understand
**pigiste** [piʒist] nm/f freelance(r)
**pignon** [piɲɔ̃] nm (de mur) gable
**pile** [pil] nf (tas) pile; (Élec) battery
▷ adv (fam: s'arrêter etc) dead; **à deux heures ~** at two on the dot; **jouer à ~ ou face** to toss up (for it); **~ ou face?** heads or tails?
**piler** [pile] vt to crush, pound
**pilier** [pilje] nm pillar
**piller** [pije] vt to pillage, plunder, loot
**pilote** [pilɔt] nm pilot; (de voiture) driver ▷ adj pilot cpd; **pilote de course** racing driver; **pilote de ligne** airline pilot; **piloter** vt (avion) to pilot, fly; (voiture) to drive
**pilule** [pilyl] nf pill; **prendre la ~** to be on the pill
**piment** [pimɑ̃] nm (aussi: **~ rouge**) chilli; (fig) spice, piquancy; **~ doux** pepper, capsicum; **pimenté, e** adj (plat) hot, spicy
**pin** [pɛ̃] nm pine
**pinard** [pinaʀ] (fam) nm (cheap) wine, plonk (BRIT)
**pince** [pɛ̃s] nf (outil) pliers pl; (de homard, crabe) pincer, claw; (Couture: pli) dart; **pince à épiler** tweezers pl; **pince à linge** clothes peg (BRIT) ou pin (US)
**pincé, e** [pɛ̃se] adj (air) stiff
**pinceau, x** [pɛ̃so] nm (paint)brush
**pincer** [pɛ̃se] vt to pinch; (fam) to nab
**pinède** [pinɛd] nf pinewood, pine forest
**pingouin** [pɛ̃gwɛ̃] nm penguin
**ping-pong®** [piŋpɔ̃g] nm table tennis
**pinson** [pɛ̃sɔ̃] nm chaffinch
**pintade** [pɛ̃tad] nf guinea-fowl
**pion** [pjɔ̃] nm (Échecs) pawn; (Dames) piece; (Scol) supervisor
**pionnier** [pjɔnje] nm pioneer
**pipe** [pip] nf pipe; **fumer la ~** to smoke a pipe
**piquant, e** [pikɑ̃, ɑ̃t] adj (barbe, rosier etc) prickly; (saveur, sauce) hot, pungent; (détail) titillating; (froid) biting ▷ nm (épine) thorn, prickle; (fig) spiciness, spice
**pique** [pik] nf pike; (fig) cutting remark

▷ nm (Cartes) spades pl
**pique-nique** [piknik] nm picnic; **pique-niquer** vi to have a picnic
**piquer** [pike] vt (suj: guêpe, fumée, orties) to sting; (: moustique) to bite; (: barbe) to prick; (: froid) to bite; (Méd) to give a jab to; (: chien, chat) to put to sleep; (intérêt) to arouse; (fam: voler) to pinch ▷ vi (avion) to go into a dive
**piquet** [pikɛ] nm (pieu) post, stake; (de tente) peg
**piqûre** [pikyʀ] nf (d'épingle) prick; (d'ortie) sting; (de moustique) bite; (Méd) injection, shot (US); **faire une ~ à qn** to give sb an injection
**pirate** [piʀat] nm, adj pirate; **pirate de l'air** hijacker
**pire** [piʀ] adj worse; (superlatif): **le(la) ~ ...** the worst ... ▷ nm: **le ~ (de)** the worst (of); **au ~** at the (very) worst
**pis** [pi] nm (de vache) udder ▷ adj, adv worse; **de mal en ~** from bad to worse
**piscine** [pisin] nf (swimming) pool; **piscine couverte** indoor (swimming) pool
**pissenlit** [pisɑ̃li] nm dandelion
**pistache** [pistaʃ] nf pistachio (nut)
**piste** [pist] nf (d'un animal, sentier) track, trail; (indice) lead; (de stade) track; (de cirque) ring; (de danse) floor; (de patinage) rink; (de ski) run; (Aviat) runway; **piste cyclable** cycle track
**pistolet** [pistɔlɛ] nm (arme) pistol, gun; (à peinture) spray gun; **pistolet-mitrailleur** nm submachine gun
**piston** [pistɔ̃] nm (Tech) piston; **avoir du ~** (fam) to have friends in the right places; **pistonner** vt (candidat) to pull strings for
**piteux, -euse** [pitø, øz] adj pitiful, sorry (avant le nom); **en ~ état** in a sorry state
**pitié** [pitje] nf pity; **il me fait ~** I feel sorry for him; **avoir ~ de** (compassion) to pity, feel sorry for; (merci) to have pity ou mercy on
**pitoyable** [pitwajabl] adj pitiful
**pittoresque** [pitɔʀɛsk] adj

picturesque

**PJ** sigle f (= police judiciaire) ≈ CID (BRIT), ≈ FBI (US)

**placard** [plakaʀ] nm (armoire) cupboard; (affiche) poster, notice

**place** [plas] nf (emplacement, classement) place; (de ville, village) square; (espace libre) room, space; (de parking) space; (siège: de train, cinéma, voiture) seat; (emploi) job; **en ~** (mettre) in its place; **sur ~** on the spot; **faire ~ à** to give way to; **ça prend de la ~** it takes up a lot of room ou space; **à la ~ de** in place of, instead of; **à votre ~...** if I were you ...; **je voudrais réserver deux ~s** I'd like to book two seats; **la ~ est prise?** is this seat taken?; **se mettre à la ~ de qn** to put o.s. in sb's place ou in sb's shoes

**placé, e** [plase] adj: **haut ~** (fig) high-ranking; **être bien/mal ~** (spectateur) to have a good/a poor seat; (concurrent) to be in a good/bad position; **il est bien ~ pour le savoir** he is in a position to know

**placement** [plasmɑ̃] nm (Finance) investment; **agence** ou **bureau de ~** employment agency

**placer** [plase] vt to place; (convive, spectateur) to seat; (argent) to place, invest; **se ~ au premier rang** to go and stand (ou sit) in the first row

**plafond** [plafɔ̃] nm ceiling

**plage** [plaʒ] nf beach; **plage arrière** (Auto) parcel ou back shelf

**plaider** [plede] vi (avocat) to plead ▷ vt to plead; **~ pour** (fig) to speak for; **plaidoyer** nm (Jur) speech for the defence; (fig) plea

**plaie** [plɛ] nf wound

**plaignant, e** [plɛɲɑ̃, ɑ̃t] nm/f plaintiff

**plaindre** [plɛ̃dʀ] vt to pity, feel sorry for; **se plaindre** vi (gémir) to moan; (protester): **se ~ (à qn) (de)** to complain (to sb) (about); (souffrir): **se ~ de** to complain of

**plaine** [plɛn] nf plain

**plain-pied** [plɛ̃pje] adv: **de ~ (avec)** on the same level (as)

**plainte** [plɛ̃t] nf (gémissement) moan, groan; (doléance) complaint; **porter ~** to lodge a complaint

**plaire** [plɛʀ] vi to be a success, be successful; **ça plaît beaucoup aux jeunes** it's very popular with young people; **~ à: cela me plaît** I like it; **se ~ quelque part** to like being somewhere ou like it somewhere; **s'il vous plaît** please

**plaisance** [plɛzɑ̃s] nf (aussi: **navigation de ~**) (pleasure) sailing, yachting

**plaisant, e** [plɛzɑ̃, ɑ̃t] adj pleasant; (histoire, anecdote) amusing

**plaisanter** [plɛzɑ̃te] vi to joke; **plaisanterie** nf joke

**plaisir** [plɛziʀ] nm pleasure; **faire ~ à qn** (délibérément) to be nice to sb, please sb; **ça me fait ~** I like (doing) it; **j'espère que ça te fera ~** I hope you'll like it; **pour le ~** for pleasure

**plaît** [plɛ] vb voir **plaire**

**plan, e** [plɑ̃, an] adj flat ▷ nm plan; (fig) level, plane; (Cinéma) shot; **au premier/second ~** in the foreground/middle distance; **à l'arrière ~** in the background; **plan d'eau** lake

**planche** [plɑ̃ʃ] nf (pièce de bois) plank, (wooden) board; (illustration) plate; **planche à repasser** ironing board; **planche (à roulettes)** skateboard; **planche (à voile)** (sport) windsurfing

**plancher** [plɑ̃ʃe] nm floor; floorboards pl ▷ vi (fam) to work hard

**planer** [plane] vi (oiseau, avion) to glide; (fam: rêveur) to have one's head in the clouds; **~ sur** (fig: danger) to hang over

**planète** [planɛt] nf planet

**planeur** [planœʀ] nm glider

**planifier** [planifje] vt to plan

**planning** [planiŋ] nm programme, schedule; **planning familial** family planning

**plant** [plɑ̃] nm seedling, young plant

**plante** [plɑ̃t] nf plant; **la plante du pied** the sole (of the foot); **plante verte** ou **d'appartement** house plant

**planter** [plɑ̃te] vt (plante) to plant; (enfoncer) to hammer ou drive in; (tente) to put up, pitch; (fam: personne) to dump; **se planter** (fam: se tromper) to get it wrong

**plaque** [plak] nf plate; (de verglas, d'eczéma) patch; (avec inscription) plaque; **plaque chauffante** hotplate; **plaque de chocolat** bar of chocolate; **plaque tournante** (fig) centre

**plaqué, e** [plake] adj: **~ or/argent** gold-/silver-plated

**plaquer** [plake] vt (Rugby) to bring down; (fam: laisser tomber) to drop

**plaquette** [plaket] nf (de chocolat) bar; (beurre) pack(et); **plaquette de frein** brake pad

**plastique** [plastik] adj, nm plastic; **plastiquer** vt to blow up (with a plastic bomb)

**plat, e** [pla, -at] adj flat; (cheveux) straight; (style) flat, dull ▷ nm (récipient, Culin) dish; (d'un repas) course; **à ~ ventre** face down; **à ~** (pneu, batterie) flat; (fam: personne) dead beat; **plat cuisiné** pre-cooked meal; **plat de résistance** main course; **plat du jour** dish of the day

**platane** [platan] nm plane tree

**plateau, x** [plato] nm (support) tray; (Géo) plateau; (Cinéma) set; **plateau à fromages** cheese board

**plate-bande** [platbɑ̃d] nf flower bed

**plate-forme** [platfɔrm] nf platform; **plate-forme de forage/pétrolière** drilling/oil rig

**platine** [platin] nm platinum ▷ nf (d'un tourne-disque) turntable; **platine laser** compact disc ou CD player

**plâtre** [plɑtR] nm (matériau) plaster; (statue) plaster statue; (Méd) (plaster) cast; **avoir un bras dans le ~** to have an arm in plaster

**plein, e** [plɛ̃, plɛn] adj full ▷ nm: **faire le ~ (d'essence)** to fill up (with petrol); **à ~es mains** (ramasser) in handfuls; **à ~ temps** full-time; **en ~ air** in the open air; **en ~ soleil** in direct sunlight; **en ~e**

**nuit/rue** in the middle of the night/ street; **en ~ jour** in broad daylight; **le ~, s'il vous plaît** fill it up, please

**pleurer** [plœre] vi to cry; (yeux) to water ▷ vt to mourn (for); **~ sur** to lament (over), to bemoan

**pleurnicher** [plœrniʃe] vi to snivel, whine

**pleurs** [plœr] nmpl: **en ~** in tears

**pleut** [plø] vb voir **pleuvoir**

**pleuvoir** [pløvwaR] vb impers to rain ▷ vi (coups) to rain down; (critiques, invitations) to shower down; **il pleut** it's raining; **il pleut des cordes** it's pouring (down), it's raining cats and dogs

**pli** [pli] nm fold; (de jupe) pleat; (de pantalon) crease

**pliant, e** [plijɑ̃, plijɑ̃t] adj folding

**plier** [plije] vt to fold; (pour ranger) to fold up; (genou, bras) to bend ▷ vi to bend; (fig) to yield; **se ~ à** to submit to

**plisser** [plise] vt (jupe) to put pleats in; (yeux) to screw up; (front) to crease

**plomb** [plɔ̃] nm (métal) lead; (d'une cartouche) (lead) shot; (Pêche) sinker; (Élec) fuse; **sans ~** (essence etc) unleaded

**plomberie** [plɔ̃bRi] nf plumbing

**plombier** [plɔ̃bje] nm plumber

**plonge** [plɔ̃ʒ] nf washing-up

**plongeant, e** [plɔ̃ʒɑ̃, ɑ̃t] adj (vue) from above; (décolleté) plunging

**plongée** [plɔ̃ʒe] nf (Sport) diving no pl; (sans scaphandre) skin diving; **~ sous-marine** diving

**plongeoir** [plɔ̃ʒwaR] nm diving board

**plongeon** [plɔ̃ʒɔ̃] nm dive

**plonger** [plɔ̃ʒe] vi to dive ▷ vt: **~ qch dans** to plunge sth into; **se ~ dans** (études, lecture) to bury ou immerse o.s. in; **plongeur** nm diver

**plu** [ply] pp de **plaire**; de **pleuvoir**

**pluie** [plɥi] nf rain

**plume** [plym] nf feather; (pour écrire) (pen) nib; (fig) pen

**plupart** [plypaR]: **la ~** pron the majority, most (of them); **la ~ des** most, the majority of; **la ~ du temps/ d'entre nous** most of the time/of us;

**pour la ~** for the most part, mostly
**pluriel** [plyʀjɛl] *nm* plural
**plus¹** [ply] *vb voir* **plaire**

⬤ MOT-CLÉ

**plus²** [ply] *adv* **1** (*forme négative*): **ne ... plus** no more, no longer; **je n'ai plus d'argent** I've got no more money *ou* no money left; **il ne travaille plus** he's no longer working, he doesn't work any more
**2** [ply, plyz + *voyelle*] (*comparatif*) more, ...+er; (*superlatif*): **le plus** the most, the ...+est; **plus grand/intelligent (que)** bigger/more intelligent (than); **le plus grand/intelligent** the biggest/most intelligent; **tout au plus** at the very most
**3** [plys, plyz + *voyelle*] (*davantage*) more; **il travaille plus (que)** he works more (than); **plus il travaille, plus il est heureux** the more he works, the happier he is; **plus de 10 personnes/3 heures** more than *ou* over 10 people/3 hours; **3 heures de plus que** 3 hours more than; **de plus** what's more, moreover; **il a 3 ans de plus que moi** he's 3 years older than me; **3 kilos en plus** 3 kilos more; **en plus de** in addition to; **de plus en plus** more and more; **plus ou moins** more or less; **ni plus ni moins** no more, no less
▷ *prép* [plys]: **4 plus 2** 4 plus 2

**plusieurs** [plyzjœʀ] *dét, pron* several; **ils sont ~** there are several of them
**plus-value** [plyvaly] *nf* (*bénéfice*) surplus
**plutôt** [plyto] *adv* rather; **je préfère ~ celui-ci** I'd rather have this one; **~ que (de) faire** rather than *ou* instead of doing
**pluvieux, -euse** [plyvjø, jøz] *adj* rainy, wet
**PME** *sigle f* (= *petite(s) et moyenne(s) entreprise(s)*) small business(es)
**PMU** *sigle m* (= *Pari mutuel urbain*) system

of betting on horses; (*café*) betting agency
**PNB** *sigle m* (= *produit national brut*) GNP
**pneu** [pnø] *nm* tyre (BRIT), tire (US); **j'ai un ~ crevé** I've got a flat tyre
**pneumonie** [pnømɔni] *nf* pneumonia
**poche** [pɔʃ] *nf* pocket; (*sous les yeux*) bag, pouch; **argent de ~** pocket money
**pochette** [pɔʃɛt] *nf* (*d'aiguilles etc*) case; (*mouchoir*) breast pocket handkerchief; (*sac à main*) clutch bag; **pochette de disque** record sleeve
**poêle** [pwal] *nm* stove ▷ *nf*: **~ (à frire)** frying pan
**poème** [pɔɛm] *nm* poem
**poésie** [pɔezi] *nf* (*poème*) poem; (*art*): **la ~** poetry
**poète** [pɔɛt] *nm* poet
**poids** [pwa] *nm* weight; (*Sport*) shot; **vendre au ~** to sell by weight; **perdre/prendre du ~** to lose/put on weight; **poids lourd** (*camion*) lorry (BRIT), truck (US)
**poignant, e** [pwaɲã, ãt] *adj* poignant
**poignard** [pwaɲaʀ] *nm* dagger; **poignarder** *vt* to stab, knife
**poigne** [pwaɲ] *nf* grip; **avoir de la ~** (*fig*) to rule with a firm hand
**poignée** [pwaɲe] *nf* (*de sel etc, fig*) handful; (*de couvercle, porte*) handle; **poignée de main** handshake
**poignet** [pwaɲɛ] *nm* (*Anat*) wrist; (*de chemise*) cuff
**poil** [pwal] *nm* (*Anat*) hair; (*de pinceau, brosse*) bristle; (*de tapis*) strand; (*pelage*) coat; **à ~** (*fam*) starkers; **au ~** (*fam*) hunky-dory; **poilu, e** *adj* hairy
**poinçonner** [pwɛ̃sɔne] *vt* (*bijou*) to hallmark; (*billet*) to punch
**poing** [pwɛ̃] *nm* fist; **coup de ~** punch
**point** [pwɛ̃] *nm* point; (*endroit*) spot; (*marque, signe*) dot; (: *de ponctuation*) full stop, period (US); (*Couture, Tricot*) stitch ▷ *adv* = **pas²**; **faire le ~** (*fig*) to take stock (of the situation); **sur le ~ de faire** (just) about to do; **à tel ~ que** so much so that; **mettre au ~** (*procédé*) to develop; (*affaire*) to settle; **à ~** (*Culin: viande*) medium; **à ~ (nommé)**

just at the right time; **deux ~s** colon; **point de côté** stitch (*pain*); **point d'exclamation/d'interrogation** exclamation/question mark; **point de repère** landmark; (*dans le temps*) point of reference; **point de vente** retail outlet; **point de vue** viewpoint; (*fig: opinion*) point of view; **point faible** weak spot; **point final** full stop, period (*US*); **point mort**: **au point mort** (*Auto*) in neutral; **points de suspension** suspension points

**pointe** [pwɛ̃t] *nf* point; (*clou*) tack; (*fig*): **une ~ de** a hint of; **être à la ~ de** (*fig*) to be in the forefront of; **sur la ~ des pieds** on tiptoe; **en ~** pointed, tapered; **de ~** (*technique etc*) leading; **heures de ~** peak hours

**pointer** [pwɛ̃te] *vt* (*diriger: canon, doigt*): **~ sur qch** to point at sth ▷ *vi* (*employé*) to clock in

**pointillé** [pwɛ̃tije] *nm* (*trait*) dotted line

**pointilleux, -euse** [pwɛ̃tijø, øz] *adj* particular, pernickety

**pointu, e** [pwɛ̃ty] *adj* pointed; (*voix*) shrill; (*analyse*) precise

**pointure** [pwɛ̃tyʀ] *nf* size

**point-virgule** [pwɛ̃viʀɡyl] *nm* semi-colon

**poire** [pwaʀ] *nf* pear; (*fam: péj*) mug

**poireau, x** [pwaʀo] *nm* leek

**poirier** [pwaʀje] *nm* pear tree

**pois** [pwɑ] *nm* (*Bot*) pea; (*sur une étoffe*) dot, spot; **~ chiche** chickpea; **à ~** (*cravate etc*) spotted, polka-dot *cpd*

**poison** [pwazɔ̃] *nm* poison

**poisseux, -euse** [pwasø, øz] *adj* sticky

**poisson** [pwasɔ̃] *nm* fish *gén inv*; (*Astrol*): **P~s** Pisces; **~ d'avril** April fool; (*blague*) April Fool's Day trick; *see note*; **poisson rouge** goldfish; **poissonnerie** *nf* fish-shop; **poissonnier, -ière** *nm/f* fishmonger (*BRIT*), fish merchant (*US*)

● **POISSON D'AVRIL**

● 
● The traditional April Fools' Day prank
● in France involves attaching a cut-

● out paper fish, known as a 'poisson
● d'avril', to the back of one's victim,
● without being caught.

**poitrine** [pwatʀin] *nf* chest; (*seins*) bust, bosom; (*Culin*) breast

**poivre** [pwavʀ] *nm* pepper

**poivron** [pwavʀɔ̃] *nm* pepper, capsicum

**polaire** [pɔlɛʀ] *adj* polar

**pôle** [pol] *nm* (*Géo, Élec*) pole; **le ~ Nord/Sud** the North/South Pole

**poli, e** [pɔli] *adj* polite; (*lisse*) smooth

**police** [pɔlis] *nf* police; **police judiciaire** ≈ Criminal Investigation Department (*BRIT*), ≈ Federal Bureau of Investigation (*US*); **police secours** ≈ emergency services *pl* (*BRIT*), ≈ paramedics *pl* (*US*); **policier, -ière** *adj* police *cpd* ▷ *nm* policeman; (*aussi*: **roman policier**) detective novel

**polir** [pɔliʀ] *vt* to polish

**politesse** [pɔlites] *nf* politeness

**politicien, ne** [pɔlitisjɛ̃, jɛn] (*péj*) *nm/f* politician

**politique** [pɔlitik] *adj* political ▷ *nf* politics *sg*; (*mesures, méthode*) policies *pl*

**politiquement** [pɔlitikmɑ̃] *adv* politically; **~ correct** politically correct

**pollen** [pɔlɛn] *nm* pollen

**polluant, e** [pɔlɥɑ̃, ɑ̃t] *adj* polluting ▷ *nm* (*produit*) pollutant; **non ~** non-polluting

**polluer** [pɔlɥe] *vt* to pollute; **pollution** *nf* pollution

**polo** [pɔlo] *nm* (*chemise*) polo shirt

**Pologne** [pɔlɔɲ] *nf*: **la ~** Poland; **polonais, e** *adj* Polish ▷ *nm/f*: **Polonais, e** Pole ▷ *nm* (*Ling*) Polish

**poltron, ne** [pɔltʀɔ̃, ɔn] *adj* cowardly

**polycopier** [pɔlikɔpje] *vt* to duplicate

**Polynésie** [pɔlinezi] *nf*: **la ~** Polynesia; **la ~ française** French Polynesia

**polyvalent, e** [pɔlivalɑ̃, ɑ̃t] *adj* (*rôle*) varied; (*salle*) multi-purpose

**pommade** [pɔmad] *nf* ointment, cream

**pomme** [pɔm] *nf* apple; **tomber**

**dans les ~s** (fam) to pass out; **pomme d'Adam** Adam's apple; **pomme de pin** pine ou fir cone; **pomme de terre** potato

**pommette** [pɔmɛt] nf cheekbone

**pommier** [pɔmje] nm apple tree

**pompe** [pɔ̃p] nf pump; (faste) pomp (and ceremony); **pompe (à essence)** petrol pump; **pompes funèbres** funeral parlour sg, undertaker's sg;

**pomper** vt to pump; (aspirer) to pump up; (absorber) to soak up

**pompeux, -euse** [pɔ̃pø, øz] adj pompous

**pompier** [pɔ̃pje] nm fireman

**pompiste** [pɔ̃pist] nm/f petrol (BRIT) ou gas (US) pump attendant

**poncer** [pɔ̃se] vt to sand (down)

**ponctuation** [pɔ̃ktɥasjɔ̃] nf punctuation

**ponctuel, le** [pɔ̃ktɥɛl] adj punctual

**pondéré, e** [pɔ̃dere] adj level-headed, composed

**pondre** [pɔ̃dr] vt to lay

**poney** [pɔnɛ] nm pony

**pont** [pɔ̃] nm bridge; (Navig) deck; **faire le ~** to take the extra day off; see note; **pont suspendu** suspension bridge; **pont-levis** nm drawbridge

○ **PONT**
○
○ The expression 'faire le pont' refers
○ to the practice of taking a Monday
○ or Friday off to make a long weekend
○ if a public holiday falls on a Tuesday
○ or Thursday. The French commonly
○ take an extra day off work to give
○ four consecutive days' holiday at
○ 'l'Ascension', 'le 14 juillet' and 'le
○ 15 août'.

**pop** [pɔp] adj inv pop

**populaire** [pɔpylɛr] adj popular; (manifestation) mass cpd; (milieux, quartier) working-class; (expression) vernacular

**popularité** [pɔpylarite] nf popularity

**population** [pɔpylasjɔ̃] nf population

**populeux, -euse** [pɔpylø, øz] adj densely populated

**porc** [pɔr] nm pig; (Culin) pork

**porcelaine** [pɔrsəlɛn] nf porcelain, china; piece of china(ware)

**porc-épic** [pɔrkepik] nm porcupine

**porche** [pɔrʃ] nm porch

**porcherie** [pɔrʃəri] nf pigsty

**pore** [pɔr] nm pore

**porno** [pɔrno] adj porno ▷ nm porn

**port** [pɔr] nm harbour, port; (ville) port; (de l'uniforme etc) wearing; (pour lettre) postage; (pour colis, aussi: posture) carriage; **port d'arme** (Jur) carrying of a firearm; **port payé** postage paid

**portable** [pɔrtabl] adj (portatif) portable; (téléphone) mobile ▷ nm (Comput) laptop (computer); (téléphone) mobile (phone)

**portail** [pɔrtaj] nm gate

**portant, e** [pɔrtɑ̃, ɑ̃t] adj: **bien/mal ~** in good/poor health

**portatif, -ive** [pɔrtatif, iv] adj portable

**porte** [pɔrt] nf door; (de ville, jardin) gate; **mettre à la ~** to throw out; **porte-avions** nm inv aircraft carrier; **porte-bagages** nm inv luggage rack; **porte-bonheur** nm inv lucky charm; **porte-clefs** nm inv key ring; **porte-documents** nm inv attaché ou document case

**porté, e** [pɔrte] adj: **être ~ à faire** to be inclined to do; **être ~ sur qch** to be keen on sth; **portée** nf (d'une arme) range; (fig: effet) impact, import; (: capacité) scope, capability; (de chatte etc) litter; (Mus) stave, staff; **à/hors de portée (de)** within/out of reach (of); **à portée de (la) main** within (arm's) reach; **à la portée de qn** (fig) at sb's level, within sb's capabilities

**porte...**: **portefeuille** nm wallet; **portemanteau, x** nm (cintre) coat hanger; (au mur) coat rack; **porte-monnaie** nm inv purse; **porte-parole** nm inv spokesman

**porter** [pɔʀte] vt to carry; (sur soi:
vêtement, barbe, bague) to wear; (fig:
responsabilité etc) to bear, carry;
(inscription, nom, fruits) to bear; (coup)
to deal; (attention) to turn; (apporter):
**~ qch à qn** to take sth to sb ▷ vi (voix)
to carry; (coup, argument) to hit home;
**se porter** vi (se sentir): **se ~ bien/mal**
to be well/unwell; **~ sur** (recherches) to
be concerned with; **se faire ~ malade**
to report sick

**porteur, -euse** [pɔʀtœʀ, øz] nm/f (de
bagages) porter; (de chèque) bearer

**porte-voix** [pɔʀtəvwa] nm inv
megaphone

**portier** [pɔʀtje] nm doorman

**portière** [pɔʀtjɛʀ] nf door

**portion** [pɔʀsjɔ̃] nf (part) portion,
share; (partie) portion, section

**porto** [pɔʀto] nm port (wine)

**portrait** [pɔʀtʀɛ] nm (peinture)
portrait; (photo) photograph; **portrait-
robot** nm Identikit® ou photo-fit®
picture

**portuaire** [pɔʀtɥɛʀ] adj port cpd,
harbour cpd

**portugais, e** [pɔʀtɥgɛ, ɛz] adj
Portuguese ▷ nm/f: **P~, e** Portuguese
▷ nm (Ling) Portuguese

**Portugal** [pɔʀtɥgal] nm: **le ~** Portugal

**pose** [poz] nf (de moquette) laying;
(attitude, d'un modèle) pose; (Photo)
exposure

**posé, e** [poze] adj serious

**poser** [poze] vt to put; (installer:
moquette, carrelage) to lay; (rideaux,
papier peint) to hang; (question) to
ask; (principe, conditions) to lay ou set
down; (difficulté) to pose; (formuler:
problème) to formulate ▷ vi (modèle)
to pose; **se poser** vi (oiseau, avion) to
land; (question) to arise; **~ qch (sur)**
(déposer) to put sth down (on); **~ qch
sur/quelque part** (placer) to put sth
on/somewhere; **~ sa candidature à
un poste** to apply for a post

**positif, -ive** [pozitif, iv] adj positive

**position** [pozisjɔ̃] nf position; **prendre**

**~** (fig) to take a stand

**posologie** [pozɔlɔʒi] nf dosage

**posséder** [pɔsede] vt to own, possess;
(qualité, talent) to have, possess;
(sexuellement) to possess; **possession** nf
ownership no pl, possession; **prendre
possession de qch** to take possession
of sth

**possibilité** [pɔsibilite] nf possibility;
**possibilités** nfpl (potentiel) potential sg

**possible** [pɔsibl] adj possible; (projet,
entreprise) feasible ▷ nm: **faire son ~** to
do all one can, do one's utmost; **le plus/
moins de livres ~** as many/few books
as possible; **le plus vite ~** as quickly as
possible; **aussitôt/dès que ~** as soon
as possible

**postal, e, -aux** [pɔstal, o] adj postal

**poste¹** [pɔst] nf (service) postal
service; (administration, bureau) post
office; **mettre à la ~** to post; **poste
restante** poste restante (BRIT), general
delivery (US)

**poste²** [pɔst] nm (fonction, Mil) post;
(Tél) extension; (de radio etc) set;
**poste (de police)** police station;
**poste de secours** first-aid post;
**poste d'essence** filling station;
**poste d'incendie** fire point; **poste de
pilotage** cockpit, flight deck

**poster** [pɔste] vt to post; **où est-ce que
je peux ~ ces cartes postales?** where
can I post these cards?

**postérieur, e** [pɔsterjœʀ] adj (date)
later; (partie) back ▷ nm (fam) behind

**postuler** [pɔstyle] vi: **~ à** ou **pour un
emploi** to apply for a job

**pot** [po] nm (en verre) jar; (en terre) pot;
(en plastique, carton) carton; (en métal)
tin; (fam: chance) luck; **avoir du ~** (fam)
to be lucky; **boire** ou **prendre un ~** (fam)
to have a drink; **petit ~ (pour bébé)** (jar
of) baby food; **~ catalytique** catalytic
converter; **pot d'échappement**
exhaust pipe

**potable** [pɔtabl] adj: **eau (non) ~**
(non-)drinking water

**potage** [pɔtaʒ] nm soup; **potager,**

**-ère** adj: **(jardin) potager** kitchen ou vegetable garden

**pot-au-feu** [pɔtofø] nm inv (beef) stew

**pot-de-vin** [podvɛ̃] nm bribe

**pote** [pɔt] (fam) nm pal

**poteau, x** [pɔto] nm post; **poteau indicateur** signpost

**potelé, e** [pɔt(ə)le] adj plump, chubby

**potentiel, le** [pɔtɑ̃sjɛl] adj, nm potential

**poterie** [pɔtri] nf pottery; (objet) piece of pottery

**potier, -ière** [pɔtje, jɛR] nm/f potter

**potiron** [pɔtiRɔ̃] nm pumpkin

**pou, x** [pu] nm louse

**poubelle** [pubɛl] nf (dust)bin

**pouce** [pus] nm thumb

**poudre** [pudR] nf powder; (fard) (face) powder; (explosif) gunpowder; **en ~**: **café en ~** instant coffee; **lait en ~** dried ou powdered milk; **poudreuse** nf powder snow; **poudrier** nm (powder) compact

**pouffer** [pufe] vi: **~ (de rire)** to burst out laughing

**poulailler** [pulaje] nm henhouse

**poulain** [pulɛ̃] nm foal; (fig) protégé

**poule** [pul] nf hen; (Culin) (boiling) fowl; **poule mouillée** coward

**poulet** [pulɛ] nm chicken; (fam) cop

**poulie** [puli] nf pulley

**pouls** [pu] nm pulse; **prendre le ~ de qn** to feel sb's pulse

**poumon** [pumɔ̃] nm lung

**poupée** [pupe] nf doll

**pour** [puR] prép for ▷ nm: **le ~ et le contre** the pros and cons; **~ faire** (so as) to do, in order to do; **~ avoir fait** for having done; **~ que** so that, in order that; **fermé ~ (cause de) travaux** closed for refurbishment ou alterations; **c'est ~ ça que ...** that's why ...; **~ quoi faire?** what for?; **~ 20 euros d'essence** 20 euros' worth of petrol; **~ cent** per cent; **~ ce qui est de** as for

**pourboire** [puRbwaR] nm tip; **combien de ~ est-ce qu'il faut laisser?** how much should I tip?

**pourcentage** [puRsɑ̃taʒ] nm percentage

**pourchasser** [puRʃase] vt to pursue

**pourparlers** [puRpaRle] nmpl talks, negotiations

**pourpre** [puRpR] adj crimson

**pourquoi** [puRkwa] adv, conj why ▷ nm inv: **le ~ (de)** the reason (for)

**pourrai** etc [puRe] vb voir **pouvoir**

**pourri, e** [puRi] adj rotten

**pourrir** [puRiR] vi to rot; (fruit) to go rotten ou bad ▷ vt to rot; (fig) to spoil thoroughly; **pourriture** nf rot

**poursuite** [puRsɥit] nf pursuit, chase; **poursuites** nfpl (Jur) legal proceedings

**poursuivre** [puRsɥivR] vt to pursue, chase (after); (obséder) to haunt; (Jur) to bring proceedings against, prosecute; (: au civil) to sue; (but) to strive towards; (continuer: études etc) to carry on with, continue; **se poursuivre** vi to go on, continue

**pourtant** [puRtɑ̃] adv yet; **c'est ~ facile** (and) yet it's easy

**pourtour** [puRtuR] nm perimeter

**pourvoir** [puRvwaR] vt: **~ qch/qn de** to equip sth/sb with ▷ vi: **~ à** to provide for; **pourvu, e** adj: **pourvu de** equipped with; **pourvu que** (si) provided that, so long as; (espérons que) let's hope (that)

**pousse** [pus] nf growth; (bourgeon) shoot

**poussée** [puse] nf thrust; (d'acné) eruption; (fig: prix) upsurge

**pousser** [puse] vt to push; (émettre: cri, soupir) to give; (stimuler: élève) to urge on; (poursuivre: études, discussion) to carry on (further) ▷ vi to push; (croître) to grow; **se pousser** vi to move over; **~ qn à** (inciter) to urge ou press sb to; (acculer) to drive sb to; **faire ~** (plante) to grow

**poussette** [pusɛt] nf push chair (BRIT), stroller (US)

**poussière** [pusjɛR] nf dust; **poussiéreux, -euse** adj dusty

**poussin** [pusɛ̃] nm chick
**poutre** [putʀ] nf beam

O **MOT-CLÉ**

**pouvoir** [puvwaʀ] nm power; (Pol:
*dirigeants*): **le pouvoir** those in power;
**les pouvoirs publics** the authorities;
**pouvoir d'achat** purchasing power
▷ vb semi-aux **1** (*être en état de*) can,
be able to; **je ne peux pas le réparer**
I can't ou I am not able to repair it;
**déçu de ne pas pouvoir le faire**
disappointed not to be able to do it
**2** (*avoir la permission*) can, may, be
allowed to; **vous pouvez aller au
cinéma** you can ou may go to the
pictures
**3** (*probabilité, hypothèse*) may, might,
could; **il a pu avoir un accident** he
may ou might ou could have had an
accident; **il aurait pu le dire!** he might
ou could have said (so)!
▷ vb impers may, might, could; **il peut
arriver que** it may ou might ou could
happen that; **il pourrait pleuvoir** it
might rain
▷ vt can, be able to; **j'ai fait tout ce que
j'ai pu** I did all I could; **je n'en peux plus**
(*épuisé*) I'm exhausted; (*à bout*) I can't
take any more
▷ vi: **se pouvoir: il se peut que** it may
ou might be that; **cela se pourrait**
that's quite possible

**prairie** [pʀeʀi] nf meadow
**praline** [pʀalin] nf sugared almond
**praticable** [pʀatikabl] adj passable,
practicable
**pratiquant, e** [pʀatikɑ̃, ɑ̃t] nm/f
(regular) churchgoer
**pratique** [pʀatik] nf practice ▷ adj
practical; **pratiquement** adv (*pour ainsi
dire*) practically, virtually; **pratiquer**
vt to practise; (*l'équitation, la pêche*)
to go in for; (*le golf, football*) to play;
(*intervention, opération*) to carry out
**pré** [pʀe] nm meadow

**préalable** [pʀealabl] adj preliminary;
**au ~** beforehand
**préambule** [pʀeɑ̃byl] nm preamble;
(*fig*) prelude; **sans ~** straight away
**préau** [pʀeo] nm (Scol) covered
playground
**préavis** [pʀeavi] nm notice
**précaution** [pʀekosjɔ̃] nf precaution;
**avec ~** cautiously; **par ~** as a
precaution
**précédemment** [pʀesedamɑ̃] adv
before, previously
**précédent, e** [pʀesedɑ̃, ɑ̃t] adj
previous ▷ nm precedent; **sans ~**
unprecedented; **le jour ~** the day
before, the previous day
**précéder** [pʀesede] vt to precede
**prêcher** [pʀeʃe] vt to preach
**précieux, -euse** [pʀesjø, jøz] adj
precious; (*aide, conseil*) invaluable
**précipice** [pʀesipis] nm drop, chasm
**précipitamment** [pʀesipitamɑ̃] adv
hurriedly, hastily
**précipitation** [pʀesipitasjɔ̃] nf (*hâte*)
haste
**précipité, e** [pʀesipite] adj hurried,
hasty
**précipiter** [pʀesipite] vt (*hâter: départ*)
to hasten; (*faire tomber*): **~ qn/qch du
haut de** to throw ou hurl sb/sth off ou
from; **se précipiter** vi to speed up; **se ~
sur/vers** to rush at/towards
**précis, e** [pʀesi, iz] adj precise;
(*mesures*) accurate, precise; **à 4 heures
~es** at 4 o'clock sharp; **précisément**
adv precisely; **préciser** vt (*expliquer*)
to be more specific about, clarify;
(*spécifier*) to state, specify; **se préciser**
vi to become clear(er); **précision**
nf precision; (*détail*) point ou detail;
**demander des précisions** to ask for
further explanation
**précoce** [pʀekɔs] adj early; (*enfant*)
precocious
**préconçu, e** [pʀekɔ̃sy] adj
preconceived
**préconiser** [pʀekɔnize] vt to advocate
**prédécesseur** [pʀedesesœʀ] nm

predecessor

**prédilection** [pʀedilɛksjɔ̃] nf: **avoir une ~ pour** to be partial to

**prédire** [pʀediʀ] vt to predict

**prédominer** [pʀedɔmine] vi to predominate

**préface** [pʀefas] nf preface

**préfecture** [pʀefɛktyʀ] nf prefecture; **préfecture de police** police headquarters pl

**préférable** [pʀefeʀabl] adj preferable

**préféré, e** [pʀefeʀe] adj, nm/f favourite

**préférence** [pʀefeʀɑ̃s] nf preference; **de ~** preferably

**préférer** [pʀefeʀe] vt: **~ qn/qch (à)** to prefer sb/sth (to), to like sb/sth better (than); **~ faire** to prefer to do; **je préférerais du thé** I would rather have tea, I'd prefer tea

**préfet** [pʀefɛ] nm prefect

**préhistorique** [pʀeistɔʀik] adj prehistoric

**préjudice** [pʀeʒydis] nm (matériel) loss; (moral) harm no pl; **porter ~ à** to harm, be detrimental to; **au ~ de** at the expense of

**préjugé** [pʀeʒyʒe] nm prejudice; **avoir un ~ contre** to be prejudiced ou biased against

**prélasser** [pʀelɑse]: **se prélasser** vi to lounge

**prélèvement** [pʀelɛvmɑ̃] nm (montant) deduction; **faire un ~ de sang** to take a blood sample

**prélever** [pʀel(ə)ve] vt (échantillon) to take; **~ (sur)** (montant) to deduct (from); (argent: sur son compte) to withdraw (from)

**prématuré, e** [pʀematyʀe] adj premature ▷ nm premature baby

**premier, -ière** [pʀəmje, jɛʀ] adj first; (rang) front; (fig: objectif) basic; **le ~ venu** the first person to come along; **de ~ ordre** first-rate; **Premier ministre** Prime Minister; **première** nf (Scol) year 12 (BRIT), eleventh grade (US); (Aviat, Rail etc) first class; **premièrement** adv firstly

**prémonition** [pʀemɔnisjɔ̃] nf premonition

**prenant, e** [pʀənɑ̃, ɑ̃t] adj absorbing, engrossing

**prénatal, e** [pʀenatal] adj (Méd) antenatal

**prendre** [pʀɑ̃dʀ] vt to take; (repas) to have; (se procurer) to get; (malfaiteur, poisson) to catch; (passager) to pick up; (personnel) to take on; (traiter: personne) to handle; (voix, ton) to put on; (ôter): **~ qch à** to take sth from; (coincer): **se ~ les doigts dans** to get one's fingers caught in ▷ vi (liquide, ciment) to set; (greffe, vaccin) to take; (feu: foyer) to go; (se diriger): **~ à gauche** to turn (to the) left; **~ froid** to catch cold; **se ~ pour** to think one is; **s'en ~ à** to attack; **se ~ d'amitié pour** to befriend; **s'y ~** (procéder) to set about it

**preneur** [pʀənœʀ] nm: **être/trouver ~** to be willing to buy/find a buyer

**prénom** [pʀenɔ̃] nm first ou Christian name

**préoccupation** [pʀeɔkypasjɔ̃] nf (souci) concern; (idée fixe) preoccupation

**préoccuper** [pʀeɔkype] vt (inquiéter) to worry; (absorber) to preoccupy; **se ~ de** to be concerned with

**préparatifs** [pʀepaʀatif] nmpl preparations

**préparation** [pʀepaʀasjɔ̃] nf preparation

**préparer** [pʀepaʀe] vt to prepare; (café, thé) to make; (examen) to prepare for; (voyage, entreprise) to plan; **se préparer** vi (orage, tragédie) to brew, be in the air; **~ qch à qn** (surprise etc) to have sth in store for sb; **se ~ (à qch/faire)** to prepare (o.s.) ou get ready (for sth/to do)

**prépondérant, e** [pʀepɔ̃deʀɑ̃, ɑ̃t] adj major, dominating

**préposé, e** [pʀepoze] nm/f employee; (facteur) postman

**préposition** [pʀepozisjɔ̃] nf preposition

**près** [pRɛ] *adv* near, close; **~ de** near.
(to), close to; (*environ*) nearly, almost;
**de ~** closely; **à 5 kg ~** to within about 5
kg; **il n'est pas à 10 minutes ~** he can
spare 10 minutes; **est-ce qu'il y a une
banque ~ d'ici?** is there a bank nearby?
**présage** [pReza3] *nm* omen
**presbyte** [pRɛsbit] *adj* long-sighted
**presbytère** [pRɛsbiteR] *nm* presbytery
**prescription** [pRɛskRipsjɔ̃] *nf*
prescription
**prescrire** [pRɛskRiR] *vt* to prescribe
**présence** [pRezɑ̃s] *nf* presence; (*au
bureau, à l'école*) attendance
**présent, e** [pRezɑ̃, ɑ̃t] *adj, nm* present;
**à ~ (que)** now (that)
**présentation** [pRezɑ̃tasjɔ̃] *nf*
presentation; (*de nouveau venu*)
introduction; (*allure*) appearance; **faire
les ~s** to do the introductions
**présenter** [pRezɑ̃te] *vt* to present;
(*excuses, condoléances*) to offer; (*invité,
conférencier*): **~ qn (à)** to introduce
sb (to) ▷ *vi*: **~ bien** to have a pleasing
appearance; **se présenter** *vi* (*occasion*)
to arise; **se ~ à** (*examen*) to sit; (*élection*)
to stand at, run for; **je vous présente
Nadine** this is Nadine, could I
introduce you to Nadine?
**préservatif** [pRezeRvatif] *nm*
condom, sheath
**préserver** [pRezeRve] *vt*: **~ de** (*protéger*)
to protect from
**président** [pRezidɑ̃] *nm* (*Pol*)
president; (*d'une assemblée, Comm*)
chairman; **président directeur
général** chairman and managing
director; **présidentielles** *nfpl*
presidential elections
**présider** [pRezide] *vt* to preside over;
(*dîner*) to be the guest of honour at
**presque** [pRɛsk] *adv* almost, nearly; **~
personne** hardly anyone; **~ rien** hardly
anything; **~ pas** hardly (at all); **~ pas
(de)** hardly any
**presqu'île** [pRɛskil] *nf* peninsula
**pressant, e** [pResɑ̃, ɑ̃t] *adj* urgent
**presse** [pRɛs] *nf* press; (*affluence*):

**heures de ~** busy times
**pressé, e** [pRese] *adj* in a hurry; (*travail*)
urgent; **orange ~e** freshly-squeezed
orange juice
**pressentiment** [pResɑ̃timɑ̃] *nm*
foreboding, premonition
**pressentir** [pResɑ̃tiR] *vt* to sense
**presse-papiers** [pRɛspapje] *nm inv*
paperweight
**presser** [pRese] *vt* (*fruit, éponge*) to
squeeze; (*bouton*) to press; (*allure*) to
speed up; (*inciter*): **~ qn de faire** to urge
*ou* press sb to do ▷ *vi* to be urgent; **se
presser** *vi* (*se hâter*) to hurry (up); **se ~
contre qn** to squeeze up against sb; **le
temps presse** there's not much time;
**rien ne presse** there's no hurry
**pressing** [pResiŋ] *nm* (*magasin*)
dry-cleaner's
**pression** [pResjɔ̃] *nf* pressure; (*bouton*)
press stud; (*fam: bière*) draught beer;
**faire ~ sur** to put pressure on; **sous ~**
pressurized, under pressure; (*fig*) under
pressure; **pression artérielle** blood
pressure
**prestataire** [pRɛstateR] *nm/f* supplier
**prestation** [pRɛstasjɔ̃] *nf* (*allocation*)
benefit; (*d'une entreprise*) service
provided; (*d'un artiste*) performance
**prestidigitateur, -trice**
[pRɛstidiʒitatœR, tRis] *nm/f* conjurer
**prestige** [pRɛstiʒ] *nm* prestige;
**prestigieux, -euse** *adj* prestigious
**présumer** [pRezyme] *vt*: **~ que** to
presume *ou* assume that
**prêt, e** [pRɛ, pRɛt] *adj* ready ▷ *nm*
(*somme*) loan; **quand est-ce que mes
photos seront ~es?** when will my
photos be ready?; **prêt-à-porter** *nm*
ready-to-wear *ou* off-the-peg (*BRIT*)
clothes *pl*
**prétendre** [pRetɑ̃dR] *vt* (*affirmer*): **~
que** to claim that; (*avoir l'intention de*): **~
faire qch** to mean *ou* intend to do sth;
**prétendu, e** *adj* (*supposé*) so-called

> Attention à ne pas traduire
> *prétendre* par **to pretend**.

**prétentieux, -euse** [pRetɑ̃sjø, jøz]

*adj* pretentious

**prétention** [pretɑ̃sjɔ̃] *nf* claim; *(vanité)* pretentiousness

**prêter** [prete] *vt (livres, argent):* **~ qch (à)** to lend sth (to); *(supposer):* **~ à qn** *(caractère, propos)* to attribute to sb; **pouvez-vous me ~ de l'argent?** can you lend me some money?

**prétexte** [pretɛkst] *nm* pretext, excuse; **sous aucun ~** on no account; **prétexter** *vt* to give as a pretext *ou* an excuse

**prêtre** [prɛtr] *nm* priest

**preuve** [prœv] *nf* proof; *(indice)* proof, evidence *no pl;* **faire ~ de** to show; **faire ses ~s** to prove o.s. *(ou* itself)

**prévaloir** [prevalwar] *vi* to prevail

**prévenant, e** [prev(ə)nɑ̃, ɑ̃t] *adj* thoughtful, kind

**prévenir** [prev(ə)nir] *vt (éviter: catastrophe etc)* to avoid, prevent; *(anticiper: désirs, besoins)* to anticipate; **~ qn (de)** *(avertir)* to warn sb (about); *(informer)* to tell *ou* inform sb (about)

**préventif, -ive** [prevɑ̃tif, iv] *adj* preventive

**prévention** [prevɑ̃sjɔ̃] *nf* prevention; **prévention routière** road safety

**prévenu, e** [prev(ə)ny] *nm/f (Jur)* defendant, accused

**prévision** [previzjɔ̃] *nf:* **~s** predictions; *(Écon)* forecast *sg;* **en ~ de** in anticipation of; **prévisions météorologiques** weather forecast *sg*

**prévoir** [prevwar] *vt (anticiper)* to foresee; *(s'attendre à)* to expect, reckon on; *(organiser: voyage etc)* to plan; *(envisager)* to allow; **comme prévu** as planned; **prévoyant, e** *adj* gifted with *(ou* showing) foresight; **prévu, e** *pp de* **prévoir**

**prier** [prije] *vi* to pray ▷ *vt (Dieu)* to pray to; *(implorer)* to beg; *(demander):* **~ qn de faire** to ask sb to do; **se faire ~** to need coaxing *ou* persuading; **je vous en prie** *(allez-y)* please do; *(de rien)* don't mention it; **prière** *nf* prayer; **"prière de ..."** "please ..."

**primaire** [primɛr] *adj* primary ▷ *nm (Scol)* primary education

**prime** [prim] *nf (bonus)* bonus; *(subvention)* premium; *(Comm: cadeau)* free gift; *(Assurances, Bourse)* premium ▷ *adj:* **de ~ abord** at first glance; **primer** *vt (récompenser)* to award a prize to ▷ *vi* to dominate; to be most important

**primevère** [primvɛr] *nf* primrose

**primitif, -ive** [primitif, iv] *adj* primitive; *(originel)* original

**prince** [prɛ̃s] *nm* prince; **princesse** *nf* princess

**principal, e, -aux** [prɛ̃sipal, o] *adj* principal, main ▷ *nm (Scol)* principal, head(master); *(essentiel)* main thing

**principe** [prɛ̃sip] *nm* principle; **par ~** on principle; **en ~** *(habituellement)* as a rule; *(théoriquement)* in principle

**printemps** [prɛ̃tɑ̃] *nm* spring

**priorité** [prijɔrite] *nf* priority; *(Auto)* right of way; **priorité à droite** right of way to vehicles coming from the right

**pris, e** [pri, priz] *pp de* **prendre** ▷ *adj (place)* taken; *(mains)* full; *(personne)* busy; **avoir le nez/la gorge ~(e)** to have a stuffy nose/a hoarse throat; **être ~ de panique** to be panic-stricken

**prise** [priz] *nf (d'une ville)* capture; *(Pêche, Chasse)* catch; *(point d'appui ou pour empoigner)* hold; *(Élec: fiche)* plug; *(: femelle)* socket; **être aux ~s avec** to be grappling with; **prise de courant** power point; **prise de sang** blood test; **prise multiple** adaptor

**priser** [prize] *vt (estimer)* to prize, value

**prison** [prizɔ̃] *nf* prison; **aller/être en ~** to go to/be in prison *ou* jail; **prisonnier, -ière** *nm/f* prisoner ▷ *adj* captive

**privé, e** [prive] *adj* private; *(en punition):* **tu es ~ de télé!** no TV for you! ▷ *nm (Comm)* private sector; **en ~** in private

**priver** [prive] *vt:* **~ qn de** to deprive sb of; **se priver de** to go *ou* do without

**privilège** [privilɛʒ] *nm* privilege

**prix** [pri] *nm* price; *(récompense, Scol)* prize; **hors de ~** exorbitantly priced;

**à aucun ~** not at any price; **à tout ~** at all costs

**probable** [pʀɔbabl] adj likely, probable; **probablement** adv probably

**problème** [pʀɔblɛm] nm problem

**procédé** [pʀɔsede] nm (méthode) process; (comportement) behaviour no pl

**procéder** [pʀɔsede] vi to proceed; (moralement) to behave; **~ à** to carry out

**procès** [pʀɔsɛ] nm trial; (poursuites) proceedings pl; **être en ~ avec** to be involved in a lawsuit with

**processus** [pʀɔsesys] nm process

**procès-verbal, -aux** [pʀɔsɛvɛʀbal, o] nm (de réunion) minutes pl; (aussi: **P.-V.**) parking ticket

**prochain, e** [pʀɔʃɛ̃, ɛn] adj next; (proche: départ, arrivée) impending ▷ nm fellow man; **la ~e fois/semaine ~e** next time/week; **prochainement** adv soon, shortly

**proche** [pʀɔʃ] adj nearby; (dans le temps) imminent; (parent, ami) close; **proches** nmpl (parents) close relatives; **être ~ (de)** to be near, be close (to)

**proclamer** [pʀɔklame] vt to proclaim

**procuration** [pʀɔkyʀasjɔ̃] nf proxy

**procurer** [pʀɔkyʀe] vt: **~ qch à qn** (fournir) to obtain sth for sb; (causer: plaisir etc) to bring sb sth; **se procurer** vt to get; **procureur** nm public prosecutor

**prodige** [pʀɔdiʒ] nm marvel, wonder; (personne) prodigy; **prodiguer** vt (soins, attentions): **prodiguer qch à qn** to give sb sth

**producteur, -trice** [pʀɔdyktœʀ, tʀis] nm/f producer

**productif, -ive** [pʀɔdyktif, iv] adj productive

**production** [pʀɔdyksjɔ̃] nf production; (rendement) output

**productivité** [pʀɔdyktivite] nf productivity

**produire** [pʀɔdɥiʀ] vt to produce; **se produire** vi (événement) to happen, occur; (acteur) to perform, appear

**produit** [pʀɔdɥi] nm product;

**produit chimique** chemical; **produits agricoles** farm produce sg; **produits de beauté** beauty products, cosmetics; **produits d'entretien** cleaning products

**prof** [pʀɔf] (fam) nm teacher

**proférer** [pʀɔfeʀe] vt to utter

**professeur, e** [pʀɔfesœʀ] nm/f teacher; (de faculté) (university) lecturer; (: titulaire d'une chaire) professor

**profession** [pʀɔfesjɔ̃] nf occupation; **~ libérale** (liberal) profession; **sans ~** unemployed; **professionnel, le** adj, nm/f professional

**profil** [pʀɔfil] nm profile; **de ~** in profile

**profit** [pʀɔfi] nm (avantage) benefit, advantage; (Comm, Finance) profit; **au ~ de** in aid of; **tirer ~ de** to profit from; **profitable** adj (utile) beneficial; (lucratif) profitable; **profiter** vi: **profiter de** (situation, occasion) to take advantage of; (vacances, jeunesse etc) to make the most of

**profond, e** [pʀɔfɔ̃, ɔ̃d] adj deep; (sentiment, intérêt) profound; **profondément** adv deeply; **il dort profondément** he is sound asleep; **profondeur** nf depth; **l'eau a quelle profondeur?** how deep is the water?

**programme** [pʀɔgʀam] nm programme; (Scol) syllabus, curriculum; (Inform) program; **programmer** vt (émission) to schedule; (Inform) to program; **programmeur, -euse** nm/f programmer

**progrès** [pʀɔgʀɛ] nm progress no pl; **faire des ~** to make progress; **progresser** vi to progress; **progressif, -ive** adj progressive

**proie** [pʀwa] nf prey no pl

**projecteur** [pʀɔʒɛktœʀ] nm (pour film) projector; (de théâtre, cirque) spotlight

**projectile** [pʀɔʒɛktil] nm missile

**projection** [pʀɔʒɛksjɔ̃] nf projection; (séance) showing

**projet** [pʀɔʒɛ] nm plan; (ébauche) draft; **projet de loi** bill; **projeter** vt (envisager) to plan; (film, photos) to project; (ombre, lueur) to throw, cast; (jeter) to throw up (ou off ou out)

**prolétaire** [pʁɔletɛʁ] adj, nmf proletarian

**prolongement** [pʁɔlɔ̃ʒmɑ̃] nm extension; **dans le ~ de** running on from

**prolonger** [pʁɔlɔ̃ʒe] vt (débat, séjour) to prolong; (délai, billet, rue) to extend; **se prolonger** vi to go on

**promenade** [pʁɔm(ə)nad] nf walk (ou drive ou ride); **faire une ~** to go for a walk; **une ~ en voiture/à vélo** a drive/(bicycle) ride

**promener** [pʁɔm(ə)ne] vt (chien) to take out for a walk; (doigts, regard): **~ qch sur** to run sth over; **se promener** vi to go for (ou be out for) a walk

**promesse** [pʁɔmɛs] nf promise

**promettre** [pʁɔmɛtʁ] vt to promise ▷ vi to be ou look promising; **~ à qn de faire** to promise sb that one will do

**promiscuité** [pʁɔmiskɥite] nf (chambre) lack of privacy

**promontoire** [pʁɔmɔ̃twaʁ] nm headland

**promoteur, -trice** [pʁɔmɔtœʁ, tʁis] nm/f: **promoteur (immobilier)** property developer (BRIT), real estate promoter (US)

**promotion** [pʁɔmosjɔ̃] nf promotion; **en ~** on special offer

**promouvoir** [pʁɔmuvwaʁ] vt to promote

**prompt, e** [pʁɔ̃(pt), pʁɔ̃(p)t] adj swift, rapid

**prôner** [pʁone] vt (préconiser) to advocate

**pronom** [pʁɔnɔ̃] nm pronoun

**prononcer** [pʁɔnɔ̃se] vt to pronounce; (dire) to utter; (discours) to deliver; **se prononcer** vi to be pronounced; **comment est-ce que ça se prononce?** how do you pronounce ou say it?; **se ~ (sur)** (se décider) to reach a decision (on ou about), give a verdict (on); **prononciation** nf pronunciation;

**pronostic** [pʁɔnɔstik] nm (Méd) prognosis; (fig: aussi: **~s**) forecast

**propagande** [pʁɔpagɑ̃d] nf propaganda

**propager** [pʁɔpaʒe] vt to spread; **se propager** vi to spread

**prophète** [pʁɔfɛt] nm prophet

**prophétie** [pʁɔfesi] nf prophecy

**propice** [pʁɔpis] adj favourable

**proportion** [pʁɔpɔʁsjɔ̃] nf proportion; **toute(s) ~(s) gardée(s)** making due allowance(s)

**propos** [pʁɔpo] nm (intention) intention, aim; (sujet): **à quel ~?** what about? ▷ nmpl (paroles) talk no pl, remarks; **à ~ de** about, regarding; **à tout ~** for the slightest thing ou reason; **à ~** by the way; (opportunément) at the right moment

**proposer** [pʁɔpoze] vt to propose; **~ qch (à qn)** (suggérer) to suggest sth (to sb), propose sth (to sb); (offrir) to offer (sb) sth; **se ~ (pour faire)** to offer one's services (to do); **proposition** (suggestion) nf proposal, suggestion; (Ling) clause

**propre** [pʁɔpʁ] adj clean; (net) neat, tidy; (possessif) own; (sens) literal; (particulier): **~ à** peculiar to; (approprié): **~ à** suitable for ▷ nm: **recopier au ~** to make a fair copy of; **proprement** adv (avec propreté) cleanly; **le village proprement dit** the village itself; **à proprement parler** strictly speaking; **propreté** nf cleanliness

**propriétaire** [pʁɔpʁijetɛʁ] nm/f owner; (pour le locataire) landlord(-lady)

**propriété** [pʁɔpʁijete] nf property; (droit) ownership

**propulser** [pʁɔpylse] vt to propel

**prose** [pʁoz] nf (style) prose

**prospecter** [pʁɔspɛkte] vt to prospect; (Comm) to canvass

**prospectus** [pʁɔspɛktys] nm leaflet

**prospère** [pʁɔspɛʁ] adj prosperous; **prospérer** vi to prosper

**prosterner** [pʁɔstɛʁne]: **se prosterner** vi to bow low, prostrate o.s.

**prostituée** [pʀɔstitɥe] *nf* prostitute

**prostitution** [pʀɔstitysjɔ̃] *nf* prostitution

**protecteur, -trice** [pʀɔtɛktœʀ, tʀis] *adj* protective; (*air, ton: péj*) patronizing ▷ *nm/f* protector

**protection** [pʀɔtɛksjɔ̃] *nf* protection; (*d'un personnage influent: aide*) patronage

**protéger** [pʀɔteʒe] *vt* to protect; **se ~ de/contre** to protect o.s. from

**protège-slip** [pʀɔtɛʒslip] *nm* panty liner

**protéine** [pʀɔtein] *nf* protein

**protestant, e** [pʀɔtɛstɑ̃, ɑ̃t] *adj, nm/f* Protestant

**protestation** [pʀɔtɛstasjɔ̃] *nf* (*plainte*) protest

**protester** [pʀɔtɛste] *vi*: **~ (contre)** to protest (against *ou* about); **~ de** (*son innocence*) to protest

**prothèse** [pʀɔtɛz] *nf*: **prothèse dentaire** denture

**protocole** [pʀɔtɔkɔl] *nm* (*fig*) etiquette

**proue** [pʀu] *nf* bow(s *pl*), prow

**prouesse** [pʀues] *nf* feat

**prouver** [pʀuve] *vt* to prove

**provenance** [pʀɔv(ə)nɑ̃s] *nf* origin; **avion en ~ de** plane (arriving) from

**provenir** [pʀɔv(ə)niʀ]: **~ de** *vt* to come from

**proverbe** [pʀɔvɛʀb] *nm* proverb

**province** [pʀɔvɛ̃s] *nf* province

**proviseur** [pʀɔvizœʀ] *nm* ≈ head(teacher) (*BRIT*), ≈ principal (*US*)

**provision** [pʀɔvizjɔ̃] *nf* (*réserve*) stock, supply; **provisions** *nfpl* (*vivres*) provisions, food *no pl*

**provisoire** [pʀɔvizwaʀ] *adj* temporary; **provisoirement** *adv* temporarily

**provocant, e** [pʀɔvɔkɑ̃, ɑ̃t] *adj* provocative

**provoquer** [pʀɔvɔke] *vt* (*défier*) to provoke; (*causer*) to cause, bring about; (*inciter*): **~ qn à** to incite sb to

**proxénète** [pʀɔksenɛt] *nm* procurer

**proximité** [pʀɔksimite] *nf* nearness,

closeness; (*dans le temps*) imminence, closeness; **à ~** near *ou* close by; **à ~ de** near (to), close to

**prudemment** [pʀydamɑ̃] *adv* carefully; wisely, sensibly

**prudence** [pʀydɑ̃s] *nf* carefulness; **avec ~** carefully; **par ~** as a precaution

**prudent, e** [pʀydɑ̃, ɑ̃t] *adj* (*pas téméraire*) careful; (: *en général*) safety-conscious; (*sage, conseillé*) wise, sensible; **c'est plus ~** it's wiser

**prune** [pʀyn] *nf* plum

**pruneau, x** [pʀyno] *nm* prune

**prunier** [pʀynje] *nm* plum tree

**PS** *sigle m* = **parti socialiste**

**pseudonyme** [psødɔnim] *nm* (*gén*) fictitious name; (*d'écrivain*) pseudonym, pen name

**psychanalyse** [psikanaliz] *nf* psychoanalysis

**psychiatre** [psikjatʀ] *nm/f* psychiatrist; **psychiatrique** *adj* psychiatric

**psychique** [psiʃik] *adj* psychological

**psychologie** [psikɔlɔʒi] *nf* psychology; **psychologique** *adj* psychological; **psychologue** *nm/f* psychologist

**pu** [py] *pp de* **pouvoir**

**puanteur** [pɥɑ̃tœʀ] *nf* stink, stench

**pub** [pyb] *nf* (*fam: annonce*) ad, advert; (*pratique*) advertising

**public, -ique** [pyblik] *adj* public; (*école, instruction*) state *cpd* ▷ *nm* public; (*assistance*) audience; **en ~** in public

**publicitaire** [pyblisitɛʀ] *adj* advertising *cpd*; (*film*) publicity *cpd*

**publicité** [pyblisite] *nf* (*méthode, profession*) advertising; (*annonce*) advertisement; (*révélations*) publicity

**publier** [pyblije] *vt* to publish

**publipostage** [pyblipɔstaʒ] *nm* mailing *m*

**publique** [pyblik] *adj voir* **public**

**puce** [pys] *nf* flea; (*Inform*) chip; **carte à ~** smart card; **(marché aux) ~s** flea market *sg*

**pudeur** [pydœʀ] *nf* modesty; **pudique**

*adj (chaste)* modest; *(discret)* discreet

**puer** [pɥe] *(péj) vi* to stink

**puéricultrice** [pɥerikyltris] *nf* p(a)ediatric nurse

**puéril, e** [pɥeril] *adj* childish

**puis** [pɥi] *vb voir* **pouvoir** ▷ *adv* then

**puiser** [pɥize] *vt*: **~ (dans)** to draw (from)

**puisque** [pɥisk] *conj* since

**puissance** [pɥisɑ̃s] *nf* power; **en ~** *adj* potential

**puissant, e** [pɥisɑ̃, ɑ̃t] *adj* powerful

**puits** [pɥi] *nm* well

**pull(-over)** [pyl(ɔvɛʀ)] *nm* sweater

**pulluler** [pylyle] *vi* to swarm

**pulpe** [pylp] *nf* pulp

**pulvériser** [pylveʀize] *vt* to pulverize; *(liquide)* to spray

**punaise** [pynɛz] *nf (Zool)* bug; *(clou)* drawing pin *(BRIT)*, thumbtack *(US)*

**punch** [pɔ̃ʃ] *nm (boisson)* punch

**punir** [pyniʀ] *vt* to punish; **punition** *nf* punishment

**pupille** [pypij] *nf (Anat)* pupil ▷ *nm/f (enfant)* ward

**pupitre** [pypitʀ] *nm (Scol)* desk

**pur, e** [pyʀ] *adj* pure; *(vin)* undiluted; *(whisky)* neat; **en ~e perte** to no avail; **c'est de la folie ~e** it's sheer madness

**purée** [pyʀe] *nf*: **~ (de pommes de terre)** mashed potatoes *pl*; **purée de marrons** chestnut purée

**purement** [pyʀmɑ̃] *adv* purely

**purgatoire** [pyʀgatwaʀ] *nm* purgatory

**purger** [pyʀʒe] *vt (Méd, Pol)* to purge; *(Jur: peine)* to serve

**pur-sang** [pyʀsɑ̃] *nm inv* thoroughbred

**pus** [py] *nm* pus

**putain** [pytɛ̃] *(fam!) nf* whore (!)

**puzzle** [pœzl] *nm* jigsaw (puzzle)

**P.-V.** [peve] *sigle m* = **procès-verbal**

**pyjama** [piʒama] *nm* pyjamas *pl (BRIT)*, pajamas *pl (US)*

**pyramide** [piʀamid] *nf* pyramid

**Pyrénées** [piʀene] *nfpl*: **les ~** the Pyrenees

**QI** *sigle m (= quotient intellectuel)* IQ

**quadragénaire** [k(w)adʀaʒenɛʀ] *nm/f* man/woman in his/her forties

**quadruple** [k(w)adʀypl] *nm*: **le ~ de** four times as much as

**quai** [ke] *nm (de port)* quay; *(de gare)* platform; **être à ~** *(navire)* to be alongside; **de quel ~ part le train pour Paris?** which platform does the Paris train go from?

**qualification** [kalifikasjɔ̃] *nf (aptitude)* qualification

**qualifier** [kalifje] *vt* to qualify; **se qualifier** *vi* to qualify; **~ qch/qn de** to describe sth/sb as

**qualité** [kalite] *nf* quality

**quand** [kɑ̃] *conj, adv* when; **~ je serai riche** when I'm rich; **~ même** all the same; **~ même, il exagère!** really, he overdoes it!; **~ bien même** even though

**quant** [kɑ̃]: **~ à** *prép (pour ce qui est de)* as for, as to; *(au sujet de)* regarding

**quantité** [kɑ̃tite] *nf* quantity, amount; *(grand nombre)*: **une** *ou* **des ~(s) de** a

great deal of

**quarantaine** [kaʀɑ̃tɛn] *nf* (*Méd*) quarantine; **avoir la ~** (*âge*) to be around forty; **une ~ (de)** forty or so, about forty

**quarante** [kaʀɑ̃t] *num* forty

**quart** [kaʀ] *nm* (*fraction*) quarter; (*surveillance*) watch; **un ~ de vin** a quarter litre of wine; **le ~ de** a quarter of; **quart d'heure** quarter of an hour; **quarts de finale** quarter finals

**quartier** [kaʀtje] *nm* (*de ville*) district, area; (*de bœuf*) quarter; (*de fruit*) piece; **cinéma de ~** local cinema; **avoir ~ libre** (*fig*) to be free; **quartier général** headquarters *pl*

**quartz** [kwaʀts] *nm* quartz

**quasi** [kazi] *adv* almost, nearly; **quasiment** *adv* almost, nearly; **quasiment jamais** hardly ever

**quatorze** [katɔʀz] *num* fourteen

**quatorzième** [katɔʀzjɛm] *num* fourteenth

**quatre** [katʀ] *num* four; **à ~ pattes** on all fours; **se mettre en ~ pour qn** to go out of one's way for sb; **~ à ~** (*monter, descendre*) four at a time; **quatre-vingt-dix** *num* ninety; **quatre-vingts** *num* eighty; **quatrième** *num* fourth ▷ *nf* (*Scol*) year 9 (*BRIT*), eighth grade (*US*)

**quatuor** [kwatɥɔʀ] *nm* quartet(te)

 **MOT-CLÉ**

**que** [kə] *conj* **1** (*introduisant complétive*) that; **il sait que tu es là** he knows (that) you're here; **je veux que tu acceptes** I want you to accept; **il a dit que oui** he said he would (*ou* it was *etc*) **2** (*reprise d'autres conjonctions*): **quand il rentrera et qu'il aura mangé** when he gets back and (when) he has eaten; **si vous y allez et que vous …** if you go there and if you … **3** (*en tête de phrase: hypothèse, souhait etc*): **qu'il le veuille ou non** whether he likes it or not; **qu'il fasse ce qu'il voudra!** let him do as he pleases!

**4** (*après comparatif*) than, as; *voir aussi* **plus**; **aussi**; **autant** *etc* **5** (*seulement*): **ne … que** only; **il ne boit que de l'eau** he only drinks water **6** (*temps*): **il y a 4 ans qu'il est parti** it is 4 years since he left, he left 4 years ago ▷ *adv* (*exclamation*): **qu'il** *ou* **qu'est-ce qu'il est bête/court vite!** he's so silly!/he runs so fast!; **que de livres!** what a lot of books! ▷ *pron* **1** (*relatif: personne*) whom; (*: chose*) that, which; **l'homme que je vois** the man (whom) I see; **le livre que tu vois** the book (that *ou* which) you see; **un jour que j'étais …** a day when I was … **2** (*interrogatif*) what; **que fais-tu?**, **qu'est-ce que tu fais?** what are you doing?; **qu'est-ce que c'est?** what is it?, what's that?; **que faire?** what can one do?

**Québec** [kebɛk] *n*: **le ~** Quebec; **québecois, e** *adj* Quebec ▷ *nm/f*: **Québecois, e** Quebecker ▷ *nm* (*Ling*) Quebec French

 **MOT-CLÉ**

**quel, quelle** [kɛl] *adj* **1** (*interrogatif: personne*) who; (*: chose*) what; **quel est cet homme?** who is this man?; **quel est ce livre?** what is this book?; **quel livre/homme?** what book/man?; (*parmi un certain choix*) which book/man?; **quels acteurs préférez-vous?** which actors do you prefer?; **dans quels pays êtes-vous allé?** which *ou* what countries did you go to? **2** (*exclamatif*): **quelle surprise!** what a surprise! **3**: **quel que soit le coupable** whoever is guilty; **quel que soit votre avis** whatever your opinion

**quelconque** [kɛlkɔ̃k] *adj* (*indéfini*): **un ami/prétexte ~** some friend/pretext or other; (*médiocre: repas*) indifferent, poor; (*laid: personne*) plain-looking

**MOT-CLÉ**

**quelque** [kɛlk] *adj* **1** (*au singulier*) some; (*au pluriel*) a few, some; (*tournure interrogative*) any; **quelque espoir** some hope; **il a quelques amis** he has a few *ou* some friends; **a-t-il quelques amis?** does he have any friends?; **les quelques livres qui** the few books which; **20 kg et quelque(s)** a bit over 20 kg

**2**: **quelque ... que**: **quelque livre qu'il choisisse** whatever (*ou* whichever) book he chooses

**3**: **quelque chose** something; (*tournure interrogative*) anything; **quelque chose d'autre** something else; anything else; **quelque part** somewhere; anywhere; **en quelque sorte** as it were

▷ *adv* **1** (*environ*): **quelque 100 mètres** some 100 metres

**2**: **quelque peu** rather, somewhat

**quelquefois** [kɛlkəfwa] *adv* sometimes

**quelques-uns, -unes** [kɛlkəzœ̃, yn] *pron* a few, some

**quelqu'un** [kɛlkœ̃] *pron* someone, somebody; (+ *tournure interrogative*) anyone, anybody; **quelqu'un d'autre** someone *ou* somebody else; (+ *tournure interrogative*) anybody else

**qu'en dira-t-on** [kɑ̃diʁatɔ̃] *nm inv*: **le qu'en dira-t-on** gossip, what people say

**querelle** [kəʁɛl] *nf* quarrel; **quereller**: **se quereller** *vi* to quarrel

**qu'est-ce que** [kɛskə] *vb + conj voir* **que**

**qu'est-ce qui** [kɛski] *vb + conj voir* **qui**

**question** [kɛstjɔ̃] *nf* question; (*fig*) matter, issue; **il a été ~ de** we (*ou* they) spoke about; **de quoi est-il ~?** what is it about?; **il n'en est pas ~** there's no question of it; **en ~** in question; **hors de ~** out of the question; **remettre**

**en ~** to question; **questionnaire** *nm* questionnaire; **questionner** *vt* to question

**quête** [kɛt] *nf* collection; (*recherche*) quest, search; **faire la ~** (*à l'église*) to take the collection; (*artiste*) to pass the hat round

**quetsche** [kwɛtʃ] *nf* kind of dark-red plum

**queue** [kø] *nf* tail; (*fig: du classement*) bottom; (: *de poêle*) handle; (: *de fruit, feuille*) stalk; (: *de train, colonne, file*) rear; **faire la ~** to queue (up) (BRIT), line up (US); **queue de cheval** ponytail; **queue de poisson** (*Auto*): **faire une queue de poisson à qn** to cut in front of sb

**MOT-CLÉ**

**qui** [ki] *pron* **1** (*interrogatif: personne*) who; (: *chose*): **qu'est-ce qui est sur la table?** what is on the table?; **qui est-ce qui?** who?; **qui est-ce que?** who?; **à qui est ce sac?** whose bag is this?; **à qui parlais-tu?** who were you talking to?, to whom were you talking?; **chez qui allez-vous?** whose house are you going to?

**2** (*relatif: personne*) who; (+*prép*) whom; **l'ami de qui je vous ai parlé** the friend I told you about; **la dame chez qui je suis allé** the lady whose house I went to

**3** (*sans antécédent*): **amenez qui vous voulez** bring who you like; **qui que ce soit** whoever it may be

**quiconque** [kikɔ̃k] *pron* (*celui qui*) whoever, anyone who; (*n'importe qui*) anyone, anybody

**quille** [kij] *nf*: (**jeu de**) **~s** skittles *sg* (BRIT), bowling (US)

**quincaillerie** [kɛ̃kajʁi] *nf* (*ustensiles*) hardware; (*magasin*) hardware shop

**quinquagénaire** [kɛ̃kaʒenɛʁ] *nm/f* man/woman in his/her fifties

**quinquennat** [kɛ̃kena] *nm five year term of office (of French President)*

**quinte** [kɛ̃t] *nf*: **~ (de toux)** coughing fit

**quintuple** [kɛ̃typl] *nm*: **le ~ de** five times as much as

**quinzaine** [kɛ̃zɛn] *nf*: **une ~ (de)** about fifteen, fifteen or so; **une ~ (de jours)** a fortnight (BRIT), two weeks

**quinze** [kɛ̃z] *num* fifteen; **dans ~ jours** in a fortnight('s time), in two weeks(' time)

**quinzième** [kɛ̃zjɛm] *num* fifteenth

**quiproquo** [kiprɔko] *nm* misunderstanding

**quittance** [kitɑ̃s] *nf* (*reçu*) receipt

**quitte** [kit] *adj*: **être ~ envers qn** to be no longer in sb's debt; (*fig*) to be quits with sb; **~ à faire** even if it means doing

**quitter** [kite] *vt* to leave; (*vêtement*) to take off; **se quitter** *vi* (*couples, interlocuteurs*) to part; **ne quittez pas** (*au téléphone*) hold the line

**qui-vive** [kiviv] *nm*: **être sur le ~** to be on the alert

 MOT-CLÉ

**quoi** [kwa] *pron interrog* **1** what; **quoi de neuf?** what's new?; **quoi?** (*qu'est-ce que tu dis?*) what?
**2** (*avec prép*): **à quoi tu penses?** what are you thinking about?; **de quoi parlez-vous?** what are you talking about?; **à quoi bon?** what's the use?
▷ *pron rel*: **as-tu de quoi écrire?** do you have anything to write with?; **il n'y a pas de quoi** (please) don't mention it; **il n'y a pas de quoi rire** there's nothing to laugh about
▷ *pron* (*locutions*): **quoi qu'il arrive** whatever happens; **quoi qu'il en soit** be that as it may; **quoi que ce soit** anything at all
▷ *excl* what!

**quoique** [kwak] *conj* (al)though

**quotidien, ne** [kɔtidjɛ̃, jɛn] *adj* daily; (*banal*) everyday ▷ *nm* (*journal*) daily (paper); **quotidiennement** *adv* daily

**r.** *abr* = **route; rue**

**rab** [ʀab] (*fam*) *nm* (*nourriture*) extra; **est-ce qu'il y a du ~?** are there any seconds?

**rabâcher** [ʀabɑʃe] *vt* to keep on repeating

**rabais** [ʀabɛ] *nm* reduction, discount; **rabaisser** *vt* (*dénigrer*) to belittle; (*rabattre: prix*) to reduce

**Rabat** [ʀaba(t)] *n* Rabat

**rabattre** [ʀabatʀ] *vt* (*couvercle, siège*) to pull down; (*déduire*) to reduce; **se rabattre** *vi* (*se refermer: couvercle*) to fall shut; (*véhicule, coureur*) to cut in; **se ~ sur** to fall back on

**rabbin** [ʀabɛ̃] *nm* rabbi

**rabougri, e** [ʀabugʀi] *adj* stunted

**raccommoder** [ʀakɔmɔde] *vt* to mend, repair

**raccompagner** [ʀakɔ̃paɲe] *vt* to take *ou* see back

**raccord** [ʀakɔʀ] *nm* link; (*retouche*) touch up; **raccorder** *vt* to join (up), link up; (*suj: pont etc*) to connect, link

**raccourci** [Rakursi] nm short cut
**raccourcir** [Rakursir] vt to shorten
▷ vi (jours) to grow shorter, draw in
**raccrocher** [Rakrɔʃe] vt (tableau) to
hang back up; (récepteur) to put down
▷ vi (Tél) to hang up, ring off
**race** [Ras] nf race; (d'animaux, fig) breed;
**de ~** purebred, pedigree
**rachat** [Raʃa] nm buying; (du même
objet) buying back
**racheter** [Raʃ(ə)te] vt (article perdu) to
buy another; (après avoir vendu) to buy
back; (d'occasion) to buy; (Comm: part,
firme) to buy up; (davantage): **~ du lait/3
œufs** to buy more milk/another 3 eggs
ou 3 more eggs; **se racheter** vi (fig) to
make amends
**racial, e, -aux** [Rasjal, jo] adj racial
**racine** [Rasin] nf root; **racine carrée/
cubique** square/cube root
**racisme** [Rasism] nm racism
**raciste** [Rasist] adj, nm/f racist
**racket** [Raket] nm racketeering no pl
**raclée** [Rɑkle] (fam) nf hiding,
thrashing
**racler** [Rɑkle] vt (surface) to scrape; **se ~
la gorge** to clear one's throat
**racontars** [Rakɔ̃tar] nmpl story, lie
**raconter** [Rakɔ̃te] vt: **~ (à qn)** (décrire)
to relate (to sb), tell (sb) about; (dire de
mauvaise foi) to tell (sb); **~ une histoire**
to tell a story
**radar** [Radar] nm radar
**rade** [Rad] nf (natural) harbour; **rester
en ~** (fig) to be left stranded
**radeau, x** [Rado] nm raft
**radiateur** [Radjatœr] nm radiator,
heater; (Auto) radiator; **radiateur
électrique** electric heater ou fire
**radiation** [Radjasjɔ̃] nf (Physique)
radiation
**radical, e, -aux** [Radikal, o] adj
radical
**radieux, -euse** [Radjø, jøz] adj radiant
**radin, e** [Radɛ̃, in] (fam) adj stingy
**radio** [Radjo] nf radio; (Méd) X-ray
▷ nm radio operator; **à la ~** on the
radio; **radioactif, -ive** adj radioactive;

**radiocassette** nm cassette radio,
radio cassette player; **radiographie** nf
radiography; (photo) X-ray photograph;
**radiophonique** adj radio cpd; **radio-
réveil** (pl **radios-réveils**) nm radio
alarm clock
**radis** [Radi] nm radish
**radoter** [Radɔte] vi to ramble on
**radoucir** [Radusir]: **se radoucir** vi
(temps) to become milder; (se calmer)
to calm down
**rafale** [Rafal] nf (vent) gust (of wind);
(tir) burst of gunfire
**raffermir** [Rafermir] vt to firm up
**raffiner** [Rafine] vt to refine; **raffinerie**
nf refinery
**raffoler** [Rafɔle]: **~ de** vt to be very
keen on
**rafle** [Rɑfl] nf (de police) raid; **rafler** (fam)
vt to swipe, nick
**rafraîchir** [Rafreʃir] vt (atmosphère,
température) to cool (down); (aussi:
**mettre à ~**) to chill; (fig: rénover) to
brighten up; **se rafraîchir** vi (temps)
to grow cooler; (en se lavant) to
freshen up; (en buvant) to refresh o.s.;
**rafraîchissant, e** adj refreshing;
**rafraîchissement** nm (boisson) cool
drink; **rafraîchissements** nmpl
(boissons, fruits etc) refreshments
**rage** [Raʒ] nf (Méd): **la ~** rabies; (fureur)
rage, fury; **faire ~** to rage; **rage de
dents** (raging) toothache
**ragot** [Rago] (fam) nm malicious
gossip no pl
**ragoût** [Ragu] nm stew
**raide** [Red] adj stiff; (câble) taut, tight;
(escarpé) steep; (droit: cheveux) straight;
(fam: sans argent) flat broke; (osé)
daring, bold ▷ adv (en pente) steeply; **~
mort** stone dead; **raideur** nf (rigidité)
stiffness; **avec raideur** (répondre) stiffly,
abruptly; **raidir** vt (muscles) to stiffen;
**se raidir** vi (tissu) to stiffen; (personne)
to tense up; (: se préparer moralement) to
brace o.s.; (fig: position) to harden
**raie** [Re] nf (Zool) skate, ray; (rayure)
stripe; (des cheveux) parting

**raifort** [ʀɛfɔʀ] *nm* horseradish

**rail** [ʀɑj] *nm* rail; (*chemins de fer*) railways *pl*; **par ~** by rail

**railler** [ʀɑje] *vt* to scoff at, jeer at

**rainure** [ʀɛnyʀ] *nf* groove

**raisin** [ʀɛzɛ̃] *nm* (*aussi*: **~s**) grapes *pl*; **raisins secs** raisins

**raison** [ʀɛzɔ̃] *nf* reason; **avoir ~** to be right; **donner ~ à qn** to agree with sb; (*événement*) to prove sb right; **perdre la ~** to become insane; **se faire une ~** to learn to live with it; **~ de plus** all the more reason; **à plus forte ~** all the more so; **en ~ de** because of; **à ~ de** at the rate of; **sans ~** for no reason; **raison sociale** corporate name; **raisonnable** *adj* reasonable, sensible

**raisonnement** [ʀɛzɔnmɑ̃] *nm* (*façon de réfléchir*) reasoning; (*argumentation*) argument

**raisonner** [ʀɛzɔne] *vi* (*penser*) to reason; (*argumenter, discuter*) to argue ▷ *vt* (*personne*) to reason with

**rajeunir** [ʀaʒœniʀ] *vt* (*suj: coiffure, robe*): **~ qn** to make sb look younger; (*fig: personnel*) to inject new blood into ▷ *vi* to become (*ou* look) younger

**rajouter** [ʀaʒute] *vt* to add

**rajuster** [ʀaʒyste] *vt* (*vêtement*) to straighten, tidy; (*salaires*) to adjust

**ralenti** [ʀalɑ̃ti] *nm*: **au ~** (*fig*) at a slower pace; **tourner au ~** (*Auto*) to tick over, idle

**ralentir** [ʀalɑ̃tiʀ] *vt* to slow down

**râler** [ʀale] *vi* to groan; (*fam*) to grouse, moan (and groan)

**rallier** [ʀalje] *vt* (*rejoindre*) to rejoin; (*gagner à sa cause*) to win over

**rallonge** [ʀalɔ̃ʒ] *nf* (*de table*) (extra) leaf

**rallonger** [ʀalɔ̃ʒe] *vt* to lengthen

**rallye** [ʀali] *nm* rally; (*Pol*) march

**ramassage** [ʀamɑsaʒ] *nm*: **ramassage scolaire** school bus service

**ramasser** [ʀamɑse] *vt* (*objet tombé ou par terre, fam*) to pick up; (*recueillir: copies, ordures*) to collect; (*récolter*) to gather; **ramassis** (*péj*) *nm* (*de voyous*) bunch; (*d'objets*) jumble

**rambarde** [ʀɑ̃baʀd] *nf* guardrail

**rame** [ʀam] *nf* (*aviron*) oar; (*de métro*) train; (*de papier*) ream

**rameau, x** [ʀamo] *nm* (small) branch; **les Rameaux** (*Rel*) Palm Sunday *sg*

**ramener** [ʀam(ə)ne] *vt* to bring back; (*reconduire*) to take back; **~ qch à** (*réduire à*) to reduce sth to

**ramer** [ʀame] *vi* to row

**ramollir** [ʀamɔliʀ] *vt* to soften; **se ramollir** *vi* to go soft

**rampe** [ʀɑ̃p] *nf* (*d'escalier*) banister(s *pl*); (*dans un garage*) ramp; (*Théâtre*): **la ~** the footlights *pl*; **rampe de lancement** launching pad

**ramper** [ʀɑ̃pe] *vi* to crawl

**rancard** [ʀɑ̃kaʀ] (*fam*) *nm* (*rendez-vous*) date

**rancart** [ʀɑ̃kaʀ] *nm*: **mettre au ~** (*fam*) to scrap

**rance** [ʀɑ̃s] *adj* rancid

**rancœur** [ʀɑ̃kœʀ] *nf* rancour

**rançon** [ʀɑ̃sɔ̃] *nf* ransom

**rancune** [ʀɑ̃kyn] *nf* grudge, rancour; **garder ~ à qn (de qch)** to bear sb a grudge (for sth); **sans ~!** no hard feelings!; **rancunier, -ière** *adj* vindictive, spiteful

**randonnée** [ʀɑ̃dɔne] *nf* (*pédestre*) walk, ramble; (: *en montagne*) hike, hiking *no pl*; **la ~** (*activité*) hiking, walking; **une ~ à cheval** a pony trek

**rang** [ʀɑ̃] *nm* (*rangée*) row; (*grade, classement*) rank; **rangs** *nmpl* (*Mil*) ranks; **se mettre en ~s** to get into *ou* form rows; **au premier ~** in the first row; (*fig*) ranking first

**rangé, e** [ʀɑ̃ʒe] *adj* (*vie*) well-ordered; (*personne*) steady

**rangée** [ʀɑ̃ʒe] *nf* row

**ranger** [ʀɑ̃ʒe] *vt* (*mettre de l'ordre dans*) to tidy up; (*classer, grouper*) to order, arrange; (*mettre à sa place*) to put away; (*fig: classer*): **~ qn/qch parmi** to rank sb/sth among; **se ranger** *vi* (*véhicule, conducteur*) to pull over *ou* in; (*piéton*) to step aside; (*s'assagir*) to settle down; **se ~ à** (*avis*) to come round to

**ranimer**[Ranime] vt (personne) to bring round; (douleur, souvenir) to revive; (feu) to rekindle

**rapace**[Rapas] nm bird of prey

**râpe**[Rɑp] nf (Culin) grater; **râper** vt (Culin) to grate

**rapide**[Rapid] adj fast; (prompt: coup d'œil, mouvement) quick ▷ nm express (train); (de cours d'eau) rapid; **rapidement** adv fast; quickly

**rapiécer**[Rapjese] vt to patch

**rappel**[Rapɛl] nm (Théâtre) curtain call; (Méd: vaccination) booster; (deuxième avis) reminder; **rappeler** vt to call back; (ambassadeur, Mil) to recall; (faire se souvenir): **rappeler qch à qn** to remind sb of sth; **se rappeler** vt (se souvenir de) to remember, recall; **pouvez-vous rappeler plus tard?** can you call back later?

**rapport**[RapɔR] nm (lien, analogie) connection; (compte rendu) report; (profit) yield, return; **rapports** nmpl (entre personnes, pays) relations; **avoir ~ à** to have something to do with; **être/se mettre en ~ avec qn** to be/get in touch with sb; **par ~ à** in relation to; **rapports (sexuels)** (sexual) intercourse sg; **rapport qualité-prix** value (for money)

**rapporter**[RapɔRte] vt (rendre, ramener) to bring back; (bénéfice) to yield, bring in; (mentionner, répéter) to report ▷ vi (investissement) to give a good return ou yield; (activité) to be very profitable; **se ~ à** to relate to

**rapprochement**[RapRɔʃmɑ̃] nm (de nations) reconciliation; (rapport) parallel

**rapprocher**[RapRɔʃe] vt (deux objets) to bring closer together; (fig: ennemis, partis etc) to bring together; (comparer) to establish a parallel between; (chaise d'une table): **~ qch (de)** to bring sth closer (to); **se rapprocher** vi to draw closer ou nearer; **se ~ de** to come closer to; (présenter une analogie avec) to be close to

**raquette**[Rakɛt] nf (de tennis) racket; (de ping-pong) bat

**rare**[RɑR] adj rare; **se faire ~** to become scarce; **rarement** adv rarely, seldom

**ras, e**[Rɑ, Rɑz] adj (poil, herbe) short; (tête) close-cropped ▷ adv short; **en ~e campagne** in open country; **à ~ bords** to the brim; **en avoir ~ le bol** (fam) to be fed up

**raser**[Rɑze] vt (barbe, cheveux) to shave off; (menton, personne) to shave; (fam: ennuyer) to bore; (démolir) to raze (to the ground); (frôler) to graze, skim; **se raser** vi to shave; (fam) to be bored (to tears); **rasoir** nm razor

**rassasier**[Rasazje] vt: **être rassasié** to have eaten one's fill

**rassemblement**[Rasɑ̃bləmɑ̃] nm (groupe) gathering; (Pol) union

**rassembler**[Rasɑ̃ble] vt (réunir) to assemble, gather; (documents, notes) to gather together, collect; **se rassembler** vi to gather

**rassurer**[RasyRe] vt to reassure; **se rassurer** vi to reassure o.s.; **rassure-toi** don't worry

**rat**[Ra] nm rat

**rate**[Rat] nf spleen

**raté, e**[Rate] adj (tentative) unsuccessful, failed ▷ nm/f (fam: personne) failure

**râteau, x**[Rɑto] nm rake

**rater**[Rate] vi (affaire, projet etc) to go wrong, fail ▷ vt (fam: cible, train, occasion) to miss; (plat) to spoil; (fam: examen) to fail; **nous avons raté notre train** we missed our train

**ration**[Rasjɔ̃] nf ration

**RATP** sigle f (= Régie autonome des transports parisiens) Paris transport authority

**rattacher**[Rataʃe] vt (animal, cheveux) to tie up again; (fig: relier): **~ qch à** to link sth with

**rattraper**[RatRape] vt (fugitif) to recapture; (empêcher de tomber) to catch (hold of); (atteindre, rejoindre) to catch up with; (réparer: erreur) to make up for; **se rattraper** vi to make up for it; **se ~**

**(à)** *(se raccrocher)* to stop o.s. falling (by catching hold of)

**rature** [RatyR] *nf* deletion, erasure

**rauque** [Rok] *adj* *(voix)* hoarse

**ravages** [Ravaʒ] *nmpl*: **faire des ~** to wreak havoc

**ravi, e** [Ravi] *adj*: **être ~ de/que** to be delighted with/that

**ravin** [Ravɛ̃] *nm* gully, ravine

**ravir** [RaviR] *vt* *(enchanter)* to delight; **à ~** *adv* beautifully

**raviser** [Ravize]: **se raviser** *vi* to change one's mind

**ravissant, e** [Ravisɑ̃, ɑ̃t] *adj* delightful

**ravisseur, -euse** [RavisœR, øz] *nm/f* abductor, kidnapper

**ravitailler** [Ravitaje] *vt* *(en vivres, munitions)* to provide with fresh supplies; *(avion)* to refuel; **se ~ (en)** to get fresh supplies (of)

**raviver** [Ravive] *vt* *(feu, douleur)* to revive; *(couleurs)* to brighten up

**rayé, e** [Reje] *adj* *(à rayures)* striped

**rayer** [Reje] *vt* *(érafler)* to scratch; *(barrer)* to cross out; *(d'une liste)* to cross off

**rayon** [Rejɔ̃] *nm* *(de soleil etc)* ray; *(Géom)* radius; *(de roue)* spoke; *(étagère)* shelf; *(de grand magasin)* department; **dans un ~ de** within a radius of; **rayon de soleil** sunbeam; **rayons X** X-rays

**rayonnement** [Rejɔnmɑ̃] *nm* *(fig: d'une culture)* influence

**rayonner** [Rejɔne] *vi* *(fig)* to shine forth; *(personne: de joie, de beauté)* to be radiant; *(touriste)* to go touring *(from one base)*

**rayure** [RejyR] *nf* *(motif)* stripe; *(éraflure)* scratch; **à ~s** striped

**raz-de-marée** [Radmare] *nm inv* tidal wave

**ré** [Re] *nm* *(Mus)* D; *(en chantant la gamme)* re

**réaction** [Reaksjɔ̃] *nf* reaction

**réadapter** [Readapte]: **se réadapter (à)** *vi* to readjust (to)

**réagir** [ReaʒiR] *vi* to react

**réalisateur, -trice** [RealizatœR, tRis]

*nm/f* *(TV, Cinéma)* director

**réalisation** [Realizasjɔ̃] *nf* realization; *(cinéma)* production; **en cours de ~** under way

**réaliser** [Realize] *vt* *(projet, opération)* to carry out, realize; *(rêve, souhait)* to realize, fulfil; *(exploit)* to achieve; *(film)* to produce; *(se rendre compte de)* to realize; **se réaliser** *vi* to be realized

**réaliste** [Realist] *adj* realistic

**réalité** [Realite] *nf* reality; **en ~** in (actual) fact; **dans la ~** in reality

**réanimation** [Reanimasjɔ̃] *nf* resuscitation; **service de ~** intensive care unit

**rébarbatif, -ive** [RebaRbatif, iv] *adj* forbidding

**rebattu, e** [R(ə)baty] *adj* hackneyed

**rebelle** [Rəbɛl] *nm/f* rebel ▷ *adj* *(troupes)* rebel; *(enfant)* rebellious; *(mèche etc)* unruly

**rebeller** [R(ə)bele]: **se rebeller** *vi* to rebel

**rebondir** [R(ə)bɔ̃diR] *vi* *(ballon: au sol)* to bounce; *(: contre un mur)* to rebound; *(fig)* to get moving again

**rebord** [R(ə)bɔR] *nm* edge; **le ~ de la fenêtre** the windowsill

**rebours** [R(ə)buR]: **à ~** *adv* the wrong way

**rebrousser** [R(ə)bRuse] *vt*: **~ chemin** to turn back

**rebuter** [Rəbyte] *vt* to put off

**récalcitrant, e** [Rekalsitrɑ̃, ɑ̃t] *adj* refractory

**récapituler** [Rekapityle] *vt* to recapitulate, sum up

**receler** [R(ə)səle] *vt* *(produit d'un vol)* to receive; *(fig)* to conceal; **receleur, -euse** *nm/f* receiver

**récemment** [Resamɑ̃] *adv* recently

**recensement** [R(ə)sɑ̃smɑ̃] *nm* *(population)* census

**recenser** [R(ə)sɑ̃se] *vt* *(population)* to take a census of; *(inventorier)* to list

**récent, e** [Resɑ̃, ɑ̃t] *adj* recent

**récépissé** [Resepise] *nm* receipt

**récepteur** [ReseptœR] *nm* receiver

**réception** [Resεpsjɔ̃] *nf* receiving *no pl*; (*accueil*) reception, welcome; (*bureau*) reception desk; (*réunion mondaine*) reception, party; **réceptionniste** *nm/f* receptionist

**recette** [R(ə)sεt] *nf* recipe; (*Comm*) takings *pl*; **recettes** *nfpl* (*Comm: rentrées*) receipts; **faire ~** (*spectacle, exposition*) to be a winner

**recevoir** [R(ə)səvwaR] *vt* to receive; (*client, patient*) to see; **être reçu** (*à un examen*) to pass

**rechange** [R(ə)ʃɑ̃ʒ]: **de ~** *adj* (*pièces, roue*) spare; (*fig: solution*) alternative; **des vêtements de ~** a change of clothes

**recharge** [R(ə)ʃaRʒ] *nf* refill; **rechargeable** *adj* (*stylo etc*) refillable; **recharger** *vt* (*stylo*) to refill; (*batterie*) to recharge

**réchaud** [Reʃo] *nm* (portable) stove

**réchauffer** [Reʃofe] *vt* (*plat*) to reheat; (*mains, personne*) to warm; **se réchauffer** *vi* (*température*) to get warmer; (*personne*) to warm o.s. (up)

**rêche** [RεʃJ] *adj* rough

**recherche** [R(ə)ʃεRʃ] *nf* (*action*) search; (*raffinement*) studied elegance; (*scientifique etc*): **la ~** research; **recherches** *nfpl* (*de la police*) investigations; (*scientifiques*) research *sg*; **la ~ de** the search for; **être à la ~ de qch** to be looking for sth

**recherché, e** [R(ə)ʃεRʃe] *adj* (*rare, demandé*) much sought-after; (*raffiné: style*) mannered; (*: tenue*) elegant

**rechercher** [R(ə)ʃεRʃe] *vt* (*objet égaré, personne*) to look for; (*causes, nouveau procédé*) to try to find; (*bonheur, compliments*) to seek

**rechute** [R(ə)ʃyt] *nf* (*Méd*) relapse

**récidiver** [Residive] *vi* to commit a subsequent offence; (*fig*) to do it again

**récif** [Resif] *nm* reef

**récipient** [Resipjɑ̃] *nm* container

**réciproque** [ResipRɔk] *adj* reciprocal

**récit** [Resi] *nm* story; **récital** *nm* recital; **réciter** *vt* to recite

**réclamation** [Reklamasjɔ̃] *nf* complaint; **(service des) ~s** complaints department

**réclame** [Reklam] *nf* ad, advert(isement); **en ~** on special offer; **réclamer** *vt* to ask for; (*revendiquer*) to claim, demand ▷ *vi* to complain

**réclusion** [Reklyzjɔ̃] *nf* imprisonment

**recoin** [Rəkwɛ̃] *nm* nook, corner

**reçois** *etc* [Rəswa] *vb voir* **recevoir**

**récolte** [Rekɔlt] *nf* harvesting, gathering; (*produits*) harvest, crop; **récolter** *vt* to harvest, gather (in); (*fig*) to collect

**recommandé** [R(ə)kɔmɑ̃de] *nm* (*Postes*): **en ~** by registered mail

**recommander** [R(ə)kɔmɑ̃de] *vt* to recommend; (*Postes*) to register

**recommencer** [R(ə)kɔmɑ̃se] *vt* (*reprendre: lutte, séance*) to resume, start again; (*refaire: travail, explications*) to start afresh, start (over) again ▷ *vi* to start again; (*récidiver*) to do it again

**récompense** [Rekɔ̃pɑ̃s] *nf* reward; (*prix*) award; **récompenser** *vt*: **récompenser qn (de** *ou* **pour)** to reward sb (for)

**réconcilier** [Rekɔ̃silje] *vt* to reconcile; **se réconcilier (avec)** to make up (with)

**reconduire** [R(ə)kɔ̃dɥiR] *vt* (*raccompagner*) to take *ou* see back; (*renouveler*) to renew

**réconfort** [Rekɔ̃fɔR] *nm* comfort; **réconforter** *vt* (*consoler*) to comfort

**reconnaissance** [R(ə)kɔnεsɑ̃s] *nf* (*gratitude*) gratitude, gratefulness; (*action de reconnaître*) recognition; (*Mil*) reconnaissance, recce; **reconnaissant, e** *adj* grateful; **je vous serais reconnaissant de bien vouloir ...** I would be most grateful if you would (kindly) ...

**reconnaître** [R(ə)kɔnεtR] *vt* to recognize; (*Mil: lieu*) to reconnoitre; (*Jur: enfant, torts*) to acknowledge; **~ que** to admit *ou* acknowledge that; **~ qn/qch à** (*l'identifier grâce à*) to recognize sb/sth by; **reconnu, e** adj (indiscuté, connu) recognized

**reconstituer** [R(ə)kɔ̃stitɥe] vt (événement, accident) to reconstruct; (fresque, vase brisé) to piece together, reconstitute

**reconstruire** [R(ə)kɔ̃stRɥiR] vt to rebuild

**reconvertir** [R(ə)kɔ̃vɛRtiR]: **se reconvertir dans** vr (un métier, une branche) to go into

**record** [R(ə)kɔR] nm, adj record

**recoupement** [R(ə)kupmɑ̃] nm: **par ~** by cross-checking

**recouper** [R(ə)kupe]: **se recouper** vi (témoignages) to tie ou match up

**recourber** [R(ə)kuRbe]: **se recourber** vi to curve (up), bend (up)

**recourir** [R(ə)kuRiR]: **~ à** vt (ami, agence) to turn ou appeal to; (force, ruse, emprunt) to resort to

**recours** [R(ə)kuR] nm: **avoir ~ à** = recourir à; **en dernier ~** as a last resort

**recouvrer** [R(ə)kuvRe] vt (vue, santé etc) to recover, regain

**recouvrir** [R(ə)kuvRiR] vt (couvrir à nouveau) to re-cover; (couvrir entièrement, aussi fig) to cover

**récréation** [RekReasjɔ̃] nf (Scol) break

**recroqueviller** [R(ə)kRɔkvije]: **se recroqueviller** vi (personne) to huddle up

**recrudescence** [R(ə)kRydesɑ̃s] nf fresh outbreak

**recruter** [R(ə)kRyte] vt to recruit

**rectangle** [Rɛktɑ̃gl] nm rectangle; **rectangulaire** adj rectangular

**rectificatif** [Rɛktifikatif] nm correction

**rectifier** [Rɛktifje] vt (calcul, adresse, paroles) to correct; (erreur) to rectify

**rectiligne** [Rɛktiliɲ] adj straight

**recto** [Rɛkto] nm front (of a page); **~ verso** on both sides (of the page)

**reçu, e** [R(ə)sy] pp de **recevoir** ▷ adj (candidat) successful; (admis, consacré) accepted ▷ nm (Comm) receipt; **je peux**

**avoir un ~, s'il vous plaît?** can I have a receipt, please?

**recueil** [Rəkœj] nm collection; **recueillir** vt to collect; (voix, suffrages) to win; (accueillir: réfugiés, chat) to take in; **se recueillir** vi to gather one's thoughts, meditate

**recul** [R(ə)kyl] nm (éloignement) distance; (déclin) decline; **être en ~** to be on the decline; **avec du ~** with hindsight; **avoir un mouvement de ~** to recoil; **prendre du ~** to stand back; **reculé, e** adj remote; **reculer** vi to move back, back away; (Auto) to reverse, back (up); (fig) to (be on the) decline ▷ vt to move back; (véhicule) to reverse, back (up); (date, décision) to postpone; **reculer devant** (danger, difficulté) to shrink from; **reculons: à reculons** adv backwards

**récupérer** [Rekypere] vt to recover, get back; (heures de travail) to make up; (déchets) to salvage ▷ vi to recover

**récurer** [RekyRe] vt to scour; **poudre à ~** scouring powder

**reçut** [Rəsy] vb voir **recevoir**

**recycler** [R(ə)sikle] vt (Tech) to recycle; **se recycler** vi to retrain

**rédacteur, -trice** [Redaktœr, tRis] nm/f (journaliste) writer; subeditor; (d'ouvrage de référence) editor, compiler

**rédaction** [Redaksjɔ̃] nf writing; (rédacteurs) editorial staff; (Scol: devoir) essay, composition

**redescendre** [R(ə)desɑ̃dR] vi to go back down ▷ vt (pente etc) to go down

**rédiger** [Redize] vt to write; (contrat) to draw up

**redire** [R(ə)diR] vt to repeat; **trouver à ~ à** to find fault with

**redoubler** [R(ə)duble] vi (tempête, violence) to intensify; (Scol) to repeat a year; **~ de patience/prudence** to be doubly patient/careful

**redoutable** [R(ə)dutabl] adj formidable, fearsome

**redouter** [R(ə)dute] vt to dread

**redressement** [R(ə)dRɛsmɑ̃] nm

(*économique*) recovery

**redresser** [ʀ(ə)dʀese] *vt* (*relever*) to set upright; (*pièce tordue*) to straighten out; (*situation, économie*) to put right; **se redresser** *vi* (*personne*) to sit (*ou* stand) up (straight); (*économie*) to recover

**réduction** [ʀedyksjɔ̃] *nf* reduction; **y a-t-il une ~ pour les étudiants?** is there a reduction for students?

**réduire** [ʀedɥiʀ] *vt* to reduce; (*prix, dépenses*) to cut, reduce; **réduit** *nm* (*pièce*) tiny room

**rééducation** [ʀeedykasjɔ̃] *nf* (*d'un membre*) re-education; (*de délinquants, d'un blessé*) rehabilitation

**réel, le** [ʀeɛl] *adj* real; **réellement** *adv* really

**réexpédier** [ʀeɛkspedje] *vt* (*à l'envoyeur*) to return, send back; (*au destinataire*) to send on, forward

**refaire** [ʀ(ə)fɛʀ] *vt* to do again; (*faire de nouveau: sport*) to take up again; (*réparer, restaurer*) to do up

**réfectoire** [ʀefɛktwaʀ] *nm* refectory

**référence** [ʀefeʀɑ̃s] *nf* reference; **références** *nfpl* (*recommandations*) reference *sg*

**référer** [ʀefeʀe]: **se référer à** *vt* to refer to

**refermer** [ʀ(ə)fɛʀme] *vt* to close *ou* shut again; **se refermer** *vi* (*porte*) to close *ou* shut (again)

**refiler** [ʀ(ə)file] *vi* (*fam*) to palm off

**réfléchi, e** [ʀefleʃi] *adj* (*caractère*) thoughtful; (*action*) well-thought-out; (*Ling*) reflexive; **c'est tout ~** my mind's made up

**réfléchir** [ʀefleʃiʀ] *vt* to reflect ▷ *vi* to think; **~ à** to think about

**reflet** [ʀ(ə)flɛ] *nm* reflection; (*sur l'eau etc*) sheen *no pl*, glint; **refléter** *vt* to reflect; **se refléter** *vi* to be reflected

**réflexe** [ʀeflɛks] *nm, adj* reflex

**réflexion** [ʀeflɛksjɔ̃] *nf* (*de la lumière etc*) reflection; (*fait de penser*) thought; (*remarque*) remark; **~ faite, à la ~** on reflection

**réflexologie** [ʀeflɛksɔlɔʒi] *nf* reflexology

**réforme** [ʀefɔʀm] *nf* reform; (*Rel*): **la R~** the Reformation; **réformer** *vt* to reform; (*Mil*) to declare unfit for service

**refouler** [ʀ(ə)fule] *vt* (*envahisseurs*) to drive back; (*larmes*) to force back; (*désir, colère*) to repress

**refrain** [ʀ(ə)fʀɛ̃] *nm* refrain, chorus

**refréner** [ʀəfʀene], **réfréner** [ʀefʀene] *vt* to curb, check

**réfrigérateur** [ʀefʀiʒeʀatœʀ] *nm* refrigerator, fridge

**refroidir** [ʀ(ə)fʀwadiʀ] *vt* to cool; (*fig: personne*) to put off ▷ *vi* to cool (down); **se refroidir** *vi* (*temps*) to get cooler *ou* colder; (*fig: ardeur*) to cool (off); **refroidissement** *nm* (*grippe etc*) chill

**refuge** [ʀ(ə)fyʒ] *nm* refuge; **réfugié, e** *adj, nm/f* refugee; **réfugier: se réfugier** *vi* to take refuge

**refus** [ʀ(ə)fy] *nm* refusal; **ce n'est pas de ~** I won't say no, it's welcome; **refuser** *vt* to refuse; (*Scol: candidat*) to fail; **refuser qch à qn** to refuse sb sth; **refuser du monde** to have to turn people away; **se refuser à faire** to refuse to do

**regagner** [ʀ(ə)ɡaɲe] *vt* (*faveur*) to win back; (*lieu*) to get back to

**régal** [ʀeɡal] *nm* treat; **régaler: se régaler** *vi* to have a delicious meal; (*fig*) to enjoy o.s.

**regard** [ʀ(ə)ɡaʀ] *nm* (*coup d'œil*) look, glance; (*expression*) look (in one's eye); **au ~ de** (*loi, morale*) from the point of view of; **en ~ de** in comparison with

**regardant, e** [ʀ(ə)ɡaʀdɑ̃, ɑ̃t] *adj* (*économe*) tight-fisted; **peu ~ (sur)** very free (about)

**regarder** [ʀ(ə)ɡaʀde] *vt* to look at; (*film, télévision, match*) to watch; (*concerner*) to concern ▷ *vi* to look; **ne pas ~ à la dépense** to spare no expense; **~ qn/qch comme** to regard sb/sth as

**régie** [ʀeʒi] *nf* (*Comm, Industrie*) state-owned company; (*Théâtre, Cinéma*) production; (*Radio, TV*) control room

**régime** [ʀeʒim] nm (Pol) régime; (Méd) diet; (Admin: carcéral, fiscal etc) system; (de bananes, dattes) bunch; **se mettre au/suivre un ~** to go on/be on a diet

**régiment** [ʀeʒimɑ̃] nm regiment

**région** [ʀeʒjɔ̃] nf region; **régional, e, -aux** adj regional

**régir** [ʀeʒiʀ] vt to govern

**régisseur** [ʀeʒisœʀ] nm (d'un domaine) steward; (Cinéma, TV) assistant director; (Théâtre) stage manager

**registre** [ʀaʒistʀ] nm register

**réglage** [ʀeɡlaʒ] nm adjustment

**règle** [ʀɛɡl] nf (instrument) ruler; (loi) rule; **règles** nfpl (menstruation) period sg; **en ~** (papiers d'identité) in order; **en ~ générale** as a (general) rule

**réglé, e** [ʀeɡle] adj (vie) well-ordered; (arrangé) settled

**règlement** [ʀɛɡləmɑ̃] nm (paiement) settlement; (arrêté) regulation; (règles, statuts) regulations pl, rules pl; **réglementaire** adj conforming to the regulations; (tenue) regulation cpd; **réglementation** nf (règles) regulations; **réglementer** vt to regulate

**régler** [ʀeɡle] vt (conflit, facture) to settle; (personne) to settle up with; (mécanisme, machine) to regulate, adjust; (thermostat etc) to set, adjust

**réglisse** [ʀeɡlis] nf liquorice

**règne** [ʀɛɲ] nm (d'un roi etc, fig) reign; **le ~ végétal/animal** the vegetable/animal kingdom; **régner** vi (roi) to rule, reign; (fig) to reign

**regorger** [ʀ(ə)ɡɔʀʒe] vi: **~ de** to overflow with, be bursting with

**regret** [ʀ(ə)ɡʀɛ] nm regret; **à ~** with regret; **sans ~** with no regrets; **regrettable** adj regrettable; **regretter** vt to regret; (personne) to miss; **je regrette mais …** I'm sorry but …

**regrouper** [ʀ(ə)ɡʀupe] vt (grouper) to group together; (contenir) to include, comprise; **se regrouper** vi to gather (together)

**régulier, -ière** [ʀeɡylje, jɛʀ] adj (gén)

regular; (vitesse, qualité) steady; (égal: couche, ligne) even; (Transports: ligne, service) scheduled, regular; (légal) lawful, in order; (honnête) straight, on the level; **régulièrement** adv regularly; (uniformément) evenly

**rehausser** [ʀaose] vt (relever) to heighten, raise; (fig: souligner) to set off, enhance

**rein** [ʀɛ̃] nm kidney; **reins** nmpl (dos) back sg

**reine** [ʀɛn] nf queen

**reine-claude** [ʀɛnklod] nf greengage

**réinscriptible** [ʀeɛ̃skʀiptibl] adj (CD, DVD) rewritable

**réinsertion** [ʀeɛ̃sɛʀsjɔ̃] nf (de délinquant) reintegration, rehabilitation

**réintégrer** [ʀeɛ̃teɡʀe] vt (lieu) to return to; (fonctionnaire) to reinstate

**rejaillir** [ʀ(ə)ʒajiʀ] vi to splash up; **~ sur** (fig: scandale) to rebound on; (: gloire) to be reflected on

**rejet** [ʀəʒɛ] nm rejection; **rejeter** vt (relancer) to throw back; (écarter) to reject; (déverser) to throw out, discharge; (vomir) to bring ou throw up; **rejeter la responsabilité de qch sur qn** to lay the responsibility for sth at sb's door

**rejoindre** [ʀ(ə)ʒwɛ̃dʀ] vt (famille, régiment) to rejoin, return to; (lieu) to get (back) to; (suj: route etc) to meet, join; (rattraper) to catch up (with); **se rejoindre** vi to meet; **je te rejoins à la gare** I'll see ou meet you at the station

**réjouir** [ʀeʒwiʀ] vt to delight; **se ~ (de qch/de faire)** to be delighted (about sth/to do); **réjouissances** nfpl (fête) festivities

**relâche** [ʀəlɑʃ] nm ou nf: **sans ~** without respite ou a break; **relâché, e** adj loose, lax; **relâcher** vt (libérer) to release; (desserrer) to loosen; **se relâcher** vi (discipline) to become slack ou lax; (élève etc) to slacken off

**relais** [ʀ(ə)lɛ] nm (Sport): **(course de) ~** relay (race); **prendre le ~ (de)** to take over (from); **relais routier** ≈ transport café (BRIT), ≈ truck stop (US)

**relancer** [R(ə)lɑ̃se] vt (balle) to throw back; (moteur) to restart; (fig) to boost, revive; (harceler): **~ qn** to pester sb

**relatif, -ive** [R(ə)latif, iv] adj relative

**relation** [R(ə)lasjɔ̃] nf (rapport) relation(ship); (connaissance) acquaintance; **relations** nfpl (rapports) relations; (connaissances) connections; **être/entrer en ~(s) avec** to be/get in contact with

**relaxer** [Rəlakse]: **se relaxer** vi to relax

**relayer** [R(ə)leje] vt (collaborateur, coureur etc) to relieve; **se relayer** vi (dans une activité) to take it in turns

**reléguer** [R(ə)lege] vt to relegate

**relevé, e** [Rəl(ə)ve] adj (manches) rolled-up; (sauce) highly-seasoned ▷ nm (de compteur) reading; **relevé bancaire** ou **de compte** bank statement

**relève** [Rəlεv] nf (personne) relief; **prendre la ~** to take over

**relever** [Rəl(ə)ve] vt (meuble) to stand up again; (personne tombée) to help up; (vitre, niveau de vie) to raise; (inf) to turn up; (style) to elevate; (plat, sauce) to season; (sentinelle, équipe) to relieve; (fautes) to pick out; (défi) to accept, take up; (noter: adresse etc) to take down, note; (: plan) to sketch; (compteur) to read; (ramasser: cahiers) to collect, take in; **se relever** vi (se remettre debout) to get up; **~ de** (maladie) to be recovering from; (être du ressort de) to be a matter for; (fig) to pertain to; **~ qn de** (fonctions) to relieve sb of; **~ la tête** to look up

**relief** [Rəljεf] nm relief; **mettre en ~** (fig) to bring out, highlight

**relier** [Rəlje] vt to link up; (livre) to bind; **~ qch à** to link sth to

**religieux, -euse** [R(ə)liʒjø, jøz] adj religious ▷ nm monk

**religion** [R(ə)liʒjɔ̃] nf religion

**relire** [R(ə)liR] vt (à nouveau) to reread, read again; (vérifier) to read over

**reluire** [R(ə)lɥiR] vi to gleam

**remanier** [R(ə)manje] vt to reshape, recast; (Pol) to reshuffle

**remarquable** [R(ə)maRkabl] adj remarkable

**remarque** [R(ə)maRk] nf remark; (écrite) note

**remarquer** [R(ə)maRke] vt (voir) to notice; **se remarquer** vi to be noticeable; **faire ~ (à qn) que** to point out (to sb) that; **faire ~ qch (à qn)** to point sth out (to sb); **remarquez, ...** mind you ...; **se faire ~** to draw attention to o.s.

**rembourrer** [Rɑ̃buRe] vt to stuff

**remboursement** [Rɑ̃buRsəmɑ̃] nm (de dette, d'emprunt) repayment; (de frais) refund; **rembourser** vt to pay back, repay; (frais, billet etc) to refund; **se faire rembourser** to get a refund

**remède** [R(ə)mεd] nm (médicament) medicine; (traitement, fig) remedy, cure

**remémorer** [R(ə)memɔRe]: **se remémorer** vt to recall, recollect

**remerciements** [RəmεRsimɑ̃] nmpl thanks; **(avec) tous mes ~** (with) grateful ou many thanks

**remercier** [R(ə)mεRsje] vt to thank; (congédier) to dismiss; **~ qn de/d'avoir fait** to thank sb for/for having done

**remettre** [R(ə)mεtR] vt (replacer) to put back; (vêtement) to put back on; (ajouter) to add; (ajourner): **~ qch (à)** to postpone (until); **se remettre** vi: **se ~ (de)** to recover (from); **~ qch à qn** (donner: lettre, clé etc) to hand over sth to sb; (: prix, décoration) to present sb with sth; **se ~ à faire qch** to start doing sth again; **s'en ~ à** to leave it (up) to

**remise** [R(ə)miz] nf (rabais) discount; (local) shed; **remise de peine** reduction of sentence; **remise des prix** prize-giving; **remise en cause** ou **question** calling into question, challenging; **remise en jeu** (Football) throw-in

**remontant** [R(ə)mɔ̃tɑ̃] nm tonic, pick-me-up

**remonte-pente** [R(ə)mɔ̃tpɑ̃t] nm ski-lift

**remonter** [R(ə)mɔ̃te] vi to go back

up; (*prix, température*) to go up again
▷ *vt* (*pente*) to go up; (*fleuve*) to sail (*ou* swim *etc*) up; (*manches, pantalon*) to roll up; (*col*) to turn up; (*niveau, limite*) to raise; (*fig: personne*) to buck up; (*qch de démonté*) to put back together, reassemble; (*montre*) to wind up; **~ le moral à qn** to raise sb's spirits; **~ à** (*dater de*) to date *ou* go back to

**remords** [ʀ(ə)mɔʀ] *nm* remorse *no pl*; **avoir des ~** to feel remorse

**remorque** [ʀ(ə)mɔʀk] *nf* trailer; **remorquer** *vt* to tow; **remorqueur** *nm* tug(boat)

**remous** [ʀəmu] *nm* (*d'un navire*) (back)wash *no pl*; (*de rivière*) swirl, eddy ▷ *nmpl* (*fig*) stir *sg*

**remparts** [ʀɑ̃paʀ] *nmpl* walls, ramparts

**remplaçant, e** [ʀɑ̃plasɑ̃, ɑ̃t] *nm/f* replacement, stand-in; (*Scol*) supply teacher

**remplacement** [ʀɑ̃plasmɑ̃] *nm* replacement; **faire des ~s** (*professeur*) to do supply teaching; (*secrétaire*) to temp

**remplacer** [ʀɑ̃plase] *vt* to replace; **~ qch/qn** to replace sth/sb with

**rempli, e** [ʀɑ̃pli] *adj* (*emploi du temps*) full, busy; **~ de** full of, filled with

**remplir** [ʀɑ̃pliʀ] *vt* to fill (up); (*questionnaire*) to fill out *ou* up; (*obligations, fonction, condition*) to fulfil; **se remplir** *vi* to fill up

**remporter** [ʀɑ̃pɔʀte] *vt* (*marchandise*) to take away; (*fig*) to win, achieve

**remuant, e** [ʀəmɥɑ̃, ɑ̃t] *adj* restless

**remue-ménage** [ʀ(ə)mymenaʒ] *nm inv* commotion

**remuer** [ʀəmɥe] *vt* to move; (*café, sauce*) to stir ▷ *vi* to move; **se remuer** *vi* to move; (*fam: s'activer*) to get a move on

**rémunérer** [ʀemyneʀe] *vt* to remunerate

**renard** [ʀ(ə)naʀ] *nm* fox

**renchérir** [ʀɑ̃ʃeʀiʀ] *vi* (*fig*): **~ (sur)** (*en paroles*) to add something (to)

**rencontre** [ʀɑ̃kɔ̃tʀ] *nf* meeting; (*imprévue*) encounter; **aller à la ~ de qn**
to go and meet sb; **rencontrer** *vt* to meet; (*mot, expression*) to come across; (*difficultés*) to meet with; **se rencontrer** *vi* to meet

**rendement** [ʀɑ̃dmɑ̃] *nm* (*d'un travailleur, d'une machine*) output; (*d'un champ*) yield

**rendez-vous** [ʀɑ̃devu] *nm* appointment; (*d'amoureux*) date; (*lieu*) meeting place; **donner ~ à qn** to arrange to meet sb; **avoir/ prendre ~ (avec)** to have/make an appointment (with); **j'ai ~ avec ...** I have an appointment with ...; **je voudrais prendre ~** I'd like to make an appointment

**rendre** [ʀɑ̃dʀ] *vt* (*restituer*) to give back, return; (*invitation*) to return, repay; (*vomir*) to bring up; (*exprimer, traduire*) to render; (*faire devenir*): **~ qn célèbre/qch possible** to make sb famous/sth possible; **se rendre** *vi* (*capituler*) to surrender, give o.s. up; (*aller*): **se ~ quelque part** to go somewhere; **se ~ la monnaie à qn** to give sb his change; **se ~ compte de qch** to realize sth

**rênes** [ʀɛn] *nfpl* reins

**renfermé, e** [ʀɑ̃fɛʀme] *adj* (*fig*) withdrawn ▷ *nm*: **sentir le ~** to smell stuffy

**renfermer** [ʀɑ̃fɛʀme] *vt* to contain

**renforcer** [ʀɑ̃fɔʀse] *vt* to reinforce; **renfort: renforts** *nmpl* reinforcements; **à grand renfort de** with a great deal of

**renfrogné, e** [ʀɑ̃fʀɔɲe] *adj* sullen

**renier** [ʀənje] *vt* (*personne*) to disown, repudiate; (*foi*) to renounce

**renifler** [ʀ(ə)nifle] *vi, vt* to sniff

**renne** [ʀɛn] *nm* reindeer *inv*

**renom** [ʀənɔ̃] *nm* reputation; (*célébrité*) renown; **renommé, e** *adj* celebrated, renowned; **renommée** *nf* fame

**renoncer** [ʀ(ə)nɔ̃se] **~ à** *vt* to give up; **~ à faire** to give up the idea of doing

**renouer** [ʀənwe] *vt*: **~ avec** (*habitude*) to take up again

**renouveler** [ʀ(ə)nuv(ə)le] *vt* to

renew; (*exploit, méfait*) to repeat; **se
renouveler** vi (*incident*) to recur,
happen again; **renouvellement** nm
(*remplacement*) renewal

**rénover** [ʀenɔve] vt (*immeuble*) to
renovate, do up; (*quartier*) to redevelop

**renseignement** [ʀɑ̃sɛɲmɑ̃] nm
information no pl, piece of information;
**(guichet des) ~s** information office;
**(service des) ~s** (*Tél*) directory
enquiries (*BRIT*), information (*US*)

**renseigner** [ʀɑ̃seɲe] vt: **~ qn (sur)**
to give information to sb (about); **se
renseigner** vi to ask for information,
make inquiries

**rentabilité** [ʀɑ̃tabilite] nf profitability

**rentable** [ʀɑ̃tabl] adj profitable

**rente** [ʀɑ̃t] nf private income; (*pension*)
pension

**rentrée** [ʀɑ̃tʀe] nf: **~ (d'argent)** cash
no pl coming in; **la ~ (des classes)** the
start of the new school year

**rentrer** [ʀɑ̃tʀe] vi (*revenir chez soi*) to
go (*ou* come) (back) home; (*entrer de
nouveau*) to go (*ou* come) back in; (*entrer*)
to go (*ou* come) in; (*air, clou: pénétrer*) to
go in; (*revenu*) to come in ▷ vt to bring
in; (*véhicule*) to put away; (*chemise dans
pantalon etc*) to tuck in; (*griffes*) to draw
in; **~ le ventre** to pull in one's stomach;
**~ dans** (*heurter*) to crash into; **~ dans
l'ordre** to be back to normal; **~ dans
ses frais** to recover one's expenses;
**je rentre mardi** I'm going *ou* coming
home on Tuesday

**renverse** [ʀɑ̃vɛʀs]: **à la ~** adv
backwards

**renverser** [ʀɑ̃vɛʀse] vt (*faire tomber:
chaise, verre*) to knock over, overturn;
(*liquide, contenu*) to spill, upset; (*piéton*)
to knock down; (*retourner*) to turn
upside down; (*: ordre des mots etc*)
to reverse; (*fig: gouvernement etc*) to
overthrow; (*fam: stupéfier*) to bowl over;
**se renverser** vi (*verre, vase*) to fall over;
(*contenu*) to spill

**renvoi** [ʀɑ̃vwa] nm (*d'employé*)
dismissal; (*d'élève*) expulsion; (*référence*)

cross-reference; (*éructation*) belch;
**renvoyer** vt to send back; (*congédier*) to
dismiss; (*élève: définitivement*) to expel;
(*lumière*) to reflect; (*ajourner*): **renvoyer
qch (à)** to put sth off *ou* postpone
sth (until)

**repaire** [ʀ(ə)pɛʀ] nm den

**répandre** [ʀepɑ̃dʀ] vt (*renverser*) to
spill; (*étaler, diffuser*) to spread; (*odeur*)
to give off; **se répandre** vi to spill; (*se
propager*) to spread; **répandu, e** adj
(*opinion, usage*) widespread

**réparation** [ʀepaʀasjɔ̃] nf repair

**réparer** [ʀepaʀe] vt to repair; (*fig:
offense*) to make up for, atone for;
(*: oubli, erreur*) to put right; **où est-ce
que je peux le faire ~?** where can I
get it fixed?

**repartie** [ʀepaʀti] nf retort; **avoir de
la ~** to be quick at repartee

**repartir** [ʀ(ə)paʀtiʀ] vi to leave again;
(*voyageur*) to set off again; (*fig*) to get
going again; **~ à zéro** to start from
scratch (again)

**répartir** [ʀepaʀtiʀ] vt (*pour attribuer*)
to share out; (*pour disperser, disposer*)
to divide up; (*poids*) to distribute; **se
répartir** vt (*travail, rôles*) to share out
between themselves; **répartition** nf
(*des richesses etc*) distribution

**repas** [ʀ(ə)pɑ] nm meal

**repassage** [ʀ(ə)pɑsaʒ] nm ironing

**repasser** [ʀ(ə)pɑse] vi to come (*ou*
go) back ▷ vt (*vêtement, tissu*) to iron;
(*examen*) to retake, resit; (*film*) to show
again; (*leçon: revoir*) to go over (again)

**repentir** [ʀəpɑ̃tiʀ] nm repentance; **se
repentir** vi to repent; **se ~ d'avoir fait
qch** (*regretter*) to regret having done sth

**répercussions** [ʀepɛʀkysjɔ̃] nfpl (*fig*)
repercussions

**répercuter** [ʀepɛʀkyte]: **se répercuter**
vi (*bruit*) to reverberate; (*fig*): **se ~ sur** to
have repercussions on

**repère** [ʀ(ə)pɛʀ] nm mark; (*monument,
événement*) landmark

**repérer** [ʀ(ə)peʀe] vt (*fam: erreur,
personne*) to spot; (*: endroit*) to locate; **se**

**repérer** *vi* to find one's way about

**répertoire** [ʀepɛʀtwaʀ] *nm* (*liste*) (alphabetical) list; (*carnet*) index notebook; (*Inform*) folder, directory; (*d'un artiste*) repertoire

**répéter** [ʀepete] *vt* to repeat; (*préparer: leçon*) to learn, go over; (*Théâtre*) to rehearse; **se répéter** *vi* (*redire*) to repeat o.s.; (*se reproduire*) to be repeated, recur; **pouvez-vous ~, s'il vous plaît?** can you repeat that, please?

**répétition** [ʀepetisjɔ̃] *nf* repetition; (*Théâtre*) rehearsal; **~ générale** (final) dress rehearsal

**répit** [ʀepi] *nm* respite; **sans ~** without letting up

**replier** [ʀ(ə)plije] *vt* (*rabattre*) to fold down *ou* over; **se replier** *vi* (*troupes, armée*) to withdraw, fall back; (*sur soi-même*) to withdraw into o.s.

**réplique** [ʀeplik] *nf* (*repartie, fig*) reply; (*Théâtre*) line; (*copie*) replica; **répliquer** *vi* to reply; (*riposter*) to retaliate

**répondeur** [ʀepɔ̃dœʀ] *nm*: **~ (automatique)** (*Tél*) answering machine

**répondre** [ʀepɔ̃dʀ] *vi* to answer, reply; (*freins*) to respond; **~ à** to reply to, answer; (*affection, salut*) to return; (*provocation*) to respond to; (*correspondre à: besoin*) to answer; (: *conditions*) to meet; (: *description*) to match; (*avec impertinence*): **~ à qn** to answer sb back; **~ de** to answer for

**réponse** [ʀepɔ̃s] *nf* answer, reply; **en ~ à** in reply to

**reportage** [ʀ(ə)pɔʀtaʒ] *nm* report

**reporter**[1] [ʀəpɔʀtɛʀ] *nm* reporter

**reporter**[2] [ʀəpɔʀte] *vt* (*ajourner*): **~ qch (à)** to postpone sth (until); (*transférer*): **~ qch sur** to transfer sth to; **se reporter à** (*époque*) to think back to; (*document*) to refer to

**repos** [ʀ(ə)po] *nm* rest; (*tranquillité*) peace (and quiet); (*Mil*) **~!** stand at ease!; **ce n'est pas de tout ~!** it's no picnic!

**reposant, e** [ʀ(ə)pozɑ̃, ɑ̃t] *adj* restful

**reposer** [ʀ(ə)poze] *vt* (*verre, livre*) to put down; (*délasser*) to rest ▷ *vi*: **laisser ~** (*pâte*) to leave to stand; **se reposer** *vi* to rest; **se ~ sur qn** to rely on sb; **~ sur** (*fig*) to rest on

**repoussant, e** [ʀ(ə)pusɑ̃, ɑ̃t] *adj* repulsive

**repousser** [ʀ(ə)puse] *vi* to grow again ▷ *vt* to repel, repulse; (*offre*) to turn down, reject; (*personne*) to push back; (*différer*) to put back

**reprendre** [ʀ(ə)pʀɑ̃dʀ] *vt* (*objet prêté, donné*) to take back; (*prisonnier, ville*) to recapture; (*firme, entreprise*) to take over; (*le travail*) to resume; (*emprunter: argument, idée*) to take up, use; (*refaire: article etc*) to go over again; (*vêtement*) to alter; (*réprimander*) to tell off; (*corriger*) to correct; (*chercher*) **je viendrai te ~ à 4 h** I'll come and fetch you at 4; (*se resservir de*): **~ du pain/un œuf** to take (*ou* eat) more bread/another egg ▷ *vi* (*classes, pluie*) to start (up) again; (*activités, travaux, combats*) to resume, start (up) again; (*affaires*) to pick up; (*dire*): **reprit-il** he went on; **~ des forces** to recover one's strength; **~ courage** to take new heart; **~ la route** to resume one's journey, set off again; **~ haleine** *ou* **son souffle** to get one's breath back

**représentant, e** [ʀ(ə)pʀezɑ̃tɑ̃, ɑ̃t] *nm/f* representative

**représentation** [ʀ(ə)pʀezɑ̃tasjɔ̃] *nf* (*symbole, image*) representation; (*spectacle*) performance

**représenter** [ʀ(ə)pʀezɑ̃te] *vt* to represent; (*donner: pièce, opéra*) to perform; **se représenter** *vt* (*se figurer*) to imagine

**répression** [ʀepʀesjɔ̃] *nf* repression

**réprimer** [ʀepʀime] *vt* (*émotions*) to suppress; (*peuple etc*) to repress

**repris** [ʀ(ə)pʀi] *nm*: **~ de justice** ex-prisoner, ex-convict

**reprise** [ʀ(ə)pʀiz] *nf* (*recommencement*) resumption; (*économique*) recovery; (*TV*) repeat; (*Comm*) trade-in, part exchange; (raccommodage) mend; **à plusieurs ~s** on several occasions

**repriser** [ʀ(ə)pʀize] vt (chaussette, lainage) to darn; (tissu) to mend

**reproche** [ʀ(ə)pʀɔʃ] nm (remontrance) reproach; **faire des ~s à qn** to reproach sb; **sans ~(s)** beyond reproach;

**reprocher** vt: **reprocher qch à qn** to reproach ou blame sb for sth; **reprocher qch à** (critiquer) to have sth against

**reproduction** [ʀ(ə)pʀɔdyksjɔ̃] nf reproduction

**reproduire** [ʀ(ə)pʀɔdɥiʀ] vt to reproduce; **se reproduire** vi (Bio) to reproduce; (recommencer) to recur, re-occur

**reptile** [ʀɛptil] nm reptile

**république** [ʀepyblik] nf republic

**répugnant, e** [ʀepyɲɑ̃, ɑ̃t] adj disgusting

**répugner** [ʀepyɲe]: **~ à** vt: **~ à qn** to repel ou disgust sb; **~ à faire** to be loath ou reluctant to do

**réputation** [ʀepytasjɔ̃] nf reputation; **réputé, e** adj renowned

**requérir** [ʀəkeʀiʀ] vt (nécessiter) to require, call for

**requête** [ʀəkɛt] nf request

**requin** [ʀəkɛ̃] nm shark

**requis, e** [ʀəki, iz] adj required

**RER** sigle m (= réseau express régional) Greater Paris high-speed train service

**rescapé, e** [ʀɛskape] nm/f survivor

**rescousse** [ʀɛskus] nf: **aller à la ~ de qn** to go to sb's aid ou rescue

**réseau, x** [ʀezo] nm network

**réservation** [ʀezɛʀvasjɔ̃] nf booking, reservation; **j'ai confirmé ma ~ par fax/e-mail** I confirmed my booking by fax/e-mail

**réserve** [ʀezɛʀv] nf (retenue) reserve; (entrepôt) storeroom; (restriction, d'Indiens) reservation; (de pêche, chasse) preserve; **de ~** (provisions etc) in reserve

**réservé, e** [ʀezɛʀve] adj reserved; **chasse/pêche ~e** private hunting/ fishing

**réserver** [ʀezɛʀve] vt to reserve;

(chambre, billet etc) to book, reserve; (fig: destiner) to have in store; (garder): **~ qch pour/à** to keep ou save sth for; **je voudrais ~ une chambre pour deux personnes** I'd like to book a double room; **j'ai réservé une table au nom de ...** I booked a table in the name of ...

**réservoir** [ʀezɛʀvwaʀ] nm tank

**résidence** [ʀezidɑ̃s] nf residence; **résidence secondaire** second home; **résidence universitaire** hall of residence (BRIT), dormitory (US); **résidentiel, le** adj residential; **résider** vi: **résider à/dans/en** to reside in; **résider dans** (fig) to lie in

**résidu** [ʀezidy] nm residue no pl

**résigner** [ʀeziɲe]: **se résigner** vi: **se ~ (à qch/à faire)** to resign o.s. (to sth/to doing)

**résilier** [ʀezilje] vt to terminate

**résistance** [ʀezistɑ̃s] nf resistance; (de réchaud, bouilloire: fil) element

**résistant, e** [ʀezistɑ̃, ɑ̃t] adj (personne) robust, tough; (matériau) strong, hard-wearing

**résister** [ʀeziste] vi to resist; **~ à** (assaut, tentation) to resist; (supporter: gel etc) to withstand; (désobéir à) to stand up to, oppose

**résolu, e** [ʀezɔly] pp de **résoudre** ▷ adj: **être ~ à qch/faire** to be set upon sth/doing

**résolution** [ʀezɔlysjɔ̃] nf (fermeté, décision) resolution; (d'un problème) solution

**résolve** etc [ʀezɔlv] vb voir **résoudre**

**résonner** [ʀezɔne] vi (cloche, pas) to reverberate, resound; (salle) to be resonant

**résorber** [ʀezɔʀbe]: **se résorber** vi (fig: chômage) to be reduced; (: déficit) to be absorbed

**résoudre** [ʀezudʀ] vt to solve; **se ~ à faire** to bring o.s. to do

**respect** [ʀɛspɛ] nm respect; **tenir en ~** to keep at bay; **présenter ses ~s à qn** to pay one's respects to sb; **respecter** vt to respect; **respectueux, -euse** adj respectful

**respiration** [rɛspirasjɔ̃] nf
breathing no pl

**respirer** [rɛspire] vi to breathe; (fig: se
détendre) to get one's breath;
(: se rassurer) to breathe again ▷ vt to
breathe (in), inhale; (manifester: santé,
calme etc) to exude

**resplendir** [rɛsplɑ̃dir] vi to shine;
(fig): ~ **(de)** to be radiant (with)

**responsabilité** [rɛspɔ̃sabilite] nf
responsibility; (légale) liability

**responsable** [rɛspɔ̃sabl] adj
responsible ▷ nm/f (coupable) person
responsible; (personne compétente)
person in charge; (de parti, syndicat)
official; ~ **de** responsible for

**ressaisir** [r(ə)sezir]: **se ressaisir** vi to
regain one's self-control

**ressasser** [r(ə)sase] vt to keep going
over

**ressemblance** [r(ə)sɑ̃blɑ̃s] nf
resemblance, similarity, likeness

**ressemblant, e** [r(ə)sɑ̃blɑ̃, ɑ̃t] adj
(portrait) lifelike, true to life

**ressembler** [r(ə)sɑ̃ble]: ~ **à** vt to
be like, resemble; (visuellement) to
look like; **se ressembler** vi to look (ou
look) alike

**ressentiment** [r(ə)sɑ̃timɑ̃] nm
resentment

**ressentir** [r(ə)sɑ̃tir] vt to feel; **se ~ de**
to feel (ou show) the effects of

**resserrer** [r(ə)sere] vt (nœud, boulon)
to tighten (up); (fig: liens) to strengthen

**resservir** [r(ə)servir] vi to do ou serve
again; ~ **qn (d'un plat)** to give sb a
second helping (of a dish); **se ~ de** (plat)
to take a second helping of; (outil etc)
to use again

**ressort** [rəsɔr] nm (pièce) spring;
(énergie) spirit; (recours): **en dernier ~** as
a last resort; (compétence): **être du ~ de**
to fall within the competence of

**ressortir** [rəsɔrtir] vi to go (ou come)
out (again); (contraster) to stand out;
~ **de** to emerge from; **faire ~** (fig:
souligner) to bring out

**ressortissant, e** [r(ə)sɔrtisɑ̃, ɑ̃t]
nm/f national

**ressources** [r(ə)surs] nfpl (moyens)
resources

**ressusciter** [resysite] vt (fig) to revive,
bring back ▷ vi to rise (from the dead)

**restant, e** [rɛstɑ̃, ɑ̃t] adj remaining
▷ nm: **le ~ (de)** the remainder (of); **un ~
de** (de trop) some left-over

**restaurant** [rɛstɔrɑ̃] nm restaurant;
**pouvez-vous m'indiquer un bon
~?** can you recommend a good
restaurant?

**restauration** [rɛstɔrasjɔ̃] nf
restoration; (hôtellerie) catering;
**restauration rapide** fast food

**restaurer** [rɛstɔre] vt to restore; **se
restaurer** vi to have something to eat

**reste** [rɛst] nm (restant): **le ~ (de)** the
rest (of); (de trop): **un ~ (de)** some
left-over; **restes** nmpl (nourriture) left-
overs; (d'une cité etc, dépouille mortelle)
remains; **du ~, au ~** besides, moreover

**rester** [rɛste] vi to stay, remain;
(subsister) to remain, be left; (durer)
to last, live on ▷ vb impers: **il reste du
pain/2 œufs** there's some bread/there
are 2 eggs left (over); **restons-en là** let's
leave it at that; **il me reste assez de
temps** I have enough time left; **il ne me
reste plus qu'à ...** I've just got to ...

**restituer** [rɛstitɥe] vt (objet, somme): ~
**qch (à qn)** to return sth (to sb)

**restreindre** [rɛstrɛ̃dr] vt to restrict,
limit

**restriction** [rɛstriksjɔ̃] nf restriction

**résultat** [rezylta] nm result; **résultats**
nmpl (d'examen, d'élection) results pl

**résulter** [rezylte]: ~ **de** vt to result
from, be the result of

**résumé** [rezyme] nm summary,
résumé; **en ~** in brief; (pour conclure)
to sum up

**résumer** [rezyme] vt (texte) to
summarize; (récapituler) to sum up
▌ Attention à ne pas traduire **résumer**
par **to resume**.

**résurrection** [rezyrɛksjɔ̃] nf

resurrection

**rétablir** [Retabliʀ] vt to restore, re-establish; **se rétablir** vi (guérir) to recover; (silence, calme) to return, be restored; **rétablissement** nm restoring; (guérison) recovery

**retaper** [R(ə)tape] (fam) vt (maison, voiture etc) to do up; (revigorer) to buck up

**retard** [R(ə)taʀ] nm (d'une personne attendue) lateness no pl; (sur l'horaire, un programme) delay; (fig: scolaire, mental etc) backwardness; **en ~ (de 2 heures)** (2 hours) late; **avoir du ~** to be late; (sur un programme) to be behind (schedule); **prendre du ~** (train, avion) to be delayed; **sans ~** without delay; **désolé d'être en ~** sorry I'm late; **le vol a deux heures de ~** the flight is two hours late

**retardataire** [R(ə)taʀdatɛʀ] nm/f latecomer

**retardement** [R(ə)taʀdəmɑ̃]: **à ~** adj delayed action cpd; **bombe à ~** time bomb

**retarder** [R(ə)taʀde] vt to delay; (montre) to put back ▷ vi (montre) to be slow; **~ qn (d'une heure)** (sur un horaire) to delay sb (an hour); **~ qch (de 2 jours)** (départ, date) to put sth back (2 days)

**retenir** [Rət(ə)niʀ] vt (garder, retarder) to keep, detain; (maintenir: objet qui glisse, fig: colère, larmes) to hold back; (se rappeler) to retain; (réserver) to reserve; (accepter: proposition etc) to accept; (fig: empêcher d'agir): **~ qn (de faire)** to hold sb back (from doing); (prélever): **~ qch (sur)** to deduct sth (from); **se retenir** vi (se raccrocher): **se ~ à** to hold onto; (se contenir): **se ~ de faire** to restrain o.s. from doing; **~ son souffle** to hold one's breath

**retentir** [R(ə)tɑ̃tiʀ] vi to ring out; **retentissant, e** adj resounding

**retenue** [Rət(ə)ny] nf (prélèvement) deduction; (Scol) detention; (modération) (self-)restraint

**réticence** [Retisɑ̃s] nf hesitation, reluctance no pl; **réticent, e** adj

hesitant, reluctant

**rétine** [Retin] nf retina

**retiré, e** [R(ə)tiʀe] adj (vie) secluded; (lieu) remote

**retirer** [R(ə)tiʀe] vt (vêtement, lunettes) to take off, remove; (argent, plainte) to withdraw; (reprendre: bagages, billets) to collect, pick up; (extraire): **~ qch de** to take sth out of, remove sth from

**retomber** [R(ə)tɔ̃be] vi (à nouveau) to fall again; (atterrir: après un saut etc) to land; (échoir): **~ sur qn** to fall on sb

**rétorquer** [Retɔʀke] vt: **~ (à qn) que** to retort (to sb) that

**retouche** [R(ə)tuʃ] nf (sur vêtement) alteration; **retoucher** vt (photographie) to touch up; (texte, vêtement) to alter

**retour** [R(ə)tuʀ] nm return; **au ~** (en route) on the way back; **à mon ~** when I get/got back; **être de ~ (de)** to be back (from); **par ~ du courrier** by return of post; **quand serons-nous de ~?** when do we get back?

**retourner** [R(ə)tuʀne] vt (dans l'autre sens: matelas, crêpe etc) to turn (over); (: sac, vêtement) to turn inside out; (fam: bouleverser) to shake; (renvoyer, restituer): **~ qch à qn** to return sth to sb ▷ vi (aller, revenir): **~ quelque part/à** to go back ou return somewhere/to; **se retourner** vi (tourner la tête) to turn round; **~ à** (état, activité) to return to, go back to; **se ~ contre** (fig) to turn against

**retrait** [R(ə)tʀɛ] nm (d'argent) withdrawal; **en ~** set back; **retrait du permis (de conduire)** disqualification from driving (BRIT), revocation of driver's license (US)

**retraite** [R(ə)tʀɛt] nf (d'un employé) retirement; (revenu) pension; (d'une armée, Rel) retreat; **prendre sa ~** to retire; **retraite anticipée** early retirement; **retraité, e** adj retired ▷ nm/f pensioner

**retrancher** [R(ə)tʀɑ̃ʃe] vt (nombre, somme): **~ qch de** to take ou deduct sth from; **se ~ derrière/dans** to take refuge behind/in

**rétrécir** [ʀetʀesiʀ] vt (vêtement) to take in ▷ vi to shrink; **se rétrécir** (route, vallée) to narrow

**rétro** [ʀetʀo] adj inv: **la mode ~** the nostalgia vogue

**rétroprojecteur** [ʀetʀopʀɔʒɛktœʀ] nm overhead projector

**rétrospective** [ʀetʀospɛktiv] nf (Art) retrospective; (Cinéma) season, retrospective; **rétrospectivement** adv in retrospect

**retrousser** [ʀ(ə)tʀuse] vt to roll up

**retrouvailles** [ʀ(ə)tʀuvaj] nfpl reunion sg

**retrouver** [ʀ(ə)tʀuve] vt (fugitif, objet perdu) to find; (calme, santé) to regain; (revoir) to see again; (rejoindre) to meet (again), join; **se retrouver** vi to meet; (s'orienter) to find one's way; **se ~ quelque part** to find o.s. somewhere; **s'y ~** (y voir clair) to make sense of it; (rentrer dans ses frais) to break even; **je ne retrouve plus mon portefeuille** I can't find my wallet (BRIT) ou billfold (US)

**rétroviseur** [ʀetʀɔvizœʀ] nm (rear-view) mirror

**réunion** [ʀeynjɔ̃] nf (séance) meeting

**réunir** [ʀeyniʀ] vt (rassembler) to gather together; (inviter: amis, famille) to have round, have in; (cumuler: qualités etc) to combine; (rapprocher: ennemis) to bring together (again), reunite; (rattacher: parties) to join (together); **se réunir** vi (se rencontrer) to meet

**réussi, e** [ʀeysi] adj successful

**réussir** [ʀeysiʀ] vi to succeed, be successful; (à un examen) to pass ▷ vt to make a success of; **~ à faire** to succeed in doing; **~ à qn** (être bénéfique à) to agree with sb; **réussite** nf success; (Cartes) patience

**revaloir** [ʀ(ə)valwaʀ] vt: **je vous revaudrai cela** I'll repay you some day; (en mal) I'll pay you back for this

**revanche** [ʀ(ə)vɑ̃ʃ] nf revenge; (sport) revenge match; **en ~** on the other hand

**rêve** [ʀɛv] nm dream; **de ~** dream cpd;

**faire un ~** to have a dream

**réveil** [ʀevɛj] nm waking up no pl; (fig) awakening; (pendule) alarm (clock); **au ~** on waking (up); **réveiller** vt (personne) to wake up; (fig) to awaken, revive; **se réveiller** vi to wake up; **pouvez-vous me réveiller à 7 heures, s'il vous plaît?** could I have an alarm call at 7am, please?

**réveillon** [ʀevɛjɔ̃] nm Christmas Eve; (de la Saint-Sylvestre) New Year's Eve; **réveillonner** vi to celebrate Christmas Eve (ou New Year's Eve)

**révélateur, -trice** [ʀevelatœʀ, tʀis] adj: **~ (de qch)** revealing (sth)

**révéler** [ʀevele] vt to reveal; **se révéler** vi to be revealed, reveal itself ▷ vb +attrib: **se ~ difficile/aisé** to prove difficult/easy

**revenant, e** [ʀ(ə)vənɑ̃, ɑ̃t] nm/f ghost

**revendeur, -euse** [ʀ(ə)vɑ̃dœʀ, øz] nm/f (détaillant) retailer; (de drogue) (drug-)dealer

**revendication** [ʀ(ə)vɑ̃dikasjɔ̃] nf claim, demand

**revendiquer** [ʀ(ə)vɑ̃dike] vt to claim, demand; (responsabilité) to claim

**revendre** [ʀ(ə)vɑ̃dʀ] vt (d'occasion) to resell; (détailler) to sell; **à ~** (en abondance) to spare

**revenir** [ʀəv(ə)niʀ] vi to come back; (coûter): **~ cher/à 100 euros (à qn)** to cost (sb) a lot/100 euros; **~ à** (reprendre: études, projet) to return to, go back to; (équivaloir à) to amount to; **~ à qn** (part, honneur) to go to sb, be sb's; (souvenir, nom) to come back to sb; **~ sur** (question, sujet) to go back over; (engagement) to go back on; **~ à soi** to come round; **n'en pas ~: je n'en reviens pas** I can't get over it; **~ sur ses pas** to retrace one's steps; **cela revient à dire que/au même** it amounts to saying that/the same thing; **faire ~** (Culin) to brown

**revenu** [ʀəv(ə)ny] nm income; **revenus** nmpl income sg

**rêver** [ʀeve] vi, vt to dream; **~ de/à** to dream of

**réverbère** [ʀevɛʀbɛʀ] *nm* street lamp *ou* light; **réverbérer** *vt* to reflect

**revers** [ʀ(ə)vɛʀ] *nm* (*de feuille, main*) back; (*d'étoffe*) wrong side; (*de pièce, médaille*) back, reverse; (*Tennis, Ping-Pong*) backhand; (*de veste*) lapel; (*fig: échec*) setback

**revêtement** [ʀ(ə)vɛtmɑ̃] *nm* (*des sols*) flooring; (*de chaussée*) surface

**revêtir** [ʀ(ə)vetiʀ] *vt* (*habit*) to don, put on; (*prendre: importance, apparence*) to take on; **~ qch de** to cover sth with

**rêveur, -euse** [ʀɛvœʀ, øz] *adj* dreamy ▷ *nm/f* dreamer

**revient** [ʀəvjɛ̃] *vb voir* **revenir**

**revigorer** [ʀ(ə)vigɔʀe] *vt* (*air frais*) to invigorate, brace up; (*repas, boisson*) to revive, buck up

**revirement** [ʀ(ə)viʀmɑ̃] *nm* change of mind; (*d'une situation*) reversal

**réviser** [ʀevize] *vt* to revise; (*machine*) to overhaul, service

**révision** [ʀevizjɔ̃] *nf* revision; (*de voiture*) servicing *no pl*

**revivre** [ʀ(ə)vivʀ] *vi* (*reprendre des forces*) to come alive again ▷ *vt* (*épreuve, moment*) to relive

**revoir** [ʀəvwaʀ] *vt* to see again; (*réviser*) to revise ▷ *nm*: **au ~** goodbye

**révoltant, e** [ʀevɔltɑ̃, ɑ̃t] *adj* revolting, appalling

**révolte** [ʀevɔlt] *nf* rebellion, revolt

**révolter** [ʀevɔlte] *vt* to revolt; **se révolter (contre)** to rebel (against)

**révolu, e** [ʀevɔly] *adj* past; (*Admin*): **âgé de 18 ans ~s** over 18 years of age

**révolution** [ʀevɔlysjɔ̃] *nf* revolution; **révolutionnaire** *adj, nm/f* revolutionary

**revolver** [ʀevɔlvɛʀ] *nm* gun; (*à barillet*) revolver

**révoquer** [ʀevɔke] *vt* (*fonctionnaire*) to dismiss; (*arrêt, contrat*) to revoke

**revue** [ʀ(ə)vy] *nf* review; (*périodique*) review, magazine; (*de music-hall*) variety show; **passer en ~** (*mentalement*) to go through

**rez-de-chaussée** [ʀed(ə)ʃose] *nm inv* ground floor

**RF** *sigle f* = **République française**

**Rhin** [ʀɛ̃] *nm* Rhine

**rhinocéros** [ʀinɔseʀɔs] *nm* rhinoceros

**Rhône** [ʀon] *nm* Rhone

**rhubarbe** [ʀybaʀb] *nf* rhubarb

**rhum** [ʀɔm] *nm* rum

**rhumatisme** [ʀymatism] *nm* rheumatism *no pl*

**rhume** [ʀym] *nm* cold; **rhume de cerveau** head cold; **le rhume des foins** hay fever

**ricaner** [ʀikane] *vi* (*avec méchanceté*) to snigger; (*bêtement*) to giggle

**riche** [ʀiʃ] *adj* rich; (*personne, pays*) rich, wealthy; **~ en** rich in; **richesse** *nf* wealth; (*fig: de sol, musée etc*) richness; **richesses** *nfpl* (*ressources, argent*) wealth *sg*; (*fig: trésors*) treasures

**ricochet** [ʀikɔʃɛ] *nm*: **faire des ~s** to skip stones

**ride** [ʀid] *nf* wrinkle

**rideau, x** [ʀido] *nm* curtain; **rideau de fer** (*boutique*) metal shutter(s)

**rider** [ʀide] *vt* to wrinkle; **se rider** *vi* to become wrinkled

**ridicule** [ʀidikyl] *adj* ridiculous ▷ *nm*: **le ~** ridicule; **ridiculiser** *vt* to ridicule; **se ridiculiser** *vi* to make a fool of o.s.

**MOT-CLÉ**

**rien** [ʀjɛ̃] *pron* **1: (ne) ... rien** nothing, *tournure négative* + *anything*; **qu'est-ce que vous avez? — rien** what have you got? — nothing; **il n'a rien dit/fait** he said/did nothing; he hasn't said/done anything; **n'avoir peur de rien** to be afraid *ou* frightened of nothing, not to be afraid *ou* frightened of anything; **il n'a rien** (*n'est pas blessé*) he's all right; **ça ne fait rien** it doesn't matter; **de rien!** not at all!

**2: rien de: rien d'intéressant** nothing interesting; **rien d'autre** nothing else; **rien du tout** nothing at all

**3: rien que** just, only; nothing but; **rien que pour lui faire plaisir** only *ou* just to please him; **rien que la vérité** nothing but the truth; **rien que cela** that alone ▷ *nm:* **un petit rien** (*cadeau*) a little something; **des riens** trivia *pl;* **un rien de** a hint of; **en un rien de temps** in no time at all

**rieur, -euse** [R(i)jœR, R(i)jøz] *adj* cheerful

**rigide** [Riʒid] *adj* stiff; (*fig*) rigid; strict

**rigoler** [Rigɔle] *vi* (*fam: rire*) to laugh; (*s'amuser*) to have (some) fun; (*plaisanter*) to be joking *ou* kidding; **rigolo, -ote** (*fam*) *adj* funny ▷ *nm/f* comic; (*péj*) fraud, phoney

**rigoureusement** [RiguRøzmɑ̃] *adv* (*vrai*) absolutely; (*interdit*) strictly

**rigoureux, -euse** [RiguRø, øz] *adj* rigorous; (*hiver*) hard, harsh

**rigueur** [RigœR] *nf* rigour; **"tenue de soirée de ~"** "formal dress only"; **à la ~** at a pinch; **tenir ~ à qn de qch** to hold sth against sb

**rillettes** [Rijɛt] *nfpl* potted meat (*made from pork or goose*)

**rime** [Rim] *nf* rhyme

**rinçage** [Rɛ̃saʒ] *nm* rinsing (out); (*opération*) rinse

**rincer** [Rɛ̃se] *vt* to rinse; (*récipient*) to rinse out

**ringard, e** [Rɛ̃gaR, aRd] (*fam*) *adj* old-fashioned

**riposter** [Ripɔste] *vi* to retaliate ▷ *vt:* **~ que** to retort that

**rire** [RiR] *vi* to laugh; (*se divertir*) to have fun ▷ *nm* laugh; **le ~** laughter; **~ de** to laugh at; **pour ~** (*pas sérieusement*) for a joke *ou* a laugh

**risible** [Rizibl] *adj* laughable

**risque** [Risk] *nm* risk; **le ~** danger; **à ses ~s et périls** at his own risk; **risqué, e** *adj* risky; (*plaisanterie*) risqué, daring; **risquer** *vt* to risk; (*allusion, question*) to venture, hazard; **ça ne risque rien** it's quite safe; **risquer de: il risque de se tuer** he could get himself killed; **ce qui risque de se produire** what might *ou* could well happen; **il ne risque pas**

**de recommencer** there's no chance of him doing that again; **se risquer à faire** (*tenter*) to venture *ou* dare to do

**rissoler** [Risɔle] *vi, vt:* **(faire) ~** to brown

**ristourne** [RistuRn] *nf* discount

**rite** [Rit] *nm* rite; (*fig*) ritual

**rivage** [Rivaʒ] *nm* shore

**rival, e, -aux** [Rival, o] *adj, nm/f* rival; **rivaliser** *vi:* **rivaliser avec** (*personne*) to rival, vie with; **rivalité** *nf* rivalry

**rive** [Riv] *nf* shore; (*de fleuve*) bank; **riverain, e** *nm/f* riverside (*ou* lakeside) resident; (*d'une route*) local resident

**rivière** [RivjɛR] *nf* river

**riz** [Ri] *nm* rice; **rizière** *nf* paddy-field, ricefield

**RMI** *sigle m* (= *revenu minimum d'insertion*) ≈ income support (BRIT), ≈ welfare (US)

**RN** *sigle f* = **route nationale**

**robe** [Rɔb] *nf* dress; (*de juge*) robe; (*pelage*) coat; **robe de chambre** dressing gown; **robe de mariée** wedding dress; **robe de soirée** evening dress

**robinet** [Rɔbinɛ] *nm* tap (BRIT), faucet (US)

**robot** [Rɔbo] *nm* robot; **robot de cuisine** food processor

**robuste** [Rɔbyst] *adj* robust, sturdy; **robustesse** *nf* robustness, sturdiness

**roc** [Rɔk] *nm* rock

**rocade** [Rɔkad] *nf* bypass

**rocaille** [Rɔkaj] *nf* loose stones *pl;* (*jardin*) rockery, rock garden

**roche** [Rɔʃ] *nf* rock

**rocher** [Rɔʃe] *nm* rock

**rocheux, -euse** [Rɔʃø, øz] *adj* rocky

**rôdage** [Rodaʒ] *nm:* **en ~** running in

**rôder** [Rode] *vi* to roam about; (*de façon suspecte*) to lurk (about *ou* around); **rôdeur, -euse** *nm/f* prowler

**rogne** [Rɔɲ] (*fam*) *nf:* **être en ~** to be in a temper

**rogner** [Rɔɲe] *vt* to clip; **~ sur** (*fig*) to cut down *ou* back on

**rognons** [Rɔɲɔ̃] *nmpl* (*Culin*) kidneys

**roi** [Rwa] *nm* king; **la fête des Rois, les**

**Rois** Twelfth Night

**rôle** [Rol] nm role, part

**rollers** [RolœR] nmpl Rollerblades®

**romain, e** [Romɛ̃, ɛn] adj Roman
▷ nm/f: **R~, e** Roman

**roman, e** [Romã, an] adj (Archit)
Romanesque ▷ nm novel; **roman
policier** detective story

**romancer** [Romãse] vt (agrémenter) to
romanticize; **romancier, -ière** nm/f
novelist; **romanesque** adj (amours,
aventures) storybook cpd; (sentimental:
personne) romantic

**roman-feuilleton** [Romãfœjtɔ̃] nm
serialized novel

**romanichel, le** [Romaniʃɛl] (péj)
nm/f gipsy

**romantique** [Romãtik] adj romantic

**romarin** [RomaRɛ̃] nm rosemary

**Rome** [Rom] n Rome

**rompre** [Rɔ̃pR] vt to break; (entretien,
fiançailles) to break off ▷ vi (fiancés) to
break it off; **se rompre** vi to break;
**rompu, e** (fourbu) exhausted

**ronces** [Rɔ̃s] nfpl brambles

**ronchonner** [Rɔ̃ʃone] (fam) vi to
grouse, grouch

**rond, e** [Rɔ̃, Rɔ̃d] adj round; (joues,
mollets) well-rounded; (fam: ivre) tight
▷ nm (cercle) ring; (fam: sou): **je n'ai
plus un ~** I haven't a penny left; **en ~**
(s'asseoir, danser) in a ring; **ronde** nf
(gén: de surveillance) rounds pl, patrol;
(danse) round (dance); (Mus) semibreve
(BRIT), whole note (US); **à la ronde**
(alentour): **à 10 km à la ronde** for 10 km
round; **rondelet, te** adj plump

**rondelle** [Rɔ̃dɛl] nf (tranche) slice,
round; (Tech) washer

**rond-point** [Rɔ̃pwɛ̃] nm roundabout

**ronflement** [Rɔ̃fləmã] nm snore,
snoring

**ronfler** [Rɔ̃fle] vi to snore; (moteur,
poêle) to hum

**ronger** [Rɔ̃ʒe] vt to gnaw (at); (suj: vers,
rouille) to eat into; **se ~ les ongles** to
bite one's nails; **se ~ les sangs** to worry
o.s. sick; **rongeur** nm rodent

**ronronner** [Rɔ̃Rone] vi to purr

**rosbif** [Rɔsbif] nm: **du ~** roasting beef;
(cuit) roast beef

**rose** [Roz] nf rose ▷ adj pink; **rose
bonbon** adj inv candy pink

**rosé, e** [Roze] adj pinkish; **(vin) ~** rosé

**roseau, x** [Rozo] nm reed

**rosée** [Roze] nf dew

**rosier** [Rozje] nm rosebush, rose tree

**rossignol** [Rosiɲɔl] nm (Zool)
nightingale

**rotation** [Rotasjɔ̃] nf rotation

**roter** [Rote] (fam) vi to burp, belch

**rôti** [Roti] nm: **du ~** roasting meat; (cuit)
roast meat; **un ~ de bœuf/porc** a joint
of beef/pork

**rotin** [Rotɛ̃] nm rattan (cane); **fauteuil
en ~** cane (arm)chair

**rôtir** [RotiR] vi, vt (aussi: **faire ~**)
to roast; **rôtisserie** nf (restaurant)
steakhouse; (traiteur) roast meat shop;
**rôtissoire** nf (roasting) spit

**rotule** [Rotyl] nf kneecap

**rouage** [Rwaʒ] nm cog(wheel),
gearwheel; **les ~s de l'État** the wheels
of State

**roue** [Ru] nf wheel; **roue de secours**
spare wheel

**rouer** [Rwe] vt: **~ qn de coups** to give
sb a thrashing

**rouge** [Ruʒ] adj, nm/f red ▷ nm red;
**(vin) ~** red wine; **sur la liste ~** ex-
directory (BRIT), unlisted (US); **passer
au ~** (signal) to go red; (automobiliste)
to go through a red light; **rouge à joue**
blusher; **rouge (à lèvres)** lipstick;
**rouge-gorge** nm robin (redbreast)

**rougeole** [Ruʒɔl] nf measles sg

**rougeoyer** [Ruʒwaje] vi to glow red

**rouget** [Ruʒɛ] nm mullet

**rougeur** [RuʒœR] nf redness; (Méd:
tache) red blotch

**rougir** [RuʒiR] vi to turn red; (de honte,
timidité) to blush, flush; (de plaisir, colère)
to flush

**rouille** [Ruj] nf rust; **rouillé, e** adj rusty;
**rouiller** vt to rust ▷ vi to rust, go rusty

**roulant, e** [Rulã, ãt] adj (meuble) on

wheels; (*tapis etc*) moving; **escalier ~** escalator

**rouleau, x** [Rulo] *nm* roll; (*à mise en plis, à peinture, vague*) roller; **rouleau à pâtisserie** rolling pin

**roulement** [Rulmã] *nm* (*rotation*) rotation; (*bruit*) rumbling *no pl*, rumble; **travailler par ~** to work on a rota (BRIT) *ou* rotation (US) basis; **roulement (à billes)** ball bearings *pl*; **roulement de tambour** drum roll

**rouler** [Rule] *vt* to roll; (*papier, tapis*) to roll up; (*Culin: pâte*) to roll out; (*fam: duper*) to do, con ▷ *vi* (*bille, boule*) to roll; (*voiture, train*) to go, run; (*automobiliste*) to drive; (*bateau*) to roll; **se ~ dans** (*boue*) to roll in; (*couverture*) to roll o.s. (up) in

**roulette** [Rulɛt] *nf* (*de table, fauteuil*) castor; (*de dentiste*) drill; (*jeu*) roulette; **à ~s** on castors; **ça a marché comme sur des ~s** (*fam*) it went off very smoothly

**roulis** [Ruli] *nm* roll(ing)

**roulotte** [Rulɔt] *nf* caravan

**roumain, e** [Rumɛ̃, ɛn] *adj* Rumanian ▷ *nm/f*: **R~, e** Rumanian

**Roumanie** [Rumani] *nf* Rumania

**rouquin, e** [Rukɛ̃, in] (*péj*) *nm/f* redhead

**rouspéter** [Ruspete] (*fam*) *vi* to moan

**rousse** [Rus] *adj voir* **roux**

**roussir** [Rusir] *vt* to scorch ▷ *vi* (*Culin*): **faire ~** to brown

**route** [Rut] *nf* road; (*fig: chemin*) way; (*itinéraire, parcours*) route; (*fig: voie*) road, path; **il y a 3h de ~** it's a 3-hour ride *ou* journey; **en ~** on the way; **en ~!** let's go!; **mettre en ~** to start up; **se mettre en ~** to set off; **quelle ~ dois-je prendre pour aller à ...?** which road do I take for ...?; **route nationale** ≈ A road (BRIT), ≈ state highway (US); **routier, -ière** *adj* road *cpd* ▷ *nm* (*camionneur*) (long-distance) lorry (BRIT) *ou* truck (US) driver; (*restaurant*) ≈ transport café (BRIT), ≈ truck stop (US)

**routine** [Rutin] *nf* routine; **routinier, -ière** (*péj*) *adj* (*activité*) humdrum;

(*personne*) addicted to routine

**rouvrir** [Ruvrir] *vt, vi* to reopen, open again; **se rouvrir** *vi* to reopen, open again

**roux, rousse** [Ru, Rus] *adj* red; (*personne*) red-haired ▷ *nm/f* redhead

**royal, e, -aux** [Rwajal, o] *adj* royal; (*cadeau etc*) fit for a king

**royaume** [Rwajom] *nm* kingdom; (*fig*) realm; **le Royaume-Uni** the United Kingdom

**royauté** [Rwajote] *nf* (*régime*) monarchy

**ruban** [Rybã] *nm* ribbon; **ruban adhésif** adhesive tape

**rubéole** [Rybeɔl] *nf* German measles *sg*, rubella

**rubis** [Rybi] *nm* ruby

**rubrique** [Rybrik] *nf* (*titre, catégorie*) heading; (*Presse: article*) column

**ruche** [Ryʃ] *nf* hive

**rude** [Ryd] *adj* (*au toucher*) rough; (*métier, tâche*) hard, tough; (*climat*) severe, harsh; (*bourru*) harsh, rough; (*fruste: manières*) rugged, tough; (*fam: fameux*) jolly good; **rudement** (*fam*) *adv* (*très*) terribly

**rudimentaire** [Rydimãtɛr] *adj* rudimentary, basic

**rudiments** [Rydimã] *nmpl*: **avoir des ~ d'anglais** to have a smattering of English

**rue** [Ry] *nf* street

**ruée** [Rɥe] *nf* rush

**ruelle** [Rɥɛl] *nf* alley(-way)

**ruer** [Rɥe] *vi* (*cheval*) to kick out; **se ruer** *vi*: **se ~ sur** to pounce on; **se ~ vers/dans/hors de** to rush *ou* dash towards/into/out of

**rugby** [Rygbi] *nm* rugby (football)

**rugir** [Ryʒir] *vi* to roar

**rugueux, -euse** [Rygø, øz] *adj* rough

**ruine** [Rɥin] *nf* ruin; **ruiner** *vt* to ruin; **ruineux, -euse** *adj* ruinous

**ruisseau, x** [Rɥiso] *nm* stream, brook

**ruisseler** [Rɥis(ə)le] *vi* to stream

**rumeur** [Rymœr] *nf* (*nouvelle*) rumour; (*bruit confus*) rumbling

**ruminer** [Rymine] *vt* (*herbe*) to ruminate; (*fig*) to ruminate on *ou* over, chew over

**rupture** [RyptyR] *nf* (*séparation, désunion*) break-up, split; (*de négociations etc*) breakdown; (*de contrat*) breach; (*dans continuité*) break

**rural, e, -aux** [RyRal, o] *adj* rural, country *cpd*

**ruse** [Ryz] *nf*: **la ~** cunning, craftiness; (*pour tromper*) trickery; **une ~** a trick, a ruse; **rusé, e** *adj* cunning, crafty

**russe** [Rys] *adj* Russian ▷ *nm/f*: **R~** Russian ▷ *nm* (*Ling*) Russian

**Russie** [Rysi] *nf*: **la ~** Russia

**rustine®** [Rystin] *nf* rubber repair patch (*for bicycle tyre*)

**rustique** [Rystik] *adj* rustic

**rythme** [Ritm] *nm* rhythm; (*vitesse*) rate; (: *de la vie*) pace, tempo; **rythmé, e** *adj* rhythmic(al)

**s'** [s] *pron voir* **se**

**sa** [sa] *adj voir* **son¹**

**sable** [sabl] *nm* sand

**sablé** [sable] *nm* shortbread biscuit

**sabler** [sable] *vt* (*contre le verglas*) to grit; **~ le champagne** to drink champagne

**sabot** [sabo] *nm* clog; (*de cheval*) hoof; **sabot de frein** brake shoe

**saboter** [sabote] *vt* to sabotage; (*bâcler*) to make a mess of, botch

**sac** [sak] *nm* bag; (*à charbon etc*) sack; **mettre à ~** to sack; **sac à dos** rucksack; **sac à main** handbag; **sac de couchage** sleeping bag; **sac de voyage** travelling bag

**saccadé, e** [sakade] *adj* jerky; (*respiration*) spasmodic

**saccager** [sakaʒe] *vt* (*piller*) to sack; (*dévaster*) to create havoc in

**saccharine** [sakarin] *nf* saccharin

**sachet** [saʃɛ] *nm* (small) bag; (*de sucre, café*) sachet; **du potage en ~** packet soup; **sachet de thé** tea bag

**sacoche** [sakɔʃ] nf (gén) bag; (de bicyclette) saddlebag

**sacré, e** [sakʀe] adj sacred; (fam: satané) blasted; (: fameux): **un ~ toupet** a heck of a cheek

**sacrement** [sakʀəmɑ̃] nm sacrament

**sacrifice** [sakʀifis] nm sacrifice; **sacrifier** vt to sacrifice

**sacristie** [sakʀisti] nf (catholique) sacristy; (protestante) vestry

**sadique** [sadik] adj sadistic

**safran** [safʀɑ̃] nm saffron

**sage** [saʒ] adj wise; (enfant) good

**sage-femme** [saʒfam] nf midwife

**sagesse** [saʒɛs] nf wisdom

**Sagittaire** [saʒitɛʀ] nm: **le ~** Sagittarius

**Sahara** [saaʀa] nm: **le ~** the Sahara (desert)

**saignant, e** [sɛɲɑ̃, ɑ̃t] adj (viande) rare

**saigner** [seɲe] vi to bleed ▷ vt to bleed; (animal) to kill (by bleeding); **~ du nez** to have a nosebleed

**saillir** [sajiʀ] vi to project, stick out; (veine, muscle) to bulge

**sain, e** [sɛ̃, sɛn] adj healthy; **~ et sauf** safe and sound, unharmed; **~ d'esprit** sound in mind, sane

**saindoux** [sɛ̃du] nm lard

**saint, e** [sɛ̃, sɛ̃t] adj holy ▷ nm/f saint; **le Saint Esprit** the Holy Ghost; **la Sainte Vierge** the Blessed Virgin; **la Saint-Sylvestre** New Year's Eve; **sainteté** nf holiness

**sais** etc [sɛ] vb voir **savoir**

**saisie** [sezi] nf seizure; **saisie (de données)** (data) capture

**saisir** [seziʀ] vt to take hold of, grab; (fig: occasion) to seize; (comprendre) to grasp; (entendre) to get, catch; (données) to capture; (Culin) to fry quickly; (Jur: biens, publication) to seize; **saisissant, e** adj startling, striking

**saison** [sɛzɔ̃] nf season; **haute/basse/morte ~** high/low/slack season; **saisonnier, -ière** adj seasonal

**salade** [salad] nf (Bot) lettuce etc; (Culin) (green) salad; (fam: confusion) tangle, muddle; **salade composée** mixed salad; **salade de fruits** fruit salad; **saladier** nm (salad) bowl

**salaire** [salɛʀ] nm (annuel, mensuel) salary; (hebdomadaire, journalier) pay, wages pl; **salaire minimum interprofessionnel de croissance** index-linked guaranteed minimum wage

**salarié, e** [salaʀje] nm/f salaried employee; wage-earner

**salaud** [salo] (fam!) nm sod (!), bastard (!)

**sale** [sal] adj dirty, filthy; (fam: mauvais) nasty

**salé, e** [sale] adj (mer, goût) salty; (Culin: amandes, beurre etc) salted; (: gâteaux) savoury; (fam: grivois) spicy; (: facture) steep

**saler** [sale] vt to salt

**saleté** [salte] nf (état) dirtiness; (crasse) dirt, filth; (tache etc) dirt no pl; (fam: méchanceté) dirty trick; (: camelote) rubbish no pl; (: obscénité) filthy thing (to say)

**salière** [saljɛʀ] nf saltcellar

**salir** [saliʀ] vt to (make) dirty; (fig: quelqu'un) to soil the reputation of; **se salir** vi to get dirty; **salissant, e** adj (tissu) which shows the dirt; (travail) dirty, messy

**salle** [sal] nf room; (d'hôpital) ward; (de restaurant) dining room; (d'un cinéma) auditorium; (: public) audience; **salle à manger** dining room; **salle d'attente** waiting room; **salle de bain(s)** bathroom; **salle de classe** classroom; **salle de concert** concert hall; **salle d'eau** shower-room; **salle d'embarquement** (à l'aéroport) departure lounge; **salle de jeux** (pour enfants) playroom; **salle de séjour** living room; **salle des ventes** saleroom

**salon** [salɔ̃] nm lounge, sitting room; (mobilier) lounge suite; (exposition) exhibition, show; **salon de coiffure** hairdressing salon; **salon de thé** tearoom

**salope** [salɔp] (fam!) nf bitch (!);

**saloperie** (*fam!*) *nf* (*action*) dirty trick; (*chose sans valeur*) rubbish *no pl*

**salopette** [salɔpɛt] *nf* dungarees *pl*; (*d'ouvrier*) overall(s)

**salsifis** [salsifi] *nm* salsify

**salubre** [salybʀ] *adj* healthy, salubrious

**saluer** [salɥe] *vt* (*pour dire bonjour, fig*) to greet; (*pour dire au revoir*) to take one's leave; (*Mil*) to salute

**salut** [saly] *nm* (*geste*) wave; (*parole*) greeting; (*Mil*) salute; (*sauvegarde*) safety; (*Rel*) salvation ▷ *excl* (*fam: bonjour*) hi (there); (: *au revoir*) see you, bye

**salutations** [salytasjɔ̃] *nfpl* greetings; **Veuillez agréer, Monsieur, mes ~ distinguées** yours faithfully

**samedi** [samdi] *nm* Saturday

**SAMU** [samy] *sigle m* (= *service d'assistance médicale d'urgence*) ≈ ambulance (service) (*BRIT*), ≈ paramedics *pl* (*US*)

**sanction** [sɑ̃ksjɔ̃] *nf* sanction; **sanctionner** *vt* (*loi, usage*) to sanction; (*punir*) to punish

**sandale** [sɑ̃dal] *nf* sandal

**sandwich** [sɑ̃dwi(t)ʃ] *nm* sandwich; **je voudrais un ~ au jambon/fromage** I'd like a ham/cheese sandwich

**sang** [sɑ̃] *nm* blood; **en ~** covered in blood; **se faire du mauvais ~** to fret, get in a state; **sang-froid** *nm* calm, sangfroid; **de sang-froid** in cold blood; **sanglant, e** *adj* bloody

**sangle** [sɑ̃gl] *nf* strap

**sanglier** [sɑ̃glije] *nm* (wild) boar

**sanglot** [sɑ̃glo] *nm* sob; **sangloter** *vi* to sob

**sangsue** [sɑ̃sy] *nf* leech

**sanguin, e** [sɑ̃gɛ̃, in] *adj* blood *cpd*

**sanitaire** [sanitɛʀ] *adj* health *cpd*; **sanitaires** *nmpl* (*lieu*) bathroom *sg*

**sans** [sɑ̃] *prép* without; **un pull ~ manches** a sleeveless jumper; **~ faute** without fail; **~ arrêt** without a break; **~ ça** (*fam*) otherwise; **~ qu'il s'en aperçoive** without him

ou his noticing; **sans-abri** *nmpl* homeless; **sans-emploi** *nm/f inv* unemployed person; **les sans-emploi** the unemployed; **sans-gêne** *adj inv* inconsiderate

**santé** [sɑ̃te] *nf* health; **en bonne ~** in good health; **boire à la ~ de qn** to drink (to) sb's health; **à ta/votre ~!** cheers!

**saoudien, ne** [saudjɛ̃, jɛn] *adj* Saudi Arabian ▷ *nm/f*: **S~, ne** Saudi Arabian

**saoul, e** [su, sul] *adj* = **soûl**

**saper** [sape] *vt* to undermine, sap

**sapeur-pompier** [sapœʀpɔ̃pje] *nm* fireman

**saphir** [safiʀ] *nm* sapphire

**sapin** [sapɛ̃] *nm* fir (tree); (*bois*) fir; **sapin de Noël** Christmas tree

**sarcastique** [saʀkastik] *adj* sarcastic

**Sardaigne** [saʀdɛɲ] *nf*: **la ~** Sardinia

**sardine** [saʀdin] *nf* sardine

**SARL** *sigle f* (= *société à responsabilité limitée*) ≈ plc (*BRIT*), ≈ Inc. (*US*)

**sarrasin** [saʀazɛ̃] *nm* buckwheat

**satané, e** [satane] (*fam*) *adj* confounded

**satellite** [satelit] *nm* satellite

**satin** [satɛ̃] *nm* satin

**satire** [satiʀ] *nf* satire; **satirique** *adj* satirical

**satisfaction** [satisfaksjɔ̃] *nf* satisfaction

**satisfaire** [satisfɛʀ] *vt* to satisfy; **~ à** (*conditions*) to meet; **satisfaisant, e** *adj* (*acceptable*) satisfactory; **satisfait, e** *adj* satisfied; **satisfait de** happy *ou* satisfied with

**saturer** [satyʀe] *vt* to saturate

**sauce** [sos] *nf* sauce; (*avec un rôti*) gravy; **sauce tomate** tomato sauce; **saucière** *nf* sauceboat

**saucisse** [sosis] *nf* sausage

**saucisson** [sosisɔ̃] *nm* (slicing) sausage

**sauf, sauve** [sof, sov] *adj* unharmed, unhurt; (*fig: honneur*) intact, saved ▷ *prép* except; **laisser la vie sauve à qn** to spare sb's life; **~ si** (*à moins que*) unless; **~ erreur** if I'm not mistaken;

~ **avis contraire** unless you hear to the contrary

**sauge** [soʒ] nf sage

**saugrenu, e** [sogrəny] adj preposterous

**saule** [sol] nm willow (tree)

**saumon** [somɔ̃] nm salmon inv

**saupoudrer** [supudʀe] vt: ~ **qch de** to sprinkle sth with

**saur** [sɔʀ] adj m: **hareng** ~ smoked herring, kipper

**saut** [so] nm jump; (discipline sportive) jumping; **faire un ~ chez qn** to pop over to sb's (place); **saut à l'élastique** bungee jumping; **saut à la perche** pole vaulting; **saut en hauteur/longueur** high/long jump; **saut périlleux** somersault

**sauter** [sote] vi to jump, leap; (exploser) to blow up, explode; (: fusibles) to blow; (se détacher) to pop out (ou off) ▷ vt to jump (over), leap (over); (fig: omettre) to skip, miss (out); **faire ~** to blow up; (Culin) to sauté; **~ à la corde** to skip; **~ au cou de qn** to fly into sb's arms; **~ sur une occasion** to jump at an opportunity; **~ aux yeux** to be (quite) obvious

**sauterelle** [sotʀɛl] nf grasshopper

**sautiller** [sotije] vi (oiseau) to hop; (enfant) to skip

**sauvage** [sovaʒ] adj (gén) wild; (peuplade) savage; (farouche: personne) unsociable; (barbare) wild, savage; (non officiel) unauthorized, unofficial; **faire du camping ~** to camp in the wild ▷ nm/f savage; (timide) unsociable type

**sauve** [sov] adj f voir **sauf**

**sauvegarde** [sovgaʀd] nf safeguard; (Inform) backup; **sauvegarder** vt to safeguard; (Inform: enregistrer) to save; (: copier) to back up

**sauve-qui-peut** [sovkipø] excl run for your life!

**sauver** [sove] vt to save; (porter secours à) to rescue; (récupérer) to salvage, rescue; **se sauver** vi (s'enfuir) to run away; (fam: partir) to be off; **sauvetage**

nm rescue; **sauveteur** nm rescuer; **sauvette: à la sauvette** adv (se marier etc) hastily, hurriedly; **sauveur** nm saviour (BRIT), savior (US)

**savant, e** [savɑ̃, ɑ̃t] adj scholarly, learned ▷ nm scientist

**saveur** [savœʀ] nf flavour; (fig) savour

**savoir** [savwaʀ] vt to know; (être capable de): **il sait nager** he can swim ▷ nm knowledge; **se savoir** vi (être connu) to be known; **je ne sais pas** I don't know; **je ne sais pas parler français** I don't speak French; **savez-vous où je peux …?** do you know where I can …?; **je n'en sais rien** I (really) don't know; **à ~** that is, namely; **faire ~ qch à qn** to let sb know sth; **pas que je sache** not as far as I know

**savon** [savɔ̃] nm (produit) soap; (morceau) bar of soap; (fam): **passer un ~ à qn** to give sb a good dressing-down; **savonner** vt to soap; **savonnette** nf bar of soap

**savourer** [savuʀe] vt to savour; **savoureux, -euse** adj tasty; (fig: anecdote) spicy, juicy

**saxo(phone)** [saksɔ(fɔn)] nm sax(ophone)

**scabreux, -euse** [skabʀø, øz] adj risky; (indécent) improper, shocking

**scandale** [skɑ̃dal] nm scandal; **faire un ~** (scène) to make a scene; (Jur) to create a disturbance; **faire ~** to scandalize people; **scandaleux, -euse** adj scandalous, outrageous

**scandinave** [skɑ̃dinav] adj Scandinavian ▷ nm/f: **S~** Scandinavian

**Scandinavie** [skɑ̃dinavi] nf Scandinavia

**scarabée** [skaʀabe] nm beetle

**scarlatine** [skaʀlatin] nf scarlet fever

**scarole** [skaʀɔl] nf endive

**sceau, x** [so] nm seal

**sceller** [sele] vt to seal

**scénario** [senaʀjo] nm scenario

**scène** [sɛn] nf (gén) scene; (estrade, fig: théâtre) stage; **entrer en ~** to come on stage; **mettre en ~** (Théâtre) to stage;

(*Cinéma*) to direct; **faire une ~ (à qn)**
to make a scene (with sb); **scène de
ménage** domestic scene
**sceptique** [sɛptik] *adj* sceptical
**schéma** [ʃema] *nm* (*diagramme*)
diagram, sketch; **schématique** *adj*
diagrammatic(al), schematic; (*fig*)
oversimplified
**sciatique** [sjatik] *nf* sciatica
**scie** [si] *nf* saw
**sciemment** [sjamɑ̃] *adv* knowingly
**science** [sjɑ̃s] *nf* science; (*savoir*)
knowledge; **sciences humaines/
sociales** social sciences; **sciences
naturelles** (*Scol*) natural science
*sg*, biology *sg*; **sciences po** political
science *ou* studies *pl*; **science-fiction**
*nf* science fiction; **scientifique** *adj*
scientific ▷ *nm/f* scientist; (*étudiant*)
science student
**scier** [sje] *vt* to saw; (*retrancher*) to saw
off; **scierie** *nf* sawmill
**scintiller** [sɛ̃tije] *vi* to sparkle; (*étoile*)
to twinkle
**sciure** [sjyʀ] *nf*: **~ (de bois)** sawdust
**sclérose** [skleʀoz] *nf*: **sclérose en
plaques** multiple sclerosis
**scolaire** [skɔlɛʀ] *adj* school *cpd*;
**scolariser** *vt* to provide with
schooling/schools; **scolarité** *nf*
schooling
**scooter** [skutœʀ] *nm* (motor) scooter
**score** [skɔʀ] *nm* score
**scorpion** [skɔʀpjɔ̃] *nm* (*signe*): **le S~**
Scorpio
**scotch** [skɔtʃ] *nm* (*whisky*) scotch,
whisky; **S~®** (*adhésif*) Sellotape® (BRIT),
Scotch® tape (US)
**scout, e** [skut] *adj, nm* scout
**script** [skʀipt] *nm* (*écriture*) printing;
(*Cinéma*) (shooting) script
**scrupule** [skʀypyl] *nm* scruple
**scruter** [skʀyte] *vt* to scrutinize;
(*l'obscurité*) to peer into
**scrutin** [skʀytɛ̃] *nm* (*vote*) ballot;
(*ensemble des opérations*) poll
**sculpter** [skylte] *vt* to sculpt; (*bois*)
to carve; **sculpteur** *nm* sculptor;

**sculpture** *nf* sculpture
**SDF** *sigle m*: **sans domicile fixe**
homeless person; **les ~** the homeless

○ **MOT-CLÉ**

**se** [sə], **s'** *pron* **1** (*emploi réfléchi*) oneself;
(*: masc*) himself; (*: fém*) herself; (*: sujet
non humain*) itself; (*: pl*) themselves; **se
savonner** to soap o.s.
**2** (*réciproque*) one another, each other;
**ils s'aiment** they love one another *ou*
each other
**3** (*passif*): **cela se répare facilement** it
is easily repaired
**4** (*possessif*): **se casser la jambe/se
laver les mains** to break one's leg/
wash one's hands

**séance** [seɑ̃s] *nf* (*d'assemblée*) meeting,
session; (*de tribunal*) sitting, session;
(*musicale, Théâtre*) performance
**seau, x** [so] *nm* bucket, pail
**sec, sèche** [sɛk, sɛʃ] *adj* dry; (*raisins,
figues*) dried; (*cœur: insensible*) hard, cold
▷ *nm*: **tenir au ~** to keep in a dry place
▷ *adv* hard; **je le bois ~** I drink it straight
*ou* neat; **à ~** (*puits*) dried up
**sécateur** [sekatœʀ] *nm* secateurs *pl*
(BRIT), shears *pl*
**sèche** [sɛʃ] *adj f voir* **sec**; **sèche-
cheveux** *nm inv* hair-drier; **sèche-
linge** *nm inv* tumble dryer; **sèchement**
*adv* (*répondre*) drily
**sécher** [seʃe] *vt* to dry; (*dessécher: peau,
blé*) to dry (out); (*: étang*) to dry up; (*fam:
cours*) to skip ▷ *vi* to dry; to dry out; to
dry up; (*fam: candidat*) to be stumped;
**se sécher** (*après le bain*) to dry o.s.;
**sécheresse** *nf* dryness; (*absence de
pluie*) drought; **séchoir** *nm* drier
**second, e** [s(ə)gɔ̃, ɔ̃d] *adj* second ▷ *nm*
(*assistant*) second in command; (*Navig*)
first mate ▷ *nf* (*Scol*) year 11 (BRIT), tenth
grade (US); (*Aviat, Rail etc*) second class;
**voyager en ~e** to travel second-class;
**secondaire** *adj* secondary; **seconde²**
*nf* second; **seconder** *vt* to assist

**secouer** [s(ə)kwe] vt to shake; (*passagers*) to rock; (*traumatiser*) to shake (up)

**secourir** [s(ə)kuʀiʀ] vt (*venir en aide à*) to assist, aid; **secourisme** nm first aid; **secouriste** nm/f first-aid worker

**secours** [s(ə)kuʀ] nm help, aid, assistance ▷ nmpl aid sg; **au ~!** help!; **appeler au ~** to shout ou call for help; **porter ~ à qn** to give sb assistance, help sb; **les premiers ~** first aid sg

● **ÉQUIPES DE SECOURS**
●
● Emergency phone numbers can
● be dialled free from public phones.
● For the police ('la police') dial 17; for
● medical services ('le SAMU') dial
● 15; for the fire brigade ('les sapeurs
● pompiers'), dial 18.

**secousse** [s(ə)kus] nf jolt, bump; (*électrique*) shock; (*fig: psychologique*) jolt, shock

**secret, -ète** [səkʀɛ, ɛt] adj secret; (*fig: renfermé*) reticent, reserved ▷ nm secret; (*discrétion absolue*): **le ~** secrecy; **en ~** in secret, secretly; **secret professionel** professional secrecy

**secrétaire** [s(ə)kʀetɛʀ] nm/f secretary ▷ nm (*meuble*) writing desk; **secrétaire de direction** private ou personal secretary; **secrétaire d'État** junior minister; **secrétariat** nm (*profession*) secretarial work; (*bureau*) office; (: *d'organisation internationale*) secretariat

**secteur** [sɛktœʀ] nm sector; (*zone*) area; (*Élec*): **branché sur ~** plugged into the mains (supply)

**section** [sɛksjɔ̃] nf section; (*de parcours d'autobus*) fare stage; (*Mil: unité*) platoon; **sectionner** vt to sever

**sécu** [seky] abr f = **sécurité sociale**

**sécurité** [sekyʀite] nf (*absence de danger*) safety; (*absence de troubles*) security; **système de ~** security system; **être en ~** to be safe; **la sécurité routière** road safety; **la sécurité sociale** ≈ (the) Social Security (BRIT), ≈ Welfare (US)

**sédentaire** [sedɑ̃tɛʀ] adj sedentary

**séduction** [sedyksjɔ̃] nf seduction; (*charme, attrait*) appeal, charm

**séduire** [seduiʀ] vt to charm; (*femme: abuser de*) to seduce; **séduisant, e** adj (*femme*) seductive; (*homme, offre*) very attractive

**ségrégation** [segʀegasjɔ̃] nf segregation

**seigle** [sɛgl] nm rye

**seigneur** [sɛɲœʀ] nm lord

**sein** [sɛ̃] nm breast; (*entrailles*) womb; **au ~ de** (*équipe, institution*) within

**séisme** [seism] nm earthquake

**seize** [sɛz] num sixteen; **seizième** num sixteenth

**séjour** [seʒuʀ] nm stay; (*pièce*) living room; **séjourner** vi to stay

**sel** [sɛl] nm salt; (*fig: piquant*) spice

**sélection** [selɛksjɔ̃] nf selection; **sélectionner** vt to select

**self-service** [sɛlfsɛʀvis] adj, nm self-service

**selle** [sɛl] nf saddle; **selles** nfpl (*Méd*) stools; **seller** vt to saddle

**selon** [s(ə)lɔ̃] prép according to; (*en se conformant à*) in accordance with; **~ que** according to whether; **~ moi** as I see it

**semaine** [s(ə)mɛn] nf week; **en ~** during the week, on weekdays

**semblable** [sɑ̃blabl] adj similar; (*de ce genre*): **de ~s mésaventures** such mishaps ▷ nm fellow creature ou man; **~ à** similar to, like

**semblant** [sɑ̃blɑ̃] nm: **un ~ de ...** a semblance of ...; **faire ~ (de faire)** to pretend (to do)

**sembler** [sɑ̃ble] vb +attrib to seem ▷ vb impers: **il semble (bien) que/inutile de** it (really) seems ou appears that/ useless to; **il me semble que** it seems to me that; **comme bon lui semble** as he sees fit

**semelle** [s(ə)mɛl] nf sole; (*intérieure*) insole, inner sole

**semer** [s(ə)me] *vt* to sow; (*fig: éparpiller*) to scatter; (: *confusion*) to spread; (*fam: poursuivants*) to lose, shake off; **semé de** (*difficultés*) riddled with

**semestre** [s(ə)mɛstʀ] *nm* half-year; (*Scol*) semester

**séminaire** [seminɛʀ] *nm* seminar

**semi-remorque** [səmiʀəmɔʀk] *nm* articulated lorry (BRIT), semi(trailer) (US)

**semoule** [s(ə)mul] *nf* semolina

**sénat** [sena] *nm* senate; **sénateur** *nm* senator

**Sénégal** [senegal] *nm*: **le ~** Senegal

**sens** [sɑ̃s] *nm* (*Physiol.*) sense; (*signification*) meaning, sense; (*direction*) direction; **à mon ~** to my mind; **dans le ~ des aiguilles d'une montre** clockwise; **dans le ~ contraire des aiguilles d'une montre** anticlockwise; **dans le mauvais ~** (*aller*) the wrong way, in the wrong direction; **le bon ~** common sense; **sens dessus dessous** upside down; **sens interdit/unique** one-way street

**sensation** [sɑ̃sasjɔ̃] *nf* sensation; **à ~** (*péj*) sensational; **faire ~** to cause *ou* create a sensation; **sensationnel, le** *adj* (*fam*) fantastic, terrific

**sensé, e** [sɑ̃se] *adj* sensible

**sensibiliser** [sɑ̃sibilize] *vt*: **~ qn à** to make sb sensitive to

**sensibilité** [sɑ̃sibilite] *nf* sensitivity

**sensible** [sɑ̃sibl] *adj* sensitive; (*aux sens*) perceptible; (*appréciable: différence, progrès*) appreciable, noticeable; **~ à** sensitive to; **sensiblement** *adv* (*à peu près*): **ils sont sensiblement du même âge** they are approximately the same age; **sensiblerie** *nf* sentimentality

  Attention à ne pas traduire *sensible* par le mot anglais *sensible*.

**sensuel, le** [sɑ̃sɥɛl] *adj* (*personne*) sensual; (*musique*) sensuous

**sentence** [sɑ̃tɑ̃s] *nf* (*jugement*) sentence

**sentier** [sɑ̃tje] *nm* path

**sentiment** [sɑ̃timɑ̃] *nm* feeling; **recevez mes ~s respectueux**

(*personne nommée*) yours sincerely; (*personne non nommée*) yours faithfully; **sentimental, e, -aux** *adj* sentimental; (*vie, aventure*) love *cpd*

**sentinelle** [sɑ̃tinɛl] *nf* sentry

**sentir** [sɑ̃tiʀ] *vt* (*par l'odorat*) to smell; (*par le goût*) to taste; (*au toucher, fig*) to feel; (*répandre une odeur de*) to smell of; (: *ressemblance*) to smell like ▷ *vi* to smell; **~ mauvais** to smell bad; **se ~ bien** to feel good; **se ~ mal** (*être indisposé*) to feel unwell *ou* ill; **se ~ le courage/la force de faire** to feel brave/strong enough to do; **il ne peut pas le ~** (*fam*) he can't stand him; **je ne me sens pas bien** I don't feel well

**séparation** [separasjɔ̃] *nf* separation; (*cloison*) division, partition

**séparé, e** [separe] *adj* (*distinct*) separate; (*époux*) separated; **séparément** *adv* separately

**séparer** [separe] *vt* to separate; (*désunir*) to drive apart; (*détacher*): **~ qch de** to pull sth (off) from; **se séparer** *vi* (*époux, amis*) to separate, part; (*se diviser: route etc*) to divide; **se ~ de** (*époux*) to separate *ou* part from; (*employé, objet personnel*) to part with

**sept** [sɛt] *num* seven; **septante** (BELGIQUE, SUISSE) *adj inv* seventy

**septembre** [sɛptɑ̃bʀ] *nm* September

**septicémie** [sɛptisemi] *nf* blood poisoning, septicaemia

**septième** [sɛtjɛm] *num* seventh

**séquelles** [sekɛl] *nfpl* after-effects; (*fig*) aftermath *sg*

**serbe** [sɛʀb(ə)] *adj* Serbian

**Serbie** [sɛʀbi] *nf*: **la ~** Serbia

**serein, e** [səʀɛ̃, ɛn] *adj* serene

**sergent** [sɛʀʒɑ̃] *nm* sergeant

**série** [seʀi] *nf* series *inv*; (*de clés, casseroles, outils*) set; (*catégorie: Sport*) rank; **en ~** in quick succession; (*Comm*) mass *cpd*; **de ~** (*voiture*) standard; **hors ~** (*Comm*) custom-built; **série noire** (*crime*) thriller

**sérieusement** [seʀjøzmɑ̃] *adv* seriously

**sérieux, -euse** [serjø, jøz] *adj* serious; (*élève, employé*) reliable, responsible; (*client, maison*) reliable, dependable ▷ *nm* seriousness; (*d'une entreprise etc*) reliability; **garder son ~** to keep a straight face; **prendre qch/qn au ~** to take sth/sb seriously

**serin** [s(ə)rɛ̃] *nm* canary

**seringue** [s(ə)rɛ̃g] *nf* syringe

**serment** [sermɑ̃] *nm* (*juré*) oath; (*promesse*) pledge, vow

**sermon** [sermɔ̃] *nm* sermon

**séropositif, -ive** [seropozitif, iv] *adj* (*Méd*) HIV positive

**serpent** [serpɑ̃] *nm* snake; **serpenter** *vi* to wind

**serpillière** [serpijɛr] *nf* floorcloth

**serre** [ser] *nf* (*Agr*) greenhouse; **serres** *nfpl* (*griffes*) claws, talons

**serré, e** [sere] *adj* (*habits*) tight; (*fig: lutte, match*) tight, close-fought; (*passagers etc*) (tightly) packed; (*réseau*) dense; **avoir le cœur ~** to have a heavy heart

**serrer** [sere] *vt* (*tenir*) to grip *ou* hold tight; (*comprimer, coincer*) to squeeze; (*poings, mâchoires*) to clench; (*suj: vêtement*) to be too tight for; (*ceinture, nœud, vis*) to tighten ▷ *vi*: **~ à droite** to keep *ou* get over to the right

**serrure** [seryr] *nf* lock; **serrurier** *nm* locksmith

**sert** *etc* [ser] *vb voir* **servir**

**servante** [servɑ̃t] *nf* (maid) servant

**serveur, -euse** [servœr, øz] *nm/f* waiter (waitress)

**serviable** [servjabl] *adj* obliging, willing to help

**service** [servis] *nm* service; (*assortiment de vaisselle*) set, service; (*bureau: de la vente etc*) department, section; (*travail*) duty; **premier ~** (*série de repas*) first sitting; **être de ~** to be on duty; **faire le ~** to serve; **rendre un ~ à qn** to do sb a favour; (*objet: s'avérer utile*) to come in useful *ou* handy for sb; **mettre en ~** to put into service *ou* operation; **~ compris/non compris** service included/not included; **hors ~** out of order; **service après vente** after sales service; **service d'ordre** police (*ou* stewards) in charge of maintaining order; **service militaire** military service; *see note*; **services secrets** secret service *sg*

**serviette** [servjɛt] *nf* (*de table*) (table) napkin, serviette; (*de toilette*) towel; (*porte-documents*) briefcase; **serviette hygiénique** sanitary towel

**servir** [servir] *vt* to serve; (*au restaurant*) to wait on; (*au magasin*) to serve, attend to ▷ *vi* (*Tennis*) to serve; (*Cartes*) to deal; **se servir** *vi* (*prendre d'un plat*) to help o.s.; **vous êtes servi?** are you being served?; **~ à qn** (*diplôme, livre*) to be of use to sb; **~ à qch/faire** (*outil etc*) to be used for sth/doing; **ça ne sert à rien** it's no use; **~ (à qn) de** to serve as (for sb); **se ~ de** (*plat*) to help o.s. to;

(*voiture, outil, relations*) to use; **sers-toi!** help yourself!

**serviteur** [sɛʁvitœʁ] nm servant

**ses** [se] adj voir **son¹**

**seuil** [sœj] nm doorstep; (*fig*) threshold

**seul, e** [sœl] adj (*sans compagnie*) alone; (*unique*): **un ~ livre** only one book, a single book ▷ adv (*vivre*) alone, on one's own ▷ nm, nf: **il en reste un(e) ~(e)** there's only one left; **le ~ livre** the only book; **parler tout ~** to talk to oneself; **faire qch (tout) ~** to do sth (all) on one's own ou (all) by oneself; **à lui (tout) ~** single-handed, on his own; **se sentir ~** to feel lonely; **seulement** adv only; **non seulement ... mais aussi** ou **encore** not only ... but also

**sève** [sɛv] nf sap

**sévère** [sevɛʁ] adj severe

**sexe** [sɛks] nm sex; (*organes génitaux*) genitals, sex organs; **sexuel, le** adj sexual

**shampooing** [ʃɑ̃pwɛ̃] nm shampoo

**Shetland** [ʃɛtlɑ̃d] n: **les îles ~** the Shetland Islands, Shetland

**short** [ʃɔʁt] nm (pair of) shorts pl

○ **MOT-CLÉ**

**si** [si] adv **1** (*oui*) yes; **"Paul n'est pas venu" — "si!"** "Paul hasn't come" — "yes, he has!"; **je vous assure que si** I assure you he did ou she is etc
**2** (*tellement*) so; **si gentil/rapidement** so kind/fast; **(tant et) si bien que** so much so that; **si rapide qu'il soit** however fast he may be
▷ conj if; **si tu veux** if you want; **je me demande si** I wonder if ou whether; **si seulement** if only
▷ nm (*Mus*) B; (*en chantant la gamme*) ti

**Sicile** [sisil] nf: **la ~** Sicily

**SIDA** [sida] sigle m (= syndrome immuno-déficitaire acquis) AIDS sg

**sidéré, e** [sideʁe] adj staggered

**sidérurgie** [sideʁyʁʒi] nf steel industry

**siècle** [sjɛkl] nm century

**siège** [sjɛʒ] nm seat; (*d'entreprise*) head office; (*d'organisation*) headquarters pl; (*Mil*) siege; **siège social** registered office; **siéger** vi to sit

**sien, ne** [sjɛ̃, sjɛn] pron: **le(la) ~(ne), les ~(ne)s** (*homme*) his; (*femme*) hers; (*chose, animal*) its

**sieste** [sjɛst] nf (afternoon) snooze ou nap; **faire la ~** to have a snooze ou nap

**sifflement** [sifləmɑ̃] nm: **un ~** a whistle

**siffler** [sifle] vi (*gén*) to whistle; (*en respirant, vapeur*) to wheeze; (*serpent, vapeur*) to hiss ▷ vt (*chanson*) to whistle; (*chien etc*) to whistle for; (*fille*) to whistle at; (*pièce, orateur*) to hiss, boo; (*fin du match, départ*) to blow one's whistle for; (*fam: verre*) to guzzle

**sifflet** [siflɛ] nm whistle; **coup de ~** whistle

**siffloter** [siflɔte] vi, vt to whistle

**sigle** [sigl] nm acronym

**signal, -aux** [siɲal, o] nm signal; (*indice, écriteau*) sign; **donner le ~ de** to give the signal for; **signal d'alarme** alarm signal; **signalement** nm description, particulars pl

**signaler** [siɲale] vt to indicate; (*personne: faire un signe*) to signal; (*vol, perte*) to report; (*faire remarquer*): **~ qch à qn/(à qn) que** to point out sth to sb/(to sb) that; **je voudrais ~ un vol** I'd like to report a theft

**signature** [siɲatyʁ] nf signature; (*action*) signing

**signe** [siɲ] nm sign; (*Typo*) mark; **faire un ~ de la main** to give a sign with one's hand; **faire ~ à qn** (*fig: contacter*) to get in touch with sb; **faire ~ à qn d'entrer** to motion (to) sb to come in; **signer** vt to sign; **se signer** vi to cross o.s.; **où dois-je signer?** where do I sign?

**significatif, -ive** [siɲifikatif, iv] adj significant

**signification** [siɲifikasjɔ̃] nf meaning

**signifier** [siɲifje] vt (*vouloir dire*) to mean; (*faire connaître*): **~ qch (à qn)** to make sth known (to sb)

**silence** [silɑ̃s] *nm* silence; (*Mus*) rest; **garder le ~** to keep silent, say nothing; **silencieux, -euse** *adj* quiet, silent ▷ *nm* silencer

**silhouette** [silwɛt] *nf* outline, silhouette; (*allure*) figure

**sillage** [sijaʒ] *nm* wake

**sillon** [sijɔ̃] *nm* furrow; (*de disque*) groove; **sillonner** *vt* to criss-cross

**simagrées** [simagʀe] *nfpl* fuss *sg*

**similaire** [similɛʀ] *adj* similar; **similicuir** *nm* imitation leather; **similitude** *nf* similarity

**simple** [sɛ̃pl] *adj* simple; (*non multiple*) single ▷ *nm*: **~ messieurs/dames** men's/ladies' singles *sg* ▷ *nm/f*: **~ d'esprit** simpleton

**simplicité** [sɛ̃plisite] *nf* simplicity; **en toute ~** quite simply

**simplifier** [sɛ̃plifje] *vt* to simplify

**simuler** [simyle] *vt* to sham, simulate

**simultané, e** [simyltane] *adj* simultaneous

**sincère** [sɛ̃sɛʀ] *adj* sincere; **sincèrement** *adv* sincerely; (*pour parler franchement*) honestly, really; **sincérité** *nf* sincerity

**Singapour** [sɛ̃gapuʀ] *nm* Singapore

**singe** [sɛ̃ʒ] *nm* monkey; (*de grande taille*) ape; **singer** *vt* to ape, mimic; **singeries** *nfpl* antics

**singulariser** [sɛ̃gylaʀize]: **se singulariser** *vi* to call attention to o.s.

**singularité** [sɛ̃gylaʀite] *nf* peculiarity

**singulier, -ière** [sɛ̃gylje, jɛʀ] *adj* remarkable, singular ▷ *nm* singular

**sinistre** [sinistʀ] *adj* sinister ▷ *nm* (*incendie*) blaze; (*catastrophe*) disaster; (*Assurances*) damage (*giving rise to a claim*); **sinistré, e** *adj* disaster-stricken ▷ *nm/f* disaster victim

**sinon** [sinɔ̃] *conj* (*autrement, sans quoi*) otherwise, or else; (*sauf*) except, other than; (*si ce n'est*) if not

**sinueux, -euse** [sinɥø, øz] *adj* winding

**sinus** [sinys] *nm* (*Anat*) sinus; (*Géom*)

sine; **sinusite** *nf* sinusitis

**sirène** [siʀɛn] *nf* siren; **sirène d'alarme** fire alarm; (*en temps de guerre*) air-raid siren

**sirop** [siʀo] *nm* (*à diluer: de fruit etc*) syrup; (*pharmaceutique*) syrup, mixture; **~ pour la toux** cough mixture

**siroter** [siʀote] *vt* to sip

**sismique** [sismik] *adj* seismic

**site** [sit] *nm* (*paysage, environnement*) setting; (*d'une ville etc: emplacement*) site; **site (pittoresque)** beauty spot; **sites touristiques** places of interest; **site Web** (*Inform*) website

**sitôt** [sito] *adv*: **~ parti** as soon as he *etc* had left; **~ que** as soon as; **pas de ~** not for a long time

**situation** [sitɥasjɔ̃] *nf* situation; (*d'un édifice, d'une ville*) position, location; **situation de famille** marital status

**situé, e** [sitɥe] *adj* situated

**situer** [sitɥe] *vt* to site, situate; (*en pensée*) to set, place; **se situer** *vi* to be situated

**six** [sis] *num* six; **sixième** *num* sixth ▷ *nf* (*Scol*) year 7 (BRIT), sixth grade (US)

**skaï®** [skaj] *nm* Leatherette®

**ski** [ski] *nm* (*objet*) ski; (*sport*) skiing; **faire du ~** to ski; **ski de fond** cross-country skiing; **ski nautique** water-skiing; **ski de piste** downhill skiing; **ski de randonnée** cross-country skiing; **skier** *vi* to ski; **skieur, -euse** *nm/f* skier

**slip** [slip] *nm* (*sous-vêtement*) pants *pl*, briefs *pl*; (*de bain: d'homme*) trunks *pl*; (*: du bikini*) (bikini) briefs *pl*

**slogan** [slogɑ̃] *nm* slogan

**Slovaquie** [slɔvaki] *nf*: **la ~** Slovakia

**SMIC** [smik] *sigle m* = **salaire minimum interprofessionnel de croissance**

**smoking** [smɔkiŋ] *nm* dinner *ou* evening suit

**SMS** *sigle m* (= *short message service*) (*service*) SMS; (*message*) text message

**SNCF** *sigle f* (= *Société nationale des chemins de fer français*) French railways

**snob** [snɔb] *adj* snobbish ▷ *nm/f* snob; **snobisme** *nm* snobbery, snobbishness

**sobre** [sɔbʀ] *adj* (*personne*) temperate, abstemious; (*élégance, style*) sober

**sobriquet** [sɔbʀikɛ] *nm* nickname

**social, e, -aux** [sɔsjal, jo] *adj* social

**socialisme** [sɔsjalism] *nm* socialism; **socialiste** *nm/f* socialist

**société** [sɔsjete] *nf* society; (*sportive*) club; (*Comm*) company; **la ~ de consommation** the consumer society; **société anonyme** ≈ limited (BRIT) *ou* incorporated (US) company

**sociologie** [sɔsjɔlɔʒi] *nf* sociology

**socle** [sɔkl] *nm* (*de colonne, statue*) plinth, pedestal; (*de lampe*) base

**socquette** [sɔkɛt] *nf* ankle sock

**sœur** [sœʀ] *nf* sister; (*religieuse*) nun, sister

**soi** [swa] *pron* oneself; **en ~** (*intrinsèquement*) in itself; **cela va de ~** that *ou* it goes without saying; **soi-disant** *adj inv* so-called ▷ *adv* supposedly

**soie** [swa] *nf* silk; **soierie** *nf* (*tissu*) silk

**soif** [swaf] *nf* thirst; **avoir ~** to be thirsty; **donner ~ à qn** to make sb thirsty

**soigné, e** [swaɲe] *adj* (*tenue*) well-groomed, neat; (*travail*) careful, meticulous

**soigner** [swaɲe] *vt* (*malade, maladie: suj: docteur*) to treat; (*suj: infirmière, mère*) to nurse, look after; (*travail, détails*) to take care over; (*jardin, invités*) to look after; **soigneux, -euse** *adj* (*propre*) tidy, neat; (*appliqué*) painstaking, careful

**soi-même** [swamɛm] *pron* oneself

**soin** [swɛ̃] *nm* (*application*) care; (*propreté, ordre*) tidiness, neatness; **soins** *nmpl* (*à un malade, blessé*) treatment *sg*, medical attention *sg*; (*hygiène*) care *sg*; **prendre ~ de** to take care of, look after; **prendre ~ de faire** to take care to do; **les premiers ~s** first aid *sg*

**soir** [swaʀ] *nm* evening; **ce ~** this evening, tonight; **à ce ~!** see you this evening (*ou* tonight)!; **sept/dix heures du ~** seven in the evening/ten at night; **demain ~** tomorrow evening, tomorrow night; **soirée** *nf* evening; (*réception*) party

**soit**[1] [swa] *vb voir* **être** ▷ *conj* (*à savoir*) namely; (*ou*) **~ ... ~** either ... or; **~ que ... ~ que ou ou que** whether ... or whether

**soit**[2] [swat] *adv* so be it, very well

**soixantaine** [swasɑ̃tɛn] *nf*: **une ~ (de)** sixty or so, about sixty; **avoir la ~** (*âge*) to be around sixty

**soixante** [swasɑ̃t] *num* sixty; **soixante-dix** *num* seventy

**soja** [sɔʒa] *nm* soya; (*graines*) soya beans *pl*; **germes de ~** beansprouts

**sol** [sɔl] *nm* ground; (*de logement*) floor; (*Agr*) soil; (*Mus*) G; (: *en chantant la gamme*) so(h)

**solaire** [sɔlɛʀ] *adj* (*énergie etc*) solar; (*crème etc*) sun *cpd*

**soldat** [sɔlda] *nm* soldier

**solde** [sɔld] *nf* pay ▷ *nm* (*Comm*) balance; **soldes** *nm ou f pl* (*articles*) sale goods; (*vente*) sales; **en ~** at sale price; **solder** *vt* (*marchandise*) to sell at sale price, sell off

**sole** [sɔl] *nf* sole *inv* (*fish*)

**soleil** [sɔlɛj] *nm* sun; (*lumière*) sun(light); (*temps ensoleillé*) sun(shine); **il fait du ~** it's sunny; **au ~** in the sun

**solennel, le** [sɔlanɛl] *adj* solemn

**solfège** [sɔlfɛʒ] *nm* musical theory

**solidaire** [sɔlidɛʀ] *adj*: **être ~s** to show solidarity, stand *ou* stick together; **être ~ de** (*collègues*) to stand by; **solidarité** *nf* solidarity; **par solidarité (avec)** in sympathy (with)

**solide** [sɔlid] *adj* solid; (*mur, maison, meuble*) solid, sturdy; (*connaissances, argument*) sound; (*personne, estomac*) robust, sturdy ▷ *nm* solid

**soliste** [sɔlist] *nm/f* soloist

**solitaire** [sɔlitɛʀ] *adj* (*sans compagnie*) solitary, lonely; (*lieu*) lonely ▷ *nm/f* (*ermite*) recluse; (*fig: ours*) loner

**solitude** [sɔlityd] *nf* loneliness; (*tranquillité*) solitude

**solliciter** [sɔlisite] *vt* (*personne*) to appeal to; (*emploi, faveur*) to seek

**sollicitude** [sɔlisityd] *nf* concern

**soluble** [sɔlybl] *adj* soluble

**solution** [sɔlysjɔ̃] *nf* solution; **solution de facilité** easy way out

**solvable** [sɔlvabl] *adj* solvent

**sombre** [sɔ̃bʀ] *adj* dark; (*fig*) gloomy; **sombrer** *vi* (*bateau*) to sink; **sombrer dans** (*misère, désespoir*) to sink into

**sommaire** [sɔmɛʀ] *adj* (*simple*) basic; (*expéditif*) summary ▷ *nm* summary

**somme** [sɔm] *nf* (*Math*) sum; (*quantité*) amount; (*argent*) sum, amount ▷ *nm*: **faire un ~** to have a (short) nap; **en ~** all in all; **~ toute** all in all

**sommeil** [sɔmɛj] *nm* sleep; **avoir ~** to be sleepy; **sommeiller** *vi* to doze

**sommet** [sɔmɛ] *nm* top; (*d'une montagne*) summit, top; (*fig: de la perfection, gloire*) height

**sommier** [sɔmje] *nm* (bed) base

**somnambule** [sɔmnɑ̃byl] *nm/f* sleepwalker

**somnifère** [sɔmnifɛʀ] *nm* sleeping drug *no pl* (*ou* pill)

**somnoler** [sɔmnɔle] *vi* to doze

**somptueux, -euse** [sɔ̃ptɥø, øz] *adj* sumptuous

**son¹, sa** [sɔ̃, sa] (*pl* **ses**) *adj* (*antécédent humain: mâle*) his; (: *femelle*) her; (: *valeur indéfinie*) one's, his/her; (*antécédent non humain*) its

**son²** [sɔ̃] *nm* sound; (*de blé*) bran

**sondage** [sɔ̃daʒ] *nm*: **sondage (d'opinion)** (opinion) poll

**sonde** [sɔ̃d] *nf* (*Navig*) lead *ou* sounding line; (*Méd*) probe; (*Tech: de forage*) borer, driller

**sonder** [sɔ̃de] *vt* (*Navig*) to sound; (*Tech*) to bore, drill; (*fig: personne*) to sound out; **~ le terrain** (*fig*) to test the ground

**songe** [sɔ̃ʒ] *nm* dream; **songer** *vi*: **songer à** (*penser à*) to think over; (*envisager*) to consider, think of; **songer que** to think that; **songeur, -euse** *adj* pensive

**sonnant, e** [sɔnɑ̃, ɑ̃t] *adj*: **à 8 heures ~es** on the stroke of 8

**sonné, e** [sɔne] *adj* (*fam*) cracked; **il est**

**midi ~** it's gone twelve

**sonner** [sɔne] *vi* to ring ▷ *vt* (*cloche*) to ring; (*glas, tocsin*) to sound; (*portier, infirmière*) to ring for; **~ faux** (*instrument*) to sound out of tune; (*rire*) to ring false

**sonnerie** [sɔnʀi] *nf* (*son*) ringing; (*sonnette*) bell; (*de portable*) ringtone; **sonnerie d'alarme** alarm bell

**sonnette** [sɔnɛt] *nf* bell; **sonnette d'alarme** alarm bell

**sonore** [sɔnɔʀ] *adj* (*voix*) sonorous, ringing; (*salle*) resonant; (*film, signal*) sound *cpd*; **sonorisation** *nf* (*équipement: de salle de conférences*) public address system, P.A. system; (: *de discothèque*) sound system; **sonorité** *nf* (*de piano, violon*) tone; (*d'une salle*) acoustics *pl*

**sophistiqué, e** [sɔfistike] *adj* sophisticated

**sorbet** [sɔʀbɛ] *nm* water ice, sorbet

**sorcier** [sɔʀsje] *nm* sorcerer

**sordide** [sɔʀdid] *adj* (*lieu*) squalid; (*action*) sordid

**sort** [sɔʀ] *nm* (*destinée*) fate; (*condition*) lot; (*magique*) curse, spell; **tirer au ~** to draw lots

**sorte** [sɔʀt] *nf* sort, kind; **de la ~** in that way; **de (telle) ~ que** so that; **en quelque ~** in a way; **faire en ~ que** to see to it that; **quelle ~ de ...?** what kind of ...?

**sortie** [sɔʀti] *nf* (*issue*) way out, exit; (*remarque drôle*) sally; (*promenade*) outing; (*le soir: au restaurant etc*) night out; (*Comm: d'un disque*) release; (: *d'un livre*) publication; (: *d'un modèle*) launching; **où est la ~?** where's the exit?; **sortie de bain** (*vêtement*) bathrobe

**sortilège** [sɔʀtilɛʒ] *nm* (magic) spell

**sortir** [sɔʀtiʀ] *vi* (*gén*) to come out; (*partir, se promener, aller au spectacle*) to go out; (*numéro gagnant*) to come up ▷ *vt* (*gén*) to take out; (*produit, modèle*) to bring out; (*fam: dire*) to come out with; **~ avec qn** to be going out with sb; **s'en ~** (*malade*) to pull through;

(d'une difficulté etc) to get through; **~ de** (endroit) to go (ou come) out of, leave; (provenir de) to come from; (compétence) to be outside

**sosie** [sɔzi] nm double

**sot, sotte** [so, sɔt] adj silly, foolish ▷ nm/f fool; **sottise** nf (caractère) silliness, foolishness; (action) silly ou foolish thing

**sou** [su] nm: **près de ses ~s** tight-fisted; **sans le ~** penniless

**soubresaut** [subʀəso] nm start; (cahot) jolt

**souche** [suʃ] nf (d'arbre) stump; (de carnet) counterfoil (BRIT), stub

**souci** [susi] nm (inquiétude) worry; (préoccupation) concern; (Bot) marigold; **se faire du ~** to worry; **soucier: se soucier de** vt to care about; **soucieux, -euse** adj concerned, worried

**soucoupe** [sukup] nf saucer; **soucoupe volante** flying saucer

**soudain, e** [sudɛ̃, ɛn] adj (douleur, mort) sudden ▷ adv suddenly, all of a sudden

**Soudan** [sudɑ̃] nm: **le ~** Sudan

**soude** [sud] nf soda

**souder** [sude] vt (avec fil à souder) to solder; (par soudure autogène) to weld; (fig) to bind together

**soudure** [sudyʀ] nf soldering; welding; (joint) soldered joint; weld

**souffle** [sufl] nm (en expirant) breath; (en soufflant) puff, blow; (respiration) breathing; (d'explosion, de ventilateur) blast; (du vent) blowing; **être à bout de ~** to be out of breath; **un ~ d'air** a breath of air

**soufflé, e** [sufle] adj (fam: stupéfié) staggered ▷ nm (Culin) soufflé

**souffler** [sufle] vi (gén) to blow; (haleter) to puff (and blow) ▷ vt (feu, bougie) to blow out; (chasser: poussière etc) to blow away; (Tech: verre) to blow; (dire): **~ qch à qn** to whisper sth to sb

**souffrance** [sufʀɑ̃s] nf suffering; **en ~** (affaire) pending

**souffrant, e** [sufʀɑ̃, ɑ̃t] adj unwell

**souffre-douleur** [sufʀədulœʀ] nm inv butt, underdog

**souffrir** [sufʀiʀ] vi to suffer, be in pain ▷ vt to suffer, endure; (supporter) to bear, stand; **~ de** (maladie, froid) to suffer from; **elle ne peut pas le ~** she can't stand ou bear him

**soufre** [sufʀ] nm sulphur

**souhait** [swɛ] nm wish; **tous nos ~s pour la nouvelle année** (our) best wishes for the New Year; **à vos ~s!** bless you!; **souhaitable** adj desirable

**souhaiter** [swete] vt to wish for; **~ la bonne année à qn** to wish sb a happy New Year; **~ que** to hope that

**soûl, e** [su, sul] adj drunk ▷ nm: **tout son ~** to one's heart's content

**soulagement** [sulaʒmɑ̃] nm relief

**soulager** [sulaʒe] vt to relieve

**soûler** [sule] vt: **~ qn** to get sb drunk; (suj: boisson) to make sb drunk; (fig) to make sb's head spin ou reel; **se soûler** vi to get drunk

**soulever** [sul(ə)ve] vt to lift; (poussière) to send up; (enthousiasme) to arouse; (question, débat) to raise; **se soulever** vi (peuple) to rise up; (personne couchée) to lift o.s. up

**soulier** [sulje] nm shoe

**souligner** [suliɲe] vt to underline; (fig) to emphasize, stress

**soumettre** [sumɛtʀ] vt (pays) to subject, subjugate; (rebelle) to put down, subdue; **~ qch à qn** (projet etc) to submit sth to sb; **se soumettre (à)** to submit (to)

**soumis, e** [sumi, iz] adj submissive; **soumission** nf submission

**soupçon** [supsɔ̃] nm suspicion; (petite quantité): **un ~ de** a hint ou touch of; **soupçonner** vt to suspect; **soupçonneux, -euse** adj suspicious

**soupe** [sup] nf soup

**souper** [supe] vi to have supper ▷ nm supper

**soupeser** [supəze] vt to weigh in one's hand(s); (fig) to weigh up

**soupière** [supjɛʀ] nf (soup) tureen

**soupir** [supiʀ] nm sigh; **pousser un**

**~ de soulagement** to heave a sigh of relief

**soupirer** [supiʀe] *vi* to sigh

**souple** [supl] *adj* supple; (*fig: règlement, caractère*) flexible; (: *démarche, taille*) lithe, supple; **souplesse** *nf* suppleness; (*de caractère*) flexibility

**source** [suʀs] *nf* (*point d'eau*) spring; (*d'un cours d'eau, fig*) source; **de bonne ~** on good authority

**sourcil** [suʀsi] *nm* (eye)brow; **sourciller** *vi:* **sans sourciller** without turning a hair *ou* batting an eyelid

**sourd, e** [suʀ, suʀd] *adj* deaf; (*bruit*) muffled; (*douleur*) dull ▷ *nm/f* deaf person; **faire la ~e oreille** to turn a deaf ear; **sourdine** *nf* (*Mus*) mute; **en sourdine** softly, quietly; **sourd-muet, sourde-muette** *adj* deaf-and-dumb ▷ *nm/f* deaf-mute

**souriant, e** [suʀjɑ̃, jɑ̃t] *adj* cheerful

**sourire** [suʀiʀ] *nm* smile ▷ *vi* to smile; **~ à qn** to smile at sb; (*fig: plaire à*) to appeal to sb; (*suj: chance*) to smile on sb; **garder le ~** to keep smiling

**souris** [suʀi] *nf* mouse

**sournois, e** [suʀnwa, waz] *adj* deceitful, underhand

**sous** [su] *prép* under; **~ la pluie** in the rain; **~ terre** underground; **~ peu** shortly, before long; **sous-bois** *nm inv* undergrowth

**souscrire** [suskʀiʀ]: **~ à** *vt* to subscribe to

**sous...:** **sous-directeur, -trice** *nm/f* assistant manager(-manageress); **sous-entendre** *vt* to imply, infer; **sous-entendu, e** *adj* implied ▷ *nm* innuendo, insinuation; **sous-estimer** *vt* to underestimate; **sous-jacent, e** *adj* underlying; **sous-louer** *vt* to sublet; **sous-marin, e** *adj* (*flore, faune*) submarine; (*pêche*) underwater ▷ *nm* submarine; **sous-pull** *nm* thin poloneck jersey; **soussigné, e** *adj:* **je soussigné** I the undersigned; **sous-sol** *nm* basement; **sous-titre** *nm* subtitle

**soustraction** [sustʀaksjɔ̃] *nf* subtraction

**soustraire** [sustʀɛʀ] *vt* to subtract, take away; (*dérober*) **~ qch à qn** to remove sth from sb; **se soustraire à** (*autorité etc*) to elude, escape from

**sous...:** **sous-traitant** *nm* sub-contractor; **sous-traiter** *vt* to sub-contract; **sous-vêtements** *nmpl* underwear *sg*

**soutane** [sutan] *nf* cassock, soutane

**soute** [sut] *nf* hold

**soutenir** [sut(ə)niʀ] *vt* to support; (*assaut, choc*) to stand up to, withstand; (*intérêt, effort*) to keep up; (*assurer*) **~ que** to maintain that; **soutenu, e** *adj* (*efforts*) sustained, unflagging; (*style*) elevated

**souterrain, e** [suteʀɛ̃, ɛn] *adj* underground ▷ *nm* underground passage

**soutien** [sutjɛ̃] *nm* support; **soutien-gorge** *nm* bra

**soutirer** [sutiʀe] *vt:* **~ qch à qn** to squeeze *ou* get sth out of sb

**souvenir** [suv(ə)niʀ] *nm* (*réminiscence*) memory; (*objet*) souvenir ▷ *vb:* **se ~ de** to remember; **se ~ que** to remember that; **en ~ de** in memory *ou* remembrance of; **avec mes affectueux/meilleurs ~s, ...** with love from, .../regards, ...

**souvent** [suvɑ̃] *adv* often; **peu ~** seldom, infrequently

**souverain, e** [suv(ə)ʀɛ̃, ɛn] *nm/f* sovereign, monarch

**soyeux, -euse** [swajø, øz] *adj* silky

**spacieux, -euse** [spasjø, jøz] *adj* spacious, roomy

**spaghettis** [spageti] *nmpl* spaghetti *sg*

**sparadrap** [spaʀadʀa] *nm* sticking plaster (BRIT), Bandaid® (US)

**spatial, e, -aux** [spasjal, jo] *adj* (*Aviat*) space *cpd*

**speaker, ine** [spikœʀ, kʀin] *nm/f* announcer

**spécial, e, -aux** [spesjal, jo] *adj* special; (*bizarre*) peculiar; **spécialement** *adv* especially,

particularly; (*tout exprès*) specially;
**spécialiser: se spécialiser** vi to
specialize; **spécialiste** nm/f specialist;
**spécialité** nf speciality; (*branche*)
special field
**spécifier** [spesifje] vt to specify, state
**spécimen** [spesimɛn] nm specimen
**spectacle** [spɛktakl] nm (*scène*)
sight; (*représentation*) show; (*industrie*)
show business; **spectaculaire** adj
spectacular
**spectateur, -trice** [spɛktatœʀ,
tʀis] nm/f (*Cinéma etc*) member of
the audience; (*Sport*) spectator; (*d'un
événement*) onlooker, witness
**spéculer** [spekyle] vi to speculate
**spéléologie** [speleɔlɔʒi] nf potholing
**sperme** [spɛʀm] nm semen, sperm
**sphère** [sfɛʀ] nf sphere
**spirale** [spiʀal] nf spiral
**spirituel, le** [spiʀitɥɛl] adj spiritual;
(*fin, piquant*) witty
**splendide** [splãdid] adj splendid
**spontané, e** [spɔ̃tane] adj
spontaneous; **spontanéité** nf
spontaneity
**sport** [spɔʀ] nm sport ▷ adj inv
(*vêtement*) casual; **faire du ~** to do sport;
**sports d'hiver** winter sports; **sportif,
-ive** adj (*journal, association, épreuve*)
sports cpd; (*allure, démarche*) athletic;
(*attitude, esprit*) sporting
**spot** [spɔt] nm (*lampe*) spot(light);
(*annonce*); **spot (publicitaire)**
commercial (break)
**square** [skwaʀ] nm public garden(s)
**squelette** [skəlɛt] nm skeleton;
**squelettique** adj scrawny
**SRAS** [sʀas] sigle m (= *syndrome
respiratoire aigu sévère*) SARS
**Sri Lanka** [sʀilãka] nm: **le ~** Sri Lanka
**stabiliser** [stabilize] vt to stabilize
**stable** [stabl] adj stable, steady
**stade** [stad] nm (*Sport*) stadium; (*phase,
niveau*) stage
**stage** [staʒ] nm (*cours*) training course;
**~ de formation (professionnelle)**
vocational (training) course; **~ de**

**perfectionnement** advanced training
course; **stagiaire** nm/f, adj trainee
▌ Attention à ne pas traduire *stage*
par le mot anglais *stage*.
**stagner** [stagne] vi to stagnate
**stand** [stɑ̃d] nm (*d'exposition*) stand; (*de
foire*) stall; **stand de tir** (à la foire, Sport)
shooting range
**standard** [stɑ̃daʀ] adj inv standard
▷ nm switchboard; **standardiste** nm/f
switchboard operator
**standing** [stɑ̃diŋ] nm standing; **de
grand ~** luxury
**starter** [staʀtɛʀ] nm (*Auto*) choke
**station** [stasjɔ̃] nf station; (*de
bus*) stop; (*de villégiature*) resort;
**station de ski** ski resort; **station
de taxis** taxi rank (BRIT) ou stand
(US); **stationnement** nm parking;
**stationner** vi to park; **station-service**
nf service station
**statistique** [statistik] nf (*science*)
statistics sg; (*rapport, étude*) statistic
▷ adj statistical
**statue** [staty] nf statue
**statu quo** [statykwo] nm status quo
**statut** [staty] nm status; **statuts** nmpl
(*Jur, Admin*) statutes; **statutaire** adj
statutory
**Sté** abr = **société**
**steak** [stɛk] nm steak; **~ haché**
hamburger
**sténo(graphie)** [stenɔ(gʀafi)] nf
shorthand
**stérile** [steʀil] adj sterile
**stérilet** [steʀilɛ] nm coil, loop
**stériliser** [steʀilize] vt to sterilize
**stimulant** [stimylɑ̃] nm (*fig*) stimulus,
incentive; (*physique*) stimulant
**stimuler** [stimyle] vt to stimulate
**stipuler** [stipyle] vt to stipulate
**stock** [stɔk] nm stock; **stocker** vt to
stock
**stop** [stɔp] nm (*Auto: écriteau*) stop sign;
(: *feu arrière*) brake-light; **faire du ~**
(*fam*) to hitch(hike); **stopper** vt, vi to
stop, halt
**store** [stɔʀ] nm blind; (*de magasin*)

shade, awning

**strabisme** [strabism] nm squinting

**strapontin** [strapɔ̃tɛ̃] nm jump ou foldaway seat

**stratégie** [strateʒi] nf strategy; **stratégique** adj strategic

**stress** [stres] nm stress; **stressant, e** adj stressful; **stresser** vt: **stresser qn** to make sb (feel) tense

**strict, e** [strikt] adj strict; (tenue, décor) severe, plain; **le ~ nécessaire/ minimum** the bare essentials/ minimum

**strident, e** [stridɑ̃, ɑ̃t] adj shrill, strident

**strophe** [strof] nf verse, stanza

**structure** [stryktyr] nf structure; **~s d'accueil** reception facilities

**studieux, -euse** [stydjø, jøz] adj studious

**studio** [stydjo] nm (logement) (one-roomed) flatlet (BRIT) ou apartment (US); (d'artiste, TV etc) studio

**stupéfait, e** [stypefɛ, ɛt] adj astonished

**stupéfiant, e** [stypefjɑ̃, jɑ̃t] adj (étonnant) stunning, astounding ▷ nm (Méd) drug, narcotic

**stupéfier** [stypefje] vt (étonner) to stun, astonish

**stupeur** [stypœr] nf astonishment

**stupide** [stypid] adj stupid; **stupidité** nf stupidity; (parole, acte) stupid thing (to do ou say)

**style** [stil] nm style

**stylé, e** [stile] adj well-trained

**styliste** [stilist] nm/f designer

**stylo** [stilo] nm: **~ (à encre)** (fountain) pen; **stylo (à) bille** ball-point pen

**su, e** [sy] pp de **savoir** ▷ nm: **au su de** with the knowledge of

**suave** [sɥav] adj sweet

**subalterne** [sybaltɛrn] adj (employé, officier) junior; (rôle) subordinate, subsidiary ▷ nm/f subordinate

**subconscient** [sypkɔ̃sjɑ̃] nm subconscious

**subir** [sybir] vt (affront, dégâts) to suffer;

(opération, châtiment) to undergo

**subit, e** [sybi, it] adj sudden; **subitement** adv suddenly, all of a sudden

**subjectif, -ive** [sybʒɛktif, iv] adj subjective

**subjonctif** [sybʒɔ̃ktif] nm subjunctive

**subjuguer** [sybʒyge] vt to captivate

**submerger** [sybmɛrʒe] vt to submerge; (fig) to overwhelm

**subordonné, e** [sybɔrdɔne] adj, nm/f subordinate

**subrepticement** [sybrɛptismɑ̃] adv surreptitiously

**subside** [sybzid] nm grant

**subsidiaire** [sybzidjɛr] adj: **question ~** deciding question

**subsister** [sybziste] vi (rester) to remain, subsist; (survivre) to live on

**substance** [sypstɑ̃s] nf substance

**substituer** [sypstitɥe] vt: **~ qn/qch à** to substitute sb/sth for; **se ~ à qn** (évincer) to substitute o.s. for sb

**substitut** [sypstity] nm (succédané) substitute

**subterfuge** [sybtɛrfyʒ] nm subterfuge

**subtil, e** [sybtil] adj subtle

**subvenir** [sybvənir] vt: **~ à** to meet

**subvention** [sybvɑ̃sjɔ̃] nf subsidy, grant; **subventionner** vt to subsidize

**suc** [syk] nm (Bot) sap; (de viande, fruit) juice

**succéder** [syksede] vt: **~ à** vt to succeed; **se succéder** vi (accidents, années) to follow one another

**succès** [syksɛ] nm success; **avoir du ~** to be a success, be successful; **à ~** successful; **succès de librairie** bestseller

**successeur** [syksesœr] nm successor

**successif, -ive** [syksesif, iv] adj successive

**succession** [syksesjɔ̃] nf (série, Pol) succession; (Jur: patrimoine) estate, inheritance

**succomber** [sykɔ̃be] vi to die, succumb; (fig): **~ à** to succumb to

**succulent, e** [sykylɑ̃, ɑ̃t] adj (repas,

*mets*) delicious
**succursale** [sykyʀsal] *nf* branch
**sucer** [syse] *vt* to suck; **sucette** *nf* (*bonbon*) lollipop; (*de bébé*) dummy (BRIT), pacifier (US)
**sucre** [sykʀ] *nm* (*substance*) sugar; (*morceau*) lump of sugar, sugar lump *ou* cube; **sucre d'orge** barley sugar; **sucre en morceaux/cristallisé/en poudre** lump/granulated/caster sugar; **sucre glace** icing sugar (BRIT), confectioner's sugar (US); **sucré, e** *adj* (*produit alimentaire*) sweetened; (*au goût*) sweet; **sucrer** *vt* (*thé, café*) to sweeten, put sugar in; **sucreries** *nfpl* (*bonbons*) sweets, sweet things; **sucrier** *nm* (*récipient*) sugar bowl
**sud** [syd] *nm*: **le ~** the south ▷ *adj inv* south; (*côte*) south, southern; **au ~** (*situation*) in the south; (*direction*) to the south; **au ~ de** (to the) south of; **sud-africain, e** *adj* South African ▷ *nm/f*: **Sud-Africain, e** South African; **sud-américain, e** *adj* South American ▷ *nm/f*: **Sud-Américain, e** South American; **sud-est** *nm, adj inv* south-east; **sud-ouest** *nm, adj inv* south-west
**Suède** [sɥɛd] *nf*: **la ~** Sweden; **suédois, e** *adj* Swedish ▷ *nm/f*: **Suédois, e** Swede ▷ *nm* (*Ling*) Swedish
**suer** [sɥe] *vi* to sweat; (*suinter*) to ooze; **sueur** *nf* sweat; **en sueur** sweating, in a sweat; **donner des sueurs froides à qn** to put sb in(to) a cold sweat
**suffire** [syfiʀ] *vi* (*être assez*): **~ (à qn/ pour qch/pour faire)** to be enough *ou* sufficient (for sb/for sth/to do); **il suffit d'une négligence ...** it only takes an act of carelessness ...; **il suffit qu'on oublie pour que ...** one only needs to forget for ...; **ça suffit!** that's enough!
**suffisamment** [syfizamɑ̃] *adv* sufficiently, enough; **~ de** sufficient, enough
**suffisant, e** [syfizɑ̃, ɑ̃t] *adj* sufficient; (*résultats*) satisfactory; (*vaniteux*) self-important, bumptious
**suffixe** [syfiks] *nm* suffix

**suffoquer** [syfɔke] *vt* to choke, suffocate; (*stupéfier*) to stagger, astound ▷ *vi* to choke, suffocate
**suffrage** [syfʀaʒ] *nm* (*Pol: voix*) vote
**suggérer** [sygʒeʀe] *vt* to suggest; **suggestion** *nf* suggestion
**suicide** [sɥisid] *nm* suicide; **suicider**: **se suicider** *vi* to commit suicide
**suie** [sɥi] *nf* soot
**suisse** [sɥis] *adj* Swiss ▷ *nm*: **S~** Swiss *pl inv* ▷ *nf*: **la S~** Switzerland; **la S~ romande/allemande** French-speaking/German-speaking Switzerland
**suite** [sɥit] *nf* (*continuation: d'énumération etc*) rest, remainder; (: *de feuilleton*) continuation; (: *film etc sur le même thème*) sequel; (*série*) series, succession; (*conséquence*) result; (*ordre, liaison logique*) coherence; (*appartement, Mus*) suite; (*escorte*) retinue, suite; **suites** *nfpl* (*d'une maladie etc*) effects; **prendre la ~ de** (*directeur etc*) to succeed, take over from; **donner ~ à** (*requête, projet*) to follow up; **faire ~ à** to follow; **(faisant) ~ à votre lettre du ...** further to your letter of the ...; **de ~** (*d'affilée*) in succession; (*immédiatement*) at once; **par la ~** afterwards, subsequently; **à la ~** one after the other; **à la ~ de** (*derrière*) behind; (*en conséquence de*) following
**suivant, e** [sɥivɑ̃, ɑ̃t] *adj* next, following ▷ *prép* (*selon*) according to; **au ~!** next!
**suivi, e** [sɥivi] *adj* (*effort, qualité*) consistent; (*cohérent*) coherent; **très/ peu ~** (*cours*) well-/poorly-attended
**suivre** [sɥivʀ] *vt* (*gén*) to follow; (*Scol: cours*) to attend; (*comprendre*) to keep up with; (*Comm: article*) to continue to stock ▷ *vi* to follow; (*élève: assimiler*) to keep up; **se suivre** *vi* (*accidents etc*) to follow one after the other; **faire ~** (*lettre*) to forward; **"à ~"** "to be continued"
**sujet, te** [syʒɛ, ɛt] *adj*: **être ~ à** (*vertige etc*) to be liable *ou* subject to ▷ *nm/f*

(*d'un souverain*) subject ▷ *nm* subject;
**au ~ de** about; **sujet de conversation**
topic *ou* subject of conversation;
**sujet d'examen** (*Scol*) examination
question

**super** [sypɛʀ] (*fam*) *adj inv* terrific,
great, fantastic, super

**superbe** [sypɛʀb] *adj* magnificent,
superb

**superficie** [sypɛʀfisi] *nf* (surface) area

**superficiel, le** [sypɛʀfisjɛl] *adj*
superficial

**superflu, e** [sypɛʀfly] *adj* superfluous

**supérieur, e** [sypeʀjœʀ] *adj* (*lèvre,*
*étages, classes*) upper; (*plus élevé:*
*température, niveau, enseignement*): **~ (à)**
higher (than); (*meilleur: qualité, produit*):
**~ (à)** superior (to); (*excellent, hautain*)
superior ▷ *nm, nf* superior; **supériorité**
*nf* superiority

**supermarché** [sypɛʀmaʀʃe] *nm*
supermarket

**superposer** [sypɛʀpoze] *vt* (*faire*
*chevaucher*) to superimpose; **lits**
**superposés** bunk beds

**superpuissance** [sypɛʀpɥisɑ̃s] *nf*
super-power

**superstitieux, -euse** [sypɛʀstisjø,
jøz] *adj* superstitious

**superviser** [sypɛʀvize] *vt* to
supervise

**supplanter** [syplɑ̃te] *vt* to supplant

**suppléant, e** [sypleɑ̃, -ɑ̃t] *adj*
(*professeur*) supply *cpd*; (*juge,*
*fonctionnaire*) deputy *cpd* ▷ *nm/f*
(*professeur*) supply teacher

**suppléer** [syplee] *vt* (*ajouter: mot*
*manquant etc*) to supply, provide;
(*compenser: lacune*) to fill in; **~ à** to
make up for

**supplément** [syplemɑ̃] *nm*
supplement; (*de frites etc*) extra portion;
**un ~ de travail** extra *ou* additional
work; **payer un ~** to pay an additional
charge; **le vin est en ~** wine is extra;
**supplémentaire** *adj* additional,
further; (*train, bus*) relief *cpd*, extra

**supplications** [syplikasjɔ̃] *nfpl* pleas,

entreaties

**supplice** [syplis] *nm* torture *no pl*

**supplier** [syplije] *vt* to implore,
beseech

**support** [sypɔʀ] *nm* support;
(*publicitaire*) medium; (*audio-visuel*) aid

**supportable** [sypɔʀtabl] *adj* (*douleur*)
bearable

**supporter¹** [sypɔʀtɛʀ] *nm* supporter,
fan

**supporter²** [sypɔʀte] *vt* (*conséquences,*
*épreuve*) to bear, endure; (*défauts,*
*personne*) to put up with; (*suj: chose:*
*chaleur etc*) to withstand; (: *personne:*
*chaleur, vin*) to be able to take

⎸ Attention à ne pas traduire
*supporter* par *to support*.

**supposer** [sypoze] *vt* to suppose;
(*impliquer*) to presuppose; **à ~ que**
supposing (that)

**suppositoire** [sypozitwaʀ] *nm*
suppository

**suppression** [sypʀesjɔ̃] *nf* (*voir*
*supprimer*) cancellation; removal;
deletion

**supprimer** [sypʀime] *vt* (*congés,*
*service d'autobus etc*) to cancel; (*emplois,*
*privilèges, témoin gênant*) to do away
with; (*cloison, cause, anxiété*) to remove;
(*clause, mot*) to delete

**suprême** [sypʀɛm] *adj* supreme

⬤ **MOT-CLÉ**

**sur** [syʀ] *prép* **1** (*position*) on; (*par-dessus*)
over; (*au-dessus*) above; **pose-le sur**
**la table** put it on the table; **je n'ai**
**pas d'argent sur moi** I haven't any
money on me
**2** (*direction*) towards; **en allant sur**
**Paris** going towards Paris; **sur votre**
**droite** on *ou* to your right
**3** (*à propos de*) on, about; **un livre/une**
**conférence sur Balzac** a book/lecture
on *ou* about Balzac
**4** (*proportion*) out of; **un sur 10** one in
10; (*Scol*) one out of 10
**5** (*mesures*) by; **4 m sur 2** 4 m by 2

**6** (*succession*): **avoir accident sur accident** to have one accident after the other

**sûr, e** [syʀ] *adj* sure, certain; (*digne de confiance*) reliable; (*sans danger*) safe; (*diagnostic, goût*) reliable; **le plus ~ est de** the safest thing is to; **sûr de soi** self-assured, self-confident
**surcharge** [syʀʃaʀʒ] *nf* (*de passagers, marchandises*) excess load; **surcharger** *vt* to overload
**surcroît** [syʀkʀwa] *nm*: **un ~ de** additional +*nom*; **par** *ou* **de ~** moreover; **en ~** in addition
**surdité** [syʀdite] *nf* deafness
**sûrement** [syʀmã] *adv* (*certainement*) certainly; (*sans risques*) safely
**surenchère** [syʀɑ̃ʃɛʀ] *nf* (*aux enchères*) higher bid; **surenchérir** *vi* to bid higher; (*fig*) to try and outbid each other
**surestimer** [syʀɛstime] *vt* to overestimate
**sûreté** [syʀte] *nf* (*sécurité*) safety; (*exactitude: de renseignements etc*) reliability; (*d'un geste*) steadiness; **mettre en ~** to put in a safe place; **pour plus de ~** as an extra precaution, to be on the safe side
**surf** [sœʀf] *nm* surfing
**surface** [syʀfas] *nf* surface; (*superficie*) surface area; **une grande ~** a supermarket; **faire ~** to surface; **en ~** near the surface; (*fig*) superficially
**surfait, e** [syʀfɛ, ɛt] *adj* overrated
**surfer** [syʀfe] *vi*: **~ sur Internet** to surf *ou* browse the Internet
**surgelé, e** [syʀʒəle] *adj* (deep-)frozen ▷ *nm*: **les ~s** (deep-)frozen food
**surgir** [syʀʒiʀ] *vi* to appear suddenly; (*fig: problème, conflit*) to arise
**sur...**: **surhumain, e** *adj* superhuman; **sur-le-champ** *adv* immediately; **surlendemain** *nm*: **le surlendemain (soir)** two days later (in the evening); **le surlendemain de** two days after; **surmenage** *nm* overwork(ing);

**surmener**: **se surmener** *vi* to overwork
**surmonter** [syʀmɔ̃te] *vt* (*vaincre*) to overcome; (*être au-dessus de*) to top
**surnaturel, le** [syʀnatyʀɛl] *adj, nm* supernatural
**surnom** [syʀnɔ̃] *nm* nickname
**surnombre** [syʀnɔ̃bʀ] *nm*: **être en ~** to be too many (*ou* one too many)
**surpeuplé, e** [syʀpœple] *adj* overpopulated
**surplace** [syʀplas] *nm*: **faire du ~** to mark time
**surplomber** [syʀplɔ̃be] *vt, vi* to overhang
**surplus** [syʀply] *nm* (*Comm*) surplus; (*reste*): **~ de bois** wood left over
**surprenant, e** [syʀpʀənɑ̃, ɑ̃t] *adj* amazing
**surprendre** [syʀpʀɑ̃dʀ] *vt* (*étonner*) to surprise; (*tomber sur: intrus etc*) to catch; (*entendre*) to overhear
**surpris, e** [syʀpʀi, iz] *adj*: **~ (de/que)** surprised (at/that); **surprise** *nf* surprise; **faire une surprise à qn** to give sb a surprise; **surprise-partie** *nf* party
**sursaut** [syʀso] *nm* start, jump; **~ de** (*énergie, indignation*) sudden fit *ou* burst of; **en ~** with a start; **sursauter** *vi* to (give a) start, jump
**sursis** [syʀsi] *nm* (*Jur: gén*) suspended sentence; (*fig*) reprieve
**surtout** [syʀtu] *adv* (*avant tout, d'abord*) above all; (*spécialement, particulièrement*) especially; **~, ne dites rien!** whatever you do don't say anything!; **~ pas!** certainly *ou* definitely not!; **~ que** especially as ...
**surveillance** [syʀvejɑ̃s] *nf* watch; (*Police, Mil*) surveillance; **sous ~ médicale** under medical supervision
**surveillant, e** [syʀvejɑ̃, ɑ̃t] *nm/f* (*de prison*) warder; (*Scol*) monitor
**surveiller** [syʀveje] *vt* (*enfant, élèves, bagages*) to watch, keep an eye on; (*prisonnier, suspect*) to keep (a) watch on; (*territoire, bâtiment*) to (keep) watch

over; (*travaux, cuisson*) to supervise;
(*Scol: examen*) to invigilate; **~ son
langage/sa ligne** to watch one's
language/figure
**survenir** [syrvənir] *vi* (*incident, retards*)
to occur, arise; (*événement*) to take place
**survêtement** [syrvɛtmã] *nm*
tracksuit
**survie** [syrvi] *nf* survival; **survivant, e**
*nm/f* survivor; **survivre** *vi* to survive;
**survivre à** (*accident etc*) to survive
**survoler** [syrvɔle] *vt* to fly over; (*fig:
livre*) to skim through
**survolté, e** [syrvɔlte] *adj* (*fig*)
worked up
**sus** [sy(s)]: **en ~ de** *prép* in addition to,
over and above; **en ~** in addition
**susceptible** [sysɛptibl] *adj* touchy,
sensitive; **~ de faire** (*hypothèse*) liable
to do
**susciter** [sysite] *vt* (*admiration*) to
arouse; (*ennuis*): **~ (à qn)** to create
(for sb)
**suspect, e** [syspɛ(kt), ɛkt] *adj*
suspicious; (*témoignage, opinions*)
suspect ▷ *nm/f* suspect; **suspecter**
*vt* to suspect; (*honnêteté de qn*) to
question, have one's suspicions about
**suspendre** [syspãdr] *vt* (*accrocher:
vêtement*): **~ qch (à)** to hang sth up (on);
(*interrompre, démettre*) to suspend
**suspendu, e** [syspãdy] *adj* (*accroché*):
**~ à** hanging on (ou from); (*perché*): **~
au-dessus de** suspended over
**suspens** [syspã]: **en ~** *adv* (*affaire*)
in abeyance; **tenir en ~** to keep in
suspense
**suspense** [syspɛns, syspãs] *nm*
suspense
**suspension** [syspãsjõ] *nf* suspension;
(*lustre*) light fitting *ou* fitment
**suture** [sytyr] *nf* (*Méd*): **point de ~**
stitch
**svelte** [svɛlt] *adj* slender, svelte
**SVP** *abr* (= *s'il vous plaît*) please
**sweat** [swit] *nm* (*fam*) sweatshirt
**sweat-shirt** [switʃœrt] (*pl* **~s**) *nm*
sweatshirt

**syllabe** [si(l)lab] *nf* syllable
**symbole** [sɛbɔl] *nm* symbol;
**symbolique** *adj* symbolic(al); (*geste,
offrande*) token *cpd*; **symboliser** *vt* to
symbolize
**symétrique** [simetrik] *adj*
symmetrical
**sympa** [sɛpa] (*fam*) *adj inv* nice; **sois ~,
prête-le moi** be a pal and lend it to me
**sympathie** [sɛpati] *nf* (*inclination*)
liking; (*affinité*) friendship;
(*condoléances*) sympathy; **j'ai
beaucoup de ~ pour lui** I like him a lot;
**sympathique** *adj* nice, friendly
  Attention à ne pas traduire
  *sympathique* par *sympathetic*.
**sympathisant, e** [sɛpatizã, ãt] *nm/f*
sympathizer
**sympathiser** [sɛpatize] *vi* (*voisins
etc: s'entendre*) to get on (BRIT) *ou* along
(US) (well)
**symphonie** [sɛfɔni] *nf* symphony
**symptôme** [sɛptom] *nm* symptom
**synagogue** [sinagɔg] *nf* synagogue
**syncope** [sɛkɔp] *nf* (*Méd*) blackout;
**tomber en ~** to faint, pass out
**syndic** [sɛdik] *nm* (*d'immeuble*)
managing agent
**syndical, e, -aux** [sɛdikal, o] *adj*
(trade) union *cpd*; **syndicaliste** *nm/f*
trade unionist
**syndicat** [sɛdika] *nm* (*d'ouvriers,
employés*) (trade) union; **syndicat
d'initiative** tourist office; **syndiqué, e**
*adj* belonging to a (trade) union;
**syndiquer: se syndiquer** *vi* to form
a trade union; (*adhérer*) to join a trade
union
**synonyme** [sinɔnim] *adj* synonymous
▷ *nm* synonym; **~ de** synonymous with
**syntaxe** [sɛtaks] *nf* syntax
**synthèse** [sɛtez] *nf* synthesis
**synthétique** [sɛtetik] *adj* synthetic
**Syrie** [siri] *nf*: **la ~** Syria
**systématique** [sistematik] *adj*
systematic
**système** [sistɛm] *nm* system; **le ~ D**
resourcefulness

**t**

**t'** [t] *pron voir* **te**

**ta** [ta] *adj voir* **ton¹**

**tabac** [taba] *nm* tobacco; (*magasin*) tobacconist's (shop)

**tabagisme** [tabaʒism] *nm*: **tabagisme passif** passive smoking

**table** [tabl] *nf* table; **à ~!** dinner *etc* is ready!; **se mettre à ~** to sit down to eat; **mettre la ~** to lay the table; **une ~ pour 4, s'il vous plaît** a table for 4, please; **table à repasser** ironing board; **table de cuisson** hob; **table de nuit** *ou* **de chevet** bedside table; **table des matières** (table of) contents *pl*; **table d'orientation** viewpoint indicator; **table roulante** trolley (*BRIT*), tea wagon (*US*)

**tableau, x** [tablo] *nm* (*peinture*) painting; (*reproduction, fig*) picture; (*panneau*) board; (*schéma*) table, chart; **tableau d'affichage** notice board; **tableau de bord** dashboard; (*Aviat*) instrument panel; **tableau noir** blackboard

**tablette** [tablɛt] *nf* (*planche*) shelf; **tablette de chocolat** bar of chocolate

**tablier** [tablije] *nm* apron

**tabou** [tabu] *nm* taboo

**tabouret** [taburɛ] *nm* stool

**tac** [tak] *nm*: **il m'a répondu du ~ au ~** he answered me right back

**tache** [taʃ] *nf* (*saleté*) stain, mark; (*Art, de couleur, lumière*) spot; **tache de rousseur** freckle

**tâche** [taʃ] *nf* task

**tacher** [taʃe] *vt* to stain, mark

**tâcher** [taʃe] *vi*: **~ de faire** to try *ou* endeavour to do

**tacheté, e** [taʃte] *adj* spotted

**tact** [takt] *nm* tact; **avoir du ~** to be tactful

**tactique** [taktik] *adj* tactical ▷ *nf* (*technique*) tactics *sg*; (*plan*) tactic

**taie** [tɛ] *nf*: **~ (d'oreiller)** pillowslip, pillowcase

**taille** [taj] *nf* cutting; (*d'arbre etc*) pruning; (*milieu du corps*) waist; (*hauteur*) height; (*grandeur*) size; **de ~ à faire** capable of doing; **de ~** sizeable; **taille-crayon(s)** *nm* pencil sharpener

**tailler** [taje] *vt* (*pierre, diamant*) to cut; (*arbre, plante*) to prune; (*vêtement*) to cut out; (*crayon*) to sharpen

**tailleur** [tajœr] *nm* (*couturier*) tailor; (*vêtement*) suit; **en ~** (*assis*) cross-legged

**taillis** [taji] *nm* copse

**taire** [tɛr] *vi*: **faire ~ qn** to make sb be quiet; **se taire** *vi* to be silent *ou* quiet; **taisez-vous!** be quiet!

**Taiwan** [tajwan] *nf* Taiwan

**talc** [talk] *nm* talc, talcum powder

**talent** [talɑ̃] *nm* talent

**talkie-walkie** [tokiwoki] *nm* walkie-talkie

**talon** [talɔ̃] *nm* heel; (*de chèque, billet*) stub, counterfoil (*BRIT*); **talons plats/aiguilles** flat/stiletto heels

**talus** [taly] *nm* embankment

**tambour** [tɑ̃bur] *nm* (*Mus, aussi Tech*) drum; (*musicien*) drummer; (*porte*) revolving door(s *pl*); **tambourin** *nm* tambourine

**Tamise** [tamiz] *nf*: **la ~** the Thames
**tamisé, e** [tamize] *adj* (*fig*) subdued, soft
**tampon** [tɑ̃pɔ̃] *nm* (*de coton, d'ouate*) wad, pad; (*amortisseur*) buffer; (*bouchon*) plug, stopper; (*cachet, timbre*) stamp; **(mémoire) ~** (*Inform*) buffer; **tampon (hygiénique)** tampon; **tamponner** *vt* (*timbres*) to stamp; (*heurter*) to crash *ou* ram into; **tamponneuse** *adj f*: **autos tamponneuses** dodgems
**tandem** [tɑ̃dɛm] *nm* tandem
**tandis** [tɑ̃di]: **~ que** *conj* while
**tanguer** [tɑ̃ge] *vi* to pitch (and toss)
**tant** [tɑ̃] *adv* so much; **~ de** (*sable, eau*) so much; (*gens, livres*) so many; **~ que** as long as; (*autant que*) as much as; **~ mieux** that's great; (*avec une certaine réserve*) so much the better; **~ pis** too bad; (*conciliant*) never mind; **~ bien que mal** as well as can be expected
**tante** [tɑ̃t] *nf* aunt
**tantôt** [tɑ̃to] *adv* (*parfois*): **~ ... ~** now ... now; (*cet après-midi*) this afternoon
**taon** [tɑ̃] *nm* horsefly
**tapage** [tapaʒ] *nm* uproar, din
**tapageur, -euse** [tapaʒœʀ, øz] *adj* noisy; (*voyant*) loud, flashy
**tape** [tap] *nf* slap
**tape-à-l'œil** [tapalœj] *adj inv* flashy, showy
**taper** [tape] *vt* (*porte*) to bang, slam; (*enfant*) to slap; (*dactylographier*) to type (out); (*fam: emprunter*): **~ qn de 10 euros** to touch sb for 10 euros ▷ *vi* (*soleil*) to beat down; **se taper** *vt* (*repas*) to put away; (*fam: corvée*) to get landed with; **~ sur qn** to thump sb; (*fig*) to run sb down; **~ sur un clou** to hit a nail; **~ sur la table** to bang on the table; **~ à** (*porte etc*) to knock on; **~ dans** (*se servir*) to dig into; **~ des mains/pieds** to clap one's hands/stamp one's feet; **~ (à la machine)** to type
**tapi, e** [tapi] *adj* (*blotti*) crouching; (*caché*) hidden away
**tapis** [tapi] *nm* carpet; (*petit*) rug; **tapis de sol** (*de tente*) groundsheet;

**tapis de souris** (*Inform*) mouse mat; **tapis roulant** (*pour piétons*) moving walkway; (*pour bagages*) carousel
**tapisser** [tapise] *vt* (*avec du papier peint*) to paper; (*recouvrir*): **~ qch (de)** to cover sth (with); **tapisserie** *nf* (*tenture, broderie*) tapestry; (*papier peint*) wallpaper; **tapissier-décorateur** *nm* interior decorator
**tapoter** [tapote] *vt* (*joue, main*) to pat; (*objet*) to tap
**taquiner** [takine] *vt* to tease
**tard** [taʀ] *adv* late; **plus ~** later (on); **au plus ~** at the latest; **sur le ~** late in life; **il est trop ~** it's too late
**tarder** [taʀde] *vi* (*chose*) to be a long time coming; (*personne*): **~ à faire** to delay doing; **il me tarde d'être** I am longing to be; **sans (plus) ~** without (further) delay
**tardif, -ive** [taʀdif, iv] *adj* late
**tarif** [taʀif] *nm*: **~ des consommations** price list; **~s postaux/douaniers** postal/customs rates; **~ des taxis** taxi fares; **~ plein/réduit** (*train*) full/reduced fare; (*téléphone*) peak/off-peak rate
**tarir** [taʀiʀ] *vi* to dry up, run dry
**tarte** [taʀt] *nf* tart; **~ aux fraises** strawberry tart; **~ Tatin** ≈ apple upside-down tart
**tartine** [taʀtin] *nf* slice of bread; **tartine de miel** slice of bread and honey; **tartiner** *vt* to spread; **fromage à tartiner** cheese spread
**tartre** [taʀtʀ] *nm* (*des dents*) tartar; (*de bouilloire*) fur, scale
**tas** [tɑ] *nm* heap, pile; (*fig*): **un ~ de** heaps of, lots of; **en ~** in a heap *ou* pile; **formé sur le ~** trained on the job
**tasse** [tɑs] *nf* cup; **tasse à café** coffee cup
**tassé, e** [tɑse] *adj*: **bien ~** (*café etc*) strong
**tasser** [tɑse] *vt* (*terre, neige*) to pack down; (*entasser*): **~ qch dans** to cram sth into; **se tasser** *vi* (*se serrer*) to squeeze up; (*s'affaisser*) to settle; (*fig*) to

settle down

**tâter** [tate] vt to feel; (fig) to try out; **se tâter** (hésiter) to be in two minds; **~ de** (prison etc) to have a taste of

**tatillon, ne** [tatijɔ̃, ɔn] adj pernickety

**tâtonnement** [tatɔnmɑ̃] nm: **par ~s** (fig) by trial and error

**tâtonner** [tatɔne] vi to grope one's way along

**tâtons** [tatɔ̃]: **à ~** adv: **chercher/ avancer à ~** to grope around for/grope one's way forward

**tatouage** [tatwaʒ] nm tattoo

**tatouer** [tatwe] vt to tattoo

**taudis** [todi] nm hovel, slum

**taule** [tol] (fam) nf nick (fam), prison

**taupe** [top] nf mole

**taureau, x** [tɔʀo] nm bull; (signe): **le T~** Taurus

**taux** [to] nm rate; (d'alcool) level; **taux d'intérêt** interest rate

**taxe** [taks] nf tax; (douanière) duty; **toutes ~s comprises** inclusive of tax; **la boutique hors ~s** the duty-free shop; **taxe à la valeur ajoutée** value-added tax; **taxe de séjour** tourist tax

**taxer** [takse] vt (personne) to tax; (produit) to put a tax on, tax

**taxi** [taksi] nm taxi; (chauffeur: fam) taxi driver; **pouvez-vous m'appeler un ~, s'il vous plaît?** can you call me a taxi, please?

**Tchécoslovaquie** [tʃekɔslɔvaki] nf Czechoslovakia; **tchèque** adj Czech ▷ nm/f: **Tchèque** Czech ▷ nm (Ling) Czech; **la République tchèque** the Czech Republic

**Tchétchénie** [tʃetʃeni] nf: **la ~** Chechnya

**te, t'** [tə] pron you; (réfléchi) yourself

**technicien, ne** [tɛknisjɛ̃, jɛn] nm/f technician

**technico-commercial, e, -aux** [tɛknikokɔmɛʀsjal, jo] adj: **agent ~** sales technician

**technique** [tɛknik] adj technical ▷ nf technique; **techniquement** adv technically

**techno** [tɛkno] nf (Mus) techno (music)

**technologie** [tɛknɔlɔʒi] nf technology; **technologique** adj technological

**teck** [tɛk] nm teak

**tee-shirt** [tiʃœʀt] nm T-shirt, tee-shirt

**teindre** [tɛ̃dʀ] vt to dye; **se ~ les cheveux** to dye one's hair; **teint, e** adj dyed ▷ nm (du visage) complexion; (momentané) colour ▷ nf shade; **grand teint** colourfast

**teinté, e** [tɛ̃te] adj: **~ de** (fig) tinged with

**teinter** [tɛ̃te] vt (verre, papier) to tint; (bois) to stain

**teinture** [tɛ̃tyʀ] nf dye; **teinture d'iode** tincture of iodine; **teinturerie** nf dry cleaner's; **teinturier** nm dry cleaner

**tel, telle** [tɛl] adj (pareil) such; (comme): **~ un/des ...** like a/like ...; (indéfini) such-and-such a; (intensif): **un ~/de ~s ...** such (a)/such ...; **rien de ~** nothing like it; **~ que** like, such as; **~ quel** as it is ou stands (ou was etc); **venez ~ jour** come on such-and-such a day

**télé** [tele] (fam) nf TV; **à la ~** on TV ou telly

**télé...**: **télécabine** nf (benne) cable car; **télécarte** nf phonecard; **téléchargeable** adj downloadable; **téléchargement** nm (action) downloading; (fichier) download; **télécharger** vt to download; **télécommande** nf remote control; **télécopieur** nm fax machine; **télédistribution** nf cable TV; **télégramme** nm telegram; **télégraphier** vt to telegraph, cable; **téléguider** vt to radio-control; **télématique** nf telematics sg; **téléobjectif** nm telephoto lens sg; **télépathie** nf telepathy; **téléphérique** nm cable car

**téléphone** [telefɔn] nm telephone; **avoir le ~** to be on the (tele)phone; **au ~** on the phone; **téléphoner** vi to make a phone call; **téléphoner à** to phone,

call up; **est-ce que je peux téléphoner d'ici?** can I make a call from here?; **téléphonique** adj (tele)phone cpd
**télé...: téléréalité** nf reality TV
**télescope** [teleskɔp] nm telescope
**télescoper** [teleskɔpe] vt to smash up; **se télescoper** (véhicules) to concertina
**télé...: téléscripteur** nm teleprinter; **télésiège** nm chairlift; **téléski** nm ski-tow; **téléspectateur, -trice** nm/f (television) viewer; **télétravail** nm telecommuting; **télévente** nf telesales; **téléviseur** nm television set; **télévision** nf television; **à la télévision** on television; **télévision numérique** digital TV; **télévision par câble/satellite** cable/satellite television
**télex** [teleks] nm telex
**telle** [tɛl] adj voir **tel**; **tellement** adv (tant) so much; (si) so; **tellement de** (sable, eau) so much; (gens, livres) so many; **il s'est endormi tellement il était fatigué** he was so tired (that) he fell asleep; **pas tellement** not (all) that much; not (all) that +adjectif
**téméraire** [temeʀɛʀ] adj reckless, rash
**témoignage** [temwaɲaʒ] nm (Jur: déclaration) testimony no pl, evidence no pl; (rapport, récit) account; (fig: d'affection etc: cadeau) token, mark; (: geste) expression
**témoigner** [temwaɲe] vt (intérêt, gratitude) to show ▷ vi (Jur) to testify, give evidence; **~ de** to bear witness to, testify to
**témoin** [temwɛ̃] nm witness ▷ adj: **appartement ~** show flat (BRIT); **être ~ de** to witness; **témoin oculaire** eyewitness
**tempe** [tɑ̃p] nf temple
**tempérament** [tɑ̃peʀamɑ̃] nm temperament, disposition; **à ~** (vente) on deferred (payment) terms; (achat) by instalments, hire purchase cpd
**température** [tɑ̃peʀatyʀ] nf temperature; **avoir** ou **faire de la ~** to be running ou have a temperature

**tempête** [tɑ̃pɛt] nf storm; **tempête de sable/neige** sand/snowstorm
**temple** [tɑ̃pl] nm temple; (protestant) church
**temporaire** [tɑ̃pɔʀɛʀ] adj temporary
**temps** [tɑ̃] nm (atmosphérique) weather; (durée) time; (époque) time, times pl; (Ling) tense; (Mus) beat; (Tech) stroke; **un ~ de chien** (fam) rotten weather; **quel ~ fait-il?** what's the weather like?; **il fait beau/mauvais** the weather is fine/bad; **avoir le ~/tout son ~** to have time/plenty of time; **en ~ de paix/guerre** in peacetime/wartime; **en ~ utile** ou **voulu** in due time ou course; **ces derniers ~** lately; **dans quelque ~** in a (little) while; **de ~ en ~, de ~ à autre** from time to time; **à ~** (partir, arriver) in time; **à ~ complet, à plein ~** full-time; **à ~ partiel, à mi-~** part-time; **dans le ~** at one time; **temps d'arrêt** pause, halt; **temps libre** free ou spare time; **temps mort** (Comm) slack period
**tenable** [t(ə)nabl] adj bearable
**tenace** [tənas] adj persistent
**tenant, e** [tənɑ̃, ɑ̃t] nm/f (Sport): **~ du titre** title-holder
**tendance** [tɑ̃dɑ̃s] nf tendency; (opinions) leanings pl, sympathies pl; (évolution) trend; **avoir ~ à** to have a tendency to, tend to
**tendeur** [tɑ̃dœʀ] nm (attache) elastic strap
**tendre** [tɑ̃dʀ] adj tender; (bois, roche, couleur) soft ▷ vt (élastique, peau) to stretch; (corde) to tighten; (muscle) to tense; (fig: piège) to set, lay; (donner): **~ qch à qn** to hold sth out to sb; (offrir) to offer sb sth; **se tendre** vi (corde) to tighten; (relations) to become strained; **~ à qch/à faire** to tend towards sth/to do; **~ l'oreille** to prick up one's ears; **~ la main/le bras** to hold out one's hand/ stretch out one's arm; **tendrement** adv tenderly; **tendresse** nf tenderness
**tendu, e** [tɑ̃dy] pp de **tendre** ▷ adj (corde) tight; (muscles) tensed; (relations) strained

**ténèbres** [tenɛbʀ] *nfpl* darkness *sg*

**teneur** [tənœʀ] *nf* content; (*d'une lettre*) terms *pl*, content

**tenir** [t(ə)niʀ] *vt* to hold; (*magasin, hôtel*) to run; (*promesse*) to keep ▷ *vi* to hold; (*neige, gel*) to last; **se tenir** *vi* (*avoir lieu*) to be held, take place; (*être: personne*) to stand; **~ à** (*personne, objet*) to be attached to; (*réputation*) to care about; **~ à faire** to be determined to do; **~ de** (*ressembler à*) to take after; **ça ne tient qu'à lui** it is entirely up to him; **~ qn pour** to regard sb as; **~ qch de qn** (*histoire*) to have heard *ou* learnt sth from sb; (*qualité, défaut*) to have inherited *ou* got sth from sb; **~ dans** to fit into; **~ compte de qch** to take sth into account; **~ les comptes** to keep the books; **~ bon** to stand fast; **~ le coup** to hold out; **~ au chaud** (*café, plat*) to keep hot; **un manteau qui tient chaud** a warm coat; **tiens/tenez, voilà le stylo** there's the pen!; **tiens, voilà Alain!** here's Alain!; **tiens?** (*surprise*) really?; **se ~ droit** to stand (*ou* sit) up straight; **bien se ~** to behave well; **se ~ à qch** to hold on to sth; **s'en ~ à qch** to confine o.s. to sth

**tennis** [tenis] *nm* tennis; (*court*) tennis court ▷ *nm ou f pl* (*aussi:* **chaussures de ~**) tennis *ou* gym shoes; **tennis de table** table tennis; **tennisman** *nm* tennis player

**tension** [tɑ̃sjɔ̃] *nf* tension; (*Méd*) blood pressure; **avoir de la ~** to have high blood pressure

**tentation** [tɑ̃tasjɔ̃] *nf* temptation

**tentative** [tɑ̃tativ] *nf* attempt

**tente** [tɑ̃t] *nf* tent

**tenter** [tɑ̃te] *vt* (*éprouver, attirer*) to tempt; (*essayer*): **~ qch/de faire** to attempt *ou* try sth/to do; **~ sa chance** to try one's luck

**tenture** [tɑ̃tyʀ] *nf* hanging

**tenu, e** [t(ə)ny] *pp de* **tenir** ▷ *adj* (*maison, comptes*): **bien ~** well-kept; (*obligé*): **~ de faire** obliged to do ▷ *nf* (*vêtements*) clothes *pl*; (*comportement*)

(good) manners *pl*, good behaviour; (*d'une maison*) upkeep; **en petite ~e** scantily dressed *ou* clad

**ter** [tɛʀ] *adj*: **16 ~** 16b *ou* B

**terme** [tɛʀm] *nm* term; (*fin*) end; **à court/long ~** *adj* short-/long-term ▷ *adv* in the short/long term; **avant ~** (*Méd*) prematurely; **mettre un ~ à** to put an end *ou* a stop to; **en bons ~s** on good terms

**terminaison** [tɛʀminɛzɔ̃] *nf* (*Ling*) ending

**terminal, -aux** [tɛʀminal, o] *nm* terminal; **terminale** *nf* (*Scol*) ≈ year 13 (*BRIT*), ≈ twelfth grade (*US*)

**terminer** [tɛʀmine] *vt* to finish; **se terminer** *vi* to end; **quand est-ce que le spectacle se termine?** when does the show finish?

**terne** [tɛʀn] *adj* dull

**ternir** [tɛʀniʀ] *vt* to dull; (*fig*) to sully, tarnish; **se ternir** *vi* to become dull

**terrain** [teʀɛ̃] *nm* (*sol, fig*) ground; (*Comm: étendue de terre*) land *no pl*; (*parcelle*) plot (of land); (*à bâtir*) site; **sur le ~** (*fig*) on the field; **terrain d'aviation** airfield; **terrain de camping** campsite; **terrain de football/rugby** football/rugby pitch (*BRIT*) *ou* field (*US*); **terrain de golf** golf course; **terrain de jeu** games field; (*pour les petits*) playground; **terrain de sport** sports ground; **terrain vague** waste ground *no pl*

**terrasse** [teʀas] *nf* terrace; **à la ~** (*café*) outside; **terrasser** *vt* (*adversaire*) to floor; (*suj: maladie etc*) to strike down

**terre** [tɛʀ] *nf* (*gén, aussi Élec*) earth; (*substance*) soil, earth; (*opposé à mer*) land *no pl*; (*contrée*) land; **terres** *nfpl* (*terrains*) lands, land *sg*; **en ~** (*pipe, poterie*) clay *cpd*; **à ~ ou par ~** (*mettre, être, s'asseoir*) on the ground (*ou* floor); (*jeter, tomber*) to the ground, down; **terre à terre** *adj inv* (*considération, personne*) down-to-earth; **terre cuite** terracotta; **la terre ferme** dry land; **terre glaise** clay

**terreau** [teʀo] *nm* compost

**terre-plein** [tɛʀplɛ̃] nm platform; (sur chaussée) central reservation

**terrestre** [tɛʀɛstʀ] adj (surface) earth's, of the earth; (Bot, Zool, Mil) land cpd; (Rel) earthly

**terreur** [tɛʀœʀ] nf terror no pl

**terrible** [tɛʀibl] adj terrible, dreadful; (fam) terrific; **pas ~** nothing special

**terrien, ne** [tɛʀjɛ̃, jɛn] adj: **propriétaire ~** landowner ▷ nm/f (non martien etc) earthling

**terrier** [tɛʀje] nm burrow, hole; (chien) terrier

**terrifier** [tɛʀifje] vt to terrify

**terrine** [tɛʀin] nf (récipient) terrine; (Culin) pâté

**territoire** [tɛʀitwaʀ] nm territory

**terroriser** [tɛʀɔʀize] vt to terrorize

**terrorisme** [tɛʀɔʀism] nm terrorism; **terroriste** nm/f terrorist

**tertiaire** [tɛʀsjɛʀ] adj tertiary ▷ nm (Écon) service industries pl

**tes** [te] adj voir **ton¹**

**test** [tɛst] nm test

**testament** [tɛstamɑ̃] nm (Jur) will; (Rel) Testament; (fig) legacy

**tester** [tɛste] vt to test

**testicule** [tɛstikyl] nm testicle

**tétanos** [tetanos] nm tetanus

**têtard** [tɛtaʀ] nm tadpole

**tête** [tɛt] nf head; (cheveux) hair no pl; (visage) face; **de ~** (comme adj: wagon etc) front cpd; (comme adv: calculer) in one's head, mentally; **perdre la ~** (fig: s'affoler) to lose one's head; (: devenir fou) to go off one's head; **tenir ~ à qn** to stand up to sb; **la ~ en bas** with one's head down; **la ~ la première** (tomber) headfirst; **faire une ~** (Football) to head the ball; **faire la ~** (fig) to sulk; **en ~** at the front; (Sport) in the lead; **à la ~ de** at the head of; **à ~ reposée** in a more leisurely moment; **n'en faire qu'à sa ~** to do as one pleases; **en avoir par-dessus la ~** to be fed up; **en ~ à ~** in private, alone together; **de la ~ aux pieds** from head to toe; **tête de lecture** (playback) head; **tête de liste** (Pol) chief candidate; **tête**

**de mort** skull and crossbones; **tête de série** (Tennis) seeded player, seed; **tête de Turc** (fig) whipping boy (BRIT), butt; **tête-à-queue** nm inv: **faire un tête-à-queue** to spin round

**téter** [tete] vt: **~ (sa mère)** to suck at one's mother's breast, feed

**tétine** [tetin] nf teat; (sucette) dummy (BRIT), pacifier (US)

**têtu, e** [tety] adj stubborn, pigheaded

**texte** [tɛkst] nm text; (morceau choisi) passage

**textile** [tɛkstil] adj textile cpd ▷ nm textile; **le ~** the textile industry

**Texto®** [tɛksto] nm text message

**texture** [tɛkstyʀ] nf texture

**TGV** sigle m (= train à grande vitesse) high-speed train

**thaïlandais, e** [tajlɑ̃dɛ, ɛz] adj Thai ▷ nm/f: **T~, e** Thai

**Thaïlande** [tailɑ̃d] nf Thailand

**thé** [te] nm tea; **~ au citron** lemon tea; **~ au lait** tea with milk; **prendre le ~** to have tea; **faire le ~** to make the tea

**théâtral, e, -aux** [teɑtʀal, o] adj theatrical

**théâtre** [teɑtʀ] nm theatre; (péj: simulation) playacting; (fig: lieu): **le ~ de** the scene of; **faire du ~** to act

**théière** [tejɛʀ] nf teapot

**thème** [tɛm] nm theme; (Scol: traduction) prose (composition)

**théologie** [teɔlɔʒi] nf theology

**théorie** [teɔʀi] nf theory; **théorique** adj theoretical

**thérapie** [teʀapi] nf therapy

**thermal, e, -aux** [tɛʀmal, o] adj: **station ~e** spa; **cure ~e** water cure

**thermomètre** [tɛʀmɔmɛtʀ] nm thermometer

**thermos®** [tɛʀmos] nm ou nf: **(bouteille) thermos** vacuum ou Thermos® flask

**thermostat** [tɛʀmɔsta] nm thermostat

**thèse** [tɛz] nf thesis

**thon** [tɔ̃] nm tuna (fish)

**thym** [tɛ̃] nm thyme

**Tibet** [tibɛ] nm: **le ~** Tibet

**tibia** [tibja] nm shinbone, tibia; (*partie antérieure de la jambe*) shin

**TIC** sigle fpl (= *technologies de l'information et de la communication*) ICT sg

**tic** [tik] nm tic, (nervous) twitch; (*de langage etc*) mannerism

**ticket** [tikɛ] nm ticket; **ticket de caisse** receipt; **je peux avoir un ticket de caisse, s'il vous plaît?** can I have a receipt, please?

**tiède** [tjɛd] adj lukewarm; (*vent, air*) mild, warm; **tiédir** vi to cool; (*se réchauffer*) to grow warmer

**tien, ne** [tjɛ̃, tjɛn] pron: **le(la) ~(ne), les ~(ne)s** yours; **à la ~ne!** cheers!

**tiens** [tjɛ̃] vb, excl voir **tenir**

**tiercé** [tjɛʀse] nm system of forecast betting giving first 3 horses

**tiers, tierce** [tjɛʀ, tjɛʀs] adj third ▷ nm (Jur) third party; (*fraction*) third; **le tiers monde** the Third World

**tige** [tiʒ] nf stem; (*baguette*) rod

**tignasse** [tiɲas] (*péj*) nf mop of hair

**tigre** [tigʀ] nm tiger; **tigré, e** adj (*rayé*) striped; (*tacheté*) spotted; (*chat*) tabby; **tigresse** nf tigress

**tilleul** [tijœl] nm lime (tree), linden (tree); (*boisson*) lime(-blossom) tea

**timbre** [tɛ̃bʀ] nm (*tampon*) stamp; (*aussi:* **~-poste**) (postage) stamp; (*Mus: de voix, instrument*) timbre, tone

**timbré, e** [tɛ̃bʀe] (*fam*) adj cracked

**timide** [timid] adj shy; (*timoré*) timid; **timidement** adv shyly; timidly; **timidité** nf shyness; timidity

**tintamarre** [tɛ̃tamaʀ] nm din, uproar

**tinter** [tɛ̃te] vi to ring, chime; (*argent, clefs*) to jingle

**tique** [tik] nf (*parasite*) tick

**tir** [tiʀ] nm (*sport*) shooting; (*fait ou manière de tirer*) firing no pl; (*rafale*) fire; (*stand*) shooting gallery; **tir à l'arc** archery

**tirage** [tiʀaʒ] nm (*action*) printing; (Photo) print; (*de journal*) circulation; (*de livre: nombre d'exemplaires*) (print) run; (: *édition*) edition; (*de loterie*) draw; **par ~**

**au sort** by drawing lots

**tire** [tiʀ] nf: **vol à la ~** pickpocketing

**tiré, e** [tiʀe] adj (*traits*) drawn; **~ par les cheveux** far-fetched

**tire-bouchon** [tiʀbuʃɔ̃] nm corkscrew

**tirelire** [tiʀliʀ] nf moneybox

**tirer** [tiʀe] vt (*gén*) to pull; (*trait, rideau, carte, conclusion, chèque*) to draw; (*langue*) to stick out; (*en faisant feu: balle, coup*) to fire; (: *animal*) to shoot; (*journal, livre, photo*) to print; (Football: *corner etc*) to take ▷ vi (*faire feu*) to fire; (*faire du tir, Football*) to shoot; **se tirer** vi (*fam*) to push off; **s'en ~** (*éviter le pire*) to get off; (*survivre*) to pull through; (*se débrouiller*) to manage; **~ qch de** (*extraire*) to take ou pull sth out of; **~ qn de** (*embarras etc*) to help ou get sb out of; **~ sur** (*corde*) to pull on ou at; (*faire feu sur*) to shoot ou fire at; (*pipe*) to draw on; (*approcher de: couleur*) to verge ou border on; **~ à l'arc/la carabine** to shoot with a bow and arrow/with a rifle; **~ à sa fin** to be drawing to a close; **~ qch au clair** to clear sth up; **~ au sort** to draw lots; **~ parti de** to take advantage of; **~ profit de** to profit from; **~ les cartes** to read ou tell the cards

**tiret** [tiʀɛ] nm dash

**tireur** [tiʀœʀ] nm gunman; **tireur d'élite** marksman

**tiroir** [tiʀwaʀ] nm drawer; **tiroir-caisse** nm till

**tisane** [tizan] nf herb tea

**tisser** [tise] vt to weave

**tissu** [tisy] nm fabric, material, cloth no pl; (*Anat, Bio*) tissue; **tissu-éponge** nm (terry) towelling no pl

**titre** [titʀ] nm (*gén*) title; (*de journal*) headline; (*diplôme*) qualification; (Comm) security; **en ~** (*champion*) official; **à juste ~** rightly; **à quel ~?** on what grounds?; **à aucun ~** on no account; **au même ~ (que)** in the same way (as); **à ~ d'information** for (your) information; **à ~ gracieux** free of charge; **à ~ d'essai** on a trial basis; **à ~ privé** in a private capacity;

**titre de propriété** title deed; **titre de transport** ticket

**tituber** [titybe] *vi* to stagger (along)

**titulaire** [titylɛʀ] *adj* (*Admin*) with tenure ▷ *nm/f* (*de permis*) holder; **être ~ de** (*diplôme, permis*) to hold

**toast** [tost] *nm* slice *ou* piece of toast; (*de bienvenue*) (welcoming) toast; **porter un ~ à qn** to propose *ou* drink a toast to sb

**toboggan** [tɔbɔgã] *nm* slide; (*Auto*) flyover

**toc** [tɔk] *excl*: **~, ~** knock knock ▷ *nm*: **en ~** fake

**tocsin** [tɔksɛ̃] *nm* alarm (bell)

**tohu-bohu** [tɔybɔy] *nm* hubbub

**toi** [twa] *pron* you

**toile** [twal] *nf* (*tableau*) canvas; **de** *ou* **en ~** (*pantalon*) cotton; (*sac*) canvas; **la T~** (*Internet*) the Web; **toile cirée** oilcloth; **toile d'araignée** cobweb; **toile de fond** (*fig*) backdrop

**toilette** [twalɛt] *nf* (*habits*) outfit; **toilettes** *nfpl* (*w.-c.*) toilet *sg*; **faire sa ~** to have a wash, get washed; **articles de ~** toiletries; **où sont les ~s?** where's the toilet?

**toi-même** [twamɛm] *pron* yourself

**toit** [twa] *nm* roof; **toit ouvrant** sunroof

**toiture** [twatyʀ] *nf* roof

**Tokyo** [tɔkjo] *n* Tokyo

**tôle** [tol] *nf* (*plaque*) steel *ou* iron sheet; **tôle ondulée** corrugated iron

**tolérable** [tɔleʀabl] *adj* tolerable

**tolérant, e** [tɔleʀɑ̃, ɑ̃t] *adj* tolerant

**tolérer** [tɔleʀe] *vt* to tolerate; (*Admin: hors taxe etc*) to allow

**tollé** [tɔ(l)le] *nm* outcry

**tomate** [tɔmat] *nf* tomato; **~s farcies** stuffed tomatoes

**tombe** [tɔ̃b] *nf* (*sépulture*) grave; (*avec monument*) tomb

**tombeau, x** [tɔ̃bo] *nm* tomb

**tombée** [tɔ̃be] *nf*: **à la ~ de la nuit** at nightfall

**tomber** [tɔ̃be] *vi* to fall; (*fièvre, vent*) to drop; **laisser ~** (*objet*) to drop; (*personne*) to let down; (*activité*) to give up; **laisse ~!** forget it!; **faire ~** to knock over; **~ sur** (*rencontrer*) to bump into; **~ de fatigue/sommeil** to drop from exhaustion/be falling asleep on one's feet; **ça tombe bien** that's come at the right time; **il est bien tombé** he's been lucky; **~ à l'eau** (*projet*) to fall through; **~ en panne** to break down

**tombola** [tɔ̃bɔla] *nf* raffle

**tome** [tɔm] *nm* volume

**ton¹, ta** [tɔ̃, ta] (*pl* **tes**) *adj* your

**ton²** [tɔ̃] *nm* (*gén*) tone; (*couleur*) shade, tone; **de bon ~** in good taste

**tonalité** [tɔnalite] *nf* (*au téléphone*) dialling tone

**tondeuse** [tɔ̃døz] *nf* (*à gazon*) (lawn)mower; (*du coiffeur*) clippers *pl*; (*pour les moutons*) shears *pl*

**tondre** [tɔ̃dʀ] *vt* (*pelouse, herbe*) to mow; (*haie*) to cut, clip; (*mouton, toison*) to shear; (*cheveux*) to crop

**tongs** [tɔ̃g] *nfpl* flip-flops

**tonifier** [tɔnifje] *vt* (*peau, organisme*) to tone up

**tonique** [tɔnik] *adj* fortifying ▷ *nm* tonic

**tonne** [tɔn] *nf* metric ton, tonne

**tonneau, x** [tɔno] *nm* (*à vin, cidre*) barrel; **faire des ~x** (*voiture, avion*) to roll over

**tonnelle** [tɔnɛl] *nf* bower, arbour

**tonner** [tɔne] *vi* to thunder; **il tonne** it is thundering, there's some thunder

**tonnerre** [tɔnɛʀ] *nm* thunder

**tonus** [tɔnys] *nm* energy

**top** [tɔp] *nm*: **au 3ème ~** at the 3rd stroke ▷ *adj*: **~ secret** top secret

**topinambour** [tɔpinãbuʀ] *nm* Jerusalem artichoke

**torche** [tɔʀʃ] *nf* torch

**torchon** [tɔʀʃɔ̃] *nm* cloth; (*à vaisselle*) tea towel *ou* cloth

**tordre** [tɔʀdʀ] *vt* (*chiffon*) to wring; (*barre, fig: visage*) to twist; **se tordre** *vi*: **se ~ le poignet/la cheville** to twist one's wrist/ankle; **se ~ de douleur/rire** to be doubled up with pain/laughter;

**tordu, e** adj bent; (fig) crazy

**tornade** [tɔʀnad] nf tornado

**torrent** [tɔʀɑ̃] nm mountain stream

**torsade** [tɔʀsad] nf: **un pull à ~s** a cable sweater

**torse** [tɔʀs] nm chest; (Anat, Sculpture) torso; **~ nu** stripped to the waist

**tort** [tɔʀ] nm (défaut) fault; **torts** nmpl (Jur) fault sg; **avoir ~** to be wrong; **être dans son ~** to be in the wrong; **donner ~ à qn** to lay the blame on sb; **causer du ~ à qn** to harm sb; **à ~** wrongly; **à ~ et à travers** wildly

**torticolis** [tɔʀtikɔli] nm stiff neck

**tortiller** [tɔʀtije] vt to twist; (moustache) to twirl; **se tortiller** vi to wriggle; (en dansant) to wiggle

**tortionnaire** [tɔʀsjɔnɛʀ] nm torturer

**tortue** [tɔʀty] nf tortoise; (d'eau douce) terrapin; (d'eau de mer) turtle

**tortueux, -euse** [tɔʀtɥø, øz] adj (rue) twisting; (fig) tortuous

**torture** [tɔʀtyʀ] nf torture; **torturer** vt to torture; (fig) to torment

**tôt** [to] adv early; **~ ou tard** sooner or later; **si ~** so early; (déjà) so soon; **plus ~** earlier; **au plus ~** at the earliest

**total, e, -aux** [tɔtal, o] adj, nm total; **au ~** in total; (fig) on the whole; **faire le ~** to work out the total; **totalement** adv totally; **totaliser** vt to total; **totalitaire** adj totalitarian; **totalité** nf: **la totalité de** all (of); the whole +sg; **en totalité** entirely

**toubib** [tubib] (fam) nm doctor

**touchant, e** [tuʃɑ̃, ɑ̃t] adj touching

**touche** [tuʃ] nf (de piano, de machine à écrire) key; (de téléphone) button; (Peinture etc) stroke, touch; (fig: de nostalgie) touch; (Football: aussi: **remise en ~**) throw-in; (aussi: **ligne de ~**) touch-line; **touche dièse** (de téléphone, clavier) hash key

**toucher** [tuʃe] nm touch ▷ vt to touch; (palper) to feel; (atteindre: d'un coup de feu etc) to hit; (concerner) to concern, affect; (contacter) to reach, contact; (recevoir: récompense) to receive, get; (: salaire) to draw, get; (: chèque) to cash; **se toucher** (être en contact) to touch; **au ~** to the touch; **~ à** to touch; (concerner) to have to do with, concern; **je vais lui en ~ un mot** I'll have a word with him about it; **~ au but** (fig) to near one's goal; **~ à sa fin** to be drawing to a close

**touffe** [tuf] nf tuft

**touffu, e** [tufy] adj thick, dense

**toujours** [tuʒuʀ] adv always; (encore) still; (constamment) forever; **~ plus** more and more; **pour ~** forever; **~ est-il que** the fact remains that; **essaie ~** (you can) try anyway

**toupie** [tupi] nf (spinning) top

**tour¹** [tuʀ] nf tower; (immeuble) high-rise block (BRIT) ou building (US); (Échecs) castle, rook; **tour de contrôle** nf control tower; **la tour Eiffel** the Eiffel Tower

**tour²** [tuʀ] nm (excursion) trip; (à pied) stroll, walk; (en voiture) run, ride; (Sport: aussi: **~ de piste**) lap; (d'être servi ou de jouer etc) turn; (de roue etc) revolution; (Pol: aussi: **~ de scrutin**) ballot; (ruse, de prestidigitation) trick; (de taille, hanches) measurement; (Tech) lathe; (circonférence): **de 3 m de ~** 3 m round, with a circumference ou girth of 3 m; **faire le ~ de** to go round; (à pied) to walk round; **c'est au ~ de Renée** it's Renée's turn; **à ~ de rôle, ~ à ~** in turn; **tour de chant** nm song recital; **tour de force** tour de force; **tour de garde** nm spell of duty; **tour d'horizon** nm (fig) general survey; **tour de taille/tête** nm waist/head measurement; **un 33 tours** an LP; **un 45 tours** a single

**tourbe** [tuʀb] nf peat

**tourbillon** [tuʀbijɔ̃] nm whirlwind; (d'eau) whirlpool; (fig) whirl, swirl; **tourbillonner** vi to whirl (round)

**tourelle** [tuʀɛl] nf turret

**tourisme** [tuʀism] nm tourism; **agence de ~** tourist agency; **faire du ~** to go touring; (en ville) to go sightseeing; **touriste** nm/f tourist; **touristique** adj tourist cpd; (région) touristic

**tourment** [tuʀmɑ̃] nm torment;
**tourmenter** vt to torment; **se
tourmenter** to fret, worry o.s.

**tournage** [tuʀnaʒ] nm (Cinéma)
shooting

**tournant** [tuʀnɑ̃] nm (de route) bend;
(fig) turning point

**tournée** [tuʀne] nf (du facteur etc)
round; (d'artiste, politicien) tour; (au café)
round (of drinks)

**tourner** [tuʀne] vt to turn; (sauce,
mélange) to stir; (Cinéma: faire les prises
de vues) to shoot; (: produire) to shoot
▷ vi to turn; (moteur) to run; (taximètre)
to tick away; (lait etc) to turn (sour); **se
tourner** vi to turn round; **tournez à
gauche/droite au prochain carrefour**
turn left/right at the next junction;
**mal ~** to go wrong; **~ autour de** to go
round; (péj) to hang round; **~ à/en** to
turn into; **~ qn en ridicule** to make
sb; **~ le dos à** (mouvement) to turn one's
back on; (position) to have one's back
to; **~ de l'œil** to pass out; **se ~ vers** to
turn towards; (fig) to turn to; **se ~ les
pouces** to twiddle one's thumbs

**tournesol** [tuʀnəsɔl] nm sunflower

**tournevis** [tuʀnəvis] nm screwdriver

**tournoi** [tuʀnwa] nm tournament

**tournure** [tuʀnyʀ] nf (Ling) turn of
phrase; (évolution): **la ~ de qch** the way
sth is developing; **tournure d'esprit**
turn ou cast of mind

**tourte** [tuʀt] nf pie

**tourterelle** [tuʀtəʀɛl] nf turtledove

**tous** [tu] adj, pron voir **tout**

**Toussaint** [tusɛ̃] nf: **la ~** All Saints' Day

**tousser** [tuse] vi to cough

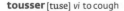 **MOT-CLÉ**

**tout, e** [tu, tut] (mpl **tous**, fpl **toutes**)
adj **1** (avec article singulier) all; **tout le
lait** all the milk; **toute la nuit** all night,
the whole night; **tout le livre** the whole
book; **tout un pain** a whole loaf; **tout
le temps** all the time; the whole time;
**tout le monde** everybody; **c'est tout
le contraire** it's quite the opposite
**2** (avec article pluriel) every, all; **tous les
livres** all the books; **toutes les nuits**
every night; **toutes les fois** every time;
**toutes les trois/deux semaines** every
third/other ou second week, every
three/two weeks; **tous les deux** both
ou each of us (ou them ou you); **toutes
les trois** all three of us (ou them ou you)
**3** (sans article): **à tout âge** at any age;
**pour toute nourriture, il avait ...** his
only food was ...
▷ pron everything, all; **il a tout fait**
he's done everything; **je les vois tous**
I can see them all ou all of them; **nous y
sommes tous allés** all of us went, we
all went; **c'est tout** that's all; **en tout** in
all; **tout ce qu'il sait** all he knows
▷ nm whole; **le tout** all of it (ou them);
**le tout est de ...** the main thing is to ...;
**pas du tout** not at all
▷ adv **1** (très, complètement) very; **tout
près** very near; **le tout premier** the
very first; **tout seul** all alone; **le livre
tout entier** the whole book; **tout
en haut** right at the top; **tout droit**
straight ahead
**2**: **tout en** while; **tout en travaillant**
while working, as he etc works ou worked
**3**: **tout d'abord** first of all; **tout à coup**
suddenly; **tout à fait** absolutely; **tout
à l'heure** a short while ago; (futur) in a
short while, shortly; **à tout à l'heure!**
see you later!; **tout de même** all the
same; **tout de suite** immediately,
straight away; **tout simplement**
quite simply

**toutefois** [tutfwa] adv however

**toutes** [tut] *adj, pron voir* **tout**

**tout-terrain** [tuterɛ̃] *adj:* **vélo ~** mountain bike; **véhicule ~** four-wheel drive

**toux** [tu] *nf* cough

**toxicomane** [tɔksikɔman] *nm/f* drug addict

**toxique** [tɔksik] *adj* toxic

**trac** [tʀak] *nm (au théâtre, en public)* stage fright; *(aux examens)* nerves *pl;* **avoir le ~** *(au théâtre, en public)* to have stage fright; *(aux examens)* to be feeling nervous

**tracasser** [tʀakase] *vt* to worry, bother; **se tracasser** to worry

**trace** [tʀas] *nf (empreintes)* tracks *pl;* *(marques, aussi fig)* mark; *(quantité infime, indice, vestige)* trace; **traces de pas** footprints

**tracer** [tʀase] *vt* to draw; *(piste)* to open up

**tract** [tʀakt] *nm* tract, pamphlet

**tracteur** [tʀaktœʀ] *nm* tractor

**traction** [tʀaksjɔ̃] *nf:* **~ avant/arrière** front-wheel/rear-wheel drive

**tradition** [tʀadisjɔ̃] *nf* tradition; **traditionnel, le** *adj* traditional

**traducteur, -trice** [tʀadyktœʀ, tʀis] *nm/f* translator

**traduction** [tʀadyksjɔ̃] *nf* translation

**traduire** [tʀadɥiʀ] *vt* to translate; *(exprimer)* to convey; **~ qn en justice** to bring sb before the courts; **pouvez-vous me ~ ceci?** can you translate this for me?

**trafic** [tʀafik] *nm* traffic; **trafic d'armes** arms dealing; **trafiquant, e** *nm/f* trafficker; *(d'armes)* dealer; **trafiquer** *(péj) vt (vin)* to doctor; *(moteur, document)* to tamper with

**tragédie** [tʀaʒedi] *nf* tragedy; **tragique** *adj* tragic

**trahir** [tʀaiʀ] *vt* to betray; **trahison** *nf* betrayal; *(Jur)* treason

**train** [tʀɛ̃] *nm (Rail)* train; *(allure)* pace; **être en ~ de faire qch** to be doing sth; **c'est bien le ~ pour ...?** is this the train for ...?; **train d'atterrissage** undercarriage; **train de vie** lifestyle; **train électrique** *(jouet)* (electric) train set

**traîne** [tʀɛn] *nf (de robe)* train; **être à la ~** to lag behind

**traîneau, x** [tʀɛno] *nm* sleigh, sledge

**traîner** [tʀene] *vt (remorque)* to pull; *(enfant, chien)* to drag *ou* trail along ▷ *vi (robe, manteau)* to trail; *(être en désordre)* to lie around; *(aller lentement)* to dawdle (along); *(vagabonder, agir lentement)* to hang about; *(durer)* to drag on; **se traîner** *vi:* **se ~ par terre** to crawl (on the ground); **~ les pieds** to drag one's feet

**train-train** [tʀɛ̃tʀɛ̃] *nm* humdrum routine

**traire** [tʀɛʀ] *vt* to milk

**trait** [tʀɛ] *nm (ligne)* line; *(de dessin)* stroke; *(caractéristique)* feature, trait; **traits** *nmpl (du visage)* features; **d'un ~** *(boire)* in one gulp; **de ~** *(animal)* draught; **avoir ~ à** to concern; **trait d'union** hyphen

**traitant, e** [tʀɛtɑ̃, ɑ̃t] *adj (shampooing)* medicated; **votre médecin ~** your usual *ou* family doctor

**traite** [tʀɛt] *nf (Comm)* draft; *(Agr)* milking; **d'une ~** without stopping

**traité** [tʀete] *nm* treaty

**traitement** [tʀɛtmɑ̃] *nm* treatment; *(salaire)* salary; **traitement de données** data processing; **traitement de texte** word processing; *(logiciel)* word processing package

**traiter** [tʀete] *vt* to treat; *(qualifier):* **~ qn d'idiot** to call sb a fool ▷ *vi* to deal; **~ de** to deal with

**traiteur** [tʀɛtœʀ] *nm* caterer

**traître, -esse** [tʀɛtʀ, tʀɛtʀɛs] *adj (dangereux)* treacherous ▷ *nm* traitor

**trajectoire** [tʀaʒɛktwaʀ] *nf* path

**trajet** [tʀaʒɛ] *nm (parcours, voyage)* journey; *(itinéraire)* route; *(distance à parcourir)* distance; **il y a une heure de ~** the journey takes one hour

**trampoline** [tʀɑ̃pɔlin] *nm* trampoline

**tramway** [tʀamwɛ] *nm* tram(way);

(voiture) tram(car) (BRIT), streetcar (US)

**tranchant, e** [tʀɑ̃ʃɑ̃, ɑ̃t] adj sharp; (fig) peremptory ▷ nm (d'un couteau) cutting edge; (de la main) edge; **à double ~** double-edged

**tranche** [tʀɑ̃ʃ] nf (morceau) slice; (arête) edge; **~ d'âge/de salaires** age/wage bracket

**tranché, e** [tʀɑ̃ʃe] adj (couleurs) distinct; (opinions) clear-cut

**trancher** [tʀɑ̃ʃe] vt to cut, sever ▷ vi to take a decision; **~ avec** to contrast sharply with

**tranquille** [tʀɑ̃kil] adj quiet; (rassuré) easy in one's mind, with one's mind at rest; **se tenir ~** (enfant) to be quiet; **laisse-moi/laisse-ça ~** leave me/it alone; **avoir la conscience ~** to have a clear conscience; **tranquillisant** nm tranquillizer; **tranquillité** nf peace (and quiet); (d'esprit) peace of mind

**transférer** [tʀɑ̃sfeʀe] vt to transfer; **transfert** nm transfer

**transformation** [tʀɑ̃sfɔʀmasjɔ̃] nf change, alteration; (radicale) transformation; (Rugby) conversion; **transformations** nfpl (travaux) alterations

**transformer** [tʀɑ̃sfɔʀme] vt to change; (radicalement) to transform; (vêtement) to alter; (matière première, appartement, Rugby) to convert; **(se) ~ en** to turn into

**transfusion** [tʀɑ̃sfyzjɔ̃] nf: **~ sanguine** blood transfusion

**transgénique** [tʀɑ̃sʒenik] adj transgenic

**transgresser** [tʀɑ̃sgʀese] vt to contravene

**transi, e** [tʀɑ̃zi] adj numb (with cold), chilled to the bone

**transiger** [tʀɑ̃ziʒe] vi to compromise

**transit** [tʀɑ̃zit] nm transit; **transiter** vi to pass in transit

**transition** [tʀɑ̃zisjɔ̃] nf transition; **transitoire** adj transitional

**transmettre** [tʀɑ̃smɛtʀ] vt (passer): **~ qch à qn** to pass sth on to sb;

(Tech, Tél, Méd) to transmit; (TV, Radio: retransmettre) to broadcast; **transmission** nf transmission

**transparent, e** [tʀɑ̃spaʀɑ̃, ɑ̃t] adj transparent

**transpercer** [tʀɑ̃spɛʀse] vt (froid, pluie) to go through, pierce; (balle) to go through

**transpiration** [tʀɑ̃spiʀasjɔ̃] nf perspiration

**transpirer** [tʀɑ̃spiʀe] vi to perspire

**transplanter** [tʀɑ̃splɑ̃te] vt (Méd, Bot) to transplant

**transport** [tʀɑ̃spɔʀ] nm transport; **transports en commun** public transport sg; **transporter** vt to carry, move; (Comm) to transport, convey; **transporteur** nm haulage contractor (BRIT), trucker (US)

**transvaser** [tʀɑ̃svɑze] vt to decant

**transversal, e, -aux** [tʀɑ̃svɛʀsal, o] adj (rue) which runs across; **coupe ~e** cross section

**trapèze** [tʀapɛz] nm (au cirque) trapeze

**trappe** [tʀap] nf trap door

**trapu, e** [tʀapy] adj squat, stocky

**traquenard** [tʀaknaʀ] nm trap

**traquer** [tʀake] vt to track down; (harceler) to hound

**traumatiser** [tʀomatize] vt to traumatize

**travail, -aux** [tʀavaj] nm (gén) work; (tâche, métier) work no pl, job; (Écon, Méd) labour; **être sans ~** (employé) to be unemployed; voir aussi **travaux**; **travail (au) noir** moonlighting

**travailler** [tʀavaje] vi to work; (bois) to warp ▷ vt (bois, métal) to work; (objet d'art, discipline) to work on; **cela le travaille** it is on his mind; **travailleur, -euse** adj hard-working ▷ nm/f worker; **travailleur social** social worker; **travailliste** adj ≈ Labour cpd

**travaux** [tʀavo] nmpl (de réparation, agricoles etc) work sg; (sur route) roadworks pl; (de construction) building (work); **travaux des champs** farmwork sg; **travaux dirigés** (Scol) tutorial sg; **travaux forcés** hard labour no pl; **travaux manuels** (Scol) handicrafts; **travaux ménagers** housework no pl; **travaux pratiques** (Scol) practical work; (en laboratoire) lab work

**travers** [tʀavɛʀ] nm fault, failing; **en ~ (de)** across; **au ~ (de)/à ~** through; **de ~** (nez, bouche) crooked; (chapeau) askew; **comprendre de ~** to misunderstand; **regarder de ~** (fig) to look askance at

**traverse** [tʀavɛʀs] nf (de voie ferrée) sleeper; **chemin de ~** shortcut

**traversée** [tʀavɛʀse] nf crossing; **combien de temps dure la ~?** how long does the crossing take?

**traverser** [tʀavɛʀse] vt (gén) to cross; (ville, tunnel, aussi: percer, fig) to go through; (suj: ligne, trait) to run across

**traversin** [tʀavɛʀsɛ̃] nm bolster

**travesti** [tʀavɛsti] nm transvestite

**trébucher** [tʀebyʃe] vi: **~ (sur)** to stumble (over), trip (against)

**trèfle** [tʀɛfl] nm (Bot) clover; (Cartes: couleur) clubs pl; (: carte) club; **~ à quatre feuilles** four-leaf clover

**treize** [tʀɛz] num thirteen; **treizième** num thirteenth

**tréma** [tʀema] nm diaeresis

**tremblement** [tʀɑ̃bləmɑ̃] nm: **tremblement de terre** earthquake

**trembler** [tʀɑ̃ble] vi to tremble, shake; **~ de** (froid, fièvre) to shiver ou tremble with; (peur) to shake ou tremble with; **~ pour qn** to fear for sb

**trémousser** [tʀemuse]: **se trémousser** vi to jig about, wriggle about

**trempé, e** [tʀɑ̃pe] adj soaking (wet), drenched; (Tech) tempered

**tremper** [tʀɑ̃pe] vt to soak, drench; (aussi: **faire ~, mettre à ~**) to soak; (plonger): **~ qch dans** to dip sth in(to) ▷ vi to soak; (fig): **~ dans** to be involved ou have a hand in; **se tremper** vi to have a quick dip

**tremplin** [tʀɑ̃plɛ̃] nm springboard; (Ski) ski-jump

**trentaine** [tʀɑ̃tɛn] nf: **une ~ (de)** thirty or so, about thirty; **avoir la ~** (âge) to be around thirty

**trente** [tʀɑ̃t] num thirty; **être sur son ~ et un** to be wearing one's Sunday best; **trentième** num thirtieth

**trépidant, e** [tʀepidɑ̃, ɑ̃t] adj (fig: rythme) pulsating; (: vie) hectic

**trépigner** [tʀepiɲe] vi to stamp (one's feet)

**très** [tʀɛ] adv very; much +pp, highly +pp

**trésor** [tʀezɔʀ] nm treasure; **Trésor (public)** public revenue; **trésorerie** nf (gestion) accounts pl; (bureaux) accounts department; **difficultés de trésorerie** cash problems, shortage of cash ou funds; **trésorier, -ière** nm/f treasurer

**tressaillir** [tʀesajiʀ] vi to shiver, shudder

**tressauter** [tʀesote] vi to start, jump

**tresse** [tʀɛs] nf braid, plait; **tresser** vt (cheveux) to braid, plait; (fil, jonc) to plait; (corbeille) to weave; (corde) to twist

**tréteau, x** [tʀeto] nm trestle

**treuil** [tʀœj] nm winch

**trêve** [tʀɛv] nf (Mil, Pol) truce; (fig) respite; **~ de ...** enough of this ...

**tri** [tʀi] nm: **faire le ~ (de)** to sort out; **le (bureau de) ~** (Postes) the sorting office

**triangle** [tʀijɑ̃gl] nm triangle; **triangulaire** adj triangular

**tribord** [tʀibɔʀ] nm: **à ~** to starboard, on the starboard side

**tribu** [tʀiby] nf tribe

**tribunal, -aux** [tʀibynal, o] nm (Jur) court; (Mil) tribunal

**tribune** [tʀibyn] nf (estrade) platform, rostrum; (débat) forum; (d'église, de tribunal) gallery; (de stade) stand

**tribut** [tʀiby] nm tribute

**tributaire** [tʀibytɛʀ] adj: **être ~ de** to be dependent on

**tricher** [tʀiʃe] vi to cheat; **tricheur, -euse** nm/f cheat(er)

**tricolore** [tʀikɔlɔʀ] adj three-coloured; (français) red, white and blue

**tricot** [tʀiko] nm (technique, ouvrage) knitting no pl; (vêtement) jersey, sweater; **~ de peau** vest; **tricoter** vt to knit

**tricycle** [tʀisikl] nm tricycle

**trier** [tʀije] vt to sort out; (Postes, fruits) to sort

**trimestre** [tʀimɛstʀ] nm (Scol) term; (Comm) quarter; **trimestriel, le** adj quarterly; (Scol) end-of-term

**trinquer** [tʀɛ̃ke] vi to clink glasses

**triomphe** [tʀijɔ̃f] nm triumph; **triompher** vi to triumph, win; **triompher de** to triumph over, overcome

**tripes** [tʀip] nfpl (Culin) tripe sg

**triple** [tʀipl] adj triple ▷ nm: **le ~ (de)** (comparaison) three times as much (as); **en ~ exemplaire** in triplicate; **tripler** vi, vt to triple, treble

**triplés, -ées** [tʀiple] nm/fpl triplets

**tripoter** [tʀipɔte] vt to fiddle with

**triste** [tʀist] adj sad; (couleur, temps, journée) dreary; (péj): **~ personnage/ affaire** sorry individual/affair; **tristesse** nf sadness

**trivial, e, -aux** [tʀivjal, jo] adj coarse, crude; (commun) mundane

**troc** [tʀɔk] nm barter

**trognon** [tʀɔɲɔ̃] nm (de fruit) core; (de légume) stalk

**trois** [tʀwɑ] num three; **troisième** num third ▷ nf (Scol) year 10 (BRIT), ninth grade (US); **le troisième âge** (période de vie) one's retirement years; (personnes âgées) senior citizens pl

**trombe** [tʀɔ̃b] nf: **des ~s d'eau** a downpour; **en ~** like a whirlwind

**trombone** [tʀɔ̃bɔn] nm (Mus) trombone; (de bureau) paper clip

**trompe** [tʀɔ̃p] nf (d'éléphant) trunk; (Mus) trumpet, horn

**tromper** [tʀɔ̃pe] vt to deceive; (vigilance, poursuivants) to elude; **se tromper** vi to make a mistake, be mistaken; **se ~ de voiture/jour** to take the wrong car/get the day wrong; **se ~ de 3 cm/20 euros** to be out by 3 cm/20

euros; **je me suis trompé de route** I took the wrong road

**trompette** [tʀɔ̃pɛt] nf trumpet; **en ~** (nez) turned-up

**trompeur, -euse** [tʀɔ̃pœʀ, øz] adj deceptive

**tronc** [tʀɔ̃] nm (Bot, Anat) trunk; (d'église) collection box

**tronçon** [tʀɔ̃sɔ̃] nm section; **tronçonner** vt to saw up; **tronçonneuse** nf chainsaw

**trône** [tʀon] nm throne

**trop** [tʀo] adv (+vb) too much; (+adjectif, adverbe) too; **~ (nombreux)** too many; **~ peu (nombreux)** too few; **~ (souvent)** too often; **~ (longtemps)** (for) too long; **~ de** (nombre) too many; (quantité) too much; **de ~, en ~: des livres en ~** a few books too many; **du lait en ~** too much milk; **3 livres/3 euros de ~** 3 books too many/3 euros too much; **ça coûte ~ cher** it's too expensive

**tropical, e, -aux** [tʀɔpikal, o] adj tropical

**tropique** [tʀɔpik] nm tropic

**trop-plein** [tʀoplɛ̃] nm (tuyau) overflow ou outlet (pipe); (liquide) overflow

**troquer** [tʀɔke] vt: **~ qch contre** to barter ou trade sth for; (fig) to swap sth for

**trot** [tʀo] nm trot; **trotter** vi to trot

**trottinette** [tʀɔtinɛt] nf (child's) scooter

**trottoir** [tʀɔtwaʀ] nm pavement (BRIT), sidewalk (US); **faire le ~** (péj) to walk the streets; **trottoir roulant** moving walkway, travellator

**trou** [tʀu] nm hole; (fig) gap; (Comm) deficit; **trou d'air** air pocket; **trou de mémoire** blank, lapse of memory

**troublant, e** [tʀublɑ̃, ɑ̃t] adj disturbing

**trouble** [tʀubl] adj (liquide) cloudy; (image, photo) blurred; (affaire) shady, murky ▷ adv: **voir ~** to have blurred vision ▷ nm agitation; **troubles** nmpl (Pol) disturbances, troubles, unrest sg;

(*Méd*) trouble *sg*, disorders; **trouble-fête** *nm* spoilsport

**troubler** [tʀuble] *vt* to disturb; (*liquide*) to make cloudy; (*intriguer*) to bother; **se troubler** *vi* (*personne*) to become flustered *ou* confused

**trouer** [tʀue] *vt* to make a hole (*ou* holes) in

**trouille** [tʀuj] (*fam*) *nf*: **avoir la ~** to be scared to death

**troupe** [tʀup] *nf* troop; **troupe (de théâtre)** (theatrical) company

**troupeau, x** [tʀupo] *nm* (*de moutons*) flock; (*de vaches*) herd

**trousse** [tʀus] *nf* case, kit; (*d'écolier*) pencil case; **aux ~s de** (*fig*) on the heels *ou* tail of; **trousse à outils** toolkit; **trousse de toilette** toilet bag

**trousseau, x** [tʀuso] *nm* (*de mariée*) trousseau; **trousseau de clefs** bunch of keys

**trouvaille** [tʀuvaj] *nf* find

**trouver** [tʀuve] *vt* to find; (*rendre visite*): **aller/venir ~ qn** to go/come and see sb; **se trouver** *vi* (*être*) to be; **je trouve que** I find *ou* think that; **~ à boire/critiquer** to find something to drink/criticize; **se ~ mal** to pass out

**truand** [tʀyɑ̃] *nm* gangster; **truander** *vt*: **se faire truander** to be swindled

**truc** [tʀyk] *nm* (*astuce*) way, trick; (*de cinéma, prestidigitateur*) trick, effect; (*chose*) thing, thingumajig; **avoir le ~** to have the knack; **c'est pas mon ~** (*fam*) it's not really my thing

**truffe** [tʀyf] *nf* truffle; (*nez*) nose

**truffé, e** [tʀyfe] *adj* (*Culin*) garnished with truffles; **~ de** (*fig: citations*) peppered with; (*: fautes*) riddled with; (*: pièges*) bristling with

**truie** [tʀɥi] *nf* sow

**truite** [tʀɥit] *nf* trout *inv*

**truquage** [tʀykaʒ] *nm* special effects *pl*

**truquer** [tʀyke] *vt* (*élections, serrure, dés*) to fix

**TSVP** *sigle* (= *tournez svp*) PTO

**TTC** *sigle* (= *toutes taxes comprises*) inclusive of tax

**tu¹** [ty] *pron* you; **dire tu à qn** to use the "tu" form to sb

**tu², e** [ty] *pp de* **taire**

**tuba** [tyba] *nm* (*Mus*) tuba; (*Sport*) snorkel

**tube** [tyb] *nm* tube; (*chanson*) hit

**tuberculose** [tybɛʀkyloz] *nf* tuberculosis

**tuer** [tɥe] *vt* to kill; **se tuer** *vi* to be killed; (*suicide*) to kill o.s.; **se ~ au travail** (*fig*) to work o.s. to death; **tuerie** *nf* slaughter *no pl*

**tue-tête** [tytɛt] : **à ~** *adv* at the top of one's voice

**tueur** [tɥœʀ] *nm* killer; **tueur à gages** hired killer

**tuile** [tɥil] *nf* tile; (*fam*) spot of bad luck, blow

**tulipe** [tylip] *nf* tulip

**tuméfié, e** [tymefje] *adj* puffed-up, swollen

**tumeur** [tymœʀ] *nf* growth, tumour

**tumulte** [tymylt] *nm* commotion; **tumultueux, -euse** *adj* stormy, turbulent

**tunique** [tynik] *nf* tunic

**Tunis** [tynis] *n* Tunis

**Tunisie** [tynizi] *nf*: **la ~** Tunisia; **tunisien, ne** *adj* Tunisian ▷ *nm/f*: **Tunisien, ne** Tunisian

**tunnel** [tynɛl] *nm* tunnel; **le ~ sous la Manche** the Channel Tunnel

**turbulent, e** [tyʀbylɑ̃, ɑ̃t] *adj* boisterous, unruly

**turc, turque** [tyʀk] *adj* Turkish ▷ *nm/f*: **T~, Turque** Turk/Turkish woman ▷ *nm* (*Ling*) Turkish

**turf** [tyʀf] *nm* racing; **turfiste** *nm/f* racegoer

**Turquie** [tyʀki] *nf*: **la ~** Turkey

**turquoise** [tyʀkwaz] *nf* turquoise ▷ *adj inv* turquoise

**tutelle** [tytɛl] *nf* (*Jur*) guardianship; (*Pol*) trusteeship; **sous la ~ de** (*fig*) under the supervision of

**tuteur** [tytœʀ] *nm* (*Jur*) guardian; (*de plante*) stake, support

**tutoyer** [tytwaje] *vt*: **~ qn** to address

sb as "tu"

**tuyau, x** [tɥijo] *nm* pipe; (*flexible*) tube;
(*fam*) tip; **tuyau d'arrosage** hosepipe;
**tuyau d'échappement** exhaust pipe;
**tuyauterie** *nf* piping *no pl*

**TVA** *sigle f* (= *taxe à la valeur ajoutée*) VAT

**tympan** [tɛ̃pɑ̃] *nm* (*Anat*) eardrum

**type** [tip] *nm* type; (*fam*) chap, guy ▷ *adj*
typical, classic

**typé, e** [tipe] *adj* ethnic

**typique** [tipik] *adj* typical

**tyran** [tirɑ̃] *nm* tyrant; **tyrannique** *adj*
tyrannical

**tzigane** [dzigan] *adj* gipsy, tzigane

**ulcère** [ylsɛʀ] *nm* ulcer

**ultérieur, e** [ylteʀjœʀ] *adj* later,
subsequent; **remis à une date
~e** postponed to a later date;
**ultérieurement** *adv* later,
subsequently

**ultime** [yltim] *adj* final

**○ MOT-CLÉ**

**un, une** [œ̃, yn] *art indéf* a; (*devant
voyelle*) an; **un garçon/vieillard** a
boy/an old man; **une fille** a girl
▷ *pron* one; **l'un des meilleurs** one of
the best; **l'un ..., l'autre** (the) one ...,
the other; **les uns ..., les autres**
some ..., others; **l'un et l'autre** both
(of them); **l'un ou l'autre** either (of
them); **l'un l'autre** each other; **les
uns les autres** one another; **pas un
seul** not a single one; **un par un** one
by one
▷ *num* one; **un pamplemousse
seulement** one grapefruit only, just

one grapefruit
▷ *nf*: **la une** (*Presse*) the front page

**unanime** [ynanim] *adj* unanimous;
**unanimité** *nf*: **à l'unanimité**
unanimously

**uni, e** [yni] *adj* (*ton, tissu*) plain; (*surface*)
smooth, even; (*famille*) close(-knit);
(*pays*) united

**unifier** [ynifje] *vt* to unite, unify

**uniforme** [yniform] *adj* uniform;
(*surface, ton*) even ▷ *nm* uniform;
**uniformiser** *vt* (*systèmes*) to
standardize

**union** [ynjɔ̃] *nf* union; **union de
consommateurs** consumers'
association; **union libre**: **vivre en
union libre** (*en concubinage*) to cohabit;
**Union européenne** European Union;
**Union soviétique** Soviet Union

**unique** [ynik] *adj* (*seul*) only;
(*exceptionnel*) unique; (*le même*): **un
prix/système ~** a single price/system;
**fils/fille ~** only son/daughter,
only child; **sens ~** one-way street;
**uniquement** *adv* only, solely; (*juste*)
only, merely

**unir** [ynir] *vt* (*nations*) to unite; (*en
mariage*) to unite, join together; **s'unir**
*vi* to unite; (*en mariage*) to be joined
together

**unitaire** [yniter] *adj*: **prix ~** unit price

**unité** [ynite] *nf* unit; (*harmonie,
cohésion*) unity

**univers** [yniver] *nm* universe;
**universel, le** *adj* universal

**universitaire** [yniversiter] *adj*
university *cpd*; (*diplôme, études*)
academic, university *cpd* ▷ *nm/f*
academic

**université** [yniversite] *nf* university

**urbain, e** [yrbɛ̃, ɛn] *adj* urban, city
*cpd*, town *cpd*; **urbanisme** *nm* town
planning

**urgence** [yrʒɑ̃s] *nf* urgency; (*Méd etc*)
emergency; **d'~** *adj* emergency *cpd*
▷ *adv* as a matter of urgency; **(service
des) ~s** casualty

**urgent, e** [yrʒɑ̃, ɑ̃t] *adj* urgent

**urine** [yrin] *nf* urine; **urinoir** *nm*
(public) urinal

**urne** [yrn] *nf* (*électorale*) ballot box;
(*vase*) urn

**urticaire** [yrtiker] *nf* nettle rash

**us** [ys] *nmpl*: **us et coutumes** (habits
and) customs

**usage** [yzaʒ] *nm* (*emploi, utilisation*) use;
(*coutume*) custom; **à l'~** with use; **à l'~
de** (*pour*) (for use of); **en ~** in use; **hors
d'~** out of service; **à ~ interne** (*Méd*) to
be taken (internally); **à ~ externe** (*Méd*)
for external use only; **usagé, e** *adj* (*usé*)
worn; **usager, -ère** *nm/f* user

**usé, e** [yze] *adj* worn; (*banal: argument
etc*) hackneyed

**user** [yze] *vt* (*outil*) to wear down;
(*vêtement*) to wear out; (*matière*) to wear
away; (*consommer: charbon etc*) to use;
**s'user** *vi* (*tissu, vêtement*) to wear out;
**~ de** (*moyen, procédé*) to use, employ;
(*droit*) to exercise

**usine** [yzin] *nf* factory

**usité, e** [yzite] *adj* common

**ustensile** [ystɑ̃sil] *nm* implement;
**ustensile de cuisine** kitchen utensil

**usuel, le** [yzɥɛl] *adj* everyday, common

**usure** [yzyr] *nf* wear

**utérus** [yterys] *nm* uterus, womb

**utile** [ytil] *adj* useful

**utilisation** [ytilizasjɔ̃] *nf* use

**utiliser** [ytilize] *vt* to use

**utilitaire** [ytiliter] *adj* utilitarian

**utilité** [ytilite] *nf* usefulness *no pl*; **de
peu d'~** of little use *ou* help

**utopie** [ytɔpi] *nf* utopia

# V

**va** [va] *vb voir* **aller**

**vacance** [vakɑ̃s] *nf* (*Admin*) vacancy; **vacances** *nfpl* holiday(s *pl* (*BRIT*)), vacation *sg* (*US*); **les grandes ~s** the summer holidays; **prendre des/ses ~s** to take a holiday/one's holiday(s); **aller en ~s** to go on holiday; **je suis ici en ~s** I'm here on holiday; **vacancier, -ière** *nm/f* holiday-maker

**vacant, e** [vakɑ̃, ɑ̃t] *adj* vacant

**vacarme** [vakaʀm] *nm* (*bruit*) racket

**vaccin** [vaksɛ̃] *nm* vaccine; (*opération*) vaccination; **vaccination** *nf* vaccination; **vacciner** *vt* to vaccinate; **être vacciné contre qch** (*fam*) to be cured of sth

**vache** [vaʃ] *nf* (*Zool*) cow; (*cuir*) cowhide ▷ *adj* (*fam*) rotten, mean; **vachement** (*fam*) *adv* (*très*) really; (*pleuvoir, travailler*) a hell of a lot; **vacherie** *nf* (*action*) dirty trick; (*remarque*) nasty remark

**vaciller** [vasije] *vi* to sway, wobble; (*bougie, lumière*) to flicker; (*fig*) to be failing, falter

**va-et-vient** [vaevjɛ̃] *nm inv* (*de personnes, véhicules*) comings and goings *pl*, to-ings and fro-ings *pl*

**vagabond** [vagabɔ̃] *nm* (*rôdeur*) tramp, vagrant; (*voyageur*) wanderer; **vagabonder** *vi* to roam, wander

**vagin** [vaʒɛ̃] *nm* vagina

**vague** [vag] *nf* wave ▷ *adj* vague; (*regard*) faraway; (*manteau, robe*) loose(-fitting); (*quelconque*): **un ~ bureau/cousin** some office/cousin or other; **vague de fond** ground swell; **vague de froid** cold spell

**vaillant, e** [vajɑ̃, ɑ̃t] *adj* (*courageux*) gallant; (*robuste*) hale and hearty

**vain, e** [vɛ̃, vɛn] *adj* vain; **en ~** in vain

**vaincre** [vɛ̃kʀ] *vt* to defeat; (*fig*) to conquer, overcome; **vaincu, e** *nm/f* defeated party; **vainqueur** *nm* victor; (*Sport*) winner

**vaisseau, x** [vɛso] *nm* (*Anat*) vessel; (*Navig*) ship, vessel; **vaisseau spatial** spaceship

**vaisselier** [vɛsəlje] *nm* dresser

**vaisselle** [vɛsɛl] *nf* (*service*) crockery; (*plats etc à laver*) (dirty) dishes *pl*; **faire la ~** to do the washing-up (*BRIT*) *ou* the dishes

**valable** [valabl] *adj* valid; (*acceptable*) decent, worthwhile

**valet** [valɛ] *nm* manservant; (*Cartes*) jack

**valeur** [valœʀ] *nf* (*gén*) value; (*mérite*) worth, merit; (*Comm: titre*) security; **valeurs** *nfpl* (*morales*) values; **mettre en ~** (*détail*) to highlight; (*objet décoratif*) to show off to advantage; **avoir de la ~** to be valuable; **sans ~** worthless; **prendre de la ~** to go up *ou* gain in value

**valide** [valid] *adj* (*en bonne santé*) fit; (*valable*) valid; **valider** *vt* to validate

**valise** [valiz] *nf* (suit)case; **faire ses ~s** to pack one's bags

**vallée** [vale] *nf* valley

**vallon** [valɔ̃] *nm* small valley

**valoir** [valwaʀ] *vi* (*être valable*) to hold, apply ▷ *vt* (*prix, valeur, effort*)

to be worth; (*causer*): **~ qch à qn** to earn sb sth; **se valoir** *vi* to be of equal merit; (*péj*) to be two of a kind; **faire ~** (*droits, prérogatives*) to assert; **se faire ~** to make the most of o.s.; **à ~ sur** to be deducted from; **vaille que vaille** somehow or other; **cela ne me dit rien qui vaille** I don't like the look of it at all; **ce climat ne me vaut rien** this climate doesn't suit me; **~ le coup** *ou* **la peine** to be worth the trouble *ou* worth it; **~ mieux: il vaut mieux se taire** it's better to say nothing; **ça ne vaut rien** it's worthless; **que vaut ce candidat?** how good is this applicant?
**valse** [vals] *nf* waltz
**vandalisme** [vɑ̃dalism] *nm* vandalism
**vanille** [vanij] *nf* vanilla
**vanité** [vanite] *nf* vanity; **vaniteux, -euse** *adj* vain, conceited
**vanne** [van] *nf* gate; (*fig*) joke
**vannerie** [vanʀi] *nf* basketwork
**vantard, e** [vɑ̃taʀ, aʀd] *adj* boastful
**vanter** [vɑ̃te] *vt* to speak highly of, praise; **se vanter** *vi* to boast, brag; **se ~ de** to pride o.s. on; (*péj*) to boast of
**vapeur** [vapœʀ] *nf* steam; (*émanation*) vapour, fumes *pl*; **vapeurs** *nfpl* (*bouffées*) vapours; **à ~** steam-powered, steam *cpd*; **cuit à la ~** steamed; **vapoureux, -euse** *adj* (*flou*) hazy, misty; (*léger*) filmy; **vaporisateur** *nm* spray; **vaporiser** *vt* (*parfum etc*) to spray
**varappe** [vaʀap] *nf* rock climbing
**vareuse** [vaʀøz] *nf* (*blouson*) pea jacket; (*d'uniforme*) tunic
**variable** [vaʀjabl] *adj* variable; (*temps, humeur*) changeable; (*divers: résultats*) varied, various
**varice** [vaʀis] *nf* varicose vein
**varicelle** [vaʀisɛl] *nf* chickenpox
**varié, e** [vaʀje] *adj* varied; (*divers*) various; **hors d'œuvre ~s** selection of hors d'œuvres
**varier** [vaʀje] *vi* to vary; (*temps, humeur*) to change ▷ *vt* to vary; **variété** *nf* variety; **variétés** *nfpl*: **spectacle/ émission de variétés** variety show

**variole** [vaʀjɔl] *nf* smallpox
**Varsovie** [vaʀsɔvi] *n* Warsaw
**vas** [va] *vb voir* **aller; ~-y!** [vazi] go on!
**vase** [vɑz] *nm* vase ▷ *nf* silt, mud; **vaseux, -euse** *adj* silty, muddy; (*fig: confus*) woolly, hazy; (: *fatigué*) woozy
**vasistas** [vazistɑs] *nm* fanlight
**vaste** [vast] *adj* vast, immense
**vautour** [votuʀ] *nm* vulture
**vautrer** [votʀe] *vb*: **se ~ dans/sur** to wallow in/sprawl on
**va-vite** [vavit]: **à la ~** *adv* in a rush *ou* hurry
**VDQS** *sigle* (= *vin délimité de qualité supérieure*) *label guaranteeing the quality of wine*
**veau, x** [vo] *nm* (*Zool*) calf; (*Culin*) veal; (*peau*) calfskin
**vécu, e** [veky] *pp de* **vivre**
**vedette** [vədɛt] *nf* (*artiste etc*) star; (*canot*) motor boat; (*police*) launch
**végétal, e, -aux** [veʒetal, o] *adj* vegetable ▷ *nm* vegetable, plant; **végétalien, ne** *adj, nm/f* vegan
**végétarien, ne** [veʒetaʀjɛ̃, jɛn] *adj, nm/f* vegetarian; **avez-vous des plats ~s?** do you have any vegetarian dishes?
**végétation** [veʒetasjɔ̃] *nf* vegetation; **végétations** *nfpl* (*Méd*) adenoids
**véhicule** [veikyl] *nm* vehicle; **véhicule utilitaire** commercial vehicle
**veille** [vɛj] *nf* (*état*) wakefulness; (*jour*): **la ~ (de)** the day before; **la ~ au soir** the previous evening; **à la ~ de** on the eve of; **la ~ de Noël** Christmas Eve; **la ~ du jour de l'An** New Year's Eve
**veillée** [veje] *nf* (*soirée*) evening; (*réunion*) evening gathering; **veillée (funèbre)** wake
**veiller** [veje] *vi* to stay up ▷ *vt* (*malade, mort*) to watch over, sit up with; **~ à** to attend to, see to; **~ à ce que** to make sure that; **~ sur** to watch over; **veilleur** *nm*: **veilleur de nuit** night watchman; **veilleuse** *nf* (*lampe*) night light; (*Auto*) sidelight; (*flamme*) pilot light
**veinard, e** [vɛnaʀ, aʀd] *nm/f* lucky devil

**veine** [vɛn] nf (Anat, du bois etc) vein; (filon) vein, seam; (fam: chance): **avoir de la ~** to be lucky

**véliplanchiste** [veliplɑ̃ʃist] nm/f windsurfer

**vélo** [velo] nm bike, cycle; **faire du ~** to go cycling; **vélomoteur** nm moped

**velours** [v(ə)luʀ] nm velvet; **velours côtelé** corduroy; **velouté, e** adj velvety ▷ nm: **velouté de tomates** cream of tomato soup

**velu, e** [vəly] adj hairy

**vendange** [vɑ̃dɑ̃ʒ] nf (aussi: **~s**) grape harvest; **vendanger** vi to harvest the grapes

**vendeur, -euse** [vɑ̃dœʀ, øz] nm/f shop assistant ▷ nm (Jur) vendor, seller

**vendre** [vɑ̃dʀ] vt to sell; **~ qch à qn** to sell sb sth; **"à ~"** "for sale"

**vendredi** [vɑ̃dʀədi] nm Friday; **vendredi saint** Good Friday

**vénéneux, -euse** [venenø, øz] adj poisonous

**vénérien, ne** [veneʀjɛ̃, jɛn] adj venereal

**vengeance** [vɑ̃ʒɑ̃s] nf vengeance no pl, revenge no pl

**venger** [vɑ̃ʒe] vt to avenge; **se venger** vi to avenge o.s.; **se ~ de qch** to avenge o.s. for sth, take one's revenge for sth; **se ~ de qn** to take revenge on sb; **se ~ sur** to take revenge on

**venimeux, -euse** [vənimø, øz] adj poisonous, venomous; (fig: haineux) venomous, vicious

**venin** [vənɛ̃] nm venom, poison

**venir** [v(ə)niʀ] vi to come; **~ de** to come from; **~ de faire: je viens d'y aller/de le voir** I've just been there/seen him; **s'il vient à pleuvoir** if it should rain; **j'en viens à croire que** I have come to believe that; **où veux-tu en ~?** what are you getting at?; **faire ~** (docteur, plombier) to call (out)

**vent** [vɑ̃] nm wind; **il y a du ~** it's windy; **c'est du ~** it's all hot air; **dans le ~** (fam) trendy

**vente** [vɑ̃t] nf sale; **la ~** (activité) selling;

(secteur) sales pl; **mettre en ~** (produit) to put on sale; (maison, objet personnel) to put up for sale; **vente aux enchères** auction sale; **vente de charité** jumble sale

**venteux, -euse** [vɑ̃tø, øz] adj windy

**ventilateur** [vɑ̃tilatœʀ] nm fan

**ventiler** [vɑ̃tile] vt to ventilate

**ventouse** [vɑ̃tuz] nf (de caoutchouc) suction pad

**ventre** [vɑ̃tʀ] nm (Anat) stomach; (légèrement péj) belly; (utérus) womb; **avoir mal au ~** to have stomach ache (BRIT) ou a stomach ache (US)

**venu, e** [v(ə)ny] pp de **venir** ▷ adj: **bien ~** timely; **mal ~** out of place; **être mal ~ à ou de faire** to have no grounds for doing, be in no position to do

**ver** [vɛʀ] nm worm; (des fruits etc) maggot; (du bois) woodworm no pl; voir aussi **vers**; **ver à soie** silkworm; **ver de terre** earthworm; **ver luisant** glow-worm; **ver solitaire** tapeworm

**verbe** [vɛʀb] nm verb

**verdâtre** [vɛʀdɑtʀ] adj greenish

**verdict** [vɛʀdik(t)] nm verdict

**verdir** [vɛʀdiʀ] vi, vt to turn green; **verdure** nf greenery

**véreux, -euse** [veʀø, øz] adj worm-eaten; (malhonnête) shady, corrupt

**verge** [vɛʀʒ] nf (Anat) penis

**verger** [vɛʀʒe] nm orchard

**verglacé, e** [vɛʀglase] adj icy, iced-over

**verglas** [vɛʀglɑ] nm (black) ice

**véridique** [veʀidik] adj truthful

**vérification** [veʀifikasjɔ̃] nf (action) checking no pl; (contrôle) check

**vérifier** [veʀifje] vt to check; (corroborer) to confirm, bear out

**véritable** [veʀitabl] adj real; (ami, amour) true; **un ~ désastre** an absolute disaster

**vérité** [veʀite] nf truth; **en ~** really, actually

**verlan** [vɛʀlɑ̃] nm (fam) (back) slang

**vermeil, le** [vɛʀmɛj] adj ruby red

**vermine** [vɛʀmin] nf vermin pl

**vermoulu, e** [vɛʀmuly] *adj* worm-eaten

**verni, e** [vɛʀni] *adj* (*fam*) lucky; **cuir ~** patent leather

**vernir** [vɛʀniʀ] *vt* (*bois, tableau, ongles*) to varnish; (*poterie*) to glaze; **vernis** *nm* (*enduit*) varnish; glaze; (*fig*) veneer; **vernis à ongles** nail polish *ou* varnish; **vernissage** *nm* (*d'une exposition*) preview

**vérole** [veʀɔl] *nf* (*variole*) smallpox

**verre** [vɛʀ] *nm* glass; (*de lunettes*) lens *sg*; **boire** *ou* **prendre un ~** to have a drink; **verres de contact** contact lenses; **verrière** *nf* (*paroi vitrée*) glass wall; (*toit vitré*) glass roof

**verrou** [veʀu] *nm* (*targette*) bolt; **mettre qn sous les ~s** to put sb behind bars; **verrouillage** *nm* locking; **verrouillage centralisé** central locking; **verrouiller** *vt* (*porte*) to bolt; (*ordinateur*) to lock

**verrue** [veʀy] *nf* wart

**vers** [vɛʀ] *nm* line ▷ *nmpl* (*poésie*) verse *sg* ▷ *prép* (*en direction de*) toward(s); (*près de*) around (about); (*temporel*) about, around

**versant** [vɛʀsɑ̃] *nm* slopes *pl*, side

**versatile** [vɛʀsatil] *adj* fickle, changeable

**verse** [vɛʀs]: **à ~** *adv*: **il pleut à ~** it's pouring (with rain)

**Verseau** [vɛʀso] *nm*: **le ~** Aquarius

**versement** [vɛʀsəmɑ̃] *nm* payment; **en 3 ~s** in 3 instalments

**verser** [vɛʀse] *vt* (*liquide, grains*) to pour; (*larmes, sang*) to shed; (*argent*) to pay; **~ qch sur un compte** to pay sth into an account

**version** [vɛʀsjɔ̃] *nf* version; (*Scol*) translation (*into the mother tongue*); **film en ~ originale** film in the original language

**verso** [vɛʀso] *nm* back; **voir au ~** see over(leaf)

**vert, e** [vɛʀ, vɛʀt] *adj* green; (*vin*) young; (*vigoureux*) sprightly ▷ *nm* green; **les V~s** (*Pol*) the Greens

**vertèbre** [vɛʀtɛbʀ] *nf* vertebra

**vertement** [vɛʀtəmɑ̃] *adv* (*réprimander*) sharply

**vertical, e, -aux** [vɛʀtikal, o] *adj* vertical; **verticale** *nf* vertical; **à la verticale** vertically; **verticalement** *adv* vertically

**vertige** [vɛʀtiʒ] *nm* (*peur du vide*) vertigo; (*étourdissement*) dizzy spell; (*fig*) fever; **vertigineux, -euse** *adj* breathtaking

**vertu** [vɛʀty] *nf* virtue; **en ~ de** in accordance with; **vertueux, -euse** *adj* virtuous

**verve** [vɛʀv] *nf* witty eloquence; **être en ~** to be in brilliant form

**verveine** [vɛʀvɛn] *nf* (*Bot*) verbena, vervain; (*infusion*) verbena tea

**vésicule** [vezikyl] *nf* vesicle; **vésicule biliaire** gall-bladder

**vessie** [vesi] *nf* bladder

**veste** [vɛst] *nf* jacket; **veste droite/croisée** single-/double-breasted jacket

**vestiaire** [vɛstjɛʀ] *nm* (*au théâtre etc*) cloakroom; (*de stade etc*) changing-room (BRIT), locker-room (US)

**vestibule** [vɛstibyl] *nm* hall

**vestige** [vɛstiʒ] *nm* relic; (*fig*) vestige; **vestiges** *nmpl* (*de ville*) remains

**vestimentaire** [vɛstimɑ̃tɛʀ] *adj* (*détail*) of dress; (*élégance*) sartorial; **dépenses ~s** clothing expenditure

**veston** [vɛstɔ̃] *nm* jacket

**vêtement** [vɛtmɑ̃] *nm* garment, item of clothing; **vêtements** *nmpl* clothes

**vétérinaire** [veteʀinɛʀ] *nm/f* vet, veterinary surgeon

**vêtir** [vetiʀ] *vt* to clothe, dress

**vêtu, e** [vety] *pp de* **vêtir** ▷ *adj*: **~ de** dressed in, wearing

**vétuste** [vetyst] *adj* ancient, timeworn

**veuf, veuve** [vœf, vœv] *adj* widowed ▷ *nm* widower

**veuve** [vœv] *nf* widow

**vexant, e** [vɛksɑ̃, ɑ̃t] *adj* (*contrariant*) annoying; (*blessant*) hurtful

**vexation** [vɛksasjɔ̃] *nf* humiliation

**vexer** [vɛkse] vt: **~ qn** to hurt sb's feelings; **se vexer** vi to be offended
**viable** [vjabl] adj viable; (économie, industrie etc) sustainable
**viande** [vjɑ̃d] nf meat; **je ne mange pas de ~** I don't eat meat
**vibrer** [vibʀe] vi to vibrate; (son, voix) to be vibrant; (fig) to be stirred; **faire ~** to (cause to) vibrate; (fig) to stir, thrill
**vice** [vis] nm vice; (défaut) fault ▷ préfixe: **~...** vice-; **vice de forme** legal flaw ou irregularity
**vicié, e** [visje] adj (air) polluted, tainted; (Jur) invalidated
**vicieux, -euse** [visjø, jøz] adj (pervers) lecherous; (rétif) unruly ▷ nm/f lecher
**vicinal, e, -aux** [visinal, o] adj: **chemin ~** by-road, byway
**victime** [viktim] nf victim; (d'accident) casualty
**victoire** [viktwaʀ] nf victory
**victuailles** [viktɥaj] nfpl provisions
**vidange** [vidɑ̃ʒ] nf (d'un fossé, réservoir) emptying; (Auto) oil change; (de lavabo: bonde) waste outlet; **vidanges** nfpl (matières) sewage sg; **vidanger** vt to empty
**vide** [vid] adj empty ▷ nm (Physique) vacuum; (espace) (empty) space, gap; (futilité, néant) void; **avoir peur du ~** to be afraid of heights; **emballé sous ~** vacuum packed; **à ~** (sans occupants) empty; (sans charge) unladen
**vidéo** [video] nf video ▷ adj: **cassette ~** video cassette; **jeu ~** video game; **vidéoclip** nm music video; **vidéoconférence** nf videoconference
**vide-ordures** [vidɔʀdyʀ] nm inv (rubbish) chute
**vider** [vide] vt to empty; (Culin: volaille, poisson) to gut, clean out; **se vider** vi to empty; **~ les lieux** to quit ou vacate the premises; **videur** nm (de boîte de nuit) bouncer, doorman
**vie** [vi] nf life; **être en ~** to be alive; **sans ~** lifeless; **à ~** for life; **que faites-vous dans la ~?** what do you do?
**vieil** [vjɛj] adj m voir **vieux**; **vieillard**

nm old man; **vieille** adj, nf voir **vieux**; **vieilleries** nfpl old things; **vieillesse** nf old age; **vieillir** vi (prendre de l'âge) to grow old; (population, vin) to age; (doctrine, auteur) to become dated ▷ vt to age; **vieillissement** nm growing old; ageing
**Vienne** [vjɛn] nf Vienna
**viens** [vjɛ̃] vb voir **venir**
**vierge** [vjɛʀʒ] adj virgin; (page) clean, blank ▷ nf virgin; (signe): **la V~** Virgo
**Vietnam, Viet-Nam** [vjɛtnam] nm Vietnam; **vietnamien, ne** adj Vietnamese ▷ nm/f: **Vietnamien, ne** Vietnamese
**vieux, vieil, vieille** [vjø, vjɛj] adj old ▷ nm/f old man (woman); **les vieux** nmpl old people; **un petit ~** a little old man; **mon ~/ma vieille** (fam) old man/girl; **prendre un coup de ~** to put years on; **vieux garçon** bachelor; **vieux jeu** adj inv old-fashioned
**vif, vive** [vif, viv] adj (animé) lively; (alerte, brusque, aigu) sharp; (lumière, couleur) bright; (air) crisp; (vent, émotion) keen; (fort: regret, déception) great, deep; (vivant): **brûlé ~** burnt alive; **de vive voix** personally; **avoir l'esprit ~** to be quick-witted; **piquer qn au ~** to cut sb to the quick; **à ~** (plaie) open; **avoir les nerfs à ~** to be on edge
**vigne** [viɲ] nf (plante) vine; (plantation) vineyard; **vigneron** nm wine grower
**vignette** [viɲɛt] nf (Admin) ≈ (road) tax disc (BRIT), ≈ license plate sticker (US); (de médicament) price label (used for reimbursement)
**vignoble** [viɲɔbl] nm (plantation) vineyard; (vignes d'une région) vineyards pl
**vigoureux, -euse** [viguʀø, øz] adj vigorous, robust
**vigueur** [vigœʀ] nf vigour; **entrer en ~** to come into force; **en ~** current
**vilain, e** [vilɛ̃, ɛn] adj (laid) ugly; (affaire, blessure) nasty; (pas sage: enfant) naughty; **vilain mot** naughty ou bad word

**villa** [villa] *nf* (detached) house; **~ en multipropriété** time-share villa

**village** [vilaʒ] *nm* village; **villageois, e** *adj* village *cpd* ▷ *nm/f* villager

**ville** [vil] *nf* town; (*importante*) city; (*administration*): **la ~** the (town) council, the local authority; **ville d'eaux** spa; **ville nouvelle** new town

**vin** [vɛ̃] *nm* wine; **avoir le ~ gai** to get happy after a few drinks; **vin d'honneur** reception (*with wine and snacks*); **vin de pays** local wine; **vin ordinaire** *ou* **de table** table wine

**vinaigre** [vinɛgʁ] *nm* vinegar; **vinaigrette** *nf* vinaigrette, French dressing

**vindicatif, -ive** [vɛ̃dikatif, iv] *adj* vindictive

**vingt** [vɛ̃] *num* twenty; **~-quatre heures sur ~-quatre** twenty-four hours a day, round the clock; **vingtaine** *nf*: **une vingtaine (de)** about twenty, twenty or so; **vingtième** *num* twentieth

**vinicole** [vinikɔl] *adj* wine *cpd*, wine-growing

**vinyle** [vinil] *nm* vinyl

**viol** [vjɔl] *nm* (*d'une femme*) rape; (*d'un lieu sacré*) violation

**violacé, e** [vjɔlase] *adj* purplish, mauvish

**violemment** [vjɔlamɑ̃] *adv* violently

**violence** [vjɔlɑ̃s] *nf* violence

**violent, e** [vjɔlɑ̃, ɑ̃t] *adj* violent; (*remède*) drastic

**violer** [vjɔle] *vt* (*femme*) to rape; (*sépulture, loi, traité*) to violate

**violet, te** [vjɔlɛ, ɛt] *adj, nm* purple, mauve; **violette** *nf* (*fleur*) violet

**violon** [vjɔlɔ̃] *nm* violin; (*fam: prison*) lock-up; **violon d'Ingres** hobby; **violoncelle** *nm* cello; **violoniste** *nm/f* violinist

**vipère** [vipɛʁ] *nf* viper, adder

**virage** [viʁaʒ] *nm* (*d'un véhicule*) turn; (*d'une route, piste*) bend

**virée** [viʁe] *nf* trip; (*à pied*) walk; (*longue*) walking tour; (*dans les cafés*) tour

**virement** [viʁmɑ̃] *nm* (*Comm*) transfer

**virer** [viʁe] *vt* (*Comm*): **~ qch (sur)** to transfer sth (into); (*fam: expulser*): **~ qn** to kick sb out ▷ *vi* to turn; (*Chimie*) to change colour: **~ au bleu/rouge** to turn blue/red; **~ de bord** to tack

**virevolter** [viʁvɔlte] *vi* to twirl around

**virgule** [viʁgyl] *nf* comma; (*Math*) point

**viril, e** [viʁil] *adj* (*propre à l'homme*) masculine; (*énergique, courageux*) manly, virile

**virtuel, le** [viʁtɥɛl] *adj* potential; (*théorique*) virtual

**virtuose** [viʁtɥoz] *nm/f* (*Mus*) virtuoso; (*gén*) master

**virus** [viʁys] *nm* virus

**vis¹** [vi] *vb voir* **voir; vivre**

**vis²** [vis] *nf* screw

**visa** [viza] *nm* (*sceau*) stamp; (*validation de passeport*) visa

**visage** [vizaʒ] *nm* face

**vis-à-vis** [vizavi] *prép*: **~ de qn** to(wards) sb; **en ~** facing each other

**visées** [vize] *nfpl* (*intentions*) designs

**viser** [vize] *vi* to aim ▷ *vt* to aim at; (*concerner*) to be aimed *ou* directed at; (*apposer un visa sur*) to stamp, visa; **~ à qch/faire** to aim at sth/at doing *ou* to do

**visibilité** [vizibilite] *nf* visibility

**visible** [vizibl] *adj* visible; (*disponible*): **est-il ~?** can he see me?, will he see visitors?

**visière** [vizjɛʁ] *nf* (*de casquette*) peak; (*qui s'attache*) eyeshade

**vision** [vizjɔ̃] *nf* vision; (*sens*) (eye)sight, vision; (*fait de voir*): **la ~ de** the sight of; **visionneuse** *nf* viewer

**visiophone** [vizjɔfɔn] *nm* videophone

**visite** [vizit] *nf* visit; **~ médicale** medical examination; **~ accompagnée** *ou* **guidée** guided tour; **la ~ guidée commence à quelle heure?** what time does the guided tour start?; **faire une ~ à qn** to call on sb, pay sb a visit; **rendre ~ à qn** to visit sb, pay sb a visit; **être en ~ (chez qn)** to be visiting (sb); **avoir**

**de la ~** to have visitors; **heures de ~** (*hôpital, prison*) visiting hours

**visiter** [vizite] *vt* to visit; **visiteur, -euse** *nm/f* visitor

**vison** [vizɔ̃] *nm* mink

**visser** [vise] *vt*: **~ qch** (*fixer, serrer*) to screw sth on

**visuel, le** [vizɥɛl] *adj* visual

**vital, e, -aux** [vital, o] *adj* vital

**vitamine** [vitamin] *nf* vitamin

**vite** [vit] *adv* (*rapidement*) quickly, fast; (*sans délai*) quickly; (*sous peu*) soon; **~!** quick!; **faire ~** to be quick; **le temps passe ~** time flies

**vitesse** [vitɛs] *nf* speed; (*Auto: dispositif*) gear; **prendre de la ~** to pick up *ou* gather speed; **à toute ~** at full *ou* top speed; **en ~** (*rapidement*) quickly; (*en hâte*) in a hurry

- **LIMITE DE VITESSE**
-
- The speed limit in France is 50 km/h
- in built-up areas, 90 km/h on main
- roads, and 130 km/h on motorways
- (110 km/h when it is raining).

**viticulteur** [vitikyltœr] *nm* wine grower

**vitrage** [vitraʒ] *nm*: **double ~** double glazing

**vitrail, -aux** [vitraj, o] *nm* stained-glass window

**vitre** [vitr] *nf* (*window*) pane; (*de portière, voiture*) window; **vitré, e** *adj* glass *cpd*

**vitrine** [vitrin] *nf* (*shop*) window; (*petite armoire*) display cabinet; **en ~** in the window

**vivable** [vivabl] *adj* (*personne*) livable-with; (*maison*) fit to live in

**vivace** [vivas] *adj* (*arbre, plante*) hardy; (*fig*) indestructible, inveterate

**vivacité** [vivasite] *nf* liveliness, vivacity

**vivant, e** [vivɑ̃, ɑ̃t] *adj* (*qui vit*) living, alive; (*animé*) lively; (*preuve, exemple*) living ▷ *nm*: **du ~ de qn** in sb's lifetime;

**les ~s** the living

**vive** [viv] *adj voir* **vif** ▷ *vb voir* **vivre** ▷ *excl*: **~ le roi!** long live the king!; **vivement** *adv* deeply ▷ *excl*: **vivement les vacances!** roll on the holidays!

**vivier** [vivje] *nm* (*étang*) fish tank; (*réservoir*) fishpond

**vivifiant, e** [vivifjɑ̃, jɑ̃t] *adj* invigorating

**vivoter** [vivɔte] *vi* (*personne*) to scrape a living, get by; (*fig: affaire etc*) to struggle along

**vivre** [vivr] *vi, vt* to live; (*période*) to live through; **vivres** *nmpl* provisions, food supplies; **~ de** to live on; **il vit encore** he is still alive; **se laisser ~** to take life as it comes; **ne plus ~** (*être anxieux*) to live on one's nerves; **il a vécu** (*eu une vie aventureuse*) he has seen life; **être facile à ~** to be easy to get on with; **faire ~ qn** (*pourvoir à sa subsistance*) to provide (a living) for sb

**vlan** [vlɑ̃] *excl* wham!, bang!

**VO** [veo] *nf*: **film en VO** film in the original version; **en VO sous-titrée** in the original version with subtitles

**vocabulaire** [vɔkabylɛr] *nm* vocabulary

**vocation** [vɔkasjɔ̃] *nf* vocation, calling

**vœu, x** [vø] *nm* wish; (*promesse*) vow; **faire ~ de** to take a vow of; **tous nos ~x de bonne année, meilleurs ~x** best wishes for the New Year

**vogue** [vɔg] *nf* fashion, vogue; **en ~** in fashion, in vogue

**voici** [vwasi] *prép* (*pour introduire, désigner*) here is +*sg*, here are +*pl*; **et ~ que ...** and now it (*ou* he) ...; *voir aussi* **voilà**

**voie** [vwa] *nf* way; (*Rail*) track, line; (*Auto*) lane; **être en bonne ~** to be going well; **mettre qn sur la ~** to put sb on the right track; **pays en ~ de développement** developing country; **être en ~ d'achèvement/de rénovation** to be nearing completion/in the process of renovation; **par ~ buccale** *ou* **orale** orally; **route à ~**

**unique** single-track road; **route à 2/3 ~s** 2-/3-lane road; **voie de garage** (*Rail*) siding; **voie express** expressway; **voie ferrée** track; railway line (*BRIT*), railroad (*US*); **la voie lactée** the Milky Way; **la voie publique** the public highway

**voilà** [vwala] *prép* (*en désignant*) there is +*sg*, there are +*pl*; **les ~** *ou* **voici** here *ou* there they are; **en ~** *ou* **voici un** here's one, there's one; **voici mon frère et ~ ma sœur** this is my brother and that's my sister; **~** *ou* **voici deux ans** two years ago; **~** *ou* **voici deux ans que** it's two years since; **et ~!** there we are!; **~ tout** that's all; **~** *ou* **voici** (*en offrant etc*) there *ou* here you are; **tiens! ~ Paul** look! there's Paul

**voile** [vwal] *nm* veil; (*tissu léger*) net ▷ *nf* sail; (*sport*) sailing; **voiler** *vt* to veil; (*fausser: roue*) to buckle; (: *bois*) to warp; **se voiler** *vi* (*lune, regard*) to mist over; (*voix*) to become husky; (*roue, disque*) to buckle; (*planche*) to warp; **voilier** *nm* sailing ship; (*de plaisance*) sailing boat; **voilure** *nf* (*de voilier*) sails *pl*

**voir** [vwar] *vi, vt* to see; **se voir** *vi* (*être visible*) to show; (*se fréquenter*) to see each other; (*se produire*) to happen; **cela se voit** (*c'est visible*) that's obvious, it shows; **faire ~ qch à qn** to show sb sth; **en faire ~ à qn** (*fig*) to give sb a hard time; **ne pas pouvoir ~ qn** not to be able to stand sb; **voyons!** let's see now; (*indignation etc*) come on!; **ça n'a rien à ~ avec lui** that has nothing to do with him

**voire** [vwar] *adv* even

**voisin, e** [vwazɛ̃, in] *adj* (*proche*) neighbouring; (*contigu*) next; (*ressemblant*) connected ▷ *nm/f* neighbour; **voisinage** *nm* (*proximité*) proximity; (*environs*) vicinity; (*quartier, voisins*) neighbourhood

**voiture** [vwatyr] *nf* car; (*wagon*) coach, carriage; **voiture de course** racing car; **voiture de sport** sports car

**voix** [vwa] *nf* voice; (*Pol*) vote; **à haute ~**

aloud; **à ~ basse** in a low voice; **à 2/4 ~** (*Mus*) in 2/4 parts; **avoir ~ au chapitre** to have a say in the matter

**vol** [vɔl] *nm* (*d'oiseau, d'avion*) flight; (*larcin*) theft; **~ régulier** scheduled flight; **à ~ d'oiseau** as the crow flies; **au ~: attraper qch au ~** to catch sth as it flies past; **en ~** in flight; **je voudrais signaler un ~** I'd like to report a theft; **vol à main armée** armed robbery; **vol à voile** gliding; **vol libre** hang-gliding

**volage** [vɔlaʒ] *adj* fickle

**volaille** [vɔlaj] *nf* (*oiseaux*) poultry *pl*; (*viande*) poultry *no pl*; (*oiseau*) fowl

**volant, e** [vɔlɑ̃, ɑ̃t] *adj* **voir feuille** *etc* ▷ *nm* (*d'automobile*) (steering) wheel; (*de commande*) wheel; (*objet lancé*) shuttlecock; (*bande de tissu*) flounce

**volcan** [vɔlkɑ̃] *nm* volcano

**volée** [vɔle] *nf* (*Tennis*) volley; **à la ~: rattraper à la ~** to catch in mid-air; **à toute ~** (*sonner les cloches*) vigorously; (*lancer un projectile*) with full force

**voler** [vɔle] *vi* (*avion, oiseau, fig*) to fly; (*voleur*) to steal ▷ *vt* (*objet*) to steal; (*personne*) to rob; **~ qch à qn** to steal sth from sb; **on m'a volé mon portefeuille** my wallet (*BRIT*) *ou* billfold (*US*) has been stolen; **il ne l'a pas volé!** he asked for it!

**volet** [vɔle] *nm* (*de fenêtre*) shutter; (*de feuillet, document*) section

**voleur, -euse** [vɔlœr, øz] *nm/f* thief ▷ *adj* thieving; **"au ~!"** "stop thief!"

**volontaire** [vɔlɔ̃ter] *adj* (*acte, enrôlement, prisonnier*) voluntary; (*oubli*) intentional; (*caractère, personne: décidé*) self-willed ▷ *nm/f* volunteer

**volonté** [vɔlɔ̃te] *nf* (*faculté de vouloir*) will; (*énergie, fermeté*) will(power); (*souhait, désir*) wish; **à ~** as much as one likes; **bonne ~** goodwill, willingness; **mauvaise ~** lack of goodwill, unwillingness

**volontiers** [vɔlɔ̃tje] *adv* (*avec plaisir*) willingly, gladly; (*habituellement, souvent*) readily, willingly; **voulez-vous boire quelque chose? — ~!** would you like something to drink? — yes, please!

**volt** [vɔlt] *nm* volt

**volte-face** [vɔltəfas] *nf inv*: **faire ~** to turn round

**voltige** [vɔltiʒ] *nf* (*Équitation*) trick riding; (*au cirque*) acrobatics *sg*; **voltiger** *vi* to flutter (about)

**volubile** [vɔlybil] *adj* voluble

**volume** [vɔlym] *nm* volume; (*Géom: solide*) solid; **volumineux, -euse** *adj* voluminous, bulky

**volupté** [vɔlypte] *nf* sensual delight *ou* pleasure

**vomi** [vɔmi] *nm* vomit; **vomir** *vi* to vomit, be sick ▷ *vt* to vomit, bring up; (*fig*) to belch out, spew out; (*exécrer*) to loathe, abhor

**vorace** [vɔras] *adj* voracious

**vos** [vo] *adj voir* **votre**

**vote** [vɔt] *nm* vote; **vote par correspondance/procuration** postal/proxy vote; **voter** *vi* to vote ▷ *vt* (*projet de loi*) to vote for; (*loi, réforme*) to pass

**votre** [vɔtʀ] (*pl* **vos**) *adj* your

**vôtre** [votʀ] *pron*: **le ~, la ~, les ~s** yours; **les ~s** (*fig*) your family *ou* folks; **à la ~** (*toast*) your (good) health!

**vouer** [vwe] *vt*: **~ sa vie à** (*étude, cause etc*) to devote one's life to; **~ une amitié éternelle à qn** to vow undying friendship to sb

○ MOT-CLÉ

**vouloir** [vulwaʀ] *nm*: **le bon vouloir de qn** sb's goodwill; sb's pleasure
▷ *vt* 1 (*exiger, désirer*) to want; **vouloir faire/que qn fasse** to want to do/sb to do; **voulez-vous du thé?** would you like *ou* do you want some tea?; **que me veut-il?** what does he want with me?; **sans le vouloir** (*involontairement*) without meaning to, unintentionally; **je voudrais ceci/faire** I would *ou* I'd like this/to do; **le hasard a voulu que ...** as fate would have it ...; **la tradition veut que ...** it is a tradition that ...

2 (*consentir*): **je veux bien** (*bonne volonté*) I'll be happy to; (*concession*) fair enough, that's fine; **je peux le faire, si vous voulez** I can do it if you like; **oui, si on veut** (*en quelque sorte*) yes, if you like; **veuillez attendre** please wait; **veuillez agréer ...** (*formule épistolaire: personne nommée*) yours sincerely; (*personne non nommée*) yours faithfully

3: **en vouloir à qn** to bear sb a grudge; **s'en vouloir (de)** to be annoyed with o.s. (for); **il en veut à mon argent** he's after my money

4: **vouloir de**: **l'entreprise ne veut plus de lui** the firm doesn't want him any more; **elle ne veut pas de son aide** she doesn't want his help

5: **vouloir dire** to mean

**voulu, e** [vuly] *adj* (*requis*) required, requisite; (*délibéré*) deliberate, intentional; *voir aussi* **vouloir**

**vous** [vu] *pron you*; (*objet indirect*) (to) you; (*réfléchi: sg*) yourself; (: *pl*) yourselves; (*réciproque*) each other ▷ *nm*: **employer le ~** (*vouvoyer*) to use the "vous" form; **~-même** yourself; **~-mêmes** yourselves

**vouvoyer** [vuvwaje] *vt*: **~ qn** to address sb as "vous"

**voyage** [vwajaʒ] *nm* journey, trip; (*fait de voyager*): **le ~** travel(ling); **partir/être en ~** to go off/be away on a journey *ou* trip; **faire bon ~** to have a good journey; **votre ~ s'est bien passé?** how was your journey?; **voyage d'affaires/d'agrément** business/pleasure trip; **voyage de noces** honeymoon; **nous sommes en voyage de noces** we're on honeymoon; **voyage organisé** package tour

**voyager** [vwajaʒe] *vi* to travel; **voyageur, -euse** *nm/f* traveller; (*passager*) passenger; **voyageur de commerce** sales representative, commercial traveller

**voyant, e** [vwajã, ãt] *adj* (*couleur*) loud, gaudy ▷ *nm* (*signal*) (warning) light

**voyelle** [vwajɛl] *nf* vowel

**voyou** [vwaju] *nm* hooligan

**vrac** [vʀak]: **en ~** *adv* (*au détail*) loose; (*en gros*) in bulk; (*en désordre*) in a jumble

**vrai, e** [vʀɛ] *adj* (*véridique: récit, faits*) true; (*non factice, authentique*) real; **à ~ dire** to tell the truth; **vraiment** *adv* really; **vraisemblable** *adj* likely; (*excuse*) convincing; **vraisemblablement** *adj* probably; **vraisemblance** *nf* likelihood; (*romanesque*) verisimilitude

**vrombir** [vʀɔ̃biʀ] *vi* to hum

**VRP** *sigle m* (= *voyageur, représentant, placier*) sales rep (*fam*)

**VTT** *sigle m* (= *vélo tout-terrain*) mountain bike

**vu, e** [vy] *pp de* **voir** ▷ *adj*: **bien/mal vu** (*fig: personne*) popular/unpopular; (: *chose*) approved/disapproved of ▷ *prép* (*en raison de*) in view of; **vu que** in view of the fact that

**vue** [vy] *nf* (*fait de voir*): **la ~ de** the sight of; (*sens, faculté*) (eye)sight; (*panorama, image, photo*) view; **vues** *nfpl* (*idées*) views; (*dessein*) designs; **hors de ~** out of sight; **avoir en ~** to have in mind; **tirer à ~** to shoot on sight; **à ~ d'œil** visibly; **à première ~** at first sight; **de ~** by sight; **perdre de ~** to lose sight of; **en ~** (*visible*) in sight; (*célèbre*) in the public eye; **en ~ de faire** with a view to doing; **perdre la ~** to lose one's (eye)sight; **avoir ~ sur** (*suj: fenêtre*) to have a view of; **vue d'ensemble** overall view

**vulgaire** [vylgɛʀ] *adj* (*grossier*) vulgar, coarse; (*ordinaire*) commonplace, mundane; (*péj: quelconque*): **de ~s touristes** common tourists; (*Bot, Zool: non latin*) common; **vulgariser** *vt* to popularize

**vulnérable** [vylneʀabl] *adj* vulnerable

**wagon** [vagɔ̃] *nm* (*de voyageurs*) carriage; (*de marchandises*) truck, wagon; **wagon-lit** *nm* sleeper, sleeping car; **wagon-restaurant** *nm* restaurant *ou* dining car

**wallon, ne** [walɔ̃, ɔn] *adj* Walloon ▷ *nm* (*Ling*) Walloon ▷ *nm/f*: **W~, ne** Walloon

**watt** [wat] *nm* watt

**w-c** *sigle mpl* (= *water-closet(s)*) toilet

**Web** [wɛb] *nm inv*: **le ~** the (World Wide) Web; **webmaster** [-mastœʀ], **webmestre** [-mɛstʀ] *nm/f* webmaster

**week-end** [wikɛnd] *nm* weekend

**western** [wɛstɛʀn] *nm* western

**whisky** [wiski] (*pl* **whiskies**) *nm* whisky

**xénophobe** [gzenɔfɔb] *adj*
xenophobic ▷ *nm/f* xenophobe
**xérès** [gzeʀɛs] *nm* sherry
**xylophone** [gzilɔfɔn] *nm* xylophone

**y** [i] *adv (à cet endroit)* there; *(dessus)* on
it *(ou* them); *(dedans)* in it *(ou* them)
▷ *pron (about ou* on *ou* of) it *(d'après le
verbe employé)*; **j'y pense** I'm thinking
about it; **ça y est!** that's it!; *voir aussi*
**aller**; **avoir**
**yacht** [jɔt] *nm* yacht
**yaourt** [jauʀt] *nm* yoghourt; **~ nature/
aux fruits** plain/fruit yogurt
**yeux** [jø] *nmpl de* **œil**
**yoga** [jɔga] *nm* yoga
**yoghourt** [jɔguʀt] *nm* = **yaourt**
**yougoslave** [jugɔslav] *(Histoire) adj*
Yugoslav(ian) ▷ *nm/f*: **Y~** Yugoslav
**Yougoslavie** [jugɔslavi] *nf (Histoire)*
Yugoslavia; **l'ex-~** the former
Yugoslavia

# Z

≈ restricted parking area; **zone industrielle** industrial estate
**zoo** [zo(o)] *nm* zoo
**zoologie** [zɔɔlɔʒi] *nf* zoology; **zoologique** *adj* zoological
**zut** [zyt] *excl* dash (it)! (*BRIT*), nuts! (*US*)

**zapper** [zape] *vi* to zap
**zapping** [zapiŋ] *nm*: **faire du ~** to flick through the channels
**zèbre** [zɛbʀ(ə)] *nm* (*Zool*) zebra; **zébré, e** *adj* striped, streaked
**zèle** [zɛl] *nm* zeal; **faire du ~** (*péj*) to be over-zealous; **zélé, e** *adj* zealous
**zéro** [zeʀo] *nm* zero, nought (*BRIT*); **au-dessous de ~** below zero (Centigrade) ou freezing; **partir de ~** to start from scratch; **trois (buts) à ~** 3 (goals to) nil
**zeste** [zɛst] *nm* peel, zest
**zézayer** [zezeje] *vi* to have a lisp
**zigzag** [zigzag] *nm* zigzag; **zigzaguer** *vi* to zigzag
**Zimbabwe** [zimbabwe] *nm*: **le ~** Zimbabwe
**zinc** [zɛ̃g] *nm* (*Chimie*) zinc
**zipper** [zipe] *vt* (*Inform*) to zip
**zizi** [zizi] *nm* (*langage enfantin*) willy
**zodiaque** [zɔdjak] *nm* zodiac
**zona** [zona] *nm* shingles *sg*
**zone** [zon] *nf* zone, area; (*fam: quartiers pauvres*): **la ~** the slums; **zone bleue**

# French in focus

# Introduction

*French in focus* gives you a fascinating introduction to the French-speaking world. The following pages look at where French is spoken throughout the world, helping you to get to know the language and the people that speak it. Practical language tips and notes on common translation difficulties will allow you to become more confident in French and a useful correspondence section gives you all the information you need to be able to communicate effectively.

We've also included a number of links to useful websites, which will give you the opportunity to read and learn more about French-speaking countries and the French language.

We hope that you will enjoy using your *French in focus* supplement. We are sure that it will help you to find out more about French-speaking countries and become more confident in writing and speaking French.

*Allez-y!*

# France and its regions

# France and its regions

## The six biggest French cities

| City | Name of inhabitants | Population |
| --- | --- | --- |
| Paris | les Parisiens | 9,645,000 (Paris area) |
| | | 2,125,000 (the city proper) |
| Marseille–Aix-en-Provence | les Marseillais | 1,350,000 |
| | les Aixois | |
| Lyon | les Lyonnais | 1,349,000 |
| Lille | les Lillois | 1,001,000 |
| Nice | les Niçois | 889,000 |
| Toulouse | les Toulousains | 761,000 |

Note that the names of the city inhabitants start with a capital letter, but when they are used as adjectives, they begin with a small letter: *les musées parisiens* (Paris museums), *la cuisine lyonnaise* (cooking from Lyons).

French speakers often refer to mainland France as *l'Hexagone* because of its shape. The head of state is the President (*le Président de la République*), who is elected for five years. The President appoints a Prime Minister (*le Premier Ministre*), who heads the government.

France is organized into twenty-two areas called *régions*. Each *région* is made up of several smaller *départements*, four of which lie far beyond Europe's borders.

**Useful links:**
www.premier-ministre.gouv.fr
   *Office of the Prime Minister.*
www.service-public.fr
   *Links to most government departments.*

The overseas *Départements* (*Départements d'outre-mer – DOM* and *Régions d'outre-mer – ROM*) consist of:
• the Caribbean islands of *Martinique* and *Guadeloupe*
• *Réunion* in the Indian Ocean
• *Guyane française* in South America
They have the same legal system as mainland France.

France's overseas territories (*Collectivités d'outre-mer – COM*) include:
• *Polynésie française, Wallis-et-Futuna* and *Nouvelle-Calédonie* in the South Pacific
• *Mayotte* in the Indian Ocean
• *Saint-Pierre et Miquelon*
• polar territories in the Antarctic

**A useful link:**
www.outre-mer.gouv.fr
   *Information on the DOM-ROM.*

# A snapshot of France

- France is the biggest country by area in Western Europe, covering 549 000 km² (well over twice the size of the UK).

- The Loire is the longest river in France, and is around 1010 km long. It rises in the Cévennes mountains and flows into the Atlantic Ocean at Saint-Nazaire.

- The highest mountain in the Alps, Mont Blanc (4807 m), lies just within France's border with Italy.

- 59.3 million people live in metropolitan France, and there are another 1.7 million in the overseas *départements*.

- France is the world's fifth largest economy after the US, Japan, Germany and the UK.

- The main religion in France is Roman Catholicism; Islam is the second largest religion.

- After Italy, France is the world's biggest wine-producing country.

- The Tour de France is the world's most famous cycle race. Competitors cover approximately 3500 km nationwide.

**A useful link:**
www.insee.fr
   *The French statistical office.*

# The French-speaking world

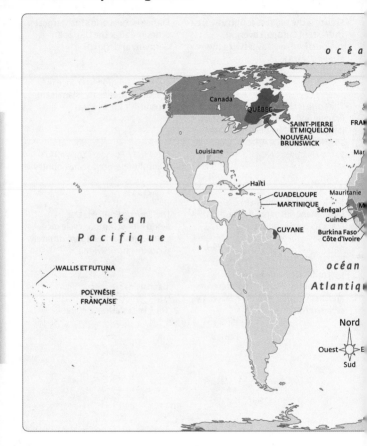

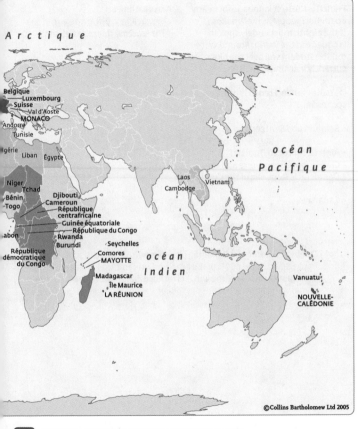

Arctique

Belgique
Luxembourg
Suisse
Val d'Aoste
MONACO
Andorre
Tunisie
Algérie  Liban  Égypte

océan
Pacifique

Niger  Tchad
Bénin
Togo
Djibouti
Cameroun
République
centrafricaine
Guinée équatoriale
République du Congo
Rwanda
Burundi
Gabon
République
démocratique
du Congo

Laos
Cambodge  Vietnam

Seychelles
Comores
MAYOTTE
Madagascar
Île Maurice
LA RÉUNION

océan
Indien

Vanuatu

NOUVELLE-
CALÉDONIE

©Collins Bartholomew Ltd 2005

COUNTRIES OR REGIONS WHERE FRENCH IS THE MOTHER TONGUE

Countries where French is one of the official languages

Countries or regions where French is used

7

## Varieties of French

French is the first language for nearly 80 million people, which makes it the eighth most widely spoken language in the world. Around 57 million students all over the globe are currently learning French.

Outside France, French is mostly spoken in:

• Belgium and Switzerland

• Algeria, Morocco, Tunisia, Cameroon, Côte d'Ivoire and the Democratic Republic of the Congo

• Canada

**A useful link :**
www.academie-francaise.fr
*The Académie française web site.*

*Le Québec*
Québec is the largest Canadian province, with an area of around 1 540 680 km². Over 80% of the province's inhabitants speak French as their first language, although it is rather different from the language of mainland France. The French spoken in Québec is called *Québécois*.

# French regional languages

Other languages spoken within France:

| Language | French name | Brief description | Where spoken |
|----------|-------------|-------------------|--------------|
| Alsatian | l'alsacien | Close to German | Near the border with Germany |
| Breton | le breton | A Celtic language | Brittany in north-west France |
| Basque | le basque | Not related to any other known language | Near the border with Spain |
| Catalan | le catalan | Close to Spanish | Near the border with Spain |
| Corsican | le corse | Close to Italian | The island of Corsica |
| Flemish | le flamand | Close to Dutch | Near the border with Belgium |
| Occitan | l'occitan | Close to Spanish and French | The southern part of France |

# Words that have crossed the Channel

When the Normans invaded England in 1066, French became the language of the ruling classes. Since then, it has played a central part in the development of English.

English has absorbed thousands of French words over time, for example, 'beef' comes from *bœuf*, 'marriage' comes from *mariage* and so on.

However, English also uses words that come directly from French and don't change at all: for example, 'au pair', 'eau de toilette' and 'rendez-vous'.

With the spread of English as a global means of communication, English terms have become more widespread in the French language.

Some of these terms mean the same in both languages:

| | |
|---|---|
| *le brunch* | *un cocktail* |
| *le hit-parade* | *une interview* |
| *un self-service* | *le stress* |
| *un tee-shirt* | *les WC* |
| *le Web* | *le week-end* |
| *un western* | *un yacht* |

Others have different meanings in French and English:

| | |
|---|---|
| *un agenda* | diary |
| *les baskets* | trainers (BRIT), sneakers (US) |
| *les chips* | crisps (BRIT), chips (US) |
| *la lecture* | reading |
| *un parking* | a car park |
| *un smoking* | a dinner jacket |
| *un stop* | a stop sign, a brake-light |

---

*Be careful!*
Some words are singular in French but plural in English and vice versa:

*un jean* (a pair of) jeans
*un short* (a pair of) shorts
*les WC* the WC

---

**A useful link:**
www.academie-francaise.fr
   *The Académie française web site.*

# Some informal French

We all use different language styles – more relaxed, more formal – depending on the situation we find ourselves in.

When you visit a French-speaking country, you're sure to hear some informal expressions in everyday situations.

Here are some examples of French informal words:

| | |
|---|---|
| *la bagnole* | car |
| *le boulot* | work |
| *dingue* | crazy |
| *génial* | fantastic |
| *le mec* | guy |
| *moche* | ugly, rotten |
| *le prof* | teacher |

Informal language is marked very clearly in the dictionary to help you choose the appropriate word or phrase.

Be careful when using items marked 'informal' (*fam*) in your dictionary, and avoid ones marked 'offensive' (*fam!*) altogether.

> *Le verlan*
> *Verlan* is a kind of slang in which words are invented by swapping round syllables and often chopping off the end of the new word: for example, *femme* becomes *meuf*, and *Arabe* becomes *beur*.

# Improving your pronunciation

There are a number of different methods you can use to improve your pronunciation and increase your confidence in speaking French:

- read out loud to yourself to improve your confidence
- listen to French radio
- watch French-language films
- chat with French-speakers

**Useful links:**

www.radiofrance.fr
*France Info, France Inter and France Culture.*

www.rfi.fr
*Radio France Internationale,' the equivalent of the BBC World Service.*

---

**Some points to help you with your pronunciation**

- **U and ou.** For *ou*, round your lips as for English 'oo!' For *u*, round your lips but say 'ee'.

- **Silent consonant endings and *liaison*.** Consonants at the end of words are not normally pronounced but you do pronounce them when the following word starts with a vowel (*mes amis* sounds like 'may**z**amee', *c'est ici* sounds like 'se**t**eesee'). This is called *liaison*.

- **Elision.** When the words *je, le, la, me, te, se* and *ne* are immediately followed by a word starting with any vowel, the *e* is dropped (and replaced by an apostrophe in writing): *j'adore l'été, elle s'habille, je t'aime*.

- **Letter *h*.** The letter *h* is never pronounced at the beginning of French words. So, *haricot* is pronounced 'areeko' and *hôtel* as 'otel'.

Words beginning with *h* can behave in one of two ways as regards pronunciation.

In some cases, the word behaves as if it began with a vowel, and preceding words like *le* and *la* are shortened: *à l'hôtel, l'huile, ils l'hébergent*. For such words liaison also takes place: *les hôtels* is pronounced as 'layzotel'.

In other cases, *le, la* and similar words are not shortened: *la Hollande, le haricot*, and liaison does not happen: *les haricots* is pronounced as 'lay ariko' and not 'layzariko '. Words which behave like this are preceded by an apostrophe in the dictionary: '*hasard*.

# Improving your fluency

## Conversational words and phrases

In English we insert lots of words and phrases, such as *so*, *then*, *by the way*, into our conversation, to give our thoughts a structure and often to show our attitude. The French words shown below do the same thing. If you use them they will make you sound more fluent and natural.

- *alors*

  *Tu as fini?* **Alors** *je m'en vais.* (= then)

  **Alors** *tu viens (oui ou non)?* (= well, then)

- *bon*

  **Bon**! *J'y vais.* (= right!)

  **Bon**! *Ça suffit maintenant.* (= OK!)

- *ah bon*

  *Je pars aux États-Unis demain.* – **Ah bon**? (= really?)

- *c'est ça*

  *Vous avez vingt-cinq ans, alors?* – *Oui,* **c'est ça**. (= that's right)

- *donc*

  *Voilà* **donc** *la solution.* (= so, then)

  *C'était* **donc** *un espion?* (= then, so)

- *enfin*

  **Enfin**, *vous voyez, c'est la catastrophe!* (= in a word)

  **Enfin**, *tu aurais pu le faire!* (= even so)

- *de toute façon*

  **De toute façon,** *je ne veux pas y aller.* (= anyway)

  *Tu peux m'appeler, je serai à la maison* **de toute façon**. (= in any case)

- *au fait*

  **Au fait**, *est-ce que tu as aimé le film?* (= by the way)

  *C'est quand,* **au fait**, *ton anniversaire?* (= in fact)

- *en fait*

  **En fait**, *je n'ai pas beaucoup de temps.* (= actually)

  **En fait**, *on devrait partir maintenant.* (= in fact)

- *quand même*

  *C'est* **quand même** *ennuyeux.* (= after all)

  *Merci* **quand même**. (= all the same)

# Improving your fluency

Varying the words you use to get your message across will make you sound more fluent in French. For example, you already know *J'aime* *bien les gâteaux*, but for a change you could say *J'adore les gâteaux* to mean the same thing. Here are some other suggestions:

### Saying what you like or dislike

| | |
|---|---|
| *J'ai bien aimé le film.* | I liked … |
| *La visite des vignobles m'a beaucoup plu.* | I really enjoyed … |
| *Je n'aime pas (du tout) le poisson.* | I don't like … (at all). |
| *J'ai horreur du sport.* | I loathe … |

### Expressing your opinion

| | |
|---|---|
| *Je pense que c'est trop cher.* | I think … |
| *Je trouve que c'est normal.* | I think … |
| *Je crois que c'est un peu tard.* | I think … |
| *Je suis certain/sûr que Marc va gagner.* | I'm sure … |
| *À mon avis, il n'a pas changé.* | In my opinion … |

### Agreeing or disagreeing

| | |
|---|---|
| *Je trouve que vous avez raison.* | I think you're right. |
| *Je suis d'accord avec vous.* | I agree with you. |
| *Il a tort.* | He's wrong. |
| *Je ne suis pas d'accord.* | I disagree. |

# Correspondence

The following section on correspondence has been designed to help you communicate confidently in written as well as spoken French. Sample letters, e-mails and sections on text messaging and making telephone calls will ensure that you have all the vocabulary you need to correspond successfully in French.

## Text messaging

| Texto | French | English |
|---|---|---|
| @+ | à plus tard | see you later |
| @2m1 | à demain | see you tomorrow |
| bi1to | bientôt | soon |
| cpg | c'est pas grave | it's no big deal |
| dsl | désolé | I'm sorry |
| entouk | en tout cas | in any case |
| G la N | J'ai la haine | I'm gutted |
| je t'M | je t'aime | I love you |
| mdr | mort de rire | rolling on the floor laughing |
| mr6 | merci | thanks |
| MSG | message | message |
| p2k | pas de quoi | you're welcome |
| parske | parce que | because |
| qqn | quelqu'un | someone |
| ri1 | rien | nothing |
| svp | s'il vous plaît | please |
| TOK | t'es OK? | are you OK? |
| TOQP | t'es occupé? | are you busy? |
| we | week-end | weekend |
| Xlnt | excellent | excellent |

## Writing an e-mail

| Fichier | Edition | Affichage | Outils | **Composer** | Aide | Envoyer |
|---------|---------|-----------|--------|--------------|------|---------|

| | |
|---|---|
| A: | michel@europost.fr |
| Cc: | |
| Copie cachée: | |
| Object: | Demain soir |

**Composer menu:**
- Nouveau message
- Répondre
- Répondre à tous
- Faire suivre
- Fichier joint

Tu veux sortir demain soir? Le nouveau James Bond passe à l'Odéon, si ça t'intéresse.

Si tu ne peux pas demain, je suis libre samedi midi. On pourrait déjeuner ensemble.

Grosses bises

Nadia

**Saying your e-mail address**
In French, when you tell someone your e-mail address, you say:
*michel arobase europost point ef-ayr*

| | | | |
|---|---|---|---|
| *fichier (m)* | file | *répondre à tous* | reply to all |
| *édition (f)* | edit | *faire suivre* | forward |
| *affichage (m)* | view | *fichier (m) joint* | attachment |
| *outils (mpl)* | tools | *à* | to |
| *composer* | compose | *cc* | cc (carbon copy) |
| *aide (f)* | help | *copie (f) cachée* | bcc (blind carbon copy) |
| *envoyer* | send | *objet (m)* | subject |
| *nouveau message (m)* | new | *de* | from |
| *répondre* | reply to sender | *date (f)* | sent |

Here is some additional useful Internet vocabulary:

| | | | |
|---|---|---|---|
| *barre (f) de défilement* | scroll bar | *icône (f)* | icon |
| *base (f) de données* | database | *imprimer* | to print |
| *clavier (m)* | keyboard | *l'Internet (m)* | the Internet |
| *clic (m) droit* | right click | *liens (mpl)* | links |
| *cliquer* | to click | *menu (m)* | menu |
| *clore une session* | to log off | *moniteur (m)* | monitor |
| *coller* | to paste | *moteur (m) de recherche* | search engine |
| *copier* | to copy | *navigateur (m)* | browser |
| *corbeille (f)* | recycle bin | *ouvrir une session* | to log on |
| *couper* | to cut | *page (f) d'accueil* | home page |
| *dossier (m)* | folder | *page (f) Web* | web page |
| *double-cliquer* | to double click | *précédente* | back |
| *envoyé* | sent | *rechercher* | to search |
| *FAQ* | FAQs | *sauvegarder* | to save |
| *favoris* | favourites | *site (m) Web* | website |
| *fenêtre (f)* | window | *suivante* | forward |
| *feuille (f) de calcul* | spreadsheet | *surfer sur Internet* | to surf the Net |
| *fournisseur (m) d'accès à Internet* | Internet Service Provider | *télécharger* | to download |
| *historique* | history | *transmission (f) à haut débit* | broadband |

## Writing a personal letter

Your own name and address ➝ Guy Leduc
18, rue des Tulipes
65004 Gervais

Town/city you are writing from, and the date ➝ Gervais, le 14 février 2006

Salut Frédéric !

Merci beaucoup pour les CD que tu m'as envoyés. Tu as vraiment bien choisi puisqu'il s'agit de mes deux chanteurs préférés: je n'arrête pas de les écouter!

Sinon, rien de nouveau ici. Je passe presque tout mon temps à préparer mes examens qui commencent dans quinze jours. J'espère que je les réussirai tous, mais j'ai le trac pour mon examen de maths: c'est la matière que j'aime le moins.

Maman m'a dit que tu pars en Crète avec ta famille la semaine prochaine. Je te souhaite de très bonnes vacances, et je suis sûr que tu reviendras tout bronzé.

À bientôt!

Maxime

# Writing a personal letter

| Other ways of starting a personal letter | Other ways of ending a personal letter |
|---|---|
| Chers Jean et Sylvie<br>Chère tante Laure<br>Mon cher Laurent | Affectueusement<br>Je t'embrasse<br>Grosses bises (informal) |

### Some useful phrases

| | |
|---|---|
| Je te remercie de ta lettre. | Thank you for your letter. |
| J'ai été très content d'avoir de tes nouvelles. | It was great to hear from you. |
| Je suis désolé de ne pas vous avoir répondu plus vite. | I'm sorry I didn't reply sooner. |
| Transmettez mes amitiés à Sophie. | Give my regards to Sophie. |
| Dis bonjour à Martin de ma part. | Say hello to Martin for me. |
| Maman t'embrasse. | Mum sends her love. |

## Writing a formal letter

Jeanne Judon ← *Your own name and address*
89, bd des Tertres
75008 Paris

*Name and address of the person/company you are writing to* →
Hôtel Renoir
15, av. Jean Médecin
06000 Nice

Paris, le 2 juin 2006 ← *Town/city you are writing from, and the date*

Madame ou Monsieur,

Suite à notre conversation téléphonique de
ce matin, je vous écris afin de confirmer ma
réservation pour une chambre avec salle de bains
pour deux nuits du mercredi 1er au jeudi 2 juillet
2007 inclus.

Comme convenu, veuillez trouver ci-joint un
chèque de 30€ correspondant au montant des
arrhes.

Je vous prie de croire, Madame, Monsieur, à
l'assurance de mes sentiments distingués.

*Jeanne Judon*

# Writing a formal letter

| Other ways of starting a formal letter | Other ways of ending a formal letter |
| --- | --- |
| *Monsieur le Directeur (or le Maire etc)* *Madame le Directeur* *Messieurs* *Madame* *Cher Monsieur* *Chère Madame* | *Veuillez accepter, [...]\*, l'expression de mes sentiments distingués.* \*Fill in the brackets with the words you used to start your letter: *Messieurs, chère Madame* etc. |

### Some useful phrases

| | |
| --- | --- |
| *Je vous serais reconnaissant(e) de ...* | I would be grateful if you would ... |
| *Je vous prie de ...* | Please ... |
| *Nous vous remercions de votre lettre.* | Thank you for your letter. |
| *Dans l'attente de votre réponse ...* | I look forward to hearing from you ... |
| *Je vous remercie dès à présent de ...* | Thank you in advance for ... |

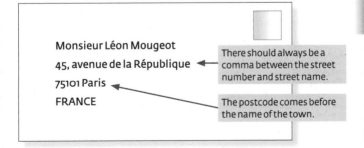

Monsieur Léon Mougeot
45, avenue de la République ← There should always be a comma between the street number and street name.
75101 Paris ← The postcode comes before the name of the town.
FRANCE

# Making a call

### Asking for information

Quel est l'indicatif de Bordeaux? — What's the code for Bordeaux?

Comment fait-on pour avoir une ligne extérieure? — How do I get an outside line?

Pouvez-vous me donner le numéro du poste de M Durand? — Could you give me the extension number for Mr Durand?

### When your number answers

Bonjour! J'aimerais parler à Valérie. — Hello! Could I speak to Valérie, please?

Pourriez-vous me passer le docteur Leduc, s'il vous plaît? — Could you put me through to Dr Leduc, please?

Pourriez-vous lui demander de me rappeler, s'il vous plaît? — Would you ask him/her to call me back, please?

Je rappellerai dans une demi-heure. — I'll call back in half an hour.

Je peux laisser un message, s'il vous plaît? — Could I leave a message, please?

### When you answer the telephone

Allô! C'est Marc à l'appareil. — Hello! It's Marc speaking.

C'est moi. — Speaking.

Qui est à l'appareil? — Who's speaking?

### What you may hear

C'est de la part de qui? — Who shall I say is calling?

Je vous le/la passe. — I'm putting you through.

Ne quittez pas. — Please hold.

Ça ne répond pas. — There's no reply.

Voulez-vous laisser un message? — Would you like to leave a message?

## Making a call

### If you have a problem

*Je suis désolé, j'ai dû faire un faux numéro.*
I'm sorry, I must have dialled the wrong number.

*La ligne est très mauvaise.*
This is a very bad line.

*Ça coupe.*
You're breaking up.

*Ma batterie est presque à plat.*
My battery's low.

*Je ne t'entends plus.*
I can't hear you.

---

### Saying your phone number

To tell someone your phone number in French, you divide the number up into pairs instead of saying each digit separately. For example:

01 40 32 37 12

*zéro-un / quarante / trente-deux / trente-sept / douze*

If there's one extra number, you say that first:

0 26 23 84 47 46

*zéro / vingt-six / vingt-trois / quatre-vingt-quatre / quarante-sept / quarante-six*

# French phrases and sayings

In French, as in many languages, people use vivid expressions based on images from their experience of real life. We've grouped the common expressions below according to the type of image they use. For fun, we have given you the word-for-word translation as well as the true English equivalent.

## Fruit and vegetables

**Ce ne sont pas mes oignons!** → This is none of my business!
    word for word: *these aren't my onions*

**C'est la fin des haricots.** → It's the last straw.
    word for word: *it's the end of beans*

**être haut comme trois pommes** → to be knee-high to a grasshopper
    word for word: *to be high as three apples*

**tomber dans les pommes** → to faint
    word for word: *to fall into the apples*

## Animals and Insects

**donner sa langue au chat** → to give in or up (*when guessing*)
    word for word: *to give one's tongue to the cat*

**appeler un chat un chat** → to call a spade a spade
    word for word: *to call a cat a cat*

**quand les poules auront des dents** → pigs might fly
    word for word: *when hens have teeth*

**passer du coq à l'âne** → to jump from one subject to another
    word for word: *to go from the cockerel to the donkey*

**avoir un chat dans la gorge** → to have a frog in one's throat
    word for word: *to have a cat in one's throat*

# French phrases and sayings

## The weather

**Ce n'est pas la mer à boire.** → It's not the end of the world.

    word for word: *it's not like having to drink the sea*

**Je ne suis pas tombé de la dernière pluie.** → I wasn't born yesterday.

    word for word: *I didn't come down with the last shower of rain*

**passer entre les gouttes** → to come through without a scratch

    word for word: *to run between the raindrops*

**pleuvoir des cordes** → to be bucketing down

    word for word: *to be raining ropes*

**Ça ne me fait ni chaud ni froid.** → It doesn't make any difference to me.

    word for word: *it makes me neither hot nor cold*

## Parts of the body

**avoir une dent contre quelqu'un** → to have a grudge against somebody

    word for word: *to have a tooth against somebody*

**Il n'a pas la langue dans sa poche.** → He's never at a loss for words.

    word for word: *he doesn't keep his tongue in his pocket*

**avoir un poil dans la main** → to be bone idle

    word for word: *to have a hair growing on one's palm*

**gagner les doigts dans le nez** → to win hands down

    word for word: *to win with one's fingers up one's nose*

# French phrases and sayings

## Clothes

**changer d'avis comme de chemise** → to be always changing one's mind

    word for word: *to change one's mind as often as one's shirt*

**trouver chaussure à son pied** → to find a suitable match

    word for word: *to find a shoe for one's foot*

**Lâche-moi la chemise!** or **Lâche-moi** → Get off my back!
**les baskets!**

    word for word: *let go of my shirt, let go of my trainers*

**C'est bonnet blanc et blanc bonnet.** → It's six of one and half a dozen of the other.

    word for word: *it's white hat and hat white*

## Colours

**voir tout en rose** → to see life through rose-tinted spectacles

    word for word: *to see everything in pink*

**avoir une peur bleue de quelque chose** → to be scared stiff of something

    word for word: *to have a blue fear of something*

**regarder qn dans le blanc des yeux** → to look somebody straight in the eye

    word for word: *to look into the whites of somebody's eyes*

# Some common translation difficulties

On the following pages we have shown some of the translation difficulties that you are most likely to come across. We hope that the tips we have given will help you to avoid these common pitfalls when writing and speaking French.

## Tu or *vous*?

In French the word for 'you' depends on who you are talking to:

• To a person you know well, use *tu*:

Will **you** lend me this CD? → *Tu me prêtes ce CD?*

• To a person you do not know so well, use *vous*:

Have **you** met my wife? → *Vous connaissez ma femme?*

• To more than one person, whether you know them well or not, use *vous*:

Do **you** understand, children? → *Vous comprenez, les enfants?*

---

**Getting friendly**

When you get to know someone, they may ask you:

*On se tutoie?* → Shall we use 'tu' to each other?

*On* is the usual way of saying 'we' in conversation.

*On est allé voir la Tour Eiffel.* → We went to see the Eiffel Tower.

---

# Some common translation difficulties

In English -**'s** is a common way of showing who or what something belongs to. In French you have to use *de*:

| | | |
|---|---|---|
| my brother**'s** car | → | *la voiture **de** mon frère* |
| the children**'s** bedroom | → | *la chambre **des** enfants* |

### Singular versus plural

A word that is singular in English may be plural in French, and vice versa. Check in the dictionary if you are not sure:

*Singular:*  
luggage

*Plural:*  
→ ***les** bagage**s***

*Plural:*  
my trousers

*Singular:*  
→ ***mon** pantalon*

### 'There is' and 'there are'

In French these are both translated by *il y a*:

**There is** someone at the door. → *Il y a quelqu'un à la porte.*

**There are** five books on the table. → *Il y a cinq livres sur la table.*

# Some common translation difficulties

### Using *en*

When the word *en* is used with numbers, it is often not translated in English but it can <u>never</u> be missed out in French:

I want **two** (**of them**). → J'**en** veux **deux**.

Have you got a dictionary? – Yes, → Tu as un dictionnaire? – Oui,
I've got **one**.                       j'**en** ai **un**.

### Translating 'to'

'To' is generally translated by *à*, but remember:

• When you are talking about the time, use *moins*:

    five **to** ten → dix heures **moins** cinq

• In front of verbs, it is shown by the verb ending:

    **to** eat → mang**er**
    **to** leave → part**ir**
    **to** wait → attend**re**

• When you mean 'in order to', use *pour*:

    He's going into town **(in order)** → Il va en ville **pour** acheter
    **to** buy a present.                  un cadeau.

### Using *ne … pas* and other negatives

You often find the verb 'do' in English negatives, but *faire* is never used like this. You use set word pairs instead:

English negative with 'do':          French negative word pair:

I do**n't** smoke. → Je **ne** fume **pas**.

Do**n't** change **anything**. → **Ne** changez **rien**.

# Some common translation difficulties

## Translating 'to be'

'To be' usually corresponds to être, but remember:

- In phrases describing how you feel, use **avoir**:

| | | |
|---|---|---|
| **to be** warm/cold | → | **avoir** chaud/froid |
| **to be** hungry/thirsty | → | **avoir** faim/soif |
| **to be** afraid | → | **avoir** peur |

- To describe the weather, use **faire**:

| | | |
|---|---|---|
| It**'s** lovely weather today. | → | Il **fait** beau aujourd'hui. |

- To say your age, use **avoir**:

| | | |
|---|---|---|
| I**'m** fifteen. | → | J'**ai** quinze ans. |

- To talk about your health, use **aller**:

| | | |
|---|---|---|
| I**'m** very well, thank you. | → | Je **vais** très bien, merci. |

## Translating verbs

Many English verbs can be followed by a preposition or adverb such as 'on' or 'back' – 'to go on', 'to give back'. These additions often give the verb a new meaning. There is no similar way of doing this in French – you just use a different word, for example:

| Verb (+ preposition/adverb): | | Translation: |
|---|---|---|
| to go | → | aller |
| to go on | → | continuer |
| | | |
| to give | → | donner |
| to give back | → | rendre |

# Some common translation difficulties

Sentences that contain a verb and preposition in English might not contain a preposition in French, and vice versa. The dictionary can help you with these. For example:

- Verb + preposition:                    Verb without preposition:

    to pay **for** something      →      *payer quelque chose*

- Verb without preposition:              Verb + preposition:

    to change something           →      *changer **de** quelque chose*

**A** [eɪ] n (Mus) la m

○ **KEYWORD**

**a** [eɪ, ə] (before vowel or silent h **an**) indef art **1** un(e); **a book** un livre; **an apple** une pomme; **she's a doctor** elle est médecin

**2** (instead of the number "one") un(e); **a year ago** il y a un an; **a hundred/ thousand** etc **pounds** cent/mille etc livres

**3** (in expressing ratios, prices etc): **3 a day/week** 3 par jour/semaine; **10 km an hour** 10 km à l'heure; **£5 a person** 5£ par personne; **30p a kilo** 30p le kilo

**A2** n (BRIT: Scol) deuxième partie de l'examen équivalent au baccalauréat

**A.A.** n abbr (BRIT: = Automobile Association) ≈ ACF m; (= Alcoholics Anonymous) AA

**A.A.A.** n abbr (= American Automobile Association) ≈ ACF m

**aback** [ə'bæk] adv: **to be taken ~** être décontenancé(e)

**abandon** [ə'bændən] vt abandonner

**abattoir** ['æbətwɑːʳ] n (BRIT) abattoir m

**abbey** ['æbɪ] n abbaye f

**abbreviation** [əbriːvɪ'eɪʃən] n abréviation f

**abdomen** ['æbdəmən] n abdomen m

**abduct** [æb'dʌkt] vt enlever

**abide** [ə'baɪd] vt souffrir, supporter; **I can't ~ it/him** je ne le supporte pas; **abide by** vt fus observer, respecter

**ability** [ə'bɪlɪtɪ] n compétence f; capacité f; (skill) talent m

**able** ['eɪbl] adj compétent(e); **to be ~ to do sth** pouvoir faire qch, être capable de faire qch

**abnormal** [æb'nɔːməl] adj anormal(e)

**aboard** [ə'bɔːd] adv à bord ▷ prep à bord de; (train) dans

**abolish** [ə'bɔlɪʃ] vt abolir

**abolition** [æbə'lɪʃən] n abolition f

**abort** [ə'bɔːt] vt (Med) faire avorter; (Comput, fig) abandonner; **abortion** [ə'bɔːʃən] n avortement m; **to have an abortion** se faire avorter

○ **KEYWORD**

**about** [ə'baut] adv **1** (approximately) environ, à peu près; **about a hundred/ thousand** etc environ cent/mille etc; **it takes about 10 hours** ça prend environ or à peu près 10 heures; **at about 2 o'clock** vers 2 heures; **I've just about finished** j'ai presque fini

**2** (referring to place) çà et là, de-ci de-là; **to run about** courir çà et là; **to walk about** se promener, aller et venir; **they left all their things lying about** ils ont laissé traîner toutes leurs affaires

**3**: **to be about to do sth** être sur le point de faire qch

▷ prep **1** (relating to) au sujet de, à propos de; **a book about London** un livre sur Londres; **what is it about?** de quoi s'agit-il?; **we talked about it** nous en avons parlé; **what** or **how about doing this?** et si nous faisions ceci? 2 (*referring to place*) dans; **to walk about the town** se promener dans la ville

**above** [ə'bʌv] *adv* au-dessus ▷ *prep* au-dessus de; (*more than*) plus de; **mentioned ~** mentionné ci-dessus; **~ all** par-dessus tout, surtout

**abroad** [ə'brɔːd] *adv* à l'étranger

**abrupt** [ə'brʌpt] *adj* (*steep, blunt*) abrupt(e); (*sudden, gruff*) brusque

**abscess** ['æbsɪs] *n* abcès *m*

**absence** ['æbsəns] *n* absence *f*

**absent** ['æbsənt] *adj* absent(e); **absent-minded** *adj* distrait(e)

**absolute** ['æbsəluːt] *adj* absolu(e); **absolutely** [æbsə'luːtlɪ] *adv* absolument

**absorb** [əb'zɔːb] *vt* absorber; **to be ~ed in a book** être plongé(e) dans un livre; **absorbent cotton** *n* (*US*) coton *m* hydrophile; **absorbing** *adj* absorbant(e); (*book, film etc*) captivant(e)

**abstain** [əb'steɪn] *vi*: **to ~ (from)** s'abstenir (de)

**abstract** ['æbstrækt] *adj* abstrait(e)

**absurd** [əb'səːd] *adj* absurde

**abundance** [ə'bʌndəns] *n* abondance *f*

**abundant** [ə'bʌndənt] *adj* abondant(e)

**abuse** *n* [ə'bjuːs] (*insults*) insultes *fpl*, injures *fpl*; (*ill-treatment*) mauvais traitements *mpl*; (*of power etc*) abus *m* ▷ *vt* [ə'bjuːz] (*insult*) insulter; (*ill-treat*) malmener; (*power etc*) abuser de; **abusive** *adj* grossier(-ière), injurieux(-euse)

**abysmal** [ə'bɪzməl] *adj* exécrable; (*ignorance etc*) sans bornes

**academic** [ækə'dɛmɪk] *adj* universitaire; (*person: scholarly*) intellectuel(-le); (*pej: issue*) oiseux(-euse), purement théorique ▷ *n* universitaire *m/f*; **academic year** *n*

(*University*) année *f* universitaire; (*Scol*) année scolaire

**academy** [ə'kædəmɪ] *n* (*learned body*) académie *f*; (*school*) collège *m*; **~ of music** conservatoire *m*

**accelerate** [æk'sɛləreɪt] *vt, vi* accélérer; **acceleration** [æksɛlə'reɪʃən] *n* accélération *f*; **accelerator** *n* (*BRIT*) accélérateur *m*

**accent** ['æksɛnt] *n* accent *m*

**accept** [ək'sɛpt] *vt* accepter; **acceptable** *adj* acceptable; **acceptance** *n* acceptation *f*

**access** ['æksɛs] *n* accès *m*; **to have ~ to** (*information, library etc*) avoir accès à, pouvoir utiliser or consulter; (*person*) avoir accès auprès de; **accessible** [æk'sɛsəbl] *adj* accessible

**accessory** [æk'sɛsərɪ] *n* accessoire *m*; **~ to** (*Law*) accessoire à

**accident** ['æksɪdənt] *n* accident *m*; (*chance*) hasard *m*; **I've had an ~** j'ai eu un accident; **by ~** (*by chance*) par hasard; (*not deliberately*) accidentellement; **accidental** [æksɪ'dɛntl] *adj* accidentel(le); **accidentally** [æksɪ'dɛntəlɪ] *adv* accidentellement; **Accident and Emergency Department** *n* (*BRIT*) service *m* des urgences; **accident insurance** *n* assurance *f* accident

**acclaim** [ə'kleɪm] *vt* acclamer ▷ *n* acclamations *fpl*

**accommodate** [ə'kɔmədeɪt] *vt* loger, recevoir; (*oblige, help*) obliger; (*car etc*) contenir

**accommodation** (*US* **accommodations**) [əkɔmə'deɪʃən(z)] *n(pl)* logement *m*

**accompaniment** [ə'kʌmpənɪmənt] *n* accompagnement *m*

**accompany** [ə'kʌmpənɪ] *vt* accompagner

**accomplice** [ə'kʌmplɪs] *n* complice *m/f*

**accomplish** [ə'kʌmplɪʃ] *vt* accomplir; **accomplishment** *n* (*skill: gen pl*) talent *m*; (*completion*) accomplissement *m*;

(*achievement*) réussite f

**accord** [əˈkɔːd] n accord m ▷ vt accorder; **of his own ~** de son plein gré; **accordance** n: **in accordance with** conformément à; **according**: **according to** prep selon; **accordingly** adv (*appropriately*) en conséquence; (*as a result*) par conséquent

**account** [əˈkaʊnt] n (Comm) compte m; (*report*) compte rendu, récit m; **accounts** npl (Comm: *records*) comptabilité f, comptes; **of no ~** sans importance; **on ~** en acompte; **to buy sth on ~** acheter qch à crédit; **on no ~** en aucun cas; **on ~ of** à cause de; **to take into ~, take ~ of** tenir compte de; **account for** vt fus (*explain*) expliquer, rendre compte de; (*represent*) représenter; **accountable** adj: **accountable (to)** responsable (devant); **accountant** n comptable m/f; **account number** n numéro m de compte

**accumulate** [əˈkjuːmjʊleɪt] vt accumuler, amasser ▷ vi s'accumuler, s'amasser

**accuracy** [ˈækjʊrəsɪ] n exactitude f, précision f

**accurate** [ˈækjʊrɪt] adj exact(e), précis(e); (*device*) précis; **accurately** adv avec précision

**accusation** [ækjuˈzeɪʃən] n accusation f

**accuse** [əˈkjuːz] vt: **to ~ sb (of sth)** accuser qn (de qch); **accused** n (Law) accusé(e)

**accustomed** [əˈkʌstəmd] adj: **~ to** habitué(e) or accoutumé(e) à

**ace** [eɪs] n as m

**ache** [eɪk] n mal m, douleur f ▷ vi (be sore) faire mal, être douloureux(-euse); **my head ~s** j'ai mal à la tête

**achieve** [əˈtʃiːv] vt (*aim*) atteindre; (*victory, success*) remporter, obtenir; **achievement** n exploit m, réussite f; (*of aims*) réalisation f

**acid** [ˈæsɪd] adj, n acide (m)

**acknowledge** [əkˈnɒlɪdʒ] vt (also: ~

**receipt of**) accuser réception de; (*fact*) reconnaître; **acknowledgement** n (*of letter*) accusé m de réception

**acne** [ˈæknɪ] n acné m

**acorn** [ˈeɪkɔːn] n gland m

**acoustic** [əˈkuːstɪk] adj acoustique

**acquaintance** [əˈkweɪntəns] n connaissance f

**acquire** [əˈkwaɪəʳ] vt acquérir; **acquisition** [ækwɪˈzɪʃən] n acquisition f

**acquit** [əˈkwɪt] vt acquitter; **to ~ o.s. well** s'en tirer très honorablement

**acre** [ˈeɪkəʳ] n acre f (= 4047 m²)

**acronym** [ˈækrənɪm] n acronyme m

**across** [əˈkrɒs] prep (*on the other side*) de l'autre côté de; (*crosswise*) en travers de ▷ adv de l'autre côté; en travers; **to run/swim ~** traverser en courant/à la nage; **~ from** en face de

**acrylic** [əˈkrɪlɪk] adj, n acrylique (m)

**act** [ækt] n acte m, action f; (Theat: *part of play*) acte; (: *of performer*) numéro m; (Law) loi f ▷ vi agir; (Theat) jouer; (*pretend*) jouer la comédie ▷ vt (*role*) jouer, tenir; **to catch sb in the ~** prendre qn le fait or en flagrant délit; **to ~ as** servir de; **act up** (inf) ▷ vi (*person*) se conduire mal; (*knee, back, injury*) jouer des tours; (*machine*) être capricieux(-ieuse); **acting** adj suppléant(e), par intérim ▷ n (*activity*): **to do some acting** faire du théâtre (or du cinéma)

**action** [ˈækʃən] n action f; (Mil) combat(s) m(pl); (Law) procès m, action en justice; **out of ~** hors de combat; (*machine etc*) hors d'usage; **to take ~** agir, prendre des mesures; **action replay** n (BRIT TV) ralenti m

**activate** [ˈæktɪveɪt] vt (*mechanism*) actionner, faire fonctionner

**active** [ˈæktɪv] adj actif(-ive); (*volcano*) en activité; **actively** adv activement; (*discourage*) vivement

**activist** [ˈæktɪvɪst] n activiste m/f

**activity** [ækˈtɪvɪtɪ] n activité f; **activity holiday** n vacances actives

**actor** ['æktər] n acteur m

**actress** ['æktrɪs] n actrice f

**actual** ['æktjuəl] adj réel(le), véritable; (*emphatic use*) lui-même (elle-même)

▮ Be careful not to translate *actual* by the French word *actuel*.

**actually** ['æktjuəlɪ] adv réellement, véritablement; (*in fact*) en fait

▮ Be careful not to translate *actually* by the French word *actuellement*.

**acupuncture** ['ækjupʌŋktʃər] n acuponcture f

**acute** [ə'kjuːt] adj aigu(ë); (*mind, observer*) pénétrant(e)

**A.D.** adv abbr (= *Anno Domini*) ap. J.-C.

**ad** [æd] n abbr = **advertisement**

**adamant** ['ædəmənt] adj inflexible

**adapt** [ə'dæpt] vt adapter ▷ vi: **to ~ (to)** s'adapter (à); **adapter, adaptor** n (*Elec*) adaptateur m; (*for several plugs*) prise f multiple

**add** [æd] vt ajouter; (*figures: also: **to ~ up***) additionner ▷ vi (*fig*): **it doesn't ~ up** cela ne rime à rien; **add up to** vt fus (*Math*) s'élever à; (*fig: mean*) signifier

**addict** ['ædɪkt] n toxicomane m/f; (*fig*) fanatique m/f; **addicted** [ə'dɪktɪd] adj: **to be addicted to** (*drink, drugs*) être adonné(e) à; (*fig: football etc*) être un(e) fanatique de; **addiction** [ə'dɪkʃən] n (*Med*) dépendance f; **addictive** [ə'dɪktɪv] adj qui crée une dépendance

**addition** [ə'dɪʃən] n (*adding up*) addition f; (*thing added*) ajout m; **in ~** de plus, de surcroît; **in ~ to** en plus de; **additional** adj supplémentaire

**additive** ['ædɪtɪv] n additif m

**address** [ə'drɛs] n adresse f; (*talk*) discours m, allocution f ▷ vt adresser; (*speak to*) s'adresser à; **my ~ is ...** mon adresse, c'est ...; **address book** n carnet m d'adresses

**adequate** ['ædɪkwɪt] adj (*enough*) suffisant(e); (*satisfactory*) satisfaisant(e)

**adhere** [əd'hɪər] vi: **to ~ to** adhérer à; (*fig: rule, decision*) se tenir à

**adhesive** [əd'hiːzɪv] n adhésif m;

**adhesive tape** n (*BRIT*) ruban m adhésif; (*US Med*) sparadrap m

**adjacent** [ə'dʒeɪsənt] adj adjacent(e), contigu(ë); **~ to** adjacent à

**adjective** ['ædʒɛktɪv] n adjectif m

**adjoining** [ə'dʒɔɪnɪŋ] adj voisin(e), adjacent(e), attenant(e)

**adjourn** [ə'dʒəːn] vt ajourner ▷ vi suspendre la séance; lever la séance; clore la session

**adjust** [ə'dʒʌst] vt (*machine*) ajuster, régler; (*prices, wages*) rajuster ▷ vi: **to ~ (to)** s'adapter (à); **adjustable** adj réglable; **adjustment** n (*of machine*) ajustage m, réglage m; (*of prices, wages*) rajustement m; (*of person*) adaptation f

**administer** [əd'mɪnɪstər] vt administrer; **administration** [ədmɪnɪs'treɪʃən] n (*management*) administration f; (*government*) gouvernement m; **administrative** [əd'mɪnɪstrətɪv] adj administratif(-ive)

**administrator** [əd'mɪnɪstreɪtər] n administrateur(-trice)

**admiral** ['ædmərəl] n amiral m

**admiration** [ædmə'reɪʃən] n admiration f

**admire** [əd'maɪər] vt admirer; **admirer** n (*fan*) admirateur(-trice)

**admission** [əd'mɪʃən] n admission f; (*to exhibition, night club etc*) entrée f; (*confession*) aveu m

**admit** [əd'mɪt] vt laisser entrer; admettre; (*agree*) reconnaître, admettre; (*crime*) reconnaître avoir commis; **"children not ~ted"** "entrée interdite aux enfants"; **admit to** vt fus reconnaître, avouer; **admittance** n admission f, (droit m d')entrée f; **admittedly** adv il faut en convenir

**adolescent** [ædəu'lɛsnt] adj, n adolescent(e)

**adopt** [ə'dɔpt] vt adopter; **adopted** adj adoptif(-ive), adopté(e); **adoption** [ə'dɔpʃən] n adoption f

**adore** [ə'dɔːr] vt adorer

**adorn** [ə'dɔːn] vt orner

**Adriatic (Sea)** [eɪdrɪ'ætɪk-] n, adj:
the **Adriatic (Sea)** la mer Adriatique,
l'Adriatique f

**adrift** [ə'drɪft] adv à la dérive

**adult** ['ædʌlt] n adulte m/f ▷ adj
(grown-up) adulte; (for adults) pour
adultes; **adult education** n éducation
f des adultes

**adultery** [ə'dʌltərɪ] n adultère m

**advance** [əd'vɑ:ns] n avance f ▷ vt
avancer ▷ vi s'avancer; **in ~** en avance,
d'avance; **to make ~s to sb** (gen) faire
des propositions à qn; (amorously) faire
des avances à qn; **~ booking** location f;
**~ notice, ~ warning** préavis m; (verbal)
avertissement m; **do I need to book in
~?** est-ce qu'il faut réserver à l'avance?;
**advanced** adj avancé(e); (Scol: studies)
supérieur(e)

**advantage** [əd'vɑ:ntɪdʒ] n (also Tennis)
avantage m; **to take ~ of** (person)
exploiter; (opportunity) profiter de

**advent** ['ædvɛnt] n avènement m,
venue f; **A~** (Rel) avent m

**adventure** [əd'vɛntʃəʳ] n aventure f;
**adventurous** [əd'vɛntʃərəs] adj
aventureux(-euse)

**adverb** ['ædvə:b] n adverbe m

**adversary** ['ædvəsərɪ] n adversaire
m/f

**adverse** ['ædvə:s] adj adverse; (effect)
négatif(-ive); (weather, publicity)
mauvais(e); (wind) contraire

**advert** ['ædvə:t] n abbr (BRIT)
= **advertisement**

**advertise** ['ædvətaɪz] vi faire de la
publicité or de la réclame; (in classified
ads etc) mettre une annonce ▷ vt faire
de la publicité or de la réclame pour; (in
classified ads etc) mettre une annonce
pour vendre; **to ~ for** (staff) recruter
par (voie d')annonce; **advertisement**
[əd'və:tɪsmənt] n (Comm) publicité
f, réclame f; (in classified ads etc)
annonce f; **advertiser** n annonceur m;
**advertising** n publicité f

**advice** [əd'vaɪs] n conseils mpl;
(notification) avis m; **a piece of ~** un

conseil; **to take legal ~** consulter
un avocat

**advisable** [əd'vaɪzəbl] adj
recommandable, indiqué(e)

**advise** [əd'vaɪz] vt conseiller; **to ~ sb
of sth** aviser or informer qn de qch; **to
~ against sth/doing sth** déconseiller
qch/conseiller de ne pas faire qch;
**adviser, advisor** n conseiller(-ère);
**advisory** adj consultatif(-ive)

**advocate** n ['ædvəkɪt] (lawyer)
avocat (plaidant); (upholder) défenseur
m, avocat(e) ▷ vt ['ædvəkeɪt]
recommander, prôner; **to be an ~ of**
être partisan(ne) de

**Aegean** [i:'dʒi:ən] n, adj: **the ~ (Sea)** la
mer Égée, l'Égée f

**aerial** ['ɛərɪəl] n antenne f ▷ adj
aérien(ne)

**aerobics** [ɛə'rəubɪks] n aérobic m

**aeroplane** ['ɛərəpleɪn] n (BRIT) avion m

**aerosol** ['ɛərəsɔl] n aérosol m

**affair** [ə'fɛəʳ] n affaire f; (also: **love ~**)
liaison f; aventure f

**affect** [ə'fɛkt] vt affecter; (subj: disease)
atteindre; **affected** adj affecté(e);
**affection** n affection f; **affectionate**
adj affectueux(-euse)

**afflict** [ə'flɪkt] vt affliger

**affluent** ['æfluənt] adj (person, family,
surroundings) aisé(e), riche; **the ~
society** la société d'abondance

**afford** [ə'fɔ:d] vt (behaviour) se
permettre; (provide) fournir, procurer;
**can we ~ a car?** avons-nous de quoi
acheter or les moyens d'acheter une
voiture?; **affordable** adj abordable

**Afghanistan** [æf'gænɪstæn] n
Afghanistan m

**afraid** [ə'freɪd] adj effrayé(e); **to be ~
of** or **to** avoir peur de; **I am ~ that** je
crains que + sub; **I'm ~ so/not** oui/non,
malheureusement

**Africa** ['æfrɪkə] n Afrique f; **African** adj
africain(e) ▷ n Africain(e); **African-
American** adj afro-américain(e) ▷ n
Afro-Américain(e)

**after** ['ɑ:ftəʳ] prep, adv après ▷ conj

après que; **it's quarter ~ two** (US) il est deux heures et quart; **~ having done/~ he left** après avoir fait/ après son départ; **to name sb ~ sb** donner à qn le nom de qn; **to ask ~ sb** demander des nouvelles de qn; **what/who are you ~?** que/qui cherchez-vous?; **~ you!** après vous!; **~ all** après tout; **after-effects** npl (of disaster, radiation, drink etc) répercussions fpl; (of illness) séquelles fpl, suites fpl; **aftermath** n conséquences fpl; **afternoon** n après-midi m or f; **after-shave (lotion)** n lotion f après-rasage; **aftersun (lotion/cream)** n après-soleil m inv; **afterwards** (US **afterward**) adv après

**again** [ə'gɛn] adv de nouveau, encore (une fois); **to do sth ~** refaire qch; **~ and ~** à plusieurs reprises

**against** [ə'gɛnst] prep contre; (compared to) par rapport à

**age** [eɪdʒ] n âge m ▷ vt, vi vieillir; **he is 20 years of ~** il a 20 ans; **to come of ~** atteindre sa majorité; **it's been ~s since I saw you** ça fait une éternité que je ne t'ai pas vu; **~d 10** âgé(e) de 10 ans; **age group** n tranche f d'âge; **age limit** n limite f d'âge

**agency** ['eɪdʒənsɪ] n agence f

**agenda** [ə'dʒɛndə] n ordre m du jour

> Be careful not to translate agenda by the French word agenda.

**agent** ['eɪdʒənt] n agent m; (firm) concessionnaire m

**aggravate** ['æɡrəveɪt] vt (situation) aggraver; (annoy) exaspérer, agacer

**aggression** [ə'ɡrɛʃən] n agression f

**aggressive** [ə'ɡrɛsɪv] adj agressif(-ive)

**agile** ['ædʒaɪl] adj agile

**agitated** ['ædʒɪteɪtɪd] adj inquiet(-ète)

**AGM** n abbr (= annual general meeting) AG f

**ago** [ə'ɡəʊ] adv: **2 days ~** il y a 2 jours; **not long ~** il n'y a pas longtemps; **how long ~?** il y a combien de temps (de cela)?

**agony** ['æɡənɪ] n (pain) douleur f atroce; (distress) angoisse f; **to be in ~**

souffrir le martyre

**agree** [ə'ɡriː] vt (price) convenir de ▷ vi: **to ~ with** (person) être d'accord avec; (statements etc) concorder avec; (Ling) s'accorder avec; **to ~ to do** accepter de or consentir à faire; **to ~ to sth** consentir à qch; **to ~ that** (admit) convenir or reconnaître que; **garlic doesn't ~ with me** je ne supporte pas l'ail; **agreeable** adj (pleasant) agréable; (willing) consentant(e), d'accord; **agreed** adj (time, place) convenu(e); **agreement** n accord m; **in agreement** d'accord

**agricultural** [æɡrɪ'kʌltʃərəl] adj agricole

**agriculture** ['æɡrɪkʌltʃər] n agriculture f

**ahead** [ə'hɛd] adv en avant; devant; **go right** or **straight ~** (direction) allez tout droit; **go ~!** (permission) allez-y!; **~ of** devant; (fig: schedule etc) en avance sur; **~ of time** en avance

**aid** [eɪd] n aide f; (device) appareil m ▷ vt aider; **in ~ of** en faveur de

**aide** [eɪd] n (person) assistant(e)

**AIDS** [eɪdz] n abbr (= acquired immune (or immuno-)deficiency syndrome) SIDA m

**ailing** ['eɪlɪŋ] adj (person) souffreteux(euse); (economy) malade

**ailment** ['eɪlmənt] n affection f

**aim** [eɪm] vt: **to ~ sth (at)** (gun, camera) braquer or pointer qch (sur); (missile) lancer qch (à or contre or en direction de); (remark, blow) destiner or adresser qch (à) ▷ vi (also: **to take ~**) viser ▷ n (objective) but m; (skill): **his ~ is bad** il vise mal; **to ~ at** viser; (fig) viser (à); **to ~ to do** avoir l'intention de faire

**ain't** [eɪnt] (inf) = **am not**; **aren't**; **isn't**

**air** [ɛər] n air m ▷ vt aérer; (idea, grievance, views) mettre sur le tapis ▷ cpd (currents, attack etc) aérien(ne); **to throw sth into the ~** (ball etc) jeter qch en l'air; **by ~** par avion; **to be on the ~** (Radio, TV: programme) être diffusé(e); (: station) émettre; **airbag** n airbag m; **airbed** n (BRIT) matelas *m* pneumatique; **airborne** *adj* (*plane*) en vol; **as soon as the plane was airborne** dès que l'avion eut décollé; **air-conditioned** *adj* climatisé(e), à air conditionné; **air conditioning** *n* climatisation *f*; **aircraft** *n inv* avion *m*; **airfield** *n* terrain *m* d'aviation; **Air Force** *n* Armée *f* de l'air; **air hostess** *n* (BRIT) hôtesse *f* de l'air; **airing cupboard** *n* (BRIT) placard qui contient la chaudière et dans lequel on met le linge à sécher; **airlift** *n* pont aérien; **airline** *n* ligne aérienne, compagnie aérienne; **airliner** *n* avion *m* de ligne; **airmail** *n*: **by airmail** par avion; **airplane** *n* (US) avion *m*; **airport** *n* aéroport *m*; **air raid** *n* attaque aérienne; **airsick** *adj*: **to be airsick** avoir le mal de l'air; **airspace** *n* espace *m* aérien; **airstrip** *n* terrain *m* d'atterrissage; **air terminal** *n* aérogare *f*; **airtight** *adj* hermétique; **air-traffic controller** *n* aiguilleur *m* du ciel; **airy** *adj* bien aéré(e); (*manners*) dégagé(e)

**aisle** [aɪl] *n* (*of church: central*) allée *f* centrale; (*: side*) nef *f* latérale, bas-côté *m*; (*in theatre, supermarket*) allée; (*on plane*) couloir *m*; **aisle seat** *n* place *f* côté couloir

**ajar** [ə'dʒɑːʳ] *adj* entrouvert(e)

**à la carte** [ælæˈkɑːt] *adv* à la carte

**alarm** [ə'lɑːm] *n* alarme *f* ▷ *vt* alarmer; **alarm call** *n* coup *m* de fil pour réveiller; **could I have an alarm call at 7 am, please?** pouvez-vous me réveiller à 7 heures, s'il vous plaît?; **alarm clock** *n* réveille-matin *m inv*, réveil *m*; **alarmed** *adj* (*frightened*) alarmé(e); (*protected by an alarm*) protégé(e) par un système d'alarme; **alarming** *adj* alarmant(e)

**Albania** [æl'beɪnɪə] *n* Albanie *f*

**albeit** [ɔːl'biːɪt] *conj* bien que + *sub*, encore que + *sub*

**album** ['ælbəm] *n* album *m*

**alcohol** ['ælkəhɒl] *n* alcool *m*; **alcohol-free** *adj* sans alcool; **alcoholic** [ælkə'hɒlɪk] *adj, n* alcoolique (*m/f*)

**alcove** ['ælkəʊv] *n* alcôve *f*

**ale** [eɪl] *n* bière *f*

**alert** [ə'ləːt] *adj* alerte, vif (vive); (*watchful*) vigilant(e) ▷ *n* alerte *f* ▷ *vt* alerter; **on the ~** sur le qui-vive; (*Mil*) en état d'alerte

**algebra** ['ældʒɪbrə] *n* algèbre *m*

**Algeria** [æl'dʒɪərɪə] *n* Algérie *f*

**Algerian** [æl'dʒɪərɪən] *adj* algérien(ne) ▷ *n* Algérien(ne)

**Algiers** [æl'dʒɪəz] *n* Alger

**alias** ['eɪlɪəs] *adv* alias ▷ *n* faux nom, nom d'emprunt

**alibi** ['ælɪbaɪ] *n* alibi *m*

**alien** ['eɪlɪən] *n* (*from abroad*) étranger(-ère); (*from outer space*) extraterrestre ▷ *adj*: **~ (to)** étranger(-ère) (à); **alienate** *vt* aliéner; (*subj: person*) s'aliéner

**alight** [ə'laɪt] *adj* en feu ▷ *vi* mettre pied à terre; (*passenger*) descendre; (*bird*) se poser

**align** [ə'laɪn] *vt* aligner

**alike** [ə'laɪk] *adj* semblable, pareil(le) ▷ *adv* de même; **to look ~** se ressembler

**alive** [ə'laɪv] *adj* vivant(e); (*active*) plein(e) de vie

🔘 **KEYWORD**

**all** [ɔːl] *adj* (*singular*) tout(e); (*plural*) tous (toutes); **all day** toute la journée; **all night** toute la nuit; **all men** tous les hommes; **all five** tous les cinq; **all the books** tous les livres; **all his life** toute sa vie

▷ *pron* **1** tout; **I ate it all, I ate all of it** j'ai tout mangé; **all of us went** nous y sommes tous allés; **all of the boys went** tous les garçons y sont allés; **is that all?** c'est tout?; (*in shop*) ce sera tout?

**2** (*in phrases*): **above all** surtout, par-dessus tout; **after all** après tout; **at all**: **not at all** (*in answer to question*) pas du tout; (*in answer to thanks*) je vous en prie!; **I'm not at all tired** je ne suis pas du tout fatigué(e); **anything at all will**

**do** n'importe quoi fera l'affaire; **all in all** tout bien considéré, en fin de compte ▷ *adv*: **all alone** tout(e) seul(e); **it's not as hard as all that** ce n'est pas si difficile que ça; **all the more/the better** d'autant plus/mieux; **all but** presque, pratiquement; **the score is 2 all** le score est de 2 partout

**Allah** ['ælə] *n* Allah *m*
**allegation** [ælɪ'geɪʃən] *n* allégation *f*
**alleged** [ə'lɛdʒd] *adj* prétendu(e);
   **allegedly** *adv* à ce que l'on prétend, paraît-il
**allegiance** [ə'liːdʒəns] *n* fidélité *f*, obéissance *f*
**allergic** [ə'ləːdʒɪk] *adj*: **~ to** allergique à; **I'm ~ to penicillin** je suis allergique à la pénicilline
**allergy** ['ælədʒɪ] *n* allergie *f*
**alleviate** [ə'liːvɪeɪt] *vt* soulager, adoucir
**alley** ['ælɪ] *n* ruelle *f*
**alliance** [ə'laɪəns] *n* alliance *f*
**allied** ['ælaɪd] *adj* allié(e)
**alligator** ['ælɪgeɪtəʳ] *n* alligator *m*
**all-in** ['ɔːlɪn] *adj*, *adv* (BRIT: *charge*) tout compris
**allocate** ['æləkeɪt] *vt* (*share out*) répartir, distribuer; **to ~ sth to** (*duties*) assigner *or* attribuer qch à; (*sum, time*) allouer qch à
**allot** [ə'lɔt] *vt* (*share out*) répartir, distribuer; **to ~ sth to** (*time*) allouer qch à; (*duties*) assigner qch à
**all-out** ['ɔːlaut] *adj* (*effort etc*) total(e)
**allow** [ə'lau] *vt* (*practice, behaviour*) permettre, autoriser; (*sum to spend etc*) accorder, allouer; (*sum, time estimated*) compter, prévoir; (*claim, goal*) admettre; (*concede*): **to ~ that** convenir que; **to ~ sb to do** permettre à qn de faire, autoriser qn à faire; **he is ~ed to ...** on lui permet de ...; **allow for** *vt fus* tenir compte de; **allowance** *n* (*money received*) allocation *f*; (: *from parent etc*) subside *m*; (: *for expenses*) indemnité *f*; (US: *pocket money*) argent *m*

de poche; (*Tax*) somme *f* déductible du revenu imposable, abattement *m*; **to make allowances for** (*person*) essayer de comprendre; (*thing*) tenir compte de
**all right** *adv* (*feel, work*) bien; (*as answer*) d'accord
**ally** *n* ['ælaɪ] allié *m* ▷ *vt* [ə'laɪ]: **to ~ o.s. with** s'allier avec
**almighty** [ɔːl'maɪtɪ] *adj* tout(e)-puissant(e); (*tremendous*) énorme
**almond** ['ɑːmənd] *n* amande *f*
**almost** ['ɔːlməust] *adv* presque
**alone** [ə'ləun] *adj*, *adv* seul(e); **to leave sb ~** laisser qn tranquille; **to leave sth ~** ne pas toucher à qch; **let ~ ...** sans parler de ...; encore moins ...
**along** [ə'lɔŋ] *prep* le long de ▷ *adv*: **is he coming ~ with us?** vient-il avec nous?; **he was hopping/limping ~** il venait *or* avançait en sautillant/boitant; **~ with** avec, en plus de; (*person*) en compagnie de; **all ~** (*all the time*) depuis le début; **alongside** *prep* (*along*) le long de; (*beside*) à côté de ▷ *adv* bord à bord; côte à côte
**aloof** [ə'luːf] *adj* distant(e) ▷ *adv*: **to stand ~** se tenir à l'écart *or* à distance
**aloud** [ə'laud] *adv* à haute voix
**alphabet** ['ælfəbɛt] *n* alphabet *m*
**Alps** [ælps] *npl*: **the ~** les Alpes *fpl*
**already** [ɔːl'rɛdɪ] *adv* déjà
**alright** ['ɔːl'raɪt] *adv* (BRIT) = **all right**
**also** ['ɔːlsəu] *adv* aussi
**altar** ['ɔltəʳ] *n* autel *m*
**alter** ['ɔltəʳ] *vt*, *vi* changer; **alteration** [ɔltə'reɪʃən] *n* changement *m*, modification *f*; **alterations** *npl* (*Sewing*) retouches *fpl*; (*Archit*) modifications *fpl*
**alternate** *adj* [ɔl'təːnɪt] alterné(e), alternant(e), alternatif(-ive); (*us*) = **alternative** ▷ *vi* ['ɔltəːneɪt] alterner; **to ~ with** alterner avec; **on ~ days** un jour sur deux, tous les deux jours
**alternative** [ɔl'təːnətɪv] *adj* (*solution, plan*) autre, de remplacement; (*lifestyle*) parallèle ▷ *n* (*choice*) alternative *f*; (*other possibility*) autre possibilité *f*;

**~ medicine** médecine alternative, médecine douce; **alternatively** adv: **alternatively one could ...** une autre or l'autre solution serait de ...

**although** [ɔːl'ðəu] conj bien que + sub

**altitude** ['æltɪtjuːd] n altitude f

**altogether** [ɔːltə'ɡeðə<sup>r</sup>] adv entièrement, tout à fait; (on the whole) tout compte fait; (in all) en tout

**aluminium** [ælju'mɪnɪəm] (BRIT **aluminum**) [ə'luːmɪnəm] (US) n aluminium m

**always** ['ɔːlweɪz] adv toujours

**Alzheimer's (disease)** ['æltshaɪməz-] n maladie f d'Alzheimer

**am** [æm] vb see **be**

**a.m.** adv abbr (= ante meridiem) du matin

**amalgamate** [ə'mælɡəmeɪt] vt, vi fusionner

**amass** [ə'mæs] vt amasser

**amateur** ['æmətə<sup>r</sup>] n amateur m

**amaze** [ə'meɪz] vt stupéfier; **to be ~d (at)** être stupéfait(e) (de); **amazed** adj stupéfait(e); **amazement** n surprise f, étonnement m; **amazing** adj étonnant(e), incroyable; (bargain, offer) exceptionnel(le)

**Amazon** ['æməzən] n (Geo) Amazone f

**ambassador** [æm'bæsədə<sup>r</sup>] n ambassadeur m

**amber** ['æmbə<sup>r</sup>] n ambre m; **at ~** (BRIT Aut) à l'orange

**ambiguous** [æm'bɪɡjuəs] adj ambigu(ë)

**ambition** [æm'bɪʃən] n ambition f; **ambitious** [æm'bɪʃəs] adj ambitieux(-euse)

**ambulance** ['æmbjuləns] n ambulance f; **call an ~!** appelez une ambulance!

**ambush** ['æmbuʃ] n embuscade f ▷ vt tendre une embuscade à

**amen** ['ɑː'mɛn] excl amen

**amend** [ə'mɛnd] vt (law) amender; (text) corriger; **to make ~s** réparer ses torts, faire amende honorable; **amendment** n (to law) amendement m; (to text) correction f

**amenities** [ə'miːnɪtɪz] npl aménagements mpl, équipements mpl

**America** [ə'mɛrɪkə] n Amérique f; **American** adj américain(e) ▷ n Américain(e); **American football** n (BRIT) football m américain

**amicable** ['æmɪkəbl] adj amical(e); (Law) à l'amiable

**amid(st)** [ə'mɪd(st)] prep parmi, au milieu de

**ammunition** [æmju'nɪʃən] n munitions fpl

**amnesty** ['æmnɪstɪ] n amnistie f

**among(st)** [ə'mʌŋ(st)] prep parmi, entre

**amount** [ə'maunt] n (sum of money) somme f; (total) montant m; (quantity) quantité f; nombre m ▷ vi: **to ~ to** (total) s'élever à; (be same as) équivaloir à, revenir à

**amp(ère)** ['æmp(ɛə<sup>r</sup>)] n ampère m

**ample** ['æmpl] adj ample, spacieux(-euse); (enough): **this is ~** c'est largement suffisant; **to have ~ time/ room** avoir bien assez de temps/place

**amplifier** ['æmplɪfaɪə<sup>r</sup>] n amplificateur m

**amputate** ['æmpjuteɪt] vt amputer

**Amtrak** ['æmtræk] (US) n société mixte de transports ferroviaires interurbains pour voyageurs

**amuse** [ə'mjuːz] vt amuser; **amusement** n amusement m; (pastime) distraction f; **amusement arcade** n salle f de jeu; **amusement park** n parc m d'attractions

**amusing** [ə'mjuːzɪŋ] adj amusant(e), divertissant(e)

**an** [æn, ən, n] indef art see **a**

**anaemia** [ə'niːmɪə] (US **anemia**) n anémie f

**anaemic** [ə'niːmɪk] (US **anemic**) adj anémique

**anaesthetic** [ænɪs'θɛtɪk] (US **anesthetic**) n anesthésique m

**analog(ue)** ['ænəlɒɡ] adj (watch, computer) analogique

**analogy** [ə'nælədʒɪ] n analogie f

**analyse** ['ænəlaɪz] (*US* **analyze**) *vt*
analyser; **analysis** (*pl* **analyses**)
[ə'næləsɪs, -siːz] *n* analyse *f*; **analyst**
['ænəlɪst] *n* (*political analyst etc*)
analyste *m/f*; (*US*) psychanalyste *m/f*
**analyze** ['ænəlaɪz] *vt* (*US*) = **analyse**
**anarchy** ['ænəkɪ] *n* anarchie *f*
**anatomy** [ə'nætəmɪ] *n* anatomie *f*
**ancestor** ['ænsɪstər] *n* ancêtre *m*,
aïeul *m*
**anchor** ['æŋkər] *n* ancre *f* ▷ *vi* (*also:*
**to drop ~**) jeter l'ancre, mouiller ▷ *vt*
mettre à l'ancre; (*fig*): **to ~ sth to**
fixer qch à
**anchovy** ['æntʃəvɪ] *n* anchois *m*
**ancient** ['eɪnʃənt] *adj* ancien(ne),
antique; (*person*) d'un âge vénérable;
(*car*) antédiluvien(ne)
**and** [ænd] *conj* et; **~ so on** et ainsi de
suite; **try ~ come** tâchez de venir;
**come ~ sit here** venez vous asseoir ici;
**he talked ~ talked** il a parlé pendant
des heures; **better ~ better** de mieux
en mieux; **more ~ more** de plus en plus
**Andorra** [æn'dɔːrə] *n* (principauté *f*
d')Andorre *f*
**anemia** *etc* [ə'niːmɪə] (*US*) = **anaemia**
*etc*
**anesthetic** [ænɪs'θetɪk] (*US*)
= **anaesthetic**
**angel** ['eɪndʒəl] *n* ange *m*
**anger** ['æŋgər] *n* colère *f*
**angina** [æn'dʒaɪnə] *n* angine *f* de
poitrine
**angle** ['æŋgl] *n* angle *m*; **from their ~** de
leur point de vue
**angler** ['æŋglər] *n* pêcheur(-euse) à
la ligne
**Anglican** ['æŋglɪkən] *adj*, *n* anglican(e)
**angling** ['æŋglɪŋ] *n* pêche *f* à la ligne
**angrily** ['æŋgrɪlɪ] *adv* avec colère
**angry** ['æŋgrɪ] *adj* en colère,
furieux(-euse); (*wound*) enflammé(e); **to
be ~ with sb/at sth** être furieux contre
qn/de qch; **to get ~** se fâcher, se mettre
en colère
**anguish** ['æŋgwɪʃ] *n* angoisse *f*
**animal** ['ænɪməl] *n* animal *m* ▷ *adj*
animal(e)
**animated** ['ænɪmeɪtɪd] *adj* animé(e)
**animation** [ænɪ'meɪʃən] *n* (*of person*)
entrain *m*; (*of street, Cine*) animation *f*
**aniseed** ['ænɪsiːd] *n* anis *m*
**ankle** ['æŋkl] *n* cheville *f*
**annex** ['æneks] *n* (*BRIT: also:* **~e**) annexe
*f* ▷ *vt* [ə'neks] annexer
**anniversary** [ænɪ'vəːsərɪ] *n*
anniversaire *m*
**announce** [ə'nauns] *vt* annoncer;
(*birth, death*) faire part de;
**announcement** *n* annonce *f*; (*for births
etc: in newspaper*) avis *m* de faire-part;
(: *letter, card*) faire-part *m*; **announcer**
*n* (*Radio, TV: between programmes*)
speaker(ine); (: *in a programme*)
présentateur(-trice)
**annoy** [ə'nɔɪ] *vt* agacer, ennuyer,
contrarier; **don't get ~ed!** ne vous
fâchez pas!; **annoying** *adj* agaçant(e),
contrariant(e)
**annual** ['ænjuəl] *adj* annuel(le) ▷ *n*
(*Bot*) plante annuelle; (*book*) album *m*;
**annually** *adv* annuellement
**annum** ['ænəm] *n see* **per**
**anonymous** [ə'nɔnɪməs] *adj*
anonyme
**anorak** ['ænəræk] *n* anorak *m*
**anorexia** [ænə'reksɪə] *n* (*also:* **~
nervosa**) anorexie *f*
**anorexic** [ænə'reksɪk] *adj*, *n*
anorexique (*m/f*)
**another** [ə'nʌðər] *adj*: **~ book** (*one more*)
un autre livre, encore un livre, un livre
de plus; (*a different one*) un autre livre
▷ *pron* un(e) autre, encore un(e), un(e)
de plus; *see also* **one**
**answer** ['ɑːnsər] *n* réponse *f*; (*to
problem*) solution *f* ▷ *vi* répondre ▷ *vt*
(*reply to*) répondre à; (*problem*) résoudre;
(*prayer*) exaucer; **in ~ to your letter**
suite *or* en réponse à votre lettre; **to
~ the phone** répondre (au téléphone);
**to ~ the bell** *or* **the door** aller *or* venir
ouvrir (la porte); **answer back** *vi*
répondre, répliquer; **answerphone** *n*
(*esp BRIT*) répondeur *m* (téléphonique)

**ant** [ænt] n fourmi f
**Antarctic** [ænt'ɑ:ktɪk] n: **the ~**
l'Antarctique m
**antelope** ['æntɪləup] n antilope f
**antenatal** ['æntɪ'neɪtl] adj prénatal(e)
**antenna** (pl **~e**) [æn'tɛnə, -niː] n
antenne f
**anthem** ['ænθəm] n: **national ~** hymne
national
**anthology** [æn'θɔlədʒɪ] n anthologie f
**anthrax** ['ænθræks] n anthrax m
**anthropology** [ænθrə'pɔlədʒɪ] n
anthropologie f
**anti** ['æntɪ] prefix anti-; **antibiotic**
['æntɪbaɪ'ɔtɪk] n antibiotique m;
**antibody** ['æntɪbɔdɪ] n anticorps m
**anticipate** [æn'tɪsɪpeɪt] vt s'attendre
à, prévoir; (wishes, request) aller au
devant de, devancer; **anticipation**
[æntɪsɪ'peɪʃən] n attente f
**anticlimax** ['æntɪ'klaɪmæks] n
déception f
**anticlockwise** ['æntɪ'klɔkwaɪz] (BRIT)
adv dans le sens inverse des aiguilles
d'une montre
**antics** ['æntɪks] npl singeries fpl
**anti**: **antidote** ['æntɪdəut] n antidote
m, contrepoison m; **antifreeze**
['æntɪfriːz] n antigel m; **anti-
globalization** n antimondialisation f;
**antihistamine** [æntɪ'hɪstəmɪn] n
antihistaminique m; **antiperspirant**
[æntɪ'pə:spɪrənt] n déodorant m
**antique** [æn'tiːk] n (ornament) objet m
d'art ancien; (furniture) meuble ancien
▷ adj ancien(ne); **antique shop** n
magasin m d'antiquités
**antiseptic** [æntɪ'sɛptɪk] adj, n
antiseptique (m)
**antisocial** ['æntɪ'səuʃəl] adj (unfriendly)
peu liant(e), insociable; (against society)
antisocial(e)
**antlers** ['æntləz] npl bois mpl, ramure f
**anxiety** [æŋ'zaɪətɪ] n anxiété f;
(keenness): **~ to do** grand désir or
impatience f de faire
**anxious** ['æŋkʃəs] adj (très)
inquiet(-ète); (always worried)

anxieux(-euse); (worrying)
angoissant(e); (keen): **~ to do/that** qui
tient beaucoup à faire/à ce que + sub;
impatient(e) de faire/que + sub

🅞 KEYWORD

**any** ['ɛnɪ] adj 1 (in questions etc: singular)
du, de l', de la; (: plural) des; **do you have
any butter/children/ink?** avez-vous
du beurre/des enfants/de l'encre?
2 (with negative) de, d'; **I don't have any
money/books** je n'ai pas d'argent/de
livres
3 (no matter which) n'importe quel(le);
(each and every) tout(e), chaque; **choose
any book you like** vous pouvez choisir
n'importe quel livre; **any teacher
you ask will tell you** n'importe quel
professeur vous le dira
4 (in phrases): **in any case** de toute
façon; **any day now** d'un jour à l'autre;
**at any moment** à tout moment, d'un
instant à l'autre; **at any rate** en tout
cas; **any time** n'importe quand; **he
might come (at) any time** il pourrait
venir n'importe quand; **come (at) any
time** venez quand vous voulez
▷ pron 1 (in questions etc) en; **have you
got any?** est-ce que vous en avez?; **can
any of you sing?** est-ce que parmi vous
il y en a qui savent chanter?
2 (with negative) en; **I don't have any
(of them)** je n'en ai pas, je n'en ai aucun
3 (no matter which one(s)) n'importe
lequel (or laquelle); (anybody) n'importe
qui; **take any of those books (you
like)** vous pouvez prendre n'importe
lequel de ces livres
▷ adv 1 (in questions etc): **do you
want any more soup/sandwiches?**
voulez-vous encore de la soupe/des
sandwichs?; **are you feeling any
better?** est-ce que vous vous sentez
mieux?
2 (with negative): **I can't hear him
any more** je ne l'entends plus; **don't
wait any longer** n'attendez pas plus

longtemps; **anybody** pron n'importe qui; (in interrogative sentences) quelqu'un; (in negative sentences): **I don't see anybody** je ne vois personne; **if anybody should phone ...** si quelqu'un téléphone ...; **anyhow** adv quoi qu'il en soit; (haphazardly) n'importe comment; **do it anyhow you like** faites-le comme vous voulez; **she leaves things just anyhow** elle laisse tout traîner; **I shall go anyhow** j'irai de toute façon; **anyone** pron = **anybody**; **anything** pron (no matter what) n'importe quoi; (in questions) quelque chose; (with negative) ne ... rien; **can you see anything?** tu vois quelque chose?; **if anything happens to me ...** s'il m'arrive quoi que ce soit ...; **you can say anything you like** vous pouvez dire ce que vous voulez; **anything will do** n'importe quoi fera l'affaire; **he'll eat anything** il mange de tout; **anytime** adv (at any moment) à un moment à l'autre; (whenever) n'importe quand; **anyway** adv de toute façon; **anyway, I couldn't come even if I wanted to** de toute façon, je ne pouvais pas venir même si je le voulais; **I shall go anyway** j'irai quand même; **why are you phoning, anyway?** au fait, pourquoi tu me téléphones?; **anywhere** adv n'importe où; (in interrogative sentences) quelque part; (in negative sentences): **I can't see him anywhere** je ne le vois nulle part; **can you see him anywhere?** tu le vois quelque part?; **put the books down anywhere** pose les livres n'importe où; **anywhere in the world** (no matter where) n'importe où dans le monde

**apart** [əˈpɑːt] adv (to one side) à part; de côté; à l'écart; (separately) séparément; **to take/pull ~** démonter; **10 miles/a long way ~** à 10 miles/très éloignés l'un de l'autre; **~ from** prep à part, excepté

**apartment** [əˈpɑːtmənt] n (us) appartement m, logement m; (room) chambre f; **apartment building** n (us) immeuble m; maison divisée en appartements

**apathy** [ˈæpəθɪ] n apathie f, indifférence f

**ape** [eɪp] n (grand) singe ▷ vt singer

**aperitif** [əˈperitif] n apéritif m

**aperture** [ˈæpətʃjʊəʳ] n orifice m, ouverture f; (Phot) ouverture (du diaphragme)

**APEX** [ˈeɪpeks] n abbr (Aviat: = advance purchase excursion) APEX m

**apologize** [əˈpɒlədʒaɪz] vi: **to ~ (for sth to sb)** s'excuser (de qch auprès de qn), présenter des excuses (à qn pour qch)

**apology** [əˈpɒlədʒɪ] n excuses fpl

**apostrophe** [əˈpɒstrəfɪ] n apostrophe f

**appal** [əˈpɔːl] (us **appall**) vt consterner, atterrer; horrifier; **appalling** adj épouvantable; (stupidity) consternant(e)

**apparatus** [æpəˈreɪtəs] n appareil m, dispositif m; (in gymnasium) agrès mpl

**apparent** [əˈpærənt] adj apparent(e); **apparently** adv apparemment

**appeal** [əˈpiːl] vi (Law) faire or interjeter appel ▷ n (Law) appel m; (request) appel; prière f; (charm) attrait m, charme m; **to ~ for** demander (instamment); implorer; **to ~ to** (beg) faire appel à; (be attractive) plaire à; **it doesn't ~ to me** cela ne m'attire pas; **appealing** adj (attractive) attrayant(e)

**appear** [əˈpɪəʳ] vi apparaître, se montrer; (Law) comparaître; (publication) paraître, sortir, être publié(e); (seem) paraître, sembler; **it would ~ that** il semble que; **to ~ in Hamlet** jouer dans Hamlet; **to ~ on TV** passer à la télé; **appearance** n apparition f; parution f; (look, aspect) apparence f, aspect m

**appendices** [əˈpendisiːz] npl of **appendix**

**appendicitis** [əpendɪˈsaɪtɪs] n appendicite f

**appendix** (pl **appendices**) [əˈpendɪks,

-si:z) n appendice m
**appetite** ['æpɪtaɪt] n appétit m
**appetizer** ['æpɪtaɪzə'] n (food) amuse-
gueule m; (drink) apéritif m
**applaud** [ə'plɔ:d] vt, vi applaudir
**applause** [ə'plɔ:z] n
applaudissements mpl
**apple** ['æpl] n pomme f; **apple pie** n
tarte f aux pommes
**appliance** [ə'plaɪəns] n appareil m
**applicable** [ə'plɪkəbl] adj applicable;
**to be ~ to** (relevant) valoir pour
**applicant** ['æplɪkənt] n: **~ (for)**
candidat(e) (à)
**application** [æplɪ'keɪʃən] n
application f; (for a job, a grant etc)
demande f; candidature f; **application
form** n formulaire m de demande
**apply** [ə'plaɪ] vt: **to ~ (to)** (paint,
ointment) appliquer (sur); (law,
etc) appliquer (à) ▷ vi: **to ~ to** (ask)
s'adresser à; (be suitable for, relevant to)
s'appliquer à; **to ~ (for)** (permit, grant)
faire une demande (en vue d'obtenir);
(job) poser sa candidature (pour), faire
une demande d'emploi (concernant);
**to ~ o.s. to** s'appliquer à
**appoint** [ə'pɔɪnt] vt (to post) nommer,
engager; (date, place) fixer, désigner;
**appointment** n (to post) nomination
f; (job) poste m; (arrangement to
meet) rendez-vous m; **to have an
appointment** avoir un rendez-vous;
**to make an appointment (with)**
prendre rendez-vous (avec); **I'd like to
make an appointment** je voudrais
prendre rendez-vous
**appraisal** [ə'preɪzl] n évaluation f
**appreciate** [ə'pri:ʃɪeɪt] vt (like)
apprécier, faire cas de; (be grateful
for) être reconnaissant(e) de; (be
aware of) comprendre, se rendre
compte de ▷ vi (Finance) prendre
de la valeur; **appreciation**
[əpri:ʃɪ'eɪʃən] n appréciation f;
(gratitude) reconnaissance f; (Finance)
hausse f, valorisation f
**apprehension** [æprɪ'hɛnʃən] n

appréhension f, inquiétude f
**apprehensive** [æprɪ'hɛnsɪv] adj
inquiet(-ète), appréhensif(-ive)
**apprentice** [ə'prɛntɪs] n apprenti m
**approach** [ə'prəʊtʃ] vi approcher ▷ vt
(come near) approcher de; (ask, apply to)
s'adresser à; (subject, passer-by) aborder
▷ n approche f; accès m, abord m;
démarche f (intellectuelle)
**appropriate** adj [ə'prəʊprɪɪt] (tool etc)
qui convient, approprié(e); (moment,
remark) opportun(e) ▷ vt [ə'prəʊprɪeɪt]
(take) s'approprier
**approval** [ə'pru:vəl] n approbation f;
**on ~** (Comm) à l'examen
**approve** [ə'pru:v] vt approuver;
**approve of** vt fus (thing) approuver;
(person): **they don't ~ of her** ils n'ont
pas bonne opinion d'elle
**approximate** [ə'prɔksɪmɪt] adj
approximatif(-ive); **approximately** adv
approximativement
**Apr.** abbr = **April**
**apricot** ['eɪprɪkɔt] n abricot m
**April** ['eɪprəl] n avril m; **April Fools' Day**
n le premier avril

● **APRIL FOOLS' DAY**
●
● **April Fools' Day** est le 1er avril, à
● l'occasion duquel on fait des farces
● de toutes sortes. Les victimes de
● ces farces sont les "April fools".
● Traditionnellement, on n'est censé
● faire des farces que jusqu'à midi.

**apron** ['eɪprən] n tablier m
**apt** [æpt] adj (suitable) approprié(e);
(likely): **~ to do** susceptible de faire;
ayant tendance à faire
**aquarium** [ə'kwɛərɪəm] n aquarium m
**Aquarius** [ə'kwɛərɪəs] n le Verseau
**Arab** ['ærəb] n Arabe m/f ▷ adj arabe
**Arabia** [ə'reɪbɪə] n Arabie f; **Arabian**
adj arabe; **Arabic** ['ærəbɪk] adj, n
arabe (m)
**arbitrary** ['ɑ:bɪtrərɪ] adj arbitraire
**arbitration** [ɑ:bɪ'treɪʃən] n

arbitrage *m*

**arc** [ɑːk] *n* arc *m*

**arcade** [ɑːˈkeɪd] *n* arcade *f*; (*passage with shops*) passage *m*, galerie *f*; (*with games*) salle *f* de jeu

**arch** [ɑːtʃ] *n* arche *f*; (*of foot*) cambrure *f*, voûte *f* plantaire ▷ *vt* arquer, cambrer

**archaeology** [ɑːkɪˈɔlədʒɪ] (*Us* **archeology**) *n* archéologie *f*

**archbishop** [ɑːtʃˈbɪʃəp] *n* archevêque *m*

**archeology** [ɑːkɪˈɔlədʒɪ] (*Us*) = **archaeology**

**architect** [ˈɑːkɪtɛkt] *n* architecte *m*; **architectural** [ɑːkɪˈtɛktʃərəl] *adj* architectural(e); **architecture** *n* architecture *f*

**archive** [ˈɑːkaɪv] *n* (*often pl*) archives *fpl*

**Arctic** [ˈɑːktɪk] *adj* arctique ▷ *n*: **the ~** l'Arctique *m*

**are** [ɑːʳ] *vb see* **be**

**area** [ˈɛərɪə] *n* (*Geom*) superficie *f*; (*zone*) région *f*; (: *smaller*) secteur *m*; (*in room*) coin *m*; (*knowledge, research*) domaine *m*; **area code** (*Us*) *n* (*Tel*) indicatif *m* de zone

**arena** [əˈriːnə] *n* arène *f*

**aren't** [ɑːnt] = **are not**

**Argentina** [ɑːdʒənˈtiːnə] *n* Argentine *f*; **Argentinian** [ɑːdʒənˈtɪnɪən] *adj* argentin(e) ▷ *n* Argentin(e)

**arguably** [ˈɑːgjuəblɪ] *adv*: **it is ~ ...** on peut soutenir que c'est ...

**argue** [ˈɑːgjuː] *vi* (*quarrel*) se disputer; (*reason*) argumenter; **to ~ that** objecter *or* alléguer que, donner comme argument que

**argument** [ˈɑːgjumənt] *n* (*quarrel*) dispute *f*, discussion *f*; (*reasons*) argument *m*

**Aries** [ˈɛərɪz] *n* le Bélier

**arise** (*pt* **arose**, *pp* **~n**) [əˈraɪz, əˈrəuz, əˈrɪzn] *vi* survenir, se présenter

**arithmetic** [əˈrɪθmətɪk] *n* arithmétique *f*

**arm** [ɑːm] *n* bras *m* ▷ *vt* armer; **arms** *npl* (*weapons, Heraldry*) armes *fpl*; **~ in ~** bras dessus bras dessous; **armchair**

[ˈɑːmtʃɛəʳ] *n* fauteuil *m*

**armed** [ɑːmd] *adj* armé(e); **armed forces** *npl*: **the armed forces** les forces armées; **armed robbery** *n* vol *m* à main armée

**armour** (*Us* **armor**) [ˈɑːməʳ] *n* armure *f*; (*Mil: tanks*) blindés *mpl*

**armpit** [ˈɑːmpɪt] *n* aisselle *f*

**armrest** [ˈɑːmrɛst] *n* accoudoir *m*

**army** [ˈɑːmɪ] *n* armée *f*

**A road** *n* (*BRIT*) ≈ route nationale

**aroma** [əˈrəumə] *n* arôme *m*; **aromatherapy** *n* aromathérapie *f*

**arose** [əˈrəuz] *pt of* **arise**

**around** [əˈraund] *adv* (*tout*) autour; (*nearby*) dans les parages ▷ *prep* autour de; (*near*) près de; (*fig: about*) environ; (: *date, time*) vers; **is he ~?** est-il dans les parages *or* là?

**arouse** [əˈrauz] *vt* (*sleeper*) éveiller; (*curiosity, passions*) éveiller, susciter; (*anger*) exciter

**arrange** [əˈreɪndʒ] *vt* arranger; **to ~ to do sth** prévoir de faire qch; **arrangement** *n* arrangement *m*; **arrangements** *npl* (*plans etc*) arrangements *mpl*, dispositions *fpl*

**array** [əˈreɪ] *n* (*of objects*) déploiement *m*, étalage *m*

**arrears** [əˈrɪəz] *npl* arriéré *m*; **to be in ~ with one's rent** devoir un arriéré de loyer

**arrest** [əˈrɛst] *vt* arrêter; (*sb's attention*) retenir, attirer ▷ *n* arrestation *f*; **under ~** en état d'arrestation

**arrival** [əˈraɪvl] *n* arrivée *f*; **new ~** nouveau venu/nouvelle venue; (*baby*) nouveau-né(e)

**arrive** [əˈraɪv] *vi* arriver; **arrive at** *vt fus* (*decision, solution*) parvenir à

**arrogance** [ˈærəgəns] *n* arrogance *f*

**arrogant** [ˈærəgənt] *adj* arrogant(e)

**arrow** [ˈærəu] *n* flèche *f*

**arse** [ɑːs] *n* (*BRIT inf!*) cul *m* (!)

**arson** [ˈɑːsn] *n* incendie criminel

**art** [ɑːt] *n* art *m*; **Arts** *npl* (*Scol*) les lettres *fpl*; **art college** *n* école *f* des beaux-arts

**artery** [ˈɑːtərɪ] n artère f
**art gallery** n musée m d'art; (saleroom) galerie f de peinture
**arthritis** [ɑːˈθraɪtɪs] n arthrite f
**artichoke** [ˈɑːtɪtʃəuk] n artichaut m; **Jerusalem ~** topinambour m
**article** [ˈɑːtɪkl] n article m
**articulate** adj [ɑːˈtɪkjulɪt] (person) qui s'exprime clairement et aisément; (speech) bien articulé(e), prononcé(e) clairement ⊳ vb [ɑːˈtɪkjuleɪt] ⊳ vi articuler, parler distinctement ⊳ vt articuler
**artificial** [ɑːtɪˈfɪʃəl] adj artificiel(le)
**artist** [ˈɑːtɪst] n artiste m/f; **artistic** [ɑːˈtɪstɪk] adj artistique
**art school** n ≈ école f des beaux-arts

**KEYWORD**

**as** [æz] conj 1 (time: moment) comme, alors que; à mesure que; **he came in as I was leaving** il est arrivé comme je partais; **as the years went by** à mesure que les années passaient; **as from tomorrow** à partir de demain
2 (since, because) comme, puisque; **he left early as he had to be home by 10** comme il or puisqu'il devait être de retour avant 10h, il est parti de bonne heure
3 (referring to manner, way) comme; **do as you wish** faites comme vous voudrez; **as she said** comme elle disait ⊳ adv 1 (in comparisons): **as big as** aussi grand que; **twice as big as** deux fois plus grand que; **as much** or **many as** autant que; **as much money/many books as** autant d'argent/de livres que; **as soon as** dès que
2 (concerning): **as for** or **to that** quant à cela, pour ce qui est de cela
3: **as if** or **though** comme si; **he looked as if he was ill** il avait l'air d'être malade; see also **long; such; well** ⊳ prep (in the capacity of) en tant que, en qualité de; **he works as a driver** il travaille comme chauffeur; **as chairman of the company, he ...** en tant que président de la société, il ...; **he gave me it as a present** il me l'a offert, il m'en a fait cadeau

**a.s.a.p.** abbr = **as soon as possible**
**asbestos** [æzˈbɛstəs] n asbeste m, amiante m
**ascent** [əˈsɛnt] n (climb) ascension f
**ash** [æʃ] n (dust) cendre f; (also: **~ tree**) frêne m
**ashamed** [əˈʃeɪmd] adj honteux(-euse), confus(e); **to be ~ of** avoir honte de
**ashore** [əˈʃɔːʳ] adv à terre
**ashtray** [ˈæʃtreɪ] n cendrier m
**Ash Wednesday** n mercredi m des Cendres
**Asia** [ˈeɪʃə] n Asie f; **Asian** n (from Asia) Asiatique m/f; (BRIT: from Indian subcontinent) Indo-Pakistanais(-e) ⊳ adj asiatique; indo-pakistanais(-e)
**aside** [əˈsaɪd] adv de côté; à l'écart ⊳ n aparté m
**ask** [ɑːsk] vt demander; (invite) inviter; **to ~ sb sth/to do sth** demander à qn qch/de faire qch; **to ~ sb about sth** questionner qn au sujet de qch; se renseigner auprès de qn au sujet de qch; **to ~ (sb) a question** poser une question (à qn); **to ~ sb out to dinner** inviter qn au restaurant; **ask for** vt fus demander; **it's just ~ing for trouble** or **for it** ce serait chercher des ennuis
**asleep** [əˈsliːp] adj endormi(e); **to fall ~** s'endormir
**AS level** n abbr (= Advanced Subsidiary level) première partie de l'examen équivalent au baccalauréat
**asparagus** [əsˈpærəgəs] n asperges fpl
**aspect** [ˈæspɛkt] n aspect m; (direction in which a building etc faces) orientation f, exposition f
**aspirations** [æspəˈreɪʃənz] npl (hopes, ambition) aspirations fpl
**aspire** [əsˈpaɪəʳ] vi: **to ~ to** aspirer à
**aspirin** [ˈæsprɪn] n aspirine f
**ass** [æs] n âne m; (inf) imbécile m/f; (us

*infl)* cul *m* (!)
**assassin** [ə'sæsɪn] *n* assassin *m*;
**assassinate** *vt* assassiner
**assault** [ə'sɔːlt] *n* (*Mil*) assaut *m*; (*gen*:
*attack*) agression *f* ▷ *vt* attaquer;
(*sexually*) violenter
**assemble** [ə'sɛmbl] *vt* assembler ▷ *vi*
s'assembler, se rassembler
**assembly** [ə'sɛmblɪ] *n* (*meeting*)
rassemblement *m*; (*parliament*)
assemblée *f*; (*construction*)
assemblage *m*
**assert** [ə'səːt] *vt* affirmer, déclarer;
(*authority*) faire valoir; (*innocence*)
protester de; **assertion** [ə'səːʃən] *n*
assertion *f*, affirmation *f*
**assess** [ə'sɛs] *vt* évaluer, estimer; (*tax*,
*damages*) établir *or* fixer le montant de;
(*person*) juger la valeur de; **assessment**
*n* évaluation *f*, estimation *f*; (*of tax*)
fixation *f*
**asset** ['æsɛt] *n* avantage *m*, atout *m*;
(*person*) atout; **assets** *npl* (*Comm*)
capital *m*; avoir(s) *m(pl)*; actif *m*
**assign** [ə'saɪn] *vt* (*date*) fixer, arrêter; **to
~ sth to** (*task*) assigner qch à; (*resources*)
affecter qch à; **assignment** *n* (*task*)
mission *f*; (*homework*) devoir *m*
**assist** [ə'sɪst] *vt* aider, assister;
**assistance** *n* aide *f*, assistance *f*;
**assistant** *n* assistant(e), adjoint(e);
(*BRIT: also*: **shop assistant**)
vendeur(-euse)
**associate** [adj, n ə'səuʃɪɪt] *associé(e)*
▷ *vb* [ə'səuʃɪeɪt] ▷ *vt* associer ▷ *vi*: **to ~
with sb** fréquenter qn
**association** [əsəuʃɪ'eɪʃən] *n*
association *f*
**assorted** [ə'sɔːtɪd] *adj* assorti(e)
**assortment** [ə'sɔːtmənt] *n*
assortiment *m*; (*of people*) mélange *m*
**assume** [ə'sjuːm] *vt* supposer;
(*responsibilities etc*) assumer; (*attitude*,
*name*) prendre, adopter
**assumption** [ə'sʌmpʃən] *n*
supposition *f*, hypothèse *f*; (*of power*)
assomption *f*, prise *f*
**assurance** [ə'ʃuərəns] *n* assurance *f*

**assure** [ə'ʃuər] *vt* assurer
**asterisk** ['æstərɪsk] *n* astérisque *m*
**asthma** ['æsmə] *n* asthme *m*
**astonish** [ə'stɔnɪʃ] *vt* étonner,
stupéfier; **astonished** *adj* étonné(e);
**to be astonished at** être étonné(e)
de; **astonishing** *adj* étonnant(e),
stupéfiant(e); **I find it astonishing
that ...** je trouve incroyable que ... + *sub*;
**astonishment** *n* (grand) étonnement,
stupéfaction *f*
**astound** [ə'staund] *vt* stupéfier,
sidérer
**astray** [ə'streɪ] *adv*: **to go ~** s'égarer;
(*fig*) quitter le droit chemin; **to lead ~**
(*morally*) détourner du droit chemin
**astrology** [əs'trɔlədʒɪ] *n* astrologie *f*
**astronaut** ['æstrənɔːt] *n*
astronaute *m/f*
**astronomer** [əs'trɔnəmər] *n*
astronome *m*
**astronomical** [æstrə'nɔmɪkl] *adj*
astronomique
**astronomy** [əs'trɔnəmɪ] *n*
astronomie *f*
**astute** [əs'tjuːt] *adj* astucieux(-euse),
malin(-igne)
**asylum** [ə'saɪləm] *n* asile *m*; **asylum
seeker** [-siːkər] *n* demandeur(-euse)
d'asile

〇 KEYWORD

**at** [æt] *prep* **1** (*referring to position,
direction*) à; **at the top** au sommet; **at
home/school** à la maison *or* chez soi/à
l'école; **at the baker's** à la boulangerie,
chez le boulanger; **to look at sth**
regarder qch
**2** (*referring to time*): **at 4 o'clock** à 4
heures; **at Christmas** à Noël; **at night**
la nuit; **at times** par moments, parfois
**3** (*referring to rates, speed etc*) à; **at £1
a kilo** une livre le kilo; **two at a time**
deux à la fois; **at 50 km/h** à 50 km/h
**4** (*referring to manner*): **at a stroke** d'un
seul coup; **at peace** en paix
**5** (*referring to activity*): **to be at work** (in

*the office etc*) être au travail; (*working*) travailler; **to play at cowboys** jouer aux cowboys; **to be good at sth** être bon en qch

6 (*referring to cause*): **shocked/ surprised/annoyed at sth** choqué par/étonné de/agacé par qch; **I went at his suggestion** j'y suis allé sur son conseil

7 (*symbol*) arobase *f*

**ate** [eɪt] *pt of* **eat**
**atheist** ['eɪθɪɪst] *n* athée *m/f*
**Athens** ['æθɪnz] *n* Athènes
**athlete** ['æθliːt] *n* athlète *m/f*
**athletic** [æθ'lɛtɪk] *adj* athlétique;
**athletics** *n* athlétisme *m*
**Atlantic** [ət'læntɪk] *adj* atlantique ▷ *n*:
**the ~ (Ocean)** l'(océan *m*) Atlantique *m*
**atlas** ['ætləs] *n* atlas *m*
**A.T.M.** *n abbr* (= *Automated Telling Machine*) guichet *m* automatique
**atmosphere** ['ætməsfɪə<sup>r</sup>] *n* (*air*) atmosphère *f*; (*fig: of place etc*) atmosphère, ambiance *f*
**atom** ['ætəm] *n* atome *m*; **atomic** [ə'tɒmɪk] *adj* atomique; **atom(ic) bomb** *n* bombe *f* atomique
**A to Z®** *n* (*map*) plan *m* des rues
**atrocity** [ə'trɒsɪtɪ] *n* atrocité *f*
**attach** [ə'tætʃ] *vt* (*gen*) attacher; (*document, letter*) joindre; **to be ~ed to sb/sth** (*to like*) être attaché à qn/qch; **attachment** *n* (*tool*) accessoire *m*; (*Comput*) fichier *m* joint; (*love*): **attachment (to)** affection *f* (pour), attachement *m* (à)
**attack** [ə'tæk] *vt* attaquer; (*task etc*) s'attaquer à ▷ *n* attaque *f*; **heart ~** crise *f* cardiaque; **attacker** *n* attaquant *m*; agresseur *m*
**attain** [ə'teɪn] *vt* (*also:* **to ~ to**) parvenir à, atteindre; (*knowledge*) acquérir
**attempt** [ə'tɛmpt] *n* tentative *f* ▷ *vt* essayer, tenter
**attend** [ə'tɛnd] *vt* (*course*) suivre; (*meeting, talk*) assister à; (*school, church*) aller à, fréquenter; (*patient*) soigner;

s'occuper de; **attend to** *vt fus* (*needs, affairs etc*) s'occuper de; (*customer*) s'occuper de, servir; **attendance** *n* (*being present*) présence *f*; (*people present*) assistance *f*; **attendant** *n* employé(e); gardien(ne) ▷ *adj* concomitant(e), qui accompagne *or* s'ensuit

> Be careful not to translate *to attend* by the French word *attendre*.

**attention** [ə'tɛnʃən] *n* attention *f* ▷ *excl* (*Mil*) garde-à-vous!; **for the ~ of** (*Admin*) à l'attention de
**attic** ['ætɪk] *n* grenier *m*, combles *mpl*
**attitude** ['ætɪtjuːd] *n* attitude *f*
**attorney** [ə'tɜːnɪ] *n* (*US: lawyer*) avocat *m*; **Attorney General** *n* (*BRIT*) ≈ procureur général; (*US*) ≈ garde *m* des Sceaux, ministre *m* de la Justice
**attract** [ə'trækt] *vt* attirer; **attraction** [ə'trækʃən] *n* (*gen pl: pleasant things*) attraction *f*, attrait *m*; (*Physics*) attraction; (*fig: towards sb, sth*) attirance *f*; **attractive** *adj* séduisant(e), attrayant(e)
**attribute** *n* ['ætrɪbjuːt] attribut *m* ▷ *vt* [ə'trɪbjuːt]: **to ~ sth to** attribuer qch à
**aubergine** ['əʊbəʒiːn] *n* aubergine *f*
**auburn** ['ɔːbən] *adj* auburn *inv*, châtain roux *inv*
**auction** ['ɔːkʃən] *n* (*also:* **sale by ~**) vente *f* aux enchères ▷ *vt* (*also:* **to sell by ~**) vendre aux enchères
**audible** ['ɔːdɪbl] *adj* audible
**audience** ['ɔːdɪəns] *n* (*people*) assistance *f*, public *m*; (*on radio*) auditeurs *mpl*; (*at theatre*) spectateurs *mpl*; (*interview*) audience *f*
**audit** ['ɔːdɪt] *vt* vérifier
**audition** [ɔː'dɪʃən] *n* audition *f*
**auditor** ['ɔːdɪtə<sup>r</sup>] *n* vérificateur *m* des comptes
**auditorium** [ɔːdɪ'tɔːrɪəm] *n* auditorium *m*, salle *f* de concert *or* de spectacle
**Aug.** *abbr* = **August**
**August** ['ɔːgəst] *n* août *m*
**aunt** [ɑːnt] *n* tante *f*; **auntie, aunty** *n* diminutive of **aunt**

**au pair** [ˈəuˈpɛəʳ] n (also: **~ girl**) jeune fille f au pair

**aura** [ˈɔːrə] n atmosphère f; (of person) aura f

**austerity** [ɔsˈtɛrɪtɪ] n austérité f

**Australia** [ɔsˈtreɪlɪə] n Australie f; **Australian** adj australien(ne) ▷ n Australien(ne)

**Austria** [ˈɔstrɪə] n Autriche f; **Austrian** adj autrichien(ne) ▷ n Autrichien(ne)

**authentic** [ɔːˈθɛntɪk] adj authentique

**author** [ˈɔːθəʳ] n auteur m

**authority** [ɔːˈθɔrɪtɪ] n autorité f; (permission) autorisation (formelle); **the authorities** les autorités fpl, l'administration f

**authorize** [ˈɔːθəraɪz] vt autoriser

**auto** [ˈɔːtəu] n (us) auto f, voiture f; **autobiography** [ɔːtəbaɪˈɔgrəfɪ] n autobiographie f; **autograph** [ˈɔːtəgrɑːf] n autographe m ▷ vt signer, dédicacer; **automatic** [ɔːtəˈmætɪk] adj automatique ▷ n (gun) automatique m; (car) voiture f à transmission automatique; **automatically** adv automatiquement; **automobile** [ˈɔːtəməbiːl] n (us) automobile f; **autonomous** [ɔːˈtɔnəməs] adj autonome; **autonomy** [ɔːˈtɔnəmɪ] n autonomie f

**autumn** [ˈɔːtəm] n automne m

**auxiliary** [ɔːgˈzɪlɪərɪ] adj, n auxiliaire (m/f)

**avail** [əˈveɪl] vt: **to ~ o.s. of** user de; profiter de ▷ n: **to no ~** sans résultat, en vain, en pure perte

**availability** [əveɪləˈbɪlɪtɪ] n disponibilité f

**available** [əˈveɪləbl] adj disponible

**avalanche** [ˈævəlɑːnʃ] n avalanche f

**Ave.** abbr = **avenue**

**avenue** [ˈævənjuː] n avenue f; (fig) moyen m

**average** [ˈævərɪdʒ] n moyenne f ▷ adj moyen(ne) ▷ vt (a certain figure) atteindre or faire etc en moyenne; **on ~** en moyenne

**avert** [əˈvəːt] vt (danger) prévenir, écarter; (one's eyes) détourner

**avid** [ˈævɪd] adj avide

**avocado** [ævəˈkɑːdəu] n (BRIT: also: **~ pear**) avocat m

**avoid** [əˈvɔɪd] vt éviter

**await** [əˈweɪt] vt attendre

**awake** [əˈweɪk] adj éveillé(e) ▷ vb (pt **awoke**, pp **awoken**) ▷ vt éveiller ▷ vi s'éveiller; **to be ~** être réveillé(e)

**award** [əˈwɔːd] n (for bravery) récompense f; (prize) prix m; (Law: damages) dommages-intérêts mpl ▷ vt (prize) décerner; (Law: damages) accorder

**aware** [əˈwɛəʳ] adj: **~ of** (conscious) conscient(e) de; (informed) au courant de; **to become ~ of/that** prendre conscience de/que; se rendre compte de/que; **awareness** n conscience f, connaissance f

**away** [əˈweɪ] adv (au) loin; (movement): **she went ~** elle est partie ▷ adj (not in, not here) absent(e); **far ~** (au) loin; **two kilometres ~** à (une distance de) deux kilomètres, à deux kilomètres de distance; **two hours ~ by car** à deux heures de voiture or de route; **the holiday was two weeks ~** il restait deux semaines jusqu'aux vacances; **he's ~ for a week** il est parti (pour) une semaine; **to take sth ~ from sb** prendre qch à qn; **to take sth ~ from sth** (subtract) ôter qch de qch; **to work/pedal ~** travailler/pédaler à cœur joie; **to fade ~** (colour) s'estomper; (sound) s'affaiblir

**awe** [ɔː] n respect mêlé de crainte, effroi mêlé d'admiration; **awesome** [ˈɔːsəm] (us) adj (inf: excellent) génial(e)

**awful** [ˈɔːfəl] adj affreux(-euse); **an ~ lot of** énormément de; **awfully** adv (very) terriblement, vraiment

**awkward** [ˈɔːkwəd] adj (clumsy) gauche, maladroit(e); (inconvenient) peu pratique; (embarrassing) gênant

**awoke** [əˈwəuk] pt of **awake**

**awoken** [əˈwəukən] pp of **awake**

**axe** [æks] (*us* **ax**) *n* hache *f* ▷ *vt (project etc)* abandonner; *(jobs)* supprimer
**axle** ['æksl] *n* essieu *m*
**ay(e)** [aɪ] *excl (yes)* oui
**azalea** [ə'zeɪlɪə] *n* azalée *f*

**B** [biː] *n (Mus)*: **B** si *m*
**B.A.** *abbr (Scol)* = **Bachelor of Arts**
**baby** ['beɪbɪ] *n* bébé *m*; **baby carriage** *n (us)* voiture *f* d'enfant; **baby-sit** *vi* garder les enfants; **baby-sitter** *n* baby-sitter *m/f*; **baby wipe** *n* lingette *f (pour bébé)*
**bachelor** ['bætʃələʳ] *n* célibataire *m*; **B~ of Arts/Science (BA/BSc)** ≈ licencié(e) ès *or* en lettres/sciences
**back** [bæk] *n (of person, horse)* dos *m*; *(of hand)* dos, revers *m*; *(of house)* derrière *m*; *(of car, train)* arrière *m*; *(of chair)* dossier *m*; *(of page)* verso *m*; *(of crowd)*: **can the people at the ~ hear me properly?** est-ce que les gens du fond peuvent m'entendre?; *(Football)* arrière *m*; **~ to front** à l'envers ▷ *vt (financially)* soutenir (financièrement); *(candidate: also: ~ up)* soutenir, appuyer; *(horse: at races)* parier *or* miser sur; *(car)* (faire) reculer ▷ *vi* reculer; *(car etc)* faire marche arrière ▷ *adj (in compounds)* de derrière, à l'arrière; **~ seat/wheel** *(Aut)*

siège m/roue f arrière inv; **~ payments/ rent** arriéré m de paiements/loyer; **~ garden/room** jardin/pièce sur l'arrière ▷ adv (not forward) en arrière; (returned): **he's ~** il est rentré, il est de retour; **he ran ~** il est revenu en courant; (restitution): **throw the ball ~** renvoie la balle; **can I have it ~?** puis-je le ravoir?, peux-tu me le rendre?; (again): **he called ~** il a rappelé; **back down** vi rabattre de ses prétentions; **back out** vi (of promise) se dédire; **back up** vt (person) soutenir; (Comput) faire une copie de sauvegarde de; **backache** n mal m au dos; **backbencher** (BRIT) n membre du parlement sans portefeuille; **backbone** n colonne vertébrale, épine dorsale; **back door** n porte f de derrière; **backfire** vi (Aut) pétarader; (plans) mal tourner; **backgammon** n trictrac m; **background** n arrière-plan m; (of events) situation f, conjoncture f; (basic knowledge) éléments mpl de base; (experience) formation f; **family background** milieu familial; **backing** n (fig) soutien m, appui m; **backlog** n: **backlog of work** travail m en retard; **backpack** n sac m à dos; **backpacker** n randonneur(-euse); **backslash** n barre oblique inversée; **backstage** adv dans les coulisses; **backstroke** n dos crawlé; **backup** adj (train, plane) supplémentaire, de réserve; (Comput) de sauvegarde ▷ n (support) appui m, soutien m; (Comput: also: **backup file**) sauvegarde f; **backward** adj (movement) en arrière; (person, country) arriéré(e), attardé(e); **backwards** adv (move, go) en arrière; (read a list) à l'envers, à rebours; (fall) à la renverse; (walk) à reculons; **backyard** n arrière-cour f

**bacon** ['beɪkən] n bacon m, lard m

**bacteria** [bæk'tɪərɪə] npl bactéries fpl

**bad** [bæd] adj mauvais(e); (child) vilain(e); (mistake, accident) grave; (meat, food) gâté(e), avarié(e); **his ~ leg** sa jambe malade; **to go ~** (meat, food) se gâter; (milk) tourner

**bade** [bæd] pt of **bid**

**badge** [bædʒ] n insigne m; (of policeman) plaque f; (stick-on, sew-on) badge m

**badger** ['bædʒəʳ] n blaireau m

**badly** ['bædlɪ] adv (work, dress etc) mal; **to reflect ~ on sb** donner une mauvaise image de qn; **~ wounded** grièvement blessé; **he needs it ~** il en a absolument besoin; **~ off** adj, adv dans la gêne

**bad-mannered** ['bæd'mænəd] adj mal élevé(e)

**badminton** ['bædmɪntən] n badminton m

**bad-tempered** ['bæd'tɛmpəd] adj (by nature) ayant mauvais caractère; (on one occasion) de mauvaise humeur

**bag** [bæg] n sac m; **~s of** (inf: lots of) des tas de; **baggage** n bagages mpl; **baggage allowance** n franchise f de bagages; **baggage reclaim** n (at airport) livraison f des bagages; **baggy** adj avachi(e), qui fait des poches; **bagpipes** npl cornemuse f

**bail** [beɪl] n caution f ▷ vt (prisoner: also: **grant ~ to**) mettre en liberté sous caution; (boat: also: **~ out**) écoper; **to be released on ~** être libéré(e) sous caution; **bail out** vt (prisoner) payer la caution de

**bait** [beɪt] n appât m ▷ vt appâter; (fig: tease) tourmenter

**bake** [beɪk] vt (faire) cuire au four ▷ vi (bread etc) cuire (au four); (make cakes etc) faire de la pâtisserie; **baked beans** npl haricots blancs à la sauce tomate; **baked potato** n pomme f de terre en robe des champs; **baker** n boulanger m; **bakery** n boulangerie f; **baking** n (process) cuisson f; **baking powder** n levure f (chimique)

**balance** ['bæləns] n équilibre m; (Comm: sum) solde m; (remainder) reste m; (scales) balance f ▷ vt mettre or faire tenir en équilibre; (pros and cons) peser; (budget) équilibrer; (account) balancer; (compensate) compenser,

contrebalancer; **~ of trade/payments**
balance commerciale/des comptes or
paiements; **balanced** adj (personality,
diet) équilibré(e); (report) objectif(-ive);
**balance sheet** n bilan m

**balcony** ['bælkənɪ] n balcon m; **do you
have a room with a ~?** avez-vous une
chambre avec balcon?

**bald** [bɔːld] adj chauve; (tyre) lisse

**ball** [bɔːl] n boule f; (football) ballon m;
(for tennis, golf) balle f; (dance) bal m; **to
play ~** jouer au ballon (or à la balle);
(fig) coopérer

**ballerina** [bælə'riːnə] n ballerine f

**ballet** ['bæleɪ] n ballet m; (art)
danse f (classique); **ballet dancer** n
danseur(-euse) de ballet

**balloon** [bə'luːn] n ballon m

**ballot** ['bælət] n scrutin m

**ballpoint (pen)** ['bɔːlpɔɪnt-] n stylo
m à bille

**ballroom** ['bɔːlrʊm] n salle f de bal

**Baltic** [bɔːltɪk] n: **the ~ (Sea)** la (mer)
Baltique

**bamboo** [bæm'buː] n bambou m

**ban** [bæn] n interdiction f ▷ vt interdire

**banana** [bə'nɑːnə] n banane f

**band** [bænd] n bande f; (at a dance)
orchestre m; (Mil) musique f, fanfare f

**bandage** ['bændɪdʒ] n bandage m,
pansement m ▷ vt (wound, leg) mettre
un pansement or un bandage sur

**Band-Aid®** ['bændeɪd] n (us)
pansement adhésif

**B. & B.** n abbr = **bed and breakfast**

**bandit** ['bændɪt] n bandit m

**bang** [bæŋ] n détonation f; (of door)
claquement m; (blow) coup (violent)
▷ vt frapper (violemment); (door)
claquer ▷ vi détoner; claquer

**Bangladesh** [bæŋglə'dɛʃ] n
Bangladesh m

**Bangladeshi** [bæŋglə'dɛʃɪ] adj du
Bangladesh ▷ n habitant(e) du
Bangladesh

**bangle** ['bæŋgl] n bracelet m

**bangs** [bæŋz] npl (us: fringe) frange f

**banish** ['bænɪʃ] vt bannir

**banister(s)** ['bænɪstə(z)] n(pl) rampe
f (d'escalier)

**banjo** (pl **~es** or **~s**) ['bændʒəʊ] n
banjo m

**bank** [bæŋk] n banque f; (of river, lake)
bord m, rive f; (of earth) talus m, remblai
m ▷ vt (Aviat) virer sur l'aile; **bank on** vt
fus miser or tabler sur; **bank account**
n compte m en banque; **bank balance**
n solde m bancaire; **bank card** (BRIT)
n carte f d'identité bancaire; **bank
charges** npl (BRIT) frais mpl de banque;
**banker** n banquier m; **bank holiday**
n (BRIT) jour férié (où les banques
sont fermées); voir encadré; **banking** n
opérations fpl bancaires; profession
f de banquier; **bank manager** n
directeur m d'agence (bancaire);
**banknote** n billet m de banque

● **BANK HOLIDAY**
●
● Le terme **bank holiday** s'applique
● au Royaume-Uni aux jours fériés
● pendant lesquels banques et
● commerces sont fermés. Les
● principaux **bank holidays** à part
● Noël et Pâques se situent au mois
● de mai et fin août, et contrairement
● aux pays de tradition catholique, ne
● coïncident pas nécessairement avec
● une fête religieuse.

**bankrupt** ['bæŋkrʌpt] adj en faillite;
**to go ~** faire faillite; **bankruptcy** n
faillite f

**bank statement** n relevé m de
compte

**banner** ['bænər] n bannière f

**bannister(s)** ['bænɪstə(z)] n(pl)
= **banister(s)**

**banquet** ['bæŋkwɪt] n banquet m,
festin m

**baptism** ['bæptɪzəm] n baptême m

**baptize** [bæp'taɪz] vt baptiser

**bar** [bɑːr] n (pub) bar m; (counter)
comptoir m, bar; (rod: of metal etc) barre
f; (of window etc) barreau m; (of chocolate)

tablette f, plaque f; (fig: obstacle)
obstacle m; (prohibition) mesure f
d'exclusion; (Mus) mesure f ▷ vt (road)
barrer; (person) exclure; (activity)
interdire; **~ of soap** savonnette
f; **behind ~s** (prisoner) derrière les
barreaux; **the B~** (Law) le barreau; **~
none** sans exception
**barbaric** [bɑːˈbærɪk] adj barbare
**barbecue** [ˈbɑːbɪkjuː] n barbecue m
**barbed wire** [ˈbɑːbd-] n fil m de fer
barbelé
**barber** [ˈbɑːbəʳ] n coiffeur m (pour
hommes); **barber's (shop)** (us **barber
(shop)**) n salon m de coiffure (pour
hommes)
**bar code** n code m à barres, code-
barre m
**bare** [bɛəʳ] adj nu(e) ▷ vt mettre à nu,
dénuder; (teeth) montrer; **barefoot** adj,
adv nu-pieds, (les) pieds nus; **barely**
adv à peine
**bargain** [ˈbɑːgɪn] n (transaction)
marché m; (good buy) affaire f, occasion
f ▷ vi (haggle) marchander; (negotiate)
négocier, traiter; **into the ~** par-dessus
le marché; **bargain for** vt fus (inf): **he
got more than he ~ed for!** il en a eu
pour son argent!
**barge** [bɑːdʒ] n péniche f; **barge in** vi
(walk in) faire irruption; (interrupt talk)
intervenir mal à propos
**bark** [bɑːk] n (of tree) écorce f; (of dog)
aboiement m ▷ vi aboyer
**barley** [ˈbɑːlɪ] n orge f
**barmaid** [ˈbɑːmeɪd] n serveuse f (de
bar), barmaid f
**barman** [ˈbɑːmən] n serveur m (de bar),
barman m
**barn** [bɑːn] n grange f
**barometer** [bəˈrɒmɪtəʳ] n baromètre m
**baron** [ˈbærən] n baron m; **baroness**
n baronne f
**barracks** [ˈbærəks] npl caserne f
**barrage** [ˈbærɑːʒ] n (Mil) tir m de
barrage; (dam) barrage m; (of criticism)
feu m
**barrel** [ˈbærəl] n tonneau m; (of gun)

canon m
**barren** [ˈbærən] adj stérile
**barrette** [bəˈrɛt] (us) n barrette f
**barricade** [bærɪˈkeɪd] n barricade f
**barrier** [ˈbærɪəʳ] n barrière f
**barring** [ˈbɑːrɪŋ] prep sauf
**barrister** [ˈbærɪstəʳ] n (BRIT) avocat
(plaidant)
**barrow** [ˈbærəu] n (cart) charrette
f à bras
**bartender** [ˈbɑːtɛndəʳ] n (us) serveur
m (de bar), barman m
**base** [beɪs] n base f ▷ vt (opinion, belief):
**to ~ sth on** baser or fonder qch sur ▷ adj
vil(e), bas(se)
**baseball** [ˈbeɪsbɔːl] n base-ball m;
**baseball cap** n casquette f de base-ball
**Basel** [bɑːl] n = **Basle**
**basement** [ˈbeɪsmənt] n sous-sol m
**bases** [ˈbeɪsiːz] npl of **basis**
**bash** [bæʃ] vt (inf) frapper, cogner
**basic** [ˈbeɪsɪk] adj (precautions, rules)
élémentaire; (principles, research)
fondamental(e); (vocabulary, salary) de
base; (minimal) réduit(e) au minimum,
rudimentaire; **basically** adv (in fact) en
fait; (essentially) fondamentalement;
**basics** npl: **the basics** l'essentiel m
**basil** [ˈbæzl] n basilic m
**basin** [ˈbeɪsn] n (vessel, also Geo) cuvette
f, bassin m; (BRIT: for food) bol m; (also:
**wash~**) lavabo m
**basis** (pl **bases**) [ˈbeɪsɪs, -siːz] n base
f; **on a part-time/trial ~** à temps
partiel/à l'essai
**basket** [ˈbɑːskɪt] n corbeille f; (with
handle) panier m; **basketball** n
basket-ball m
**Basle** [bɑːl] n Bâle
**Basque** [bæsk] adj basque ▷ n Basque
m/f; **the ~ Country** le Pays basque
**bass** [beɪs] n (Mus) basse f
**bastard** [ˈbɑːstəd] n enfant naturel(le),
bâtard(e); (inf!) salaud m (!)
**bat** [bæt] n chauve-souris f; (for baseball
etc) (BRIT: for table tennis)
raquette f ▷ vt: **he didn't ~ an eyelid** il
n'a pas sourcillé or bronché

**batch** [bætʃ] n (of bread) fournée f; (of papers) liasse f; (of applicants, letters) paquet m

**bath** (pl **~s**) [baːθ, baːðz] n bain m; (bathtub) baignoire f ▷ vt baigner, donner un bain à; **to have a ~** prendre un bain; see also **baths**

**bathe** [beɪð] vi se baigner ▷ vt baigner; (wound etc) laver

**bathing** ['beɪðɪŋ] n baignade f; **bathing costume** (us **bathing suit**) n maillot m (de bain)

**bath**: **bathrobe** n peignoir m de bain; **bathroom** n salle f de bains; **baths** [baːðz] npl (BRIT: also: **swimming baths**) piscine f; **bath towel** n serviette f de bain; **bathtub** n baignoire f

**baton** ['bætən] n bâton m; (Mus) baguette f; (club) matraque f

**batter** ['bætəʳ] vt battre ▷ n pâte f à frire; **battered** adj (hat, pan) cabossé(e); **battered wife/child** épouse/enfant maltraité(e) or martyr(e)

**battery** ['bætərɪ] n (for torch, radio) pile f; (Aut, Mil) batterie f; **battery farming** n élevage m en batterie

**battle** ['bætl] n bataille f, combat m ▷ vi se battre, lutter; **battlefield** n champ m de bataille

**bay** [beɪ] n (of sea) baie f; (BRIT: for parking) place f de stationnement; (: for loading) aire f de chargement; **B~ of Biscay** golfe m de Gascogne; **to hold sb at ~** tenir qn à distance or en échec

**bay leaf** n laurier m

**bazaar** [bəˈzaːʳ] n (shop, market) bazar m; (sale) vente f de charité

**BBC** n abbr (= British Broadcasting Corporation) office de la radiodiffusion et télévision britannique

**B.C.** adv abbr (= before Christ) av. J.-C.

 **KEYWORD**

**be** [biː] (pt **was, were**, pp **been**) aux vb **1** (with present participle: forming continuous tenses): **what are you doing?** que faites-vous?; **they're coming tomorrow** ils viennent demain; **I've been waiting for you for 2 hours** je t'attends depuis 2 heures

**2** (with pp: forming passives) être; **to be killed** être tué(e); **the box had been opened** la boîte avait été ouverte; **he was nowhere to be seen** on ne le voyait nulle part

**3** (in tag questions): **it was fun, wasn't it?** c'était drôle, n'est-ce pas?; **he's good-looking, isn't he?** il est beau, n'est-ce pas?; **she's back, is she?** elle est rentrée, n'est-ce pas or alors?

**4** (+to +infinitive): **the house is to be sold** (necessity) la maison doit être vendue; (future) la maison va être vendue; **he's not to open it** il ne doit pas l'ouvrir

▷ vb + complement **1** (gen) être; **I'm English** je suis anglais(e); **I'm tired** je suis fatigué(e); **I'm hot/cold** j'ai chaud/froid; **he's a doctor** il est médecin; **be careful/good/quiet!** faites attention/soyez sages/taisez-vous!; **2 and 2 are 4** 2 et 2 font 4

**2** (of health) aller; **how are you?** comment allez-vous?; **I'm better now** je vais mieux maintenant; **he's very ill** il est très malade

**3** (of age) avoir; **how old are you?** quel âge avez-vous?; **I'm sixteen (years old)** j'ai seize ans

**4** (cost) coûter; **how much was the meal?** combien a coûté le repas?; **that'll be £5, please** ça fera 5 livres, s'il vous plaît; **this shirt is £17** cette chemise coûte 17 livres

▷ vi **1** (exist, occur etc) être, exister; **the prettiest girl that ever was** la fille la plus jolie qui ait jamais existé; **is there a God?** y a-t-il un dieu?; **be that as it may** quoi qu'il en soit; **so be it** soit

**2** (referring to place) être, se trouver; **I won't be here tomorrow** je ne serai pas là demain

**3** (referring to movement) aller; **where have you been?** où êtes-vous allé(s)?

▷ *impers vb* **1** (*referring to time*) être; **it's 5 o'clock** il est 5 heures; **it's the 28th of April** c'est le 28 avril
**2** (*referring to distance*): **it's 10 km to the village** le village est à 10 km
**3** (*referring to the weather*) faire; **it's too hot/cold** il fait trop chaud/froid; **it's windy today** il y a du vent aujourd'hui
**4** (*emphatic*): **it's me/the postman** c'est moi/le facteur; **it was Maria who paid the bill** c'est Maria qui a payé la note

**beach** [biːtʃ] *n* plage *f* ▷ *vt* échouer
**beacon** ['biːkən] *n* (*lighthouse*) fanal *m*; (*marker*) balise *f*
**bead** [biːd] *n* perle *f*; (*of dew, sweat*) goutte *f*; **beads** *npl* (*necklace*) collier *m*
**beak** [biːk] *n* bec *m*
**beam** [biːm] *n* (*Archit*) poutre *f*; (*of light*) rayon *m* ▷ *vi* rayonner
**bean** [biːn] *n* haricot *m*; (*of coffee*) grain *m*; **beansprouts** *npl* pousses *fpl* or germes *mpl* de soja
**bear** [bɛəʳ] *n* ours *m* ▷ *vb* (*pt* **bore**, *pp* **borne**) ▷ *vt* porter; (*endure*) supporter, rapporter ▷ *vi*: **to ~ right/left** obliquer à droite/gauche, se diriger vers la droite/gauche
**beard** [bɪəd] *n* barbe *f*
**bearer** ['bɛərəʳ] *n* porteur *m*; (*of passport etc*) titulaire *m/f*
**bearing** ['bɛərɪŋ] *n* maintien *m*, allure *f*; (*connection*) rapport *m*; (*Tech*): **(ball) bearings** *npl* roulement *m* (à billes)
**beast** [biːst] *n* bête *f*; (*inf: person*) brute *f*
**beat** [biːt] *n* battement *m*; (*Mus*) temps *m*, mesure *f*; (*of policeman*) ronde *f* ▷ *vt, vi* (*pt* **~**, *pp* **~en**) battre; **off the ~en track** hors des chemins *or* sentiers battus; **to ~ it** (*inf*) ficher le camp; **beat up** *vt* (*inf: person*) tabasser; **beating** *n* raclée *f*
**beautiful** ['bjuːtɪful] *adj* beau (belle); **beautifully** *adv* admirablement
**beauty** ['bjuːtɪ] *n* beauté *f*; **beauty parlour** (*US* **beauty parlor**) [-'pɑːləʳ] *n* institut *m* de beauté; **beauty salon** *n* institut *m* de beauté; **beauty spot**

*n* (*on skin*) grain *m* de beauté; (*BRIT Tourism*) site naturel (d'une grande beauté)
**beaver** ['biːvəʳ] *n* castor *m*
**became** [bɪ'keɪm] *pt of* **become**
**because** [bɪ'kɔz] *conj* parce que; **~ of** *prep* à cause de
**beckon** ['bɛkən] *vt* (*also*: **~ to**) faire signe (de venir) à
**become** [bɪ'kʌm] *vi* devenir; **to ~ fat/thin** grossir/maigrir; **to ~ angry** se mettre en colère
**bed** [bɛd] *n* lit *m*; (*of flowers*) parterre *m*; (*of coal, clay*) couche *f*; (*of sea, lake*) fond *m*; **to go to ~** aller se coucher; **bed and breakfast** *n* (*terms*) chambre et petit déjeuner; (*place*) ≈ chambre *f* d'hôte; *voir encadré*; **bedclothes** *npl* couvertures *fpl* et draps *mpl*; **bedding** *n* literie *f*; **bed linen** *n* draps *mpl* de lit (et taies *fpl* d'oreillers), literie *f*; **bedroom** *n* chambre *f* (à coucher); **bedside** *n*: **at sb's bedside** au chevet de qn; **bedside lamp** *n* lampe *f* de chevet; **bedside table** *n* table *f* de chevet; **bedsit(ter)** *n* (*BRIT*) chambre meublée, studio *m*; **bedspread** *n* couvre-lit *m*, dessus-de-lit *m*; **bedtime** *n*: **it's bedtime** c'est l'heure de se coucher

○ **BED AND BREAKFAST**
○
○ Un **bed and breakfast** est une
○ petite pension dans une maison
○ particulière ou une ferme où l'on
○ peut louer une chambre avec
○ petit déjeuner compris pour un
○ prix modique par rapport à ce que
○ l'on paierait dans un hôtel. Ces
○ établissements sont communément
○ appelés "B & B", et sont signalés par
○ une pancarte dans le jardin ou au-
○ dessus de la porte.

**bee** [biː] *n* abeille *f*
**beech** [biːtʃ] *n* hêtre *m*
**beef** [biːf] *n* bœuf *m*; **roast ~** rosbif *m*; **beefburger** *n* hamburger *m*;

**Beefeater** n hallebardier m (de la tour de Londres)

**been** [bi:n] pp of **be**

**beer** [bɪəʳ] n bière f; **beer garden** n (BRIT) jardin m d'un pub (où l'on peut emmener ses consommations)

**beet** [bi:t] n (vegetable) betterave f; (US: also: **red ~**) betterave (potagère)

**beetle** [ˈbi:tl] n scarabée m, coléoptère m

**beetroot** [ˈbi:tru:t] n (BRIT) betterave f

**before** [bɪˈfɔːʳ] prep (of time) avant; (of space) devant ▷ conj avant que + sub; avant de ▷ adv avant; **~ going** avant de partir; **~ she goes** avant qu'elle (ne) parte; **the week ~** la semaine précédente or d'avant; **I've never seen it ~** c'est la première fois que je le vois; **beforehand** adv au préalable, à l'avance

**beg** [bɛg] vi mendier ▷ vt mendier; (forgiveness, mercy etc) demander; (entreat) supplier; **to ~ sb to do sth** supplier qn de faire qch; see also **pardon**

**began** [bɪˈgæn] pt of **begin**

**beggar** [ˈbɛgəʳ] n mendiant(e)

**begin** [bɪˈgɪn] (pt **began**, pp **begun**) vt, vi commencer; **to ~ doing** or **to do sth** commencer à faire qch; **beginner** n débutant(e); **beginning** n commencement m, début m

**begun** [bɪˈgʌn] pp of **begin**

**behalf** [bɪˈhɑːf] n: **on ~ of**, (US) **in ~ of** (representing) de la part de; (for benefit of) pour le compte de; **on my/his ~ de ma/sa part**

**behave** [bɪˈheɪv] vi se conduire, se comporter; (well: also: **~ o.s.**) se conduire bien or comme il faut; **behaviour** (US **behavior**) n comportement m, conduite f

**behind** [bɪˈhaɪnd] prep derrière; (time) en retard sur; (supporting): **to be ~ sb** soutenir qn ▷ adv derrière; en retard ▷ n derrière m; **~ the scenes** dans les coulisses; **to be ~ (schedule) with sth** être en retard dans qch

**beige** [beɪʒ] adj beige

**Beijing** [ˈbeɪˈdʒɪŋ] n Pékin

**being** [ˈbiːɪŋ] n être m; **to come into ~** prendre naissance

**belated** [bɪˈleɪtɪd] adj tardif(-ive)

**belch** [bɛltʃ] vi avoir un renvoi, roter ▷ vt (also: **~ out**: smoke etc) vomir, cracher

**Belgian** [ˈbɛldʒən] adj belge, de Belgique ▷ n Belge m/f

**Belgium** [ˈbɛldʒəm] n Belgique f

**belief** [bɪˈliːf] n (opinion) conviction f; (trust, faith) foi f

**believe** [bɪˈliːv] vt, vi croire, estimer; **to ~ in** (God) croire en; (ghosts, method) croire à; **believer** n (in idea, activity) partisan(e); (Rel) croyant(e)

**bell** [bɛl] n cloche f; (small) clochette f, grelot m; (on door) sonnette f; (electric) sonnerie f

**bellboy** [ˈbɛlbɔɪ] (US **bellhop** [ˈbɛlhɔp]) n groom m, chasseur m

**bellow** [ˈbɛləu] vi (bull) meugler; (person) brailler

**bell pepper** n (esp US) poivron m

**belly** [ˈbɛlɪ] n ventre m; **belly button** (inf) n nombril m

**belong** [bɪˈlɔŋ] vi: **to ~ to** appartenir à; (club etc) faire partie de; **this book ~s here** ce livre va ici, la place de ce livre est ici; **belongings** npl affaires fpl, possessions fpl

**beloved** [bɪˈlʌvɪd] adj (bien-)aimé(e), chéri(e)

**below** [bɪˈləu] prep sous, au-dessous de ▷ adv en dessous; en contre-bas; **see ~** voir plus bas or plus loin or ci-dessous

**belt** [bɛlt] n ceinture f; (Tech) courroie f ▷ vt (thrash) donner une raclée à; **beltway** n (US Aut) route f de ceinture; (: motorway) périphérique m

**bemused** [bɪˈmjuːzd] adj médusé(e)

**bench** [bɛntʃ] n banc m; (in workshop) établi m; **the B~** (Law: judges) la magistrature, la Cour

**bend** [bɛnd] vb (pt, pp **bent**) ▷ vt courber; (leg, arm) plier ▷ vi se courber ▷ n (BRIT: in road) virage m, tournant m; (in pipe, river) coude m; **bend down** vi se baisser; **bend over** vi se pencher

**beneath** [bɪˈniːθ] prep sous, au-dessous de; (unworthy of) indigne de ▷ adv dessous, au-dessous, en bas

**beneficial** [bɛnɪˈfɪʃəl] adj: **~ (to)** salutaire (pour), bénéfique (à)

**benefit** [ˈbɛnɪfɪt] n avantage m, profit m; (allowance of money) allocation f ▷ vt faire du bien à, profiter à ▷ vi: **he'll ~ from it** cela lui fera du bien, il y gagnera or s'en trouvera bien

**Benelux** [ˈbɛnɪlʌks] n Bénélux m

**benign** [bɪˈnaɪn] adj (person, smile) bienveillant(e), affable; (Med) bénin(-igne)

**bent** [bɛnt] pt, pp of **bend** ▷ n inclination f, penchant m ▷ adj: **to be ~ on** être résolu(e) à

**bereaved** [bɪˈriːvd] n: **the ~** la famille du disparu

**beret** [ˈbɛreɪ] n béret m

**Berlin** [bəːˈlɪn] n Berlin

**Bermuda** [bəːˈmjuːdə] n Bermudes fpl

**Bern** [bəːn] n Berne

**berry** [ˈbɛrɪ] n baie f

**berth** [bəːθ] n (bed) couchette f; (for ship) poste m d'amarrage, mouillage m ▷ vi (in harbour) venir à quai; (at anchor) mouiller

**beside** [bɪˈsaɪd] prep à côté de; (compared with) par rapport à; **that's ~ the point** ça n'a rien à voir; **to be ~ o.s. (with anger)** être hors de soi; **besides** adv en outre, de plus ▷ prep en plus de; (except) excepté

**best** [bɛst] adj meilleur(e) ▷ adv le mieux; **the ~ part of** (quantity) le plus clair de, la plus grande partie de; **at ~** au mieux; **to make the ~ of sth** s'accommoder de qch (du mieux que l'on peut); **to do one's ~** faire de son mieux; **to the ~ of my knowledge** pour autant que je sache; **to the ~ of my ability** du mieux que je pourrai; **best-before date** n date f de limite d'utilisation or de consommation; **best man** (irreg) n garçon m d'honneur; **bestseller** n best-seller m, succès m

de librairie

**bet** [bɛt] n pari m ▷ vt, vi (pt, pp ~ or **~ted**) parier; **to ~ sb sth** parier qch à qn

**betray** [bɪˈtreɪ] vt trahir

**better** [ˈbɛtəʳ] adj meilleur(e) ▷ adv mieux ▷ vt améliorer ▷ n: **to get the ~ of** triompher de, l'emporter sur; **you had ~ do it** vous feriez mieux de le faire; **he thought ~ of it** il s'est ravisé; **to get ~** (Med) aller mieux; (improve) s'améliorer

**betting** [ˈbɛtɪŋ] n paris mpl; **betting shop** n (BRIT) bureau m de paris

**between** [bɪˈtwiːn] prep entre ▷ adv au milieu, dans l'intervalle

**beverage** [ˈbɛvərɪdʒ] n boisson f (gén sans alcool)

**beware** [bɪˈwɛəʳ] vi: **to ~ (of)** prendre garde (à); **"~ of the dog"** "(attention) chien méchant"

**bewildered** [bɪˈwɪldəd] adj dérouté(e), ahuri(e)

**beyond** [bɪˈjɔnd] prep (in space, time) au-delà de; (exceeding) au-dessus de ▷ adv au-delà; **~ doubt** hors de doute; **~ repair** irréparable

**bias** [ˈbaɪəs] n (prejudice) préjugé m, parti pris; (preference) prévention f; **bias(s)ed** adj partial(e), montrant un parti pris

**bib** [bɪb] n bavoir m

**Bible** [ˈbaɪbl] n Bible f

**bicarbonate of soda** [baɪˈkɑːbənɪt-] n bicarbonate m de soude

**biceps** [ˈbaɪsɛps] n biceps m

**bicycle** [ˈbaɪsɪkl] n bicyclette f; **bicycle pump** n pompe f à vélo

**bid** [bɪd] n offre f; (at auction) enchère f; (attempt) tentative f ▷ vb (pt ~ or **bade**, pp ~ or **~den**) ▷ vi faire une enchère or offre ▷ vt faire une enchère or offre de; **to ~ sb good day** souhaiter le bonjour à qn; **bidder** n: **the highest bidder** le plus offrant

**bidet** [ˈbiːdeɪ] n bidet m

**big** [bɪg] adj (in height: person, building, tree) grand(e); (in bulk, amount: person, parcel, book) gros(se); **bigheaded** adj prétentieux(-euse); **big toe** n gros orteil

● **BIG APPLE**
●
● Si l'on sait que "The Big Apple"
● désigne la ville de New York ("apple"
● est en réalité un terme d'argot
● signifiant "grande ville"), on connaît
● moins les surnoms donnés aux
● autres grandes villes américaines.
● Chicago est surnommée "Windy
● City" à cause des rafales soufflant du
● lac Michigan, La Nouvelle-Orléans
● doit son sobriquet de "Big Easy"
● à son style de vie décontracté, et
● l'industrie automobile a donné à
● Detroit son surnom de "Motown".

**bike** [baɪk] n vélo m; **bike lane** n piste f cyclable
**bikini** [bɪˈkiːnɪ] n bikini m
**bilateral** [baɪˈlætərl] adj bilatéral(e)
**bilingual** [baɪˈlɪŋɡwəl] adj bilingue
**bill** [bɪl] n boîte f, facture f; (in restaurant) addition f, note f; (Pol) projet m de loi; (US: banknote) billet m (de banque); (notice) affiche f; (of bird) bec m; **put it on my** ~ mettez-le sur mon compte; **"post no ~s"** "défense d'afficher"; **to fit** or **fill the ~** (fig) faire l'affaire; **billboard** (US) n panneau m d'affichage; **billfold** [ˈbɪlfəʊld] n (US) portefeuille m
**billiards** [ˈbɪljədz] n (jeu m de) billard m
**billion** [ˈbɪljən] n (BRIT) billion m (million de millions); (US) milliard m
**bin** [bɪn] n boîte f; (BRIT: also: **dust~**, **litter ~**) poubelle f; (for coal) coffre m
**bind** (pt, pp **bound**) [baɪnd, baʊnd] vt attacher; (book) relier; (oblige) obliger, contraindre ▷ n (inf: nuisance) scie f
**binge** [bɪndʒ] n (inf): **to go on a** ~ faire la bringue
**bingo** [ˈbɪŋɡəʊ] n sorte de jeu de loto pratiqué dans des établissements publics
**binoculars** [bɪˈnɒkjʊləz] npl jumelles fpl
**bio...** [baɪə'] prefix: **biochemistry**
n biochimie f; **biodegradable** [ˈbaɪəʊdɪˈɡreɪdəbl] adj biodégradable; **biography** [baɪˈɒɡrəfɪ] n biographie f; **biological** adj biologique; **biology** [baɪˈɒlədʒɪ] n biologie f; **biometric** [baɪəˈmɛtrɪk] adj biométrique
**birch** [bəːtʃ] n bouleau m
**bird** [bəːd] n oiseau m; (BRIT inf: girl) nana f; **bird flu** n grippe f aviaire; **bird of prey** n oiseau m de proie; **birdwatching** n ornithologie f (d'amateur)
**Biro®** [ˈbaɪərəʊ] n stylo m à bille
**birth** [bəːθ] n naissance f; **to give ~ to** donner naissance à, mettre au monde; (subj: animal) mettre bas; **birth certificate** n acte m de naissance; **birth control** n (policy) limitation f des naissances; (methods) méthode(s) contraceptive(s); **birthday** n anniversaire m ▷ cpd (cake, card etc) d'anniversaire; **birthmark** n envie f, tache f de vin; **birthplace** n lieu m de naissance
**biscuit** [ˈbɪskɪt] n (BRIT) biscuit m; (US) petit pain au lait
**bishop** [ˈbɪʃəp] n évêque m; (Chess) fou m
**bistro** [ˈbiːstrəʊ] n petit restaurant m, bistrot m
**bit** [bɪt] pt of **bite** ▷ n morceau m; (Comput) bit m, élément m binaire; (of tool) mèche f; (of horse) mors m; **a ~ of** un peu de; **a ~ mad/dangerous** un peu fou/risqué; ~ **by** ~ petit à petit
**bitch** [bɪtʃ] n (dog) chienne f; (inf!) salope f (!), garce f
**bite** [baɪt] vt, vi (pt **bit**, pp **bitten**) mordre; (insect) piquer ▷ n morsure f; (insect bite) piqûre f; (mouthful) bouchée f; **let's have a ~ (to eat)** mangeons un morceau; **to ~ one's nails** se ronger les ongles
**bitten** [ˈbɪtn] pp of **bite**
**bitter** [ˈbɪtər] adj amer(-ère); (criticism) cinglant(e); (icy: weather, wind) glacial(e) ▷ n (BRIT: beer) bière f (à forte teneur en houblon)
**bizarre** [bɪˈzɑːr] adj bizarre

**black** [blæk] *adj* noir(e) ▷ *n* (*colour*)
noir *m*; (*person*): **B~** noir(e) ▷ *vt* (BRIT
*Industry*) boycotter; **to give sb a ~
eye** pocher l'œil à qn, faire un œil
au beurre noir à qn; **to be in the ~**
(*in credit*) avoir un compte créditeur;
**~ and blue** (*bruised*) couvert(e) de
bleus; **black out** *vi* (*faint*) s'évanouir;
**blackberry** *n* mûre *f*; **blackbird** *n*
merle *m*; **blackboard** *n* tableau noir;
**black coffee** *n* café noir; **blackcurrant**
*n* cassis *m*; **black ice** *n* verglas *m*;
**blackmail** *n* chantage *m* ▷ *vt* faire
chanter, soumettre au chantage; **black
market** *n* marché noir; **blackout** *n*
panne *f* d'électricité; (*in wartime*) blackout *m*; (*TV*) interruption *f* d'émission;
(*fainting*) syncope *f*; **black pepper** *n*
poivre noir; **black pudding** *n* boudin
(noir); **Black Sea** *n*: **the Black Sea** la
mer Noire

**bladder** ['blædə'] *n* vessie *f*

**blade** [bleɪd] *n* lame *f*; (*of propeller*) pale
*f*; **a ~ of grass** un brin d'herbe

**blame** [bleɪm] *n* faute *f*, blâme *m* ▷ *vt*:
**to ~ sb/sth for sth** attribuer à qn/qch
la responsabilité de qch; reprocher
qch à qn/qch; **I'm not to ~** ce n'est pas
ma faute

**bland** [blænd] *adj* (*taste, food*) doux
(douce), fade

**blank** [blæŋk] *adj* blanc (blanche);
(*look*) sans expression, dénué(e)
d'expression ▷ *n* espace *m* vide, blanc
*m*; (*cartridge*) cartouche *f* à blanc; **his
mind was a ~** il avait la tête vide

**blanket** ['blæŋkɪt] *n* couverture *f*; (*of
snow, cloud*) couche *f*

**blast** [blɑːst] *n* explosion *f*; (*shock wave*)
souffle *m*; (*of air, steam*) bouffée *f* ▷ *vt*
faire sauter or exploser

**blatant** ['bleɪtənt] *adj* flagrant(e),
criant(e)

**blaze** [bleɪz] *n* (*fire*) incendie *m*; (*fig*)
flamboiement *m* ▷ *vi* (*fire*) flamber; (*fig*)
flamboyer, resplendir ▷ *vt*: **to ~ a trail**
(*fig*) montrer la voie; **in a ~ of publicity**
à grand renfort de publicité

**blazer** ['bleɪzə'] *n* blazer *m*

**bleach** [bliːtʃ] *n* (*also*: **household ~**)
eau *f* de Javel ▷ *vt* (*linen*) blanchir;
**bleachers** *npl* (US *Sport*) gradins *mpl*
(en plein soleil)

**bleak** [bliːk] *adj* morne, désolé(e);
(*weather*) triste, maussade; (*smile*)
lugubre; (*prospect, future*) morose

**bled** [blɛd] *pt, pp of* **bleed**

**bleed** (*pt, pp* **bled**) [bliːd, blɛd] *vt*
saigner; (*brakes, radiator*) purger ▷ *vi*
saigner; **my nose is ~ing** je saigne
du nez

**blemish** ['blɛmɪʃ] *n* défaut *m*; (*on
reputation*) tache *f*

**blend** [blɛnd] *n* mélange *m* ▷ *vt*
mélanger ▷ *vi* (*colours etc: also:* **~ in**)
se mélanger, se fondre, s'allier; **blender** *n*
(*Culin*) mixeur *m*

**bless** (*pt, pp* **~ed** *or* **blest**) [blɛs, blɛst]
*vt* bénir; **~ you!** (*after sneeze*) à tes
souhaits!; **blessing** *n* bénédiction *f*;
(*godsend*) bienfait *m*

**blew** [bluː] *pt of* **blow**

**blight** [blaɪt] *vt* (*hopes etc*) anéantir,
briser

**blind** [blaɪnd] *adj* aveugle ▷ *n* (*for
window*) store *m* ▷ *vt* aveugler; **the
blind** *npl* les aveugles *mpl*; **blind alley**
*n* impasse *f*; **blindfold** *n* bandeau *m*
▷ *adj, adv* les yeux bandés ▷ *vt* bander
les yeux à

**blink** [blɪŋk] *vi* cligner des yeux; (*light*)
clignoter

**bliss** [blɪs] *n* félicité *f*, bonheur *m* sans
mélange

**blister** ['blɪstə'] *n* (*on skin*) ampoule *f*,
cloque *f*; (*on paintwork*) boursouflure *f*
▷ *vi* (*paint*) se boursoufler, se cloquer

**blizzard** ['blɪzəd] *n* blizzard *m*, tempête
*f* de neige

**bloated** ['bləʊtɪd] *adj* (*face*) bouffi(e);
(*stomach, person*) gonflé(e)

**blob** [blɔb] *n* (*drop*) goutte *f*; (*stain,
spot*) tache *f*

**block** [blɔk] *n* bloc *m*; (*in pipes*)
obstruction *f*; (*toy*) cube *m*; (*of buildings*)
pâté *m* (de maisons) ▷ *vt* bloquer;

(*fig*) faire obstacle à; **the sink is ~ed** l'évier est bouché; **~ of flats** (*BRIT*) immeuble (locatif); **mental ~** blocage *m*; **block up** *vt* boucher; **blockade** [blɔˈkeɪd] *n* blocus *m* ▷ *vt* faire le blocus de; **blockage** *n* obstruction *f*; **blockbuster** *n* (*film, book*) grand succès; **block capitals** *npl* majuscules *fpl* d'imprimerie; **block letters** *npl* majuscules *fpl*

**blog** [blɔɡ] *n* blog *m*, blogue *m*

**bloke** [bləuk] *n* (*BRIT inf*) type *m*

**blond(e)** [blɔnd] *adj, n* blond(e)

**blood** [blʌd] *n* sang *m*; **blood donor** *n* donneur(-euse) de sang; **blood group** *n* groupe sanguin; **blood poisoning** *n* empoisonnement *m* du sang; **blood pressure** *n* tension (artérielle); **bloodshed** *n* effusion *f* de sang, carnage *m*; **bloodshot** *adj*: **bloodshot eyes** yeux injectés de sang; **bloodstream** *n* sang *m*, système sanguin; **blood test** *n* analyse *f* de sang; **blood transfusion** *n* transfusion *f* de sang; **blood type** *n* groupe sanguin; **blood vessel** *n* vaisseau sanguin; **bloody** *adj* sanglant(e); (*BRIT inf!*): **this bloody ...** ce foutu ..., ce putain de ... (!) ▷ *adv*: **bloody strong/good** (*BRIT*: *inf!*) vachement *or* sacrément fort/bon

**bloom** [blu:m] *n* fleur *f* ▷ *vi* être en fleur

**blossom** [ˈblɔsəm] *n* fleur(s) *f(pl)* ▷ *vi* être en fleurs; (*fig*) s'épanouir

**blot** [blɔt] *n* tache *f* ▷ *vt* tacher; (*ink*) sécher

**blouse** [blauz] *n* (*feminine garment*) chemisier *m*, corsage *m*

**blow** [bləu] *n* coup *m* ▷ *vb* (*pt* **blew**, *pp* **~n**) ▷ *vi* souffler ▷ *vt* (*instrument*) jouer de; (*fuse*) faire sauter; **to ~ one's nose** se moucher; **blow away** *vi* s'envoler ▷ *vt* chasser, faire s'envoler; **blow out** *vi* (*fire, flame*) s'éteindre; (*tyre*) éclater; (*fuse*) sauter; **blow up** *vi* exploser, sauter ▷ *vt* faire sauter; (*tyre*) gonfler; (*Phot*) agrandir; **blow-dry** *n* (*hairstyle*) brushing *m*

**blown** [bləun] *pp of* **blow**

**blue** [blu:] *adj* bleu(e); (*depressed*) triste; **~ film/joke** film *m*/histoire *f* pornographique; **out of the ~** (*fig*) à l'improviste, sans qu'on s'y attende; **bluebell** *n* jacinthe *f* des bois; **blueberry** *n* myrtille *f*, airelle *f*; **blue cheese** *n* (*fromage*) bleu *m*; **blues** *npl*: **the blues** (*Mus*) le blues; **to have the blues** (*inf*: *feeling*) avoir le cafard; **bluetit** *n* mésange bleue

**bluff** [blʌf] *vi* bluffer ▷ *n* bluff *m*; **to call sb's ~** mettre qn au défi d'exécuter ses menaces

**blunder** [ˈblʌndər] *n* gaffe *f*, bévue *f* ▷ *vi* faire une gaffe *or* une bévue

**blunt** [blʌnt] *adj* (*knife*) émoussé(e), peu tranchant(e); (*pencil*) mal taillé(e); (*person*) brusque, ne mâchant pas ses mots

**blur** [blə:r] *n* (*shape*): **to become a ~** devenir flou ▷ *vt* brouiller, rendre flou(e); **blurred** *adj* flou(e)

**blush** [blʌʃ] *vi* rougir ▷ *n* rougeur *f*; **blusher** *n* rouge *m* à joues

**board** [bɔ:d] *n* (*wooden*) planche *f*; (*on wall*) panneau *m*; (*for chess etc*) plateau *m*; (*cardboard*) carton *m*; (*committee*) conseil *m*, comité *m*; (*in firm*) conseil d'administration; (*Naut, Aviat*): **on ~** à bord ▷ *vt* (*ship*) monter à bord de; (*train*) monter dans; **full ~** (*BRIT*) pension complète; **half ~** (*BRIT*) demi-pension *f*; **~ and lodging** *n* chambre *f* avec pension; **to go by the ~** (*hopes, principles*) être abandonné(e); **board game** *n* jeu *m* de société; **boarding card** *n* (*Aviat, Naut*) carte *f* d'embarquement; **boarding pass** *n* (*BRIT*) = **boarding card**; **boarding school** *n* internat *m*, pensionnat *m*; **board room** *n* salle *f* du conseil d'administration

**boast** [bəust] *vi*: **to ~ (about** *or* **of)** se vanter (de)

**boat** [bəut] *n* bateau *m*; (*small*) canot *m*; barque *f*

**bob** [bɔb] *vi* (*boat, cork on water*: *also*: **~**

**up and down**) danser, se balancer
**bobby pin** ['bɒbɪ-] n (US) pince f à
cheveux
**body** ['bɒdɪ] n corps m; (of car)
carrosserie f; (fig: society) organe m,
organisme m; **body-building** n body-
building m, culturisme m; **bodyguard**
n garde m du corps; **bodywork** n
carrosserie f
**bog** [bɒg] n tourbière f ▷ vt: **to get ~ged
down (in)** (fig) s'enliser (dans)
**bogus** ['bəʊgəs] adj bidon inv; fantôme
**boil** [bɔɪl] vt (faire) bouillir ▷ vi bouillir
▷ n (Med) furoncle m; **to come to the
or** (US) **a ~** bouillir; **boil down** vi (fig):
**to ~ down to** se réduire or ramener à;
**boil over** vi déborder; **boiled egg** n
œuf m à la coque; **boiled potatoes** n
pommes fpl à l'anglaise or à l'eau; **boiler**
n chaudière f; **boiling** ['bɔɪlɪŋ] adj: **I'm
boiling (hot)** (inf) je crève de chaud;
**boiling point** n point m d'ébullition
**bold** [bəʊld] adj hardi(e),
audacieux(-euse), (pej) effronté(e),
(outline, colour) franc (franche),
tranché(e), marqué(e)
**bollard** ['bɒləd] n (BRIT Aut) borne
lumineuse or de signalisation
**bolt** [bəʊlt] n verrou m; (with nut)
boulon m ▷ adv: **~ upright** droit(e)
comme un piquet ▷ vt (door)
verrouiller; (food) engloutir ▷ vi se
sauver, filer (comme une flèche); (horse)
s'emballer
**bomb** [bɒm] n bombe f ▷ vt bombarder;
**bombard** [bɒm'bɑːd] vt bombarder;
**bomber** n (Aviat) bombardier m;
(terrorist) poseur m de bombes; **bomb
scare** n alerte f à la bombe
**bond** [bɒnd] n lien m; (binding promise)
engagement m, obligation f; (Finance)
obligation; **bonds** npl (chains) chaînes
fpl; **in ~** (of goods) en entrepôt
**bone** [bəʊn] n os m; (of fish) arête f ▷ vt
désosser, ôter les arêtes de
**bonfire** ['bɒnfaɪər] n feu m (de joie); (for
rubbish) feu
**bonnet** ['bɒnɪt] n bonnet m; (BRIT: of

car) capot m
**bonus** ['bəʊnəs] n (money) prime f;
(advantage) avantage m
**boo** [buː] excl hou!, peuh! ▷ vt huer
**book** [bʊk] n livre m; (of stamps,
tickets etc) carnet m; (Comm): **books**
npl comptes mpl, comptabilité f ▷ vt
(ticket) prendre; (seat, room) réserver;
(football player) prendre le nom de,
donner un carton à; **I ~ed a table in
the name of ...** j'ai réservé une table
au nom de ...; **book in** vi (BRIT: at
hotel) prendre sa chambre; **book up** vt
réserver; **the hotel is ~ed up** l'hôtel est
complet; **bookcase** n bibliothèque f
(meuble); **booking** (BRIT) réservation
f; **I confirmed my booking by
fax/e-mail** j'ai confirmé ma
réservation par fax/e-mail; **booking
office** n (BRIT) bureau m de location;
**book-keeping** n comptabilité f;
**booklet** n brochure f; **bookmaker** n
bookmaker m; **bookmark** n (for book)
marque-page m; (Comput) signet m;
**bookseller** n libraire m/f; **bookshelf**
n (single) étagère f (à livres); (bookcase)
bibliothèque f; **bookshop, bookstore**
n librairie f
**boom** [buːm] n (noise) grondement
m; (in prices, population) forte
augmentation; (busy period) boom m,
vague f de prospérité ▷ vi gronder;
prospérer
**boost** [buːst] n stimulant m, remontant
m ▷ vt stimuler
**boot** [buːt] n botte f; (for hiking)
chaussure f (de marche); (ankle boot)
bottine f; (BRIT: of car) coffre m ▷ vt
(Comput) lancer, mettre en route; **to
~** (in addition) par-dessus le marché,
en plus
**booth** [buːð] n (at fair) baraque
(foraine); (of telephone etc) cabine f;
(also: **voting ~**) isoloir m
**booze** [buːz] (inf) n boissons fpl
alcooliques, alcool m
**border** ['bɔːdər] n bordure f; bord m; (of
a country) frontière f; **borderline** n (fig)

ligne f de démarcation

**bore** [bɔːʳ] pt of **bear** ▷ vt (person) ennuyer, raser; (hole) percer; (well, tunnel) creuser ▷ n (person) raseur(-euse); (boring thing) barbe f; (of gun) calibre m; **bored** adj: **to be bored** s'ennuyer; **boredom** n ennui m

**boring** ['bɔːrɪŋ] adj ennuyeux(-euse)

**born** [bɔːn] adj: **to be ~** naître; **I was ~ in 1960** je suis né en 1960

**borne** [bɔːn] pp of **bear**

**borough** ['bʌrə] n municipalité f

**borrow** ['bɔrəu] vt: **to ~ sth (from sb)** emprunter qch (à qn)

**Bosnia(-Herzegovina)** ['bɔːsnɪə(hɜːrzə'gəuvɪːnə)] n Bosnie-Herzégovine f; **Bosnian** ['bɔznɪən] adj bosniaque, bosnien(ne) ▷ n Bosniaque m/f, Bosnien(ne)

**bosom** ['buzəm] n poitrine f; (fig) sein m

**boss** [bɔs] n patron(ne) ▷ vt (also: **~ about, ~ around**) mener à la baguette; **bossy** adj autoritaire

**both** [bəuθ] adj les deux, l'un(e) et l'autre ▷ pron: **~ (of them)** les deux, tous (toutes) (les) deux, l'un(e) et l'autre; **~ of us went, we ~ went** nous y sommes allés tous les deux ▷ adv: **~ A and B** A et B

**bother** ['bɔðəʳ] vt (worry) tracasser; (needle, bait) importuner, ennuyer; (disturb) déranger ▷ vi (also: **~ o.s.**) se tracasser, se faire du souci ▷ n (trouble) ennuis mpl; **to ~ doing** prendre la peine de faire; **don't ~** ce n'est pas la peine; **it's no ~** aucun problème

**bottle** ['bɔtl] n bouteille f; (baby's) biberon m; (of perfume, medicine) flacon m ▷ vt mettre en bouteille(s); **bottle bank** n conteneur m (de bouteilles); **bottle-opener** n ouvre-bouteille m

**bottom** ['bɔtəm] n (of container, sea etc) fond m; (buttocks) derrière m; (of page, list) bas m; (of mountain, tree, hill) pied m ▷ adj (shelf, step) du bas

**bought** [bɔːt] pt, pp of **buy**

**boulder** ['bəuldəʳ] n gros rocher (gén lisse, arrondi)

**bounce** [bauns] vi (ball) rebondir; (cheque) être refusé (étant sans provision) ▷ vt faire rebondir ▷ n (rebound) rebond m; **bouncer** n (inf: at dance, club) videur m

**bound** [baund] pt, pp of **bind** ▷ n (gen pl) limite f; (leap) bond m ▷ vi (leap) bondir ▷ vt (limit) borner ▷ adj: **to be ~ to do sth** (obliged) être obligé(e) or avoir obligation de faire qch; **he's ~ to fail** (likely) il est sûr d'échouer, son échec est inévitable or assuré; **~ by** (law, regulation) engagé(e) par; **~ for** à destination de; **out of ~s** dont l'accès est interdit

**boundary** ['baundrɪ] n frontière f

**bouquet** ['bukeɪ] n bouquet m

**bourbon** ['buəbən] n (us: also: **~ whiskey**) bourbon m

**bout** [baut] n période f; (of malaria etc) accès m, crise f, attaque f; (Boxing etc) combat m, match m

**boutique** [buː'tiːk] n boutique f

**bow¹** [bəu] n nœud m; (weapon) arc m; (Mus) archet m

**bow²** [bau] n (with body) révérence f, inclination f (du buste or corps); (Naut: also: **~s**) proue f ▷ vi faire une révérence, s'incliner

**bowels** [bauəlz] npl intestins mpl; (fig) entrailles fpl

**bowl** [bəul] n (for eating) bol m; (for washing) cuvette f; (ball) boule f ▷ vi (Cricket) lancer (la balle); **bowler** n (Cricket) lanceur m (de la balle); (BRIT: also: **bowler hat**) (chapeau m) melon m; **bowling** n (game) jeu m de boules, jeu de quilles; **bowling alley** n bowling m; **bowling green** n terrain m de boules (gazonné et carré); **bowls** n (jeu m de) boules fpl

**bow tie** [bəu-] n nœud m papillon

**box** [bɔks] n boîte f; (also: **cardboard ~**) carton m; (Theat) loge f ▷ vt mettre en boîte ▷ vi boxer, faire de la boxe; **boxer** ['bɔksəʳ] n (person) boxeur m; **boxer shorts** npl caleçon m; **boxing** ['bɔksɪŋ] n (sport) boxe f; **Boxing Day**

n (BRIT) le lendemain de Noël; voir encadré; **boxing gloves** npl gants mpl de boxe; **boxing ring** n ring m; **box junction** n (BRIT Aut) zone f (de carrefour) d'accès réglementé; **box office** n bureau m de location

**boy** [bɔɪ] n garçon m; **boy band** n boys band m
**boycott** [ˈbɔɪkɔt] n boycottage m ▷ vt boycotter
**boyfriend** [ˈbɔɪfrɛnd] n (petit) ami
**bra** [brɑː] n soutien-gorge m
**brace** [breɪs] n (support) attache f, agrafe f; (BRIT: also: **~s**: on teeth) appareil m (dentaire); (tool) vilebrequin m ▷ vt (support) consolider, soutenir; **braces** npl (BRIT: for trousers) bretelles fpl; **to ~ o.s.** (fig) se préparer mentalement
**bracelet** [ˈbreɪslɪt] n bracelet m
**bracket** [ˈbrækɪt] n (Tech) tasseau m, support m; (group) classe f, tranche f; (also: **brace ~**) accolade f; (also: **round ~**) parenthèse f; (also: **square ~**) crochet m ▷ vt mettre entre parenthèses; **in ~s** entre parenthèses or crochets
**brag** [bræg] vi se vanter
**braid** [breɪd] n (trimming) galon m; (of hair) tresse f, natte f
**brain** [breɪn] n cerveau m; **brains** npl (intellect, food) cervelle f
**braise** [breɪz] vt braiser
**brake** [breɪk] n frein m ▷ vt, vi freiner; **brake light** n feu m de stop
**bran** [bræn] n son m
**branch** [brɑːntʃ] n branche f; (Comm) succursale f; (: of bank) agence f; **branch off** vi (road) bifurquer; **branch out** vi diversifier ses activités

**brand** [brænd] n marque (commerciale) ▷ vt (cattle) marquer (au fer rouge); **brand name** n nom m de marque; **brand-new** adj tout(e) neuf (neuve), flambant neuf (neuve)
**brandy** [ˈbrændɪ] n cognac m
**brash** [bræʃ] adj effronté(e)
**brass** [brɑːs] n cuivre m (jaune), laiton m; **the ~** (Mus) les cuivres; **brass band** n fanfare f
**brat** [bræt] n (pej) mioche m/f, môme m/f
**brave** [breɪv] adj courageux(-euse), brave ▷ vt braver, affronter; **bravery** n bravoure f, courage m
**brawl** [brɔːl] n rixe f, bagarre f
**Brazil** [brəˈzɪl] n Brésil m; **Brazilian** adj brésilien(ne) ▷ n Brésilien(ne)
**breach** [briːtʃ] vt ouvrir une brèche dans ▷ n (gap) brèche f; (breaking): **~ of contract** rupture f de contrat; **~ of the peace** attentat m à l'ordre public
**bread** [brɛd] n pain m; **breadbin** n (BRIT) boîte f or huche f à pain; **breadbox** n (US) boîte f or huche f à pain; **breadcrumbs** npl miettes fpl de pain; (Culin) chapelure f, panure f
**breadth** [brɛtθ] n largeur f
**break** [breɪk] (pt **broke**, pp **broken**) vt casser, briser; (promise) rompre; (law) violer ▷ vi se casser, se briser; (weather) tourner; (storm) éclater; (day) se lever ▷ n (gap) brèche f; (fracture) cassure f; (rest) interruption f, arrêt m; (: short) pause f; (: at school) récréation f; (chance) chance f, occasion f favorable; **to ~ one's leg** etc se casser la jambe etc; **to ~ a record** battre un record; **to ~ the news to sb** annoncer la nouvelle à qn; **break down** vt (door etc) enfoncer; (figures, data) décomposer, analyser ▷ vi s'effondrer; (Med) faire une dépression (nerveuse); (Aut) tomber en panne; **my car has broken down** ma voiture est en panne; **break in** vt (horse etc) dresser ▷ vi (burglar) entrer par effraction; (interrupt) interrompre; **break into** vt fus (house) s'introduire or pénétrer par

effraction dans; **break off** vi (speaker) s'interrompre; (branch) se rompre ▷ vt (talks, engagement) rompre; **break out** vi éclater, se déclarer; (prisoner) s'évader; **to ~ out in spots** se couvrir de boutons; **break up** vi (partnership) cesser, prendre fin; (marriage) se briser; (crowd, meeting) se séparer; (ship) se disloquer; (Scol: pupils) être en vacances; (line) couper; **the line's** or **you're ~ing up** ça coupe ▷ vt fracasser, casser; (fight etc) interrompre, faire cesser; (marriage) désunir; **breakdown** n (Aut) panne f; (in communications, marriage) rupture f; (Med: also: **nervous breakdown**) dépression (nerveuse); (of figures) ventilation f, répartition f; **breakdown truck** (us **breakdown van**) n dépanneuse f

**breakfast** ['brɛkfəst] n petit déjeuner m; **what time is ~?** le petit déjeuner est à quelle heure?

**break**: **break-in** n cambriolage m; **breakthrough** n percée f

**breast** [brɛst] n (of woman) sein m; (chest) poitrine f; (of chicken, turkey) blanc m; **breast-feed** vt, vi (irreg: like **feed**) allaiter; **breast-stroke** n brasse f

**breath** [brɛθ] n haleine f, souffle m; **to take a deep ~** respirer à fond; **out of ~** à bout de souffle, essoufflé(e)

**Breathalyser®** ['brɛθəlaɪzə'] (BRIT) n alcootest m

**breathe** [briːð] vt, vi respirer; **breathe in** vi inspirer ▷ vt aspirer; **breathe out** vt, vi expirer; **breathing** n respiration f

**breath**: **breathless** adj essoufflé(e), haletant(e); **breathtaking** adj stupéfiant(e), à vous couper le souffle; **breath test** n alcootest m

**bred** [brɛd] pt, pp of **breed**

**breed** [briːd] (pt, pp **bred**) vt élever, faire l'élevage de ▷ vi se reproduire ▷ n race f, variété f

**breeze** [briːz] n brise f

**breezy** [briːzɪ] adj (day, weather) venteux(-euse); (manner) désinvolte; (person) jovial(e)

**brew** [bruː] vt (tea) faire infuser; (beer) brasser ▷ vi (fig) se préparer, couver; **brewery** n brasserie f (fabrique)

**bribe** [braɪb] n pot-de-vin m ▷ vt acheter; soudoyer; **bribery** n corruption f

**bric-a-brac** ['brɪkəbræk] n bric-à-brac m

**brick** [brɪk] n brique f; **bricklayer** n maçon m

**bride** [braɪd] n mariée f, épouse f; **bridegroom** n marié m, époux m; **bridesmaid** n demoiselle f d'honneur

**bridge** [brɪdʒ] n pont m; (Naut) passerelle f (de commandement); (of nose) arête f; (Cards, Dentistry) bridge m ▷ vt (gap) combler

**bridle** ['braɪdl] n bride f

**brief** [briːf] adj bref (brève) ▷ n (Law) dossier m, cause f; (gen) tâche f ▷ vt mettre au courant; **briefs** npl slip m; **briefcase** n serviette f; porte-documents m inv; **briefing** n instructions fpl; (Press) briefing m; **briefly** adv brièvement

**brigadier** [brɪgə'dɪə'] n brigadier général

**bright** [braɪt] adj brillant(e); (room, weather) clair(e); (person: clever) intelligent(e), doué(e); (: cheerful) gai(e); (idea) génial(e); (colour) vif (vive)

**brilliant** ['brɪljənt] adj brillant(e); (light, sunshine) éclatant(e); (: inf: great) super

**brim** [brɪm] n bord m

**brine** [braɪn] n (Culin) saumure f

**bring** (pt, pp **brought**) [brɪŋ, brɔːt] vt (thing) apporter; (person) amener; **bring about** vt provoquer, entraîner; **bring back** vt rapporter; (person) ramener; **bring down** vt (lower) abaisser; (shoot down) abattre; (government) faire s'effondrer; **bring in** vt (person) faire entrer; (object) rentrer; (Pol: legislation) introduire; (produce: income) rapporter; **bring on** vt (illness, attack) provoquer; (player, substitute) amener; **bring out** vt sortir; (meaning) faire ressortir, mettre en relief; **bring up** vt élever; (carry up) monter; (*question*) soulever; (*food: vomit*) vomir, rendre

**brink** [brɪŋk] n bord m

**brisk** [brɪsk] adj vif (vive); (*abrupt*) brusque; (*trade etc*) actif(-ive)

**bristle** ['brɪsl] n poil m ▷ vi se hérisser

**Brit** [brɪt] n abbr (inf: = *British person*) Britannique m/f

**Britain** ['brɪtən] n (also: **Great ~**) la Grande-Bretagne

**British** ['brɪtɪʃ] adj britannique ▷ npl: **the ~** les Britanniques mpl; **British Isles** npl: **the British Isles** les îles fpl Britanniques

**Briton** ['brɪtən] n Britannique m/f

**Brittany** ['brɪtənɪ] n Bretagne f

**brittle** ['brɪtl] adj cassant(e), fragile

**B road** n (BRIT) ≈ route départementale

**broad** [brɔːd] adj large; (*distinction*) général(e); (*accent*) prononcé(e); **in ~ daylight** en plein jour; **broadband** n transmission f à haut débit; **broad bean** n fève f; **broadcast** n émission f ▷ vb (pt, pp **broadcast**) ▷ vt (Radio) radiodiffuser; (*TV*) téléviser ▷ vi émettre; **broaden** vt élargir; **to broaden one's mind** élargir ses horizons ▷ vi s'élargir; **broadly** adv en gros, généralement; **broad-minded** adj large d'esprit

**broccoli** ['brɔkəlɪ] n brocoli m

**brochure** ['brəʊʃjuər] n prospectus m, dépliant m

**broil** [brɔɪl] (US) vt rôtir

**broiler** ['brɔɪlər] n (*fowl*) poulet m (à rôtir); (US: *grill*) gril m

**broke** [brəʊk] pt of **break** ▷ adj (inf) fauché(e)

**broken** ['brəʊkn] pp of **break** ▷ adj (*stick, leg etc*) cassé(e); (*machine: also: ~ down*) fichu(e); **in ~ French/English** dans un français/anglais approximatif or hésitant

**broker** ['brəʊkər] n courtier m

**bronchitis** [brɔŋ'kaɪtɪs] n bronchite f

**bronze** [brɔnz] n bronze m

**brooch** [brəʊtʃ] n broche f

**brood** [bruːd] n couvée f ▷ vi (*person*)

méditer (sombrement), ruminer

**broom** [brum] n balai m; (*Bot*) genêt m

**Bros.** abbr (Comm: = *brothers*) Frères

**broth** [brɔθ] n bouillon m de viande et de légumes

**brothel** ['brɔθl] n maison close, bordel m

**brother** ['brʌðər] n frère m; **brother-in-law** n beau-frère m

**brought** [brɔːt] pt, pp of **bring**

**brow** [brau] n front m; (*eyebrow*) sourcil m; (*of hill*) sommet m

**brown** [braun] adj brun(e), marron inv; (*hair*) châtain inv; (*tanned*) bronzé(e) ▷ n (*colour*) brun m, marron m ▷ vt brunir; (Culin) faire dorer, faire roussir; **brown bread** n pain m bis

**Brownie** ['braunɪ] n jeannette f, éclaireuse (cadette)

**brown rice** n riz m complet

**brown sugar** n cassonade f

**browse** [brauz] vi (*in shop*) regarder (sans acheter); **to ~ through a book** feuilleter un livre; **browser** n (Comput) navigateur m

**bruise** [bruːz] n bleu m, ecchymose f, contusion f ▷ vt contusionner, meurtrir

**brunette** [bruː'nɛt] n (femme) brune

**brush** [brʌʃ] n brosse f; (*for painting*) pinceau m; (*for shaving*) blaireau m; (*quarrel*) accrochage m, prise f de bec ▷ vt brosser; (*also: ~ past, ~ against*) effleurer, frôler

**Brussels** ['brʌslz] n Bruxelles

**Brussels sprout** [-spraut] n chou m de Bruxelles

**brutal** ['bruːtl] adj brutal(e)

**B.Sc.** n abbr = **Bachelor of Science**

**BSE** n abbr (= *bovine spongiform encephalopathy*) ESB f, BSE f

**bubble** ['bʌbl] n bulle f ▷ vi bouillonner, faire des bulles; (*sparkle, fig*) pétiller; **bubble bath** n bain moussant; **bubble gum** n chewing-gum m; **bubblejet printer** ['bʌbldʒɛt-] n imprimante f à bulle d'encre

**buck** [bʌk] n mâle m (*d'un lapin, lièvre*,

*daim etc*); (*us inf*) dollar *m* ▷ *vi* ruer, lancer une ruade; **to pass the ~ (to sb)** se décharger de la responsabilité (sur qn)

**bucket** ['bʌkɪt] *n* seau *m*

**buckle** ['bʌkl] *n* boucle *f* ▷ *vt* (*belt etc*) boucler, attacher ▷ *vi* (*warp*) tordre, gauchir; (: *wheel*) se voiler

**bud** [bʌd] *n* bourgeon *m*; (*of flower*) bouton *m* ▷ *vi* bourgeonner; (*flower*) éclore

**Buddhism** ['budɪzəm] *n* bouddhisme *m*

**Buddhist** ['budɪst] *adj* bouddhiste ▷ *n* Bouddhiste *m/f*

**buddy** ['bʌdɪ] *n* (*us*) copain *m*

**budge** [bʌdʒ] *vt* faire bouger ▷ *vi* bouger

**budgerigar** ['bʌdʒərɪgɑːʳ] *n* perruche *f*

**budget** ['bʌdʒɪt] *n* budget *m* ▷ *vi*: **to ~ for sth** inscrire qch au budget

**budgie** ['bʌdʒɪ] *n* = **budgerigar**

**buff** [bʌf] *adj* (*couleur f*) chamois *m* ▷ *n* (*inf: enthusiast*) mordu(e)

**buffalo** (*pl* **~** *or* **~es**) ['bʌfələu] *n* (*BRIT*) buffle *m*; (*us*) bison *m*

**buffer** ['bʌfəʳ] *n* tampon *m*; (*Comput*) mémoire *f* tampon

**buffet** *n* ['bufeɪ] (*food BRIT: bar*) buffet *m* ▷ *vt* ['bʌfɪt] secouer, ébranler; **buffet car** *n* (*BRIT Rail*) voiture-bar *f*

**bug** [bʌg] *n* (*bedbug etc*) punaise *f*; (*esp us: any insect*) insecte *m*, bestiole *f*; (*fig: germ*) virus *m*, microbe *m*; (*spy device*) dispositif *m* d'écoute (électronique), micro clandestin; (*Comput: of program*) erreur *f* ▷ *vt* (*room*) poser des micros dans; (*inf: annoy*) embêter

**buggy** ['bʌgɪ] *n* poussette *f*

**build** [bɪld] *n* (*of person*) carrure *f*, charpente *f* ▷ *vt* (*pt*, *pp* **built**) construire, bâtir; **build up** *vt* accumuler, amasser; (*business*) développer; (*reputation*) bâtir; **builder** *n* entrepreneur *m*; **building** *n* (*trade*) construction *f*; (*structure*) bâtiment *m*, construction *f*; (: *residential, offices*) immeuble *m*; **building site** *n* chantier

*m* (de construction); **building society** *n* (*BRIT*) société *f* de crédit immobilier

**built** [bɪlt] *pt*, *pp* *of* **build**; **built-in** *adj* (*cupboard*) encastré(e); (*device*) incorporé(e); intégré(e); **built-up** *adj*: **built-up area** zone urbanisée

**bulb** [bʌlb] *n* (*Bot*) bulbe *m*, oignon *m*; (*Elec*) ampoule *f*

**Bulgaria** [bʌl'gɛərɪə] *n* Bulgarie *f*; **Bulgarian** *adj* bulgare ▷ *n* Bulgare *m/f*

**bulge** [bʌldʒ] *n* renflement *m*, gonflement *m* ▷ *vi* faire saillie; présenter un renflement; (*pocket, file*): **to be bulging with** être plein(e) à craquer de

**bulimia** [bə'lɪmɪə] *n* boulimie *f*

**bulimic** [bju:'lɪmɪk] *adj*, *n* boulimique (*m/f*)

**bulk** [bʌlk] *n* masse *f*, volume *m*; **in ~** (*Comm*) en gros, en vrac; **the ~ of** la plus grande *or* grosse partie de; **bulky** *adj* volumineux(-euse), encombrant(e)

**bull** [bul] *n* taureau *m*; (*male elephant, whale*) mâle *m*

**bulldozer** ['buldəuzəʳ] *n* bulldozer *m*

**bullet** ['bulɪt] *n* balle *f* (de fusil etc)

**bulletin** ['bulɪtɪn] *n* bulletin *m*, communiqué *m*; (*also*: **news ~**) (bulletin d')informations *fpl*; **bulletin board** *n* (*Comput*) messagerie *f* (électronique)

**bullfight** ['bulfaɪt] *n* corrida *f*, course *f* de taureaux; **bullfighter** *n* torero *m*; **bullfighting** *n* tauromachie *f*

**bully** ['bulɪ] *n* brute *f*, tyran *m* ▷ *vt* tyranniser, rudoyer

**bum** [bʌm] *n* (*inf: BRIT: backside*) derrière *m*; (: *esp us: tramp*) vagabond(e), traîne-savates *m/f inv*; (: *idler*) glandeur *m*

**bumblebee** ['bʌmblbiː] *n* bourdon *m*

**bump** [bʌmp] *n* (*blow*) coup *m*, choc *m*; (*jolt*) cahot *m*; (*on road etc, on head*) bosse *f* ▷ *vt* heurter, cogner; (*car*) emboutir; **bump into** *vt fus* rentrer dans, tamponner; (*inf: meet*) tomber sur; **bumper** *n* pare-chocs *m inv* ▷ *adj*: **bumper crop/harvest** récolte/moisson exceptionnelle; **bumpy** *adj* (*road*) cahoteux(-euse); **it was a**

**bumpy flight/ride** on a été secoués dans l'avion/la voiture

**bun** [bʌn] n (cake) petit gâteau; (bread) petit pain au lait; (of hair) chignon m

**bunch** [bʌntʃ] n (of flowers) bouquet m; (of keys) trousseau m; (of bananas) régime m; (of people) groupe m; **bunches** npl (in hair) couettes fpl; **~ of grapes** grappe f de raisin

**bundle** ['bʌndl] n paquet m ▷ vt (also: **~ up**) faire un paquet de; (put): **to ~ sth/sb into** fourrer or enfourner qch/qn dans

**bungalow** ['bʌŋgələu] n bungalow m

**bungee jumping** ['bʌndʒi:'dʒʌmpɪŋ] n saut m à l'élastique

**bunion** ['bʌnjən] n oignon m (au pied)

**bunk** [bʌŋk] n couchette f; **bunk beds** npl lits superposés

**bunker** ['bʌŋkə'] n (coal store) soute f à charbon; (Mil, Golf) bunker m

**bunny** ['bʌnɪ] n (also: **~ rabbit**) lapin m

**buoy** [bɔɪ] n bouée f; **buoyant** adj (ship) flottable; (carefree) gai(e), plein(e) d'entrain; (Comm: market, economy) actif(-ive)

**burden** ['bə:dn] n fardeau m, charge f ▷ vt charger; (oppress) accabler, surcharger

**bureau** (pl **-x**) ['bjuərəu, -z] n (BRIT: writing desk) bureau m, secrétaire m; (US: chest of drawers) commode f; (office) bureau, office m

**bureaucracy** [bjuə'rɔkrəsɪ] n bureaucratie f

**bureaucrat** ['bjuərəkræt] n bureaucrate m/f, rond-de-cuir m

**bureau de change** [-də'ʃɑ̃ʒ] (pl **bureaux de change**) n bureau m de change

**bureaux** ['bjuərəuz] npl of **bureau**

**burger** ['bə:gə'] n hamburger m

**burglar** ['bə:glə'] n cambrioleur m; **burglar alarm** n sonnerie f d'alarme; **burglary** n cambriolage m

**Burgundy** ['bə:gəndɪ] n Bourgogne f

**burial** ['bɛrɪəl] n enterrement m

**burn** [bə:n] vt, vi (pt, pp **~ed** or **~t**) brûler

▷ n brûlure f; **burn down** vt incendier, détruire par le feu; **burn out** vt (writer etc): **to ~ o.s. out** s'user (à force de travailler); **burning** adj (building, forest) en flammes; (issue, question) brûlant(e); (ambition) dévorant(e)

**Burns' Night** [bə:nz-] n fête écossaise à la mémoire du poète Robert Burns

● **BURNS NIGHT**
●
● **Burns Night** est une fête qui a lieu
● le 25 janvier, à la mémoire du poète
● écossais Robert Burns (1759 - 1796),
● à l'occasion de laquelle les Écossais
● partout dans le monde organisent
● un souper, en général arrosé de
● whisky. Le plat principal est toujours
● le haggis, servi avec de la purée de
● pommes de terre et de la purée de
● rutabagas. On apporte le haggis au
● son des cornemuses et au cours du
● repas on lit des poèmes de Burns et
● on chante des chansons.

**burnt** [bə:nt] pt, pp of **burn**

**burp** [bə:p] (inf) n rot m ▷ vi roter

**burrow** ['bʌrəu] n terrier m ▷ vi (rabbit) creuser un terrier; (rummage) fouiller

**burst** [bə:st] (pt, pp **~**) vt faire éclater; (river: banks etc) rompre ▷ vi éclater; (tyre) crever ▷ n explosion f; (also: **~ pipe**) fuite f (due à une rupture); **a ~ of enthusiasm/energy** un accès d'enthousiasme/d'énergie; **to ~ into flames** s'enflammer soudainement; **to ~ out laughing** éclater de rire; **to ~ into tears** fondre en larmes; **to ~ open** vi s'ouvrir violemment or soudainement; **to be ~ing with** (container) être plein(e) (à craquer) de, regorger de; (fig) être débordant(e) de; **burst into** vt fus (room etc) faire irruption dans

**bury** ['bɛrɪ] vt enterrer

**bus** (pl **~es**) [bʌs, 'bʌsɪz] n autobus m; **bus conductor** n receveur(-euse) m/f de bus

**bush** [buʃ] n buisson m; (scrub land)

brousse f; **to beat about the ~** tourner autour du pot

**business** ['bɪznɪs] n (matter, firm) affaire f; (trading) affaires fpl; (job, duty) travail m; **to be away on ~** être en déplacement d'affaires; **it's none of my ~** cela ne me regarde pas, ce ne sont pas mes affaires; **he means ~** il ne plaisante pas, il est sérieux; **business class** n (on plane) classe f affaires; **businesslike** adj sérieux(-euse), efficace; **businessman** (irreg) n homme m d'affaires; **business trip** n voyage m d'affaires; **businesswoman** (irreg) n femme f d'affaires

**busker** ['bʌskəʳ] n (BRIT) artiste ambulant(e)

**bus**: **bus pass** n carte f de bus; **bus shelter** n abribus m; **bus station** n gare routière; **bus-stop** n arrêt m d'autobus

**bust** [bʌst] n buste m; (measurement) tour m de poitrine ▷ adj (inf: broken) fichu(e), fini(e); **to go ~** faire faillite

**bustling** ['bʌslɪŋ] adj (town) très animé(e)

**busy** ['bɪzɪ] adj occupé(e); (shop, street) très fréquenté(e); (us: telephone, line) occupé ▷ vt: **to ~ o.s.** s'occuper; **busy signal** n (us) tonalité f occupé inv

○ **KEYWORD**

**but** [bʌt] conj mais; **I'd love to come, but I'm busy** j'aimerais venir mais je suis occupé; **he's not English but French** il n'est pas anglais mais français; **but that's far too expensive!** mais c'est bien trop cher!
▷ prep (apart from, except) sauf, excepté; **nothing but** rien d'autre que; **we've had nothing but trouble** nous n'avons eu que des ennuis; **no-one but him can do it** lui seul peut le faire; **who but a lunatic would do such a thing?** qui sinon un fou ferait une chose pareille?; **but for you/your help** sans toi/ton aide; **anything but that** tout sauf or

excepté ça, tout mais pas ça
▷ adv (just, only) ne ... que; **she's but a child** elle n'est qu'une enfant; **had I but known** si seulement j'avais su; **I can but try** je peux toujours essayer; **all but finished** pratiquement terminé

**butcher** ['butʃəʳ] n boucher m ▷ vt massacrer; (cattle etc for meat) tuer; **butcher's (shop)** n boucherie f

**butler** ['bʌtləʳ] n maître m d'hôtel

**butt** [bʌt] n (cask) gros tonneau; (of gun) crosse f; (of cigarette) mégot m; (BRIT fig: target) cible f ▷ vt donner un coup de tête à

**butter** ['bʌtəʳ] n beurre m ▷ vt beurrer; **buttercup** n bouton m d'or

**butterfly** ['bʌtəflaɪ] n papillon m; (Swimming: also: **~ stroke**) brasse f papillon

**buttocks** ['bʌtəks] npl fesses fpl

**button** ['bʌtn] n bouton m; (us: badge) pin m ▷ vt (also: **~ up**) boutonner ▷ vi se boutonner

**buy** [baɪ] (pt, pp **bought**) vt acheter ▷ n achat m; **to ~ sb sth/sth from sb** acheter qch à qn; **to ~ sb a drink** offrir un verre or à boire à qn; **can I ~ you a drink?** je vous offre un verre?; **where can I ~ some postcards?** où est-ce que je peux acheter des cartes postales?; **buy out** vt (partner) désintéresser; **buy up** vt acheter en bloc, rafler; **buyer** n acheteur(-euse) m/f

**buzz** [bʌz] n bourdonnement m; (inf: phone call): **to give sb a ~** passer un coup de fil à qn ▷ vi bourdonner; **buzzer** n timbre m électrique

○ **KEYWORD**

**by** [baɪ] prep **1** (referring to cause, agent) par, de; **killed by lightning** tué par la foudre; **surrounded by a fence** entouré d'une barrière; **a painting by Picasso** un tableau de Picasso
**2** (referring to method, manner, means): **by bus/car** en autobus/voiture; **by train**

par le *or* en train; **to pay by cheque**
payer par chèque; **by moonlight/**
**candlelight** à la lueur de la lune/d'une
bougie; **by saving hard, he ...** à force
d'économiser, il ...
**3** (*via, through*) par; **we came by Dover**
nous sommes venus par Douvres
**4** (*close to, past*) à côté de; **the house by**
**the school** la maison à côté de l'école;
**a holiday by the sea** des vacances au
bord de la mer; **she went by me** elle est
passée à côté de moi; **I go by the post**
**office every day** je passe devant la
poste tous les jours
**5** (*with time: not later than*) avant;
(: *during*): **by daylight** à la lumière du
jour; **by night** la nuit, de nuit; **by 4**
**o'clock** avant 4 heures; **by this time**
**tomorrow** d'ici demain à la même
heure; **by the time I got here it was**
**too late** lorsque je suis arrivé il était
déjà trop tard
**6** (*amount*) à; **by the kilo/metre** au
kilo/au mètre; **paid by the hour** payé
à l'heure
**7** (*Math: measure*): **to divide/multiply**
**by 3** diviser/multiplier par 3; **a room 3**
**metres by 4** une pièce de 3 mètres sur
4; **it's broader by a metre** c'est plus
large d'un mètre
**8** (*according to*) d'après, selon; **it's 3**
**o'clock by my watch** il est 3 heures à
ma montre; **it's all right by me** je n'ai
rien contre
**9**: **(all) by oneself** *etc* tout(e) seul(e)
▷ *adv* **1** *see* **go**; **pass** *etc*
**2**: **by and by** un peu plus tard, bientôt;
**by and large** dans l'ensemble

**bye(-bye)** ['baɪ('baɪ)] *excl* au revoir!,
salut!
**by-election** ['baɪɪlɛkʃən] *n* (BRIT)
élection (législative) partielle
**bypass** ['baɪpɑːs] *n* rocade *f*; (*Med*)
pontage *m* ▷ *vt* éviter
**byte** [baɪt] *n* (*Comput*) octet *m*

# C

**C** [siː] *n* (*Mus*): **C** do *m*
**cab** [kæb] *n* taxi *m*; (*of train, truck*)
cabine *f*
**cabaret** ['kæbəreɪ] *n* (*show*) spectacle
*m* de cabaret
**cabbage** ['kæbɪdʒ] *n* chou *m*
**cabin** ['kæbɪn] *n* (*house*) cabane *f*,
hutte *f*; (*on ship*) cabine *f*; (*on plane*)
compartiment *m*; **cabin crew** *n* (*Aviat*)
équipage *m*
**cabinet** ['kæbɪnɪt] *n* (*Pol*) cabinet *m*;
(*furniture*) petit meuble à tiroirs et
rayons; (*also*: **display ~**) vitrine *f*, petite
armoire vitrée; **cabinet minister** *n*
ministre *m* (*membre du cabinet*)
**cable** ['keɪbl] *n* câble *m* ▷ *vt*
câbler, télégraphier; **cable car** *n*
téléphérique *m*; **cable television** *n*
télévision *f* par câble
**cactus** (*pl* **cacti**) ['kæktəs, -taɪ] *n*
cactus *m*
**café** ['kæfeɪ] *n* ≈ café(-restaurant) *m*
(*sans alcool*)
**cafeteria** [kæfɪ'tɪərɪə] *n* cafétéria *f*

**caffein(e)** ['kæfi:n] n caféine f
**cage** [keɪdʒ] n cage f
**cagoule** [kə'gu:l] n K-way® m
**Cairo** ['kaɪərəʊ] n le Caire
**cake** [keɪk] n gâteau m; **~ of soap** savonnette f
**calcium** ['kælsɪəm] n calcium m
**calculate** ['kælkjuleɪt] vt calculer; (estimate: chances, effect) évaluer; **calculation** [kælkju'leɪʃən] n calcul m; **calculator** n calculatrice f
**calendar** ['kæləndər] n calendrier m
**calf** (pl **calves**) [kɑ:f, kɑ:vz] n (of cow) veau m; (of other animals) petit m; (also: **~skin**) veau m, vachette f; (Anat) mollet m
**calibre** (US **caliber**) ['kælɪbər] n calibre m
**call** [kɔ:l] vt appeler; (meeting) convoquer ▷ vi appeler; (visit: also: **~ in, ~ round**) passer ▷ n (shout) appel m, cri m; (also: **telephone ~**) coup m de téléphone; **to be on ~** être de permanence; **to be ~ed** s'appeler; **can I make a ~ from here?** est-ce que je peux téléphoner d'ici?; **call back** vi (return) repasser; (Tel) rappeler ▷ vt (Tel) rappeler; **can you ~ back later?** pouvez-vous rappeler plus tard?; **call for** vt fus (demand) demander; (fetch) passer prendre; **call in** vt (doctor, expert, police) appeler, faire venir; **call off** vt annuler; **call on** vt fus (visit) rendre visite à, passer voir; (request): **to ~ on sb to do** inviter qn à faire; **call out** vi pousser un cri or des cris; **call up** vt (Mil) appeler, mobiliser; (Tel) appeler; **callbox** n (BRIT) cabine f téléphonique; **call centre** (US **call center**) n centre m d'appels; **caller** n (Tel) personne f qui appelle; (visitor) visiteur m
**callous** ['kæləs] adj dur(e), insensible
**calm** [kɑ:m] adj calme ▷ n calme m ▷ vt calmer, apaiser; **calm down** vi se calmer, s'apaiser ▷ vt calmer, apaiser; **calmly** ['kɑ:mlɪ] adv calmement, avec calme
**Calor gas®** ['kælər-] n (BRIT) butane m,

butagaz® m
**calorie** ['kælərɪ] n calorie f
**calves** [kɑ:vz] npl of **calf**
**Cambodia** [kæm'bəʊdɪə] n Cambodge m
**camcorder** ['kæmkɔ:dər] n caméscope m
**came** [keɪm] pt of **come**
**camel** ['kæməl] n chameau m
**camera** ['kæmərə] n appareil-photo m; (Cine, TV) caméra f; **in ~** à huis clos, en privé; **cameraman** n caméraman m; **camera phone** n téléphone m avec appareil photo numérique intégré
**camouflage** ['kæməflɑ:ʒ] n camouflage m ▷ vt camoufler
**camp** [kæmp] n camp m ▷ vi camper ▷ adj (man) efféminé(e)
**campaign** [kæm'peɪn] n (Mil, Pol etc) campagne f ▷ vi (also fig) faire campagne; **campaigner** n: **campaigner for** partisan(e) de; **campaigner against** opposant(e) à
**camp: campbed** [kæmpbed] n (BRIT) lit m de camp; **camper** n campeur(-euse); (vehicle) camping-car m; **campground** (US) n (terrain m de) camping m; **camping** n camping m; **to go camping** faire du camping; **campsite** n (terrain m de) camping m
**campus** ['kæmpəs] n campus m
**can¹** [kæn] n (of milk, oil, water) bidon m; (tin) boîte f (de conserve) ▷ vt mettre en conserve

**KEYWORD**

**can²** [kæn] (negative **cannot, can't**, conditional and pt **could**) aux vb **1** (be able to) pouvoir; **you can do it if you try** vous pouvez le faire si vous essayez; **I can't hear you** je ne t'entends pas
**2** (know how to) savoir; **I can swim/play tennis/drive** je sais nager/jouer au tennis/conduire; **can you speak French?** parlez-vous français?
**3** (may) pouvoir; **can I use your phone?** puis-je me servir de votre téléphone?

**4** (expressing disbelief, puzzlement etc):
**it can't be true!** ce n'est pas possible!;
**what can he want?** qu'est-ce qu'il peut
bien vouloir?
**5** (expressing possibility, suggestion etc):
**he could be in the library** il est peut-
être dans la bibliothèque; **she could
have been delayed** il se peut qu'elle ait
été retardée

**Canada** ['kænədə] n Canada m;
**Canadian** [kə'neɪdɪən] adj
canadien(ne) ⊳ n Canadien(ne)
**canal** [kə'næl] n canal m
**canary** [kə'nɛərɪ] n canari m, serin m
**cancel** ['kænsəl] vt annuler; (train)
supprimer; (party, appointment)
décommander; (cross out) barrer, rayer;
(cheque) faire opposition à; **I would
like to ~ my booking** je voudrais
annuler ma réservation; **cancellation**
[kænsə'leɪʃən] n annulation f;
suppression f
**Cancer** ['kænsər] n (Astrology) le Cancer
**cancer** ['kænsər] n cancer m
**candidate** ['kændɪdeɪt] n candidat(e)
**candle** ['kændl] n bougie f; (in church)
cierge m; **candlestick** n (also: **candle
holder**) bougeoir m; (bigger, ornate)
chandelier m
**candy** ['kændɪ] n sucre candi; (US)
bonbon m; **candy bar** (US) n barre f
chocolatée; **candyfloss** n (BRIT) barbe
f à papa
**cane** [keɪn] n canne f; (for baskets, chairs
etc) rotin m ⊳ vt (BRIT Scol) administrer
des coups de bâton à
**canister** ['kænɪstər] n boîte f (gén en
métal); (of gas) bombe f
**cannabis** ['kænəbɪs] n (drug)
cannabis m
**canned** ['kænd] adj (food) en boîte,
en conserve; (inf: music) enregistré(e);
(BRIT inf: drunk) bourré(e); (US inf: worker)
mis(e) à la porte
**cannon** (pl ~ or ~**s**) ['kænən] n (gun)
canon m
**cannot** ['kænɔt] = **can not**

**canoe** [kə'nuː] n pirogue f; (Sport)
canoë m; **canoeing** n (sport) canoë m
**canon** ['kænən] n (clergyman) chanoine
m; (standard) canon m
**can-opener** [-'əupnər] n ouvre-boîte m
**can't** [kɑːnt] = **can not**
**canteen** [kæn'tiːn] n (eating place)
cantine f; (BRIT: of cutlery) ménagère f
**canter** ['kæntər] vi aller au petit galop
**canvas** ['kænvəs] n toile f
**canvass** ['kænvəs] vi (Pol): **to ~ for**
faire campagne pour ⊳ vt (citizens,
opinions) sonder
**canyon** ['kænjən] n cañon m, gorge
(profonde)
**cap** [kæp] n casquette f; (for swimming)
bonnet m de bain; (of pen) capuchon m;
(of bottle) capsule f; (BRIT: contraceptive:
also: **Dutch ~**) diaphragme m ⊳ vt
(outdo) surpasser; (put limit on)
plafonner
**capability** [keɪpə'bɪlɪtɪ] n aptitude
f, capacité f
**capable** ['keɪpəbl] adj capable
**capacity** [kə'pæsɪtɪ] n (of container)
capacité f, contenance f; (ability)
aptitude f
**cape** [keɪp] n (garment) cape f; (Geo)
cap m
**caper** ['keɪpər] n (Culin: gen pl) câpre f;
(prank) farce f
**capital** ['kæpɪtl] n (also: **~ city**)
capitale f; (money) capital m; (also:
**~ letter**) majuscule f; **capitalism**
n capitalisme m; **capitalist** adj, n
capitaliste m/f; **capital punishment** n
peine capitale
**Capitol** ['kæpɪtl] n: **the ~** le Capitole
**Capricorn** ['kæprɪkɔːn] n le Capricorne
**capsize** [kæp'saɪz] vt faire chavirer
⊳ vi chavirer
**capsule** ['kæpsjuːl] n capsule f
**captain** ['kæptɪn] n capitaine m
**caption** ['kæpʃən] n légende f
**captivity** [kæp'tɪvɪtɪ] n captivité f
**capture** ['kæptʃər] vt (prisoner, animal)
capturer; (town) prendre; (attention)
capter; (Comput) saisir ⊳ n capture f; (of

*data*) saisie *f* de données
**car** [kɑːʳ] *n* voiture *f*, auto *f*; (*us Rail*) wagon *m*, voiture
**carafe** [kəˈræf] *n* carafe *f*
**caramel** [ˈkærəməl] *n* caramel *m*
**carat** [ˈkærət] *n* carat *m*
**caravan** [ˈkærəvæn] *n* caravane *f*;
  **caravan site** *n* (*BRIT*) camping *m* pour caravanes
**carbohydrate** [kɑːbəuˈhaɪdreɪt] *n* hydrate *m* de carbone; (*food*) féculent *m*
**carbon** [ˈkɑːbən] *n* carbone *m*;
  **carbon dioxide** [-daɪˈɔksaɪd] *n* gaz *m* carbonique, dioxyde *m* de carbone;
  **carbon monoxide** [-mɔˈnɔksaɪd] *n* oxyde *m* de carbone
**car boot sale** *n* voir encadré

○ **CAR BOOT SALE**
○
○ Type de brocante très populaire, où
○ chacun vide sa cave ou son grenier.
○ Les articles sont présentés dans
○ des coffres de voitures et la vente
○ a souvent lieu sur un parking ou
○ dans un champ. Les brocanteurs
○ d'un jour doivent s'acquitter d'une
○ petite contribution pour participer
○ à la vente.

**carburettor** (*us* **carburetor**) [kɑːbjuˈrɛtəʳ] *n* carburateur *m*
**card** [kɑːd] *n* carte *f*; (*material*) carton *m*;
  **cardboard** *n* carton *m*; **card game** *n* jeu *m* de cartes
**cardigan** [ˈkɑːdɪgən] *n* cardigan *m*
**cardinal** [ˈkɑːdɪnl] *adj* cardinal(e);
  (*importance*) capital(e) ▷ *n* cardinal *m*
**cardphone** [ˈkɑːdfəun] *n* téléphone *m* à carte (magnétique)
**care** [kɛəʳ] *n* soin *m*, attention *f*;
  (*worry*) souci *m* ▷ *vi*: **to ~ about** (*feel interest for*) se soucier de, s'intéresser à; (*person: love*) être attaché(e) à; **in sb's ~** à la garde de qn, confié à qn; **~ of** (*on letter*) chez; **to take ~ (to do)** faire attention (à faire); **to take ~ of** *vt* s'occuper de; **I don't ~** ça m'est bien

égal, peu m'importe; **I couldn't ~ less** cela m'est complètement égal, je m'en fiche complètement; **care for** *vt fus* s'occuper de; (*like*) aimer
**career** [kəˈrɪəʳ] *n* carrière *f* ▷ *vi* (*also: ~ along*) aller à toute allure
**care**: **carefree** *adj* sans souci, insouciant(e); **careful** *adj* soigneux(-euse); (*cautious*) prudent(e); **(be) careful!** (fais) attention!; **carefully** *adv* avec soin, soigneusement; prudemment;
  **caregiver** (*us*) *n* (*professional*) travailleur social; (*unpaid*) *personne qui s'occupe d'un proche qui est malade*;
  **careless** *adj* négligent(e); (*heedless*) insouciant(e); **carelessness** *n* manque *m* de soin, négligence *f*; insouciance *f*;
  **carer** [ˈkɛərəʳ] *n* (*professional*) travailleur social; (*unpaid*) *personne qui s'occupe d'un proche qui est malade*;
  **caretaker** *n* gardien(ne), concierge *m/f*
**car-ferry** [ˈkɑːfɛrɪ] *n* (*on sea*) ferry(-boat) *m*; (*on river*) bac *m*
**cargo** (*pl* **~es**) [ˈkɑːgəu] *n* cargaison *f*, chargement *m*
**car hire** *n* (*BRIT*) location *f* de voitures
**Caribbean** [kærɪˈbiːən] *adj*, *n*: **the ~ (Sea)** la mer des Antilles *or* des Caraïbes
**caring** [ˈkɛərɪŋ] *adj* (*person*) bienveillant(e); (*society, organization*) humanitaire
**carnation** [kɑːˈneɪʃən] *n* œillet *m*
**carnival** [ˈkɑːnɪvl] *n* (*public celebration*) carnaval *m*; (*us: funfair*) fête foraine
**carol** [ˈkærəl] *n*: **(Christmas) ~** chant *m* de Noël
**carousel** [kærəˈsɛl] *n* (*for luggage*) carrousel *m*; (*us*) manège *m*
**car park** (*BRIT*) *n* parking *m*, parc *m* de stationnement
**carpenter** [ˈkɑːpɪntəʳ] *n* charpentier *m*; (*joiner*) menuisier *m*
**carpet** [ˈkɑːpɪt] *n* tapis *m* ▷ *vt* recouvrir (d'un tapis); **fitted ~** (*BRIT*) moquette *f*
**car rental** *n* (*us*) location *f* de voitures
**carriage** [ˈkærɪdʒ] *n* (*BRIT Rail*)

wagon m; (horse-drawn) voiture f; (of goods) transport m; (: cost) port m; **carriageway** n (BRIT: part of road) chaussée f

**carrier** ['kærɪər] n transporteur m, camionneur m; (company) entreprise f de transport; (Med) porteur(-euse); **carrier bag** n (BRIT) sac m en papier or en plastique

**carrot** ['kærət] n carotte f

**carry** ['kærɪ] vt (subj: person) porter; (: vehicle) transporter; (involve: responsibilities etc) comporter, impliquer; (Med: disease) être porteur de ▷ vi (sound) porter; **to get carried away** (fig) s'emballer, s'enthousiasmer; **carry on** vi (continue) continuer ▷ vt (conduct: business) diriger; (: conversation) entretenir; (continue: business, conversation) continuer; **to ~ on with sth/doing** continuer qch/à faire; **carry out** vt (orders) exécuter; (investigation) effectuer

**cart** [kɑːt] n charrette f ▷ vt (inf) transporter

**carton** ['kɑːtən] n (box) carton m; (of yogurt) pot m (en carton)

**cartoon** [kɑːˈtuːn] n (Press) dessin m (humoristique); (satirical) caricature f; (comic strip) bande dessinée; (Cine) dessin animé

**cartridge** ['kɑːtrɪdʒ] n (for gun, pen) cartouche f

**carve** [kɑːv] vt (meat: also: ~ up) découper; (wood, stone) tailler, sculpter; **carving** n (in wood etc) sculpture f

**car wash** n station f de lavage (de voitures)

**case** [keɪs] n cas m; (Law) affaire f, procès m; (box) caisse f, boîte f; (for glasses) étui m; (BRIT: also: **suit~**) valise f; **in ~ of** en cas de; **in ~ he** au cas où il; **just in ~** à tout hasard; **in any ~** en tout cas, de toute façon

**cash** [kæʃ] n argent m; (Comm) (argent m) liquide m ▷ vt encaisser; **to pay (in) ~** payer (en argent) comptant or en espèces; **~ with order/on delivery**

(Comm) payable or paiement à la commande/livraison; **I haven't got any ~** je n'ai pas de liquide; **cashback** n (discount) remise f; (at supermarket etc) retrait m (à la caisse); **cash card** n carte f de retrait; **cash desk** n (BRIT) caisse f; **cash dispenser** n distributeur m automatique de billets

**cashew** [kæˈʃuː] n (also: ~ **nut**) noix f de cajou

**cashier** [kæˈʃɪər] n caissier(-ère)

**cashmere** ['kæʃmɪər] n cachemire m

**cash point** n distributeur m automatique de billets

**cash register** n caisse enregistreuse

**casino** [kəˈsiːnəu] n casino m

**casket** ['kɑːskɪt] n coffret m; (US: coffin) cercueil m

**casserole** ['kæsərəul] n (pot) cocotte f; (food) ragoût m (en cocotte)

**cassette** [kæˈset] n cassette f; **cassette player** n lecteur m de cassettes

**cast** [kɑːst] (vb: pt, pp ~) vt (throw) jeter; (shadow: lit) projeter; (: fig) jeter; (glance) jeter ▷ n (Theat) distribution f; (also: **plaster ~**) plâtre m; **to ~ sb as Hamlet** attribuer à qn le rôle d'Hamlet; **to ~ one's vote** voter, exprimer son suffrage; **to ~ doubt on** jeter un doute sur; **cast off** vi (Naut) larguer les amarres; (Knitting) arrêter les mailles

**castanets** [kæstəˈnets] npl castagnettes fpl

**caster sugar** ['kɑːstə-] n (BRIT) sucre m semoule

**cast-iron** ['kɑːstaɪən] adj (lit) de or en fonte; (fig: will) de fer; (alibi) en béton

**castle** ['kɑːsl] n château m; (fortress) château-fort m; (Chess) tour f

**casual** ['kæʒjul] adj (by chance) de hasard, fait(e) au hasard, fortuit(e); (irregular: work etc) temporaire; (unconcerned) désinvolte; ~ **wear** vêtements mpl sport inv

**casualty** ['kæʒjultɪ] n accidenté(e), blessé(e); (dead) victime f, mort(e); (BRIT: Med: department) urgences fpl

**cat** [kæt] n chat m

**Catalan** [ˈkætələn] *adj* catalan(e)
**catalogue** (*US* **catalog**) [ˈkætələg] *n* catalogue *m* ▷ *vt* cataloguer
**catalytic converter** [kætəˈlɪtɪkkənˈvɜːtə<sup>r</sup>] *n* pot *m* catalytique
**cataract** [ˈkætərækt] *n* (*also Med*) cataracte *f*
**catarrh** [kəˈtɑː<sup>r</sup>] *n* rhume *m* chronique, catarrhe *f*
**catastrophe** [kəˈtæstrəfɪ] *n* catastrophe *f*
**catch** [kætʃ] (*pt, pp* **caught**) *vt* attraper; (*person: by surprise*) prendre, surprendre; (*understand*) saisir; (*get entangled*) accrocher ▷ *vi* (*fire*) prendre; (*get entangled*) s'accrocher ▷ *n* (*fish etc*) prise *f*; (*hidden problem*) attrape *f*; (*Tech*) loquet *m*; cliquet *m*; **to ~ sb's attention** *or* **eye** attirer l'attention de qn; **to ~ fire** prendre feu; **to ~ sight of** apercevoir; **catch up** *vi* (*with work*) se rattraper, combler son retard ▷ *vt* (*also:* **~ up with**) rattraper; **catching** [ˈkætʃɪŋ] *adj* (*Med*) contagieux(-euse)
**category** [ˈkætɪgərɪ] *n* catégorie *f*
**cater** [ˈkeɪtə<sup>r</sup>] *vi*: **to ~ for** (*BRIT: needs*) satisfaire, pourvoir à; (*: readers, consumers*) s'adresser à, pourvoir aux besoins de; (*Comm: parties etc*) préparer des repas pour
**caterpillar** [ˈkætəpɪlə<sup>r</sup>] *n* chenille *f*
**cathedral** [kəˈθiːdrəl] *n* cathédrale *f*
**Catholic** [ˈkæθəlɪk] (*Rel*) *adj* catholique ▷ *n* catholique *m/f*
**Catseye®** [ˈkætsˈaɪ] *n* (*BRIT Aut*) (clou *m* à) catadioptre *m*
**cattle** [ˈkætl] *npl* bétail *m*, bestiaux *mpl*
**catwalk** [ˈkætwɔːk] *n* passerelle *f*; (*for models*) podium *m* (*de défilé de mode*)
**caught** [kɔːt] *pt, pp of* **catch**
**cauliflower** [ˈkɔlɪflauə<sup>r</sup>] *n* chou-fleur *m*
**cause** [kɔːz] *n* cause *f* ▷ *vt* causer
**caution** [ˈkɔːʃən] *n* prudence *f*; (*warning*) avertissement *m* ▷ *vt* avertir, donner un avertissement à; **cautious** *adj* prudent(e)

**cave** [keɪv] *n* caverne *f*, grotte *f*; **cave in** *vi* (*roof etc*) s'effondrer
**caviar(e)** [ˈkævɪɑː<sup>r</sup>] *n* caviar *m*
**cavity** [ˈkævɪtɪ] *n* cavité *f*; (*Med*) carie *f*
**cc** *abbr* (= *cubic centimetre*) cm³; (*on letter etc*) = **carbon copy**
**CCTV** *n abbr* = **closed-circuit television**
**CD** *n abbr* (= *compact disc*) CD *m*; **CD burner** *n* graveur *m* de CD; **CD player** *n* platine *f* laser; **CD-ROM** [siːdiːˈrɔm] *n abbr* (= *compact disc read-only memory*) CD-ROM *m inv*; **CD writer** *n* graveur *m* de CD
**cease** [siːs] *vt, vi* cesser; **ceasefire** *n* cessez-le-feu *m*
**cedar** [ˈsiːdə<sup>r</sup>] *n* cèdre *m*
**ceilidh** [ˈkeɪlɪ] *n* bal *m* folklorique écossais *or* irlandais
**ceiling** [ˈsiːlɪŋ] *n* (*also fig*) plafond *m*
**celebrate** [ˈsɛlɪbreɪt] *vt, vi* célébrer; **celebration** [sɛlɪˈbreɪʃən] *n* célébration *f*
**celebrity** [sɪˈlɛbrɪtɪ] *n* célébrité *f*
**celery** [ˈsɛlərɪ] *n* céleri *m* (*en branches*)
**cell** [sɛl] *n* (*gen*) cellule *f*; (*Elec*) élément *m* (*de pile*)
**cellar** [ˈsɛlə<sup>r</sup>] *n* cave *f*
**cello** [ˈtʃɛləu] *n* violoncelle *m*
**Cellophane®** [ˈsɛləfeɪn] *n* cellophane® *f*
**cellphone** [ˈsɛlfəun] *n* téléphone *m* cellulaire
**Celsius** [ˈsɛlsɪəs] *adj* Celsius *inv*
**Celtic** [ˈkɛltɪk, ˈsɛltɪk] *adj* celte, celtique
**cement** [səˈmɛnt] *n* ciment *m*
**cemetery** [ˈsɛmɪtrɪ] *n* cimetière *m*
**censor** [ˈsɛnsə<sup>r</sup>] *n* censeur *m* ▷ *vt* censurer; **censorship** *n* censure *f*
**census** [ˈsɛnsəs] *n* recensement *m*
**cent** [sɛnt] *n* (*unit of dollar, euro*) cent *m* (= *un centième du dollar, de l'euro*); *see also* **per**
**centenary** [sɛnˈtiːnərɪ] (*US* **centennial**) [sɛnˈtɛnɪəl] *n* centenaire *m*
**center** [ˈsɛntə<sup>r</sup>] (*US*) = **centre**
**centi…** [sɛntɪ] *prefix*: **centigrade** *adj* centigrade; **centimetre** (*US*

**centimeter**) n centimètre m;
**centipede** ['sɛntɪpiːd] n mille-
pattes m inv
**central** ['sɛntrəl] adj central(e);
**Central America** n Amérique centrale;
**central heating** n chauffage central;
**central reservation** n (BRIT Aut) terre-
plein central
**centre** (US **center**) ['sɛntə'] n centre m
▷ vt centrer; **centre-forward** n (Sport)
avant-centre m; **centre-half** n (Sport)
demi-centre m
**century** ['sɛntjuri] n siècle m; **in the
twentieth ~** au vingtième siècle
**CEO** n abbr (US) = **chief executive
officer**
**ceramic** [sɪ'ræmɪk] adj céramique
**cereal** ['siːriəl] n céréale f
**ceremony** ['sɛrɪmənɪ] n cérémonie f;
**to stand on ~** faire des façons
**certain** ['səːtən] adj certain(e);
**to make ~ of** s'assurer de; **for ~**
certainement, sûrement; **certainly**
adv certainement; **certainty** n
certitude f
**certificate** [sə'tɪfɪkɪt] n certificat m
**certify** ['səːtɪfaɪ] vt certifier; (award
diploma to) conférer un diplôme etc
à; (declare insane) déclarer malade
mental(e)
**cf.** abbr (= compare) cf., voir
**CFC** n abbr (= chlorofluorocarbon) CFC m
**chain** [tʃeɪn] n (gen) chaîne f ▷ vt
(also: ~ **up**) enchaîner, attacher (avec
une chaîne); **chain-smoke** vi fumer
cigarette des façons
**chair** [tʃeə'] n chaise f; (armchair)
fauteuil m; (of university) chaire f; (of
meeting) présidence f ▷ vt (meeting)
présider; **chairlift** n télésiège m;
**chairman** n président m; **chairperson**
n président(e); **chairwoman** n
présidente f
**chalet** ['ʃæleɪ] n chalet m
**chalk** [tʃɔːk] n craie f; **chalkboard** (US)
n tableau noir
**challenge** ['tʃælɪndʒ] n défi m ▷ vt
défier; (statement, right) mettre en

question, contester; **to ~ sb to do**
mettre qn au défi de faire; **challenging**
adj (task, career) qui représente un défi
or une gageure; (tone, look) de défi,
provocateur(-trice)
**chamber** ['tʃeɪmbə'] n chambre f; (BRIT
Law: gen pl) cabinet m; **~ of commerce**
chambre de commerce; **chambermaid**
n femme f de chambre
**champagne** [ʃæm'peɪn] n
champagne m
**champion** ['tʃæmpɪən] n (also of cause)
champion(ne); **championship** n
championnat m
**chance** [tʃɑːns] n (luck) hasard m;
(opportunity) occasion f, possibilité f;
(hope, likelihood) chance f; (risk) risque
m ▷ vt (risk) risquer ▷ adj fortuit(e), de
hasard; **to take a ~** prendre un risque;
**by ~** par hasard; **to ~ it** risquer le coup,
essayer
**chancellor** ['tʃɑːnsələ'] n chancelier m;
**Chancellor of the Exchequer**
[-ɪks'tʃɛkə'] (BRIT) n chancelier m de
l'Échiquier
**chandelier** [ʃændə'lɪə'] n lustre m
**change** [tʃeɪndʒ] vt (alter, replace:
Comm: money) changer; (switch,
substitute: hands, trains, clothes,
one's name etc) changer de ▷ vi (gen)
changer; (change clothes) se changer;
(be transformed): **to ~ into** se changer
or transformer en ▷ n changement
m; (money) monnaie f; **to ~ gear** (Aut)
changer de vitesse; **to ~ one's mind**
changer d'avis; **a ~ of clothes** des
vêtements de rechange; **for a ~** pour
changer; **do you have ~ for £10?** vous
avez la monnaie de 10 livres?; **where
can I ~ some money?** où est-ce que je
peux changer de l'argent?; **keep the
~!** gardez la monnaie!; **change over**
vi (swap) échanger; (change: drivers
etc) changer; (change sides: players etc)
changer de côté; **to ~ over from sth to
sth** passer de qch à qch; **changeable**
adj (weather) variable; **change
machine** n distributeur m de monnaie;

**changing room** n (BRIT: in shop) salon m d'essayage; (: Sport) vestiaire m

**channel** ['tʃænl] n (TV) chaîne f; (waveband, groove, fig: medium) canal m; (of river, sea) chenal m ▷ vt canaliser; **the (English) C~** la Manche; **Channel Islands** npl: **the Channel Islands** les îles fpl Anglo-Normandes; **Channel Tunnel** n: **the Channel Tunnel** le tunnel sous la Manche

**chant** [tʃɑːnt] n chant m; (Rel) psalmodie f ▷ vt chanter, scander

**chaos** ['keɪɔs] n chaos m

**chaotic** [keɪ'ɔtɪk] adj chaotique

**chap** [tʃæp] n (BRIT inf: man) type m

**chapel** ['tʃæpl] n chapelle f

**chapped** [tʃæpt] adj (skin, lips) gercé(e)

**chapter** ['tʃæptər] n chapitre m

**character** ['kærɪktər] n caractère m; (in novel, film) personnage m; (eccentric person) numéro m, phénomène m; **characteristic** ['kærɪktə'rɪstɪk] adj, n caractéristique (f); **characterize** ['kærɪktəraɪz] vt caractériser

**charcoal** ['tʃɑːkəul] n charbon m de bois; (Art) charbon

**charge** [tʃɑːdʒ] n (accusation) accusation f; (Law) inculpation f; (cost) prix (demandé) ▷ vt (gun, battery, Mil: enemy) charger; (customer, sum) faire payer ▷ vi foncer; **charges** npl (costs) frais mpl; (BRIT Tel): **to reverse the ~s** téléphoner en PCV; **to take ~ of** se charger de; **to be in ~ of** être responsable de, s'occuper de; **to ~ sb (with)** (Law) inculper qn (de); **charge card** n carte f de client (émise par un grand magasin); **charger** n (also: **battery charger**) chargeur m

**charismatic** [kærɪz'mætɪk] adj charismatique

**charity** ['tʃærɪtɪ] n charité f; (organization) institution f charitable or de bienfaisance, œuvre f (de charité); **charity shop** n (BRIT) boutique vendant des articles d'occasion au profit d'une organisation caritative

**charm** [tʃɑːm] n charme m; (on bracelet)

breloque f ▷ vt charmer, enchanter; **charming** adj charmant(e)

**chart** [tʃɑːt] n tableau m, diagramme m; graphique m; (map) carte marine ▷ vt dresser or établir la carte de; (sales, progress) établir la courbe de; **charts** npl (Mus) hit-parade m; **to be in the ~s** (record, pop group) figurer au hit-parade

**charter** ['tʃɑːtər] vt (plane) affréter ▷ n (document) charte f; **chartered accountant** n (BRIT) expert-comptable m; **charter flight** n charter m

**chase** [tʃeɪs] vt poursuivre, pourchasser; (also: **~ away**) chasser ▷ n poursuite f, chasse f

**chat** [tʃæt] vi (also: **have a ~**) bavarder, causer; (on Internet) chatter ▷ n conversation f; **chat up** vt (BRIT inf: girl) baratiner; **chat room** n (Internet) forum m de discussion; **chat show** n (BRIT) talk-show m

**chatter** ['tʃætər] vi (person) bavarder, papoter ▷ n bavardage m, papotage m; **my teeth are ~ing** je claque des dents

**chauffeur** ['ʃəufər] n chauffeur m (de maître)

**chauvinist** ['ʃəuvɪnɪst] n (also: **male ~**) phallocrate m, macho m; (nationalist) chauvin(e)

**cheap** [tʃiːp] adj bon marché inv, pas cher (chère); (reduced: ticket) à prix réduit; (: fare) réduit(e); (joke) facile, d'un goût douteux; (poor quality) à bon marché, de qualité médiocre ▷ adv à bon marché, pour pas cher; **can you recommend a ~ hotel/restaurant, please?** pourriez-vous m'indiquer un hôtel/restaurant bon marché?; **cheap day return** n billet m d'aller et retour réduit (valable pour la journée); **cheaply** adv à bon marché, à bon compte

**cheat** [tʃiːt] vi tricher; (in exam) copier ▷ vt tromper, duper; (rob): **to ~ sb out of sth** escroquer qch à qn ▷ n tricheur(-euse) m/f; escroc m; **cheat on** vt fus tromper

**Chechnya** [tʃɪtʃ'njɑː] n Tchétchénie f

**check** [tʃɛk] vt vérifier; (*passport, ticket*) contrôler; (*halt*) enrayer; (*restrain*) maîtriser ▷ vi (*official etc*) se renseigner ▷ n vérification f; contrôle m; (*curb*) frein m; (BRIT: *bill*) addition f; (US) = **cheque**; (*pattern: gen pl*) carreaux mpl; **to ~ with sb** demander à qn; **check in** vi (*in hotel*) remplir sa fiche (d'hôtel); (*at airport*) se présenter à l'enregistrement ▷ vt (*luggage*) (faire) enregistrer; **check off** vt (*tick off*) cocher; **check out** vi (*in hotel*) régler sa note ▷ vt (*investigate: story*) vérifier; **check up** vi: **to ~ up (on sth)** vérifier (qch); **to ~ up on sb** se renseigner sur le compte de qn; **checkbook** (US) = **chequebook**; **checked** adj (*pattern, cloth*) à carreaux; **checkers** n (US) jeu m de dames; **check-in** n (also: **check-in desk**: *at airport*) enregistrement m; **checking account** n (US) compte courant; **checklist** n liste f de contrôle; **checkmate** n échec et mat m; **checkout** n (*in supermarket*) caisse f; **checkpoint** n contrôle m; **checkroom** (US) n consigne f; **checkup** n (*Med*) examen médical, check-up m

**cheddar** [ˈtʃɛdəʳ] n (also: **~ cheese**) cheddar m

**cheek** [tʃiːk] n joue f; (*impudence*) toupet m, culot m; **what a ~!** quel toupet!; **cheekbone** n pommette f; **cheeky** adj effronté(e), culotté(e)

**cheer** [tʃɪəʳ] vt acclamer, applaudir; (*gladden*) réjouir, réconforter ▷ vi applaudir ▷ n (*gen pl*) acclamations fpl, applaudissements mpl; bravos mpl, hourras mpl; **~s!** à la vôtre!; **cheer up** vi se dérider, reprendre courage ▷ vt remonter le moral à or de, dérider, égayer; **cheerful** adj gai(e), joyeux(-euse)

**cheerio** [tʃɪərɪˈəu] excl (BRIT) salut!, au revoir!

**cheerleader** [ˈtʃɪəliːdəʳ] n membre d'un groupe de majorettes qui chantent et dansent pour soutenir leur équipe pendant les matchs de football américain

**cheese** [tʃiːz] n fromage m; **cheeseburger** n cheeseburger m; **cheesecake** n tarte f au fromage

**chef** [ʃɛf] n chef (cuisinier)

**chemical** [ˈkɛmɪkl] adj chimique ▷ n produit m chimique

**chemist** [ˈkɛmɪst] n (BRIT: *pharmacist*) pharmacien(ne); (*scientist*) chimiste m/f; **chemistry** n chimie f; **chemist's (shop)** n (BRIT) pharmacie f

**cheque** (US **check**) [tʃɛk] n chèque m; **chequebook** (US **checkbook**) n chéquier m, carnet m de chèques; **cheque card** n (BRIT) carte f (d'identité) bancaire

**cherry** [ˈtʃɛrɪ] n cerise f; (also: **~ tree**) cerisier m

**chess** [tʃɛs] n échecs mpl

**chest** [tʃɛst] n poitrine f; (*box*) coffre m, caisse f

**chestnut** [ˈtʃɛsnʌt] n châtaigne f; (also: **~ tree**) châtaignier m

**chest of drawers** n commode f

**chew** [tʃuː] vt mâcher; **chewing gum** n chewing-gum m

**chic** [ʃiːk] adj chic inv, élégant(e)

**chick** [tʃɪk] n poussin m; (*inf*) pépée f

**chicken** [ˈtʃɪkɪn] n poulet m; (*inf: coward*) poule mouillée; **chicken out** vi (*inf*) se dégonfler; **chickenpox** n varicelle f

**chickpea** [ˈtʃɪkpiː] n pois m chiche

**chief** [tʃiːf] n chef m ▷ adj principal(e); **chief executive** (US **chief executive officer**) n directeur(-trice) général(e); **chiefly** adv principalement, surtout

**child** (pl **~ren**) [tʃaɪld, ˈtʃɪldrən] n enfant m/f; **child abuse** n maltraitance f d'enfants; (*sexual*) abus mpl sexuels sur des enfants; **child benefit** n (BRIT) ≈ allocations familiales; **childbirth** n accouchement m; **child-care** n (*for working parents*) garde f des enfants (*pour les parents qui travaillent*); **childhood** n enfance f; **childish** adj puéril(e), enfantin(e); **child minder** n (BRIT) garde f d'enfants; **children** [ˈtʃɪldrən] npl of **child**

**Chile** ['tʃɪlɪ] n Chili m
**chill** [tʃɪl] n (of water) froid m; (of air) fraîcheur f; (Med) refroidissement m, coup m de froid ▷ vt (person) faire frissonner; (Culin) mettre au frais, rafraîchir; **chill out** vi (inf: esp US) se relaxer
**chil(l)i** ['tʃɪlɪ] n piment m (rouge)
**chilly** ['tʃɪlɪ] adj froid(e), glacé(e); (sensitive to cold) frileux(-euse)
**chimney** ['tʃɪmnɪ] n cheminée f
**chimpanzee** [tʃɪmpæn'ziː] n chimpanzé m
**chin** [tʃɪn] n menton m
**China** ['tʃaɪnə] n Chine f
**china** ['tʃaɪnə] n (material) porcelaine f; (crockery) (vaisselle f en) porcelaine f
**Chinese** [tʃaɪ'niːz] adj chinois(e) ▷ n (pl inv) Chinois(e); (Ling) chinois m
**chip** [tʃɪp] n (gen pl: Culin: BRIT) frite f; (: US: also: **potato ~**) chip m; (of wood) copeau m; (of glass, stone) éclat m; (also: **micro~**) puce f; (in gambling) fiche f ▷ vt (cup, plate) ébrécher; **chip shop** n (BRIT) friterie f

**chiropodist** [kɪ'rɔpədɪst] n (BRIT) pédicure m/f
**chisel** ['tʃɪzl] n ciseau m
**chives** [tʃaɪvz] npl ciboulette f, civette f
**chlorine** ['klɔːriːn] n chlore m

**choc-ice** ['tʃɔkaɪs] n (BRIT) esquimau® m
**chocolate** ['tʃɔklɪt] n chocolat m
**choice** [tʃɔɪs] n choix m ▷ adj de choix
**choir** ['kwaɪə'] n chœur m, chorale f
**choke** [tʃəuk] vi étouffer ▷ vt étrangler; étouffer; (block) boucher, obstruer ▷ n (Aut) starter m
**cholesterol** [kə'lɛstərɔl] n cholestérol m
**choose** (pt **chose**, pp **chosen**) [tʃuːz, tʃəuz, 'tʃəuzn] vt choisir; **to ~ to do** décider de faire, juger bon de faire
**chop** [tʃɔp] vt (wood) couper (à la hache); (Culin: also: **~ up**) couper (fin), émincer, hacher (en morceaux) ▷ n (Culin) côtelette f; **chop down** vt (tree) abattre; **chop off** vt trancher; **chopsticks** ['tʃɔpstɪks] npl baguettes fpl
**chord** [kɔːd] n (Mus) accord m
**chore** [tʃɔː'] n travail m de routine; **household ~s** travaux mpl du ménage
**chorus** ['kɔːrəs] n chœur m; (repeated part of song, also fig) refrain m
**chose** [tʃəuz] pt of **choose**
**chosen** ['tʃəuzn] pp of **choose**
**Christ** [kraɪst] n Christ m
**christen** ['krɪsn] vt baptiser; **christening** n baptême m
**Christian** ['krɪstɪən] adj, n chrétien(ne); **Christianity** [krɪstɪ'ænɪtɪ] n christianisme m; **Christian name** n prénom m
**Christmas** ['krɪsməs] n Noël m or f; **happy** or **merry ~!** joyeux Noël!; **Christmas card** n carte f de Noël; **Christmas carol** n chant m de Noël; **Christmas Day** n le jour de Noël; **Christmas Eve** n la veille de Noël; la nuit de Noël; **Christmas pudding** n (esp BRIT) Christmas m pudding; **Christmas tree** n arbre m de Noël
**chrome** [krəum] n chrome m
**chronic** ['krɔnɪk] adj chronique
**chrysanthemum** [krɪ'sænθəməm] n chrysanthème m
**chubby** ['tʃʌbɪ] adj potelé(e),

**chuck** [tʃʌk] vt (inf) lancer, jeter; (BRIT: also: **~ up**: job) lâcher; **chuck out** vt (inf: person) flanquer dehors or à la porte; (: rubbish etc) jeter

**chuckle** ['tʃʌkl] vi glousser

**chum** [tʃʌm] n copain (copine)

**chunk** [tʃʌŋk] n gros morceau

**church** [tʃɜːtʃ] n église f; **churchyard** n cimetière m

**churn** [tʃɜːn] n (for butter) baratte f; (also: **milk ~**) (grand) bidon à lait

**chute** [ʃuːt] n goulotte f; (also: **rubbish ~**) vide-ordures m inv; (BRIT: children's slide) toboggan m

**chutney** ['tʃʌtnɪ] n chutney m

**CIA** n abbr (= Central Intelligence Agency) CIA f

**CID** n abbr (= Criminal Investigation Department) ≈ P.J. f

**cider** ['saɪdə<sup>r</sup>] n cidre m

**cigar** [sɪ'gɑː<sup>r</sup>] n cigare m

**cigarette** [sɪgə'rɛt] n cigarette f; **cigarette lighter** n briquet m

**cinema** ['sɪnəmə] n cinéma m

**cinnamon** ['sɪnəmən] n cannelle f

**circle** ['sɜːkl] n cercle m; (in cinema) balcon m ⊳ vi faire ou décrire des cercles ⊳ vt (surround) entourer, encercler; (move round) faire le tour de, tourner autour de

**circuit** ['sɜːkɪt] n circuit m; (lap) tour m

**circular** ['sɜːkjulə<sup>r</sup>] adj circulaire ⊳ n circulaire f; (as advertisement) prospectus m

**circulate** ['sɜːkjuleɪt] vi circuler ⊳ vt faire circuler; **circulation** [sɜːkju'leɪʃən] n circulation f; (of newspaper) tirage m

**circumstances** ['sɜːkəmstənsɪz] npl circonstances fpl; (financial condition) moyens mpl, situation financière

**circus** ['sɜːkəs] n cirque m

**cite** [saɪt] vt citer

**citizen** ['sɪtɪzn] n (Pol) citoyen(ne); (resident): **the ~s of this town** les habitants de cette ville; **citizenship** n citoyenneté f; (BRIT: Scol) ≈ éducation f civique

**citrus fruits** ['sɪtrəs-] npl agrumes mpl

**city** ['sɪtɪ] n (grande) ville f; **the C~** la Cité de Londres (centre des affaires); **city centre** n centre ville m; **city technology college** n (BRIT) établissement m d'enseignement technologique (situé dans un quartier défavorisé)

**civic** ['sɪvɪk] adj civique; (authorities) municipal(e)

**civil** ['sɪvɪl] adj civil(e); (polite) poli(e), civil(e); **civilian** [sɪ'vɪlɪən] adj, n civil(e)

**civilization** [sɪvɪlaɪ'zeɪʃən] n civilisation f

**civilized** ['sɪvɪlaɪzd] adj civilisé(e); (fig) où règnent les bonnes manières

**civil**: **civil law** n code civil; (study) droit civil; **civil rights** npl droits mpl civiques; **civil servant** n fonctionnaire m/f; **Civil Service** n fonction publique, administration f; **civil war** n guerre civile

**CJD** n abbr (= Creutzfeldt-Jakob disease) MCJ f

**claim** [kleɪm] vt (rights etc) revendiquer; (compensation) réclamer; (assert) déclarer, prétendre ⊳ vi (for insurance) faire une déclaration de sinistre ⊳ n revendication f; prétention f; (right) droit m; **(insurance) ~** demande f d'indemnisation, déclaration f de sinistre; **claim form** n (gen) formulaire m de demande

**clam** [klæm] n palourde f

**clamp** [klæmp] n crampon m; (on workbench) valet m; (on car) sabot m de Denver ⊳ vt attacher; (car) mettre un sabot à; **clamp down on** vt fus sévir contre, prendre des mesures draconiennes à l'égard de

**clan** [klæn] n clan m

**clap** [klæp] vi applaudir

**claret** ['klærət] n (vin m de) bordeaux m (rouge)

**clarify** ['klærɪfaɪ] vt clarifier

**clarinet** [klærɪ'nɛt] n clarinette f

**clarity** ['klærɪtɪ] n clarté f

**clash** [klæʃ] n (*sound*) choc m, fracas m; (*with police*) affrontement m; (*fig*) conflit m ▷ vi se heurter; être or entrer en conflit; (*colours*) jurer; (*dates, events*) tomber en même temps

**clasp** [klɑːsp] n (*of necklace, bag*) fermoir m ▷ vt serrer, étreindre

**class** [klɑːs] n (*gen*) classe f; (*group, category*) catégorie f ▷ vt classer, classifier

**classic** ['klæsɪk] adj classique ▷ n (*author, work*) classique m; **classical** adj classique

**classification** [klæsɪfɪ'keɪʃən] n classification f

**classify** ['klæsɪfaɪ] vt classifier, classer

**classmate** ['klɑːsmeɪt] n camarade m/f de classe

**classroom** ['klɑːsrum] n (*salle f de*) classe f; **classroom assistant** n assistant(-e) d'éducation

**classy** ['klɑːsɪ] (*inf*) adj classe (*inf*)

**clatter** ['klætər] n cliquetis m ▷ vi cliqueter

**clause** [klɔːz] n clause f; (*Ling*) proposition f

**claustrophobic** [klɔːstrə'fəubɪk] adj (*person*) claustrophobe; (*place*) où l'on se sent claustrophobe

**claw** [klɔː] n griffe f; (*of bird of prey*) serre f; (*of lobster*) pince f

**clay** [kleɪ] n argile f

**clean** [kliːn] adj propre; (*clear, smooth*) net(te); (*record, reputation*) sans tache; (*joke, story*) correct(e) ▷ vt nettoyer; **clean up** vt nettoyer; (*fig*) remettre de l'ordre dans; **cleaner** n (*person*) nettoyeur(-euse), femme f de ménage; (*product*) détachant m; **cleaner's** n (*also:* **dry cleaner's**) teinturier m; **cleaning** n nettoyage m

**cleanser** ['klɛnzər] n (*for face*) démaquillant m

**clear** [klɪər] adj clair(e); (*glass, plastic*) transparent(e); (*road, way*) libre, dégagé(e); (*profit, majority*) net(te); (*conscience*) tranquille; (*skin*) frais (fraîche); (*sky*) dégagé(e) ▷ vt (*road*) dégager, déblayer; (*table*) débarrasser; (*room etc: of people*) faire évacuer; (*cheque*) compenser; (*Law: suspect*) innocenter; (*obstacle*) franchir or sauter sans heurter ▷ vi (*weather*) s'éclaircir; (*fog*) se dissiper ▷ adv: **~ of** à distance de, à l'écart de; **to ~ the table** débarrasser la table, desservir; **clear away** vt (*things, clothes etc*) enlever, retirer; **to ~ away the dishes** débarrasser la table; **clear up** vt ranger, mettre en ordre; (*mystery*) éclaircir, résoudre; **clearance** n (*removal*) déblayage m; (*permission*) autorisation f; **clear-cut** adj précis(e), nettement défini(e); **clearing** n (*in forest*) clairière f; **clearly** adv clairement; (*obviously*) de toute évidence; **clearway** n (*BRIT*) route f à stationnement interdit

**clench** [klɛntʃ] vt serrer

**clergy** ['klɜːdʒɪ] n clergé m

**clerk** [klɑːk, US klɜːrk] n (*BRIT*) employé(e) de bureau; (*US: salesman/woman*) vendeur(-euse)

**clever** ['klɛvər] adj (*intelligent*) intelligent(e); (*skilful*) habile, adroit(e); (*device, arrangement*) ingénieux(-euse), astucieux(-euse)

**cliché** ['kliːʃeɪ] n cliché m

**click** [klɪk] vi (*Comput*) cliquer ▷ vt: **to ~ one's tongue** faire claquer sa langue; **to ~ one's heels** claquer des talons; **to ~ on an icon** cliquer sur une icône

**client** ['klaɪənt] n client(e)

**cliff** [klɪf] n falaise f

**climate** ['klaɪmɪt] n climat m; **climate change** n changement m climatique

**climax** ['klaɪmæks] n apogée m, point culminant; (*sexual*) orgasme m

**climb** [klaɪm] vi grimper, monter; (*plane*) prendre de l'altitude ▷ vt (*stairs*) monter; (*mountain*) escalader; (*tree*) grimper à ▷ n montée f, escalade f; **to ~ over a wall** passer par dessus un mur; **climb down** vi (re)descendre; (*BRIT fig*) rabattre de ses prétentions; **climber** n (*also:* **rock climber**) grimpeur(-euse), varappeur(-euse); (*plant*) plante grimpante; **climbing** *n* (*also:* **rock climbing**) escalade *f*, varappe *f*

**clinch** [klɪntʃ] *vt* (*deal*) conclure, sceller

**cling** (*pt, pp* **clung**) [klɪŋ, klʌŋ] *vi*: **to ~ (to)** se cramponner (à), s'accrocher (à); (*clothes*) coller (à)

**Clingfilm®** ['klɪŋfɪlm] *n* film *m* alimentaire

**clinic** ['klɪnɪk] *n* clinique *f*; centre médical

**clip** [klɪp] *n* (*for hair*) barrette *f*; (*also:* **paper ~**) trombone *m*; (*TV, Cinema*) clip *m* ▷ *vt* (*also:* **~ together**: *papers*) attacher; (*hair, nails*) couper; (*hedge*) tailler; **clipping** *n* (*from newspaper*) coupure *f* de journal

**cloak** [kləuk] *n* grande cape ▷ *vt* (*fig*) masquer, cacher; **cloakroom** *n* (*for coats etc*) vestiaire *m*; (*BRIT:* W.C.) toilettes *fpl*

**clock** [klɔk] *n* (*large*) horloge *f*; (*small*) pendule *f*; **clock in** *or* **on** (*BRIT*) *vi* (*with card*) pointer (en arrivant); (*start work*) commencer à travailler; **clock off** *or* **out** (*BRIT*) *vi* (*with card*) pointer (en partant); (*leave work*) quitter le travail; **clockwise** *adv* dans le sens des aiguilles d'une montre; **clockwork** *n* rouages *mpl*, mécanisme *m*; (*of clock*) mouvement *m* (d'horlogerie) ▷ *adj* (*toy, train*) mécanique

**clog** [klɔg] *n* sabot *m* ▷ *vt* boucher, encrasser ▷ *vi* (*also:* **~ up**) se boucher, s'encrasser

**clone** [kləun] *n* clone *m* ▷ *vt* cloner

**close¹** [kləus] *adj* (*near*): **~ (to)** près (de), proche (de); (*contact, link, watch*) étroit(e); (*examination*) attentif(-ive), minutieux(-euse); (*contest*) très serré(e); (*weather*) lourd(e), étouffant(e) ▷ *adv* près, à proximité; **~ to** *prep* près de; **~ by, ~ at hand** *adj, adv* tout(e) près; **a ~ friend** un ami intime; **to have a ~ shave** (*fig*) l'échapper belle

**close²** [kləuz] *vt* fermer ▷ *vi* (*shop etc*) fermer; (*lid, door etc*) se fermer; (*end*) se terminer, se conclure ▷ *n* (*end*)

conclusion *f*; **what time do you ~?** à quelle heure fermez-vous?; **close down** *vi* fermer (définitivement); **closed** *adj* (*shop etc*) fermé(e)

**closely** ['kləuslɪ] *adv* (*examine, watch*) de près

**closet** ['klɔzɪt] *n* (*cupboard*) placard *m*, réduit *m*

**close-up** ['kləusʌp] *n* gros plan

**closing time** *n* heure *f* de fermeture

**closure** ['kləuʒəʳ] *n* fermeture *f*

**clot** [klɔt] *n* (*of blood, milk*) caillot *m*; (*inf: person*) ballot *m* ▷ *vi* (: *external bleeding*) se coaguler

**cloth** [klɔθ] *n* (*material*) tissu *m*, étoffe *f*; (*BRIT: also:* **tea ~**) torchon *m*; lavette *f*; (*also:* **table~**) nappe *f*

**clothes** [kləuðz] *npl* vêtements *mpl*, habits *mpl*; **clothes line** *n* corde *f* (à linge); **clothes peg** (*us* **clothes pin**) *n* pince *f* à linge

**clothing** ['kləuðɪŋ] *n* = **clothes**

**cloud** [klaud] *n* nuage *m*; **cloud over** *vi* se couvrir; (*fig*) s'assombrir; **cloudy** *adj* nuageux(-euse), couvert(e); (*liquid*) trouble

**clove** [kləuv] *n* clou *m* de girofle; **a ~ of garlic** une gousse d'ail

**clown** [klaun] *n* clown *m* ▷ *vi* (*also:* **~ about, ~ around**) faire le clown

**club** [klʌb] *n* (*society*) club *m*; (*weapon*) massue *f*, matraque *f*; (*also:* **golf ~**) club ▷ *vt* matraquer ▷ *vi*: **to ~ together** s'associer; **clubs** *npl* (*Cards*) trèfle *m*; **club class** *n* (*Aviat*) classe *f* club

**clue** [klu:] *n* indice *m*; (*in crosswords*) définition *f*; **I haven't a ~** je n'en ai pas la moindre idée

**clump** [klʌmp] *n*: **~ of trees** bouquet *m* d'arbres

**clumsy** ['klʌmzɪ] *adj* (*person*) gauche, maladroit(e); (*object*) malcommode, peu maniable

**clung** [klʌŋ] *pt, pp of* **cling**

**cluster** ['klʌstəʳ] *n* (petit) groupe; (*of flowers*) grappe *f* ▷ *vi* se rassembler

**clutch** [klʌtʃ] *n* (*Aut*) embrayage *m*; (*grasp*): **~es** étreinte *f*, prise *f* ▷ *vt* (*grasp*)

agripper; (*hold tightly*) serrer fort; (*hold on to*) se cramponner à
**cm** *abbr* (= *centimetre*) cm
**Co.** *abbr* = **company, county**
**c/o** *abbr* (= *care of*) c/o, aux bons soins de
**coach** [kəutʃ] *n* (*bus*) autocar *m*; (*horse-drawn*) diligence *f*; (*of train*) voiture *f*, wagon *m*; (*Sport: trainer*) entraîneur(-euse) (*school: tutor*) répétiteur(-trice) ▷ *vt* (*Sport*) entraîner; (*student*) donner des leçons particulières à; **coach station** (*BRIT*) *n* gare routière; **coach trip** *n* excursion *f* en car
**coal** [kəul] *n* charbon *m*
**coalition** [kəuə'lɪʃən] *n* coalition *f*
**coarse** [kɔːs] *adj* grossier(-ère), rude; (*vulgar*) vulgaire
**coast** [kəust] *n* côte *f* ▷ *vi* (*car, cycle*) descendre en roue libre; **coastal** *adj* côtier(-ère); **coastguard** *n* garde-côte *m*; **coastline** *n* côte *f*, littoral *m*
**coat** [kəut] *n* manteau *m*; (*of animal*) pelage *m*, poil *m*; (*of paint*) couche *f* ▷ *vt* couvrir, enduire; **coat hanger** *n* cintre *m*; **coating** *n* couche *f*, enduit *m*
**coax** [kəuks] *vt* persuader par des cajoleries
**cob** [kɔb] *n* see **corn**
**cobbled** ['kɔbld] *adj* pavé(e)
**cobweb** ['kɔbwɛb] *n* toile *f* d'araignée
**cocaine** [kə'keɪn] *n* cocaïne *f*
**cock** [kɔk] *n* (*rooster*) coq *m*; (*male bird*) mâle *m* ▷ *vt* (*gun*) armer; **cockerel** *n* jeune coq *m*
**cockney** ['kɔknɪ] *n* cockney *m/f* (*habitant des quartiers populaires de l'East End de Londres*), ≈ faubourien(ne)
**cockpit** ['kɔkpɪt] *n* (*in aircraft*) poste *m* de pilotage, cockpit *m*
**cockroach** ['kɔkrəutʃ] *n* cafard *m*, cancrelat *m*
**cocktail** ['kɔkteɪl] *n* cocktail *m*
**cocoa** ['kəukəu] *n* cacao *m*
**coconut** ['kəukənʌt] *n* noix *f* de coco
**C.O.D.** *abbr* = **cash on delivery**
**cod** [kɔd] *n* morue fraîche, cabillaud *m*
**code** [kəud] *n* code *m*; (*Tel: area code*)

indicatif *m*
**coeducational** ['kəuɛdju'keɪʃənl] *adj* mixte
**coffee** ['kɔfɪ] *n* café *m*; **coffee bar** *n* (*BRIT*) café *m*; **coffee bean** *n* grain *m* de café; **coffee break** *n* pause-café *f*; **coffee maker** *n* cafetière *f*; **coffeepot** *n* cafetière *f*; **coffee shop** *n* café *m*; **coffee table** *n* (*petite*) table basse
**coffin** ['kɔfɪn] *n* cercueil *m*
**cog** [kɔg] *n* (*wheel*) roue dentée; (*tooth*) dent *f* (d'engrenage)
**cognac** ['kɔnjæk] *n* cognac *m*
**coherent** [kəu'hɪərənt] *adj* cohérent(e)
**coil** [kɔɪl] *n* rouleau *m*, bobine *f*; (*contraceptive*) stérilet *m* ▷ *vt* enrouler
**coin** [kɔɪn] *n* pièce *f* (de monnaie) ▷ *vt* (*word*) inventer
**coincide** [kəuɪn'saɪd] *vi* coïncider; **coincidence** [kəu'ɪnsɪdəns] *n* coïncidence *f*
**Coke®** [kəuk] *n* coca *m*
**coke** [kəuk] *n* (*coal*) coke *m*
**colander** ['kɔləndə<sup>r</sup>] *n* passoire *f* (à légumes)
**cold** [kəuld] *adj* froid(e) ▷ *n* froid *m*; (*Med*) rhume *m*; **it's ~** il fait froid; **to be ~** (*person*) avoir froid; **to catch a ~** s'enrhumer, attraper un rhume; **in ~ blood** de sang-froid; **cold cuts** (*US*) *npl* viandes froides; **cold sore** *n* bouton *m* de fièvre
**coleslaw** ['kəulslɔː] *n* sorte de salade de chou crue
**colic** ['kɔlɪk] *n* colique(s) *f(pl)*
**collaborate** [kə'læbəreɪt] *vi* collaborer
**collapse** [kə'læps] *vi* s'effondrer, s'écrouler; (*Med*) avoir un malaise ▷ *n* effondrement *m*, écroulement *m*; (*of government*) chute *f*
**collar** ['kɔlə<sup>r</sup>] *n* (*of coat, shirt*) col *m*; (*for dog*) collier *m*; **collarbone** *n* clavicule *f*
**colleague** ['kɔliːg] *n* collègue *m/f*
**collect** [kə'lɛkt] *vt* rassembler; (*pick up*) ramasser; (*as a hobby*) collectionner; (*BRIT: call for*) (passer) prendre; (*mail*) faire la levée de, ramasser; (*money owed*)

encaisser; (*donations, subscriptions*) recueillir ▷ vi (*people*) se rassembler; (*dust, dirt*) s'amasser; **to call ~** (*US Tel*) téléphoner en PCV; **collection** [kə'lɛkʃən] n collection f; (*of mail*) levée f; (*for money*) collecte f, quête f; **collective** [kə'lɛktɪv] adj collectif(-ive); **collector** n collectionneur m

**college** ['kɔlɪdʒ] n collège m; (*of technology, agriculture etc*) institut m

**collide** [kə'laɪd] vi: **to ~ (with)** entrer en collision (avec)

**collision** [kə'lɪʒən] n collision f, heurt m

**cologne** [kə'ləun] n (*also:* **eau de ~**) eau f de cologne

**colon** ['kəulən] n (*sign*) deux-points mpl; (*Med*) côlon m

**colonel** ['kə:nl] n colonel m

**colonial** [kə'ləunɪəl] adj colonial(e)

**colony** ['kɔlənɪ] n colonie f

**colour** etc (*US* **color** etc) ['kʌləʳ] n couleur f ▷ vt colorer; (*dye*) teindre; (*paint*) peindre; (*with crayons*) colorier; (*news*) fausser, exagérer ▷ vi (*blush*) rougir; **I'd like a different ~** je le voudrais dans un autre coloris; **colour in** vt colorier; **colour-blind** adj daltonien(ne); **coloured** adj coloré(e); (*photo*) en couleur; **colour film** n (*for camera*) pellicule f (en) couleur; **colourful** adj coloré(e), vif (vive); (*personality*) pittoresque, haut(e) en couleurs; **colouring** n colorant m; (*complexion*) teint m; **colour television** n télévision f (en) couleur

**column** ['kɔləm] n colonne f; (*fashion column, sports column etc*) rubrique f

**coma** ['kəumə] n coma m

**comb** [kəum] n peigne m ▷ vt (*hair*) peigner; (*area*) ratisser, passer au peigne fin

**combat** ['kɔmbæt] n combat m ▷ vt combattre, lutter contre

**combination** [kɔmbɪ'neɪʃən] n (*gen*) combinaison f

**combine** vb [kəm'baɪn] ▷ vt combiner ▷ vi s'associer; (*Chem*) se combiner ▷ n ['kɔmbaɪn] (*Econ*) trust m; **to ~ sth with sth** (*one quality with another*) joindre ou allier qch à qch

**come** (*pt* **came**, *pp* **~**) [kʌm, keɪm] vi **1** (*movement towards*) venir; **to ~ running** arriver en courant; **he's ~ here to work** il est venu ici pour travailler; **~ with me** suivez-moi
**2** (*arrive*) arriver; **to ~ home** rentrer (chez soi *or* à la maison); **we've just ~ from Paris** nous arrivons de Paris
**3** (*reach*): **to ~ to** (*decision etc*) parvenir à, arriver à; **the bill came to £40** la note s'est élevée à 40 livres
**4** (*occur*): **an idea came to me** il m'est venu une idée
**5** (*be, become*): **to ~ loose/undone** se défaire/desserrer; **I've ~ to like him** j'ai fini par bien l'aimer; **come across** vt fus rencontrer par hasard, tomber sur; **come along** vi (*BRIT: pupil, work*) faire des progrès, avancer; **come back** vi revenir; **come down** vi descendre; (*prices*) baisser; (*buildings*) s'écrouler; (*: be demolished*) être démoli(e); **come from** vt fus (*source*) venir de; (*place*) venir de, être originaire de; **come in** vi entrer; (*train*) arriver; (*fashion*) entrer en vogue; (*on deal etc*) participer; **come off** vi (*button*) se détacher; (*attempt*) réussir; **come on** vi (*lights, electricity*) s'allumer; (*central heating*) se mettre en marche; (*pupil, work, project*) faire des progrès, avancer; **~ on!** viens!; allons!, allez!; **come out** vi sortir; (*sun*) se montrer; (*book*) paraître; (*stain*) s'enlever; (*strike*) cesser le travail, se mettre en grève; **come round** vi (*after faint, operation*) revenir à soi, reprendre connaissance; **come to** vi revenir à soi; **come up** vi monter; (*sun*) se lever; (*problem*) se poser; (*event*) survenir; (*in conversation*) être soulevé; **come up with** vt fus (*money*) fournir; **he came up with an idea** il a eu une idée, il a proposé quelque chose

**comeback** ['kʌmbæk] n (*Theat etc*) rentrée f

**comedian** [kə'miːdɪən] n (comic) comique m; (Theat) comédien m

**comedy** ['kɔmɪdɪ] n comédie f; (humour) comique m

**comet** ['kɔmɪt] n comète f

**comfort** ['kʌmfət] n confort m, bien-être m; (solace) consolation f, réconfort m ▷ vt consoler, réconforter; **comfortable** adj confortable; (person) à l'aise; (financially) aisé(e); (patient) dont l'état est stationnaire; **comfort station** n (US) toilettes fpl

**comic** ['kɔmɪk] adj (also: ~al) comique ▷ n (person) comique m; (BRIT: magazine: for children) magazine m de bandes dessinées or de BD; (: for adults) illustré m; **comic book** (US) n (for children) magazine m de bandes dessinées or de BD; (for adults) illustré m; **comic strip** n bande dessinée

**comma** ['kɔmə] n virgule f

**command** [kə'mɑːnd] n ordre m, commandement m; (Mil: authority) commandement m; (mastery) maîtrise f ▷ vt (troops) commander; **to ~ sb to do** donner l'ordre or commander à qn de faire; **commander** n (Mil) commandant m

**commemorate** [kə'mɛməreɪt] vt commémorer

**commence** [kə'mɛns] vt, vi commencer; **commencement** (US) n (University) remise f des diplômes

**commend** [kə'mɛnd] vt louer; (recommend) recommander

**comment** ['kɔmɛnt] n commentaire m ▷ vi: **to ~ on** faire des remarques sur; **"no ~"** "je n'ai rien à déclarer"; **commentary** ['kɔməntərɪ] n commentaire m; (Sport) reportage m (en direct); **commentator** ['kɔməntəɪtə'] n commentateur m; (Sport) reporter m

**commerce** ['kɔməːs] n commerce m

**commercial** [kə'məːʃəl] adj commercial(e) ▷ n (Radio, TV) annonce f publicitaire, spot m (publicitaire); **commercial break** n (Radio, TV) spot m (publicitaire)

**commission** [kə'mɪʃən] n (committee, fee) commission f ▷ vt (work of art) commander, charger un artiste de l'exécution de; **out of ~** (machine) hors service; **commissioner** n (Police) préfet m (de police)

**commit** [kə'mɪt] vt (act) commettre; (resources) consacrer; (to sb's care) confier (à); **to ~ o.s. (to do)** s'engager (à faire); **to ~ suicide** se suicider; **commitment** n engagement m; (obligation) responsabilité(s) (fpl)

**committee** [kə'mɪtɪ] n comité m; commission f

**commodity** [kə'mɔdɪtɪ] n produit m, marchandise f, article m

**common** ['kɔmən] adj (gen) commun(e); (usual) courant(e) ▷ n terrain communal; **commonly** adv communément, généralement; couramment; **commonplace** adj banal(e), ordinaire; **Commons** npl (BRIT Pol): **the (House of) Commons** la chambre des Communes; **common sense** n bon sens; **Commonwealth** n: **the Commonwealth** le Commonwealth

**communal** ['kɔmjuːnl] adj (life) communautaire; (for common use) commun(e)

**commune** n ['kɔmjuːn] (group) communauté f ▷ vi [kə'mjuːn]: **to ~ with** (nature) communier avec

**communicate** [kə'mjuːnɪkeɪt] vt communiquer, transmettre ▷ vi: **to ~ (with)** communiquer (avec)

**communication** [kəmjuːnɪ'keɪʃən] n communication f

**communion** [kə'mjuːnɪən] n (also: **Holy C~**) communion f

**communism** ['kɔmjunɪzəm] n communisme m; **communist** adj, n communiste m/f

**community** [kə'mjuːnɪtɪ] n communauté f; **community centre** (US **community center**) n foyer socio-éducatif, centre m de loisirs;

**community service** n ≈ travail m d'intérêt général, TIG m

**commute** [kəˈmjuːt] vi faire le trajet journalier (de son domicile à un lieu de travail assez éloigné) ▷ vt (Law) commuer; **commuter** n banlieusard(e) (qui fait un trajet journalier pour se rendre à son travail)

**compact** adj [kəmˈpækt] compact(e) ▷ n [ˈkɔmpækt] (also: **powder ~**) poudrier m; **compact disc** n disque compact; **compact disc player** n lecteur m de disques compacts

**companion** [kəmˈpænjən] n compagnon (-compagne)

**company** [ˈkʌmpənɪ] n compagnie f; **to keep sb ~** tenir compagnie à qn; **company car** n voiture f de fonction; **company director** n administrateur(-trice)

**comparable** [ˈkɔmpərəbl] adj comparable

**comparative** [kəmˈpærətɪv] adj (study) comparatif(-ive); (relative) relatif(-ive); **comparatively** adv (relatively) relativement

**compare** [kəmˈpɛər] vt: **to ~ sth/sb with** or **to** comparer qch/qn avec or à ▷ vi: **to ~ (with)** se comparer (à); être comparable (à); **comparison** [kəmˈpærɪsn] n comparaison f

**compartment** [kəmˈpɑːtmənt] n (also Rail) compartiment m; **a non-smoking ~** un compartiment non-fumeurs

**compass** [ˈkʌmpəs] n boussole f; **compasses** npl (Math) compas m

**compassion** [kəmˈpæʃən] n compassion f, humanité f

**compatible** [kəmˈpætɪbl] adj compatible

**compel** [kəmˈpɛl] vt contraindre, obliger; **compelling** adj (fig: argument) irrésistible

**compensate** [ˈkɔmpənseɪt] vt indemniser, dédommager ▷ vi: **to ~ for** compenser; **compensation** [kɔmpənˈseɪʃən] n compensation f; (money) dédommagement m, indemnité f

**compete** [kəmˈpiːt] vi (take part) concourir; (vie): **to ~ (with)** rivaliser (avec), faire concurrence (à)

**competent** [ˈkɔmpɪtənt] adj compétent(e), capable

**competition** [kɔmpɪˈtɪʃən] n (contest) compétition f, concours m; (Econ) concurrence f

**competitive** [kəmˈpɛtɪtɪv] adj (Econ) concurrentiel(le); (sports) de compétition; (person) qui a l'esprit de compétition

**competitor** [kəmˈpɛtɪtər] n concurrent(e)

**complacent** [kəmˈpleɪsnt] adj (trop) content(e) de soi

**complain** [kəmˈpleɪn] vi: **to ~ (about)** se plaindre (de); (in shop etc) réclamer (au sujet de); **complaint** n plainte f; (in shop etc) réclamation f; (Med) affection f

**complement** [ˈkɔmplɪmənt] n complément m; (esp of ship's crew etc) effectif complet ▷ vt (enhance) compléter; **complementary** [kɔmplɪˈmɛntərɪ] adj complémentaire

**complete** [kəmˈpliːt] adj complet(-ète); (finished) achevé(e) ▷ vt achever, parachever; (set, group) compléter; (a form) remplir; **completely** adv complètement; **completion** [kəmˈpliːʃən] n achèvement m; (of contract) exécution f

**complex** [ˈkɔmplɛks] adj complexe ▷ n (Psych, buildings etc) complexe m

**complexion** [kəmˈplɛkʃən] n (of face) teint m

**compliance** [kəmˈplaɪəns] n (submission) docilité f; (agreement): **~ with** le fait de se conformer à; **in ~ with** en conformité avec, conformément à

**complicate** [ˈkɔmplɪkeɪt] vt compliquer; **complicated** adj compliqué(e); **complication** [kɔmplɪˈkeɪʃən] n complication f

**compliment** n [ˈkɔmplɪmənt] compliment m ▷ vt [ˈkɔmplɪmɛnt]

complimenter; **complimentary**
[kɒmplɪ'mɛntərɪ] *adj* flatteur(-euse);
(*free*) à titre gracieux

**comply** [kəm'plaɪ] *vi*: **to ~ with** se
soumettre à, se conformer à

**component** [kəm'pəʊnənt] *adj*
composant(e), constituant(e) ▷ *n*
composant *m*, élément *m*

**compose** [kəm'pəʊz] *vt* composer;
(*form*): **to be ~d of** se composer de; **to ~
o.s.** se calmer, se maîtriser; **composer**
*n* (*Mus*) compositeur *m*; **composition**
[kɒmpə'zɪʃən] *n* composition *f*

**composure** [kəm'pəʊʒə<sup>r</sup>] *n* calme *m*,
maîtrise *f* de soi

**compound** ['kɒmpaʊnd] *n* (*Chem*,
*Ling*) composé *m*; (*enclosure*) enclos *m*,
enceinte *f* ▷ *adj* composé(e); (*fracture*)
compliqué(e)

**comprehension** [kɒmprɪ'hɛnʃən] *n*
compréhension *f*

**comprehensive** [kɒmprɪ'hɛnsɪv]
*adj* (très) complet(-ète); **~ policy**
(*Insurance*) assurance *f* tous risques;
**comprehensive (school)** *n* (BRIT)
école secondaire non sélective avec libre
circulation d'une section à l'autre, ≈ CES *m*

▐ Be careful not to translate
*comprehensive* by the French word
*compréhensif*.

**compress** *vt* [kəm'prɛs] comprimer;
(*text, information*) condenser ▷ *n*
['kɒmprɛs] (*Med*) compresse *f*

**comprise** [kəm'praɪz] *vt* (*also*: **be ~d
of**) comprendre; (*constitute*) constituer,
représenter

**compromise** ['kɒmprəmaɪz] *n*
compromis *m* ▷ *vt* compromettre ▷ *vi*
transiger, accepter un compromis

**compulsive** [kəm'pʌlsɪv] *adj* (*Psych*)
compulsif(-ive); (*book, film etc*)
captivant(e)

**compulsory** [kəm'pʌlsərɪ] *adj*
obligatoire

**computer** [kəm'pju:tə<sup>r</sup>] *n*
ordinateur *m*; **computer game** *n* jeu
*m* vidéo; **computer-generated** *adj*
de synthèse; **computerize** *vt* (*data*)

traiter par ordinateur; (*system, office*)
informatiser; **computer programmer**
*n* programmeur(-euse); **computer
programming** *n* programmation *f*;
**computer science** *n* informatique *f*;
**computer studies** *npl* informatique *f*;
**computing** [kəm'pju:tɪŋ] *n*
informatique *f*

**con** [kɒn] *vt* duper; (*cheat*) escroquer ▷ *n*
escroquerie *f*

**conceal** [kən'si:l] *vt* cacher, dissimuler

**concede** [kən'si:d] *vt* concéder ▷ *vi*
céder

**conceited** [kən'si:tɪd] *adj*
vaniteux(-euse), suffisant(e)

**conceive** [kən'si:v] *vt, vi* concevoir

**concentrate** ['kɒnsəntreɪt] *vi* se
concentrer ▷ *vt* concentrer

**concentration** [kɒnsən'treɪʃən] *n*
concentration *f*

**concept** ['kɒnsɛpt] *n* concept *m*

**concern** [kən'sə:n] *n* affaire *f*;
(*Comm*) entreprise *f*, firme *f*; (*anxiety*)
inquiétude *f*, souci *m* ▷ *vt* (*worry*)
inquiéter; (*involve*) concerner; (*relate
to*) se rapporter à; **to be ~ed (about)**
s'inquiéter (de), être inquiet(-ète) (au
sujet de); **concerning** *prep* en ce qui
concerne, à propos de

**concert** ['kɒnsət] *n* concert *m*; **concert
hall** *n* salle *f* de concert

**concerto** [kən'tʃə:təʊ] *n* concerto *m*

**concession** [kən'sɛʃən] *n* (*compromise*)
concession *f*; (*reduced price*) réduction
*f*; **tax ~** dégrèvement fiscal; **"~s"** tarif
réduit

**concise** [kən'saɪs] *adj* concis(e)

**conclude** [kən'klu:d] *vt* conclure;
**conclusion** [kən'klu:ʒən] *n*
conclusion *f*

**concrete** ['kɒnkri:t] *n* béton *m* ▷ *adj*
concret(-ète); (*Constr*) en béton

**concussion** [kən'kʌʃən] *n* (*Med*)
commotion (cérébrale)

**condemn** [kən'dɛm] *vt* condamner

**condensation** [kɒndɛn'seɪʃən] *n*
condensation *f*

**condense** [kən'dɛns] *vi* se condenser

▷ *vt* condenser

**condition** [kən'dɪʃən] *n* condition *f*; (*disease*) maladie *f* ▷ *vt* déterminer, conditionner; **on ~ that** à condition que + *sub*, à condition de; **conditional** [kən'dɪʃənl] *adj* conditionnel(le); **conditioner** *n* (*for hair*) baume démêlant; (*for fabrics*) assouplissant *m*

**condo** ['kɔndəu] *n* (*US inf*) = **condominium**

**condom** ['kɔndəm] *n* préservatif *m*

**condominium** [kɔndə'mɪnɪəm] *n* (*US: building*) immeuble *m* (en copropriété); (*: rooms*) appartement *m* (dans un immeuble en copropriété)

**condone** [kən'dəun] *vt* fermer les yeux sur, approuver (tacitement)

**conduct** *n* ['kɔndʌkt] conduite *f* ▷ *vt* [kən'dʌkt] conduire; (*manage*) mener, diriger; (*Mus*) diriger; **to ~ o.s.** se conduire, se comporter; **conducted tour** (*BRIT*) *n* voyage organisé; (*of building*) visite guidée; **conductor** *n* (*of orchestra*) chef *m* d'orchestre; (*on bus*) receveur *m*; (*US: on train*) chef *m* de train; (*Elec*) conducteur *m*

**cone** [kəun] *n* cône *m*; (*for ice-cream*) cornet *m*; (*Bot*) pomme *f* de pin, cône

**confectionery** [kən'fɛkʃənri] *n* (*sweets*) confiserie *f*

**confer** [kən'fəːʳ] *vt*: **to ~ sth on** conférer qch à ▷ *vi* conférer, s'entretenir

**conference** ['kɔnfərns] *n* conférence *f*

**confess** [kən'fɛs] *vt* confesser, avouer ▷ *vi* (*admit sth*) avouer; (*Rel*) se confesser; **confession** [kən'fɛʃən] *n* confession *f*

**confide** [kən'faɪd] *vi*: **to ~ in** s'ouvrir à, se confier à

**confidence** ['kɔnfɪdns] *n* confiance *f*; (*also*: **self-~**) assurance *f*, confiance en soi; (*secret*) confidence *f*; **in ~** (*speak, write*) en confidence, confidentiellement; **confident** *adj* (*self-assured*) sûr(e) de soi; (*sure*) sûr; **confidential** [kɔnfɪ'dɛnʃəl] *adj* confidentiel(le)

**confine** [kən'faɪn] *vt* limiter, borner; (*shut up*) confiner, enfermer; **confined** *adj* (*space*) restreint(e), réduit(e)

**confirm** [kən'fəːm] *vt* (*report, Rel*) confirmer; (*appointment*) ratifier; **confirmation** [kɔnfə'meɪʃən] *n* confirmation *f*; ratification *f*

**confiscate** ['kɔnfɪskeɪt] *vt* confisquer

**conflict** *n* ['kɔnflɪkt] conflit *m*, lutte *f* ▷ *vi* [kən'flɪkt] (*opinions*) s'opposer, se heurter

**conform** [kən'fɔːm] *vi*: **to ~ (to)** se conformer (à)

**confront** [kən'frʌnt] *vt* (*two people*) confronter; (*enemy, danger*) affronter, faire face à; (*problem*) faire face à; **confrontation** [kɔnfrən'teɪʃən] *n* confrontation *f*

**confuse** [kən'fjuːz] *vt* (*person*) troubler; (*situation*) embrouiller; (*one thing with another*) confondre; **confused** *adj* (*person*) dérouté(e), désorienté(e); (*situation*) embrouillé(e); **confusing** *adj* peu clair(e), déroutant(e); **confusion** [kən'fjuːʒən] *n* confusion *f*

**congestion** [kən'dʒɛstʃən] *n* (*Med*) congestion *f*; (*fig: traffic*) encombrement *m*

**congratulate** [kən'grætjuleɪt] *vt*: **to ~ sb (on)** féliciter qn (de); **congratulations** [kəngrætju'leɪʃənz] *npl*: **congratulations (on)** félicitations *fpl* (pour) ▷ *excl*: **congratulations!** (toutes mes) félicitations!

**congregation** [kɔngrɪ'geɪʃən] *n* assemblée *f* (des fidèles)

**congress** ['kɔngrɛs] *n* congrès *m*; (*Pol*): **C~** Congrès *m*; **congressman** *n* membre *m* du Congrès; **congresswoman** *n* membre *m* du Congrès

**conifer** ['kɔnɪfəʳ] *n* conifère *m*

**conjugate** ['kɔndʒugeɪt] *vt* conjuguer

**conjugation** [kɔndʒə'geɪʃən] *n* conjugaison *f*

**conjunction** [kən'dʒʌŋkʃən] *n* conjonction *f*; **in ~ with** (conjointement) avec

**conjure** ['kʌndʒəʳ] *vi* faire des tours de

passe-passe

**connect** [kə'nɛkt] vt joindre, relier;
(Elec) connecter; (Tel: caller) mettre
en connexion; (: subscriber) brancher;
(fig) établir un rapport entre, faire un
rapprochement entre ▷ vi (train): **to ~
with** assurer la correspondance avec;
**to be ~ed with** avoir un rapport avec;
(have dealings with) avoir des rapports
avec, être en relation avec; **connecting
flight** n (vol m de) correspondance
f; **connection** [kə'nɛkʃən] n
relation f, lien m; (Elec) connexion
f; (Tel) communication f; (train etc)
correspondance f

**conquer** ['kɔŋkər] vt conquérir;
(feelings) vaincre, surmonter

**conquest** ['kɔŋkwɛst] n conquête f

**cons** [kɔnz] npl see **convenience**; **pro**

**conscience** ['kɔnʃəns] n conscience f

**conscientious** [kɔnʃɪ'ɛnʃəs] adj
consciencieux(-euse)

**conscious** ['kɔnʃəs] adj conscient(e);
(deliberate: insult, error) délibéré(e);
**consciousness** n conscience f; (Med)
connaissance f

**consecutive** [kən'sɛkjutɪv] adj
consécutif(-ive); **on three ~ occasions**
trois fois de suite

**consensus** [kən'sɛnsəs] n
consensus m

**consent** [kən'sɛnt] n consentement m
▷ vi: **to ~ (to)** consentir (à)

**consequence** ['kɔnsɪkwəns] n
suites fpl, conséquence f; (significance)
importance f

**consequently** ['kɔnsɪkwəntlɪ] adv
par conséquent, donc

**conservation** [kɔnsə'veɪʃən] n
préservation f, protection f; (also:
**nature ~**) défense f de l'environnement

**conservative** [kən'sə:vətɪv] adj
conservateur(-trice); (cautious)
prudent(e); **Conservative** adj, n (BRIT
Pol) conservateur(-trice)

**conservatory** [kən'sə:vətrɪ] n (room)
jardin m d'hiver; (Mus) conservatoire m

**consider** [kən'sɪdər] vt (study)

considérer, réfléchir à; (take into
account) penser à, prendre en
considération; (regard, judge)
considérer, estimer; **to ~ doing sth**
envisager de faire qch; **considerable**
adj considérable; **considerably**
adv nettement; **considerate** adj
prévenant(e), plein(e) d'égards;
**consideration** [kənsɪdə'reɪʃən] n
considération f; (reward) rétribution
f, rémunération f; **considering** prep:
**considering (that)** étant donné (que)

**consignment** [kən'saɪnmənt] n
arrivage m, envoi m

**consist** [kən'sɪst] vi: **to ~ of** consister
en, se composer de

**consistency** [kən'sɪstənsɪ] n
(thickness) consistance f; (fig)
cohérence f

**consistent** [kən'sɪstənt] adj logique,
cohérent(e)

**consolation** [kɔnsə'leɪʃən] n
consolation f

**console¹** [kən'səul] vt consoler

**console²** ['kɔnsəul] n console f

**consonant** ['kɔnsənənt] n consonne f

**conspicuous** [kən'spɪkjuəs] adj
voyant(e), qui attire l'attention

**conspiracy** [kən'spɪrəsɪ] n
conspiration f, complot m

**constable** ['kʌnstəbl] n (BRIT) ≈ agent
m de police, gendarme m; **chief ~**
≈ préfet m de police

**constant** ['kɔnstənt] adj constant(e);
incessant(e); **constantly** adv
constamment, sans cesse

**constipated** ['kɔnstɪpeɪtɪd]
adj constipé(e); **constipation**
[kɔnstɪ'peɪʃən] n constipation f

**constituency** [kən'stɪtjuənsɪ] n (Pol:
area) circonscription électorale;
(: electors) électorat m

**constitute** ['kɔnstɪtjuːt] vt constituer

**constitution** [kɔnstɪ'tjuːʃən] n
constitution f

**constraint** [kən'streɪnt] n contrainte f

**construct** [kən'strʌkt] vt construire;
**construction** [kən'strʌkʃən] n

construction f; **constructive** adj
constructif(-ive)

**consul** ['kɔnsl] n consul m; **consulate**
['kɔnsjulɪt] n consulat m

**consult** [kən'sʌlt] vt consulter;
**consultant** n (Med) médecin
consultant; (other specialist) consultant
m, (expert-)conseil m; **consultation**
[kɔnsəl'teɪʃən] n consultation f;
**consulting room** n (BRIT) cabinet m de
consultation

**consume** [kən'sju:m] vt consommer;
(subj: flames, hatred, desire) consumer;
**consumer** n consommateur(-trice)

**consumption** [kən'sʌmpʃən] n
consommation f

**cont.** abbr (= continued) suite

**contact** ['kɔntækt] n contact m;
(person) connaissance f, relation f ▷ vt
se mettre en contact or en rapport
avec; **contact lenses** npl verres mpl
de contact

**contagious** [kən'teɪdʒəs] adj
contagieux(-euse)

**contain** [kən'teɪn] vt contenir;
**to ~ o.s.** se contenir, se maîtriser;
**container** n récipient m; (for shipping
etc) conteneur m

**contaminate** [kən'tæmɪneɪt] vt
contaminer

**cont'd** abbr (= continued) suite

**contemplate** ['kɔntəmpleɪt] vt
contempler; (consider) envisager

**contemporary** [kən'tempərərɪ] adj
contemporain(e); (design, wallpaper)
moderne ▷ n contemporain(e)

**contempt** [kən'tempt] n mépris m,
dédain m; **~ of court** (Law) outrage m à
l'autorité de la justice

**contend** [kən'tend] vt: **to ~ that**
soutenir or prétendre que ▷ vi: **to ~
with** (compete) rivaliser avec; (struggle)
lutter avec

**content** [kən'tent] adj content(e),
satisfait(e) ▷ vt contenter, satisfaire
▷ n ['kɔntent] contenu m; (of fat,
moisture) teneur f; **contents** npl (of
container etc) contenu m; **(table of) ~s**

table f des matières; **contented** adj
content(e), satisfait(e)

**contest** n ['kɔntest] combat m, lutte f;
(competition) concours m ▷ vt [kən'test]
contester, discuter; (compete for)
disputer; (Law) attaquer; **contestant**
[kən'testənt] n concurrent(e); (in fight)
adversaire m/f

**context** ['kɔntekst] n contexte m

**continent** ['kɔntɪnənt] n continent
m; **the C~** (BRIT) l'Europe continentale;
**continental** [kɔntɪ'nentl] adj
continental(e); **continental breakfast**
n café (or thé) complet; **continental
quilt** n (BRIT) couette f

**continual** [kən'tɪnjuəl] adj
continuel(le); **continually** adv
continuellement, sans cesse

**continue** [kən'tɪnju:] vi continuer ▷ vt
continuer; (start again) reprendre

**continuity** [kɔntɪ'nju:ɪtɪ] n continuité
f; (TV etc) enchaînement m

**continuous** [kən'tɪnjuəs] adj
continu(e), permanent(e); (Ling)
progressif(-ive); **continuous
assessment** (BRIT) n contrôle
continu; **continuously** adv
continuellement; (uninterruptedly) sans
interruption

**contour** ['kɔntuər] n contour m, profil
m; (also: **~ line**) courbe f de niveau

**contraception** [kɔntrə'sepʃən] n
contraception f

**contraceptive** [kɔntrə'septɪv]
adj contraceptif(-ive),
anticonceptionnel(le) ▷ n
contraceptif m

**contract** n ['kɔntrækt] contrat m ▷ vb
[kən'trækt] ▷ vi (become smaller) se
contracter, se resserrer ▷ vt contracter;
(Comm): **to ~ to do sth** s'engager (par
contrat) à faire qch; **contractor** n
entrepreneur m

**contradict** [kɔntrə'dɪkt] vt contredire;
**contradiction** [kɔntrə'dɪkʃən] n
contradiction f

**contrary¹** ['kɔntrərɪ] adj contraire,
opposé(e) ▷ n contraire m; **on the ~** au

contraire; **unless you hear to the ~** sauf avis contraire

**contrary²** [kən'trɛərɪ] adj (perverse) contrariant(e), entêté(e)

**contrast** n ['kɒntrɑːst] contraste m ▷ vt [kən'trɑːst] mettre en contraste, contraster; **in ~ to** or **with** contrairement à, par opposition à

**contribute** [kən'trɪbjuːt] vi contribuer ▷ vt: **to ~ £10/an article to** donner 10 livres/un article à; **to ~ to** (gen) contribuer à; (newspaper) collaborer à; (discussion) prendre part à; **contribution** [kɒntrɪ'bjuːʃən] n contribution f; (BRIT: for social security) cotisation f; (to publication) article m; **contributor** n (to newspaper) collaborateur(-trice); (of money, goods) donateur(-trice)

**control** [kən'trəul] vt (process, machinery) commander; (temper) maîtriser; (disease) enrayer ▷ n maîtrise f; (power) autorité f; **controls** npl (of machine etc) commandes fpl; (on radio) boutons mpl de réglage; **to be in ~ of** être maître de, maîtriser; (in charge of) être responsable de; **everything is under ~** j'ai (or il a etc) la situation en main; **the car went out of ~** j'ai (or il a etc) perdu le contrôle du véhicule; **control tower** n (Aviat) tour f de contrôle

**controversial** [kɒntrə'vəːʃl] adj discutable, controversé(e)

**controversy** ['kɒntrəvəːsɪ] n controverse f, polémique f

**convenience** [kən'viːnɪəns] n commodité f; **at your ~** quand or comme cela vous convient; **all modern ~s, all mod cons** (BRIT) avec tout le confort moderne, tout confort

**convenient** [kən'viːnɪənt] adj commode

**convent** ['kɒnvənt] n couvent m

**convention** [kən'vɛnʃən] n convention f; (custom) usage m; **conventional** adj conventionnel(le)

**conversation** [kɒnvə'seɪʃən] n conversation f

**conversely** [kɒn'vəːslɪ] adv inversement, réciproquement

**conversion** [kən'vəːʃən] n conversion f; (BRIT: of house) transformation f, aménagement m; (Rugby) transformation f

**convert** vt [kən'vəːt] (Rel, Comm) convertir; (alter) transformer; (house) aménager ▷ n ['kɒnvəːt] converti(e); **convertible** adj convertible ▷ n (voiture f) décapotable f

**convey** [kən'veɪ] vt transporter; (thanks) transmettre; (idea) communiquer; **conveyor belt** n convoyeur m tapis roulant

**convict** vt [kən'vɪkt] déclarer (or reconnaître) coupable ▷ n ['kɒnvɪkt] forçat m, convict m; **conviction** [kən'vɪkʃən] n (Law) condamnation f; (belief) conviction f

**convince** [kən'vɪns] vt convaincre, persuader; **convinced** adj: **convinced of/that** convaincu(e) de/que; **convincing** adj persuasif(-ive), convaincant(e)

**convoy** ['kɒnvɔɪ] n convoi m

**cook** [kuk] vt (faire) cuire ▷ vi cuire; (person) faire la cuisine ▷ n cuisinier(-ière); **cookbook** n livre m de cuisine; **cooker** n cuisinière f; **cookery** n cuisine f; **cookery book** n (BRIT) = **cookbook**; **cookie** n (US) biscuit m, petit gâteau sec; **cooking** n cuisine f

**cool** [kuːl] adj frais (fraîche); (not afraid) calme; (unfriendly) froid(e); (inf: trendy) cool inv (inf); (: great) super inv (inf) ▷ vt, vi rafraîchir, refroidir; **cool down** vi refroidir; (fig: person, situation) se calmer; **cool off** vi (become calmer) se calmer; (lose enthusiasm) perdre son enthousiasme

**cop** [kɒp] n (inf) flic m

**cope** [kəup] vi s'en sortir, tenir le coup; **to ~ with** (problem) faire face à

**copper** ['kɒpə'] n cuivre m; (BRIT: inf: policeman) flic m

**copy** ['kɒpɪ] n copie f; (book etc)

exemplaire *m* ▷ *vt* copier; (*imitate*) imiter; **copyright** *n* droit *m* d'auteur, copyright *m*

**coral** ['kɔrəl] *n* corail *m*

**cord** [kɔːd] *n* corde *f*; (*fabric*) velours côtelé; (*Elec*) cordon *m* (d'alimentation), fil *m* (électrique); **cords** *npl* (*trousers*) pantalon *m* de velours côtelé; **cordless** *adj* sans fil

**corduroy** ['kɔːdərɔɪ] *n* velours côtelé

**core** [kɔːʳ] *n* (*of fruit*) trognon *m*, cœur *m*; (*fig: of problem etc*) cœur *m* ▷ *vt* enlever le trognon *or* le cœur de

**coriander** [kɔrɪ'ændəʳ] *n* coriandre *f*

**cork** [kɔːk] *n* (*material*) liège *m*; (*of bottle*) bouchon *m*; **corkscrew** *n* tire-bouchon *m*

**corn** [kɔːn] *n* (BRIT: *wheat*) blé *m*; (US: *maize*) maïs *m*; (*on foot*) cor *m*; **~ on the cob** (*Culin*) épi *m* de maïs au naturel

**corned beef** ['kɔːnd-] *n* corned-beef *m*

**corner** ['kɔːnəʳ] *n* coin *m*; (*in road*) tournant *m*, virage *m*; (*Football*) corner *m* ▷ *vt* (*trap: prey*) acculer; (*fig*) coincer; (*Comm: market*) accaparer ▷ *vi* prendre un virage; **corner shop** (BRIT) *n* magasin *m* du coin

**cornflakes** ['kɔːnfleɪks] *npl* cornflakes *mpl*

**cornflour** ['kɔːnflauəʳ] *n* (BRIT) farine *f* de maïs, maïzena® *f*

**cornstarch** ['kɔːnstɑːtʃ] *n* (US) farine *f* de maïs, maïzena® *f*

**Cornwall** ['kɔːnwəl] *n* Cornouailles *f*

**coronary** ['kɔrənərɪ] *n*: **~ (thrombosis)** infarctus *m* (du myocarde), thrombose *f* coronaire

**coronation** [kɔrə'neɪʃən] *n* couronnement *m*

**coroner** ['kɔrənəʳ] *n* coroner *m*, officier *de police judiciaire chargé de déterminer les causes d'un décès*

**corporal** ['kɔːpərl] *n* caporal *m*, brigadier *m* ▷ *adj*: **~ punishment** châtiment corporel

**corporate** ['kɔːpərɪt] *adj* (*action, ownership*) en commun; (*Comm*) de la société

**corporation** [kɔːpə'reɪʃən] *n* (*of town*) municipalité *f*, conseil municipal; (*Comm*) société *f*

**corps** [kɔːʳ, *pl* kɔːz] *n* corps *m*; **the diplomatic ~** le corps diplomatique; **the press ~** la presse

**corpse** [kɔːps] *n* cadavre *m*

**correct** [kə'rɛkt] *adj* (*accurate*) correct(e), exact(e); (*proper*) correct, convenable ▷ *vt* corriger; **correction** [kə'rɛkʃən] *n* correction *f*

**correspond** [kɔrɪs'pɔnd] *vi* correspondre; **to ~ to sth** (*be equivalent to*) correspondre à qch; **correspondence** *n* correspondance *f*; **correspondent** *n* correspondant(e); **corresponding** *adj* correspondant(e)

**corridor** ['kɔrɪdɔːʳ] *n* couloir *m*, corridor *m*

**corrode** [kə'rəud] *vt* corroder, ronger ▷ *vi* se corroder

**corrupt** [kə'rʌpt] *adj* corrompu(e); (*Comput*) altéré(e) ▷ *vt* corrompre; (*Comput*) altérer; **corruption** *n* corruption *f*; (*Comput*) altération *f* (de données)

**Corsica** ['kɔːsɪkə] *n* Corse *f*

**cosmetic** [kɔz'mɛtɪk] *n* produit *m* de beauté, cosmétique *m* ▷ *adj* (*fig: reforms*) symbolique, superficiel(le); **cosmetic surgery** *n* chirurgie *f* esthétique

**cosmopolitan** [kɔzmə'pɔlɪtn] *adj* cosmopolite

**cost** [kɔst] *n* coût *m* ▷ *vb* (*pt, pp* ~) ▷ *vi* coûter ▷ *vt* établir *or* calculer le prix de revient de; **costs** *npl* (*Comm*) frais *mpl*; (*Law*) dépens *mpl*; **how much does it ~?** combien ça coûte?; **to ~ sb time/effort** demander du temps/un effort à qn; **it ~ him his life/job** ça lui a coûté la vie/son emploi; **at all ~s** coûte que coûte, à tout prix

**co-star** ['kəustɑːʳ] *n* partenaire *m/f*

**costly** ['kɔstlɪ] *adj* coûteux(-euse)

**cost of living** *n* coût *m* de la vie

**costume** ['kɔstjuːm] *n* costume *m*; (BRIT: *also*: **swimming ~**) maillot *m*

(de bain)

**cosy** (us **cozy**) ['kəʊzɪ] adj (room, bed) douillet(te); **to be ~** (person) être bien (au chaud)

**cot** [kɒt] n (BRIT: child's) lit m d'enfant, petit lit; (us: campbed) lit m de camp

**cottage** ['kɒtɪdʒ] n petite maison (à la campagne), cottage m; **cottage cheese** n fromage blanc (maigre)

**cotton** ['kɒtn] n coton m; (thread) fil m (de coton); **cotton on** vi (inf): **to ~ on (to sth)** piger (qch); **cotton bud** (BRIT) n coton-tige ® m; **cotton candy** (us) n barbe f à papa; **cotton wool** n (BRIT) ouate f, coton m hydrophile

**couch** [kaʊtʃ] n canapé m; divan m

**cough** [kɒf] vi tousser ▷ vt toux f; **I've got a ~** j'ai la toux; **cough mixture, cough syrup** n sirop m pour la toux

**could** [kʊd] pt of **can²**; **couldn't = could not**

**council** ['kaʊnsl] n conseil m; **city or town ~** conseil municipal; **council estate** n (BRIT) (quartier m or zone f de) logements loués à/par la municipalité; **council house** n (BRIT) maison f (à loyer modéré) louée par la municipalité; **councillor** (us **councilor**) n conseiller(-ère); **council tax** n (BRIT) impôts locaux

**counsel** ['kaʊnsl] n conseil m; (lawyer) avocat(e) ▷ vt: **to ~ (sb to do sth)** conseiller (à qn de faire qch); **counselling** (us **counseling**) n (Psych) aide psychosociale; **counsellor** (us **counselor**) n conseiller(-ère); (us Law) avocat m

**count** [kaʊnt] vt, vi compter ▷ n compte m; (nobleman) comte m; **count in** vt (inf): **to ~ sb in on sth** inclure qn dans qch; **count on** vt fus compter sur; **countdown** n compte m à rebours

**counter** ['kaʊntə'] n comptoir m; (in post office, bank) guichet m; (in game) jeton m ▷ vt aller à l'encontre de, opposer ▷ adv: **~ to** à l'encontre de; contrairement à; **counterclockwise** (us) adv en sens inverse des aiguilles d'une montre

**counterfeit** ['kaʊntəfɪt] n faux m, contrefaçon f ▷ vt contrefaire ▷ adj faux (fausse)

**counterpart** ['kaʊntəpɑːt] n (of person) homologue m/f

**countess** ['kaʊntɪs] n comtesse f

**countless** ['kaʊntlɪs] adj innombrable

**country** ['kʌntrɪ] n pays m; (native land) patrie f; (as opposed to town) campagne f; (region) région f, pays; **country and western (music)** n musique f country; **country house** n manoir m, (petit) château; **countryside** n campagne f

**county** ['kaʊntɪ] n comté m

**coup** [kuː, pl kuːz] n (achievement) beau coup; (also: **~ d'état**) coup d'État

**couple** ['kʌpl] n couple m; **a ~ of** (two) deux; (a few) deux ou trois

**coupon** ['kuːpɒn] n (voucher) bon m de réduction; (detachable form) coupon m détachable, coupon-réponse m

**courage** ['kʌrɪdʒ] n courage m; **courageous** [kə'reɪdʒəs] adj courageux(-euse)

**courgette** [kuə'ʒɛt] n (BRIT) courgette f

**courier** ['kʊrɪə'] n messager m, courrier m; (for tourists) accompagnateur(-trice)

**course** [kɔːs] n cours m; (of ship) route f; (for golf) terrain m; (part of meal) plat m; **of ~** adv bien sûr; **(no,) of ~ not!** bien sûr que non!, évidemment que non!; **~ of treatment** (Med) traitement m

**court** [kɔːt] n cour f; (Law) cour, tribunal m; (Tennis) court m ▷ vt (woman) courtiser, faire la cour à; **to take to ~** actionner or poursuivre en justice

**courtesy** ['kəːtəsɪ] n courtoisie f, politesse f; **(by) ~ of** avec l'aimable autorisation de; **courtesy bus, courtesy coach** n navette gratuite

**court**: **court-house** ['kɔːthaʊs] n (us) palais m de justice; **courtroom** ['kɔːtrʊm] n salle f de tribunal; **courtyard** ['kɔːtjɑːd] n cour f

**cousin** ['kʌzn] n cousin(e); **first ~** cousin(e) germain(e)

**cover** ['kʌvə'] vt couvrir; (Press: report

*on)* faire un reportage sur; *(feelings, mistake)* cacher; *(include)* englober; *(discuss)* traiter ▷ n *(of book, Comm)* couverture f; *(of pan)* couvercle m; *(over furniture)* housse f; *(shelter)* abri m; **covers** npl *(on bed)* couvertures; **to take ~** se mettre à l'abri; **under ~** à l'abri; **under ~ of darkness** à la faveur de la nuit; **under separate ~** *(Comm)* sous pli séparé; **cover up** vi: **to ~ up for sb** *(fig)* couvrir qn; **coverage** n *(in media)* reportage m; **cover charge** n couvert m *(supplément à payer)*; **cover-up** n tentative f pour étouffer une affaire

**cow** [kau] n vache f ▷ vt effrayer, intimider

**coward** ['kauəd] n lâche m/f; **cowardly** adj lâche

**cowboy** ['kaubɔɪ] n cow-boy m

**cozy** ['kəuzɪ] adj *(US)* = **cosy**

**crab** [kræb] n crabe m

**crack** [kræk] n *(split)* fente f, fissure f; *(in cup, bone)* fêlure f; *(in wall)* lézarde f; *(noise)* craquement m, coup *(sec)*; *(Drugs)* crack m ▷ vt fendre, fissurer; *(nut)* casser; *(problem)* résoudre; *(code)* déchiffrer ▷ cpd *(athlete)* de première classe, d'élite; **crack down on** vt fus *(crime)* sévir contre, réprimer; **cracked** adj *(cup, bone)* fêlé(e); *(broken)* cassé(e); *(wall)* lézardé(e); *(surface)* craquelé(e); *(inf)* toqué(e), timbré(e); **cracker** n *(also:* **Christmas cracker***)* pétard m; *(biscuit)* biscuit *(salé)*, craquelin m

**crackle** ['krækl] vi crépiter, grésiller

**cradle** ['kreɪdl] n berceau m

**craft** [krɑːft] n métier *(artisanal)*; *(cunning)* ruse f, astuce f; *(boat: pl inv)* embarcation f, barque f; *(plane: pl inv)* appareil m; **craftsman** *(irreg)* n artisan m ouvrier *(qualifié)*; **craftsmanship** n métier m, habileté f

**cram** [kræm] vt *(fill)*: **to ~ sth with** bourrer qch de; *(put)*: **to ~ sth into** fourrer qch dans ▷ vi *(for exams)* bachoter

**cramp** [kræmp] n crampe f; **I've got ~ in my leg** j'ai une crampe à la jambe; **cramped** adj à l'étroit, très serré(e)

**cranberry** ['krænbərɪ] n canneberge f

**crane** [kreɪn] n grue f

**crap** [kræp] n *(infl: nonsense)* conneries fpl *(!)*; *(: excrement)* merde f *(!)*

**crash** [kræʃ] n *(noise)* fracas m; *(of car, plane)* collision f; *(of business)* faillite f ▷ vt *(plane)* écraser ▷ vi *(plane)* s'écraser; *(two cars)* se percuter, s'emboutir; *(business)* s'effondrer; **to ~ into** se jeter or se fracasser contre; **crash course** n cours intensif; **crash helmet** n casque *(protecteur)*

**crate** [kreɪt] n cageot m; *(for bottles)* caisse f

**crave** [kreɪv] vt, vi: **to ~ (for)** avoir une envie irrésistible de

**crawl** [krɔːl] vi ramper; *(vehicle)* avancer au pas ▷ n *(Swimming)* crawl m

**crayfish** ['kreɪfɪʃ] n *(pl inv: freshwater)* écrevisse f; *(saltwater)* langoustine f

**crayon** ['kreɪən] n crayon m *(de couleur)*

**craze** [kreɪz] n engouement m

**crazy** ['kreɪzɪ] adj fou *(folle)*; **to be ~ about sb/sth** *(inf)* être fou de qn/qch

**creak** [kriːk] vi *(hinge)* grincer; *(floor, shoes)* craquer

**cream** [kriːm] n crème f ▷ adj *(colour)* crème inv; **cream cheese** n fromage m à la crème, fromage blanc; **creamy** adj crémeux(-euse)

**crease** [kriːs] n pli m ▷ vt froisser, chiffonner ▷ vi se froisser, se chiffonner

**create** [kriː'eɪt] vt créer; **creation** [kriː'eɪʃən] n création f; **creative** adj créatif(-ive); **creator** n créateur(-trice)

**creature** ['kriːtʃər] n créature f

**crèche** [kreʃ] n garderie f, crèche f

**credentials** [krɪ'dɛnʒlz] npl *(references)* références fpl; *(identity papers)* pièce f d'identité

**credibility** [krɛdɪ'bɪlɪtɪ] n crédibilité f

**credible** ['krɛdɪbl] adj digne de foi, crédible

**credit** ['krɛdɪt] n crédit m; *(recognition)*

honneur m; (Scol) unité f de valeur ▷ vt (Comm) créditer; (believe: also: **give ~ to**) ajouter foi à, croire; **credits** npl (Cine) générique m; **to be in ~** (person, bank account) être créditeur(-trice); **to ~ sb with** (fig) prêter or attribuer à qn; **credit card** n carte f de crédit; **do you take credit cards?** acceptez-vous les cartes de crédit?

**creek** [kriːk] n (inlet) crique f, anse f; (US: stream) ruisseau m, petit cours d'eau

**creep** (pt, pp **crept**) [kriːp, krɛpt] vi ramper

**cremate** [krɪˈmeɪt] vt incinérer

**crematorium** (pl **crematoria**) [krɛməˈtɔːrɪəm, -ˈtɔːrɪə] n four m crématoire

**crept** [krɛpt] pt, pp of **creep**

**crescent** [ˈkrɛsnt] n croissant m; (street) rue f (en arc de cercle)

**cress** [krɛs] n cresson m

**crest** [krɛst] n crête f; (of coat of arms) timbre m

**crew** [kruː] n équipage m; (Cine) équipe f (de tournage); **crew-neck** n col ras

**crib** [krɪb] n lit m d'enfant; (for baby) berceau m ▷ vt (inf) copier

**cricket** [ˈkrɪkɪt] n (insect) grillon m, cri-cri m inv; (game) cricket m; **cricketer** n joueur m de cricket

**crime** [kraɪm] n crime m; **criminal** [ˈkrɪmɪnl] adj, n criminel(le)

**crimson** [ˈkrɪmzn] adj cramoisi(e)

**cringe** [krɪndʒ] vi avoir un mouvement de recul

**cripple** [ˈkrɪpl] n boiteux(-euse), infirme m/f ▷ vt (person) estropier, paralyser; (ship, plane) immobiliser; (production, exports) paralyser

**crisis** (pl **crises**) [ˈkraɪsɪs, -siːz] n crise f

**crisp** [krɪsp] adj croquant(e); (weather) vif (vive); (manner etc) brusque; **crisps** (BRIT) npl (pommes fpl) chips fpl; **crispy** adj croustillant(e)

**criterion** (pl **criteria**) [kraɪˈtɪərɪən, -ˈtɪərɪə] n critère m

**critic** [ˈkrɪtɪk] n critique m/f; **critical** adj critique; **criticism** [ˈkrɪtɪsɪzəm]

n critique f; **criticize** [ˈkrɪtɪsaɪz] vt critiquer

**Croat** [ˈkrəʊæt] adj, n = **Croatian**

**Croatia** [krəʊˈeɪʃə] n Croatie f; **Croatian** adj croate ▷ n Croate m/f; (Ling) croate m

**crockery** [ˈkrɒkərɪ] n vaisselle f

**crocodile** [ˈkrɒkədaɪl] n crocodile m

**crocus** [ˈkrəʊkəs] n crocus m

**croissant** [ˈkrwɑːsã] n croissant m

**crook** [kruk] n escroc m; (of shepherd) houlette f; **crooked** [ˈkrʊkɪd] adj courbé(e), tordu(e); (action) malhonnête

**crop** [krɒp] n (produce) culture f; (amount produced) récolte f; (riding crop) cravache f ▷ vt (hair) tondre; **crop up** vi surgir, se présenter, survenir

**cross** [krɒs] n croix f; (Biol) croisement m ▷ vt (street etc) traverser; (arms, legs, Biol) croiser; (cheque) barrer ▷ adj en colère, fâché(e); **cross off** or **out** vt barrer, rayer; **cross over** vi traverser; **cross-Channel ferry** [ˈkrɒsˈtʃænl-] n ferry m qui fait la traversée de la Manche; **crosscountry (race)** n cross(-country) m; **crossing** n (sea passage) traversée f; (also: **pedestrian crossing**) passage clouté; **how long does the crossing take?** combien de temps dure la traversée?; **crossing guard** (US) n contractuel qui fait traverser la rue aux enfants; **crossroads** n carrefour m; **crosswalk** n (US) passage clouté; **crossword** n mots mpl croisés

**crotch** [krɒtʃ] n (of garment) entrejambe m; (Anat) entrecuisse m

**crouch** [krautʃ] vi s'accroupir; (hide) se tapir; (before springing) se ramasser

**crouton** [ˈkruːtɒn] n croûton m

**crow** [krəʊ] n (bird) corneille f; (of cock) chant m du coq, cocorico m ▷ vi (cock) chanter

**crowd** [kraud] n foule f ▷ vt bourrer, remplir ▷ vi affluer, s'attrouper, s'entasser; **crowded** adj bondé(e), plein(e)

**crown** [kraun] n couronne f; (of head)

sommet *m* de la tête; (*of hill*) sommet *m* ▷ *vt* (*also tooth*) couronner; **crown jewels** *npl* joyaux *mpl* de la Couronne

**crucial** ['kru:ʃl] *adj* crucial(e), décisif(-ive)

**crucifix** ['kru:sıfıks] *n* crucifix *m*

**crude** [kru:d] *adj* (*materials*) brut(e); non raffiné(e); (*basic*) rudimentaire, sommaire; (*vulgar*) cru(e), grossier(-ière); **crude (oil)** *n* (pétrole) brut *m*

**cruel** ['kruəl] *adj* cruel(le); **cruelty** *n* cruauté *f*

**cruise** [kru:z] *n* croisière *f* ▷ *vi* (*ship*) croiser; (*car*) rouler; (*aircraft*) voler

**crumb** [krʌm] *n* miette *f*

**crumble** ['krʌmbl] *vt* émietter ▷ *vi* (*plaster etc*) s'effriter; (*land, earth*) s'ébouler; (*building*) s'écrouler, crouler; (*fig*) s'effondrer

**crumpet** ['krʌmpıt] *n* petite crêpe (épaisse)

**crumple** ['krʌmpl] *vt* froisser, friper

**crunch** [krʌntʃ] *vt* croquer; (*underfoot*) faire craquer, écraser; faire crisser ▷ *n* (*fig*) instant *m* or moment *m* critique, moment de vérité; **crunchy** *adj* croquant(e), croustillant(e)

**crush** [krʌʃ] *n* (*crowd*) foule *f*, cohue *f*; (*love*): **to have a ~ on sb** avoir le béguin pour qn; (*drink*): **lemon ~** citron pressé ▷ *vt* écraser; (*crumple*) froisser; (*grind, break up: garlic, ice*) piler; (*: grapes*) presser; (*hopes*) anéantir

**crust** [krʌst] *n* croûte *f*; **crusty** *adj* (*bread*) croustillant(e); (*inf: person*) revêche, bourru(e)

**crutch** [krʌtʃ] *n* béquille *f*; (*also:* **crotch**) entrejambe *m*

**cry** [kraı] *vi* pleurer; (*shout: also:* **~ out**) crier ▷ *n* cri *m*; **cry out** *vi* (*call out, shout*) pousser un cri ▷ *vt* crier

**crystal** ['krıstl] *n* cristal *m*

**cub** [kʌb] *n* petit *m* (*d'un animal*); (*also:* **~ scout**) louveteau *m*

**Cuba** ['kju:bə] *n* Cuba *m*

**cube** [kju:b] *n* cube *m* ▷ *vt* (*Math*) élever au cube

**cubicle** ['kju:bıkl] *n* (*in hospital*) box *m*; (*at pool*) cabine *f*

**cuckoo** ['kuku:] *n* coucou *m*

**cucumber** ['kju:kʌmbə<sup>r</sup>] *n* concombre *m*

**cuddle** ['kʌdl] *vt* câliner, caresser ▷ *vi* se blottir l'un contre l'autre

**cue** [kju:] *n* queue *f* de billard; (*Theat etc*) signal *m*

**cuff** [kʌf] *n* (*BRIT: of shirt, coat etc*) poignet *m*, manchette *f*; (*US: on trousers*) revers *m*; (*blow*) gifle *f*; **off the ~** *adv* à l'improviste; **cufflinks** *n* boutons *m* de manchette

**cuisine** [kwı'zi:n] *n* cuisine *f*

**cul-de-sac** ['kʌldəsæk] *n* cul-de-sac *m*, impasse *f*

**cull** [kʌl] *vt* sélectionner ▷ *n* (*of animals*) abattage sélectif

**culminate** ['kʌlmıneıt] *vi*: **to ~ in** finir or se terminer par; (*lead to*) mener à

**culprit** ['kʌlprıt] *n* coupable *m/f*

**cult** [kʌlt] *n* culte *m*

**cultivate** ['kʌltıveıt] *vt* cultiver

**cultural** ['kʌltʃərəl] *adj* culturel(le)

**culture** ['kʌltʃə<sup>r</sup>] *n* culture *f*

**cumin** ['kʌmın] *n* (*spice*) cumin *m*

**cunning** ['kʌnıŋ] *n* ruse *f*, astuce *f* ▷ *adj* rusé(e), malin(-igne); (*clever: device, idea*) astucieux(-euse)

**cup** [kʌp] *n* tasse *f*; (*prize, event*) coupe *f*; (*of bra*) bonnet *m*

**cupboard** ['kʌbəd] *n* placard *m*

**cup final** *n* (*BRIT Football*) finale *f* de la coupe

**curator** [kjuə'reıtə<sup>r</sup>] *n* conservateur *m* (*d'un musée etc*)

**curb** [kə:b] *vt* refréner, mettre un frein à ▷ *n* (*fig*) frein *m*; (*US*) bord *m* du trottoir

**curdle** ['kə:dl] *vi* (se) cailler

**cure** [kjuə<sup>r</sup>] *vt* guérir; (*Culin: salt*) saler; (*: smoke*) fumer; (*: dry*) sécher ▷ *n* remède *m*

**curfew** ['kə:fju:] *n* couvre-feu *m*

**curiosity** [kjuərı'ɔsıtı] *n* curiosité *f*

**curious** ['kjuərıəs] *adj* curieux(-euse); **I'm ~ about him** il m'intrigue

**curl** [kə:l] *n* boucle *f* (de cheveux) ▷ *vt*,

*vi* boucler; (*tightly*) friser; **curl up** *vi* s'enrouler; (*person*) se pelotonner; **curler** *n* bigoudi *m*, rouleau *m*; **curly** *adj* bouclé(e); (*tightly curled*) frisé(e)

**currant** ['kʌrnt] *n* raisin *m* de Corinthe, raisin sec; (*fruit*) groseille *f*

**currency** ['kʌrnsɪ] *n* monnaie *f*; **to gain ~** (*fig*) s'accréditer

**current** ['kʌrnt] *n* courant *m* ▷ *adj* (*common*) courant(e); (*tendency, price, event*) actuel(le); **current account** *n* (*BRIT*) compte courant; **current affairs** *npl* (questions *fpl* d')actualité *f*; **currently** *adv* actuellement

**curriculum** (*pl* **~s** or **curricula**) [kə'rɪkjuləm, -lə] *n* programme *m* d'études; **curriculum vitae** [-'viːtaɪ] *n* curriculum vitae (CV) *m*

**curry** ['kʌrɪ] *n* curry *m* ▷ *vt*: **to ~ favour with** chercher à gagner la faveur or à s'attirer les bonnes grâces de; **curry powder** *n* poudre *f* de curry

**curse** [kəːs] *vi* jurer, blasphémer ▷ *vt* maudire ▷ *n* (*spell*) malédiction *f*; (*problem, scourge*) fléau *m*; (*swearword*) juron *m*

**cursor** ['kəːsəʳ] *n* (*Comput*) curseur *m*

**curt** [kəːt] *adj* brusque, sec(-sèche)

**curtain** ['kəːtn] *n* rideau *m*

**curve** [kəːv] *n* courbe *f*; (*in the road*) tournant *m*, virage *m* ▷ *vi* se courber; (*road*) faire une courbe; **curved** *adj* courbe

**cushion** ['kuʃən] *n* coussin *m* ▷ *vt* (*fall, shock*) amortir

**custard** ['kʌstəd] *n* (*for pouring*) crème anglaise

**custody** ['kʌstədɪ] *n* (*of child*) garde *f*; (*for offenders*): **to take sb into ~** placer qn en détention préventive

**custom** ['kʌstəm] *n* coutume *f*, usage *m*; (*Comm*) clientèle *f*

**customer** ['kʌstəməʳ] *n* client(e)

**customized** ['kʌstəmaɪzd] *adj* personnalisé(e); (*car etc*) construit(e) sur commande

**customs** ['kʌstəmz] *npl* douane *f*; **customs officer** *n* douanier *m*

**cut** [kʌt] *vb* (*pt, pp* **~**) ▷ *vt* couper; (*meat*) découper; (*reduce*) réduire ▷ *vi* couper ▷ *n* (*gen*) coupure *f*; (*of clothes*) coupe *f*; (*in salary etc*) réduction *f*; (*of meat*) morceau *m*; **to ~ a tooth** percer une dent; **to ~ one's finger** se couper le doigt; **to get one's hair ~** se faire couper les cheveux; **I've ~ myself** je me suis coupé; **cut back** *vt* (*plants*) tailler; (*production, expenditure*) réduire; **cut down** *vt* (*tree*) abattre; (*reduce*) réduire; **cut off** *vt* couper; (*fig*) isoler; **cut out** *vt* (*picture etc*) découper; (*remove*) supprimer; **cut up** *vt* découper; **cutback** *n* réduction *f*

**cute** [kjuːt] *adj* mignon(ne), adorable

**cutlery** ['kʌtlərɪ] *n* couverts *mpl*

**cutlet** ['kʌtlɪt] *n* côtelette *f*

**cut-price** ['kʌt'praɪs] (*us* **cut-rate** ['kʌt'reɪt]) *adj* au rabais, à prix réduit

**cutting** ['kʌtɪŋ] *adj* (*fig*) cinglant(e) ▷ *n* (*BRIT: from newspaper*) coupure *f* (de journal); (*from plant*) bouture *f*

**CV** *n abbr* = **curriculum vitae**

**cwt** *abbr* = **hundredweight(s)**

**cyberspace** ['saɪbəspeɪs] *n* cyberespace *m*

**cycle** ['saɪkl] *n* cycle *m*; (*bicycle*) bicyclette *f*, vélo *m* ▷ *vi* faire de la bicyclette; **cycle hire** *n* location *f* de vélos; **cycle lane, cycle path** *n* piste *f* cyclable; **cycling** *n* cyclisme *m*; **cyclist** *n* cycliste *m/f*

**cyclone** ['saɪkləun] *n* cyclone *m*

**cylinder** ['sɪlɪndəʳ] *n* cylindre *m*

**cymbals** ['sɪmblz] *npl* cymbales *fpl*

**cynical** ['sɪnɪkl] *adj* cynique

**Cypriot** ['sɪprɪət] *adj* cypriote, chypriote ▷ *n* Cypriote *m/f*, Chypriote *m/f*

**Cyprus** ['saɪprəs] *n* Chypre *f*

**cyst** [sɪst] *n* kyste *m*; **cystitis** [sɪs'taɪtɪs] *n* cystite *f*

**czar** [zaːʳ] *n* tsar *m*

**Czech** [tʃɛk] *adj* tchèque ▷ *n* Tchèque *m/f*; (*Ling*) tchèque *m*; **Czech Republic** *n*: **the Czech Republic** la République tchèque

**D** [diː] n (Mus): **D** ré m

**dab** [dæb] vt (eyes, wound) tamponner; (paint, cream) appliquer (par petites touches or rapidement)

**dad, daddy** [dæd, 'dædɪ] n papa m

**daffodil** ['dæfədɪl] n jonquille f

**daft** [dɑːft] adj (inf) idiot(e), stupide

**dagger** ['dægər] n poignard m

**daily** ['deɪlɪ] adj quotidien(ne), journalier(-ière) ▷ adv tous les jours

**dairy** ['dɛərɪ] n (shop) crémerie f, laiterie f; (on farm) laiterie f; **dairy produce** n produits laitiers

**daisy** ['deɪzɪ] n pâquerette f

**dam** [dæm] n (wall) barrage m; (water) réservoir m, lac m de retenue ▷ vt endiguer

**damage** ['dæmɪdʒ] n dégâts mpl, dommages mpl; (fig) tort m ▷ vt endommager, abîmer; (fig) faire du tort à; **damages** npl (Law) dommages-intérêts mpl

**damn** [dæm] vt condamner; (curse) maudire ▷ n (inf): **I don't give a ~** je m'en fous ▷ adj (inf: also: **~ed**): **this ~ ...** ce sacré or foutu ...; **~ (it)!** zut!

**damp** [dæmp] adj humide ▷ n humidité f ▷ vt (also: **~en**) (cloth, rag) humecter; (: enthusiasm etc) refroidir

**dance** [dɑːns] n danse f; (ball) bal m ▷ vi danser; **dance floor** n piste f de danse; **dancer** n danseur(-euse); **dancing** n danse f

**dandelion** ['dændɪlaɪən] n pissenlit m

**dandruff** ['dændrəf] n pellicules fpl

**D & T** n abbr (BRIT: Scol) = **design and technology**

**Dane** [deɪn] n Danois(e)

**danger** ['deɪndʒər] n danger m; **~!** (on sign) danger!; **in ~** en danger; **he was in ~ of falling** il risquait de tomber; **dangerous** adj dangereux(-euse)

**dangle** ['dæŋgl] vt balancer ▷ vi pendre, se balancer

**Danish** ['deɪnɪʃ] adj danois(e) ▷ n (Ling) danois m

**dare** [dɛər] vt: **to ~ sb to do** défier qn or mettre qn au défi de faire ▷ vi: **to ~ (to) do sth** oser faire qch; **I ~ say he'll turn up** il est probable qu'il viendra; **daring** adj hardi(e), audacieux(-euse) ▷ n audace f, hardiesse f

**dark** [dɑːk] adj (night, room) obscur(e), sombre; (colour, complexion) foncé(e), sombre ▷ n: **in the ~** dans le noir; **to be in the ~ about** (fig) ignorer tout de; **after ~** après la tombée de la nuit; **darken** vt obscurcir, assombrir ▷ vi s'obscurcir, s'assombrir; **darkness** n obscurité f; **darkroom** n chambre noire

**darling** ['dɑːlɪŋ] adj, n chéri(e)

**dart** [dɑːt] n fléchette f; (in sewing) pince f ▷ vi: **to ~ towards** se précipiter or s'élancer vers; **dartboard** n cible f (de jeu de fléchettes); **darts** n jeu m de fléchettes

**dash** [dæʃ] n (sign) tiret m; (small quantity) goutte f, larme f ▷ vt (throw) jeter or lancer violemment; (hopes) anéantir ▷ vi: **to ~ towards** se précipiter or se ruer vers

**dashboard** ['dæʃbɔːd] n (Aut) tableau m de bord

**data** ['deɪtə] npl données fpl; **database** n base f de données; **data processing** n traitement m (électronique) de l'information

**date** [deɪt] n date f; (with sb) rendez-vous m; (fruit) datte f ▷ vt dater; (person) sortir avec; **~ of birth** date de naissance; **to ~** adv à ce jour; **out of ~** périmé(e); **up to ~** à la page, mis(e) à jour, moderne; **dated** adj démodé(e)

**daughter** ['dɔːtər] n fille f; **daughter-in-law** n belle-fille f, bru f

**daunting** ['dɔːntɪŋ] adj décourageant(e), intimidant(e)

**dawn** [dɔːn] n aube f, aurore f ▷ vi (day) se lever, poindre; **it ~ed on him that ...** il lui vint à l'esprit que ...

**day** [deɪ] n jour m; (as duration) journée f; (period of time, age) époque f, temps m; **the ~ before** la veille, le jour précédent; **the ~ after** le lendemain, le jour suivant; **the following ~** le lendemain, le jour suivant; **the ~ before yesterday** avant-hier; **the ~ after tomorrow** après-demain; **by ~** de jour; **day-care centre** ['deɪkeə-] n (for elderly people) centre m d'accueil de jour; (for children) garderie f; **daydream** vi rêver (tout éveillé); **daylight** n (lumière f du) jour m; **day return** n (BRIT) billet m d'aller-retour (valable pour la journée); **daytime** n jour m, journée f; **day-to-day** adj (routine, expenses) journalier(-ière); **day trip** n excursion f (d'une journée)

**dazed** [deɪzd] adj abruti(e)

**dazzle** ['dæzl] vt éblouir, aveugler; **dazzling** adj (light) aveuglant(e), éblouissant(e); (fig) éblouissant(e)

**DC** abbr (Elec) = **direct current**

**dead** [dɛd] adj mort(e); (numb) engourdi(e), insensible; (battery) à plat ▷ adv (completely) absolument, complètement; (exactly) juste; **he was shot ~** il a été tué d'un coup de revolver; **~ tired** éreinté(e), complètement fourbu(e); **to stop ~** s'arrêter pile or net;

**the line is ~** (Tel) la ligne est coupée; **dead end** n impasse f; **deadline** n date f or heure f limite; **deadly** adj mortel(le); (weapon) meurtrier(-ière); **Dead Sea** n: **the Dead Sea** la mer Morte

**deaf** [dɛf] adj sourd(e); **deafen** vt rendre sourd(e); **deafening** adj assourdissant(e)

**deal** [diːl] n affaire f, marché m ▷ vt (pt, pp ~t) (blow) porter; (cards) donner, distribuer; **a great ~ of** beaucoup de; **deal with** vt fus (handle) s'occuper or se charger de; (be about: book etc) traiter de; **dealer** n (Comm) marchand m; (Cards) donneur m; **dealings** npl (in goods, shares) opérations fpl, transactions fpl; (relations) relations fpl, rapports mpl

**dealt** [dɛlt] pt, pp of **deal**

**dean** [diːn] n (Rel, BRIT Scol) doyen m; (US Scol) conseiller principal (conseillère principale) d'éducation

**dear** [dɪər] adj cher (chère); (expensive) cher, coûteux(-euse) ▷ n: **my ~** mon cher (ma chère) ▷ excl: **~ me!** mon Dieu!; **D~ Sir/Madam** (in letter) Monsieur/Madame; **D~ Mr/Mrs X** Cher Monsieur X (Chère Madame X); **dearly** adv (love) tendrement; (pay) cher

**death** [dɛθ] n mort f; (Admin) décès m; **death penalty** n peine f de mort; **death sentence** n condamnation f à mort

**debate** [dɪ'beɪt] n discussion f, débat m ▷ vt discuter, débattre

**debit** ['dɛbɪt] n débit m ▷ vt: **to ~ a sum to sb or to sb's account** porter une somme au débit de qn, débiter qn d'une somme; **debit card** n carte f de paiement

**debris** ['debriː] n débris mpl, décombres mpl

**debt** [dɛt] n dette f; **to be in ~** avoir des dettes, être endetté(e)

**debut** ['deɪbjuː] n début(s) m(pl)

**Dec.** abbr (= December) déc

**decade** ['dɛkeɪd] n décennie f, décade f

**decaffeinated** [dɪ'kæfɪneɪtɪd] *adj* décaféiné(e)

**decay** [dɪ'keɪ] *n* (*of building*) délabrement *m*; (*also:* **tooth ~**) carie *f* (dentaire) ▷ *vi* (*rot*) se décomposer, pourrir; (: *teeth*) se carier

**deceased** [dɪ'siːst] *n*: **the ~** le (la) défunt(e)

**deceit** [dɪ'siːt] *n* tromperie *f*, supercherie *f*; **deceive** [dɪ'siːv] *vt* tromper

**December** [dɪ'sɛmbə'] *n* décembre *m*

**decency** ['diːsənsɪ] *n* décence *f*

**decent** ['diːsənt] *adj* (*proper*) décent(e), convenable

**deception** [dɪ'sɛpʃən] *n* tromperie *f*

**deceptive** [dɪ'sɛptɪv] *adj* trompeur(-euse)

**decide** [dɪ'saɪd] *vt* (*subj: person*) décider; (*question, argument*) trancher, régler ▷ *vi* se décider, décider; **to ~ to do/that** décider de faire/que; **to ~ on** décider, se décider pour

**decimal** ['dɛsɪməl] *adj* décimal(e) ▷ *n* décimale *f*

**decision** [dɪ'sɪʒən] *n* décision *f*

**decisive** [dɪ'saɪsɪv] *adj* décisif(-ive); (*manner, person*) décidé(e), catégorique

**deck** [dɛk] *n* (*Naut*) pont *m*; (*of cards*) jeu *m*; (*record deck*) platine *f*; (*of bus*): **top ~** impériale *f*; **deckchair** *n* chaise longue

**declaration** [dɛklə'reɪʃən] *n* déclaration *f*

**declare** [dɪ'klɛə'] *vt* déclarer

**decline** [dɪ'klaɪn] *n* (*in decay*) déclin *m*; (*lessening*) baisse *f* ▷ *vt* refuser, décliner ▷ *vi* décliner; (*business*) baisser

**decorate** ['dɛkəreɪt] *vt* (*adorn, give a medal to*) décorer; (*paint and paper*) peindre et tapisser; **decoration** [dɛkə'reɪʃən] *n* (*medal etc, adornment*) décoration *f*; **decorator** *n* peintre *m* en bâtiment

**decrease** *n* ['diːkriːs] diminution *f* ▷ *vt, vi* [diː'kriːs] diminuer

**decree** [dɪ'kriː] *n* (*Pol, Rel*) décret *m*; (*Law*) arrêt *m*, jugement *m*

**dedicate** ['dɛdɪkeɪt] *vt* consacrer; (*book etc*) dédier; **dedicated** *adj* (*person*) dévoué(e); (*Comput*) spécialisé(e), dédié(e); **dedicated word processor** station *f* de traitement de texte; **dedication** [dɛdɪ'keɪʃən] *n* (*devotion*) dévouement *m*; (*in book*) dédicace *f*

**deduce** [dɪ'djuːs] *vt* déduire, conclure

**deduct** [dɪ'dʌkt] *vt*: **to ~ sth (from)** déduire qch (de), retrancher qch (de); **deduction** [dɪ'dʌkʃən] *n* (*deducting, deducing*) déduction *f*; (*from wage etc*) prélèvement *m*, retenue *f*

**deed** [diːd] *n* action *f*, acte *m*; (*Law*) acte notarié, contrat *m*

**deem** [diːm] *vt* (*formal*) juger, estimer

**deep** [diːp] *adj* profond(e); (*voice*) grave ▷ *adv*: **spectators stood 20 ~** il y avait 20 rangs de spectateurs; **4 metres ~** de 4 mètres de profondeur; **how ~ is the water?** l'eau à quelle profondeur?; **deep-fry** *vt* faire frire (dans une friteuse); **deeply** *adv* profondément; (*regret, interested*) vivement

**deer** [dɪə'] *n* (*pl inv*): (**red**) **~** cerf *m*; (**fallow**) **~** daim *m*; (**roe**) **~** chevreuil *m*

**default** [dɪ'fɔːlt] *n* (*Comput: also:* **~ value**) valeur *f* par défaut; **by ~** (*Law*) par défaut, par contumace; (*Sport*) par forfait

**defeat** [dɪ'fiːt] *n* défaite *f* ▷ *vt* (*team, opponents*) battre

**defect** *n* ['diːfɛkt] défaut *m* ▷ *vi* [dɪ'fɛkt]: **to ~ to the enemy/the West** passer à l'ennemi/l'Ouest; **defective** [dɪ'fɛktɪv] *adj* défectueux(-euse)

**defence** (*US* **defense**) [dɪ'fɛns] *n* défense *f*

**defend** [dɪ'fɛnd] *vt* défendre; **defendant** *n* défendeur(-deresse); (*in criminal case*) accusé(e), prévenu(e); **defender** *n* défenseur *m*

**defense** [dɪ'fɛns] (*US*) = **defence**

**defensive** [dɪ'fɛnsɪv] *adj* défensif(-ive) ▷ *n*: **on the ~** sur la défensive

**defer** [dɪ'fə:'] *vt* (*postpone*) différer, ajourner

**defiance** [dɪ'faɪəns] *n* défi *m*; **in ~ of** au mépris de; **defiant** [dɪ'faɪənt] *adj* provocant(e), de défi; (*person*) rebelle, intraitable

**deficiency** [dɪ'fɪʃənsɪ] *n* (*lack*) insuffisance *f*; (: *Med*) carence *f*; (*flaw*) faiblesse *f*; **deficient** [dɪ'fɪʃənt] *adj* (*inadequate*) insuffisant(e); **to be deficient in** manquer de

**deficit** ['dɛfɪsɪt] *n* déficit *m*

**define** [dɪ'faɪn] *vt* définir

**definite** ['dɛfɪnɪt] *adj* (*fixed*) défini(e), (bien) déterminé(e); (*clear, obvious*) net(te), manifeste; (*certain*) sûr(e); **he was ~ about it** il a été catégorique; **definitely** *adv* sans aucun doute

**definition** [dɛfɪ'nɪʃən] *n* définition *f*; (*clearness*) netteté *f*

**deflate** [di:'fleɪt] *vt* dégonfler

**deflect** [dɪ'flɛkt] *vt* détourner, faire dévier

**defraud** [dɪ'frɔːd] *vt*: **to ~ sb of sth** escroquer qch à qn

**defrost** [di:'frɒst] *vt* (*fridge*) dégivrer; (*frozen food*) décongeler

**defuse** [di:'fjuːz] *vt* désamorcer

**defy** [dɪ'faɪ] *vt* défier; (*efforts etc*) résister à; **it defies description** cela défie toute description

**degree** [dɪ'griː] *n* degré *m*; (*Scol*) diplôme *m* (universitaire); **a (first) ~ in maths** (*BRIT*) une licence en maths; **by ~s** (*gradually*) par degrés; **to some ~** jusqu'à un certain point, dans une certaine mesure

**dehydrated** [di:haɪ'dreɪtɪd] *adj* déshydraté(e); (*milk, eggs*) en poudre

**de-icer** ['di:'aɪsər] *n* dégivreur *m*

**delay** [dɪ'leɪ] *vt* retarder; (*payment*) différer ▷ *vi* s'attarder ▷ *n* délai *m*, retard *m*; **to be ~ed** être en retard

**delegate** *n* ['dɛlɪgɪt] délégué(e) ▷ *vt* ['dɛlɪgeɪt] déléguer

**delete** [dɪ'liːt] *vt* rayer, supprimer; (*Comput*) effacer

**deli** ['dɛlɪ] *n* épicerie fine

**deliberate** *adj* [dɪ'lɪbərɪt] (*intentional*) délibéré(e); (*slow*) mesuré(e) ▷ *vi* [dɪ'lɪbəreɪt] délibérer, réfléchir; **deliberately** *adv* (*on purpose*) exprès,

délibérément

**delicacy** ['dɛlɪkəsɪ] *n* délicatesse *f*; (*choice food*) mets fin *or* délicat, friandise *f*

**delicate** ['dɛlɪkɪt] *adj* délicat(e)

**delicatessen** [dɛlɪkə'tɛsn] *n* épicerie fine

**delicious** [dɪ'lɪʃəs] *adj* délicieux(-euse)

**delight** [dɪ'laɪt] *n* (grande) joie, grand plaisir ▷ *vt* enchanter; **she's a ~ to work with** c'est un plaisir de travailler avec elle; **to take ~ in** prendre grand plaisir à; **delighted** *adj*: **delighted (at** *or* **with sth)** ravi(e) (de qch); **to be delighted to do sth/that** être enchanté(e) *or* ravi(e) de faire qch/que; **delightful** *adj* (*person*) adorable; (*meal, evening*) merveilleux(-euse)

**delinquent** [dɪ'lɪŋkwənt] *adj, n* délinquant(e)

**deliver** [dɪ'lɪvər] *vt* (*mail*) distribuer; (*goods*) livrer; (*message*) remettre; (*speech*) prononcer; (*Med: baby*) mettre au monde; **delivery** *n* (*of mail*) distribution *f*; (*of goods*) livraison *f*; (*of speaker*) élocution *f*; (*Med*) accouchement *m*; **to take delivery of** prendre livraison de

**delusion** [dɪ'luːʒən] *n* illusion *f*

**de luxe** [də'lʌks] *adj* de luxe

**delve** [dɛlv] *vi*: **to ~ into** fouiller dans

**demand** [dɪ'mɑːnd] *vt* réclamer, exiger ▷ *n* exigence *f*; (*claim*) revendication *f*; (*Econ*) demande *f*; **in ~** demandé(e), recherché(e); **on ~** sur demande; **demanding** *adj* (*person*) exigeant(e); (*work*) astreignant(e)

> Be careful not to translate **to demand** by the French word **demander**.

**demise** [dɪ'maɪz] *n* décès *m*

**demo** ['dɛməu] *n abbr* (*inf*) = **demonstration** (*protest*) manif *f*; (*Comput*) démonstration *f*

**democracy** [dɪ'mɔkrəsɪ] *n* démocratie *f*; **democrat** ['dɛməkræt] *n* démocrate *m/f*; **democratic** [dɛmə'krætɪk] *adj* démocratique

**demolish** [dɪ'mɔlɪʃ] vt démolir
**demolition** [dɛmə'lɪʃən] n
démolition f
**demon** ['diːmən] n démon m
**demonstrate** ['dɛmənstreɪt] vt
démontrer, prouver; (show) faire
une démonstration de ▷ vi: **to
~ (for/against)** manifester (en
faveur de/contre); **demonstration**
[dɛmən'streɪʃən] n démonstration
f; (Pol etc) manifestation f;
**demonstrator** n (Pol etc)
manifestant(e)
**demote** [dɪ'məut] vt rétrograder
**den** [dɛn] n (of lion) tanière f; (room)
repaire m
**denial** [dɪ'naɪəl] n (of accusation)
démenti m; (of rights, guilt, truth)
dénégation f
**denim** ['dɛnɪm] n jean m; **denims** npl
(blue-)jeans mpl
**Denmark** ['dɛnmaːk] n Danemark m
**denomination** [dɪnɔmɪ'neɪʃən] n
(money) valeur f; (Rel) confession f
**denounce** [dɪ'nauns] vt dénoncer
**dense** [dɛns] adj dense; (inf: stupid)
obtus(e)
**density** ['dɛnsɪtɪ] n densité f;
**single-/double-~ disk** (Comput)
disquette f (à) simple/double densité
**dent** [dɛnt] n bosse f ▷ vt (also: **make a
~ in**) cabosser
**dental** ['dɛntl] adj dentaire; **dental
floss** [-flɔs] n fil m dentaire; **dental
surgery** n cabinet m de dentiste
**dentist** ['dɛntɪst] n dentiste m/f
**dentures** ['dɛntʃəz] npl dentier msg
**deny** [dɪ'naɪ] vt nier; (refuse) refuser
**deodorant** [diːˈəudərənt] n
déodorant m
**depart** [dɪ'paːt] vi partir; **to ~ from** (fig:
differ from) s'écarter de
**department** [dɪ'paːtmənt] n (Comm)
rayon m; (Scol) section f; (Pol) ministère
m, département m; **department store**
n grand magasin
**departure** [dɪ'paːtʃəʳ] n départ m; (fig):
**a new ~** une nouvelle voie; **departure

**lounge** n salle f de départ
**depend** [dɪ'pɛnd] vi: **to ~ (up)on**
dépendre de; (rely on) compter sur; **it
~s** cela dépend; **~ing on the result …**
selon le résultat …; **dependant** n
personne f à charge; **dependent** adj: **to
be dependent (on)** dépendre (de) ▷ n
= **dependant**
**depict** [dɪ'pɪkt] vt (in picture)
représenter; (in words) (dé)peindre,
décrire
**deport** [dɪ'pɔːt] vt déporter, expulser
**deposit** [dɪ'pɔzɪt] n (Chem, Comm, Geo)
dépôt m; (of ore, oil) gisement m; (part
payment) arrhes fpl, acompte m; (on
bottle etc) consigne f; (for hired goods
etc) cautionnement m, garantie f ▷ vt
déposer; **deposit account** n compte
m sur livret
**depot** ['dɛpəu] n dépôt m; (US: Rail)
gare f
**depreciate** [dɪ'priːʃɪeɪt] vi se déprécier,
se dévaloriser
**depress** [dɪ'prɛs] vt déprimer; (press
down) appuyer sur, abaisser; (wages etc)
faire baisser; **depressed** adj (person)
déprimé(e); (area) en déclin, touché(e)
par le sous-emploi; **depressing** adj
déprimant(e); **depression** [dɪ'prɛʃən]
n dépression f
**deprive** [dɪ'praɪv] vt: **to ~ sb of** priver
qn de; **deprived** adj déshérité(e)
**dept.** abbr (= department) dép, dépt
**depth** [dɛpθ] n profondeur f; **to be in
the ~s of despair** être au plus profond
du désespoir; **to be out of one's ~**
(BRIT: swimmer) ne plus avoir pied; (fig)
être dépassé(e), nager
**deputy** ['dɛpjutɪ] n (second in command)
adjoint(e); (Pol) député m; (US: also: ~
**sheriff**) shérif adjoint ▷ adj: **~ head**
(Scol) directeur(-trice) adjoint(e), sous-
directeur(-trice)
**derail** [dɪ'reɪl] vt: **to be ~ed** dérailler
**derelict** ['dɛrɪlɪkt] adj abandonné(e),
à l'abandon
**derive** [dɪ'raɪv] vt: **to ~ sth from** tirer
qch de; trouver qch dans ▷ vi: **to ~ from**

provenir de, dériver de

**descend** [dɪ'sɛnd] *vt, vi* descendre; **to ~ from** descendre de, être issu(e) de; **to ~ to** s'abaisser à; **descendant** *n* descendant(e); **descent** *n* descente *f*; (*origin*) origine *f*

**describe** [dɪs'kraɪb] *vt* décrire; **description** [dɪs'krɪpʃən] *n* description *f*; (*sort*) sorte *f*, espèce *f*

**desert** *n* ['dɛzət] désert *m* ▷ *vb* [dɪ'zɔ:t] ▷ *vt* déserter, abandonner ▷ *vi* (*Mil*) déserter; **deserted** [dɪ'zɔ:tɪd] *adj* désert(e)

**deserve** [dɪ'zɔ:v] *vt* mériter

**design** [dɪ'zaɪn] *n* (*sketch*) plan *m*, dessin *m*; (*layout, shape*) conception *f*, ligne *f*; (*pattern*) dessin, motif(s) *m(pl)*; (*of dress, car*) modèle *m*; (*art*) design *m*, stylisme *m*; (*intention*) dessein *m* ▷ *vt* dessiner; (*plan*) concevoir; **design and technology** *n* (BRIT: *Scol*) technologie *f*

**designate** *vt* ['dɛzɪgneɪt] désigner ▷ *adj* ['dɛzɪgnɪt] désigné(e)

**designer** [dɪ'zaɪnə<sup>r</sup>] *n* (*Archit, Art*) dessinateur(-trice); (*Industry*) concepteur *m*, designer *m*; (*Fashion*) styliste *m/f*

**desirable** [dɪ'zaɪərəbl] *adj* (*property, location, purchase*) attrayant(e)

**desire** [dɪ'zaɪə<sup>r</sup>] *n* désir *m* ▷ *vt* désirer, vouloir

**desk** [dɛsk] *n* (*in office*) bureau *m*; (*for pupil*) pupitre *m*; (BRIT: *in shop, restaurant*) caisse *f*; (*in hotel, at airport*) réception *f*; **desk-top publishing** ['dɛsktɔp-] *n* publication assistée par ordinateur, PAO *f*

**despair** [dɪs'pɛə<sup>r</sup>] *n* désespoir *m* ▷ *vi*: **to ~ of** désespérer de

**despatch** [dɪs'pætʃ] *n, vt* = **dispatch**

**desperate** ['dɛspərɪt] *adj* désespéré(e); (*fugitive*) prêt(e) à tout; **to be ~ for sth/ to do sth** avoir désespérément besoin de qch/de faire qch; **desperately** *adv* désespérément; (*very*) terriblement, extrêmement; **desperation** [dɛspə'reɪʃən] *n* désespoir *m*; **in (sheer) desperation** en désespoir

de cause

**despise** [dɪs'paɪz] *vt* mépriser

**despite** [dɪs'paɪt] *prep* malgré, en dépit de

**dessert** [dɪ'zɔ:t] *n* dessert *m*; **dessertspoon** *n* cuiller *f* à dessert

**destination** [dɛstɪ'neɪʃən] *n* destination *f*

**destined** ['dɛstɪnd] *adj*: **~ for London** à destination de Londres

**destiny** ['dɛstɪnɪ] *n* destinée *f*, destin *m*

**destroy** [dɪs'trɔɪ] *vt* détruire; (*injured horse*) abattre; (*dog*) faire piquer

**destruction** [dɪs'trʌkʃən] *n* destruction *f*

**destructive** [dɪs'trʌktɪv] *adj* destructeur(-trice)

**detach** [dɪ'tætʃ] *vt* détacher; **detached** *adj* (*attitude*) détaché(e); **detached house** *n* pavillon *m* maison(nette) (individuelle)

**detail** ['di:teɪl] *n* détail *m* ▷ *vt* raconter en détail, énumérer; **in ~** en détail; **detailed** *adj* détaillé(e)

**detain** [dɪ'teɪn] *vt* retenir; (*in captivity*) détenir

**detect** [dɪ'tɛkt] *vt* déceler, percevoir; (*Med, Police*) dépister; (*Mil, Radar, Tech*) détecter; **detection** [dɪ'tɛkʃən] *n* découverte *f*; **detective** *n* policier *m*; **private detective** détective privé; **detective story** *n* roman policier

**detention** [dɪ'tɛnʃən] *n* détention *f*; (*Scol*) retenue *f*, consigne *f*

**deter** [dɪ'tə:<sup>r</sup>] *vt* dissuader

**detergent** [dɪ'tə:dʒənt] *n* détersif *m*, détergent *m*

**deteriorate** [dɪ'tɪərɪəreɪt] *vi* se détériorer, se dégrader

**determination** [dɪtə:mɪ'neɪʃən] *n* détermination *f*

**determine** [dɪ'tə:mɪn] *vt* déterminer; **to ~ to do** résoudre de faire, se déterminer à faire; **determined** *adj* (*person*) déterminé(e), décidé(e); **determined to do** bien décidé à faire

**deterrent** [dɪ'tɛrənt] *n* effet *m* de dissuasion; force *f* de dissuasion

**detest** [dɪ'tɛst] vt détester, avoir
horreur de

**detour** ['di:tuə'] n détour m; (us Aut:
diversion) déviation f

**detract** [dɪ'trækt] vt: **to ~ from** (quality,
pleasure) diminuer; (reputation) porter
atteinte à

**detrimental** [dɛtrɪ'mɛntl] adj: **~ to**
préjudiciable or nuisible à

**devastating** ['dɛvəsteɪtɪŋ] adj
dévastateur(-trice); (news) accablant(e)

**develop** [dɪ'vɛləp] vt (gen) développer;
(disease) commencer à souffrir
de; (resources) mettre en valeur,
exploiter; (land) aménager ▷ vi se
développer; (situation, disease: evolve)
évoluer; (facts, symptoms: appear) se
manifester, se produire; **can you ~
this film?** pouvez-vous développer
cette pellicule?; **developing country**
n pays m en voie de développement;
**development** n développement m;
(of land) exploitation f; (new fact, event)
rebondissement m, fait(s) nouveau(x)

**device** [dɪ'vaɪs] n (apparatus) appareil
m, dispositif m

**devil** ['dɛvl] n diable m; démon m

**devious** ['di:vɪəs] adj (person)
sournois(e), dissimulé(e)

**devise** [dɪ'vaɪz] vt imaginer, concevoir

**devote** [dɪ'vəut] vt: **to ~ sth to**
consacrer qch à; **devoted** adj
dévoué(e); **to be devoted to** être
dévoué(e) or très attaché(e) à; (book
etc) être consacré(e) à; **devotion** n
dévouement m, attachement m; (Rel)
dévotion f, piété f

**devour** [dɪ'vauə'] vt dévorer

**devout** [dɪ'vaut] adj pieux(-euse),
dévot(e)

**dew** [dju:] n rosée f

**diabetes** [daɪə'bi:ti:z] n diabète m

**diabetic** [daɪə'bɛtɪk] n diabétique m/f
▷ adj (person) diabétique

**diagnose** [daɪəg'nəuz] vt
diagnostiquer

**diagnosis** (pl **diagnoses**)
[daɪəg'nəusɪs, -si:z] n diagnostic m

**diagonal** [daɪ'ægənl] adj diagonal(e)
▷ n diagonale f

**diagram** ['daɪəgræm] n diagramme
m, schéma m

**dial** ['daɪəl] n cadran m ▷ vt (number)
faire, composer

**dialect** ['daɪəlɛkt] n dialecte m

**dialling code** ['daɪəlɪŋ-] (us **dial code**)
n indicatif m (téléphonique); **what's
the ~ for Paris?** quel est l'indicatif
de Paris?

**dialling tone** ['daɪəlɪŋ-] (us **dial tone**)
n tonalité f

**dialogue** (us **dialog**) ['daɪəlɔg] n
dialogue m

**diameter** [daɪ'æmɪtə'] n diamètre m

**diamond** ['daɪəmənd] n diamant
m; (shape) losange m; **diamonds** npl
(Cards) carreau m

**diaper** ['daɪəpə'] n (us) couche f

**diarrhoea** (us **diarrhea**) [daɪə'ri:ə] n
diarrhée f

**diary** ['daɪərɪ] n (daily account) journal
m; (book) agenda m

**dice** [daɪs] n (pl inv) dé m ▷ vt (Culin)
couper en dés or en cubes

**dictate** [dɪk'teɪt] vt dicter; **dictation**
[dɪk'teɪʃən] n dictée f

**dictator** [dɪk'teɪtə'] n dictateur m

**dictionary** ['dɪkʃənrɪ] n dictionnaire m

**did** [dɪd] pt of **do**

**didn't** [dɪdnt] = **did not**

**die** [daɪ] vi mourir; **to be dying for
sth** avoir une envie folle de qch; **to be
dying to do sth** mourir d'envie de faire
qch; **die down** vi se calmer, s'apaiser;
**die out** vi disparaître, s'éteindre

**diesel** ['di:zl] n (vehicle) diesel m; (also: ~
oil) carburant m diesel, gas-oil m

**diet** ['daɪət] n alimentation f; (restricted
food) régime m ▷ vi (also: **be on a ~**)
suivre un régime

**differ** ['dɪfə'] vi: **to ~ from sth** (be
different) être différent(e) de qch,
différer de qch; **to ~ from sb over sth**
ne pas être d'accord avec qn au sujet de
qch; **difference** n différence f; (quarrel)
différend m, désaccord m; **different**

*adj* différent(e); **differentiate**
[dɪfəˈrɛnʃɪeɪt] *vi*: **to differentiate
between** faire une différence entre;
**differently** *adv* différemment
**difficult** [ˈdɪfɪkəlt] *adj* difficile;
**difficulty** *n* difficulté *f*
**dig** [dɪg] *vt* (*pt, pp* **dug**) (*hole*) creuser;
(*garden*) bêcher ▷ *n* (*prod*) coup *m* de
coude; (*fig: remark*) coup de griffe *or* de
patte; (*Archaeology*) fouille *f*; **to ~ one's
nails into** enfoncer ses ongles dans;
**dig up** *vt* déterrer
**digest** *vt* [daɪˈdʒɛst] digérer ▷ *n*
[ˈdaɪdʒɛst] sommaire *m*, résumé *m*;
**digestion** [dɪˈdʒɛstʃən] *n* digestion *f*
**digit** [ˈdɪdʒɪt] *n* (*number*) chiffre *m* (*de o
à 9*); (*finger*) doigt *m*; **digital** *adj* (*system,
recording, radio*) numérique, digital(e);
(*watch*) à affichage numérique *or*
digital; **digital camera** *n* appareil
*m* photo numérique; **digital TV** *n*
télévision *f* numérique
**dignified** [ˈdɪgnɪfaɪd] *adj* digne
**dignity** [ˈdɪgnɪtɪ] *n* dignité *f*
**digs** [dɪgz] *npl* (*BRIT inf*) piaule *f*,
chambre meublée
**dilemma** [daɪˈlɛmə] *n* dilemme *m*
**dill** [dɪl] *n* aneth *m*
**dilute** [daɪˈluːt] *vt* diluer
**dim** [dɪm] *adj* (*light, eyesight*) faible;
(*memory, outline*) vague, indécis(e);
(*room*) sombre; (*inf: stupid*) borné(e),
obtus(e) ▷ *vt* (*light*) réduire, baisser; (*us
Aut*) mettre en code, baisser
**dime** [daɪm] *n* (*us*) pièce *f* de 10 cents
**dimension** [daɪˈmɛnʃən] *n*
dimension *f*
**diminish** [dɪˈmɪnɪʃ] *vt, vi* diminuer
**din** [dɪn] *n* vacarme *m*
**dine** [daɪn] *vi* dîner; **diner** *n* (*person*)
dîneur(-euse); (*us: eating place*) petit
restaurant
**dinghy** [ˈdɪŋgɪ] *n* youyou *m*; (*inflatable*)
canot *m* pneumatique; (*also*: **sailing ~**)
voilier *m*, dériveur *m*
**dingy** [ˈdɪndʒɪ] *adj* miteux(-euse),
minable
**dining car** [ˈdaɪnɪŋ-] *n* (*BRIT*) voiture-

restaurant *f*, wagon-restaurant *m*
**dining room** [ˈdaɪnɪŋ-] *n* salle *f* à
manger
**dining table** [daɪnɪŋ-] *n* table *f* de (la)
salle à manger
**dinner** [ˈdɪnər] *n* (*evening meal*) dîner *m*;
(*lunch*) déjeuner *m*; (*public*) banquet *m*;
**dinner jacket** *n* smoking *m*; **dinner
party** *n* dîner *m*; **dinner time** *n*
(*evening*) heure *f* du dîner; (*midday*)
heure du déjeuner
**dinosaur** [ˈdaɪnəsɔːr] *n* dinosaure *m*
**dip** [dɪp] *n* (*slope*) déclivité *f*; (*in sea*)
baignade *f*, bain *m*; (*Culin*) ≈ sauce *f*
▷ *vt* tremper, plonger; (*BRIT Aut: lights*)
mettre en code, baisser ▷ *vi* plonger
**diploma** [dɪˈpləʊmə] *n* diplôme *m*
**diplomacy** [dɪˈpləʊməsɪ] *n*
diplomatie *f*
**diplomat** [ˈdɪpləmæt] *n* diplomate *m*;
**diplomatic** [dɪpləˈmætɪk] *adj*
diplomatique
**dipstick** [ˈdɪpstɪk] *n* (*BRIT Aut*) jauge *f*
de niveau d'huile
**dire** [daɪər] *adj* (*poverty*) extrême; (*awful*)
affreux(-euse)
**direct** [daɪˈrɛkt] *adj* direct(e) ▷ *vt* (*tell
way*) diriger, orienter; (*letter, remark*)
adresser; (*Cine, TV*) réaliser; (*Theat*)
mettre en scène; (*order*): **to ~ sb to do
sth** ordonner à qn de faire qch ▷ *adv*
directement; **can you ~ me to ...?**
pouvez-vous m'indiquer le chemin
de ...?; **direct debit** *n* (*BRIT Banking*)
prélèvement *m* automatique
**direction** [dɪˈrɛkʃən] *n* direction *f*;
**directions** *npl* (*to a place*) indications
*fpl*; **~s for use** mode *m* d'emploi; **sense
of ~** sens *m* de l'orientation
**directly** [dɪˈrɛktlɪ] *adv* (*in straight line*)
directement, tout droit; (*at once*) tout
de suite, immédiatement
**director** [dɪˈrɛktər] *n* directeur *m*;
(*Theat*) metteur *m* en scène; (*Cine, TV*)
réalisateur(-trice)
**directory** [dɪˈrɛktərɪ] *n* annuaire
*m*; (*Comput*) répertoire *m*; **directory
enquiries** (*us* **directory assistance**) *n*

(Tel: service) renseignements mpl

**dirt** [dɜːt] n saleté f; (mud) boue f; **dirty** adj sale; (joke) cochon(ne) ▷ vt salir

**disability** [dɪsə'bɪlɪtɪ] n invalidité f, infirmité f

**disabled** [dɪs'eɪbld] adj handicapé(e); (maimed) mutilé(e)

**disadvantage** [dɪsəd'vɑːntɪdʒ] n désavantage m, inconvénient m

**disagree** [dɪsə'griː] vi (differ) ne pas concorder; (be against, think otherwise): **to ~ (with)** ne pas être d'accord (avec); **disagreeable** adj désagréable; **disagreement** n désaccord m, différend m

**disappear** [dɪsə'pɪər] vi disparaître; **disappearance** n disparition f

**disappoint** [dɪsə'pɔɪnt] vt décevoir; **disappointed** adj déçu(e); **disappointing** adj décevant(e); **disappointment** n déception f

**disapproval** [dɪsə'pruːvəl] n désapprobation f

**disapprove** [dɪsə'pruːv] vi: **to ~ of** désapprouver

**disarm** [dɪs'ɑːm] vt désarmer; **disarmament** [dɪs'ɑːməmənt] n désarmement m

**disaster** [dɪ'zɑːstər] n catastrophe f, désastre m; **disastrous** adj désastreux(-euse)

**disbelief** ['dɪsbə'liːf] n incrédulité f

**disc** [dɪsk] n disque m; (Comput) = **disk**

**discard** [dɪs'kɑːd] vt (old things) se débarrasser de; (fig) écarter, renoncer à

**discharge** vt [dɪs'tʃɑːdʒ] (duties) s'acquitter de; (waste etc) déverser; décharger; (patient) renvoyer (chez lui); (employee, soldier) congédier, licencier ▷ n ['dɪstʃɑːdʒ] (Elec, Med) émission f; (dismissal) renvoi m; licenciement m

**discipline** ['dɪsɪplɪn] n discipline f ▷ vt discipliner; (punish) punir

**disc jockey** n disque-jockey m (DJ)

**disclose** [dɪs'kləuz] vt révéler, divulguer

**disco** ['dɪskəu] n abbr discothèque f

**discoloured** [dɪs'kʌləd] (US

**discolored**) adj décoloré(e), jauni(e)

**discomfort** [dɪs'kʌmfət] n malaise m, gêne f; (lack of comfort) manque m de confort

**disconnect** [dɪskə'nɛkt] vt (Elec, Radio) débrancher; (gas, water) couper

**discontent** [dɪskən'tɛnt] n mécontentement m

**discontinue** [dɪskən'tɪnjuː] vt cesser, interrompre; **"~d"** (Comm) "fin de série"

**discount** n ['dɪskaunt] remise f, rabais m ▷ vt [dɪs'kaunt] (report etc) ne pas tenir compte de

**discourage** [dɪs'kʌrɪdʒ] vt décourager

**discover** [dɪs'kʌvər] vt découvrir; **discovery** n découverte f

**discredit** [dɪs'krɛdɪt] vt (idea) mettre en doute; (person) discréditer

**discreet** [dɪ'skriːt] adj discret(-ète)

**discrepancy** [dɪ'skrɛpənsɪ] n divergence f, contradiction f

**discretion** [dɪ'skrɛʃən] n discrétion f; **at the ~ of** à la discrétion de

**discriminate** [dɪ'skrɪmɪneɪt] vi: **to ~ between** établir une distinction entre, faire la différence entre; **to ~ against** pratiquer une discrimination contre; **discrimination** [dɪskrɪmɪ'neɪʃən] n discrimination f; (judgment) discernement m

**discuss** [dɪ'skʌs] vt discuter de; (debate) discuter; **discussion** [dɪ'skʌʃən] n discussion f

**disease** [dɪ'ziːz] n maladie f

**disembark** [dɪsɪm'bɑːk] vt, vi débarquer

**disgrace** [dɪs'greɪs] n honte f; (disfavour) disgrâce f ▷ vt déshonorer, couvrir de honte; **disgraceful** adj scandaleux(-euse), honteux(-euse)

**disgruntled** [dɪs'grʌntld] adj mécontent(e)

**disguise** [dɪs'gaɪz] n déguisement m ▷ vt déguiser; **in ~** déguisé(e)

**disgust** [dɪs'gʌst] n dégoût m, aversion f ▷ vt dégoûter, écœurer

**disgusted** [dɪs'gʌstɪd] adj dégoûté(e), écœuré(e)

**disgusting** [dɪs'gʌstɪŋ] *adj*
dégoûtant(e)

**dish** [dɪʃ] *n* plat *m*; **to do** *or* **wash the
~es** faire la vaisselle; **dishcloth** *n* (*for
drying*) torchon *m*; (*for washing*) lavette *f*

**dishonest** [dɪs'ɔnɪst] *adj* malhonnête

**dishtowel** ['dɪʃtauəl] *n* (*US*) torchon *m*
(à vaisselle)

**dishwasher** ['dɪʃwɔʃə<sup>r</sup>] *n* lave-
vaisselle *m*

**disillusion** [dɪsɪ'luːʒən] *vt* désabuser,
désenchanter

**disinfectant** [dɪsɪn'fɛktənt] *n*
désinfectant *m*

**disintegrate** [dɪs'ɪntɪgreɪt] *vi* se
désintégrer

**disk** [dɪsk] *n* (*Comput*) disquette *f*;
**single-/double-sided ~** disquette une
face/double face; **disk drive** *n* lecteur
*m* de disquette; **diskette** *n* (*Comput*)
disquette *f*

**dislike** [dɪs'laɪk] *n* aversion *f*,
antipathie *f* ▷ *vt* ne pas aimer

**dislocate** ['dɪsləkeɪt] *vt* disloquer,
déboîter

**disloyal** [dɪs'lɔɪəl] *adj* déloyal(e)

**dismal** ['dɪzml] *adj* (*gloomy*) lugubre,
maussade; (*very bad*) lamentable

**dismantle** [dɪs'mæntl] *vt* démonter

**dismay** [dɪs'meɪ] *n* consternation *f* ▷ *vt*
consterner

**dismiss** [dɪs'mɪs] *vt* congédier,
renvoyer; (*idea*) écarter; (*Law*) rejeter;
**dismissal** *n* renvoi *m*

**disobedient** [dɪsə'biːdɪənt] *adj*
désobéissant(e), indiscipliné(e)

**disobey** [dɪsə'beɪ] *vt* désobéir à

**disorder** [dɪs'ɔːdə<sup>r</sup>] *n* désordre
*m*; (*rioting*) désordres *mpl*; (*Med*)
troubles *mpl*

**disorganized** [dɪs'ɔːgənaɪzd] *adj*
désorganisé(e)

**disown** [dɪs'əun] *vt* renier

**dispatch** [dɪs'pætʃ] *vt* expédier,
envoyer ▷ *n* envoi *m*, expédition *f*; (*Mil*,
*Press*) dépêche *f*

**dispel** [dɪs'pɛl] *vt* dissiper, chasser

**dispense** [dɪs'pɛns] *vt* (*medicine*)

préparer (et vendre); **dispense with** *vt
fus* se passer de; **dispenser** *n* (*device*)
distributeur *m*

**disperse** [dɪs'pəːs] *vt* disperser ▷ *vi* se
disperser

**display** [dɪs'pleɪ] *n* (*of goods*) étalage
*m*; affichage *m*; (*Comput: information*)
visualisation *f*; (: *device*) visuel *m*; (*of
feeling*) manifestation *f* ▷ *vt* montrer;
(*goods*) mettre à l'étalage, exposer;
(*results, departure times*) afficher; (*pej*)
faire étalage de

**displease** [dɪs'pliːz] *vt* mécontenter,
contrarier

**disposable** [dɪs'pəuzəbl] *adj* (*pack etc*)
jetable; (*income*) disponible

**disposal** [dɪs'pəuzl] *n* (*of rubbish*)
évacuation *f*, destruction *f*; (*of property
etc: by selling*) vente *f*; (: *by giving away*)
cession *f*; **at one's ~** à sa disposition

**dispose** [dɪs'pəuz] *vi*: **to ~ of** (*unwanted
goods*) se débarrasser de, se défaire
de; (*problem*) expédier; **disposition**
[dɪspə'zɪʃən] *n* disposition *f*;
(*temperament*) naturel *m*

**disproportionate** [dɪsprə'pɔːʃənət]
*adj* disproportionné(e)

**dispute** [dɪs'pjuːt] *n* discussion *f*; (*also:
**industrial ~**) conflit *m* ▷ *vt* (*question*)
contester; (*matter*) discuter

**disqualify** [dɪs'kwɔlɪfaɪ] *vt* (*Sport*)
disqualifier; **to ~ sb for sth/from
doing** rendre qn inapte à qch/à faire

**disregard** [dɪsrɪ'gɑːd] *vt* ne pas tenir
compte de

**disrupt** [dɪs'rʌpt] *vt* (*plans, meeting,
lesson*) perturber, déranger; **disruption**
[dɪs'rʌpʃən] *n* perturbation *f*,
dérangement *m*

**dissatisfaction** [dɪssætɪs'fækʃən] *n*
mécontentement *m*, insatisfaction *f*

**dissatisfied** [dɪs'sætɪsfaɪd] *adj*: **~
(with)** insatisfait(e) (de)

**dissect** [dɪ'sɛkt] *vt* disséquer

**dissent** [dɪ'sɛnt] *n* dissentiment *m*,
différence *f* d'opinion

**dissertation** [dɪsə'teɪʃən] *n* (*Scol*)
mémoire *m*

**dissolve** [dɪ'zɔlv] *vt* dissoudre ▷ *vi* se dissoudre, fondre; **to ~ in(to) tears** fondre en larmes

**distance** ['dɪstns] *n* distance *f*; **in the ~** au loin

**distant** ['dɪstnt] *adj* lointain(e), éloigné(e); (*manner*) distant(e), froid(e)

**distil** (*us* **distill**) [dɪs'tɪl] *vt* distiller; **distillery** *n* distillerie *f*

**distinct** [dɪs'tɪŋkt] *adj* distinct(e); (*clear*) marqué(e); **as ~ from** par opposition à; **distinction** [dɪs'tɪŋkʃən] *n* distinction *f*; (*in exam*) mention *f* très bien; **distinctive** *adj* distinctif(-ive)

**distinguish** [dɪs'tɪŋgwɪʃ] *vt* distinguer; **to ~ o.s.** se distinguer; **distinguished** *adj* (*eminent, refined*) distingué(e)

**distort** [dɪs'tɔːt] *vt* déformer

**distract** [dɪs'trækt] *vt* distraire, déranger; **distracted** *adj* (*not concentrating*) distrait(e); (*worried*) affolé(e); **distraction** [dɪs'trækʃən] *n* distraction *f*

**distraught** [dɪs'trɔːt] *adj* éperdu(e)

**distress** [dɪs'trɛs] *n* détresse *f* ▷ *vt* affliger; **distressing** *adj* douloureux(-euse), pénible

**distribute** [dɪs'trɪbjuːt] *vt* distribuer; **distribution** [dɪstrɪ'bjuːʃən] *n* distribution *f*; **distributor** *n* (*gen: Tech*) distributeur *m*; (*Comm*) concessionnaire *m/f*

**district** ['dɪstrɪkt] *n* (*of country*) région *f*; (*of town*) quartier *m*; (*Admin*) district *m*; **district attorney** *n* (*us*) ≈ procureur *m* de la République

**distrust** [dɪs'trʌst] *n* méfiance *f*, doute *m* ▷ *vt* se méfier de

**disturb** [dɪs'təːb] *vt* troubler; (*inconvenience*) déranger; **disturbance** *n* dérangement *m*; (*political etc*) troubles *mpl*; **disturbed** *adj* (*worried, upset*) agité(e), troublé(e); **to be emotionally disturbed** avoir des problèmes affectifs; **disturbing** *adj* troublant(e), inquiétant(e)

**ditch** [dɪtʃ] *n* fossé *m*; (*for irrigation*)

rigole *f* ▷ *vt* (*inf*) abandonner; (*person*) plaquer

**ditto** ['dɪtəu] *adv* idem

**dive** [daɪv] *n* plongeon *m*; (*of submarine*) plongée *f* ▷ *vi* plonger; **to ~ into** (*bag etc*) plonger la main dans; (*place*) se précipiter dans; **diver** *n* plongeur *m*

**diverse** [daɪ'vəːs] *adj* divers(e)

**diversion** [daɪ'vəːʃən] *n* (*BRIT Aut*) déviation *f*; (*distraction, Mil*) diversion *f*

**diversity** [daɪ'vəːsɪtɪ] *n* diversité *f*, variété *f*

**divert** [daɪ'vəːt] *vt* (*BRIT: traffic*) dévier; (*plane*) dérouter; (*train, river*) détourner

**divide** [dɪ'vaɪd] *vt* diviser; (*separate*) séparer ▷ *vi* se diviser; **divided highway** (*us*) *n* route *f* à quatre voies

**divine** [dɪ'vaɪn] *adj* divin(e)

**diving** ['daɪvɪŋ] *n* plongée (sous-marine); **diving board** *n* plongeoir *m*

**division** [dɪ'vɪʒən] *n* division *f*; (*separation*) séparation *f*; (*Comm*) service *m*

**divorce** [dɪ'vɔːs] *n* divorce *m* ▷ *vt* divorcer d'avec; **divorced** *adj* divorcé(e); **divorcee** [dɪvɔː'siː] *n* divorcé(e)

**D.I.Y.** *adj, n abbr* (*BRIT*) = **do-it-yourself**

**dizzy** ['dɪzɪ] *adj*: **I feel ~** la tête me tourne, j'ai la tête qui tourne

**DJ** *n abbr* = **disc jockey**

**DNA** *n abbr* (= deoxyribonucleic acid) ADN *m*

**KEYWORD**

**do** [duː] (*pt* **did**, *pp* **done**) *n* (*inf: party etc*) soirée *f*, fête *f*
▷ *vb* **1** (*in negative constructions*) non traduit; **I don't understand** je ne comprends pas
**2** (*to form questions*) non traduit; **didn't you know?** vous ne le saviez pas?; **what do you think?** qu'en pensez-vous?
**3** (*for emphasis, in polite expressions*): **people do make mistakes sometimes** on peut toujours se tromper; **she does seem rather late** je

trouve qu'elle est bien en retard; **do sit down/help yourself** asseyez-vous/servez-vous je vous en prie; **do take care!** faites bien attention à vous!
**4** (*used to avoid repeating vb*): **she swims better than I do** elle nage mieux que moi; **do you agree? - yes, I do/no I don't** vous êtes d'accord? - oui/non; **she lives in Glasgow - so do I** elle habite Glasgow - moi aussi; **he didn't like it and neither did we** il n'a pas aimé ça, et nous non plus; **who broke it? - I did** qui l'a cassé? - c'est moi; **he asked me to help him and I did** il m'a demandé de l'aider, et c'est ce que j'ai fait
**5** (*in question tags*): **you like him, don't you?** vous l'aimez bien, n'est-ce pas?; **I don't know him, do I?** je ne crois pas le connaître
▷ *vt* **1** (*gen: carry out, perform etc*) faire; (*visit: city, museum*) faire, visiter; **what are you doing tonight?** qu'est-ce que vous faites ce soir?; **what do you do?** (*job*) que faites-vous dans la vie?; **what can I do for you?** que puis-je faire pour vous?; **to do the cooking/washing-up** faire la cuisine/la vaisselle; **to do one's teeth/hair/nails** se brosser les dents/se coiffer/se faire les ongles
**2** (*Aut etc: distance*) faire; (: *speed*) faire du; **we've done 200 km already** nous avons déjà fait 200 km; **the car was doing 100** la voiture faisait du 100 (à l'heure); **he can do 100 in that car** il peut faire du 100 (à l'heure) dans cette voiture-là
▷ *vi* **1** (*act, behave*) faire; **do as I do** faites comme moi
**2** (*get on, fare*) marcher; **the firm is doing well** l'entreprise marche bien; **he's doing well/badly at school** ça marche bien/mal pour lui à l'école; **how do you do?** comment allez-vous?; (*on being introduced*) enchanté(e)!
**3** (*suit*) aller; **will it do?** est-ce que ça ira?
**4** (*be sufficient*) suffire, aller; **will £10**

do? est-ce que 10 livres suffiront?; **that'll do** ça suffit, ça ira; **that'll do!** (*in annoyance*) ça va or suffit comme ça!; **to make do (with)** se contenter (de)
**do up** *vt* (*laces, dress*) attacher; (*buttons*) boutonner; (*zip*) fermer; (*renovate: room*) refaire; (: *house*) remettre à neuf
**do with** *vt fus* (*need*): **I could do with a drink/some help** quelque chose à boire/un peu d'aide ne serait pas de refus; **it could do with a wash** ça ne lui ferait pas de mal d'être lavé; (*be connected with*): **that has nothing to do with you** cela ne vous concerne pas; **I won't have anything to do with it** je ne veux pas m'en mêler
**do without** *vi* s'en passer; **if you're late for tea then you'll do without** si vous êtes en retard pour le dîner il faudra vous en passer
▷ *vt fus* se passer de; **I can do without a car** je peux me passer de voiture

**dock** [dɔk] *n* dock *m*; (*wharf*) quai *m*; (*Law*) banc *m* des accusés ▷ *vi* se mettre à quai; (*Space*) s'arrimer; **docks** *npl* (*Naut*) docks
**doctor** ['dɔktər] *n* médecin *m*, docteur *m*; (*PhD etc*) docteur ▷ *vt* (*drink*) frelater; **call a ~!** appelez un docteur or un médecin!; **Doctor of Philosophy (PhD)** *n* (*degree*) doctorat *m*; (*person*) titulaire *m/f* d'un doctorat
**document** ['dɔkjumənt] *n* document *m*; **documentary** [dɔkju'mɛntərɪ] *adj, n* documentaire (*m*); **documentation** [dɔkjumən'teɪʃən] *n* documentation *f*
**dodge** [dɔdʒ] *n* truc *m*; combine *f* ▷ *vt* esquiver, éviter
**dodgy** ['dɔdʒɪ] *adj* (*inf: uncertain*) douteux(-euse); (: *shady*) louche
**does** [dʌz] *vb see* **do**
**doesn't** ['dʌznt] = **does not**
**dog** [dɔg] *n* chien(ne) ▷ *vt* (*follow closely*) suivre de près; (*fig: memory etc*) poursuivre, harceler; **doggy bag** ['dɔgɪ-] *n* petit sac pour emporter les restes

**do-it-yourself**['duːɪtjɔː'sɛlf] n
bricolage m

**dole**[dəul] n (BRIT: payment) allocation f
de chômage; **on the ~** au chômage

**doll**[dɔl] n poupée f

**dollar**['dɔləʳ] n dollar m

**dolphin**['dɔlfɪn] n dauphin m

**dome**[dəum] n dôme m

**domestic**[də'mɛstɪk] adj (duty,
happiness) familial(e); (policy,
affairs, flight) intérieur(e); (animal)
domestique; **domestic appliance** n
appareil ménager

**dominant**['dɔmɪnənt] adj
dominant(e)

**dominate**['dɔmɪneɪt] vt dominer

**domino**['dɔmɪnəu] (pl **~es**) n
domino m; **dominoes** n (game)
dominos mpl

**donate**[də'neɪt] vt faire don de,
donner; **donation**[də'neɪʃən] n
donation f, don m

**done**[dʌn] pp of **do**

**donkey**['dɔŋkɪ] n âne m

**donor**['dəunəʳ] n (of blood etc)
donneur(-euse); (to charity)
donateur(-trice); **donor card** n carte f
de don d'organes

**don't**[dəunt] = **do not**

**donut**['dəunʌt] (US) n = **doughnut**

**doodle**['duːdl] vi griffonner, gribouiller

**doom**[duːm] n (fate) destin m ▷ vt: **to
be ~ed to failure** être voué(e) à l'échec

**door**[dɔːʳ] n porte f; (Rail, car) portière f;
**doorbell** n sonnette f; **door handle**
n poignée f de porte; (of car) poignée
de portière; **doorknob** n poignée f or
bouton m de porte; **doorstep** n pas
m de (la) porte, seuil m; **doorway** n
(embrasure f de) porte f

**dope**[dəup] n (inf: drug) drogue f;
(: person) andouille f ▷ vt (horse etc)
doper

**dormitory**['dɔːmɪtrɪ] n (BRIT) dortoir
m; (US: hall of residence) résidence f
universitaire

**DOS**[dɔs] n abbr (= disk operating system)
DOS m

**dosage**['dəusɪdʒ] n dose f; dosage m;
(on label) posologie f

**dose**[dəus] n dose f

**dot**[dɔt] n point m; (on material) pois m
▷ vt: **~ted with** parsemé(e) de; **on the
~** à l'heure tapante; **dotcom**[dɔt'kɔm]
n point com m, pointcom m; **dotted
line**['dɔtɪd-] n ligne pointillée; **to sign
on the dotted line** signer à l'endroit
indiqué or sur la ligne pointillée

**double**['dʌbl] adj double ▷ adv (twice):
**to cost ~ (sth)** coûter le double
(de qch) or deux fois plus (que qch) ▷ n
double m; (Cine) doublure f ▷ vt
doubler; (fold) plier en deux ▷ vi
doubler; **on the ~**, **at the ~** au pas
de course; **double back** vi (person)
revenir sur ses pas; **double bass** n
contrebasse f; **double bed** n grand
lit; **double-check** vt, vi revérifier;
**double-click** vi (Comput) double-
cliquer; **double-cross** vt doubler,
trahir; **doubledecker** n autobus m à
impériale; **double glazing** n (BRIT)
double vitrage m; **double room** n
chambre f pour deux; **doubles** n
(Tennis) double m; **double yellow
lines** npl (BRIT: Aut) double bande jaune
marquant l'interdiction de stationner

**doubt**[daut] n doute m ▷ vt douter
de; **no ~** sans doute; **to ~ that** douter
que + sub; **doubtful** adj douteux(-euse);
(person) incertain(e); **doubtless** adv
sans doute, sûrement

**dough**[dəu] n pâte f; **doughnut** (US)
**donut**) n beignet m

**dove**[dʌv] n colombe f

**Dover**['dəuvəʳ] n Douvres

**down**[daun] n (fluff) duvet m ▷ adv
en bas, vers le bas; (on the ground) par
terre ▷ prep en bas de; (along) le long
de ▷ vt (inf: drink) siffler; **to walk ~ a
hill** descendre une colline; **to run ~ the
street** descendre la rue en courant;
**~ with X!** à bas X!; **down-and-out** n
(tramp) clochard(e); **downfall** n chute
f; ruine f; **downhill** adv: **to go downhill**
descendre; (business) péricliter

**Downing Street** ['daunɪŋ-] n (BRIT):
**10 ~** résidence du Premier ministre

- **DOWNING STREET**
-
- **Downing Street** est une rue de
- Westminster (à Londres) où se
- trouvent la résidence officielle
- du Premier ministre et celle du
- ministre des Finances. Le nom
- **Downing Street** est souvent utilisé
- pour désigner le gouvernement
- britannique.

**down**: **download** vt (Comput)
télécharger; **downright** adj (lie etc)
effronté(e); (refusal) catégorique
**Down's syndrome** [daunz-] n
trisomie f
**down**: **downstairs** adv (on or to
ground floor) au rez-de-chaussée; (on
or to floor below) à l'étage inférieur;
**down-to-earth** adj terre à terre inv;
**downtown** adv en ville; **down under**
adv en Australie or Nouvelle Zélande;
**downward** ['daunwəd] adj, adv vers
le bas; **downwards** ['daunwədz] adv
vers le bas
**doz.** abbr = **dozen**
**doze** [dəuz] vi sommeiller
**dozen** ['dʌzn] n douzaine f; **a ~ books**
une douzaine de livres; **~s of** des
centaines de
**Dr.** abbr (= doctor) Dr; (in street names)
= **drive**
**drab** [dræb] adj terne, morne
**draft** [drɑːft] n (of letter, school
work) brouillon m; (of literary work)
ébauche f; (Comm) traite f; (US: call-up)
conscription f ▷ vt faire le brouillon de;
(Mil: send) détacher; see also **draught**
**drag** [dræg] vt traîner; (river) draguer
▷ vi traîner ▷ n (inf) casse-pieds m/f;
(women's clothing): **in ~** (en) travesti; **to
~ and drop** (Comput) glisser-poser
**dragon** ['drægn] n dragon m
**dragonfly** ['drægənflaɪ] n libellule f
**drain** [dreɪn] n égout m; (on resources)

saignée f ▷ vt (land, marshes) drainer,
assécher; (vegetables) égoutter;
(reservoir etc) vider ▷ vi (water) s'écouler;
**drainage** n (system) système m
d'égouts; (act) drainage m; **drainpipe** n
tuyau m d'écoulement
**drama** ['drɑːmə] n (art) théâtre m, art
m dramatique; (play) pièce f; (event)
drame m; **dramatic** [drə'mætɪk]
adj (Theat) dramatique; (impressive)
spectaculaire
**drank** [dræŋk] pt of **drink**
**drape** [dreɪp] vt draper; **drapes** npl (US)
rideaux mpl
**drastic** ['dræstɪk] adj (measures)
d'urgence, énergique; (change)
radical(e)
**draught** (US **draft**) [drɑːft] n courant m
d'air; **on ~** (beer) à la pression; **draught
beer** n bière f (à la) pression; **draughts**
n (BRIT: game) (jeu m de) dames fpl
**draw** [drɔː] (vb: pt **drew**, pp **~n**) vt tirer;
(picture) dessiner; (attract) attirer; (line,
circle) tracer; (money) retirer; (wages)
toucher ▷ vi (Sport) faire match nul ▷ n
match nul; (lottery) loterie f; (: picking
of ticket) tirage m au sort; **draw out**
vi (lengthen) s'allonger ▷ vt (money)
retirer; **draw up** vi (stop) s'arrêter
▷ vt (document) établir, dresser; (plan)
formuler, dessiner; (chair) approcher;
**drawback** n inconvénient m,
désavantage m
**drawer** [drɔːr] n tiroir m
**drawing** ['drɔːɪŋ] n dessin m; **drawing
pin** n (BRIT) punaise f; **drawing room**
n salon m
**drawn** [drɔːn] pp of **draw**
**dread** [drɛd] n épouvante f, effroi m ▷ vt
redouter, appréhender; **dreadful** adj
épouvantable, affreux(-euse)
**dream** [driːm] n rêve m ▷ vt, vi (pt,
pp **~ed** or **~t**) rêver; **dreamer** n
rêveur(-euse)
**dreamt** [drɛmt] pt, pp of **dream**
**dreary** ['drɪərɪ] adj triste; monotone
**drench** [drɛntʃ] vt tremper
**dress** [drɛs] n robe f; (clothing)

habillement m, tenue f ▷ vt habiller; (wound) panser ▷ vi: **to get ~ed** s'habiller; **dress up** vi s'habiller; (in fancy dress) se déguiser; **dress circle** n (BRIT) premier balcon; **dresser** n (furniture) vaisselier m; (: US) coiffeuse f, commode f; **dressing** n (Med) pansement m; (Culin) sauce f, assaisonnement m; **dressing gown** n (BRIT) robe f de chambre; **dressing room** n (Theat) loge f; (Sport) vestiaire m; **dressing table** n coiffeuse f; **dressmaker** n couturière f

**drew** [druː] pt of **draw**

**dribble** ['drɪbl] vi (baby) baver ▷ vt (ball) dribbler

**dried** [draɪd] adj (fruit, beans) sec (sèche); (eggs, milk) en poudre

**drier** ['draɪə<sup>r</sup>] n = **dryer**

**drift** [drɪft] n (of current etc) force f; direction f; (of snow) rafale f; coulée f; (: on ground) congère f; (general meaning) sens général ▷ vi (boat) aller à la dérive, dériver; (sand, snow) s'amonceler, s'entasser

**drill** [drɪl] n perceuse f; (bit) foret m; (of dentist) roulette f, fraise f; (Mil) exercice m ▷ vt percer; (troops) entraîner ▷ vi (for oil) faire un or des forage(s)

**drink** [drɪŋk] n boisson f; (alcoholic) verre m ▷ vt, vi (pt **drank**, pp **drunk**) boire; **to have a ~** boire quelque chose, boire un verre; **a ~ of water** un verre d'eau; **would you like a ~?** tu veux boire quelque chose?; **drink-driving** n conduite f en état d'ivresse; **drinker** n buveur(-euse); **drinking water** n eau f potable

**drip** [drɪp] n (drop) goutte f; (Med: device) goutte-à-goutte m inv; (: liquid) perfusion f ▷ vi tomber goutte à goutte; (tap) goutter

**drive** [draɪv] n (ride) promenade f or trajet m en voiture; (also: **~way**) allée f; (energy) dynamisme m, énergie f; (push) effort (concerté); campagne f; (Comput: also: **disk ~**) lecteur m de disquette ▷ vb (pt **drove**, pp **~n**) ▷ vt conduire; (nail)

enfoncer; (push) chasser, pousser; (Tech: motor) actionner; entraîner ▷ vi (be at the wheel) conduire; (travel by car) aller en voiture; **left-/right-hand ~** (Aut) conduite f à gauche/droite; **to ~ sb mad** rendre qn fou (folle); **drive out** vt (force out) chasser; **drive-in** adj, n (esp US) drive-in m

**driven** ['drɪvn] pp of **drive**

**driver** ['draɪvə<sup>r</sup>] n conducteur(-trice); (of taxi, bus) chauffeur m; **driver's license** n (US) permis m de conduire

**driveway** ['draɪvweɪ] n allée f

**driving** ['draɪvɪŋ] n conduite f; **driving instructor** n moniteur m d'auto-école; **driving lesson** n leçon f de conduite; **driving licence** n (BRIT) permis m de conduire; **driving test** n examen m du permis de conduire

**drizzle** ['drɪzl] n bruine f, crachin m

**droop** [druːp] vi (flower) commencer à se faner; (shoulders, head) tomber

**drop** [drɔp] n (of liquid) goutte f; (fall) baisse f; (also: **parachute ~**) saut m ▷ vt laisser tomber; (voice, eyes, price) baisser; (passenger) déposer ▷ vi tomber; **drop in** vi (inf: visit): **to ~ in (on)** faire un saut (chez), passer (chez); **drop off** vi (sleep) s'assoupir ▷ vt (passenger) déposer; **drop out** vi (withdraw) se retirer; (student etc) abandonner, décrocher

**drought** [draʊt] n sécheresse f

**drove** [drəʊv] pt of **drive**

**drown** [draʊn] vt noyer ▷ vi se noyer

**drowsy** ['draʊzɪ] adj somnolent(e)

**drug** [drʌg] n médicament m; (narcotic) drogue f ▷ vt droguer; **to be on ~s** se droguer; **drug addict** n toxicomane m/f; **drug dealer** n revendeur(-euse) de drogue; **druggist** n (US) pharmacien(ne)-droguiste; **drugstore** n (US) pharmacie-droguerie f, drugstore m

**drum** [drʌm] n tambour m; (for oil, petrol) bidon m; **drums** npl (Mus) batterie f; **drummer** n (joueur m de) tambour m

**drunk** [drʌŋk] *pp of* **drink** ▷ *adj* ivre, soûl(e) ▷ *n* (*also*: **~ard**) ivrogne *m/f*; **to get ~** se soûler; **drunken** *adj* ivre, soûl(e), d'ivrogne; *(rage, stupor)* d'ivrogne

**dry** [draɪ] *adj* sec (sèche); *(day)* sans pluie ▷ *vt* sécher; *(clothes)* faire sécher ▷ *vi* sécher; **dry off** *vi, vt* sécher; **dry up** *vi* (*river, supplies*) se tarir; **dry-cleaner's** *n* teinturerie *f*; **dry-cleaning** *n* (*process*) nettoyage *m* à sec; **dryer** *n* (*tumble-dryer*) sèche-linge *m inv*; *(for hair)* sèche-cheveux *m inv*

**DSS** *n abbr* (BRIT) = **Department of Social Security**

**DTP** *n abbr* (= *desktop publishing*) PAO *f*

**dual** ['djuəl] *adj* double; **dual carriageway** *n* (BRIT) route *f* à quatre voies

**dubious** ['dju:biəs] *adj* hésitant(e), incertain(e); *(reputation, company)* douteux(-euse)

**duck** [dʌk] *n* canard *m* ▷ *vi* se baisser vivement, baisser subitement la tête

**due** [dju:] *adj* (*money, payment*) dû (due); *(expected)* attendu(e); *(fitting)* qui convient ▷ *adv*: **~ north** droit vers le nord; **~ to** (*because of*) en raison de; *(caused by)* dû à; **the train is ~ at 8 a.m.** le train est attendu à 8 h; **she is ~ back tomorrow** elle doit rentrer demain; **he is ~** on lui doit 10 livres; **to give sb his** *or* **her ~** être juste envers qn

**duel** ['djuəl] *n* duel *m*

**duet** [dju:'ɛt] *n* duo *m*

**dug** [dʌg] *pt, pp of* **dig**

**duke** [dju:k] *n* duc *m*

**dull** [dʌl] *adj* (*boring*) ennuyeux(-euse); *(not bright)* morne, terne; *(sound, pain)* sourd(e); *(weather, day)* gris(e), maussade ▷ *vt* (*pain, grief*) atténuer; *(mind, senses)* engourdir

**dumb** [dʌm] *adj* muet(te); *(stupid)* bête

**dummy** ['dʌmɪ] *n* (*tailor's model*) mannequin *m*; *(mock-up)* factice *m*, maquette *f*; (BRIT: *for baby*) tétine *f* ▷ *adj* faux (fausse), factice

**dump** [dʌmp] *n* (*also*: **rubbish ~**) décharge (publique); *(inf: place)* trou *m* ▷ *vt* (*put down*) déposer; déverser; *(get rid of)* se débarrasser de; *(Comput)* lister

**dumpling** ['dʌmplɪŋ] *n* boulette *f* (de pâte)

**dune** [dju:n] *n* dune *f*

**dungarees** [dʌŋgə'ri:z] *npl* bleu(s) *m(pl)*; *(for child, woman)* salopette *f*

**dungeon** ['dʌndʒən] *n* cachot *m*

**duplex** ['dju:plɛks] *n* (US: *also*: **~ apartment**) duplex *m*

**duplicate** *n* ['dju:plɪkət] double *m* ▷ *vt* ['dju:plɪkeɪt] faire un double de; *(on machine)* polycopier; **in ~** en deux exemplaires, en double

**durable** ['djuərəbl] *adj* durable; *(clothes, metal)* résistant(e), solide

**duration** [djuə'reɪʃən] *n* durée *f*

**during** ['djuərɪŋ] *prep* pendant, au cours de

**dusk** [dʌsk] *n* crépuscule *m*

**dust** [dʌst] *n* poussière *f* ▷ *vt* (*furniture*) essuyer, épousseter; *(cake etc)*: **to ~ with** saupoudrer de; **dustbin** *n* (BRIT) poubelle *f*; **duster** *n* chiffon *m*; **dustman** *n* (BRIT: *irreg*) boueux *m*, éboueur *m*; **dustpan** *n* pelle *f* à poussière; **dusty** *adj* poussiéreux(-euse)

**Dutch** [dʌtʃ] *adj* hollandais(e), néerlandais(e) ▷ *n* (Ling) hollandais *m*, néerlandais *m* ▷ *adv*: **to go ~** *or* **dutch** *(inf)* partager les frais; **the Dutch** *npl* les Hollandais, les Néerlandais; **Dutchman** (*irreg*) *n* Hollandais *m*; **Dutchwoman** (*irreg*) *n* Hollandaise *f*

**duty** ['dju:tɪ] *n* devoir *m*; *(tax)* droit *m*, taxe *f*; **on ~** de service; *(at night etc)* de garde; **off ~** libre, pas de service *or* de garde; **duty-free** *adj* exempté(e) de douane, hors-taxe

**duvet** ['du:veɪ] *n* (BRIT) couette *f*

**DVD** *n abbr* (= *digital versatile or video disc*) DVD *m*; **DVD burner** *n* graveur *m* de DVD; **DVD player** *n* lecteur *m* de DVD; **DVD writer** *n* graveur *m* de DVD

**dwarf** (*pl* **dwarves**) [dwɔ:f, dwɔ:vz] *n* nain(e) ▷ *vt* écraser

**dwell** (*pt, pp* **dwelt**) [dwɛl, dwɛlt] *vi*

demeurer; **dwell on** vt fus s'étendre sur

**dwelt** [dwɛlt] pt, pp of **dwell**

**dwindle** ['dwɪndl] vi diminuer, décroître

**dye** [daɪ] n teinture f ▷ vt teindre

**dying** ['daɪɪŋ] adj mourant(e), agonisant(e)

**dynamic** [daɪ'næmɪk] adj dynamique

**dynamite** ['daɪnəmaɪt] n dynamite f

**dyslexia** [dɪs'lɛksɪə] n dyslexie f

**dyslexic** [dɪs'lɛksɪk] adj, n dyslexique m/f

**E** [i:] n (Mus): **E** mi m

**E111** n abbr (= form E111) formulaire m E111

**each** [i:tʃ] adj chaque ▷ pron chacun(e); **~ other** l'un l'autre; **they hate ~ other** ils se détestent (mutuellement); **they have 2 books ~** ils ont 2 livres chacun; **they cost £5 ~** ils coûtent 5 livres (la) pièce

**eager** ['i:gəʳ] adj (person, buyer) empressé(e); (keen: pupil, worker) enthousiaste; **to be ~ to do sth** (impatient) brûler de faire qch; (keen) désirer vivement faire qch; **to be ~ for** (event) désirer vivement; (vengeance, affection, information) être avide de

**eagle** ['i:gl] n aigle m

**ear** [ɪəʳ] n oreille f; (of corn) épi m; **earache** n mal m aux oreilles; **eardrum** n tympan m

**earl** [əːl] n comte m

**earlier** ['əːlɪəʳ] adj (date etc) plus rapproché(e); (edition etc) plus ancien(ne), antérieur(e) ▷ adv plus tôt

**early** ['əːlɪ] adv tôt, de bonne heure;

(*ahead of time*) en avance; (*near the beginning*) au début ▷ *adj* précoce, qui se manifeste (*or* se fait) tôt *or* de bonne heure; (*Christians, settlers*) premier(-ière); (*reply*) rapide; (*death*) prématuré(e); (*work*) de jeunesse; **to have an ~ night/start** se coucher/partir tôt *or* de bonne heure; **in the ~** *or* **~ in the spring/19th century** au début *or* commencement du printemps/19ème siècle; **early retirement** *n* retraite anticipée

**earmark** ['ɪəmɑːk] *vt*: **to ~ sth for** réserver *or* destiner qch à

**earn** [əːn] *vt* gagner; (*Comm: yield*) rapporter; **to ~ one's living** gagner sa vie

**earnest** ['əːnɪst] *adj* sérieux(-euse) ▷ *n*: **in ~** *adv* sérieusement, pour de bon

**earnings** ['əːnɪŋz] *npl* salaire *m*; gains *mpl*; (*of company etc*) profits *mpl*, bénéfices *mpl*

**ear: earphones** *npl* écouteurs *mpl*; **earplugs** *npl* boules *fpl* Quiès®; (*to keep out water*) protège-tympans *mpl*; **earring** *n* boucle *f* d'oreille

**earth** [əːθ] *n* (*gen, also* BRIT *Elec*) terre *f* ▷ *vt* (BRIT *Elec*) relier à la terre; **earthquake** *n* tremblement *m* de terre, séisme *m*

**ease** [iːz] *n* facilité *f*, aisance *f*; (*comfort*) bien-être *m* ▷ *vt* (*soothe: mind*) tranquilliser; (*reduce: pain, problem*) atténuer; (: *tension*) réduire; (*loosen*) relâcher, détendre; (*help pass*): **to ~ sth in/out** faire pénétrer/sortir qch délicatement *or* avec douceur, faciliter la pénétration/la sortie de qch; **at ~** à l'aise; (*Mil*) au repos

**easily** ['iːzɪlɪ] *adv* facilement; (*by far*) de loin

**east** [iːst] *n* est *m* ▷ *adj* (*wind*) d'est; (*side*) est *inv* ▷ *adv* à l'est, vers l'est; **the E~** l'Orient *m*; (*Pol*) les pays *mpl* de l'Est; **eastbound** *adj* en direction de l'est; (*carriageway*) est *inv*

**Easter** ['iːstər] *n* Pâques *fpl*; **Easter egg** *n* œuf *m* de Pâques

**eastern** ['iːstən] *adj* de l'est, oriental(e)

**Easter Sunday** *n* le dimanche de Pâques

**easy** ['iːzɪ] *adj* facile; (*manner*) aisé(e) ▷ *adv*: **to take it** *or* **things ~** (*rest*) ne pas se fatiguer; (*not worry*) ne pas (trop) s'en faire; **easy-going** *adj* accommodant(e), facile à vivre

**eat** (*pt* **ate**, *pp* **~en**) [iːt, eɪt, 'iːtn] *vt*, *vi* manger; **can we have something to ~?** est-ce qu'on peut manger quelque chose?; **eat out** *vi* manger au restaurant

**eavesdrop** ['iːvzdrɒp] *vi*: **to ~ (on)** écouter de façon indiscrète

**e-book** ['iːbuk] *n* livre *m* électronique

**e-business** ['iːbɪznɪs] *n* (*company*) entreprise *f* électronique; (*commerce*) commerce *m* électronique

**EC** *n abbr* (= *European Community*) CE *f*

**eccentric** [ɪk'sɛntrɪk] *adj*, *n* excentrique *m/f*

**echo, echoes** ['ɛkəu] *n* écho *m* ▷ *vt* répéter ▷ *vi* résonner; faire écho

**eclipse** [ɪ'klɪps] *n* éclipse *f*

**eco-friendly** [iːkə'frɛndlɪ] *adj* non nuisible à *or* qui ne nuit pas à l'environnement

**ecological** [iːkə'lɒdʒɪkəl] *adj* écologique

**ecology** [ɪ'kɒlədʒɪ] *n* écologie *f*

**e-commerce** [iːkɒməːs] *n* commerce *m* électronique

**economic** [iːkə'nɒmɪk] *adj* économique; (*profitable*) rentable; **economical** *adj* économique; (*person*) économe; **economics** *n* (*Scol*) économie *f* politique ▷ *npl* (*of project etc*) côté *m or* aspect *m* économique

**economist** [ɪ'kɒnəmɪst] *n* économiste *m/f*

**economize** [ɪ'kɒnəmaɪz] *vi* économiser, faire des économies

**economy** [ɪ'kɒnəmɪ] *n* économie *f*; **economy class** *n* (*Aviat*) classe *f* touriste; **economy class syndrome** *n* syndrome *m* de la classe économique

**ecstasy** ['ɛkstəsɪ] *n* extase *f*; (*Drugs*)

ecstasy m; **ecstatic** [ɛks'tætɪk] adj extatique, en extase

**eczema** ['ɛksɪmə] n eczéma m

**edge** [ɛdʒ] n bord m; (of knife etc) tranchant m, fil m ▷ vt border; **on ~** (fig) crispé(e), tendu(e)

**edgy** ['ɛdʒɪ] adj crispé(e), tendu(e)

**edible** ['ɛdɪbl] adj comestible; (meal) mangeable

**Edinburgh** ['ɛdɪnbərə] n Édimbourg

- **EDINBURGH FESTIVAL**
- 
- Le Festival d'Édimbourg, qui se tient
- chaque année durant trois semaines
- au mois d'août, est l'un des grands
- festivals européens. Il est réputé
- pour son programme officiel mais
- aussi pour son festival "off" (the
- Fringe) qui propose des spectacles
- aussi bien traditionnels que
- résolument d'avant-garde. Pendant
- la durée du Festival se tient par
- ailleurs, sur l'esplanade du château,
- un grand spectacle de musique
- militaire, le "Military Tattoo".

**edit** ['ɛdɪt] vt (text, book) éditer; (report) préparer; (film) monter; (magazine) diriger; (newspaper) être le rédacteur or la rédactrice en chef de; **edition** [ɪ'dɪʃən] n édition f; **editor** n (of newspaper) rédacteur(-trice), rédacteur(-trice) en chef; (of sb's work) éditeur(-trice); (also: **film editor**) monteur(-euse); **political/ foreign editor** rédacteur politique/au service étranger; **editorial** [ɛdɪ'tɔːrɪəl] adj de la rédaction, éditorial(e) ▷ n éditorial m

**educate** ['ɛdjukeɪt] vt (teach) instruire; (bring up) éduquer; **educated** ['ɛdjukeɪtɪd] adj (person) cultivé(e)

**education** [ɛdju'keɪʃən] n éducation f; (studies) études fpl; (teaching) enseignement m, instruction f; **educational** adj pédagogique; (institution) scolaire; (game, toy) éducatif(-ive)

**eel** [iːl] n anguille f

**eerie** ['ɪərɪ] adj inquiétant(e), spectral(e), surnaturel(le)

**effect** [ɪ'fɛkt] n effet m ▷ vt effectuer; **effects** npl (property) effets, affaires fpl; **to take ~** (Law) entrer en vigueur, prendre effet; (drug) agir, faire son effet; **in ~** en fait; **effective** adj efficace; (actual) véritable; **effectively** adv efficacement; (in reality) effectivement, en fait

**efficiency** [ɪ'fɪʃənsɪ] n efficacité f; (of machine, car) rendement m

**efficient** [ɪ'fɪʃənt] adj efficace; (machine, car) d'un bon rendement; **efficiently** adv efficacement

**effort** ['ɛfət] n effort m; **effortless** adj sans effort, aisé(e); (achievement) facile

**e.g.** adv abbr (= exempli gratia) par exemple, p. ex.

**egg** [ɛg] n œuf m; **hard-boiled/soft-boiled ~** œuf dur/à la coque; **eggcup** n coquetier m; **egg plant** (US) n aubergine f; **eggshell** n coquille f d'œuf; **egg white** n blanc m d'œuf; **egg yolk** n jaune m d'œuf

**ego** ['iːgəu] n (self-esteem) amour-propre m; (Psych) moi m

**Egypt** ['iːdʒɪpt] n Égypte f; **Egyptian** [ɪ'dʒɪpʃən] adj égyptien(ne) ▷ n Égyptien(ne)

**Eiffel Tower** ['aɪfəl-] n tour f Eiffel

**eight** [eɪt] num huit; **eighteen** num dix-huit; **eighteenth** num dix-huitième; **eighth** num huitième; **eightieth** ['eɪtɪɪθ] num quatre-vingtième

**eighty** ['eɪtɪ] num quatre-vingt(s)

**Eire** ['ɛərə] n République f d'Irlande

**either** ['aɪðə'] adj l'un ou l'autre; (both, each) chaque ▷ pron: **~ (of them)** l'un ou l'autre ▷ adv non plus ▷ conj: **~ good or bad** soit bon soit mauvais; **on ~ side** de chaque côté; **I don't like ~** je n'aime ni l'un ni l'autre; **no, I don't ~** moi non plus; **which bike do you want? - ~ will do** quel vélo voulez-vous? - n'importe lequel; **answer with ~ yes or no** répondez par oui ou par non

**eject** [ɪ'dʒɛkt] *vt* (*tenant etc*) expulser; (*object*) éjecter

**elaborate** *adj* [ɪ'læbərɪt] compliqué(e), recherché(e), minutieux(-euse) ▷ *vb* [ɪ'læbəreɪt] ▷ *vt* élaborer ▷ *vi* entrer dans les détails

**elastic** [ɪ'læstɪk] *adj, n* élastique (*m*); **elastic band** *n* (*BRIT*) élastique *m*

**elbow** ['ɛlbəu] *n* coude *m*

**elder** ['ɛldə'] *adj* aîné(e) ▷ *n* (*tree*) sureau *m*; **one's ~s** ses aînés; **elderly** *adj* âgé(e) ▷ *npl*: **the elderly** les personnes âgées

**eldest** ['ɛldɪst] *adj, n*: **the ~ (child)** l'aîné(e) (des enfants)

**elect** [ɪ'lɛkt] *vt* élire; (*choose*): **to ~ to do** choisir de faire ▷ *adj*: **the president ~** le président désigné; **election** *n* élection *f*; **electoral** *adj* électoral(e); **electorate** *n* électorat *m*

**electric** [ɪ'lɛktrɪk] *adj* électrique; **electrical** *adj* électrique; **electric blanket** *n* couverture chauffante; **electric fire** *n* (*BRIT*) radiateur *m* électrique; **electrician** [ɪlɛk'trɪʃən] *n* électricien *m*; **electricity** [ɪlɛk'trɪsɪtɪ] *n* électricité *f*; **electric shock** *n* choc *m or* décharge *f* électrique; **electrify** [ɪ'lɛktrɪfaɪ] *vt* (*Rail*) électrifier; (*audience*) électriser

**electronic** [ɪlɛk'trɔnɪk] *adj* électronique; **electronic mail** *n* courrier *m* électronique; **electronics** *n* électronique *f*

**elegance** ['ɛlɪgəns] *n* élégance *f*

**elegant** ['ɛlɪgənt] *adj* élégant(e)

**element** ['ɛlɪmənt] *n* (*gen*) élément *m*; (*of heater, kettle etc*) résistance *f*

**elementary** [ɛlɪ'mɛntərɪ] *adj* élémentaire; (*school, education*) primaire; **elementary school** *n* (*US*) école *f* primaire

**elephant** ['ɛlɪfənt] *n* éléphant *m*

**elevate** ['ɛlɪveɪt] *vt* élever

**elevator** ['ɛlɪveɪtə'] *n* (*in warehouse etc*) élévateur *m*, monte-charge *m inv*; (*US: lift*) ascenseur *m*

**eleven** [ɪ'lɛvn] *num* onze; **eleventh** *num* onzième

**eligible** ['ɛlɪdʒəbl] *adj* éligible; (*for membership*) admissible; **an ~ young man** un beau parti; **to be ~ for sth** remplir les conditions requises pour qch

**eliminate** [ɪ'lɪmɪneɪt] *vt* éliminer

**elm** [ɛlm] *n* orme *m*

**eloquent** ['ɛləkwənt] *adj* éloquent(e)

**else** [ɛls] *adv*: **something ~** quelque chose d'autre, autre chose; **somewhere ~** ailleurs, autre part; **everywhere ~** partout ailleurs; **everyone ~** tous les autres; **nothing ~** rien d'autre; **where ~?** à quel autre endroit?; **little ~** pas grand-chose d'autre; **elsewhere** *adv* ailleurs, autre part

**elusive** [ɪ'lu:sɪv] *adj* insaisissable

**e-mail** ['i:meɪl] *n abbr* (= *electronic mail*) e-mail *m*, courriel *m* ▷ *vt*: **to ~ sb** envoyer un e-mail or un courriel à qn; **e-mail address** *n* adresse *f* e-mail

**embankment** [ɪm'bæŋkmənt] *n* (*of road, railway*) remblai *m*, talus *m*; (*of river*) berge *f*, quai *m*; (*dyke*) digue *f*

**embargo, embargoes** [ɪm'ba:gəu] *n* (*Comm, Naut*) embargo *m*; (*prohibition*) interdiction *f*

**embark** [ɪm'ba:k] *vi* embarquer ▷ *vt* embarquer; **to ~ on** (*journey etc*) commencer, entreprendre; (*fig*) se lancer or s'embarquer dans

**embarrass** [ɪm'bærəs] *vt* embarrasser, gêner; **embarrassed** *adj* gêné(e); **embarrassing** *adj* gênant(e), embarrassant(e); **embarrassment** *n* embarras *m*, gêne *f*; (*embarrassing thing, person*) source *f* d'embarras

**embassy** ['ɛmbəsɪ] *n* ambassade *f*

**embrace** [ɪm'breɪs] *vt* embrasser, étreindre; (*include*) embrasser ▷ *vi* s'embrasser, s'étreindre ▷ *n* étreinte *f*

**embroider** [ɪm'brɔɪdə'] *vt* broder; **embroidery** *n* broderie *f*

**embryo** ['ɛmbrɪəu] *n* (*also fig*) embryon *m*

**emerald** ['ɛmərəld] *n* émeraude *f*

**emerge** [ɪˈmɜːdʒ] vi apparaître; (from room, car) surgir; (from sleep, imprisonment) sortir

**emergency** [ɪˈmɜːdʒənsɪ] n (crisis) cas m d'urgence; (Med) urgence f; **in an ~** en cas d'urgence; **state of ~** état m d'urgence; **emergency brake** (us) n frein m à main; **emergency exit** n sortie f de secours; **emergency landing** n atterrissage forcé; **emergency room** n (us: Med) urgences fpl; **emergency services** npl: **the emergency services** (fire, police, ambulance) les services mpl d'urgence

**emigrate** [ˈɛmɪɡreɪt] vi émigrer; **emigration** [ɛmɪˈɡreɪʃən] n émigration f

**eminent** [ˈɛmɪnənt] adj éminent(e)

**emissions** [ɪˈmɪʃənz] npl émissions fpl

**emit** [ɪˈmɪt] vt émettre

**emotion** [ɪˈməʊʃən] n sentiment m; **emotional** adj (person) émotif(-ive), très sensible; (needs) affectif(-ive); (scene) émouvant(e); (tone, speech) qui fait appel aux sentiments

**emperor** [ˈɛmpərər] n empereur m

**emphasis** (pl **-ases**) [ˈɛmfəsɪs, -siːz] n accent m; **to lay** or **place ~ on sth** (fig) mettre l'accent sur, insister sur

**emphasize** [ˈɛmfəsaɪz] vt (syllable, word, point) appuyer or insister sur; (feature) souligner, accentuer

**empire** [ˈɛmpaɪər] n empire m

**employ** [ɪmˈplɔɪ] vt employer; **employee** [ɪmplɔɪˈiː] n employé(e); **employer** n employeur(-euse); **employment** n emploi m; **employment agency** n agence f or bureau m de placement

**empower** [ɪmˈpaʊər] vt: **to ~ sb to do** autoriser or habiliter qn à faire

**empress** [ˈɛmprɪs] n impératrice f

**emptiness** [ˈɛmptɪnɪs] n vide m; (of area) aspect m désertique

**empty** [ˈɛmptɪ] adj vide; (street, area) désert(e); (threat, promise) en l'air, vain(e) ▷ vt vider ▷ vi se vider; (liquid) s'écouler; **empty-handed** adj les mains vides

**EMU** n abbr (= European Monetary Union) UME f

**emulsion** [ɪˈmʌlʃən] n émulsion f; (also: **~ paint**) peinture mate

**enable** [ɪˈneɪbl] vt: **to ~ sb to do** permettre à qn de faire

**enamel** [ɪˈnæməl] n émail m; (also: **~ paint**) (peinture f) laque f

**enchanting** [ɪnˈtʃɑːntɪŋ] adj ravissant(e), enchanteur(-eresse)

**encl.** abbr (on letters etc: = enclosed) ci-joint(e); (= enclosure) PJ f

**enclose** [ɪnˈkləʊz] vt (land) clôturer; (space, object) entourer; (letter etc): **to ~ (with)** joindre (à); **please find ~d** veuillez trouver ci-joint

**enclosure** [ɪnˈkləʊʒər] n enceinte f

**encore** [ɔŋˈkɔːr] excl, n bis (m)

**encounter** [ɪnˈkaʊntər] n rencontre f ▷ vt rencontrer

**encourage** [ɪnˈkʌrɪdʒ] vt encourager; **encouragement** n encouragement m

**encouraging** [ɪnˈkʌrɪdʒɪŋ] adj encourageant(e)

**encyclop(a)edia** [ɛnsaɪkləʊˈpiːdɪə] n encyclopédie f

**end** [ɛnd] n fin f; (of table, street, rope etc) bout m, extrémité f ▷ vt terminer; (also: **bring to an ~, put an ~ to**) mettre fin à ▷ vi se terminer, finir; **in the ~** finalement; **on ~** (object) debout, dressé(e); **to stand on ~** (hair) se dresser sur la tête; **for hours on ~** pendant des heures (et des heures); **end up** vi: **to ~ up in** (condition) finir or se terminer par; (place) finir or aboutir à

**endanger** [ɪnˈdeɪndʒər] vt mettre en danger; **an ~ed species** une espèce en voie de disparition

**endearing** [ɪnˈdɪərɪŋ] adj attachant(e)

**endeavour** (us **endeavor**) [ɪnˈdɛvər] n effort m; (attempt) tentative f ▷ vt: **to ~ to do** tenter or s'efforcer de faire

**ending** [ˈɛndɪŋ] n dénouement m, conclusion f; (Ling) terminaison f

**endless** [ˈɛndlɪs] adj sans fin, interminable

**endorse** [ɪnˈdɔːs] vt (cheque) endosser;
(approve) appuyer, approuver,
sanctionner; **endorsement** n
(approval) appui m, aval m; (BRIT: on
driving licence) contravention f (portée au
permis de conduire)

**endurance** [ɪnˈdjuərəns] n
endurance f

**endure** [ɪnˈdjuəʳ] vt (bear) supporter,
endurer ▷ vi (last) durer

**enemy** [ˈɛnəmɪ] adj, n ennemi(e)

**energetic** [ɛnəˈdʒɛtɪk] adj énergique;
(activity) très actif(-ive), qui fait se
dépenser (physiquement)

**energy** [ˈɛnədʒɪ] n énergie f

**enforce** [ɪnˈfɔːs] vt (law) appliquer,
faire respecter

**engaged** [ɪnˈɡeɪdʒd] adj (BRIT: busy, in
use) occupé(e); (betrothed) fiancé(e); **to
get ~** se fiancer; **the line's ~** la ligne est
occupée; **engaged tone** n (BRIT Tel)
tonalité f occupé ligne

**engagement** [ɪnˈɡeɪdʒmənt] n
(undertaking) obligation f, engagement
m; (appointment) rendez-vous m inv; (to
marry) fiançailles fpl; **engagement ring**
n bague f de fiançailles

**engaging** [ɪnˈɡeɪdʒɪŋ] adj
engageant(e), attirant(e)

**engine** [ˈɛndʒɪn] n (Aut) moteur m;
(Rail) locomotive f

  ▌ Be careful not to translate engine
  by the French word engin.

**engineer** [ɛndʒɪˈnɪəʳ] n ingénieur m;
(BRIT: repairer) dépanneur m; (Navy, US
Rail) mécanicien m; **engineering** n
engineering m, ingénierie f; (of bridges,
ships) génie m; (of machine) mécanique f

**England** [ˈɪŋɡlənd] n Angleterre f

**English** [ˈɪŋɡlɪʃ] adj anglais(e) ▷ n
(Ling) anglais m; **the ~** npl les Anglais;
**English Channel** n: **the English
Channel** la Manche; **Englishman**
(irreg) n Anglais m; **Englishwoman**
(irreg) n Anglaise f

**engrave** [ɪnˈɡreɪv] vt graver

**engraving** [ɪnˈɡreɪvɪŋ] n gravure f

**enhance** [ɪnˈhɑːns] vt rehausser,
mettre en valeur

**enjoy** [ɪnˈdʒɔɪ] vt aimer, prendre plaisir
à; (have benefit of: health, fortune) jouir
de; (: success) connaître; **to ~ o.s.**
s'amuser; **enjoyable** adj agréable;
**enjoyment** n plaisir m

**enlarge** [ɪnˈlɑːdʒ] vt accroître;
(Phot) agrandir ▷ vi: **to ~ on** (subject)
s'étendre sur; **enlargement** n (Phot)
agrandissement m

**enlist** [ɪnˈlɪst] vt recruter; (support)
s'assurer ▷ vi s'engager

**enormous** [ɪˈnɔːməs] adj énorme

**enough** [ɪˈnʌf] adj: **~ time/books** assez
or suffisamment de temps/livres ▷ adv:
**big ~** assez or suffisamment grand
▷ pron: **have you got ~?** (en) avez-vous
assez?; **~ to eat** assez à manger; **that's
~, thanks** cela suffit or c'est assez,
merci; **I've had ~ of him** j'en ai assez
de lui; **he has not worked ~** il n'a pas
assez or suffisamment travaillé, il n'a
pas travaillé assez or suffisamment;
**... which, funnily** or **oddly ~ ...** qui,
chose curieuse

**enquire** [ɪnˈkwaɪəʳ] vt, vi = **inquire**

**enquiry** [ɪnˈkwaɪərɪ] n = **inquiry**

**enrage** [ɪnˈreɪdʒ] vt mettre en fureur or
en rage, rendre furieux(-euse)

**enrich** [ɪnˈrɪtʃ] vt enrichir

**enrol** (US **enroll**) [ɪnˈrəul] vt inscrire ▷ vi
s'inscrire; **enrolment** (US **enrollment**)
n inscription f

**en route** [ɔnˈruːt] adv en route, en
chemin

**en suite** [ˈɔnswiːt] adj: **with ~
bathroom** avec salle de bains en
attenante

**ensure** [ɪnˈʃuəʳ] vt assurer, garantir

**entail** [ɪnˈteɪl] vt entraîner, nécessiter

**enter** [ˈɛntəʳ] vt (room) entrer dans,
pénétrer dans; (club, army) entrer à;
(competition) s'inscrire à or pour; (sb
for a competition) (faire) inscrire; (write
down) inscrire, noter; (Comput) entrer,
introduire ▷ vi entrer

**enterprise** [ˈɛntəpraɪz] n (company,
undertaking) entreprise f; (initiative)

(esprit m d')initiative f; **free ~** libre entreprise; **private ~** entreprise privée; **enterprising** adj entreprenant(e), dynamique; (scheme) audacieux(-euse)

**entertain** [ɛntə'teɪn] vt amuser, distraire; (invite) recevoir (à dîner); (idea, plan) envisager; **entertainer** n artiste m/f de variétés; **entertaining** adj amusant(e), distrayant(e); **entertainment** n (amusement) distraction f, divertissement m, amusement m; (show) spectacle m

**enthusiasm** [ɪn'θu:zɪæzəm] n enthousiasme m

**enthusiast** [ɪn'θu:zɪæst] n enthousiaste m/f; **enthusiastic** [ɪnθu:zɪ'æstɪk] adj enthousiaste; **to be enthusiastic about** être enthousiasmé(e) par

**entire** [ɪn'taɪər] adj (tout) entier(-ère); **entirely** adv entièrement, complètement

**entitle** [ɪn'taɪtl] vt: **to ~ sb to sth** donner droit à qch à qn; **entitled** adj (book) intitulé(e); **to be entitled to do** avoir le droit de faire

**entrance** n ['ɛntrns] entrée f ▷ vt [ɪn'trɑ:ns] enchanter, ravir; **where's the ~?** où est l'entrée?; **to gain ~ to** (university etc) être admis à; **entrance examination** n examen m d'entrée or d'admission; **entrance fee** n (to museum etc) prix m d'entrée; (to join club etc) droit m d'inscription; **entrance ramp** n (us Aut) bretelle f d'accès; **entrant** n (in race etc) participant(e), concurrent(e); (BRIT: in exam) candidat(e)

**entrepreneur** ['ɔntrəprə'nə:r] n entrepreneur m

**entrust** [ɪn'trʌst] vt: **to ~ sth to** confier qch à

**entry** ['ɛntrɪ] n entrée f; (in register, diary) inscription f; **"no ~"** "défense d'entrer", "entrée interdite"; (Aut) "sens interdit"; **entry phone** n (BRIT) interphone m (à l'entrée d'un immeuble)

**envelope** ['ɛnvələup] n enveloppe f

**envious** ['ɛnvɪəs] adj envieux(-euse)

**environment** [ɪn'vaɪərnmənt] n (social, moral) milieu m; (natural world): **the ~** l'environnement m; **environmental** [ɪnvaɪərn'mɛntl] adj (of surroundings) du milieu; (issue, disaster) écologique; **environmentally** [ɪnvaɪərn'mɛntlɪ] adv: **environmentally sound/friendly** qui ne nuit pas à l'environnement

**envisage** [ɪn'vɪzɪdʒ] vt (foresee) prévoir

**envoy** ['ɛnvɔɪ] n envoyé(e); (diplomat) ministre m plénipotentiaire

**envy** ['ɛnvɪ] n envie f ▷ vt envier; **to ~ sb sth** envier qch à qn

**epic** ['ɛpɪk] n épopée f ▷ adj épique

**epidemic** [ɛpɪ'dɛmɪk] n épidémie f

**epilepsy** ['ɛpɪlɛpsɪ] n épilepsie f; **epileptic** adj, n épileptique m/f; **epileptic fit** n crise f d'épilepsie

**episode** ['ɛpɪsəud] n épisode m

**equal** ['i:kwl] adj égal(e) ▷ vt égaler; **~ to** (task) à la hauteur de; **equality** [i:'kwɔlɪtɪ] n égalité f; **equalize** vt, vi (Sport) égaliser; **equally** adv également; (share) en parts égales; (treat) de la même façon; (pay) autant; (just as) tout aussi

**equation** [ɪ'kweɪʃən] n (Math) équation f

**equator** [ɪ'kweɪtər] n équateur m

**equip** [ɪ'kwɪp] vt équiper; **to ~ sb/sth with** équiper or munir qn/qch de; **equipment** n équipement m; (electrical etc) appareillage m, installation f

**equivalent** [ɪ'kwɪvəlnt] adj équivalent(e) ▷ n équivalent m; **to be ~ to** équivaloir à, être équivalent(e) à

**ER** abbr (BRIT: = Elizabeth Regina) la reine Élisabeth; (US: Med: = emergency room) urgences fpl

**era** ['ɪərə] n ère f, époque f

**erase** [ɪ'reɪz] vt effacer; **eraser** n gomme f

**erect** [ɪ'rɛkt] adj droit(e) ▷ vt construire; (monument) ériger, élever; (tent etc) dresser; **erection** [ɪ'rɛkʃən] n (Physiol) érection f; (of building) construction f

**ERM** n abbr (= Exchange Rate Mechanism) mécanisme m des taux de change

**erode** [ɪˈrəud] vt éroder; (metal) ronger

**erosion** [ɪˈrəuʒən] n érosion f

**erotic** [ɪˈrɔtɪk] adj érotique

**errand** [ˈɛrnd] n course f, commission f

**erratic** [ɪˈrætɪk] adj irrégulier(-ière), inconstant(e)

**error** [ˈɛrəʳ] n erreur f

**erupt** [ɪˈrʌpt] vi entrer en éruption; (fig) éclater; **eruption** [ɪˈrʌpʃən] n éruption f; (of anger, violence) explosion f

**escalate** [ˈɛskəleɪt] vi s'intensifier; (costs) monter en flèche

**escalator** [ˈɛskəleɪtəʳ] n escalier roulant

**escape** [ɪˈskeɪp] n évasion f, fuite f; (of gas etc) fuite ▷ vi s'échapper, fuir; (from jail) s'évader; (fig) s'en tirer; (leak) s'échapper ▷ vt échapper à; **to ~ from** (person) échapper à; (place) s'échapper de; (fig) fuir; **his name ~s me** son nom m'échappe

**escort** vt [ɪˈskɔːt] escorter ▷ n [ˈɛskɔːt] (Mil) escorte f

**especially** [ɪˈspɛʃlɪ] adv (particularly) particulièrement; (above all) surtout

**espionage** [ˈɛspɪənɑːʒ] n espionnage m

**essay** [ˈɛseɪ] n (Scol) dissertation f; (Literature) essai m

**essence** [ˈɛsns] n essence f; (Culin) extrait m

**essential** [ɪˈsɛnʃl] adj essentiel(le); (basic) fondamental(e); **essentials** npl éléments essentiels; **essentially** adv essentiellement

**establish** [ɪˈstæblɪʃ] vt établir; (business) fonder, créer; (one's power etc) asseoir, affermir; **establishment** n établissement m; (founding) création f; (institution) établissement m; **the Establishment** les pouvoirs établis; l'ordre établi

**estate** [ɪˈsteɪt] n (land) domaine m, propriété f; (Law) biens mpl, succession f; (BRIT: also: **housing ~**)

lotissement m; **estate agent** n (BRIT) agent immobilier; **estate car** n (BRIT) break m

**estimate** n [ˈɛstɪmət] estimation f; (Comm) devis m ▷ vb [ˈɛstɪmeɪt] ▷ vt estimer

**etc** abbr (= et cetera) etc

**eternal** [ɪˈtəːnl] adj éternel(le)

**eternity** [ɪˈtəːnɪtɪ] n éternité f

**ethical** [ˈɛθɪkl] adj moral(e); **ethics** [ˈɛθɪks] n éthique f ▷ npl moralité f

**Ethiopia** [iːθɪˈəupɪə] n Éthiopie f

**ethnic** [ˈɛθnɪk] adj ethnique; (clothes, food) folklorique, exotique, propre aux minorités ethniques non-occidentales; **ethnic minority** n minorité f ethnique

**e-ticket** [ˈiːtɪkɪt] n billet m électronique

**etiquette** [ˈɛtɪkɛt] n convenances fpl, étiquette f

**EU** n abbr (= European Union) UE f

**euro** [ˈjuərəu] n (currency) euro m

**Europe** [ˈjuərəp] n Europe f; **European** [juərəˈpiːən] adj européen(ne) ▷ n Européen(ne); **European Community** n Communauté européenne; **European Union** n Union européenne

**Eurostar®** [ˈjuərəustɑːʳ] n Eurostar® m

**evacuate** [ɪˈvækjueɪt] vt évacuer

**evade** [ɪˈveɪd] vt échapper à; (question etc) éluder; (duties) se dérober à

**evaluate** [ɪˈvæljueɪt] vt évaluer

**evaporate** [ɪˈvæpəreɪt] vi s'évaporer; (fig: hopes, fear) s'envoler; (anger) se dissiper

**eve** [iːv] n: **on the ~ of** à la veille de

**even** [ˈiːvn] adj (level, smooth) régulier(-ière); (equal) égal(e); (number) pair(e) ▷ adv même; **~ if** même si + indic; **~ though** alors même que + cond; **~ more** encore plus; **~ faster** encore plus vite; **~ so** quand même; **not ~** pas même; **~ he was there** même lui était là; **~ on Sundays** même le dimanche; **to get ~ with sb** prendre sa revanche sur qn

**evening** [ˈiːvnɪŋ] n soir m; (as duration,

*event*) soirée *f*; **in the ~** le soir; **evening class** *n* cours *m* du soir; **evening dress** *n* (*man's*) tenue *f* de soirée, smoking *m*; (*woman's*) robe *f* de soirée

**event** [ɪ'vɛnt] *n* événement *m*; (*Sport*) épreuve *f*; **in the ~ of** en cas de; **eventful** *adj* mouvementé(e)

**eventual** [ɪ'vɛntʃuəl] *adj* final(e)

> Be careful not to translate *eventual* by the French word *éventuel*.

**eventually** [ɪ'vɛntʃuəlɪ] *adv* finalement

> Be careful not to translate *eventually* by the French word *éventuellement*.

**ever** ['ɛvə'] *adv* jamais; (*at all times*) toujours; (*in questions*): **why ~ not?** mais enfin, pourquoi pas?; **the best ~** le meilleur qu'on ait jamais vu; **have you ~ seen it?** l'as-tu déjà vu?, as-tu eu l'occasion *or* t'est-il arrivé de le voir?; **~ since** (*as adv*) depuis; (*as conj*) depuis que; **~ so pretty** si joli; **evergreen** *n* arbre *m* à feuilles persistantes

○ **KEYWORD**

**every** ['ɛvrɪ] *adj* **1** (*each*) chaque; **every one of them** tous (sans exception); **every shop in town was closed** tous les magasins en ville étaient fermés
**2** (*all possible*) tous (toutes) les; **I gave you every assistance** j'ai fait tout mon possible pour vous aider; **I have every confidence in him** j'ai entièrement *or* pleinement confiance en lui; **we wish you every success** nous vous souhaitons beaucoup de succès
**3** (*showing recurrence*) tous les; **every day** tous les jours, chaque jour; **every other car** une voiture sur deux; **every other/third day** tous les deux/trois jours; **every now and then** de temps en temps; **everybody = everyone**; **everyday** *adj* (*expression*) courant(e), d'usage courant; (*use*) courant; (*clothes, life*) de tous les jours; (*occurrence,*

*problem*) quotidien(ne); **everyone** *pron* tout le monde, tous *pl*; **everything** *pron* tout; **everywhere** *adv* partout; **everywhere you go you meet ...** où qu'on aille, on rencontre ...

**evict** [ɪ'vɪkt] *vt* expulser

**evidence** ['ɛvɪdns] *n* (*proof*) preuve(s) *f(pl)*; (*of witness*) témoignage *m*; (*sign*): **to show ~ of** donner des signes de; **to give ~** témoigner, déposer

**evident** [ɛvɪdnt] *adj* évident(e); **evidently** *adv* de toute évidence; (*apparently*) apparemment

**evil** ['i:vl] *adj* mauvais(e) ▷ *n* mal *m*

**evoke** [ɪ'vəuk] *vt* évoquer

**evolution** [i:və'lu:ʃən] *n* évolution *f*

**evolve** [ɪ'vɔlv] *vt* élaborer ▷ *vi* évoluer, se transformer

**ewe** [ju:] *n* brebis *f*

**ex** [ɛks] *n* (*inf*): **my ex** mon ex

**ex-** [ɛks] *prefix* ex-

**exact** [ɪg'zækt] *adj* exact(e) ▷ *vt*: **to ~ sth (from)** (*signature, confession*) extorquer qch (à); (*apology*) exiger qch (de); **exactly** *adv* exactement

**exaggerate** [ɪg'zædʒəreɪt] *vt, vi* exagérer; **exaggeration** [ɪgzædʒə'reɪʃən] *n* exagération *f*

**exam** [ɪg'zæm] *n abbr* (*Scol*) = **examination**

**examination** [ɪgzæmɪ'neɪʃən] *n* (*Scol, Med*) examen *m*; **to take** *or* **sit an ~** (*BRIT*) passer un examen

**examine** [ɪg'zæmɪn] *vt* (*gen*) examiner; (*Scol, Law: person*) interroger; **examiner** *n* examinateur(-trice)

**example** [ɪg'zɑ:mpl] *n* exemple *m*; **for ~** par exemple

**exasperated** [ɪg'zɑ:spəreɪtɪd] *adj* exaspéré(e)

**excavate** ['ɛkskəveɪt] *vt* (*site*) fouiller, excaver; (*object*) mettre au jour

**exceed** [ɪk'si:d] *vt* dépasser; (*one's powers*) outrepasser; **exceedingly** *adv* extrêmement

**excel** [ɪk'sɛl] *vi* exceller ▷ *vt* surpasser; **to ~ o.s.** se surpasser

**excellence** ['ɛksələns] n excellence f
**excellent** ['ɛksələnt] adj excellent(e)
**except** [ik'sɛpt] prep (also: **~ for, ~ing**)
sauf, excepté, à l'exception de ▷ vt
excepter; **~ if/when** sauf si/quand;
**~ that** excepté que, si ce n'est que;
**exception** [ik'sɛpʃən] n exception
f; **to take exception to** s'offusquer
de; **exceptional** [ik'sɛpʃənl] adj
exceptionnel(le); **exceptionally**
[ik'sɛpʃənəli] adv exceptionnellement
**excerpt** ['ɛksə:pt] n extrait m
**excess** [ik'sɛs] n excès m; **excess**
**baggage** n excédent m de bagages;
**excessive** adj excessif(-ive)
**exchange** [iks'tʃeɪndʒ] n échange m;
(also: **telephone ~**) central m ▷ vt: **to ~**
**(for)** échanger (contre); **could I ~ this,**
**please?** est-ce que je peux échanger
ceci, s'il vous plaît?; **exchange rate** n
taux m de change
**excite** [ik'saɪt] vt exciter; **excited** adj
(tout (toute)) excité(e); **to get excited**
s'exciter; **excitement** n excitation f;
**exciting** adj passionnant(e)
**exclaim** [ik'skleɪm] vi s'exclamer;
**exclamation** [ɛksklə'meɪʃən] n
exclamation f; **exclamation mark**
(US **exclamation point**) n point m
d'exclamation
**exclude** [ik'sklu:d] vt exclure
**excluding** [ik'sklu:diŋ] prep: **~ VAT** la
TVA non comprise
**exclusion** [ik'sklu:ʒən] n exclusion f
**exclusive** [ik'sklu:siv] adj
exclusif(-ive); (club, district) sélect(e);
(item of news) en exclusivité; **~ of VAT**
TVA non comprise; **exclusively** adv
exclusivement
**excruciating** [ik'skru:ʃieitiŋ]
adj (pain) atroce, déchirant(e);
(embarrassing) pénible
**excursion** [ik'skə:ʃən] n excursion f
**excuse** n [ik'skju:s] excuse f ▷ vt
[ik'skju:z] (forgive) excuser; **to ~ sb**
**from** (activity) dispenser qn de; **~ me!**
excusez-moi!, pardon!; **now if you**
**will ~ me, ...** maintenant, si vous (le)

permettez ...
**ex-directory** ['ɛksdi'rɛktəri] adj (BRIT)
sur la liste rouge
**execute** ['ɛksikju:t] vt exécuter;
**execution** [ɛksi'kju:ʃən] n exécution f
**executive** [ig'zɛkjutiv] n (person) cadre
m; (managing group) bureau m; (Pol)
exécutif m ▷ adj exécutif(-ive); (position,
job) de cadre
**exempt** [ig'zɛmpt] adj: **~ from**
exempté(e) or dispensé(e) de ▷ vt: **to ~**
**sb from** exempter or dispenser qn de
**exercise** ['ɛksəsaiz] n exercice m ▷ vt
exercer; (patience etc) faire preuve de;
(dog) promener ▷ vi (also: **to take ~**)
prendre de l'exercice; **exercise book**
n cahier m
**exert** [ig'zə:t] vt exercer, employer; **to**
**~ o.s.** se dépenser; **exertion** [ig'zə:ʃən]
n effort m
**exhale** [ɛks'heil] vt exhaler ▷ vi expirer
**exhaust** [ig'zɔ:st] n (also: **~ fumes**)
gaz mpl d'échappement; (also: **~ pipe**)
tuyau m d'échappement ▷ vt épuiser;
**exhausted** adj épuisé(e); **exhaustion**
[ig'zɔ:stʃən] n épuisement m; **nervous**
**exhaustion** fatigue nerveuse
**exhibit** [ig'zibit] n (Art) pièce f or objet
m exposé(e); (Law) pièce à conviction
▷ vt (Art) exposer; (courage, skill) faire
preuve de; **exhibition** [ɛksi'biʃən] n
exposition f
**exhilarating** [ig'ziləreitiŋ] adj
grisant(e), stimulant(e)
**exile** ['ɛksail] n exil m; (person) exilé(e)
▷ vt exiler
**exist** [ig'zist] vi exister; **existence** n
existence f; **existing** adj actuel(le)
**exit** ['ɛksit] n sortie f ▷ vi (Comput,
Theat) sortir; **where's the ~?** où est la
sortie?; **exit ramp** n (US Aut) bretelle
f d'accès
**exotic** [ig'zɔtik] adj exotique
**expand** [ik'spænd] vt (area) agrandir;
(quantity) accroître ▷ vi (trade, etc) se
développer, s'accroître; (gas, metal)
se dilater
**expansion** [ik'spænʃən] n (territorial,

*economic)* expansion f; *(of trade, influence etc)* développement m; *(of production)* accroissement m; *(of population)* croissance f; *(of gas, metal)* expansion, dilatation f

**expect** [ɪkˈspɛkt] vt *(anticipate)* s'attendre à, s'attendre à ce que + sub; *(count on)* compter sur, escompter; *(require)* demander, exiger; *(suppose)* supposer; *(await: also baby)* attendre ▷ vi: **to be ~ing** *(pregnant woman)* être enceinte; **expectation** [ɛkspɛkˈteɪʃən] n *(hope)* attente f, espérance(s) f(pl); *(belief)* attente f

**expedition** [ɛkspəˈdɪʃən] n expédition f

**expel** [ɪkˈspɛl] vt chasser, expulser; *(Scol)* renvoyer, exclure

**expenditure** [ɪkˈspɛndɪtʃəʳ] n *(act of spending)* dépense f; *(money spent)* dépenses fpl

**expense** [ɪkˈspɛns] n *(high cost)* coût m; *(spending)* dépense f, frais mpl; **expenses** npl frais mpl; dépenses; **at the ~ of** *(fig)* aux dépens de; **expense account** n *(note f de)* frais mpl

**expensive** [ɪkˈspɛnsɪv] adj cher *(chère)*, coûteux(-euse); **it's too ~** ça coûte trop cher

**experience** [ɪkˈspɪərɪəns] n expérience f ▷ vt connaître; *(feeling)* éprouver; **experienced** adj expérimenté(e)

**experiment** [ɪkˈspɛrɪmənt] n expérience f ▷ vi faire une expérience; **experimental** [ɪkspɛrɪˈmɛntl] adj expérimental(e)

**expert** [ˈɛkspəːt] adj expert(e) ▷ n expert m; **expertise** [ɛkspəːˈtiːz] n *(grande)* compétence f

**expire** [ɪkˈspaɪəʳ] vi expirer; **expiry** n expiration f; **expiry date** n date f d'expiration; *(on label)* à utiliser avant …

**explain** [ɪkˈspleɪn] vt expliquer; **explanation** [ɛkspləˈneɪʃən] n explication f

**explicit** [ɪkˈsplɪsɪt] adj explicite; *(definite)* formel(le)

**explode** [ɪkˈspləud] vi exploser

**exploit** n [ˈɛksplɔɪt] exploit m ▷ vt [ɪkˈsplɔɪt] exploiter; **exploitation** [ɛksplɔɪˈteɪʃən] n exploitation f

**explore** [ɪkˈsplɔːʳ] vt explorer; *(possibilities)* étudier, examiner; **explorer** n explorateur(-trice)

**explosion** [ɪkˈspləuʒən] n explosion f; **explosive** [ɪkˈspləusɪv] adj explosif(-ive) ▷ n explosif m

**export** vt [ɛkˈspɔːt] exporter ▷ n [ˈɛkspɔːt] exportation f ▷ cpd d'exportation; **exporter** n exportateur m

**expose** [ɪkˈspəuz] vt exposer; *(unmask)* démasquer, dévoiler; **exposed** adj *(land, house)* exposé(e); **exposure** [ɪkˈspəuʒəʳ] n exposition f; *(publicity)* couverture f; *(Phot: speed)* *(temps m de)* pose f; *(: shot)* pose f; **to die of exposure** *(Med)* mourir de froid

**express** [ɪkˈsprɛs] adj *(definite)* formel(le), exprès(-esse); *(BRIT: letter etc)* exprès inv ▷ n *(train)* rapide m ▷ vt exprimer; **expression** [ɪkˈsprɛʃən] n expression f; **expressway** n *(US)* voie f express *(à plusieurs files)*

**exquisite** [ɛkˈskwɪzɪt] adj exquis(e)

**extend** [ɪkˈstɛnd] vt *(visit, street)* prolonger, remettre; *(building)* agrandir; *(offer)* présenter, offrir; *(hand, arm)* tendre ▷ vi *(land)* s'étendre; **extension** n *(of visit, street)* prolongation f; *(building)* annexe f; *(telephone: in offices)* poste m; *(: in private house)* téléphone m supplémentaire; **extension cable, extension lead** n *(Elec)* rallonge f; **extensive** adj étendu(e), vaste; *(damage, alterations)* considérable; *(inquiries)* approfondi(e)

**extent** [ɪkˈstɛnt] n étendue f; **to some ~** dans une certaine mesure; **to the ~ of …** au point de …; **to what ~?** dans quelle mesure?, jusqu'à quel point?; **to such an ~ that …** à tel point que …

**exterior** [ɛkˈstɪərɪəʳ] adj extérieur(e) ▷ n extérieur m

**external** [ɛkˈstəːnl] adj externe

**extinct** [ɪk'stɪŋkt] *adj* (*volcano*) éteint(e); (*species*) disparu(e); **extinction** *n* extinction *f*

**extinguish** [ɪk'stɪŋgwɪʃ] *vt* éteindre

**extra** ['ɛkstrə] *adj* supplémentaire, de plus ▷ *adv* (*in addition*) en plus ▷ *n* supplément *m*; (*perk*) à-coté *m*; (*Cine, Theat*) figurant(e)

**extract** *vt* [ɪk'strækt] extraire; (*tooth*) arracher; (*money, promise*) soutirer ▷ *n* ['ɛkstrækt] extrait *m*

**extradite** ['ɛkstrədaɪt] *vt* extrader

**extraordinary** [ɪk'strɔːdnrɪ] *adj* extraordinaire

**extravagance** [ɪk'strævəgəns] *n* (*excessive spending*) prodigalités *fpl*; (*thing bought*) folie *f*, dépense excessive; **extravagant** *adj* extravagant(e); (*in spending: person*) prodigue, dépensier(-ière); (: *tastes*) dispendieux(-euse)

**extreme** [ɪk'striːm] *adj, n* extrême (*m*); **extremely** *adv* extrêmement

**extremist** [ɪk'striːmɪst] *adj, n* extrémiste *m/f*

**extrovert** ['ɛkstrəvəːt] *n* extraverti(e)

**eye** [aɪ] *n* œil *m* ((*yeux*) *pl*); (*of needle*) trou *m*, chas *m* ▷ *vt* examiner; **to keep an ~ on** surveiller; **eyeball** *n* globe *m* oculaire; **eyebrow** *n* sourcil *m*; **eyedrops** *npl* gouttes *fpl* pour les yeux; **eyelash** *n* cil *m*; **eyelid** *n* paupière *f*; **eyeliner** *n* eye-liner *m*; **eyeshadow** *n* ombre *f* à paupières; **eyesight** *n* vue *f*; **eye witness** *n* témoin *m* oculaire

**F** [ɛf] *n* (*Mus*): **F** fa *m*

**fabric** ['fæbrɪk] *n* tissu *m*

**fabulous** ['fæbjuləs] *adj* fabuleux(-euse); (*inf: super*) formidable, sensationnel(le)

**face** [feɪs] *n* visage *m*, figure *f*; (*expression*) air *m*; (*of clock*) cadran *m*; (*of cliff*) paroi *f*; (*of mountain*) face *f*; (*of building*) façade *f* ▷ *vt* faire face à; (*facts etc*) accepter; **~ down** (*person*) à plat ventre; (*card*) face en dessous; **to lose/save ~** perdre/sauver la face; **to pull a ~** faire une grimace; **in the ~ of** (*difficulties etc*) face à, devant; **on the ~ of it** à première vue; **~ to ~** face à face; **face up to** *vt fus* faire face à, affronter; **face cloth** *n* (*BRIT*) gant *m* de toilette; **face pack** *n* (*BRIT*) masque *m* (de beauté)

**facial** ['feɪʃl] *adj* facial(e) ▷ *n* soin complet du visage

**facilitate** [fə'sɪlɪteɪt] *vt* faciliter

**facilities** [fə'sɪlɪtɪz] *npl* installations *fpl*, équipement *m*; **credit ~** facilités de paiement

**fact** [fækt] n fait m; **in ~** en fait

**faction** ['fækʃən] n faction f

**factor** ['fæktər] n facteur m; (of sun cream) indice m (de protection); **I'd like a ~ 15 suntan lotion** je voudrais une crème solaire d'indice 15

**factory** ['fæktəri] n usine f, fabrique f

**factual** ['fæktjuəl] adj basé(e) sur les faits

**faculty** ['fækəltı] n faculté f; (us: teaching staff) corps enseignant

**fad** [fæd] n (personal) manie f; (craze) engouement m

**fade** [feɪd] vi se décolorer, passer; (light, sound) s'affaiblir; (flower) se faner; **fade away** vi (sound) s'affaiblir

**fag** [fæg] n (BRIT inf: cigarette) clope f

**Fahrenheit** ['fɑːrənhaɪt] n Fahrenheit m inv

**fail** [feɪl] vt (exam) échouer à; (candidate) recaler; (subj: courage, memory) faire défaut à ▷ vi échouer; (eyesight, health, light: also: **be ~ing**) baisser, s'affaiblir; (brakes) lâcher; **to ~ to do sth** (neglect) négliger de or ne pas faire qch; (be unable) ne pas arriver or parvenir à faire qch; **without ~** à coup sûr; sans faute; **failing** n défaut m ▷ prep faute de; **failing that** à défaut, sinon; **failure** ['feɪljər] n échec m; (person) raté(e); (mechanical etc) défaillance f

**faint** [feɪnt] adj faible; (recollection) vague; (mark) à peine visible ▷ n évanouissement m ▷ vi s'évanouir; **to feel ~** défaillir; **faintest** adj: **I haven't the faintest idea** je n'en ai pas la moindre idée; **faintly** adv faiblement; (vaguely) vaguement

**fair** [fɛər] adj équitable, juste; (hair) blond(e); (skin, complexion) pâle, blanc (blanche); (weather) beau (belle); (good enough) assez bon(ne); (sizeable) considérable ▷ adv: **to play ~** jouer franc jeu ▷ n foire f; (BRIT: funfair) fête (foraine); **fairground** n champ m de foire; **fair-haired** adj (person) aux cheveux clairs, blond(e); **fairly** adv

(justly) équitablement; (quite) assez;

**fair trade** n commerce m équitable;

**fairway** n (Golf) fairway m

**fairy** ['fɛərı] n fée f; **fairy tale** n conte m de fées

**faith** [feɪθ] n foi f; (trust) confiance f; (sect) culte m, religion f; **faithful** adj fidèle; **faithfully** adv fidèlement; **yours faithfully** (BRIT: in letters) veuillez agréer l'expression de mes salutations les plus distinguées

**fake** [feɪk] n (painting etc) faux m; (person) imposteur m ▷ adj faux (fausse) ▷ vt (emotions) simuler; (painting) faire un faux m

**falcon** ['fɔːlkən] n faucon m

**fall** [fɔːl] n chute f; (decrease) baisse f; (us: autumn) automne m ▷ vi (pt fell, pp **~en**) tomber; (price, temperature, dollar) baisser; **falls** npl (waterfall) chute f d'eau, cascade f; **to ~ flat** vi (on one's face) tomber de tout son long, s'étaler; (joke) tomber à plat; (plan) échouer; **fall apart** vi (object) tomber en morceaux; **fall down** vi (person) tomber; (building) s'effondrer, s'écrouler; **fall for** vt fus (trick) se laisser prendre à; (person) tomber amoureux(-euse) de; **fall off** vi tomber; (diminish) baisser, diminuer; **fall out** vi (friends etc) se brouiller; (hair, teeth) tomber; **fall over** vi tomber (par terre); **fall through** vi (plan, project) tomber à l'eau

**fallen** ['fɔːlən] pp of **fall**

**fallout** ['fɔːlaut] n retombées (radioactives)

**false** [fɔːls] adj faux (fausse); **under ~ pretences** sous un faux prétexte; **false alarm** n fausse alerte; **false teeth** npl (BRIT) fausses dents, dentier m

**fame** [feɪm] n renommée f, renom m

**familiar** [fə'mɪlɪər] adj familier(-ière); **to be ~ with sth** connaître qch; **familiarize** [fə'mɪlɪəraɪz] vt: **to familiarize o.s. with** se familiariser avec

**family** ['fæmɪlı] n famille f; **family doctor** n médecin m de famille; **family**

**planning** n planning familial
**famine** ['fæmɪn] n famine f
**famous** ['feɪməs] adj célèbre
**fan** [fæn] n (folding) éventail m;
(Elec) ventilateur m; (person) fan m,
admirateur(-trice); (Sport) supporter
m/f ▷ vt éventer; (fire, quarrel) attiser
**fanatic** [fə'nætɪk] n fanatique m/f
**fan belt** n courroie f de ventilateur
**fan club** n fan-club m
**fancy** ['fænsɪ] n (whim) fantaisie f,
envie f; (imagination) imagination
f ▷ adj (luxury) de luxe; (elaborate:
jewellery, packaging) fantaisie inv ▷ vt
(feel like, want) avoir envie de; (imagine)
imaginer; **to take a ~ to** se prendre
d'affection pour; s'enticher de; **he
fancies her** elle lui plaît; **fancy dress** n
déguisement m, travesti m
**fan heater** n (BRIT) radiateur soufflant
**fantasize** ['fæntəsaɪz] vi fantasmer
**fantastic** [fæn'tæstɪk] adj fantastique
**fantasy** ['fæntəsɪ] n imagination f,
fantaisie f; (unreality) fantasme m
**fanzine** ['fænzi:n] n fanzine m
**FAQ** n abbr (= frequently asked question)
FAQ f inv, faq f inv
**far** [fɑː<sup>r</sup>] adj (distant) lointain(e),
éloigné(e) ▷ adv loin; **the ~ side/end**
l'autre côté/bout; **it's not ~ (from
here)** ce n'est pas loin (d'ici); **~ away,
~ off** au loin, dans le lointain; **~ better**
beaucoup mieux; **~ from** loin de; **by ~**
de loin, de beaucoup; **go as ~ as the
bridge** allez jusqu'au pont; **as ~ as I
know** pour autant que je sache; **how ~
is it to ...?** combien y a-t-il jusqu'à ...?;
**how ~ have you got with your work?**
où en êtes-vous dans votre travail?
**farce** [fɑːs] n farce f
**fare** [fɛə<sup>r</sup>] n (on trains, buses) prix m du
billet; (in taxi) prix de la course; (food)
table f, chère f; **half ~** demi-tarif; **full
~** plein tarif
**Far East** n: **the ~** l'Extrême-Orient m
**farewell** [fɛə'wɛl] excl, n adieu m
**farm** [fɑːm] n ferme f ▷ vt cultiver;
**farmer** n fermier(-ière); **farmhouse**

n (maison f de) ferme f; **farming** n
agriculture f; (of animals) élevage m;
**farmyard** n cour f de ferme
**far-reaching** ['fɑː'riːtʃɪŋ] adj d'une
grande portée
**fart** [fɑːt] (inf!) vi péter
**farther** ['fɑːðə<sup>r</sup>] adv plus loin ▷ adj plus
éloigné(e), plus lointain(e)
**farthest** ['fɑːðɪst] superlative of **far**
**fascinate** ['fæsɪneɪt] vt fasciner,
captiver; **fascinated** adj fasciné(e)
**fascinating** ['fæsɪneɪtɪŋ] adj
fascinant(e)
**fascination** [fæsɪ'neɪʃən] n
fascination f
**fascist** ['fæʃɪst] adj, n fasciste m/f
**fashion** ['fæʃən] n mode f; (manner)
façon f, manière f ▷ vt façonner; **in
~** à la mode; **out of ~** démodé(e);
**fashionable** adj à la mode; **fashion
show** n défilé m de mannequins or
de mode
**fast** [fɑːst] adj rapide; (clock): **to be ~**
avancer; (dye, colour) grand or bon teint
inv ▷ adv vite, rapidement; (stuck, held)
solidement ▷ n jeûne m ▷ vi jeûner; **~
asleep** profondément endormi
**fasten** ['fɑːsn] vt attacher, fixer;
(coat) attacher, fermer ▷ vi se fermer,
s'attacher
**fast food** n fast food m, restauration
f rapide
**fat** [fæt] adj gros(se) ▷ n graisse f; (on
meat) gras m; (for cooking) matière
grasse
**fatal** ['feɪtl] adj (mistake) fatal(e); (injury)
mortel(le); **fatality** [fə'tælɪtɪ] n (road
death etc) victime f, décès m; **fatally** adv
fatalement; (injured) mortellement
**fate** [feɪt] n destin m; (of person) sort m
**father** ['fɑːðə<sup>r</sup>] n père m; **Father
Christmas** n le Père Noël; **father-in-
law** n beau-père m
**fatigue** [fə'tiːg] n fatigue f
**fattening** ['fætnɪŋ] adj (food) qui
fait grossir
**fatty** ['fætɪ] adj (food) gras(se) ▷ n (inf)
gros (grosse)

**faucet** ['fɔːsɪt] n (US) robinet m

**fault** [fɔːlt] n faute f; (defect) défaut m; (Geo) faille f ▷ vt trouver des défauts à, prendre en défaut; **it's my ~** c'est de ma faute; **to find ~ with** trouver à redire or à critiquer à; **at ~** fautif(-ive), coupable; **faulty** adj défectueux(-euse)

**fauna** ['fɔːnə] n faune f

**favour** etc (us **favor** etc) ['feɪvər] n faveur f; (help) service m ▷ vt (proposition) être en faveur de; (pupil etc) favoriser; (team, horse) donner gagnant; **to do sb a ~** rendre un service à qn; **in ~ of** en faveur de; **to find ~ with sb** trouver grâce aux yeux de qn; **favourable** adj favorable; **favourite** ['feɪvrɪt] adj, n favori(te)

**fawn** [fɔːn] n (deer) faon m ▷ adj (also: **~-coloured**) fauve ▷ vi: **to ~ (up)on** flatter servilement

**fax** [fæks] n (document) télécopie f; (machine) télécopieur m ▷ vt envoyer par télécopie

**FBI** n abbr (US: = Federal Bureau of Investigation) FBI m

**fear** [fɪər] n crainte f, peur f ▷ vt craindre; **for ~ of** de peur que + sub or de + infinitive; **fearful** adj craintif(-ive); (sight, noise) affreux(-euse), épouvantable; **fearless** adj intrépide

**feasible** ['fiːzəbl] adj faisable, réalisable

**feast** [fiːst] n festin m, banquet m; (Rel: also: **~ day**) fête f ▷ vi festoyer

**feat** [fiːt] n exploit m, prouesse f

**feather** ['fɛðər] n plume f

**feature** ['fiːtʃər] n caractéristique f; (article) chronique f, rubrique f ▷ vt (film) avoir pour vedette(s) ▷ vi figurer (en bonne place); **features** npl (of face) traits mpl; **a (special) ~ on sth/sb** un reportage sur qch/qn; **feature film** n long métrage

**Feb.** abbr (= February) fév

**February** ['fɛbruərɪ] n février m

**fed** [fɛd] pt, pp of **feed**

**federal** ['fɛdərəl] adj fédéral(e)

**federation** [fɛdə'reɪʃən] n fédération f

**fed up** adj: **to be ~ (with)** en avoir marre or plein le dos (de)

**fee** [fiː] n rémunération f; (of doctor, lawyer) honoraires mpl; (of school, college etc) frais mpl de scolarité; (for examination) droits mpl

**feeble** ['fiːbl] adj faible; (attempt, excuse) pauvre; (joke) piteux(-euse)

**feed** [fiːd] n (of animal) nourriture f, pâture f; (on printer) mécanisme m d'alimentation f ▷ vt (pt, pp **fed**) (person) nourrir; (BRIT: baby: breastfeed) allaiter; (: with bottle) donner le biberon à; (horse etc) donner à manger à; (machine) alimenter; (data etc): **to ~ sth into** enregistrer qch dans; **feedback** n (Elec) effet m Larsen; (from person) réactions fpl

**feel** [fiːl] n (sensation) sensation f; (impression) impression f ▷ vt (pt, pp **felt**) (touch) toucher; (explore) tâter, palper; (cold, pain) sentir; (grief, anger) ressentir, éprouver; (think, believe): **to ~ (that)** trouver que; **to ~ hungry/cold** avoir faim/froid; **to ~ lonely/better** se sentir seul/mieux; **I don't ~ well** je ne me sens pas bien; **it ~s soft** c'est doux au toucher; **to ~ like** (want) avoir envie de; **feeling** n (physical) sensation f; (emotion, impression) sentiment m; **to hurt sb's feelings** froisser qn

**feet** [fiːt] npl of **foot**

**fell** [fɛl] pt of **fall** ▷ vt (tree) abattre

**fellow** ['fɛləu] n type m; (comrade) compagnon m; (of learned society) membre m ▷ cpd: **their ~ prisoners/students** leurs camarades prisonniers/étudiants; **fellow citizen** n concitoyen(ne); **fellow countryman** n (irreg) compatriote m; **fellow men** npl semblables mpl; **fellowship** n (society) association f; (comradeship) amitié f, camaraderie f; (Scol) sorte de bourse universitaire

**felony** ['fɛlənɪ] n crime m, forfait m

**felt** [fɛlt] pt, pp of **feel** ▷ n feutre m; **felt-tip** n (also: **felt-tip pen**) stylo-feutre m

**female** ['fiːmeɪl] n (Zool) femelle f;

(*pej: woman*) bonne femme ▷ *adj* (*Biol*) femelle; (*sex, character*) féminin(e); (*vote etc*) des femmes

**feminine** ['fɛmɪnɪn] *adj* féminin(e)

**feminist** ['fɛmɪnɪst] *n* féministe *m/f*

**fence** [fɛns] *n* barrière *f* ▷ *vi* faire de l'escrime; **fencing** *n* (*sport*) escrime *m*

**fend** [fɛnd] *vi*: **to ~ for o.s.** se débrouiller (tout seul); **fend off** *vt* (*attack etc*) parer; (*questions*) éluder

**fender** ['fɛndə$^r$] *n* garde-feu *m inv*; (*on boat*) défense *f*; (*us: of car*) aile *f*

**fennel** ['fɛnl] *n* fenouil *m*

**ferment** *vi* [fə'mɛnt] fermenter ▷ *n* ['fəːmɛnt] (*fig*) agitation *f*, effervescence *f*

**fern** [fəːn] *n* fougère *f*

**ferocious** [fə'rəuʃəs] *adj* féroce

**ferret** ['fɛrɪt] *n* furet *m*

**ferry** ['fɛrɪ] *n* (*small*) bac *m*; (*large: also: ~boat*) ferry(-boat *m*) *m* ▷ *vt* transporter

**fertile** ['fəːtaɪl] *adj* fertile; (*Biol*) fécond(e); **fertilize** ['fəːtɪlaɪz] *vt* fertiliser; (*Biol*) féconder; **fertilizer** *n* engrais *m*

**festival** ['fɛstɪvəl] *n* (*Rel*) fête *f*; (*Art, Mus*) festival *m*

**festive** ['fɛstɪv] *adj* de fête; **the ~ season** (*BRIT: Christmas*) la période des fêtes

**fetch** [fɛtʃ] *vt* aller chercher; (*BRIT: sell for*) rapporter

**fête** [feɪt] *n* fête *f*, kermesse *f*

**fetus** ['fiːtəs] *n* (*us*) = **foetus**

**feud** [fjuːd] *n* querelle *f*, dispute *f*

**fever** ['fiːvə$^r$] *n* fièvre *f*; **feverish** *adj* fiévreux(-euse), fébrile

**few** [fjuː] *adj* (*not many*) peu de ▷ *pron* peu; **a ~** (*as adj*) quelques; (*as pron*) quelques-uns(-unes); **quite a ~ ...** *adj* un certain nombre de ..., pas mal de ...; **in the past ~ days** ces derniers jours; **fewer** *adj* moins de; **fewest** *adj* le moins nombreux

**fiancé** [fɪ'ɑːnseɪ] *n* fiancé *m*; **fiancée** *n* fiancée *f*

**fiasco** [fɪ'æskəu] *n* fiasco *m*

**fib** [fɪb] *n* bobard *m*

**fibre** (*us* **fiber**) ['faɪbə$^r$] *n* fibre *f*; **fibreglass** (*us* **Fiberglass®**) *n* fibre *f* de verre

**fickle** ['fɪkl] *adj* inconstant(e), volage, capricieux(-euse)

**fiction** ['fɪkʃən] *n* romans *mpl*, littérature *f* romanesque; (*invention*) fiction *f*; **fictional** *adj* fictif(-ive)

**fiddle** ['fɪdl] *n* (*Mus*) violon *m*; (*cheating*) combine *f*; escroquerie *f* ▷ *vt* (*BRIT: accounts*) falsifier, maquiller; **fiddle with** *vt fus* tripoter

**fidelity** [fɪ'dɛlɪtɪ] *n* fidélité *f*

**fidget** ['fɪdʒɪt] *vi* se trémousser, remuer

**field** [fiːld] *n* champ *m*; (*fig*) domaine *m*, champ; (*Sport: ground*) terrain *m*; **field marshal** *n* maréchal *m*

**fierce** [fɪəs] *adj* (*look, animal*) féroce, sauvage; (*wind, attack, person*) (très) violent(e); (*fighting, enemy*) acharné(e)

**fifteen** [fɪf'tiːn] *num* quinze; **fifteenth** *num* quinzième

**fifth** [fɪfθ] *num* cinquième

**fiftieth** ['fɪftɪɪθ] *num* cinquantième

**fifty** ['fɪftɪ] *num* cinquante; **fifty-fifty** *adv* moitié-moitié ▷ *adj*: **to have a fifty-fifty chance (of success)** avoir une chance sur deux (de réussir)

**fig** [fɪg] *n* figue *f*

**fight** [faɪt] *n* (*between persons*) bagarre *f*; (*argument*) dispute *f*; (*Mil*) combat *m*; (*against cancer etc*) lutte *f* ▷ *vb* (*pt, pp* **fought**) ▷ *vt* se battre contre; (*cancer, alcoholism, emotion*) combattre, lutter contre; (*election*) se présenter à ▷ *vi* se battre; (*argue*) se disputer; (*fig*): **to ~ (for/against)** lutter (pour/contre); **fight back** *vi* rendre les coups; (*after illness*) reprendre le dessus ▷ *vt* (*tears*) réprimer; **fight off** *vt* repousser; (*disease, sleep, urge*) lutter contre; **fighting** *n* combats *mpl*; (*brawls*) bagarres *fpl*

**figure** ['fɪgə$^r$] *n* (*Drawing, Geom*) figure *f*; (*number*) chiffre *m*; (*body, outline*) silhouette *f*; (*person's shape*) ligne *f*, formes *fpl*; (*person*) personnage *m*

▷ vt (US: think) supposer ▷ vi (appear) figurer; (US: make sense) s'expliquer; **figure out** vt (understand) arriver à comprendre; (plan) calculer

**file** [faɪl] n (tool) lime f; (dossier) dossier m; (folder) dossier, chemise f; (: binder) classeur m; (Comput) fichier m; (row) file f ▷ vt (nails, wood) limer; (papers) classer; (Law: claim) faire enregistrer; déposer; **filing cabinet** n classeur m (meuble)

**Filipino** [fɪlɪˈpiːnəu] adj philippin(e) ▷ n (person) Philippin(e)

**fill** [fɪl] vt remplir; (vacancy) pourvoir à ▷ n: **to eat one's** ~ manger à sa faim; **to ~ with** remplir de; **fill in** vt (hole) boucher; (form) remplir; **fill out** vt (form, receipt) remplir; **fill up** vt remplir ▷ vi (Aut) faire le plein

**fillet** [ˈfɪlɪt] n filet m; **fillet steak** n filet m de bœuf, tournedos m

**filling** [ˈfɪlɪŋ] n (Culin) garniture f, farce f; (for tooth) plombage m; **filling station** n station-service f, station d'essence

**film** [fɪlm] n film m; (Phot) pellicule f, film; (of powder, liquid) couche f, pellicule ▷ vt (scene) filmer ▷ vi tourner; **I'd like a 36-exposure** ~ je voudrais une pellicule de 36 poses; **film star** n vedette f de cinéma

**filter** [ˈfɪltəʳ] n filtre m ▷ vt filtrer; **filter lane** n (BRIT Aut: at traffic lights) voie f de dégagement; (: on motorway) voie f de sortie

**filth** [fɪlθ] n saleté f; **filthy** adj sale, dégoûtant(e); (language) ordurier(-ière), grossier(-ière)

**fin** [fɪn] n (of fish) nageoire f; (of shark) aileron m; (of diver) palme f

**final** [ˈfaɪnl] adj final(e), dernier(-ière); (decision, answer) définitif(-ive) ▷ n (BRIT Sport) finale f; **finals** npl (Scol) examens mpl de dernière année; (US Sport) finale f; **finale** [fɪˈnɑːlɪ] n finale m; **finalist** n (Sport) finaliste m/f; **finalize** vt mettre au point; **finally** adv (eventually) enfin, finalement; (lastly) en dernier lieu

**finance** [faɪˈnæns] n finance f ▷ vt financer; **finances** npl finances fpl; **financial** [faɪˈnænʃəl] adj financier(-ière); **financial year** n année f budgétaire

**find** [faɪnd] vt (pt, pp **found**) trouver; (lost object) retrouver ▷ n trouvaille f, découverte f; **to ~ sb guilty** (Law) déclarer qn coupable; **find out** vt se renseigner sur; (truth, secret) découvrir; (person) démasquer ▷ vi: **to ~ out about** (make enquiries) se renseigner sur; (by chance) apprendre; **findings** npl (Law) conclusions fpl, verdict m; (of report) constatations fpl

**fine** [faɪn] adj (weather) beau (belle); (excellent) excellent(e); (thin, subtle, not coarse) fin(e); (acceptable) bien inv ▷ adv (well) très bien; (small) fin, finement ▷ n (Law) amende f, contravention f ▷ vt (Law) condamner à une amende; donner une contravention à; **he's** ~ il va bien; **the weather is** ~ il fait beau; **fine arts** npl beaux-arts mpl

**finger** [ˈfɪŋɡəʳ] n doigt m ▷ vt palper, toucher; **index** ~ index m; **fingernail** n ongle m (de la main); **fingerprint** n empreinte digitale; **fingertip** n bout m du doigt

**finish** [ˈfɪnɪʃ] n fin f; (Sport) arrivée f; (polish etc) finition f ▷ vt finir, terminer ▷ vi finir, se terminer; **to ~ doing sth** finir de faire qch; **to ~ third** arriver or terminer troisième; **when does the show ~?** quand est-ce que le spectacle se termine?; **finish off** vt finir, terminer; (kill) achever; **finish up** vi, vt finir

**Finland** [ˈfɪnlənd] n Finlande f; **Finn** n Finnois(e), Finlandais(e); **Finnish** adj finnois(e), finlandais(e) ▷ n (Ling) finnois m

**fir** [fəːʳ] n sapin m

**fire** [ˈfaɪəʳ] n feu m; (accidental) incendie m; (heater) radiateur m ▷ vt (discharge): **to ~ a gun** tirer un coup de feu; (fig: interest) enflammer, animer; (inf: dismiss) mettre à la porte, renvoyer ▷ vi (*shoot*) tirer, faire feu; **~!** au feu!; **on ~** en feu; **to set ~ to sth**, **set sth on ~** mettre le feu à qch; **fire alarm** *n* avertisseur *m* d'incendie; **firearm** *n* arme *f* à feu; **fire brigade** *n* (*us* **fire department**) (régiment *m* de sapeurs-)pompiers *mpl*; **fire engine** (*BRIT*) pompe *f* à incendie; **fire escape** *n* escalier *m* de secours; **fire exit** *n* issue *f* or sortie *f* de secours; **fire extinguisher** *n* extincteur *m*; **fireman** (*irreg*) *n* pompier *m*; **fireplace** *n* cheminée *f*; **fire station** *n* caserne *f* de pompiers; **fire truck** (*us*) *n* = **fire engine**; **firewall** *n* (*Internet*) pare-feu *m*; **firewood** *n* bois *m* de chauffage; **fireworks** *npl* (*display*) feu(x) *m*(*pl*) d'artifice

**firm** [fəːm] *adj* ferme ▷ *n* compagnie *f*, firme *f*; **firmly** *adv* fermement

**first** [fəːst] *adj* premier(-ière) ▷ *adv* (*before other people*) le premier, la première; (*before other things*) en premier, d'abord; (*when listing reasons etc*) en premier lieu, premièrement; (*in the beginning*) au début ▷ *n* (*person: in race*) premier(-ière); (*BRIT Scol*) mention *f* très bien; (*Aut*) première *f*; **the ~ of January** le premier janvier; **at ~** au commencement, au début; **~ of all** tout d'abord, pour commencer; **first aid** *n* premiers secours *or* soins; **first-aid kit** *n* trousse *f* à pharmacie; **first-class** *adj* (*ticket etc*) de première classe; (*excellent*) excellent(e), exceptionnel(le); (*post*) en tarif prioritaire; **first-hand** *adj* de première main; **first lady** *n* (*us*) femme *f* du président; **firstly** *adv* premièrement, en premier lieu; **first name** *n* prénom *m*; **first-rate** *adj* excellent(e)

**fiscal** [ˈfɪskl] *adj* fiscal(e); **fiscal year** *n* exercice financier

**fish** [fɪʃ] *n* (*pl inv*) poisson *m* ▷ *vt, vi* pêcher; **~ and chips** poisson frit et frites; **fisherman** (*irreg*) *n* pêcheur *m*; **fish fingers** *npl* (*BRIT*) bâtonnets de poisson (congelés); **fishing** *n* pêche *f*; **to go fishing** aller à la pêche;

**fishing boat** *n* barque *f* de pêche; **fishing line** *n* ligne *f* (de pêche); **fishmonger** *n* (*BRIT*) marchand *m* de poisson; **fishmonger's (shop)** *n* (*BRIT*) poissonnerie *f*; **fish sticks** *npl* (*us*) = **fish fingers**; **fishy** *adj* (*inf*) suspect(e), louche

**fist** [fɪst] *n* poing *m*

**fit** [fɪt] *adj* (*Med, Sport*) en (bonne) forme; (*proper*) convenable; approprié(e) ▷ *vt* (*subj: clothes*) aller à; (*put in, attach*) installer, poser; (*equip*) équiper, garnir, munir; (*suit*) convenir à ▷ *vi* (*clothes*) aller; (*parts*) s'adapter; (*in space, gap*) entrer, s'adapter ▷ *n* (*Med*) accès *m*, crise *f*; (*of anger*) accès; (*of hysterics, jealousy*) crise; **~ to** (*ready to*) en état de; **~ for** (*worthy*) digne de; (*capable*) apte à; **to keep ~** se maintenir en forme; **this dress is a tight/good ~** cette robe est un peu juste/(me) va très bien; **a ~ of coughing** une quinte de toux; **by ~s and starts** par à-coups; **fit in** *vi* (*add up*) cadrer; (*integrate*) s'intégrer; (*to new situation*) s'adapter; **fitness** *n* (*Med*) forme *f* physique; **fitted** *adj* (*jacket, shirt*) ajusté(e); **fitted carpet** *n* moquette *f*; **fitted kitchen** *n* (*BRIT*) cuisine équipée; **fitted sheet** *n* drap-housse *m*; **fitting** *adj* approprié(e) ▷ *n* (*of dress*) essayage *m*; (*of piece of equipment*) pose *f*, installation *f*; **fitting room** *n* (*in shop*) cabine *f* d'essayage; **fittings** *npl* installations *fpl*

**five** [faɪv] *num* cinq; **fiver** *n* (*inf: BRIT*) billet *m* de cinq livres; (: *us*) billet de cinq dollars

**fix** [fɪks] *vt* (*date, amount etc*) fixer; (*sort out*) arranger; (*mend*) réparer; (*make ready: meal, drink*) préparer ▷ *n*: **to be in a ~** être dans le pétrin; **fix up** *vt* (*meeting*) arranger; **to ~ sb up with sth** faire avoir qch à qn; **fixed** *adj* (*prices etc*) fixe; **fixture** *n* installation *f* (fixe); (*Sport*) rencontre *f* (au programme)

**fizzy** [ˈfɪzɪ] *adj* pétillant(e), gazeux(-euse)

**flag** [flæg] *n* drapeau *m*; (*also*: **~stone**)

dalle f ▷ vi faiblir; fléchir; **flag down**
vt héler, faire signe (de s'arrêter) à;
**flagpole** n mât m

**flair** [flɛəʳ] n flair m

**flak** [flæk] n (Mil) tir antiaérien; (inf:
criticism) critiques fpl

**flake** [fleɪk] n (of rust, paint) écaille f; (of
snow, soap powder) flocon m ▷ vi (also: ~
**off**) s'écailler

**flamboyant** [flæm'bɔɪənt] adj
flamboyant(e), éclatant(e); (person)
haut(e) en couleur

**flame** [fleɪm] n flamme f

**flamingo** [flə'mɪŋgəʊ] n flamant
m (rose)

**flammable** ['flæməbl] adj
inflammable

**flan** [flæn] n (BRIT) tarte f

**flank** [flæŋk] n flanc m ▷ vt flanquer

**flannel** ['flænl] n (BRIT: also: **face ~**)
gant m de toilette; (fabric) flanelle f

**flap** [flæp] n (of pocket, envelope) rabat
m ▷ vt (wings) battre (de) ▷ vi (sail,
flag) claquer

**flare** [flɛəʳ] n (signal) signal lumineux;
(Mil) fusée éclairante; (in skirt etc)
évasement m; **flares** npl (trousers)
pantalon m à pattes d'éléphant; **flare
up** vi s'embraser; (fig: person) se mettre
en colère, s'emporter; (: revolt) éclater

**flash** [flæʃ] n éclair m; (also: **news ~**)
flash m (d'information); (Phot) flash
▷ vt (switch on) allumer (brièvement);
(direct): **to ~ sth at** braquer qch sur;
(send: message) câbler; (smile) lancer
▷ vi briller; jeter des éclairs; (light
on ambulance etc) clignoter; **a ~ of
lightning** un éclair; **in a ~** en un clin
d'œil; **to ~ one's headlights** faire un
appel de phares; **he ~ed by** or **past** il
passa (devant nous) comme un éclair;
**flashback** n flashback m, retour m en
arrière; **flashbulb** n ampoule f de flash;
**flashlight** n lampe f de poche

**flask** [flɑːsk] n flacon m, bouteille f;
(also: **vacuum ~**) bouteille f thermos®

**flat** [flæt] adj plat(e); (tyre) dégonflé(e),
à plat; (beer) éventé(e); (battery) à plat;

(denial) catégorique; (Mus) bémol inv;
(: voice) faux (fausse) ▷ n (BRIT:
apartment) appartement m; (Aut)
crevaison f, pneu crevé; (Mus) bémol m;
**~ out** (work) sans relâche; (race) à fond;
**flatten** vt (also: **flatten out**) aplatir;
(crop) coucher; (building, city) raser

**flatter** ['flætəʳ] vt flatter; **flattering** adj
flatteur(-euse); (clothes etc) seyant(e)

**flaunt** [flɔːnt] vt faire étalage de

**flavour** etc (US **flavor** etc) ['fleɪvəʳ]
n goût m, saveur f; (of ice cream etc)
parfum m ▷ vt parfumer, aromatiser;
**vanilla-~ed** à l'arôme de vanille,
vanillé(e); **what ~s do you have?** quels
parfums avez-vous?; **flavouring** n
arôme m (synthétique)

**flaw** [flɔː] n défaut m; **flawless** adj
sans défaut

**flea** [fliː] n puce f; **flea market** n
marché m aux puces

**flee** (pt, pp **fled**) [fliː, flɛd] vt fuir, s'enfuir
de ▷ vi fuir, s'enfuir

**fleece** [fliːs] n (of sheep) toison f; (top)
(laine f) polaire f ▷ vt (inf) voler, filouter

**fleet** [fliːt] n flotte f; (of lorries, cars etc)
parc m; convoi m

**fleeting** ['fliːtɪŋ] adj fugace,
fugitif(-ive); (visit) très bref (brève)

**Flemish** ['flɛmɪʃ] adj flamand(e)
▷ n (Ling) flamand m; **the ~** npl les
Flamands

**flesh** [flɛʃ] n chair f

**flew** [fluː] pt of **fly**

**flex** [flɛks] n fil m or câble m électrique
(souple) ▷ vt (knee) fléchir; (muscles)
tendre; **flexibility** n flexibilité f;
**flexible** adj flexible; (person, schedule)
souple; **flexitime** (US **flextime**) n
horaire m variable or à la carte

**flick** [flɪk] n petit coup; (with finger)
chiquenaude f ▷ vt donner un petit
coup à; (switch) appuyer sur; **flick
through** vt fus feuilleter

**flicker** ['flɪkəʳ] vi (light, flame) vaciller

**flies** [flaɪz] npl of **fly**

**flight** [flaɪt] n vol m; (escape) fuite f;
(also: **~ of steps**) escalier m; **flight**

**attendant** n steward m, hôtesse f
de l'air

**flimsy** ['flɪmzɪ] adj peu solide; (clothes)
trop léger(-ère); (excuse) pauvre, mince

**flinch** [flɪntʃ] vi tressaillir; **to ~ from** se
dérober à, reculer devant

**fling** [flɪŋ] vt (pt, pp **flung**) jeter, lancer

**flint** [flɪnt] n silex m; (in lighter) pierre
f (à briquet)

**flip** [flɪp] vt (throw) donner une
chiquenaude à; (switch) appuyer sur;
(US: pancake) faire sauter; **to ~ sth over**
retourner qch

**flip-flops** ['flɪpflɒps] npl (esp BRIT)
tongs fpl

**flipper** ['flɪpə'] n (of animal) nageoire f;
(for swimmer) palme f

**flirt** [flɜːt] vi flirter ▷ n flirteur(-euse)

**float** [fləut] n flotteur m; (in procession)
char m; (sum of money) réserve f ▷ vi
flotter

**flock** [flɒk] n (of sheep) troupeau m; (of
birds) vol m; (of people) foule f

**flood** [flʌd] n inondation f; (of letters,
refugees etc) flot m ▷ vt inonder ▷ vi
(place) être inondé; (people): **to ~ into**
envahir; **flooding** n inondation f;
**floodlight** n projecteur m

**floor** [flɔː'] n sol m; (storey) étage m;
(of sea, valley) fond m ▷ vt (knock down)
terrasser; (baffle) désorienter; **ground
~**, (US) **first ~** rez-de-chaussée m; **first
~**, (US) **second ~** premier étage; **what ~
is it on?** c'est à quel étage?; **floorboard**
n planche f (du plancher); **flooring**
n sol m; (wooden) plancher m; (covering)
revêtement m de sol; **floor show** n
spectacle m de variétés

**flop** [flɒp] n fiasco m ▷ vi (fail) faire
fiasco; (fall) s'affaler, s'effondrer; **floppy**
adj lâche, flottant(e) ▷ n (Comput: also:
**floppy disk**) disquette f

**flora** ['flɔːrə] n flore f

**floral** ['flɔːrl] adj floral(e); (dress) à fleurs

**florist** ['flɒrɪst] n fleuriste m/f; **florist's
(shop)** n magasin m or boutique f de
fleuriste

**flotation** [fləu'teɪʃən] n (of shares)

émission f; (of company) lancement m
(en Bourse)

**flour** ['flauə'] n farine f

**flourish** ['flʌrɪʃ] vi prospérer ▷ n
(gesture) moulinet m

**flow** [fləu] n (of water, traffic etc)
écoulement m; (tide, influx) flux m;
(of blood, Elec) circulation f; (of river)
courant m ▷ vi couler; (traffic) s'écouler;
(robes, hair) flotter

**flower** ['flauə'] n fleur f ▷ vi fleurir;
**flower bed** n plate-bande f; **flowerpot**
n pot m (à fleurs)

**flown** [fləun] pp of **fly**

**fl. oz.** abbr = **fluid ounce**

**flu** [fluː] n grippe f

**fluctuate** ['flʌktjueɪt] vi varier,
fluctuer

**fluent** ['fluːənt] adj (speech, style)
coulant(e), aisé(e); **he speaks ~
French, he's ~ in French** il parle le
français couramment

**fluff** [flʌf] n duvet m; (on jacket, carpet)
peluche f; **fluffy** adj duveteux(-euse);
(toy) en peluche

**fluid** ['fluːɪd] n fluide m; (in diet) liquide
m ▷ adj fluide; **fluid ounce** n (BRIT) =
0.028 l; 0.05 pints

**fluke** [fluːk] n coup m de veine

**flung** [flʌŋ] pt, pp of **fling**

**fluorescent** [fluə'resnt] adj
fluorescent(e)

**fluoride** ['fluəraɪd] n fluor m

**flurry** ['flʌrɪ] n (of snow) rafale f,
bourrasque f; **a ~ of activity** un
affairement soudain

**flush** [flʌʃ] n (on face) rougeur f; (fig: of
youth etc) éclat m ▷ vt nettoyer à grande
eau ▷ vi rougir ▷ adj (level): **~ with** au
ras de, de niveau avec; **to ~ the toilet**
tirer la chasse (d'eau)

**flute** [fluːt] n flûte f

**flutter** ['flʌtə'] n (of panic, excitement)
agitation f; (of wings) battement m ▷ vi
(bird) battre des ailes, voleter

**fly** [flaɪ] n (insect) mouche f; (on trousers:
also: **flies**) braguette f ▷ vb (pt **flew**, pp
**flown**) ▷ vt (plane) piloter; (passengers,

*cargo*) transporter (par avion); (*distance*) parcourir ▷ *vi* voler; (*passengers*) aller en avion; (*escape*) s'enfuir, fuir; (*flag*) se déployer; **fly away, fly off** *vi* s'envoler; **fly-drive** *n* formule *f* avion plus voiture; **flying** *n* (*activity*) aviation *f*; (*action*) vol *m* ▷ *adj*: **flying visit** visite *f* éclair *inv*; **with flying colours** haut la main; **flying saucer** *n* soucoupe *f* volante; **flyover** *n* (BRIT: *overpass*) pont routier

**FM** *abbr* (*Radio*: = *frequency modulation*) FM

**foal** [fəul] *n* poulain *m*

**foam** [fəum] *n* écume *f*; (*on beer*) mousse *f*; (*also*: = **rubber**) caoutchouc *m* mousse ▷ *vi* (*liquid*) écumer; (*soapy water*) mousser

**focus** ['fəukəs] *n* (*pl* ~**es**) foyer *m*; (*of interest*) centre *m* ▷ *vt* (*field glasses etc*) mettre au point ▷ *vi*: **to ~ (on)** (*with camera*) régler la mise au point (sur); (*with eyes*) fixer son regard (sur); (*fig: concentrate*) se concentrer; **out of/in ~** (*picture*) flou(e)/net(te); (*camera*) pas au point/au point

**foetus** (US **fetus**) ['fi:təs] *n* fœtus *m*

**fog** [fɔg] *n* brouillard *m*; **foggy** *adj*: **it's foggy** il y a du brouillard; **fog lamp** (US **fog light**) *n* (*Aut*) phare *m* anti-brouillard

**foil** [fɔil] *vt* déjouer, contrecarrer ▷ *n* feuille *f* de métal; (*kitchen foil*) papier *m* d'alu(minium); **to act as a ~ to** (*fig*) servir de repoussoir *or* de faire-valoir à

**fold** [fəuld] *n* (*bend, crease*) pli *m*; (*Agr*) parc *m* à moutons; (*fig*) bercail *m* ▷ *vt* plier; **to ~ one's arms** croiser les bras; **fold up** *vi* (*map etc*) se plier, se replier; (*business*) fermer boutique ▷ *vt* (*map etc*) plier, replier; **folder** *n* (*for papers*) chemise *f*; (*: binder*) classeur *m*; (*Comput*) dossier *m*; **folding** *adj* (*chair, bed*) pliant(e)

**foliage** ['fəulɪɪdʒ] *n* feuillage *m*

**folk** [fəuk] *npl* gens *mpl* ▷ *cpd* folklorique; **folks** *npl* (*inf: parents*) famille *f*, parents *mpl*; **folklore**

['fəuklɔːʳ] *n* folklore *m*; **folk music** *n* musique *f* folklorique; (*contemporary*) musique folk, folk *m*; **folk song** *n* chanson *f* folklorique; (*contemporary*) chanson folk *inv*

**follow** ['fɔləu] *vt* suivre ▷ *vi* suivre; (*result*) s'ensuivre; **to ~ suit** (*fig*) faire de même; **follow up** *vt* (*letter, offer*) donner suite à; (*case*) suivre; **follower** *n* disciple *m/f*, partisan(e); **following** *adj* suivant(e) ▷ *n* partisans *mpl*, disciples *mpl*; **follow-up** *n* suite *f*; (*on file, case*) suivi *m*

**fond** [fɔnd] *adj* (*memory, look*) tendre, affectueux(-euse); (*hopes, dreams*) un peu fou (folle); **to be ~ of** aimer beaucoup

**food** [fu:d] *n* nourriture *f*; **food mixer** *n* mixeur *m*; **food poisoning** *n* intoxication *f* alimentaire; **food processor** *n* robot *m* de cuisine; **food stamp** *n* (US) bon *m* de nourriture (*pour indigents*)

**fool** [fu:l] *n* idiot(e); (*Culin*) mousse *f* de fruits ▷ *vt* berner, duper; **fool about, fool around** *vi* (*pej: waste time*) traînasser, glandouiller; (*: behave foolishly*) faire l'idiot *or* l'imbécile; **foolish** *adj* idiot(e), stupide; (*rash*) imprudent(e); **foolproof** *adj* (*plan etc*) infaillible

**foot** (*pl* **feet**) [fut, fi:t] *n* pied *m*; (*of animal*) patte *f*; (*measure*) pied (= 30.48 cm; 12 inches) ▷ *vt* (*bill*) payer; **on ~** à pied; **footage** *n* (*Cine: length*) métrage *m*; (*: material*) séquences *fpl*; **foot-and-mouth (disease)** [futənd'mauθ-] *n* fièvre aphteuse; **football** *n* (*ball*) ballon *m* (de football; (*sport*: BRIT) football *m*; (*: US*) football américain; **footballer** *n* (BRIT) = **football player**; **football match** *n* (BRIT) match *m* de foot(ball); **football player** *n* footballeur(-euse), joueur(-euse) de football; (US) joueur(-euse) de football américain; **footbridge** *n* passerelle *f*; **foothills** *npl* contreforts *mpl*; **foothold** *n* prise *f* (de pied); **footing** *n* (*fig*) position *f*; **to lose**

one's footing perdre pied; **footnote**
n note f (en bas de page); **footpath**
n sentier m; **footprint** n trace f (de
pied); **footstep** n pas m; **footwear** n
chaussures fpl

O **KEYWORD**

**for** [fɔːʳ] prep **1** (indicating destination,
intention, purpose) pour; **the train for
London** le train pour (or à destination
de) Londres; **he left for Rome** il est
parti pour Rome; **he went for the
paper** il est allé chercher le journal; **is
this for me?** c'est pour moi?; **it's time
for lunch** c'est l'heure du déjeuner;
**what's it for?** ça sert à quoi?; **what for?**
(why) pourquoi?; (to what end) pour quoi
faire?, à quoi bon?; **for sale** n à vendre; **to
pray for peace** prier pour la paix
**2** (on behalf of, representing) pour;
**the MP for Hove** le député de Hove;
**to work for sb/sth** travailler pour
qn/qch; **I'll ask him for you** je vais lui
demander pour toi; **G for George** G
comme Georges
**3** (because of) pour; **for this reason**
pour cette raison; **for fear of being
criticized** de peur d'être critiqué
**4** (with regard to) pour; **it's cold for
July** il fait froid pour juillet; **a gift for
languages** un don pour les langues
**5** (in exchange for): **I sold it for £5** je l'ai
vendu 5 livres; **to pay 50 pence for a
ticket** payer un billet 50 pence
**6** (in favour of) pour; **are you for or
against us?** êtes-vous pour ou contre
nous?; **I'm all for it** je suis tout à fait
pour; **vote for X** votez pour X
**7** (referring to distance) pendant, sur;
**there are roadworks for 5 km** il y a
des travaux sur or pendant 5 km; **we
walked for miles** nous avons marché
pendant des kilomètres
**8** (referring to time) pendant; depuis;
pour; **he was away for 2 years** il a
été absent pendant 2 ans; **she will be
away for a month** elle sera absente

(pendant) un mois; **it hasn't rained for
3 weeks** ça fait 3 semaines qu'il ne pleut
pas, il ne pleut pas depuis 3 semaines;
**I have known her for years** je la
connais depuis des années; **can you do
it for tomorrow?** est-ce que tu peux le
faire pour demain?
**9** (with infinitive clauses): **it is not for
me to decide** ce n'est pas à moi de
décider; **it would be best for you to
leave** le mieux serait que vous partiez;
**there is still time for you to do it** vous
avez encore le temps de le faire; **for
this to be possible ...** pour que cela
soit possible ..
**10** (in spite of): **for all that** malgré cela,
néanmoins; **for all his work/efforts**
malgré tout son travail/tous ses
efforts; **for all his complaints, he's
very fond of her** il a beau se plaindre, il
l'aime beaucoup
▷ conj (since, as: rather formal) car

**forbid** (pt **forbad(e)**, pp **~den**) [fəˈbɪd,
-ˈbæd, -ˈbɪdn] vt défendre, interdire; **to
~ sb to do** défendre or interdire à qn de
faire; **forbidden** adj défendu(e)
**force** [fɔːs] n force f ▷ vt forcer; (push)
pousser (de force); **to ~ o.s. to do** se
forcer à faire; **in ~** (being used: rule, law,
prices) en vigueur; (in large numbers) en
force; **forced** adj forcé(e); **forceful** adj
énergique
**ford** [fɔːd] n gué m
**fore** [fɔːʳ] n: **to the ~** en évidence;
**forearm** n avant-bras m inv; **forecast**
n prévision f; (also: **weather forecast**)
prévisions fpl météorologiques, météo
f ▷ vt (irreg: like **cast**) prévoir; **forecourt**
n (of garage) devant m; **forefinger** n
index m; **forefront** n: **in the forefront
of** au premier rang or plan de;
**foreground** n premier plan m; **forehead**
[ˈfɒrɪd] n front m
**foreign** [ˈfɒrɪn] adj étranger(-ère);
(trade) extérieur(e); (travel) à l'étranger;
**foreign currency** n devises
étrangères; **foreigner** n étranger(-ère);

**foreign exchange** n (system) change m; (money) devises fpl; **Foreign Office** n (BRIT) ministère m des Affaires étrangères; **Foreign Secretary** n (BRIT) ministre m des Affaires étrangères

**fore**: **foreman** (irreg) n (in construction) contremaître m; **foremost** adj le (la) plus en vue, premier(-ière) ▷ adv: **first and foremost** avant tout, tout d'abord; **forename** n prénom m

**forensic** [fə'rɛnsɪk] adj: **~ medicine** médecine légale

**foresee** (pt **foresaw**, pp **~n**) [fɔː'siː, -'sɔː, -'siːn] vt prévoir; **foreseeable** adj prévisible

**forest** ['fɒrɪst] n forêt f; **forestry** n sylviculture f

**forever** [fə'rɛvər] adv pour toujours; (fig: endlessly) continuellement

**foreword** ['fɔːwəːd] n avant-propos m inv

**forfeit** ['fɔːfɪt] vt perdre

**forgave** [fə'geɪv] pt of **forgive**

**forge** [fɔːdʒ] n forge f ▷ vt (signature) contrefaire; (wrought iron) forger; **to ~ money** (BRIT) fabriquer de la fausse monnaie; **forger** n faussaire m; **forgery** n faux m, contrefaçon f

**forget** (pt **forgot**, pp **forgotten**) [fə'gɛt, -'gɒt, -'gɒtn] vt, vi oublier; **I've forgotten my key/passport** j'ai oublié ma clé/mon passeport; **forgetful** adj distrait(e), étourdi(e)

**forgive** (pt **forgave**, pp **~n**) [fə'gɪv, -'geɪv, -'gɪvn] vt pardonner; **to ~ sb for sth/for doing sth** pardonner qch à qn/à qn de faire qch

**forgot** [fə'gɒt] pt of **forget**

**forgotten** [fə'gɒtn] pp of **forget**

**fork** [fɔːk] n (for eating) fourchette f; (for gardening) fourche f; (of roads) bifurcation f ▷ vi (road) bifurquer

**forlorn** [fə'lɔːn] adj (deserted) abandonné(e); (hope, attempt) désespéré(e)

**form** [fɔːm] n forme f; (Scol) classe f; (questionnaire) formulaire m ▷ vt former; (habit) contracter; **to ~ part**

**of sth** faire partie de qch; **on top ~** en pleine forme

**formal** ['fɔːməl] adj (offer, receipt) en bonne et due forme; (person) cérémonieux(-euse); (occasion, dinner) officiel(le); (garden) à la française; (clothes) de soirée; **formality** [fɔː'mælɪtɪ] n formalité f

**format** ['fɔːmæt] n format m ▷ vt (Comput) formater

**formation** [fɔː'meɪʃən] n formation f

**former** ['fɔːmər] adj ancien(ne); (before n) précédent(e); **the ~ ... the latter** le premier ... le second, celui-là ... celui-ci; **formerly** adv autrefois

**formidable** ['fɔːmɪdəbl] adj redoutable

**formula** ['fɔːmjulə] n formule f

**fort** [fɔːt] n fort m

**forthcoming** [fɔːθ'kʌmɪŋ] adj qui va paraître or avoir lieu prochainement; (character) ouvert(e), communicatif(-ive); (available) disponible

**fortieth** ['fɔːtɪɪθ] num quarantième

**fortify** ['fɔːtɪfaɪ] vt (city) fortifier; (person) remonter

**fortnight** ['fɔːtnaɪt] n (BRIT) quinzaine f, quinze jours mpl; **fortnightly** adj bimensuel(le) ▷ adv tous les quinze jours

**fortress** ['fɔːtrɪs] n forteresse f

**fortunate** ['fɔːtʃənɪt] adj heureux(-euse); (person) chanceux(-euse); **it is ~ that** c'est une chance que, il est heureux que; **fortunately** adv heureusement, par bonheur

**fortune** ['fɔːtʃən] n chance f; (wealth) fortune f; **fortune-teller** n diseuse f de bonne aventure

**forty** ['fɔːtɪ] num quarante

**forum** ['fɔːrəm] n forum m, tribune f

**forward** ['fɔːwəd] adj (movement, position) en avant, vers l'avant; (not shy) effronté(e); (in time) en avance ▷ adv (also: **~s**) en avant ▷ n (Sport) avant m ▷ vt (letter) faire suivre; (parcel, goods) expédier; (*fig*) promouvoir, favoriser; **to move ~** avancer; **forwarding address** *n* adresse *f* de réexpédition

**forward slash** *n* barre *f* oblique

**fossil** ['fɒsl] *adj*, *n* fossile *m*

**foster** ['fɒstər] *vt* (*encourage*) encourager, favoriser; (*child*) élever (*sans adopter*); **foster child** *n* enfant élevé dans une famille d'accueil

**foster parent** *n* parent qui élève un enfant sans l'adopter

**fought** [fɔːt] *pt*, *pp* of **fight**

**foul** [faul] *adj* (*weather, smell, food*) infect(e); (*language*) ordurier(-ière) ▷ *n* (*Football*) faute *f* ▷ *vt* (*dirty*) salir, encrasser; **he's got a ~ temper** il a un caractère de chien; **foul play** *n* (*Law*) acte criminel

**found** [faund] *pt*, *pp* of **find** ▷ *vt* (*establish*) fonder; **foundation** [faun'deɪʃən] *n* (*act*) fondation *f*; (*base*) fondement *m*; (*also:* **foundation cream**) fond *m* de teint; **foundations** *npl* (*of building*) fondations *fpl*

**founder** ['faundər] *n* fondateur *m* ▷ *vi* couler, sombrer

**fountain** ['fauntɪn] *n* fontaine *f*; **fountain pen** *n* stylo *m* (à encre)

**four** [fɔːr] *num* quatre; **on all ~s** à quatre pattes; **four-letter word** *n* obscénité *f*, gros mot; **four-poster** *n* (*also:* **four-poster bed**) lit *m* à baldaquin; **fourteen** *num* quatorze; **fourteenth** *num* quatorzième; **fourth** *num* quatrième ▷ *n* (*Aut: also:* **fourth gear**) quatrième *f*; **four-wheel drive** *n* (*Aut: car*) voiture *f* à quatre roues motrices

**fowl** [faul] *n* volaille *f*

**fox** [fɒks] *n* renard *m* ▷ *vt* mystifier

**foyer** ['fɔɪeɪ] *n* (*in hotel*) vestibule *m*; (*Theat*) foyer *m*

**fraction** ['frækʃən] *n* fraction *f*

**fracture** ['fræktʃər] *n* fracture *f* ▷ *vt* fracturer

**fragile** ['frædʒaɪl] *adj* fragile

**fragment** ['frægmənt] *n* fragment *m*

**fragrance** ['freɪgrəns] *n* parfum *m*

**frail** [freɪl] *adj* fragile, délicat(e); (*person*) frêle

**frame** [freɪm] *n* (*of building*) charpente *f*; (*of human, animal*) charpente, ossature *f*; (*of picture*) cadre *m*; (*of door, window*) encadrement *m*, chambranle *m*; (*of spectacles: also:* **~s**) monture *f* ▷ *vt* (*picture*) encadrer; **~ of mind** disposition *f* d'esprit; **framework** *n* structure *f*

**France** [frɑːns] *n* la France

**franchise** ['fræntʃaɪz] *n* (*Pol*) droit *m* de vote; (*Comm*) franchise *f*

**frank** [fræŋk] *adj* franc (franche) ▷ *vt* (*letter*) affranchir; **frankly** *adv* franchement

**frantic** ['fræntɪk] *adj* (*hectic*) frénétique; (*distraught*) hors de soi

**fraud** [frɔːd] *n* supercherie *f*, fraude *f*, tromperie *f*; (*person*) imposteur *m*

**fraught** [frɔːt] *adj* (*tense: person*) très tendu(e); (: *situation*) pénible; **~ with** (*difficulties etc*) chargé(e) de, plein(e) de

**fray** [freɪ] *vt* effilocher ▷ *vi* s'effilocher

**freak** [friːk] *n* (*eccentric person*) phénomène *m*; (*unusual event*) hasard *m* extraordinaire; (*pej: fanatic*): **health freak ~** fana *m/f* ou obsédé(e) de l'alimentation saine ▷ *adj* (*storm*) exceptionnel(le); (*accident*) bizarre

**freckle** ['frɛkl] *n* tache *f* de rousseur

**free** [friː] *adj* libre; (*gratis*) gratuit(e) ▷ *vt* (*prisoner etc*) libérer; (*jammed object or person*) dégager; **is this seat ~?** la place est libre?; **~ (of charge)** gratuitement; **freedom** *n* liberté *f*; **Freefone®** *n* numéro vert; **free gift** *n* prime *f*; **free kick** *n* (*Sport*) coup franc; **freelance** *adj* (*journalist etc*) indépendant(e), free-lance *inv* ▷ *adv* en free-lance; **freely** *adv* librement; (*liberally*) libéralement; **Freepost®** *n* (*BRIT*) port payé; **free-range** *adj* (*egg*) de ferme; (*chicken*) fermier; **freeway** *n* (*US*) autoroute *f*; **free will** *n* libre arbitre *m*; **of one's own free will** de son plein gré

**freeze** [friːz] *vb* (*pt* **froze**, *pp* **frozen**) ▷ *vi* geler ▷ *vt* geler; (*food*) congeler; (*prices, salaries*) bloquer, geler ▷ *n* gel *m*;

(*of prices, salaries*) blocage *m*; **freezer** *n* congélateur *m*; **freezing** *adj*: **freezing (cold)** (*room etc*) glacial(e); (*person, hands*) gelé(e), glacé(e) ▷ *n*: **3 degrees below freezing** 3 degrés au-dessous de zéro; **it's freezing** il fait un froid glacial; **freezing point** *n* point *m* de congélation

**freight** [freɪt] *n* (*goods*) fret *m*, cargaison *f*; (*money charged*) fret, prix *m* du transport; **freight train** *n* (*us*) train *m* de marchandises

**French** [frɛntʃ] *adj* français(e) ▷ *n* (*Ling*) français *m*; **the ~** *npl* les Français; **what's the ~ (word) for ...?** comment dit-on ... en français?; **French bean** *n* (*BRIT*) haricot vert; **French bread** *n* pain *m* français; **French dressing** *n* (*Culin*) vinaigrette *f*; **French fried potatoes** (*us* **French fries**) *npl* (pommes de terre *fpl*) frites *fpl*; **Frenchman** (*irreg*) *n* Français *m*; **French stick** *n* ≈ baguette *f*; **French window** *n* porte-fenêtre *f*; **Frenchwoman** (*irreg*) *n* Française *f*

**frenzy** ['frɛnzɪ] *n* frénésie *f*

**frequency** ['friːkwənsɪ] *n* fréquence *f*

**frequent** *adj* ['friːkwənt] fréquent(e) ▷ *vt* [frɪ'kwɛnt] fréquenter; **frequently** ['friːkwəntlɪ] *adv* fréquemment

**fresh** [frɛʃ] *adj* frais (fraîche); (*new*) nouveau (nouvelle); (*cheeky*) familier(-ière), culotté(e); **freshen** *vi* (*wind, air*) fraîchir; **freshen up** *vi* faire un brin de toilette; **fresher** *n* (*BRIT University: inf*) bizuth *m*, étudiant(e) de première année; **freshly** *adv* nouvellement, récemment; **freshman** (*us: irreg*) *n* = **fresher**; **freshwater** *adj* (*fish*) d'eau douce

**fret** [frɛt] *vi* s'agiter, se tracasser

**Fri** *abbr* (= *Friday*) ve

**friction** ['frɪkʃən] *n* friction *f*, frottement *m*

**Friday** ['fraɪdɪ] *n* vendredi *m*

**fridge** [frɪdʒ] *n* (*BRIT*) frigo *m*, frigidaire® *m*

**fried** [fraɪd] *adj* frit(e); **~ egg** œuf *m* sur le plat

**friend** [frɛnd] *n* ami(e); **friendly** *adj* amical(e); (*kind*) sympathique, gentil(le); (*place*) accueillant(e); (*Pol: country*) ami(e) ▷ *n* (*also*: **friendly match**) match amical; **friendship** *n* amitié *f*

**fries** [fraɪz] (*esp us*) *npl* = **French fried potatoes**

**frigate** ['frɪgɪt] *n* frégate *f*

**fright** [fraɪt] *n* peur *f*, effroi *m*; **to give sb a ~** faire peur à qn; **to take ~** prendre peur, s'effrayer; **frighten** *vt* effrayer, faire peur à; **frightened** *adj*: **to be frightened (of)** avoir peur (de); **frightening** *adj* effrayant(e); **frightful** *adj* affreux(-euse)

**frill** [frɪl] *n* (*of dress*) volant *m*; (*of shirt*) jabot *m*

**fringe** [frɪndʒ] *n* (*BRIT: of hair*) frange *f*; (*edge: of forest etc*) bordure *f*

**Frisbee®** ['frɪzbɪ] *n* Frisbee® *m*

**fritter** ['frɪtər] *n* beignet *m*

**frivolous** ['frɪvələs] *adj* frivole

**fro** [frəu] *see* **to**

**frock** [frɔk] *n* robe *f*

**frog** [frɔg] *n* grenouille *f*; **frogman** (*irreg*) *n* homme-grenouille *m*

○ **KEYWORD**

**from** [frɔm] *prep* **1** (*indicating starting place, origin etc*) de; **where do you come from?**, **where are you from?** d'où venez-vous?; **where has he come from?** d'où arrive-t-il?; **from London to Paris** de Londres à Paris; **to escape from sb/sth** échapper à qn/qch; **a letter/telephone call from my sister** une lettre/un appel de ma sœur; **to drink from the bottle** boire à (même) la bouteille; **tell him from me that ...** dites-lui de ma part que ...
**2** (*indicating time*) (à partir) de; **from one o'clock to** *or* **until** *or* **till two** d'une heure à deux heures; **from January (on)** à partir de janvier

**3** (*indicating distance*) de; **the hotel is one kilometre from the beach** l'hôtel est à un kilomètre de la plage
**4** (*indicating price, number etc*) de; **prices range from £10 to £50** les prix varient entre 10 livres et 50 livres; **the interest rate was increased from 9% to 10%** le taux d'intérêt est passé de 9% à 10%
**5** (*indicating difference*) de; **he can't tell red from green** il ne peut pas distinguer le rouge du vert; **to be different from sb/sth** être différent de qn/qch
**6** (*because of, on the basis of*): **from what he says** d'après ce qu'il dit; **weak from hunger** affaibli par la faim

**front** [frʌnt] *n* (*of house, dress*) devant *m*; (*of coach, train*) avant *m*; (*promenade: also*: **sea ~**) bord *m* de mer; (*Mil, Pol, Meteorology*) front *m*; (*fig: appearances*) contenance *f*, façade *f* ▷ *adj* de devant; (*seat, wheel*) avant *inv* ▷ *vi*: **in ~ (of)** devant; **front door** *n* porte *f* d'entrée; (*of car*) portière *f* avant; **frontier** ['frʌntɪəʳ] *n* frontière *f*; **front page** *n* première page *f*; **front-wheel drive** *n* traction *f* avant
**frost** [frɔst] *n* gel *m*, gelée *f*; (*also*: **hoar~**) givre *m*; **frostbite** *n* gelures *fpl*; **frosting** (*esp US: on cake*) glaçage *m*; **frosty** *adj* (*window*) couvert(e) de givre; (*weather, welcome*) glacial(e)
**froth** [frɔθ] *n* mousse *f*; écume *f*
**frown** [fraun] *n* froncement *m* de sourcils ▷ *vi* froncer les sourcils
**froze** [frəuz] *pt of* **freeze**
**frozen** ['frəuzn] *pp of* **freeze** ▷ *adj* (*food*) congelé(e); (*very cold: person: Comm: assets*) gelé(e)
**fruit** [fru:t] *n* (*pl inv*) fruit *m*; **fruit juice** *n* jus *m* de fruit; **fruit machine** *n* (*BRIT*) machine *f* à sous; **fruit salad** *n* salade *f* de fruits
**frustrate** [frʌsˈtreɪt] *vt* frustrer; **frustrated** *adj* frustré(e)
**fry** (*pt, pp* **fried**) [fraɪ, -d] *vt* (*faire*) frire;

**small ~** le menu fretin; **frying pan** *n* poêle *f* (à frire)
**ft.** *abbr* = **foot**; **feet**
**fudge** [fʌdʒ] *n* (*Culin*) sorte de confiserie à base de sucre, de beurre et de lait
**fuel** [fjuəl] *n* (*for heating*) combustible *m*; (*for engine*) carburant *m*; **fuel tank** *n* (*in vehicle*) réservoir *m* de *or* à carburant
**fulfil** (*US* **fulfill**) [fulˈfɪl] *vt* (*function, condition*) remplir; (*order*) exécuter; (*wish, desire*) satisfaire, réaliser
**full** [ful] *adj* plein(e); (*details, hotel, bus*) complet(-ète); (*busy: day*) chargé(e); (*skirt*) ample, large ▷ *adv*: **to know ~ well that** savoir fort bien que; **I'm ~ (up)** j'ai bien mangé; **~ employment/ fare** plein emploi/tarif; **a ~ two hours** deux bonnes heures; **at ~ speed** à toute vitesse; **in ~** (*reproduce, quote, pay*) intégralement; (*write name etc*) en toutes lettres; **full-length** *adj* (*portrait*) en pied; (*coat*) long(ue); **full-length film** long métrage *m*; **full moon** *n* pleine lune; **full-scale** *adj* (*model*) grandeur nature *inv*; (*search, retreat*) complet(-ète), total(e); **full stop** *n* point *m*; **full-time** *adj, adv* (*work*) à plein temps; **fully** *adv* entièrement, complètement; (*at least*)
**fumble** ['fʌmbl] *vi* fouiller, tâtonner; **fumble with** *vt fus* tripoter
**fume** [fju:m] *vi* (*rage*) rager; **fumes** *npl* vapeurs *fpl*, émanations *fpl*, gaz *mpl*
**fun** [fʌn] *n* amusement *m*, divertissement *m*; **to have ~** s'amuser; **for ~** pour rire; **to make ~ of** se moquer de
**function** ['fʌŋkʃən] *n* fonction *f*; (*reception, dinner*) cérémonie *f*, soirée officielle ▷ *vi* fonctionner
**fund** [fʌnd] *n* caisse *f*, fonds *m*; (*source, store*) source *f*, mine *f*; **funds** *npl* (*money*) fonds *mpl*
**fundamental** [fʌndəˈmɛntl] *adj* fondamental(e)
**funeral** ['fju:nərəl] *n* enterrement *m*, obsèques *fpl* (*more formal occasion*); **funeral director** *n* entrepreneur *m*

des pompes funèbres; **funeral parlour** [-'pɑːləʳ] n (BRIT) dépôt m mortuaire

**funfair** ['fʌnfɛəʳ] n (BRIT) fête (foraine)

**fungus** (pl **fungi**) ['fʌŋgəs, -gaɪ] n champignon m; (mould) moisissure f

**funnel** ['fʌnl] n entonnoir m; (of ship) cheminée f

**funny** ['fʌnɪ] adj amusant(e), drôle; (strange) curieux(-euse), bizarre

**fur** [fəːʳ] n fourrure f; (BRIT: in kettle etc) (dépôt m de) tartre m; **fur coat** n manteau m de fourrure

**furious** ['fjuərɪəs] adj furieux(-euse); (effort) acharné(e)

**furnish** ['fəːnɪʃ] vt meubler; (supply) fournir; **furnishings** npl mobilier m, articles mpl d'ameublement

**furniture** ['fəːnɪtʃəʳ] n meubles mpl, mobilier m; **piece of ~** meuble m

**furry** ['fəːrɪ] adj (animal) à fourrure; (toy) en peluche

**further** ['fəːðəʳ] adj supplémentaire, autre; nouveau (nouvelle) ▷ adv plus loin; (more) davantage; (moreover) de plus ▷ vt faire avancer or progresser, promouvoir; **further education** n enseignement m postscolaire (recyclage, formation professionnelle); **furthermore** adv de plus, en outre

**furthest** ['fəːðɪst] superlative of **far**

**fury** ['fjuərɪ] n fureur f

**fuse** (US **fuze**) [fjuːz] n fusible m; (for bomb etc) amorce f, détonateur m ▷ vt, vi (metal) fondre; (BRIT: Elec): **to ~ the lights** faire sauter les fusibles or les plombs; **fuse box** n boîte f à fusibles

**fusion** ['fjuːʒən] n fusion f

**fuss** [fʌs] n (anxiety, excitement) chichis mpl, façons fpl; (commotion) tapage m; (complaining, trouble) histoire(s) f(pl); **to make a ~** faire des façons (or des histoires); **to make a ~ of sb** dorloter qn; **fussy** adj (person) tatillon(ne), difficile, chichiteux(-euse); (dress, style) tarabiscoté(e)

**future** ['fjuːtʃəʳ] adj futur(e) ▷ n avenir m; (Ling) futur m; **futures** npl (Comm) opérations fpl à terme; **in (the) ~** à l'avenir

**fuze** [fjuːz] n, vt, vi (US) = **fuse**

**fuzzy** ['fʌzɪ] adj (Phot) flou(e); (hair) crépu(e)

**G** [dʒiː] n (Mus): **G** sol m

**g.** abbr (= gram) g

**gadget** ['gædʒɪt] n gadget m

**Gaelic** ['geɪlɪk] adj, n (Ling) gaélique (m)

**gag** [gæg] n (on mouth) bâillon m; (joke) gag m ▷ vt (prisoner etc) bâillonner

**gain** [geɪn] n (improvement) gain m; (profit) gain, profit m ▷ vt gagner ▷ vi (watch) avancer; **to ~ from/by** gagner de/à; **to ~ on sb** (catch up) rattraper qn; **to ~ 3lbs (in weight)** prendre 3 livres; **to ~ ground** gagner du terrain

**gal.** abbr = **gallon**

**gala** ['gɑːlə] n gala m

**galaxy** ['gæləksɪ] n galaxie f

**gale** [geɪl] n coup m de vent

**gall bladder** ['gɔːl-] n vésicule f biliaire

**gallery** ['gælərɪ] n (also: **art ~**) musée m; (: private) galerie f; (: in theatre) dernier balcon

**gallon** ['gæln] n gallon m (BRIT = 4.543 l; US = 3.785 l)

**gallop** ['gæləp] n galop m ▷ vi galoper

**gallstone** ['gɔːlstəun] n calcul m

(biliaire)

**gamble** ['gæmbl] n pari m, risque calculé ▷ vt, vi jouer; **to ~ on** (fig) miser sur; **gambler** n joueur m; **gambling** n jeu m

**game** [geɪm] n jeu m; (event) match m; (of tennis, chess, cards) partie f; (Hunting) gibier m ▷ adj (willing): **to be ~ (for)** être prêt(e) (à or pour); **big ~** gros gibier; **games** npl (Scol) sport m; (sport event) jeux; **games console** ['geɪmz-] n console f de jeux vidéo; **game show** n jeu télévisé

**gammon** ['gæmən] n (bacon) quartier m de lard fumé; (ham) jambon fumé or salé

**gang** [gæŋ] n bande f; (of workmen) équipe f

**gangster** ['gæŋstəʳ] n gangster m, bandit m

**gap** [gæp] n trou m; (in time) intervalle m; (difference): **~ (between)** écart m (entre)

**gape** [geɪp] vi (person) être or rester bouche bée; (hole, shirt) être ouvert(e)

**gap year** n année que certains étudiants prennent pour voyager ou pour travailler avant d'entrer à l'université

**garage** ['gærɑːʒ] n garage m; **garage sale** n vide-grenier m

**garbage** ['gɑːbɪdʒ] n (US: rubbish) ordures fpl, détritus mpl; (inf: nonsense) âneries fpl; **garbage can** n (US) poubelle f, boîte f à ordures; **garbage collector** n (US) éboueur m

**garden** ['gɑːdn] n jardin m; **gardens** npl (public) jardin public; (private) parc m; **garden centre** (BRIT) n pépinière f, jardinerie f; **gardener** n jardinier m; **gardening** n jardinage m

**garlic** ['gɑːlɪk] n ail m

**garment** ['gɑːmənt] n vêtement m

**garnish** ['gɑːnɪʃ] (Culin) vt garnir ▷ n décoration f

**garrison** ['gærɪsn] n garnison f

**gas** [gæs] n gaz m; (US: gasoline) essence f ▷ vt asphyxier; **I can smell ~** ça sent le gaz; **gas cooker** n (BRIT) cuisinière f à gaz; **gas cylinder** n bouteille f de gaz; **gas fire** n (BRIT) radiateur m à gaz

**gasket** ['gæskɪt] n (Aut) joint m de culasse

**gasoline** ['gæsəli:n] n (US) essence f

**gasp** [gɑ:sp] n halètement m; (of shock etc): **she gave a small ~ of pain** la douleur lui coupa le souffle ▷ vi haleter; (fig) avoir le souffle coupé

**gas**: **gas pedal** n (US) accélérateur m; **gas station** n (US) station-service f; **gas tank** n (US Aut) réservoir m d'essence

**gate** [geɪt] n (of garden) portail m; (of field, at level crossing) barrière f; (of building, town, at airport) porte f

**gateau** (pl **~x**) ['gætəu, -z] n gros gâteau à la crème

**gatecrash** ['geɪtkræʃ] vt s'introduire sans invitation dans

**gateway** ['geɪtweɪ] n porte f

**gather** ['gæðər] vt (flowers, fruit) cueillir; (pick up) ramasser; (assemble: objects) rassembler; (: people) réunir; (: information) recueillir; (understand) comprendre; (Sewing) froncer ▷ vi (assemble) se rassembler; **to ~ speed** prendre de la vitesse; **gathering** n rassemblement m

**gauge** [geɪdʒ] n (instrument) jauge f ▷ vt jauger; (fig) juger de

**gave** [geɪv] pt of **give**

**gay** [geɪ] adj (homosexual) homosexuel(le); (colour) gai, vif (vive) ·

**gaze** [geɪz] n regard m fixe ▷ vi: **to ~ at** vt fixer du regard

**GB** abbr = **Great Britain**

**GCSE** n abbr (= General Certificate of Secondary Education) examen passé à l'âge de 16 ans sanctionnant les connaissances de l'élève

**gear** [giər] n matériel m, équipement m; (Tech) engrenage m; (Aut) vitesse f ▷ vt (fig: adapt) adapter; **top** or (US) **high/low ~** quatrième (or cinquième)/ première vitesse; **in ~** en prise; **gear up** vi: **to ~ up (to do)** se préparer (à faire); **gear box** n boîte f de vitesse; **gear**

**lever** n levier m de vitesse; **gear shift** (US) n = **gear lever**; **gear stick** (BRIT) n = **gear lever**

**geese** [gi:s] npl of **goose**

**gel** [dʒɛl] n gelée f

**gem** [dʒɛm] n pierre précieuse

**Gemini** ['dʒɛmɪnaɪ] n les Gémeaux mpl

**gender** ['dʒɛndər] n genre m; (person's sex) sexe m

**gene** [dʒi:n] n (Biol) gène m

**general** ['dʒɛnərl] n général m ▷ adj général(e); **in ~** en général; **general anaesthetic** (US **general anesthetic**) n anesthésie générale; **general election** n élection(s) législative(s); **generalize** vi généraliser; **generally** adv généralement; **general practitioner** n généraliste m/f; **general store** n épicerie f

**generate** ['dʒɛnəreɪt] vt engendrer; (electricity) produire

**generation** [dʒɛnə'reɪʃən] n génération f; (of electricity etc) production f

**generator** ['dʒɛnəreɪtər] n générateur m

**generosity** [dʒɛnə'rɔsɪtɪ] n générosité f

**generous** ['dʒɛnərəs] adj généreux(-euse); (copious) copieux(-euse)

**genetic** [dʒɪ'nɛtɪk] adj génétique; **~ engineering** ingénierie m génétique; **~ fingerprinting** système m d'empreinte génétique; **genetically modified** adj (food etc) génétiquement modifié(e); **genetics** n génétique f

**Geneva** [dʒɪ'ni:və] n Genève

**genitals** ['dʒɛnɪtlz] npl organes génitaux

**genius** ['dʒi:nɪəs] n génie m

**gent** [dʒɛnt] n abbr (BRIT inf) = **gentleman**

**gentle** ['dʒɛntl] adj doux (douce); (breeze, touch) léger(-ère)

**gentleman** (irreg) ['dʒɛntlmən] n monsieur m; (well-bred man) gentleman m

**gently** ['dʒɛntlɪ] adv doucement
**gents** [dʒɛnts] n W.-C. mpl (pour hommes)
**genuine** ['dʒɛnjuɪn] adj véritable, authentique; (person, emotion) sincère;
   **genuinely** adv sincèrement, vraiment
**geographic(al)** [dʒɪə'græfɪk(l)] adj géographique
**geography** [dʒɪ'ɔgrəfɪ] n géographie f
**geology** [dʒɪ'ɔlədʒɪ] n géologie f
**geometry** [dʒɪ'ɔmətrɪ] n géométrie f
**geranium** [dʒɪ'reɪnɪəm] n géranium m
**geriatric** [dʒɛrɪ'ætrɪk] adj gériatrique
   ▷ n patient(e) gériatrique
**germ** [dʒəːm] n (Med) microbe m
**German** ['dʒəːmən] adj allemand(e)
   ▷ n Allemand(e); (Ling) allemand m;
   **German measles** n rubéole f
**Germany** ['dʒəːmənɪ] n Allemagne f
**gesture** ['dʒɛstjəʳ] n geste m

**KEYWORD**

**get** [gɛt] (pt, pp **got**, pp **gotten** (us)) vi
1 (become, be) devenir; **to get old/tired** devenir vieux/fatigué, vieillir/se fatiguer; **to get drunk** s'enivrer; **to get dirty** se salir; **to get married** se marier; **when do I get paid?** quand est-ce que je serai payé?; **it's getting late** il se fait tard
2 (go): **to get to/from** aller à/de; **to get home** rentrer chez soi; **how did you get here?** comment es-tu arrivé ici?
3 (begin) commencer or se mettre à; **to get to know sb** apprendre à connaître qn; **I'm getting to like him** je commence à l'apprécier; **let's get going** or **started** allons-y
4 (modal aux vb): **you've got to do it** il faut que vous le fassiez; **I've got to tell the police** je dois le dire à la police
   ▷ vt 1: **to get sth done** (do) faire qch; (have done) faire faire qch; **to get sth/sb ready** préparer qch/qn; **to get one's hair cut** se faire couper les cheveux; **to get the car going** or **to go** (faire) démarrer la voiture; **to get sb to do sth**

faire faire qch à qn
2 (obtain: money, permission, results) obtenir, avoir; (buy) acheter; (find: job, flat) trouver; (fetch: person, doctor, object) aller chercher; **to get sth for sb** procurer qch à qn; **get me Mr Jones, please** (on phone) passez-moi Mr Jones, s'il vous plaît; **can I get you a drink?** est-ce que je peux vous servir à boire?
3 (receive: present, letter) recevoir, avoir; (acquire: reputation) avoir; (prize) obtenir; **what did you get for your birthday?** qu'est-ce que tu as eu pour ton anniversaire?; **how much did you get for the painting?** combien avez-vous vendu le tableau?
4 (catch) prendre, saisir, attraper; (hit: target etc) atteindre; **to get sb by the arm/throat** prendre or saisir or attraper qn par le bras/à la gorge; **get him!** arrête-le!; **the bullet got him in the leg** il a pris la balle dans la jambe
5 (take, move): **to get sth to sb** faire parvenir qch à qn; **do you think we'll get it through the door?** on arrivera à le faire passer par la porte?
6 (catch, take: plane, bus etc) prendre; **where do I get the train for Birmingham?** où prend-on le train pour Birmingham?
7 (understand) comprendre, saisir; (hear) entendre; **I've got it!** j'ai compris!; **I don't get your meaning** je ne vois or comprends pas ce que vous voulez dire; **I didn't get your name** je n'ai pas entendu votre nom
8 (have, possess): **to have got** avoir; **how many have you got?** vous en avez combien?
9 (illness) avoir; **I've got a cold** j'ai le rhume; **she got pneumonia and died** elle a fait une pneumonie et elle en est morte
**get away** vi partir, s'en aller; (escape) s'échapper
**get away with** vt fus (punishment) en être quitte pour; (crime etc) se faire pardonner

**get back** vi (return) rentrer
▷ vt récupérer, recouvrer; **when do we get back?** quand serons-nous de retour?
**get in** vi entrer; (arrive home) rentrer; (train) arriver
**get into** vt fus entrer dans; (car, train etc) monter dans; (clothes) mettre, enfiler, endosser; **to get into bed/a rage** se mettre au lit/en colère
**get off** vi (from train etc) descendre; (depart: person, car) s'en aller
▷ vt (remove: clothes, stain) enlever
▷ vt fus (train, bus) descendre de; **where do I get off?** où est-ce que je dois descendre?
**get on** vi (at exam etc) se débrouiller; (agree): **to get on (with)** s'entendre (avec); **how are you getting on?** comment ça va?
▷ vt fus monter dans; (horse) monter sur
**get out** vi sortir; (of vehicle) descendre
▷ vt sortir
**get out of** vt fus sortir de; (duty etc) échapper à, se soustraire à
**get over** vt fus (illness) se remettre de
**get through** vi (Tel) avoir la communication; **to get through to sb** atteindre qn
**get up** vi (rise) se lever
▷ vt fus monter

**getaway** ['gɛtəweɪ] n fuite f
**Ghana** ['gɑːnə] n Ghana m
**ghastly** ['gɑːstlɪ] adj atroce, horrible
**ghetto** ['gɛtəu] n ghetto m
**ghost** [gəust] n fantôme m, revenant m
**giant** ['dʒaɪənt] n géant(e) ▷ adj géant(e), énorme
**gift** [gɪft] n cadeau m; (donation, talent) don m; **gifted** adj doué(e); **gift shop** (us **gift store**) n boutique f de cadeaux; **gift token, gift voucher** n chèque-cadeau m
**gig** [gɪg] n (inf: concert) concert m
**gigabyte** ['dʒɪgəbaɪt] n gigaoctet m
**gigantic** [dʒaɪ'gæntɪk] adj gigantesque

**giggle** ['gɪgl] vi pouffer, ricaner sottement
**gills** [gɪlz] npl (of fish) ouïes fpl, branchies fpl
**gilt** [gɪlt] n dorure f ▷ adj doré(e)
**gimmick** ['gɪmɪk] n truc m
**gin** [dʒɪn] n gin m
**ginger** ['dʒɪndʒər] n gingembre m
**gipsy** ['dʒɪpsɪ] n = **gypsy**
**giraffe** [dʒɪ'rɑːf] n girafe f
**girl** [gəːl] n fille f, fillette f; (young unmarried woman) jeune fille; (daughter) fille; **an English ~** une jeune Anglaise; **girl band** n girls band m; **girlfriend** n (of girl) amie f; (of boy) petite amie; **Girl Guide** n (BRIT) éclaireuse f; (Roman Catholic) guide f; **Girl Scout** n (US) = **Girl Guide**
**gist** [dʒɪst] n essentiel m
**give** [gɪv] vb (pt **gave**, pp **~n**) ▷ vt donner ▷ vi (break) céder; (stretch: fabric) se prêter; **to ~ sb sth, ~ sth to sb** donner qch à qn; (gift) offrir qch à qn; (message) transmettre qch à qn; **to ~ sb a call/kiss** appeler/embrasser qn; **to ~ a cry/sigh** pousser un cri/un soupir; **give away** vt donner; (give free) faire cadeau de; (betray) donner, trahir; (disclose) révéler; **give back** vt rendre; **give in** vi céder ▷ vt donner; **give out** vt (food etc) distribuer; **give up** vi renoncer ▷ vt renoncer à; **to ~ up smoking** arrêter de fumer; **to ~ o.s. up** se rendre
**given** ['gɪvn] pp of **give** ▷ adj (fixed: time, amount) donné(e), déterminé(e) ▷ conj: **~ the circumstances ...** étant donné les circonstances ..., vu les circonstances ...; **~ that ...** étant donné que ...
**glacier** ['glæsɪər] n glacier m
**glad** [glæd] adj content(e); **gladly** ['glædlɪ] adv volontiers
**glamorous** ['glæmərəs] adj (person) séduisant(e); (job) prestigieux(-euse)
**glamour** (us **glamor**) ['glæmər] n éclat m, prestige m
**glance** [glɑːns] n coup m d'œil ▷ vi: **to ~**

**at** jeter un coup d'œil à
**gland** [glænd] n glande f
**glare** [glɛəʳ] n (of anger) regard furieux; (of light) lumière éblouissante; (of publicity) feux mpl ▷ vi briller d'un éclat aveuglant; **to ~ at** lancer un regard or des regards furieux à; **glaring** adj (mistake) criant(e), qui saute aux yeux
**glass** [glɑːs] n verre m; **glasses** npl (spectacles) lunettes fpl
**glaze** [gleɪz] vt (door) vitrer; (pottery) vernir ▷ n vernis m
**gleam** [gliːm] vi luire, briller
**glen** [glɛn] n vallée f
**glide** [glaɪd] vi glisser; (Aviat, bird) planer; **glider** n (Aviat) planeur m
**glimmer** ['glɪməʳ] n lueur f
**glimpse** [glɪmps] n vision passagère, aperçu m ▷ vt entrevoir, apercevoir
**glint** [glɪnt] vi étinceler
**glisten** ['glɪsn] vi briller, luire
**glitter** ['glɪtəʳ] vi scintiller, briller
**global** ['gləubl] adj (world-wide) mondial(e); (overall) global(e); **globalization** n mondialisation f; **global warming** n réchauffement m de la planète
**globe** [gləub] n globe m
**gloom** [gluːm] n obscurité f; (sadness) tristesse f, mélancolie f; **gloomy** adj (person) morose; (place, outlook) sombre
**glorious** ['glɔːrɪəs] adj glorieux(-euse); (beautiful) splendide
**glory** ['glɔːrɪ] n gloire f; splendeur f
**gloss** [glɔs] n (shine) brillant m, vernis m; (also: ~ **paint**) peinture brillante or laquée
**glossary** ['glɔsərɪ] n glossaire m, lexique m
**glossy** ['glɔsɪ] adj brillant(e), luisant(e) ▷ n (also: ~ **magazine**) revue f de luxe
**glove** [glʌv] n gant m; **glove compartment** n (Aut) boîte f à gants, vide-poches m inv
**glow** [gləu] vi rougeoyer; (face) rayonner; (eyes) briller
**glucose** ['gluːkəus] n glucose m
**glue** [gluː] n colle f ▷ vt coller

**GM** abbr (= genetically modified) génétiquement modifié(e)
**gm** abbr (= gram) g
**GMO** n abbr (= genetically modified organism) OGM m
**GMT** abbr (= Greenwich Mean Time) GMT
**gnaw** [nɔː] vt ronger
**go** [gəu] vb (pt **went**, pp **gone**) ▷ vi aller; (depart) partir, s'en aller; (work) marcher; (break) céder; (time) passer; (be sold): **to go for £10** se vendre 10 livres; (become): **to go pale/mouldy** pâlir/moisir ▷ n (pl **goes**): **to have a go (at)** essayer (de faire); **to be on the go** être en mouvement; **whose go is it?** à qui est-ce de jouer?; **he's going to do it** il va le faire, il est sur le point de le faire; **to go for a walk** aller se promener; **to go dancing/shopping** aller danser/faire les courses; **to go and see sb, go to see sb** aller voir qn; **how did it go?** comment est-ce que ça s'est passé?; **to go round the back/by the shop** passer par derrière/devant le magasin; **... to go** (us: food) ... à emporter; **go ahead** vi (take place) avoir lieu; (get going) y aller; **go away** vi partir, s'en aller; **go back** vi rentrer; revenir; (go again) retourner; **go by** vi (years, time) passer, s'écouler ▷ vt fus s'en tenir à; (believe) en croire; **go down** vi descendre; (number, price, amount) baisser; (ship) couler; (sun) se coucher ▷ vt fus descendre; **go for** vt fus (fetch) aller chercher; (like) aimer; (attack) s'en prendre à; attaquer; **go in** vi entrer; **go into** vt fus entrer dans; (investigate) étudier, examiner; (embark on) se lancer dans; **go off** vi partir, s'en aller; (food) se gâter; (milk) tourner; (bomb) sauter; (alarm clock) sonner; (alarm) se déclencher; (lights etc) s'éteindre; (event) se dérouler ▷ vt fus ne plus aimer; **the gun went off** le coup est parti; **go on** vi continuer; (happen) se passer; (lights) s'allumer ▷ vt fus: **to go on doing** continuer à faire; **go out** vi sortir; (fire, light) s'éteindre;

(*tide*) descendre; **to go out with sb** sortir avec qn; **go over** *vi*, *vt fus* (*check*) revoir, vérifier; **go past** *vt fus*: **to go past sth** passer devant qch; **go round** *vi* (*circulate: news, rumour*) circuler; (*revolve*) tourner; (*suffice*) suffire (pour tout le monde); (*visit*): **to go round to sb's** passer chez qn; aller chez qn; (*make a detour*): **to go round (by)** faire un détour (par); **go through** *vt fus* (*town etc*) traverser; (*search through*) fouiller; (*suffer*) subir; **go up** *vi* monter; (*price*) augmenter ▷ *vt fus* gravir; **go with** *vt fus* aller avec; **go without** *vt fus* se passer de

**go-ahead** ['gəʊəhɛd] *adj* dynamique, entreprenant(e) ▷ *n* feu vert

**goal** [gəʊl] *n* but *m*; **goalkeeper** *n* gardien *m* de but; **goal-post** *n* poteau *m* de but

**goat** [gəʊt] *n* chèvre *f*

**gobble** ['gɔbl] *vt* (*also:* **~ down, ~ up**) engloutir

**god** [gɔd] *n* dieu *m*; **G~** Dieu; **godchild** *n* filleul(e); **goddaughter** *n* filleule *f*; **goddess** *n* déesse *f*; **godfather** *n* parrain *m*; **godmother** *n* marraine *f*; **godson** *n* filleul *m*

**goggles** ['gɔglz] *npl* (*for skiing etc*) lunettes (protectrices); (*for swimming*) lunettes de piscine

**going** ['gəʊɪŋ] *n* (*conditions*) état *m* du terrain ▷ *adj*: **the ~ rate** le tarif (en vigueur)

**gold** [gəʊld] *n* or *m* ▷ *adj* en or; (*reserves*) d'or; **golden** *adj* (*made of gold*) en or; (*gold in colour*) doré(e); **goldfish** *n* poisson *m* rouge; **goldmine** *n* mine *f* d'or; **gold-plated** *adj* plaqué(e) or *inv*

**golf** [gɔlf] *n* golf *m*; **golf ball** *n* balle *f* de golf; (*on typewriter*) boule *f*; **golf club** *n* club *m* de golf; (*stick*) club *m*, crosse *f* de golf; **golf course** *n* terrain *m* de golf; **golfer** *n* joueur(-euse) de golf

**gone** [gɔn] *pp of* **go**

**gong** [gɔŋ] *n* gong *m*

**good** [gʊd] *adj* bon(ne); (*kind*) gentil(le); (*child*) sage; (*weather*) beau (belle) ▷ *n*

bien *m*; **goods** *npl* marchandise *f*, articles *mpl*; **~!** bon!, très bien!; **to be ~ at** être bon, fort en; **to be ~ for** être bon pour; **it's no ~ complaining** cela ne sert à rien de se plaindre; **to make ~** (*deficit*) combler; (*losses*) compenser; **for ~** (*for ever*) pour de bon, une fois pour toutes; **would you be ~ enough to ...?** auriez-vous la bonté *or* l'amabilité de ...?; **is this any ~?** (*will it do?*) est-ce que ceci fera l'affaire?, est-ce que cela peut vous rendre service?; (*what's it like?*) qu'est-ce que ça vaut?; **a ~ deal (of)** beaucoup (de); **a ~ many** beaucoup (de); **~ morning/afternoon!** bonjour!; **~ evening!** bonsoir!; **~ night!** bonsoir!; (*on going to bed*) bonne nuit!; **goodbye** *excl* au revoir!; **to say goodbye to sb** dire au revoir à qn; **Good Friday** *n* Vendredi saint; **good-looking** *adj* beau (belle), bien *inv*; **good-natured** *adj* (*person*) qui a un bon naturel; **goodness** *n* (*of person*) bonté *f*; **for goodness sake!** je vous en prie!; **goodness gracious!** mon Dieu!; **goods train** *n* (*BRIT*) train *m* de marchandises; **goodwill** *n* bonne volonté

**goose** (*pl* **geese**) [guːs, giːs] *n* oie *f*

**gooseberry** ['gʊzbərɪ] *n* groseille *f* à maquereau; **to play ~** (*BRIT*) tenir la chandelle

**goose bumps, goose pimples** *npl* chair *f* de poule

**gorge** [gɔːdʒ] *n* gorge *f* ▷ *vt*: **to ~ o.s. (on)** se gorger (de)

**gorgeous** ['gɔːdʒəs] *adj* splendide, superbe

**gorilla** [gə'rɪlə] *n* gorille *m*

**gosh** (*inf*) [gɔʃ] *excl* mince alors!

**gospel** ['gɔspl] *n* évangile *m*

**gossip** ['gɔsɪp] *n* (*chat*) bavardages *mpl*; (*malicious*) commérage *m*, cancans *mpl*; (*person*) commère *f* ▷ *vi* bavarder; cancaner, faire des commérages; **gossip column** *n* (*Press*) échos *mpl*

**got** [gɔt] *pt*, *pp of* **get**

**gotten** ['gɔtn] (*US*) *pp of* **get**

**gourmet** ['gʊəmeɪ] *n* gourmet *m*,

gastronome *m/f*

**govern** ['gʌvən] *vt* gouverner;
(*influence*) déterminer; **government**
*n* gouvernement *m*; (*BRIT: ministers*)
ministère *m*; **governor** *n* (*of colony,
state, bank*) gouverneur *m*; (*of school,
hospital etc*) administrateur(-trice);
(*BRIT: of prison*) directeur(-trice)

**gown** [gaun] *n* robe *f*; (*of teacher, BRIT:
of judge*) toge *f*

**G.P.** *n abbr* (*Med*) = **general practitioner**

**grab** [græb] *vt* saisir, empoigner ▷ *vi*: **to
~ at** essayer de saisir

**grace** [greɪs] *n* grâce *f* ▷ *vt* (*honour*)
honorer; (*adorn*) orner; **5 days' ~**
un répit de 5 jours; **graceful** *adj*
gracieux(-euse), élégant(e); **gracious**
['greɪʃəs] *adj* bienveillant(e)

**grade** [greɪd] *n* (*Comm: quality*) qualité
*f*; (*size*) calibre *m*; (*type*) catégorie
*f*; (*in hierarchy*) grade *m*, échelon *m*;
(*Scol*) note *f*; (*US: school class*) classe
*f*; (: *gradient*) pente *f* ▷ *vt* classer; (*by
size*) calibrer; **grade crossing** *n* (*US*)
passage *m* à niveau; **grade school** *n*
(*US*) école *f* primaire

**gradient** ['greɪdɪənt] *n* inclinaison
*f*, pente *f*

**gradual** ['grædjuəl] *adj* graduel(le),
progressif(-ive); **gradually** *adv* peu à
peu, graduellement

**graduate** *n* ['grædjuɪt] diplômé(e)
d'université; (*US: of high school*)
diplômé(e) de fin d'études ▷ *vi*
['grædjueɪt] obtenir un diplôme
d'université (*or de fin d'études*);
**graduation** [grædju'eɪʃən] *n*
cérémonie *f* de remise des diplômes

**graffiti** [grə'fi:tɪ] *npl* graffiti *mpl*

**graft** [grɑːft] *n* (*Agr, Med*) greffe *f*;
(*bribery*) corruption *f* ▷ *vt* greffer; **hard
~** (*BRIT: inf*) boulot acharné

**grain** [greɪn] *n* (*single piece*) grain *m*; (*no
pl: cereals*) céréales *fpl*; (*US: corn*) blé *m*

**gram** [græm] *n* gramme *m*

**grammar** ['græmə'] *n* grammaire *f*;
**grammar school** *n* (*BRIT*) ≈ lycée *m*

**gramme** [græm] *n* = **gram**

**gran** (*inf*) [græn] *n* (*BRIT*) mamie *f* (*inf*),
mémé *f* (*inf*)

**grand** [grænd] *adj* magnifique,
splendide; (*gesture etc*) noble; **grandad**
(*inf*) *n* = **granddad**; **grandchild** (*pl
~ren*) *n* petit-fils *m*, petite-fille *f*;
**grandchildren** *npl* petits-enfants;
**granddad** *n* (*inf*) papy *m* (*inf*), papi
*m* (*inf*), pépé *m* (*inf*); **granddaughter**
*n* petite-fille *f*; **grandfather** *n*
grand-père *m*; **grandma** *n* (*inf*)
= **gran**; **grandmother** *n* grand-
mère *f*; **grandpa** *n* (*inf*) = **granddad**;
**grandparents** *npl* grands-parents *mpl*;
**grand piano** *n* piano *m* à queue; **Grand
Prix** ['grɑ̃:'priː] *n* (*Aut*) grand prix
automobile; **grandson** *n* petit-fils *m*

**granite** ['grænɪt] *n* granit *m*

**granny** ['grænɪ] *n* (*inf*) = **gran**

**grant** [grɑːnt] *vt* accorder; (*a request*)
accéder à; (*admit*) concéder ▷ *n* (*Scol*)
bourse *f*; (*Admin*) subside *m*, subvention
*f*; **to take sth for ~ed** considérer qch
comme acquis; **to take sb for ~ed**
considérer qn comme faisant partie
du décor

**grape** [greɪp] *n* raisin *m*

**grapefruit** ['greɪpfruːt] *n*
pamplemousse *m*

**graph** [grɑːf] *n* graphique *m*, courbe *f*;
**graphic** ['græfɪk] *adj* graphique; (*vivid*)
vivant(e); **graphics** *n* (*art*) arts *mpl*
graphiques; (*process*) graphisme *m*
▷ *npl* (*drawings*) illustrations *fpl*

**grasp** [grɑːsp] *vt* saisir ▷ *n* (*grip*) prise *f*;
(*fig*) compréhension *f*, connaissance *f*

**grass** [grɑːs] *n* herbe *f*; (*lawn*) gazon *m*;
**grasshopper** *n* sauterelle *f*

**grate** [greɪt] *n* grille *f* de cheminée ▷ *vi*
grincer ▷ *vt* (*Culin*) râper

**grateful** ['greɪtful] *adj*
reconnaissant(e)

**grater** ['greɪtə'] *n* râpe *f*

**gratitude** ['grætɪtjuːd] *n* gratitude *f*

**grave** [greɪv] *n* tombe *f* ▷ *adj* grave,
sérieux(-euse)

**gravel** ['grævl] *n* gravier *m*

**gravestone** ['greɪvstəun] *n* pierre

tombale
**graveyard** ['greɪvjɑːd] n cimetière m
**gravity** ['grævɪtɪ] n (Physics) gravité f;
pesanteur f; (seriousness) gravité
**gravy** ['greɪvɪ] n jus m (de viande),
sauce f (au jus de viande)
**gray** [greɪ] adj (US) = **grey**
**graze** [greɪz] vi paître, brouter ▷ vt
(touch lightly) frôler, effleurer; (scrape)
écorcher ▷ n écorchure f
**grease** [griːs] n (fat) graisse f; (lubricant)
lubrifiant m ▷ vt graisser; lubrifier;
**greasy** adj gras(se), graisseux(-euse);
(hands, clothes) graisseux
**great** [greɪt] adj grand(e); (heat, pain etc)
très fort(e), intense; (inf) formidable;
**Great Britain** n Grande-Bretagne f;
**great-grandfather** n arrière-grand-
père m; **great-grandmother** n
arrière-grand-mère f; **greatly** adv très,
grandement; (with verbs) beaucoup
**Greece** [griːs] n Grèce f
**greed** [griːd] n (also: ~iness) avidité f;
(for food) gourmandise f; **greedy** adj
avide; (for food) gourmand(e)
**Greek** [griːk] adj grec (grecque) ▷ n
Grec (Grecque); (Ling) grec m
**green** [griːn] adj vert(e); (inexperienced)
(bien) jeune, naïf(-ïve); (ecological:
product etc) écologique ▷ n (colour) vert
m; (on golf course) green m; (stretch of
grass) pelouse f; **greens** npl (vegetables)
légumes verts; **green card** n (Aut)
carte verte; (US: work permit) permis m
de travail; **greengage** n reine-claude f;
**greengrocer** n (BRIT) marchand m
de fruits et légumes; **greengrocer's
(shop)** n magasin m de fruits et
légumes; **greenhouse** n serre f;
**greenhouse effect** n: **the greenhouse
effect** l'effet m de serre
**Greenland** ['griːnlənd] n Groenland m
**green salad** n salade verte
**greet** [griːt] vt accueillir; **greeting** n
salutation f; **Christmas/birthday
greetings** souhaits mpl de Noël/de
bon anniversaire; **greeting(s) card** n
carte f de vœux

**grew** [gruː] pt of **grow**
**grey** (US **gray**) [greɪ] adj gris(e); (dismal)
sombre; **grey-haired** adj aux cheveux
gris; **greyhound** n lévrier m
**grid** [grɪd] n grille f; (Elec)
réseau m; **gridlock** n (traffic jam)
embouteillage m
**grief** [griːf] n chagrin m, douleur f
**grievance** ['griːvəns] n doléance f,
grief m; (cause for complaint) grief
**grieve** [griːv] vi avoir du chagrin; se
désoler ▷ vt faire de la peine à, affliger;
**to ~ for sb** pleurer qn
**grill** [grɪl] n (on cooker) gril m; (also:
**mixed ~**) grillade(s) f(pl) ▷ vt (Brit)
griller; (inf: question) cuisiner
**grille** [grɪl] n grillage m; (Aut) calandre f
**grim** [grɪm] adj sinistre, lugubre;
(serious, stern) sévère
**grime** [graɪm] n crasse f
**grin** [grɪn] n large sourire m ▷ vi sourire
**grind** [graɪnd] vb (pt, pp **ground**) ▷ vt
écraser; (coffee, pepper etc) moudre; (US:
meat) hacher ▷ n (work) corvée f
**grip** [grɪp] n (handclasp) poigne f;
(control) prise f; (handle) poignée f;
(holdall) sac m de voyage ▷ vt saisir,
empoigner; (viewer, reader) captiver;
**to come to ~s with** se colleter avec,
en venir aux prises avec; **to ~ the road**
(Aut) adhérer à la route; **gripping** adj
prenant(e), palpitant(e)
**grit** [grɪt] n gravillon m; (courage) cran
m ▷ vt (road) sabler; **to ~ one's teeth**
serrer les dents
**grits** [grɪts] npl (US) gruau m de maïs
**groan** [grəʊn] n (of pain) gémissement
m ▷ vi gémir
**grocer** ['grəʊsər] n épicier m; **groceries**
npl provisions fpl; **grocer's (shop),
grocery** n épicerie f
**groin** [grɔɪn] n aine f
**groom** [gruːm] n (for horses) palefrenier
m; (also: **bride~**) marié m ▷ vt (horse)
panser; (fig): **to ~ sb for** former qn pour
**groove** [gruːv] n sillon m, rainure f
**grope** [grəʊp] vi tâtonner; **to ~ for**
chercher à tâtons

**gross** [grəus] *adj* grossier(-ière); (*Comm*) brut(e); **grossly** *adv* (*greatly*) très, grandement

**grotesque** [grə'tɛsk] *adj* grotesque

**ground** [graund] *pt, pp of* **grind** ▷ *n* sol *m*, terre *f*; (*land*) terrain *m*, terres *fpl*; (*Sport*) terrain; (*reason: gen pl*) raison *f*; (*us: also:* **~ wire**) terre *f* ▷ *vt* (*plane*) empêcher de décoller, retenir au sol; (*us Elec*) équiper d'une prise de terre; **grounds** *npl* (*gardens etc*) parc *m*, domaine *m*; (*of coffee*) marc *m*; **on the ~, to the ~** par terre; **to gain/lose ~** gagner/perdre du terrain; **ground floor** *n* (*BRIT*) rez-de-chaussée *m*; **groundsheet** *n* (*BRIT*) tapis *m* de sol; **groundwork** *n* préparation *f*

**group** [gru:p] *n* groupe *m* ▷ *vt* (*also:* **~ together**) grouper ▷ *vi* (*also:* **~ together**) se grouper

**grouse** [graus] *n* (*pl inv: bird*) grouse *f* (*sorte de coq de bruyère*) ▷ *vi* (*complain*) rouspéter, râler

**grovel** ['grɔvl] *vi* (*fig*): **to ~ (before)** ramper (devant)

**grow** (*pt* **grew**, *pp* **~n**) [grəu, gru:, grəun] *vi* (*plant*) pousser, croître; (*person*) grandir; (*increase*) augmenter, se développer; (*become*) devenir; **to ~ rich/weak** s'enrichir/s'affaiblir ▷ *vt* cultiver, faire pousser; (*hair, beard*) laisser pousser; **grow on** *vt fus*: **that painting is ~ing on me** je finirai par aimer ce tableau; **grow up** *vi* grandir

**growl** [graul] *vi* grogner

**grown** [grəun] *pp of* **grow**; **grown-up** *n* adulte *m/f*, grande personne

**growth** [grəuθ] *n* croissance *f*, développement *m*; (*what has grown*) pousse *f*; poussée *f*; (*Med*) grosseur *f*, tumeur *f*

**grub** [grʌb] *n* larve *f*; (*inf: food*) bouffe *f*

**grubby** ['grʌbɪ] *adj* crasseux(-euse)

**grudge** [grʌdʒ] *n* rancune *f* ▷ *vt*: **to ~ sb sth** (*in giving*) donner qch à qn à contre-cœur; (*resent*) reprocher qch à qn; **to bear sb a ~ (for)** garder rancune *or* en vouloir à qn (de)

**gruelling** (*us* **grueling**) ['gruəlɪŋ] *adj* exténuant(e)

**gruesome** ['gru:səm] *adj* horrible

**grumble** ['grʌmbl] *vi* rouspéter, ronchonner

**grumpy** ['grʌmpɪ] *adj* grincheux(-euse)

**grunt** [grʌnt] *vi* grogner

**guarantee** [gærən'ti:] *n* garantie *f* ▷ *vt* garantir

**guard** [ga:d] *n* garde *f*; (*one man*) garde *m*; (*BRIT Rail*) chef *m* de train; (*safety device: on machine*) dispositif *m* de sûreté; (*also:* **fire~**) garde-feu *m inv* ▷ *vt* garder, surveiller; (*protect*): **to ~ sb/sth (against** *or* **from)** protéger qn/qch (contre); **to be on one's ~** (*fig*) être sur ses gardes; **guardian** *n* gardien(ne); (*of minor*) tuteur(-trice)

**guerrilla** [gə'rɪlə] *n* guérillero *m*

**guess** [gɛs] *vi* deviner ▷ *vt* deviner; (*estimate*) évaluer; (*us*) croire, penser ▷ *n* supposition *f*, hypothèse *f*; **to take** *or* **have a ~** essayer de deviner

**guest** [gɛst] *n* invité(e); (*in hotel*) client(e); **guest house** *n* pension *f*; **guest room** *n* chambre *f* d'amis

**guidance** ['gaɪdəns] *n* (*advice*) conseils *mpl*

**guide** [gaɪd] *n* (*person*) guide *m/f*; (*book*) guide *m*; (*also:* **Girl G~**) éclaireuse *f*; (*Roman Catholic*) guide *f* ▷ *vt* guider; **is there an English-speaking ~?** est-ce que l'un des guides parle anglais?; **guidebook** *n* guide *m*; **guide dog** *n* chien *m* d'aveugle; **guided tour** *n* visite guidée; **what time does the guided tour start?** la visite guidée commence à quelle heure?; **guidelines** *npl* (*advice*) instructions générales, conseils *mpl*

**guild** [gɪld] *n* (*History*) corporation *f*; (*sharing interests*) cercle *m*, association *f*

**guilt** [gɪlt] *n* culpabilité *f*; **guilty** *adj* coupable

**guinea pig** ['gɪnɪ-] *n* cobaye *m*

**guitar** [gɪ'ta:'] *n* guitare *f*; **guitarist** *n* guitariste *m/f*

**gulf** [gʌlf] *n* golfe *m*; (*abyss*) gouffre *m*

**gull** [gʌl] *n* mouette *f*

**gulp** [gʌlp] vi avaler sa salive; (from emotion) avoir la gorge serrée, s'étrangler ▷ vt (also: **~ down**) avaler

**gum** [gʌm] n (Anat) gencive f; (glue) colle f; (also: **chewing-~**) chewing-gum m ▷ vt coller

**gun** [gʌn] n (small) revolver m, pistolet m; (rifle) fusil m, carabine f; (cannon) canon m; **gunfire** n fusillade f; **gunman** (irreg) n bandit armé; **gunpoint** n: **at gunpoint** sous la menace du pistolet (or fusil); **gunpowder** n poudre f à canon; **gunshot** n coup m de feu

**gush** [gʌʃ] vi jaillir; (fig) se répandre en effusions

**gust** [gʌst] n (of wind) rafale f

**gut** [gʌt] n intestin m, boyau m; **guts** npl (Anat) boyaux mpl; (inf: courage) cran m

**gutter** ['gʌtər] n (of roof) gouttière f; (in street) caniveau m

**guy** [gaɪ] n (inf: man) type m; (also: **~rope**) corde f; (figure) effigie de Guy Fawkes

**Guy Fawkes' Night** [gaɪˈfɔːks-] n voir encadré

- **GUY FAWKES' NIGHT**
-
- **Guy Fawkes' Night**, que l'on
- appelle également "bonfire night",
- commémore l'échec du complot (le
- "Gunpowder Plot") contre James Ist
- et son parlement le 5 novembre 1605.
- L'un des conspirateurs, Guy Fawkes,
- avait été surpris dans les caves du
- parlement alors qu'il s'apprêtait à y
- mettre le feu. Chaque année pour le
- 5 novembre, les enfants préparent à
- l'avance une effigie de Guy Fawkes
- et ils demandent aux passants "un
- penny pour le guy" avec lequel ils
- pourront s'acheter des fusées de feu
- d'artifice. Beaucoup de gens font
- encore un feu dans leur jardin sur
- lequel ils brûlent le "guy".

**gym** [dʒɪm] n (also: **~nasium**) gymnase m; (also: **~nastics**) gym f; **gymnasium** n gymnase m; **gymnast** n gymnaste m/f; **gymnastics** n, npl gymnastique f; **gym shoes** npl chaussures fpl de gym(nastique)

**gynaecologist** (US **gynecologist**) [gaɪnɪˈkɒlədʒɪst] n gynécologue m/f

**gypsy** ['dʒɪpsɪ] n gitan(e), bohémien(ne)

# h

_animal_) poil _m_; **to do one's ~** se coiffer; **hairband** _n_ (_elasticated_) bandeau _m_; (_plastic_) serre-tête _m_; **hairbrush** _n_ brosse _f_ à cheveux; **haircut** _n_ coupe _f_ (de cheveux); **hairdo** _n_ coiffure _f_; **hairdresser** _n_ coiffeur(-euse); **hairdresser's** _n_ salon _m_ de coiffure, coiffeur _m_; **hair dryer** _n_ sèche-cheveux _m_, séchoir _m_; **hair gel** _n_ gel _m_ pour cheveux; **hair spray** _n_ laque _f_ (pour les cheveux); **hairstyle** _n_ coiffure _f_; **hairy** _adj_ poilu(e), chevelu(e); (_inf: frightening_) effrayant(e)

**hake** (_pl_ ~ _or_ ~**s**) [heɪk] _n_ colin _m_, merlu _m_

**half** [hɑːf] _n_ (_pl_ **halves**) moitié _f_; (_of beer: also:_ **~ pint**) ≈ demi _m_; (_Rail, bus: also:_ **~ fare**) demi-tarif _m_; (_Sport: of match_) mi-temps _f_ ▷ _adj_ demi(e) ▷ _adv_ (à) moitié, à demi; **~ an hour** une demi-heure; **~ a dozen** une demi-douzaine; **~ a pound** une demi-livre, ≈ 250 g; **two and a ~** deux et demi; **to cut sth in ~** couper qch en deux; **half board** _n_ (_BRIT: in hotel_) demi-pension _f_; **half-brother** _n_ demi-frère _m_; **half day** _n_ demi-journée _f_; **half fare** _n_ demi-tarif _m_; **half-hearted** _adj_ tiède, sans enthousiasme; **half-hour** _n_ demi-heure _f_; **half-price** _adj_ à moitié prix ▷ _adv_ (_also:_ **at half-price**) à moitié prix; **half term** _n_ (_BRIT Scol_) vacances _fpl_ (de demi-trimestre); **half-time** _n_ mi-temps _f_; **halfway** _adv_ à mi-chemin; **halfway through sth** au milieu de qch

**hall** [hɔːl] _n_ salle _f_; (_entrance way: big_) hall _m_; (_small_) entrée _f_; (_US: corridor_) couloir _m_; (_mansion_) château _m_, manoir _m_

**hallmark** ['hɔːlmɑːk] _n_ poinçon _m_; (_fig_) marque _f_

**hallo** [hə'ləʊ] _excl_ = **hello**

**hall of residence** _n_ (_BRIT_) pavillon _m_ or résidence _f_ universitaire

**Halloween, Hallowe'en** ['hæləʊ'iːn] _n_ veille _f_ de la Toussaint; _voir encadré_

**haberdashery** [hæbə'dæʃərɪ] _n_ (_BRIT_) mercerie _f_

**habit** ['hæbɪt] _n_ habitude _f_; (_costume: Rel_) habit _m_

**habitat** ['hæbɪtæt] _n_ habitat _m_

**hack** [hæk] _vt_ hacher, tailler ▷ _n_ (_pej: writer_) nègre _m_; **hacker** _n_ (_Comput_) pirate _m_ (informatique)

**had** [hæd] _pt, pp of_ **have**

**haddock** (_pl_ ~ _or_ ~**s**) ['hædək] _n_ églefin _m_; **smoked ~** haddock _m_

**hadn't** ['hædnt] = **had not**

**haemorrhage** (_US_ **hemorrhage**) ['hɛmərɪdʒ] _n_ hémorragie _f_

**haemorrhoids** (_US_ **hemorrhoids**) ['hɛmərɔɪdz] _npl_ hémorroïdes _fpl_

**haggle** ['hægl] _vi_ marchander

**Hague** [heɪg] _n:_ **The ~** La Haye

**hail** [heɪl] _n_ grêle _f_ ▷ _vt_ (_call_) héler; (_greet_) acclamer ▷ _vi_ grêler; **hailstone** _n_ grêlon _m_

**hair** [hɛər] _n_ cheveux _mpl_; (_on body_) poils _mpl_; (_of animal_) pelage _m_; (_single hair: on head_) cheveu _m_; (: _on body, of_

- **HALLOWEEN**

Selon la tradition, **Halloween** est la nuit des fantômes et des sorcières. En Écosse et aux États-Unis surtout (et de plus en plus en Angleterre) les enfants, pour fêter **Halloween**, se déguisent ce soir-là et ils vont ainsi de porte en porte en demandant de petits cadeaux (du chocolat, une pomme etc).

**hallucination** [həluːsɪ'neɪʃən] *n* hallucination *f*

**hallway** ['hɔːlweɪ] *n* (*entrance*) vestibule *m*; (*corridor*) couloir *m*

**halo** ['heɪləʊ] *n* (*of saint etc*) auréole *f*

**halt** [hɔːlt] *n* halte *f*, arrêt *m* ▷ *vt* faire arrêter; (*progress etc*) interrompre ▷ *vi* faire halte, s'arrêter

**halve** [hɑːv] *vt* (*apple etc*) partager *or* diviser en deux; (*reduce by half*) réduire de moitié

**halves** [hɑːvz] *npl of* **half**

**ham** [hæm] *n* jambon *m*

**hamburger** ['hæmbəːgəʳ] *n* hamburger *m*

**hamlet** ['hæmlɪt] *n* hameau *m*

**hammer** ['hæməʳ] *n* marteau *m* ▷ *vt* (*nail*) enfoncer; (*fig*) éreinter, démolir ▷ *vi* (*at door*) frapper à coups redoublés; **to ~ a point home to sb** faire rentrer qch dans la tête de qn

**hammock** ['hæmək] *n* hamac *m*

**hamper** ['hæmpəʳ] *vt* gêner ▷ *n* panier *m* (d'osier)

**hamster** ['hæmstəʳ] *n* hamster *m*

**hamstring** ['hæmstrɪŋ] *n* (*Anat*) tendon *m* du jarret

**hand** [hænd] *n* main *f*; (*of clock*) aiguille *f*; (*handwriting*) écriture *f*; (*at cards*) jeu *m*; (*worker*) ouvrier(-ière) ▷ *vt* passer, donner; **to give sb a ~** donner un coup de main à qn; **at ~** à portée de la main; **in ~** (*situation*) en main; (*work*) en cours; **to be on ~** (*person*) être disponible; (*emergency services*) se tenir prêt(e) (à intervenir); **to ~** (*information etc*) sous

la main, à portée de la main; **on the one ~ ..., on the other ~** d'une part ..., d'autre part; **hand down** *vt* passer; (*tradition, heirloom*) transmettre; (*us: sentence, verdict*) prononcer; **hand in** *vt* remettre; **hand out** *vt* distribuer; **hand over** *vt* remettre; (*powers etc*) transmettre; **handbag** *n* sac *m* à main; **hand baggage** *n* = **hand luggage**; **handbook** *n* manuel *m*; **handbrake** *n* frein *m* à main; **handcuffs** *npl* menottes *fpl*; **handful** *n* poignée *f*

**handicap** ['hændɪkæp] *n* handicap *m* ▷ *vt* handicaper; **mentally/physically ~ped** handicapé(e) mentalement/ physiquement

**handkerchief** ['hæŋkətʃɪf] *n* mouchoir *m*

**handle** ['hændl] *n* (*of door etc*) poignée *f*; (*of cup etc*) anse *f*; (*of knife etc*) manche *m*; (*of saucepan*) queue *f*; (*for winding*) manivelle *f* ▷ *vt* toucher, manier; (*deal with*) s'occuper de; (*treat: people*) prendre; **"~ with care"** "fragile"; **to fly off the ~** s'énerver; **handlebar(s)** *n(pl)* guidon *m*

**hand**: **hand luggage** *n* bagages *mpl* à main; **handmade** *adj* fait(e) à la main; **handout** *n* (*money*) aide *f*, don *m*; (*leaflet*) prospectus *m*; (*at lecture*) polycopié *m*; **hands-free** *adj* (*phone*) mains libres *inv* ▷ *n* (*also*: **hands-free kit**) kit *m* mains libres *inv*

**handsome** ['hænsəm] *adj* beau (belle); (*profit*) considérable

**handwriting** ['hændraɪtɪŋ] *n* écriture *f*

**handy** ['hændɪ] *adj* (*person*) adroit(e); (*close at hand*) sous la main; (*convenient*) pratique

**hang** (*pt, pp* **hung**) [hæŋ, hʌŋ] *vt* accrocher; (*criminal: pt, pp* **~ed**) pendre ▷ *vi* pendre; (*hair, drapery*) tomber ▷ *n*: **to get the ~ of (doing) sth** (*inf*) attraper le coup pour faire qch; **hang about, hang around** *vi* traîner; **hang down** *vi* pendre; **hang on** *vi* (*wait*) attendre; **hang out** *vt* (*washing*) étendre (dehors) ▷ *vi* (*inf*: *live*) habiter, percher; (: *spend time*) traîner; **hang round** *vi* = **hang around**; **hang up** *vi* (*Tel*) raccrocher ▷ *vt* (*coat, painting etc*) accrocher, suspendre

**hanger** ['hæŋər] *n* cintre *m*, portemanteau *m*

**hang-gliding** ['hæŋɡlaɪdɪŋ] *n* vol *m* libre *or* sur aile delta

**hangover** ['hæŋəʊvər] *n* (*after drinking*) gueule *f* de bois

**hankie, hanky** ['hæŋkɪ] *n abbr* = **handkerchief**

**happen** ['hæpən] *vi* arriver, se passer, se produire; **what's ~ing?** que se passe-t-il?; **she ~ed to be free** il s'est trouvé (*or* se trouvait) qu'elle était libre; **as it ~s** justement

**happily** ['hæpɪlɪ] *adv* heureusement; (*cheerfully*) joyeusement

**happiness** ['hæpɪnɪs] *n* bonheur *m*

**happy** ['hæpɪ] *adj* heureux(-euse); **~ with** (*arrangements etc*) satisfait(e) de; **to be ~ to do** faire volontiers; **~ birthday!** bon anniversaire!

**harass** ['hærəs] *vt* accabler, tourmenter; **harassment** *n* tracasseries *fpl*

**harbour** (*us* **harbor**) ['hɑːbər] *n* port *m* ▷ *vt* héberger, abriter; (*hopes, suspicions*) entretenir

**hard** [hɑːd] *adj* dur(e); (*question, problem*) difficile; (*facts, evidence*) concret(-ète) ▷ *adv* (*work*) dur; (*think, try*) sérieusement; **to look ~ at** regarder fixement; (*thing*) regarder de près; **no ~ feelings!** sans rancune!; **to be ~ of hearing** être dur(e) d'oreille; **to be ~ done by** être traité(e) injustement; **hardback** *n* livre relié; **hardboard** *n* Isorel® *m*; **hard disk** *n* (*Comput*) disque dur; **harden** *vt* durcir; (*fig*) endurcir ▷ *vi* (*substance*) durcir

**hardly** ['hɑːdlɪ] *adv* (*scarcely*) à peine; (*harshly*) durement; **~ anywhere/ever** presque nulle part/jamais

**hard**: **hardship** *n* (*difficulties*) épreuves *fpl*; (*deprivation*) privations *fpl*; **hard**

**shoulder** *n* (*BRIT Aut*) accotement stabilisé; **hard-up** *adj* (*inf*) fauché(e); **hardware** *n* quincaillerie *f*; (*Comput, Mil*) matériel *m*; **hardware shop** (*us* **hardware store**) *n* quincaillerie *f*; **hard-working** *adj* travailleur(-euse), consciencieux(-euse)

**hardy** ['hɑːdɪ] *adj* robuste; (*plant*) résistant(e) au gel

**hare** [heər] *n* lièvre *m*

**harm** [hɑːm] *n* mal *m*; (*wrong*) tort *m* ▷ *vt* (*person*) faire du mal ou du tort à; (*thing*) endommager; **out of ~'s way** à l'abri du danger, en lieu sûr; **harmful** *adj* nuisible; **harmless** *adj* inoffensif(-ive)

**harmony** ['hɑːmənɪ] *n* harmonie *f*

**harness** ['hɑːnɪs] *n* harnais *m* ▷ *vt* (*horse*) harnacher; (*resources*) exploiter

**harp** [hɑːp] *n* harpe *f* ▷ *vi*: **to ~ on about** revenir toujours sur

**harsh** [hɑːʃ] *adj* (*hard*) dur(e); (*severe*) sévère; (*unpleasant: sound*) discordant(e); (: *light*) cru(e)

**harvest** ['hɑːvɪst] *n* (*of corn*) moisson *f*; (*of fruit*) récolte *f*; (*of grapes*) vendange *f* ▷ *vt* moissonner; récolter; vendanger

**has** [hæz] *vb see* **have**

**hasn't** ['hæznt] = **has not**

**hassle** ['hæsl] *n* (*inf*: *fuss*) histoire(s) *f(pl)*

**haste** [heɪst] *n* hâte *f*, précipitation *f*; **hasten** ['heɪsn] *vt* hâter, accélérer ▷ *vi* se hâter, s'empresser; **hastily** *adv* à la hâte; (*leave*) précipitamment; **hasty** *adj* (*decision, action*) hâtif(-ive); (*departure, escape*) précipité(e)

**hat** [hæt] *n* chapeau *m*

**hatch** [hætʃ] *n* (*Naut: also:* **~way**) écoutille *f*; (*BRIT: also:* **service ~**) passe-plats *m inv* ▷ *vi* éclore

**hatchback** ['hætʃbæk] *n* (*Aut*) modèle *m* avec hayon arrière

**hate** [heɪt] *vt* haïr, détester ▷ *n* haine *f*; **hatred** ['heɪtrɪd] *n* haine *f*

**haul** [hɔːl] *vt* traîner, tirer ▷ *n* (*of fish*) prise *f*; (*of stolen goods etc*) butin *m*

**haunt** [hɔːnt] *vt* (*subj*: *ghost, fear*)

hanter; (: *person*) fréquenter ▷ *n*
repaire *m*; **haunted** *adj* (*castle etc*)
hanté(e); (*look*) égaré(e), hagard(e)

⬤ **KEYWORD**

**have** [hæv] (*pt, pp* **had**) *aux vb* **1** (*gen*)
avoir; être; **to have eaten/slept** avoir
mangé/dormi; **to have arrived/gone**
être arrivé(e)/allé(e); **having finished**
*or* **when he had finished, he left**
quand il a eu fini, il est parti; **we'd
already eaten** nous avions déjà mangé
**2** (*in tag questions*): **you've done it,
haven't you?** vous l'avez fait, n'est-ce
pas?
**3** (*in short answers and questions*): **no I
haven't!/yes we have!** mais non!/
mais si!; **so I have!** ah oui!, oui c'est
vrai!; **I've been there before, have
you?** j'y suis déjà allé, et vous?
▷ *modal aux vb* (*be obliged*): **to have
(got) to do sth** devoir faire qch, être
obligé(e) de faire qch; **she has (got)
to do it** elle doit le faire, il faut qu'elle
le fasse; **you haven't to tell her** vous
n'êtes pas obligé de le lui dire; (*must not*)
ne le lui dites surtout pas; **do you have
to book?** il faut réserver?
▷ *vt* **1** (*possess*): **he has (got) blue
eyes/dark hair** il a les yeux bleus/les
cheveux bruns
**2** (*referring to meals etc*): **to have
breakfast** prendre le petit déjeuner; **to
have dinner/lunch** dîner/déjeuner; **to
have a drink** prendre un verre; **to have
a cigarette** fumer une cigarette
**3** (*receive*) avoir, recevoir; (*obtain*) avoir;
**may I have your address?** puis-je
avoir votre adresse?; **you can have it
for £5** vous pouvez l'avoir pour 5 livres;
**I must have it for tomorrow** il me
le faut pour demain; **to have a baby**
avoir un bébé
**4** (*maintain, allow*): **I won't have it!** ça
ne se passera pas comme ça!; **we can't
have that** nous ne tolérerons pas ça
**5** (*by sb else*): **to have sth done** faire

faire qch; **to have one's hair cut** se
faire couper les cheveux; **to have sb do
sth** faire faire qch à qn
**6** (*experience, suffer*) avoir; **to have a
cold/flu** avoir un rhume/la grippe;
**to have an operation** se faire opérer;
**she had her bag stolen** elle s'est fait
voler son sac
**7** (*+noun*): **to have a swim/walk** nager/
se promener; **to have a bath/shower**
prendre un bain/une douche; **let's
have a look** regardons; **to have a
meeting** se réunir; **to have a party**
organiser une fête; **let me have a try**
laissez-moi essayer

**haven** ['heɪvn] *n* port *m*; (*fig*) havre *m*
**haven't** ['hævnt] = **have not**
**havoc** ['hævək] *n* ravages *mpl*
**Hawaii** [hə'waɪ:] *n* (îles *fpl*) Hawaï *m*
**hawk** [hɔ:k] *n* faucon *m*
**hawthorn** ['hɔ:θɔ:n] *n* aubépine *f*
**hay** [heɪ] *n* foin *m*; **hay fever** *n* rhume *m*
des foins; **haystack** *n* meule *f* de foin
**hazard** ['hæzəd] *n* (*risk*) danger *m*,
risque *m* ▷ *vt* risquer, hasarder;
**hazardous** *adj* hasardeux(-euse),
risqué(e); **hazard warning lights** *npl*
(*Aut*) feux *mpl* de détresse
**haze** [heɪz] *n* brume *f*
**hazel** ['heɪzl] *n* (*tree*) noisetier *m*
▷ *adj* (*eyes*) noisette *inv*; **hazelnut** *n*
noisette *f*
**hazy** ['heɪzɪ] *adj* brumeux(-euse); (*idea*) vague
**he** [hi:] *pron* il; **it is he who ...** c'est lui
qui ...; **here he is** le voici
**head** [hɛd] *n* tête *f*; (*leader*) chef *m*; (*of
school*) directeur(-trice); (*of secondary
school*) proviseur *m* ▷ *vt* (*list*) être
en tête de; (*group, company*) être à
la tête de; **~s or tails** pile ou face; **~
first** la tête la première; **~ over heels
in love** follement *or* éperdument
amoureux(-euse); **to ~ the ball** faire
une tête; **head for** *vt fus* se diriger vers;
(*disaster*) aller à; **head off** *vt* (*threat,
danger*) détourner; **headache** *n* mal *m*

de tête; **to have a headache** avoir mal
à la tête; **heading** n titre m; (subject
title) rubrique f; **headlamp** (BRIT) n
= **headlight**; **headlight** n phare m;
**headline** n titre m; **head office** n siège
m, bureau m central; **headphones** npl
casque m (à écouteurs); **headquarters**
npl (of business) bureau or siège central;
(Mil) quartier général; **headroom** n
(in car) hauteur f de plafond; (under
bridge) hauteur limite; **headscarf** n
foulard m; **headset** n = **headphones**;
**headteacher** n directeur(-trice);
(of secondary school) proviseur m; **head
waiter** n maître m d'hôtel

**heal** [hi:l] vt, vi guérir

**health** [hɛlθ] n santé f; **health care** n
services médicaux; **health centre** n
(BRIT) centre m de santé; **health food** n
aliment(s) naturel(s); **Health Service**
n: **the Health Service** (BRIT) ≈ la
Sécurité Sociale; **healthy** adj (person)
en bonne santé; (climate, food, attitude
etc) sain(e)

**heap** [hi:p] n tas m ▷ vt (also: ~ **up**)
entasser, amonceler; **she ~ed her plate
with cakes** elle a chargé son assiette
de gâteaux; **~s (of)** (inf: lots) des tas (de)

**hear** (pt, pp ~**d**) [hɪər, hə:d] vt entendre;
(news) apprendre ▷ vi entendre; **to ~
about** entendre parler de; (have news
of) avoir des nouvelles de; **to ~ from sb**
recevoir des nouvelles de qn

**heard** [hə:d] pt, pp of **hear**

**hearing** ['hɪərɪŋ] n (sense) ouïe f;
(of witnesses) audition f; (of a case)
audience f; **hearing aid** n appareil m
acoustique

**hearse** [hə:s] n corbillard m

**heart** [hɑ:t] n cœur m; **hearts** npl
(Cards) cœur m; **at ~** au fond; **by ~**
(learn, know) par cœur; **to lose/take
~** perdre/prendre courage; **heart
attack** n crise f cardiaque; **heartbeat**
n battement m de cœur; **heartbroken**
adj: **to be heartbroken** avoir beaucoup
de chagrin; **heartburn** n brûlures fpl
d'estomac; **heart disease** n maladie

f cardiaque

**hearth** [hɑ:θ] n foyer m, cheminée f

**heartless** ['hɑ:tlɪs] adj (person) sans
cœur, insensible; (treatment) cruel(le)

**hearty** ['hɑ:tɪ] adj chaleureux(-euse);
(appetite) solide; (dislike) cordial(e);
(meal) copieux(-euse)

**heat** [hi:t] n chaleur f; (Sport:
also: **qualifying ~**) éliminatoire
f ▷ vt chauffer; **heat up** vi (liquid)
chauffer; (room) se réchauffer ▷ vt
réchauffer; **heated** adj chauffé(e); (fig)
passionné(e), échauffé(e), excité(e);
**heater** n appareil m de chauffage;
radiateur m; (in car) chauffage m; (water
heater) chauffe-eau m

**heather** ['hɛðər] n bruyère f

**heating** ['hi:tɪŋ] n chauffage m

**heatwave** ['hi:tweɪv] n vague f de
chaleur

**heaven** ['hɛvn] n ciel m, paradis m; (fig)
paradis; **heavenly** adj céleste, divin(e)

**heavily** ['hɛvɪlɪ] adv lourdement;
(drink, smoke) beaucoup; (sleep, sigh)
profondément

**heavy** ['hɛvɪ] adj lourd(e); (work, rain,
user, eater) gros(se); (drinker, smoker)
grand(e); (schedule, week) chargé(e)

**Hebrew** ['hi:bru:] adj hébraïque ▷ n
(Ling) hébreu m

**Hebrides** ['hɛbrɪdi:z] npl: **the ~** les
Hébrides fpl

**hectare** ['hɛktɑ:r] n (BRIT) hectare m

**hectic** ['hɛktɪk] adj (schedule) très
chargé(e); (day) mouvementé(e);
(lifestyle) trépidant(e)

**he'd** [hi:d] = **he would**; **he had**

**hedge** [hɛdʒ] n haie f ▷ vi se dérober
▷ vt: **to ~ one's bets** (fig) se couvrir

**hedgehog** ['hɛdʒhɔg] n hérisson m

**heed** [hi:d] vt (also: **take ~ of**) tenir
compte de, prendre garde à

**heel** [hi:l] n talon m ▷ vt retalonner

**hefty** ['hɛftɪ] adj (person) costaud(e);
(parcel) lourd(e); (piece, price) gros(se)

**height** [haɪt] n (of person) taille f,
grandeur f; (of object) hauteur f; (of
plane, mountain) altitude f; (high ground)

hauteur, éminence f; (fig: of glory, fame, power) sommet m; (: of luxury, stupidity) comble m; **at the ~ of summer** au cœur de l'été; **heighten** vt hausser, surélever; (fig) augmenter

**heir** [ɛəʳ] n héritier m; **heiress** n héritière f

**held** [hɛld] pt, pp of **hold**

**helicopter** ['hɛlɪkɔptəʳ] n hélicoptère m

**hell** [hɛl] n enfer m; **oh ~!** (inf) merde!

**he'll** [hiːl] = **he will**; **he shall**

**hello** [hə'ləu] excl bonjour!; (to attract attention) hé!; (surprise) tiens!

**helmet** ['hɛlmɪt] n casque m

**help** [hɛlp] n aide f; (cleaner etc) femme f de ménage ▷ vt, vi aider; **~!** au secours!; **~ yourself** servez-vous; **can you ~ me?** pouvez-vous m'aider?; **can I ~ you?** (in shop) vous désirez?; **he can't ~ it** il n'y peut rien; **help out** vi aider ▷ vt: **to ~ sb out** aider qn; **helper** n aide m/f, assistant(e); **helpful** adj serviable, obligeant(e); (useful) utile; **helping** n portion f; **helpless** adj impuissant(e); (baby) sans défense; **helpline** n service m d'assistance téléphonique; (free) ≈ numéro vert

**hem** [hɛm] n ourlet m ▷ vt ourler

**hemisphere** ['hɛmɪsfɪəʳ] n hémisphère m

**hemorrhage** ['hɛmərɪdʒ] n (US) = **haemorrhage**

**hemorrhoids** ['hɛmərɔɪdz] npl (US) = **haemorrhoids**

**hen** [hɛn] n poule f; (female bird) femelle f

**hence** [hɛns] adv (therefore) d'où, de là; **2 years ~** d'ici 2 ans

**hen night, hen party** n soirée f entre filles (avant le mariage de l'une d'elles)

**hepatitis** [hɛpə'taɪtɪs] n hépatite f

**her** [həːʳ] pron (direct) la, l' + vowel or h mute; (indirect) lui; (stressed, after prep) elle ▷ adj son (sa), ses pl; see also **me; my**

**herb** [həːb] n herbe f; **herbal** adj à base de plantes; **herbal tea** n tisane f

**herd** [həːd] n troupeau m

**here** [hɪəʳ] adv ici; (time) alors ▷ excl tiens!, tenez!; **~!** (present) présent!; **~ is, ~ are** voici; **~ he/she is** le (la) voici

**hereditary** [hɪ'rɛdɪtrɪ] adj héréditaire

**heritage** ['hɛrɪtɪdʒ] n héritage m, patrimoine m

**hernia** ['həːnɪə] n hernie f

**hero** (pl **~es**) ['hɪərəu] n héros m; **heroic** [hɪ'rəuɪk] adj héroïque

**heroin** ['hɛrəuɪn] n héroïne f (drogue)

**heroine** ['hɛrəuɪn] n héroïne f (femme)

**heron** ['hɛrən] n héron m

**herring** ['hɛrɪŋ] n hareng m

**hers** [həːz] pron le (la) sien(ne), les siens (siennes); see also **mine**[1]

**herself** [həː'sɛlf] pron (reflexive) se; (emphatic) elle-même; (after prep) elle; see also **oneself**

**he's** [hiːz] = **he is**; **he has**

**hesitant** ['hɛzɪtənt] adj hésitant(e), indécis(e)

**hesitate** ['hɛzɪteɪt] vi: **to ~ (about/to do)** hésiter (sur/à faire); **hesitation** [hɛzɪ'teɪʃən] n hésitation f

**heterosexual** ['hɛtərəu'sɛksjuəl] adj, n hétérosexuel(le)

**hexagon** ['hɛksəgən] n hexagone m

**hey** [heɪ] excl hé!

**heyday** ['heɪdeɪ] n: **the ~ of** l'âge m d'or de, les beaux jours de

**HGV** n abbr = **heavy goods vehicle**

**hi** [haɪ] excl salut!; (to attract attention) hé!

**hibernate** ['haɪbəneɪt] vi hiberner

**hiccough, hiccup** ['hɪkʌp] vi hoqueter ▷ n: **to have (the) ~s** avoir le hoquet

**hid** [hɪd] pt of **hide**

**hidden** ['hɪdn] pp of **hide** ▷ adj: **~ agenda** intentions non déclarées

**hide** [haɪd] n (skin) peau f ▷ vb (pt **hid**, pp **hidden**) ▷ vt cacher ▷ vi: **to ~ (from sb)** se cacher (de qn)

**hideous** ['hɪdɪəs] adj hideux(-euse), atroce

**hiding** ['haɪdɪŋ] n (beating) correction f, volée f de coups; **to be in ~** (concealed) se tenir caché(e)

**hi-fi** ['haɪfaɪ] *adj, n abbr* (= high fidelity) hi-fi *f inv*

**high** [haɪ] *adj* haut(e); (*speed, respect, number*) grand(e); (*price*) élevé(e); (*wind*) fort(e), violent(e); (*voice*) aigu(ë) ▷ *adv* haut, en haut; **20 m ~** haut(e) de 20 m; **~ in the air** haut dans le ciel; **highchair** *n* (*child's*) chaise haute; **high-class** *adj* (*neighbourhood, hotel*) chic *inv*, de grand standing; **higher education** *n* études supérieures; **high heels** *npl* talons hauts, hauts talons; **high jump** *n* (*Sport*) saut *m* en hauteur; **highlands** ['haɪləndz] *npl* région montagneuse; **the Highlands** (*in Scotland*) les Highlands *mpl*; **highlight** *n* (*fig: of event*) point culminant ▷ *vt* (*emphasize*) faire ressortir, souligner; **highlights** *npl* (*in hair*) reflets *mpl*; **highlighter** *n* (*pen*) surligneur (lumineux); **highly** *adv* extrêmement, très; (*unlikely*) fort; (*recommended, skilled, qualified*) hautement; **to speak highly of** dire beaucoup de bien de; **highness** *n*: **His/Her Highness** son Altesse *f*; **high-rise** *n* (*also*: **high-rise block, high-rise building**) tour *f* (d'habitation); **high school** *n* lycée *m*; (*US*) établissement *m* d'enseignement supérieur; **high season** *n* (*BRIT*) haute saison; **high street** *n* (*BRIT*) grand-rue *f*; **high-tech** (*inf*) *adj* de pointe; **highway** *n* (*BRIT*) route *f*; (*US*) route nationale; **Highway Code** *n* (*BRIT*) code *m* de la route

**hijack** ['haɪdʒæk] *vt* détourner (*par la force*); **hijacker** *n* auteur *m* d'un détournement d'avion, pirate *m* de l'air

**hike** [haɪk] *vi* faire des excursions à pied ▷ *n* excursion *f* à pied, randonnée *f*; **hiker** *n* promeneur(-euse), excursionniste *m/f*; **hiking** *n* excursions *fpl* à pied, randonnée *f*

**hilarious** [hɪ'lɛərɪəs] *adj* (*behaviour, event*) désopilant(e)

**hill** [hɪl] *n* colline *f*; (*fairly high*) montagne *f*; (*on road*) côte *f*; **hillside** *n* (flanc *m* de) coteau *m*; **hill walking** *n*

randonnée *f* de basse montagne; **hilly** *adj* vallonné(e), montagneux(-euse)

**him** [hɪm] *pron* (*direct*) le, l' + *vowel or h mute*; (*stressed, indirect, after prep*) lui; *see also* **me**; **himself** *pron* (*reflexive*) se; (*emphatic*) lui-même; (*after prep*) lui; *see also* **oneself**

**hind** [haɪnd] *adj* de derrière

**hinder** ['hɪndə'] *vt* gêner; (*delay*) retarder

**hindsight** ['haɪndsaɪt] *n*: **with (the benefit of) ~** avec du recul, rétrospectivement

**Hindu** ['hɪndu:] *n* Hindou(e); **Hinduism** *n* (*Rel*) hindouisme *m*

**hinge** [hɪndʒ] *n* charnière *f* ▷ *vi* (*fig*): **to ~ on** dépendre de

**hint** [hɪnt] *n* allusion *f*; (*advice*) conseil *m*; (*clue*) indication *f* ▷ *vt*: **to ~ that** insinuer que ▷ *vi*: **to ~ at** faire une allusion à

**hip** [hɪp] *n* hanche *f*

**hippie, hippy** ['hɪpɪ] *n* hippie *m/f*

**hippo** ['hɪpəʊ] (*pl ~s*) *n* hippopotame *m*

**hippopotamus** [hɪpə'pɔtəməs] (*pl ~es or* **hippopotami**) *n* hippopotame *m*

**hippy** ['hɪpɪ] *n* = **hippie**

**hire** ['haɪə'] *vt* (*BRIT: car, equipment*) louer; (*worker*) embaucher, engager ▷ *n* location *f*; **for ~** à louer; (*taxi*) libre; **I'd like to ~ a car** je voudrais louer une voiture; **hire(d) car** *n* (*BRIT*) voiture *f* de location; **hire purchase** *n* (*BRIT*) achat *m* (*or* vente *f*) à tempérament *or* crédit

**his** [hɪz] *pron* le (la) sien(ne), les siens (siennes) ▷ *adj* son (sa), ses *pl*; *see also* **mine¹**; **my**

**Hispanic** [hɪs'pænɪk] *adj* (*in US*) hispano-américain(e) ▷ *n* Hispano-Américain(e)

**hiss** [hɪs] *vi* siffler

**historian** [hɪ'stɔːrɪən] *n* historien(ne)

**historic(al)** [hɪ'stɔrɪk(l)] *adj* historique

**history** ['hɪstərɪ] *n* histoire *f*

**hit** [hɪt] *vt* (*pt, pp ~*) frapper; (*reach: target*) atteindre, toucher; (*collide with: car*) entrer en collision avec, heurter;

*(fig: affect)* toucher ▷ *n* coup *m*; *(success)* succès *m*; *(song)* tube *m*; *(to website)* visite *f*; *(on search engine)* résultat *m* de recherche; **to ~ it off with sb** bien s'entendre avec qn; **hit back** *vi*: **to ~ back at sb** prendre sa revanche sur qn

**hitch** [hɪtʃ] *vt (fasten)* accrocher, attacher; *(also:* **~ up**) remonter d'une saccade ▷ *vi* faire de l'autostop ▷ *n (difficulty)* anicroche *f*, contretemps *m*; **to ~ a lift** faire du stop; **hitch-hike** *vi* faire de l'auto-stop; **hitch-hiker** *n* auto-stoppeur(-euse); **hitch-hiking** *n* auto-stop *m*, stop *m* (*inf*)

**hi-tech** [ˈhaɪˈtek] *adj* de pointe

**hitman** [ˈhɪtmæn] *(irreg) n (inf)* tueur *m* à gages

**HIV** *n abbr (= human immunodeficiency virus)* HIV *m*, VIH *m*; **~-negative/positive** séronégatif(-ive)/positif(-ive)

**hive** [haɪv] *n* ruche *f*

**hoard** [hɔːd] *n (of food)* provisions *fpl*, réserves *fpl*; *(of money)* trésor *m* ▷ *vt* amasser

**hoarse** [hɔːs] *adj* enroué(e)

**hoax** [həʊks] *n* canular *m*

**hob** [hɔb] *n* plaque chauffante

**hobble** [ˈhɔbl] *vi* boitiller

**hobby** [ˈhɔbɪ] *n* passe-temps favori

**hobo** [ˈhəʊbəʊ] *n (US)* vagabond *m*

**hockey** [ˈhɔkɪ] *n* hockey *m*; **hockey stick** *n* crosse *f* de hockey

**hog** [hɔg] *n* porc (châtré) ▷ *vt (fig)* accaparer; **to go the whole ~** aller jusqu'au bout

**Hogmanay** [hɔgməˈneɪ] *n* réveillon *m* du jour de l'An, Saint-Sylvestre *f*; *voir encadré*

● **HOGMANAY**
●
● La Saint-Sylvestre ou "New Year's
● Eve" se nomme **Hogmanay** en
● Écosse. En cette occasion, la famille
● et les amis se réunissent pour
● entendre sonner les douze coups de
● minuit et pour fêter le "first-footing",
● une coutume qui veut qu'on se

● rende chez ses amis et voisins en
● apportant quelque chose à boire (du
● whisky en général) et un morceau de
● charbon en gage de prospérité pour
● la nouvelle année.

**hoist** [hɔɪst] *n* palan *m* ▷ *vt* hisser

**hold** [həʊld] *(pt, pp* **held**) *vt* tenir; *(contain)* contenir; *(meeting)* tenir; *(keep back)* retenir; *(believe)* considérer; *(possess)* avoir ▷ *vi (withstand pressure)* tenir (bon); *(be valid)* valoir; *(on telephone)* attendre ▷ *n* prise *f*; *(find)* influence *f*; *(Naut)* cale *f*; **to catch** *or* **get (a) ~ of** saisir; **to get ~ of** *(find)* trouver; **~ the line!** *(Tel)* ne quittez pas!; **to ~ one's own** *(fig)* (bien) se défendre; **hold back** *vt* retenir; *(secret)* cacher; **hold on** *vi* tenir bon; *(wait)* attendre; **~ on!** *(Tel)* ne quittez pas!; **to ~ on to sth** *(grasp)* se cramponner à qch; *(keep)* conserver *or* garder qch; **hold out** *vt* offrir ▷ *vi (resist)*: **to ~ out (against)** résister (devant), tenir bon (devant); **hold up** *vt (raise)* lever; *(support)* soutenir; *(delay)* retarder; *(: traffic)* ralentir; *(rob)* braquer; **holdall** *n (BRIT)* fourre-tout *m inv*; **holder** *n (container)* support *m*; *(of ticket, record)* détenteur(-trice); *(of office, title, passport etc)* titulaire *m/f*

**hole** [həʊl] *n* trou *m*

**holiday** [ˈhɔlədɪ] *n (BRIT: vacation)* vacances *fpl*; *(day off)* jour *m* de congé; *(public)* jour férié; **to be on ~** être en vacances; **I'm here on ~** je suis ici en vacances; **holiday camp** *n (also:* **holiday centre**) camp *m* de vacances; **holiday job** *n (BRIT)* boulot *m (inf)* de vacances; **holiday-maker** *n (BRIT)* vacancier(-ière); **holiday resort** *n* centre *m* de villégiature *or* de vacances

**Holland** [ˈhɔlənd] *n* Hollande *f*

**hollow** [ˈhɔləʊ] *adj* creux(-euse); *(fig)* faux (fausse) ▷ *n* creux *m*; *(in land)* dépression *f* (de terrain), cuvette *f* ▷ *vt*: **to ~ out** creuser, évider

**holly** [ˈhɔlɪ] *n* houx *m*

**Hollywood** [ˈhɔlɪwʊd] *n* Hollywood

**holocaust** ['hɔləkɔːst] n holocauste m
**holy** ['həʊlɪ] adj saint(e); (bread, water) bénit(e); (ground) sacré(e)
**home** [həʊm] n foyer m, maison f; (country) pays natal, patrie f; (institution) maison ▷ adj de famille; (Econ, Pol) national(e), intérieur(e); (Sport: team) qui reçoit; (: match, win) sur leur (or notre) terrain ▷ adv chez soi, à la maison; au pays natal; (right in: nail etc) à fond; **at ~** chez soi, à la maison; **to go (or come) ~** rentrer (chez soi), rentrer à la maison (or au pays); **make yourself at ~** faites comme chez vous; **home address** n domicile permanent; **homeland** n patrie f; **homeless** adj sans foyer, sans abri; **homely** adj (plain) simple, sans prétention; (welcoming) accueillant(e); **home-made** adj fait(e) à la maison; **home match** n match m à domicile; **Home Office** n (BRIT) ministère m de l'Intérieur; **home owner** n propriétaire occupant; **home page** n (Comput) page f d'accueil; **Home Secretary** n (BRIT) ministre m de l'Intérieur; **homesick** adj: **to be homesick** avoir le mal du pays; (missing one's family) s'ennuyer de sa famille; **home town** n ville natale; **homework** n devoirs mpl
**homicide** ['hɔmɪsaɪd] n (US) homicide m
**homoeopathic** (US **homeopathic**) [həʊmɪ'pæθɪk] adj (medicine) homéopathique; (doctor) homéopathe
**homoeopathy** (US **homeopathy**) [həʊmɪ'ɔpəθɪ] n homéopathie f
**homosexual** [hɔməʊ'sɛksjʊəl] adj, n homosexuel(le)
**honest** ['ɔnɪst] adj honnête; (sincere) franc (franche); **honestly** adv honnêtement; franchement; **honesty** n honnêteté f
**honey** ['hʌnɪ] n miel m; **honeymoon** n lune f de miel, voyage m de noces; **we're on honeymoon** nous sommes en voyage de noces; **honeysuckle** n chèvrefeuille m

**Hong Kong** ['hɔŋ'kɔŋ] n Hong Kong
**honorary** ['ɔnərərɪ] adj honoraire; (duty, title) honorifique; **~ degree** diplôme m honoris causa
**honour** (US **honor**) ['ɔnə'] vt honorer ▷ n honneur m; **to graduate with ~s** obtenir sa licence avec mention; **honourable** (US **honorable**) adj honorable; **honours degree** n (Scol) ≈ licence f avec mention
**hood** [hud] n capuchon m; (of cooker) hotte f; (BRIT Aut) capote f; (US Aut) capot m; **hoodie** ['hudɪ] n (top) sweat m à capuche
**hoof** (pl **~s** or **hooves**) [huːf, huːvz] n sabot m
**hook** [huk] n crochet m; (on dress) agrafe f; (for fishing) hameçon m ▷ vt accrocher; **off the ~** (Tel) décroché
**hooligan** ['huːlɪɡən] n voyou m
**hoop** [huːp] n cerceau m
**hooray** [huː'reɪ] excl = **hurray**
**hoot** [huːt] vi (BRIT: Aut) klaxonner; (siren) mugir; (owl) hululer
**Hoover®** ['huːvə'] n (BRIT) aspirateur m ▷ vt: **to hoover** (room) passer l'aspirateur dans; (carpet) passer l'aspirateur sur
**hooves** [huːvz] npl of **hoof**
**hop** [hɔp] vi sauter; (on one foot) sauter à cloche-pied; (bird) sautiller
**hope** [həʊp] vt, vi espérer ▷ n espoir m; **I ~ so** je l'espère; **I ~ not** j'espère que non; **hopeful** adj (person) plein(e) d'espoir; (situation) prometteur(-euse), encourageant(e); **hopefully** adv (expectantly) avec espoir, avec optimisme; (one hopes) avec un peu de chance; **hopeless** adj désespéré(e); (useless) nul(le)
**hops** [hɔps] npl houblon m
**horizon** [hə'raɪzn] n horizon m; **horizontal** [hɔrɪ'zɔntl] adj horizontal(e)
**hormone** ['hɔːməʊn] n hormone f
**horn** [hɔːn] n corne f; (Mus) cor m; (Aut) klaxon m
**horoscope** ['hɔrəskəʊp] n

horoscope m
**horrendous** [hə'rɛndəs] adj horrible,
affreux(-euse)
**horrible** ['hɔrɪbl] adj horrible,
affreux(-euse)
**horrid** ['hɔrɪd] adj (person) détestable;
(weather, place, smell) épouvantable
**horrific** [hɔ'rɪfɪk] adj horrible
**horrifying** ['hɔrɪfaɪɪŋ] adj horrifiant(e)
**horror** ['hɔrər] n horreur f; **horror film**
n film m d'épouvante
**hors d'œuvre** [ɔː'dəːvrə] n hors
d'œuvre m
**horse** [hɔːs] n cheval m; **horseback:
on horseback** adv à cheval;
**horse chestnut** n (nut) marron m
(d'Inde); (tree) marronnier m (d'Inde);
**horsepower** n puissance f (en
chevaux); (unit) cheval-vapeur m (CV);
**horse-racing** n courses fpl de chevaux;
**horseradish** n raifort m; **horse riding**
n (BRIT) équitation f
**hose** [həuz] n (also: **~pipe**) tuyau m;
(also: **garden ~**) tuyau d'arrosage;
**hosepipe** n tuyau m; (in garden) tuyau
d'arrosage
**hospital** ['hɔspɪtl] n hôpital m; **in** ~ à
l'hôpital; **where's the nearest ~?** où
est l'hôpital le plus proche?
**hospitality** [hɔspɪ'tælɪtɪ] n
hospitalité f
**host** [həust] n hôte m; (TV,
Radio) présentateur(-trice),
animateur(-trice); (large number): **a ~ of**
une foule de; (Rel) hostie f
**hostage** ['hɔstɪdʒ] n otage m
**hostel** ['hɔstl] n foyer m; (also: **youth ~**)
auberge f de jeunesse
**hostess** ['həustɪs] n hôtesse f; (BRIT:
also: **air ~**) hôtesse de l'air; (TV, Radio)
animatrice f
**hostile** ['hɔstaɪl] adj hostile
**hostility** [hɔ'stɪlɪtɪ] n hostilité f
**hot** [hɔt] adj chaud(e); (as opposed to only
warm) très chaud(e); (spicy) fort(e); (fig:
contest) acharné(e); (topic) brûlant(e);
(temper) violent(e), passionné(e); **to be
~** (person) avoir chaud; (thing) être (très)

chaud; (weather) faire chaud; **hot dog**
n hot-dog m
**hotel** [həu'tɛl] n hôtel m
**hot-water bottle** [hɔt'wɔːtə-] n
bouillotte f
**hound** [haund] vt poursuivre avec
acharnement ▷ n chien courant
**hour** ['auər] n heure f; **hourly** adj toutes
les heures; (rate) horaire
**house** n [haus] maison f; (Pol) chambre
f; (Theat) salle f; auditoire m ▷ vt [hauz]
(person) loger, héberger; **on the ~** (fig)
aux frais de la maison; **household**
n (Admin etc) ménage m; (people)
famille f, maisonnée f; **householder**
n propriétaire m/f; (head of house)
chef m de famille; **housekeeper** n
gouvernante f; **housekeeping** n
(work) ménage m; **housewife** (irreg) n
ménagère f; femme f au foyer; **house
wine** n cuvée f maison or du patron;
**housework** n (travaux mpl du)
ménage m
**housing** ['hauzɪŋ] n logement m;
**housing development** (BRIT **housing
estate**) n (blocks of flats) cité f; (houses)
lotissement m
**hover** ['hɔvər] vi planer; **hovercraft** n
aéroglisseur m, hovercraft m
**how** [hau] adv comment; **~ are you?**
comment allez-vous?; **~ do you
do?** bonjour; (on being introduced)
enchanté(e); **~ long have you been
here?** depuis combien de temps êtes-
vous là?; **~ lovely/awful!** que or comme
c'est joli/affreux!; **~ much time/many
people?** combien de temps/gens?; **~
much does it cost?** ça coûte combien?;
**~ old are you?** quel âge avez-vous?; **~
tall is he?** combien mesure-t-il?; **~ is
school?** ça va à l'école?; **~ was the film?**
comment était le film?
**however** [hau'ɛvər] conj pourtant,
cependant ▷ adv: **~ I do it** de quelque
manière que je m'y prenne; **~ cold it is**
même s'il fait très froid; **~ did you do it?**
comment y êtes-vous donc arrivé?
**howl** [haul] n hurlement m ▷ vi hurler;

(*wind*) mugir

**H.P.** *n abbr* (BRIT) = **hire purchase**

**h.p.** *abbr* (*Aut*) = **horsepower**

**HQ** *n abbr* (= *headquarters*) QG *m*

**hr(s)** *abbr* (= *hour(s)*) h

**HTML** *n abbr* (= *hypertext markup language*) HTML *m*

**hubcap** [hʌbkæp] *n* (*Aut*) enjoliveur *m*

**huddle** ['hʌdl] *vi*: **to ~ together** se blottir les uns contre les autres

**huff** [hʌf] *n*: **in a ~** fâché(e)

**hug** [hʌg] *vt* serrer dans ses bras; (*shore, kerb*) serrer ▷ *n*: **to give sb a ~** serrer qn dans ses bras

**huge** [hju:dʒ] *adj* énorme, immense

**hull** [hʌl] *n* (*of ship*) coque *f*

**hum** [hʌm] *vt* (*tune*) fredonner ▷ *vi* fredonner; (*insect*) bourdonner; (*plane, tool*) vrombir

**human** ['hju:mən] *adj* humain(e) ▷ *n* (*also*: **~ being**) être humain

**humane** [hju:'meɪn] *adj* humain(e), humanitaire

**humanitarian** [hju:mænɪ'tɛərɪən] *adj* humanitaire

**humanity** [hju:'mænɪtɪ] *n* humanité *f*

**human rights** *npl* droits *mpl* de l'homme

**humble** ['hʌmbl] *adj* humble, modeste

**humid** ['hju:mɪd] *adj* humide; **humidity** [hju:'mɪdɪtɪ] *n* humidité *f*

**humiliate** [hju:'mɪlɪeɪt] *vt* humilier

**humiliating** [hju:'mɪlɪeɪtɪŋ] *adj* humiliant(e)

**humiliation** [hju:mɪlɪ'eɪʃən] *n* humiliation *f*

**hummus** ['huməs] *n* houm(m)ous *m*

**humorous** ['hju:mərəs] *adj* humoristique

**humour** (*us* **humor**) ['hju:məʳ] *n* humour *m*; (*mood*) humeur *f* ▷ *vt* (*person*) faire plaisir à; se prêter aux caprices de

**hump** [hʌmp] *n* bosse *f*

**hunch** [hʌntʃ] *n* (*premonition*) intuition *f*

**hundred** ['hʌndrəd] *num* cent; **~s of** des centaines de; **hundredth** [-ɪdθ]

*num* centième

**hung** [hʌŋ] *pt, pp* of **hang**

**Hungarian** [hʌŋ'gɛərɪən] *adj* hongrois(e) ▷ *n* Hongrois(e); (*Ling*) hongrois *m*

**Hungary** ['hʌŋgərɪ] *n* Hongrie *f*

**hunger** ['hʌŋgəʳ] *n* faim *f* ▷ *vi*: **to ~ for** avoir faim de, désirer ardemment

**hungry** ['hʌŋgrɪ] *adj* affamé(e); **to be ~** avoir faim; **~ for** (*fig*) avide de

**hunt** [hʌnt] *vt* (*seek*) chercher; (*Sport*) chasser ▷ *vi* (*search*): **to ~ for** chercher (partout); (*Sport*) chasser ▷ *n* (*Sport*) chasse *f*; **hunter** *n* chasseur *m*; **hunting** *n* chasse *f*

**hurdle** ['hə:dl] *n* (*Sport*) haie *f*; (*fig*) obstacle *m*

**hurl** [hə:l] *vt* lancer (avec violence); (*abuse, insults*) lancer

**hurrah, hurray** [hu'rɑ:, hu'reɪ] *excl* hourra!

**hurricane** ['hʌrɪkən] *n* ouragan *m*

**hurry** ['hʌrɪ] *n* hâte *f*, précipitation *f* ▷ *vi* se presser, se dépêcher ▷ *vt* (*person*) faire presser, faire se dépêcher; (*work*) presser; **to be in a ~** être pressé(e); **to do sth in a ~** faire qch en vitesse; **hurry up** *vi* se dépêcher

**hurt** [hə:t] (*pt, pp* **~**) *vt* (*cause pain to*) faire mal à; (*injure, fig*) blesser ▷ *vi* faire mal ▷ *adj* blessé(e); **my arm ~s** j'ai mal au bras; **to ~ o.s.** se faire mal

**husband** ['hʌzbənd] *n* mari *m*

**hush** [hʌʃ] *n* calme *m*, silence *m* ▷ *vt* faire taire; **~!** chut!

**husky** ['hʌskɪ] *adj* (*voice*) rauque ▷ *n* chien *m* esquimau *or* de traîneau

**hut** [hʌt] *n* hutte *f*; (*shed*) cabane *f*

**hyacinth** ['haɪəsɪnθ] *n* jacinthe *f*

**hydrangea** [haɪ'dreɪndʒə] *n* hortensia *m*

**hydrofoil** ['haɪdrəfɔɪl] *n* hydrofoil *m*

**hydrogen** ['haɪdrədʒən] *n* hydrogène *m*

**hygiene** ['haɪdʒi:n] *n* hygiène *f*; **hygienic** [haɪ'dʒi:nɪk] *adj* hygiénique

**hymn** [hɪm] *n* hymne *m*; cantique *m*

**hype** [haɪp] *n* (*inf*) matraquage *m*

publicitaire *or* médiatique
**hypermarket** ['haɪpəmɑːkɪt] (*BRIT*) *n*
hypermarché *m*
**hyphen** ['haɪfn] *n* trait *m* d'union
**hypnotize** ['hɪpnətaɪz] *vt* hypnotiser
**hypocrite** ['hɪpəkrɪt] *n* hypocrite *m/f*
**hypocritical** [hɪpə'krɪtɪkl] *adj*
hypocrite
**hypothesis** (*pl* **hypotheses**)
[haɪ'pɔθɪsɪs, -siːz] *n* hypothèse *f*
**hysterical** [hɪ'stɛrɪkl] *adj* hystérique;
(*funny*) hilarant(e)
**hysterics** [hɪ'stɛrɪks] *npl*: **to be in/
have ~** (*anger, panic*) avoir une crise de
nerfs; (*laughter*) attraper un fou rire

**I** [aɪ] *pron* je; (*before vowel*) j'; (*stressed*)
moi
**ice** [aɪs] *n* glace *f*; (*on road*) verglas *m*
▷ *vt* (*cake*) glacer ▷ *vi* (*also:* **~ over**)
geler; (*also:* **~ up**) se givrer; **iceberg**
*n* iceberg *m*; **ice cream** *n* glace *f*; **ice
cube** *n* glaçon *m*; **ice hockey** *n* hockey
*m* sur glace
**Iceland** ['aɪslənd] *n* Islande *f*; **Icelander**
*n* Islandais(e); **Icelandic** [aɪs'lændɪk]
*adj* islandais(e) ▷ *n* (*Ling*) islandais *m*
**ice**: **ice lolly** *n* (*BRIT*) esquimau *m*;
**ice rink** *n* patinoire *f*; **ice skating** *n*
patinage *m* (sur glace)
**icing** ['aɪsɪŋ] *n* (*Culin*) glaçage *m*; **icing
sugar** *n* (*BRIT*) sucre *m* glace
**icon** ['aɪkɔn] *n* icône *f*
**ICT** *n abbr* (*BRIT: Scol:* = *information and
communications technology*) TIC *fpl*
**icy** ['aɪsɪ] *adj* glacé(e); (*road*) verglacé(e);
(*weather, temperature*) glacial(e)
**I'd** [aɪd] = **I would**; **I had**
**ID card** *n* carte *f* d'identité
**idea** [aɪ'dɪə] *n* idée *f*

**ideal** [aɪˈdɪəl] n idéal m ▷ adj idéal(e); **ideally** [aɪˈdɪəlɪ] adv (preferably) dans l'idéal; (perfectly): **he is ideally suited to the job** il est parfait pour ce poste

**identical** [aɪˈdɛntɪkl] adj identique

**identification** [aɪdɛntɪfɪˈkeɪʃən] n identification f; **means of ~** pièce f d'identité

**identify** [aɪˈdɛntɪfaɪ] vt identifier

**identity** [aɪˈdɛntɪtɪ] n identité f; **identity card** n carte f d'identité; **identity theft** n usurpation f d'identité

**ideology** [aɪdɪˈɔlədʒɪ] n idéologie f

**idiom** [ˈɪdɪəm] n (phrase) expression f idiomatique; (style) style m

**idiot** [ˈɪdɪət] n idiot(e), imbécile m/f

**idle** [ˈaɪdl] adj (doing nothing) sans occupation, désœuvré(e); (lazy) oisif(-ive), paresseux(-euse); (unemployed) au chômage; (machinery) au repos; (question, pleasures) vain(e), futile ▷ vi (engine) tourner au ralenti

**idol** [ˈaɪdl] n idole f

**idyllic** [ɪˈdɪlɪk] adj idyllique

**i.e.** abbr (= id est: that is) c. à d., c'est-à-dire

**if** [ɪf] conj si; **if necessary** si nécessaire, le cas échéant; **if so** si c'est le cas; **if not** sinon; **if only I could!** si seulement je pouvais!; see also **as; even**

**ignite** [ɪɡˈnaɪt] vt mettre le feu à, enflammer ▷ vi s'enflammer

**ignition** [ɪɡˈnɪʃən] n (Aut) allumage m; **to switch on/off the ~** mettre/couper le contact

**ignorance** [ˈɪɡnərəns] n ignorance f

**ignorant** [ˈɪɡnərənt] adj ignorant(e); **to be ~ of** (subject) ne rien connaître en; (events) ne pas être au courant de

**ignore** [ɪɡˈnɔːʳ] vt ne tenir aucun compte de; (mistake) ne pas relever; (person: pretend to not see) faire semblant de ne pas reconnaître; (: pay no attention to) ignorer

**ill** [ɪl] adj (sick) malade; (bad) mauvais(e) ▷ n mal m ▷ adv: **to speak/think ~ of sb** dire/penser du mal de qn; **to be**

**taken ~** tomber malade

**I'll** [aɪl] = **I will; I shall**

**illegal** [ɪˈliːgl] adj illégal(e)

**illegible** [ɪˈlɛdʒɪbl] adj illisible

**illegitimate** [ɪlɪˈdʒɪtɪmət] adj illégitime

**ill health** n mauvaise santé

**illiterate** [ɪˈlɪtərət] adj illettré(e)

**illness** [ˈɪlnɪs] n maladie f

**illuminate** [ɪˈluːmɪneɪt] vt (room, street) éclairer; (for special effect) illuminer

**illusion** [ɪˈluːʒən] n illusion f

**illustrate** [ˈɪləstreɪt] vt illustrer

**illustration** [ɪləˈstreɪʃən] n illustration f

**I'm** [aɪm] = **I am**

**image** [ˈɪmɪdʒ] n image f; (public face) image de marque

**imaginary** [ɪˈmædʒɪnərɪ] adj imaginaire

**imagination** [ɪmædʒɪˈneɪʃən] n imagination f

**imaginative** [ɪˈmædʒɪnətɪv] adj imaginatif(-ive); (person) plein(e) d'imagination

**imagine** [ɪˈmædʒɪn] vt s'imaginer; (suppose) imaginer, supposer

**imbalance** [ɪmˈbæləns] n déséquilibre m

**imitate** [ˈɪmɪteɪt] vt imiter; **imitation** [ɪmɪˈteɪʃən] n imitation f

**immaculate** [ɪˈmækjulət] adj impeccable; (Rel) immaculé(e)

**immature** [ɪməˈtjuəʳ] adj (fruit) qui n'est pas mûr(e); (person) qui manque de maturité

**immediate** [ɪˈmiːdɪət] adj immédiat(e); **immediately** adv (at once) immédiatement; **immediately next to** juste à côté de

**immense** [ɪˈmɛns] adj immense, énorme; **immensely** adv (+adj) extrêmement; (+vb) énormément

**immerse** [ɪˈməːs] vt immerger, plonger; **to be ~d in** (fig) être plongé dans

**immigrant** [ˈɪmɪgrənt] n

immigrant(e); (already established)
immigré(e); **immigration** [ɪmɪˈɡreɪʃən]
n immigration f
**imminent** [ˈɪmɪnənt] adj imminent(e)
**immoral** [ɪˈmɔrl] adj immoral(e)
**immortal** [ɪˈmɔːtl] adj, n immortel(le)
**immune** [ɪˈmjuːn] adj: **~ (to)**
immunisé(e) (contre); **immune
system** n système m immunitaire
**immunize** [ˈɪmjunaɪz] vt immuniser
**impact** [ˈɪmpækt] n choc m, impact m;
(fig) impact m
**impair** [ɪmˈpɛər] vt détériorer,
diminuer
**impartial** [ɪmˈpɑːʃl] adj impartial(e)
**impatience** [ɪmˈpeɪʃəns] n
impatience f
**impatient** [ɪmˈpeɪʃənt] adj
impatient(e); **to get** or **grow ~**
s'impatienter
**impeccable** [ɪmˈpɛkəbl] adj
impeccable, parfait(e)
**impending** [ɪmˈpɛndɪŋ] adj
imminent(e)
**imperative** [ɪmˈpɛrətɪv] adj (need)
urgent(e), pressant(e); (tone)
impérieux(-euse) ▷ n (Ling) impératif m
**imperfect** [ɪmˈpəːfɪkt] adj
imparfait(e); (goods etc)
défectueux(-euse) ▷ n (Ling: also: ~
**tense**) imparfait m
**imperial** [ɪmˈpɪərɪəl] adj impérial(e);
(BRIT: measure) légal(e)
**impersonal** [ɪmˈpəːsənl] adj
impersonnel(le)
**impersonate** [ɪmˈpəːsəneɪt] vt se
faire passer pour; (Theat) imiter
**impetus** [ˈɪmpətəs] n impulsion f; (of
runner) élan m
**implant** [ɪmˈplɑːnt] vt (Med) implanter;
(fig: idea, principle) inculquer
**implement** n [ˈɪmplɪmənt] outil m,
instrument m; (for cooking) ustensile m
▷ vt [ˈɪmplɪmɛnt] exécuter
**implicate** [ˈɪmplɪkeɪt] vt impliquer,
compromettre
**implication** [ɪmplɪˈkeɪʃən] n
implication f; **by ~** indirectement

**implicit** [ɪmˈplɪsɪt] adj implicite;
(complete) absolu(e), sans réserve
**imply** [ɪmˈplaɪ] vt (hint) suggérer,
laisser entendre; (mean) indiquer,
supposer
**impolite** [ɪmpəˈlaɪt] adj impoli(e)
**import** vt [ɪmˈpɔːt] importer ▷ n
[ˈɪmpɔːt] (Comm) importation f;
(meaning) portée f, signification f
**importance** [ɪmˈpɔːtns] n
importance f
**important** [ɪmˈpɔːtnt] adj
important(e); **it's not ~** c'est sans
importance, ce n'est pas important
**importer** [ɪmˈpɔːtər] n
importateur(-trice)
**impose** [ɪmˈpəuz] vt imposer ▷ vi:
**to ~ on sb** abuser de la gentillesse
de qn; **imposing** adj imposant(e),
impressionnant(e)
**impossible** [ɪmˈpɔsɪbl] adj impossible
**impotent** [ˈɪmpətnt] adj
impuissant(e)
**impoverished** [ɪmˈpɔvərɪʃt] adj
pauvre, appauvri(e)
**impractical** [ɪmˈpræktɪkl] adj pas
pratique; (person) qui manque d'esprit
pratique
**impress** [ɪmˈprɛs] vt impressionner,
faire impression sur; (mark) imprimer,
marquer; **to ~ sth on sb** faire bien
comprendre qch à qn
**impression** [ɪmˈprɛʃən] n impression
f; (of stamp, seal) empreinte f; (imitation)
imitation f; **to be under the ~ that**
avoir l'impression que
**impressive** [ɪmˈprɛsɪv] adj
impressionnant(e)
**imprison** [ɪmˈprɪzn] vt emprisonner,
mettre en prison; **imprisonment**
n emprisonnement m; (period):
**to sentence sb to 10 years'
imprisonment** condamner qn à 10
ans de prison
**improbable** [ɪmˈprɔbəbl] adj
improbable; (excuse) peu plausible
**improper** [ɪmˈprɔpər] adj (unsuitable)
déplacé(e), de mauvais goût; (indecent)

indécent(e); (*dishonest*) malhonnête

**improve** [ɪmˈpruːv] *vt* améliorer ▷ *vi* s'améliorer; (*pupil etc*) faire des progrès; **improvement** *n* amélioration *f*; (*of pupil etc*) progrès *m*

**improvise** [ˈɪmprəvaɪz] *vt*, *vi* improviser

**impulse** [ˈɪmpʌls] *n* impulsion *f*; **on ~** impulsivement, sur un coup de tête; **impulsive** [ɪmˈpʌlsɪv] *adj* impulsif(-ive)

O **KEYWORD**

**in** [ɪn] *prep* **1** (*indicating place, position*) dans; **in the house/the fridge** dans la maison/le frigo; **in the garden** dans le *or* au jardin; **in town** en ville; **in the country** à la campagne; **in school** à l'école; **in here/there** ici/là

**2** (*with place names: of town, region, country*): **in London** à Londres; **in England** en Angleterre; **in Japan** au Japon; **in the United States** aux États-Unis

**3** (*indicating time: during*): **in spring** au printemps; **in summer** en été; **in May/2005** en mai/2005; **in the afternoon** (dans) l'après-midi; **at 4 o'clock in the afternoon** à 4 heures de l'après-midi

**4** (*indicating time: in the space of*) en; (: *future*) dans; **I did it in 3 hours/days** je l'ai fait en 3 heures/jours; **I'll see you in 2 weeks** *or* **in 2 weeks' time** je te verrai dans 2 semaines

**5** (*indicating manner etc*) à; **in a loud/soft voice** à voix haute/basse; **in pencil** au crayon; **in writing** par écrit; **in French** en français; **the boy in the blue shirt** le garçon à *or* avec la chemise bleue

**6** (*indicating circumstances*): **in the sun** au soleil; **in the shade** à l'ombre; **in the rain** sous la pluie; **a change in policy** un changement de politique

**7** (*indicating mood, state*): **in tears** en larmes; **in anger** sous le coup de la colère; **in despair** au désespoir; **in good condition** en bon état; **to live in luxury** vivre dans le luxe

**8** (*with ratios, numbers*): **1 in 10 households, 1 household in 10** 1 ménage sur 10; **20 pence in the pound** 20 pence par livre sterling; **they lined up in twos** ils se mirent en rangs (deux) par deux; **in hundreds** par centaines

**9** (*referring to people, works*) chez; **the disease is common in children** c'est une maladie courante chez les enfants; **in (the works of) Dickens** chez Dickens, dans (l'œuvre de) Dickens

**10** (*indicating profession etc*) dans; **to be in teaching** être dans l'enseignement

**11** (*after superlative*) de; **the best pupil in the class** le meilleur élève de la classe

**12** (*with present participle*): **in saying this** en disant ceci

▷ *adv*: **to be in** (*person: at home, work*) être là; (*train, ship, plane*) être arrivé(e); (*in fashion*) être à la mode; **to ask sb in** inviter qn à entrer; **to run/limp** *etc* **in** entrer en courant/boitant *etc*

▷ *n*: **the ins and outs (of)** (*of proposal, situation etc*) les tenants et aboutissants (de)

**inability** [ɪnəˈbɪlɪtɪ] *n* incapacité *f*; **~ to pay** incapacité de payer

**inaccurate** [ɪnˈækjʊrət] *adj* inexact(e); (*person*) qui manque de précision

**inadequate** [ɪnˈædɪkwət] *adj* insuffisant(e), inadéquat(e)

**inadvertently** [ɪnədˈvɜːtntlɪ] *adv* par mégarde

**inappropriate** [ɪnəˈprəʊprɪət] *adj* inopportun(e), mal à propos; (*word, expression*) impropre

**inaugurate** [ɪˈnɔːgjʊreɪt] *vt* inaugurer; (*president, official*) investir de ses fonctions

**Inc.** *abbr* = **incorporated**

**incapable** [ɪnˈkeɪpəbl] *adj*: **~ (of)** incapable (de)

**incense** n ['ɪnsɛns] encens m ▷ vt
[ɪn'sɛns] (anger) mettre en colère
**incentive** [ɪn'sɛntɪv] n
encouragement m, raison f de se
donner de la peine
**inch** [ɪntʃ] n pouce m (=25 mm; 12 in a
foot); **within an ~ of** à deux doigts de;
**he wouldn't give an ~** (fig) il n'a pas
voulu céder d'un pouce
**incidence** ['ɪnsɪdns] n (of crime, disease)
fréquence f
**incident** ['ɪnsɪdnt] n incident m
**incidentally** [ɪnsɪ'dɛntəlɪ] adv (by the
way) à propos
**inclination** [ɪnklɪ'neɪʃən] n
inclination f; (desire) envie f
**incline** n ['ɪnklaɪn] pente f, plan
incliné ▷ vb [ɪn'klaɪn] ▷ vt incliner ▷ vi
(surface) s'incliner; **to be ~d to do** (have
a tendency to do) avoir tendance à faire
**include** [ɪn'kluːd] vt inclure,
comprendre; **service is/is not ~d** le
service est compris/n'est pas compris;
**including** prep y compris; **inclusion**
n inclusion f; **inclusive** adj inclus(e),
compris(e); **inclusive of tax** taxes
comprises
**income** ['ɪnkʌm] n revenu m; (from
property etc) rentes fpl; **income
support** n (BRIT) ≈ revenu m minimum
d'insertion, RMI m; **income tax** n
impôt m sur le revenu
**incoming** ['ɪnkʌmɪŋ] adj (passengers,
mail) à l'arrivée; (government, tenant)
nouveau (nouvelle)
**incompatible** [ɪnkəm'pætɪbl] adj
incompatible
**incompetence** [ɪn'kɔmpɪtns] n
incompétence f, incapacité f
**incompetent** [ɪn'kɔmpɪtnt] adj
incompétent(e), incapable
**incomplete** [ɪnkəm'pliːt] adj
incomplet(-ète)
**inconsistent** [ɪnkən'sɪstnt] adj
qui manque de constance; (work)
irrégulier(-ière); (statement) peu
cohérent(e); **~ with** en contradiction
avec

**inconvenience** [ɪnkən'viːnjəns] n
inconvénient m; (trouble) dérangement
m ▷ vt déranger
**inconvenient** [ɪnkən'viːnjənt]
adj malcommode; (time, place) mal
choisi(e), qui ne convient pas; (visitor)
importun(e)
**incorporate** [ɪn'kɔːpəreɪt] vt
incorporer; (contain) contenir
**incorrect** [ɪnkə'rɛkt] adj incorrect(e);
(opinion, statement) inexact(e)
**increase** n ['ɪnkriːs] augmentation
f ▷ vi, vt [ɪn'kriːs] augmenter;
**increasingly** adv de plus en plus
**incredible** [ɪn'krɛdɪbl] adj incroyable;
**incredibly** adv incroyablement
**incur** [ɪn'kəː'] vt (expenses) encourir;
(anger, risk) s'exposer à; (debt)
contracter; (loss) subir
**indecent** [ɪn'diːsnt] adj indécent(e),
inconvenant(e)
**indeed** [ɪn'diːd] adv (confirming,
agreeing) en effet, effectivement; (for
emphasis) vraiment; (furthermore)
d'ailleurs; **yes ~!** certainement!
**indefinitely** [ɪn'dɛfɪnɪtlɪ] adv (wait)
indéfiniment
**independence** [ɪndɪ'pɛndns] n
indépendance f; **Independence Day**
n (US) fête de l'Indépendance américaine;
voir encadré

● **INDEPENDENCE DAY**
●
● L'**Independence Day** est la fête
● nationale aux États-Unis, le 4
● juillet. Il commémore l'adoption
● de la déclaration d'Indépendance,
● en 1776, écrite par Thomas Jefferson
● et proclamant la séparation des 13
● colonies américaines de la Grande-
● Bretagne.

**independent** [ɪndɪ'pɛndnt]
adj indépendant(e); (radio) libre;
**independent school** n (BRIT) école
privée
**index** ['ɪndɛks] n (pl **~es**) (in book)

index *m*; (: *in library etc*) catalogue *m* (*pl* **indices**) (*ratio, sign*) indice *m*
**India** ['ɪndɪə] *n* Inde *f*; **Indian** *adj* indien(ne) ▷ *n* Indien(ne); **(American) Indian** Indien(ne) (d'Amérique)
**indicate** ['ɪndɪkeɪt] *vt* indiquer ▷ *vi* (*BRIT Aut*): **to ~ left/right** mettre son clignotant à gauche/à droite; **indication** [ɪndɪ'keɪʃən] *n* indication *f*, signe *m*; **indicative** [ɪn'dɪkətɪv] *adj*: **to be indicative of sth** être symptomatique de qch ▷ *n* (*Ling*) indicatif *m*; **indicator** *n* (*sign*) indicateur *m*; (*Aut*) clignotant *m*
**indices** [ɪndɪsiːz] *npl of* **index**
**indict** [ɪn'daɪt] *vt* accuser; **indictment** *n* accusation *f*
**indifference** [ɪn'dɪfrəns] *n* indifférence *f*
**indifferent** [ɪn'dɪfrənt] *adj* indifférent(e); (*poor*) médiocre, quelconque
**indigenous** [ɪn'dɪdʒɪnəs] *adj* indigène
**indigestion** [ɪndɪ'dʒɛstʃən] *n* indigestion *f*, mauvaise digestion
**indignant** [ɪn'dɪgnənt] *adj*: **~ (at sth/ with sb)** indigné (e) (de qch/contre qn)
**indirect** [ɪndɪ'rɛkt] *adj* indirect(e)
**indispensable** [ɪndɪ'spɛnsəbl] *adj* indispensable
**individual** [ɪndɪ'vɪdjuəl] *n* individu *m* ▷ *adj* individuel(le); (*characteristic*) particulier(-ière), original(e); **individually** *adv* individuellement
**Indonesia** [ɪndə'niːzɪə] *n* Indonésie *f*
**indoor** ['ɪndɔːʳ] *adj* d'intérieur; (*plant*) d'appartement; (*swimming pool*) couvert(e); (*sport, games*) pratiqué(e) en salle; **indoors** [ɪn'dɔːz] *adv* à l'intérieur
**induce** [ɪn'djuːs] *vt* (*persuade*) persuader; (*bring about*) provoquer; (*labour*) déclencher
**indulge** [ɪn'dʌldʒ] *vt* (*whim*) céder à, satisfaire; (*child*) gâter ▷ *vi*: **to ~ in sth** (*luxury*) s'offrir qch, se permettre qch; (*fantasies etc*) se livrer à qch; **indulgent** *adj* indulgent(e)
**industrial** [ɪn'dʌstrɪəl] *adj*

industriel(le); (*injury*) du travail; (*dispute*) ouvrier(-ière); **industrial estate** *n* (*BRIT*) zone industrielle; **industrialist** *n* industriel *m*; **industrial park** *n* (*US*) zone industrielle
**industry** ['ɪndəstrɪ] *n* industrie *f*; (*diligence*) zèle *m*, application *f*
**inefficient** [ɪnɪ'fɪʃənt] *adj* inefficace
**inequality** [ɪnɪ'kwɔlɪtɪ] *n* inégalité *f*
**inevitable** [ɪn'evɪtəbl] *adj* inévitable; **inevitably** *adv* inévitablement, fatalement
**inexpensive** [ɪnɪk'spɛnsɪv] *adj* bon marché *inv*
**inexperienced** [ɪnɪk'spɪərɪənst] *adj* inexpérimenté(e)
**inexplicable** [ɪnɪk'splɪkəbl] *adj* inexplicable
**infamous** ['ɪnfəməs] *adj* infâme, abominable
**infant** ['ɪnfənt] *n* (*baby*) nourrisson *m*; (*young child*) petit(e) enfant
**infantry** ['ɪnfəntrɪ] *n* infanterie *f*
**infant school** *n* (*BRIT*) classes *fpl* préparatoires (*entre 5 et 7 ans*)
**infect** [ɪn'fɛkt] *vt* (*wound*) infecter; (*person, blood*) contaminer; **infection** [ɪn'fɛkʃən] *n* infection *f*; (*contagion*) contagion *f*; **infectious** [ɪn'fɛkʃəs] *adj* infectieux(-euse); (*also fig*) contagieux(-euse)
**infer** [ɪn'fəːʳ] *vt*: **to ~ (from)** conclure (de), déduire (de)
**inferior** [ɪn'fɪərɪəʳ] *adj* inférieur(e); (*goods*) de qualité inférieure ▷ *n* inférieur(e); (*in rank*) subalterne *m/f*
**infertile** [ɪn'fəːtaɪl] *adj* stérile
**infertility** [ɪnfəː'tɪlɪtɪ] *n* infertilité *f*, stérilité *f*
**infested** [ɪn'fɛstɪd] *adj*: **~ (with)** infesté(e) (de)
**infinite** ['ɪnfɪnɪt] *adj* infini(e); (*time, money*) illimité(e); **infinitely** *adv* infiniment
**infirmary** [ɪn'fəːmərɪ] *n* hôpital *m*; (*in school, factory*) infirmerie *f*
**inflamed** [ɪn'fleɪmd] *adj* enflammé(e)
**inflammation** [ɪnflə'meɪʃən] *n*

inflammation f

**inflatable** [ɪnˈfleɪtəbl] *adj* gonflable

**inflate** [ɪnˈfleɪt] *vt* (*tyre, balloon*) gonfler; (*fig: exaggerate*) grossir; (*: increase*) gonfler; **inflation** [ɪnˈfleɪʃən] *n* (*Econ*) inflation f

**inflexible** [ɪnˈflɛksɪbl] *adj* inflexible, rigide

**inflict** [ɪnˈflɪkt] *vt*: **to ~ on** infliger à

**influence** [ˈɪnfluəns] *n* influence f ▷ *vt* influencer; **under the ~ of alcohol** en état d'ébriété; **influential** [ɪnfluˈɛnʃl] *adj* influent(e)

**influenza** [ɪnfluˈɛnzə] *n* grippe f

**influx** [ˈɪnflʌks] *n* afflux m

**info** (*inf*) [ˈɪnfəu] *n* (= information) renseignements *mpl*

**inform** [ɪnˈfɔ:m] *vt*: **to ~ sb (of)** informer or avertir qn (de) ▷ *vi*: **to ~ on sb** dénoncer qn, informer contre qn

**informal** [ɪnˈfɔ:ml] *adj* (*person, manner, party*) simple; (*visit, discussion*) dénué(e) de formalités; (*announcement, invitation*) non officiel(le); (*colloquial*) familier(-ère)

**information** [ɪnfəˈmeɪʃən] *n* information(s) f(pl); renseignements *mpl*; (*knowledge*) connaissances *fpl*; **a piece of ~** un renseignement; **information office** *n* bureau *m* de renseignements; **information technology** *n* informatique f

**informative** [ɪnˈfɔ:mətɪv] *adj* instructif(-ive)

**infra-red** [ɪnfrəˈrɛd] *adj* infrarouge

**infrastructure** [ˈɪnfrəstrʌktʃər] *n* infrastructure f

**infrequent** [ɪnˈfri:kwənt] *adj* peu fréquent(e), rare

**infuriate** [ɪnˈfjuərɪeɪt] *vt* mettre en fureur

**infuriating** [ɪnˈfjuərɪeɪtɪŋ] *adj* exaspérant(e)

**ingenious** [ɪnˈdʒi:njəs] *adj* ingénieux(-euse)

**ingredient** [ɪnˈgri:dɪənt] *n* ingrédient *m*; (*fig*) élément *m*

**inhabit** [ɪnˈhæbɪt] *vt* habiter;

**inhabitant** *n* habitant(e)

**inhale** [ɪnˈheɪl] *vt* inhaler; (*perfume*) respirer; (*smoke*) avaler ▷ *vi* (*breathe in*) aspirer; (*in smoking*) avaler la fumée; **inhaler** *n* inhalateur *m*

**inherent** [ɪnˈhɪərənt] *adj*: **~ (in or to)** inhérent(e) (à)

**inherit** [ɪnˈhɛrɪt] *vt* hériter (de); **inheritance** *n* héritage *m*

**inhibit** [ɪnˈhɪbɪt] *vt* (*Psych*) inhiber; (*growth*) freiner; **inhibition** [ɪnhɪˈbɪʃən] *n* inhibition f

**initial** [ɪˈnɪʃl] *adj* initial(e) ▷ *n* initiale f ▷ *vt* parafer; **initials** *npl* initiales *fpl*; (*as signature*) parafe *m*; **initially** *adv* initialement, au début

**initiate** [ɪˈnɪʃɪeɪt] *vt* (*start*) entreprendre; amorcer; (*enterprise*) lancer; (*person*) initier; **to ~ proceedings against sb** (*Law*) intenter une action à qn, engager des poursuites contre qn

**initiative** [ɪˈnɪʃətɪv] *n* initiative f

**inject** [ɪnˈdʒɛkt] *vt* injecter; (*person*): **to ~ sb with sth** faire une piqûre de qch à qn; **injection** [ɪnˈdʒɛkʃən] *n* injection f, piqûre f

**injure** [ˈɪndʒər] *vt* blesser; (*damage: reputation etc*) compromettre; **to ~ o.s.** se blesser; **injured** *adj* (*person, leg etc*) blessé(e); **injury** *n* blessure f; (*wrong*) tort *m*

**injustice** [ɪnˈdʒʌstɪs] *n* injustice f

**ink** [ɪŋk] *n* encre f; **ink-jet printer** [ˈɪŋkdʒɛt-] *n* imprimante f à jet d'encre

**inland** *adj* [ˈɪnlənd] intérieur(e) ▷ *adv* [ɪnˈlænd] à l'intérieur, dans les terres; **Inland Revenue** *n* (*BRIT*) fisc *m*

**in-laws** [ˈɪnlɔ:z] *npl* beaux-parents *mpl*; belle famille

**inmate** [ˈɪnmeɪt] *n* (*in prison*) détenu(e); (*in asylum*) interné(e)

**inn** [ɪn] *n* auberge f

**inner** [ˈɪnər] *adj* intérieur(e); **inner-city** *adj* (*schools, problems*) de quartiers déshérités

**inning** [ˈɪnɪŋ] *n* (*US: Baseball*) tour *m* de batte; **innings** *npl* (*Cricket*) tour de batte

**innocence** ['ɪnəsns] n innocence f

**innocent** ['ɪnəsnt] adj innocent(e)

**innovation** [ɪnəʊ'veɪʃən] n
innovation f

**innovative** ['ɪnəʊveɪtɪv] adj
novateur(-trice); (product) innovant(e)

**in-patient** ['ɪnpeɪʃənt] n malade
hospitalisé(e)

**input** ['ɪnpʊt] n (contribution)
contribution f; (resources) ressources
fpl; (Comput) entrée f (de données);
(: data) données fpl ▷ vt (Comput)
introduire, entrer

**inquest** ['ɪnkwɛst] n enquête
(criminelle); (coroner's) enquête
judiciaire

**inquire** [ɪn'kwaɪər] vi demander
▷ vt demander; **to ~ about**
s'informer de, se renseigner sur; **to ~
when/where/whether** demander
quand/où/si; **inquiry** n demande f
de renseignements; (Law) enquête
f, investigation f; **"inquiries"**
"renseignements"

**ins.** abbr = **inches**

**insane** [ɪn'seɪn] adj fou (folle); (Med)
aliéné(e)

**insanity** [ɪn'sænɪtɪ] n folie f; (Med)
aliénation (mentale)

**insect** ['ɪnsɛkt] n insecte m; **insect
repellent** n crème f anti-insectes

**insecure** [ɪnsɪ'kjʊər] adj (person)
anxieux(-euse); (job) précaire; (building
etc) peu sûr(e)

**insecurity** [ɪnsɪ'kjʊərɪtɪ] n insécurité f

**insensitive** [ɪn'sɛnsɪtɪv] adj insensible

**insert** vt [ɪn'səːt] insérer ▷ n
['ɪnsəːt] insertion f

**inside** ['ɪn'saɪd] n intérieur m ▷ adj
intérieur(e) ▷ adv à l'intérieur, dedans
▷ prep à l'intérieur de; (of time): **~ 10
minutes** en moins de 10 minutes; **to go
~ rentrer**; **inside lane** n (Aut: in Britain)
voie f de gauche; (: in US, Europe) voie
f de droite; **inside out** adv à l'envers;
(know) à fond; **to turn sth inside out**
retourner qch

**insight** ['ɪnsaɪt] n perspicacité f;
(glimpse, idea) aperçu m

**insignificant** [ɪnsɪg'nɪfɪkɪnt] adj
insignifiant(e)

**insincere** [ɪnsɪn'sɪər] adj hypocrite

**insist** [ɪn'sɪst] vi insister; **to ~ on doing**
insister pour faire; **to ~ on sth** exiger
qch; **to ~ that** insister pour que + sub;
(claim) maintenir or soutenir que;
**insistent** adj insistant(e), pressant(e);
(noise, action) ininterrompu(e)

**insomnia** [ɪn'sɔmnɪə] n insomnie f

**inspect** [ɪn'spɛkt] vt inspecter;
(BRIT: ticket) contrôler; **inspection**
[ɪn'spɛkʃən] n inspection f; (BRIT:
of tickets) contrôle m; **inspector** n
inspecteur(-trice); (BRIT: on buses,
trains) contrôleur(-euse)

**inspiration** [ɪnspə'reɪʃən] n
inspiration f; **inspire** [ɪn'spaɪər] vt
inspirer; **inspiring** adj inspirant(e)

**instability** [ɪnstə'bɪlɪtɪ] n instabilité f

**install** (US **instal**) [ɪn'stɔːl] vt
installer; **installation** [ɪnstə'leɪʃən] n
installation f

**instalment** (US **installment**)
[ɪn'stɔːlmənt] n (payment) acompte
m, versement partiel; (of TV serial etc)
épisode m; **in ~s** (pay) à tempérament;
(receive) en plusieurs fois

**instance** ['ɪnstəns] n exemple m; **for ~**
par exemple; **in the first ~** tout d'abord,
en premier lieu

**instant** ['ɪnstənt] n instant m ▷ adj
immédiat(e), urgent(e); (coffee, food)
instantané(e), en poudre; **instantly**
adv immédiatement, tout de suite;
**instant messaging** n messagerie f
instantanée

**instead** [ɪn'stɛd] adv au lieu de cela; **~
of** au lieu de; **~ of sb** à la place de qn

**instinct** ['ɪnstɪŋkt] n instinct m;
**instinctive** adj instinctif(-ive)

**institute** ['ɪnstɪtjuːt] n institut m
▷ vt instituer, établir; (inquiry) ouvrir;
(proceedings) entamer

**institution** [ɪnstɪ'tjuːʃən] n
institution f; (school) établissement

*m* (scolaire); (*for care*) établissement (psychiatrique *etc*)

**instruct** [ɪn'strʌkt] *vt*: **to ~ sb in sth** enseigner qch à qn; **to ~ sb to do** charger qn or ordonner à qn de faire; **instruction** [ɪn'strʌkʃən] *n* instruction *f*; **instructions** *npl* (*orders*) directives *fpl*; **instructions for use** mode *m* d'emploi; **instructor** *n* professeur *m*; (*for skiing, driving*) moniteur *m*

**instrument** ['ɪnstrumənt] *n* instrument *m*; **instrumental** [ɪnstru'mɛntl] *adj* (*Mus*) instrumental(e); **to be instrumental in sth/in doing sth** contribuer à qch/à faire qch

**insufficient** [ɪnsə'fɪʃənt] *adj* insuffisant(e)

**insulate** ['ɪnsjuleɪt] *vt* isoler; (*against sound*) insonoriser; **insulation** [ɪnsju'leɪʃən] *n* isolation *f*; (*against sound*) insonorisation *f*

**insulin** ['ɪnsjulɪn] *n* insuline *f*

**insult** *n* ['ɪnsʌlt] insulte *f*, affront *m* ▷ *vt* [ɪn'sʌlt] insulter, faire un affront à; **insulting** *adj* insultant(e), injurieux(-euse)

**insurance** [ɪn'ʃuərəns] *n* assurance *f*; **fire/life ~** assurance-incendie/-vie; **insurance company** *n* compagnie *f* or société *f* d'assurances; **insurance policy** *n* police *f* d'assurance

**insure** [ɪn'ʃuə] *vt* assurer; **to ~ (o.s.) against** (*fig*) parer à

**intact** [ɪn'tækt] *adj* intact(e)

**intake** ['ɪnteɪk] *n* (*Tech*) admission *f*; (*consumption*) consommation *f*; (*BRIT Scol*): **an ~ of 200 a year** 200 admissions par an

**integral** ['ɪntɪɡrəl] *adj* (*whole*) intégral(e); (*part*) intégrant(e)

**integrate** ['ɪntɪɡreɪt] *vt* intégrer ▷ *vi* s'intégrer

**integrity** [ɪn'tɛɡrɪtɪ] *n* intégrité *f*

**intellect** ['ɪntəlɛkt] *n* intelligence *f*; **intellectual** [ɪntə'lɛktjuəl] *adj*, *n* intellectuel(le)

**intelligence** [ɪn'tɛlɪdʒəns] *n*

intelligence *f*; (*Mil etc*) informations *fpl*, renseignements *mpl*

**intelligent** [ɪn'tɛlɪdʒənt] *adj* intelligent(e)

**intend** [ɪn'tɛnd] *vt* (*gift etc*): **to ~ sth for** destiner qch à; **to ~ to do** avoir l'intention de faire

**intense** [ɪn'tɛns] *adj* intense; (*person*) véhément(e)

**intensify** [ɪn'tɛnsɪfaɪ] *vt* intensifier

**intensity** [ɪn'tɛnsɪtɪ] *n* intensité *f*

**intensive** [ɪn'tɛnsɪv] *adj* intensif(-ive); **intensive care** *n*: **to be in intensive care** être en réanimation; **intensive care unit** *n* service *m* de réanimation

**intent** [ɪn'tɛnt] *n* intention *f* ▷ *adj* attentif(-ive), absorbé(e); **to all ~s and purposes** en fait, pratiquement; **to be ~ on doing sth** être (bien) décidé à faire qch

**intention** [ɪn'tɛnʃən] *n* intention *f*; **intentional** *adj* intentionnel(le), délibéré(e)

**interact** [ɪntər'ækt] *vi* avoir une action réciproque; (*people*) communiquer; **interaction** [ɪntər'ækʃən] *n* interaction *f*; **interactive** *adj* (*Comput*) interactif, conversationnel(le)

**intercept** [ɪntə'sɛpt] *vt* intercepter; (*person*) arrêter au passage

**interchange** *n* ['ɪntətʃeɪndʒ] (*exchange*) échange *m*; (*on motorway*) échangeur *m*

**intercourse** ['ɪntəkɔːs] *n*: **sexual ~** rapports sexuels

**interest** ['ɪntrɪst] *n* intérêt *m*; (*Comm*: *stake, share*) participation *f*, intérêts *mpl* ▷ *vt* intéresser; **interested** *adj* intéressé(e); **to be interested in sth** s'intéresser à qch; **I'm interested in going** ça m'intéresse d'y aller; **interesting** *adj* intéressant(e); **interest rate** *n* taux *m* d'intérêt

**interface** ['ɪntəfeɪs] *n* (*Comput*) interface *f*

**interfere** [ɪntə'fɪə] *vi*: **to ~ in** (*quarrel*) s'immiscer dans; (*other people's business*) se mêler de; **to ~ with** (*object*) tripoter, toucher à; (*plans*) contrecarrer; (*duty*) être en conflit avec; **interference** *n* (*gen*) ingérence *f*; (*Radio, TV*) parasites *mpl*

**interim** ['ɪntərɪm] *adj* provisoire; (*post*) intérimaire ▷ *n*: **in the ~** dans l'intérim

**interior** [ɪn'tɪərɪər] *n* intérieur *m* ▷ *adj* intérieur(e); (*minister, department*) de l'intérieur; **interior design** *n* architecture *f* d'intérieur

**intermediate** [ɪntə'miːdɪət] *adj* intermédiaire; (*Scol: course, level*) moyen(ne)

**intermission** [ɪntə'mɪʃən] *n* pause *f*; (*Theat, Cine*) entracte *m*

**intern** *vt* [ɪn'təːn] interner ▷ *n* ['ɪntəːn] (*US*) interne *m/f*

**internal** [ɪn'təːnl] *adj* interne; (*dispute, reform etc*) intérieur(e); **Internal Revenue Service** *n* (*US*) fisc *m*

**international** [ɪntə'næʃənl] *adj* international(e) ▷ *n* (*BRIT Sport*) international *m*

**Internet** [ɪntə'nɛt] *n*: **the ~** l'Internet *m*; **Internet café** *n* cybercafé *m*; **Internet Service Provider** *n* fournisseur *m* d'accès à Internet; **Internet user** *n* internaute *m/f*

**interpret** [ɪn'təːprɪt] *vt* interpréter ▷ *vi* servir d'interprète; **interpretation** [ɪntəːprɪ'teɪʃən] *n* interprétation *f*; **interpreter** *n* interprète *m/f*; **could you act as an interpreter for us?** pourriez-vous nous servir d'interprète?

**interrogate** [ɪn'tɛrəʊgeɪt] *vt* interroger; (*suspect etc*) soumettre à un interrogatoire; **interrogation** [ɪntɛrəʊ'geɪʃən] *n* interrogation *f*; (*by police*) interrogatoire *m*

**interrogative** [ɪntə'rɔgətɪv] *adj* interrogateur(-trice) ▷ *n* (*Ling*) interrogatif *m*

**interrupt** [ɪntə'rʌpt] *vt, vi* interrompre; **interruption** [ɪntə'rʌpʃən] *n* interruption *f*

**intersection** [ɪntə'sɛkʃən] *n* (*of roads*) croisement *m*

**interstate** ['ɪntərsteɪt] (*US*) *n*

autoroute *f* (qui relie plusieurs États)

**interval** ['ɪntəvl] *n* intervalle *m*; (*BRIT: Theat*) entracte *m*; (: *Sport*) mi-temps *f*; **at ~s** par intervalles

**intervene** [ɪntə'viːn] *vi* (*time*) s'écouler (entre-temps); (*event*) survenir; (*person*) intervenir

**interview** ['ɪntəvjuː] *n* (*Radio, TV etc*) interview *f*; (*for job*) entrevue *f* ▷ *vt* interviewer; avoir une entrevue avec; **interviewer** *n* (*Radio, TV etc*) interviewer *m*

**intimate** *adj* ['ɪntɪmət] intime; (*friendship*) profond(e); (*knowledge*) approfondi(e) ▷ *vt* ['ɪntɪmeɪt] suggérer, laisser entendre; (*announce*) faire savoir

**intimidate** [ɪn'tɪmɪdeɪt] *vt* intimider

**intimidating** [ɪn'tɪmɪdeɪtɪŋ] *adj* intimidant(e)

**into** ['ɪntu] *prep* dans; **~ pieces/French** en morceaux/français

**intolerant** [ɪn'tɔlərnt] *adj*: **~ (of)** intolérant(e) (de)

**intranet** [ɪn'trənet] *n* intranet *m*

**intransitive** [ɪn'trænsɪtɪv] *adj* intransitif(-ive)

**intricate** ['ɪntrɪkət] *adj* complexe, compliqué(e)

**intrigue** [ɪn'triːg] *n* intrigue *f* ▷ *vt* intriguer; **intriguing** *adj* fascinant(e)

**introduce** [ɪntrə'djuːs] *vt* introduire; (*TV show etc*) présenter; **to ~ sb (to sb)** présenter qn (à qn); **to ~ sb to** (*pastime, technique*) initier qn à; **introduction** [ɪntrə'dʌkʃən] *n* introduction *f*; (*of person*) présentation *f*; (*to new experience*) initiation *f*; **introductory** [ɪntrə'dʌktərɪ] *adj* préliminaire, introductif(-ive)

**intrude** [ɪn'truːd] *vi* (*person*) être importun(e); **to ~ on** *or* **into** (*conversation etc*) s'immiscer dans; **intruder** *n* intrus *m*

**intuition** [ɪntjuː'ɪʃən] *n* intuition *f*

**inundate** ['ɪnʌndeɪt] *vt*: **to ~ with** inonder de

**invade** [ɪn'veɪd] *vt* envahir

**invalid** n ['ɪnvəlɪd] malade m/f; (with disability) invalide m/f ▷ adj [ɪn'vælɪd] (not valid) invalide, non valide

**invaluable** [ɪn'væljuəbl] adj inestimable, inappréciable

**invariably** [ɪn'vɛərɪəblɪ] adv invariablement; **she is ~ late** elle est toujours en retard

**invasion** [ɪn'veɪʒən] n invasion f

**invent** [ɪn'vɛnt] vt inventer; **invention** [ɪn'vɛnʃən] n invention f; **inventor** n inventeur(-trice)

**inventory** ['ɪnvəntrɪ] n inventaire m

**inverted commas** [ɪn'və:tɪd-] npl (BRIT) guillemets mpl

**invest** [ɪn'vɛst] vt investir ▷ vi: **to ~ in** placer de l'argent or investir dans; (fig: acquire) s'offrir, faire l'acquisition de

**investigate** [ɪn'vɛstɪgeɪt] vt étudier, examiner; (crime) faire une enquête sur; **investigation** [ɪnvɛstɪ'geɪʃən] n (of crime) enquête f, investigation f

**investigator** [ɪn'vɛstɪgeɪtə'] n investigateur(-trice); **private ~** détective privé

**investment** [ɪn'vɛstmənt] n investissement m, placement m

**investor** [ɪn'vɛstə'] n épargnant(e); (shareholder) actionnaire m/f

**invisible** [ɪn'vɪzɪbl] adj invisible

**invitation** [ɪnvɪ'teɪʃən] n invitation f

**invite** [ɪn'vaɪt] vt inviter; (opinions etc) demander; **inviting** adj engageant(e), attrayant(e)

**invoice** ['ɪnvɔɪs] n facture f ▷ vt facturer

**involve** [ɪn'vɔlv] vt (entail) impliquer; (concern) concerner; (require) nécessiter; **to ~ sb in** (theft etc) impliquer qn dans; (activity, meeting) faire participer qn à; **involved** adj (complicated) complexe; **to be involved in** (take part) participer à; **involvement** n (personal role) rôle m; (participation) participation f; (enthusiasm) enthousiasme m

**inward** ['ɪnwəd] adj (movement) vers l'intérieur; (thought, feeling) profond(e), intime ▷ adv = **inwards**; **inwards** adv vers l'intérieur

**IQ** n abbr (= intelligence quotient) Q.I. m

**IRA** n abbr (= Irish Republican Army) IRA f

**Iran** [ɪ'rɑ:n] n Iran m; **Iranian** [ɪ'reɪnɪən] adj iranien(ne) ▷ n Iranien(ne)

**Iraq** [ɪ'rɑ:k] n Irak m; **Iraqi** adj irakien(ne) ▷ n Irakien(ne)

**Ireland** ['aɪələnd] n Irlande f

**iris, irises** ['aɪrɪs, -ɪz] n iris m

**Irish** ['aɪrɪʃ] adj irlandais(e) ▷ npl: **the ~** les Irlandais; **Irishman** (irreg) n Irlandais m; **Irishwoman** (irreg) n Irlandaise f

**iron** ['aɪən] n fer m; (for clothes) fer m à repasser ▷ adj de or en fer ▷ vt (clothes) repasser

**ironic(al)** [aɪ'rɔnɪk(l)] adj ironique; **ironically** adv ironiquement

**ironing** ['aɪənɪŋ] n (activity) repassage m; (clothes: ironed) linge repassé; (: to be ironed) linge à repasser; **ironing board** n planche f à repasser

**irony** ['aɪrənɪ] n ironie f

**irrational** [ɪ'ræʃənl] adj irrationnel(le); (person) qui n'est pas rationnel

**irregular** [ɪ'rɛgjulə'] adj irrégulier(-ière); (surface) inégal(e); (action, event) peu orthodoxe

**irrelevant** [ɪ'rɛləvənt] adj sans rapport, hors de propos

**irresistible** [ɪrɪ'zɪstɪbl] adj irrésistible

**irresponsible** [ɪrɪ'spɔnsɪbl] adj (act) irréfléchi(e); (person) qui n'a pas le sens des responsabilités

**irrigation** [ɪrɪ'geɪʃən] n irrigation f

**irritable** ['ɪrɪtəbl] adj irritable

**irritate** ['ɪrɪteɪt] vt irriter; **irritating** adj irritant(e); **irritation** [ɪrɪ'teɪʃən] n irritation f

**IRS** n abbr (US) = **Internal Revenue Service**

**is** [ɪz] vb see **be**

**ISDN** n abbr (= Integrated Services Digital Network) RNIS m

**Islam** ['ɪzlɑ:m] n Islam m; **Islamic** [ɪz'lɑ:mɪk] adj islamique

**island** ['aɪlənd] n île f; (also: **traffic ~**) refuge m (pour piétons); **islander** n

habitant(e) d'une île, insulaire *m/f*
**isle** [aɪl] *n* île *f*
**isn't** ['ɪznt] = **is not**
**isolated** ['aɪsəleɪtɪd] *adj* isolé(e)
**isolation** [aɪsə'leɪʃən] *n* isolement *m*
**ISP** *n abbr* = **Internet Service Provider**
**Israel** ['ɪzreɪl] *n* Israël *m*; **Israeli** [ɪz'reɪlɪ] *adj* israélien(ne) ▷ *n* Israélien(ne)
**issue** ['ɪʃuː] *n* question *f*, problème *m*; (*of banknotes*) émission *f*; (*of newspaper*) numéro *m*; (*of book*) publication *f*, parution *f* ▷ *vt* (*rations, equipment*) distribuer; (*orders*) donner; (*statement*) publier, faire; (*certificate, passport*) délivrer; (*banknotes, cheques, stamps*) émettre, mettre en circulation; **at ~** en jeu, en cause; **to take ~ with sb (over sth)** exprimer son désaccord avec qn (sur qch)
**IT** *n abbr* = **information technology**

○ **KEYWORD**

**it** [ɪt] *pron* **1** (*specific: subject*) il (elle); (*: direct object*) le (la, l'); (*: indirect object*) lui; **it's on the table** c'est *or* il (or elle) est sur la table; **I can't find it** je n'arrive pas à le trouver; **give it to me** donne-le-moi
**2** (*after prep*): **about/from/of it** en; **I spoke to him about it** je lui en ai parlé; **what did you learn from it?** qu'est-ce que vous en avez retiré?; **I'm proud of it** j'en suis fier; **in/to it** y; **put the book in it** mettez-y le livre; **he agreed to it** il y a consenti; **did you go to it?** (*party, concert etc*) est-ce que vous y êtes allé(s)?
**3** (*impersonal*) il; ce, cela, ça; **it's raining** il pleut; **it's Friday tomorrow** demain, c'est vendredi *or* nous sommes, vendredi; **it's 6 o'clock** il est 6 heures; **how far is it? — it's 10 miles** c'est loin? — c'est à 10 miles; **who is it? — it's me** qui est-ce? — c'est moi

**Italian** [ɪ'tæljən] *adj* italien(ne) ▷ *n* Italien(ne); (*Ling*) italien *m*

**italics** [ɪ'tælɪks] *npl* italique *m*
**Italy** ['ɪtəlɪ] *n* Italie *f*
**itch** [ɪtʃ] *n* démangeaison *f* ▷ *vi* (*person*) éprouver des démangeaisons; (*part of body*) démanger; **I'm ~ing to do** l'envie me démange de faire; **itchy** *adj*: **my back is itchy** j'ai le dos qui me démange
**it'd** ['ɪtd] = **it would**; **it had**
**item** ['aɪtəm] *n* (*gen*) article *m*; (*on agenda*) question *f*, point *m*; (*also*: **news ~**) nouvelle *f*
**itinerary** [aɪ'tɪnərərɪ] *n* itinéraire *m*
**it'll** ['ɪtl] = **it will**; **it shall**
**its** [ɪts] *adj* son (sa), ses *pl*
**it's** [ɪts] = **it is**; **it has**
**itself** [ɪt'sɛlf] *pron* (*reflexive*) se; (*emphatic*) lui-même (elle-même)
**ITV** *n abbr* (BRIT: = *Independent Television*) chaîne de télévision commerciale
**I've** [aɪv] = **I have**
**ivory** ['aɪvərɪ] *n* ivoire *m*
**ivy** ['aɪvɪ] *n* lierre *m*

**jab** [dʒæb] *vt*: **to ~ sth into** enfoncer *or* planter qch dans ▷ *n* (*Med: inf*) piqûre *f*

**jack** [dʒæk] *n* (*Aut*) cric *m*; (*Cards*) valet *m*

**jacket** ['dʒækɪt] *n* veste *f*, veston *m*; (*of book*) couverture *f*, jaquette *f*; **jacket potato** *n* pomme *f* de terre en robe des champs

**jackpot** ['dʒækpɔt] *n* gros lot

**Jacuzzi®** [dʒə'kuːzɪ] *n* jacuzzi® *m*

**jagged** ['dʒægɪd] *adj* dentelé(e)

**jail** [dʒeɪl] *n* prison *f* ▷ *vt* emprisonner, mettre en prison; **jail sentence** *n* peine *f* de prison

**jam** [dʒæm] *n* confiture *f*; (*also*: **traffic ~**) embouteillage *m* ▷ *vt* (*passage etc*) encombrer, obstruer; (*mechanism, drawer etc*) bloquer, coincer; (*Radio*) brouiller ▷ *vi* (*mechanism, sliding part*) se coincer, se bloquer; (*gun*) s'enrayer; **to be in a ~** (*inf*) être dans le pétrin; **to ~ sth into** (*stuff*) entasser *or* comprimer qch dans; (*thrust*) enfoncer qch dans

**Jamaica** [dʒə'meɪkə] *n* Jamaïque *f*

**jammed** [dʒæmd] *adj* (*window etc*) coincé(e)

**Jan** *abbr* (= *January*) janv

**janitor** ['dʒænɪtər] *n* (*caretaker*) concierge *m*

**January** ['dʒænjuərɪ] *n* janvier *m*

**Japan** [dʒə'pæn] *n* Japon *m*; **Japanese** [dʒæpə'niːz] *adj* japonais(e) ▷ *n* (*pl inv*) Japonais(e); (*Ling*) japonais *m*

**jar** [dʒɑːr] *n* (*stone, earthenware*) pot *m*; (*glass*) bocal *m* ▷ *vi* (*sound*) produire un son grinçant *or* discordant; (*colours etc*) détonner, jurer

**jargon** ['dʒɑːgən] *n* jargon *m*

**javelin** ['dʒævlɪn] *n* javelot *m*

**jaw** [dʒɔː] *n* mâchoire *f*

**jazz** [dʒæz] *n* jazz *m*

**jealous** ['dʒɛləs] *adj* jaloux(-ouse); **jealousy** *n* jalousie *f*

**jeans** [dʒiːnz] *npl* jean *m*

**Jello®** ['dʒɛləu] (*US*) *n* gelée *f*

**jelly** ['dʒɛlɪ] *n* (*dessert*) gelée *f*; (*US: jam*) confiture *f*; **jellyfish** *n* méduse *f*

**jeopardize** ['dʒɛpədaɪz] *vt* mettre en danger *or* péril

**jerk** [dʒəːk] *n* secousse *f*, saccade *f*; (*of muscle*) spasme *m*; (*inf*) pauvre type *m* ▷ *vt* (*shake*) donner une secousse à; (*pull*) tirer brusquement ▷ *vi* (*vehicles*) cahoter

**jersey** ['dʒəːzɪ] *n* tricot *m*; (*fabric*) jersey *m*

**Jesus** ['dʒiːzəs] *n* Jésus

**jet** [dʒɛt] *n* (*of gas, liquid*) jet *m*; (*Aviat*) avion *m* à réaction, jet *m*; **jet lag** *n* décalage *m* horaire; **jet-ski** *vi* faire du jet-ski *or* scooter des mers

**jetty** ['dʒɛtɪ] *n* jetée *f*, digue *f*

**Jew** [dʒuː] *n* Juif *m*

**jewel** ['dʒuːəl] *n* bijou *m*, joyau *m*; (*in watch*) rubis *m*; **jeweller** (*US* **jeweler**) *n* bijoutier(-ière), joaillier *m*; **jeweller's (shop)** (*US* **jewelry store**) *n* bijouterie *f*, joaillerie *f*; **jewellery** (*US* **jewelry**) *n* bijoux *mpl*

**Jewish** ['dʒuːɪʃ] *adj* juif (juive)

**jigsaw** ['dʒɪgsɔː] *n* (*also*: **~ puzzle**) puzzle *m*

**job** [dʒɔb] *n* (*chore, task*) travail *m*, tâche

f; (*employment*) emploi *m*, poste *m*, place f; **it's a good ~ that ...** c'est heureux *or* c'est une chance que ... + *sub*; **just the ~!** (c'est) juste *or* exactement ce qu'il faut!; **job centre** (BRIT) *n* ≈ ANPE *f*, ≈ Agence nationale pour l'emploi; **jobless** *adj* sans travail, au chômage

**jockey** ['dʒɔkɪ] *n* jockey *m* ▷ *vi*: **to ~ for position** manœuvrer pour être bien placé

**jog** [dʒɔg] *vt* secouer ▷ *vi* (Sport) faire du jogging; **to ~ sb's memory** rafraîchir la mémoire de qn; **jogging** *n* jogging *m*

**join** [dʒɔɪn] *vt* (*put together*) unir, assembler; (*become member of*) s'inscrire à; (*meet*) rejoindre, retrouver; (*queue*) se joindre à ▷ *vi* (*roads, rivers*) se rejoindre, se rencontrer ▷ *n* raccord *m*; **join in** *vi* se mettre de la partie ▷ *vt fus* se mêler à; **join up** *vi* (*meet*) se rejoindre; (*Mil*) s'engager

**joiner** ['dʒɔɪnəʳ] (BRIT) *n* menuisier *m*

**joint** [dʒɔɪnt] *n* (Tech) jointure *f*; joint *m*; (Anat) articulation *f*, jointure; (BRIT Culin) rôti *m*; (*inf: place*) boîte *f*; (*of cannabis*) joint ▷ *adj* commun(e); (*committee*) mixte, paritaire; (*winner*) ex aequo; **joint account** *n* compte joint; **jointly** *adv* ensemble, en commun

**joke** [dʒəʊk] *n* plaisanterie *f*; (*also*: **practical ~**) farce *f* ▷ *vi* plaisanter; **to play a ~ on** jouer un tour à, faire une farce à; **joker** *n* (Cards) joker *m*

**jolly** ['dʒɔlɪ] *adj* gai(e), enjoué(e); (*enjoyable*) amusant(e), plaisant(e) ▷ *adv* (BRIT inf) rudement, drôlement

**jolt** [dʒəʊlt] *n* cahot *m*, secousse *f*; (*shock*) choc *m* ▷ *vt* cahoter, secouer

**Jordan** ['dʒɔːdən] *n* (*country*) Jordanie *f*

**journal** ['dʒəːnl] *n* journal *m*; **journalism** *n* journalisme *m*; **journalist** *n* journaliste *m/f*

**journey** ['dʒəːnɪ] *n* voyage *m*; (*distance covered*) trajet *m*; **the ~ takes two hours** le trajet dure deux heures; **how was your ~?** votre voyage s'est bien passé?

**joy** [dʒɔɪ] *n* joie *f*; **joyrider** *n*

voleur(-euse) de voiture (*qui fait une virée dans le véhicule volé*); **joy stick** *n* (Aviat) manche *m* à balai; (Comput) manche à balai, manette *f* (de jeu)

**Jr** *abbr* = **junior**

**judge** [dʒʌdʒ] *n* juge *m* ▷ *vt* juger; (*estimate: weight, size etc*) apprécier; (*consider*) estimer

**judo** ['dʒuːdəʊ] *n* judo *m*

**jug** [dʒʌg] *n* pot *m*, cruche *f*

**juggle** ['dʒʌgl] *vi* jongler; **juggler** *n* jongleur *m*

**juice** [dʒuːs] *n* jus *m*; **juicy** *adj* juteux(-euse)

**Jul** *abbr* (= *July*) juil

**July** [dʒuː'laɪ] *n* juillet *m*

**jumble** ['dʒʌmbl] *n* fouillis *m* ▷ *vt* (*also*: **~ up, ~ together**) mélanger, brouiller; **jumble sale** *n* (BRIT) vente *f* de charité

⬤ **JUMBLE SALE**
⬤
⬤ Les **jumble sales** ont lieu dans les
⬤ églises, salles des fêtes ou halls
⬤ d'écoles, et l'on y vend des articles
⬤ de toutes sortes, en général bon
⬤ marché et surtout d'occasion, pour
⬤ collecter des fonds pour une œuvre
⬤ de charité, une école (par exemple,
⬤ pour acheter un ordinateur), ou
⬤ encore une église (pour réparer un
⬤ toit etc).

**jumbo** ['dʒʌmbəʊ] *adj* (*also*: **~ jet**) (avion) gros porteur (à réaction)

**jump** [dʒʌmp] *vi* sauter, bondir; (*with fear etc*) sursauter; (*increase*) monter en flèche ▷ *vt* sauter, franchir ▷ *n* saut *m*, bond *m*; (*with fear etc*) sursaut *m*; (*fence*) obstacle *m*; **to ~ the queue** (BRIT) passer avant son tour

**jumper** ['dʒʌmpəʳ] *n* (BRIT: *pullover*) pull-over *m*; (US: *pinafore dress*) robe-chasuble *f*

**jump leads** (US **jumper cables**) *npl* câbles *mpl* de démarrage

**Jun.** *abbr* = **June**; **junior**

**junction** ['dʒʌŋkʃən] *n* (BRIT:

*of roads)* carrefour *m*; *(of rails)*
embranchement *m*

**June** [dʒuːn] *n* juin *m*

**jungle** ['dʒʌŋgl] *n* jungle *f*

**junior** ['dʒuːnɪəʳ] *adj, n*: **he's ~ to me
(by 2 years), he's my ~ (by 2 years)**
il est mon cadet (de 2 ans), il est plus
jeune que moi (de 2 ans); **he's ~ to me**
*(seniority)* il est en dessous de moi (dans
la hiérarchie), j'ai plus d'ancienneté que
lui; **junior high school** *n (US)* ≈ collège
*m* d'enseignement secondaire; *see also*
**high school**; **junior school** *n (BRIT)*
école *f* primaire, cours moyen

**junk** [dʒʌŋk] *n (rubbish)* camelote *f*;
*(cheap goods)* bric-à-brac *m inv*; **junk
food** *n* snacks vite prêts *(sans valeur
nutritive)*

**junkie** ['dʒʌŋkɪ] *n (inf)* junkie *m*,
drogué(e)

**junk mail** *n* prospectus *mpl*; *(Comput)*
messages *mpl* publicitaires

**Jupiter** ['dʒuːpɪtəʳ] *n (planet)* Jupiter *f*

**jurisdiction** [dʒuərɪs'dɪkʃən] *n*
juridiction *f*; **it falls** *or* **comes within/
outside our ~** cela est/n'est pas de
notre compétence *or* ressort

**jury** ['dʒuərɪ] *n* jury *m*

**just** [dʒʌst] *adj* juste ▷ *adv*: **he's ~ done
it/left** il vient de le faire/partir; **~
right/two o'clock** exactement *or* juste
ce qu'il faut/deux heures; **we were ~
going** nous partions; **I was ~ about to
phone** j'allais téléphoner; **~ as he was
leaving** au moment *or* à l'instant précis
où il partait; **~ before/enough/here**
juste avant/assez/là; **it's ~ me/a
mistake** ce n'est que moi/(rien) qu'une
erreur; **~ missed/caught** manqué/
attrapé de justesse; **~ listen to this!**
écoutez un peu ça!; **she's ~ as clever
as you** elle est tout aussi intelligente
que vous; **it's ~ as well that you ...**
heureusement que vous ...; **~ a
minute!, ~ one moment!** un instant
(s'il vous plaît)!

**justice** ['dʒʌstɪs] *n* justice *f*; *(US: judge)*
juge *m* de la Cour suprême

**justification** [dʒʌstɪfɪ'keɪʃən] *n*
justification *f*

**justify** ['dʒʌstɪfaɪ] *vt* justifier

**jut** [dʒʌt] *vi (also: ~ out)* dépasser,
faire saillie

**juvenile** ['dʒuːvənaɪl] *adj* juvénile;
*(court, books)* pour enfants ▷ *n*
adolescent(e)

# K

**K, k** [keɪ] *abbr* (= *one thousand*) K;
(= *kilobyte*) Ko
**kangaroo** [kæŋgəˈruː] *n* kangourou *m*
**karaoke** [kɑːrəˈəʊkɪ] *n* karaoké *m*
**karate** [kəˈrɑːtɪ] *n* karaté *m*
**kebab** [kəˈbæb] *n* kébab *m*
**keel** [kiːl] *n* quille *f*; **on an even ~**
(*fig*) à flot
**keen** [kiːn] *adj* (*eager*) plein(e)
d'enthousiasme; (*interest, desire,
competition*) vif (vive); (*eye, intelligence*)
pénétrant(e); (*edge*) effilé(e); **to be ~ to
do** *or* **on doing sth** désirer vivement
faire qch, tenir beaucoup à faire qch;
**to be ~ on sth/sb** aimer beaucoup
qch/qn
**keep** [kiːp] (*pt, pp* **kept**) *vt* (*retain,
preserve*) garder; (*hold back*) retenir;
(*shop, accounts, promise, diary*) tenir;
(*support*) entretenir; (*chickens, bees,
pigs etc*) élever ▷ *vi* (*food*) se conserver;
(*remain: in a certain state or place*)
rester ▷ *n* (*of castle*) donjon *m*; (*food
etc*): **enough for his ~** assez pour

(assurer) sa subsistance; **to ~ doing
sth** (*continue*) continuer à faire qch;
(*repeatedly*) ne pas arrêter de faire
qch; **to ~ sb from doing/sth from
happening** empêcher qn de faire *or* que
qn (ne) fasse/que qch (n')arrive; **to ~ sb
happy/a place tidy** faire qn soit
content/qu'un endroit reste propre; **to
~ sth to o.s.** garder qch pour soi, tenir
qch secret; **to ~ sth from sb** cacher qch
à qn; **to ~ time** (*clock*) être à l'heure,
ne pas retarder; **for ~s** (*inf*) pour de
bon, pour toujours; **keep away** *vt*: **to
~ sth/sb away from sb** tenir qch/qn
éloigné de qn ▷ *vi*: **to ~ away (from)**
ne pas s'approcher (de); **keep back** *vt*
(*crowds, tears, money*) retenir; (*conceal:
information*): **to ~ sth back from sb**
cacher qch à qn ▷ *vi* rester en arrière;
**keep off** *vt* (*dog, person*) éloigner ▷ *vi*: **if
the rain ~s off** s'il ne pleut pas; **~
your hands off!** pas touche! (*inf*); "**~
off the grass**" "pelouse interdite"; **keep on** *vi*
continuer; **to ~ on doing** continuer à
faire; **don't ~ on about it!** arrête (d'en
parler)!; **keep out** *vt* empêcher d'entrer
▷ *vi* (*stay out*) rester en dehors; "**~ out**"
"défense d'entrer"; **keep up** *vi* (*fig: in
comprehension*) suivre ▷ *vt* continuer,
maintenir; **to ~ up with sb** (*in work
etc*) se maintenir au même niveau
que qn; (*in race etc*) aller aussi vite que
qn; **keeper** *n* gardien(ne); **keep-fit** *n*
gymnastique *f* (d'entretien); **keeping**
*n* (*care*) garde *f*; **in keeping with** en
harmonie avec
**kennel** ['kɛnl] *n* niche *f*; **kennels** *npl*
(*for boarding*) chenil *m*
**Kenya** ['kɛnjə] *n* Kenya *m*
**kept** [kɛpt] *pt, pp of* **keep**
**kerb** [kəːb] *n* (*BRIT*) bordure *f* du trottoir
**kerosene** ['kɛrəsiːn] *n* kérosène *m*
**ketchup** ['kɛtʃəp] *n* ketchup *m*
**kettle** ['kɛtl] *n* bouilloire *f*
**key** [kiː] *n* (*gen, Mus*) clé *f*; (*of piano,
typewriter*) touche *f*; (*on map*) légende
*f* ▷ *adj* (*factor, role, area*) clé *inv* ▷ *vt*
(*also: ~ in: text*) saisir; **can I have my**

**~?** je peux avoir ma clé?; **a ~ issue** un problème fondamental; **keyboard** n clavier m; **keyhole** n trou m de la serrure; **keyring** n porte-clés m

**kg** abbr (= kilogram) K

**khaki** ['kɑːkɪ] adj, n kaki m

**kick** [kɪk] vt donner un coup de pied à ▷ vi (horse) ruer ▷ n coup m de pied; (inf: thrill): **he does it for ~s** il le fait parce que ça l'excite, il le fait pour le plaisir; **to ~ the habit** (inf) arrêter; **kick off** vi (Sport) donner le coup d'envoi; **kick-off** n (Sport) coup m d'envoi

**kid** [kɪd] n (inf: child) gamin(e), gosse m/f; (animal, leather) chevreau m ▷ vi (inf) plaisanter, blaguer

**kidnap** ['kɪdnæp] vt enlever, kidnapper; **kidnapping** n enlèvement m

**kidney** ['kɪdnɪ] n (Anat) rein m; (Culin) rognon m; **kidney bean** n haricot m rouge

**kill** [kɪl] vt tuer ▷ n mise f à mort; **to ~ time** tuer le temps; **killer** n tueur(-euse); (murderer) meurtrier(-ière); **killing** n meurtre m; (of group of people) tuerie f, massacre m; (inf): **to make a killing** se remplir les poches, réussir un beau coup

**kiln** [kɪln] n four m

**kilo** ['kiːləʊ] n kilo m; **kilobyte** n (Comput) kilo-octet m; **kilogram(me)** n kilogramme m; **kilometre** (us **kilometer**) ['kɪləmiːtəʳ] n kilomètre m; **kilowatt** n kilowatt m

**kilt** [kɪlt] n kilt m

**kin** [kɪn] n see **next-of-kin**

**kind** [kaɪnd] adj gentil(le), aimable ▷ n sorte f, espèce f; (species) genre m; **to be two of a ~** se ressembler; **in ~** (Comm) en nature; **~ of** (inf: rather) plutôt; **a ~ of** une sorte de; **what ~ of ...?** quelle sorte de ...?

**kindergarten** ['kɪndəɡɑːtn] n jardin m d'enfants

**kindly** ['kaɪndlɪ] adj bienveillant(e), plein(e) de gentillesse ▷ adv avec bonté; **will you ~ ...** auriez-vous la bonté or l'obligeance de ...

**kindness** ['kaɪndnɪs] n (quality) bonté f, gentillesse f

**king** [kɪŋ] n roi m; **kingdom** n royaume m; **kingfisher** n martin-pêcheur m; **king-size(d) bed** n grand lit (de 1,95 m de large)

**kiosk** ['kiːɔsk] n kiosque m; (BRIT: also: **telephone ~**) cabine f (téléphonique)

**kipper** ['kɪpəʳ] n hareng fumé et salé

**kiss** [kɪs] n baiser m ▷ vt embrasser; **to ~ (each other)** s'embrasser; **kiss of life** n (BRIT) bouche à bouche m

**kit** [kɪt] n équipement m, matériel m; (set of tools etc) trousse f; (for assembly) kit m

**kitchen** ['kɪtʃɪn] n cuisine f

**kite** [kaɪt] n (toy) cerf-volant m

**kitten** ['kɪtn] n petit chat, chaton m

**kitty** ['kɪtɪ] n (money) cagnotte f

**kiwi** ['kiːwiː] n (also: **~ fruit**) kiwi m

**km** abbr (= kilometre) km

**km/h** abbr (= kilometres per hour) km/h

**knack** [næk] n: **to have the ~ (of doing)** avoir le coup (pour faire)

**knee** [niː] n genou m; **kneecap** n rotule f

**kneel** (pt, pp **knelt**) [niːl, nɛlt] vi (also: **~ down**) s'agenouiller

**knelt** [nɛlt] pt, pp of **kneel**

**knew** [njuː] pt of **know**

**knickers** ['nɪkəz] npl (BRIT) culotte f (de femme)

**knife** [naɪf] n (pl **knives**) couteau m ▷ vt poignarder, frapper d'un coup de couteau

**knight** [naɪt] n chevalier m; (Chess) cavalier m

**knit** [nɪt] vt tricoter ▷ vi tricoter; (broken bones) se ressouder; **to ~ one's brows** froncer les sourcils; **knitting** n tricot m; **knitting needle** n aiguille f à tricoter; **knitwear** n tricots mpl, lainages mpl

**knives** [naɪvz] npl of **knife**

**knob** [nɔb] n bouton m; (BRIT): **a ~ of butter** une noix de beurre

**knock** [nɔk] vt frapper; (bump into) heurter; (fig: col) dénigrer ▷ vi (at *door etc*): **to ~ at/on** frapper à/sur ▷ *n* coup *m*; **knock down** *vt* renverser; (*price*) réduire; **knock off** *vi* (*inf: finish*) s'arrêter (de travailler) ▷ *vt* (*vase, object*) faire tomber; (*inf: steal*) piquer; (*fig: from price etc*): **to ~ off £10** faire une remise de 10 livres; **knock out** *vt* assommer; (*Boxing*) mettre k.-o.; (*in competition*) éliminer; **knock over** *vt* (*object*) faire tomber; (*pedestrian*) renverser; **knockout** *n* (*Boxing*) knock-out *m*, K.-O. *m*; **knockout competition** (*BRIT*) compétition *f* avec épreuves éliminatoires

**knot** [nɔt] *n* (*gen*) nœud *m* ▷ *vt* nouer

**know** [nəu] *vt* (*pt* **knew**, *pp* **~n**) savoir; (*person, place*) connaître; **to ~ that** savoir que; **to ~ how to do** savoir faire; **to ~ how to swim** savoir nager; **to ~ about/of sth** (*event*) être au courant de qch; (*subject*) connaître qch; **I don't ~** je ne sais pas; **do you ~ where I can ...?** savez-vous où je peux ...?; **know-all** *n* (*BRIT pej*) je-sais-tout *m/f*; **know-how** *n* savoir-faire *m*, technique *f*, compétence *f*; **knowing** *adj* (*look etc*) entendu(e); **knowingly** *adv* (*on purpose*) sciemment; (*smile, look*) d'un air entendu; **know-it-all** *n* (*US*) = **know-all**

**knowledge** ['nɔlɪdʒ] *n* connaissance *f*; (*learning*) connaissances, savoir *m*; **without my ~** à mon insu; **knowledgeable** *adj* bien informé(e)

**known** [nəun] *pp of* **know** ▷ *adj* (*thief, facts*) notoire; (*expert*) célèbre

**knuckle** ['nʌkl] *n* articulation *f* (des phalanges), jointure *f*

**koala** [kəu'ɑːlə] *n* (*also*: **~ bear**) koala *m*

**Koran** [kɔ'rɑːn] *n* Coran *m*

**Korea** [kə'rɪə] *n* Corée *f*; **Korean** *adj* coréen(ne) ▷ *n* Coréen(ne)

**kosher** ['kəuʃə'] *adj* kascher *inv*

**Kosovar, Kosovan** ['kɔsəvɑː', 'kɔsəvən] *adj* kosovar(e)

**Kosovo** ['kɔsəvəu] *n* Kosovo *m*

**Kuwait** [ku'weɪt] *n* Koweït *m*

**L** *abbr* (*BRIT Aut*: = *learner*) *signale un conducteur débutant*

**l.** *abbr* (= *litre*) l

**lab** [læb] *n abbr* (= *laboratory*) labo *m*

**label** ['leɪbl] *n* étiquette *f*; (*brand: of record*) marque *f* ▷ *vt* étiqueter

**labor** *etc* ['leɪbə'] (*US*) = **labour** *etc*

**laboratory** [lə'bɔrətərɪ] *n* laboratoire *m*

**Labor Day** *n* (*US, CANADA*) fête *f* du travail (*le premier lundi de septembre*)

- **LABOR DAY**
-
- La fête du Travail aux États-Unis et au
- Canada est fixée au premier lundi de
- septembre. Instituée par le Congrès
- en 1894 après avoir été réclamée par
- les mouvements ouvriers pendant
- douze ans, elle a perdu une grande
- partie de son caractère politique
- pour devenir un jour férié assez
- ordinaire et l'occasion de partir pour
- un long week-end avant la rentrée
- des classes.

**labor union** n (US) syndicat m
**Labour** ['leɪbər] n (BRIT Pol: also:
**the ~ Party**) le parti travailliste, les
travaillistes mpl
**labour** (US **labor**) ['leɪbər] n (work)
travail m; (workforce) main-d'œuvre f
▷ vi: **to ~ (at)** travailler dur (à), peiner
(sur) ▷ vt: **to ~ a point** insister sur un
point; **in ~** (Med) en travail; **labourer** n
manœuvre m; **farm labourer** ouvrier
m agricole
**lace** [leɪs] n dentelle f; (of shoe etc) lacet
m ▷ vt (shoe: also: ~ **up**) lacer
**lack** [læk] n manque m ▷ vt manquer
de; **through** or **for ~ of** faute de, par
manque de; **to be ~ing** manquer, faire
défaut; **to be ~ing in** manquer de
**lacquer** ['lækər] n laque f
**lacy** ['leɪsɪ] adj (of lace) en dentelle; (like
lace) comme de la dentelle
**lad** [læd] n garçon m, gars m
**ladder** ['lædər] n échelle f; (BRIT:
in tights) maille filée ▷ vt, vi (BRIT:
tights) filer
**ladle** ['leɪdl] n louche f
**lady** ['leɪdɪ] n dame f; **"ladies and
gentlemen ..."** "Mesdames (et)
Messieurs ..."; **young ~** jeune fille f;
(married) jeune femme f; **the ladies'
(room)** les toilettes fpl des dames;
**ladybird** (US **ladybug**) n coccinelle f
**lag** [læg] n retard m ▷ vi (also: ~ **behind**)
rester en arrière, traîner; (fig) rester à la
traîne ▷ vt (pipes) calorifuger
**lager** ['lɑːgər] n bière blonde
**lagoon** [lə'guːn] n lagune f
**laid** [leɪd] pt, pp of **lay**; **laid back** adj (inf)
relaxe, décontracté(e)
**lain** [leɪn] pp of **lie**
**lake** [leɪk] n lac m
**lamb** [læm] n agneau m
**lame** [leɪm] adj (also fig) boiteux(-euse)
**lament** [lə'mɛnt] n lamentation f ▷ vt
pleurer, se lamenter sur
**lamp** [læmp] n lampe f; **lamppost**
n (BRIT) réverbère m; **lampshade** n
abat-jour m inv
**land** [lænd] n (as opposed to sea)

terre f (ferme); (country) pays m; (soil)
terre; (piece of land) terrain m; (estate)
terre(s), domaine(s) m(pl) ▷ vi (from
ship) débarquer; (Aviat) atterrir; (fig:
fall) (re)tomber ▷ vt (passengers,
goods) débarquer; (obtain) décrocher;
**to ~ sb with sth** (inf) coller qch à qn;
**landing** n (from ship) débarquement
m; (Aviat) atterrissage m; (of staircase)
palier m; **landing card** n carte f
de débarquement; **landlady** n
propriétaire f, logeuse f; (of pub)
patronne f; **landlord** n propriétaire
m, logeur m; (of pub etc) patron m;
**landmark** n (point m de) repère m;
**to be a landmark** (fig) faire date or
époque; **landowner** n propriétaire
foncier or terrien; **landscape**
n paysage m; **landslide** n (Geo)
glissement m (de terrain); (fig: Pol) raz-
de-marée (électoral)
**lane** [leɪn] n (in country) chemin m; (Aut:
of road) voie f; (: line of traffic) file f; (in
race) couloir m
**language** ['læŋgwɪdʒ] n langue f; (way
one speaks) langage m; **what ~s do you
speak?** quelles langues parlez-vous?;
**bad ~** grossièretés fpl, langage grossier;
**language laboratory** n laboratoire m
de langues; **language school** n école
f de langue
**lantern** ['læntn] n lanterne f
**lap** [læp] n (of track) tour m (de piste); (of
body): **in** or **on one's ~** sur les genoux
▷ vt (also: ~ **up**) laper ▷ vi (waves)
clapoter
**lapel** [lə'pɛl] n revers m
**lapse** [læps] n défaillance f; (in
behaviour) écart m (de conduite) ▷ vi
(Law) cesser d'être en vigueur; (contract)
expirer; **to ~ into bad habits** prendre
de mauvaises habitudes; **~ of time** laps
m de temps, intervalle m
**laptop (computer)** ['læptɒp-] n
portable m
**lard** [lɑːd] n saindoux m
**larder** ['lɑːdər] n garde-manger m inv
**large** [lɑːdʒ] adj grand(e); (person,

*animal*) gros (grosse); **at ~** (*free*) en liberté; (*generally*) en général; pour la plupart; *see also* **by**; **largely** *adv* en grande partie; (*principally*) surtout; **large-scale** *adj* (*map, drawing etc*) à grande échelle; (*fig*) important(e)

**lark** [lɑːk] *n* (*bird*) alouette *f*; (*joke*) blague *f*, farce *f*

**laryngitis** [lærɪnˈdʒaɪtɪs] *n* laryngite *f*

**lasagne** [ləˈzænjə] *n* lasagne *f*

**laser** [ˈleɪzəʳ] *n* laser *m*; **laser printer** *n* imprimante *f* laser

**lash** [læʃ] *n* coup *m* de fouet; (*also:* **eye~**) cil *m* ▷ *vt* fouetter; (*tie*) attacher; **lash out** *vi*: **to ~ out (at** or **against sb/sth)** attaquer violemment (qn/qch)

**lass** [læs] (*BRIT*) *n* (jeune) fille *f*

**last** [lɑːst] *adj* dernier(-ière) ▷ *adv* en dernier; (*most recently*) la dernière fois; (*finally*) finalement ▷ *vi* durer; **~ week** la semaine dernière; **~ night** (*evening*) hier soir; (*night*) la nuit dernière; **at ~** enfin; **~ but one** avant-dernier(-ière); **lastly** *adv* en dernier lieu, pour finir; **last-minute** *adj* de dernière minute

**latch** [lætʃ] *n* loquet *m*; **latch onto** *vt fus* (*cling to: person, group*) s'accrocher à; (*idea*) se mettre en tête

**late** [leɪt] *adj* (*not on time*) en retard; (*far on in day etc*) tardif(-ive); (*: edition, delivery*) dernier(-ière); (*dead*) défunt(e) ▷ *adv* tard; (*behind time, schedule*) en retard; **to be 10 minutes ~** avoir 10 minutes de retard; **sorry I'm ~** désolé d'être en retard; **it's too ~** il est trop tard; **of ~** dernièrement; **in ~ May** vers la fin (du mois) de mai, fin mai; **the ~ Mr X** feu M. X; **latecomer** *n* retardataire *m/f*; **lately** *adv* récemment; **later** *adj* (*date etc*) ultérieur(e); (*version etc*) plus récent(e) ▷ *adv* plus tard; **latest** [ˈleɪtɪst] *adj* tout(e) dernier(-ière); **at the latest** au plus tard

**lather** [ˈlɑːðəʳ] *n* mousse *f* (de savon) ▷ *vt* savonner

**Latin** [ˈlætɪn] *n* latin *m* ▷ *adj* latin(e); **Latin America** *n* Amérique latine;

**Latin American** *adj* latino-américain(e), d'Amérique latine ▷ *n* Latino-Américain(e)

**latitude** [ˈlætɪtjuːd] *n* (*also fig*) latitude *f*

**latter** [ˈlætəʳ] *adj* deuxième, dernier(-ière) ▷ *n*: **the ~** ce dernier, celui-ci

**laugh** [lɑːf] *n* rire *m* ▷ *vi* rire; **(to do sth) for a ~** (faire qch) pour rire; **laugh at** *vt fus* se moquer de; (*joke*) rire de; **laughter** *n* rire *m*; (*of several people*) rires *mpl*

**launch** [lɔːntʃ] *n* lancement *m*; (*also: motor ~*) vedette *f* ▷ *vt* (*ship, rocket, plan*) lancer; **launch into** *vt fus* se lancer dans

**launder** [ˈlɔːndəʳ] *vt* laver; (*fig: money*) blanchir

**Launderette®** [lɔːnˈdrɛt] (*BRIT*) (*US* **Laundromat®** [ˈlɔːndrəmæt]) *n* laverie *f* (automatique)

**laundry** [ˈlɔːndrɪ] *n* (*clothes*) linge *m*; (*business*) blanchisserie *f*; (*room*) buanderie *f*; **to do the ~** faire la lessive

**lava** [ˈlɑːvə] *n* lave *f*

**lavatory** [ˈlævətərɪ] *n* toilettes *fpl*

**lavender** [ˈlævəndəʳ] *n* lavande *f*

**lavish** [ˈlævɪʃ] *adj* (*amount*) copieux(-euse); (*person: giving freely*): **~ with** prodigue de ▷ *vt*: **to ~ sth on sb** prodiguer qch à qn; (*money*) dépenser qch sans compter pour qn

**law** [lɔː] *n* loi *f*; (*science*) droit *m*; **lawful** *adj* légal(e), permis(e); **lawless** *adj* (*action*) illégal(e); (*place*) sans loi

**lawn** [lɔːn] *n* pelouse *f*; **lawnmower** *n* tondeuse *f* à gazon

**lawsuit** [ˈlɔːsuːt] *n* procès *m*

**lawyer** [ˈlɔːjəʳ] *n* (*consultant, with company*) juriste *m*; (*for sales, wills etc*) ≈ notaire *m*; (*partner, in court*) ≈ avocat *m*

**lax** [læks] *adj* relâché(e)

**laxative** [ˈlæksətɪv] *n* laxatif *m*

**lay** [leɪ] *pt of* **lie** ▷ *adj* laïque; (*not expert*) profane ▷ *vt* (*pt, pp* **laid**) poser, mettre; (*eggs*) pondre; (*trap*) tendre; (*plans*) élaborer; **to ~ the table** mettre la table;

**lay down** vt poser; (*rules etc*) établir; **to ~ down the law** (*fig*) faire la loi; **lay off** vt (*workers*) licencier; (*provide: meal etc*) fournir; **lay out** vt (*design*) dessiner, concevoir; (*display*) disposer; (*spend*) dépenser; **lay-by** n (BRIT) aire f de stationnement (sur le bas-côté)

**layer** ['leɪə'] n couche f

**layman** ['leɪmən] (*irreg*) n (*Rel*) laïque m; (*non-expert*) profane m

**layout** ['leɪaʊt] n disposition f, plan m, agencement m; (*Press*) mise f en page

**lazy** ['leɪzɪ] adj paresseux(-euse)

**lb.** abbr (*weight*) = **pound**

**lead¹** [liːd] n (*front position*) tête f; (*distance, time ahead*) avance f; (*clue*) piste f; (*Elec*) fil m; (*for dog*) laisse f; (*Theat*) rôle principal ▷ vb (*pt, pp* **led**) ▷ vt (*guide*) mener, conduire; (*be leader of*) être à la tête de ▷ vi (*Sport*) mener, être en tête; **to ~ to** (*road, pipe*) mener à, conduire à; (*result in*) conduire à; aboutir à; **to be in the ~** (*Sport: in race*) mener, être en tête; (*: in match*) mener (à la marque); **to ~ sb to do sth** amener qn à faire qch; **to ~ the way** montrer le chemin; **lead up to** vt conduire à; (*in conversation*) en venir à

**lead²** [lɛd] n (*metal*) plomb m; (*in pencil*) mine f

**leader** ['liːdə'] n (*of team*) chef m; (*of party etc*) dirigeant(e), leader m; (*Sport: in league*) leader; (*: in race*) coureur m de tête; **leadership** n (*position*) direction f; **under the leadership of ...** sous la direction de ...; **qualities of leadership** qualités fpl de chef or de meneur

**lead-free** ['lɛdfriː] adj sans plomb

**leading** ['liːdɪŋ] adj de premier plan; (*main*) principal(e); (*in race*) de tête

**lead singer** [liːd-] n (*in pop group*) (chanteur m) vedette f

**leaf** (*pl* **leaves**) [liːf, liːvz] n feuille f; (*of table*) rallonge f; **to turn over a new ~** (*fig*) changer de conduite or d'existence; **leaf through** vt (*book*) feuilleter

**leaflet** ['liːflɪt] n prospectus m, brochure f; (*Pol, Rel*) tract m

**league** [liːg] n ligue f; (*Football*) championnat m; **to be in ~ with** avoir partie liée avec, être de mèche avec

**leak** [liːk] n (*out: also fig*) fuite f ▷ vi (*pipe, liquid etc*) fuir; (*shoes*) prendre l'eau; (*ship*) faire eau ▷ vt (*liquid*) répandre; (*information*) divulguer

**lean** [liːn] adj maigre ▷ vb (*pt, pp* **~ed** or **~t**) ▷ vt: **to ~ sth on** appuyer qch sur ▷ vi (*slope*) pencher; (*rest*): **to ~ against** s'appuyer contre; être appuyé(e) contre; **to ~ on** s'appuyer sur; **lean forward** vi se pencher en avant; **lean over** vi se pencher; **leaning** n: **leaning (towards)** penchant m (pour)

**leant** [lɛnt] pt, pp of **lean**

**leap** [liːp] n bond m, saut m ▷ vi (*pt, pp* **~ed** or **~t**) bondir, sauter

**leapt** [lɛpt] pt, pp of **leap**

**leap year** n année f bissextile

**learn** (*pt, pp* **~ed** or **~t**) [ləːn, -t] vt, vi apprendre; **to ~ (how) to do sth** apprendre à faire qch; **to ~ about sth** (*Scol*) étudier qch; (*hear, read*) apprendre qch; **learner** n débutant(e); (BRIT: *also*: **learner driver**) (conducteur(-trice)) débutant(e); **learning** n savoir m

**learnt** [ləːnt] pp of **learn**

**lease** [liːs] n bail m ▷ vt louer à bail

**leash** [liːʃ] n laisse f

**least** [liːst] adj: **the ~** (+ *noun*) le (la) plus petit(e), le (la) moindre; (*smallest amount of*) le moins de ▷ pron: **(the) ~** le moins ▷ adv (+ *verb*) le moins; (+ *adj*): **the ~** le (la) moins; **the ~ money** le moins d'argent; **the ~ expensive** le (la) moins cher (chère); **the ~ possible effort** le moins d'effort possible; **at ~** au moins; (*or rather*) du moins; **you could at ~ have written** tu aurais au moins pu écrire; **not in the ~** pas le moins du monde

**leather** ['lɛðə'] n cuir m

**leave** [liːv] (vb: *pt, pp* **left**) vt laisser; (*go away from*) quitter; (*forget*) oublier ▷ vi partir, s'en aller ▷ n (*time off*) congé m; (*Mil, also: consent*) permission f; **what time does the train/bus ~?** le train/le bus part à quelle heure?; **to ~ sth to sb** (money etc) laisser qch à qn; **to be left** rester; **there's some milk left over** il reste du lait; **~ it to me!** laissez-moi faire!, je m'en occupe!; **on ~** en permission; **leave behind** vt (also fig) laisser; (forget) laisser, oublier; **leave out** vt oublier, omettre

**leaves** [liːvz] npl of **leaf**

**Lebanon** ['lɛbənən] n Liban m

**lecture** ['lɛktʃəʳ] n conférence f; (Scol) cours (magistral) ▷ vi donner des cours; enseigner ▷ vt (scold) sermonner, réprimander; **to give a ~ (on)** faire une conférence (sur), faire un cours (sur); **lecture hall** n amphithéâtre m; **lecturer** n (speaker) conférencier(-ière); (BRIT: at university) professeur m (d'université), prof m/f de fac (inf); **lecture theatre** n = **lecture hall**

> Be careful not to translate **lecture** by the French word **lecture**.

**led** [lɛd] pt, pp of **lead¹**

**ledge** [lɛdʒ] n (of window, on wall) rebord m; (of mountain) saillie f, corniche f

**leek** [liːk] n poireau m

**left** [lɛft] pt, pp of **leave** ▷ adj gauche ▷ adv à gauche ▷ n gauche f; **there are two ~** il en reste deux; **on the ~, to the ~** à gauche; **the L~** (Pol) la gauche; **left-hand** adj: **the left-hand side** la gauche; **left-hand drive** n (BRIT: vehicle) véhicule m avec la conduite à gauche; **left-handed** adj gaucher(-ère); (scissors etc) pour gauchers; **left-luggage locker** n (BRIT) (casier m à) consigne f automatique; **left-luggage (office)** n (BRIT) consigne f; **left-overs** npl restes mpl; **left-wing** adj (Pol) de gauche

**leg** [lɛg] n jambe f; (of animal) patte f; (of furniture) pied m; (Culin: of chicken) cuisse f; (of journey) étape f; **1st/2nd ~** (Sport) match m aller/retour; **~ of lamb** (Culin) gigot m d'agneau

**legacy** ['lɛgəsɪ] n (also fig) héritage m, legs m

**legal** ['liːgl] adj (permitted by law) légal(e); (relating to law) juridique; **legal holiday** (US) n jour férié; **legalize** vt légaliser; **legally** adv légalement

**legend** ['lɛdʒənd] n légende f; **legendary** ['lɛdʒəndərɪ] adj légendaire

**leggings** ['lɛgɪŋz] npl caleçon m

**legible** ['lɛdʒəbl] adj lisible

**legislation** [lɛdʒɪs'leɪʃən] n législation f

**legislative** ['lɛdʒɪslətɪv] adj législatif(-ive)

**legitimate** [lɪ'dʒɪtɪmət] adj légitime

**leisure** ['lɛʒəʳ] n (free time) temps libre, loisirs mpl; **at ~** (tout) à loisir; **at your ~** (later) à tête reposée; **leisure centre** n (BRIT) centre m de loisirs; **leisurely** adj tranquille, fait(e) sans se presser

**lemon** ['lɛmən] n citron m; **lemonade** n (fizzy) limonade f; **lemon tea** n thé m au citron

**lend** [lɛnd] (pt, pp **lent**) [lɛnd, lɛnt] vt: **to ~ sth (to sb)** prêter qch (à qn); **could you ~ me some money?** pourriez-vous me prêter de l'argent?

**length** [lɛŋθ] n longueur f; (section: of road, pipe etc) morceau m, bout m; **~ of time** durée f; **it is 2 metres in ~** cela fait 2 mètres de long; **at ~** (at last) enfin, à la fin; (lengthily) longuement; **lengthen** vt allonger, prolonger ▷ vi s'allonger; **lengthways** adv dans le sens de la longueur, en long; **lengthy** adj (très) long (longue)

**lens** [lɛnz] n lentille f; (of spectacles) verre m; (of camera) objectif m

**Lent** [lɛnt] n carême m

**lent** [lɛnt] pt, pp of **lend**

**lentil** ['lɛntl] n lentille f

**Leo** ['liːəu] n le Lion

**leopard** ['lɛpəd] n léopard m

**leotard** ['liːətɑːd] n justaucorps m

**leprosy** ['lɛprəsɪ] n lèpre f

**lesbian** ['lɛzbɪən] n lesbienne f ▷ adj lesbien(ne)

**less** [lɛs] adj moins de ▷ pron, adv moins ▷ prep: **~ tax/10% discount** avant impôt/moins 10% de remise; **~ than**

**that/you** moins que cela/vous; **~ than half** moins de la moitié; **~ than ever** moins que jamais; **~ and ~** de moins en moins; **the ~ he works ...** moins il travaille ...; **lessen** vi diminuer, s'amoindrir, s'atténuer ▷ vt diminuer, réduire, atténuer; **lesser** ['lɛsə<sup>r</sup>] adj moindre; **to a lesser extent** or **degree** à un degré moindre

**lesson** ['lɛsn] n leçon f; **to teach sb a ~** (fig) donner une bonne leçon à qn

**let** (pt, pp ~) [lɛt] vt laisser; (BRIT: lease) louer; **to ~ sb do sth** laisser qn faire qch; **to ~ sb know sth** faire savoir qch à qn, prévenir qn de qch; **~ go** lâcher prise; **to ~ go of sth**, **to ~ sth go** lâcher qch; **~'s go** allons-y; **~ him come** qu'il vienne; **"to ~"** (BRIT) "à louer"; **let down** vt (lower) baisser; (BRIT: tyre) dégonfler; (disappoint) décevoir; **let in** vt laisser entrer; (visitor etc) faire entrer; **let off** vt (allow to leave) laisser partir; (not punish) ne pas punir; (firework etc) faire partir; (bomb) faire exploser; **let out** vt laisser sortir; (scream) laisser échapper; (BRIT: rent out) louer

**lethal** ['li:θl] adj mortel(le), fatal(e); (weapon) meurtrier(-ère)

**letter** ['lɛtə<sup>r</sup>] n lettre f; **letterbox** n (BRIT) boîte f aux or à lettres

**lettuce** ['lɛtɪs] n laitue f, salade f

**leukaemia** (US **leukemia**) [luː'kiːmɪə] n leucémie f

**level** ['lɛvl] adj (flat) plat(e), plan(e), uni(e); (horizontal) horizontal(e) ▷ n niveau m ▷ vt niveler, aplanir; **"A" ~s** npl (BRIT) ≈ baccalauréat m; **to be ~ with** être au même niveau que; **to draw ~ with** (runner, car) arriver à la hauteur de, rattraper; **on the ~** (fig: honest) régulier(-ière); **level crossing** n (BRIT) passage m à niveau

**lever** ['liːvə<sup>r</sup>] n levier m; **leverage** n (influence): **leverage (on** or **with)** prise f (sur)

**levy** ['lɛvɪ] n taxe f, impôt m ▷ vt (tax) lever; (fine) infliger

**liability** [laɪə'bɪlɪtɪ] n responsabilité f;

(handicap) handicap m

**liable** ['laɪəbl] adj (subject): **~ to** sujet(te) à, passible de; (responsible): **~ (for)** responsable (de); (likely): **~ to do** susceptible de faire

**liaise** [liː'eɪz] vi: **to ~ with** assurer la liaison avec

**liar** ['laɪə<sup>r</sup>] n menteur(-euse)

**libel** ['laɪbl] n diffamation f; (document) écrit m diffamatoire ▷ vt diffamer

**liberal** ['lɪbərl] adj libéral(e); (generous): **~ with** prodigue de, généreux(-euse) avec ▷ n: **L~** (Pol) libéral(e); **Liberal Democrat** n (BRIT) libéral(e)-démocrate m/f

**liberate** ['lɪbəreɪt] vt libérer

**liberation** [lɪbə'reɪʃən] n libération f

**liberty** ['lɪbətɪ] n liberté f; **to be at ~** (criminal) être en liberté; **at ~ to do** libre de faire; **to take the ~ of** prendre la liberté de, se permettre de

**Libra** ['liːbrə] n la Balance

**librarian** [laɪ'brɛərɪən] n bibliothécaire m/f

**library** ['laɪbrərɪ] n bibliothèque f

> Be careful not to translate **library** by the French word **librairie**.

**Libya** ['lɪbɪə] n Libye f

**lice** [laɪs] npl of **louse**

**licence** (US **license**) ['laɪsns] n autorisation f, permis m; (Comm) licence f; (Radio, TV) redevance f; (also: **driving ~**, US: also: **driver's license**) permis m (de conduire)

**license** ['laɪsns] n (US) = **licence**; **licensed** adj (for alcohol) patenté(e) pour la vente des spiritueux, qui a une patente de débit de boissons; (car) muni(e) de la vignette; **license plate** n (US Aut) plaque f minéralogique; **licensing hours** (BRIT) npl heures fpl d'ouvertures (des pubs)

**lick** [lɪk] vt lécher; (inf: defeat) écraser, flanquer une piquette or raclée à; **to ~ one's lips** (fig) se frotter les mains

**lid** [lɪd] n couvercle m; (eyelid) paupière f

**lie** [laɪ] n mensonge m ▷ vi (pt, pp ~d) (tell lies) mentir; (pt **lay**, pp **lain**) (*rest*) être étendu(e) or allongé(e) or couché(e); (*object: be situated*) se trouver, être; **to ~ low** (*fig*) se cacher, rester caché(e); **to tell ~s** mentir; **lie about, lie around** vi (*things*) traîner; (BRIT: *person*) traînasser, flemmarder; **lie down** vi se coucher, s'étendre

**Liechtenstein** ['lɪktənstaɪn] n Liechtenstein m

**lie-in** ['laɪɪn] n (BRIT): **to have a ~** faire la grasse matinée

**lieutenant** [lɛf'tɛnənt, US luː'tɛnənt] n lieutenant m

**life** (pl **lives**) [laɪf, laɪvz] n vie f; **to come to ~** (*fig*) s'animer; **life assurance** n (BRIT) = **life insurance**; **lifeboat** n canot m or chaloupe f de sauvetage; **lifeguard** n surveillant m de baignade; **life insurance** n assurance vie f; **life jacket** n gilet m or ceinture f de sauvetage; **lifelike** adj qui semble vrai(e) or vivant(e), ressemblant(e); (*painting*) réaliste; **life preserver** n (US) gilet m or ceinture f de sauvetage; **life sentence** n condamnation f à vie or à perpétuité; **lifestyle** n style m de vie; **lifetime** n: **in his lifetime** de son vivant

**lift** [lɪft] vt soulever, lever; (*end*) supprimer, lever ▷ vi (*fog*) se lever ▷ n (BRIT: *elevator*) ascenseur m; **to give sb a ~** (BRIT) emmener or prendre qn en voiture; **can you give me a ~ to the station?** pouvez-vous m'emmener à la gare?; **lift up** vt soulever; **lift-off** n décollage m

**light** [laɪt] n lumière f; (*lamp*) lampe f; (Aut: *rear light*) feu m; (: *headlamp*) phare m; (*for cigarette etc*): **have you got a ~?** avez-vous du feu? ▷ vt (pt, pp **~ed** or **lit**) (*candle, cigarette, fire*) allumer; (*room*) éclairer ▷ adj (*room, colour*) clair(e); (*not heavy, also fig*) léger(-ère); (*not strenuous*) peu fatigant(e); **lights** npl (*traffic lights*) feux mpl; **to come to ~** être dévoilé(e) or découvert(e); **in the ~ of** à la lumière de; étant donné; **light up** vi s'allumer; (*face*) s'éclairer; (*smoke*) allumer une cigarette or une pipe etc ▷ vt (*illuminate*)

éclairer, illuminer; **light bulb** n ampoule f; **lighten** vt (*light up*) éclairer; (*make lighter*) éclaircir; (*make less heavy*) alléger; **lighter** n (*also:* **cigarette lighter**) briquet m; **light-hearted** adj gai(e), joyeux(-euse), enjoué(e); **lighthouse** n phare m; **lighting** n éclairage m; (*in theatre*) éclairages; **lightly** adv légèrement; **to get off lightly** s'en tirer à bon compte

**lightning** ['laɪtnɪŋ] n foudre f; (*flash*) éclair m

**lightweight** ['laɪtweɪt] adj (*suit*) léger(-ère) ▷ n (*Boxing*) poids léger

**like** [laɪk] vt aimer (bien) ▷ prep comme ▷ adj semblable, pareil(le) ▷ n: **the ~** (*pej*) (d')autres du même genre or acabit; **his ~s and dislikes** ses goûts mpl or préférences fpl; **I would ~**, **I'd ~** je voudrais, j'aimerais; **would you ~ a coffee?** voulez-vous du café?; **to be/look ~ sb/sth** ressembler à qn/qch; **what's he ~?** comment est-il?; **what does it look ~?** de quoi est-ce que ça a l'air?; **what does it taste ~?** quel goût est-ce que ça a?; **that's just ~ him** c'est bien de lui, ça lui ressemble; **do it ~ this** fais-le comme ceci; **it's nothing ~ ...** ce n'est pas du tout comme ...; **likeable** adj sympathique, agréable

**likelihood** ['laɪklɪhud] n probabilité f

**likely** ['laɪklɪ] adj (*result, outcome*) probable; (*excuse*) plausible; **he's ~ to leave** il va sûrement partir, il risque fort de partir; **not ~!** (*inf*) pas de danger!

**likewise** ['laɪkwaɪz] adv de même, pareillement

**liking** ['laɪkɪŋ] n (*for person*) affection f; (*for thing*) penchant m, goût m; **to be to sb's ~** être au goût de qn, plaire à qn

**lilac** ['laɪlək] n lilas m

**Lilo®** ['laɪləu] n matelas m pneumatique

**lily** ['lɪlɪ] n lis m; **~ of the valley** muguet m

**limb** [lɪm] n membre m

**limbo** ['lɪmbəu] n: **to be in ~** (*fig*) être tombé(e) dans l'oubli

**lime** [laɪm] n (tree) tilleul m; (fruit) citron vert, lime f; (Geo) chaux f

**limelight** ['laɪmlaɪt] n: **in the ~** (fig) en vedette, au premier plan

**limestone** ['laɪmstəun] n pierre f à chaux; (Geo) calcaire m

**limit** ['lɪmɪt] n limite f ▷ vt limiter; **limited** adj limité(e), restreint(e); **to be limited to** se limiter à, ne concerner que

**limousine** ['lɪməziːn] n limousine f

**limp** [lɪmp] n: **to have a ~** boiter ▷ vi boiter ▷ adj mou (molle)

**line** [laɪn] n (gen) ligne f; (stroke) trait m; (wrinkle) ride f; (rope) corde f; (wire) fil m; (of poem) vers m; (row, series) rangée f; (of people) file f, queue f; (railway track) voie f; (Comm: series of goods) article(s) m(pl), ligne de produits; (work) métier m ▷ vt: **to ~ (with)** (clothes) doubler (de); (box) garnir or tapisser (de); (subj: trees, crowd) border; **to stand in ~** (us) faire la queue; **in his ~ of business** dans sa partie, dans son rayon; **to be in ~ for sth** (fig) être en lice pour qch; **in ~ with** en accord avec, en conformité avec; **in a ~** aligné(e); **line up** vi s'aligner, se mettre en rang(s); (in queue) faire la queue ▷ vt aligner; (event) prévoir; (find) trouver; **to have sb/sth ~d up** avoir qn/qch en vue or de prévu(e)

**linear** ['lɪnɪə\*] adj linéaire

**linen** ['lɪnɪn] n linge m (de corps or de maison); (cloth) lin m

**liner** ['laɪnə\*] n (ship) paquebot m de ligne; (for bin) sac-poubelle m

**line-up** ['laɪnʌp] n (us: queue) file f; (also: **police ~**) parade f d'identification; (Sport) (composition f de l')équipe f

**linger** ['lɪŋgə\*] vi s'attarder; traîner; (smell, tradition) persister

**lingerie** ['lænʒəriː] n lingerie f

**linguist** ['lɪŋgwɪst] n linguiste m/f; **to be a good ~** être doué(e) pour les langues; **linguistic** adj linguistique

**lining** ['laɪnɪŋ] n doublure f; (of brakes) garniture f

**link** [lɪŋk] n (connection) lien m, rapport m; (Internet) lien m; (of a chain) maillon m ▷ vt relier, lier, unir; **links** npl (Golf) (terrain m de) golf m; **link up** vt relier ▷ vi (people) se rejoindre; (companies etc) s'associer

**lion** ['laɪən] n lion m; **lioness** n lionne f

**lip** [lɪp] n lèvre f; (of cup etc) rebord m; **lipread** vi lire sur les lèvres; **lip salve** [-sælv] n pommade f pour les lèvres, pommade rosat; **lipstick** n rouge m à lèvres

**liqueur** [lɪˈkjuə\*] n liqueur f

**liquid** ['lɪkwɪd] n liquide m ▷ adj liquide; **liquidizer** ['lɪkwɪdaɪzə\*] n (BRIT Culin) mixer m

**liquor** ['lɪkə\*] n spiritueux m, alcool m; **liquor store** (us) n magasin m de vins et spiritueux

**Lisbon** ['lɪzbən] n Lisbonne

**lisp** [lɪsp] n zézaiement m ▷ vi zézayer

**list** [lɪst] n liste f ▷ vt (write down) inscrire; (make list of) faire la liste de; (enumerate) énumérer

**listen** ['lɪsn] vi écouter; **to ~ to** écouter; **listener** n auditeur(-trice)

**lit** [lɪt] pt, pp of **light**

**liter** ['liːtə\*] n (us) = **litre**

**literacy** ['lɪtərəsɪ] n degré m d'alphabétisation, fait m de savoir lire et écrire

**literal** ['lɪtərl] adj littéral(e); **literally** adv littéralement; (really) réellement

**literary** ['lɪtərərɪ] adj littéraire

**literate** ['lɪtərət] adj qui sait lire et écrire; (educated) instruit(e)

**literature** ['lɪtrɪtʃə\*] n littérature f; (brochures etc) copie f publicitaire, prospectus m

**litre** (us **liter**) ['liːtə\*] n litre m

**litter** ['lɪtə\*] n (rubbish) détritus mpl; (dirtier) ordures fpl; (young animals) portée f; **litter bin** (BRIT) poubelle f; **littered** adj: **littered with** (scattered) jonché(e) de

**little** ['lɪtl] adj (small) petit(e); (not much): **~ milk** peu de lait ▷ adv peu; **a ~** un peu (de); **a ~ milk** un peu de lait; **a ~ bit** un peu; **as ~ as possible**

le moins possible; **~ by ~** petit à petit, peu à peu; **little finger** n auriculaire m, petit doigt

**live**[^1] [laɪv] adj (animal) vivant(e), en vie; (wire) sous tension; (broadcast) (transmis(e)) en direct; (unexploded) non explosé(e)

**live**[^2] [lɪv] vi vivre; (reside) vivre, habiter; **to ~ in London** habiter (à) Londres; **where do you ~?** où habitez-vous?; **live together** vivre ensemble, cohabiter; **live up to** vt fus se montrer à la hauteur de

**livelihood** ['laɪvlɪhʊd] n moyens mpl d'existence

**lively** ['laɪvlɪ] adj vif (vive), plein(e) d'entrain; (place, book) vivant(e)

**liven up** ['laɪvn-] vt (room etc) égayer; (discussion, evening) animer ▷ vi s'animer

**liver** ['lɪvəʳ] n foie m

**lives** [laɪvz] npl of **life**

**livestock** ['laɪvstɔk] n cheptel m, bétail m

**living** ['lɪvɪŋ] adj vivant(e), en vie ▷ n: **to earn** or **make a ~** gagner sa vie; **living room** n salle f de séjour

**lizard** ['lɪzəd] n lézard m

**load** [ləʊd] n (weight) poids m; (thing carried) chargement m, charge f; (Elec, Tech) charge f ▷ vt (also: **~ up**): **to ~ (with)** (lorry, ship) charger (de); (gun, camera) charger (avec); (Comput) charger; **a ~ of, ~s of** (fig) un or des tas de, des masses de; **to talk a ~ of rubbish** (inf) dire des bêtises; **loaded** adj (dice) pipé(e); (question) insidieux(-euse); (inf: rich) bourré(e) de fric

**loaf** (pl loaves) [ləʊf, ləʊvz] n pain m, miche f ▷ vi (also: **~ about, ~ around**) fainéanter, traîner

**loan** [ləʊn] n prêt m ▷ vt prêter; **on ~** prêté(e), en prêt

**loathe** [ləʊð] vt détester, avoir en horreur

**loaves** [ləʊvz] npl of **loaf**

**lobby** ['lɔbɪ] n hall m, entrée f; (Pol) groupe m de pression, lobby m ▷ vt faire pression sur

**lobster** ['lɔbstəʳ] n homard m

**local** ['ləʊkl] adj local(e) ▷ n (BRIT: pub) pub m or café m du coin; **the locals** npl les gens mpl du pays or du coin; **local anaesthetic** n anesthésie locale; **local authority** n collectivité locale, municipalité f; **local government** n administration locale or municipale; **locally** ['ləʊkəlɪ] adv localement; dans les environs or la région

**locate** [ləʊ'keɪt] vt (find) trouver, repérer; (situate) situer; **to be ~d in** être situé à or en

**location** [ləʊ'keɪʃən] n emplacement m; **on ~** (Cine) en extérieur

  Be careful not to translate **location** by the French word **location**.

**loch** [lɔx] n lac m, loch m

**lock** [lɔk] n (of door, box) serrure f; (of canal) écluse f; (of hair) mèche f, boucle f ▷ vt (with key) fermer à clé ▷ vi (door etc) fermer à clé; (wheels) se bloquer; **lock in** vt enfermer; **lock out** vt enfermer dehors; (on purpose) mettre à la porte; **lock up** vt (person) enfermer; (house) fermer à clé ▷ vi tout fermer à clé

**locker** ['lɔkəʳ] n casier m; (in station) consigne f automatique; **locker-room** (US) n (Sport) vestiaire m

**locksmith** ['lɔksmɪθ] n serrurier m

**locomotive** [ləʊkə'məʊtɪv] n locomotive f

**locum** ['ləʊkəm] n (Med) suppléant(e) de médecin etc

**lodge** [lɔdʒ] n pavillon m (de gardien); (also: **hunting ~**) pavillon de chasse ▷ vi (person): **to ~ with** être logé(e) chez, être en pension chez; (bullet) se loger ▷ vt (appeal etc) présenter; déposer; **to ~ a complaint** porter plainte; **lodger** n locataire m/f; (with room and meals) pensionnaire m/f

**lodging** ['lɔdʒɪŋ] n logement m

**loft** [lɔft] n grenier m; (apartment) grenier aménagé (en appartement) (gén dans ancien entrepôt ou fabrique)

**log** [lɔg] n (of wood) bûche f; (Naut) livre m or journal m de bord; (of car) ≈ carte grise ▷ vt enregistrer; **log in, log on** vi (Comput) ouvrir une session, entrer dans le système; **log off, log out** vi (Comput) clore une session, sortir du système

**logic** ['lɔdʒɪk] n logique f; **logical** adj logique

**logo** ['ləugəu] n logo m

**Loire** [lwɑː] n: **the (River) ~** la Loire

**lollipop** ['lɔlɪpɔp] n sucette f; **lollipop man/lady** (BRIT: irreg) n contractuel qui fait traverser la rue aux enfants

**lolly** ['lɔlɪ] n (inf: ice) esquimau m; (: lollipop) sucette f

**London** ['lʌndən] n Londres; **Londoner** n Londonien(ne)

**lone** [ləun] adj solitaire

**loneliness** ['ləunlɪnɪs] n solitude f, isolement m

**lonely** ['ləunlɪ] adj seul(e); (childhood etc) solitaire; (place) solitaire, isolé(e)

**long** [lɔŋ] adj long (longue) ▷ adv longtemps ▷ vi: **to ~ for sth/to do sth** avoir très envie de qch/de faire qch, attendre qch avec impatience/ attendre avec impatience de faire qch; **how ~ is this river/course?** quelle est la longueur de ce fleuve/la durée de ce cours?; **6 metres ~** (long) de 6 mètres; **6 months ~** qui dure 6 mois, de 6 mois; **all night ~** toute la nuit; **he no ~er comes** il ne vient plus; **I can't stand it any ~er** je ne peux plus le supporter; **~ before** longtemps avant; **before ~** (+ future) avant peu, dans peu de temps; (+ past) peu de temps après; **don't be ~!** fais vite!, dépêche-toi!; **I shan't be ~** je n'en ai pas pour longtemps; **at ~ last** enfin; **so** or **as ~ as** à condition que + sub; **long-distance** adj (race) de fond; (call) interurbain(e); **long-haul** adj (flight) long-courrier; **longing** n désir m, envie f; (nostalgia) nostalgie f ▷ adj plein(e) d'envie or de nostalgie

**longitude** ['lɔŋgɪtjuːd] n longitude f

**long: long jump** n saut m en longueur;

**long-life** adj (batteries etc) longue durée inv; (milk) longue conservation; **long-sighted** adj (BRIT) presbyte; (fig) prévoyant(e); **long-standing** adj de longue date; **long-term** adj à long terme

**loo** [luː] n (BRIT inf) w.-c mpl, petit coin

**look** [luk] vi regarder; (seem) sembler, paraître, avoir l'air; (building etc): **to ~ south/on to the sea** donner au sud/ sur la mer ▷ n regard m; (appearance) air m, allure f, aspect m; **looks** npl (good looks) physique m, beauté f; **to ~ like** ressembler à; **to have a ~** regarder; **to have a ~ at sth** jeter un coup d'œil à qch; **~ (here)!** (annoyance) écoutez!; **look after** vt fus s'occuper de; (luggage etc: watch over) garder, surveiller; **look around** vi regarder autour de soi; **look at** vt fus regarder; (problem etc) examiner; **look back** vi: **to ~ back at sth/sb** se retourner pour regarder qch/qn; **to ~ back on** (event, period) évoquer, repenser à; **look down on** vt fus (fig) regarder de haut, dédaigner; **look for** vt fus chercher; **we're ~ing for a hotel/restaurant** nous cherchons un hôtel/restaurant; **look forward to** vt fus attendre avec impatience; **~ing forward to hearing from you** (in letter) dans l'attente de vous lire; **look into** vt fus (matter, possibility) examiner, étudier; **look out** vi (beware): **to ~ out (for)** prendre garde (à), faire attention (à); **~ out!** attention!; **look out for** vt fus (seek) être à la recherche de; (try to spot) guetter; **look round** vt fus (house, shop) faire le tour de ▷ vi (turn) regarder derrière soi, se retourner; **look through** vt fus (papers, book) examiner; (: briefly) parcourir; **look up** vi lever les yeux; (improve) s'améliorer ▷ vt (word) chercher; **look up to** vt fus avoir du respect pour; **lookout** n (tower etc) poste m de guet; (person) guetteur m; **to be on the lookout (for)** guetter

**loom** [luːm] vi (also: ~ up) surgir; (event) paraître imminent(e); (threaten) menacer

**loony** ['lu:nɪ] *adj, n* (*inf*) timbré(e), cinglé(e) *m/f*

**loop** [lu:p] *n* boucle *f* ▷ *vt*: **to ~ sth round sth** passer qch autour de qch; **loophole** *n* (*fig*) porte *f* de sortie; échappatoire *f*

**loose** [lu:s] *adj* (*knot, screw*) desserré(e); (*clothes*) vague, ample, lâche; (*hair*) dénoué(e), épars(e); (*not firmly fixed*) pas solide; (*morals, discipline*) relâché(e); (*translation*) approximatif(-ive) ▷ *n*: **to be on the ~** être en liberté; **~ connection** (*Elec*) mauvais contact; **to be at a ~ end** or (*US*) **at ~ ends** (*fig*) ne pas trop savoir quoi faire; **loosely** *adv* sans serrer; (*imprecisely*) approximativement; **loosen** *vt* desserrer, relâcher, défaire

**loot** [lu:t] *n* butin *m* ▷ *vt* piller

**lop-sided** ['lɔp'saɪdɪd] *adj* de travers, asymétrique

**lord** [lɔ:d] *n* seigneur *m*; **L~ Smith** lord Smith; **the L~** (*Rel*) le Seigneur; **my L~** (*to noble*) Monsieur le comte/le baron; (*to judge*) Monsieur le juge; (*to bishop*) Monseigneur; **good L~!** mon Dieu!; **Lords** *npl* (*BRIT: Pol*): **the (House of) Lords** (*BRIT*) la Chambre des Lords

**lorry** ['lɔrɪ] *n* (*BRIT*) camion *m*; **lorry driver** *n* (*BRIT*) camionneur *m*, routier *m*

**lose** (*pt, pp* **lost**) [lu:z, lɔst] *vt* perdre ▷ *vi* perdre; **I've lost my wallet/passport** j'ai perdu mon portefeuille/passeport; **to ~ (time)** (*clock*) retarder; **lose out** *vi* être perdant(e); **loser** *n* perdant(e)

**loss** [lɔs] *n* perte *f*; **to make a ~** enregistrer une perte; **to be at a ~** être perplexe or embarrassé(e)

**lost** [lɔst] *pt, pp of* **lose** ▷ *adj* perdu(e); **to get ~** *vi* se perdre; **I'm ~** je me suis perdu; **~ and found property** *n* (*US*) objets trouvés; **~ and found** *n* (*US*) (bureau *m* des) objets trouvés; **lost property** *n* (*BRIT*) objets trouvés; **lost property office** or **department** (bureau *m* des) objets trouvés

**lot** [lɔt] *n* (*at auctions, set*) lot *m*; (*destiny*) sort *m*, destinée *f*; **the ~** (*everything*) le tout; (*everyone*) tous *mpl*, toutes *fpl*; **a ~** beaucoup; **a ~ of** beaucoup de; **~s of** des tas de; **to draw ~s (for sth)** tirer (qch) au sort

**lotion** ['ləuʃən] *n* lotion *f*

**lottery** ['lɔtərɪ] *n* loterie *f*

**loud** [laud] *adj* bruyant(e), sonore; (*voice*) fort(e); (*condemnation etc*) vigoureux(-euse); (*gaudy*) voyant(e), tapageur(-euse) ▷ *adv* (*speak etc*) fort; **out ~** tout haut; **loudly** *adv* fort, bruyamment; **loudspeaker** *n* haut-parleur *m*

**lounge** [laundʒ] *n* salon *m*; (*of airport*) salle *f*; (*BRIT: also*: **~ bar**) (salle de) café *m* or bar *m* ▷ *vi* (*also*: **~ about** or **around**) se prélasser, paresser

**louse** (*pl* **lice**) [laus, laɪs] *n* pou *m*

**lousy** ['lauzɪ] (*inf*) *adj* (*bad quality*) infect(e), moche; **I feel ~** je suis mal fichu(e)

**love** [lʌv] *n* amour *m* ▷ *vt* aimer; (*caringly, kindly*) aimer beaucoup; **I ~ chocolate** j'adore le chocolat; **to ~ to do** aimer beaucoup or adorer faire; **"15 ~"** (*Tennis*) "15 à rien or zéro"; **to be/fall in ~ with** être/tomber amoureux(-euse) de; **to make ~** faire l'amour; **~ from Anne, ~, Anne** affectueusement, Anne; **I ~ you** je t'aime; **love affair** *n* liaison (amoureuse); **love life** *n* vie sentimentale

**lovely** ['lʌvlɪ] *adj* (*pretty*) ravissant(e); (*friend, wife*) charmant(e); (*holiday, surprise*) très agréable, merveilleux(-euse)

**lover** ['lʌvə'] *n* amant *m*; (*person in love*) amoureux(-euse); (*amateur*): **a ~ of** un(e) ami(e) de, un(e) amoureux(-euse) de

**loving** ['lʌvɪŋ] *adj* affectueux(-euse), tendre, aimant(e)

**low** [ləu] *adj* bas (basse); (*quality*) mauvais(e), inférieur(e) ▷ *adv* bas ▷ *n* (*Meteorology*) dépression *f*; **to feel ~** se sentir déprimé(e); **he's very ~** (ill) il est bien bas or très affaibli; **to turn (down)** **~** vt baisser; **to be ~ on** (supplies etc) être à court de; **to reach a new** or **an all-time ~** tomber au niveau le plus bas; **low-alcohol** adj à faible teneur en alcool, peu alcoolisé(e); **low-calorie** adj hypocalorique

**lower** ['ləuəʳ] adj inférieur(e) ▷ vt baisser; (resistance) diminuer; **to ~ o.s. to** s'abaisser à

**low-fat** ['ləu'fæt] adj maigre

**loyal** ['lɔɪəl] adj loyal(e), fidèle; **loyalty** n loyauté f, fidélité f; **loyalty card** n carte f de fidélité

**L.P.** n abbr = **long-playing record**

**L-plates** ['ɛlpleɪts] npl (BRIT) plaques fpl (obligatoires) d'apprenti conducteur

**Lt** abbr (= lieutenant) Lt.

**Ltd** abbr (Comm: company: = limited) ≈ S.A.

**luck** [lʌk] n chance f; **bad ~** malchance f, malheur m; **good ~!** bonne chance!; **bad** or **hard** or **tough ~!** pas de chance!; **luckily** adv heureusement, par bonheur; **lucky** adj (person) qui a de la chance; (coincidence) heureux(-euse); (number etc) qui porte bonheur

**lucrative** ['lu:krətɪv] adj lucratif(-ive), rentable, qui rapporte

**ludicrous** ['lu:dɪkrəs] adj ridicule, absurde

**luggage** ['lʌgɪdʒ] n bagages mpl; **our ~ hasn't arrived** nos bagages ne sont pas arrivés; **could you send someone to collect our ~?** pourriez-vous envoyer quelqu'un chercher nos bagages?; **luggage rack** n (in train) porte-bagages m inv; (: on car) galerie f

**lukewarm** ['lu:kwɔ:m] adj tiède

**lull** [lʌl] n accalmie f; (in conversation) pause f ▷ vt: **to ~ sb to sleep** bercer qn pour qu'il s'endorme; **to be ~ed into a false sense of security** s'endormir dans une fausse sécurité

**lullaby** ['lʌləbaɪ] n berceuse f

**lumber** ['lʌmbəʳ] n (wood) bois m de charpente; (junk) bric-à-brac m inv ▷ vt (BRIT inf): **to ~ sb with sth/sb** coller or

refiler qch/qn à qn

**luminous** ['lu:mɪnəs] adj lumineux(-euse)

**lump** [lʌmp] n morceau m; (in sauce) grumeau m; (swelling) grosseur f ▷ vt (also: **~ together**) réunir, mettre en tas; **lump sum** n somme globale or forfaitaire; **lumpy** adj (sauce) qui a des grumeaux; (bed) défoncé(e), peu confortable

**lunatic** ['lu:nətɪk] n fou (folle), dément(e) ▷ adj fou (folle), dément(e)

**lunch** [lʌntʃ] n déjeuner m ▷ vi déjeuner; **lunch break, lunch hour** n pause f de midi, heure f du déjeuner; **lunchtime** n: **it's lunchtime** c'est l'heure du déjeuner

**lung** [lʌŋ] n poumon m

**lure** [luəʳ] n (attraction) attrait m, charme m; (in hunting) appât m, leurre m ▷ vt attirer or persuader par la ruse

**lurk** [lə:k] vi se tapir, se cacher

**lush** [lʌʃ] adj luxuriant(e)

**lust** [lʌst] n (sexual) désir (sexuel); (Rel) luxure f; (fig): **~ for** soif f de

**Luxembourg** ['lʌksəmbə:g] n Luxembourg m

**luxurious** [lʌg'zjuəriəs] adj luxueux(-euse)

**luxury** ['lʌkʃəri] n luxe m ▷ cpd de luxe

**Lycra®** ['laɪkrə] n Lycra® m

**lying** ['laɪɪŋ] n mensonge(s) m(pl) ▷ adj (statement, story) mensonger(-ère), faux (fausse); (person) menteur(-euse)

**Lyons** ['ljɔ̃] n Lyon

**lyrics** ['lɪrɪks] npl (of song) paroles fpl

m

**m.** *abbr* (= *metre*) m; (= *million*) M; (= *mile*) mi

**M.A.** *n abbr* (*Scol*) = **Master of Arts**

**ma** [mɑː] (*inf*) *n* maman *f*

**mac** [mæk] *n* (*BRIT*) imper(méable *m*) *m*

**macaroni** [mækə'rəʊnɪ] *n* macaronis *mpl*

**Macedonia** [mæsɪ'dəʊnɪə] *n* Macédoine *f*; **Macedonian** [mæsɪ'dəʊnɪən] *adj* macédonien(ne) ▷ *n* Macédonien(ne); (*Ling*) macédonien *m*

**machine** [mə'ʃiːn] *n* machine *f* ▷ *vt* (*dress etc*) coudre à la machine; (*Tech*) usiner; **machine gun** *n* mitrailleuse *f*; **machinery** *n* machinerie *f*, machines *fpl*; (*fig*) mécanisme(s) *m(pl)*; **machine washable** *adj* (*garment*) lavable en machine

**macho** [ˈmætʃəʊ] *adj* macho *inv*

**mackerel** [ˈmækrl] *n* (*pl inv*) maquereau *m*

**mackintosh** [ˈmækɪntɒʃ] *n* (*BRIT*) imperméable *m*

**mad** [mæd] *adj* fou (folle); (*foolish*) insensé(e); (*angry*) furieux(-euse); **to be ~ (keen) about** *or* **on sth** (*inf*) être follement passionné de qch, être fou de qch

**Madagascar** [mædə'gæskəʳ] *n* Madagascar *m*

**madam** [ˈmædəm] *n* madame *f*

**mad cow disease** *n* maladie *f* des vaches folles

**made** [meɪd] *pt, pp of* **make**; **made-to-measure** *adj* (*BRIT*) fait(e) sur mesure; **made-up** [ˈmeɪdʌp] *adj* (*story*) inventé(e), fabriqué(e)

**madly** [ˈmædlɪ] *adv* follement; **~ in love** éperdument amoureux(-euse)

**madman** [ˈmædmən] (*irreg*) *n* fou *m*, aliéné *m*

**madness** [ˈmædnɪs] *n* folie *f*

**Madrid** [mə'drɪd] *n* Madrid

**Mafia** [ˈmæfɪə] *n* maf(f)ia *f*

**mag** [mæg] *n abbr* (*BRIT inf*: = *magazine*) magazine *m*

**magazine** [mægə'ziːn] *n* (*Press*) magazine *m*, revue *f*; (*Radio, TV*) magazine

**maggot** [ˈmægət] *n* ver *m*, asticot *m*

**magic** [ˈmædʒɪk] *n* magie *f* ▷ *adj* magique; **magical** *adj* magique; (*experience, evening*) merveilleux(-euse); **magician** [mə'dʒɪʃən] *n* magicien(ne)

**magistrate** [ˈmædʒɪstreɪt] *n* magistrat *m*; juge *m*

**magnet** [ˈmægnɪt] *n* aimant *m*; **magnetic** [mæg'nɛtɪk] *adj* magnétique

**magnificent** [mæg'nɪfɪsnt] *adj* superbe, magnifique; (*splendid: robe, building*) somptueux(-euse), magnifique

**magnify** [ˈmægnɪfaɪ] *vt* grossir; (*sound*) amplifier; **magnifying glass** *n* loupe *f*

**magpie** [ˈmægpaɪ] *n* pie *f*

**mahogany** [mə'hɔgənɪ] *n* acajou *m*

**maid** [meɪd] *n* bonne *f*; (*in hotel*) femme *f* de chambre; **old ~** (*pej*) vieille fille

**maiden name** *n* nom *m* de jeune fille

**mail** [meɪl] n poste f; (letters) courrier m ▷ vt envoyer (par la poste); **by ~** par la poste; **mailbox** n (us: also Comput) boîte f aux lettres; **mailing list** n liste f d'adresses; **mailman** (irreg) n (us) facteur m; **mail-order** n vente f or achat m par correspondance

**main** [meɪn] adj principal(e) ▷ n (pipe) conduite principale, canalisation f; **the ~s** (Elec) le secteur; **the ~ thing** l'essentiel m; **in the ~** dans l'ensemble; **main course** n (Culin) plat m de résistance; **mainland** n continent m; **mainly** adv principalement, surtout; **main road** n grand axe, route nationale; **mainstream** n (fig) courant principal; **main street** n rue f principale

**maintain** [meɪn'teɪn] vt entretenir; (continue) maintenir, préserver; (affirm) soutenir; **maintenance** ['meɪntənəns] n entretien m; (Law: alimony) pension f alimentaire

**maisonette** [meɪzə'nɛt] n (BRIT) appartement m en duplex

**maize** [meɪz] n (BRIT) maïs m

**majesty** ['mædʒɪstɪ] n majesté f; (title): **Your M~** Votre Majesté

**major** ['meɪdʒə'] n (Mil) commandant m ▷ adj (important) important(e); (most important) principal(e); (Mus) majeur(e) ▷ vi (us Scol): **to ~ (in)** se spécialiser (en)

**Majorca** [mə'jɔːkə] n Majorque f

**majority** [mə'dʒɔrɪtɪ] n majorité f

**make** [meɪk] vt (pt, pp made) faire; (manufacture) faire, fabriquer; (earn) gagner; (decision) prendre; (friend) se faire; (speech) faire, prononcer; (cause to be): **to ~ sb sad** etc rendre qn triste etc; (force): **to ~ sb do sth** obliger qn à faire qch, faire faire qch à qn; (equal): **2 and 2 ~ 4** 2 et 2 font 4 ▷ n (manufacture) fabrication f; (brand) marque f; **to ~ the bed** faire le lit; **to ~ a fool of sb** (ridicule) ridiculiser qn; (trick) avoir or duper qn; **to ~ a profit** faire un or des bénéfice(s); **to ~ a loss** essuyer une perte; **to ~ it** (in time etc) y arriver; (succeed) réussir;

**what time do you ~ it?** quelle heure avez-vous?; **I ~ it £249** d'après mes calculs ça fait 249 livres; **to be made of** être en; **to ~ do with** se contenter de; se débrouiller avec; **make off** vi filer; **make out** vt (write out: cheque) faire; (decipher) déchiffrer; (understand) comprendre; (see) distinguer; (claim, imply) prétendre, vouloir faire croire; **make up** vt (invent) inventer, imaginer; (constitute) constituer; (parcel, bed) faire ▷ vi se réconcilier; (with cosmetics) se maquiller, se farder; **to be made up of** se composer de; **make up for** vt fus compenser; (lost time) rattraper; **makeover** ['meɪkəʊvə'] n (by beautician) soins mpl de maquillage; (change of image) changement m d'image; **maker** n fabricant m; (of film, programme) réalisateur(-trice); **makeshift** adj provisoire, improvisé(e); **make-up** n maquillage m

**making** ['meɪkɪn] n (fig): **in the ~** en formation or gestation; **to have the ~s of** (actor, athlete) avoir l'étoffe de

**malaria** [mə'lɛərɪə] n malaria f, paludisme m

**Malaysia** [mə'leɪzɪə] n Malaisie f

**male** [meɪl] n (Biol, Elec) mâle m ▷ adj (sex, attitude) masculin(e); (animal) mâle; (child etc) du sexe masculin

**malicious** [mə'lɪʃəs] adj méchant(e), malveillant(e)

> Be careful not to translate *malicious* by the French word *malicieux*.

**malignant** [mə'lɪgnənt] adj (Med) malin(-igne)

**mall** [mɔːl] n (also: **shopping ~**) centre commercial

**mallet** ['mælɪt] n maillet m

**malnutrition** [mælnjuː'trɪʃən] n malnutrition f

**malpractice** [mæl'præktɪs] n faute professionnelle; négligence f

**malt** [mɔːlt] n malt m ▷ cpd (whisky) pur malt

**Malta** ['mɔːltə] n Malte f; **Maltese**
[mɔːl'tiːz] adj maltais(e) ▷ n (pl inv)
Maltais(e)

**mammal** ['mæml] n mammifère m

**mammoth** ['mæməθ] n mammouth m
▷ adj géant(e), monstre

**man** (pl **men**) [mæn, mɛn] n homme
m; (Sport) joueur m; (Chess) pièce f ▷ vt
(Naut: ship) garnir d'hommes; (machine)
assurer le fonctionnement de; (Mil: gun)
servir; (: post) être de service à; **an old ~**
un vieillard; **~ and wife** mari et femme

**manage** ['mænɪdʒ] vi se débrouiller;
(succeed) y arriver, réussir ▷ vt (business)
gérer; (team, operation) diriger;
(control: ship) manier, manœuvrer;
(: person) savoir s'y prendre avec; **to**
**~ to do** se débrouiller pour faire;
(succeed) réussir à faire; **manageable**
adj maniable; (task etc) faisable;
(number) raisonnable; **management**
n (running) administration f, direction
f; (people in charge: of business, firm)
dirigeants mpl, cadres mpl; (: of hotel,
shop, theatre) direction; **manager** n
(of business) directeur m; (of institution
etc) administrateur m; (of department,
unit) responsable m/f, chef m; (of hotel
etc) gérant m; (Sport) manager m; (of
artist) impresario m; **manageress**
n directrice f; (of hotel etc) gérante f;
**managerial** [mænɪ'dʒɪərɪəl] adj
directorial(e); (skills) de cadre, de
gestion; **managing director** n
directeur général

**mandarin** ['mændərɪn] n (also: **~**
**orange**) mandarine f

**mandate** ['mændeɪt] n mandat m

**mandatory** ['mændətərɪ] adj
obligatoire

**mane** [meɪn] n crinière f

**maneuver** [mə'nuːvəʳ] (US)
= **manoeuvre**

**mangetout** ['mɔnʒ'tuː] n mangetout m inv

**mango** (pl **~es**) ['mæŋgəu] n mangue f

**man**: **manhole** n trou m d'homme;
**manhood** n (age) âge m d'homme;

(manliness) virilité f

**mania** ['meɪnɪə] n manie f; **maniac**
['meɪnɪæk] n maniaque m/f; (fig)
fou (folle)

**manic** ['mænɪk] adj maniaque

**manicure** ['mænɪkjuəʳ] n manucure f

**manifest** ['mænɪfɛst] vt manifester
▷ adj manifeste, évident(e)

**manifesto** [mænɪ'fɛstəu] n (Pol)
manifeste m

**manipulate** [mə'nɪpjuleɪt] vt
manipuler; (system, situation) exploiter

**man**: **mankind** [mæn'kaɪnd] n
humanité f, genre humain; **manly** adj
viril(e); **man-made** adj artificiel(le);
(fibre) synthétique

**manner** ['mænəʳ] n manière f, façon f;
(behaviour) attitude f, comportement
m; **manners** npl: **(good) ~s** (bonnes)
manières; **bad ~s** mauvaises manières;
**all ~ of** toutes sortes de

**manoeuvre** (US **maneuver**)
[mə'nuːvəʳ] vt (move) manœuvrer;
(manipulate: person) manipuler;
(: situation) exploiter ▷ n manœuvre f

**manpower** ['mænpauəʳ] n main-
d'œuvre f

**mansion** ['mænʃən] n château m,
manoir m

**manslaughter** ['mænslɔːtəʳ] n
homicide m involontaire

**mantelpiece** ['mæntlpiːs] n
cheminée f

**manual** ['mænjuəl] adj manuel(le)
▷ n manuel m

**manufacture** [mænju'fæktʃəʳ]
vt fabriquer ▷ n fabrication f;
**manufacturer** n fabricant m

**manure** [mə'njuəʳ] n fumier m;
(artificial) engrais m

**manuscript** ['mænjuskrɪpt] n
manuscrit m

**many** ['mɛnɪ] adj beaucoup de, de
nombreux(-euses) ▷ pron beaucoup,
un grand nombre; **a great ~** un grand
nombre (de); **~ a ...** bien des ..., plus
d'un(e) ...

**map** [mæp] n carte f; (of town) plan

*m*; **can you show it to me on the ~?**
pouvez-vous me l'indiquer sur la carte?;
**map out** *vt* tracer; (*fig: task*) planifier

**maple** ['meɪpl] *n* érable *m*

**Mar** *abbr* = **March**

**mar** [mɑːʳ] *vt* gâcher, gâter

**marathon** ['mærəθən] *n* marathon *m*

**marble** ['mɑːbl] *n* marbre *m*; (*toy*) bille *f*

**March** [mɑːtʃ] *n* mars *m*

**march** [mɑːtʃ] *vi* marcher au pas;
(*demonstrators*) défiler ▷ *n* marche *f*;
(*demonstration*) manifestation *f*

**mare** [mɛəʳ] *n* jument *f*

**margarine** [mɑːdʒəˈriːn] *n* margarine *f*

**margin** ['mɑːdʒɪn] *n* marge *f*; **marginal**
*adj* marginal(e); **marginal seat** (*Pol*)
siège disputé; **marginally** *adv* très
légèrement, sensiblement

**marigold** ['mærɪɡəuld] *n* souci *m*

**marijuana** [mærɪˈwɑːnə] *n*
marijuana *f*

**marina** [məˈriːnə] *n* marina *f*

**marinade** *n* [mærɪˈneɪd] marinade *f*

**marinate** ['mærɪneɪt] *vt* (faire)
mariner

**marine** [məˈriːn] *adj* marin(e) ▷ *n*
fusilier marin; (*US*) marine *m*

**marital** ['mærɪtl] *adj* matrimonial(e);
**marital status** *n* situation *f* de famille

**maritime** ['mærɪtaɪm] *adj* maritime

**marjoram** ['mɑːdʒərəm] *n*
marjolaine *f*

**mark** [mɑːk] *n* marque *f*; (*of skid
etc*) trace *f*; (*BRIT Scol*) note *f*; (*oven
temperature*): **(gas) ~ 4** thermostat *m* 4
▷ *vt* (*also Sport: player*) marquer; (*stain*)
tacher; (*BRIT Scol*) corriger, noter; **to
~ time** marquer le pas; **marked** *adj*
(*obvious*) marqué(e), net(te); **marker** *n*
(*sign*) jalon *m*; (*bookmark*) signet *m*

**market** ['mɑːkɪt] *n* marché *m* ▷ *vt*
(*Comm*) commercialiser; **marketing** *n*
marketing *m*; **marketplace** *n* place *f*
du marché; (*Comm*) marché *m*; **market
research** *n* étude *f* de marché

**marmalade** ['mɑːməleɪd] *n* confiture
*f* d'oranges

**maroon** [məˈruːn] *vt*: **to be ~ed** être

abandonné(e); (*fig*) être bloqué(e) ▷ *adj*
(*colour*) bordeaux *inv*

**marquee** [mɑːˈkiː] *n* chapiteau *m*

**marriage** ['mærɪdʒ] *n* mariage *m*;
**marriage certificate** *n* extrait *m*
d'acte de mariage

**married** ['mærɪd] *adj* marié(e); (*life,
love*) conjugal(e)

**marrow** ['mærəu] *n* (*of bone*) moelle *f*;
(*vegetable*) courge *f*

**marry** ['mærɪ] *vt* épouser, se marier
avec; (*subj: father, priest etc*) marier ▷ *vi*
(*also*: **get married**) se marier

**Mars** [mɑːz] *n* (*planet*) Mars *f*

**Marseilles** [mɑːˈseɪ] *n* Marseille

**marsh** [mɑːʃ] *n* marais *m*, marécage *m*

**marshal** ['mɑːʃl] *n* maréchal *m*; (*US: fire,
police*) ≈ capitaine *m*; (*for demonstration,
meeting*) membre *m* du service d'ordre
▷ *vt* rassembler

**martyr** ['mɑːtəʳ] *n* martyr(e)

**marvel** ['mɑːvl] *n* merveille *f* ▷ *vi*: **to ~
(at)** s'émerveiller (de); **marvellous** (*US*
**marvelous**) *adj* merveilleux(-euse)

**Marxism** ['mɑːksɪzəm] *n* marxisme *m*

**Marxist** ['mɑːksɪst] *adj*, *n* marxiste
(*m/f*)

**marzipan** ['mɑːzɪpæn] *n* pâte *f*
d'amandes

**mascara** [mæsˈkɑːrə] *n* mascara *m*

**mascot** ['mæskət] *n* mascotte *f*

**masculine** ['mæskjulɪn] *adj*
masculin(e) ▷ *n* masculin *m*

**mash** [mæʃ] *vt* (*Culin*) faire une purée
de; **mashed potato(es)** *n(pl)* purée *f* de
pommes de terre

**mask** [mɑːsk] *n* masque *m* ▷ *vt*
masquer

**mason** ['meɪsn] *n* (*also*: **stone~**)
maçon *m*; (*also*: **free~**) franc-maçon *m*;
**masonry** *n* maçonnerie *f*

**mass** [mæs] *n* multitude *f*, masse
*f*; (*Physics*) masse *f*; (*Rel*) messe *f*
▷ *cpd* (*communication*) de masse;
(*unemployment*) massif(-ive) ▷ *vi* se
masser; **masses** *npl*: **the ~es** les
masses; **~es of** (*inf*) des tas de

**massacre** ['mæsəkəʳ] *n* massacre *m*

**massage** ['mæsɑːʒ] n massage m
▷ vt masser

**massive** ['mæsɪv] adj énorme,
massif(-ive)

**mass media** npl mass-media mpl

**mass-produce** ['mæsprə'djuːs] vt
fabriquer en série

**mast** [mɑːst] n mât m; (Radio, TV)
pylône m

**master** ['mɑːstər] n maître m; (in
secondary school) professeur m; (in
primary school) instituteur m; (title for
boys): **M~ X** Monsieur X ▷ vt maîtriser;
(learn) apprendre à fond; **M~ of Arts/
Science (MA/MSc)** n ≈ titulaire m/f
d'une maîtrise (en lettres/science); **M~
of Arts/Science degree (MA/MSc)**
n ≈ maîtrise f; **mastermind** n esprit
supérieur ▷ vt diriger, être le cerveau
de; **masterpiece** n chef-d'œuvre m

**masturbate** ['mæstəbeɪt] vi se
masturber

**mat** [mæt] n petit tapis; (also: **door~**)
paillasson m; (also: **table~**) set m de
table ▷ adj = **matt**

**match** [mætʃ] n allumette f; (game)
match m, partie f; (fig) égal(e) ▷ vt (also:
**~ up**) assortir à; (go well with) aller bien
avec, s'assortir à; (equal) égaler, valoir
▷ vi être assorti(e); **to be a good ~** être
bien assorti(e); **matchbox** n boîte f
d'allumettes; **matching** adj assorti(e)

**mate** [meɪt] n (inf) copain (copine);
(animal) partenaire m/f, mâle (femelle);
(in merchant navy) second m ▷ vi
s'accoupler

**material** [mə'tɪərɪəl] n (substance)
matière f, matériau m; (cloth) tissu m,
étoffe f; (information, data) données fpl
▷ adj matériel(le); (relevant: evidence)
pertinent(e); **materials** npl (equipment)
matériaux mpl

**materialize** [mə'tɪərɪəlaɪz] vi se
matérialiser, se réaliser

**maternal** [mə'təːnl] adj maternel(le)

**maternity** [mə'təːnɪtɪ] n maternité f;
**maternity hospital** n maternité f;
**maternity leave** n congé m de

maternité

**math** [mæθ] n (US: = mathematics)
maths fpl

**mathematical** [mæθə'mætɪkl] adj
mathématique

**mathematician** [mæθəmə'tɪʃən] n
mathématicien(ne)

**mathematics** [mæθə'mætɪks] n
mathématiques fpl

**maths** [mæθs] n abbr (BRIT:
= mathematics) maths fpl

**matinée** ['mætɪneɪ] n matinée f

**matron** ['meɪtrən] n (in hospital)
infirmière-chef f; (in school) infirmière f

**matt** [mæt] adj mat(e)

**matter** ['mætər] n question f; (Physics)
matière f, substance f; (Med: pus) pus
m ▷ vi importer; **matters** npl (affairs,
situation) la situation; **it doesn't ~** cela
n'a pas d'importance; (I don't mind) cela
ne fait rien; **what's the ~?** qu'est-ce
qu'il y a?, qu'est-ce qui ne va pas?; **no ~
what** quoi qu'il arrive; **as a ~ of course**
tout naturellement; **as a ~ of fact** en
fait; **reading ~** (BRIT) de quoi lire, de
la lecture

**mattress** ['mætrɪs] n matelas m

**mature** [mə'tjuər] adj mûr(e); (cheese)
fait(e); (wine) arrive(e) à maturité ▷ vi
mûrir; (cheese, wine) se faire; **mature
student** n étudiant(e) plus âgé(e) que la
moyenne; **maturity** n maturité f

**maul** [mɔːl] vt lacérer

**mauve** [məʊv] adj mauve

**max** abbr = **maximum**

**maximize** ['mæksɪmaɪz] vt (profits etc,
chances) maximiser

**maximum** ['mæksɪməm] (pl **maxima**)
adj maximum ▷ n maximum m

**May** [meɪ] n mai m

**may** [meɪ] (conditional **might**) vi
(indicating possibility): **he ~ come** il se
peut qu'il vienne; (be allowed to): **~ I
smoke?** puis-je fumer?; (wishes): **~ God
bless you!** (que) Dieu vous bénisse!;
**you ~ as well go** vous feriez aussi
bien d'y aller

**maybe** ['meɪbiː] adv peut-être; **~**

**he'll ...** peut-être qu'il ...

**May Day** n le Premier mai

**mayhem** ['meɪhɛm] n grabuge m

**mayonnaise** [meɪə'neɪz] n mayonnaise f

**mayor** [mɛəʳ] n maire m; **mayoress** n (*female mayor*) maire m; (*wife of mayor*) épouse f du maire

**maze** [meɪz] n labyrinthe m, dédale m

**MD** n abbr (Comm) = **managing director**

**me** [miː] pron me, m' + *vowel or h mute*; (*stressed, after prep*) moi; **it's me** c'est moi; **he heard me** il m'a entendu; **give me a book** donnez-moi un livre; **it's for me** c'est pour moi

**meadow** ['mɛdəʊ] n prairie f, pré m

**meagre** (*US* **meager**) ['miːgəʳ] adj maigre

**meal** [miːl] n repas m; (*flour*) farine f; **mealtime** n heure f du repas

**mean** [miːn] adj (*with money*) avare, radin(e); (*unkind*) mesquin(e), méchant(e); (*shabby*) misérable; (*average*) moyen(ne) ▷ vt (pt, pp **~t**) (*signify*) signifier, vouloir dire; (*refer to*) faire allusion à, parler de; (*intend*): **to ~ to do** avoir l'intention de faire ▷ n moyenne f; **means** npl (*way, money*) moyens mpl; **by ~s of** (*instrument*) au moyen de; **by all ~s** je vous en prie; **to be ~t for** être destiné(e) à; **do you ~ it?** vous êtes sérieux?; **what do you ~?** que voulez-vous dire?

**meaning** ['miːnɪŋ] n signification f, sens m; **meaningful** adj significatif(-ive); (*relationship*) valable; **meaningless** adj dénué(e) de sens

**meant** [mɛnt] pt, pp of **mean**

**meantime** ['miːntaɪm] adv (*also:* **in the ~**) pendant ce temps

**meanwhile** ['miːnwaɪl] adv = **meantime**

**measles** ['miːzlz] n rougeole f

**measure** ['mɛʒəʳ] vt, vi mesurer ▷ n mesure f; (*ruler*) règle (graduée)

**measurements** ['mɛʒəmənts] npl mesures fpl; **chest/hip ~** tour m de poitrine/hanches

**meat** [miːt] n viande f; **I don't eat ~** je ne mange pas de viande; **cold ~s** (*BRIT*) viandes froides; **meatball** n boulette f de viande

**Mecca** ['mɛkə] n la Mecque

**mechanic** [mɪ'kænɪk] n mécanicien m; **can you send a ~?** pouvez-vous nous envoyer un mécanicien?; **mechanical** adj mécanique

**mechanism** ['mɛkənɪzəm] n mécanisme m

**medal** ['mɛdl] n médaille f; **medallist** (*US* **medalist**) n (*Sport*) médaillé(e)

**meddle** ['mɛdl] vi: **to ~ in** se mêler de, s'occuper de; **to ~ with** toucher à

**media** ['miːdɪə] npl media mpl ▷ npl of **medium**

**mediaeval** [mɛdɪ'iːvl] adj = **medieval**

**mediate** ['miːdɪeɪt] vi servir d'intermédiaire

**medical** ['mɛdɪkl] adj médical(e) ▷ n (*also:* **~ examination**) visite médicale; (*private*) examen médical; **medical certificate** n certificat médical

**medicated** ['mɛdɪkeɪtɪd] adj traitant(e), médicamenteux(-euse)

**medication** [mɛdɪ'keɪʃən] n (*drugs etc*) médication f

**medicine** ['mɛdsɪn] n médecine f; (*drug*) médicament m

**medieval** [mɛdɪ'iːvl] adj médiéval(e)

**mediocre** [miːdɪ'əʊkəʳ] adj médiocre

**meditate** ['mɛdɪteɪt] vi: **to ~ (on)** méditer (sur)

**meditation** [mɛdɪ'teɪʃən] n méditation f

**Mediterranean** [mɛdɪtə'reɪnɪən] adj méditerranéen(ne); **the ~ (Sea)** la (mer) Méditerranée

**medium** ['miːdɪəm] adj moyen(ne) ▷ n (*pl* **media**: *means*) moyen m; (*pl* **~s**: *person*) médium m; **the happy ~** le juste milieu; **medium-sized** adj de taille moyenne; **medium wave** n (*Radio*) ondes moyennes, petites ondes

**meek** [miːk] adj doux (douce), humble

**meet** (pt, pp **met**) [miːt, mɛt] vt rencontrer; (*by arrangement*) retrouver, rejoindre; (*for the first time*) faire la connaissance de; (*go and fetch*): **I'll ~ you at the station** j'irai te chercher à la gare; (*opponent, danger, problem*) faire face à; (*requirements*) satisfaire à, répondre à ▷ *vi* (*friends*) se rencontrer; se retrouver; (*in session*) se réunir; (*join: lines, roads*) se joindre; **nice ~ing you** ravi d'avoir fait votre connaissance; **meet up** *vi*: **to ~ up with sb** rencontrer qn; **meet with** *vt fus* (*difficulty*) rencontrer; **to ~ with success** être couronné(e) de succès; **meeting** *n* (*of group of people*) réunion *f*; (*between individuals*) rendez-vous *m*; **she's at or in a meeting** (*Comm*) elle est en réunion; **meeting place** *n* lieu *m* de (la) réunion; (*for appointment*) lieu de rendez-vous

**megabyte** ['mɛɡəbaɪt] *n* (*Comput*) méga-octet *m*

**megaphone** ['mɛɡəfəʊn] *n* porte-voix *m inv*

**megapixel** ['mɛɡəpɪksl] *n* mégapixel *m*

**melancholy** ['mɛlənkəlɪ] *n* mélancolie *f* ▷ *adj* mélancolique

**melody** ['mɛlədɪ] *n* mélodie *f*

**melon** ['mɛlən] *n* melon *m*

**melt** [mɛlt] *vi* fondre ▷ *vt* faire fondre

**member** ['mɛmbəʳ] *n* membre *m*; **Member of Congress** (*US*) *n* membre *m* du Congrès, ≈ député *m*; **Member of Parliament (MP)** *n* (*BRIT*) député *m*; **Member of the European Parliament (MEP)** *n* Eurodéputé *m*; **Member of the House of Representatives (MHR)** *n* (*US*) membre *m* de la Chambre des représentants; **Member of the Scottish Parliament (MSP)** *n* (*BRIT*) député *m* au Parlement écossais; **membership** *n* (*becoming a member*) adhésion *f*; admission *f*; (*the members*) membres *mpl*, adhérents *mpl*; **membership card** *n* carte *f* de membre

**memento** [mə'mɛntəʊ] *n* souvenir *m*

**memo** ['mɛməʊ] *n* note *f* (de service)

**memorable** ['mɛmərəbl] *adj* mémorable

**memorandum** (*pl* **memoranda**) [mɛmə'rændəm, -də] *n* note *f* (de service)

**memorial** [mɪ'mɔːrɪəl] *n* mémorial *m* ▷ *adj* commémoratif(-ive)

**memorize** ['mɛməraɪz] *vt* apprendre or retenir par cœur

**memory** ['mɛmərɪ] *n* (*also Comput*) mémoire *f*; (*recollection*) souvenir *m*; **in ~ of** à la mémoire de; **memory card** *n* (*for digital camera*) carte *f* mémoire

**men** [mɛn] *npl of* **man**

**menace** ['mɛnɪs] *n* menace *f*; (*inf: nuisance*) peste *f*, plaie *f* ▷ *vt* menacer

**mend** [mɛnd] *vt* réparer; (*darn*) raccommoder, repriser ▷ *n*: **on the ~** en voie de guérison; **to ~ one's ways** s'amender

**meningitis** [mɛnɪn'dʒaɪtɪs] *n* méningite *f*

**menopause** ['mɛnəʊpɔːz] *n* ménopause *f*

**men's room** (*US*) *n*: **the men's room** les toilettes *fpl* pour hommes

**menstruation** [mɛnstru'eɪʃən] *n* menstruation *f*

**menswear** ['mɛnzwɛəʳ] *n* vêtements *mpl* d'hommes

**mental** ['mɛntl] *adj* mental(e); **mental hospital** *n* hôpital *m* psychiatrique; **mentality** [mɛn'tælɪtɪ] *n* mentalité *f*; **mentally** *adv*: **to be mentally handicapped** être handicapé(e) mental(e); **the mentally ill** les malades mentaux

**menthol** ['mɛnθɒl] *n* menthol *m*

**mention** ['mɛnʃən] *n* mention *f* ▷ *vt* mentionner, faire mention de; **don't ~ it!** je vous en prie, il n'y a pas de quoi!

**menu** ['mɛnjuː] *n* (*set menu, Comput*) menu *m*; (*list of dishes*) carte *f*; **could we see the ~?** est-ce qu'on peut voir la carte?

**MEP** *n abbr* = **Member of the European Parliament**

**mercenary** ['məːsɪnərɪ] *adj* (*person*) intéressé(e), mercenaire ▷ *n* mercenaire *m*

**merchandise** [ˈmɜːtʃəndaɪz] *n* marchandises *fpl*

**merchant** [ˈmɜːtʃənt] *n* négociant *m*, marchand *m*; **merchant bank** *n* (*BRIT*) banque *f* d'affaires; **merchant navy** (*US* **merchant marine**) *n* marine marchande

**merciless** [ˈmɜːsɪlɪs] *adj* impitoyable, sans pitié

**mercury** [ˈmɜːkjʊrɪ] *n* mercure *m*

**mercy** [ˈmɜːsɪ] *n* pitié *f*, merci *f*; (*Rel*) miséricorde *f*; **at the ~ of** à la merci de

**mere** [mɪə'] *adj* simple; (*chance*) pur(e); **a ~ two hours** seulement deux heures; **merely** *adv* simplement, purement

**merge** [mɜːdʒ] *vt* unir; (*Comput*) fusionner, interclasser ▷ *vi* (*colours, shapes, sounds*) se mêler; (*roads*) se joindre; (*Comm*) fusionner; **merger** *n* (*Comm*) fusion *f*

**meringue** [məˈræŋ] *n* meringue *f*

**merit** [ˈmɛrɪt] *n* mérite *m*, valeur *f* ▷ *vt* mériter

**mermaid** [ˈmɜːmeɪd] *n* sirène *f*

**merry** [ˈmɛrɪ] *adj* gai(e); **M~ Christmas!** joyeux Noël!; **merry-go-round** *n* manège *m*

**mesh** [mɛʃ] *n* mailles *fpl*

**mess** [mɛs] *n* désordre *m*, fouillis *m*, pagaille *f*; (*muddle: of life*) gâchis *m*; (*: of economy*) pagaille *f*; (*dirt*) saleté *f*; (*Mil*) mess *m*, cantine *f*; **to be (in) a ~** être en désordre; **to be/get o.s. in a ~** (*fig*) être/se mettre dans le pétrin; **mess about** *or* **around** (*inf*) *vi* perdre son temps; **mess up** *vt* (*dirty*) salir; (*spoil*) gâcher; **mess with** (*inf*) *vt fus* (*challenge, confront*) se frotter à; (*interfere with*) toucher à

**message** [ˈmɛsɪdʒ] *n* message *m*; **can I leave a ~?** est-ce que je peux laisser un message?; **are there any ~s for me?** est-ce que j'ai des messages?

**messenger** [ˈmɛsɪndʒə'] *n* messager *m*

**Messrs, Messrs.** [ˈmɛsəz] *abbr* (*on letters: = messieurs*) MM

**messy** [ˈmɛsɪ] *adj* (*dirty*) sale; (*untidy*) en désordre

**met** [mɛt] *pt, pp of* **meet**

**metabolism** [mɛˈtæbəlɪzəm] *n* métabolisme *m*

**metal** [ˈmɛtl] *n* métal *m* ▷ *cpd* en métal; **metallic** [mɛˈtælɪk] *adj* métallique

**metaphor** [ˈmɛtəfə'] *n* métaphore *f*

**meteor** [ˈmiːtɪə'] *n* météore *m*; **meteorite** [ˈmiːtɪəraɪt] *n* météorite *m or f*

**meteorology** [miːtɪəˈrɔlədʒɪ] *n* météorologie *f*

**meter** [ˈmiːtə'] *n* (*instrument*) compteur *m*; (*also*: **parking ~**) parc(o)mètre *m*; (*US: unit*) = **metre** ▷ *vt* (*US Post*) affranchir à la machine

**method** [ˈmɛθəd] *n* méthode *f*; **methodical** [mɪˈθɔdɪkl] *adj* méthodique

**methylated spirit** [ˈmɛθɪleɪtɪd-] *n* (*BRIT: also*: **meths**) alcool *m* à brûler

**meticulous** [mɛˈtɪkjuləs] *adj* méticuleux(-euse)

**metre** (*US* **meter**) [ˈmiːtə'] *n* mètre *m*

**metric** [ˈmɛtrɪk] *adj* métrique

**metro** [ˈmɛtrəu] *n* métro *m*

**metropolitan** [mɛtrəˈpɔlɪtən] *adj* métropolitain(e); **the M~ Police** (*BRIT*) la police londonienne

**Mexican** [ˈmɛksɪkən] *adj* mexicain(e) ▷ *n* Mexicain(e)

**Mexico** [ˈmɛksɪkəu] *n* Mexique *m*

**mg** *abbr* (= *milligram*) mg

**mice** [maɪs] *npl of* **mouse**

**micro...** [maɪkrəu] *prefix*: **microchip** *n* (*Elec*) puce *f*; **microphone** *n* microphone *m*; **microscope** *n* microscope *m*; **microwave** *n* (*also*: **microwave oven**) four *m* à micro-ondes

**mid** [mɪd] *adj*: **~ May** la mi-mai; **~ afternoon** le milieu de l'après-midi; **in ~ air** en plein ciel; **he's in his ~ thirties** il a dans les trente-cinq ans; **midday** *n* midi *m*

**middle** [ˈmɪdl] *n* milieu *m*; (*waist*) ceinture *f*, taille *f* ▷ *adj* du milieu; (*average*) moyen(ne); **in the ~ of the night** au milieu de la nuit; **middle-**

**aged** adj d'un certain âge, ni vieux ni jeune; **Middle Ages** npl: **the Middle Ages** le moyen âge; **middle-class** adj bourgeois(e); **middle class(es)** n(pl): **the middle class(es)** ≈ les classes moyennes; **Middle East** n: **the Middle East** le Proche-Orient, le Moyen-Orient; **middle name** n second prénom; **middle school** n (us) école pour les enfants de 12 à 14 ans, ≈ collège m; (BRIT) école pour les enfants de 8 à 14 ans

**midge** [mɪdʒ] n moucheron m

**midget** ['mɪdʒɪt] n nain(e)

**midnight** ['mɪdnaɪt] n minuit m

**midst** [mɪdst] n: **in the ~ of** au milieu de

**midsummer** [mɪd'sʌmər] n milieu m de l'été

**midway** [mɪd'weɪ] adj, adv: **~ (between)** à mi-chemin (entre); **~ through ...** au milieu de ..., en plein(e) ...

**midweek** [mɪd'wiːk] adv au milieu de la semaine, en pleine semaine

**midwife** (pl **midwives**) ['mɪdwaɪf, -vz] n sage-femme f

**midwinter** [mɪd'wɪntər] n milieu m de l'hiver

**might** [maɪt] vb see **may** ▷ n puissance f, force f; **mighty** adj puissant(e)

**migraine** ['miːɡreɪn] n migraine f

**migrant** ['maɪɡrənt] n (bird, animal) migrateur m; (person) migrant(e) ▷ adj migrateur(-trice); migrant(e); (worker) saisonnier(-ière)

**migrate** [maɪ'ɡreɪt] vi migrer

**migration** [maɪ'ɡreɪʃən] n migration f

**mike** [maɪk] n abbr (= microphone) micro m

**mild** [maɪld] adj doux (douce); (reproach, infection) léger(-ère); (illness) bénin(-igne); (interest) modéré(e); (taste) peu relevé(e); **mildly** ['maɪldlɪ] adv doucement; légèrement; **to put it mildly** (inf) c'est le moins qu'on puisse dire

**mile** [maɪl] n mil(l)e m (= 1609 m); **mileage** n distance f en milles, ≈ kilométrage m; **mileometer**

[maɪ'lɒmɪtər] n compteur m kilométrique; **milestone** n borne f; (fig) jalon m

**military** ['mɪlɪtərɪ] adj militaire

**militia** [mɪ'lɪʃə] n milice f

**milk** [mɪlk] n lait m ▷ vt (cow) traire; (fig: person) dépouiller, plumer; (: situation) exploiter à fond; **milk chocolate** n chocolat m au lait; **milkman** (irreg) n laitier m; **milky** adj (drink) au lait; (colour) laiteux(-euse)

**mill** [mɪl] n moulin m; (factory) usine f, fabrique f; (spinning mill) filature f; (flour mill) minoterie f ▷ vt moudre, broyer ▷ vi (also: **~ about**) grouiller

**millennium** (pl **~s** or **millennia**) [mɪ'lɛnɪəm, -'lɛnɪə] n millénaire m

**milli...** ['mɪlɪ] prefix milli...; **milligram(me)** n milligramme m; **millilitre** (us **milliliter**) ['mɪlɪliːtər] n millilitre m; **millimetre** (us **millimeter**) n millimètre m

**million** ['mɪljən] n million m; **a ~ pounds** un million de livres sterling; **millionaire** [mɪljə'nɛər] n millionnaire m; **millionth** [-θ] num millionième

**milometer** [maɪ'lɒmɪtər] n = **mileometer**

**mime** [maɪm] n mime m ▷ vt, vi mimer

**mimic** ['mɪmɪk] n imitateur(-trice) ▷ vt, vi imiter, contrefaire

**min.** abbr (= minute(s)) mn.; (= minimum) min.

**mince** [mɪns] vt hacher ▷ n (BRIT Culin) viande hachée, hachis m; **mincemeat** n hachis de fruits secs utilisés en pâtisserie; (us) viande hachée, hachis m; **mince pie** n sorte de tarte aux fruits secs

**mind** [maɪnd] n esprit m ▷ vt (attend to, look after) s'occuper de; (be careful) faire attention à; (object to): **I don't ~ the noise** je ne crains pas le bruit, le bruit ne me dérange pas; **it is on my ~** cela me préoccupe; **to change one's ~** changer d'avis; **to my ~** à mon avis, selon moi; **to bear sth in ~** tenir compte de qch; **to have sb/sth**

in ~ avoir qn/qch en tête; **to make
up one's ~** se décider; **do you ~ if ...?**
est-ce que cela vous gêne si ...?; **I don't
~** cela ne me dérange pas; *(don't care)*
ça m'est égal; **~ you, ...** remarquez, ...;
**never ~** peu importe, ça ne fait rien;
*(don't worry)* ne vous en faîtes pas; **"~
the step"** "attention à la marche";
**mindless** *adj* irréfléchi(e); *(violence,
crime)* insensé(e); *(boring: job)* idiot(e)

**mine¹** [maɪn] *pron* le (la) mien(ne), les
miens (miennes); **a friend of ~** un de
mes amis, un ami à moi; **this book is ~**
ce livre est à moi

**mine²** [maɪn] *n* mine *f* ▷ *vt (coal)*
extraire; *(ship, beach)* miner; **minefield**
*n* champ *m* de mines; **miner** *n*
mineur *m*

**mineral** ['mɪnərəl] *adj* minéral(e)
▷ *n* minéral *m*; **mineral water** *n* eau
minérale

**mingle** ['mɪŋgl] *vi*: **to ~ with** se mêler à
**miniature** ['mɪnətʃə'] *adj (en)*
miniature ▷ *n* miniature *f*

**minibar** ['mɪnɪbɑː'] *n* minibar *m*
**minibus** ['mɪnɪbʌs] *n* minibus *m*
**minicab** ['mɪnɪkæb] *n (BRIT)* taxi *m*
indépendant

**minimal** ['mɪnɪml] *adj* minimal(e)
**minimize** ['mɪnɪmaɪz] *vt (reduce)*
réduire au minimum; *(play down)*
minimiser

**minimum** ['mɪnɪməm] *n (pl* **minima)**
minimum *m* ▷ *adj* minimum

**mining** ['maɪnɪŋ] *n* exploitation
minière

**miniskirt** ['mɪnɪskəːt] *n* mini-jupe *f*
**minister** ['mɪnɪstə'] *n (BRIT Pol)*
ministre *m*; *(Rel)* pasteur *m*

**ministry** ['mɪnɪstrɪ] *n (BRIT Pol)*
ministère *m*; *(Rel):* **to go into the ~**
devenir pasteur

**minor** ['maɪnə'] *adj* petit(e), de peu
d'importance; *(Mus, poet, problem)*
mineur(e) ▷ *n (Law)* mineur(e)

**minority** [maɪ'nɔrɪtɪ] *n* minorité *f*
**mint** [mɪnt] *n (plant)* menthe *f*; *(sweet)*
bonbon *m* à la menthe ▷ *vt (coins)*

battre; **the (Royal) M~, the (US)
M~** ≈ l'hôtel *m* de la Monnaie; **in ~
condition** à l'état de neuf

**minus** ['maɪnəs] *n (also:* **~ sign)** signe *m*
moins ▷ *prep* moins; **12 ~ 6 equals 6** 12
moins 6 égal 6; **~ 24˚C** moins 24˚C

**minute¹** *n* ['mɪnɪt] minute *f*; **minutes**
*npl (of meeting)* procès-verbal *m*,
compte rendu; **wait a ~!** (attendez)
un instant!; **at the last ~** à la dernière
minute

**minute²** *adj* [maɪ'njuːt] minuscule;
*(detailed)* minutieux(-euse); **in ~ detail**
par le menu

**miracle** ['mɪrəkl] *n* miracle *m*
**miraculous** [mɪ'rækjuləs] *adj*
miraculeux(-euse)

**mirage** ['mɪrɑːʒ] *n* mirage *m*
**mirror** ['mɪrə'] *n* miroir *m*, glace *f*; *(in
car)* rétroviseur *m*

**misbehave** [mɪsbɪ'heɪv] *vi* mal se
conduire

**misc.** *abbr* = **miscellaneous**
**miscarriage** ['mɪskærɪdʒ] *n (Med)*
fausse couche; **~ of justice** erreur *f*
judiciaire

**miscellaneous** [mɪsɪ'leɪnɪəs] *adj
(items, expenses)* divers(es); *(selection)*
varié(e)

**mischief** ['mɪstʃɪf] *n (naughtiness)*
sottises *fpl*; *(playfulness)* espièglerie
*f*; *(harm)* mal *m*, dommage *m*;
*(maliciousness)* méchanceté *f*;
**mischievous** ['mɪstʃɪvəs] *adj (playful,
naughty)* coquin(e), espiègle

**misconception** ['mɪskən'sɛpʃən] *n*
idée fausse

**misconduct** [mɪs'kɔndʌkt] *n*
inconduite *f*; **professional ~** faute
professionnelle

**miser** ['maɪzə'] *n* avare *m/f*
**miserable** ['mɪzərəbl] *adj (person,
expression)* malheureux(-euse);
*(conditions)* misérable; *(weather)*
maussade; *(offer, donation)* minable;
*(failure)* pitoyable

**misery** ['mɪzərɪ] *n (unhappiness)*
tristesse *f*; *(pain)* souffrances *fpl*;

(*wretchedness*) misère f

**misfortune** [mɪsˈfɔːtʃən] n malchance f, malheur m

**misgiving** [mɪsˈgɪvɪŋ] n (*apprehension*) craintes fpl; **to have ~s about sth** avoir des doutes quant à qch

**misguided** [mɪsˈgaɪdɪd] adj malavisé(e)

**mishap** [ˈmɪshæp] n mésaventure f

**misinterpret** [mɪsɪnˈtəːprɪt] vt mal interpréter

**misjudge** [mɪsˈdʒʌdʒ] vt méjuger, se méprendre sur le compte de

**mislay** [mɪsˈleɪ] vt (*irreg: like* **lay**) égarer

**mislead** [mɪsˈliːd] vt (*irreg: like* **lead**) induire en erreur; **misleading** adj trompeur(-euse)

**misplace** [mɪsˈpleɪs] vt égarer; **to be ~d** (*trust etc*) être mal placé(e)

**misprint** [ˈmɪsprɪnt] n faute f d'impression

**misrepresent** [mɪsrɛprɪˈzɛnt] vt présenter sous un faux jour

**Miss** [mɪs] n Mademoiselle

**miss** [mɪs] vt (*fail to get, attend, see*) manquer, rater; (*regret the absence of*): **I ~ him/it** il/cela me manque ▷ vi manquer ▷ n (*shot*) coup manqué; **we ~ed our train** nous avons raté notre train; **you can't ~ it** vous ne pouvez pas vous tromper; **miss out** vt (BRIT) oublier; **miss out on** vt fus (*fun, party*) rater, manquer; (*chance, bargain*) laisser passer

**missile** [ˈmɪsaɪl] n (*Aviat*) missile m; (*object thrown*) projectile m

**missing** [ˈmɪsɪŋ] adj manquant(e); (*after escape, disaster: person*) disparu(e); **to go ~** disparaître; **~ in action** (*Mil*) porté(e) disparu(e)

**mission** [ˈmɪʃən] n mission f; **on a ~ to sb** en mission auprès de qn; **missionary** n missionnaire m/f

**misspell** [ˈmɪsˈspɛl] vt (*irreg: like* **spell**) mal orthographier

**mist** [mɪst] n brume f ▷ vi (*also: ~ over, ~ up*) devenir brumeux(-euse); (BRIT: *windows*) s'embuer

f ▷ vt (*irreg: like* **take**) (*meaning*) mal comprendre; (*intentions*) se méprendre sur; **to ~ for** prendre pour; **by ~** par erreur, par inadvertance; **to make a ~** (*in writing*) faire une faute; (*in calculating etc*) faire une erreur; **there must be some ~** il doit y avoir une erreur, se tromper; **mistaken** pp of **mistake** ▷ adj (*idea etc*) erroné(e); **to be mistaken** faire erreur, se tromper

**mister** [ˈmɪstə] n (*inf*) Monsieur m; *see* **Mr**

**mistletoe** [ˈmɪsltəu] n gui m

**mistook** [mɪsˈtuk] pt of **mistake**

**mistress** [ˈmɪstrɪs] n maîtresse f; (BRIT: *in primary school*) institutrice f; (: *in secondary school*) professeur m

**mistrust** [mɪsˈtrʌst] vt se méfier de

**misty** [ˈmɪstɪ] adj brumeux(-euse); (*glasses, window*) embué(e)

**misunderstand** [mɪsʌndəˈstænd] vt, vi (*irreg: like* **stand**) mal comprendre; **misunderstanding** n méprise f, malentendu m; **there's been a misunderstanding** il y a eu un malentendu

**misunderstood** [mɪsʌndəˈstud] pt, pp of **misunderstand** ▷ adj (*person*) incompris(e)

**misuse** n [mɪsˈjuːs] mauvais emploi; (*of power*) abus m ▷ vt [mɪsˈjuːz] mal employer; abuser de

**mitt(en)** [ˈmɪt(n)] n moufle f; (*fingerless*) mitaine f

**mix** [mɪks] vt mélanger; (*sauce, drink etc*) préparer ▷ vi se mélanger; (*socialize*): **he doesn't ~ well** il est peu sociable ▷ n mélange m; **to ~ sth with sth** mélanger qch à qch; **cake ~** préparation f pour gâteau; **mix up** vt mélanger; (*confuse*) confondre; **to be ~ed up in sth** être mêlé(e) à qch ou impliqué(e) dans qch; **mixed** adj (*feelings, reactions*) contradictoire; (*school, marriage*) mixte; **mixed grill** n (BRIT) assortiment m de grillades; **mixed salad** n salade f de crudités; **mixed-up** adj (*person*) désorienté(e), embrouillé(e); **mixer**

*n* (*for food*) batteur *m*, mixeur *m*;
(*drink*) boisson gazeuse (*servant à couper un alcool*); (*person*): **he is a good mixer** il est très sociable; **mixture** *n* assortiment *m*, mélange *m*; (*Med*) préparation *f*; **mix-up** *n*: **there was a mix-up** il y a eu confusion

**ml** *abbr* (= *millilitre(s)*) ml

**mm** *abbr* (= *millimetre*) mm

**moan** [məun] *n* gémissement *m* ⊳ *vi* gémir; (*inf: complain*): **to ~ (about)** se plaindre (de)

**moat** [məut] *n* fossé *m*, douves *fpl*

**mob** [mɔb] *n* foule *f*; (*disorderly*) cohue *f* ⊳ *vt* assaillir

**mobile** ['məubaɪl] *adj* mobile ⊳ *n* (*Art*) mobile *m*; **mobile home** *n* caravane *f*; **mobile phone** *n* téléphone portatif

**mobility** [məu'bɪlɪtɪ] *n* mobilité *f*

**mobilize** ['məubɪlaɪz] *vt*, *vi* mobiliser

**mock** [mɔk] *vt* ridiculiser; (*laugh at*) se moquer de ⊳ *adj* faux (fausse); **mocks** *npl* (*BRIT: Scol*) examens blancs; **mockery** *n* moquerie *f*, raillerie *f*

**mod cons** ['mɔd'kɔnz] *npl abbr* (*BRIT*) = **modern conveniences**; *see* **convenience**

**mode** [məud] *n* mode *m*; (*of transport*) moyen *m*

**model** ['mɔdl] *n* modèle *m*; (*person: for fashion*) mannequin *m*; (: *for artist*) modèle ⊳ *vt* (*with clay etc*) modeler ⊳ *vi* travailler comme mannequin ⊳ *adj* (*railway: toy*) modèle réduit *inv*; (*child, factory*) modèle; **to ~ clothes** présenter des vêtements; **to ~ o.s. on** imiter

**modem** ['məudɛm] *n* modem *m*

**moderate** *adj* ['mɔdərət] modéré(e); (*amount, change*) peu important(e) ⊳ *vb* ['mɔdəreɪt] ⊳ *vi* se modérer, se calmer ⊳ *vt* modérer; **moderation** [mɔdə'reɪʃən] *n* modération *f*, mesure *f*; **in ~** à dose raisonnable, pris(e) or pratiqué(e) modérément

**modern** ['mɔdən] *adj* moderne; **modernize** *vt* moderniser; **modern languages** *npl* langues vivantes

**modest** ['mɔdɪst] *adj* modeste;

**modesty** *n* modestie *f*

**modification** [mɔdɪfɪ'keɪʃən] *n* modification *f*

**modify** ['mɔdɪfaɪ] *vt* modifier

**module** ['mɔdjuːl] *n* module *m*

**mohair** ['məuhɛər] *n* mohair *m*

**Mohammed** [mə'hæmɛd] *n* Mahomet *m*

**moist** [mɔɪst] *adj* humide, moite; **moisture** ['mɔɪstʃər] *n* humidité *f*; (*on glass*) buée *f*; **moisturizer** ['mɔɪstʃəraɪzər] *n* crème hydratante

**mold** *etc* [məuld] (*US*) = **mould** *etc*

**mole** [məul] *n* (*animal, spy*) taupe *f*; (*spot*) grain *m* de beauté

**molecule** ['mɔlɪkjuːl] *n* molécule *f*

**molest** [məu'lɛst] *vt* (*assault sexually*) attenter à la pudeur de

**molten** ['məultən] *adj* fondu(e); (*rock*) en fusion

**mom** [mɔm] *n* (*US*) = **mum**

**moment** ['məumənt] *n* moment *m*, instant *m*; **at the ~** en ce moment; **momentarily** ['məuməntrɪlɪ] *adv* momentanément; (*US: soon*) bientôt; **momentary** *adj* momentané(e), passager(-ère); **momentous** [məu'mɛntəs] *adj* important(e), capital(e)

**momentum** [məu'mɛntəm] *n* élan *m*, vitesse acquise; (*fig*) dynamique *f*; **to gather ~** prendre de la vitesse; (*fig*) gagner du terrain

**mommy** ['mɔmɪ] *n* (*US: mother*) maman *f*

**Mon** *abbr* (= *Monday*) l.

**Monaco** ['mɔnəkəu] *n* Monaco *f*

**monarch** ['mɔnək] *n* monarque *m*; **monarchy** *n* monarchie *f*

**monastery** ['mɔnəstərɪ] *n* monastère *m*

**Monday** ['mʌndɪ] *n* lundi *m*

**monetary** ['mʌnɪtərɪ] *adj* monétaire

**money** ['mʌnɪ] *n* argent *m*; **to make ~** (*person*) gagner de l'argent; (*business*) rapporter; **money belt** *n* ceinture-portefeuille *f*; **money order** *n* mandat *m*

**mongrel** [ˈmʌŋgrəl] n (dog) bâtard m
**monitor** [ˈmɒnɪtər] n (TV, Comput)
écran m, moniteur m ▷ vt contrôler;
(foreign station) être à l'écoute de;
(progress) suivre de près
**monk** [mʌŋk] n moine m
**monkey** [ˈmʌŋkɪ] n singe m
**monologue** [ˈmɒnəlɒg] n monologue m
**monopoly** [məˈnɒpəlɪ] n monopole m
**monosodium glutamate**
[mɒnəˈsəʊdɪəm ˈgluːtəmeɪt] n
glutamate m de sodium
**monotonous** [məˈnɒtənəs] adj
monotone
**monsoon** [mɒnˈsuːn] n mousson f
**monster** [ˈmɒnstər] n monstre m
**month** [mʌnθ] n mois m; **monthly** adj
mensuel(le) ▷ adv mensuellement
**Montreal** [mɒntrɪˈɔːl] n Montréal
**monument** [ˈmɒnjumənt] n
monument m
**mood** [muːd] n humeur f, disposition
f; **to be in a good/bad ~** être de
bonne/mauvaise humeur; **moody**
adj (variable) d'humeur changeante,
lunatique; (sullen) morose, maussade
**moon** [muːn] n lune f; **moonlight** n
clair m de lune
**moor** [muər] n lande f ▷ vt (ship)
amarrer ▷ vi mouiller
**moose** [muːs] n (pl inv) élan m
**mop** [mɒp] n balai m à laver; (for dishes)
lavette f à vaisselle ▷ vt éponger,
essuyer; **~ of hair** tignasse f; **mop up**
vt éponger
**mope** [məʊp] vi avoir le cafard, se
morfondre
**moped** [ˈməʊpɛd] n cyclomoteur m
**moral** [ˈmɒrl] adj moral(e) ▷ n morale f;
**morals** npl moralité f
**morale** [mɒˈrɑːl] n moral m
**morality** [məˈrælɪtɪ] n moralité f
**morbid** [ˈmɔːbɪd] adj morbide

**KEYWORD**

**more** [mɔːr] adj 1 (greater in number
etc) plus (de), davantage (de); **more
people/work (than)** plus de gens/de
travail (que)
2 (additional) encore (de); **do you want
(some) more tea?** voulez-vous encore
du thé?; **is there any more wine?**
reste-t-il du vin?; **I have no** or **I don't
have any more money** je n'ai plus
d'argent; **it'll take a few more weeks**
ça prendra encore quelques semaines
▷ pron plus, davantage; **more than
10** plus de 10; **it cost more than we
expected** cela a coûté plus que prévu; **I
want more** j'en veux plus or davantage;
**is there any more?** est-ce qu'il en
reste?; **there's no more** il n'y en a plus;
**a little more** un peu plus; **many/much
more** beaucoup plus, bien davantage
▷ adv plus; **more dangerous/easily
(than)** plus dangereux/facilement
(que); **more and more expensive** de
plus en plus cher; **more or less** plus
ou moins; **more than ever** plus que
jamais; **once more** encore une fois,
une fois de plus

**moreover** [mɔːˈrəʊvər] adv de plus
**morgue** [mɔːg] n morgue f
**morning** [ˈmɔːnɪŋ] n matin m; (as
duration) matinée f ▷ cpd matinal(e);
(paper) du matin; **in the ~** le matin;
**7 o'clock in the ~** 7 heures du matin;
**morning sickness** n nausées
matinales
**Moroccan** [məˈrɒkən] adj marocain(e)
▷ n Marocain(e)
**Morocco** [məˈrɒkəʊ] n Maroc m
**moron** [ˈmɔːrɒn] n idiot(e), minus m/f
**morphine** [ˈmɔːfiːn] n morphine f
**morris dancing** [ˈmɒrɪs-] n (BRIT)
danses folkloriques anglaises

● **MORRIS DANCING**
●
● Le **Morris dancing** est une
● danse folklorique anglaise
● traditionnelle réservée aux
● hommes. Habillés tout en blanc
● et portant des clochettes, ils

- exécutent différentes figures avec des mouchoirs et de longs bâtons.
- Cette danse est très populaire dans les fêtes de village.

**Morse** [mɔːs] *n* (*also:* **~ code**) morse *m*

**mortal** [ˈmɔːtl] *adj*, *n* mortel(le)

**mortar** [ˈmɔːtəʳ] *n* mortier *m*

**mortgage** [ˈmɔːgɪdʒ] *n* hypothèque *f*; (*loan*) prêt *m* (*or* crédit *m*) hypothécaire ▷ *vt* hypothéquer

**mortician** [mɔːˈtɪʃən] *n* (*us*) entrepreneur *m* de pompes funèbres

**mortified** [ˈmɔːtɪfaɪd] *adj* mort(e) de honte

**mortuary** [ˈmɔːtjuərɪ] *n* morgue *f*

**mosaic** [məuˈzeɪɪk] *n* mosaïque *f*

**Moscow** [ˈmɔskəu] *n* Moscou

**Moslem** [ˈmɔzləm] *adj*, *n* = **Muslim**

**mosque** [mɔsk] *n* mosquée *f*

**mosquito** (*pl* **~es**) [mɔsˈkiːtəu] *n* moustique *m*

**moss** [mɔs] *n* mousse *f*

**most** [məust] *adj* (*majority of*) la plupart de; (*greatest amount of*) le plus de ▷ *pron* la plupart ▷ *adv* le plus; (*very*) très, extrêmement; **the ~** le plus; **~ fish** la plupart des poissons; **the ~ beautiful woman in the world** la plus belle femme du monde; **~ of** (*with plural*) la plupart de; (*with singular*) la plus grande partie de; **~ of them** la plupart d'entre eux; **~ of the time** la plupart du temps; **I saw ~** (*a lot but not all*) j'en ai vu la plupart; (*more than anyone else*) c'est moi qui en ai vu le plus; **at the (very) ~** au plus; **to make the ~ of** profiter au maximum de; **mostly** *adv* (*chiefly*) surtout, principalement; (*usually*) généralement

**MOT** *n* *abbr* (*BRIT*) = **Ministry of Transport**; **the ~ (test)** *visite technique (annuelle) obligatoire des véhicules à moteur*

**motel** [məuˈtɛl] *n* motel *m*

**moth** [mɔθ] *n* papillon *m* de nuit; (*in clothes*) mite *f*

**mother** [ˈmʌðəʳ] *n* mère *f* ▷ *vt* (*pamper,* *protect*) dorloter; **motherhood** *n* maternité *f*; **mother-in-law** *n* belle-mère *f*; **mother-of-pearl** *n* nacre *f*; **Mother's Day** *n* fête *f* des Mères; **mother-to-be** *n* future maman; **mother tongue** *n* langue maternelle

**motif** [məuˈtiːf] *n* motif *m*

**motion** [ˈməuʃən] *n* mouvement *m*; (*gesture*) geste *m*; (*at meeting*) motion *f* ▷ *vt*, *vi*: **to ~ (to) sb to do** faire signe à qn de faire; **motionless** *adj* immobile, sans mouvement; **motion picture** *n* film *m*

**motivate** [ˈməutɪveɪt] *vt* motiver

**motivation** [məutɪˈveɪʃən] *n* motivation *f*

**motive** [ˈməutɪv] *n* motif *m*, mobile *m*

**motor** [ˈməutəʳ] *n* moteur *m*; (*BRIT inf: vehicle*) auto *f*; **motorbike** *n* moto *f*; **motorboat** *n* bateau *m* à moteur; **motorcar** *n* (*BRIT*) automobile *f*; **motorcycle** *n* moto *f*; **motorcyclist** *n* motocycliste *m/f*; **motoring** (*BRIT*) *n* tourisme *m* automobile; **motorist** *n* automobiliste *m/f*; **motor racing** *n* (*BRIT*) course *f* automobile; **motorway** *n* (*BRIT*) autoroute *f*

**motto** (*pl* **~es**) [ˈmɔtəu] *n* devise *f*

**mould** (*us* **mold**) [məuld] *n* moule *m*; (*mildew*) moisissure *f* ▷ *vt* mouler, modeler; (*fig*) façonner; **mouldy** *adj* moisi(e); (*smell*) de moisi

**mound** [maund] *n* monticule *m*, tertre *m*

**mount** [maunt] *n* (*hill*) mont *m*, montagne *f*; (*horse*) monture *f*; (*for picture*) carton *m* de montage ▷ *vt* monter; (*horse*) monter à; (*bike*) monter sur; (*picture*) monter sur carton ▷ *vi* (*inflation, tension*) augmenter; **mount up** *vi* s'élever, monter; (*bills, problems, savings*) s'accumuler

**mountain** [ˈmauntɪn] *n* montagne *f* ▷ *cpd* de (la) montagne; **mountain bike** *n* VTT *m*, vélo *m* tout terrain; **mountaineer** *n* alpiniste *m/f*; **mountaineering** *n* alpinisme *m*; **mountainous** *adj* montagneux(-euse);

**mountain range** n chaîne f de montagnes

**mourn** [mɔːn] vt pleurer ▷ vi: **to ~ for sb** pleurer qn; **to ~ for sth** se lamenter sur qch; **mourner** n parent(e) or ami(e) du défunt; personne f en deuil or venue rendre hommage au défunt; **mourning** n deuil m; **in mourning** en deuil

**mouse** (pl **mice**) [maus, maɪs] n (also Comput) souris f; **mouse mat** n (Comput) tapis m de souris

**moussaka** [mu'sɑːkə] n moussaka f

**mousse** [muːs] n mousse f

**moustache** (US **mustache**) [məs'tɑːʃ] n moustache(s) f(pl)

**mouth** [mauθ, pl -ðz] n bouche f; (of dog, cat) gueule f; (of river) embouchure f; (of hole, cave) ouverture f; **mouthful** n bouchée f; **mouth organ** n harmonica m; **mouthpiece** n (of musical instrument) bec m, embouchure f; (spokesperson) porte-parole m inv; **mouthwash** n eau f dentifrice

**move** [muːv] n (movement) mouvement m; (in game) coup m; (: turn to play) tour m; (change of house) déménagement m; (change of job) changement m d'emploi ▷ vt déplacer, bouger; (emotionally) émouvoir; (Pol: resolution etc) proposer ▷ vi (gen) bouger, remuer; (traffic) circuler; (also: ~ **house**) déménager; (in game) jouer; **can you ~ your car, please?** pouvez-vous déplacer votre voiture, s'il vous plaît?; **to ~ sb to do sth** pousser or inciter qn à faire qch; **to get a ~ on** se dépêcher, se remuer; **move back** vi revenir, retourner; **move in** vi (to a house) emménager; (police, soldiers) intervenir; **move off** vi s'éloigner, s'en aller; **move on** vi se remettre en route; **move out** vi (of house) déménager; **move over** vi se pousser, se déplacer; **move up** vi avancer; (employee) avoir de l'avancement; (pupil) passer dans la classe supérieure; **movement** n mouvement m

**movie** ['muːvɪ] n film m; **movies** npl: **the ~s** le cinéma; **movie theater** (US) n cinéma m

**moving** ['muːvɪŋ] adj en mouvement; (touching) émouvant(e)

**mow** (pt **~ed**, pp **~ed** or **~n**) [məu, -d, -n] vt faucher; (lawn) tondre; **mower** n (also: **lawnmower**) tondeuse f à gazon

**Mozambique** [məuzəm'biːk] n Mozambique m

**MP** n abbr (BRIT) = **Member of Parliament**

**MP3** n mp3 m; **MP3 player** n lecteur m mp3

**mpg** n abbr = miles per gallon (30 mpg = 9,4 l. aux 100 km)

**m.p.h.** abbr = miles per hour (60 mph = 96 km/h)

**Mr** (US **Mr.**) ['mɪstər] n: **Mr X** Monsieur X, M. X

**Mrs** (US **Mrs.**) ['mɪsɪz] n: **~ X** Madame X, Mme X

**Ms** (US **Ms.**) [mɪz] n (Miss or Mrs): **Ms X** Madame X, Mme X

**MSP** n abbr (= Member of the Scottish Parliament) député m au Parlement écossais

**Mt** abbr (Geo: = mount) Mt

**much** [mʌtʃ] adj beaucoup de ▷ adv, n or pron beaucoup; **we don't have ~ time** nous n'avons pas beaucoup de temps; **how ~ is it?** combien est-ce que ça coûte?; **it's not ~** ce n'est pas beaucoup; **too ~** trop (de); **so ~** tant (de); **I like it very/so ~** j'aime beaucoup/tellement ça; **as ~ as** autant de; **that's ~ better** c'est beaucoup mieux

**muck** [mʌk] n (mud) boue f; (dirt) ordures fpl; **muck up** vt (inf: ruin) gâcher, esquinter; (: dirty) salir; (: exam, interview) se planter à; **mucky** adj (dirty) boueux(-euse), sale

**mucus** ['mjuːkəs] n mucus m

**mud** [mʌd] n boue f

**muddle** ['mʌdl] n (mess) pagaille f, fouillis m; (mix-up) confusion f ▷ vt (also: ~ **up**) brouiller, embrouiller; **to get in a ~** (while explaining etc) s'embrouiller

**muddy** ['mʌdɪ] *adj* boueux(-euse)

**mudguard** ['mʌdgɑːd] *n* garde-boue *m inv*

**muesli** ['mjuːzlɪ] *n* muesli *m*

**muffin** ['mʌfɪn] *n* (*roll*) petit pain rond et plat; (*cake*) petit gâteau au chocolat ou aux fruits

**muffled** ['mʌfld] *adj* étouffé(e), voilé(e)

**muffler** ['mʌflər] *n* (*scarf*) cache-nez *m inv*; (*us Aut*) silencieux *m*

**mug** [mʌg] *n* (*cup*) tasse *f* (*sans soucoupe*), (: *for beer*) chope *f*; (*inf: face*) bouille *f*; (: *fool*) poire *f* ▷ *vt* (*assault*) agresser; **mugger** ['mʌgər] *n* agresseur *m*; **mugging** *n* agression *f*

**muggy** ['mʌgɪ] *adj* lourd(e), moite

**mule** [mjuːl] *n* mule *f*

**multicoloured** (*us* **multicolored**) ['mʌltɪkʌləd] *adj* multicolore

**multimedia** ['mʌltɪ'miːdɪə] *adj* multimédia *inv*

**multinational** [mʌltɪ'næʃənl] *n* multinationale *f* ▷ *adj* multinational(e)

**multiple** ['mʌltɪpl] *adj* multiple ▷ *n* multiple *m*; **multiple choice (test)** *n* QCM *m*, questionnaire *m* à choix multiple; **multiple sclerosis** [-sklɪ'rəusɪs] *n* sclérose *f* en plaques

**multiplex (cinema)** ['mʌltɪplɛks-] *n* (cinéma *m*) multisalles *m*

**multiplication** [mʌltɪplɪ'keɪʃən] *n* multiplication *f*

**multiply** ['mʌltɪplaɪ] *vt* multiplier ▷ *vi* se multiplier

**multistorey** ['mʌltɪ'stɔːrɪ] *adj* (*BRIT: building*) à étages; (: *car park*) à étages or niveaux multiples

**mum** [mʌm] *n* (*BRIT*) maman *f* ▷ *adj*: **to keep ~** ne pas souffler mot

**mumble** ['mʌmbl] *vt, vi* marmotter, marmonner

**mummy** ['mʌmɪ] *n* (*BRIT: mother*) maman *f*; (*embalmed*) momie *f*

**mumps** [mʌmps] *n* oreillons *mpl*

**munch** [mʌntʃ] *vt, vi* mâcher

**municipal** [mjuː'nɪsɪpl] *adj* municipal(e)

**mural** ['mjuərl] *n* peinture murale

**murder** ['məːdər] *n* meurtre *m*, assassinat *m* ▷ *vt* assassiner; **murderer** *n* meurtrier *m*, assassin *m*

**murky** ['məːkɪ] *adj* sombre, ténébreux(-euse); (*water*) trouble

**murmur** ['məːmər] *n* murmure *m* ▷ *vt, vi* murmurer

**muscle** ['mʌsl] *n* muscle *m*; (*fig*) force *f*; **muscular** ['mʌskjulər] *adj* musculaire; (*person, arm*) musclé(e)

**museum** [mjuː'zɪəm] *n* musée *m*

**mushroom** ['mʌʃrum] *n* champignon *m* ▷ *vi* (*fig*) pousser comme un (*or des*) champignon(s)

**music** ['mjuːzɪk] *n* musique *f*; **musical** *adj* musical(e); (*person*) musicien(ne) ▷ *n* (*show*) comédie musicale; **musical instrument** *n* instrument *m* de musique; **musician** [mjuː'zɪʃən] *n* musicien(ne)

**Muslim** ['mʌzlɪm] *adj, n* musulman(e)

**muslin** ['mʌzlɪn] *n* mousseline *f*

**mussel** ['mʌsl] *n* moule *f*

**must** [mʌst] *aux vb* (*obligation*): **I ~ do it** je dois le faire, il faut que je le fasse; (*probability*): **he ~ be there by now** il doit y être maintenant, il y est probablement maintenant; (*suggestion, invitation*): **you ~ come and see me** il faut que vous veniez me voir ▷ *n* nécessité *f*, impératif *m*; **it's a ~** c'est indispensable; **I ~ have made a mistake** j'ai dû me tromper

**mustache** ['mʌstæʃ] *n* (*us*) = **moustache**

**mustard** ['mʌstəd] *n* moutarde *f*

**mustn't** ['mʌsnt] = **must not**

**mute** [mjuːt] *adj, n* muet(te)

**mutilate** ['mjuːtɪleɪt] *vt* mutiler

**mutiny** ['mjuːtɪnɪ] *n* mutinerie *f* ▷ *vi* se mutiner

**mutter** ['mʌtər] *vt, vi* marmonner, marmotter

**mutton** ['mʌtn] *n* mouton *m*

**mutual** ['mjuːtʃuəl] *adj* mutuel(le), réciproque; (*benefit, interest*) commun(e)

**muzzle** ['mʌzl] *n* museau *m*; (*protective device*) muselière *f*; (*of gun*) gueule *f* ▷ *vt* museler

**my** [maɪ] *adj* mon (ma), mes *pl*; **my house/car/gloves** ma maison/ma voiture/mes gants; **I've washed my hair/cut my finger** je me suis lavé les cheveux/coupé le doigt; **is this my pen or yours?** c'est mon stylo ou c'est le vôtre?

**myself** [maɪ'sɛlf] *pron* (*reflexive*) me; (*emphatic*) moi-même; (*after prep*) moi; *see also* **oneself**

**mysterious** [mɪs'tɪərɪəs] *adj* mystérieux(-euse)

**mystery** ['mɪstərɪ] *n* mystère *m*

**mystical** ['mɪstɪkl] *adj* mystique

**mystify** ['mɪstɪfaɪ] *vt* (*deliberately*) mystifier; (*puzzle*) ébahir

**myth** [mɪθ] *n* mythe *m*; **mythology** [mɪ'θɔlədʒɪ] *n* mythologie *f*

**n/a** *abbr* (= *not applicable*) n.a.

**nag** [næg] *vt* (*scold*) être toujours après, reprendre sans arrêt

**nail** [neɪl] *n* (*human*) ongle *m*; (*metal*) clou *m* ▷ *vt* clouer; **to ~ sth to sth** clouer qch à qch; **to ~ sb down to a date/price** contraindre qn à accepter *or* donner une date/un prix; **nailbrush** *n* brosse *f* à ongles; **nailfile** *n* lime *f* à ongles; **nail polish** *n* vernis *m* à ongles; **nail polish remover** *n* dissolvant *m*; **nail scissors** *npl* ciseaux *mpl* à ongles; **nail varnish** *n* (BRIT) = **nail polish**

**naïve** [naɪ'iːv] *adj* naïf(-ïve)

**naked** ['neɪkɪd] *adj* nu(e)

**name** [neɪm] *n* nom *m*; (*reputation*) réputation *f* ▷ *vt* nommer; (*identify: accomplice etc*) citer; (*price, date*) fixer, donner; **by ~** par son nom; de nom; **in the ~ of** au nom de; **what's your ~?** comment vous appelez-vous?, quel est votre nom?; **namely** *adv* à savoir

**nanny** ['nænɪ] *n* bonne *f* d'enfants

**nap** [næp] *n* (*sleep*) (petit) somme

**napkin** ['næpkɪn] n serviette f (de table)

**nappy** ['næpɪ] n (BRIT) couche f

**narcotics** [nɑːˈkɒtɪkz] npl (illegal drugs) stupéfiants mpl

**narrative** ['nærətɪv] n récit m ▷ adj narratif(-ive)

**narrator** [nəˈreɪtəʳ] n narrateur(-trice)

**narrow** ['nærəʊ] adj étroit(e); (fig) restreint(e), limité(e) ▷ vi (road) devenir plus étroit, se rétrécir; (gap, difference) se réduire; **to have a ~ escape** l'échapper belle; **narrow down** vt restreindre; **narrowly** adv: **he narrowly missed injury/the tree** il a failli se blesser/rentrer dans l'arbre; **he only narrowly missed the target** il a manqué la cible de peu or de justesse; **narrow-minded** adj à l'esprit étroit, borné(e); (attitude) borné(e)

**nasal** ['neɪzl] adj nasal(e)

**nasty** ['nɑːstɪ] adj (person: malicious) méchant(e); (: rude) très désagréable; (smell) dégoûtant(e); (wound, situation) mauvais(e), vilain(e)

**nation** ['neɪʃən] n nation f

**national** ['næʃənl] adj national(e) ▷ n (abroad) ressortissant(e); (when home) national(e); **national anthem** n hymne national; **national dress** n costume national; **National Health Service** n (BRIT) service national de santé, ≈ Sécurité Sociale; **National Insurance** n (BRIT) ≈ Sécurité Sociale; **nationalist** adj, n nationaliste m/f; **nationality** [næʃəˈnælɪtɪ] n nationalité f; **nationalize** vt nationaliser; **national park** n parc national; **National Trust** n (BRIT) ≈ Caisse f nationale des monuments historiques et des sites

NATIONAL TRUST

- Le **National Trust** est un organisme
- indépendant, à but non lucratif,
- dont la mission est de protéger et
- de mettre en valeur les monuments

- et les sites britanniques en raison
- de leur intérêt historique ou de leur
- beauté naturelle.

**nationwide** ['neɪʃənwaɪd] adj s'étendant à l'ensemble du pays; (problem) à l'échelle du pays entier

**native** ['neɪtɪv] n habitant(e) du pays, autochtone m/f ▷ adj du pays, indigène; (country) natal(e); (language) maternel(le); (ability) inné(e); **Native American** ▷ n Indien(ne) d'Amérique ▷ adj amérindien(ne); **native speaker** n locuteur natif

**NATO** ['neɪtəʊ] n abbr (= North Atlantic Treaty Organization) OTAN f

**natural** ['nætʃrəl] adj naturel(le); **natural gas** n gaz naturel; **natural history** n histoire naturelle; **naturally** adv naturellement; **natural resources** npl ressources naturelles

**nature** ['neɪtʃəʳ] n nature f; **by ~** par tempérament, de nature; **nature reserve** n (BRIT) réserve naturelle

**naughty** ['nɔːtɪ] adj (child) vilain(e), pas sage

**nausea** ['nɔːsɪə] n nausée f

**naval** ['neɪvl] adj naval(e)

**navel** ['neɪvl] n nombril m

**navigate** ['nævɪgeɪt] vt (steer) diriger, piloter ▷ vi naviguer; (Aut) indiquer la route à suivre; **navigation** [nævɪˈgeɪʃən] n navigation f

**navy** ['neɪvɪ] n marine f

**navy-blue** ['neɪvɪ'bluː] adj bleu marine inv

**Nazi** ['nɑːtsɪ] n Nazi(e)

**NB** abbr (= nota bene) NB

**near** [nɪəʳ] adj proche ▷ adv près ▷ prep (also: ~ **to**) près de ▷ vt approcher de; **in the ~ future** dans un proche avenir; **nearby** [nɪəˈbaɪ] adj proche ▷ adv tout près, à proximité; **nearly** adv presque; **I nearly fell** j'ai failli tomber; **it's not nearly big enough** ce n'est vraiment pas assez grand, c'est loin d'être assez grand; **near-sighted** adj myope

**neat** [niːt] adj (person, work) soigné(e);

(*room etc*) bien tenu(e) *or* rangé(e);
(*solution, plan*) habile; (*spirits*) pur(e);
**neatly** *adv* avec soin *or* ordre; (*skilfully*)
habilement

**necessarily** ['nɛsɪsrɪlɪ] *adv*
nécessairement; **not ~** pas
nécessairement *or* forcément

**necessary** ['nɛsɪsrɪ] *adj* nécessaire; **if ~**
si besoin est, le cas échéant

**necessity** [nɪ'sɛsɪtɪ] *n* nécessité *f*;
chose nécessaire *or* essentielle

**neck** [nɛk] *n* cou *m*; (*of horse, garment*)
encolure *f*; (*of bottle*) goulot *m*; **~ and ~** à
égalité; **necklace** ['nɛklɪs] *n* collier *m*;
**necktie** ['nɛktaɪ] *n* (*esp us*) cravate *f*

**nectarine** ['nɛktərɪn] *n* brugnon *m*,
nectarine *f*

**need** [niːd] *n* besoin *m* ▷ *vt* avoir besoin
de; **to ~ to do** devoir faire; avoir besoin
de faire; **you don't ~ to go** vous n'avez
pas besoin *or* vous n'êtes pas obligé
de partir; **a signature is ~ed** il faut
une signature; **there's no ~ to do ....**
il n'y a pas lieu de faire ..., il n'est pas
nécessaire de faire ...

**needle** ['niːdl] *n* aiguille *f* ▷ *vt* (*inf*)
asticoter, tourmenter

**needless** ['niːdlɪs] *adj* inutile; **~ to**
**say, ...** inutile de dire que ...

**needlework** ['niːdlwəːk] *n* (*activity*)
travaux *mpl* d'aiguille; (*object*)
ouvrage *m*

**needn't** ['niːdnt] = **need not**

**needy** ['niːdɪ] *adj* nécessiteux(-euse)

**negative** ['nɛgətɪv] *n* (*Phot, Elec*)
négatif *m*; (*Ling*) terme *m* de négation
▷ *adj* négatif(-ive)

**neglect** [nɪ'glɛkt] *vt* négliger; (*garden*)
ne pas entretenir; (*duty*) manquer à
▷ *n* (*of person, duty, garden*) le fait de
négliger; **(state of) ~** abandon *m*; **to ~**
**to do sth** négliger *or* omettre de faire
qch; **to ~ one's appearance** se négliger

**negotiate** [nɪ'gəuʃɪeɪt] *vi* négocier ▷ *vt*
négocier; (*obstacle*) franchir, négocier;
**to ~ with sb for sth** négocier avec qn
en vue d'obtenir qch

**negotiation** [nɪgəuʃɪ'eɪʃən] *n*

négociation *f*, pourparlers *mpl*

**negotiator** [nɪ'gəuʃɪeɪtər] *n*
négociateur(-trice)

**neighbour** (*us* **neighbor** *etc*) ['neɪbər]
*n* voisin(e); **neighbourhood** *n* (*place*)
quartier *m*; (*people*) voisinage *m*;
**neighbouring** *adj* voisin(e),
avoisinant(e)

**neither** ['naɪðər] *adj, pron* aucun(e)
(des deux), ni l'un(e) ni l'autre ▷ *conj*:
**~ do I** moi non plus ▷ *adv*: **~ good nor**
**bad** ni bon ni mauvais; **~ of them** ni
l'un ni l'autre

**neon** ['niːɔn] *n* néon *m*

**Nepal** [nɪ'pɔːl] *n* Népal *m*

**nephew** ['nɛvjuː] *n* neveu *m*

**nerve** [nəːv] *n* nerf *m*; (*bravery*) sang-
froid *m*, courage *m*; (*cheek*) aplomb *m*,
toupet *m*; **nerves** *npl* (*nervousness*)
nervosité *f*; **he gets on my ~s** il
m'énerve

**nervous** ['nəːvəs] *adj* nerveux(-euse);
(*anxious*) inquiet(-ète), plein(e)
d'appréhension; (*timid*) intimidé(e);
**nervous breakdown** *n* dépression
nerveuse

**nest** [nɛst] *n* nid *m* ▷ *vi* (se) nicher,
faire son nid

**Net** [nɛt] *n* (*Comput*): **the ~** (*Internet*)
le Net

**net** [nɛt] *n* filet *m*; (*fabric*) tulle *f* ▷ *adj*
net(te) ▷ *vt* (*fish etc*) prendre au filet;
**netball** *n* netball *m*

**Netherlands** ['nɛðələndz] *npl*: **the ~**
les Pays-Bas *mpl*

**nett** [nɛt] *adj* = **net**

**nettle** ['nɛtl] *n* ortie *f*

**network** ['nɛtwəːk] *n* réseau *m*

**neurotic** [njuə'rɔtɪk] *adj* névrosé(e)

**neuter** ['njuːtər] *adj* neutre ▷ *vt* (*cat etc*)
châtrer, couper

**neutral** ['njuːtrəl] *adj* neutre ▷ *n* (*Aut*)
point mort

**never** ['nɛvər] *adv* (ne ...) jamais; **I ~**
**went** je n'y suis pas allé; **I've ~ been to**
**Spain** je ne suis jamais allé en Espagne;
**~ again** plus jamais; **~ in my life** jamais
de ma vie; *see also* **mind**; **never-ending**

*adj* interminable; **nevertheless**
[nɛvəðə'lɛs] *adv* néanmoins, malgré
tout

**new** [njuː] *adj* nouveau (nouvelle);
(*brand new*) neuf (neuve); **New Age** *n*
New Age *m*; **newborn** *adj* nouveau-
né(e); **newcomer** ['njuːkʌmər] *n*
nouveau venu (nouvelle venue); **newly**
*adv* nouvellement, récemment

**news** [njuːz] *n* nouvelle(s) *f(pl)*; (*Radio,
TV*) informations *fpl*, actualités *fpl*;
**a piece of ~** une nouvelle; **news
agency** *n* agence *f* de presse;
**newsagent** *n* (*BRIT*) marchand *m*
de journaux; **newscaster** *n* (*Radio,
TV*) présentateur(-trice); **news
dealer** *n* (*US*) marchand *m* de
journaux; **newsletter** *n* bulletin *m*;
**newspaper** *n* journal *m*; **newsreader**
*n* = **newscaster**

**newt** [njuːt] *n* triton *m*

**New Year** *n* Nouvel An; **Happy ~!**
Bonne Année!; **New Year's Day** *n*
le jour de l'An; **New Year's Eve** *n* la
Saint-Sylvestre

**New York** [-'jɔːk] *n* New York

**New Zealand** [-'ziːlənd] *n* Nouvelle-
Zélande *f*; **New Zealander** *n* Néo-
Zélandais(e)

**next** [nɛkst] *adj* (*in time*) prochain(e);
(*seat, room*) voisin(e), d'à côté; (*meeting,
bus stop*) suivant(e) ▷ *adv* la fois
suivante; la prochaine fois; (*afterwards*)
ensuite; **~ to** *prep* à côté de; **~ to
nothing** presque rien; **~ time** *adv* la
prochaine fois; **the ~ day** le lendemain,
le jour suivant *or* d'après; **~ year** l'année
prochaine; **~ please!** (*at doctor's etc*) au
suivant!; **the week after** ~ dans deux
semaines; **next door** *adv* à côté ▷ *adj*
(*neighbour*) d'à côté; **next-of-kin** *n*
parent *m* le plus proche

**NHS** *n abbr* (*BRIT*) = **National Health
Service**

**nibble** ['nɪbl] *vt* grignoter

**nice** [naɪs] *adj* (*holiday, trip, taste*)
agréable; (*flat, picture*) joli(e); (*person*)
gentil(le); (*distinction, point*) subtil(e);

**nicely** *adv* agréablement; joliment;
gentiment; subtilement

**niche** [niːʃ] *n* (*Archit*) niche *f*

**nick** [nɪk] *n* (*indentation*) encoche *f*;
(*wound*) entaille *f*; (*BRIT inf*): **in good
~** en bon état ▷ *vt* (*cut*): **to ~ o.s.** se
couper; (*inf: steal*) faucher, piquer; **in
the ~ of time** juste à temps

**nickel** ['nɪkl] *n* nickel *m*; (*US*) pièce *f*
de 5 cents

**nickname** ['nɪkneɪm] *n* surnom *m* ▷ *vt*
surnommer

**nicotine** ['nɪkətiːn] *n* nicotine *f*

**niece** [niːs] *n* nièce *f*

**Nigeria** [naɪ'dʒɪərɪə] *n* Nigéria *m or f*

**night** [naɪt] *n* nuit *f*; (*evening*) soir
*m*; **at ~** la nuit; **by ~** de nuit; **last ~**
(*evening*) hier soir; (*night-time*) la nuit
dernière; **night club** *n* boîte *f* de
nuit; **nightdress** *n* chemise *f* de nuit;
**nightie** ['naɪtɪ] *n* chemise *f* de nuit;
**nightlife** *n* vie *f* nocturne; **nightly**
*adj* (*news*) du soir; (*by night*) nocturne
▷ *adv* (*every evening*) tous les soirs; (*every
night*) toutes les nuits; **nightmare** *n*
cauchemar *m*; **night school** *n* cours
*mpl* du soir; **night shift** *n* équipe *f* de
nuit; **night-time** *n* nuit *f*

**nil** [nɪl] *n* (*BRIT Sport*) zéro *m*

**nine** [naɪn] *num* neuf; **nineteen** *num*
dix-neuf; **nineteenth** [naɪn'tiːnθ] *num*
dix-neuvième; **ninetieth** ['naɪntɪɪθ]
*num* quatre-vingt-dixième; **ninety**
*num* quatre-vingt-dix

**ninth** [naɪnθ] *num* neuvième

**nip** [nɪp] *vt* pincer ▷ *vi* (*BRIT inf*): **to
~ out/down/up** sortir/descendre/
monter en vitesse

**nipple** ['nɪpl] *n* (*Anat*) mamelon *m*, bout
*m* du sein

**nitrogen** ['naɪtrədʒən] *n* azote *m*

◯ **KEYWORD**

**no** [nəʊ] (*pl* **noes**) *adv* (*opposite of "yes"*)
non; **are you coming? — no (I'm not)**
est-ce que vous venez? — non; **would
you like some more? — no thank you**

vous en voulez encore? — non merci
▷ *adj* (*not any*) (ne ...) pas de, (ne ...)
aucun(e); **I have no money/books** je
n'ai pas d'argent/de livres; **no student
would have done it** aucun étudiant ne
l'aurait fait; **"no smoking"** "défense de
fumer"; **"no dogs"** "les chiens ne sont
pas admis"
▷ *n* non *m*

**nobility** [nəʊˈbɪlɪtɪ] *n* noblesse *f*
**noble** [ˈnəʊbl] *adj* noble
**nobody** [ˈnəʊbədɪ] *pron* (ne ...)
personne
**nod** [nɒd] *vi* faire un signe de (la) tête
(*affirmatif ou amical*); (*sleep*) somnoler
▷ *vt*: **to ~ one's head** faire un signe de
(la) tête; (*in agreement*) faire signe que
oui ▷ *n* signe *m* de (la) tête; **nod off** *vi*
s'assoupir
**noise** [nɔɪz] *n* bruit *m*; **I can't sleep for
the ~** je n'arrive pas à dormir à cause du
bruit; **noisy** *adj* bruyant(e)
**nominal** [ˈnɒmɪnl] *adj* (*rent, fee*)
symbolique; (*value*) nominal(e)
**nominate** [ˈnɒmɪneɪt] *vt* (*propose*)
proposer; (*appoint*) nommer;
**nomination** [nɒmɪˈneɪʃən] *n*
nomination *f*; **nominee** [nɒmɪˈniː] *n*
candidat agréé; personne nommée
**none** [nʌn] *pron* aucun(e); **~ of you**
aucun d'entre vous, personne parmi
vous; **I have ~ left** je n'en ai plus; **he's
~ the worse for it** il ne s'en porte pas
plus mal
**nonetheless** [ˈnʌnðəˈlɛs] *adv*
néanmoins
**non-fiction** [nɒnˈfɪkʃən] *n* littérature *f*
non-romanesque
**nonsense** [ˈnɒnsəns] *n* absurdités *fpl*,
idioties *fpl*; **~!** ne dites pas d'idioties!
**non**: **non-smoker** *n* non-fumeur *m*;
**non-smoking** *adj* non-fumeur; **non-
stick** *adj* qui n'attache pas
**noodles** [ˈnuːdlz] *npl* nouilles *fpl*
**noon** [nuːn] *n* midi *m*
**no-one** [ˈnəʊwʌn] *pron* = **nobody**
**nor** [nɔːʳ] *conj* = **neither** ▷ *adv* see

**neither**
**norm** [nɔːm] *n* norme *f*
**normal** [ˈnɔːml] *adj* normal(e);
**normally** *adv* normalement
**Normandy** [ˈnɔːməndɪ] *n* Normandie *f*
**north** [nɔːθ] *n* nord *m* ▷ *adj* nord *inv*;
(*wind*) du nord ▷ *adv* au or vers le nord;
**North Africa** *n* Afrique *f* du Nord;
**North African** *adj* nord-africain(e),
d'Afrique du Nord ▷ *n* Nord-Africain(e);
**North America** *n* Amérique *f* du Nord;
**North American** *n* Nord-Américain(e)
▷ *adj* nord-américain(e), d'Amérique
du Nord; **northbound** [ˈnɔːθbaʊnd]
*adj* (*traffic*) en direction du nord;
(*carriageway*) nord *inv*; **north-east** *n*
nord-est *m*; **northeastern** *adj* (du)
nord-est *inv*; **northern** [ˈnɔːðən] *adj*
du nord, septentrional(e); **Northern
Ireland** *n* Irlande *f* du Nord; **North
Korea** *n* Corée *f* du Nord; **North
Pole** *n*: **the North Pole** le pôle Nord;
**North Sea** *n*: **the North Sea** la mer
du Nord; **north-west** *n* nord-ouest *m*;
**northwestern** [ˈnɔːθˈwestən] *adj* (du)
nord-ouest *inv*
**Norway** [ˈnɔːweɪ] *n* Norvège *f*;
**Norwegian** [nɔːˈwiːdʒən] *adj*
norvégien(ne) ▷ *n* Norvégien(ne);
(*Ling*) norvégien *m*
**nose** [nəʊz] *n* nez *m*; (*of dog, cat*)
museau *m*; (*fig*) flair *m*; **nose about,
nose around** *vi* fouiner or fureter
(partout); **nosebleed** *n* saignement *m*
de nez; **nosey** *adj* (*inf*) curieux(-euse)
**nostalgia** [nɒsˈtældʒɪə] *n* nostalgie *f*
**nostalgic** [nɒsˈtældʒɪk] *adj*
nostalgique
**nostril** [ˈnɒstrɪl] *n* narine *f*; (*of horse*)
naseau *m*
**nosy** [ˈnəʊzɪ] (*inf*) *adj* = **nosey**
**not** [nɒt] *adv* (ne ...) pas; **he is ~ or isn't
here** il n'est pas ici; **you must ~ or
mustn't do that** tu ne dois pas faire
ça; **I hope ~** j'espère que non; **~ at
all** pas du tout; (*after thanks*) de rien;
**it's too late, isn't it?** c'est trop tard,
n'est-ce pas?; **~ yet/now** pas encore/

maintenant; *see also* **only**

**notable** ['nəʊtəbl] *adj* notable; **notably** *adv* (*particularly*) en particulier; (*markedly*) spécialement

**notch** [nɒtʃ] *n* encoche *f*

**note** [nəʊt] *n* note *f*; (*letter*) mot *m*; (*banknote*) billet *m* ▷ *vt* (*also:* **~ down**) noter; (*notice*) constater; **notebook** *n* carnet *m*; (*for shorthand etc*) blocnotes *m*; **noted** ['nəʊtɪd] *adj* réputé(e); **notepad** *n* bloc-notes *m*; **notepaper** *n* papier *m* à lettres

**nothing** ['nʌθɪŋ] *n* rien *m*; **he does ~** il ne fait rien; **~ new** rien de nouveau; **for ~** (*free*) pour rien, gratuitement; (*in vain*) pour rien; **~ at all** rien du tout; **~ much** pas grand-chose

**notice** ['nəʊtɪs] *n* (*announcement, warning*) avis *m* ▷ *vt* remarquer, s'apercevoir de; **advance ~** préavis *m*; **at short ~** dans un délai très court; **until further ~** jusqu'à nouvel ordre; **to give ~, hand in one's ~** (*employee*) donner sa démission, démissionner; **to take ~ of** prêter attention à; **to bring sth to sb's ~** porter qch à la connaissance de qn; **noticeable** *adj* visible

**notice board** *n* (BRIT) panneau *m* d'affichage

**notify** ['nəʊtɪfaɪ] *vt*: **to ~ sb of sth** avertir qn de qch

**notion** ['nəʊʃən] *n* idée *f*; (*concept*) notion *f*; **notions** *npl* (US: haberdashery) mercerie *f*

**notorious** [nəʊ'tɔːrɪəs] *adj* notoire (*souvent en mal*)

**notwithstanding** [nɒtwɪθ'stændɪŋ] *adv* néanmoins ▷ *prep* en dépit de

**nought** [nɔːt] *n* zéro *m*

**noun** [naʊn] *n* nom *m*

**nourish** ['nʌrɪʃ] *vt* nourrir; **nourishment** *n* nourriture *f*

**Nov.** *abbr* (= *November*) nov

**novel** ['nɒvl] *n* roman *m* ▷ *adj* nouveau (nouvelle), original(e); **novelist** *n* romancier *m*; **novelty** *n* nouveauté *f*

**November** [nəʊ'vɛmbər] *n*

novembre *m*

**novice** ['nɒvɪs] *n* novice *m/f*

**now** [naʊ] *adv* maintenant ▷ *conj*: **~ (that)** maintenant (que); **right ~** tout de suite; **by ~** à l'heure qu'il est; **just ~**: **that's the fashion just ~** c'est la mode en ce moment *or* maintenant; **~ and then**, **~ and again** de temps en temps; **from ~ on** dorénavant; **nowadays** ['naʊədeɪz] *adv* de nos jours

**nowhere** ['nəʊwɛər] *adv* (ne ...) nulle part

**nozzle** ['nɒzl] *n* (*of hose*) jet *m*, lance *f*; (*of vacuum cleaner*) suceur *m*

**nr** *abbr* (BRIT) = **near**

**nuclear** ['njuːklɪər] *adj* nucléaire

**nucleus** (*pl* **nuclei**) ['njuːklɪəs, 'njuːklɪaɪ] *n* noyau *m*

**nude** [njuːd] *adj* nu(e) ▷ *n* (Art) nu *m*; **in the ~** (tout(e)) nu(e)

**nudge** [nʌdʒ] *vt* donner un (petit) coup de coude à

**nudist** ['njuːdɪst] *n* nudiste *m/f*

**nudity** ['njuːdɪtɪ] *n* nudité *f*

**nuisance** ['njuːsns] *n*: **it's a ~** c'est (très) ennuyeux *or* gênant; **he's a ~** il est assommant *or* casse-pieds; **what a ~!** quelle barbe!

**numb** [nʌm] *adj* engourdi(e); (*with fear*) paralysé(e)

**number** ['nʌmbər] *n* nombre *m*; (*numeral*) chiffre *m*; (*of house, car, telephone, newspaper*) numéro *m* ▷ *vt* numéroter; (*amount to*) compter; **a ~ of** un certain nombre de; **they were seven in ~** ils étaient (au nombre de) sept; **to be ~ed among** compter parmi; **number plate** *n* (BRIT Aut) plaque *f* minéralogique *or* d'immatriculation; **Number Ten** *n* (BRIT: 10 Downing Street) résidence du Premier ministre

**numerical** [njuː'mɛrɪkl] *adj* numérique

**numerous** ['njuːmərəs] *adj* nombreux(-euse)

**nun** [nʌn] *n* religieuse *f*, sœur *f*

**nurse** [nəːs] *n* infirmière *f*; (*also:* **~maid**) bonne *f* d'enfants ▷ *vt* (*patient, cold*)

soigner

**nursery** ['nə:sərɪ] n (room) nursery f; (institution) crèche f, garderie f; (for plants) pépinière f; **nursery rhyme** n comptine f, chansonnette f pour enfants; **nursery school** n école maternelle; **nursery slope** n (BRIT Ski) piste f pour débutants

**nursing** ['nə:sɪŋ] n (profession) profession f d'infirmière; (care) soins mpl; **nursing home** n clinique f; (for convalescence) maison f de convalescence or de repos; (for old people) maison de retraite

**nurture** ['nə:tʃəʳ] vt élever

**nut** [nʌt] n (of metal) écrou m; (fruit: walnut) noix f; (: hazelnut) noisette f; (: peanut) cacahuète f (terme générique en anglais)

**nutmeg** ['nʌtmɛg] n (noix f) muscade f

**nutrient** ['nju:trɪənt] n substance nutritive

**nutrition** [nju:'trɪʃən] n nutrition f, alimentation f

**nutritious** [nju:'trɪʃəs] adj nutritif(-ive), nourrissant(e)

**nuts** [nʌts] (inf) adj dingue

**NVQ** n abbr (BRIT) = **National Vocational Qualification**

**nylon** ['naɪlɔn] n nylon m ▷ adj de or en nylon

**oak** [əuk] n chêne m ▷ cpd de or en (bois de) chêne

**O.A.P.** n abbr (BRIT) = **old age pensioner**

**oar** [ɔːʳ] n aviron m, rame f

**oasis** (pl **oases**) [əu'eɪsɪs, əu'eɪsiːz] n oasis f

**oath** [əuθ] n serment m; (swear word) juron m; **on** (BRIT) or **under ~** sous serment; assermenté(e)

**oatmeal** ['əutmiːl] n flocons mpl d'avoine

**oats** [əuts] n avoine f

**obedience** [ə'biːdɪəns] n obéissance f

**obedient** [ə'biːdɪənt] adj obéissant(e)

**obese** [əu'biːs] adj obèse

**obesity** [əu'biːsɪtɪ] n obésité f

**obey** [ə'beɪ] vt obéir à; (instructions, regulations) se conformer à ▷ vi obéir

**obituary** [ə'bɪtjuərɪ] n nécrologie f

**object** n ['ɔbdʒɪkt] objet m; (purpose) but m, objet; (Ling) complément m d'objet ▷ vi [əb'dʒɛkt]: **to ~ to** (attitude) désapprouver; (proposal) protester contre, élever une objection contre; **I ~!** je proteste!; **he ~ed that ...** il a fait valoir or a objecté que ...; **money is no ~** l'argent n'est pas un problème; **objection** [əbˈdʒekʃən] n objection f; **if you have no objection** si vous n'y voyez pas d'inconvénient; **objective** n objectif m ▷ adj objectif(-ive)

**obligation** [ɔblɪˈɡeɪʃən] n obligation f, devoir m; (debt) dette f (de reconnaissance)

**obligatory** [əˈblɪɡətərɪ] adj obligatoire

**oblige** [əˈblaɪdʒ] vt (force): **to ~ sb to do** obliger or forcer qn à faire; (do a favour) rendre service à, obliger; **to be ~d to sb for sth** être obligé(e) à qn de qch

**oblique** [əˈbliːk] adj oblique; (allusion) indirect(e)

**obliterate** [əˈblɪtəreɪt] vt effacer

**oblivious** [əˈblɪvɪəs] adj: **~ of** oublieux(-euse) de

**oblong** [ˈɔblɔŋ] adj oblong(ue) ▷ n rectangle m

**obnoxious** [əbˈnɔkʃəs] adj odieux(-euse); (smell) nauséabond(e)

**oboe** [ˈəʊbəʊ] n hautbois m

**obscene** [əbˈsiːn] adj obscène

**obscure** [əbˈskjuəʳ] adj obscur(e) ▷ vt obscurcir; (hide: sun) cacher

**observant** [əbˈzəːvnt] adj observateur(-trice)

**observation** [ɔbzəˈveɪʃən] n observation f; (by police etc) surveillance f

**observatory** [əbˈzəːvətrɪ] n observatoire m

**observe** [əbˈzəːv] vt observer; (remark) faire observer or remarquer; **observer** n observateur(-trice)

**obsess** [əbˈses] vt obséder; **obsession** [əbˈseʃən] n obsession f; **obsessive** adj obsédant(e)

**obsolete** [ˈɔbsəliːt] adj dépassé(e), périmé(e)

**obstacle** [ˈɔbstəkl] n obstacle m

**obstinate** [ˈɔbstɪnɪt] adj obstiné(e); (pain, cold) persistant(e)

**obstruct** [əbˈstrʌkt] vt (block) boucher, obstruer; (hinder) entraver; **obstruction** [əbˈstrʌkʃən] n obstruction f; (to plan, progress) obstacle m

**obtain** [əbˈteɪn] vt obtenir

**obvious** [ˈɔbvɪəs] adj évident(e), manifeste; **obviously** adv manifestement; (of course): **obviously!** bien sûr!; **obviously not!** évidemment pas!, bien sûr que non!

**occasion** [əˈkeɪʒən] n occasion f; (event) événement m; **occasional** adj pris(e) (or fait(e) etc) de temps en temps; (worker, spending) occasionnel(le); **occasionally** adv de temps en temps, quelquefois

**occult** [ɔˈkʌlt] adj occulte ▷ n: **the ~** le surnaturel

**occupant** [ˈɔkjupənt] n occupant m

**occupation** [ɔkjuˈpeɪʃən] n occupation f; (job) métier m, profession f

**occupy** [ˈɔkjupaɪ] vt occuper; **to ~ o.s. with** or **by doing** s'occuper à faire

**occur** [əˈkəːʳ] vi se produire; (difficulty, opportunity) se présenter; (phenomenon, error) se rencontrer; **to ~ to sb** venir à l'esprit de qn; **occurrence** [əˈkʌrəns] n (existence) présence f, existence f; (event) cas m, fait m

**ocean** [ˈəʊʃən] n océan m

**o'clock** [əˈklɔk] adv: **it is 5 o'clock** il est 5 heures

**Oct.** abbr (= October) oct

**October** [ɔkˈtəʊbəʳ] n octobre m

**octopus** [ˈɔktəpəs] n pieuvre f

**odd** [ɔd] adj (strange) bizarre, curieux(-euse); (number) impair(e); (not of a set) dépareillé(e); **60-~** 60 et quelques; **at ~ times** de temps en temps; **the ~ one out** l'exception f; **oddly** adv bizarrement, curieusement; **odds** npl (in betting) cote f; **it makes no odds** cela n'a pas d'importance; **odds and ends** de petites choses; **at odds** en désaccord

**odometer** [ɔˈdɔmɪtəʳ] n (US) odomètre m

**odour** (*US* **odor**) ['əudə<sup>r</sup>] *n* odeur *f*

○ **KEYWORD**

**of** [ɔv, əv] *prep* **1** (*gen*) de; **a friend of ours** un de nos amis; **a boy of 10** un garçon de 10 ans; **that was kind of you** c'était gentil de votre part
**2** (*expressing quantity, amount, dates etc*) de; **a kilo of flour** un kilo de farine; **how much of this do you need?** combien vous en faut-il?; **there were three of them** (*people*) ils étaient 3; (*objects*) il y en avait 3; **three of us went** 3 d'entre nous y sont allé(e)s; **the 5th of July** le 5 juillet; **a quarter of 4** (*US*) 4 heures moins le quart
**3** (*from, out of*) en, de; **a statue of marble** une statue de *or* en marbre; **made of wood** (fait) en bois

**off** [ɔf] *adj, adv* (*engine*) coupé(e); (*light, TV*) éteint(e); (*tap*) fermé(e); (*BRIT: food*) mauvais(e), avancé(e); (: *milk*) tourné(e); (*absent*) absent(e); (*cancelled*) annulé(e); (*removed*): **the lid was ~** le couvercle était retiré *or* n'était pas mis; (*away*): **to run/drive ~** partir en courant/en voiture ▷ *prep* de; **to be ~** (*to leave*) partir, s'en aller; **to be ~ sick** être absent pour cause de maladie; **a day ~** un jour de congé; **to have an ~ day** n'être pas en forme; **he had his coat ~** il avait enlevé son manteau; **10% ~** (*Comm*) 10% de rabais; **5 km ~ (the road)** à 5 km (de la route); **~ the coast** au large de la côte; **it's a long way ~** c'est loin (d'ici); **I'm ~ meat** je ne mange plus de viande; je n'aime plus la viande; **on the ~ chance** à tout hasard; **~ and on, on and ~** de temps à autre
**offence** (*US* **offense**) [ə'fɛns] *n* (*crime*) délit *m*, infraction *f*; **to take ~ at** se vexer de, s'offenser de
**offend** [ə'fɛnd] *vt* (*person*) offenser, blesser; **offender** *n* délinquant(e); (*against regulations*) contrevenant(e)
**offense** [ə'fɛns] *n* (*US*) = **offence**

**offensive** [ə'fɛnsɪv] *adj* offensant(e), choquant(e); (*smell etc*) très déplaisant(e); (*weapon*) offensif(-ive) ▷ *n* (*Mil*) offensive *f*
**offer** ['ɔfə<sup>r</sup>] *n* offre *f*, proposition *f* ▷ *vt* offrir, proposer; **"on ~"** (*Comm*) "en promotion"
**offhand** [ɔf'hænd] *adj* désinvolte ▷ *adv* spontanément
**office** ['ɔfɪs] *n* (*place*) bureau *m*; (*position*) charge *f*, fonction *f*; **doctor's ~** (*US*) cabinet (médical); **to take ~** entrer en fonctions; **office block** (*US* **office building**) *n* immeuble *m* de bureaux; **office hours** *npl* heures *fpl* de bureau; (*US Med*) heures de consultation
**officer** ['ɔfɪsə<sup>r</sup>] *n* (*Mil etc*) officier *m*; (*also*: **police ~**) agent *m* (de police); (*of organization*) membre *m* du bureau directeur
**office worker** *n* employé(e) de bureau
**official** [ə'fɪʃl] *adj* (*authorized*) officiel(le) ▷ *n* officiel *m*; (*civil servant*) fonctionnaire *m/f*; (*of railways, post office, town hall*) employé(e)
**off**: **off-licence** *n* (*BRIT: shop*) débit *m* de vins et de spiritueux; **off-line** *adj* (*Comput*) (en mode) autonome; (: *switched off*) non connecté(e); **off-peak** *adj* aux heures creuses; (*electricity, ticket*) au tarif heures creuses; **off-putting** *adj* (*BRIT: remark*) rébarbatif(-ive); (*person*) rebutant(e), peu engageant(e); **off-season** *adj, adv* hors-saison *inv*
**offset** ['ɔfsɛt] *vt* (*irreg: like* **set**) (*counteract*) contrebalancer, compenser
**offshore** [ɔf'ɔ:<sup>r</sup>] *adj* (*breeze*) de terre; (*island*) proche du littoral; (*fishing*) côtier(-ière)
**offside** ['ɔf'saɪd] *adj* (*Sport*) hors jeu; (*Aut: in Britain*) de droite; (: *in US, Europe*) de gauche
**offspring** ['ɔfsprɪŋ] *n* progéniture *f*
**often** ['ɔfn] *adv* souvent; **how ~ do you go?** vous y allez tous les combien?; **every so ~** de temps en temps, de temps à autre

**oh** [əu] *excl* ô!, oh!, ah!

**oil** [ɔɪl] *n* huile *f*; (*petroleum*) pétrole
*m*; (*for central heating*) mazout *m* ▷ *vt*
(*machine*) graisser; **oil filter** *n* (*Aut*)
filtre *m* à huile; **oil painting** *n* peinture
*f* à l'huile; **oil refinery** *n* raffinerie *f*
de pétrole; **oil rig** *n* derrick *m*; (*at sea*)
plate-forme pétrolière; **oil slick** *n*
nappe *f* de mazout; **oil tanker** *n* (*ship*)
pétrolier *m*; (*truck*) camion-citerne *m*;
**oil well** *n* puits *m* de pétrole; **oily** *adj*
huileux(-euse); (*food*) gras(se)

**ointment** [ˈɔɪntmənt] *n* onguent *m*

**O.K., okay** [ˈəuˈkeɪ] (*inf*) *excl* d'accord!
▷ *vt* approuver, donner son accord à
▷ *adj* (*not bad*) pas mal; **is it O.K.?, are
you O.K.?** ça va?

**old** [əuld] *adj* vieux (vieille); (*person*)
vieux, âgé(e); (*former*) ancien(ne), vieux;
**how ~ are you?** quel âge avez-vous?;
**he's 10 years ~** il a 10 ans, il est âgé de
10 ans; **~er brother/sister** frère/sœur
aîné(e); **old age** *n* vieillesse *f*; **old-
age pension** *n* (*BRIT*) (pension *f* de)
retraite *f* (*de la sécurité sociale*); **old-age
pensioner** *n* (*BRIT*) retraité(e); **old-
fashioned** *adj* démodé(e); (*person*)
vieux jeu *inv*; **old people's home** *n* (*esp
BRIT*) maison *f* de retraite

**olive** [ˈɔlɪv] *n* (*fruit*) olive *f*; (*tree*) olivier
*m* ▷ *adj* (*also*: **~-green**) (vert) olive *inv*;
**olive oil** *n* huile *f* d'olive

**Olympic** [əuˈlɪmpɪk] *adj* olympique;
**the ~ Games, the ~s** les Jeux *mpl*
olympiques

**omelet(te)** [ˈɔmlɪt] *n* omelette *f*

**omen** [ˈəumən] *n* présage *m*

**ominous** [ˈɔmɪnəs] *adj* menaçant(e),
inquiétant(e); (*event*) de mauvais
augure

**omit** [əuˈmɪt] *vt* omettre

**KEYWORD**

**on** [ɔn] *prep* 1 (*indicating position*) sur; **on
the table** sur la table; **on the wall** sur le
or au mur; **on the left** à gauche
2 (*indicating means, method, condition
etc*): **on foot** à pied; **on the train/plane**
(*be*) dans le train/l'avion; (*go*) en
train/avion; **on the telephone/radio/
television** au téléphone/à la radio/à la
télévision; **to be on drugs** se droguer;
**on holiday** (*BRIT*), **on vacation** (*US*)
en vacances
3 (*referring to time*): **on Friday** vendredi;
**on Fridays** le vendredi; **on June 20th** le
20 juin; **a week on Friday** vendredi en
huit; **on arrival** à l'arrivée; **on seeing
this** en voyant cela
4 (*about, concerning*) sur, de; **a book on
Balzac/physics** un livre sur Balzac/physique
▷ *adv* 1 (*referring to dress*): **to have one's
coat on** avoir (mis) son manteau;
**to put one's coat on** mettre son
manteau; **what's she got on?** qu'est-ce
qu'elle porte?
2 (*referring to covering*): **screw the lid on
tightly** vissez bien le couvercle
3 (*further, continuously*): **to walk** *etc* **on**
continuer à marcher *etc*; **from that day
on** depuis ce jour
▷ *adj* 1 (*in operation: machine*) en
marche; (: *radio, TV, light*) allumé(e);
(: *tap, gas*) ouvert(e); (: *brakes*) mis(e);
**is the meeting still on?** (*not cancelled*)
est-ce que la réunion a bien lieu?; (*in
progress*) la réunion dure-t-elle encore?;
**when is this film on?** quand passe
ce film?
2 (*inf*): **that's not on!** (*not acceptable*)
cela ne se fait pas!; (*not possible*) pas
question!

**once** [wʌns] *adv* une fois; (*formerly*)
autrefois ▷ *conj* une fois que + *sub*; **~ he
had left/it was done** une fois qu'il fut
parti/ que ce fut terminé; **at ~** tout de
suite, immédiatement; (*simultaneously*)
à la fois; **all at ~** *adv* tout d'un coup; **~
a week** une fois par semaine; **~ more**
encore une fois; **~ and for all** une fois
pour toutes; **~ upon a time there
was ...** il y avait une fois ..., il était
une fois ...

**oncoming** ['ɔnkʌmɪŋ] adj (traffic) venant en sens inverse

**KEYWORD**

**one** [wʌn] num un(e); **one hundred and fifty** cent cinquante; **one by one** un(e) à or par un(e); **one day** un jour
▷ adj **1** (sole) seul(e), unique; **the one book which** l'unique or le seul livre qui; **the one man who** le seul (homme) qui **2** (same) même; **they came in the one car** ils sont venus dans la même voiture
▷ pron **1**: **this one** celui-ci (celle-ci); **that one** celui-là (celle-là); **I've already got one/a red one** j'en ai déjà un(e)/un(e) rouge; **which one do you want?** lequel voulez-vous?
**2**: **one another** l'un(e) l'autre; **to look at one another** se regarder
**3** (impersonal): **one never knows** on ne sait jamais; **to cut one's finger** se couper le doigt; **one needs to eat** il faut manger

**one-off** [wʌn'ɔf] (BRIT inf) n exemplaire m unique

**oneself** [wʌn'sɛlf] pron se; (after prep, also emphatic) soi-même; **to hurt ~** se faire mal; **to keep sth for ~** garder qch pour soi; **to talk to ~** se parler à soi-même; **by ~** tout seul

**one: one-shot** [wʌn'ʃɔt] (US) n = **one-off**; **one-sided** adj (argument, decision) unilatéral(e); **one-to-one** adj (relationship) univoque; **one-way** adj (street, traffic) à sens unique

**ongoing** ['ɔngəʊɪŋ] adj en cours; (relationship) suivi(e)

**onion** ['ʌnjən] n oignon m

**on-line** ['ɔnlaɪn] adj (Comput) en ligne; (: switched on) connecté(e)

**onlooker** ['ɔnlʊkər] n spectateur(-trice)

**only** ['əʊnlɪ] adv seulement ▷ adj seul(e), unique ▷ conj seulement, mais; **an ~ child** un enfant unique; **not ~ ... but also** non seulement ... mais aussi; **I**

**~ took one** j'en ai seulement pris un, je n'en ai pris qu'un

**on-screen** [ɔn'skriːn] adj à l'écran

**onset** ['ɔnsɛt] n début m; (of winter, old age) approche f

**onto** ['ɔntu] prep = **on to**

**onward(s)** ['ɔnwəd(z)] adv (move) en avant; **from that time ~** à partir de ce moment

**oops** [ʊps] excl houp!

**ooze** [uːz] vi suinter

**opaque** [əʊ'peɪk] adj opaque

**open** ['əʊpn] adj ouvert(e); (car) découvert(e); (road, view) dégagé(e); (meeting) public(-ique); (admiration) manifeste ▷ vt ouvrir ▷ vi (flower, eyes, door, debate) s'ouvrir; (shop, bank, museum) ouvrir; (book etc: commence) commencer, débuter; **is it ~ to public?** est-ce ouvert au public?; **what time do you ~?** à quelle heure ouvrez-vous?; **in the ~ (air)** en plein air; **open up** vt ouvrir; (blocked road) dégager ▷ vi s'ouvrir; **open-air** adj en plein air; **opening** n ouverture f; (opportunity) occasion f; (work) débouché m; (job) poste vacant; **opening hours** npl heures fpl d'ouverture; **open learning** n enseignement universitaire à la carte, notamment par correspondance; (distance learning) télé-enseignement m; **openly** adv ouvertement; **open-minded** adj à l'esprit ouvert; **open-necked** adj à col ouvert; **open-plan** adj sans cloisons; **Open University** n (BRIT) cours universitaires par correspondance

○ **OPEN UNIVERSITY**
○
○ L'**Open University** a été fondée en
○ 1969. L'enseignement comprend
○ des cours (certaines plages horaires
○ sont réservées à cet effet à la
○ télévision et à la radio), des devoirs
○ qui sont envoyés par l'étudiant à son
○ directeur ou sa directrice d'études, et
○ un séjour obligatoire en université
○ d'été. Il faut préparer un certain

- nombre d'unités de valeur pendant
- une période de temps déterminée
- et obtenir la moyenne à un certain
- nombre d'entre elles pour recevoir le
- diplôme visé.

**opera** ['ɔpərə] n opéra m; **opera house** n opéra m; **opera singer** n chanteur(-euse) d'opéra

**operate** ['ɔpəreɪt] vt (machine) faire marcher, faire fonctionner ▷ vi fonctionner; **to ~ on sb (for)** (Med) opérer qn (de)

**operating room** n (US: Med) salle f d'opération

**operating theatre** n (BRIT: Med) salle f d'opération

**operation** [ɔpə'reɪʃən] n opération f; (of machine) fonctionnement m; **to have an ~ (for)** se faire opérer (de); **to be in ~** (machine) être en service; (system) être en vigueur; **operational** adj opérationnel(le); (ready for use) en état de marche

**operative** ['ɔpərətɪv] adj (measure) en vigueur ▷ n (in factory) ouvrier(-ière)

**operator** ['ɔpəreɪtər] n (of machine) opérateur(-trice); (Tel) téléphoniste m/f

**opinion** [ə'pɪnjən] n opinion f, avis m; **in my ~** à mon avis; **opinion poll** n sondage m d'opinion

**opponent** [ə'pəunənt] n adversaire m/f

**opportunity** [ɔpə'tjuːnɪtɪ] n occasion f; **to take the ~ to do** or **of doing** profiter de l'occasion pour faire

**oppose** [ə'pəuz] vt s'opposer à; **to be ~d to sth** être opposé(e) à qch; **as ~d to** par opposition à

**opposite** ['ɔpəzɪt] adj opposé(e); (house etc) d'en face ▷ adv en face ▷ prep en face de ▷ n opposé m, contraire m; (of word) contraire

**opposition** [ɔpə'zɪʃən] n opposition f

**oppress** [ə'prɛs] vt opprimer

**opt** [ɔpt] vi: **to ~ for** opter pour; **to ~ to do** choisir de faire; **opt out** vi: **to ~ out of** choisir de ne pas participer à or de

ne pas faire

**optician** [ɔp'tɪʃən] n opticien(ne)

**optimism** ['ɔptɪmɪzəm] n optimisme m

**optimist** ['ɔptɪmɪst] n optimiste m/f; **optimistic** [ɔptɪ'mɪstɪk] adj optimiste

**optimum** ['ɔptɪməm] adj optimum

**option** ['ɔpʃən] n choix m, option f; (Scol) matière f à option; **optional** adj facultatif(-ive)

**or** [ɔːr] conj ou; (with negative): **he hasn't seen or heard anything** il n'a rien vu ni entendu; **or else** sinon; ou bien

**oral** ['ɔːrəl] adj oral(e) ▷ n oral m

**orange** ['ɔrɪndʒ] n (fruit) orange f ▷ adj orange inv; **orange juice** n jus m d'orange; **orange squash** n orangeade f

**orbit** ['ɔːbɪt] n orbite f ▷ vt graviter autour de

**orchard** ['ɔːtʃəd] n verger m

**orchestra** ['ɔːkɪstrə] n orchestre m; (US: seating) (fauteuils mpl d')orchestre

**orchid** ['ɔːkɪd] n orchidée f

**ordeal** [ɔː'diːl] n épreuve f

**order** ['ɔːdər] n ordre m; (Comm) commande f ▷ vt ordonner; (Comm) commander; **in ~** en ordre; (of document) en règle; **out of ~** (not in correct order) en désordre; (machine) hors service; (telephone) en dérangement; **a machine in working ~** une machine en état de marche; **in ~ to do/that** pour faire/que + sub; **could I ~ now, please?** je peux commander, s'il vous plaît?; **to be on ~** être en commande; **to ~ sb to do** ordonner à qn de faire; **order form** n bon m de commande; **orderly** n (Mil) ordonnance f; (Med) garçon m de salle ▷ adj (room) en ordre; (mind) méthodique; (person) qui a de l'ordre

**ordinary** ['ɔːdnrɪ] adj ordinaire, normal(e); (pej) ordinaire, quelconque; **out of the ~** exceptionnel(le)

**ore** [ɔːr] n minerai m

**oregano** [ɔrɪ'gɑːnəu] n origan m

**organ** ['ɔːgən] n organe m; (Mus) orgue m, orgues fpl; **organic** [ɔː'gænɪk] adj

organique; (*crops etc*) biologique,
naturel(le); **organism** n organisme m
**organization** [ɔːɡənaɪ'zeɪʃən] n
organisation f
**organize** ['ɔːɡənaɪz] vt organiser;
**organized** ['ɔːɡənaɪzd] adj (*planned*)
organisé(e); (*efficient*) bien organisé;
**organizer** n organisateur(-trice)
**orgasm** ['ɔːɡæzəm] n orgasme m
**orgy** ['ɔːdʒɪ] n orgie f
**oriental** [ɔːrɪ'ɛntl] adj oriental(e)
**orientation** [ɔːrɪɛn'teɪʃən] n (*attitudes*)
tendance f; (*in job*) orientation f; (*of
building*) orientation, exposition f
**origin** ['ɔrɪdʒɪn] n origine f
**original** [ə'rɪdʒɪnl] adj original(e);
(*earliest*) originel(le) ▷ n original m;
**originally** adv (*at first*) à l'origine
**originate** [ə'rɪdʒɪneɪt] vi: **to ~ from**
être originaire de; (*suggestion*) provenir
de; **to ~ in** (*custom*) prendre naissance
dans, avoir son origine dans
**Orkney** ['ɔːknɪ] n (*also*: **the ~s, the ~
Islands**) les Orcades fpl
**ornament** ['ɔːnəmənt] n ornement m;
(*trinket*) bibelot m; **ornamental**
[ɔːnə'mɛntl] adj décoratif(-ive);
(*garden*) d'agrément
**ornate** [ɔː'neɪt] adj très orné(e)
**orphan** ['ɔːfn] n orphelin(e)
**orthodox** ['ɔːθədɔks] adj orthodoxe
**orthopaedic** (us **orthopedic**)
[ɔːθə'piːdɪk] adj orthopédique
**osteopath** ['ɔstɪəpæθ] n ostéopathe
m/f
**ostrich** ['ɔstrɪtʃ] n autruche f
**other** ['ʌðəʳ] adj autre ▷ pron: **the ~
(one)** l'autre; **~s** (*other people*) d'autres
▷ adv: **~ than** autrement que; à part;
**the ~ day** l'autre jour; **otherwise** adv,
conj autrement
**Ottawa** ['ɔtəwə] n Ottawa
**otter** ['ɔtəʳ] n loutre f
**ouch** [autʃ] excl aïe!
**ought** (pt **~**) [ɔːt] aux vb: **I ~ to do it** je
devrais le faire, il faudrait que je le
fasse; **this ~ to have been corrected**
cela aurait dû être corrigé; **he ~ to win**
(*probability*) il devrait gagner
**ounce** [auns] n once f (28.35g; 16 in
a pound)
**our** ['auəʳ] adj notre, nos pl; see also **my**;
**ours** pron le (la) nôtre, les nôtres; see
also **mine¹**; **ourselves** pron pl (*reflexive,
after preposition*) nous; (*emphatic*) nous-
mêmes; see also **oneself**
**oust** [aust] vt évincer
**out** [aut] adv dehors; (*published, not at
home etc*) sorti(e); (*light, fire*) éteint(e); **~
there** là-bas; **he's ~** (*absent*) il est sorti;
**to be ~ in one's calculations** s'être
trompé dans ses calculs; **to run/back**
etc **~** sortir en courant/en reculant
etc; **~ loud** adv à haute voix; **~ of** prep
(*outside*) en dehors de; (*because of: anger
etc*) par; (*from among*): **10 ~ of 10** 10 sur
10; (*without*): **~ of petrol** sans essence,
à court d'essence; **~ of order** (*machine*)
en panne; (*Tel: line*) en dérangement;
**outback** n (*in Australia*) intérieur m;
**outbound** adj: **outbound (from/for)**
en partance (de/pour); **outbreak**
n (*of violence*) éruption f, explosion
f; (*of disease*) de nombreux cas; **the
outbreak of war south of the border**
la guerre qui s'est déclarée au sud de
la frontière; **outburst** n explosion f,
accès m; **outcast** n exilé(e); (*socially*)
paria m; **outcome** n issue f, résultat m;
**outcry** n tollé (général); **outdated** adj
démodé(e); **outdoor** adj de or en plein
air; **outdoors** adv dehors; au grand air
**outer** ['autəʳ] adj extérieur(e); **outer
space** n espace m cosmique
**outfit** ['autfɪt] n (*clothes*) tenue f
**out**: **outgoing** adj (*president, tenant*)
sortant(e); (*character*) ouvert(e),
extraverti(e); **outgoings** npl (BRIT:
*expenses*) dépenses fpl; **outhouse** n
appentis m, remise f
**outing** ['autɪŋ] n sortie f; excursion f
**out**: **outlaw** n hors-la-loi m inv ▷ vt
(*person*) mettre hors la loi; (*practice*)
proscrire; **outlay** n dépenses fpl;
(*investment*) mise f de fonds; **outlet**
n (*for liquid etc*) issue f, sortie f; (*for

*emotion*) exutoire *m*; (*also*: **retail outlet**) point *m* de vente; (*US*: *Elec*) prise *f* de courant; **outline** *n* (*shape*) contour *m*; (*summary*) esquisse *f*, grandes lignes ▷ *vt* (*fig*: *theory, plan*) exposer à grands traits; **outlook** *n* perspective *f*; (*point of view*) attitude *f*; **outnumber** *vt* surpasser en nombre; **out-of-date** *adj* (*passport, ticket*) périmé(e); (*theory, idea*) dépassé(e); (*custom*) désuet(-ète); (*clothes*) démodé(e); **out-of-doors** *adv* = **outdoors**; **out-of-the-way** *adj* loin de tout; **out-of-town** *adj* (*shopping centre etc*) en périphérie; **outpatient** *n* malade *m/f* en consultation externe; **outpost** *n* avant-poste *m*; **output** *n* rendement *m*, production *f*; (*Comput*) sortie *f* ▷ *vt* (*Comput*) sortir

**outrage** ['autreɪdʒ] *n* (*anger*) indignation *f*; (*violent act*) atrocité *f*, acte *m* de violence; (*scandal*) scandale *m* ▷ *vt* outrager; **outrageous** [aut'reɪdʒəs] *adj* atroce; (*scandalous*) scandaleux(-euse)

**outright** *adv* [aut'raɪt] complètement; (*deny, refuse*) catégoriquement; (*ask*) carrément; (*kill*) sur le coup ▷ *adj* ['autraɪt] complet(-ète); catégorique

**outset** ['autsɛt] *n* début *m*

**outside** [aut'saɪd] *n* extérieur *m* ▷ *adj* extérieur(e) ▷ *adv* (au) dehors, à l'extérieur ▷ *prep* hors de, à l'extérieur de; (*in front of*) devant; **at the ~** (*fig*) au plus *or* maximum; **outside lane** *n* (*Aut*: *in Britain*) voie *f* de droite; (: *in US, Europe*) voie de gauche; **outside line** *n* (*Tel*) ligne extérieure; **outsider** *n* (*stranger*) étranger(-ère)

**out**: **outsize** *adj* énorme; (*clothes*) grande taille *inv*; **outskirts** *npl* faubourgs *mpl*; **outspoken** *adj* très franc (franche); **outstanding** *adj* remarquable, exceptionnel(le); (*unfinished*: *work, business*) en suspens, en souffrance; (*debt*) impayé(e); (*problem*) non réglé(e)

**outward** ['autwəd] *adj* (*sign, appearances*) extérieur(e); (*journey*)

(d')aller; **outwards** *adv* (*esp BRIT*) = **outward**

**outweigh** [aut'weɪ] *vt* l'emporter sur

**oval** ['əuvl] *adj*, *n* ovale *m*

**ovary** ['əuvərɪ] *n* ovaire *m*

**oven** ['ʌvn] *n* four *m*; **oven glove** *n* gant *m* de cuisine; **ovenproof** *adj* allant au four; **oven-ready** *adj* prêt(e) à cuire

**over** ['əuvər] *adv* (par-)dessus ▷ *adj* (*or adv*) (*finished*) fini(e), terminé(e); (*too much*) en plus ▷ *prep* sur; par-dessus; (*above*) au-dessus de; (*on the other side of*) de l'autre côté de; (*more than*) plus de; (*during*) pendant; (*about, concerning*): **they fell out ~ money/her** ils se sont brouillés pour des questions d'argent/à cause d'elle; **~ here** ici; **~ there** là-bas; **all ~** (*everywhere*) partout; **~ and ~ (again)** à plusieurs reprises; **~ and above** en plus de; **to ask sb ~** inviter qn (à passer); **to fall ~** tomber; **to turn sth ~** retourner qch

**overall** ['əuvərɔːl] *adj* (*length*) total(e); (*study, impression*) d'ensemble ▷ *n* (*BRIT*) blouse *f* ▷ *adv* [əuvər'ɔːl] dans l'ensemble, en général; **overalls** *npl* (*boiler suit*) bleus *mpl* (de travail)

**overboard** ['əuvəbɔːd] *adv* (*Naut*) par-dessus bord

**overcame** [əuvə'keɪm] *pt* of **overcome**

**overcast** ['əuvəkɑːst] *adj* couvert(e)

**overcharge** [əuvə'tʃɑːdʒ] *vt*: **to ~ sb for sth** faire payer qch trop cher à qn

**overcoat** ['əuvəkəut] *n* pardessus *m*

**overcome** [əuvə'kʌm] *vt* (*irreg*: *like* **come**) (*defeat*) triompher de; (*difficulty*) surmonter ▷ *adj* (*emotionally*) bouleversé(e); **~ with grief** accablé(e) de douleur

**over**: **overcrowded** *adj* bondé(e); (*city, country*) surpeuplé(e); **overdo** *vt* (*irreg*: *like* **do**) exagérer; (*overcook*) trop cuire; **to overdo it**, **to overdo things** (*work too hard*) en faire trop, se surmener; **overdone** [əuvə'dʌn] *adj* (*vegetables, steak*) trop cuit(e); **overdose** *n* dose excessive; **overdraft** *n* découvert *m*;

**overdrawn** *adj* (*account*) à découvert;
**overdue** *adj* en retard; (*bill*) impayé(e);
(*change*) qui tarde; **overestimate** *vt*
surestimer

**overflow** *vi* [əuvə'fləu] déborder
▷ *n* ['əuvəfləu] (*also*: **~ pipe**) tuyau *m*
d'écoulement, trop-plein *m*

**overgrown** [əuvə'grəun] *adj* (*garden*)
envahi(e) par la végétation

**overhaul** *vt* [əuvə'hɔːl] réviser ▷ *n*
['əuvəhɔːl] révision *f*

**overhead** *adv* [əuvə'hɛd] au-dessus
▷ *adj*, *n* ['əuvəhɛd] ▷ *adj* aérien(ne);
(*lighting*) vertical(e) ▷ *n* (*us*)
= **overheads**; **overhead projector**
*n* rétroprojecteur *m*; **overheads** *npl*
(*BRIT*) frais généraux

**over**: **overhear** *vt* (*irreg: like* **hear**)
entendre (par hasard); **overheat** *vi*
(*engine*) chauffer; **overland** *adj*, *adv* par
voie de terre; **overlap** *vi* se chevaucher;
**overleaf** *adv* au verso; **overload** *vt*
surcharger; **overlook** *vt* (*have view of*)
donner sur; (*miss*) oublier, négliger;
(*forgive*) fermer les yeux sur

**overnight** *adv* [əuvə'naɪt] (*happen*)
durant la nuit; (*fig*) soudain ▷ *adj*
['əuvənaɪt] d'une (*or* de) nuit;
soudain(e); **to stay ~ (with sb)** passer
la nuit (chez qn); **overnight bag** *n*
nécessaire *m* de voyage

**overpass** ['əuvəpaːs] *n* (*us: for cars*)
pont autoroutier; (: *for pedestrians*)
passerelle *f*, pont *m*

**overpower** [əuvə'pauə^r^] *vt* vaincre;
(*fig*) accabler; **overpowering** *adj*
irrésistible; (*heat, stench*) suffocant(e)

**over**: **overreact** [əuvəri:'ækt] *vi*
réagir de façon excessive; **overrule**
*vt* (*decision*) annuler; (*claim*) rejeter;
(*person*) rejeter l'avis de; **overrun** *vt*
(*irreg: like* **run**) (*Mil: country etc*) occuper;
(*time limit etc*) dépasser ▷ *vi* dépasser le
temps imparti

**overseas** [əuvə'siːz] *adv* outre-mer;
(*abroad*) à l'étranger ▷ *adj* (*trade*)
extérieur(e); (*visitor*) étranger(-ère)

**oversee** [əuvə'siː] *vt* (*irreg: like* **see**)

surveiller

**overshadow** [əuvə'ʃædəu] *vt* (*fig*)
éclipser

**oversight** ['əuvəsaɪt] *n* omission *f*,
oubli *m*

**oversleep** [əuvə'sliːp] *vi* (*irreg: like*
**sleep**) se réveiller (trop) tard

**overspend** [əuvə'spɛnd] *vi* (*irreg: like*
**spend**) dépenser de trop

**overt** [əu'vəːt] *adj* non dissimulé(e)

**overtake** [əuvə'teɪk] *vt* (*irreg: like* **take**)
dépasser; (*BRIT: Aut*) dépasser, doubler

**over**: **overthrow** *vt* (*irreg: like* **throw**)
(*government*) renverser; **overtime** *n*
heures *fpl* supplémentaires

**overtook** [əuvə'tuk] *pt of* **overtake**

**over**: **overturn** *vt* renverser; (*decision,
plan*) annuler ▷ *vi* se retourner;
**overweight** *adj* (*person*) trop gros(se);
**overwhelm** *vt* (*subj: emotion*) accabler,
submerger; (*enemy, opponent*) écraser;
**overwhelming** *adj* (*victory, defeat*)
écrasant(e); (*desire*) irrésistible

**ow** [au] *excl* aïe!

**owe** [əu] *vt* devoir; **to ~ sb sth, to ~ sth
to sb** devoir qch à qn; **how much do I ~
you?** combien est-ce que je vous dois?;
**owing to** *prep* à cause de, en raison de

**owl** [aul] *n* hibou *m*

**own** [əun] *vt* posséder ▷ *adj* propre;
**a room of my ~** une chambre à moi,
ma propre chambre; **to get one's ~
back** prendre sa revanche; **on one's
~** tout(e) seul(e); **own up** *vi* avouer;
**owner** *n* propriétaire *m/f*; **ownership**
*n* possession *f*

**ox** (*pl* **oxen**) [ɔks, 'ɔksn] *n* bœuf *m*

**Oxbridge** ['ɔksbrɪdʒ] *n* (*BRIT*) les
universités d'Oxford et de Cambridge

**oxen** ['ɔksən] *npl of* **ox**

**oxygen** ['ɔksɪdʒən] *n* oxygène *m*

**oyster** ['ɔɪstə^r^] *n* huître *f*

**oz.** *abbr* = **ounce(s)**

**ozone** ['əuzəun] *n* ozone *m*; **ozone
friendly** *adj* qui n'attaque pas *or* qui
préserve la couche d'ozone; **ozone
layer** *n* couche *f* d'ozone

**p** abbr (BRIT) = **penny**; **pence**
**P.A.** n abbr = **personal assistant**; **public address system**
**p.a.** abbr = **per annum**
**pace** [peɪs] n pas m; (speed) allure f; vitesse f ▷ vi: **to ~ up and down** faire les cent pas; **to keep ~ with** aller à la même vitesse que; (events) se tenir au courant de; **pacemaker** n (Med) stimulateur m cardiaque; (Sport: also: **pacesetter**) meneur(-euse) de train
**Pacific** [pə'sɪfɪk] n: **the ~ (Ocean)** le Pacifique, l'océan m Pacifique
**pacifier** ['pæsɪfaɪə'] n (US: dummy) tétine f
**pack** [pæk] n paquet m; (of hounds) meute f; (of thieves, wolves etc) bande f; (of cards) jeu m; (US: of cigarettes) paquet m; (back pack) sac m à dos ▷ vt (goods) empaqueter, emballer; (in suitcase etc) emballer; (box) remplir; (cram) entasser ▷ vi: **to ~ (one's bags)** faire ses bagages; **pack in** (BRIT inf) ▷ vi (machine) tomber en panne

▷ vt (boyfriend) plaquer; **~ it in!** laisse tomber!; **pack off** vt: **to ~ sb off to** expédier qn à; **pack up** vi (BRIT inf: machine) tomber en panne; (: person) se tirer ▷ vt (belongings) ranger; (goods, presents) empaqueter, emballer
**package** ['pækɪdʒ] n paquet m; (also: **~ deal**: agreement) marché global; (: purchase) forfait m; (Comput) progiciel m ▷ vt (goods) conditionner; **package holiday** n (BRIT) vacances organisées; **package tour** n voyage organisé
**packaging** ['pækɪdʒɪŋ] n (wrapping materials) emballage m
**packed** [pækt] adj (crowded) bondé(e); **packed lunch** (BRIT) n repas froid
**packet** ['pækɪt] n paquet m
**packing** ['pækɪŋ] n emballage m
**pact** [pækt] n pacte m, traité m
**pad** [pæd] n bloc(-notes m) m; (to prevent friction) tampon m ▷ vt rembourrer; **padded** adj (jacket) matelassé(e); (bra) rembourré(e)
**paddle** ['pædl] n (oar) pagaie f; (US: for table tennis) raquette f de ping-pong ▷ vi (with feet) barboter, faire trempette ▷ vt: **to ~ a canoe** etc pagayer; **paddling pool** n petit bassin
**paddock** ['pædək] n enclos m; (Racing) paddock m
**padlock** ['pædlɔk] n cadenas m
**paedophile** (US **pedophile**) ['piːdəufaɪl] n pédophile m
**page** [peɪdʒ] n (of book) page f; (also: **~ boy**) groom m, chasseur m; (at wedding) garçon m d'honneur ▷ vt (in hotel etc) (faire) appeler
**pager** ['peɪdʒə'] n bip m (inf), Alphapage® m
**paid** [peɪd] pt, pp of **pay** ▷ adj (work, official) rémunéré(e); (holiday) payé(e); **to put ~ to** (BRIT) mettre fin à, mettre par terre
**pain** [peɪn] n douleur f; (inf: nuisance) plaie f; **to be in ~** souffrir, avoir mal; **to take ~s to do** se donner du mal pour faire; **painful** adj douloureux(-euse); (difficult) difficile, pénible; **painkiller**

*n* calmant *m*, analgésique *m*;
**painstaking** ['peɪnzteɪkɪŋ] *adj* (*person*)
soigneux(-euse); (*work*) soigné(e)
**paint** [peɪnt] *n* peinture *f* ▷ *vt* peindre;
**to ~ the door blue** peindre la porte en
bleu; **paintbrush** *n* pinceau *m*; **painter**
*n* peintre *m*; **painting** *n* peinture *f*;
(*picture*) tableau *m*
**pair** [pɛər] *n* (*of shoes, gloves etc*) paire
*f*; (*of people*) couple *m*; **~ of scissors**
(paire de) ciseaux *mpl*; **~ of trousers**
pantalon *m*
**pajamas** [pə'dʒɑːməz] *npl* (US)
pyjama(s) *m(pl)*
**Pakistan** [pɑːkɪˈstɑːn] *n* Pakistan *m*;
**Pakistani** *adj* pakistanais(e) ▷ *n*
Pakistanais(e)
**pal** [pæl] *n* (*inf*) copain (copine)
**palace** ['pæləs] *n* palais *m*
**pale** [peɪl] *adj* pâle; **~ blue** *adj* bleu
pâle *inv*
**Palestine** ['pælɪstaɪn] *n* Palestine *f*;
**Palestinian** [pælɪsˈtɪnɪən] *adj*
palestinien(ne) ▷ *n* Palestinien(ne)
**palm** [pɑːm] *n* (*Anat*) paume *f*; (*also: ~
tree*) palmier *m* ▷ *vt*: **to ~ sth off on sb**
(*inf*) refiler qch à qn
**pamper** ['pæmpər] *vt* gâter, dorloter
**pamphlet** ['pæmflət] *n* brochure *f*
**pan** [pæn] *n* (*also: **sauce~***) casserole *f*;
(*also: **frying ~***) poêle *f*
**pancake** ['pænkeɪk] *n* crêpe *f*
**panda** ['pændə] *n* panda *m*
**pane** [peɪn] *n* carreau *m* (de fenêtre),
vitre *f*
**panel** ['pænl] *n* (*of wood, cloth etc*)
panneau *m*; (*Radio, TV*) panel *m*, invités
*mpl*; (*for interview, exams*) jury *m*
**panhandler** ['pænhændlər] *n* (US *inf*)
mendiant *m*
**panic** ['pænɪk] *n* panique *f*, affolement
*m* ▷ *vi* s'affoler, paniquer
**panorama** [pænəˈrɑːmə] *n*
panorama *m*
**pansy** ['pænzɪ] *n* (*Bot*) pensée *f*
**pant** [pænt] *vi* haleter
**panther** ['pænθər] *n* panthère *f*
**panties** ['pæntɪz] *npl* slip *m*, culotte *f*

**pantomime** ['pæntəmaɪm] *n* (BRIT)
spectacle *m* de Noël; *voir encadré*

○ **PANTOMIME**
○
○ Une **pantomime** (à ne pas confondre
○ avec le mot tel qu'on l'utilise en
○ français), que l'on appelle également
○ de façon familière "panto", est un
○ genre de farce où le personnage
○ principal est souvent un jeune
○ garçon et où il y a toujours une
○ "dame", c'est-à-dire une vieille
○ femme jouée par un homme, et
○ un méchant. La plupart du temps,
○ l'histoire est basée sur un conte de
○ fées comme Cendrillon ou Le Chat
○ botté, et le public est encouragé
○ à participer en prévenant le héros
○ d'un danger imminent. Ce genre de
○ spectacle, qui s'adresse surtout aux
○ enfants, vise également un public
○ d'adultes au travers des nombreuses
○ plaisanteries faisant allusion à des
○ faits d'actualité.

**pants** [pænts] *n* (BRIT: *woman's*) culotte
*f*, slip *m*; (: *man's*) slip, caleçon *m*; (US:
*trousers*) pantalon *m*
**pantyhose** ['pæntɪhəʊz] (US) *npl*
collant *m*
**paper** ['peɪpər] *n* papier *m*; (*also:
**wall~***) papier peint; (*also: **news~***)
journal *m*; (*academic essay*) article *m*;
(*exam*) épreuve écrite ▷ *adj* en or de
papier ▷ *vt* tapisser (de papier peint);
**papers** *npl* (*also: **identity ~s***) papiers
*mpl* (d'identité); **paperback** *n* livre
broché *or* non relié; (*small*) livre *m* de
poche; **paper bag** *n* sac *m* en papier;
**paper clip** *n* trombone *m*; **paper shop**
*n* (BRIT) marchand *m* de journaux;
**paperwork** *n* papiers *mpl*; (*pej*)
paperasserie *f*
**paprika** ['pæprɪkə] *n* paprika *m*
**par** [pɑːr] *n* pair *m*; (*Golf*) normale *f* du
parcours; **on a ~ with** à égalité avec, au
même niveau que

**paracetamol** [pærə'siːtəmɒl] (*BRIT*) *n* paracétamol *m*

**parachute** ['pærəʃuːt] *n* parachute *m*

**parade** [pə'reɪd] *n* défilé *m* ▷ *vt* (*fig*) faire étalage de ▷ *vi* défiler

**paradise** ['pærədaɪs] *n* paradis *m*

**paradox** ['pærədɒks] *n* paradoxe *m*

**paraffin** ['pærəfɪn] *n* (*BRIT*): **~ (oil)** pétrole (lampant)

**paragraph** ['pærəgrɑːf] *n* paragraphe *m*

**parallel** ['pærəlɛl] *adj*: **~ (with or to)** parallèle (à); (*fig*) analogue (à) ▷ *n* (*line*) parallèle *f*; (*fig, Geo*) parallèle *m*

**paralysed** ['pærəlaɪzd] *adj* paralysé(e)

**paralysis** (*pl* **paralyses**) [pə'rælɪsɪs, -siːz] *n* paralysie *f*

**paramedic** [pærə'mɛdɪk] *n* auxiliaire *m/f* médical(e)

**paranoid** ['pærənɔɪd] *adj* (*Psych*) paranoïaque; (*neurotic*) paranoïde

**parasite** ['pærəsaɪt] *n* parasite *m*

**parcel** ['pɑːsl] *n* paquet *m*, colis *m* ▷ *vt* (*also:* **~ up**) empaqueter

**pardon** ['pɑːdn] *n* pardon *m*; (*Law*) grâce *f* ▷ *vt* pardonner à; (*Law*) gracier; **~! pardon!; ~ me!** (*after burping etc*) excusez-moi!; **I beg your ~!** (*I'm sorry*) pardon!, je suis désolé!; **(I beg your) ~?**, (*US*) **~ me?** (*what did you say?*) pardon?

**parent** ['pɛərənt] *n* (*father*) père *m*; (*mother*) mère *f*; **parents** *npl* parents *mpl*; **parental** [pə'rɛntl] *adj* parental(e), des parents

**Paris** ['pærɪs] *n* Paris

**parish** ['pærɪʃ] *n* paroisse *f*; (*BRIT*: *civil*) ≈ commune *f*

**Parisian** [pə'rɪzɪən] *adj* parisien(ne), de Paris ▷ *n* Parisien(ne)

**park** [pɑːk] *n* parc *m*, jardin public ▷ *vt* garer ▷ *vi* se garer; **can I ~ here?** est-ce que je peux me garer ici?

**parking** ['pɑːkɪŋ] *n* stationnement *m*; **"no ~"** "stationnement interdit"; **parking lot** *n* (*US*) parking *m*, parc *m* de stationnement; **parking meter** *n* parc(o)mètre *m*; **parking ticket** *n* P.-V. *m*

> ⬛ Be careful not to translate *parking* by the French word *parking*.

**parkway** ['pɑːkweɪ] *n* (*US*) route *f* express (*en site vert ou aménagé*)

**parliament** ['pɑːləmənt] *n* parlement *m*; **parliamentary** [pɑːlə'mɛntərɪ] *adj* parlementaire

**Parmesan** [pɑːmɪ'zæn] *n* (*also:* **~ cheese**) Parmesan *m*

**parole** [pə'rəul] *n*: **on ~** en liberté conditionnelle

**parrot** ['pærət] *n* perroquet *m*

**parsley** ['pɑːslɪ] *n* persil *m*

**parsnip** ['pɑːsnɪp] *n* panais *m*

**parson** ['pɑːsn] *n* ecclésiastique *m*; (*Church of England*) pasteur *m*

**part** [pɑːt] *n* partie *f*; (*of machine*) pièce *f*; (*Theat etc*) rôle *m*; (*of serial*) épisode *m*; (*US*: *in hair*) raie *f* ▷ *adv* = **partly** ▷ *vt* séparer ▷ *vi* (*people*) se séparer; (*crowd*) s'ouvrir; **to take ~ in** participer à, prendre part à; **to take sb's ~** prendre le parti de qn, prendre parti pour qn; **for my ~** en ce qui me concerne; **for the most ~** en grande partie; dans la plupart des cas; **in ~** en partie; **to take sth in good/bad ~** prendre qch du bon/mauvais côté; **part with** *vt fus* (*person*) se séparer de; (*possessions*) se défaire de

**partial** ['pɑːʃl] *adj* (*incomplete*) partiel(le); **to be ~ to** aimer, avoir un faible pour

**participant** [pɑː'tɪsɪpənt] *n* (*in competition, campaign*) participant(e)

**participate** [pɑː'tɪsɪpeɪt] *vi*: **to ~ (in)** participer (à), prendre part (à)

**particle** ['pɑːtɪkl] *n* particule *f*; (*of dust*) grain *m*

**particular** [pə'tɪkjulər] *adj* (*specific*) particulier(-ière); (*special*) particulier, spécial(e); (*fussy*) difficile, exigeant(e); (*careful*) méticuleux(-euse); **in ~** en particulier, surtout; **particularly** *adv* particulièrement; (*in particular*) en particulier; **particulars** *npl* détails *mpl*; (*information*) renseignements *mpl*

**parting** ['pɑːtɪŋ] *n* séparation *f*; (*BRIT*:

in hair) raie f
**partition** [pɑːˈtɪʃən] n (Pol) partition f,
division f; (wall) cloison f
**partly** [ˈpɑːtlɪ] adv en partie,
partiellement
**partner** [ˈpɑːtnər] n (Comm)
associé(e); (Sport) partenaire m/f;
(spouse) conjoint(e); (friend) ami(e); (at
dance) cavalier(-ière); **partnership** n
association f
**part of speech** n (Ling) partie f du
discours
**partridge** [ˈpɑːtrɪdʒ] n perdrix f
**part-time** [ˈpɑːtˈtaɪm] adj, adv à mi-
temps, à temps partiel
**party** [ˈpɑːtɪ] n (Pol) parti m; (celebration)
fête f; (: formal) réception f; (: in evening)
soirée f; (group) groupe m; (Law) partie f
**pass** [pɑːs] vt (time, object) passer;
(place) passer devant; (friend) croiser;
(exam) être reçu(e) à, réussir; (overtake)
dépasser; (approve) approuver, accepter
▷ vi passer; (Scol) être reçu(e) ou
admis(e), réussir ▷ n (permit) laissez-
passer m inv; (membership card) carte f
d'accès ou d'abonnement; (in mountains)
col m; (Sport) passe f; (Scol: also: ~ mark):
**to get a ~** être reçu(e) (sans mention);
**to ~ sb sth** passer qch à qn; **could you
~ the salt/oil, please?** pouvez-vous
me passer le sel/l'huile, s'il vous plaît?;
**to make a ~ at sb** (inf) faire des avances
à qn; **pass away** vi mourir; **pass by** vi
passer ▷ vt (ignore) négliger; **pass on**
vt (hand on) ▷ **~ on (to)** transmettre
(à); **pass out** vi s'évanouir; **pass over**
vt (ignore) passer sous silence; **pass up**
vt (opportunity) laisser passer; **passable**
adj (road) praticable; (work) acceptable

> Be careful not to translate **to pass
> an exam** by the French expression
> **passer un examen**.

**passage** [ˈpæsɪdʒ] n (also: **~way**)
couloir m; (gen, in book) passage m; (by
boat) traversée f
**passenger** [ˈpæsɪndʒər] n
passager(-ère)
**passer-by** [pɑːsəˈbaɪ] n passant(e)

**passing place** n (Aut) aire f de
croisement
**passion** [ˈpæʃən] n passion f;
**passionate** adj passionné(e); **passion
fruit** n fruit m de la passion
**passive** [ˈpæsɪv] adj (also Ling)
passif(-ive)
**passport** [ˈpɑːspɔːt] n passeport m;
**passport control** n contrôle m des
passeports; **passport office** n bureau
m de délivrance des passeports
**password** [ˈpɑːswəːd] n mot m de
passe
**past** [pɑːst] prep (in front of) devant;
(further than) au delà de, plus loin que;
après; (later than) après ▷ adv: **to run
~** passer en courant ▷ adj passé(e);
(president etc) ancien(ne) ▷ n passé m;
**he's ~ forty** il a dépassé la quarantaine,
il a plus de ou passé quarante ans;
**ten/quarter ~ eight** huit heures
dix/un ou et quart; **for the ~ few/3 days**
depuis quelques/3 jours; ces derniers/3
derniers jours
**pasta** [ˈpæstə] n pâtes fpl
**paste** [peɪst] n pâte f; (Culin: meat)
pâté m (à tartiner); (: tomato) purée
f, concentré m; (glue) colle f (de pâte)
▷ vt coller
**pastel** [ˈpæstl] adj pastel inv ▷ n (Art:
pencil) (crayon m) pastel m; (: drawing)
(dessin m au) pastel; (: colour) ton m
pastel inv
**pasteurized** [ˈpæstəraɪzd] adj
pasteurisé(e)
**pastime** [ˈpɑːstaɪm] n passe-temps m
inv, distraction f
**pastor** [ˈpɑːstər] n pasteur m
**past participle** [-ˈpɑːtɪsɪpl] n (Ling)
participe passé
**pastry** [ˈpeɪstrɪ] n pâte f; (cake)
pâtisserie f
**pasture** [ˈpɑːstʃər] n pâturage m
**pasty¹** n [ˈpæstɪ] petit pâté (en croûte)
**pasty²** [ˈpeɪstɪ] adj (complexion)
terreux(-euse)
**pat** [pæt] vt donner une petite tape à;
(dog) caresser

**patch** [pætʃ] n (of material) pièce f;
(eye patch) cache m; (spot) tache f; (of
land) parcelle f; (on tyre) rustine f ▷ vt
(clothes) rapiécer; **a bad ~** (BRIT) une
période difficile; **patchy** adj inégal(e);
(incomplete) fragmentaire
**pâté** ['pæteɪ] n pâté m, terrine f
**patent** ['peɪtnt, US'pætnt] n brevet m
(d'invention) ▷ vt faire breveter ▷ adj
patent(e), manifeste
**paternal** [pə'tə:nl] adj paternel(le)
**paternity leave** [pə'tə:nɪtɪ-] n congé
m de paternité
**path** [pɑ:θ] n chemin m, sentier m; (in
garden) allée f; (of missile) trajectoire f
**pathetic** [pə'θεtɪk] adj (pitiful)
pitoyable; (very bad) lamentable,
minable
**pathway** ['pɑ:θweɪ] n chemin m,
sentier m; (in garden) allée f
**patience** ['peɪʃns] n patience f; (BRIT:
Cards) réussite f
**patient** ['peɪʃnt] n malade m/f; (of
dentist etc) patient(e) ▷ adj patient(e)
**patio** ['pætɪəu] n patio m
**patriotic** [pætrɪ'ɔtɪk] adj patriotique;
(person) patriote
**patrol** [pə'trəul] n patrouille f ▷ vt
patrouiller dans; **patrol car** n voiture
f de police
**patron** ['peɪtrən] n (in shop) client(e);
(of charity) patron(ne); **~ of the arts**
mécène m
**patronizing** ['pætrənaɪzɪŋ] adj
condescendant(e)
**pattern** ['pætən] n (Sewing) patron
m; (design) motif m; **patterned** adj à
motifs
**pause** [pɔ:z] n pause f, arrêt m ▷ vi faire
une pause, s'arrêter
**pave** [peɪv] vt paver, daller; **to ~ the
way for** ouvrir la voie à
**pavement** ['peɪvmənt] n (BRIT)
trottoir m; (US) chaussée f
**pavilion** [pə'vɪlɪən] n pavillon m; (Sport)
stand m
**paving** ['peɪvɪŋ] n (material) pavé
m, dalle f

**paw** [pɔ:] n patte f
**pawn** [pɔ:n] n (Chess, also fig) pion m
▷ vt mettre en gage; **pawnbroker** n
prêteur m sur gages
**pay** [peɪ] n salaire m; (of manual worker)
paie f ▷ vb (pt, pp **paid**) ▷ vt payer ▷ vi
payer; (be profitable) être rentable;
**can I ~ by credit card?** est-ce que je
peux payer par carte de crédit?; **to ~
attention (to)** prêter attention (à);
**to ~ sb a visit** rendre visite à qn; **to
~ one's respects to sb** présenter ses
respects à qn; **pay back** vt rembourser;
**pay for** vt fus payer; **pay in** vt verser;
**pay off** vt (debts) régler, acquitter;
(person) rembourser ▷ vi (scheme,
decision) se révéler payant(e); **pay out**
vt (money) payer, sortir de sa poche;
**pay up** vt (amount) payer; **payable** adj
payable; **to make a cheque payable
to sb** établir un chèque à l'ordre de
qn; **pay day** n jour m de paie; **pay
envelope** n (US) paie f; **payment** n
paiement m; (of bill) règlement m; (of
deposit, cheque) versement m; **monthly
payment** mensualité f; **payout** n
(from insurance) dédommagement m;
(in competition) prix m; **pay packet**
n (BRIT) paie f; **pay phone** n cabine
f téléphonique, téléphone public;
**pay raise** n (US) = **pay rise**; **pay rise**
n (BRIT) augmentation f (de salaire);
**payroll** n registre m du personnel; **pay
slip** n (BRIT) bulletin m de paie, feuille
f de paie; **pay television** n chaînes
fpl payantes
**PC** n abbr = **personal computer**;
(BRIT) = **police constable** ▷ adj abbr
= **politically correct**
**p.c.** abbr = **per cent**
**PDA** n abbr (= personal digital assistant)
agenda m électronique
**PE** n abbr (= physical education) EPS f
**pea** [pi:] n (petit) pois
**peace** [pi:s] n paix f; (calm) calme m,
tranquillité f; **peaceful** adj paisible,
calme
**peach** [pi:tʃ] n pêche f

**peacock** ['pi:kɔk] n paon m
**peak** [pi:k] n (mountain) pic m, cime f; (of cap) visière f; (fig: highest level) maximum m; **peak hours** npl heures fpl d'affluence or de pointe
**peanut** ['pi:nʌt] n arachide f, cacahuète f; **peanut butter** n beurre m de cacahuète
**pear** [pɛər] n poire f
**pearl** [pə:l] n perle f
**peasant** ['pɛznt] n paysan(ne)
**peat** [pi:t] n tourbe f
**pebble** ['pɛbl] n galet m, caillou m
**peck** [pɛk] vt (also: **~ at**) donner un coup de bec à; (food) picorer ▷ n coup m de bec; (kiss) bécot m; **peckish** adj (BRIT inf): **I feel peckish** je mangerais bien quelque chose, j'ai la dent
**peculiar** [pɪ'kju:lɪər] adj (odd) étrange, bizarre, curieux(-euse); (particular) particulier(-ière); **~ to** particulier à
**pedal** ['pɛdl] n pédale f ▷ vi pédaler
**pedalo** ['pɛdələu] n pédalo m
**pedestal** ['pɛdəstl] n piédestal m
**pedestrian** [pɪ'dɛstrɪən] n piéton m; **pedestrian crossing** n (BRIT) passage clouté; **pedestrianized** adj: **a pedestrianized street** une rue piétonne; **pedestrian precinct** (US **pedestrian zone**) n (BRIT) zone piétonne
**pedigree** ['pɛdɪgri:] n ascendance f; (of animal) pedigree m ▷ cpd (animal) de race
**pedophile** ['pi:dəufaɪl] (US) n = **paedophile**
**pee** [pi:] vi (inf) faire pipi, pisser
**peek** [pi:k] vi jeter un coup d'œil (furtif)
**peel** [pi:l] n pelure f, épluchure f; (of orange, lemon) écorce f ▷ vt peler, éplucher ▷ vi (paint etc) s'écailler; (wallpaper) se décoller; (skin) peler
**peep** [pi:p] n (BRIT: look) coup d'œil furtif; (sound) pépiement m ▷ vi (BRIT) jeter un coup d'œil (furtif)
**peer** [pɪər] vi: **to ~ at** regarder attentivement, scruter ▷ n (noble) pair

m; (equal) pair, égal(e)
**peg** [pɛg] n (for coat etc) patère f; (BRIT: also: **clothes ~**) pince f à linge
**pelican** ['pɛlɪkən] n pélican m; **pelican crossing** n (BRIT Aut) feu m à commande manuelle
**pelt** [pɛlt] vt: **to ~ sb (with)** bombarder qn (de) ▷ vi (rain) tomber à seaux; (inf: run) courir à toutes jambes ▷ n peau f
**pelvis** ['pɛlvɪs] n bassin m
**pen** [pɛn] n (for writing) stylo m; (for sheep) parc m
**penalty** ['pɛnltɪ] n pénalité f; sanction f; (fine) amende f; (Sport) pénalisation f; (Football) penalty m; (Rugby) pénalité f
**pence** [pɛns] npl of **penny**
**pencil** ['pɛnsl] n crayon m; **pencil in** vt noter provisoirement; **pencil case** n trousse f (d'écolier); **pencil sharpener** n taille-crayon(s) m inv
**pendant** ['pɛndnt] n pendentif m
**pending** ['pɛndɪŋ] prep en attendant ▷ adj en suspens
**penetrate** ['pɛnɪtreɪt] vt pénétrer dans; (enemy territory) entrer en
**penfriend** ['pɛnfrɛnd] n (BRIT) correspondant(e)
**penguin** ['pɛŋgwɪn] n pingouin m
**penicillin** [pɛnɪ'sɪlɪn] n pénicilline f
**peninsula** [pə'nɪnsjulə] n péninsule f
**penis** ['pi:nɪs] n pénis m, verge f
**penitentiary** [pɛnɪ'tɛnʃərɪ] n (US) prison f
**penknife** ['pɛnnaɪf] n canif m
**penniless** ['pɛnɪlɪs] adj sans le sou
**penny** (pl **pennies** or **pence**) ['pɛnɪ, 'pɛnɪz, pɛns] n (BRIT) penny m; (US) cent m
**penpal** ['pɛnpæl] n correspondant(e)
**pension** ['pɛnʃən] n (from company) retraite f; **pensioner** n (BRIT) retraité(e)
**pentagon** ['pɛntəgən] n: **the P~** (US Pol) le Pentagone
**penthouse** ['pɛnthaus] n appartement m (de luxe) en attique
**penultimate** [pɪ'nʌltɪmət] adj pénultième, avant-dernier(-ière)
**people** ['pi:pl] npl gens mpl; personnes

*fpl*; (*inhabitants*) population *f*; (*Pol*) peuple *m* ▷ *n* (*nation, race*) peuple *m*; **several ~ came** plusieurs personnes sont venues; **~ say that …** on dit *or* les gens disent que …

**pepper** ['pɛpər] *n* poivre *m*; (*vegetable*) poivron *m* ▷ *vt* (*Culin*) poivrer; **peppermint** *n* (*sweet*) pastille *f* de menthe

**per** [pər] *prep* par; **~ hour** (*miles etc*) à l'heure; (*fee*) (de) l'heure; **~ kilo** *etc* le kilo *etc*; **~ day/person** par jour/personne; **~ annum** per an

**perceive** [pə'siːv] *vt* percevoir; (*notice*) remarquer, s'apercevoir de

**per cent** *adv* pour cent

**percentage** [pə'sɛntɪdʒ] *n* pourcentage *m*

**perception** [pə'sɛpʃən] *n* perception *f*; (*insight*) sensibilité *f*

**perch** [pəːtʃ] *n* (*fish*) perche *f*; (*for bird*) perchoir *m* ▷ *vi* (se) percher

**percussion** [pə'kʌʃən] *n* percussion *f*

**perennial** [pə'rɛnɪəl] *n* (*Bot*) (plante *f*) vivace *f*, plante pluriannuelle

**perfect** ['pəːfɪkt] *adj* parfait(e) ▷ *n* (*also:* **~ tense**) parfait *m* ▷ *vt* [pə'fɛkt] (*technique, skill, work of art*) parfaire; (*method, plan*) mettre au point; **perfection** [pə'fɛkʃən] *n* perfection *f*; **perfectly** ['pəːfɪktlɪ] *adv* parfaitement

**perform** [pə'fɔːm] *vt* (*carry out*) exécuter; (*concert etc*) jouer, donner ▷ *vi* (*actor, musician*) jouer; **performance** *n* représentation *f*, spectacle *m*; (*of an artist*) interprétation *f*; (*Sport: of car, engine*) performance *f*; (*of company, economy*) résultats *mpl*; **performer** *n* artiste *m/f*

**perfume** ['pəːfjuːm] *n* parfum *m*

**perhaps** [pə'hæps] *adv* peut-être

**perimeter** [pə'rɪmɪtər] *n* périmètre *m*

**period** ['pɪərɪəd] *n* période *f*; (*History*) époque *f*; (*Scol*) cours *m*; (*full stop*) point *m*; (*Med*) règles *fpl* ▷ *adj* (*costume, furniture*) d'époque; **periodical** [pɪərɪ'ɔdɪkl] *n* périodique *m*; **periodically** *adv* périodiquement

**perish** ['pɛrɪʃ] *vi* périr, mourir; (*decay*) se détériorer

**perjury** ['pəːdʒərɪ] *n* (*Law: in court*) faux témoignage; (*breach of oath*) parjure *m*

**perk** [pəːk] *n* (*inf*) avantage *m*, à-côté *m*

**perm** [pəːm] *n* (*for hair*) permanente *f*

**permanent** ['pəːmənənt] *adj* permanent(e); **permanently** *adv* de façon permanente; (*move abroad*) définitivement; (*open, closed*) en permanence; (*tired, unhappy*) constamment

**permission** [pə'mɪʃən] *n* permission *f*, autorisation *f*

**permit** *n* ['pəːmɪt] permis *m*

**perplex** [pə'plɛks] *vt* (*person*) rendre perplexe

**persecute** ['pəːsɪkjuːt] *vt* persécuter

**persecution** [pəːsɪ'kjuːʃən] *n* persécution *f*

**persevere** [pəːsɪ'vɪər] *vi* persévérer

**Persian** ['pəːʃən] *adj* persan(e); **the ~ Gulf** le golfe Persique

**persist** [pə'sɪst] *vi*: **to ~ (in doing)** persister (à faire), s'obstiner (à faire); **persistent** *adj* persistant(e), tenace

**person** ['pəːsn] *n* personne *f*; **in ~** en personne; **personal** *adj* personnel(le); **personal assistant** *n* secrétaire personnel(le); **personal computer** *n* ordinateur individuel, PC *m*; **personality** [pəːsə'nælɪtɪ] *n* personnalité *f*; **personally** *adv* personnellement; **to take sth personally** se sentir visé(e) par qch; **personal organizer** *n* agenda (personnel) (*style Filofax®*); (*electronic*) agenda électronique; **personal stereo** *n* Walkman® *m*, baladeur *m*

**personnel** [pəːsə'nɛl] *n* personnel *m*

**perspective** [pə'spɛktɪv] *n* perspective *f*

**perspiration** [pəːspɪ'reɪʃən] *n* transpiration *f*

**persuade** [pə'sweɪd] *vt*: **to ~ sb to do sth** persuader qn de faire qch, amener *or* décider qn à faire qch

**persuasion** [pə'sweɪʒən] *n* persuasion

*f; (creed)* conviction *f*
**persuasive** [pə'sweɪsɪv] *adj*
persuasif(-ive)
**perverse** [pə'vɜːs] *adj* pervers(e);
*(contrary)* entêté(e), contrariant(e)
**pervert** *n* ['pɜːvɜːt] perverti(e) ▷ *vt*
[pə'vɜːt] pervertir; *(words)* déformer
**pessimism** ['pɛsɪmɪzəm] *n*
pessimisme *m*
**pessimist** ['pɛsɪmɪst] *n* pessimiste
*m/f*; **pessimistic** [pɛsɪ'mɪstɪk] *adj*
pessimiste
**pest** [pɛst] *n* animal *m (or* insecte *m)*
nuisible; *(fig)* fléau *m*
**pester** ['pɛstə'] *vt* importuner, harceler
**pesticide** ['pɛstɪsaɪd] *n* pesticide *m*
**pet** [pɛt] *n* animal familier ▷ *cpd*
*(favourite)* favori(e) ▷ *vt (stroke)*
caresser, câliner; **teacher's ~** chouchou
*m* du professeur; **~ hate** bête noire
**petal** ['pɛtl] *n* pétale *m*
**petite** [pə'tiːt] *adj* menu(e)
**petition** [pə'tɪʃən] *n* pétition *f*
**petrified** ['pɛtrɪfaɪd] *adj (fig)* mort(e)
de peur
**petrol** ['pɛtrəl] *n (BRIT)* essence *f*; **I've**
**run out of ~** je suis en panne d'essence
> Be careful not to translate *petrol* by
the French word *pétrole*.
**petroleum** [pə'trəʊlɪəm] *n* pétrole *m*
**petrol: petrol pump** *n (BRIT: in car,*
*at garage)* pompe *f* à essence; **petrol**
**station** *n (BRIT)* station-service *f*;
**petrol tank** *n (BRIT)* réservoir *m*
d'essence
**petticoat** ['pɛtɪkəʊt] *n* jupon *m*
**petty** ['pɛtɪ] *adj (mean)* mesquin(e);
*(unimportant)* insignifiant(e), sans
importance
**pew** [pjuː] *n* banc *m* (d'église)
**pewter** ['pjuːtə'] *n* étain *m*
**phantom** ['fæntəm] *n* fantôme *m*
**pharmacist** ['fɑːməsɪst] *n*
pharmacien(ne)
**pharmacy** ['fɑːməsɪ] *n* pharmacie *f*
**phase** [feɪz] *n* phase *f*, période *f*; **phase**
**in** *vt* introduire progressivement;
**phase out** *vt* supprimer

progressivement
**Ph.D.** *abbr* = **Doctor of Philosophy**
**pheasant** ['fɛznt] *n* faisan *m*
**phenomena** [fə'nɔmɪnə] *npl of*
**phenomenon**
**phenomenal** [fɪ'nɔmɪnl] *adj*
phénoménal(e)
**phenomenon** *(pl* **phenomena)**
[fə'nɔmɪnən, -nə] *n* phénomène *m*
**Philippines** ['fɪlɪpiːnz] *npl (also:*
**Philippine Islands)**: **the ~** les
Philippines *fpl*
**philosopher** [fɪ'lɔsəfə'] *n*
philosophe *m*
**philosophical** [fɪlə'sɔfɪkl] *adj*
philosophique
**philosophy** [fɪ'lɔsəfɪ] *n* philosophie *f*
**phlegm** [flɛm] *n* flegme *m*
**phobia** ['fəʊbjə] *n* phobie *f*
**phone** [fəʊn] *n* téléphone *m* ▷ *vt*
téléphoner à ▷ *vi* téléphoner; **to be**
**on the ~** avoir le téléphone; *(be calling)*
être au téléphone; **phone back** *vt, vi*
rappeler; **phone up** *vt* téléphoner à ▷ *vi*
téléphoner; **phone book** *n* annuaire *m*;
**phone box** *(US* **phone booth)** *n* cabine
*f* téléphonique; **phone call** *n* coup *m*
de fil *or* de téléphone; **phonecard** *n*
télécarte *f*; **phone number** *n* numéro
*m* de téléphone
**phonetics** [fə'nɛtɪks] *n* phonétique *f*
**phoney** ['fəʊnɪ] *adj* faux (fausse),
factice; *(person)* pas franc (franche)
**photo** ['fəʊtəʊ] *n* photo *f*; **photo album**
*n* album *m* de photos; **photocopier** *n*
copieur *m*; **photocopy** *n* photocopie *f*
▷ *vt* photocopier
**photograph** ['fəʊtəgræf] *n*
photographie *f* ▷ *vt* photographier;
**photographer** [fə'tɔgrəfə'] *n*
photographe *m/f*; **photography**
[fə'tɔgrəfɪ] *n* photographie *f*
**phrase** [freɪz] *n* expression *f*; *(Ling)*
locution *f* ▷ *vt* exprimer; **phrase**
**book** *n* recueil *m* d'expressions (pour
touristes)
**physical** ['fɪzɪkl] *adj* physique;
**physical education** *n* éducation

*f* physique; **physically** *adv* physiquement

**physician** [fɪ'zɪʃən] *n* médecin *m*

**physicist** ['fɪzɪsɪst] *n* physicien(ne)

**physics** ['fɪzɪks] *n* physique *f*

**physiotherapist** [fɪzɪəu'θerəpɪst] *n* kinésithérapeute *m/f*

**physiotherapy** [fɪzɪəu'θerəpɪ] *n* kinésithérapie *f*

**physique** [fɪ'ziːk] *n* (appearance) physique *m*; (health etc) constitution *f*

**pianist** ['piːənɪst] *n* pianiste *m/f*

**piano** [pɪ'ænəu] *n* piano *m*

**pick** [pɪk] *n* (tool: also: **~-axe**) pic *m*, pioche *f* ▷ *vt* choisir; (gather) cueillir; (remove) prendre; (lock) forcer; **take your ~** faites votre choix; **the ~ of** le (la) meilleur(e) de; **to ~ one's nose** se mettre les doigts dans le nez; **to ~ one's teeth** se curer les dents; **to ~ a quarrel with sb** chercher noise à qn; **pick on** *vt fus* (person) harceler; **pick out** *vt* choisir; (distinguish) distinguer; **pick up** *vi* (improve) remonter, s'améliorer ▷ *vt* ramasser; (collect) passer prendre; (Aut: give lift to) prendre; (learn) apprendre; (Radio) capter; **to ~ up speed** prendre de la vitesse; **to ~ o.s. up** se relever

**pickle** ['pɪkl] *n* (also: **~s**: as condiment) pickles *mpl* ▷ *vt* conserver dans du vinaigre or dans de la saumure; **in a ~** (fig) dans le pétrin

**pickpocket** ['pɪkpɔkɪt] *n* pickpocket *m*

**pick-up** ['pɪkʌp] *n* (also: **~ truck**) pick-up *m inv*

**picnic** ['pɪknɪk] *n* pique-nique *m* ▷ *vi* pique-niquer; **picnic area** *n* aire *f* de pique-nique

**picture** ['pɪktʃər] *n* (also TV) image *f*; (painting) peinture *f*, tableau *m*; (photograph) photo(graphie) *f*; (drawing) dessin *m*; (film) film *m*; (fig: description) description *f* ▷ *vt* (imagine) se représenter; **pictures** *npl*: **the ~s** (BRIT) le cinéma; **to take a ~ of sb/sth** prendre qn/qch en photo; **would you take a ~ of us, please?** pourriez-vous

nous prendre en photo, s'il vous plaît?; **picture frame** *n* cadre *m*; **picture messaging** *n* picture messaging *m*, messagerie *f* d'images

**picturesque** [pɪktʃə'resk] *adj* pittoresque

**pie** [paɪ] *n* tourte *f*; (of fruit) tarte *f*; (of meat) pâté *m* en croûte

**piece** [piːs] *n* morceau *m*; (item): **a ~ of furniture/advice** un meuble/conseil ▷ *vt*: **to ~ together** rassembler; **to take to ~s** démonter

**pie chart** *n* graphique *m* à secteurs, camembert *m*

**pier** [pɪər] *n* jetée *f*

**pierce** [pɪəs] *vt* percer, transpercer; **pierced** *adj* (ears) percé(e)

**pig** [pɪg] *n* cochon *m*, porc *m*; (pej: unkind person) mufle *m*; (: greedy person) goinfre *m*

**pigeon** ['pɪdʒən] *n* pigeon *m*

**piggy bank** ['pɪgɪ-] *n* tirelire *f*

**pigsty** ['pɪgstaɪ] *n* porcherie *f*

**pigtail** ['pɪgteɪl] *n* natte *f*, tresse *f*

**pike** [paɪk] *n* (fish) brochet *m*

**pilchard** ['pɪltʃəd] *n* pilchard *m* (sorte de sardine)

**pile** [paɪl] *n* (pillar, of books) pile *f*; (heap) tas *m*; (of carpet) épaisseur *f*; **pile up** *vi* (accumulate) s'entasser, s'accumuler ▷ *vt* (put in heap) empiler, entasser; (accumulate) accumuler; **piles** *npl* hémorroïdes *fpl*; **pile-up** *n* (Aut) télescopage *m*, collision *f* en série

**pilgrim** ['pɪlgrɪm] *n* pèlerin *m*

- **PILGRIM FATHERS**
-
- Les "Pères pèlerins" sont un
- groupe de puritains qui quittèrent
- l'Angleterre en 1620 pour fuir les
- persécutions religieuses. Ayant
- traversé l'Atlantique à bord du
- "Mayflower", ils fondèrent New
- Plymouth en Nouvelle-Angleterre,
- dans ce qui est aujourd'hui le
- Massachusetts. Ces Pères pèlerins
- sont considérés comme les

- fondateurs des États-Unis, et l'on
- commémore chaque année, le jour
- de "Thanksgiving", la réussite de leur
- première récolte.

**pilgrimage** ['pɪlɡrɪmɪdʒ] n
pèlerinage m

**pill** [pɪl] n pilule f; **the ~** la pilule

**pillar** ['pɪlər] n pilier m

**pillow** ['pɪləʊ] n oreiller m; **pillowcase,
pillowslip** n taie f d'oreiller

**pilot** ['paɪlət] n pilote m ▷ cpd (scheme
etc) pilote, expérimental(e) ▷ vt piloter;
**pilot light** n veilleuse f

**pimple** ['pɪmpl] n bouton m

**PIN** n abbr (= personal identification
number) code m confidentiel

**pin** [pɪn] n épingle f; (Tech) cheville f ▷ vt
épingler; **~s and needles** fourmis fpl; **to
~ sb down** (fig) coincer qn; **to ~ sth on
sb** (fig) mettre qch sur le dos de qn

**pinafore** ['pɪnəfɔːʳ] n tablier m

**pinch** [pɪntʃ] n pincement m; (of salt
etc) pincée f ▷ vt pincer; (inf: steal)
piquer, chiper ▷ vi (shoe) serrer; **at a ~**
à la rigueur

**pine** [paɪn] n (also: **~ tree**) pin m ▷ vi: **to
~ for** aspirer à, désirer ardemment

**pineapple** ['paɪnæpl] n ananas m

**ping** [pɪŋ] n (noise) tintement m; **ping-
pong®** n ping-pong® m

**pink** [pɪŋk] adj rose ▷ n (colour) rose m

**pinpoint** ['pɪnpɔɪnt] vt indiquer (avec
précision)

**pint** [paɪnt] n pinte f (BRIT = 0.57 l; US =
0.47 l); (BRIT inf) ≈ demi m, ≈ pot m

**pioneer** [paɪə'nɪəʳ] n pionnier m

**pious** ['paɪəs] adj pieux(-euse)

**pip** [pɪp] n (seed) pépin m; **pips** npl: **the
~s** (BRIT: time signal on radio) le top

**pipe** [paɪp] n tuyau m, conduite f; (for
smoking) pipe f ▷ vt amener par tuyau;
**pipeline** n (for gas) gazoduc m, pipeline
m; (for oil) oléoduc m, pipeline; **piper** n
(flautist) joueur(-euse) de pipeau; (of
bagpipes) joueur(-euse) de cornemuse

**pirate** ['paɪərət] n pirate m ▷ vt (CD,
video, book) pirater

**Pisces** ['paɪsiːz] n les Poissons mpl

**piss** [pɪs] vi (inf!) pisser (!); **pissed** (inf!)
adj (BRIT: drunk) bourré(e); (US: angry)
furieux(-euse)

**pistol** ['pɪstl] n pistolet m

**piston** ['pɪstən] n piston m

**pit** [pɪt] n trou m, fosse f; (also: **coal ~**)
puits m de mine; (also: **orchestra ~**)
fosse d'orchestre; (US: fruit stone) noyau
m ▷ vt: **to ~ o.s.** or **one's wits against**
se mesurer à

**pitch** [pɪtʃ] n (BRIT Sport) terrain m; (Mus)
ton m; (fig: degree) degré m; (tar) poix
f ▷ vt (throw) lancer; (tent) dresser ▷ vi
(fall): **to ~ into/off** tomber dans/de;
**pitch-black** adj noir(e) comme poix

**pitfall** ['pɪtfɔːl] n piège m

**pith** [pɪθ] n (of orange etc) intérieur m
de l'écorce

**pitiful** ['pɪtɪful] adj (touching) pitoyable;
(contemptible) lamentable

**pity** ['pɪtɪ] n pitié f ▷ vt plaindre; **what a
~!** quel dommage!

**pizza** ['piːtsə] n pizza f

**placard** ['plækɑːd] n affiche f; (in march)
pancarte f

**place** [pleɪs] n endroit m, lieu m;
(proper position, job, rank, seat) place
f; (home): **at/to his ~** chez lui ▷ vt
(position) placer, mettre; (identify)
situer; reconnaître; **to take ~** avoir
lieu; **to change ~s with sb** changer
de place avec qn; **out of ~** (not suitable)
déplacé(e), inopportun(e); **in the first
~** d'abord, en premier; **place mat** n set
m de table; (in linen etc) napperon m;
**placement** n (during studies) stage m

**placid** ['plæsɪd] adj placide

**plague** [pleɪg] n (Med) peste f ▷ vt (fig)
tourmenter

**plaice** [pleɪs] n (pl inv) carrelet m

**plain** [pleɪn] adj (in one colour) uni(e);
(clear) clair(e), évident(e); (simple)
simple; (not handsome) quelconque,
ordinaire ▷ adv franchement,
carrément ▷ n plaine f; **plain
chocolate** n chocolat m à croquer;
**plainly** adv clairement; (frankly)

carrément, sans détours

**plaintiff** ['pleɪntɪf] n plaignant(e)

**plait** [plæt] n tresse f, natte f

**plan** [plæn] n plan m; (scheme) projet m
▷ vt (think in advance) projeter; (prepare)
organiser ▷ vi faire des projets; **to ~ to
do** projeter de faire

**plane** [pleɪn] n (Aviat) avion m; (also:
**~ tree**) platane m; (tool) rabot m; (Art,
Math etc) plan m; (fig) niveau m, plan
▷ vt (with tool) raboter

**planet** ['plænɪt] n planète f

**plank** [plæŋk] n planche f

**planning** ['plænɪŋ] n planification f;
**family ~** planning familial

**plant** [plɑːnt] n plante f; (machinery)
matériel m; (factory) usine f ▷ vt
planter; (bomb) déposer, poser;
(microphone, evidence) cacher

**plantation** [plæn'teɪʃən] n
plantation f

**plaque** [plæk] n plaque f

**plaster** ['plɑːstər] n plâtre m; (also: **~
of Paris**) plâtre à mouler; (BRIT: also:
**sticking ~**) pansement adhésif ▷ vt
plâtrer; (cover): **to ~ with** couvrir de;
**plaster cast** n (Med) plâtre m; (model,
statue) moule m

**plastic** ['plæstɪk] n plastique m ▷ adj
(made of plastic) en plastique; **plastic
bag** n sac m en plastique; **plastic
surgery** n chirurgie f esthétique

**plate** [pleɪt] n (dish) assiette f; (sheet of
metal, on door; Phot) plaque f; (in book)
gravure f; (dental) dentier m

**plateau** (pl **~s** or **~x**) ['plætəʊ, -z] n
plateau m

**platform** ['plætfɔːm] n (at meeting)
tribune f; (stage) estrade f; (Rail) quai m;
(Pol) plateforme f

**platinum** ['plætɪnəm] n platine m

**platoon** [plə'tuːn] n peloton m

**platter** ['plætər] n plat m

**plausible** ['plɔːzɪbl] adj plausible;
(person) convaincant(e)

**play** [pleɪ] n jeu m; (Theat) pièce f (de
théâtre) ▷ vt (game) jouer à; (team,
opponent) jouer contre; (instrument)
jouer de; (part, piece of music, note)
jouer; (CD etc) passer ▷ vi jouer; **to ~
safe** ne prendre aucun risque; **play
back** vt repasser, réécouter; **play up** vi
(cause trouble) faire des siennes; **player**
n joueur(-euse); (Mus) musicien(ne);
**playful** adj enjoué(e); **playground**
n cour f de récréation; (in park) aire
f de jeux; **playgroup** n garderie f;
**playing card** n carte f à jouer;
**playing field** n terrain m de sport;
**playschool** n = **playgroup**; **playtime**
n (Scol) récréation f; **playwright** n
dramaturge m

**plc** abbr (BRIT: = public limited company)
≈ SARL f

**plea** [pliː] n (request) appel m; (Law)
défense f

**plead** [pliːd] vt plaider; (give as excuse)
invoquer ▷ vi (Law) plaider; (beg):
**to ~ with sb (for sth)** implorer qn
(d'accorder qch); **to ~ guilty/not guilty**
plaider coupable/non coupable

**pleasant** ['plɛznt] adj agréable

**please** [pliːz] excl s'il te (or vous) plaît
▷ vt plaire à ▷ vi (think fit): **do as you ~**
faites comme il vous plaira; **~ yourself!**
(inf) (faites) comme vous voulez!;
**pleased** adj: **pleased (with)** content(e)
(de); **pleased to meet you** enchanté
(de faire votre connaissance)

**pleasure** ['plɛʒər] n plaisir m; **"it's a ~"**
"je vous en prie"

**pleat** [pliːt] n pli m

**pledge** [plɛdʒ] n (promise) promesse f
▷ vt promettre

**plentiful** ['plɛntɪful] adj abondant(e),
copieux(-euse)

**plenty** ['plɛntɪ] n: **~ of** beaucoup de;
(sufficient) (bien) assez de

**pliers** ['plaɪəz] npl pinces fpl

**plight** [plaɪt] n situation f critique

**plod** [plɒd] vi avancer péniblement;
(fig) peiner

**plonk** [plɒŋk] (inf) n (BRIT: wine) pinard
m, piquette f ▷ vt: **to ~ sth down** poser
brusquement qch

**plot** [plɒt] n complot m, conspiration f;

(of story, play) intrigue f; (of land) lot m de terrain, lopin m ▷ vt (mark out) tracer point par point; (Naut) pointer; (make graph of) faire le graphique de; (conspire) comploter ▷ vi comploter

**plough** (US **plow**) [plau] n charrue f ▷ vt (earth) labourer; **to ~ money into** investir dans; **ploughman's lunch** n (BRIT) assiette froide avec du pain, du fromage et des pickles

**plow** [plau] (US) = **plough**

**ploy** [plɔɪ] n stratagème m

**pluck** [plʌk] vt (fruit) cueillir; (musical instrument) pincer; (bird) plumer; **to ~ one's eyebrows** s'épiler les sourcils; **to ~ up courage** prendre son courage à deux mains

**plug** [plʌg] n (stopper) bouchon m, bonde f; (Elec) prise f de courant; (Aut: also: **spark(ing) ~**) bougie f ▷ vt (hole) boucher; (inf: advertise) faire du battage pour, matraquer; **plug in** vt (Elec) brancher; **plughole** n (BRIT) trou m (d'écoulement)

**plum** [plʌm] n (fruit) prune f

**plumber** ['plʌmə<sup>r</sup>] n plombier m

**plumbing** ['plʌmɪŋ] n (trade) plomberie f; (piping) tuyauterie f

**plummet** ['plʌmɪt] vi (person, object) plonger; (sales, prices) dégringoler

**plump** [plʌmp] adj rondelet(te), dodu(e), bien en chair; **plump for** vt fus (inf: choose) se décider pour

**plunge** [plʌndʒ] n plongeon m; (fig) chute f ▷ vt plonger ▷ vi (fall) tomber, dégringoler; (dive) plonger; **to take the ~** se jeter à l'eau

**pluperfect** [pluːˈpəːfɪkt] n (Ling) plus-que-parfait m

**plural** ['pluərl] adj pluriel(le) ▷ n pluriel m

**plus** [plʌs] n (also: **~ sign**) signe m plus; (advantage) atout m ▷ prep plus; **ten/twenty ~** plus de dix/vingt

**ply** [plaɪ] n (of wool) fil m ▷ vt (a trade) exercer ▷ vi (ship) faire la navette; **to ~ sb with drink** donner continuellement à boire à qn; **plywood**

n contreplaqué m

**P.M.** n abbr (BRIT) = **prime minister**

**p.m.** adv abbr (= post meridiem) de l'après-midi

**PMS** n abbr (= premenstrual syndrome) syndrome prémenstruel

**PMT** n abbr (= premenstrual tension) syndrome prémenstruel

**pneumatic drill** [njuːˈmætɪk-] n marteau-piqueur m

**pneumonia** [njuːˈməunɪə] n pneumonie f

**poach** [pəutʃ] vt (cook) pocher; (steal) pêcher (or chasser) sans permis ▷ vi braconner; **poached** adj (egg) poché(e)

**P.O. Box** n abbr = **post office box**

**pocket** ['pɔkɪt] n poche f ▷ vt empocher; **to be (£5) out of ~** (BRIT) en être de sa poche (pour 5 livres); **pocketbook** n (US: wallet) portefeuille m; **pocket money** n argent m de poche

**pod** [pɔd] n cosse f

**podcast** n podcast m

**podiatrist** [pɔˈdiːətrɪst] n (US) pédicure m/f

**podium** ['pəudɪəm] n podium m

**poem** ['pəuɪm] n poème m

**poet** ['pəuɪt] n poète m; **poetic** [pəuˈɛtɪk] adj poétique; **poetry** n poésie f

**poignant** ['pɔɪnjənt] adj poignant(e)

**point** [pɔɪnt] n point m; (tip) pointe f; (in time) moment m; (in space) endroit m; (subject, idea) point, sujet m; (purpose) but m; (also: **decimal ~**): **2 ~ 3 (2.3)** 2 virgule 3 (2,3); (BRIT Elec: also: **power ~**) prise f (de courant) ▷ vt (show) indiquer; (gun etc): **to ~ sth at** braquer or diriger qch sur ▷ vi: **to ~ at** montrer du doigt; **points** npl (Rail) aiguillage m; **to make a ~ of doing sth** ne pas manquer de faire qch; **to get/miss the ~** comprendre/ne pas comprendre; **to come to the ~** en venir au fait; **there's no ~ (in doing)** cela ne sert à rien (de faire), à quoi ça sert?; **to be on the ~ of doing sth** être sur le point de faire qch; **point out** vt (mention) faire remarquer, souligner; **point-blank** adv (fig) catégoriquement; (also: **at point-blank range**) à bout portant; **pointed** adj (shape) pointu(e); (remark) plein(e) de sous-entendus; **pointer** n (needle) aiguille f; (clue) indication f; (advice) tuyau m; **pointless** adj inutile, vain(e); **point of view** n point m de vue

**poison** ['pɔɪzn] n poison m ▷ vt empoisonner; **poisonous** adj (snake) venimeux(-euse); (substance, plant) vénéneux(-euse); (fumes) toxique

**poke** [pəuk] vt (jab with finger, stick etc) piquer; pousser du doigt; (put): **to ~ sth in(to)** fourrer ou enfoncer qch dans; **poke about** vi fureter; **poke out** vi (stick out) sortir

**poker** ['pəukər] n tisonnier m; (Cards) poker m

**Poland** ['pəulənd] n Pologne f

**polar** ['pəulər] adj polaire; **polar bear** n ours blanc

**Pole** [pəul] n Polonais(e)

**pole** [pəul] n (of wood) mât m, perche f; (Elec) poteau m; (Geo) pôle m; **pole bean** n (us) haricot m (à rames); **pole vault** n saut m à la perche

**police** [pə'li:s] npl police f ▷ vt maintenir l'ordre dans; **police car** n voiture f de police; **police constable** n (BRIT) agent m de police; **police force** n police f, forces fpl de l'ordre; **policeman** (irreg) n agent m de police, policier m; **police officer** n agent m de police; **police station** n commissariat m de police; **policewoman** (irreg) n femme-agent f

**policy** ['pɔlɪsɪ] n politique f; (also: **insurance ~**) police f (d'assurance)

**polio** ['pəulɪəu] n polio f

**Polish** ['pəulɪʃ] adj polonais(e) ▷ n (Ling) polonais m

**polish** ['pɔlɪʃ] n (for shoes) cirage m; (for floor) cire f, encaustique f; (for nails) vernis m; (shine) éclat m, poli m; (fig: refinement) raffinement m ▷ vt (put polish on: shoes, wood) cirer; (make

shiny) astiquer, faire briller; **polish off** vt (food) liquider; **polished** adj (fig) raffiné(e)

**polite** [pə'laɪt] adj poli(e); **politeness** n politesse f

**political** [pə'lɪtɪkl] adj politique; **politically** adv politiquement; **politically correct** politiquement correct(e)

**politician** [pɔlɪ'tɪʃən] n homme/femme politique, politicien(ne)

**politics** ['pɔlɪtɪks] n politique f

**poll** [pəul] n scrutin m, vote m; (also: **opinion ~**) sondage m (d'opinion) ▷ vt (votes) obtenir

**pollen** ['pɔlən] n pollen m

**polling station** n (BRIT) bureau m de vote

**pollute** [pə'lu:t] vt polluer

**pollution** [pə'lu:ʃən] n pollution f

**polo** ['pəuləu] n polo m; **polo-neck** adj à col roulé ▷ n (sweater) pull m à col roulé; **polo shirt** n polo m

**polyester** [pɔlɪ'estər] n polyester m

**polystyrene** [pɔlɪ'staɪri:n] n polystyrène m

**polythene** ['pɔlɪθi:n] n (BRIT) polyéthylène m; **polythene bag** n sac m en plastique

**pomegranate** ['pɔmɪɡrænɪt] n grenade f

**pompous** ['pɔmpəs] adj pompeux(-euse)

**pond** [pɔnd] n étang m; (stagnant) mare f

**ponder** ['pɔndər] vt considérer, peser

**pony** ['pəunɪ] n poney m; **ponytail** n queue f de cheval; **pony trekking** n (BRIT) randonnée f équestre or à cheval

**poodle** ['pu:dl] n caniche m

**pool** [pu:l] n (of rain) flaque f; (pond) mare f; (artificial) bassin m; (also: **swimming ~**) piscine f; (sth shared) fonds commun; (billiards) poule f ▷ vt mettre en commun; **pools** npl (football) ≈ loto sportif

**poor** [puər] adj pauvre; (mediocre) médiocre, faible, mauvais(e) ▷ npl: **the ~** les pauvres mpl; **poorly** adv (badly) mal, médiocrement ▷ *adj* souffrant(e), malade

**pop** [pɔp] *n* (*noise*) bruit sec; (*Mus*) musique *f* pop; (*inf*: *drink*) soda *m*; (*us inf*: *father*) papa *m* ▷ *vt* (*put*) fourrer, mettre (rapidement) ▷ *vi* éclater; (*cork*) sauter; **pop in** *vi* entrer en passant; **pop out** *vi* sortir; **popcorn** *n* pop-corn *m*

**pope** [pəup] *n* pape *m*

**poplar** ['pɔplə'] *n* peuplier *m*

**popper** ['pɔpə'] *n* (*BRIT*) bouton-pression *m*

**poppy** ['pɔpɪ] *n* (*wild*) coquelicot *m*; (*cultivated*) pavot *m*

**Popsicle®** ['pɔpsɪkl] *n* (*us*) esquimau *m* (*glace*)

**pop star** *n* pop star *f*

**popular** ['pɔpjulə'] *adj* populaire; (*fashionable*) à la mode; **popularity** [pɔpju'lærɪtɪ] *n* popularité *f*

**population** [pɔpju'leɪʃən] *n* population *f*

**pop-up** *adj* (*Comput*: *menu, window*) pop up *inv* ▷ *n* pop up *m inv*, fenêtre *f* pop up

**porcelain** ['pɔːslɪn] *n* porcelaine *f*

**porch** [pɔːtʃ] *n* porche *m*; (*us*) véranda *f*

**pore** [pɔː'] *n* pore *m* ▷ *vi*: **to ~ over** s'absorber dans, être plongé(e) dans

**pork** [pɔːk] *n* porc *m*; **pork chop** *n* côte *f* de porc; **pork pie** *n* pâté *m* de porc en croûte

**porn** [pɔːn] *adj* (*inf*) porno ▷ *n* (*inf*) porno *m*; **pornographic** [pɔːnə'græfɪk] *adj* pornographique; **pornography** [pɔː'nɔɡrəfɪ] *n* pornographie *f*

**porridge** ['pɔrɪdʒ] *n* porridge *m*

**port** [pɔːt] *n* (*harbour*) port *m*; (*Naut*: *left side*) bâbord *m*; (*wine*) porto *m*; (*Comput*) port *m*, accès *m*; **~ of call** (port d')escale *f*

**portable** ['pɔːtəbl] *adj* portatif(-ive)

**porter** ['pɔːtə'] *n* (*for luggage*) porteur *m*; (*doorkeeper*) gardien(ne); portier *m*

**portfolio** [pɔːt'fəulɪəu] *n* portefeuille *m*; (*of artist*) portfolio *m*

**portion** ['pɔːʃən] *n* portion *f*, part *f*

**portrait** ['pɔːtreɪt] *n* portrait *m*

**portray** [pɔː'treɪ] *vt* faire le portrait de; (*in writing*) dépeindre, représenter; (*subj*: *actor*) jouer

**Portugal** ['pɔːtjuɡl] *n* Portugal *m*

**Portuguese** [pɔːtju'ɡiːz] *adj* portugais(e) ▷ *n* (*pl inv*) Portugais(e); (*Ling*) portugais *m*

**pose** [pəuz] *n* pose *f* ▷ *vi* poser; (*pretend*): **to ~ as** se faire passer pour ▷ *vt* poser; (*problem*) créer

**posh** [pɔʃ] *adj* (*inf*) chic *inv*

**position** [pə'zɪʃən] *n* position *f*; (*job, situation*) situation *f* ▷ *vt* mettre en place *or* en position

**positive** ['pɔzɪtɪv] *adj* positif(-ive); (*certain*) sûr(e), certain(e); (*definite*) formel(le), catégorique; **positively** *adv* (*affirmatively, enthusiastically*) de façon positive; (*inf*: *really*) carrément

**possess** [pə'zɛs] *vt* posséder; **possession** [pə'zɛʃən] *n* possession *f*; **possessions** *npl* (*belongings*) affaires *fpl*; **possessive** *adj* possessif(-ive)

**possibility** [pɔsɪ'bɪlɪtɪ] *n* possibilité *f*; (*event*) éventualité *f*

**possible** ['pɔsɪbl] *adj* possible; **as big as ~** aussi gros que possible; **possibly** *adv* (*perhaps*) peut-être; **I cannot possibly come** il m'est impossible de venir

**post** [pəust] *n* (*BRIT*: *mail*) poste *f*; (: *letters, delivery*) courrier *m*; (*job, situation*) poste *m*; (*pole*) poteau *m* ▷ *vt* (*BRIT*: *send by post*) poster; (: *appoint*): **to ~ to** affecter à; **where can I ~ these cards?** où est-ce que je peux poster ces cartes postales?; **postage** *n* tarifs *mpl* d'affranchissement; **postal** *adj* postal(e); **postal order** *n* mandat(-poste *m*) *m*; **postbox** *n* (*BRIT*) boîte *f* aux lettres (*publique*); **postcard** *n* carte postale; **postcode** *n* (*BRIT*) code postal

**poster** ['pəustə'] *n* affiche *f*

**postgraduate** ['pəust'ɡrædjuət] *n* ≈ étudiant(e) de troisième cycle

**postman** ['pəustmən] (*BRIT*: *irreg*) *n*

facteur m

**postmark** ['pəustmɑːk] n cachet m (de la poste)

**post-mortem** [pəust'mɔːtəm] n autopsie f

**post office** n (building) poste f; (organization): **the Post Office** les postes fpl

**postpone** [pəs'pəun] vt remettre (à plus tard), reculer

**posture** ['pɔstʃəʳ] n posture f; (fig) attitude f

**postwoman** [pəust'wumən] (BRIT: irreg) n factrice f

**pot** [pɔt] n (for cooking) marmite f; casserole f; (teapot) théière f; (for coffee) cafetière f; (for plants, jam) pot m; (inf: marijuana) herbe f ▷ vt (plant) mettre en pot; **to go to ~** (inf) aller à vau-l'eau

**potato** (pl **~es**) [pə'teitəu] n pomme f de terre; **potato peeler** n épluche-légumes m

**potent** ['pəutnt] adj puissant(e); (drink) fort(e), très alcoolisé(e); (man) viril

**potential** [pə'tɛnʃl] adj potentiel(le) ▷ n potentiel m

**pothole** ['pɔthəul] n (in road) nid m de poule; (BRIT: underground) gouffre m, caverne f

**pot plant** n plante f d'appartement

**potter** ['pɔtəʳ] n potier m ▷ vi (BRIT): **to ~ around** or **about** bricoler; **pottery** n poterie f

**potty** ['pɔti] n (child's) pot m

**pouch** [pautʃ] n (Zool) poche f; (for tobacco) blague f; (for money) bourse f

**poultry** ['pəultri] n volaille f

**pounce** [pauns] vi: **to ~ (on)** bondir (sur), fondre (sur)

**pound** [paund] n livre f (weight = 453g, 16 ounces; money = 100 pence); (for dogs, cars) fourrière f ▷ vt (beat) bourrer de coups, marteler; (crush) piler, pulvériser ▷ vi (heart) battre violemment, taper; **pound sterling** n livre f sterling

**pour** [pɔːʳ] vt verser ▷ vi couler à flots; (rain) pleuvoir à verse; **to ~ sb a drink** verser or servir à boire à qn; **pour in**

vi (people) affluer, se précipiter; (news, letters) arriver en masse; **pour out** vi (people) sortir en masse ▷ vt vider; (fig) déverser; (serve: a drink) verser; **pouring** adj: **pouring rain** pluie torrentielle

**pout** [paut] vi faire la moue

**poverty** ['pɔvəti] n pauvreté f, misère f

**powder** ['paudəʳ] n poudre f ▷ vt poudrer; **powdered milk** n lait m en poudre

**power** ['pauəʳ] n (strength, nation) puissance f, force f; (ability, Pol: of party, leader) pouvoir m; (of speech, thought) faculté f; (Elec) courant m; **to be in ~** être au pouvoir; **power cut** n (BRIT) coupure f de courant; **power failure** n panne f de courant; **powerful** adj puissant(e); (performance etc) très fort(e); **powerless** adj impuissant(e); **power point** n (BRIT) prise f de courant; **power station** n centrale f électrique

**p.p.** abbr (= per procurationem: by proxy) p.p.

**PR** n abbr = **public relations**

**practical** ['præktikl] adj pratique; **practical joke** n farce f; **practically** adv (almost) pratiquement

**practice** ['præktis] n pratique f; (of profession) exercice m; (at football etc) entraînement m; (business) cabinet m ▷ vt, vi (US) = **practise**; **in ~** (in reality) en pratique; **out of ~** rouillé(e)

**practise** (US **practice**) ['præktis] vt (work at: piano, backhand etc) s'exercer à, travailler; (train for: sport) s'entraîner à; (a sport, religion, method) pratiquer; (profession) exercer ▷ vi s'exercer, travailler; (train) s'entraîner; (lawyer, doctor) exercer; **practising** (US **practicing**) adj (Christian etc) pratiquant(e); (lawyer) en exercice

**practitioner** [præk'tiʃənəʳ] n praticien(ne)

**pragmatic** [præg'mætik] adj pragmatique

**prairie** ['prɛəri] n savane f

**praise** [preiz] n éloge(s) m(pl), louange(s) f(pl) ▷ vt louer, faire l'éloge de

**pram** [præm] n (BRIT) landau m, voiture f d'enfant

**prank** [præŋk] n farce f

**prawn** [prɔːn] n crevette f (rose); **prawn cocktail** n cocktail m de crevettes

**pray** [preɪ] vi prier; **prayer** [prɛəʳ] n prière f

**preach** [priːtʃ] vi prêcher; **preacher** n prédicateur m; (US: clergyman) pasteur m

**precarious** [prɪˈkɛərɪəs] adj précaire

**precaution** [prɪˈkɔːʃən] n précaution f

**precede** [prɪˈsiːd] vt, vi précéder; **precedent** [ˈprɛsɪdənt] n précédent m; **preceding** [prɪˈsiːdɪŋ] adj qui précède (or précédait)

**precinct** [ˈpriːsɪŋkt] n (US: district) circonscription f, arrondissement m; **pedestrian ~** (BRIT) zone piétonnière; **shopping ~** (BRIT) centre commercial

**precious** [ˈprɛʃəs] adj précieux(-euse)

**precise** [prɪˈsaɪs] adj précis(e); **precisely** adv précisément

**precision** [prɪˈsɪʒən] n précision f

**predator** [ˈprɛdətəʳ] n prédateur m, rapace m

**predecessor** [ˈpriːdɪsɛsəʳ] n prédécesseur m

**predicament** [prɪˈdɪkəmənt] n situation f difficile

**predict** [prɪˈdɪkt] vt prédire; **predictable** adj prévisible; **prediction** [prɪˈdɪkʃən] n prédiction f

**predominantly** [prɪˈdɔmɪnəntlɪ] adv en majeure partie; (especially) surtout

**preface** [ˈprɛfəs] n préface f

**prefect** [ˈpriːfɛkt] n (BRIT: in school) élève chargé de certaines fonctions de discipline

**prefer** [prɪˈfəːʳ] vt préférer; **preferable** [ˈprɛfrəbl] adj préférable; **preferably** [ˈprɛfrəblɪ] adv de préférence; **preference** [ˈprɛfrəns] n préférence f

**prefix** [ˈpriːfɪks] n préfixe m

**pregnancy** [ˈprɛgnənsɪ] n grossesse f

**pregnant** [ˈprɛgnənt] adj enceinte adj f; (animal) pleine

**prehistoric** [ˈpriːhɪsˈtɔrɪk] adj

préhistorique

**prejudice** [ˈprɛdʒudɪs] n préjugé m; **prejudiced** adj (person) plein(e) de préjugés; (in a matter) partial(e)

**preliminary** [prɪˈlɪmɪnərɪ] adj préliminaire

**prelude** [ˈprɛljuːd] n prélude m

**premature** [ˈprɛmətʃuəʳ] adj prématuré(e)

**premier** [ˈprɛmɪəʳ] adj premier(-ière), principal(e) ▷ n (Pol: Prime Minister) premier ministre; (Pol: President) chef m de l'État

**premiere** [ˈprɛmɪɛəʳ] n première f

**Premier League** n première division

**premises** [ˈprɛmɪsɪz] npl locaux mpl; **on the ~** sur les lieux; sur place

**premium** [ˈpriːmɪəm] n prime f; **to be at a ~** (fig: housing etc) être très demandé(e), être rarissime

**premonition** [prɛməˈnɪʃən] n prémonition f

**preoccupied** [priːˈɔkjupaɪd] adj préoccupé(e)

**prepaid** [priːˈpeɪd] adj payé(e) d'avance

**preparation** [prɛpəˈreɪʃən] n préparation f; **preparations** npl (for trip, war) préparatifs mpl

**preparatory school** n école primaire privée; (US) lycée privé

**prepare** [prɪˈpɛəʳ] vt préparer ▷ vi: **to ~ for** se préparer à

**prepared** [prɪˈpɛəd] adj: **~ for** préparé(e) à; **~ to** prêt(e) à

**preposition** [prɛpəˈzɪʃən] n préposition f

**prep school** n = **preparatory school**

**prerequisite** [priːˈrɛkwɪzɪt] n condition f préalable

**preschool** [ˈpriːˈskuːl] adj préscolaire; (child) d'âge préscolaire

**prescribe** [prɪˈskraɪb] vt prescrire

**prescription** [prɪˈskrɪpʃən] n (Med) ordonnance f; (: medicine) médicament m (obtenu sur ordonnance); **could you write me a ~?** pouvez-vous me faire une ordonnance?

**presence** [ˈprɛzns] n présence f; **in**

**sb's ~** en présence de qn; **~ of mind** présence d'esprit

**present** ['prɛznt] *adj* présent(e); (*current*) présent, actuel(le) ▷ *n* cadeau *m*; (*actuality*) présent *m* ▷ *vt* [prɪ'zɛnt] présenter; (*prize, medal*) remettre; (*give*): **to ~ sb with sth** offrir qch à qn; **at ~** en ce moment; **to give sb a ~** offrir un cadeau à qn; **presentable** [prɪ'zɛntəbl] *adj* présentable; **presentation** [prɛzn'teɪʃən] *n* présentation *f*; (*ceremony*) remise *f* du cadeau (*or* de la médaille *etc*); **present-day** *adj* contemporain(e), actuel(le); **presenter** [prɪ'zɛntər] *n* (BRIT *Radio, TV*) présentateur(-trice); **presently** *adv* (*soon*) tout à l'heure, bientôt; (*with verb in past*) peu après; (*at present*) en ce moment; **present participle** [-'pɑːtɪsɪpl] *n* participe *m* présent

**preservation** [prɛzə'veɪʃən] *n* préservation *f*, conservation *f*

**preservative** [prɪ'zəːvətɪv] *n* agent *m* de conservation

**preserve** [prɪ'zəːv] *vt* (*keep safe*) préserver, protéger; (*maintain*) conserver, garder; (*food*) mettre en conserve ▷ *n* (*for game, fish*) réserve *f*; (*often pl: jam*) confiture *f*

**preside** [prɪ'zaɪd] *vi* présider

**president** ['prɛzɪdənt] *n* président(e); **presidential** [prɛzɪ'dɛnʃl] *adj* présidentiel(le)

**press** [prɛs] *n* (*tool, machine, newspapers*) presse *f*; (*for wine*) pressoir *m* ▷ *vt* (*push*) appuyer sur; (*squeeze*) presser, serrer; (*clothes: iron*) repasser; (*insist*): **to ~ sth on sb** presser qn d'accepter qch; (*urge, entreat*): **to ~ sb to do** *or* **into doing sth** pousser qn à faire qch ▷ *vi* appuyer; **we are ~ed for time** le temps nous manque; **to ~ for sth** faire pression pour obtenir qch; **press conference** *n* conférence *f* de presse; **pressing** *adj* urgent(e), pressant(e); **press stud** *n* (BRIT) bouton-pression *m*; **press-up** *n* (BRIT) traction *f*

**pressure** ['prɛʃər] *n* pression *f*; (*stress*)

tension *f*; **to put ~ on sb (to do sth)** faire pression sur qn (pour qu'il fasse qch); **pressure cooker** *n* cocotte-minute *f*; **pressure group** *n* groupe *m* de pression

**prestige** [prɛs'tiːʒ] *n* prestige *m*

**prestigious** [prɛs'tɪdʒəs] *adj* prestigieux(-euse)

**presumably** [prɪ'zjuːməblɪ] *adv* vraisemblablement

**presume** [prɪ'zjuːm] *vt* présumer, supposer

**pretence** (US **pretense**) [prɪ'tɛns] *n* (*claim*) prétention *f*; **under false ~s** sous des prétextes fallacieux

**pretend** [prɪ'tɛnd] *vt* (*feign*) feindre, simuler ▷ *vi* (*feign*) faire semblant

**pretense** [prɪ'tɛns] *n* (US) = **pretence**

**pretentious** [prɪ'tɛnʃəs] *adj* prétentieux(-euse)

**pretext** ['priːtɛkst] *n* prétexte *m*

**pretty** ['prɪtɪ] *adj* joli(e) ▷ *adv* assez

**prevail** [prɪ'veɪl] *vi* (*win*) l'emporter, prévaloir; (*be usual*) avoir cours; **prevailing** *adj* (*widespread*) courant(e), répandu(e); (*wind*) dominant(e)

**prevalent** ['prɛvələnt] *adj* répandu(e), courant(e)

**prevent** [prɪ'vɛnt] *vt*: **to ~ (from doing)** empêcher (de faire); **prevention** [prɪ'vɛnʃən] *n* prévention *f*; **preventive** *adj* préventif(-ive)

**preview** ['priːvjuː] *n* (*of film*) avant-première *f*

**previous** ['priːvɪəs] *adj* (*last*) précédent(e); (*earlier*) antérieur(e); **previously** *adv* précédemment, auparavant

**prey** [preɪ] *n* proie *f* ▷ *vi*: **to ~ on** s'attaquer à; **it was ~ing on his mind** ça le rongeait *or* minait

**price** [praɪs] *n* prix *m* ▷ *vt* (*goods*) fixer le prix de; **priceless** *adj* sans prix, inestimable; **price list** *n* tarif *m*

**prick** [prɪk] *n* (*sting*) piqûre *f* ▷ *vt* piquer; **to ~ up one's ears** dresser *or* tendre l'oreille

**prickly** ['prɪklɪ] *adj* piquant(e),

épineux(-euse); (*fig: person*) irritable

**pride** [praɪd] *n* fierté *f*; (*pej*) orgueil *m* ▷ *vt*: **to ~ o.s. on** se flatter de; s'enorgueillir de

**priest** [priːst] *n* prêtre *m*

**primarily** ['praɪmərɪlɪ] *adv* principalement, essentiellement

**primary** ['praɪmərɪ] *adj* primaire; (*first in importance*) premier(-ière), primordial(e) ▷ *n* (*US: election*) (élection *f*) primaire *f*; **primary school** *n* (BRIT) école *f* primaire

**prime** [praɪm] *adj* primordial(e), fondamental(e); (*excellent*) excellent(e) ▷ *vt* (*fig*) mettre au courant ▷ *n*: **in the ~ of life** dans la fleur de l'âge; **Prime Minister** *n* Premier ministre

**primitive** ['prɪmɪtɪv] *adj* primitif(-ive)

**primrose** ['prɪmrəuz] *n* primevère *f*

**prince** [prɪns] *n* prince *m*

**princess** [prɪn'sɛs] *n* princesse *f*

**principal** ['prɪnsɪpl] *adj* principal(e) ▷ *n* (*head teacher*) directeur *m*, principal *m*; **principally** *adv* principalement

**principle** ['prɪnsɪpl] *n* principe *m*; **in ~** en principe; **on ~** par principe

**print** [prɪnt] *n* (*mark*) empreinte *f*; (*letters*) caractères *mpl*; (*fabric*) imprimé *m*; (*Art*) gravure *f*, estampe *f*; (*Phot*) épreuve *f* ▷ *vt* imprimer; (*publish*) publier; (*write in capitals*) écrire en majuscules; **out of ~** épuisé(e); **print out** *vt* (*Comput*) imprimer; **printer** *n* (*machine*) imprimante *f*; (*person*) imprimeur *m*; **printout** *n* (*Comput*) sortie *f* imprimante

**prior** ['praɪə'] *adj* antérieur(e), précédent(e); (*more important*) prioritaire ▷ *adv*: **~ to doing** avant de faire

**priority** [praɪ'ɔrɪtɪ] *n* priorité *f*; **to have** or **take ~ over sth/sb** avoir la priorité sur qch/qn

**prison** ['prɪzn] *n* prison *f* ▷ *cpd* pénitentiaire; **prisoner** *n* prisonnier(-ière); **prisoner of war** *n* prisonnier(-ière) de guerre

**pristine** ['prɪstiːn] *adj* virginal(e)

**privacy** ['prɪvəsɪ] *n* intimité *f*, solitude *f*

**private** ['praɪvɪt] *adj* (*not public*) privé(e); (*personal*) personnel(le); (*house, car, lesson*) particulier(-ière); (*quiet: place*) tranquille ▷ *n* soldat *m* de deuxième classe; **"~"** (*on envelope*) "personnelle"; (*on door*) "privé"; **in ~** en privé; **privately** *adv* en privé; (*within oneself*) intérieurement; **private property** *n* propriété privée; **private school** *n* école privée

**privatize** ['praɪvɪtaɪz] *vt* privatiser

**privilege** ['prɪvɪlɪdʒ] *n* privilège *m*

**prize** [praɪz] *n* prix *m* ▷ *adj* (*example, idiot*) parfait(e); (*bull, novel*) primé(e) ▷ *vt* priser, faire grand cas de; **prizegiving** *n* distribution *f* des prix; **prizewinner** *n* gagnant(e)

**pro** [prəu] *n* (*inf: Sport*) professionnel(le) ▷ *prep* pro ...; **pros** *npl*: **the ~s and cons** le pour et le contre

**probability** [prɔbə'bɪlɪtɪ] *n* probabilité *f*; **in all ~** très probablement

**probable** ['prɔbəbl] *adj* probable

**probably** ['prɔbəblɪ] *adv* probablement

**probation** [prə'beɪʃən] *n*: **on ~** (*employee*) à l'essai; (*Law*) en liberté surveillée

**probe** [prəub] *n* (*Med, Space*) sonde *f*; (*enquiry*) enquête *f*, investigation *f* ▷ *vt* sonder, explorer

**problem** ['prɔbləm] *n* problème *m*

**procedure** [prə'siːdʒə'] *n* (*Admin, Law*) procédure *f*; (*method*) marche *f* à suivre, façon *f* de procéder

**proceed** [prə'siːd] *vi* (*go forward*) avancer; (*act*) procéder; (*continue*): **to ~ (with)** continuer, poursuivre; **to ~ to do** se mettre à faire; **proceedings** *npl* (*measures*) mesures *fpl*; (*Law: against sb*) poursuites *fpl*; (*meeting*) réunion *f*, séance *f*; (*records*) compte rendu; actes *mpl*; **proceeds** ['prəusiːdz] *npl* produit *m*, recette *f*

**process** ['prəusɛs] *n* processus *m*; (*method*) procédé *m* ▷ *vt* traiter

**procession** [prə'sɛʃən] *n* défilé *m*,

cortège *m*; **funeral ~** (*on foot*) cortège funèbre; (*in cars*) convoi *m* mortuaire
**proclaim** [prə'kleɪm] *vt* déclarer, proclamer
**prod** [prɒd] *vt* pousser
**produce** *n* ['prɒdjuːs] (*Agr*) produits *mpl* ▷ *vt* [prə'djuːs] produire; (*show*) présenter; (*cause*) provoquer, causer; (*Theat*) monter, mettre en scène; (*TV: programme*) réaliser; (*: play, film*) mettre en scène; (*Radio: programme*) réaliser; (*: play*) mettre en ondes; **producer** *n* (*Theat*) metteur *m* en scène; (*Agr, Comm, Cine*) producteur *m*; (*TV: of programme*) réalisateur *m*; (*: of play, film*) metteur en scène; (*Radio: of programme*) réalisateur; (*: of play*) metteur en ondes
**product** ['prɒdʌkt] *n* produit *m*; **production** [prə'dʌkʃən] *n* production *f*; (*Theat*) mise *f* en scène; **productive** [prə'dʌktɪv] *adj* productif(-ive); **productivity** [prɒdʌk'tɪvɪtɪ] *n* productivité *f*
**Prof.** [prɒf] *abbr* (= *professor*) Prof
**profession** [prə'fɛʃən] *n* profession *f*; **professional** *n* professionnel(le) ▷ *adj* professionnel(le); (*work*) de professionnel
**professor** [prə'fɛsə'] *n* professeur *m* (*titulaire d'une chaire*); (*us: teacher*) professeur *m*
**profile** ['prəʊfaɪl] *n* profil *m*
**profit** ['prɒfɪt] *n* (*from trading*) bénéfice *m*; (*advantage*) profit *m* ▷ *vi*: **to ~ (by** *or* **from**) profiter (de); **profitable** *adj* lucratif(-ive), rentable
**profound** [prə'faʊnd] *adj* profond(e)
**programme** (*us* **program**) ['prəʊgræm] *n* (*Comput: also* BRIT: **program**) programme *m*; (*Radio, TV*) émission *f* ▷ *vt* programmer; **programmer** (*us* **programer**) *n* programmeur(-euse); **programming** (*us* **programing**) *n* programmation *f*
**progress** *n* ['prəʊgrɛs] progrès *m(pl)* ▷ *vi* [prə'grɛs] progresser, avancer; **in ~** en cours; **progressive** [prə'grɛsɪv] *adj* progressif(-ive); (*person*) progressiste

**prohibit** [prə'hɪbɪt] *vt* interdire, défendre
**project** *n* ['prɒdʒɛkt] (*plan*) projet *m*, plan *m*; (*venture*) opération *f*, entreprise *f*; (*Scol: research*) étude *f*, dossier *m* ▷ *vb* [prə'dʒɛkt] ▷ *vt* projeter ▷ *vi* (*stick out*) faire saillie, s'avancer; **projection** [prə'dʒɛkʃən] *n* projection *f*; (*overhang*) saillie *f*; **projector** [prə'dʒɛktə'] *n* projecteur *m*
**prolific** [prə'lɪfɪk] *adj* prolifique
**prolong** [prə'lɒŋ] *vt* prolonger
**prom** [prɒm] *n abbr* = **promenade** (*us: ball*) bal *m* d'étudiants; **the P-s** série de concerts de musique classique; *voir encadré*

**promenade** [prɒmə'nɑːd] *n* (*by sea*) esplanade *f*, promenade *f*
**prominent** ['prɒmɪnənt] *adj* (*standing out*) proéminent(e); (*important*) important(e)
**promiscuous** [prə'mɪskjuəs] *adj* (*sexually*) de mœurs légères
**promise** ['prɒmɪs] *n* promesse *f* ▷ *vt, vi* promettre; **promising** *adj* prometteur(-euse)
**promote** [prə'məʊt] *vt* promouvoir; (*new product*) lancer; **promotion**

[prə'məʊʃən] n promotion f
**prompt** [prɔmpt] adj rapide ▷ n
(Comput) message m (de guidage) ▷ vt
(cause) entraîner, provoquer; (Theat)
souffler (son rôle or ses répliques) à;
**at 8 o'clock ~** à 8 heures précises; **to ~
sb to do** inciter or pousser qn à faire;
**promptly** adv (quickly) rapidement,
sans délai; (on time) ponctuellement
**prone** [prəʊn] adj (lying) couché(e) (face
contre terre); (liable): **~ to** enclin(e) à
**prong** [prɔŋ] n (of fork) dent f
**pronoun** ['prəʊnaʊn] n pronom m
**pronounce** [prə'naʊns] vt prononcer;
**how do you ~ it?** comment est-ce que
ça se prononce?
**pronunciation** [prənʌnsɪ'eɪʃən] n
prononciation f
**proof** [pruːf] n preuve f ▷ adj: **~ against**
à l'épreuve de
**prop** [prɔp] n support m, étai m; (fig)
soutien m ▷ vt (also: **~ up**) étayer,
soutenir; **props** npl accessoires mpl
**propaganda** [prɔpə'gændə] n
propagande f
**propeller** [prə'pelə'] n hélice f
**proper** ['prɔpə'] adj (suited, right)
approprié(e), bon (bonne); (seemly)
correct(e), convenable; (authentic)
vrai(e), véritable; (referring to place):
**the village ~** le village proprement
dit; **properly** adv correctement,
convenablement; **proper noun** n nom
m propre
**property** ['prɔpətɪ] n (possessions)
biens mpl; (house etc) propriété f; (land)
terres fpl, domaine m
**prophecy** ['prɔfɪsɪ] n prophétie f
**prophet** ['prɔfɪt] n prophète m
**proportion** [prə'pɔːʃən] n proportion
f; (share) part f, partie f; **proportions**
npl (size) dimensions fpl; **proportional,
proportionate** adj proportionnel(le)
**proposal** [prə'pəʊzl] n proposition
f, offre f; (plan) projet m; (of marriage)
demande f en mariage
**propose** [prə'pəʊz] vt proposer,
suggérer ▷ vi faire sa demande en

mariage; **to ~ to do** avoir l'intention
de faire
**proposition** [prɔpə'zɪʃən] n
proposition f
**proprietor** [prə'praɪətə'] n
propriétaire m/f
**prose** [prəʊz] n prose f; (Scol: translation)
thème m
**prosecute** ['prɔsɪkjuːt] vt poursuivre;
**prosecution** [prɔsɪ'kjuːʃən] n
poursuites fpl judiciaires; (accusing side:
in criminal case) accusation f; (: in civil
case) la partie plaignante; **prosecutor**
n (lawyer) procureur m; (also: **public
prosecutor**) ministère public; (us:
plaintiff) plaignant(e)
**prospect** n ['prɔspɛkt] perspective
f; (hope) espoir m, chances fpl ▷ vt,
vi [prə'spɛkt] prospecter; **prospects**
npl (for work etc) possibilités fpl
d'avenir, débouchés mpl; **prospective**
[prə'spɛktɪv] adj (possible) éventuel(le);
(future) futur(e)
**prospectus** [prə'spɛktəs] n
prospectus m
**prosper** ['prɔspə'] vi prospérer;
**prosperity** [prɔ'spɛrɪtɪ] n prospérité f;
**prosperous** adj prospère
**prostitute** ['prɔstɪtjuːt] n prostituée f;
**male ~** prostitué m
**protect** [prə'tɛkt] vt protéger;
**protection** [prə'tɛkʃən] n protection f;
**protective** adj protecteur(-trice);
(clothing) de protection
**protein** ['prəʊtiːn] n protéine f
**protest** n ['prəʊtɛst] protestation
f ▷ vb [prə'tɛst] ▷ vi: **to ~ against/
about** protester contre/à propos de; **to
~ (that)** protester que
**Protestant** ['prɔtɪstənt] adj, n
protestant(e)
**protester, protestor** [prə'tɛstə'] n
(in demonstration) manifestant(e)
**protractor** [prə'træktə'] n (Geom)
rapporteur m
**proud** [praʊd] adj fier(-ère); (pej)
orgueilleux(-euse)
**prove** [pruːv] vt prouver, démontrer

▷ *vi*: **to ~ correct** *etc* s'avérer juste *etc*; **to ~ o.s.** montrer ce dont on est capable

**proverb** ['prɔvəːb] *n* proverbe *m*

**provide** [prə'vaɪd] *vt* fournir; **to ~ sb with sth** fournir qch à qn; **provide for** *vt fus* (*person*) subvenir aux besoins de; (*future event*) prévoir; **provided** *conj*: **provided (that)** à condition que + *sub*; **providing** [prə'vaɪdɪŋ] *conj* à condition que + *sub*

**province** ['prɔvɪns] *n* province *f*; (*fig*) domaine *m*; **provincial** [prə'vɪnʃəl] *adj* provincial(e)

**provision** [prə'vɪʒən] *n* (*supplying*) fourniture *f*; approvisionnement *m*; (*stipulation*) disposition *f*; **provisions** *npl* (*food*) provisions *fpl*; **provisional** *adj* provisoire

**provocative** [prə'vɔkətɪv] *adj* provocateur(-trice), provocant(e)

**provoke** [prə'vəuk] *vt* provoquer

**prowl** [praul] *vi* (*also*: **~ about, ~ around**) rôder

**proximity** [prɔk'sɪmɪtɪ] *n* proximité *f*

**proxy** ['prɔksɪ] *n*: **by ~** par procuration

**prudent** ['pruːdnt] *adj* prudent(e)

**prune** [pruːn] *n* pruneau *m* ▷ *vt* élaguer

**pry** [praɪ] *vi*: **to ~ into** fourrer son nez dans

**PS** *n abbr* (= *postscript*) PS *m*

**pseudonym** ['sjuːdənɪm] *n* pseudonyme *m*

**PSHE** *n abbr* (BRIT: Scol: = *personal, social and health education*) cours d'éducation personnelle, sanitaire et sociale préparant à la vie adulte

**psychiatric** [saɪkɪ'ætrɪk] *adj* psychiatrique

**psychiatrist** [saɪ'kaɪətrɪst] *n* psychiatre *m/f*

**psychic** ['saɪkɪk] *adj* (*also*: **~al**) (méta)psychique; (*person*) doué(e) de télépathie or d'un sixième sens

**psychoanalysis** (*pl* **-ses**) [saɪkəuə'nælɪsɪs, -siːz] *n* psychanalyse *f*

**psychological** [saɪkə'lɔdʒɪkl] *adj*

psychologique

**psychologist** [saɪ'kɔlədʒɪst] *n* psychologue *m/f*

**psychology** [saɪ'kɔlədʒɪ] *n* psychologie *f*

**psychotherapy** [saɪkəu'θɛrəpɪ] *n* psychothérapie *f*

**pt** *abbr* = **pint(s)**; **point(s)**

**PTO** *abbr* (= *please turn over*) TSVP

**pub** [pʌb] *n abbr* (= *public house*) pub *m*

**puberty** ['pjuːbətɪ] *n* puberté *f*

**public** ['pʌblɪk] *adj* public(-ique) ▷ *n* public *m*; **in ~** en public; **to make ~** rendre public

**publication** [pʌblɪ'keɪʃən] *n* publication *f*

**public**: **public company** *n* société *f* anonyme; **public convenience** *n* (BRIT) toilettes *fpl*; **public holiday** *n* (BRIT) jour férié; **public house** *n* (BRIT) pub *m*

**publicity** [pʌb'lɪsɪtɪ] *n* publicité *f*

**publicize** ['pʌblɪsaɪz] *vt* (*make known*) faire connaître, rendre public; (*advertise*) faire de la publicité pour

**public**: **public limited company** *n* ≈ société *f* anonyme (SA) (*cotée en Bourse*); **publicly** *adv* publiquement, en public; **public opinion** *n* opinion publique; **public relations** *n or npl* relations publiques (RP); **public school** *n* (BRIT) école privée; (US) école publique; **public transport** (US **public transportation**) *n* transports *mpl* en commun

**publish** ['pʌblɪʃ] *vt* publier; **publisher** *n* éditeur *m*; **publishing** *n* (*industry*) édition *f*

**pub lunch** *n* repas *m* de bistrot

**pudding** ['pudɪŋ] *n* (BRIT: *dessert*) dessert *m*, entremets *m*; (*sweet dish*) pudding *m*, gâteau *m*

**puddle** ['pʌdl] *n* flaque *f* d'eau

**puff** [pʌf] *n* bouffée *f* ▷ *vt* (*also*: **~ out**: *sails, cheeks*) gonfler ▷ *vi* (*pant*) haleter; **puff pastry** (US **puff paste**) *n* pâte feuilletée

**pull** [pul] *n* (*tug*): **to give sth a ~** tirer sur qch ▷ *vt* tirer; (*trigger*) presser;

(*strain: muscle, tendon*) se claquer ▷ vi tirer; **to ~ to pieces** mettre en morceaux; **to ~ one's punches** (*also fig*) ménager son adversaire; **to ~ one's weight** y mettre du sien; **to ~ o.s. together** se ressaisir; **to ~ sb's leg** (*fig*) faire marcher qn; **pull apart** vt (*break*) mettre en pièces, démantibuler; **pull away** vi (*vehicle: move off*) partir; (*draw back*) s'éloigner; **pull back** vt (*lever etc*) tirer sur; (*curtains*) ouvrir ▷ vi (*refrain*) s'abstenir; (*Mil: withdraw*) se retirer; **pull down** vt baisser, abaisser; (*house*) démolir; **pull in** vi (*Aut*) se ranger; (*Rail*) entrer en gare; **pull off** vt enlever, ôter; (*deal etc*) conclure; **pull out** vi démarrer, partir; (*Aut: come out of line*) déboîter ▷ vt (*from bag, pocket*) sortir; (*remove*) arracher; **pull over** vi (*Aut*) se ranger; **pull up** vi (*stop*) s'arrêter ▷ vt remonter; (*uproot*) déraciner, arracher

**pulley** ['pulɪ] n poulie f

**pullover** ['puləuvəʳ] n pull-over m, tricot m

**pulp** [pʌlp] n (*of fruit*) pulpe f; (*for paper*) pâte f à papier

**pulpit** ['pulpɪt] n chaire f

**pulse** [pʌls] n (*of blood*) pouls m; (*of heart*) battement m; **pulses** npl (*Culin*) légumineuses fpl

**puma** ['pju:mə] n puma m

**pump** [pʌmp] n pompe f; (*shoe*) escarpin m ▷ vt pomper; **pump up** vt gonfler

**pumpkin** ['pʌmpkɪn] n potiron m, citrouille f

**pun** [pʌn] n jeu m de mots, calembour m

**punch** [pʌntʃ] n (*blow*) coup m de poing; (*tool*) poinçon m; (*drink*) punch m ▷ vt (*make a hole in*) poinçonner, perforer; (*hit*): **to ~ sb/sth** donner un coup de poing à qn/sur qch; **punch-up** n (BRIT inf) bagarre f

**punctual** ['pʌŋktjuəl] adj ponctuel(le)

**punctuation** [pʌŋktju'eɪʃən] n ponctuation f

**puncture** ['pʌŋktʃəʳ] n (BRIT) crevaison f ▷ vt crever

**punish** ['pʌnɪʃ] vt punir; **punishment** n punition f, châtiment m

**punk** [pʌŋk] n (*person: also:* **~ rocker**) punk m/f; (*music: also:* **~ rock**) le punk; (US inf: *hoodlum*) voyou m

**pup** [pʌp] n chiot m

**pupil** ['pju:pl] n élève m/f; (*of eye*) pupille f

**puppet** ['pʌpɪt] n marionnette f, pantin m

**puppy** ['pʌpɪ] n chiot m, petit chien

**purchase** ['pə:tʃɪs] n achat m ▷ vt acheter

**pure** [pjuəʳ] adj pur(e); **purely** adv purement

**purify** ['pjuərɪfaɪ] vt purifier, épurer

**purity** ['pjuərɪtɪ] n pureté f

**purple** ['pə:pl] adj violet(te); (*face*) cramoisi(e)

**purpose** ['pə:pəs] n intention f, but m; **on ~** exprès

**purr** [pə:ʳ] vi ronronner

**purse** [pə:s] n (BRIT: *for money*) porte-monnaie m inv; (US: *handbag*) sac m (à main) ▷ vt serrer, pincer

**pursue** [pə'sju:] vt poursuivre

**pursuit** [pə'sju:t] n poursuite f; (*occupation*) occupation f, activité f

**pus** [pʌs] n pus m

**push** [puʃ] n poussée f ▷ vt pousser; (*button*) appuyer sur; (*fig: product*) mettre en avant, faire de la publicité pour ▷ vi pousser; **to ~ for** (*better pay, conditions*) réclamer; **push in** vi s'introduire de force; **push off** vi (*inf*) filer, ficher le camp; **push on** vi (*continue*) continuer; **push over** vt renverser; **push through** vi (*in crowd*) se frayer un chemin; **pushchair** n (BRIT) poussette f; **pusher** n (*also:* **drug pusher**) revendeur(-euse) (de drogue), ravitailleur(-euse) (en drogue); **push-up** n (US) traction f

**pussy(-cat)** ['pusɪ-] n (*inf*) minet m

**put** [put] (pt, pp **put**) vt mettre; (*place*) poser, placer; (*say*) dire, exprimer; (*a question*) poser; (*case, view*) exposer, présenter; (*estimate*) estimer; **put**

**aside** *vt* mettre de côté; **put away** *vt* (*store*) ranger; **put back** *vt* (*replace*) remettre, replacer; (*postpone*) remettre; **put by** *vt* (*money*) mettre de côté, économiser; **put down** *vt* (*parcel etc*) poser, déposer; (*in writing*) mettre par écrit, inscrire; (*suppress: revolt etc*) réprimer, écraser; (*attribute*) attribuer; (*animal*) abattre; (*cat, dog*) faire piquer; **put forward** *vt* (*ideas*) avancer, proposer; **put in** *vt* (*complaint*) soumettre; (*time, effort*) consacrer; **put off** *vt* (*postpone*) remettre à plus tard, ajourner; (*discourage*) dissuader; **put on** *vt* (*clothes, lipstick, CD*) mettre; (*light etc*) allumer; (*play etc*) monter; (*weight*) prendre; (*assume: accent, manner*) prendre; **put out** *vt* (*take outside*) mettre dehors; (*one's hand*) tendre; (*light etc*) éteindre; (*person: inconvenience*) déranger, gêner; **put through** *vt* (*Tel: caller*) mettre en communication; (: *call*) passer; (*plan*) faire accepter; **put together** *vt* mettre ensemble; (*assemble: furniture*) monter, assembler; (*meal*) préparer; **put up** *vt* (*raise*) lever, relever, remonter; (*hang*) accrocher; (*build*) construire, ériger; (*increase*) augmenter; (*accommodate*) loger; **put up with** *vt fus* supporter

**putt** [pʌt] *n* putt *m*; **putting green** *n* green *m*

**puzzle** ['pʌzl] *n* énigme *f*, mystère *m*; (*game*) jeu *m*, casse-tête *m*; (*jigsaw*) puzzle *m*; (*also:* **crossword ~**) mots croisés ▷ *vt* intriguer, rendre perplexe ▷ *vi:* **to ~ over** chercher à comprendre; **puzzled** *adj* perplexe; **puzzling** *adj* déconcertant(e), inexplicable

**pyjamas** [pɪˈdʒɑːməz] *npl* (BRIT) pyjama *m*

**pylon** ['paɪlən] *n* pylône *m*

**pyramid** ['pɪrəmɪd] *n* pyramide *f*

**Pyrenees** [pɪrəˈniːz] *npl* Pyrénées *fpl*

**quack** [kwæk] *n* (*of duck*) coin-coin *m inv*; (*pej: doctor*) charlatan *m*

**quadruple** [kwɒˈdruːpl] *vt, vi* quadrupler

**quail** [kweɪl] *n* (*Zool*) caille *f* ▷ *vi:* **to ~ at** *or* **before** reculer devant

**quaint** [kweɪnt] *adj* bizarre; (*old-fashioned*) désuet(-ète); (*picturesque*) au charme vieillot, pittoresque

**quake** [kweɪk] *vi* trembler ▷ *n abbr* = **earthquake**

**qualification** [kwɒlɪfɪˈkeɪʃən] *n* (*often pl: degree etc*) diplôme *m*; (*training*) qualification(s) *f(pl)*; (*ability*) compétence(s) *f(pl)*; (*limitation*) réserve *f*, restriction *f*

**qualified** ['kwɒlɪfaɪd] *adj* (*trained*) qualifié(e); (*professionally*) diplômé(e); (*fit, competent*) compétent(e), qualifié(e); (*limited*) conditionnel(le)

**qualify** ['kwɒlɪfaɪ] *vt* qualifier; (*modify*) atténuer, nuancer ▷ *vi:* **to ~ (as)** obtenir son diplôme (de); **to ~ (for)** remplir les conditions requises (pour);

(*Sport*) se qualifier (pour)
**quality** ['kwɒlɪtɪ] *n* qualité *f*
**qualm** [kwɑːm] *n* doute *m*; scrupule *m*
**quantify** ['kwɒntɪfaɪ] *vt* quantifier
**quantity** ['kwɒntɪtɪ] *n* quantité *f*
**quarantine** ['kwɒrntiːn] *n* quarantaine *f*
**quarrel** ['kwɒrl] *n* querelle *f*, dispute *f* ▷ *vi* se disputer, se quereller
**quarry** ['kwɒrɪ] *n* (*for stone*) carrière *f*; (*animal*) proie *f*, gibier *m*
**quart** [kwɔːt] *n* ≈ litre *m*
**quarter** ['kwɔːtər] *n* quart *m*; (*of year*) trimestre *m*; (*district*) quartier *m*; (*us, CANADA: 25 cents*) (pièce *f* de) vingt-cinq cents *mpl* ▷ *vt* partager en quartiers *or* en quatre; (*Mil*) caserner, cantonner; **quarters** *npl* logement *m*; (*Mil*) quartiers *mpl*, cantonnement *m*; **a ~ of an hour** un quart d'heure; **quarter final** *n* quart *m* de finale; **quarterly** *adj* trimestriel(le) ▷ *adv* tous les trois mois
**quartet(te)** [kwɔːˈtet] *n* quatuor *m*; (*jazz players*) quartette *m*
**quartz** [kwɔːts] *n* quartz *m*
**quay** [kiː] *n* (*also*: **~side**) quai *m*
**queasy** ['kwiːzɪ] *adj*: **to feel ~** avoir mal au cœur
**Quebec** [kwɪˈbek] *n* (*city*) Québec; (*province*) Québec *m*
**queen** [kwiːn] *n* (*gen*) reine *f*; (*Cards etc*) dame *f*
**queer** [kwɪər] *adj* étrange, curieux(-euse); (*suspicious*) louche ▷ *n* (*inf: highly offensive*) homosexuel *m*
**quench** [kwentʃ] *vt*: **to ~ one's thirst** se désaltérer
**query** ['kwɪərɪ] *n* question *f* ▷ *vt* (*disagree with, dispute*) mettre en doute, questionner
**quest** [kwest] *n* recherche *f*, quête *f*
**question** ['kwestʃən] *n* question *f* ▷ *vt* (*person*) interroger; (*plan, idea*) mettre en question *or* en doute; **beyond ~** sans aucun doute; **out of the ~** hors de question; **questionable** *adj* discutable; **question mark** *n* point *m* d'interrogation; **questionnaire**

['kwestʃəˈneər] *n* questionnaire *m*
**queue** [kjuː] (*BRIT*) *n* queue *f*, file *f* ▷ *vi* (*also*: **~ up**) faire la queue
**quiche** [kiːʃ] *n* quiche *f*
**quick** [kwɪk] *adj* rapide; (*mind*) vif (vive); (*agile*) agile, vif (vive) ▷ *n*: **cut to the ~** (*fig*) touché(e) au vif; **be ~!** dépêche-toi!; **quickly** *adv* (*fast*) vite, rapidement; (*immediately*) tout de suite
**quid** [kwɪd] *n* (*pl inv*: *BRIT inf*) livre *f*
**quiet** ['kwaɪət] *adj* tranquille, calme; (*voice*) bas(se); (*ceremony, colour*) discret(-ète) ▷ *n* tranquillité *f*, calme *m*; (*silence*) silence *m*; **quietly** *adv* tranquillement; (*silently*) silencieusement; (*discreetly*) discrètement
**quilt** [kwɪlt] *n* édredon *m*; (*continental quilt*) couette *f*
**quirky** ['kwɜːkɪ] *adj* singulier(-ère)
**quit** [kwɪt] (*pt, pp* **~** *or* **~ted**) *vt* quitter ▷ *vi* (*give up*) abandonner, renoncer; (*resign*) démissionner
**quite** [kwaɪt] *adv* (*rather*) assez, plutôt; (*entirely*) complètement, tout à fait; **~ a few of them** un assez grand nombre d'entre eux; **that's not ~ right** ce n'est pas tout à fait juste; **~ (so)!** exactement!
**quits** [kwɪts] *adj*: **~ (with)** quitte (envers); **let's call it ~** restons-en là
**quiver** ['kwɪvər] *vi* trembler, frémir
**quiz** [kwɪz] *n* (*on TV*) jeu-concours *m* (télévisé); (*in magazine etc*) test *m* de connaissances ▷ *vt* interroger
**quota** ['kwəʊtə] *n* quota *m*
**quotation** [kwəʊˈteɪʃən] *n* citation *f*; (*estimate*) devis *m*; **quotation marks** *npl* guillemets *mpl*
**quote** [kwəʊt] *n* citation *f*; (*estimate*) devis *m* ▷ *vt* (*sentence, author*) citer; (*price*) donner, soumettre ▷ *vi*: **to ~ from** citer; **quotes** *npl* (*inverted commas*) guillemets *mpl*

# r

**Rabat** [rə'bɑːt] n Rabat
**rabbi** ['ræbaɪ] n rabbin m
**rabbit** ['ræbɪt] n lapin m
**rabies** ['reɪbiːz] n rage f
**RAC** n abbr (BRIT: = Royal Automobile
Club) ≈ ACF m
**rac(c)oon** [rə'kuːn] n raton m laveur
**race** [reɪs] n (species) race f; (competition,
rush) course f ▷ vt (person) faire la
course avec ▷ vi (compete) faire la
course, courir; (pulse) battre très
vite; **race car** n (US = **racing car**;
**racecourse** n champ m de courses;
**racehorse** n cheval m de course;
**racetrack** n piste f
**racial** ['reɪʃl] adj racial(e)
**racing** ['reɪsɪŋ] n courses fpl; **racing
car** n (BRIT) voiture f de course; **racing
driver** n (BRIT) pilote m de course
**racism** ['reɪsɪzəm] n racisme m; **racist**
['reɪsɪst] adj, n raciste m/f
**rack** [ræk] n (for guns, tools) râtelier m;
(for clothes) portant m; (for bottles) casier
m; (also: **luggage ~**) filet m à bagages;

(also: **roof ~**) galerie f; (also: **dish ~**)
égouttoir m ▷ vt tourmenter; **to ~
one's brains** se creuser la cervelle
**racket** ['rækɪt] n (for tennis) raquette f;
(noise) tapage m, vacarme m; (swindle)
escroquerie f
**racquet** ['rækɪt] n raquette f
**radar** ['reɪdɑːʳ] n radar m
**radiation** [reɪdɪ'eɪʃən] n rayonnement
m; (radioactive) radiation f
**radiator** ['reɪdɪeɪtəʳ] n radiateur m
**radical** ['rædɪkl] adj radical(e)
**radio** ['reɪdɪəu] n radio f ▷ vt (person)
appeler par radio; **on the ~** à la radio;
**radioactive** adj radioactif(-ive); **radio
station** n station f de radio
**radish** ['rædɪʃ] n radis m
**RAF** n abbr (BRIT) = **Royal Air Force**
**raffle** ['ræfl] n tombola f
**raft** [rɑːft] n (craft: also: **life ~**) radeau m;
(logs) train m de flottage
**rag** [ræg] n chiffon m; (pej: newspaper)
feuille f, torchon m; (for charity)
attractions organisées par les étudiants
au profit d'œuvres de charité; **rags** npl
haillons mpl
**rage** [reɪdʒ] n (fury) rage f, fureur f ▷ vi
(person) être fou (folle) de rage; (storm)
faire rage, être déchaîné(e); **it's all the
~** cela fait fureur
**ragged** ['rægɪd] adj (edge) inégal(e),
qui accroche; (clothes) en loques;
(appearance) déguenillé(e)
**raid** [reɪd] n (Mil) raid m; (criminal) hold-
up m inv; (by police) descente f, rafle f
▷ vt faire un raid sur or un hold-up dans
or une descente dans
**rail** [reɪl] n (on stair) rampe f; (on
bridge, balcony) balustrade f; (of ship)
bastingage m; (for train) rail m; **railcard**
n (BRIT) carte f de chemin de fer;
**railing(s)** n(pl) grille f; **railway** (US
**railroad**) n chemin m de fer; (track)
voie f ferrée; **railway line** n (BRIT) ligne
f de chemin de fer; (track) voie f ferrée;
**railway station** n (BRIT) gare f
**rain** [reɪn] n pluie f ▷ vi pleuvoir; **in
the ~** sous la pluie; **it's ~ing** il pleut;

**rainbow** n arc-en-ciel m; **raincoat** n
imperméable m; **raindrop** n goutte
f de pluie; **rainfall** n chute f de
pluie; (measurement) hauteur f des
précipitations; **rainforest** n forêt
tropicale; **rainy** adj pluvieux(-euse)

**raise** [reɪz] n augmentation f ▷ vt (lift)
lever; hausser; (increase) augmenter;
(morale) remonter; (standards)
améliorer; (a protest, doubt) provoquer,
causer; (a question) soulever; (cattle,
family) élever; (crop) faire pousser;
(army, funds) rassembler; (loan) obtenir;
**to ~ one's voice** élever la voix

**raisin** ['reɪzn] n raisin sec

**rake** [reɪk] n (tool) râteau m; (person)
débauché m ▷ vt (garden) ratisser

**rally** ['rælɪ] n (Pol etc) meeting m,
rassemblement m; (Aut) rallye m;
(Tennis) échange m ▷ vt rassembler,
rallier; (support) gagner ▷ vi (sick person)
aller mieux; (Stock Exchange) reprendre

**RAM** [ræm] n abbr (Comput: = random
access memory) mémoire vive

**ram** [ræm] n bélier m ▷ vt (push)
enfoncer; (crash into: vehicle) emboutir;
(: lamppost etc) percuter

**Ramadan** [ræmə'dæn] n Ramadan m

**ramble** ['ræmbl] n randonnée f
▷ vi (walk) se promener, faire une
randonnée; (pej: also: **~ on**) discourir,
pérorer; **rambler** n promeneur(-euse),
randonneur(-euse); **rambling** adj
(speech) décousu(e); (house) plein(e) de
coins et de recoins; (Bot) grimpant(e)

**ramp** [ræmp] n (incline) rampe f; (Aut)
dénivellation f; (in garage) pont m;
**on/off ~** (US Aut) bretelle f d'accès

**rampage** [ræm'peɪdʒ] n: **to be on the
~** se déchaîner

**ran** [ræn] pt of **run**

**ranch** [rɑːntʃ] n ranch m

**random** ['rændəm] adj fait(e) or
établi(e) au hasard; (Comput, Math)
aléatoire ▷ n: **at ~** au hasard

**rang** [ræŋ] pt of **ring**

**range** [reɪndʒ] n (of mountains) chaîne
f; (of missile, voice) portée f; (of products)

choix m, gamme f; (also: **shooting
~**) champ m de tir; (also: **kitchen ~**)
fourneau m (de cuisine) ▷ vt (place)
mettre en rang, placer ▷ vi: **to ~ over**
couvrir; **to ~ from … to** aller de … à

**ranger** ['reɪndʒəʳ] n garde m forestier

**rank** [ræŋk] n rang m; (Mil) grade m;
(BRIT: also: **taxi ~**) station f de taxis
▷ vi: **to ~ among** compter or se classer
parmi ▷ adj (smell) nauséabond(e); **the
~ and file** (fig) la masse, la base

**ransom** ['rænsəm] n rançon f; **to hold
sb to ~** (fig) exercer un chantage sur qn

**rant** [rænt] vi fulminer

**rap** [ræp] n (music) rap m ▷ vt (door)
frapper sur or à; (table etc) taper sur

**rape** [reɪp] n viol m; (Bot) colza m ▷ vt
violer

**rapid** ['ræpɪd] adj rapide; **rapidly**
adv rapidement; **rapids** npl (Geo)
rapides mpl

**rapist** ['reɪpɪst] n auteur m d'un viol

**rapport** [ræ'pɔːʳ] n entente f

**rare** [rɛəʳ] adj rare; (Culin: steak)
saignant(e); **rarely** adv rarement

**rash** [ræʃ] adj imprudent(e),
irréfléchi(e) ▷ n (Med) rougeur f,
éruption f; (of events) série f (noire)

**rasher** ['ræʃəʳ] n fine tranche (de lard)

**raspberry** ['rɑːzbərɪ] n framboise f

**rat** [ræt] n rat m

**rate** [reɪt] n (ratio) taux m, pourcentage
m; (speed) vitesse f, rythme m; (price)
tarif m ▷ vt (price) évaluer, estimer;
(people) classer; **rates** npl (BRIT: property
tax) impôts locaux; **to ~ sb/sth as**
considérer qn/qch comme

**rather** ['rɑːðəʳ] adv (somewhat) assez,
plutôt; (to some extent) un peu; **it's ~
expensive** c'est assez cher; (too much)
c'est un peu cher; **there's ~ a lot** il y en a
beaucoup; **I would** or **I'd ~ go** j'aimerais
mieux or je préférerais partir; **or ~** (more
accurately) ou plutôt

**rating** ['reɪtɪŋ] n (assessment)
évaluation f; (score) classement m;
(Finance) cote f; **ratings** npl (Radio)
indice(s) m(pl) d'écoute; (TV) Audimat®

**ratio** ['reɪʃɪəu] n proportion f; **in the ~ of 100 to 1** dans la proportion de 100 contre 1

**ration** ['ræʃən] n ration f ▷ vt rationner; **rations** npl (food) vivres mpl

**rational** ['ræʃənl] adj raisonnable, sensé(e); (solution, reasoning) logique; (Med: person) lucide

**rat race** n foire f d'empoigne

**rattle** ['rætl] n (of door, window) battement m; (of coins, chain) cliquetis m; (of train, engine) bruit m de ferraille; (for baby) hochet m ▷ vi cliqueter; (car, bus): **to ~ along** rouler en faisant un bruit de ferraille ▷ vt agiter (bruyamment); (inf: disconcert) décontenancer

**rave** [reɪv] vi (in anger) s'emporter; (with enthusiasm) s'extasier; (Med) délirer ▷ n (inf: party) rave f, soirée f techno

**raven** ['reɪvən] n grand corbeau

**ravine** [rə'viːn] n ravin m

**raw** [rɔː] adj (uncooked) cru(e); (not processed) brut(e); (sore) à vif, irrité(e); (inexperienced) inexpérimenté(e); **~ materials** matières premières

**ray** [reɪ] n rayon m; **~ of hope** lueur f d'espoir

**razor** ['reɪzər] n rasoir m; **razor blade** n lame f de rasoir

**Rd** abbr = **road**

**RE** n abbr (BRIT) = **religious education**

**re** [riː] prep concernant

**reach** [riːtʃ] n portée f, atteinte f; (of river etc) étendue f ▷ vt atteindre, arriver à; (conclusion, decision) parvenir à ▷ vi s'étendre; **out of/within ~** (object) hors de/à portée; **reach out** vt tendre ▷ vi: **to ~ out (for)** allonger le bras (pour prendre)

**react** [riː'ækt] vi réagir; **reaction** [riː'ækʃən] n réaction f; **reactor** [riː'æktər] n réacteur m

**read** (pt, pp **~**) [riːd, rɛd] vi lire ▷ vt lire; (understand) comprendre, interpréter; (study) étudier; (meter) relever; (subj: instrument etc) indiquer, marquer; **read out** vt lire à haute voix; **reader** n

lecteur(-trice)

**readily** ['rɛdɪlɪ] adv volontiers, avec empressement; (easily) facilement

**reading** ['riːdɪŋ] n lecture f; (understanding) interprétation f; (on instrument) indications fpl

**ready** ['rɛdɪ] adj prêt(e); (willing) prêt, disposé(e); (available) disponible ▷ n: **at the ~** (Mil) prêt à faire feu; **when will my photos be ~?** quand est-ce que mes photos seront prêtes?; **to get ~** (as vi) se préparer; (as vt) préparer; **ready-cooked** adj précuit(e); **ready-made** adj tout(e) faite(e)

**real** [rɪəl] adj (world, life) réel(le); (genuine) véritable; (proper) vrai(e) ▷ adv (US inf: very) vraiment; **real ale** n bière traditionnelle; **real estate** n biens fonciers or immobiliers; **realistic** [rɪə'lɪstɪk] adj réaliste; **reality** [riː'ælɪtɪ] n réalité f

**reality TV** n téléréalité f

**realization** [rɪəlaɪ'zeɪʃən] n (awareness) prise f de conscience; (fulfilment: also: of asset) réalisation f

**realize** ['rɪəlaɪz] vt (understand) se rendre compte de, prendre conscience de; (a project, Comm: asset) réaliser

**really** ['rɪəlɪ] adv vraiment; **~?** vraiment?, c'est vrai?

**realm** [rɛlm] n royaume m; (fig) domaine m

**realtor** ['rɪəltɔːr] n (US) agent immobilier

**reappear** [riːə'pɪər] vi réapparaître, reparaître

**rear** [rɪər] adj de derrière, arrière inv; (Aut: wheel etc) arrière ▷ n arrière m ▷ vt (cattle, family) élever ▷ vi (also: ~ up: animal) se cabrer

**rearrange** [riːə'reɪndʒ] vt réarranger

**rear**: **rear-view mirror** n (Aut) rétroviseur m; **rear-wheel drive** n (Aut) traction f arrière

**reason** ['riːzn] n raison f ▷ vi: **to ~ with sb** raisonner qn, faire entendre raison à qn; **it stands to ~ that** il va sans dire que; **reasonable** adj raisonnable;

(not bad) acceptable; **reasonably** adv
(behave) raisonnablement; (fairly) assez;
**reasoning** n raisonnement m
**reassurance** [riːəˈʃʊərəns] n (factual)
assurance f, garantie f; (emotional)
réconfort m
**reassure** [riːəˈʃʊəʳ] vt rassurer
**rebate** [ˈriːbeɪt] n (on tax etc)
dégrèvement m
**rebel** n [ˈrɛbl] rebelle m/f ▷ vi [rɪˈbɛl]
se rebeller, se révolter; **rebellion**
[rɪˈbɛljən] n rébellion f, révolte f;
**rebellious** [rɪˈbɛljəs] adj rebelle
**rebuild** [riːˈbɪld] vt (irreg: like **build**)
reconstruire
**recall** vt [rɪˈkɔːl] rappeler; (remember)
se rappeler, se souvenir de ▷ [ˈriːkɔl]
rappel m; (ability to remember) mémoire f
**rec'd** abbr (=received)
**receipt** [rɪˈsiːt] n (document) reçu m;
(for parcel etc) accusé m de réception;
(act of receiving) réception f; **receipts**
npl (Comm) recettes fpl; **can I have a
~, please?** je peux avoir un reçu, s'il
vous plaît?
**receive** [rɪˈsiːv] vt recevoir; (guest)
recevoir, accueillir; **receiver** n (Tel)
récepteur m, combiné m; (Radio)
récepteur; (of stolen goods) receleur
m; (for bankruptcies) administrateur m
judiciaire
**recent** [ˈriːsnt] adj récent(e); **recently**
adv récemment
**reception** [rɪˈsɛpʃən] n réception
f; (welcome) accueil m, réception;
**reception desk** n réception f;
**receptionist** n réceptionniste m/f
**recession** [rɪˈsɛʃən] n (Econ) récession f
**recharge** [riːˈtʃɑːdʒ] vt (battery)
recharger
**recipe** [ˈrɛsɪpɪ] n recette f
**recipient** [rɪˈsɪpɪənt] n (of payment)
bénéficiaire m/f; (of letter) destinataire
m/f
**recital** [rɪˈsaɪtl] n récital m
**recite** [rɪˈsaɪt] vt (poem) réciter
**reckless** [ˈrɛkləs] adj (driver
etc) imprudent(e); (spender etc)

insouciant(e)
**reckon** [ˈrɛkən] vt (count) calculer,
compter; (consider) considérer, estimer;
(think): **I ~ (that) ...** je pense (que) ...,
j'estime (que) ...
**reclaim** [rɪˈkleɪm] vt (land: from sea)
assécher; (demand back) réclamer (le
remboursement or la restitution de);
(waste materials) récupérer
**recline** [rɪˈklaɪn] vi être allongé(e) or
étendu(e)
**recognition** [rɛkəgˈnɪʃən] n
reconnaissance f; **transformed
beyond ~** méconnaissable
**recognize** [ˈrɛkəgnaɪz] vt: **to ~ (by/as)**
reconnaître (à/comme étant)
**recollection** [rɛkəˈlɛkʃən] n
souvenir m
**recommend** [rɛkəˈmɛnd] vt
recommander; **can you ~ a good
restaurant?** pouvez-vous me
conseiller un bon restaurant?;
**recommendation** [rɛkəmɛnˈdeɪʃən] n
recommandation f
**reconcile** [ˈrɛkənsaɪl] vt (two people)
réconcilier; (two facts) concilier,
accorder; **to ~ o.s. to** se résigner à
**reconsider** [riːkənˈsɪdəʳ] vt
reconsidérer
**reconstruct** [riːkənˈstrʌkt] vt
(building) reconstruire; (crime, system)
reconstituer
**record** n [ˈrɛkɔːd] rapport m, récit
m; (of meeting etc) procès-verbal m;
(register) registre m; (file) dossier m;
(Comput) article m; (also: **police ~**)
casier m judiciaire; (Mus: disc) disque
m; (Sport) record m ▷ adj record inv ▷ vt
[rɪˈkɔːd] (set down) noter; (Mus: song
etc) enregistrer; **public ~s** archives
fpl; **in ~ time** dans un temps record;
**recorded delivery** n (BRIT Post): **to
send sth recorded delivery** ≈ envoyer
qch en recommandé; **recorder** n
(Mus) flûte f à bec; **recording** n (Mus)
enregistrement m; **record player** n
tourne-disque m
**recount** [rɪˈkaunt] vt raconter

**recover** [rɪ'kʌvəʳ] vt récupérer ▷ vi (from illness) se rétablir; (from shock) se remettre; **recovery** n récupération f; rétablissement m; (Econ) redressement m

**recreate** [riːkrɪ'eɪt] vt recréer

**recreation** [rɛkrɪ'eɪʃən] n (leisure) récréation f, détente f; **recreational drug** n drogue récréative; **recreational vehicle** n (US) camping-car m

**recruit** [rɪ'kruːt] n recrue f ▷ vt recruter; **recruitment** n recrutement m

**rectangle** ['rɛktæŋgl] n rectangle m; **rectangular** [rɛk'tæŋgjuləʳ] adj rectangulaire

**rectify** ['rɛktɪfaɪ] vt (error) rectifier, corriger

**rector** ['rɛktəʳ] n (Rel) pasteur m

**recur** [rɪ'kəːʳ] vi se reproduire; (idea, opportunity) se retrouver; (symptoms) réapparaître; **recurring** adj (problem) périodique, fréquent(e); (Math) périodique

**recyclable** [riː'saɪkləbl] adj recyclable

**recycle** [riː'saɪkl] vt, vi recycler

**recycling** [riː'saɪklɪŋ] n recyclage m

**red** [rɛd] n rouge m; (Pol: pej) rouge m/f ▷ adj rouge; (hair) roux (rousse); **in the ~** (account) à découvert; (business) en déficit; **Red Cross** n Croix-Rouge f; **redcurrant** n groseille f (rouge)

**redeem** [rɪ'diːm] vt (debt) rembourser; (sth in pawn) dégager; (fig, also Rel) racheter

**red**: **red-haired** adj roux (rousse); **redhead** n roux (rousse); **red-hot** adj chauffé(e) au rouge, brûlant(e); **red light** n: **to go through a red light** (Aut) brûler un feu rouge; **red-light district** n quartier mal famé

**red meat** n viande f rouge

**reduce** [rɪ'djuːs] vt réduire; (lower) abaisser; **"~ speed now"** (Aut) "ralentir"; **to ~ sb to tears** faire pleurer qn; **reduced** adj réduit(e); **"greatly reduced prices"** "gros rabais"; **at a**

**reduced price** (goods) au rabais; (ticket etc) à prix réduit; **reduction** [rɪ'dʌkʃən] n réduction f; (of price) baisse f; (discount) rabais m; réduction; **is there a reduction for children/students?** y a-t-il une réduction pour les enfants/les étudiants?

**redundancy** [rɪ'dʌndənsɪ] n (BRIT) licenciement m, mise f au chômage

**redundant** [rɪ'dʌndnt] adj (BRIT: worker) licencié(e), mis(e) au chômage; (detail, object) superflu(e); **to be made ~** (worker) être licencié, être mis au chômage

**reed** [riːd] n (Bot) roseau m

**reef** [riːf] n (at sea) récif m, écueil m

**reel** [riːl] n bobine f; (Fishing) moulinet m; (Cine) bande f; (dance) quadrille écossais ▷ vi (sway) chanceler

**ref** [rɛf] n abbr (inf: = referee) arbitre m

**refectory** [rɪ'fɛktərɪ] n réfectoire m

**refer** [rɪ'fəːʳ] vt: **to ~ sb to** (inquirer, patient) adresser qn à; (reader: to text) renvoyer qn à ▷ vi: **to ~ to** (allude to) parler de, faire allusion à; (consult) se reporter à; (apply to) s'appliquer à

**referee** [rɛfə'riː] n arbitre m; (BRIT: for job application) répondant(e) ▷ vt arbitrer

**reference** ['rɛfrəns] n référence f, renvoi m; (mention) allusion f, mention f; (for job application: letter) références; lettre f de recommandation; **with ~ to** en ce qui concerne; (Comm: in letter) me référant à; **reference number** n (Comm) numéro m de référence

**refill** vt [riː'fɪl] remplir à nouveau; (pen, lighter etc) recharger ▷ n ['riːfɪl] (for pen etc) recharge f

**refine** [rɪ'faɪn] vt (sugar, oil) raffiner; (taste) affiner; (idea, theory) peaufiner; **refined** adj (person, taste) raffiné(e); **refinery** n raffinerie f

**reflect** [rɪ'flɛkt] vt (light, image) réfléchir, refléter ▷ vi (think) réfléchir, méditer; **it ~s badly on him** cela le discrédite; **it ~s well on him** c'est tout à son honneur; **reflection** [rɪ'flɛkʃən] *n* réflexion *f*; (*image*) reflet *m*; **on reflection** réflexion faite

**reflex** ['ri:flɛks] *adj, n* réflexe (*m*)

**reform** [rɪ'fɔ:m] *n* réforme *f* ▷ *vt* réformer

**refrain** [rɪ'freɪn] *vi*: **to ~ from doing** s'abstenir de faire ▷ *n* refrain *m*

**refresh** [rɪ'frɛʃ] *vt* rafraîchir; (*subj: food, sleep etc*) redonner des forces à; **refreshing** *adj* (*drink*) rafraîchissant(e); (*sleep*) réparateur(-trice); **refreshments** *npl* rafraîchissements *mpl*

**refrigerator** [rɪ'frɪdʒəreɪtə'] *n* réfrigérateur *m*, frigidaire *m*

**refuel** [ri:'fjuəl] *vi* se ravitailler en carburant

**refuge** ['rɛfju:dʒ] *n* refuge *m*; **to take ~ in** se réfugier dans; **refugee** [rɛfju'dʒi:] *n* réfugié(e)

**refund** *n* ['ri:fʌnd] remboursement *m* ▷ *vt* [rɪ'fʌnd] rembourser

**refurbish** [ri:'fə:bɪʃ] *vt* remettre à neuf

**refusal** [rɪ'fju:zəl] *n* refus *m*; **to have first ~ on sth** avoir droit de préemption sur qch

**refuse**[1] ['rɛfju:s] *n* ordures *fpl*, détritus *mpl*

**refuse**[2] [rɪ'fju:z] *vt, vi* refuser; **to ~ to do sth** refuser de faire qch

**regain** [rɪ'geɪn] *vt* (*lost ground*) regagner; (*strength*) retrouver

**regard** [rɪ'gɑ:d] *n* respect *m*, estime *f*, considération *f* ▷ *vt* considérer; **to give one's ~s to** faire ses amitiés à; **"with kindest ~s"** "bien amicalement"; **as ~s, with ~ to** en ce qui concerne; **regarding** *prep* en ce qui concerne; **regardless** *adv* quand même; **regardless of** sans se soucier de

**regenerate** [rɪ'dʒɛnəreɪt] *vt* régénérer ▷ *vi* se régénérer

**reggae** ['rɛgeɪ] *n* reggae *m*

**regiment** ['rɛdʒɪmənt] *n* régiment *m*

**region** ['ri:dʒən] *n* région *f*; **in the ~ of** (*fig*) aux alentours de; **regional** *adj* régional(e)

**register** ['rɛdʒɪstə'] *n* registre *m*;

(*also*: **electoral ~**) liste électorale ▷ *vt* enregistrer, inscrire; (*birth*) déclarer; (*vehicle*) immatriculer; (*letter*) envoyer en recommandé; (*subj: instrument*) marquer ▷ *vi* s'inscrire; (*at hotel*) signer le registre; (*make impression*) être (bien) compris(e); **registered** *adj* (BRIT: *letter*) recommandé(e)

**registered trademark** *n* marque déposée

**registrar** ['rɛdʒɪstrɑ:'] *n* officier *m* de l'état civil

**registration** [rɛdʒɪs'treɪʃən] *n* (*act*) enregistrement *m*; (*of student*) inscription *f*; (BRIT Aut: *also*: **~ number**) numéro *m* d'immatriculation

**registry office** ['rɛdʒɪstrɪ-] *n* (BRIT) bureau *m* de l'état civil; **to get married in a ~** ≈ se marier à la mairie

**regret** [rɪ'grɛt] *n* regret *m* ▷ *vt* regretter; **regrettable** *adj* regrettable, fâcheux(-euse)

**regular** ['rɛgjulə'] *adj* régulier(-ière); (*usual*) habituel(le), normal(e); (*soldier*) de métier; (Comm: *size*) ordinaire ▷ *n* (*client etc*) habitué(e); **regularly** *adv* régulièrement

**regulate** ['rɛgjuleɪt] *vt* régler; **regulation** [rɛgju'leɪʃən] *n* (*rule*) règlement *m*; (*adjustment*) réglage *m*

**rehabilitation** ['ri:əbɪlɪ'teɪʃən] *n* (*of offender*) réhabilitation *f*; (*of addict*) réadaptation *f*

**rehearsal** [rɪ'hə:səl] *n* répétition *f*

**rehearse** [rɪ'hə:s] *vt* répéter

**reign** [reɪn] *n* règne *m* ▷ *vi* régner

**reimburse** [ri:ɪm'bə:s] *vt* rembourser

**rein** [reɪn] *n* (*for horse*) rêne *f*

**reincarnation** [ri:ɪnkɑ:'neɪʃən] *n* réincarnation *f*

**reindeer** ['reɪndɪə'] *n* (*pl inv*) renne *m*

**reinforce** [ri:ɪn'fɔ:s] *vt* renforcer; **reinforcements** *npl* (Mil) renfort(s) *m(pl)*

**reinstate** [ri:ɪn'steɪt] *vt* rétablir, réintégrer

**reject** *n* ['ri:dʒɛkt] (Comm) article *m* de rebut ▷ *vt* [rɪ'dʒɛkt] refuser; (*idea*) rejeter; **rejection** [rɪ'dʒɛkʃən] n rejet m, refus m

**rejoice** [rɪ'dʒɔɪs] vi: **to ~ (at or over)** se réjouir (de)

**relate** [rɪ'leɪt] vt (tell) raconter; (connect) établir un rapport entre ▷ vi: **to ~ to** (connect) se rapporter à; **to ~ to sb** (interact) entretenir des rapports avec qn; **related** adj apparenté(e); **related to** (subject) lié(e) à; **relating to** prep concernant

**relation** [rɪ'leɪʃən] n (person) parent(e); (link) rapport m, lien m; **relations** npl (relatives) famille f; **relationship** n rapport m, lien m; (personal ties) relations fpl, rapports; (also: **family relationship**) lien de parenté; (affair) liaison f

**relative** ['rɛlətɪv] n parent(e) ▷ adj relatif(-ive); (respective) respectif(-ive); **relatively** adv relativement

**relax** [rɪ'læks] vi (muscle) se relâcher; (person: unwind) se détendre ▷ vt relâcher; (mind, person) détendre; **relaxation** [ri:læk'seɪʃən] n relâchement m; (of mind) détente f; (recreation) détente, délassement m; **relaxed** adj relâché(e); détendu(e); **relaxing** adj délassant(e)

**relay** ['ri:leɪ] n (Sport) course f de relais ▷ vt (message) retransmettre, relayer

**release** [rɪ'li:s] n (from prison, obligation) libération f; (of gas etc) émission f; (of film etc) sortie f; (new recording) disque m ▷ vt (prisoner) libérer; (book, film) sortir; (report, news) rendre public, publier; (gas etc) émettre, dégager; (free: from wreckage etc) dégager; (Tech: catch, spring etc) déclencher; (let go: person, animal) relâcher; (: hand, object) lâcher; (: grip, brake) desserrer

**relegate** ['rɛləgeɪt] vt reléguer; (BRIT Sport): **to be ~d** descendre dans une division inférieure

**relent** [rɪ'lɛnt] vi se laisser fléchir; **relentless** adj implacable; (non-stop) continuel(le)

**relevant** ['rɛləvənt] adj (question) pertinent(e); (corresponding) approprié(e); (fact) significatif(-ive); (information) utile

**reliable** [rɪ'laɪəbl] adj (person, firm) sérieux(-euse), fiable; (method, machine) fiable; (news, information) sûr(e)

**relic** ['rɛlɪk] n (Rel) relique f; (of the past) vestige m

**relief** [rɪ'li:f] n (from pain, anxiety) soulagement m; (help, supplies) secours m(pl); (Art, Geo) relief m

**relieve** [rɪ'li:v] vt (pain, patient) soulager; (fear, worry) dissiper; (bring help) secourir; (take over from: gen) relayer; (: guard) relever; **to ~ sb of sth** débarrasser qn de qch; **to ~ o.s.** (euphemism) se soulager, faire ses besoins; **relieved** adj soulagé(e)

**religion** [rɪ'lɪdʒən] n religion f

**religious** [rɪ'lɪdʒəs] adj religieux(-euse); (book) de piété; **religious education** n instruction religieuse

**relish** ['rɛlɪʃ] n (Culin) condiment m; (enjoyment) délectation f ▷ vt (food etc) savourer; **to ~ doing** se délecter à faire

**relocate** [ri:ləu'keɪt] vt (business) transférer ▷ vi se transférer, s'installer or s'établir ailleurs

**reluctance** [rɪ'lʌktəns] n répugnance f

**reluctant** [rɪ'lʌktənt] adj peu disposé(e), qui hésite; **reluctantly** adv à contrecœur, sans enthousiasme

**rely on** [rɪ'laɪ-] vt fus (be dependent on) dépendre de; (trust) compter sur

**remain** [rɪ'meɪn] vi rester; **remainder** n reste m; (Comm) fin f de série; **remaining** adj qui reste; **remains** npl restes mpl

**remand** [rɪ'mɑ:nd] n: **on ~** en détention préventive ▷ vt: **to be ~ed in custody** être placé(e) en détention préventive

**remark** [rɪ'mɑ:k] n remarque f, observation f ▷ vt (faire) remarquer, dire; **remarkable** adj remarquable

**remarry** [ri:'mærɪ] vi se remarier

**remedy** ['rɛmədɪ] n: **~ (for)** remède m

(contre *or* à) ▷ *vt* remédier à

**remember** [rɪˈmɛmbəʳ] *vt* se rappeler, se souvenir de; (*send greetings*): ~ **me to him** saluez-le de ma part; **Remembrance Day** [rɪˈmɛmbrəns-] *n* (*BRIT*) ≈ (le jour de) l'Armistice *m*, ≈ le 11 novembre

● **REMEMBRANCE DAY**
●
● **Remembrance Day** ou
● **Remembrance Sunday** est le
● dimanche le plus proche du 11
● novembre, jour où la Première
● Guerre mondiale a officiellement
● pris fin. Il rend hommage aux
● victimes des deux guerres
● mondiales. À cette occasion, on
● observe deux minutes de silence
● à 11h, heure de la signature de
● l'armistice avec l'Allemagne en
● 1918; certaines membres de la
● famille royale et du gouvernement
● déposent des gerbes de coquelicots
● au cénotaphe de Whitehall, et des
● couronnes sont placées sur les
● monuments aux morts dans toute
● la Grande-Bretagne; par ailleurs,
● les gens portent des coquelicots
● artificiels fabriqués et vendus
● par les membres de la légion
● britannique blessés au combat, au
● profit des blessés de guerre et de
● leur famille.

**remind** [rɪˈmaɪnd] *vt*: **to ~ sb of sth** rappeler qch à qn; **to ~ sb to do** faire penser à qn à faire, rappeler à qn qu'il doit faire; **reminder** *n* (*Comm: letter*) rappel *m*; (*note etc*) pense-bête *m*; (*souvenir*) souvenir *m*

**reminiscent** [rɛmɪˈnɪsnt] *adj*: **~ of** qui rappelle, qui fait penser à

**remnant** [ˈrɛmnənt] *n* reste *m*, restant *m*; (*of cloth*) coupon *m*

**remorse** [rɪˈmɔːs] *n* remords *m*

**remote** [rɪˈməut] *adj* éloigné(e), lointain(e); (*person*) distant(e);

(*possibility*) vague; **remote control** *n* télécommande *f*; **remotely** *adv* au loin; (*slightly*) très vaguement

**removal** [rɪˈmuːvəl] *n* (*taking away*) enlèvement *m*; suppression *f*; (*BRIT: from house*) déménagement *m*; (*from office: dismissal*) renvoi *m*; (*of stain*) nettoyage *m*; (*Med*) ablation *f*; **removal man** (*irreg*) *n* (*BRIT*) déménageur *m*; **removal van** *n* (*BRIT*) camion *m* de déménagement

**remove** [rɪˈmuːv] *vt* enlever, retirer; (*employee*) renvoyer; (*stain*) faire partir; (*abuse*) supprimer; (*doubt*) chasser

**Renaissance** [rɪˈneɪsɑ̃ːs] *n*: **the ~** la Renaissance

**rename** [riːˈneɪm] *vt* rebaptiser

**render** [ˈrɛndəʳ] *vt* rendre

**rendezvous** [ˈrɔndɪvuː] *n* rendez-vous *m inv*

**renew** [rɪˈnjuː] *vt* renouveler; (*negotiations*) reprendre; (*acquaintance*) renouer

**renovate** [ˈrɛnəveɪt] *vt* rénover; (*work of art*) restaurer

**renowned** [rɪˈnaund] *adj* renommé(e)

**rent** [rɛnt] *pt, pp of* **rend** ▷ *n* loyer *m* ▷ *vt* louer; **rental** *n* (*for television, car*) (prix *m* de) location *f*

**reorganize** [riːˈɔːɡənaɪz] *vt* réorganiser

**rep** [rɛp] *n abbr* (*Comm*) = **representative**

**repair** [rɪˈpɛəʳ] *n* réparation *f* ▷ *vt* réparer; **in good/bad ~** en bon/mauvais état; **where can I get this ~ed?** où est-ce que je peux faire réparer ceci?; **repair kit** *n* trousse *f* de réparations

**repay** [riːˈpeɪ] *vt* (*irreg: like* **pay**) (*money, creditor*) rembourser; (*sb's efforts*) récompenser; **repayment** *n* remboursement *m*

**repeat** [rɪˈpiːt] *n* (*Radio, TV*) reprise *f* ▷ *vt* répéter; (*promise, attack, also Comm: order*) renouveler; (*Scol: a class*) redoubler ▷ *vi* répéter; **can you ~ that, please?** pouvez-vous répéter,

s'il vous plaît?; **repeatedly** adv
souvent, à plusieurs reprises; **repeat
prescription** n (BRIT): **I'd like a repeat
prescription** je voudrais renouveler
mon ordonnance

**repellent** [rɪˈpɛlənt] adj repoussant(e)
▷ n: **insect ~** insectifuge m

**repercussions** [riːpəˈkʌʃənz] npl
répercussions fpl

**repetition** [rɛpɪˈtɪʃən] n répétition f

**repetitive** [rɪˈpɛtɪtɪv] adj (movement,
work) répétitif(-ive); (speech) plein(e)
de redites

**replace** [rɪˈpleɪs] vt (put back)
remettre, replacer; (take the place
of) remplacer; **replacement** n
(substitution) remplacement m; (person)
remplaçant(e)

**replay** [ˈriːpleɪ] n (of match) match
rejoué; (of tape, film) répétition f

**replica** [ˈrɛplɪkə] n réplique f, copie
exacte

**reply** [rɪˈplaɪ] n réponse f ▷ vi répondre

**report** [rɪˈpɔːt] n rapport m; (Press
etc) reportage m; (BRIT: also: **school
~**) bulletin m (scolaire); (of gun)
détonation f ▷ vt rapporter, faire un
compte rendu de; (Press etc) faire un
reportage sur; (notify: accident) signaler;
(: culprit) dénoncer ▷ vi (make a report)
faire un rapport; **I'd like to ~ a theft**
je voudrais signaler un vol; (present
o.s.): **to ~ (to sb)** se présenter (chez
qn); **report card** n (US, SCOTTISH)
bulletin m (scolaire); **reportedly** adv:
**she is reportedly living in Spain** elle
habiterait en Espagne; **he reportedly
told them to ...** il leur aurait dit de ...;
**reporter** n reporter m

**represent** [rɛprɪˈzɛnt] vt représenter;
(view, belief) présenter, expliquer;
(describe): **to ~ sth as** présenter or
décrire qch comme; **representation**
[rɛprɪzɛnˈteɪʃən] n représentation f;
**representative** n représentant(e); (US
Pol) député m ▷ adj représentatif(-ive),
caractéristique

**repress** [rɪˈprɛs] vt réprimer;

**repression** [rɪˈprɛʃən] n répression f

**reprimand** [ˈrɛprɪmɑːnd] n
réprimande f ▷ vt réprimander

**reproduce** [riːprəˈdjuːs] vt reproduire
▷ vi se reproduire; **reproduction**
[riːprəˈdʌkʃən] n reproduction f

**reptile** [ˈrɛptaɪl] n reptile m

**republic** [rɪˈpʌblɪk] n république f;
**republican** adj, n républicain(e)

**reputable** [ˈrɛpjutəbl] adj de bonne
réputation; (occupation) honorable

**reputation** [rɛpjuˈteɪʃən] n
réputation f

**request** [rɪˈkwɛst] n demande f;
(formal) requête f ▷ vt: **to ~ (of or from
sb)** demander (à qn); **request stop** n
(BRIT: for bus) arrêt facultatif

**require** [rɪˈkwaɪər] vt (need: subj: person)
avoir besoin de; (: thing, situation)
nécessiter, demander; (want) exiger;
(order): **to ~ sb to do sth/sth of sb**
exiger que qn fasse qch/qch de qn;
**requirement** n (need) exigence f;
besoin m; (condition) condition f
(requise)

**resat** [riːˈsæt] pt, pp of **resit**

**rescue** [ˈrɛskjuː] n (from accident)
sauvetage m; (help) secours mpl ▷ vt
sauver

**research** [rɪˈsəːtʃ] n recherche(s) f(pl)
▷ vt faire des recherches sur

**resemblance** [rɪˈzɛmbləns] n
ressemblance f

**resemble** [rɪˈzɛmbl] vt ressembler à

**resent** [rɪˈzɛnt] vt être contrarié(e)
par; **resentful** adj irrité(e), plein(e)
de ressentiment; **resentment** n
ressentiment m

**reservation** [rɛzəˈveɪʃən] n (booking)
réservation f; **to make a ~ (in an
hotel/a restaurant/on a plane)**
réserver or retenir une chambre/une
table/une place; **reservation desk** n
(US: in hotel) réception f

**reserve** [rɪˈzəːv] n réserve f; (Sport)
remplaçant(e) ▷ vt (seats etc) réserver,
retenir; **reserved** adj réservé(e)

**reservoir** [ˈrɛzəvwɑːr] n réservoir m

**reshuffle** [riːˈʃʌfl] n: **Cabinet ~** (Pol) remaniement ministériel

**residence** [ˈrɛzɪdəns] n résidence f; **residence permit** n (BRIT) permis m de séjour

**resident** [ˈrɛzɪdənt] n (of country) résident(e); (of area, house) habitant(e); (in hotel) pensionnaire ▷ adj résidant(e); **residential** [rɛzɪˈdɛnʃəl] adj de résidence; (area) résidentiel(le); (course) avec hébergement sur place

**residue** [ˈrɛzɪdjuː] n reste m; (Chem, Physics) résidu m

**resign** [rɪˈzaɪn] vt (one's post) se démettre de ▷ vi démissionner; **to ~ o.s. to** (endure) se résigner à; **resignation** [rɛzɪɡˈneɪʃən] n (from post) démission f; (state of mind) résignation f

**resin** [ˈrɛzɪn] n résine f

**resist** [rɪˈzɪst] vt résister à; **resistance** n résistance f

**resit** (BRIT) vt [riːˈsɪt] (pt, pp **resat**) (exam) repasser ▷ n [ˈriːsɪt] deuxième session f (d'un examen)

**resolution** [rɛzəˈluːʃən] n résolution f

**resolve** [rɪˈzɔlv] n résolution f ▷ vt (decide): **to ~ to do** résoudre or décider de faire; (problem) résoudre

**resort** [rɪˈzɔːt] n (seaside town) station f balnéaire; (for skiing) station de ski; (recourse) recours m ▷ vi: **to ~ to** avoir recours à; **in the last ~** en dernier ressort

**resource** [rɪˈsɔːs] n ressource f; **resourceful** adj ingénieux(-euse), débrouillard(e)

**respect** [rɪsˈpɛkt] n respect m ▷ vt respecter; **respectable** adj respectable; (quite good: result etc) honorable; **respectful** adj respectueux(-euse); **respective** adj respectif(-ive); **respectively** adv respectivement

**respite** [ˈrɛspaɪt] n répit m

**respond** [rɪsˈpɔnd] vi répondre; (react) réagir; **response** [rɪsˈpɔns] n réponse f; (reaction) réaction f

**responsibility** [rɪspɔnsɪˈbɪlɪtɪ] n responsabilité f

**responsible** [rɪsˈpɔnsɪbl] adj (liable): **~ (for)** responsable (de); (person) digne de confiance; (job) qui comporte des responsabilités; **responsibly** adv avec sérieux

**responsive** [rɪsˈpɔnsɪv] adj (student, audience) réceptif(-ive); (brakes, steering) sensible

**rest** [rɛst] n repos m; (stop) arrêt m, pause f; (Mus) silence m; (support) support m, appui m; (remainder) reste m, restant m ▷ vi se reposer; (be supported): **to ~ on** appuyer or reposer sur ▷ vt (lean): **to ~ sth on/against** appuyer qch sur/contre; **the ~ of them** les autres

**restaurant** [ˈrɛstərɔŋ] n restaurant m; **restaurant car** n (BRIT Rail) wagon-restaurant m

**restless** [ˈrɛstlɪs] adj agité(e)

**restoration** [rɛstəˈreɪʃən] n (of building) restauration f; (of stolen goods) restitution f

**restore** [rɪˈstɔːʳ] vt (building) restaurer; (sth stolen) restituer; (peace, health) rétablir; **to ~ to** (former state) ramener à

**restrain** [rɪsˈtreɪn] vt (feeling) contenir; (person): **to ~ (from doing)** retenir (de faire); **restraint** n (restriction) contrainte f; (moderation) retenue f; (of style) sobriété f

**restrict** [rɪsˈtrɪkt] vt restreindre, limiter; **restriction** [rɪsˈtrɪkʃən] n restriction f, limitation f

**rest room** n (US) toilettes fpl

**restructure** [riːˈstrʌktʃəʳ] vt restructurer

**result** [rɪˈzʌlt] n résultat m ▷ vi: **to ~ in** aboutir à, se terminer par; **as a ~ of** à la suite de

**resume** [rɪˈzjuːm] vt (work, journey) reprendre ▷ vi (work etc) reprendre

**résumé** [ˈreɪzjuːmeɪ] n (summary) résumé m; (US: curriculum vitae) curriculum vitae m inv

**resuscitate** [rɪˈsʌsɪteɪt] vt (Med) réanimer

**retail** ['riːteɪl] *adj* de *or* au détail ▷ *adv* au détail; **retailer** *n* détaillant(e)

**retain** [rɪ'teɪn] *vt* (*keep*) garder, conserver

**retaliation** [rɪtælɪ'eɪʃən] *n* représailles *fpl*, vengeance *f*

**retarded** [rɪ'tɑːdɪd] *adj* retardé(e)

**retire** [rɪ'taɪə*] *vi* (*give up work*) prendre sa retraite; (*withdraw*) se retirer, partir; (*go to bed*) (aller) se coucher; **retired** *adj* (*person*) retraité(e); **retirement** *n* retraite *f*

**retort** [rɪ'tɔːt] *vi* riposter

**retreat** [rɪ'triːt] *n* retraite *f* ▷ *vi* battre en retraite

**retrieve** [rɪ'triːv] *vt* (*sth lost*) récupérer; (*situation, honour*) sauver; (*error, loss*) réparer; (*Comput*) rechercher

**retrospect** ['rɛtrəspɛkt] *n*: **in ~** rétrospectivement, après coup; **retrospective** [rɛtrə'spɛktɪv] *adj* rétrospectif(-ive); (*law*) rétroactif(-ive) ▷ *n* (*Art*) rétrospective *f*

**return** [rɪ'təːn] *n* (*going or coming back*) retour *m*; (*of sth stolen etc*) restitution *f*; (*Finance: from land, shares*) rapport *m* ▷ *cpd* (*journey*) de retour; (*BRIT: ticket*) aller et retour; (*match*) retour ▷ *vi* (*person etc: come back*) revenir; (: *go back*) retourner ▷ *vt* rendre; (*bring back*) rapporter; (*send back*) renvoyer; (*put back*) remettre; (*Pol: candidate*) élire; **returns** *npl* (*Comm*) recettes *fpl*; (*Finance*) bénéfices *mpl*; **many happy ~s (of the day)!** bon anniversaire!; **by ~ (of post)** par retour (du courrier); **in ~ (for)** en échange (de); **a ~ (ticket) for ...** un billet aller et retour pour ...; **return ticket** *n* (*esp BRIT*) billet *m* aller-retour

**reunion** [riː'juːnɪən] *n* réunion *f*

**reunite** [riːjuː'naɪt] *vt* réunir

**revamp** [riː'væmp] *vt* (*house*) retaper; (*firm*) réorganiser

**reveal** [rɪ'viːl] *vt* (*make known*) révéler; (*display*) laisser voir; **revealing** *adj* révélateur(-trice); (*dress*) au décolleté généreux *or* suggestif

**revel** ['rɛvl] *vi*: **to ~ in sth/in doing** se délecter de qch/à faire

**revelation** [rɛvə'leɪʃən] *n* révélation *f*

**revenge** [rɪ'vɛndʒ] *n* vengeance *f*; (*in game etc*) revanche *f* ▷ *vt* venger; **to take ~ (on)** se venger (sur)

**revenue** ['rɛvənjuː] *n* revenu *m*

**Reverend** ['rɛvərənd] *adj* (*in titles*): **the ~ John Smith** (*Anglican*) le révérend John Smith; (*Catholic*) l'abbé (John) Smith; (*Protestant*) le pasteur (John) Smith

**reversal** [rɪ'vəːsl] *n* (*of opinion*) revirement *m*; (*of order*) renversement *m*; (*of direction*) changement *m*

**reverse** [rɪ'vəːs] *n* contraire *m*, opposé *m*; (*back*) dos *m*, envers *m*; (*of paper*) verso *m*; (*of coin*) revers *m*; (*Aut: also*: **~ gear**) marche *f* arrière ▷ *adj* (*order, direction*) opposé(e), inverse ▷ *vt* (*order, position*) changer, inverser; (*direction, policy*) changer complètement de; (*decision*) annuler; (*roles*) renverser ▷ *vi* (*BRIT Aut*) faire marche arrière; **reverse-charge call** *n* (*BRIT Tel*) communication *f* en PCV; **reversing lights** *npl* (*BRIT Aut*) feux *mpl* de marche arrière *or* de recul

**revert** [rɪ'vəːt] *vi*: **to ~ to** revenir à, retourner à

**review** [rɪ'vjuː] *n* revue *f*; (*of book, film*) critique *f*; (*of situation, policy*) examen *m*, bilan *m*; (*US: examination*) examen ▷ *vt* passer en revue; faire la critique de; examiner

**revise** [rɪ'vaɪz] *vt* réviser, modifier; (*manuscript*) revoir, corriger ▷ *vi* (*study*) réviser; **revision** [rɪ'vɪʒən] *n* révision *f*

**revival** [rɪ'vaɪvəl] *n* reprise *f*; (*recovery*) rétablissement *m*; (*of faith*) renouveau *m*

**revive** [rɪ'vaɪv] *vt* (*person*) ranimer; (*custom*) rétablir; (*economy*) relancer; (*hope, courage*) raviver, faire renaître; (*play, fashion*) reprendre ▷ *vi* (*person*) reprendre connaissance; (: *from ill health*) se rétablir; (*hope etc*) renaître; (*activity*) reprendre

**revolt** [rɪ'vəult] *n* révolte *f* ▷ *vi* se

révolter, se rebeller ▷ vt révolter, dégoûter; **revolting** adj dégoûtant(e)

**revolution** [rɛvə'luːʃən] n révolution f; (of wheel etc) tour m, révolution; **revolutionary** adj, n révolutionnaire (m/f)

**revolve** [rɪ'vɒlv] vi tourner

**revolver** [rɪ'vɒlvə*] n revolver m

**reward** [rɪ'wɔːd] n récompense f ▷ vt: **to ~ (for)** récompenser (de); **rewarding** adj (fig) qui (en) vaut la peine, gratifiant(e)

**rewind** [riː'waɪnd] vt (irreg: like **wind**) (tape) réembobiner

**rewritable** [riː'raɪtəbl] adj (CD, DVD) réinscriptible

**rewrite** [riː'raɪt] (pt **rewrote**, pp **rewritten**) vt récrire

**rheumatism** ['ruːmətɪzəm] n rhumatisme m

**Rhine** [raɪn] n: **the (River) ~** le Rhin

**rhinoceros** [raɪ'nɒsərəs] n rhinocéros m

**Rhône** [rəʊn] n: **the (River) ~** le Rhône

**rhubarb** ['ruːbɑːb] n rhubarbe f

**rhyme** [raɪm] n rime f; (verse) vers mpl

**rhythm** ['rɪðm] n rythme m

**rib** [rɪb] n (Anat) côte f

**ribbon** ['rɪbən] n ruban m; **in ~s** (torn) en lambeaux

**rice** [raɪs] n riz m; **rice pudding** n riz m au lait

**rich** [rɪtʃ] adj riche; (gift, clothes) somptueux(-euse); **to be ~ in sth** être riche en qch

**rid** [rɪd] (pt, pp ~) vt: **to ~ sb of** débarrasser qn de; **to get ~ of** se débarrasser de

**riddle** ['rɪdl] n (puzzle) énigme f ▷ vt: **to be ~d with** être criblé(e) de; (fig) être en proie à

**ride** [raɪd] n promenade f, tour m; (distance covered) trajet m ▷ vb (pt **rode**, pp **ridden**) ▷ vi (as sport) monter (à cheval), faire du cheval; (go somewhere: on horse, bicycle) aller (à cheval or à bicyclette etc); (travel: on bicycle, motor cycle, bus) rouler ▷ vt (a horse) monter;

(distance) parcourir, faire; **to ~ a horse/ bicycle** monter à cheval/à bicyclette; **to take sb for a ~** (fig) faire marcher qn; (cheat) rouler qn; **rider** n cavalier(-ière); (in race) jockey m; (on bicycle) cycliste m/f; (on motorcycle) motocycliste m/f

**ridge** [rɪdʒ] n (of hill) faîte m; (of roof, mountain) arête f; (on object) strie f

**ridicule** ['rɪdɪkjuːl] n ridicule m; dérision f ▷ vt ridiculiser, tourner en dérision; **ridiculous** [rɪ'dɪkjuləs] adj ridicule

**riding** ['raɪdɪŋ] n équitation f; **riding school** n manège m, école f d'équitation

**rife** [raɪf] adj répandu(e); **~ with** abondant(e) en

**rifle** ['raɪfl] n fusil m (à canon rayé) ▷ vt vider, dévaliser

**rift** [rɪft] n fente f, fissure f; (fig: disagreement) désaccord m

**rig** [rɪg] n (also: **oil ~**: on land) derrick m; (: at sea) plate-forme pétrolière ▷ vt (election etc) truquer

**right** [raɪt] adj (true) juste, exact(e); (correct) bon (bonne); (suitable) approprié(e), convenable; (just) juste, équitable; (morally good) bien inv; (not left) droit(e) ▷ n (moral good) bien m; (title, claim) droit m; (not left) droite f ▷ adv (answer) correctement; (treat) bien, comme il faut; (not on the left) à droite ▷ vt redresser ▷ excl bon!; **do you have the ~ time?** avez-vous l'heure juste or exacte?; **to be ~** (person) avoir raison; (answer) être juste or correct(e); **by ~s** en toute justice; **on the ~** à droite; **to be in the ~** avoir raison; **~ in the middle** en plein milieu; **~ away** immédiatement; **right angle** n (Math) angle droit; **rightful** adj (heir) légitime; **right-hand** adj: **the right-hand side** la droite; **right-hand drive** n (BRIT) conduite f à droite; (vehicle) véhicule m avec la conduite à droite; **right-handed** adj (person) droitier(-ière); **rightly** adv bien, correctement; (with reason) à juste titre; **right of way** n (on path etc) droit m de passage; (Aut) priorité f; **right-wing** adj (Pol) de droite

**rigid** ['rɪdʒɪd] adj rigide; (principle, control) strict(e)

**rigorous** ['rɪgərəs] adj rigoureux(-euse)

**rim** [rɪm] n bord m; (of spectacles) monture f; (of wheel) jante f

**rind** [raɪnd] n (of bacon) couenne f; (of lemon etc) écorce f, zeste m; (of cheese) croûte f

**ring** [rɪŋ] n anneau m; (on finger) bague f; (also: **wedding ~**) alliance f; (of people, objects) cercle m; (of spies) réseau m; (of smoke etc) rond m; (arena) piste f, arène f; (for boxing) ring m; (sound of bell) sonnerie f ▷ vb (pt **rang**, pp **rung**) ▷ vi (telephone, bell) sonner; (person: by telephone) téléphoner; (ears) bourdonner; (also: ~ **out**: voice, words) retentir ▷ vt (BRIT Tel: also: ~ **up**) téléphoner à, appeler; **to ~ the bell** sonner; **to give sb a ~** (Tel) passer un coup de téléphone or de fil à qn; **ring back** vt, vi (BRIT Tel) rappeler; **ring off** vi (BRIT Tel) raccrocher; **ring up** (BRIT) ▷ vt (Tel) téléphoner à, appeler; **ringing tone** n (BRIT Tel) tonalité f d'appel; **ringleader** n (of gang) chef m, meneur m; **ring road** n (BRIT) rocade f; (motorway) périphérique m; **ringtone** n (on mobile) sonnerie f (de téléphone portable)

**rink** [rɪŋk] n (also: **ice ~**) patinoire f

**rinse** [rɪns] n rinçage m ▷ vt rincer

**riot** ['raɪət] n émeute f, bagarres fpl ▷ vi (demonstrators) manifester avec violence; (population) se soulever, se révolter; **to run ~** se déchaîner

**rip** [rɪp] n déchirure f ▷ vt déchirer ▷ vi se déchirer; **rip off** vt (inf: cheat) arnaquer; **rip up** vt déchirer

**ripe** [raɪp] adj (fruit) mûr(e); (cheese) fait(e)

**rip-off** ['rɪpɔf] n (inf): **it's a ~!** c'est du vol manifeste!, c'est de l'arnaque!

**ripple** ['rɪpl] n ride f, ondulation f; (of applause, laughter) cascade f ▷ vi se rider, onduler

**rise** [raɪz] n (slope) côte f, pente f; (hill) élévation f; (increase: in wages: BRIT) augmentation f; (: in prices, temperature) hausse f, augmentation f; (fig: to power etc) ascension f ▷ vi (pt **rose**, pp ~**n**) s'élever, monter; (prices, numbers) augmenter, monter; (waters, river) monter; (sun, wind, person: from chair, bed) se lever; (also: ~ **up**: tower, building) s'élever; (: rebel) se révolter; se rebeller; (in rank) s'élever; **to give ~ to** donner lieu à; **to ~ to the occasion** se montrer à la hauteur; **risen** ['rɪzn] pp of **rise**; **rising** adj (increasing: number, prices) en hausse; (tide) montant(e); (sun, moon) levant(e)

**risk** [rɪsk] n risque m ▷ vt risquer; **to take** or **run the ~ of doing** courir le risque de faire; **at ~** en danger; **at one's own ~** à ses risques et périls; **risky** adj risqué(e)

**rite** [raɪt] n rite m; **the last ~s** les derniers sacrements

**ritual** ['rɪtjuəl] adj rituel(le) ▷ n rituel m

**rival** ['raɪvl] n rival(e); (in business) concurrent(e) ▷ adj rival(e); qui fait concurrence ▷ vt (match) égaler; **rivalry** n rivalité f; (in business) concurrence f

**river** ['rɪvəʳ] n rivière f; (major: also fig) fleuve m ▷ cpd (port, traffic) fluvial(e); **up/down ~** en amont/aval; **riverbank** n rive f, berge f

**rivet** ['rɪvɪt] n rivet m ▷ vt (fig) river, fixer

**Riviera** [rɪvɪ'ɛərə] n: **the (French) ~** la Côte d'Azur

**road** [rəud] n route f; (in town) rue f; (fig) chemin, voie f ▷ cpd (accident) de la route; **major/minor ~** route principale or à priorité/voie secondaire; **which ~ do I take for ...?** quelle route dois-je prendre pour aller à...?; **roadblock** n barrage routier; **road map** n carte routière; **road rage** n comportement très agressif de certains usagers de la route; **road safety** n sécurité routière; **roadside** n bord m de la route, bas-côté m; **roadsign** n panneau m de signalisation; **road tax** n (BRIT Aut) taxe f sur les automobiles; **roadworks** npl travaux mpl (de réfection des routes)

**roam** [rəum] vi errer, vagabonder

**roar** [rɔːʳ] n rugissement m; (of crowd) hurlements mpl; (of vehicle, thunder, storm) grondement m ▷ vi rugir; hurler; gronder; **to ~ with laughter** rire à gorge déployée; **to do a ~ing trade** faire des affaires en or

**roast** [rəust] n rôti m ▷ vt (meat) (faire) rôtir; (coffee) griller, torréfier; **roast beef** n rôti m de bœuf, rosbif m

**rob** [rɔb] vt (person) voler; (bank) dévaliser; **to ~ sb of sth** voler or dérober qch à qn; (fig: deprive) priver qn de qch; **robber** n bandit m, voleur m; **robbery** n vol m

**robe** [rəub] n (for ceremony etc) robe f; (also: **bath~**) peignoir m; (us: rug) couverture f ▷ vt revêtir (d'une robe)

**robin** ['rɔbɪn] n rouge-gorge m

**robot** ['rəubɔt] n robot m

**robust** [rəu'bʌst] adj robuste; (material, appetite) solide

**rock** [rɔk] n (substance) roche f, roc m; (boulder) rocher m, roche; (us: small stone) caillou m; (BRIT: sweet) ≈ sucre m d'orge ▷ vt (swing gently: cradle) balancer; (: child) bercer; (shake) ébranler, secouer ▷ vi se balancer, être ébranlé(e) or secoué(e); **on the ~s** (drink) avec des glaçons; (marriage etc) en train de craquer; **rock and roll** n rock (and roll) m, rock'n'roll m; **rock climbing** n varappe f

**rocket** ['rɔkɪt] n fusée f; (Mil) fusée, roquette f; (Culin) roquette f

**rocking chair** ['rɔkɪŋ-] n fauteuil m à bascule

**rocky** ['rɔkɪ] adj (hill) rocheux(-euse); (path) rocailleux(-euse)

**rod** [rɔd] n (metallic) tringle f; (Tech) tige f; (wooden) baguette f; (also: **fishing ~**) canne f à pêche

**rode** [rəud] pt of **ride**

**rodent** ['rəudnt] n rongeur m

**rogue** [rəug] n coquin(e)

**role** [rəul] n rôle m; **role-model** n modèle m à émuler

**roll** [rəul] n rouleau m; (of banknotes) liasse f; (also: **bread ~**) petit pain; (register) liste f; (sound: of drums etc) roulement m ▷ vt rouler; (also: **~ up**: string) enrouler; (also: **~ out**: pastry) étendre au rouleau, abaisser ▷ vi rouler; **roll over** vi se retourner; **roll up** vi (inf: arrive) arriver, s'amener ▷ vt (carpet, cloth, map) rouler; (sleeves) retrousser; **roller** n rouleau m; (wheel) roulette f; (for road) rouleau compresseur; (for hair) bigoudi m; **roller coaster** n montagnes fpl russes; **roller skates** npl patins mpl à roulettes; **roller-skating** n patin m à roulettes; **to go roller-skating** faire du patin à roulettes; **rolling pin** n rouleau m à pâtisserie

**ROM** [rɔm] n abbr (Comput: = read-only memory) mémoire morte, ROM f

**Roman** ['rəumən] adj romain(e) ▷ n Romain(e); **Roman Catholic** adj, n catholique (m/f)

**romance** [rə'mæns] n (love affair) idylle f; (charm) poésie f; (novel) roman m à l'eau de rose

**Romania** etc [rəu'meɪnɪə] = **Rumania** etc

**Roman numeral** n chiffre romain

**romantic** [rə'mæntɪk] adj romantique; (novel, attachment) sentimental(e)

**Rome** [rəum] n Rome

**roof** [ruːf] n toit m; (of tunnel, cave) plafond m ▷ vt couvrir (d'un toit); **the ~ of the mouth** la voûte du palais; **roof rack** n (Aut) galerie f

**rook** [ruk] n (bird) freux m; (Chess) tour f

**room** [ruːm] n (in house) pièce f; (also: **bed~**) chambre f (à coucher); (in school etc) salle f; (space) place f; **roommate** n camarade m/f de chambre; **room service** n service m des chambres (dans un hôtel); **roomy** adj spacieux(-euse);

(*garment*) ample

**rooster** ['ru:stəʳ] n coq m

**root** [ru:t] n (*Bot, Math*) racine f; (*fig: of problem*) origine f, fond m ▷ vi (*plant*) s'enraciner

**rope** [rəup] n corde f; (*Naut*) cordage m ▷ vt (*tie up or together*) attacher; (*climbers: also:* **~ together**) encorder; (*area: also:* **~ off**) interdire l'accès de; (*: divide off*) séparer; **to know the ~s** (*fig*) être au courant, connaître les ficelles

**rose** [rəuz] pt of **rise** ▷ n rose f; (*also:* **~bush**) rosier m

**rosé** ['rəuzeɪ] n rosé m

**rosemary** ['rəuzmərɪ] n romarin m

**rosy** ['rəuzɪ] adj rose; **a ~ future** un bel avenir

**rot** [rɔt] n (*decay*) pourriture f; (*fig: pej: nonsense*) idioties fpl, balivernes fpl ▷ vt, vi pourrir

**rota** ['rəutə] n liste f, tableau m de service

**rotate** [rəu'teɪt] vt (*revolve*) faire tourner; (*change round: crops*) alterner; (*: jobs*) faire à tour de rôle ▷ vi (*revolve*) tourner

**rotten** ['rɔtn] adj (*decayed*) pourri(e); (*dishonest*) corrompu(e); (*inf: bad*) mauvais(e), moche; **to feel ~** (*ill*) être mal fichu(e)

**rough** [rʌf] adj (*cloth, skin*) rêche, rugueux(-euse); (*terrain*) accidenté(e); (*path*) rocailleux(-euse); (*voice*) rauque, rude; (*person, manner: coarse*) rude, fruste; (*: violent*) brutal(e); (*district, weather*) mauvais(e); (*sea*) houleux(-euse); (*plan*) ébauché(e); (*guess*) approximatif(-ive) ▷ n (*Golf*) rough m ▷ vt: **to ~ it** vivre à la dure; **to sleep ~** (*BRIT*) coucher à la dure; **roughly** adv (*handle*) rudement, brutalement; (*speak*) avec brusquerie; (*make*) grossièrement; (*approximately*) à peu près, en gros

**roulette** [ru:'let] n roulette f

**round** [raund] adj rond(e) ▷ n rond m, cercle m; (*BRIT: of toast*) tranche f; (*duty: of policeman, milkman etc*)

tournée f; (*: of doctor*) visites fpl; (*game: of cards, in competition*) partie f; (*Boxing*) round m; (*of talks*) série f ▷ vt (*corner*) tourner ▷ prep autour de ▷ adv: **right ~, all ~** tout autour; **~ of ammunition** cartouche f; **~ of applause** applaudissements mpl; **~ of drinks** tournée f; **~ of sandwiches** (*BRIT*) sandwich m; **the long way ~** (*par*) le chemin le plus long; **all (the) year ~** toute l'année; **it's just ~ the corner** (*fig*) c'est tout près; **to go ~ to sb's (house)** aller chez qn; **go ~ the back** passez par derrière; **enough to go ~** assez pour tout le monde; **she arrived ~ (about) noon** (*BRIT*) elle est arrivée vers midi; **~ the clock** 24 heures sur 24; **round off** vt (*speech etc*) terminer; **round up** vt rassembler; (*criminals*) effectuer une rafle de; (*prices*) arrondir (au chiffre supérieur); **roundabout** n (*BRIT Aut*) rond-point m (à sens giratoire); (*at fair*) manège m (de chevaux de bois) ▷ adj (*route, means*) détourné(e); **round trip** n (*voyage m*) aller et retour m; **roundup** n rassemblement m; (*of criminals*) rafle f

**rouse** [rauz] vt (*wake up*) réveiller; (*stir up*) susciter, provoquer; (*interest*) éveiller; (*suspicions*) susciter, éveiller

**route** [ru:t] n itinéraire m; (*of bus*) parcours m; (*of trade, shipping*) route f

**routine** [ru:'ti:n] adj (*work*) ordinaire, courant(e); (*procedure*) d'usage ▷ n (*habits*) habitudes fpl; (*pej*) train-train m; (*Theat*) numéro m

**row**[1] [rəu] n (*line*) rangée f; (*of people, seats, Knitting*) rang m; (*behind one another: of cars, people*) file f ▷ vi (*in boat*) ramer; (*as sport*) faire de l'aviron ▷ vt (*boat*) faire aller à la rame or à l'aviron; **in a ~** (*fig*) d'affilée

**row**[2] [rau] n (*noise*) vacarme m; (*dispute*) dispute f, querelle f; (*scolding*) réprimande f, savon m ▷ vi (*also:* **to have a ~**) se disputer, se quereller

**rowboat** ['rəubəut] n (*US*) canot m (à rames)

**rowing** ['rəuɪŋ] n canotage m; (as sport)
aviron m; **rowing boat** n (BRIT) canot
m (à rames)

**royal** ['rɔɪəl] adj royal(e); **royalty** n
(royal persons) (membres mpl de la)
famille royale; (payment: to author)
droits mpl d'auteur; (: to inventor)
royalties fpl

**rpm** abbr (= revolutions per minute) t/mn
(= tours/minute)

**R.S.V.P.** abbr (= répondez s'il vous plaît)
RSVP

**Rt. Hon.** abbr (BRIT: = Right Honourable)
titre donné aux députés de la Chambre des
communes

**rub** [rʌb] n: **to give sth a ~** donner un
coup de chiffon or de torchon à qch
▷ vt frotter; (person) frictionner; (hands)
se frotter; **to ~ sb up** (BRIT) or **to ~ sb**
(US) **the wrong way** prendre qn à
rebrousse-poil; **rub in** vt (ointment)
faire pénétrer; **rub off** vi partir; **rub
out** vt effacer

**rubber** ['rʌbər] n caoutchouc m; (BRIT:
eraser) gomme f (à effacer); **rubber
band** n élastique m; **rubber gloves** npl
gants mpl en caoutchouc

**rubbish** ['rʌbɪʃ] n (from household)
ordures fpl; (fig: pej) choses fpl sans
valeur; camelote f; (nonsense) bêtises
fpl, idioties fpl; **rubbish bin** n (BRIT)
boîte f à ordures, poubelle f; **rubbish
dump** n (BRIT: in town) décharge
publique, dépotoir m

**rubble** ['rʌbl] n décombres mpl; (smaller)
gravats mpl; (Constr) blocage m

**ruby** ['ruːbɪ] n rubis m

**rucksack** ['rʌksæk] n sac m à dos

**rudder** ['rʌdər] n gouvernail m

**rude** [ruːd] adj (impolite: person)
impoli(e); (: word, manners)
grossier(-ière); (shocking) indécent(e),
inconvenant(e)

**ruffle** ['rʌfl] vt (hair) ébouriffer; (clothes)
chiffonner; (fig: person): **to get ~d**
s'énerver

**rug** [rʌg] n petit tapis m; (BRIT: blanket)
couverture f

**rugby** ['rʌgbɪ] n (also: ~ **football**)
rugby m

**rugged** ['rʌgɪd] adj (landscape)
accidenté(e); (features, character) rude

**ruin** ['ruːɪn] n ruine f ▷ vt ruiner; (spoil:
clothes) abîmer; (: event) gâcher; **ruins**
npl (of building) ruine(s)

**rule** [ruːl] n règle f; (regulation)
règlement m; (government) autorité
f, gouvernement m ▷ vt (country)
gouverner; (person) dominer; (decide)
décider ▷ vi commander; (Law): **as
a ~** normalement, en règle générale;
**rule out** vt exclure; **ruler** n (sovereign)
souverain(e); (leader) chef m (d'État); (for
measuring) règle f; **ruling** adj (party) au
pouvoir; (class) dirigeant(e) ▷ n (Law)
décision f

**rum** [rʌm] n rhum m

**Rumania** [ruːˈmeɪnɪə] n Roumanie f;
**Rumanian** adj roumain(e) ▷ n
Roumain(e); (Ling) roumain m

**rumble** ['rʌmbl] n grondement m; (of
stomach, pipe) gargouillement m ▷ vi
gronder; (stomach, pipe) gargouiller

**rumour** (US **rumor**) ['ruːmər] n rumeur
f, bruit m (qui court) ▷ vt: **it is ~ed that**
le bruit court que

**rump steak** n romsteck m

**run** [rʌn] n (race) course f; (outing)
tour m or promenade f (en voiture);
(distance travelled) parcours m, trajet m;
(series) suite f, série f; (Theat) série de
représentations; (Ski) piste f; (Cricket,
Baseball) point m; (in tights, stockings)
maille filée, échelle f ▷ vb (pt ran, pp
~) ▷ vt (business) diriger; (competition,
course) organiser; (hotel, house) tenir;
(race) participer à; (Comput: program)
exécuter; (to pass: hand, finger): **to
~ sth over** promener or passer qch
sur; (water, bath) faire couler; (Press:
feature) publier ▷ vi courir; (pass: road
etc) passer; (work: machine, factory)
marcher; (bus, train) circuler; (continue:
play) se jouer, être à l'affiche; (: contract)
être valide or en vigueur; (flow: river,
bath, nose) couler; (colours, washing)

déteindre; (*in election*) être candidat, se présenter; **at a ~** au pas de course; **to go for a ~** aller courir *or* faire un peu de course à pied; (*in car*) faire un tour *or* une promenade (en voiture); **there was a ~ on** (*meat, tickets*) les gens se sont rués sur; **in the long ~** à la longue; **on the ~** en fuite; **I'll ~ you to the station** je vais vous emmener *or* conduire à la gare; **to ~ a risk** courir un risque; **run after** *vt fus* (*to catch up*) courir après; (*chase*) poursuivre; **run away** *vi* s'enfuir; **run down** *vt* (*Aut: knock over*) renverser; (*BRIT: reduce: production*) réduire progressivement; (*: factory/shop*) réduire progressivement la production/l'activité de; (*criticize*) critiquer, dénigrer; **to be ~ down** (*tired*) être fatigué(e) *or* à plat; **run into** *vt fus* (*meet: person*) rencontrer par hasard; (*: trouble*) se heurter à; (*collide with*) heurter; **run off** *vi* s'enfuir ▷ *vt* (*water*) laisser s'écouler; (*copies*) tirer; **run out** *vi* (*person*) sortir en courant; (*liquid*) couler; (*lease*) expirer; (*money*) être épuisé(e); **run out of** *vt fus* se trouver à court de; **run over** *vt* (*Aut*) écraser ▷ *vt fus* (*revise*) revoir, reprendre; **run through** *vt fus* (*recap*) reprendre, revoir; (*play*) répéter; **run up** *vi*: **to ~ up against** (*difficulties*) se heurter à; **runaway** *adj* (*horse*) emballé(e); (*truck*) fou (folle); (*person*) fugitif(-ive); (*child*) fugueur(-euse)

**rung** [rʌŋ] *pp of* **ring** ▷ *n* (*of ladder*) barreau *m*

**runner** ['rʌnəʳ] *n* (*in race: person*) coureur(-euse); (*: horse*) partant *m*; (*on sledge*) patin *m*; (*for drawer etc*) coulisseau *m*; **runner bean** *n* (*BRIT*) haricot *m* (à rames); **runner-up** *n* second(e)

**running** ['rʌnɪŋ] *n* (*in race etc*) course *f*; (*of business, organization*) direction *f*, gestion *f* ▷ *adj* (*water*) courant(e); (*commentary*) suivi(e); **6 days ~** 6 jours de suite; **to be in/out of the ~ for sth** être/ne pas être sur les rangs pour qch

**runny** ['rʌnɪ] *adj* qui coule

**run-up** ['rʌnʌp] *n* (*BRIT*): **~ to sth** période *f* précédant qch

**runway** ['rʌnweɪ] *n* (*Aviat*) piste *f* (d'envol *or* d'atterrissage)

**rupture** ['rʌptʃəʳ] *n* (*Med*) hernie *f*

**rural** ['rʊərl] *adj* rural(e)

**rush** [rʌʃ] *n* (*of crowd, Comm: sudden demand*) ruée *f*; (*hurry*) hâte *f*; (*of anger, joy*) accès *m*; (*current*) flot *m*; (*Bot*) jonc *m* ▷ *vt* (*hurry*) transporter *or* envoyer d'urgence ▷ *vi* se précipiter; **to ~ sth off** (*do quickly*) faire qch à la hâte; **rush hour** *n* heures *fpl* de pointe *or* d'affluence

**Russia** ['rʌʃə] *n* Russie *f*; **Russian** *adj* russe ▷ *n* Russe *m/f*; (*Ling*) russe *m*

**rust** [rʌst] *n* rouille *f* ▷ *vi* rouiller

**rusty** ['rʌstɪ] *adj* rouillé(e)

**ruthless** ['ruːθlɪs] *adj* sans pitié, impitoyable

**RV** *n abbr* (*US*) = **recreational vehicle**

**rye** [raɪ] *n* seigle *m*

**Sabbath** ['sæbəθ] n (Jewish) sabbat m; (Christian) dimanche m

**sabotage** ['sæbətɑːʒ] n sabotage m ▷ vt saboter

**saccharin(e)** ['sækərɪn] n saccharine f

**sachet** ['sæʃeɪ] n sachet m

**sack** [sæk] n (bag) sac m ▷ vt (dismiss) renvoyer, mettre à la porte; (plunder) piller, mettre à sac; **to get the ~** être renvoyé(e) or mis(e) à la porte

**sacred** ['seɪkrɪd] adj sacré(e)

**sacrifice** ['sækrɪfaɪs] n sacrifice m ▷ vt sacrifier

**sad** [sæd] adj (unhappy) triste; (deplorable) triste, fâcheux(-euse); (inf: pathetic: thing) triste, lamentable; (: person) minable

**saddle** ['sædl] n selle f ▷ vt (horse) seller; **to be ~d with sth** (inf) avoir qch sur les bras

**sadistic** [sə'dɪstɪk] adj sadique

**sadly** ['sædlɪ] adv tristement; (unfortunately) malheureusement; (seriously) fort

**sadness** ['sædnɪs] n tristesse f

**s.a.e.** n abbr (BRIT: = stamped addressed envelope) enveloppe affranchie pour la réponse

**safari** [sə'fɑːrɪ] n safari m

**safe** [seɪf] adj (out of danger) hors de danger, en sécurité; (not dangerous) sans danger; (cautious) prudent(e); (sure: bet etc) assuré(e) ▷ n coffre-fort m; **could you put this in the ~, please?** pourriez-vous mettre ceci dans le coffre-fort?; **~ and sound** sain(e) et sauf (sauve); **(just) to be on the ~ side** pour plus de sûreté, par précaution; **safely** adv (assume, say) sans risque d'erreur; (drive, arrive) sans accident; **safe sex** n rapports sexuels protégés

**safety** ['seɪftɪ] n sécurité f; **safety belt** n ceinture f de sécurité; **safety pin** n épingle f de sûreté or de nourrice

**saffron** ['sæfrən] n safran m

**sag** [sæg] vi s'affaisser, fléchir; (hem, breasts) pendre

**sage** [seɪdʒ] n (herb) sauge f; (person) sage m

**Sagittarius** [sædʒɪ'tɛərɪəs] n le Sagittaire

**Sahara** [sə'hɑːrə] n: **the ~ (Desert)** le (désert du) Sahara m

**said** [sɛd] pt, pp of **say**

**sail** [seɪl] n (on boat) voile f; (trip): **to go for a ~** faire un tour en bateau ▷ vt (boat) manœuvrer, piloter ▷ vi (travel: ship) avancer, naviguer; (set off) partir, prendre la mer; (Sport) faire de la voile; **they ~ed into Le Havre** ils sont entrés dans le port du Havre; **sailboat** n (US) bateau m à voiles, voilier m; **sailing** n (Sport) voile f; **to go sailing** faire de la voile; **sailing boat** n bateau m à voiles, voilier m; **sailor** n marin m, matelot m

**saint** [seɪnt] n saint(e)

**sake** [seɪk] n: **for the ~ of** (out of concern for) pour (l'amour de), dans l'intérêt de; (out of consideration for) par égard pour

**salad** ['sæləd] n salade f; **salad cream** n (BRIT) (sorte f de) mayonnaise f; **salad dressing** n vinaigrette f

**salami** [sə'lɑːmɪ] n salami m
**salary** ['sælərɪ] n salaire m, traitement m
**sale** [seɪl] n vente f; (at reduced prices) soldes mpl; **sales** npl (total amount sold) chiffre m de ventes; **"for ~"** "à vendre"; **on ~** en vente; **sales assistant** (US **sales clerk**) n vendeur(-euse); **salesman** (irreg) n (in shop) vendeur m; **salesperson** (irreg) n (in shop) vendeur(-euse); **sales rep** n (Comm) représentant(e) m/f; **saleswoman** (irreg) n (in shop) vendeuse f
**saline** ['seɪlaɪn] adj salin(e)
**saliva** [sə'laɪvə] n salive f
**salmon** ['sæmən] n (pl inv) saumon m
**salon** ['sælɔn] n salon m
**saloon** [sə'luːn] n (US) bar m; (BRIT Aut) berline f; (ship's lounge) salon m
**salt** [sɔːlt] n sel m ▷ vt saler; **saltwater** adj (fish etc) (d'eau) de mer; **salty** adj salé(e)
**salute** [sə'luːt] n salut m; (of guns) salve f ▷ vt saluer
**salvage** ['sælvɪdʒ] n (saving) sauvetage m; (things saved) biens sauvés or récupérés ▷ vt sauver, récupérer
**Salvation Army** [sæl'veɪʃən-] n Armée f du Salut
**same** [seɪm] adj même ▷ pron: **the ~** le (la) même, les mêmes; **the ~ book as** le même livre que; **at the ~ time** en même temps; (yet) néanmoins; **all** or **just the ~** tout de même, quand même; **to do the ~** faire de même, en faire autant; **to do the ~ as sb** faire comme qn; **and the ~ to you!** et à vous de même!; (after insult) toi-même!
**sample** ['sɑːmpl] n échantillon m; (Med) prélèvement m ▷ vt (food, wine) goûter
**sanction** ['sæŋkʃən] n approbation f, sanction f ▷ vt cautionner; **sanctions** npl (Pol) sanctions
**sanctuary** ['sæŋktjuərɪ] n (holy place) sanctuaire m; (refuge) asile m; (for wildlife) réserve f

**sand** [sænd] n sable m ▷ vt (also: ~ **down**: wood etc) poncer
**sandal** ['sændl] n sandale f
**sand**: **sandbox** n (US: for children) tas m de sable; **sandcastle** n château m de sable; **sand dune** n dune f de sable; **sandpaper** n papier m de verre; **sandpit** n (BRIT: for children) tas m de sable; **sands** npl plage f (de sable); **sandstone** ['sændstəun] n grès m
**sandwich** ['sændwɪtʃ] n sandwich m ▷ vt (also: ~ **in**) intercaler; **~ed between** pris en sandwich entre; **cheese/ham ~** sandwich au fromage/jambon
**sandy** ['sændɪ] adj sablonneux(-euse); (colour) sable inv, blond roux inv
**sane** [seɪn] adj (person) sain(e) d'esprit; (outlook) sensé(e), sain(e)
**sang** [sæŋ] pt of **sing**
**sanitary towel** (US **sanitary napkin**) ['sænɪtərɪ-] n serviette f hygiénique
**sanity** ['sænɪtɪ] n santé mentale; (common sense) bon sens
**sank** [sæŋk] pt of **sink**
**Santa Claus** [sæntə'klɔːz] n le Père Noël
**sap** [sæp] n (of plants) sève f ▷ vt (strength) saper, miner
**sapphire** ['sæfaɪə'] n saphir m
**sarcasm** ['sɑːkæzm] n sarcasme m, raillerie f
**sarcastic** [sɑː'kæstɪk] adj sarcastique
**sardine** [sɑː'diːn] n sardine f
**SASE** n abbr (US: = self-addressed stamped envelope) enveloppe affranchie pour la réponse
**sat** [sæt] pt, pp of **sit**
**Sat.** abbr (= Saturday) sa
**satchel** ['sætʃl] n cartable m
**satellite** ['sætəlaɪt] n satellite m; **satellite dish** n antenne f parabolique; **satellite television** n télévision f par satellite
**satin** ['sætɪn] n satin m ▷ adj en or de satin, satiné(e)
**satire** ['sætaɪə'] n satire f
**satisfaction** [sætɪs'fækʃən] n satisfaction f

**satisfactory** [sætɪsˈfæktərɪ] *adj*
satisfaisant(e)

**satisfied** [ˈsætɪsfaɪd] *adj* satisfait(e);
**to be ~ with sth** être satisfait de qch

**satisfy** [ˈsætɪsfaɪ] *vt* satisfaire,
contenter; (*convince*) convaincre,
persuader

**Saturday** [ˈsætədɪ] *n* samedi *m*

**sauce** [sɔːs] *n* sauce *f*; **saucepan** *n*
casserole *f*

**saucer** [ˈsɔːsə<sup>r</sup>] *n* soucoupe *f*

**Saudi Arabia** [ˈsaʊdɪ-] *n* Arabie *f*
Saoudite

**sauna** [ˈsɔːnə] *n* sauna *m*

**sausage** [ˈsɒsɪdʒ] *n* saucisse *f*; (*salami etc*) saucisson *m*; **sausage roll** *n*
friand *m*

**sautéed** [ˈsəʊteɪd] *adj* sauté(e)

**savage** [ˈsævɪdʒ] *adj* (*cruel, fierce*)
brutal(e), féroce; (*primitive*)
primitif(-ive), sauvage ▷ *n* sauvage *m/f*
▷ *vt* attaquer férocement

**save** [seɪv] *vt* (*person, belongings*) sauver;
(*money*) mettre de côté, économiser;
(*time*) (faire) gagner; (*keep*) garder;
(*Comput*) sauvegarder; (*Sport: stop*)
arrêter; (*avoid: trouble*) éviter ▷ *vi* (*also:
~ up*) mettre de l'argent de côté ▷ *n*
(*Sport*) arrêt *m* (du ballon) ▷ *prep* sauf, à
l'exception de

**savings** [ˈseɪvɪŋz] *npl* économies *fpl*;
**savings account** *n* compte *m*
d'épargne; **savings and loan
association** (*us*) *n* ≈ société *f* de crédit
immobilier

**savoury** (*us* **savory**) [ˈseɪvərɪ] *adj*
savoureux(-euse); (*dish: not sweet*)
salé(e)

**saw** [sɔː] *pt of* **see** ▷ *n* (*tool*) scie *f* ▷ *vt*
(*pt* **~ed**, *pp* **~ed** *or* **~n**) scier; **sawdust**
*n* sciure *f*

**sawn** [sɔːn] *pp of* **saw**

**saxophone** [ˈsæksəfəʊn] *n*
saxophone *m*

**say** [seɪ] *n*: **to have one's ~** dire ce qu'on
a à dire ▷ *vt* (*pt, pp* **said**) dire; **to have
a ~** avoir voix au chapitre; **could you ~
that again?** pourriez-vous répéter ce

que vous venez de dire?; **to ~ yes/no**
dire oui/non; **my watch ~s 3 o'clock**
ma montre indique 3 heures, il est 3
heures à ma montre; **that is to ~** c'est-
à-dire, cela va sans dire, cela va de soi;
**saying** *n* dicton *m*, proverbe *m*

**scab** [skæb] *n* croûte *f*; (*pej*) jaune *m/f*

**scaffolding** [ˈskæfəldɪŋ] *n*
échafaudage *m*

**scald** [skɔːld] *n* brûlure *f* ▷ *vt*
ébouillanter

**scale** [skeɪl] *n* (*of fish*) écaille *f*; (*Mus*)
gamme *f*; (*of ruler, thermometer etc*)
graduation *f*, échelle (graduée); (*of
salaries, fees etc*) barème *m*; (*of map,
also size, extent*) échelle ▷ *vt* (*mountain*)
escalader; **scales** *npl* balance *f*; (*larger*)
bascule *f*; (*also:* **bathroom ~s**) pèse-
personne *m inv*; **~ of charges** tableau *m*
des tarifs; **on a large ~** sur une grande
échelle, en grand

**scallion** [ˈskæljən] *n* (*us: salad onion*)
ciboule *f*

**scallop** [ˈskɒləp] *n* coquille *f* Saint-
Jacques; (*Sewing*) feston *m*

**scalp** [skælp] *n* cuir chevelu ▷ *vt*
scalper

**scalpel** [ˈskælpl] *n* scalpel *m*

**scam** [skæm] *n* (*inf*) arnaque *f*

**scampi** [ˈskæmpɪ] *npl* langoustines
(frites), scampi *mpl*

**scan** [skæn] *vt* (*examine*) scruter,
examiner; (*glance at quickly*) parcourir;
(*TV, Radar*) balayer ▷ *n* (*Med*)
scanographie *f*

**scandal** [ˈskændl] *n* scandale *m*;
(*gossip*) ragots *mpl*

**Scandinavia** [skændɪˈneɪvɪə] *n*
Scandinavie *f*; **Scandinavian** *adj*
scandinave ▷ *n* Scandinave *m/f*

**scanner** [ˈskænə<sup>r</sup>] *n* (*Radar, Med*)
scanner *m*, scanographe *m*; (*Comput*)
scanner, numériseur *m*

**scapegoat** [ˈskeɪpgəʊt] *n* bouc *m*
émissaire

**scar** [skɑː<sup>r</sup>] *n* cicatrice *f* ▷ *vt* laisser une
cicatrice *or* une marque à

**scarce** [skɛəs] *adj* rare, peu

abondant(e); **to make o.s. ~** (*inf*) se sauver; **scarcely** *adv* à peine, presque pas

**scare** [skɛəʳ] *n* peur *f*, panique *f* ▷ *vt* effrayer, faire peur à; **to ~ sb stiff** faire une peur bleue à qn; **bomb ~** alerte *f* à la bombe; **scarecrow** *n* épouvantail *m*; **scared** *adj*: **to be scared** avoir peur

**scarf** (*pl* **scarves**) [skɑːf, skɑːvz] *n* (*long*) écharpe *f*; (*square*) foulard *m*

**scarlet** ['skɑːlɪt] *adj* écarlate

**scarves** [skɑːvz] *npl of* **scarf**

**scary** ['skɛərɪ] *adj* (*inf*) effrayant(e); (*film*) qui fait peur

**scatter** ['skætəʳ] *vt* éparpiller, répandre; (*crowd*) disperser ▷ *vi* se disperser

**scenario** [sɪ'nɑːrɪəu] *n* scénario *m*

**scene** [siːn] *n* (*Theat, fig etc*) scène *f*; (*of crime, accident*) lieu(x) *m(pl)*, endroit *m*; (*sight, view*) spectacle *m*, vue *f*; **scenery** *n* (*Theat*) décor(s) *m(pl)*; (*landscape*) paysage *m*; **scenic** *adj* offrant de beaux paysages or panoramas

**scent** [sɛnt] *n* parfum *m*, odeur *f*; (*fig: track*) piste *f*

**sceptical** (*us* **skeptical**) ['skɛptɪkl] *adj* sceptique

**schedule** ['ʃɛdjuːl, *us* 'skɛdjuːl] *n* programme *m*, plan *m*; (*of trains*) horaire *m*; (*of prices etc*) barème *m*, tarif *m* ▷ *vt* prévoir; **on ~** à l'heure (prévue); à la date prévue; **to be ahead of/behind ~** avoir de l'avance/du retard; **scheduled flight** *n* vol régulier

**scheme** [skiːm] *n* plan *m*, projet *m*; (*plot*) complot *m*, combine *f*; (*arrangement*) arrangement *m*, classification *f*; (*pension scheme etc*) régime *m* ▷ *vt*, *vi* comploter, manigancer

**schizophrenic** [skɪtsə'frɛnɪk] *adj* schizophrène

**scholar** ['skɔləʳ] *n* érudit(e); (*pupil*) boursier(-ère); **scholarship** *n* érudition *f*; (*grant*) bourse *f* (d'études)

**school** [skuːl] *n* (*gen*) école *f*; (*secondary school*) collège *m*, lycée *m*; (*in university*)

faculté *f*; (*us: university*) université *f* ▷ *cpd* scolaire; **schoolbook** *n* livre *m* scolaire or de classe; **schoolboy** *n* écolier *m*; (*at secondary school*) collégien *m*, lycéen *m*; **schoolchildren** *npl* écoliers *mpl*; (*at secondary school*) collégiens *mpl*, lycéens *mpl*; **schoolgirl** *n* écolière *f*; (*at secondary school*) collégienne *f*, lycéenne *f*; **schooling** *n* instruction *f*, études *fpl*; **schoolteacher** *n* (*primary*) instituteur(-trice); (*secondary*) professeur *m*

**science** ['saɪəns] *n* science *f*; **science fiction** *n* science-fiction *f*; **scientific** [saɪən'tɪfɪk] *adj* scientifique; **scientist** *n* scientifique *m/f*; (*eminent*) savant *m*

**sci-fi** ['saɪfaɪ] *n abbr* (*inf*: = *science fiction*) SF *f*

**scissors** ['sɪzəz] *npl* ciseaux *mpl*; **a pair of ~** une paire de ciseaux

**scold** [skəuld] *vt* gronder

**scone** [skɔn] *n* sorte de petit pain rond au lait

**scoop** [skuːp] *n* pelle *f* (à main); (*for ice cream*) boule *f* à glace; (*Press*) reportage exclusif or à sensation

**scooter** ['skuːtəʳ] *n* (*motor cycle*) scooter *m*; (*toy*) trottinette *f*

**scope** [skəup] *n* (*capacity: of plan, undertaking*) portée *f*, envergure *f*; (: *of person*) compétence *f*, capacités *fpl*; (*opportunity*) possibilités *fpl*

**scorching** ['skɔːtʃɪŋ] *adj* torride, brûlant(e)

**score** [skɔːʳ] *n* score *m*, décompte *m* des points; (*Mus*) partition *f* ▷ *vt* (*goal, point*) marquer; (*success*) remporter; (*cut: leather, wood, card*) entailler, inciser ▷ *vi* marquer des points; (*Football*) marquer un but; (*keep score*) compter les points; **on that ~** sur ce chapitre, à cet égard; **a ~ of** (*twenty*) vingt; **~s of** (*fig*) des tas de; **to ~ 6 out of 10** obtenir 6 sur 10; **score out** *vt* rayer, barrer, biffer; **scoreboard** *n* tableau *m*; **scorer** *n* (*Football*) auteur *m* du but; buteur *m*; (*keeping score*) marqueur *m*

**scorn** [skɔːn] *n* mépris *m*, dédain *m*

**Scorpio** [ˈskɔːpɪəʊ] n le Scorpion
**scorpion** [ˈskɔːpɪən] n scorpion m
**Scot** [skɒt] n Écossais(e)
**Scotch** [skɒtʃ] n whisky m, scotch m
**Scotch tape®** (us) n scotch® m, ruban adhésif
**Scotland** [ˈskɒtlənd] n Écosse f
**Scots** [skɒts] adj écossais(e); **Scotsman** (irreg) n Écossais m; **Scotswoman** (irreg) n Écossaise f; **Scottish** [ˈskɒtɪʃ] adj écossais(e); **Scottish Parliament** n Parlement écossais
**scout** [skaʊt] n (Mil) éclaireur m; (also: **boy ~**) scout m; **girl ~** (us) guide f
**scowl** [skaʊl] vi se renfrogner, avoir l'air maussade; **to ~ at** regarder de travers
**scramble** [ˈskræmbl] n (rush) bousculade f, ruée f ▷ vi grimper/descendre tant bien que mal; **to ~ for** se bousculer or se disputer pour (avoir); **to go scrambling** (Sport) faire du trial; **scrambled eggs** npl œufs brouillés
**scrap** [skræp] n bout m, morceau m; (fight) bagarre f; (also: **~ iron**) ferraille f ▷ vt jeter, mettre au rebut; (fig) abandonner, laisser tomber ▷ vi se bagarrer; **scraps** npl (waste) déchets mpl; **scrapbook** n album m
**scrape** [skreɪp] vt, vi gratter, racler ▷ n: **to get into a ~** s'attirer des ennuis; **scrape through** vi (exam etc) réussir de justesse
**scrap paper** n papier m brouillon
**scratch** [skrætʃ] n égratignure f, rayure f; (on paint) éraflure f; (from claw) coup m de griffe ▷ vt (rub) (se) gratter; (paint etc) érafler; (with claw, nail) griffer ▷ vi (se) gratter; **to start from ~** partir de zéro; **to be up to ~** être à la hauteur; **scratch card** n carte f à gratter
**scream** [skriːm] n cri perçant, hurlement m ▷ vi crier, hurler
**screen** [skriːn] n écran m; (in room) paravent m; (fig) écran, rideau m ▷ vt masquer, cacher; (from the wind etc) abriter, protéger; (film) projeter; (candidates etc) filtrer; **screening** n (of film) projection f; (Med) test m (or

tests) de dépistage; **screenplay** n scénario m; **screen saver** n (Comput) économiseur m d'écran
**screw** [skruː] n vis f ▷ vt (also: **~ in**) visser; **screw up** vt (paper etc) froisser; **to ~ up one's eyes** se plisser les yeux; **screwdriver** n tournevis m
**scribble** [ˈskrɪbl] n gribouillage m ▷ vt gribouiller, griffonner
**script** [skrɪpt] n (Cine etc) scénario m, texte m; (writing) (écriture f) script m
**scroll** [skrəʊl] n rouleau m ▷ vt (Comput) faire défiler (sur l'écran)
**scrub** [skrʌb] n (land) broussailles fpl ▷ vt (floor) nettoyer à la brosse; (pan) récurer; (washing) frotter
**scruffy** [ˈskrʌfɪ] adj débraillé(e)
**scrum(mage)** [ˈskrʌm(ɪdʒ)] n mêlée f
**scrutiny** [ˈskruːtɪnɪ] n examen minutieux
**scuba diving** [ˈskuːbə-] n plongée sous-marine (autonome)
**sculptor** [ˈskʌlptəˈ] n sculpteur m
**sculpture** [ˈskʌlptʃəˈ] n sculpture f
**scum** [skʌm] n écume f, mousse f; (pej: people) rebut m, lie f
**scurry** [ˈskʌrɪ] vi filer à toute allure; **to ~ off** détaler, se sauver
**sea** [siː] n mer f ▷ cpd marin(e), de (la) mer, maritime; **by** or **beside the ~** (holiday, town) au bord de la mer; **by ~** par mer, en bateau; **out to ~** au large; **(out) at ~** en mer; **to be all at ~** (fig) nager complètement; **seafood** n fruits mpl de mer; **sea front** n bord m de mer; **seagull** n mouette f
**seal** [siːl] n (animal) phoque m; (stamp) sceau m, cachet m ▷ vt sceller; (envelope) coller; (: with seal) cacheter; **seal off** vt (forbid entry to) interdire l'accès de
**sea level** n niveau m de la mer
**seam** [siːm] n couture f; (of coal) veine f, filon m
**search** [səːtʃ] n (for person, thing, Comput) recherche(s) f(pl); (of drawer, pockets) fouille f; (Law: at sb's home) perquisition f ▷ vt fouiller; (examine)

examiner minutieusement; scruter
▷ *vi*: **to ~ for** chercher; **in ~ of** à la
recherche de; **search engine** *n*
(Comput) moteur *m* de recherche;
**search party** *n* expédition *f* de secours
**sea**: **seashore** *n* rivage *m*, plage *f*,
bord *m* de (la) mer; **seasick** *adj*: **to be
seasick** avoir le mal de mer; **seaside**
*n* bord *m* de mer; **seaside resort** *n*
station *f* balnéaire
**season** ['siːzn] *n* saison *f* ▷ *vt*
assaisonner, relever; **to be in/out of ~**
être/ne pas être de saison; **seasonal**
*adj* saisonnier(-ière); **seasoning** *n*
assaisonnement *m*; **season ticket** *n*
carte *f* d'abonnement
**seat** [siːt] *n* siège *m*; (in bus, train:
place) place *f*; (buttocks) postérieur *m*;
(of trousers) fond *m* ▷ *vt* faire asseoir,
placer; (have room for) avoir des places
assises pour, pouvoir accueillir; **I'd like
to book two ~s** je voudrais réserver
deux places; **to be ~ed** être assis; **seat
belt** *n* ceinture *f* de sécurité; **seating** *n*
sièges *fpl*, places assises
**sea**: **sea water** *n* eau *f* de mer; **seaweed**
*n* algues *fpl*
**sec.** *abbr* (= second) sec
**secluded** [sɪ'kluːdɪd] *adj* retiré(e),
à l'écart
**second** ['sɛkənd] *num* deuxième,
second(e) ▷ *adv* (in race etc) en seconde
position ▷ *n* (unit of time) seconde *f*;
(Aut: also: **~ gear**) seconde; (Comm:
imperfect) article *m* de second choix;
(BRIT Scol) ≈ licence *f* avec mention ▷ *vt*
(motion) appuyer; **seconds** *npl* (inf: food)
rab *m* (inf); **secondary** *adj* secondaire;
**secondary school** *n* collège *m*; lycée *m*;
**second-class** *adj* de deuxième classe;
(Rail) de seconde (classe); (Post) au
tarif réduit; (pej) de qualité inférieure
▷ *adv* (Rail) en seconde; (Post) au tarif
réduit; **secondhand** *adj* d'occasion;
(information) de seconde main;
**secondly** *adv* deuxièmement; **second-
rate** *adj* de deuxième ordre, de qualité
inférieure; **second thoughts** *npl*: **to**

**have second thoughts** changer d'avis;
**on second thoughts** *or* **thought** (us)
à la réflexion
**secrecy** ['siːkrəsɪ] *n* secret *m*
**secret** ['siːkrɪt] *adj* secret(-ète)
▷ *n* secret *m*; **in ~** *adv* en secret,
secrètement, en cachette
**secretary** ['sɛkrətrɪ] *n* secrétaire *m/f*;
**S~ of State (for)** (Brit Pol) ministre
*m* (de)
**secretive** ['siːkrətɪv] *adj* réservé(e);
(pej) cachottier(-ière), dissimulé(e)
**secret service** *n* services secrets
**sect** [sɛkt] *n* secte *f*
**section** ['sɛkʃən] *n* section *f*; (Comm)
rayon *m*; (of document) section, article
*m*, paragraphe *m*; (cut) coupe *f*
**sector** ['sɛktər] *n* secteur *m*
**secular** ['sɛkjulər] *adj* laïque
**secure** [sɪ'kjuər] *adj* (free from anxiety)
sans inquiétude, sécurisé(e); (firmly
fixed) solide, bien attaché(e) (or
fermé(e) etc); (in safe place) en lieu sûr,
en sûreté ▷ *vt* (fix) fixer, attacher; (get)
obtenir, se procurer
**security** [sɪ'kjuərɪtɪ] *n* sécurité *f*,
mesures *fpl* de sécurité; (for loan)
caution *f*, garantie *f*; **securities** *npl*
(Stock Exchange) valeurs *fpl*, titres *mpl*;
**security guard** *n* garde chargé
de la sécurité; (transporting money)
convoyeur *m* de fonds
**sedan** [sə'dæn] *n* (us Aut) berline *f*
**sedate** [sɪ'deɪt] *adj* calme; posé(e) ▷ *vt*
donner des sédatifs à
**sedative** ['sɛdɪtɪv] *n* calmant *m*,
sédatif *m*
**seduce** [sɪ'djuːs] *vt* séduire; **seductive**
[sɪ'dʌktɪv] *adj* séduisant(e);
(smile) séducteur(-trice); (fig: offer)
alléchant(e)
**see** [siː] *vb* (*pt* **saw**, *pp* **~n**) ▷ *vt* (gen)
voir; (accompany): **to ~ sb to the
door** reconduire *or* raccompagner qn
jusqu'à la porte ▷ *vi* voir; **to ~ that**
(ensure) veiller à ce que + *sub*, faire en
sorte que + *sub*, s'assurer que; **~ you
soon/later/tomorrow!** à bientôt/plus

tard/demain!; **see off** vt accompagner (à la gare or à l'aéroport etc); **see out** vt (take to door) raccompagner à la porte; **see through** vt mener à bonne fin ▷ vt fus voir clair dans; **see to** vt fus s'occuper de, se charger de

**seed** [siːd] n graine f; (fig) germe m; (Tennis etc) tête f de série; **to go to ~** (plant) monter en graine; (fig) se laisser aller

**seeing** ['siːɪŋ] conj: **~ (that)** vu que, étant donné que

**seek** (pt, pp **sought**) [siːk, sɔːt] vt chercher, rechercher

**seem** [siːm] vi sembler, paraître; **there ~s to be …** il semble qu'il y a …, on dirait qu'il y a …; **seemingly** adv apparemment

**seen** [siːn] pp of **see**

**seesaw** ['siːsɔː] n (jeu m de) bascule f

**segment** ['sɛgmənt] n segment m; (of orange) quartier m

**segregate** ['sɛgrɪgeɪt] vt séparer, isoler

**Seine** [seɪn] n: **the (River) ~** la Seine

**seize** [siːz] vt (grasp) saisir, attraper; (take possession of) s'emparer de; (opportunity) saisir

**seizure** ['siːʒər] n (Med) crise f, attaque f; (of power) prise f

**seldom** ['sɛldəm] adv rarement

**select** [sɪ'lɛkt] adj choisi(e), d'élite; (hotel, restaurant, club) chic inv, sélect inv ▷ vt sélectionner, choisir; **selection** n sélection f, choix m; **selective** adj sélectif(-ive); (school) à recrutement sélectif

**self** [sɛlf] n (pl **selves**): **the ~** le moi inv ▷ prefix auto-; **self-assured** adj sûr(e) de soi, plein(e) d'assurance; **self-catering** adj (BRIT: flat) avec cuisine, où l'on peut faire sa cuisine; (: holiday) en appartement (or chalet etc) loué; **self-centred** (US **self-centered**) adj égocentrique; **self-confidence** n confiance f en soi; **self-confident** adj sûr(e) de soi, plein(e) d'assurance; **self-conscious** adj timide, qui manque d'assurance; **self-contained**

adj (BRIT: flat) avec entrée particulière, indépendant(e); **self-control** n maîtrise f de soi; **self-defence** (US **self-defense**) n autodéfense f; (Law) légitime défense f; **self-drive** adj (BRIT): **self-drive car** voiture f de location; **self-employed** adj qui travaille à son compte; **self-esteem** n amour-propre m; **self-indulgent** adj qui ne se refuse rien; **self-interest** n intérêt personnel; **selfish** adj égoïste; **self-pity** n apitoiement m sur soi-même; **self-raising** [sɛlf'reɪzɪŋ] (US **self-rising** [sɛlf'raɪzɪŋ]); **self-raising flour** farine f pour gâteaux (avec levure incorporée); **self-respect** n respect m de soi, amour-propre m; **self-service** adj, n libre-service (m), self-service (m)

**sell** (pt, pp **sold**) [sɛl, səʊld] vt vendre ▷ vi se vendre; **to ~ at or for 10 euros** se vendre 10 euros; **sell off** vt liquider; **sell out** vi: **to ~ out (of sth)** (use up stock) vendre tout son stock (de qch); **sell-by date** n date f limite de vente; **seller** n vendeur(-euse), marchand(e)

**Sellotape®** ['sɛləʊteɪp] n (BRIT) scotch® m

**selves** [sɛlvz] npl of **self**

**semester** [sɪ'mɛstər] n (esp US) semestre m

**semi…** ['sɛmɪ] prefix semi-, demi-; à demi, à moitié; **semicircle** n demi-cercle m; **semidetached (house)** n (BRIT) maison jumelée or jumelle; **semi-final** n demi-finale f

**seminar** ['sɛmɪnɑːr] n séminaire m

**semi-skimmed** ['sɛmɪ'skɪmd] adj demi-écrémé(e)

**senate** ['sɛnɪt] n sénat m; (US): **the S~** le Sénat; **senator** n sénateur m

**send** (pt, pp **sent**) [sɛnd, sɛnt] vt envoyer; **send back** vt renvoyer; **send for** vt fus (by post) se faire envoyer, commander par correspondance; **send in** vt (report, application, resignation) remettre; **send off** vt (goods) envoyer, expédier; (BRIT Sport: player) expulser or renvoyer du terrain; **send on** vt

(BRIT: letter) faire suivre; (luggage etc: in advance) (faire) expédier à l'avance; **send out** vt (invitation) envoyer (par la poste); (emit: light, heat, signal) émettre; **send up** vt (person, price) faire monter; (BRIT: parody) mettre en boîte, parodier; **sender** n expéditeur(-trice); **send-off** n: **a good send-off** des adieux chaleureux

**senile** ['si:naɪl] adj sénile

**senior** ['si:nɪər] adj (high-ranking) de haut niveau; (of higher rank): **to be ~ to sb** être le supérieur de qn; **senior citizen** n personne f du troisième âge; **senior high school** n (US) ≈ lycée m

**sensation** [sɛn'seɪʃən] n sensation f; **sensational** adj qui fait sensation; (marvellous) sensationnel(le)

**sense** [sɛns] n sens m; (feeling) sentiment m; (meaning) sens, signification f; (wisdom) bon sens ▷ vt sentir, pressentir; **it makes ~** c'est logique; **senseless** adj insensé(e), stupide; (unconscious) sans connaissance; **sense of humour** (US **sense of humor**) n sens m de l'humour

**sensible** ['sɛnsɪbl] adj sensé(e), raisonnable; (shoes etc) pratique

⬛ Be careful not to translate **sensible** by the French word **sensible**.

**sensitive** ['sɛnsɪtɪv] adj: **~ (to)** sensible (à)

**sensual** ['sɛnsjuəl] adj sensuel(le)

**sensuous** ['sɛnsjuəs] adj voluptueux(-euse), sensuel(le)

**sent** [sɛnt] pt, pp of **send**

**sentence** ['sɛntns] n (Ling) phrase f; (Law: judgment) condamnation f, sentence f; (: punishment) peine f ▷ vt: **to ~ sb to death/to 5 years** condamner qn à mort/à 5 ans

**sentiment** ['sɛntɪmənt] n sentiment m; (opinion) opinion f, avis m; **sentimental** [sɛntɪ'mɛntl] adj sentimental(e)

**Sep.** abbr (= September) septembre

**separate** adj ['sɛprɪt] séparé(e); (organization) indépendant(e); (day,

occasion, issue) différent(e) ▷ vb ['sɛpəreɪt] ▷ vt séparer; (distinguish) distinguer ▷ vi se séparer; **separately** adv séparément; **separates** npl (clothes) coordonnés mpl; **separation** [sɛpə'reɪʃən] n séparation f

**September** [sɛp'tɛmbər] n septembre m

**septic** ['sɛptɪk] adj (wound) infecté(e); **septic tank** n fosse f septique

**sequel** ['si:kwl] n conséquence f; séquelles fpl; (of story) suite f

**sequence** ['si:kwəns] n ordre m, suite f; (in film) séquence f; (dance) numéro m

**sequin** ['si:kwɪn] n paillette f

**Serb** [sə:b] adj, n = **Serbian**

**Serbia** ['sə:bɪə] n Serbie f

**Serbian** ['sə:bɪən] adj serbe ▷ n Serbe m/f; (Ling) serbe m

**sergeant** ['sɑ:dʒənt] n sergent m; (Police) brigadier m

**serial** ['sɪərɪəl] n feuilleton m; **serial killer** n meurtrier m tuant en série; **serial number** n numéro m de série

**series** ['sɪəriz] n série f; (Publishing) collection f

**serious** ['sɪəriəs] adj sérieux(-euse); (accident etc) grave; **seriously** adv sérieusement; (hurt) gravement

**sermon** ['sə:mən] n sermon m

**servant** ['sə:vənt] n domestique m/f; (fig) serviteur (servante)

**serve** [sə:v] vt (employer etc) servir, être au service de; (purpose) servir à; (customer, food, meal) servir; (subj: train) desservir; (apprenticeship) faire, accomplir; (prison term) faire; purger ▷ vi (Tennis) servir; (be useful): **to ~ as/for/to do** servir de/à/à faire ▷ n (Tennis) service m; **it ~s him right** c'est bien fait pour lui; **server** n (Comput) serveur m

**service** ['sə:vɪs] n (gen) service m; (Aut) révision f; (Rel) office m ▷ vt (car etc) réviser; **services** npl (Econ: tertiary sector) (secteur m) tertiaire m, secteur des services; (BRIT: on motorway) station-service f; (Mil): **the**

**S~s** npl les forces armées; **to be of ~ to sb**, **to do sb a ~** rendre service à qn; **~ included/not included** service compris/non compris; **service area** n (on motorway) aire f de services; **service charge** n (BRIT) service m; **serviceman** (irreg) n militaire m; **service station** n station-service f

**serviette** [sə:vi'ɛt] n (BRIT) serviette f (de table)

**session** ['sɛʃən] n (sitting) séance f; **to be in ~** siéger, être en session or en séance

**set** [sɛt] n série f, assortiment m; (of tools etc) jeu m; (Radio, TV) poste m; (Tennis) set m; (group of people) cercle m, milieu m; (Cine) plateau m; (Theat: stage) scène f, (: scenery) décor m; (Math) ensemble m; (Hairdressing) mise f en plis ▷ adj (fixed) fixe, déterminé(e); (ready) prêt(e) ▷ vb (pt, pp ~) ▷ vt (place) mettre, poser, placer; (fix, establish) fixer; (: record) établir; (assign: task, homework) donner; (exam) composer; (adjust) régler; (decide: rules etc) fixer, choisir ▷ vi (sun) se coucher; (jam, jelly, concrete) prendre; (bone) se ressouder; **to be ~ on doing** être résolu(e) à faire; **to ~ to music** mettre en musique; **to ~ on fire** mettre le feu à; **to ~ free** libérer; **to ~ sth going** déclencher qch; **to ~ sail** partir, prendre la mer; **set aside** vt mettre de côté; (time) garder; **set down** vt (subj: bus, train) déposer; **set in** vi (infection, bad weather) s'installer; (complications) survenir, surgir; **set off** vi se mettre en route, partir ▷ vt (bomb) faire exploser; (cause to start) déclencher; (show up well) mettre en valeur, faire valoir; **set out** vi: **to ~ out (from)** partir (de) ▷ vt (arrange) disposer; (state) présenter, exposer; **to ~ out to do** entreprendre de faire; avoir pour but or intention de faire; **set up** vt (organization) fonder, créer; **setback** n (hitch) revers m, contretemps m; **set menu** n menu m

**settee** [sɛ'ti:] n canapé m

**setting** ['sɛtɪŋ] n cadre m; (of jewel)

monture f; (position: of controls) réglage m

**settle** ['sɛtl] vt (argument, matter, account) régler; (problem) résoudre; (Med: calm) calmer ▷ vi (bird, dust etc) se poser; **to ~ for sth** accepter qch, se contenter de qch; **to ~ on sth** opter or se décider pour qch; **settle down** vi (get comfortable) s'installer; (become calmer) se calmer; se ranger; (live quietly) se fixer; **settle in** vi s'installer; **settle up** vi: **to ~ up with sb** régler (ce que l'on doit à) qn; **settlement** n (payment) règlement m; (agreement) accord m; (village etc) village m, hameau m

**setup** ['sɛtʌp] n (arrangement) manière f dont les choses sont organisées; (situation) situation f, allure f des choses

**seven** ['sɛvn] num sept; **seventeen** num dix-sept; **seventeenth** [sɛvn'ti:nθ] num dix-septième; **seventh** num septième; **seventieth** ['sɛvntɪɪθ] num soixante-dixième; **seventy** num soixante-dix

**sever** ['sɛvə'] vt couper, trancher; (relations) rompre

**several** ['sɛvrl] adj, pron plusieurs pl; **~ of us** plusieurs d'entre nous

**severe** [sɪ'vɪə'] adj (stern) sévère, strict(e); (serious) grave, sérieux(-euse); (plain) sévère, austère

**sew** (pt **~ed**, pp **~n**) [səu, səud, səun] vt, vi coudre

**sewage** ['su:ɪdʒ] n vidange(s) f(pl)

**sewer** ['su:ə'] n égout m

**sewing** ['səuɪŋ] n couture f; (item(s)) ouvrage m; **sewing machine** n machine f à coudre

**sewn** [səun] pp of **sew**

**sex** [sɛks] n sexe m; **to have ~ with** avoir des rapports (sexuels) avec; **sexism** ['sɛksɪzəm] n sexisme m; **sexist** adj sexiste; **sexual** ['sɛksjuəl] adj sexuel(le); **sexual intercourse** n rapports sexuels; **sexuality** [sɛksju'ælɪtɪ] n sexualité f; **sexy** adj sexy inv

**shabby** ['ʃæbɪ] adj miteux(-euse);

(behaviour) mesquin(e), méprisable
**shack** [ʃæk] n cabane f, hutte f
**shade** [ʃeɪd] n ombre f; (for lamp)
abat-jour m inv; (of colour) nuance f, ton
m; (us: window shade) store m; (small
quantity): **a ~ of** un soupçon de ▷ vt
abriter du soleil, ombrager; **shades** npl
(us: sunglasses) lunettes fpl de soleil;
**in the ~** à l'ombre; **a ~ smaller** un tout
petit peu plus petit
**shadow** [ˈʃædəu] n ombre f ▷ vt (follow)
filer; **shadow cabinet** n (BRIT Pol)
cabinet parallèle formé par le parti qui n'est
pas au pouvoir
**shady** [ˈʃeɪdɪ] adj ombragé(e); (fig:
dishonest) louche, véreux(-euse)
**shaft** [ʃɑːft] n (of arrow, spear) hampe f;
(Aut, Tech) arbre m; (of mine) puits m; (of
lift) cage f; (of light) rayon m, trait m
**shake** [ʃeɪk] vb (pt **shook**, pp **~n**) ▷ vt
secouer; (bottle, cocktail) agiter; (house,
confidence) ébranler ▷ vi trembler; **to ~
one's head** (in refusal etc) dire or faire
non de la tête; (in dismay) secouer la
tête; **to ~ hands with sb** serrer la main
à qn; **shake off** vt secouer; (pursuer) se
débarrasser de; **shake up** vt secouer;
**shaky** adj (hand, voice) tremblant(e);
(building) branlant(e), peu solide
**shall** [ʃæl] aux vb: **I ~ go** j'irai; **~ I open
the door?** j'ouvre la porte?; **I'll get the
coffee, ~ I?** je vais chercher le café,
d'accord?
**shallow** [ˈʃæləu] adj peu profond(e);
(fig) superficiel(le), qui manque de
profondeur
**sham** [ʃæm] n frime f
**shambles** [ˈʃæmblz] n confusion f,
pagaïe f, fouillis m
**shame** [ʃeɪm] n honte f ▷ vt faire
honte à; **it is a ~ (that/to do)** c'est
dommage (que + sub/de faire); **what
a ~!** quel dommage!; **shameful** adj
honteux(-euse), scandaleux(-euse);
**shameless** adj éhonté(e), effronté(e)
**shampoo** [ʃæmˈpuː] n shampooing m
▷ vt faire un shampooing à
**shandy** [ˈʃændɪ] n bière panachée

**shan't** [ʃɑːnt] = **shall not**
**shape** [ʃeɪp] n forme f ▷ vt façonner,
modeler; (sb's ideas, character) former;
(sb's life) déterminer ▷ vi (also: ~ **up**:
events) prendre tournure; (: person)
faire des progrès, s'en sortir; **to take ~**
prendre forme or tournure
**share** [ʃɛəʳ] n part f; (Comm) action
f ▷ vt partager; (have in common)
avoir en commun; **to ~ out (among
or between)** partager (entre);
**shareholder** n (BRIT) actionnaire m/f
**shark** [ʃɑːk] n requin m
**sharp** [ʃɑːp] adj (razor, knife)
tranchant(e), bien aiguisé(e); (point,
voice) aigu(ë); (nose, chin) pointu(e);
(outline, increase) net(te); (cold, pain) vif
(vive); (taste) piquant(e), âcre; (Mus)
dièse; (person: quick-witted) vif (vive),
éveillé(e); (: unscrupulous) malhonnête
▷ n (Mus) dièse m ▷ adv: **at 2 o'clock
~** à 2 heures pile or tapantes; **sharpen**
vt aiguiser; (pencil) tailler; (fig) aviver;
**sharpener** n (also: **pencil sharpener**)
taille-crayon(s) m inv; **sharply** adv
(turn, stop) brusquement; (stand out)
nettement; (criticize, retort) sèchement,
vertement
**shatter** [ˈʃætəʳ] vt briser; (fig: upset)
bouleverser; (: ruin) briser, ruiner ▷ vi
voler en éclats, se briser; **shattered**
adj (overwhelmed, grief-stricken)
bouleversé(e); (inf: exhausted) éreinté(e)
**shave** [ʃeɪv] vt raser ▷ vi se raser ▷ n:
**to have a ~** se raser; **shaver** n (also:
**electric shaver**) rasoir m électrique
**shaving cream** n crème f à raser
**shaving foam** n mousse f à raser
**shavings** [ˈʃeɪvɪŋz] npl (of wood etc)
copeaux mpl
**shawl** [ʃɔːl] n châle m
**she** [ʃiː] pron elle
**sheath** [ʃiːθ] n gaine f, fourreau m, étui
m; (contraceptive) préservatif m
**shed** [ʃed] n remise f, resserre f ▷ vt
(pt, pp **~**) (leaves, fur etc) perdre; (tears)
verser, répandre; (workers) congédier
**she'd** [ʃiːd] = **she had**; **she would**

**sheep** [ʃiːp] n (pl inv) mouton m; **sheepdog** n chien m de berger; **sheepskin** n peau f de mouton

**sheer** [ʃɪəʳ] adj (utter) pur(e), pur et simple; (steep) à pic, abrupt(e); (almost transparent) extrêmement fin(e) ▷ adv à pic, abruptement

**sheet** [ʃiːt] n (on bed) drap m; (of paper) feuille f; (of glass, metal etc) feuille, plaque f

**sheik(h)** [ʃeɪk] n cheik m

**shelf** (pl **shelves**) [ʃɛlf, ʃɛlvz] n étagère f, rayon m

**shell** [ʃɛl] n (on beach) coquillage m; (of egg, nut etc) coquille f; (explosive) obus m; (of building) carcasse f ▷ vt (peas) écosser; (Mil) bombarder (d'obus)

**she'll** [ʃiːl] = **she will**; **she shall**

**shellfish** [ʃɛlfɪʃ] n (pl inv: crab etc) crustacé m; (: scallop etc) coquillage m ▷ npl (as food) fruits mpl de mer

**shelter** [ʃɛltəʳ] n abri m, refuge m ▷ vt abriter, protéger; (give lodging to) donner asile à ▷ vi s'abriter, se mettre à l'abri; **sheltered** adj (life) retiré(e), à l'abri des soucis; (spot) abrité(e)

**shelves** [ʃɛlvz] npl of **shelf**

**shelving** [ʃɛlvɪŋ] n (shelves) rayonnage(s) m(pl)

**shepherd** [ʃɛpəd] n berger m ▷ vt (guide) guider, escorter; **shepherd's pie** n ≈ hachis m Parmentier

**sheriff** [ʃɛrɪf] (us) n shérif m

**sherry** [ʃɛrɪ] n xérès m, sherry m

**she's** [ʃiːz] = **she is**; **she has**

**Shetland** [ʃɛtlənd] n (also: **the ~s, the ~ Isles** or **Islands**) les îles fpl Shetland

**shield** [ʃiːld] n bouclier m; (protection) écran m de protection ▷ vt: **to ~ (from)** protéger (de or contre)

**shift** [ʃɪft] n (change) changement m; (work period) période f de travail; (of workers) équipe f, poste m ▷ vt déplacer, changer de place; (remove) enlever ▷ vi changer de place, bouger

**shin** [ʃɪn] n tibia m

**shine** [ʃaɪn] n éclat m, brillant m ▷ vb (pt, pp **shone**) ▷ vi briller ▷ vt (torch): **to ~ on** braquer sur; (polish: pt, pp **~d**) faire briller or reluire

**shingles** [ʃɪŋglz] n (Med) zona m

**shiny** [ʃaɪnɪ] adj brillant(e)

**ship** [ʃɪp] n bateau m; (large) navire m ▷ vt transporter (par mer); (send) expédier (par mer); **shipment** n cargaison f; **shipping** n (ships) navires mpl; (traffic) navigation f; (the industry) industrie navale; (transport) transport m; **shipwreck** n épave f; (event) naufrage m ▷ vt: **to be shipwrecked** faire naufrage; **shipyard** n chantier naval

**shirt** [ʃəːt] n chemise f; (woman's) chemisier m; **in ~ sleeves** en bras de chemise

**shit** [ʃɪt] excl (inf!) merde (!)

**shiver** [ʃɪvəʳ] n frisson m ▷ vi frissonner

**shock** [ʃɔk] n choc m; (Elec) secousse f, décharge f; (Med) commotion f, choc ▷ vt (scandalize) choquer, scandaliser; (upset) bouleverser; **shocking** adj (outrageous) choquant(e), scandaleux(-euse); (awful) épouvantable

**shoe** [ʃuː] n chaussure f, soulier m; (also: **horse~**) fer m à cheval ▷ vt (pt, pp **shod**) (horse) ferrer; **shoelace** n lacet m (de soulier); **shoe polish** n cirage m; **shoeshop** n magasin m de chaussures

**shone** [ʃɔn] pt, pp of **shine**

**shook** [ʃuk] pt of **shake**

**shoot** [ʃuːt] n (on branch, seedling) pousse f ▷ vb (pt, pp **shot**) ▷ vt (game: hunt) chasser; (: aim at) tirer; (: kill) abattre; (person) blesser/tuer d'un coup de fusil (or de revolver); (execute) fusiller; (arrow) tirer; (gun) tirer un coup de; (Cine) tourner ▷ vi (with gun, bow): **to ~ (at)** tirer (sur); (Football) shooter, tirer; **shooter**, tirer; **shoot down** vt (plane) abattre; **shoot up** vi (fig: prices etc) monter en flèche; **shooting** n (shots) coups mpl de feu; (attack) fusillade f; (murder) homicide m (à l'aide d'une arme à feu); (Hunting) chasse f

**shop** [ʃɔp] n magasin m; (workshop)

atelier m ▷ vi (also: **go ~ping**) faire ses courses or ses achats; **shop assistant** n (BRIT) vendeur(-euse); **shopkeeper** n marchand(e), commerçant(e); **shoplifting** n vol m à l'étalage; **shopping** n (goods) achats mpl, provisions fpl; **shopping bag** n sac m (à provisions); **shopping centre** (US **shopping center**) n centre commercial; **shopping mall** n centre commercial; **shopping trolley** n (BRIT) Caddie® m; **shop window** n vitrine f

**shore** [ʃɔːʳ] n (of sea, lake) rivage m, rive f ▷ vt: **to ~ (up)** étayer; **on ~** à terre

**short** [ʃɔːt] adj (not long) court(e); (soon finished) court, bref (brève); (person, step) petit(e); (curt) brusque, sec (sèche); (insufficient) insuffisant(e) ▷ n (also: **~ film**) court métrage m; (Elec) court-circuit m; **to be ~ of sth** être à court de or manquer de qch; **in ~** bref; en bref; **~ of doing** à moins de faire; **everything ~ of** tout sauf; **it is ~ for** c'est l'abréviation or le diminutif de; **to cut ~** (speech, visit) abréger, écourter; **to fall ~ of** ne pas être à la hauteur de; **to run ~ of** arriver à court de, venir à manquer de; **to stop ~** s'arrêter net; **to stop ~ of** ne pas aller jusqu'à; **shortage** n manque m, pénurie f; **shortbread** n ≈ sablé m; **shortcoming** n défaut m; **short(crust) pastry** n (BRIT) pâte brisée; **shortcut** n raccourci m; **shorten** vt raccourcir; (text, visit) abréger; **shortfall** n déficit m; **shorthand** n (BRIT) sténo(graphie) f; **shortlist** n (BRIT: for job) liste f des candidats sélectionnés; **short-lived** adj de courte durée; **shortly** adv bientôt, sous peu; **shorts** npl: **(a pair of) shorts** un short; **short-sighted** adj (BRIT) myope; (fig) qui manque de clairvoyance; **short-sleeved** adj à manches courtes; **short story** n nouvelle f; **short-tempered** adj qui s'emporte facilement; **short-term** adj (effect) à court terme

**shot** [ʃɔt] pt, pp of **shoot** ▷ n coup m

(de feu); (try) coup, essai m; (injection) piqûre f; (Phot) photo f; **to be a good/poor ~** (person) tirer bien/mal; **like a ~** comme une flèche; (very readily) sans hésiter; **shotgun** n fusil m de chasse

**should** [ʃud] aux vb: **I ~ go now** je devrais partir maintenant; **he ~ be there now** il devrait être arrivé maintenant; **I ~ go if I were you** si j'étais vous j'irais; **I ~ like to** j'aimerais bien, volontiers

**shoulder** ['ʃəuldəʳ] n épaule f ▷ vt (fig) endosser, se charger de; **shoulder blade** n omoplate f

**shouldn't** ['ʃudnt] = **should not**

**shout** [ʃaut] n cri m ▷ vt crier ▷ vi crier, pousser des cris

**shove** [ʃʌv] vt pousser; (inf: put): **to ~ sth in** fourrer or ficher qch dans ▷ n poussée f

**shovel** ['ʃʌvl] n pelle f ▷ vt pelleter, enlever (or enfourner) à la pelle

**show** [ʃəu] n (of emotion) manifestation f, démonstration f; (semblance) semblant m, apparence f; (exhibition) exposition f, salon m; (Theat, TV) spectacle m; (Cine) séance f ▷ vb (pt **~ed**, pp **~n**) ▷ vt montrer; (film) passer; (courage etc) faire preuve de, manifester; (exhibit) exposer ▷ vi se voir, être visible; **can you ~ me where it is, please?** pouvez-vous me montrer où c'est?; **to be on ~** être exposé(e); **it's just for ~** c'est juste pour l'effet; **show in** vt faire entrer; **show off** vi (pej) crâner ▷ vt (display) faire valoir; (pej) faire étalage de; **show out** vt reconduire à la porte; **show up** vi (stand out) ressortir; (inf: turn up) se montrer ▷ vt (unmask) démasquer, dénoncer; (flaw) faire ressortir; **show business** n le monde du spectacle

**shower** ['ʃauəʳ] n (for washing) douche f; (rain) averse f; (of stones etc) pluie f, grêle f; (US: party) réunion organisée pour la remise de cadeaux ▷ vi prendre une douche, se doucher ▷ vt: **to ~ sb with** (gifts etc) combler qn de; **to have**

or **take a ~** prendre une douche, se doucher; **shower cap** n bonnet m de douche; **shower gel** n gel m douche
**showing** ['ʃəʊɪŋ] n (of film) projection f
**show jumping** [-dʒʌmpɪŋ] n concours m hippique
**shown** [ʃəʊn] pp of **show**
**show**: **show-off** n (inf: person) crâneur(-euse), m'as-tu-vu(e); **showroom** n magasin m or salle f d'exposition
**shrank** [ʃræŋk] pt of **shrink**
**shred** [ʃred] n (gen pl) lambeau m, petit morceau; (fig: of truth, evidence) parcelle f ▷ vt mettre en lambeaux, déchirer; (documents) détruire; (Culin: grate) râper; (: lettuce etc) couper en lanières
**shrewd** [ʃruːd] adj astucieux(-euse), perspicace; (business person) habile
**shriek** [ʃriːk] n cri perçant or aigu, hurlement m ▷ vt, vi hurler, crier
**shrimp** [ʃrɪmp] n crevette grise
**shrine** [ʃraɪn] n (place) lieu m de pèlerinage
**shrink** (pt **shrank**, pp **shrunk**) [ʃrɪŋk, ʃræŋk, ʃrʌŋk] vi rétrécir; (fig) diminuer; (also: **~ away**) reculer ▷ vt (wool) (faire) rétrécir ▷ n (inf: pej) psychanalyste m/f; **to ~ from (doing) sth** reculer devant (la pensée de faire) qch
**shrivel** ['ʃrɪvl] (also: **~ up**) vt ratatiner, flétrir ▷ vi se ratatiner, se flétrir
**shroud** [ʃraʊd] n linceul m ▷ vt: **~ed in mystery** enveloppé(e) de mystère
**Shrove Tuesday** ['ʃrəʊv-] n (le) Mardi gras
**shrub** [ʃrʌb] n arbuste m
**shrug** [ʃrʌg] n haussement m d'épaules ▷ vt, vi: **to ~ (one's shoulders)** hausser les épaules; **shrug off** vt faire fi de
**shrunk** [ʃrʌŋk] pp of **shrink**
**shudder** ['ʃʌdəʳ] n frisson m, frémissement m ▷ vi frissonner, frémir
**shuffle** ['ʃʌfl] vt (cards) battre; **to ~ (one's feet)** traîner les pieds
**shun** [ʃʌn] vt éviter, fuir
**shut** (pt, pp **~**) [ʃʌt] vt fermer ▷ vi (se) fermer; **shut down** vt fermer

définitivement ▷ vi fermer définitivement; **shut up** vi (inf: keep quiet) se taire ▷ vt (close) fermer; (silence) faire taire; **shutter** n volet m; (Phot) obturateur m
**shuttle** ['ʃʌtl] n navette f; (also: **~ service**) (service m de) navette f; **shuttlecock** n volant m (de badminton)
**shy** [ʃaɪ] adj timide
**siblings** ['sɪblɪŋz] npl (formal) frères et sœurs mpl (de mêmes parents)
**Sicily** ['sɪsɪlɪ] n Sicile f
**sick** [sɪk] adj (ill) malade; (BRIT: vomiting): **to be ~** vomir; (humour) noir(e), macabre; **to feel ~** avoir envie de vomir, avoir mal au cœur; **to be ~ of** (fig) en avoir assez de; **sickening** adj (fig) écœurant(e), révoltant(e), répugnant(e); **sick leave** n congé m de maladie; **sickly** adj maladif(-ive), souffreteux(-euse); (causing nausea) écœurant(e); **sickness** n maladie f; (vomiting) vomissement(s) m(pl)
**side** [saɪd] n côté m; (of lake, road) bord m; (of mountain) versant m; (fig: aspect) côté, aspect m; (team: Sport) équipe f; (TV: channel) chaîne f ▷ adj (door, entrance) latéral(e) ▷ vi: **to ~ with sb** prendre le parti de qn, se ranger du côté de qn; **by the ~ of** au bord de; **~ by ~** côte à côte; **to rock from ~ to ~** se balancer; **to take ~s (with)** prendre parti (pour); **sideboard** n buffet m; **sideboards** (BRIT), **sideburns** npl (whiskers) pattes fpl; **side effect** n effet m secondaire; **sidelight** n (Aut) veilleuse f; **sideline** n (Sport) (ligne f de) touche f; (fig) activité f secondaire; **side order** n garniture f; **side road** n petite route, route transversale; **side street** n rue transversale; **sidetrack** vt (fig) faire dévier de son sujet; **sidewalk** n (US) trottoir m; **sideways** adv de côté
**siege** [siːdʒ] n siège m
**sieve** [sɪv] n tamis m, passoire f ▷ vt tamiser, passer (au tamis)
**sift** [sɪft] vt passer au tamis or au crible; (fig) passer au crible

**sigh** [saɪ] n soupir m ▷ vi soupirer, pousser un soupir

**sight** [saɪt] n (faculty) vue f; (spectacle) spectacle m; (on gun) mire f ▷ vt apercevoir; **in ~** visible; (fig) en vue; **out of ~** hors de vue; **sightseeing** n tourisme m; **to go sightseeing** faire du tourisme

**sign** [saɪn] n (gen) signe m; (with hand etc) signe, geste m; (notice) panneau m, écriteau m; (also: **road ~**) panneau de signalisation ▷ vt signer; **where do I ~?** où dois-je signer?; **sign for** vt fus (item) signer le reçu pour; **sign in** vi signer le registre (en arrivant); **sign on** vi (BRIT: as unemployed) s'inscrire au chômage; (enrol) s'inscrire ▷ vt (employee) embaucher; **sign over** vt: **to ~ sth over to sb** céder qch par écrit à qn; **sign up** vi (Mil) s'engager; (for course) s'inscrire

**signal** ['sɪɡnl] n signal m ▷ vi (Aut) mettre son clignotant ▷ vt (person) faire signe à; (message) communiquer par signaux

**signature** ['sɪɡnətʃər] n signature f

**significance** [sɪɡ'nɪfɪkəns] n signification f; importance f

**significant** [sɪɡ'nɪfɪkənt] adj significatif(-ive); (important) important(e), considérable

**signify** ['sɪɡnɪfaɪ] vt signifier

**sign language** n langage m par signes

**signpost** ['saɪnpəust] n poteau indicateur

**Sikh** [siːk] adj, n Sikh m/f

**silence** ['saɪləns] n silence m ▷ vt faire taire, réduire au silence

**silent** ['saɪlnt] adj silencieux(-euse); (film) muet(te); **to keep** or **remain ~** garder le silence, ne rien dire

**silhouette** [sɪlu:'ɛt] n silhouette f

**silicon chip** ['sɪlɪkən-] n puce f électronique

**silk** [sɪlk] n soie f ▷ cpd de or en soie

**silly** ['sɪlɪ] adj stupide, sot(te), bête

**silver** ['sɪlvər] n argent m; (money) monnaie f (en pièces d'argent); (also: **~ware**) argenterie f ▷ adj (made of silver) d'argent, en argent; (in colour) argenté(e); **silver-plated** adj plaqué(e) argent

**similar** ['sɪmɪlər] adj: **~ (to)** semblable (à); **similarity** [sɪmɪ'lærɪtɪ] n ressemblance f, similarité f; **similarly** adv de la même façon, de même

**simmer** ['sɪmər] vi cuire à feu doux, mijoter

**simple** ['sɪmpl] adj simple; **simplicity** [sɪm'plɪsɪtɪ] n simplicité f; **simplify** ['sɪmplɪfaɪ] vt simplifier; **simply** adv simplement; (without fuss) avec simplicité; (absolutely) absolument

**simulate** ['sɪmjuleɪt] vt simuler, feindre

**simultaneous** [sɪməl'teɪnɪəs] adj simultané(e); **simultaneously** adv simultanément

**sin** [sɪn] n péché m ▷ vi pécher

**since** [sɪns] adv, prep depuis ▷ conj (time) depuis que; (because) puisque, étant donné que, comme; **~ then**, **ever ~** depuis ce moment-là

**sincere** [sɪn'sɪər] adj sincère; **sincerely** adv sincèrement; **Yours sincerely** (at end of letter) veuillez agréer, Monsieur (or Madame) l'expression de mes sentiments distingués or les meilleurs

**sing** (pt **sang**, pp **sung**) [sɪŋ, sæŋ, sʌŋ] vt, vi chanter

**Singapore** [sɪŋɡə'pɔːr] n Singapour m

**singer** ['sɪŋər] n chanteur(-euse)

**singing** ['sɪŋɪŋ] n (of person, bird) chant m

**single** ['sɪŋɡl] adj seul(e), unique; (unmarried) célibataire; (not double) simple ▷ n (BRIT: also: **~ ticket**) aller m (simple); (record) 45 tours m; **singles** npl (Tennis) simple m; **every ~ day** chaque jour sans exception; **single out** vt choisir; (distinguish) distinguer; **single bed** n lit m d'une personne or à une place; **single file** n: **in single file** en file indienne; **single-handed** adv tout(e) seul(e), sans (aucune) aide; **single-minded** adj résolu(e), tenace; **single parent** n parent unique (or célibataire); **single-parent family** famille monoparentale; **single room** n chambre f à un lit or pour une personne

**singular** ['sɪŋɡjuləʳ] adj singulier(-ière); (odd) singulier, étrange; (outstanding) remarquable; (Ling) (au) singulier, du singulier ▷ n (Ling) singulier m

**sinister** ['sɪnɪstəʳ] adj sinistre

**sink** [sɪŋk] n évier m; (washbasin) lavabo m ▷ vb (pt **sank**, pp **sunk**) ▷ vt (ship) (faire) couler, faire sombrer; (foundations) creuser ▷ vi couler, sombrer; (ground etc) s'affaisser; **to ~ into sth** s'enfoncer dans qch; **sink in** vi (explanation) rentrer (inf), être compris

**sinus** ['saɪnəs] n (Anat) sinus m inv

**sip** [sɪp] n petite gorgée ▷ vt boire à petites gorgées

**sir** [səʳ] n monsieur m; **S~ John Smith** sir John Smith; **yes ~** oui Monsieur

**siren** ['saɪərn] n sirène f

**sirloin** ['səːlɔɪn] n (also: **~ steak**) aloyau m

**sister** ['sɪstəʳ] n sœur f; (nun) religieuse f, (bonne) sœur; (BRIT: nurse) infirmière f en chef; **sister-in-law** n belle-sœur f

**sit** (pt, pp **sat**) [sɪt, sæt] vi s'asseoir; (be sitting) être assis(e); (assembly) être en séance, siéger; (for painter) poser ▷ vt (exam) passer, se présenter à; **sit back** vi (in seat) bien s'installer, se carrer; **sit down** vi s'asseoir; **sit on** vt fus (jury, committee) faire partie de; **sit up** vi s'asseoir; (straight) se redresser; (not go to bed) rester debout, ne pas se coucher

**sitcom** ['sɪtkɔm] n abbr (TV: = situation comedy) sitcom f, comédie f de situation

**site** [saɪt] n emplacement m, site m; (also: **building ~**) chantier m ▷ vt placer

**sitting** ['sɪtɪŋ] n (of assembly etc) séance f; (in canteen) service m; **sitting room** n salon m

**situated** ['sɪtjueɪtɪd] adj situé(e)

**situation** [sɪtju'eɪʃən] n situation f; **"~s vacant/wanted"** (BRIT) "offres/demandes d'emploi"

**six** [sɪks] num six; **sixteen** num seize; **sixteenth** [sɪks'tiːnθ] num seizième; **sixth** ['sɪksθ] num sixième; **sixth form** n (BRIT) ≈ classes fpl de première et de terminale; **sixth-form college** n lycée n'ayant que des classes de première et de terminale; **sixtieth** ['sɪkstɪɪθ] num soixantième; **sixty** num soixante

**size** [saɪz] n dimensions fpl; (of person) taille f; (of clothing) taille f; (of shoes) pointure f; (of problem) ampleur f; (glue) colle f; **sizeable** adj assez grand(e); (amount, problem, majority) assez important(e)

**sizzle** ['sɪzl] vi grésiller

**skate** [skeɪt] n patin m; (fish: pl inv) raie f ▷ vi patiner; **skateboard** n skateboard m, planche f à roulettes; **skateboarding** n skateboard m; **skater** n patineur(-euse); **skating** n patinage m; **skating rink** n patinoire f

**skeleton** ['skɛlɪtn] n squelette m; (outline) schéma m

**skeptical** ['skɛptɪkl] (US) = **sceptical**

**sketch** [skɛtʃ] n (drawing) croquis m, esquisse f; (outline plan) aperçu m; (Theat) sketch m, saynète f ▷ vt esquisser, faire un croquis or une esquisse de; (plan etc) esquisser

**skewer** ['skjuːəʳ] n brochette f

**ski** [skiː] n ski m ▷ vi skier, faire du ski; **ski boot** n chaussure f de ski

**skid** [skɪd] n dérapage m ▷ vi déraper

**ski:** **skier** n skieur(-euse); **skiing** n ski m; **to go skiing** (aller) faire du ski

**skilful** (US **skillful**) ['skɪlful] adj habile, adroit(e)

**ski lift** n remonte-pente m inv

**skill** [skɪl] n (ability) habileté f, adresse f, talent m; (requiring training) compétences fpl; **skilled** adj habile, adroit(e); (worker) qualifié(e)

**skim** [skɪm] vt (soup) écumer; (glide over) raser, effleurer ▷ vi: **to ~ through** (fig) parcourir; **skimmed milk** (US **skim milk**) n lait écrémé

**skin** [skɪn] n peau f ▷ vt (fruit etc) éplucher; (animal) écorcher; **skinhead** n *n* skinhead *m*; **skinny** *adj* maigre, maigrichon(ne)

**skip** [skɪp] *n* petit bond *or* saut; (BRIT: *container*) benne *f* ▷ *vi* gambader, sautiller; (*with rope*) sauter à la corde ▷ *vt* (*pass over*) sauter

**ski: ski pass** *n* forfait-skieur(s) *m*; **ski pole** *n* bâton *m* de ski

**skipper** ['skɪpə'] *n* (Naut, Sport) capitaine *m*; (*in race*) skipper *m*

**skipping rope** ['skɪpɪŋ-] *n* (BRIT) (*US* **skip rope**) corde *f* à sauter

**skirt** [skə:t] *n* jupe *f* ▷ *vt* longer, contourner

**skirting board** ['skə:tɪŋ-] *n* (BRIT) plinthe *f*

**ski slope** *n* piste *f* de ski

**ski suit** *n* combinaison *f* de ski

**skull** [skʌl] *n* crâne *m*

**skunk** [skʌŋk] *n* mouffette *f*

**sky** [skaɪ] *n* ciel *m*; **skyscraper** *n* gratte-ciel *m inv*

**slab** [slæb] *n* (*of stone*) dalle *f*; (*of meat, cheese*) tranche épaisse

**slack** [slæk] *adj* (*loose*) lâche, desserré(e); (*slow*) stagnant(e); (*careless*) négligent(e), peu sérieux(-euse) *or* consciencieux(-euse); **slacks** *npl* pantalon *m*

**slain** [sleɪn] *pp of* **slay**

**slam** [slæm] *vt* (*door*) (faire) claquer; (*throw*) jeter violemment, flanquer; (*inf: criticize*) éreinter, démolir ▷ *vi* claquer

**slander** ['slɑ:ndə'] *n* calomnie *f*; (Law) diffamation *f*

**slang** [slæŋ] *n* argot *m*

**slant** [slɑ:nt] *n* inclinaison *f*; (*fig*) angle *m*, point *m* de vue

**slap** [slæp] *n* claque *f*, gifle *f*; (*on the back*) tape *f* ▷ *vt* donner une claque *or* une gifle (*or* une tape) à; **to ~ on** (*paint*) appliquer rapidement ▷ *adv* (*directly*) tout droit, en plein

**slash** [slæʃ] *vt* entailler, taillader; (*fig: prices*) casser

**slate** [sleɪt] *n* ardoise *f* ▷ *vt* (*fig: criticize*) éreinter, démolir

**slaughter** ['slɔ:tə'] *n* carnage *m*,

massacre *m*; (*of animals*) abattage *m* ▷ *vt* (*animal*) abattre; (*people*) massacrer; **slaughterhouse** *n* abattoir *m*

**Slav** [slɑ:v] *adj* slave

**slave** [sleɪv] *n* esclave *m/f* ▷ *vi* (*also:* **~ away**) trimer, travailler comme un forçat; **slavery** *n* esclavage *m*

**slay** (*pt* **slew**, *pp* **slain**) [sleɪ, slu:, sleɪn] *vt* (*literary*) tuer

**sleazy** ['sli:zɪ] *adj* miteux(-euse), minable

**sled** [slɛd] (*US*) = **sledge**

**sledge** [slɛdʒ] *n* luge *f*

**sleek** [sli:k] *adj* (*hair, fur*) brillant(e), luisant(e); (*car, boat*) aux lignes pures *or* élégantes

**sleep** [sli:p] *n* sommeil *m* ▷ *vi* (*pt, pp* **slept**) dormir; **to go to ~** s'endormir; **sleep in** *vi* (*oversleep*) se réveiller trop tard; (*on purpose*) faire la grasse matinée; **sleep together** *vi* (*have sex*) coucher ensemble; **sleeper** *n* (*person*) dormeur(-euse); (BRIT Rail: *on track*) traverse *f*; (: *train*) train-couchettes *m*; (: *berth*) couchette *f*; **sleeping bag** *n* sac *m* de couchage; **sleeping car** *n* wagon-lits *m*, voiture-lits *f*; **sleeping pill** *n* somnifère *m*; **sleepover** *n* nuit *f* chez un copain *or* une copine; **we're having a sleepover at Jo's** nous allons passer la nuit chez Jo; **sleepwalk** *vi* marcher en dormant; **sleepy** *adj* (*fig*) endormi(e)

**sleet** [sli:t] *n* neige fondue

**sleeve** [sli:v] *n* manche *f*; (*of record*) pochette *f*; **sleeveless** *adj* (*garment*) sans manches

**sleigh** [sleɪ] *n* traîneau *m*

**slender** ['slɛndə'] *adj* svelte, mince; (*fig*) faible, ténu(e)

**slept** [slɛpt] *pt, pp of* **sleep**

**slew** [slu:] *pt of* **slay**

**slice** [slaɪs] *n* tranche *f*; (*round*) rondelle *f*; (*utensil*) spatule *f*; (*also:* **fish ~**) pelle *f* à poisson ▷ *vt* couper en tranches (*or* en rondelles)

**slick** [slɪk] *adj* (*skilful*) bien ficelé(e);

(*salesperson*) qui a du bagout ▷ *n* (*also:* **oil ~**) nappe *f* de pétrole, marée noire

**slide** [slaɪd] *n* (*in playground*) toboggan *m*; (*Phot*) diapositive *f*; (*BRIT: also:* **hair ~**) barrette *f*; (*in prices*) chute *f*, baisse *f* ▷ *vb* (*pt, pp* **slid**) ▷ *vt* (faire) glisser ▷ *vi* glisser; **sliding** *adj* (*door*) coulissant(e)

**slight** [slaɪt] *adj* (*slim*) mince, menu(e); (*frail*) frêle; (*trivial*) faible, insignifiant(e); (*small*) petit(e), léger(-ère) *before n* ▷ *n* offense *f*, affront *m* ▷ *vt* (*offend*) blesser, offenser; **not in the ~est** pas le moins du monde, pas du tout; **slightly** *adv* légèrement, un peu

**slim** [slɪm] *adj* mince ▷ *vi* maigrir; (*diet*) suivre un régime amaigrissant; **slimming** *n* amaigrissement *m* ▷ *adj* (*diet, pills*) amaigrissant(e), pour maigrir; (*food*) qui ne fait pas grossir

**slimy** ['slaɪmɪ] *adj* visqueux(-euse), gluant(e)

**sling** [slɪŋ] *n* (*Med*) écharpe *f*; (*for baby*) porte-bébé *m*; (*weapon*) fronde *f*, lance-pierre *m* ▷ *vt* (*pt, pp* **slung**) lancer, jeter

**slip** [slɪp] *n* faux pas; (*mistake*) erreur *f*, bévue *f*; (*underskirt*) combinaison *f*; (*of paper*) petite feuille, fiche *f* ▷ *vt* (*slide*) glisser ▷ *vi* (*slide*) glisser; (*move smoothly*): **to ~ into/out of** se glisser or se faufiler dans/hors de; (*decline*) baisser; **to ~ sth on/off** enfiler/enlever qch; **to give sb the ~** fausser compagnie à qn; **a ~ of the tongue** un lapsus; **slip up** *vi* faire une erreur, gaffer

**slipped disc** [slɪpt-] *n* déplacement *m* de vertèbre

**slipper** ['slɪpər] *n* pantoufle *f*

**slippery** ['slɪpərɪ] *adj* glissant(e)

**slip road** *n* (*BRIT: to motorway*) bretelle *f* d'accès

**slit** [slɪt] *n* fente *f*; (*cut*) incision *f* ▷ *vt* (*pt, pp* **~**) fendre; couper, inciser

**slog** [slɔg] *n* (*BRIT: effort*) gros effort; (: *work*) tâche fastidieuse ▷ *vi* travailler très dur

**slogan** ['sləʊgən] *n* slogan *m*

**slope** [sləʊp] *n* pente *f*, côte *f*; (*side of mountain*) versant *m*; (*slant*) inclinaison *f* ▷ *vi*: **to ~ down** être or descendre en pente; **to ~ up** monter; **sloping** *adj* en pente, incliné(e); (*handwriting*) penché(e)

**sloppy** ['slɔpɪ] *adj* (*work*) peu soigné(e), bâclé(e); (*appearance*) négligé(e), débraillé(e)

**slot** [slɔt] *n* fente *f* ▷ *vt*: **to ~ sth into** encastrer or insérer qch dans; **slot machine** *n* (*BRIT: vending machine*) distributeur *m* (automatique), machine *f* à sous; (*for gambling*) appareil *m* or machine à sous

**Slovakia** [sləʊ'vækɪə] *n* Slovaquie *f*

**Slovene** [sləʊ'viːn] *adj* slovène ▷ *n* Slovène *m/f*; (*Ling*) slovène *m*

**Slovenia** [sləʊ'viːnɪə] *n* Slovénie *f*; **Slovenian** *adj, n* = **Slovene**

**slow** [sləʊ] *adj* lent(e); (*watch*): **to be ~** retarder ▷ *adv* lentement ▷ *vt, vi* ralentir; **"~"** (*road sign*) "ralentir"; **slow down** *vi* ralentir; **slowly** *adv* lentement; **slow motion** *n*: **in slow motion** au ralenti

**slug** [slʌg] *n* limace *f*; (*bullet*) balle *f*; **sluggish** *adj* (*person*) mou (molle), lent(e); (*stream, engine, trading*) lent(e)

**slum** [slʌm] *n* (*house*) taudis *m*; **slums** *npl* (*area*) quartiers *mpl* pauvres

**slump** [slʌmp] *n* baisse soudaine, effondrement *m*; (*Econ*) crise *f* ▷ *vi* s'effondrer, s'affaisser

**slung** [slʌŋ] *pt, pp* of **sling**

**slur** [sləːr] *n* (*smear*): **~ (on)** atteinte *f* (à); insinuation *f* (contre) ▷ *vt* mal articuler

**slush** [slʌʃ] *n* neige fondue

**sly** [slaɪ] *adj* (*person*) rusé(e); (*smile, expression, remark*) sournois(e)

**smack** [smæk] *n* (*slap*) tape *f*; (*on face*) gifle *f* ▷ *vt* donner une tape à; (*on face*) gifler; (*on bottom*) donner la fessée à ▷ *vi*: **to ~ of** avoir des relents de, sentir

**small** [smɔːl] *adj* petit(e); **small ads** *npl* (*BRIT*) petites annonces; **small change** *n* petite or menue monnaie

**smart** [smɑːt] *adj* élégant(e), chic

*inv*; (*clever*) intelligent(e); (*quick*) vif (vive), prompt(e) ▷ *vi* faire mal, brûler; **smartcard** *n* carte *f* à puce

**smash** [smæʃ] *n* (*also*: **~-up**) collision *f*, accident *m*; (*Mus*) succès foudroyant ▷ *vt* casser, briser, fracasser; (*opponent*) écraser; (*Sport: record*) pulvériser ▷ *vi* se briser, se fracasser; s'écraser; **smashing** *adj* (*inf*) formidable

**smear** [smɪə*ʳ*] *n* (*stain*) tache *f*; (*mark*) trace *f*; (*Med*) frottis *m* ▷ *vt* enduire; (*make dirty*) salir; **smear test** *n* (BRIT Med) frottis *m*

**smell** [smɛl] *n* odeur *f*; (*sense*) odorat *m* ▷ *vb* (*pt, pp* **smelt** *or* **~ed**) ▷ *vt* sentir ▷ *vi* (*pej*) sentir mauvais; **smelly** *adj* qui sent mauvais, malodorant(e)

**smelt** [smɛlt] *pt, pp of* **smell**

**smile** [smaɪl] *n* sourire *m* ▷ *vi* sourire

**smirk** [smə:k] *n* petit sourire suffisant *or* affecté

**smog** [smɔg] *n* brouillard mêlé de fumée

**smoke** [sməuk] *n* fumée *f* ▷ *vt, vi* fumer; **do you mind if I ~?** ça ne vous dérange pas que je fume?; **smoke alarm** *n* détecteur *m* de fumée; **smoked** *adj* (*bacon, glass*) fumé(e); **smoker** *n* (*person*) fumeur(-euse); (*Rail*) wagon *m* fumeurs; **smoking** *n*: **"no smoking"** (*sign*) "défense de fumer"; **smoky** *adj* enfumé(e); (*taste*) fumé(e)

**smooth** [smu:ð] *adj* lisse; (*sauce*) onctueux(-euse); (*flavour, whisky*) moelleux(-euse); (*movement*) régulier(-ière), sans à-coups *or* heurts; (*flight*) sans secousses; (*pej: person*) doucereux(-euse), mielleux(-euse) ▷ *vt* (*also*: **~ out**) lisser, défroisser; (*creases, difficulties*) faire disparaître

**smother** ['smʌðə*ʳ*] *vt* étouffer

**SMS** *n abbr* (= *short message service*) SMS *m*; **SMS message** *n* message *m* SMS

**smudge** [smʌdʒ] *n* tache *f*, bavure *f* ▷ *vt* salir, maculer

**smug** [smʌg] *adj* suffisant(e), content(e) de soi

**smuggle** ['smʌgl] *vt* passer en contrebande *or* en fraude; **smuggling** *n* contrebande *f*

**snack** [snæk] *n* casse-croûte *m inv*; **snack bar** *n* snack(-bar) *m*

**snag** [snæg] *n* inconvénient *m*, difficulté *f*

**snail** [sneɪl] *n* escargot *m*

**snake** [sneɪk] *n* serpent *m*

**snap** [snæp] *n* (*sound*) claquement *m*, bruit sec; (*photograph*) photo *f*, instantané *m* ▷ *adj* subit(e), fait(e) sans réfléchir ▷ *vt* (*fingers*) faire claquer; (*break*) casser net ▷ *vi* se casser net *or* avec un bruit sec; (*speak sharply*) parler d'un ton brusque; **to ~ open/shut** s'ouvrir/se refermer brusquement; **snap at** *vt fus* (*subj: dog*) essayer de mordre; **snap up** *vt* sauter sur, saisir; **snapshot** *n* photo *f*, instantané *m*

**snarl** [snɑ:l] *vi* gronder

**snatch** [snætʃ] *n* (*small amount*) ▷ *vt* saisir (*d'un geste vif*); (*steal*) voler; **to ~ some sleep** arriver à dormir un peu

**sneak** [sni:k] (*US: pt* **snuck**) *vi*: **to ~ in/out** entrer/sortir furtivement *or* à la dérobée ▷ *n* (*inf: pej: informer*) faux jeton; **to ~ up on sb** s'approcher de qn sans faire de bruit; **sneakers** *npl* tennis *mpl*, baskets *fpl*

**sneer** [snɪə*ʳ*] *vi* ricaner; **to ~ at sb/sth** se moquer de qn/qch avec mépris

**sneeze** [sni:z] *vi* éternuer

**sniff** [snɪf] *vi* renifler ▷ *vt* renifler, flairer; (*glue, drug*) sniffer, respirer

**snigger** ['snɪgə*ʳ*] *vi* ricaner

**snip** [snɪp] *n* (*cut*) entaille *f*; (BRIT: *inf: bargain*) (bonne) occasion *or* affaire *f* ▷ *vt* couper

**sniper** ['snaɪpə*ʳ*] *n* (*marksman*) tireur embusqué

**snob** [snɔb] *n* snob *m/f*

**snooker** ['snu:kə*ʳ*] *n* sorte de jeu de billard

**snoop** [snu:p] *vi*: **to ~ about** fureter

**snooze** [snu:z] *n* petit somme ▷ *vi* faire un petit somme

**snore** [snɔ:*ʳ*] *vi* ronfler ▷ *n*

ronflement m

**snorkel** ['snɔːkl] n (of swimmer) tuba m

**snort** [snɔːt] n grognement m ▷ vi grogner; (horse) renâcler

**snow** [snəʊ] n neige f ▷ vi neiger; **snowball** n boule f de neige; **snowdrift** n congère f; **snowman** (irreg) n bonhomme m de neige; **snowplough** (US **snowplow**) n chasse-neige m inv; **snowstorm** n tempête f de neige

**snub** [snʌb] vt repousser, snober ▷ n rebuffade f

**snug** [snʌg] adj douillet(te), confortable; (person) bien au chaud

○ **KEYWORD**

**so** [səʊ] adv 1 (thus, likewise) ainsi, de cette façon; **if so** si oui; **so do** or **have I** moi aussi; **it's 5 o'clock - so it is!** il est 5 heures - en effet! or c'est vrai!; **I hope/think so** je l'espère/le crois; **so far** jusqu'ici, jusqu'à maintenant; (in past) jusque-là

**2** (in comparisons etc: to such a degree) si, tellement; **so big (that)** si or tellement grand (que); **she's not so clever as her brother** elle n'est pas aussi intelligente que son frère

**3**: **so much** adj, adv tant (de); **I've got so much work** j'ai tant de travail; **I love you so much** je vous aime tant; **so many** tant (de)

**4** (phrases): **10 or so** à peu près or environ 10; **so long!** (inf: goodbye) au revoir!, à un de ces jours!; **so (what)?** (inf) (bon) et alors?, et après?

▷ conj 1 (expressing purpose): **so as to do** pour faire, afin de faire; **so (that)** pour que or afin que + sub

**2** (expressing result) donc, par conséquent; **so that** si bien que, de (telle) sorte que; **so that's the reason!** c'est donc (pour) ça!; **so you see, I could have gone** alors tu vois, j'aurais pu y aller

**soak** [səʊk] vt faire or laisser tremper; (drench) tremper ▷ vi tremper; **soak up** vt absorber; **soaking** adj (also: **soaking wet**) trempé(e)

**so-and-so** ['səʊənsəʊ] n (somebody) un(e) tel(le)

**soap** [səʊp] n savon m; **soap opera** n feuilleton télévisé (quotidienneté réaliste ou embellie); **soap powder** n lessive f, détergent m

**soar** [sɔːʳ] vi monter (en flèche), s'élancer; (building) s'élancer

**sob** [sɔb] n sanglot m ▷ vi sangloter

**sober** ['səʊbəʳ] adj qui n'est pas (or plus) ivre; (serious) sérieux(-euse), sensé(e); (colour, style) sobre, discret(-ète); **sober up** vi se dégriser

**so-called** ['səʊ'kɔːld] adj soi-disant inv

**soccer** ['sɔkəʳ] n football m

**sociable** ['səʊʃəbl] adj sociable

**social** ['səʊʃl] adj social(e); (sociable) sociable ▷ n (petite) fête; **socialism** n socialisme m; **socialist** adj, n socialiste (m/f); **socialize** vi: **to socialize with** (meet often) fréquenter; (get to know) lier connaissance or parler avec; **social life** n vie sociale; **socially** adv socialement, en société; **social security** n aide sociale; **social services** npl services sociaux; **social work** n assistance sociale; **social worker** n assistant(e) sociale(e)

**society** [sə'saɪətɪ] n société f; (club) société, association f; (also: **high ~**) (haute) société, grand monde

**sociology** [səʊsɪ'ɔlədʒɪ] n sociologie f

**sock** [sɔk] n chaussette f

**socket** ['sɔkɪt] n cavité f; (Elec: also: **wall ~**) prise f de courant

**soda** ['səʊdə] n (Chem) soude f; (also: **~ water**) eau f de Seltz; (US: also: **~ pop**) soda m

**sodium** ['səʊdɪəm] n sodium m

**sofa** ['səʊfə] n sofa m, canapé m; **sofa bed** n canapé-lit m

**soft** [sɔft] adj (not rough) doux (douce); (not hard) doux, mou (molle); (not loud) doux, léger(-ère); (kind) doux, gentil(le); **soft drink** n boisson non alcoolisée;

**soft drugs** npl drogues douces; **soften**
['sɒfn] vt (r)amollir; (fig) adoucir ▷ vi
se ramollir; (fig) s'adoucir; **softly** adv
doucement; (touch) légèrement; (kiss)
tendrement; **software** n (Comput)
logiciel m, software m
**soggy** ['sɒgɪ] adj (clothes) trempé(e);
(ground) détrempé(e)
**soil** [sɔɪl] n (earth) sol m, terre f ▷ vt salir;
(fig) souiller
**solar** ['səʊləʳ] adj solaire; **solar power**
n énergie f solaire; **solar system** n
système m solaire
**sold** [səʊld] pt, pp of **sell**
**soldier** ['səʊldʒəʳ] n soldat m,
militaire m
**sold out** adj (Comm) épuisé(e)
**sole** [səʊl] n (of foot) plante f; (of shoe)
semelle f; (fish: pl inv) sole f ▷ adj
seul(e), unique; **solely** adv seulement,
uniquement
**solemn** ['sɒləm] adj solennel(le);
(person) sérieux(-euse), grave
**solicitor** [sə'lɪsɪtəʳ] n (BRIT: for wills etc)
≈ notaire m; (: in court) ≈ avocat m
**solid** ['sɒlɪd] adj (not liquid) solide; (not
hollow: mass) compact(e); (: metal, rock,
wood) massif(-ive) ▷ n solide m
**solitary** ['sɒlɪtərɪ] adj solitaire
**solitude** ['sɒlɪtjuːd] n solitude f
**solo** ['səʊləʊ] n solo m ▷ adv (fly) en
solitaire; **soloist** n soliste m/f
**soluble** ['sɒljʊbl] adj soluble
**solution** [sə'luːʃən] n solution f
**solve** [sɒlv] vt résoudre
**solvent** ['sɒlvənt] adj (Comm) solvable
▷ n (Chem) (dis)solvant m
**sombre** (US **somber**) ['sɒmbəʳ] adj
sombre, morne

O **KEYWORD**

**some** [sʌm] adj **1** (a certain amount
or number of): **some tea/water/ice
cream** du thé/de l'eau/de la glace;
**some children/apples** des enfants/
pommes; **I've got some money but
not much** j'ai de l'argent mais pas

beaucoup
**2** (certain: in contrasts): **some people
say that ...** il y a des gens qui disent
que ...; **some films were excellent,
but most were mediocre** certains
films étaient excellents, mais la plupart
étaient médiocres
**3** (unspecified): **some woman was
asking for you** il y avait une dame qui
vous demandait; **he was asking for
some book (or other)** il demandait un
livre quelconque; **some day** un de ces
jours; **some day next week** un jour la
semaine prochaine
▷ pron **1** (a certain number) quelques-
un(e)s, certain(e)s; **I've got some**
(books etc) j'en ai (quelques-uns); **some
(of them) have been sold** certains ont
été vendus
**2** (a certain amount) un peu; **I've got
some** (money, milk) j'en ai (un peu);
**would you like some?** est-ce que vous
en voulez?, en voulez-vous?; **could I
have some of that cheese?** pourrais-
je avoir un peu de ce fromage?; **I've
read some of the book** j'ai lu une
partie du livre
▷ adv: **some 10 people** quelque 10
personnes, 10 personnes environ;
**somebody** ['sʌmbədɪ] pron
= **someone**; **somehow** adv d'une
façon ou d'une autre; (for some
reason) pour une raison ou une
autre; **someone** pron quelqu'un;
**someplace** adv (US) = **somewhere**;
**something** pron quelque chose m;
**something interesting** quelque
chose d'intéressant; **something to do**
quelque chose à faire; **sometime** adv
(in future) un de ces jours, un jour ou
l'autre; (in past): **sometime last month**
au cours du mois dernier; **sometimes**
adv quelquefois, parfois; **somewhat**
adv quelque peu, un peu; **somewhere**
adv quelque part; **somewhere else**
ailleurs, autre part

**son** [sʌn] n fils m

**song** [sɒŋ] n chanson f; (of bird) chant m

**son-in-law** [ˈsʌnɪnlɔː] n gendre m, beau-fils m

**soon** [suːn] adv bientôt; (early) tôt; **~ afterwards** peu après; see also **as**; **sooner** adv (time) plus tôt; (preference): **I would sooner do that** j'aimerais autant or je préférerais faire ça; **sooner or later** tôt ou tard

**soothe** [suːð] vt calmer, apaiser

**sophisticated** [səˈfɪstɪkeɪtɪd] adj raffiné(e), sophistiqué(e); (machinery) hautement perfectionné(e), très complexe

**sophomore** [ˈsɒfəmɔːʳ] n (us) étudiant(e) de seconde année

**soprano** [səˈprɑːnəʊ] n (singer) soprano m/f

**sorbet** [ˈsɔːbeɪ] n sorbet m

**sordid** [ˈsɔːdɪd] adj sordide

**sore** [sɔːʳ] adj (painful) douloureux(-euse), sensible ▷ n plaie f

**sorrow** [ˈsɒrəʊ] n peine f, chagrin m

**sorry** [ˈsɒrɪ] adj désolé(e); (condition, excuse, tale) triste, déplorable; **~!** pardon!, excusez-moi!; **~?** pardon?; **to feel ~ for sb** plaindre qn

**sort** [sɔːt] n genre m, espèce f, sorte f; (make: of coffee, car etc) marque f ▷ vt (also: **~ out**: select which to keep) trier; (classify) classer; (tidy) ranger; **sort out** vt (problem) résoudre, régler

**SOS** n SOS m

**so-so** [ˈsəʊsəʊ] adv comme ci comme ça

**sought** [sɔːt] pt, pp of **seek**

**soul** [səʊl] n âme f

**sound** [saʊnd] adj (healthy) en bonne santé, sain(e); (safe, not damaged) solide, en bon état; (reliable, not superficial) sérieux(-euse), solide; (sensible) sensé(e) ▷ adv: **~ asleep** profondément endormi(e) ▷ n (noise, volume) son m; (louder) bruit m; (Geo) détroit m, bras m de mer ▷ vt (alarm) sonner ▷ vi sonner, retentir; (fig: seem) sembler (être); **to ~ like** ressembler à; **sound bite** n phrase toute faite (pour

être citée dans les médias); **soundtrack** n (of film) bande f sonore

**soup** [suːp] n soupe f, potage m

**sour** [ˈsaʊəʳ] adj aigre; **it's ~ grapes** c'est du dépit

**source** [sɔːs] n source f

**south** [saʊθ] n sud m ▷ adj sud inv; (wind) du sud ▷ adv au sud, vers le sud; **South Africa** n Afrique f du Sud; **South African** adj sud-africain(e) ▷ n Sud-Africain(e); **South America** n Amérique f du Sud; **South American** adj sud-américain(e) ▷ n Sud-Américain(e); **southbound** adj en direction du sud; (carriageway) sud inv; **south-east** n sud-est m; **southeastern** [saʊθˈiːstən] adj du or au sud-est; **southern** [ˈsʌðən] adj (du) sud; méridional(e); **South Korea** n Corée f du Sud; **South of France** n: **the South of France** le Sud de la France, le Midi; **South Pole** n Pôle m Sud; **southward(s)** adv vers le sud; **southwest** n sud-ouest m; **southwestern** [saʊθˈwestən] adj du or au sud-ouest

**souvenir** [suːvəˈnɪəʳ] n souvenir m (objet)

**sovereign** [ˈsɒvrɪn] adj, n souverain(e)

**sow¹** [səʊ] (pt **~ed**, pp **~n**) vt semer

**sow²** n [saʊ] truie f

**soya** [ˈsɔɪə] (us **soy** [sɔɪ]) n: **~ bean** graine f de soja; **~ sauce** sauce f au soja

**spa** [spɑː] n (town) station thermale; (us: also: **health ~**) établissement m de cure de rajeunissement

**space** [speɪs] n (gen) espace m; (room) place f; espace; (length of time) laps m de temps ▷ cpd spatial(e) ▷ vt (also: **~ out**) espacer; **spacecraft** n engin or vaisseau spatial; **spaceship** n = **spacecraft**

**spacious** [ˈspeɪʃəs] adj spacieux(-euse), grand(e)

**spade** [speɪd] n (tool) bêche f, pelle f; (child's) pelle; **spades** npl (Cards) pique m

**spaghetti** [spəˈɡetɪ] n spaghetti mpl

**Spain** [speɪn] n Espagne f

**spam** [spæm] n (Comput) spam m
**span** [spæn] n (of bird, plane) envergure f; (of arch) portée f; (in time) espace m de temps, durée f ▷ vt enjamber, franchir; (fig) couvrir, embrasser
**Spaniard** ['spænjəd] n Espagnol(e)
**Spanish** ['spænɪʃ] adj espagnol(e), d'Espagne ▷ n (Ling) espagnol m; **the Spanish** npl les Espagnols
**spank** [spæŋk] vt donner une fessée à
**spanner** ['spænər] n (Brit) clé f (de mécanicien)
**spare** [spɛər] adj de réserve, de rechange; (surplus) de or en trop, de reste ▷ n (part) pièce f de rechange, pièce détachée ▷ vt (do without) se passer de; (afford to give) donner, accorder, passer; (not hurt) épargner; **to ~** (surplus) en surplus, de trop; **spare part** n pièce f de rechange, pièce détachée; **spare room** n chambre f d'ami; **spare time** n moments mpl de loisir; **spare tyre** (US **spare tire**) n (Aut) pneu m de rechange; **spare wheel** n (Aut) roue f de secours
**spark** [spɑːk] n étincelle f; **spark(ing) plug** n bougie f
**sparkle** ['spɑːkl] n scintillement m, étincellement m, éclat m ▷ vi étinceler, scintiller
**sparkling** ['spɑːklɪŋ] adj (wine) mousseux(-euse), pétillant(e); (water) pétillant(e), gazeux(-euse)
**sparrow** ['spærəʊ] n moineau m
**sparse** [spɑːs] adj clairsemé(e)
**spasm** ['spæzəm] n (Med) spasme m
**spat** [spæt] pt, pp of **spit**
**spate** [speɪt] n (fig): **~ of** avalanche f or torrent m de
**spatula** ['spætjʊlə] n spatule f
**speak** (pt **spoke**, pp **spoken**) [spiːk, spəʊk, 'spəʊkn] vt (language) parler; (truth) dire ▷ vi parler; (make a speech) prendre la parole; **to ~ to sb/of or about sth** parler à qn/de qch; **I don't ~ French** je ne parle pas français; **do you ~ English?** parlez-vous anglais?; **can I ~ to ...?** est-ce que je peux parler à ...?; **speaker** n (in public) orateur m; (also: **loudspeaker**) haut-parleur m; (for stereo etc) baffle m, enceinte f; (Pol): **the Speaker** (Brit) le président de la Chambre des communes or des représentants; (US) le président de la Chambre
**spear** [spɪər] n lance f ▷ vt transpercer
**special** ['spɛʃl] adj spécial(e); **special delivery** n (Post): **by special delivery** en express; **special effects** npl (Cine) effets spéciaux; **specialist** n spécialiste m/f; **speciality** [spɛʃɪˈælɪtɪ] n (Brit) spécialité f; **specialize** vi: **to specialize (in)** se spécialiser (dans); **specially** adv spécialement, particulièrement; **special needs** npl (Brit) difficultés fpl d'apprentissage scolaire; **special offer** n (Comm) réclame f; **special school** n (Brit) établissement m d'enseignement spécialisé; **specialty** n (US) = **speciality**
**species** ['spiːʃiːz] n (pl inv) espèce f
**specific** [spəˈsɪfɪk] adj (not vague) précis(e), explicite; (particular) particulier(-ière); **specifically** adv explicitement, précisément; (intend, ask, design) expressément, spécialement
**specify** ['spɛsɪfaɪ] vt spécifier, préciser
**specimen** ['spɛsɪmən] n spécimen m, échantillon m; (Med: of blood) prélèvement m; (: of urine) échantillon m
**speck** [spɛk] n petite tache, petit point; (particle) grain m
**spectacle** ['spɛktəkl] n spectacle m; **spectacles** npl (Brit) lunettes fpl; **spectacular** [spɛkˈtækjulər] adj spectaculaire
**spectator** [spɛkˈteɪtər] n spectateur(-trice)
**spectrum** (pl **spectra**) ['spɛktrəm, -rə] n spectre m; (fig) gamme f
**speculate** ['spɛkjuleɪt] vi spéculer; (try to guess): **to ~ about** s'interroger sur
**sped** [spɛd] pt, pp of **speed**
**speech** [spiːtʃ] n (faculty) parole f; (talk) discours m, allocution f; (manner of speaking) façon f de parler, langage m;

(*enunciation*) élocution f; **speechless** *adj* muet(te)

**speed** [spi:d] *n* vitesse f; (*promptness*) rapidité f ▷ *vi* (*pt, pp* **sped**: *Aut: exceed speed limit*) faire un excès de vitesse; **at full** or **top ~** à toute vitesse or allure; **speed up** (*pt, pp* **~ed up**) *vi* aller plus vite, accélérer ▷ *vt* accélérer; **speedboat** *n* vedette f, hors-bord *m inv*; **speeding** *n* (*Aut*) excès *m* de vitesse; **speed limit** *n* limitation f de vitesse, vitesse maximale permise; **speedometer** [spɪ'dɔmɪtəʳ] *n* compteur *m* (de vitesse); **speedy** *adj* rapide, prompt(e)

**spell** [spɛl] *n* (*also: **magic ~***) sortilège *m*, charme *m*; (*period of time*) (courte) période ▷ *vt* (*pt, pp* **spelt** or **~ed**) (*in writing*) écrire, orthographier; (*aloud*) épeler; (*fig*) signifier; **to cast a ~ on sb** jeter un sort à qn; **he can't ~** il fait des fautes d'orthographe; **spell out** *vt* (*explain*): **to ~ sth out for sb** expliquer qch clairement à qn; **spellchecker** ['spɛltʃɛkəʳ] *n* (*Comput*) correcteur *m* or vérificateur *m* orthographique; **spelling** *n* orthographe f

**spelt** [spɛlt] *pt, pp of* **spell**

**spend** (*pt, pp* **spent**) [spɛnd, spɛnt] *vt* (*money*) dépenser; (*time, life*) passer; (*devote*) consacrer; **spending** *n*: **government spending** les dépenses publiques

**spent** [spɛnt] *pt, pp of* **spend** ▷ *adj* (*cartridge, bullets*) vide

**sperm** [spə:m] *n* spermatozoïde *m*; (*semen*) sperme *m*

**sphere** [sfɪəʳ] *n* sphère f; (*fig*) sphère, domaine *m*

**spice** [spaɪs] *n* épice f ▷ *vt* épicer

**spicy** ['spaɪsɪ] *adj* épicé(e), relevé(e); (*fig*) piquant(e)

**spider** ['spaɪdəʳ] *n* araignée f

**spike** [spaɪk] *n* pointe f; (*Bot*) épi *m*

**spill** (*pt, pp* **spilt** or **~ed**) [spɪl, -t, -d] *vt* renverser; répandre ▷ *vi* se répandre; **spill over** *vi* déborder

**spin** [spɪn] *n* (*revolution of wheel*) tour *m*; (*Aviat*) (*chute f en*) vrille f; (*trip in car*) petit tour, balade f; (*on ball*) effet *m* ▷ *vb* (*pt, pp* **spun**) ▷ *vt* (*wool etc*) filer; (*wheel*) faire tourner ▷ *vi* (*turn*) tourner, tournoyer

**spinach** ['spɪnɪtʃ] *n* épinards *mpl*

**spinal** ['spaɪnl] *adj* vertébral(e), spinal(e)

**spinal cord** *n* moelle épinière

**spin doctor** *n* (*inf*) personne employée pour présenter un parti politique sous un jour favorable

**spin-dryer** [spɪn'draɪəʳ] *n* (*BRIT*) essoreuse f

**spine** [spaɪn] *n* colonne vertébrale; (*thorn*) épine f, piquant *m*

**spiral** ['spaɪərl] *n* spirale f ▷ *vi* (*fig: prices etc*) monter en flèche

**spire** ['spaɪəʳ] *n* flèche f, aiguille f

**spirit** ['spɪrɪt] *n* (*soul*) esprit *m*, âme f; (*ghost*) esprit, revenant *m*; (*mood*) esprit, état m d'esprit; (*courage*) courage *m*, énergie f; **spirits** *npl* (*drink*) spiritueux *mpl*, alcool *m*; **in good ~s** de bonne humeur

**spiritual** ['spɪrɪtjuəl] *adj* spirituel(le); (*religious*) religieux(-euse)

**spit** [spɪt] *n* (*for roasting*) broche f; (*spittle*) crachat *m*; (*saliva*) salive f ▷ *vi* (*pt, pp* **spat**) cracher; (*sound*) crépiter; (*rain*) crachiner

**spite** [spaɪt] *n* rancune f, dépit *m* ▷ *vt* contrarier, vexer; **in ~ of** en dépit de, malgré; **spiteful** *adj* malveillant(e), rancunier(-ière)

**splash** [splæʃ] *n* (*sound*) plouf *m*; (*of colour*) tache f ▷ *vt* éclabousser ▷ *vi* (*also: ~ about*) barboter, patauger; **splash out** *vi* (*BRIT*) faire une folie

**splendid** ['splɛndɪd] *adj* splendide, superbe, magnifique

**splinter** ['splɪntəʳ] *n* (*wood*) écharde f; (*metal*) éclat *m* ▷ *vi* (*wood*) se fendre; (*glass*) se briser

**split** [splɪt] *n* fente f, déchirure f; (*fig: Pol*) scission f ▷ *vb* (*pt, pp* **~**) ▷ *vt* fendre, déchirer; (*party*) diviser; (*work, profits*) partager, répartir ▷ *vi* (*break*) se fendre, se briser; (*divide*) se diviser; **split up** *vi* (*couple*) se séparer, rompre; (*meeting*) se disperser

**spoil** (*pt, pp* **~ed** *or* **~t**) [spɔɪl, -d, -t] *vt* (*damage*) abîmer; (*mar*) gâcher; (*child*) gâter

**spoilt** [spɔɪlt] *pt, pp of* **spoil** ▷ *adj* (*child*) gâté(e); (*ballot paper*) nul(le)

**spoke** [spəuk] *pt of* **speak** ▷ *n* rayon *m*

**spoken** ['spəukn] *pp of* **speak**

**spokesman** ['spəuksmən] (*irreg*) *n* porte-parole *m*

**spokesperson** ['spəukspə:sn] *n* porte-parole *m inv*

**spokeswoman** ['spəukswumən] (*irreg*) *n* porte-parole *m inv*

**sponge** [spʌndʒ] *n* éponge *f*; (*Culin: also:* **~ cake**) ≈ biscuit *m* de Savoie ▷ *vt* éponger ▷ *vi*: **to ~ off** *or* **on** vivre aux crochets de; **sponge bag** *n* (BRIT) trousse *f* de toilette

**sponsor** ['spɔnsə<sup>r</sup>] *n* (*Radio, TV, Sport*) sponsor *m*; (*for application*) parrain *m*, marraine *f*; (BRIT: *for fund-raising event*) donateur(-trice) ▷ *vt* sponsoriser, parrainer, faire un don à; **sponsorship** *n* sponsoring *m*, parrainage *m*; dons *mpl*

**spontaneous** [spɔn'teɪnɪəs] *adj* spontané(e)

**spooky** ['spu:kɪ] *adj* (*inf*) qui donne la chair de poule

**spoon** [spu:n] *n* cuiller *f*; **spoonful** *n* cuillerée *f*

**sport** [spɔ:t] *n* sport *m*; (*person*) chic type *m*/chic fille *f* ▷ *vt* (*wear*) arborer; **sport jacket** *n* (US) = **sports jacket**; **sports car** *n* voiture *f* de sport; **sports centre** (BRIT) *n* centre sportif; **sports jacket** *n* (BRIT) veste *f* de sport; **sportsman** (*irreg*) *n* sportif *m*; **sports utility vehicle** *n* véhicule *m* de loisirs (*de type SUV*); **sportswear** *n* vêtements *mpl* de sport; **sportswoman** (*irreg*) *n* sportive *f*; **sporty** *adj* sportif(-ive)

**spot** [spɔt] *n* tache *f*; (*dot: on pattern*) pois *m*; (*pimple*) bouton *m*; (*place*) endroit *m*, coin *m*; (*small amount*): **a ~ of** un peu de ▷ *vt* (*notice*) apercevoir,

repérer; **on the ~** sur place, sur les lieux; (*immediately*) sur le champ; **spotless** *adj* immaculé(e); **spotlight** *n* projecteur *m*; (*Aut*) phare *m* auxiliaire

**spouse** [spauz] *n* époux (épouse)

**sprain** [spreɪn] *n* entorse *f*, foulure *f* ▷ *vt*: **to ~ one's ankle** se fouler *or* se tordre la cheville

**sprang** [spræŋ] *pt of* **spring**

**sprawl** [sprɔ:l] *vi* s'étaler

**spray** [spreɪ] *n* jet *m* (en fines gouttelettes); (*from sea*) embruns *mpl*; (*aerosol*) vaporisateur *m*, bombe *f*; (*for garden*) pulvérisateur *m*; (*of flowers*) petit bouquet ▷ *vt* vaporiser, pulvériser; (*crops*) traiter

**spread** [spred] *n* (*distribution*) répartition *f*; (*Culin*) pâte *f* à tartiner; (*inf: meal*) festin *m* ▷ *vb* (*pt, pp* **~**) ▷ *vt* (*paste, contents*) étendre, étaler; (*rumour, disease*) répandre, propager; (*wealth*) répartir ▷ *vi* s'étendre; se répandre; se propager; (*stain*) s'étaler; **spread out** *vi* (*people*) se disperser; **spreadsheet** *n* (*Comput*) tableur *m*

**spree** [spri:] *n*: **to go on a ~** faire la fête

**spring** [sprɪŋ] *n* (*season*) printemps *m*; (*leap*) bond *m*, saut *m*; (*coiled metal*) ressort *m*; (*of water*) source *f* ▷ *vb* (*pt* **sprang**, *pp* **sprung**) ▷ *vi* bondir, sauter; **spring up** *vi* (*problem*) se présenter, surgir; (*plant, buildings*) surgir de terre; **spring onion** *n* (BRIT) ciboule *f*, cive *f*

**sprinkle** ['sprɪŋkl] *vt*: **to ~ water** *etc* **on**, **~ with water** *etc* asperger d'eau *etc*; **to ~ sugar** *etc* **on**, **~ with sugar** *etc* saupoudrer de sucre *etc*

**sprint** [sprɪnt] *n* sprint *m* ▷ *vi* courir à toute vitesse; (*Sport*) sprinter

**sprung** [sprʌŋ] *pp of* **spring**

**spun** [spʌn] *pt, pp of* **spin**

**spur** [spə:<sup>r</sup>] *n* éperon *m*; (*fig*) aiguillon *m* ▷ *vt* (*also:* **~ on**) éperonner; aiguillonner; **on the ~ of the moment** sous l'impulsion du moment

**spurt** [spə:t] *n* jet *m*; (*of blood*) jaillissement *m*; (*of energy*) regain *m*, sursaut *m* ▷ *vi* jaillir, gicler

**spy** [spaɪ] n espion(ne) ▷ vi: **to ~ on** espionner, épier ▷ vt (see) apercevoir

**sq.** abbr = **square**

**squabble** ['skwɒbl] vi se chamailler

**squad** [skwɒd] n (Mil, Police) escouade f, groupe m; (Football) contingent m

**squadron** ['skwɒdrn] n (Mil) escadron m; (Aviat, Naut) escadrille f

**squander** ['skwɒndəʳ] vt gaspiller, dilapider

**square** [skwɛəʳ] n carré m; (in town) place f ▷ adj carré(e) ▷ vt (arrange) régler; arranger; (Math) élever au carré; (reconcile) concilier; **all ~** quitte; à égalité; **a ~ meal** un repas convenable; **2 metres ~** (de) 2 mètres sur 2; **1 ~ metre** 1 mètre carré; **square root** n racine carrée

**squash** [skwɒʃ] n (BRIT: drink): **lemon/ orange ~** citronnade f/orangeade f; (Sport) squash m; (US: vegetable) courge f ▷ vt écraser

**squat** [skwɒt] adj petit(e) et épais(se), ramassé(e) ▷ vi (also: ~ **down**) s'accroupir; **squatter** n squatter m

**squeak** [skwiːk] vi (hinge, wheel) grincer; (mouse) pousser un petit cri

**squeal** [skwiːl] vi pousser un ou des cri(s) aigu(s) or perçant(s); (brakes) grincer

**squeeze** [skwiːz] n pression f ▷ vt presser; (hand, arm) serrer

**squid** [skwɪd] n calmar m

**squint** [skwɪnt] vi loucher

**squirm** [skwəːm] vi se tortiller

**squirrel** ['skwɪrəl] n écureuil m

**squirt** [skwəːt] vi jaillir, gicler ▷ vt faire gicler

**Sr** abbr = **senior**

**Sri Lanka** [srɪ'læŋkə] n Sri Lanka m

**St** abbr = **saint**; **street**

**stab** [stæb] n (with knife etc) coup m (de couteau etc); (of pain) lancée f; (inf: try): **to have a ~ at (doing) sth** s'essayer à (faire) qch ▷ vt poignarder

**stability** [stə'bɪlɪtɪ] n stabilité f

**stable** ['steɪbl] n écurie f ▷ adj stable

**stack** [stæk] n tas m, pile f ▷ vt empiler, entasser

**stadium** ['steɪdɪəm] n stade m

**staff** [stɑːf] n (work force) personnel m; (BRIT Scol: also: **teaching ~**) professeurs mpl, enseignants mpl, personnel enseignant ▷ vt pourvoir en personnel

**stag** [stæg] n cerf m

**stage** [steɪdʒ] n scène f; (platform) estrade f; (point) étape f, stade m; (profession): **the ~** le théâtre ▷ vt (play) monter, mettre en scène; (demonstration) organiser; **in ~s** par étapes, par degrés

> Be careful not to translate **stage** by the French word **stage**.

**stagger** ['stægəʳ] vi chanceler, tituber ▷ vt (person): amaze) stupéfier; (hours, holidays) étaler, échelonner; **staggering** adj (amazing) stupéfiant(e), renversant(e)

**stagnant** ['stægnənt] adj stagnant(e)

**stag night, stag party** n enterrement m de vie de garçon

**stain** [steɪn] n tache f; (colouring) colorant m ▷ vt tacher; (wood) teindre; **stained glass** n (decorative) verre coloré; (in church) vitraux mpl; **stainless steel** n inox m, acier m inoxydable

**staircase** ['stɛəkeɪs] n = **stairway**

**stairs** [stɛəz] npl escalier m

**stairway** ['stɛəweɪ] n escalier m

**stake** [steɪk] n pieu m, poteau m; (Comm: interest) intérêts mpl; (Betting) enjeu m ▷ vt risquer, jouer; (also: ~ **out**: area) marquer, délimiter; **to be at ~** être en jeu

**stale** [steɪl] adj (bread) rassis(e); (food) pas frais (fraîche); (beer) éventé(e); (smell) de renfermé; (air) confiné(e)

**stalk** [stɔːk] n tige f ▷ vt traquer

**stall** [stɔːl] n (BRIT: in street, market etc) éventaire m, étal m; (in stable) stalle f ▷ vt (Aut: car) caler; (fig: delay) retarder ▷ vi (Aut) caler; (fig) essayer de gagner du temps; **stalls** npl (BRIT: in cinema, theatre) orchestre m

**stamina** ['stæmɪnə] n vigueur f, endurance f

**stammer** ['stæmə'] n bégaiement m
▷ vi bégayer

**stamp** [stæmp] n timbre m; (also:
**rubber ~**) tampon m; (mark, also fig)
empreinte f; (on document) cachet
m ▷ vi (also: **~ one's foot**) taper du
pied ▷ vt (letter) timbrer; (with rubber
stamp) tamponner; **stamp out** vt (fire)
piétiner; (crime) éradiquer; (opposition)
éliminer; **stamped addressed
envelope** n (BRIT) enveloppe
affranchie pour la réponse

**stampede** [stæm'pi:d] n ruée f; (of
cattle) débandade f

**stance** [stæns] n position f

**stand** [stænd] n (position) position f;
(for taxis) station f (de taxis); (Comm)
étalage m, stand m; (Sport: also: **~s**)
tribune f; (also: **music ~**) pupitre m
▷ vb (pt, pp **stood**) ▷ vi être or se tenir
(debout); (rise) se lever, se mettre
debout; (be placed) se trouver; (remain:
offer etc) rester valable ▷ vt (place)
mettre, poser; (tolerate, withstand)
supporter; (treat, invite) offrir, payer;
**to make a ~** prendre position; **to ~
for parliament** (BRIT) se présenter
aux élections (comme candidat à la
députation); **I can't ~ him** je ne peux
pas le voir; **stand back** vi (move back)
reculer, s'écarter; **stand by** vi (be ready)
se tenir prêt(e) ▷ vt fus (opinion) s'en
tenir à; (person) ne pas abandonner,
soutenir; **stand down** vi (withdraw)
se retirer; **stand for** vt fus (signify)
représenter, signifier; (tolerate)
supporter, tolérer; **stand in for** vt fus
remplacer; **stand out** vi (be prominent)
ressortir; **stand up** vi (rise) se lever,
se mettre debout; **stand up for** vt fus
défendre; **stand up to** vt fus tenir tête
à, résister à

**standard** ['stændəd] n (norm) norme
f, étalon m; (level) niveau m (voulu);
(criterion) critère m; (flag) étendard m
▷ adj (size etc) ordinaire, normal(e);
(model, feature) standard inv; (practice)
courant(e); (text) de base; **standards**

npl (morals) morale f, principes mpl;
**standard of living** n niveau m de vie

**stand-by ticket** n (Aviat) billet m
stand-by

**standing** ['stændɪŋ] adj debout
inv; (permanent) permanent(e) ▷ n
réputation f, rang m, standing m; **of
many years' ~** qui dure or existe depuis
longtemps; **standing order** n (BRIT:
at bank) virement m automatique,
prélèvement m bancaire

**stand: standpoint** n point m de vue;
**standstill** n: **at a standstill** à l'arrêt;
(fig) au point mort; **to come to a
standstill** s'immobiliser, s'arrêter

**stank** [stæŋk] pt of **stink**

**staple** ['steɪpl] n (for papers) agrafe f
▷ adj (food, crop, industry etc) de base,
principal(e) ▷ vt agrafer

**star** [stɑ:'] n étoile f; (celebrity) vedette f
▷ vt (Cine) avoir pour vedette; **stars** npl:
**the ~s** (Astrology) l'horoscope m

**starboard** ['stɑ:bəd] n tribord m

**starch** [stɑ:tʃ] n amidon m; (in food)
fécule f

**stardom** ['stɑ:dəm] n célébrité f

**stare** [steə'] n regard m fixe ▷ vi: **to ~ at**
regarder fixement

**stark** [stɑ:k] adj (bleak) désolé(e),
morne ▷ adv: **~ naked** complètement
nu(e)

**start** [stɑ:t] n commencement m,
début m; (of race) départ m; (sudden
movement) sursaut m; (advantage)
avance f, avantage m ▷ vt commencer;
(cause: fight) déclencher; (rumour)
donner naissance à; (fashion) lancer;
(found: business, newspaper) lancer, créer;
(engine) mettre en marche ▷ vi (begin)
commencer; (begin journey) partir, se
mettre en route; (jump) sursauter;
**when does the film ~?** à quelle heure
est-ce que le film commence?; **to ~
doing** or **to do sth** se mettre à faire qch;
**start off** vi commencer; (leave) partir;
**start out** vi (begin) commencer; (set
out) partir; **start up** vi commencer;
(car) démarrer ▷ vt (fight) déclencher;

(*business*) créer; (*car*) mettre en marche;
**starter** *n* (*Aut*) démarreur *m*; (*Sport:
official*) starter *m*; (*BRIT Culin*) entrée *f*;
**starting point** *n* point *m* de départ
**startle** ['stɑːtl] *vt* faire sursauter;
donner un choc à; **startling** *adj*
surprenant(e), saisissant(e)
**starvation** [stɑːˈveɪʃən] *n* faim *f*,
famine *f*
**starve** [stɑːv] *vi* mourir de faim ▷ *vt*
laisser mourir de faim
**state** [steɪt] *n* état *m*; (*Pol*) État ▷ *vt*
(*declare*) déclarer, affirmer; (*specify*)
indiquer, spécifier; **States** *npl*: **the
S~s** les États-Unis; **to be in a ~** être
dans tous ses états; **stately home**
*n* manoir *m or* château *m* (*ouvert au
public*); **statement** *n* déclaration *f*;
(*Law*) déposition *f*; **state school** *n*
école publique; **statesman** (*irreg*) *n*
homme *m* d'État
**static** ['stætɪk] *n* (*Radio*) parasites
*mpl*; (*also*: **~ electricity**) électricité *f*
statique ▷ *adj* statique
**station** ['steɪʃən] *n* gare *f*; (*also*: **police
~**) poste *m or* commissariat *m* (de
police) ▷ *vt* placer, poster
**stationary** ['steɪʃnərɪ] *adj* à l'arrêt,
immobile
**stationer's (shop)** *n* (*BRIT*)
papeterie *f*
**stationery** ['steɪʃnərɪ] *n* papier *m* à
lettres, petit matériel de bureau
**station wagon** *n* (*US*) break *m*
**statistic** [stəˈtɪstɪk] *n* statistique *f*;
**statistics** *n* (*science*) statistique *f*
**statue** ['stætjuː] *n* statue *f*
**stature** ['stætʃər] *n* stature *f*; (*fig*)
envergure *f*
**status** ['steɪtəs] *n* position *f*, situation
*f*; (*prestige*) prestige *m*; (*Admin, official
position*) statut *m*; **status quo** [-'kwəʊ]
*n*: **the status quo** le statu quo
**statutory** ['stætjutrɪ] *adj* statutaire,
prévu(e) par un article de loi
**staunch** [stɔːntʃ] *adj* sûr(e), loyal(e)
**stay** [steɪ] *n* (*period of time*) séjour *m* ▷ *vi*
rester; (*reside*) loger; (*spend some time*)

séjourner; **to ~ put** ne pas bouger;
**to ~ the night** passer la nuit; **stay
away** *vi* (*from person, building*) ne pas
s'approcher; (*from event*) ne pas venir;
**stay behind** *vi* rester en arrière; **stay
in** *vi* (*at home*) rester à la maison; **stay
on** *vi* rester; **stay out** *vi* (*of house*) ne
pas rentrer; (*strikers*) rester en grève;
**stay up** *vi* (*at night*) ne pas se coucher
**steadily** ['stedɪlɪ] *adv* (*regularly*)
progressivement; (*firmly*) fermement;
(*walk*) d'un pas ferme; (*fixedly: look*) sans
détourner les yeux
**steady** ['stedɪ] *adj* stable, solide, ferme;
(*regular*) constant(e), régulier(-ière);
(*person*) calme, pondéré(e) ▷ *vt*
assurer, stabiliser; (*nerves*) calmer; **a ~
boyfriend** un petit ami
**steak** [steɪk] *n* (*meat*) bifteck *m*, steak
*m*; (*fish, pork*) tranche *f*
**steal** (*pt* **stole**, *pp* **stolen**) [stiːl, stəʊl,
'stəʊln] *vt, vi* voler; (*move*) se faufiler,
se déplacer furtivement; **my wallet
has been stolen** on m'a volé mon
portefeuille
**steam** [stiːm] *n* vapeur *f* ▷ *vt* (*Culin*)
cuire à la vapeur ▷ *vi* fumer; **steam up**
*vi* (*window*) se couvrir de buée; **to get
~ed up about sth** (*fig: inf*) s'exciter à
propos de qch; **steamy** *adj* humide;
(*window*) embué(e); (*sexy*) torride
**steel** [stiːl] *n* acier *m* ▷ *cpd* d'acier
**steep** [stiːp] *adj* raide, escarpé(e); (*price*)
très élevé(e), excessif(-ive) ▷ *vt* (faire)
tremper
**steeple** ['stiːpl] *n* clocher *m*
**steer** [stɪər] *vt* diriger; (*boat*) gouverner;
(*lead: person*) guider, conduire ▷ *vi*
tenir le gouvernail; **steering** *n* (*Aut*)
conduite *f*; **steering wheel** *n* volant *m*
**stem** [stem] *n* (*of plant*) tige *f*; (*of glass*)
pied *m* ▷ *vt* contenir, endiguer; (*attack,
spread of disease*) juguler
**step** [step] *n* pas *m*; (*stair*) marche *f*;
(*action*) mesure *f*, disposition *f* ▷ *vi*:
**to ~ forward/back** faire un pas en
avant/arrière, avancer/reculer; **steps**
*npl* (*BRIT*) = **stepladder**; **to be in/out of**

~ **(with)** (fig) aller dans le sens (de)/être déphasé(e) (par rapport à); **step down** vi (fig) se retirer, se désister; **step in** vi (fig) intervenir; **step up** vt (production, sales) augmenter; (campaign, efforts) intensifier; **stepbrother** n demi-frère m; **stepchild** (pl **~ren**) n beau-fils m, belle-fille f; **stepdaughter** n belle-fille f; **stepfather** n beau-père m; **stepladder** n (BRIT) escabeau m; **stepmother** n belle-mère f; **stepsister** n demi-sœur f; **stepson** n beau-fils m

**stereo** ['stɛriəu] n (sound) stéréo f; (hi-fi) chaîne f stéréo ▷ adj (also: **~phonic**) stéréo(phonique)

**stereotype** ['stɪəriətaip] n stéréotype m ▷ vt stéréotyper

**sterile** ['stɛraɪl] adj stérile; **sterilize** ['stɛrɪlaɪz] vt stériliser

**sterling** ['stə:lɪŋ] adj (silver) de bon aloi, fin(e) ▷ n (currency) livre f sterling inv

**stern** [stə:n] adj sévère ▷ n (Naut) arrière m, poupe f

**steroid** ['stɪərɔɪd] n stéroïde m

**stew** [stju:] n ragoût m ▷ vt, vi cuire à la casserole

**steward** ['stju:əd] n (Aviat, Naut, Rail) steward m; **stewardess** n hôtesse f

**stick** [stɪk] n bâton m; (for walking) canne f; (of chalk etc) morceau m ▷ vb (pt, pp **stuck**) ▷ vt (glue) coller; (thrust): **to ~ sth into** piquer or planter or enfoncer qch dans; (inf: put) mettre, fourrer; (: tolerate) supporter ▷ vi (adhere) tenir, coller; (remain) rester; (get jammed: door, lift) se bloquer; **stick out** vi dépasser, sortir; **stick up** vi dépasser, sortir; **stick up for** vt fus défendre; **sticker** n auto-collant m; **sticking plaster** n sparadrap m, pansement m adhésif; **stick insect** n phasme m; **stick shift** n (us Aut) levier m de vitesses

**sticky** ['stɪkɪ] adj poisseux(-euse); (label) adhésif(-ive); (fig: situation) délicat(e)

**stiff** [stɪf] adj (gen) raide, rigide; (door, brush) dur(e); (difficult) difficile, ardu(e);

(cold) froid(e), distant(e); (strong, high) fort(e), élevé(e) ▷ adv: **to be bored/scared/frozen ~** s'ennuyer à mourir/être mort(e) de peur/froid

**stifling** ['staiflɪŋ] adj (heat) suffocant(e)

**stigma** ['stɪgmə] n stigmate m

**stiletto** [stɪ'lɛtəu] n (BRIT: also: **~ heel**) talon m aiguille

**still** [stɪl] adj immobile ▷ adv (up to this time) encore, toujours; (even) encore; (nonetheless) quand même, tout de même

**stimulate** ['stɪmjuleɪt] vt stimuler

**stimulus** (pl **stimuli**) ['stɪmjuləs, 'stɪmjulaɪ] n stimulant m; (Biol, Psych) stimulus m

**sting** [stɪŋ] n piqûre f; (organ) dard m ▷ vt, vi (pt, pp **stung**) piquer

**stink** [stɪŋk] n puanteur f ▷ vi (pt **stank**, pp **stunk**) puer, empester

**stir** [stə:ʳ] n agitation f, sensation f ▷ vt remuer ▷ vi remuer, bouger; **stir up** vt (trouble) fomenter, provoquer; **stir-fry** vt faire sauter ▷ n: **vegetable stir-fry** légumes sautés à la poêle

**stitch** [stɪtʃ] n (Sewing) point m; (Knitting) maille f; (Med) point de suture; (pain) point de côté ▷ vt coudre, piquer; (Med) suturer

**stock** [stɔk] n réserve f, provision f; (Comm) stock m; (Agr) cheptel m, bétail m; (Culin) bouillon m; (Finance) valeurs fpl, titres mpl; (descent, origin) souche f ▷ adj (fig: reply etc) classique ▷ vt (have in stock) avoir, vendre; **in ~** en stock, en magasin; **out of ~** épuisé(e); **to take ~** (fig) faire le point; **~s and shares** valeurs (mobilières), titres; **stockbroker** ['stɔkbrəukəʳ] n agent m de change; **stock cube** n (BRIT Culin) bouillon-cube m; **stock exchange** n Bourse f (des valeurs); **stockholder** ['stɔkhəuldəʳ] n (US) actionnaire m/f

**stocking** ['stɔkɪŋ] n bas m

**stock market** n Bourse f, marché financier

**stole** [stəul] pt of **steal** ▷ n étole f

**stolen** ['stəuln] pp of **steal**

**stomach** ['stʌmək] n estomac m; (abdomen) ventre m ▷ vt supporter, digérer; **stomachache** n mal m à l'estomac or au ventre

**stone** [stəʊn] n pierre f; (pebble) caillou m, galet m; (in fruit) noyau m; (Med) calcul m; (= weight): 6.348 kg; 14 pounds ▷ cpd de or en pierre ▷ vt (person) lancer des pierres sur, lapider; (fruit) dénoyauter

**stood** [stʊd] pt, pp of **stand**

**stool** [stuːl] n tabouret m

**stoop** [stuːp] vi (also: **have a ~**) être voûté(e); (also: **~ down**: bend) se baisser, se courber

**stop** [stɒp] n arrêt m; (in punctuation) point m ▷ vt arrêter; (break off) interrompre; (also: **put a ~ to**) mettre fin à; (prevent) empêcher ▷ vi s'arrêter; (rain, noise etc) cesser, s'arrêter; **to ~ doing sth** cesser or arrêter de faire qch; **to ~ sb (from) doing sth** empêcher qn de faire qch; **~ it!** arrête!; **stop by** vi s'arrêter (au passage); **stop off** vi faire une courte halte; **stopover** n halte f; (Aviat) escale f; **stoppage** n (strike) arrêt m de travail; (obstruction) obstruction f

**storage** ['stɔːrɪdʒ] n emmagasinage m

**store** [stɔːʳ] n (stock) provision f, réserve f; (depot) entrepôt m; (BRIT: large shop) grand magasin; (US: shop) magasin m ▷ vt emmagasiner; (information) enregistrer; **stores** npl (food) provisions f; **who knows what is in ~ for us?** qui sait ce que l'avenir nous réserve or ce qui nous attend?; **storekeeper** n (US) commerçant(e)

**storey** (US **story**) ['stɔːrɪ] n étage m

**storm** [stɔːm] n tempête f; (thunderstorm) orage m ▷ vi (fig) fulminer ▷ vt prendre d'assaut; **stormy** adj orageux(-euse)

**story** ['stɔːrɪ] n histoire f; (Press: article) article m; (US) = **storey**

**stout** [staʊt] adj (strong) solide; (fat) gros(se), corpulent(e) ▷ n bière brune

**stove** [stəʊv] n (for cooking) fourneau m;

(: small) réchaud m; (for heating) poêle m

**straight** [streɪt] adj droit(e); (hair) raide; (frank) honnête, franc (franche); (simple) simple ▷ adv (tout) droit; (drink) sec, sans eau; **to put** or **get ~** mettre en ordre, mettre de l'ordre dans; (fig) mettre au clair; **~ away, ~ off** (at once) tout de suite; **straighten** vt ajuster; (bed) arranger; **straighten out** vt (fig) débrouiller; **straighten up** vi (stand up) se redresser; **straightforward** adj simple; (frank) honnête, direct(e)

**strain** [streɪn] n (Tech) tension f; pression f; (physical) effort m; (mental) tension (nerveuse); (Med) entorse f; (breed: of plants) variété f; (: of animals) race f ▷ vt (fig: resources etc) mettre à rude épreuve, grever; (hurt: back etc) se faire mal à; (vegetables) égoutter; **strains** npl (Mus) accords mpl, accents mpl; **strained** adj (muscle) froissé(e); (laugh etc) forcé(e), contraint(e); (relations) tendu(e); **strainer** n passoire f

**strait** [streɪt] n (Geo) détroit m; **straits** npl: **to be in dire ~s** (fig) avoir de sérieux ennuis

**strand** [strænd] n (of thread) fil m, brin m; (of rope) toron m; (of hair) mèche f ▷ vt (boat) échouer; **stranded** adj en rade, en plan

**strange** [streɪndʒ] adj (not known) inconnu(e); (odd) étrange, bizarre; **strangely** adv étrangement, bizarrement; see also **enough**; **stranger** n (unknown) inconnu(e); (from somewhere else) étranger(-ère)

**strangle** ['stræŋgl] vt étrangler

**strap** [stræp] n lanière f, courroie f, sangle f; (of slip, dress) bretelle f

**strategic** [strə'tiːdʒɪk] adj stratégique

**strategy** ['strætɪdʒɪ] n stratégie f

**straw** [strɔː] n paille f; **that's the last ~!** ça c'est le comble!

**strawberry** ['strɔːbərɪ] n fraise f

**stray** [streɪ] adj (animal) perdu(e), errant(e); (scattered) isolé(e) ▷ vi s'égarer; **~ bullet** balle perdue

**streak** [striːk] n bande f, filet m; (in hair) raie f ▷ vt zébrer, strier

**stream** [striːm] n (brook) ruisseau m; (current) courant m, flot m; (of people) défilé ininterrompu, flot ▷ vt (Scol) répartir par niveau ▷ vi ruisseler; **to ~ in/out** entrer/sortir à flots

**street** [striːt] n rue f; **streetcar** n (us) tramway m; **street light** n réverbère m; **street map, street plan** n plan m des rues

**strength** [strεŋθ] n force f; (of girder, knot etc) solidité f; **strengthen** vt renforcer; (muscle) fortifier; (building, Econ) consolider

**strenuous** ['strεnjʊəs] adj vigoureux(-euse), énergique; (tiring) ardu(e), fatigant(e)

**stress** [strεs] n (force, pressure) pression f; (mental strain) tension (nerveuse), stress m; (accent) accent m; (emphasis) insistance f ▷ vt insister sur, souligner; (syllable) accentuer; **stressed** adj (tense) stressé(e); (syllable) accentué(e); **stressful** adj (job) stressant(e)

**stretch** [strεtʃ] n (of sand etc) étendue f ▷ vi (extend): (extend) s'étirer; **to ~ to or as far as** s'étendre jusqu'à ▷ vt tendre, étirer; (fig) pousser (au maximum); **at a ~** d'affilée; **stretch out** vi s'étendre ▷ vt (arm etc) allonger, tendre; (to spread) étendre

**stretcher** ['strεtʃər] n brancard m, civière f

**strict** [strɪkt] adj strict(e); **strictly** adv strictement

**stride** [straɪd] n grand pas, enjambée f ▷ vi (pt **strode**, pp **stridden**) marcher à grands pas

**strike** [straɪk] n grève f; (of oil etc) découverte f; (attack) raid m ▷ vb (pt, pp **struck**) ▷ vt frapper; (oil etc) trouver, découvrir; (make: agreement, deal) conclure ▷ vi faire grève; (attack) attaquer; (clock) sonner; **to go on or come out on ~** se mettre en grève, faire grève; **to ~ a match** frotter une allumette; **striker** n gréviste

m/f; (Sport) buteur m; **striking** adj frappant(e), saisissant(e); (attractive) éblouissant(e)

**string** [strɪŋ] n ficelle f, fil m; (row: of beads) rang m; (Mus) corde f ▷ vt (pt, pp **strung**): **to ~ out** échelonner; **to ~ together** enchaîner; **the strings** npl (Mus) les instruments mpl à cordes; **to pull ~s** (fig) faire jouer le piston

**strip** [strɪp] n bande f; (Sport) tenue f ▷ vt (undress) déshabiller; (paint) décaper; (fig) dégarnir, dépouiller; (also: ~ **down**: machine) démonter ▷ vi se déshabiller; **strip off** vt (paint etc) décaper ▷ vi (person) se déshabiller

**stripe** [straɪp] n raie f, rayure f; (Mil) galon m; **striped** adj rayé(e), à rayures

**stripper** ['strɪpər] n strip-teaseuse f

**strip-search** ['strɪpsəːtʃ] vt: **to ~ sb** fouiller qn (en le faisant se déshabiller)

**strive** (pt **strove**, pp **~n**) [straɪv, strəʊv, 'strɪvn] vi: **to ~ to do/for sth** s'efforcer de faire/d'obtenir qch

**strode** [strəʊd] pt of **stride**

**stroke** [strəʊk] n coup m; (Med) attaque f; (Swimming: style) (sorte f de) nage f ▷ vt caresser; **at a ~** d'un (seul) coup

**stroll** [strəʊl] n petite promenade ▷ vi flâner, se promener nonchalamment; **stroller** n (us: for child) poussette f

**strong** [strɔŋ] adj (gen) fort(e); (healthy) vigoureux(-euse); (heart, nerves) solide; **they are 50 ~** ils sont au nombre de 50; **stronghold** n forteresse f, fort m; (fig) bastion m; **strongly** adv fortement, avec force; vigoureusement; solidement

**strove** [strəʊv] pt of **strive**

**struck** [strʌk] pt, pp of **strike**

**structure** ['strʌktʃər] n structure f; (building) construction f

**struggle** ['strʌgl] n lutte f ▷ vi lutter, se battre

**strung** [strʌŋ] pt, pp of **string**

**stub** [stʌb] n (of cigarette) bout m, mégot m; (of ticket etc) talon m ▷ vt: **to ~ one's toe (on sth)** se heurter le doigt de pied (contre qch); **stub out** vt écraser

**stubble** ['stʌbl] n chaume m; (on chin) barbe f de plusieurs jours

**stubborn** ['stʌbən] adj têtu(e), obstiné(e), opiniâtre

**stuck** [stʌk] pt, pp of **stick** ▷ adj (jammed) bloqué(e), coincé(e)

**stud** [stʌd] n (on boots etc) clou m; (collar stud) bouton m de col; (earring) petite boucle d'oreille; (of horses: also: ~ **farm**) écurie f, haras m; (also: ~ **horse**) étalon m ▷ vt (fig): **~ded with** parsemé(e) or criblé(e) de

**student** ['stju:dənt] n étudiant(e) ▷ adj (life) estudiantin(e), étudiant(e), d'étudiant; (residence, restaurant) universitaire; (loan, movement) étudiant; **student driver** n (US) (conducteur(-trice)) débutant(e); **students' union** n (BRIT: association) ≈ union f des étudiants; (: building) ≈ foyer m des étudiants

**studio** ['stju:dɪəu] n studio m, atelier m; (TV etc) studio; **studio flat** (US **studio apartment**) n studio m

**study** ['stʌdɪ] n étude f; (room) bureau m ▷ vt étudier; (examine) examiner ▷ vi étudier, faire ses études

**stuff** [stʌf] n (gen) chose(s) f(pl), truc m; (belongings) affaires fpl, trucs; (substance) substance f ▷ vt rembourrer; (Culin) farcir; (inf: push) fourrer; **stuffing** n bourre f, rembourrage m; (Culin) farce f; **stuffy** adj (room) mal ventilé(e) or aéré(e); (ideas) vieux jeu inv

**stumble** ['stʌmbl] vi trébucher; **to ~ across** or **on** (fig) tomber sur

**stump** [stʌmp] n souche f; (of limb) moignon m ▷ vt: **to be ~ed** sécher, ne pas savoir que répondre

**stun** [stʌn] vt (blow) étourdir; (news) abasourdir, stupéfier

**stung** [stʌŋ] pt, pp of **sting**

**stunk** [stʌŋk] pp of **stink**

**stunned** [stʌnd] adj assommé(e); (fig) sidéré(e)

**stunning** ['stʌnɪŋ] adj (beautiful) étourdissant(e); (news etc) stupéfiant(e)

**stunt** [stʌnt] n (in film) cascade f, acrobatie f; (publicity) truc m publicitaire ▷ vt retarder, arrêter

**stupid** ['stju:pɪd] adj stupide, bête; **stupidity** [stju:'pɪdɪtɪ] n stupidité f, bêtise f

**sturdy** ['stə:dɪ] adj (person, plant) robuste, vigoureux(-euse); (object) solide

**stutter** ['stʌtər] n bégaiement m ▷ vi bégayer

**style** [staɪl] n style m; (distinction) allure f, cachet m, style; (design) modèle m; **stylish** adj élégant(e), chic inv; **stylist** n (hair stylist) coiffeur(-euse)

**sub...** [sʌb] prefix sub..., sous-; **subconscious** adj subconscient(e)

**subdued** [səb'dju:d] adj (light) tamisé(e); (person) qui a perdu de son entrain

**subject** n ['sʌbdʒɪkt] sujet m; (Scol) matière f ▷ vt [səb'dʒɛkt]: **to ~ to** soumettre à; **to be ~ to** (law) être soumis(e) à; **subjective** [səb'dʒɛktɪv] adj subjectif(-ive); **subject matter** n (content) contenu m

**subjunctive** [səb'dʒʌŋktɪv] n subjonctif m

**submarine** [sʌbmə'ri:n] n sous-marin m

**submission** [səb'mɪʃən] n soumission f

**submit** [səb'mɪt] vt soumettre ▷ vi soumettre

**subordinate** [sə'bɔ:dɪnət] adj (junior) subalterne; (Grammar) subordonné(e) ▷ n subordonné(e)

**subscribe** [səb'skraɪb] vi cotiser; **to ~ to** (opinion, fund) souscrire à; (newspaper) s'abonner à; être abonné(e) à

**subscription** [səb'skrɪpʃən] n (to magazine etc) abonnement m

**subsequent** ['sʌbsɪkwənt] adj ultérieur(e), suivant(e); **subsequently** adv par la suite

**subside** [səb'saɪd] vi (land) s'affaisser;

(*flood*) baisser; (*wind, feelings*) tomber
**subsidiary** [səb'sɪdɪərɪ] *adj*
subsidiaire; accessoire; (*BRIT Scol: subject*) complémentaire ▷ *n* filiale *f*
**subsidize** ['sʌbsɪdaɪz] *vt*
subventionner
**subsidy** ['sʌbsɪdɪ] *n* subvention *f*
**substance** ['sʌbstəns] *n* substance *f*
**substantial** [səb'stænʃl] *adj*
substantiel(le); (*fig*) important(e)
**substitute** ['sʌbstɪtjuːt] *n* (*person*)
remplaçant(e); (*thing*) succédané *m*
▷ *vt*: **to ~ sth/sb for** substituer qch/qn
à, remplacer par qch/qn; **substitution**
*n* substitution *f*
**subtitles** ['sʌbtaɪtlz] *npl* (*Cine*) sous-titres *mpl*
**subtle** ['sʌtl] *adj* subtil(e)
**subtract** [səb'trækt] *vt* soustraire,
retrancher
**suburb** ['sʌbəːb] *n* faubourg *m*; **the ~s** la
banlieue; **suburban** [sə'bəːbən] *adj* de
banlieue, suburbain(e)
**subway** ['sʌbweɪ] *n* (*BRIT: underpass*)
passage souterrain; (*US: railway*)
métro *m*
**succeed** [sək'siːd] *vi* réussir ▷ *vt*
succéder à; **to ~ in doing** réussir à faire
**success** [sək'sɛs] *n* succès *m*; réussite *f*;
**successful** *adj* (*business*) prospère,
qui réussit; (*attempt*) couronné(e) de
succès; **to be successful (in doing)**
réussir (à faire); **successfully** *adv*
avec succès
**succession** [sək'sɛʃən] *n* succession *f*
**successive** [sək'sɛsɪv] *adj*
successif(-ive)
**successor** [sək'sɛsər] *n* successeur *m*
**succumb** [sə'kʌm] *vi* succomber
**such** [sʌtʃ] *adj* tel (telle); (*of that kind*):
**~ a book** un livre de ce genre *or* pareil,
un tel livre; (*so much*): **~ courage** un
tel courage ▷ *adv* si; **~ a long trip** un
si long voyage; **~ a lot of** tellement
*or* tant de; **~ as** (*like*) tel (telle) que,
comme; **as ~** *adv* en tant que tel (telle),
à proprement parler; **such-and-such**
*adj* tel ou tel (telle ou telle)

**suck** [sʌk] *vt* sucer; (*breast, bottle*) téter
**Sudan** [su'dɑːn] *n* Soudan *m*
**sudden** ['sʌdn] *adj* soudain(e),
subit(e); **all of a ~** soudain, tout à coup;
**suddenly** *adv* brusquement, tout à
coup, soudain
**sue** [suː] *vt* poursuivre en justice,
intenter un procès à
**suede** [sweɪd] *n* daim *m*, cuir suédé
**suffer** ['sʌfər] *vt* souffrir, subir; (*bear*)
tolérer, supporter, subir ▷ *vi* souffrir;
**to ~ from** (*illness*) souffrir de, avoir;
**suffering** *n* souffrance(s) *f(pl)*
**suffice** [sə'faɪs] *vi* suffire
**sufficient** [sə'fɪʃənt] *adj* suffisant(e)
**suffocate** ['sʌfəkeɪt] *vi* suffoquer;
étouffer
**sugar** ['ʃugər] *n* sucre *m* ▷ *vt* sucrer
**suggest** [sə'dʒɛst] *vt* suggérer,
proposer; (*indicate*) sembler
indiquer; **suggestion** [sə'dʒɛstʃən] *n*
suggestion *f*
**suicide** ['suɪsaɪd] *n* suicide *m*; **~
bombing** attentat *m* suicide; *see also*
**commit**; **suicide bomber** *n* kamikaze
*m/f*
**suit** [suːt] *n* (*man's*) costume *m*, complet
*m*; (*woman's*) tailleur *m*, ensemble *m*;
(*Cards*) couleur *f*; (*lawsuit*) procès *m*
▷ *vt* (*subj: clothes, hairstyle*) aller à; (*be
convenient for*) convenir à; (*adapt*): **to
~ sth to** adapter *or* approprier qch à;
**well ~ed** (*couple*) faits l'un pour l'autre,
très bien assortis; **suitable** *adj* qui
convient; approprié(e), adéquat(e);
**suitcase** *n* valise *f*
**suite** [swiːt] *n* (*of rooms, also Mus*) suite
*f*; (*furniture*): **bedroom/dining room ~**
(ensemble *m* de) chambre *f* à coucher/
salle *f* à manger; **a three-piece ~** un
salon (canapé et deux fauteuils)
**sulfur** ['sʌlfər] (*US*) *n* = **sulphur**
**sulk** [sʌlk] *vi* bouder
**sulphur** (*US* **sulfur**) ['sʌlfər] *n* soufre *m*
**sultana** [sʌl'tɑːnə] *n* (*fruit*) raisin (sec)
de Smyrne
**sum** [sʌm] *n* somme *f*; (*Scol etc*) calcul *m*;
**sum up** *vt* résumer ▷ *vi* résumer

**summarize** ['sʌməraɪz] vt résumer

**summary** ['sʌmərɪ] n résumé m

**summer** ['sʌmər] n été m ▷ cpd d'été, estival(e); **in (the) ~** en été, pendant l'été; **summer holidays** npl grandes vacances; **summertime** n (season) été m

**summit** ['sʌmɪt] n sommet m; (also: **~ conference**) (conférence f au) sommet m

**summon** ['sʌmən] vt appeler, convoquer; **to ~ a witness** citer or assigner un témoin

**Sun.** abbr (= Sunday) dim

**sun** [sʌn] n soleil m; **sunbathe** vi prendre un bain de soleil; **sunbed** n lit pliant; (with sun lamp) lit à ultra-violets; **sunblock** n écran m total; **sunburn** n coup m de soleil; **sunburned, sunburnt** adj bronzé(e), hâlé(e); (painfully) brûlé(e) par le soleil

**Sunday** ['sʌndɪ] n dimanche m

**sunflower** ['sʌnflauər] n tournesol m

**sung** [sʌŋ] pp of **sing**

**sunglasses** ['sʌnɡlɑːsɪz] npl lunettes fpl de soleil

**sunk** [sʌŋk] pp of **sink**

**sun**: **sunlight** n (lumière f du) soleil m; **sun lounger** n chaise longue; **sunny** adj ensoleillé(e); **it is sunny** il fait (du) soleil, il y a du soleil; **sunrise** n lever m du soleil; **sun roof** n (Aut) toit ouvrant; **sunscreen** n crème f solaire; **sunset** n coucher m du soleil; **sunshade** n (over table) parasol m; **sunshine** n (lumière f du) soleil m; **sunstroke** n insolation f, coup m de soleil; **suntan** n bronzage m; **suntan lotion** n lotion f or lait m solaire; **suntan oil** n huile f solaire

**super** ['suːpər] adj (inf) formidable

**superb** [suː'pəːb] adj superbe, magnifique

**superficial** [suːpə'fɪʃəl] adj superficiel(le)

**superintendent** [suːpərɪn'tɛndənt] n directeur(-trice); (Police) ≈ commissaire m

**superior** [su'pɪərɪər] adj supérieur(e); (smug) condescendant(e), méprisant(e) ▷ n supérieur(e)

**superlative** [su'pəːlətɪv] n (Ling) superlatif m

**supermarket** ['suːpəmɑːkɪt] n supermarché m

**supernatural** [suːpə'nætʃərəl] adj surnaturel(le) ▷ n: **the ~** le surnaturel

**superpower** ['suːpəpauər] n (Pol) superpuissance f

**superstition** [suːpə'stɪʃən] n superstition f

**superstitious** [suːpə'stɪʃəs] adj superstitieux(-euse)

**superstore** ['suːpəstɔːr] n (BRIT) hypermarché m, grande surface

**supervise** ['suːpəvaɪz] vt (children etc) surveiller; (organization, work) diriger; **supervision** [suːpə'vɪʒən] n surveillance f; (monitoring) contrôle m; (management) direction f; **supervisor** n surveillant(e); (in shop) chef m de rayon

**supper** ['sʌpər] n dîner m; (late) souper m

**supple** ['sʌpl] adj souple

**supplement** n ['sʌplɪmənt] supplément m ▷ vt [sʌplɪ'mɛnt] ajouter à, compléter

**supplier** [sə'plaɪər] n fournisseur m

**supply** [sə'plaɪ] vt (provide) fournir; (equip): **to ~ (with)** approvisionner or ravitailler (en); fournir (en) ▷ n provision f, réserve f; (supplying) approvisionnement m; **supplies** npl (food) vivres mpl; (Mil) subsistances fpl

**support** [sə'pɔːt] n (moral, financial etc) soutien m, appui m; (Tech) support m, soutien m ▷ vt soutenir, supporter; (financially) subvenir aux besoins de; (uphold) être pour, être partisan de, appuyer; (Sport: team) être pour; **supporter** n (Pol etc) partisan(e); (Sport) supporter m

**suppose** [sə'pəuz] vt, vi supposer; imaginer; **to be ~d to do/be** être censé(e) faire/être; **supposedly** [sə'pəuzɪdlɪ] adv soi-disant; **supposing** conj si, à supposer que + sub

**suppress** [sə'prɛs] vt (revolt, feeling) réprimer; (information) faire disparaître; (scandal, yawn) étouffer

**supreme** [su'pri:m] adj suprême

**surcharge** ['sə:tʃɑ:dʒ] n surcharge f

**sure** [ʃuəʳ] adj (gen) sûr(e); (definite, convinced) sûr, certain(e); ~! (of course) bien sûr!; ~ **enough** effectivement; **to make** ~ **of sth/that** s'assurer de qch/que, vérifier qch/que; **surely** adv sûrement; certainement

**surf** [sə:f] n (waves) ressac m ▷ vt: **to** ~ **the Net** surfer sur Internet, surfer sur le net

**surface** ['sə:fɪs] n surface f ▷ vt (road) poser un revêtement sur ▷ vi remonter à la surface; (fig) faire surface; **by** ~ **mail** par voie de terre; (by sea) par voie maritime

**surfboard** ['sə:fbɔ:d] n planche f de surf

**surfer** ['sə:fəʳ] n (in sea) surfeur(-euse); **web** or **net** ~ internaute m/f

**surfing** ['sə:fɪŋ] n surf m

**surge** [sə:dʒ] n (of emotion) vague f ▷ vi déferler

**surgeon** ['sə:dʒən] n chirurgien m

**surgery** ['sə:dʒərɪ] n chirurgie f; (BRIT: room) cabinet m (de consultation); (also: ~ **hours**) heures fpl de consultation

**surname** ['sə:neɪm] n nom m de famille

**surpass** [sə:'pɑ:s] vt surpasser, dépasser

**surplus** ['sə:pləs] n surplus m, excédent m ▷ adj en surplus, de trop; (Comm) excédentaire

**surprise** [sə'praɪz] n (gen) surprise f; (astonishment) étonnement m ▷ vt surprendre, étonner; **surprised** adj (look, smile) surpris(e), étonné(e); **to be surprised** être surpris; **surprising** adj surprenant(e), étonnant(e); **surprisingly** adv (easy, helpful) étonnamment, étrangement; **(somewhat) surprisingly, he agreed** curieusement, il a accepté

**surrender** [sə'rɛndəʳ] n reddition f, capitulation f ▷ vi se rendre, capituler

**surround** [sə'raund] vt entourer; (Mil etc) encercler; **surrounding** adj environnant(e); **surroundings** npl environs mpl, alentours mpl

**surveillance** [sə:'veɪləns] n surveillance f

**survey** n ['sə:veɪ] enquête f, étude f; (in house buying etc) inspection f, (rapport m d')expertise f; (of land) levé m ▷ vt [sə:'veɪ] (situation) passer en revue; (examine carefully) inspecter; (building) expertiser; (land) faire le levé de; (look at) embrasser du regard; **surveyor** n (of building) expert m; (of land) (arpenteur m) géomètre m

**survival** [sə'vaɪvl] n survie f

**survive** [sə'vaɪv] vi survivre; (custom etc) subsister ▷ vt (accident etc) survivre à, réchapper de; (person) survivre à; **survivor** n survivant(e)

**suspect** adj, n ['sʌspɛkt] suspect(e) ▷ vt [səs'pɛkt] soupçonner, suspecter

**suspend** [səs'pɛnd] vt suspendre; **suspended sentence** n (Law) condamnation f avec sursis; **suspenders** npl (BRIT) jarretelles fpl; (US) bretelles fpl

**suspense** [səs'pɛns] n attente f, incertitude f; (in film etc) suspense m; **to keep sb in** ~ tenir qn en suspens, laisser qn dans l'incertitude

**suspension** [səs'pɛnʃən] n (gen, Aut) suspension f; (of driving licence) retrait m provisoire; **suspension bridge** n pont suspendu

**suspicion** [səs'pɪʃən] n soupçon(s) m(pl); **suspicious** adj (suspecting) soupçonneux(-euse), méfiant(e); (causing suspicion) suspect(e)

**sustain** [səs'teɪn] vt soutenir; (subj: food) nourrir, donner des forces à; (damage) subir; (injury) recevoir

**SUV** n abbr (esp US: = sports utility vehicle) SUV m, véhicule m de loisirs

**swallow** ['swɔləu] n (bird) hirondelle f ▷ vt avaler; (fig: story) gober

**swam** [swæm] *pt of* **swim**

**swamp** [swɔmp] *n* marais *m*, marécage *m* ▷ *vt* submerger

**swan** [swɔn] *n* cygne *m*

**swap** [swɔp] *n* échange *m*, troc *m* ▷ *vt*: **to ~ (for)** échanger (contre), troquer (contre)

**swarm** [swɔ:m] *n* essaim *m* ▷ *vi* (*bees*) essaimer; (*people*) grouiller; **to be ~ing with** grouiller de

**sway** [sweɪ] *vi* se balancer, osciller ▷ *vt* (*influence*) influencer

**swear** [swɛə<sup>r</sup>] (*pt* **swore**, *pp* **sworn**) *vt, vi* jurer; **swear in** *vt* assermenter; **swearword** *n* gros mot, juron *m*

**sweat** [swɛt] *n* sueur *f*, transpiration *f* ▷ *vi* suer

**sweater** ['swɛtə<sup>r</sup>] *n* tricot *m*, pull *m*

**sweatshirt** ['swɛtʃə:t] *n* sweat-shirt *m*

**sweaty** ['swɛtɪ] *adj* en sueur, moite *or* mouillé(e) de sueur

**Swede** [swi:d] *n* Suédois(e)

**swede** [swi:d] *n* (*BRIT*) rutabaga *m*

**Sweden** ['swi:dn] *n* Suède *f*; **Swedish** ['swi:dɪʃ] *adj* suédois(e) ▷ *n* (*Ling*) suédois *m*

**sweep** [swi:p] *n* (*curve*) grande courbe; (*also*: **chimney ~**) ramoneur *m* ▷ *vb* (*pt, pp* **swept**) ▷ *vt* balayer; (*subj: current*) emporter

**sweet** [swi:t] *n* (*BRIT: pudding*) dessert *m*; (*candy*) bonbon *m* ▷ *adj* doux (douce); (*not savoury*) sucré(e); (*kind*) gentil(le); (*baby*) mignon(ne); **sweetcorn** *n* maïs doux; **sweetener** ['swi:tnə<sup>r</sup>] *n* (*Culin*) édulcorant *m*; **sweetheart** *n* amoureux(-euse); **sweetshop** *n* (*BRIT*) confiserie *f*

**swell** [swɛl] *n* (*of sea*) houle *f* ▷ *adj* (*US: inf: excellent*) chouette ▷ *vb* (*pt* **~ed**, *pp* **swollen** *or* **~ed**) ▷ *vt* (*increase*) grossir, augmenter ▷ *vi* (*increase*) grossir, augmenter; (*sound*) s'enfler; (*Med: also*: **~ up**) enfler; **swelling** *n* (*Med*) enflure *f*; (: *lump*) grosseur *f*

**swept** [swɛpt] *pt, pp of* **sweep**

**swerve** [swə:v] *vi* (*to avoid obstacle*) faire une embardée *or* un écart; (*off the*

*road*) dévier

**swift** [swɪft] *n* (*bird*) martinet *m* ▷ *adj* rapide, prompt(e)

**swim** [swɪm] *n*: **to go for a ~** aller nager *or* se baigner ▷ *vb* (*pt* **swam**, *pp* **swum**) ▷ *vi* nager; (*Sport*) faire de la natation; (*fig: head, room*) tourner ▷ *vt* traverser (à la nage); **to ~ a length** nager une longueur; **swimmer** *n* nageur(-euse); **swimming** *n* nage *f*, natation *f*; **swimming costume** *n* (*BRIT*) maillot *m* (de bain); **swimming pool** *n* piscine *f*; **swimming trunks** *npl* maillot *m* de bain; **swimsuit** *n* maillot *m* (de bain)

**swing** [swɪŋ] *n* (*in playground*) balançoire *f*; (*movement*) balancement *m*, oscillations *fpl*; (*change in opinion etc*) revirement *m* ▷ *vb* (*pt, pp* **swung**) ▷ *vt* balancer, faire osciller; (*also*: **~ round**) tourner, faire virer ▷ *vi* se balancer, osciller; (*also*: **~ round**) virer, tourner; **to be in full ~** battre son plein

**swipe card** [swaɪp-] *n* carte *f* magnétique

**swirl** [swə:l] *vi* tourbillonner, tournoyer

**Swiss** [swɪs] *adj* suisse ▷ *n* (*pl inv*) Suisse(-esse)

**switch** [swɪtʃ] *n* (*for light, radio etc*) bouton *m*; (*change*) changement *m*, revirement *m* ▷ *vt* (*change*) changer; **switch off** *vt* éteindre; (*engine, machine*) arrêter; **could you ~ off the light?** pouvez-vous éteindre la lumière?; **switch on** *vt* allumer; (*engine, machine*) mettre en marche; **switchboard** *n* (*Tel*) standard *m*

**Switzerland** ['swɪtsələnd] *n* Suisse *f*

**swivel** ['swɪvl] *vi* (*also*: **~ round**) pivoter, tourner

**swollen** ['swəulən] *pp of* **swell**

**swoop** [swu:p] *n* (*by police etc*) rafle *f*, descente *f* ▷ *vi* (*bird: also*: **~ down**) descendre en piqué, fondre

**swop** [swɔp] *n, vt* = **swap**

**sword** [sɔ:d] *n* épée *f*; **swordfish** *n* espadon *m*

**swore** [swɔ:<sup>r</sup>] *pt of* **swear**

**sworn** [swɔ:n] *pp of* **swear** ▷ *adj*

(*statement, evidence*) donné(e) sous serment; (*enemy*) juré(e)

**swum** [swʌm] *pp of* **swim**

**swung** [swʌŋ] *pt, pp of* **swing**

**syllable** ['sɪləbl] *n* syllabe *f*

**syllabus** ['sɪləbəs] *n* programme *m*

**symbol** ['sɪmbl] *n* symbole *m*; **symbolic(al)** [sɪm'bɒlɪk(l)] *adj* symbolique

**symmetrical** [sɪ'mɛtrɪkl] *adj* symétrique

**symmetry** ['sɪmɪtrɪ] *n* symétrie *f*

**sympathetic** [sɪmpə'θɛtɪk] *adj* (*showing pity*) compatissant(e); (*understanding*) bienveillant(e), compréhensif(-ive); **~ towards** bien disposé(e) envers

> Be careful not to translate *sympathetic* by the French word *sympathique*.

**sympathize** ['sɪmpəθaɪz] *vi*: **to ~ with sb** plaindre qn; (*in grief*) s'associer à la douleur de qn; **to ~ with sth** comprendre qch

**sympathy** ['sɪmpəθɪ] *n* (*pity*) compassion *f*

**symphony** ['sɪmfənɪ] *n* symphonie *f*

**symptom** ['sɪmptəm] *n* symptôme *m*; indice *m*

**synagogue** ['sɪnəgɒg] *n* synagogue *f*

**syndicate** ['sɪndɪkɪt] *n* syndicat *m*, coopérative *f*; (*Press*) agence *f* de presse

**syndrome** ['sɪndrəʊm] *n* syndrome *m*

**synonym** ['sɪnənɪm] *n* synonyme *m*

**synthetic** [sɪn'θɛtɪk] *adj* synthétique

**Syria** ['sɪrɪə] *n* Syrie *f*

**syringe** [sɪ'rɪndʒ] *n* seringue *f*

**syrup** ['sɪrəp] *n* sirop *m*; (BRIT: *also*: **golden ~**) mélasse raffinée

**system** ['sɪstəm] *n* système *m*; (*Anat*) organisme *m*; **systematic** [sɪstə'mætɪk] *adj* systématique; méthodique; **systems analyst** *n* analyste-programmeur *m/f*

# t

**ta** [tɑː] *excl* (BRIT *inf*) merci!

**tab** [tæb] *n* (*label*) étiquette *f*; (*on drinks can etc*) languette *f*; **to keep ~s on** (*fig*) surveiller

**table** ['teɪbl] *n* table *f* ▷ *vt* (BRIT: *motion etc*) présenter; **a ~ for 4, please** une table pour 4, s'il vous plaît; **to lay** or **set the ~** mettre le couvert or la table; **tablecloth** *n* nappe *f*; **table d'hôte** [tɑːbl'dəʊt] *adj* (*meal*) à prix fixe; **table lamp** *n* lampe décorative or de table; **tablemat** *n* (*for plate*) napperon *m*, set *m*; (*for hot dish*) dessous-de-plat *m inv*; **tablespoon** *n* cuiller *f* de service; (*also*: **tablespoonful**: *as measurement*) cuillerée *f* à soupe

**tablet** ['tæblɪt] *n* (*Med*) comprimé *m*; (*of stone*) plaque *f*

**table tennis** *n* ping-pong *m*, tennis *m* de table

**tabloid** ['tæblɔɪd] *n* (*newspaper*) quotidien *m* populaire

**taboo** [tə'buː] *adj*, *n* tabou (*m*)

**tack** [tæk] *n* (*nail*) petit clou *m*; (*fig*)

direction f ▷ vt (nail) clouer; (sew) bâtir ▷ vi (Naut) tirer un or des bord(s); **to ~ sth on to (the end of) sth** (of letter, book) rajouter qch à la fin de qch

**tackle** ['tækl] n matériel m, équipement m; (for lifting) appareil m de levage; (Football, Rugby) plaquage m ▷ vt (difficulty, animal, burglar) s'attaquer à; (person: challenge) s'expliquer avec; (Football, Rugby) plaquer

**tacky** ['tækɪ] adj collant(e); (paint) pas sec (sèche); (pej: poor-quality) minable; (: showing bad taste) ringard(e)

**tact** [tækt] n tact m; **tactful** adj plein(e) de tact

**tactics** ['tæktɪks] npl tactique f

**tactless** ['tæktlɪs] adj qui manque de tact

**tadpole** ['tædpəul] n têtard m

**taffy** ['tæfɪ] n (us) (bonbon m au) caramel m

**tag** [tæg] n étiquette f

**tail** [teɪl] n queue f; (of shirt) pan m ▷ vt (follow) suivre, filer; **tails** npl (suit) habit m; see also **head**

**tailor** ['teɪlə'] n tailleur m (artisan)

**Taiwan** ['taɪ'wɑːn] n Taïwan (no article); **Taiwanese** [taɪwə'niːz] adj taïwanais(e) ▷ n inv Taïwanais(e)

**take** [teɪk] vb (pt **took**, pp **~n**) ▷ vt prendre; (gain: prize) remporter; (require: effort, courage) demander; (tolerate) accepter, supporter; (hold: passengers etc) contenir; (accompany) emmener, accompagner; (bring, carry) apporter, emporter; (exam) passer, se présenter à; **to ~ sth from** (drawer etc) prendre qch dans; (person) prendre qch à; **I ~ it that** je suppose que; **to be ~n ill** tomber malade; **it won't ~ long** ça ne prendra pas longtemps; **I was quite ~n with her/it** elle/cela m'a beaucoup plu; **take after** vt fus ressembler à; **take apart** vt démonter; **take away** vt (carry off) emporter; (remove) enlever; (subtract) soustraire; **take back** vt (return) rendre, rapporter; (one's words) retirer; **take down** vt

(building) démolir; (letter etc) prendre, écrire; **take in** vt (deceive) tromper, rouler; (understand) comprendre, saisir; (include) couvrir, inclure; (lodger) prendre; (dress, waistband) reprendre; **take off** vi (Aviat) décoller ▷ vt (remove) enlever; **take on** vt (work) accepter, se charger de; (employee) prendre, embaucher; (opponent) accepter de se battre contre; **take out** vt sortir; (remove) enlever; (invite) sortir avec; **to ~ sth out of** (out of drawer etc) prendre qch dans; **to ~ sb out to a restaurant** emmener qn au restaurant; **take over** vt (business) reprendre ▷ vi: **to ~ over from sb** prendre la relève de qn; **take up** vt (one's story) reprendre; (dress) raccourcir; (occupy: time, space) prendre, occuper; (engage in: hobby etc) se mettre à; (accept: offer, challenge) accepter; **takeaway** (BRIT) adj (food) à emporter ▷ n (shop, restaurant) ≈ magasin m qui vend des plats à emporter; **taken** pp of **take**; **is this seat taken?** la place est prise?; **takeoff** n (Aviat) décollage m; **takeout** adj, n (us) = **takeaway**; **takeover** n (Comm) rachat m; **takings** npl (Comm) recette f

**talc** [tælk] n (also: **~um powder**) talc m

**tale** [teɪl] n (story) conte m, histoire f; (account) récit m; **to tell ~s** (fig) rapporter

**talent** ['tælnt] n talent m, don m; **talented** adj doué(e), plein(e) de talent

**talk** [tɔːk] n (a speech) causerie f, exposé m; (conversation) discussion f; (interview) entretien m; (gossip) racontars mpl (pej) ▷ vi parler; (chatter) bavarder; **talks** npl (Pol etc) entretiens mpl; **to ~ about** parler de; **to ~ sb out of/into doing** persuader qn de ne pas faire/de faire; **to ~ shop** parler métier or affaires; **talk over** vt discuter (de); **talk show** n (TV, Radio) émission-débat f

**tall** [tɔːl] adj (person) grand(e); (building, tree) haut(e); **to be 6 feet ~** ≈ mesurer 1 mètre 80

**tambourine** [tæmbə'riːn] n

tambourin m

**tame** [teɪm] adj apprivoisé(e); (fig: story, style) insipide

**tamper** ['tæmpəʳ] vi: **to ~ with** toucher à (en cachette ou sans permission)

**tampon** ['tæmpən] n tampon m hygiénique or périodique

**tan** [tæn] n (also: **sun~**) bronzage m ▷ vt, vi bronzer, brunir ▷ adj (colour) marron clair inv

**tandem** ['tændəm] n tandem m

**tangerine** [tændʒə'riːn] n mandarine f

**tangle** ['tæŋgl] n enchevêtrement m; **to get in(to) a ~** s'emmêler

**tank** [tæŋk] n réservoir m; (for fish) aquarium m; (Mil) char m d'assaut, tank m

**tanker** ['tæŋkəʳ] n (ship) pétrolier m, tanker m; (truck) camion-citerne m

**tanned** [tænd] adj bronzé(e)

**tantrum** ['tæntrəm] n accès m de colère

**Tanzania** [tænzə'niːə] n Tanzanie f

**tap** [tæp] n (on sink etc) robinet m; (gentle blow) petite tape ▷ vt frapper or taper légèrement; (resources) exploiter, utiliser; (telephone) mettre sur écoute; **on ~** (fig: resources) disponible; **tap dancing** n claquettes fpl

**tape** [teɪp] n (for tying) ruban m; (also: **magnetic ~**) bande f (magnétique); (cassette) cassette f; (sticky) Scotch® m ▷ vt (record) enregistrer (au magnétoscope or sur cassette); (stick) coller avec du Scotch®; **tape measure** n mètre m à ruban; **tape recorder** n magnétophone m

**tapestry** ['tæpɪstrɪ] n tapisserie f

**tar** [tɑː] n goudron m

**target** ['tɑːgɪt] n cible f; (fig: objective) objectif m

**tariff** ['tærɪf] n (Comm) tarif m; (taxes) tarif douanier

**tarmac** ['tɑːmæk] n (BRIT: on road) macadam m; (Aviat) aire f d'envol

**tarpaulin** [tɑː'pɔːlɪn] n bâche goudronnée

**tarragon** ['tærəgən] n estragon m

**tart** [tɑːt] n (Culin) tarte f; (BRIT inf: pej:

prostitute) poule f ▷ adj (flavour) âpre, aigrelet(te)

**tartan** ['tɑːtn] n tartan m ▷ adj écossais(e)

**tartar(e) sauce** n sauce f tartare

**task** [tɑːsk] n tâche f; **to take to ~** prendre à partie

**taste** [teɪst] n goût m; (fig: glimpse, idea) idée f, aperçu m ▷ vt goûter ▷ vi: **to ~ of** (fish etc) avoir le or un goût de; **you can ~ the garlic (in it)** on sent bien l'ail; **to have a ~ of sth** goûter (à) qch; **can I have a ~?** je peux goûter?; **to be in good/bad** or **poor ~** être de bon/mauvais goût; **tasteful** adj de bon goût; **tasteless** adj (food) insipide; (remark) de mauvais goût; **tasty** adj savoureux(-euse), délicieux(-euse)

**tatters** ['tætəz] npl: **in ~** (also: **tattered**) en lambeaux

**tattoo** [tə'tuː] n tatouage m; (spectacle) parade f militaire ▷ vt tatouer

**taught** [tɔːt] pt, pp of **teach**

**taunt** [tɔːnt] n raillerie f ▷ vt railler

**Taurus** ['tɔːrəs] n le Taureau

**taut** [tɔːt] adj tendu(e)

**tax** [tæks] n (on goods etc) taxe f; (on income) impôts mpl, contributions fpl ▷ vt taxer; imposer; (fig: patience etc) mettre à l'épreuve; **tax disc** n (BRIT Aut) vignette f (automobile); **tax-free** adj exempt(e) d'impôts

**taxi** ['tæksɪ] n taxi m ▷ vi (Aviat) rouler (lentement) au sol; **can you call me a ~, please?** pouvez-vous m'appeler un taxi, s'il vous plaît?; **taxi driver** n chauffeur m de taxi; **taxi rank** (BRIT), **taxi stand** n station f de taxis

**tax payer** [-peɪəʳ] n contribuable m/f

**tax return** n déclaration f d'impôts or de revenus

**TB** n abbr = **tuberculosis**

**tea** [tiː] n thé m; (BRIT: snack: for children) goûter m; **high ~** (BRIT) collation combinant goûter et dîner; **tea bag** n sachet m de thé; **tea break** n (BRIT) pause-thé f

**teach** (pt, pp **taught**) [tiːtʃ, tɔːt] vt: **to**

~ **sb sth**, **to** ~ **sth to sb** apprendre qch à qn; (in school etc) enseigner qch à qn ▷ vi enseigner; **teacher** n (in secondary school) professeur m; (in primary school) instituteur(-trice); **teaching** n enseignement m

**tea**: **tea cloth** n (BRIT) torchon m; **teacup** n tasse f à thé

**tea leaves** npl feuilles fpl de thé

**team** [ti:m] n équipe f; (of animals) attelage m; **team up** vi: **to ~ up (with)** faire équipe (avec)

**teapot** ['ti:pɔt] n théière f

**tear**¹ [tɪə'] n larme f; **in ~s** en larmes

**tear**² n [tɛə'] déchirure f ▷ vb (pt **tore**, pp **torn**) ▷ vt déchirer ▷ vi se déchirer; **tear apart** vt (also fig) déchirer; **tear down** vt (building, statue) démolir; (poster, flag) arracher; **tear off** vt (sheet of paper etc) arracher; (one's clothes) enlever à toute vitesse; **tear up** vt (sheet of paper etc) déchirer, mettre en morceaux or pièces

**tearful** ['tɪəful] adj larmoyant(e)

**tear gas** ['tɪə-] n gaz m lacrymogène

**tearoom** ['ti:ru:m] n salon m de thé

**tease** [ti:z] vt taquiner; (unkindly) tourmenter

**tea**: **teaspoon** n petite cuiller; (also: **teaspoonful**: as measurement) ≈ cuillerée f à café; **teatime** n l'heure f du thé; **tea towel** n (BRIT) torchon m (à vaisselle)

**technical** ['tɛknɪkl] adj technique

**technician** [tɛk'nɪʃən] n technicien(ne)

**technique** [tɛk'ni:k] n technique f

**technology** [tɛk'nɔlədʒɪ] n technologie f

**teddy (bear)** ['tɛdɪ-] n ours m (en peluche)

**tedious** ['ti:dɪəs] adj fastidieux(-euse)

**tee** [ti:] n (Golf) tee m

**teen** [ti:n] adj = **teenage** ▷ n (US) = **teenager**

**teenage** ['ti:neɪdʒ] adj (fashions etc) pour jeunes, pour adolescents; (child) qui est adolescent(e); **teenager** n

adolescent(e)

**teens** [ti:nz] npl: **to be in one's ~** être adolescent(e)

**teeth** [ti:θ] npl of **tooth**

**teetotal** ['ti:'təutl] adj (person) qui ne boit jamais d'alcool

**telecommunications** ['tɛlɪkəmju:nɪ'keɪʃənz] n télécommunications fpl

**telegram** ['tɛlɪgræm] n télégramme m

**telegraph pole** ['tɛlɪgrɑ:f-] n poteau m télégraphique

**telephone** ['tɛlɪfəun] n téléphone m ▷ vt (person) téléphoner à; (message) téléphoner; **to be on the ~** (be speaking) être au téléphone; **telephone book** n = **telephone directory**; **telephone booth** (BRIT), **telephone box** n cabine f téléphonique; **telephone call** n appel m téléphonique; **telephone directory** n annuaire m (du téléphone); **telephone number** n numéro m de téléphone

**telesales** ['tɛlɪseɪlz] npl télévente f

**telescope** ['tɛlɪskəup] n télescope m

**televise** ['tɛlɪvaɪz] vt téléviser

**television** ['tɛlɪvɪʒən] n télévision f; **on ~** à la télévision; **television programme** n émission f de télévision

**tell** (pt, pp **told**) [tɛl, təuld] vt dire; (relate: story) raconter; (distinguish): **to ~ sth from** distinguer qch de ▷ vi (talk): **to ~ of** parler de; (have effect) se faire sentir, se voir; **to ~ sb to do** dire à qn de faire; **to ~ the time** (know how to) savoir lire l'heure; **tell off** vt réprimander, gronder; **teller** n (in bank) caissier(-ière)

**telly** ['tɛlɪ] n abbr (BRIT inf: = television) télé f

**temp** [tɛmp] n (BRIT = temporary worker) intérimaire m/f ▷ vi travailler comme intérimaire

**temper** ['tɛmpə'] n (nature) caractère m; (mood) humeur f; (fit of anger) colère f ▷ vt (moderate) tempérer, adoucir; **to be in a ~** être en colère; **to lose one's ~** se mettre en colère

**temperament** ['tɛmprəmənt]
n (nature) tempérament m;
**temperamental** [tɛmprə'mɛntl] adj
capricieux(-euse)

**temperature** ['tɛmprətʃər] n
température f; **to have** or **run a ~** avoir
de la fièvre

**temple** ['tɛmpl] n (building) temple m;
(Anat) tempe f

**temporary** ['tɛmpərərɪ] adj
temporaire, provisoire; (job, worker)
temporaire

**tempt** [tɛmpt] vt tenter; **to ~ sb into
doing** induire qn à faire; **temptation** n
tentation f; **tempting** adj tentant(e);
(food) appétissant(e)

**ten** [tɛn] num dix

**tenant** ['tɛnənt] n locataire m/f

**tend** [tɛnd] vt s'occuper de ▷ vi: **to ~ to
do** avoir tendance à faire; **tendency**
['tɛndənsɪ] n tendance f

**tender** ['tɛndər] adj tendre; (delicate)
délicat(e); (sore) sensible ▷ n (Comm:
offer) soumission f; (money): **legal ~**
cours légal ▷ vt offrir

**tendon** ['tɛndən] n tendon m

**tenner** ['tɛnər] n (BRIT inf) billet m de
dix livres

**tennis** ['tɛnɪs] n tennis m; **tennis ball**
n balle f de tennis; **tennis court** n
(court m de) tennis m; **tennis match**
n match m de tennis; **tennis player** n
joueur(-euse) de tennis; **tennis racket**
n raquette f de tennis

**tenor** ['tɛnər] n (Mus) ténor m

**tenpin bowling** ['tɛnpɪn-] n (BRIT)
bowling m (à 10 quilles)

**tense** [tɛns] adj tendu(e) ▷ n (Ling)
temps m

**tension** ['tɛnʃən] n tension f

**tent** [tɛnt] n tente f

**tentative** ['tɛntətɪv] adj timide,
hésitant(e); (conclusion) provisoire

**tenth** [tɛnθ] num dixième

**tent**: **tent peg** n piquet m de tente; **tent
pole** n montant m de tente

**tepid** ['tɛpɪd] adj tiède

**term** [təːm] n terme m; (Scol) trimestre

m ▷ vt appeler; **terms** npl (conditions)
conditions fpl; (Comm) tarif m; **in the
short/long ~** à court/long terme; **to
come to ~s with** (problem) faire face à;
**to be on good ~s with** bien s'entendre
avec, être en bons termes avec

**terminal** ['təːmɪnl] adj (disease) dans sa
phase terminale; (patient) incurable ▷ n
(Elec) borne f; (for oil, ore etc, also Comput)
terminal m; (also: **air ~**) aérogare f;
(BRIT: also: **coach ~**) gare routière

**terminate** ['təːmɪneɪt] vt mettre fin à;
(pregnancy) interrompre

**termini** ['təːmɪnaɪ] npl of **terminus**

**terminology** [təːmɪ'nɔlədʒɪ] n
terminologie f

**terminus** (pl **termini**) ['təːmɪnəs,
'təːmɪnaɪ] n terminus m inv

**terrace** ['tɛrəs] n terrasse f; (BRIT: row of
houses) rangée f de maisons (attenantes
les unes aux autres); **the ~s** (BRIT Sport)
les gradins mpl; **terraced** adj (garden)
en terrasses; (in a row: house, cottage etc)
attenant(e) aux maisons voisines

**terrain** [tɛ'reɪn] n terrain m (sol)

**terrestrial** [tɪ'rɛstrɪəl] adj terrestre

**terrible** ['tɛrɪbl] adj terrible, atroce;
(weather, work) affreux(-euse),
épouvantable; **terribly** adv
terriblement; (very badly) affreusement
mal

**terrier** ['tɛrɪər] n terrier m (chien)

**terrific** [tə'rɪfɪk] adj (very
great) fantastique, incroyable,
terrible; (wonderful) formidable,
sensationnel(le)

**terrified** ['tɛrɪfaɪd] adj terrifié(e); **to be
~ of sth** avoir très peur de qch

**terrify** ['tɛrɪfaɪ] vt terrifier; **terrifying**
adj terrifiant(e)

**territorial** [tɛrɪ'tɔːrɪəl] adj
territorial(e)

**territory** ['tɛrɪtərɪ] n territoire m

**terror** ['tɛrər] n terreur f; **terrorism** n
terrorisme m; **terrorist** n terroriste
m/f; **terrorist attack** n attentat m
terroriste

**test** [tɛst] n (trial, check) essai m; (: of

*courage etc*) épreuve *f*; (*Med*) examen *m*; (*Chem*) analyse *f*; (*Scol*) interrogation *f* de contrôle; (*also*: **driving ~**) (examen du) permis *m* de conduire ▷ *vt* essayer; mettre à l'épreuve; examiner; analyser; faire subir une interrogation (de contrôle) à

**testicle** ['tɛstɪkl] *n* testicule *m*

**testify** ['tɛstɪfaɪ] *vi* (*Law*) témoigner, déposer; **to ~ to sth** (*Law*) attester qch

**testimony** ['tɛstɪmənɪ] *n* (*Law*) témoignage *m*, déposition *f*

**test**: **test match** *n* (*Cricket, Rugby*) match international; **test tube** *n* éprouvette *f*

**tetanus** ['tɛtənəs] *n* tétanos *m*

**text** [tɛkst] *n* texte *m*; (*on mobile phone*) texto *m*, SMS *m inv* ▷ *vt* (*inf*) envoyer un texto *or* SMS à; **textbook** *n* manuel *m*

**textile** ['tɛkstaɪl] *n* textile *m*

**text message** *n* texto *m*, SMS *m inv*

**text messaging** [-'mɛsɪdʒɪŋ] *n* messagerie textuelle

**texture** ['tɛkstʃə*r*] *n* texture *f*; (*of skin, paper etc*) grain *m*

**Thai** [taɪ] *adj* thaïlandais(e) ▷ *n* Thaïlandais(e)

**Thailand** ['taɪlænd] *n* Thaïlande *f*

**Thames** [tɛmz] *n*: **the (River) ~** la Tamise

**than** [ðæn, ðən] *conj* que; (*with numerals*): **more ~ 10/once** plus de 10/d'une fois; **I have more/less ~ you** j'en ai plus/moins que toi; **she has more apples ~ pears** elle a plus de pommes que de poires; **it is better to phone ~ to write** il vaut mieux téléphoner (plutôt) qu'écrire; **she is older ~ you think** elle est plus âgée que tu le crois

**thank** [θæŋk] *vt* remercier, dire merci à; **thanks** *npl* remerciements *mpl* ▷ *excl* merci!; **~ you (very much)** merci (beaucoup); **~ God** Dieu merci!; **~s to** *prep* grâce à; **thankfully** *adv* (*fortunately*) heureusement; **Thanksgiving (Day)** *n* jour *m* d'action de grâce; *voir encadré*

○ **THANKSGIVING (DAY)**
○
○ **Thanksgiving (Day)** est un
○ jour de congé aux États-Unis,
○ le quatrième jeudi du mois de
○ novembre, commémorant la bonne
○ récolte que les Pèlerins venus de
○ Grande-Bretagne ont eue en 1621,
○ traditionnellement, c'était un jour
○ où l'on remerciait Dieu et où l'on
○ organisait un grand festin. Une
○ fête semblable, mais qui n'a aucun
○ rapport avec les Pères Pèlerins, a
○ lieu au Canada le deuxième lundi
○ d'octobre.

○ **KEYWORD**

**that** [ðæt] *adj* (*demonstrative*: *pl* **those**) ce, cet + *vowel or h mute*, cette *f*; **that man/woman/book** cet homme/cette femme/ce livre; (*not this*) cet homme-là/cette femme-là/ce livre-là; **that one** celui-là (celle-là)
▷ *pron* **1** (*demonstrative*: *pl* **those**) ce; (*not this one*) cela, ça; (*that one*) celui (celle); **who's that?** qui est-ce?; **what's that?** qu'est-ce que c'est?; **is that you?** c'est toi?; **I prefer this to that** je préfère ceci à cela *or* ça; **that's what he said** c'est *or* voilà ce qu'il a dit; **will you eat all that?** est-ce que tu vas manger tout ça?; **that is (to say)** c'est-à-dire, à savoir
**2** (*relative*: *subject*) qui; (: *object*) que; (: *after prep*) lequel (laquelle), lesquels (lesquelles) *pl*; **the book that I read** le livre que j'ai lu; **the books that are in the library** les livres qui sont dans la bibliothèque; **all that I have** tout ce que j'ai; **the box that I put it in** la boîte dans laquelle je l'ai mis; **the people that I spoke to** les gens auxquels *or* à qui j'ai parlé
**3** (*relative*: *of time*) où; **the day that he came** le jour où il est venu
▷ *conj* que; **he thought that I was ill** il pensait que j'étais malade

▷ adv (demonstrative): **I don't like it that much** ça ne me plaît pas tant que ça; **I didn't know it was that bad** je ne savais pas que c'était si or aussi mauvais; **it's about that high** c'est à peu près de cette hauteur

**thatched** [θætʃt] adj (roof) de chaume; **~ cottage** chaumière f
**thaw** [θɔː] n dégel m ▷ vi (ice) fondre; (food) dégeler ▷ vt (food) (faire) dégeler

○ **KEYWORD**

**the** [ðiː, ðə] def art **1** (gen) le, la f, l' + vowel or h mute, les pl (NB: à + le(s) = **au(x)**; de + le = **du**; de + les = **des**); **the boy/girl/ink** le garçon/la fille/l'encre; **the children** les enfants; **the history of the world** l'histoire du monde; **give it to the postman** donne-le au facteur; **to play the piano/flute** jouer du piano/de la flûte
**2** (+ adj to form n) le, la f, l' + vowel or h mute, les pl; **the rich and the poor** les riches et les pauvres; **to attempt the impossible** tenter l'impossible
**3** (in titles): **Elizabeth the First** Elisabeth première; **Peter the Great** Pierre le Grand
**4** (in comparisons): **the more he works, the more he earns** plus il travaille, plus il gagne de l'argent

**theatre** (US **theater**) ['θɪətər] n théâtre m; (Med: also: **operating ~**) salle f d'opération
**theft** [θɛft] n vol m (larcin)
**their** [ðɛər] adj leur, leurs pl; see also **my**; **theirs** pron le (la) leur, les leurs; see also **mine**[1]
**them** [ðɛm, ðəm] pron (direct) les; (indirect) leur; (stressed, after prep) eux (elles); **give me a few of ~** donnez m'en quelques uns (or quelques unes); see also **me**
**theme** [θiːm] n thème m; **theme park** n parc m à thème

**themselves** [ðəm'sɛlvz] pl pron (reflexive) se; (emphatic, after prep) eux-mêmes (elles-mêmes); **between ~** entre eux (elles); see also **oneself**
**then** [ðɛn] adv (at that time) alors, à ce moment-là; (next) puis, ensuite; (and also) et puis ▷ conj (therefore) alors, dans ce cas ▷ adj: **the ~ president** le président d'alors or de l'époque; **by ~** (past) à ce moment-là; (future) d'ici là; **from ~ on** dès lors; **until ~** jusqu'à ce moment-là, jusque-là
**theology** [θɪ'ɒlədʒɪ] n théologie f
**theory** ['θɪərɪ] n théorie f
**therapist** ['θɛrəpɪst] n thérapeute m/f
**therapy** ['θɛrəpɪ] n thérapie f

○ **KEYWORD**

**there** [ðɛər] adv **1**: **there is**, **there are** il y a; **there are 3 of them** (people, things) il y en a 3; **there is no-one here/no bread left** il n'y a personne/il n'y a plus de pain; **there has been an accident** il y a eu un accident
**2** (referring to place) là, là-bas; **it's there** c'est là(-bas); **in/on/up/down there** là-dedans/là-dessus/là-haut/en bas; **he went there on Friday** il y est allé vendredi; **I want that book there** je veux ce livre-là; **there he is!** le voilà!
**3**: **there, there** (esp to child) allons, allons!

**there**: **thereabouts** adv (place) par là, près de là; (amount) environ, à peu près; **thereafter** adv par la suite; **thereby** adv ainsi; **therefore** adv donc, par conséquent
**there's** ['ðɛəz] = **there is**; **there has**
**thermal** ['θəːml] adj thermique; **~ underwear** sous-vêtements mpl en Thermolactyl®
**thermometer** [θə'mɒmɪtər] n thermomètre m
**thermostat** ['θəːməustæt] n thermostat m
**these** [ðiːz] pl pron ceux-ci (celles-ci) ▷ pl adj ces; (not those): **~ books** ces

livres-ci

**thesis** (pl **theses**) ['θiːsɪs, 'θiːsiːz] n thèse f

**they** [ðeɪ] pl pron ils (elles); (stressed) eux (elles); **~ say that ...** (it is said that) on dit que ...; **they'd = they had**; **they would**; **they'll = they shall**; **they will**; **they're = they are**; **they've = they have**

**thick** [θɪk] adj épais(se); (stupid) bête, borné(e) ▷ n: **in the ~ of** au beau milieu de, en plein cœur de; **it's 20 cm ~** ça a 20 cm d'épaisseur; **thicken** vi s'épaissir ▷ vt (sauce etc) épaissir; **thickness** n épaisseur f

**thief** (pl **thieves**) [θiːf, θiːvz] n voleur(-euse)

**thigh** [θaɪ] n cuisse f

**thin** [θɪn] adj mince; (skinny) maigre; (soup) peu épais(se); (hair, crowd) clairsemé(e) ▷ vt (also: **~ down**: sauce, paint) délayer

**thing** [θɪŋ] n chose f; (object) objet m; (contraption) truc m; **things** npl (belongings) affaires fpl; **the ~ is ...** c'est que ...; **the best ~ would be to** le mieux serait de; **how are ~s?** comment ça va?; **to have a ~ about** (be obsessed by) être obsédé(e) par; (hate) détester; **poor ~!** le (or la) pauvre!

**think** (pt, pp **thought**) [θɪŋk, θɔːt] vi penser, réfléchir ▷ vt penser, croire; (imagine) s'imaginer; **what did you ~ of them?** qu'avez-vous pensé d'eux?; **to ~ about sth/sb** penser à qch/qn; **I'll ~ about it** je vais y réfléchir; **to ~ of doing** avoir l'idée de faire; **I ~ so/not** je crois or pense que oui/non; **to ~ well of** avoir une haute opinion de; **think over** vt bien réfléchir à; **think up** vt inventer, trouver

**third** [θəːd] num troisième ▷ n (fraction) tiers m; (Aut) troisième (vitesse) f; (BRIT Scol: degree) ≈ licence f avec mention passable; **thirdly** adv troisièmement; **third party insurance** n (BRIT) assurance f au tiers; **Third World** n: **the Third World** le Tiers-Monde

**thirst** [θəːst] n soif f; **thirsty** adj qui a soif, assoiffé(e); (work) qui donne soif; **to be thirsty** avoir soif

**thirteen** [θəː'tiːn] num treize; **thirteenth** [-'tiːnθ] num treizième

**thirtieth** ['θəːtɪɪθ] num trentième

**thirty** ['θəːtɪ] num trente

**KEYWORD**

**this** [ðɪs] adj (demonstrative: pl **these**) ce, cet + vowel or h mute, cette f; **this man/woman/book** cet homme/cette femme/ce livre; (not that) cet homme-ci/cette femme-ci/ce livre-ci; **this one** celui-ci (celle-ci)
▷ pron (demonstrative: pl **these**) ce; (not that one) celui-ci (celle-ci), ceci; **who's this?** qui est-ce?; **what's this?** qu'est-ce que c'est?; **I prefer this to that** je préfère ceci à cela; **this is where I live** c'est ici que j'habite; **this is what he said** voici ce qu'il a dit; **this is Mr Brown** (in introductions) je vous présente Mr Brown; (in photo) c'est Mr Brown; (on telephone) ici Mr Brown
▷ adv (demonstrative): **it was about this big** c'était à peu près de cette grandeur or grand comme ça; **I didn't know it was this bad** je ne savais pas que c'était si or aussi mauvais

**thistle** ['θɪsl] n chardon m

**thorn** [θɔːn] n épine f

**thorough** ['θʌrə] adj (search) minutieux(-euse); (knowledge, research) approfondi(e); (work, person) consciencieux(-euse); (cleaning) à fond; **thoroughly** adv (search) minutieusement; (study) en profondeur; (clean) à fond; (very) tout à fait

**those** [ðəuz] pl pron ceux-là (celles-là) ▷ pl adj ces; (not these): **~ books** ces livres-là

**though** [ðəu] conj bien que + sub, quoique + sub ▷ adv pourtant

**thought** [θɔːt] pt, pp of **think** ▷ n

pensée f; (idea) idée f; (opinion) avis m;
**thoughtful** adj (deep in thought)
pensif(-ive); (serious) réfléchi(e);
(considerate) prévenant(e); **thoughtless**
adj qui manque de considération
**thousand** ['θauzənd] num mille; **one
~** mille; **two ~** deux mille; **~s of** des
milliers de; **thousandth** num millième
**thrash** [θræʃ] vt rouer de coups; (as
punishment) donner une correction à;
(inf: defeat) battre à plate(s) couture(s)
**thread** [θred] n fil m; (of screw) pas m,
filetage m ▷ vt (needle) enfiler
**threat** [θret] n menace f; **threaten** vi
(storm) menacer ▷ vt: **to threaten sb
with sth/to do** menacer qn de qch/de
faire; **threatening** adj menaçant(e)
**three** [θri:] num trois; **three-
dimensional** adj à trois dimensions;
**three-piece suite** n salon m (canapé
et deux fauteuils); **three-quarters** npl
trois-quarts mpl; **three-quarters full**
aux trois-quarts plein
**threshold** ['θreʃhəuld] n seuil m
**threw** [θru:] pt of **throw**
**thrill** [θrɪl] n (excitement) émotion f,
sensation forte; (shudder) frisson m
▷ vt (audience) électriser; **thrilled** adj:
**thrilled (with)** ravi(e) de; **thriller**
n film m (or roman m or pièce f) à
suspense; **thrilling** adj (book, play
etc) saisissant(e); (news, discovery)
excitant(e)
**thriving** ['θraɪvɪŋ] adj (business,
community) prospère
**throat** [θrəut] n gorge f; **to have a sore
~** avoir mal à la gorge
**throb** [θrɔb] vi (heart) palpiter; (engine)
vibrer; **my head is ~bing** j'ai des
élancements dans la tête
**throne** [θrəun] n trône m
**through** [θru:] prep à travers; (time)
pendant, durant; (by means of) par, par
l'intermédiaire de; (owing to) à cause
de ▷ adj (ticket, train, passage) direct(e)
▷ adv à travers; **(from) Monday ~
Friday** (us) de lundi à vendredi; **to put
sb ~ to sb** (Tel) passer qn à qn; **to be**

~ (Brit: Tel) avoir la communication;
(esp us: have finished) avoir fini; **"no ~
traffic"** (us) "passage interdit"; **"no ~
road"** (Brit) "impasse"; **throughout**
prep (place) partout dans; (time) durant
tout(e) le (la) ▷ adv partout
**throw** [θrəu] n jet m; (Sport) lancer
m ▷ vt (pt **threw**, pp **~n**) lancer, jeter;
(Sport) lancer; (rider) désarçonner; (fig)
décontenancer; **to ~ a party** donner
une réception; **throw away** vt jeter;
(money) gaspiller; **throw in** vt (Sport:
ball) remettre en jeu; (include) ajouter;
**throw off** vt se débarrasser de; **throw
out** vt jeter; (reject) rejeter; (person)
mettre à la porte; **throw up** vi vomir
**thru** [θru:] (us) = **through**
**thrush** [θrʌʃ] n (Zool) grive f
**thrust** [θrʌst] vt (pt, pp **~**) pousser
brusquement; (push in) enfoncer
**thud** [θʌd] n bruit sourd
**thug** [θʌg] n voyou m
**thumb** [θʌm] n (Anat) pouce m ▷ vt: **to
~ a lift** faire de l'auto-stop, arrêter une
voiture; **thumbtack** n (us) punaise
f (clou)
**thump** [θʌmp] n grand coup; (sound)
bruit sourd ▷ vt cogner sur ▷ vi cogner,
frapper
**thunder** ['θʌndər] n tonnerre m ▷ vi
tonner; (train etc): **to ~ past** passer dans
un grondement or un bruit de tonnerre;
**thunderstorm** n orage m
**Thur(s)** abbr (= Thursday) jeu
**Thursday** ['θə:zdɪ] n jeudi m
**thus** [ðʌs] adv ainsi
**thwart** [θwɔ:t] vt contrecarrer
**thyme** [taɪm] n thym m
**Tibet** [tɪ'bɛt] n Tibet m
**tick** [tɪk] n (sound: of clock) tic-tac m;
(mark) coche f; (Zool) tique f; (Brit
inf): **in a ~** dans un instant ▷ vi faire
tic-tac ▷ vt (item on list) cocher; **tick
off** vt (item on list) cocher; (person)
réprimander, attraper
**ticket** ['tɪkɪt] n billet m; (for bus, tube)
ticket m; (in shop: on goods) étiquette
f; (for library) carte f; (also: **parking ~**)

contravention f, p.-v. m; **ticket barrier** n (BRIT: Rail) portillon m automatique; **ticket collector** n contrôleur(-euse); **ticket inspector** n contrôleur(-euse); **ticket machine** n billetterie f automatique; **ticket office** n guichet m, bureau m de vente des billets

**tickle** ['tɪkl] vi chatouiller ▷ vt chatouiller; **ticklish** adj (person) chatouilleux(-euse); (problem) épineux(-euse)

**tide** [taɪd] n marée f; (fig: of events) cours m

**tidy** ['taɪdɪ] adj (room) bien rangé(e); (dress, work) net (nette), soigné(e); (person) ordonné(e), qui a de l'ordre ▷ vt (also: **~ up**) ranger

**tie** [taɪ] n (string etc) cordon m; (BRIT: also: **neck~**) cravate f; (fig: link) lien m; (Sport: draw) égalité f de points; match nul ▷ vt (parcel) attacher; (ribbon) nouer ▷ vi (Sport) faire match nul; finir à égalité de points; **to ~ sth in a bow** faire un nœud à or une cocarde; **to ~ a knot in sth** faire un nœud à qch; **tie down** vt (fig): **to ~ sb down to** contraindre qn à accepter; **to feel ~d down** (by relationship) se sentir coincé(e); **tie up** vt (parcel) ficeler; (dog, boat) attacher; (prisoner) ligoter; (arrangements) conclure; **to be ~d up** (busy) être pris(e) or occupé(e)

**tier** [tɪər] n gradin m; (of cake) étage m

**tiger** ['taɪgər] n tigre m

**tight** [taɪt] adj (rope) tendu(e), raide; (clothes) étroit(e), très juste; (budget, programme, bend) serré(e); (control) strict(e), sévère; (inf: drunk) ivre, rond(e) ▷ adv (squeeze) très fort; (shut) à bloc, hermétiquement; **hold ~!** accrochez-vous bien!; **tighten** vt (rope) tendre; (screw) resserrer; (control) renforcer ▷ vi se tendre; se resserrer; **tightly** adv (grasp) bien, très fort; **tights** npl (BRIT) collant m

**tile** [taɪl] n (on roof) tuile f; (on wall or floor) carreau m

**till** [tɪl] n caisse (enregistreuse) ▷ prep,

conj = **until**

**tilt** [tɪlt] vt pencher, incliner ▷ vi pencher, être incliné(e)

**timber** ['tɪmbər] n (material) bois m de construction

**time** [taɪm] n temps m; (epoch: often pl) époque f, temps; (by clock) heure f; (moment) moment m; (occasion, also Math) fois f ▷ vt (race) chronométrer; (programme) minuter; (visit) fixer; (remark etc) choisir le moment de; **a long** ~ un long moment, longtemps; **four at a** ~ quatre à la fois; **for the** ~ **being** pour le moment; **from** ~ **to** ~ de temps en temps; **at** ~s parfois; **in** ~ (soon enough) à temps; (after some time) avec le temps, à la longue; (Mus) en mesure; **in a week's** ~ dans une semaine; **in no** ~ en un rien de temps; **any** ~ n'importe quand; **on** ~ à l'heure; **5** ~**s 5** 5 fois 5; **what** ~ **is it?** quelle heure est-il?; **what** ~ **is the museum/shop open?** à quelle heure ouvre le musée/magasin?; **to have a good** ~ bien s'amuser; **time limit** n limite f de temps, délai m; **timely** adj opportun(e); **timer** n (in kitchen) compte-minutes m inv; (Tech) minuteur m; **time-share** n maison f/appartement m en multipropriété; **timetable** n (Rail) (indicateur m) horaire m; (Scol) emploi m du temps; **time zone** n fuseau m horaire

**timid** ['tɪmɪd] adj timide; (easily scared) peureux(-euse)

**timing** ['taɪmɪŋ] n (Sport) chronométrage m; **the** ~ **of his resignation** le moment choisi pour sa démission

**tin** [tɪn] n étain m; (also: ~ **plate**) fer-blanc m; (BRIT: can) boîte f (de conserve); (: for baking) moule m (à gâteau); (for storage) boîte f; **tinfoil** n papier m d'étain or d'aluminium

**tingle** ['tɪŋgl] vi picoter; (person) avoir des picotements

**tinker** ['tɪŋkər]; **tinker with** vt fus bricoler, rafistoler

**tinned** [tɪnd] *adj* (BRIT: *food*) en boîte, en conserve

**tin opener** [-'əupnə<sup>r</sup>] *n* (BRIT) ouvre-boîte(s) *m*

**tinsel** ['tɪnsl] *n* guirlandes *fpl* de Noël (*argentées*)

**tint** [tɪnt] *n* teinte *f*; (*for hair*) shampooing colorant; **tinted** *adj* (*hair*) teint(e); (*spectacles, glass*) teinté(e)

**tiny** ['taɪnɪ] *adj* minuscule

**tip** [tɪp] *n* (*end*) bout *m*; (*gratuity*) pourboire *m*; (BRIT: *for rubbish*) décharge *f*; (*advice*) tuyau *m* ▷ *vt* (*waiter*) donner un pourboire à; (*tilt*) incliner; (*overturn: also:* **~ over**) renverser; (*empty: also:* **~ out**) déverser; **how much should I ~?** combien de pourboire est-ce qu'il faut laisser?; **tip off** *vt* prévenir, avertir

**tiptoe** ['tɪptəu] *n*: **on ~** sur la pointe des pieds

**tire** ['taɪə<sup>r</sup>] *n* (US) = **tyre** ▷ *vt* fatiguer ▷ *vi* se fatiguer; **tired** *adj* fatigué(e); **to be tired of** en avoir assez de, être las (lasse) de; **tire pressure** (US) = **tyre pressure**; **tiring** *adj* fatigant(e)

**tissue** ['tɪʃuː] *n* tissu *m*; (*paper handkerchief*) mouchoir *m* en papier, kleenex® *m*; **tissue paper** *n* papier *m* de soie

**tit** [tɪt] *n* (*bird*) mésange *f*; **to give ~ for tat** rendre coup pour coup

**title** ['taɪtl] *n* titre *m*

**T-junction** ['tiː'dʒʌŋkʃən] *n* croisement *m* en T

**TM** *n abbr* = **trademark**

 **KEYWORD**

**to** [tuː, tə] *prep* **1** (*direction*) à; (*towards*) vers; envers; **to go to France/Portugal/London/school** aller en France/au Portugal/à Londres/à l'école; **to go to Claude's/the doctor's** aller chez Claude/le docteur; **the road to Edinburgh** la route d'Édimbourg

**2** (*as far as*) (jusqu')à; **to count to 10** compter jusqu'à 10; **from 40 to 50**

people de 40 à 50 personnes

**3** (*with expressions of time*): **a quarter to 5** 5 heures moins le quart; **it's twenty to 3** il est 3 heures moins vingt

**4** (*for, of*) de; **the key to the front door** la clé de la porte d'entrée; **a letter to his wife** une lettre (adressée) à sa femme

**5** (*expressing indirect object*) à; **to give sth to sb** donner qch à qn; **to talk to sb** parler à qn; **to be a danger to sb** être dangereux(-euse) pour qn

**6** (*in relation to*) à; **3 goals to 2** 3 (buts) à 2; **30 miles to the gallon** ≈ 9,4 litres aux cent (km)

**7** (*purpose, result*): **to come to sb's aid** venir au secours de qn, porter secours à qn; **to sentence sb to death** condamner qn à mort; **to my surprise** à ma grande surprise

▷ *with vb* **1** (*simple infinitive*): **to go/eat** aller/manger

**2** (*following another vb*): **to want/try/start to do** vouloir/essayer de/commencer à faire

**3** (*with vb omitted*): **I don't want to** je ne veux pas

**4** (*purpose, result*) pour; **I did it to help you** je l'ai fait pour vous aider

**5** (*equivalent to relative clause*): **I have things to do** j'ai des choses à faire; **the main thing is to try** l'important est d'essayer

**6** (*after adjective etc*): **ready to go** prêt(e) à partir; **too old/young to ...** trop vieux/jeune pour ...

▷ *adv*: **push/pull the door to** tirez/poussez la porte

**toad** [təud] *n* crapaud *m*; **toadstool** *n* champignon (vénéneux)

**toast** [təust] *n* (Culin) pain grillé, toast *m*; (*drink, speech*) toast ▷ *vt* (Culin) faire griller; (*drink to*) porter un toast à; **toaster** *n* grille-pain *m inv*

**tobacco** [tə'bækəu] *n* tabac *m*

**toboggan** [tə'bɔgən] *n* toboggan *m*; (*child's*) luge *f*

**today** [tə'deɪ] *adv*, *n* (*also fig*) aujourd'hui (*m*)

**toddler** ['tɒdlə*ᵣ*] *n* enfant *m/f* qui commence à marcher, bambin *m*

**toe** [təʊ] *n* doigt *m* de pied, orteil *m*; (*of shoe*) bout *m* ▷ *vt*: **to ~ the line** (*fig*) obéir, se conformer; **toenail** *n* ongle *m* de l'orteil

**toffee** ['tɒfɪ] *n* caramel *m*

**together** [tə'geðə*ᵣ*] *adv* ensemble; (*at same time*) en même temps; **~ with** *prep* avec

**toilet** ['tɔɪlət] *n* (*BRIT: lavatory*) toilettes *fpl*, cabinets *mpl*; **to go to the ~** aller aux toilettes; **where's the ~?** où sont les toilettes?; **toilet bag** *n* (*BRIT*) nécessaire *m* de toilette; **toilet paper** *n* papier *m* hygiénique; **toiletries** *npl* articles *mpl* de toilette; **toilet roll** *n* rouleau *m* de papier hygiénique

**token** ['təʊkən] *n* (*sign*) marque *f*, témoignage *m*; (*metal disc*) jeton *m* ▷ *adj* (*fee, strike*) symbolique; **book/record ~** (*BRIT*) chèque-livre/-disque *m*

**Tokyo** ['təʊkjəʊ] *n* Tokyo

**told** [təʊld] *pt*, *pp* of **tell**

**tolerant** ['tɒlərnt] *adj*: **~ (of)** tolérant(e) (à l'égard de)

**tolerate** ['tɒləreɪt] *vt* supporter

**toll** [təʊl] *n* (*tax, charge*) péage *m* ▷ *vi* (*bell*) sonner; **the accident ~ on the roads** le nombre des victimes de la route; **toll call** *n* (*US Tel*) appel *m* (à) longue distance; **toll-free** *adj* (*US*) gratuit(e) ▷ *adv* gratuitement

**tomato** [tə'mɑːtəʊ] (*pl* **-es**) *n* tomate *f*; **tomato sauce** *n* sauce *f* tomate

**tomb** [tuːm] *n* tombe *f*; **tombstone** *n* pierre tombale

**tomorrow** [tə'mɒrəʊ] *adv*, *n* (*also fig*) demain (*m*); **the day after ~** après-demain; **a week ~** demain en huit; **~ morning** demain matin

**ton** [tʌn] *n* tonne *f* (*BRIT* = 1016 kg; *US* = 907 kg; *metric* = 1000 kg); **~s of** (*inf*) des tas de

**tone** [təʊn] *n* ton *m*; (*of radio*, *BRIT Tel*) tonalité *f* ▷ *vi* (*also*: **~ in**) s'harmoniser;

**tone down** *vt* (*colour, criticism*) adoucir

**tongs** [tɒŋz] *npl* pinces *fpl*; (*for coal*) pincettes *fpl*; (*for hair*) fer *m* à friser

**tongue** [tʌŋ] *n* langue *f*; **~ in cheek** *adv* ironiquement

**tonic** ['tɒnɪk] *n* (*Med*) tonique *m*; (*also*: **~ water**) Schweppes® *m*

**tonight** [tə'naɪt] *adv*, *n* cette nuit; (*this evening*) ce soir

**tonne** [tʌn] *n* (*BRIT: metric ton*) tonne *f*

**tonsil** ['tɒnsl] *n* amygdale *f*; **tonsillitis** [tɒnsɪ'laɪtɪs] *n*: **to have tonsillitis** avoir une angine *or* une amygdalite

**too** [tuː] *adv* (*excessively*) trop; (*also*) aussi; **~ much** (*as adv*) trop; (*as adj*) trop de; **~ many** *adj* trop de

**took** [tʊk] *pt* of **take**

**tool** [tuːl] *n* outil *m*; **tool box** *n* boîte *f* à outils; **tool kit** *n* trousse *f* à outils

**tooth** (*pl* **teeth**) [tuːθ, tiːθ] *n* (*Anat, Tech*) dent *f*; **to brush one's teeth** se laver les dents; **toothache** *n* mal *m* de dents; **to have toothache** avoir mal aux dents; **toothbrush** *n* brosse *f* à dents; **toothpaste** *n* (*pâte f*) dentifrice *m*; **toothpick** *n* cure-dent *m*

**top** [tɒp] *n* (*of mountain, head*) sommet *m*; (*of page, ladder*) haut *m*; (*of box, cupboard, table*) dessus *m*; (*lid: of box, jar*) couvercle *m*; (*: of bottle*) bouchon *m*; (*toy*) toupie *f*; (*Dress: blouse etc*) haut; (*: of pyjamas*) veste *f* ▷ *adj* du haut; (*in rank*) premier(-ière); (*best*) meilleur(e) ▷ *vt* (*exceed*) dépasser; (*be first in*) être en tête de; **from ~ to bottom** de fond en comble; **on ~ of** sur; (*in addition to*) en plus de; **over the ~** (*inf: behaviour etc*) qui dépasse les limites; **top up** (*US* **top off**) *vt* (*bottle*) remplir; (*salary*) compléter; **to ~ up one's mobile (phone)** recharger son compte; **top floor** *n* dernier étage; **top hat** *n* haut-de-forme *m*

**topic** ['tɒpɪk] *n* sujet *m*, thème *m*; **topical** *adj* d'actualité

**topless** ['tɒplɪs] *adj* (*bather etc*) aux seins nus

**topping** ['tɒpɪŋ] *n* (*Culin*) couche de

crème, fromage etc qui recouvre un plat

**topple** ['tɔpl] vt renverser, faire tomber ▷ vi basculer; tomber

**top-up** ['tɔpʌp] n (for mobile phone) recharge f, minutes fpl; **top-up card** n (for mobile phone) recharge f

**torch** [tɔːtʃ] n torche f; (BRIT: electric) lampe f de poche

**tore** [tɔːʳ] pt of **tear²**

**torment** n ['tɔːmɛnt] tourment m ▷ vt [tɔː'mɛnt] tourmenter; (fig: annoy) agacer

**torn** [tɔːn] pp of **tear²**

**tornado** [tɔː'neɪdəu] (pl **~es**) n tornade f

**torpedo** [tɔː'piːdəu] (pl **~es**) n torpille f

**torrent** ['tɔrnt] n torrent m; **torrential** [tɔ'rɛnʃl] adj torrentiel(le)

**tortoise** ['tɔːtəs] n tortue f

**torture** ['tɔːtʃəʳ] n torture f ▷ vt torturer

**Tory** ['tɔːrɪ] adj, n (BRIT Pol) tory m/f, conservateur(-trice)

**toss** [tɔs] vt lancer, jeter; (BRIT: pancake) faire sauter; (head) rejeter en arrière ▷ vi: **to ~ up for sth** (BRIT) jouer qch à pile ou face; **to ~ a coin** jouer à pile ou face; **to ~ and turn** (in bed) se tourner et se retourner

**total** ['təutl] adj total(e) ▷ n total m ▷ vt (add up) faire le total de, additionner; (amount to) s'élever à

**totalitarian** [təutælɪ'tɛərɪən] adj totalitaire

**totally** ['təutəlɪ] adv totalement

**touch** [tʌtʃ] n contact m, toucher m; (sense, skill: of pianist etc) toucher ▷ vt (gen) toucher; (tamper with) toucher à; **a ~ of** (fig) un petit peu de; une touche de; **to get in ~ with** prendre contact avec; **to lose ~** (friends) se perdre de vue; **touch down** vi (Aviat) atterrir; (on sea) amerrir; **touchdown** n (Aviat) atterrissage m; (on sea) amerrissage m; (US Football) essai m; **touched** adj (moved) touché(e); **touching** adj touchant(e), attendrissant(e); **touchline** n (Sport) (ligne f de) touche

f; **touch-sensitive** adj (keypad) à effleurement; (screen) tactile

**tough** [tʌf] adj dur(e); (resistant) résistant(e), solide; (meat) dur, coriace; (firm) inflexible; (task, problem, situation) difficile

**tour** ['tuəʳ] n voyage m; (also: **package ~**) voyage organisé; (of town, museum) tour m, visite f; (by band) tournée f ▷ vt visiter; **tour guide** n (person) guide m/f

**tourism** ['tuərɪzm] n tourisme m

**tourist** ['tuərɪst] n touriste m/f ▷ cpd touristique; **tourist office** n syndicat m d'initiative

**tournament** ['tuənəmənt] n tournoi m

**tour operator** n (BRIT) organisateur m de voyages, tour-opérateur m

**tow** [təu] vt remorquer; (caravan, trailer) tracter; **"on ~", (US) "in ~"** (Aut) "véhicule en remorque"; **tow away** vt (subj: police) emmener à la fourrière; (: breakdown service) remorquer

**toward(s)** [tə'wɔːd(z)] prep vers; (of attitude) envers, à l'égard de; (of purpose) pour

**towel** ['tauəl] n serviette f (de toilette); **towelling** n (fabric) tissu-éponge m

**tower** ['tauəʳ] n tour f; **tower block** n (BRIT) tour f (d'habitation)

**town** [taun] n ville f; **to go to ~** aller en ville; (fig) y mettre le paquet; **town centre** n (BRIT) centre m de la ville, centre-ville m; **town hall** n ≈ mairie f

**tow truck** n (US) dépanneuse f

**toxic** ['tɔksɪk] adj toxique

**toy** [tɔɪ] n jouet m; **toy with** vt fus jouer avec; (idea) caresser; **toyshop** n magasin m de jouets

**trace** [treɪs] n trace f ▷ vt (draw) tracer, dessiner; (follow) suivre la trace de; (locate) retrouver

**tracing paper** ['treɪsɪŋ-] n papier-calque m

**track** [træk] n (mark) trace f; (path: gen) chemin m, piste f; (: of bullet etc) trajectoire f; (: of suspect, animal) piste f; (Rail) voie ferrée, rails mpl; (on tape,

*Comput, Sport*) piste; (*on CD*) piste *f*; (*on record*) plage *f* ▷ *vt* suivre la trace *or* la piste de; **track down** *vt* (*prey*) trouver et capturer; (*sth lost*) finir par retrouver; **tracksuit** *n* survêtement *m*

**tractor** ['træktə<sup>r</sup>] *n* tracteur *m*

**trade** [treɪd] *n* commerce *m*; (*skill, job*) métier *m* ▷ *vi* faire du commerce ▷ *vt* (*exchange*): **to ~ sth (for sth)** échanger qch (contre qch); **to ~ with/in** faire du commerce avec/le commerce de; **trade in** *vt* (*old car etc*) faire reprendre; **trademark** *n* marque *f* de fabrique; **trader** *n* commerçant(e), négociant(e); **tradesman** (*irreg*) *n* (*shopkeeper*) commerçant *m*; **trade union** *n* syndicat *m*

**trading** ['treɪdɪŋ] *n* affaires *fpl*, commerce *m*

**tradition** [trə'dɪʃən] *n* tradition *f*; **traditional** *adj* traditionnel(le)

**traffic** ['træfɪk] *n* trafic *m*; (*cars*) circulation *f* ▷ *vi*: **to ~ in** (*pej: liquor, drugs*) faire le trafic de; **traffic circle** *n* (*US*) rond-point *m*; **traffic island** *n* refuge *m* (pour piétons); **traffic jam** *n* embouteillage *m*; **traffic lights** *npl* feux *mpl* (de signalisation); **traffic warden** *n* contractuel(le)

**tragedy** ['trædʒədɪ] *n* tragédie *f*

**tragic** ['trædʒɪk] *adj* tragique

**trail** [treɪl] *n* (*tracks*) trace *f*, piste *f*; (*path*) chemin *m*, piste; (*of smoke etc*) traînée *f* ▷ *vt* (*drag*) traîner, tirer; (*follow*) suivre ▷ *vi* traîner; (*in game, contest*) être en retard; **trailer** *n* (*Aut*) remorque *f*; (*US*) caravane *f*; (*Cine*) bande-annonce *f*

**train** [treɪn] *n* train *m*; (*in underground*) rame *f*; (*of dress*) traîne *f*; (*BRIT: series*): **~ of events** série *f* d'événements ▷ *vt* (*apprentice, doctor etc*) former; (*Sport*) entraîner; (*dog*) dresser; (*memory*) exercer; (*point: gun etc*): **to ~ sth on** braquer qch sur ▷ *vi* recevoir sa formation; (*Sport*) s'entraîner; **one's ~ of thought** le fil de sa pensée; **what**

**time does the ~ from Paris get in?** à quelle heure arrive le train de Paris?; **is this the ~ for ...?** c'est bien le train pour...?; **trainee** [treɪ'niː] *n* stagiaire *m/f*; (*in trade*) apprenti(e); **trainer** *n* (*Sport*) entraîneur(-euse); (*of dogs etc*) dresseur(-euse); **trainers** *npl* (*shoes*) chaussures *fpl* de sport; **training** *n* formation *f*; (*Sport*) entraînement *m*; (*of dog etc*) dressage *m*; **in training** (*Sport*) à l'entraînement; (*fit*) en forme; **training course** *n* cours *m* de formation professionnelle; **training shoes** *npl* chaussures *fpl* de sport

**trait** [treɪt] *n* trait *m* (de caractère)

**traitor** ['treɪtə<sup>r</sup>] *n* traître *m*

**tram** [træm] *n* (*BRIT: also*: **~car**) tram(way) *m*

**tramp** [træmp] *n* (*person*) vagabond(e), clochard(e); (*inf: pej: woman*): **to be a ~** être coureuse

**trample** ['træmpl] *vt*: **to ~ (underfoot)** piétiner

**trampoline** ['træmpəliːn] *n* trampoline *m*

**tranquil** ['træŋkwɪl] *adj* tranquille; **tranquillizer** (*US* **tranquilizer**) *n* (*Med*) tranquillisant *m*

**transaction** [træn'zækʃən] *n* transaction *f*

**transatlantic** ['trænzət'læntɪk] *adj* transatlantique

**transcript** ['trænskrɪpt] *n* transcription *f* (*texte*)

**transfer** *n* ['trænsfə<sup>r</sup>] (*gen, also Sport*) transfert *m*; (*Pol: of power*) passation *f*; (*of money*) virement *m*; (*picture, design*) décalcomanie *f*; (: *stick-on*) autocollant *m* ▷ *vt* [træns'fəːr] transférer; passer; virer; **to ~ the charges** (*BRIT Tel*) téléphoner en P.C.V.

**transform** [træns'fɔːm] *vt* transformer; **transformation** *n* transformation *f*

**transfusion** [træns'fjuːʒən] *n* transfusion *f*

**transit** ['trænzɪt] *n*: **in ~** en transit

**transition** [træn'zɪʃən] *n* transition *f*

**transitive** ['trænzɪtɪv] *adj* (*Ling*) transitif(-ive)

**translate** [trænz'leɪt] *vt*: **to ~ (from/into)** traduire (du/en); **can you ~ this for me?** pouvez-vous me traduire ceci?; **translation** [trænz'leɪʃən] *n* traduction *f*; (*Scol: as opposed to prose*) version *f*; **translator** *n* traducteur(-trice)

**transmission** [trænz'mɪʃən] *n* transmission *f*

**transmit** [trænz'mɪt] *vt* transmettre; (*Radio, TV*) émettre; **transmitter** *n* émetteur *m*

**transparent** [træns'pærnt] *adj* transparent(e)

**transplant** *n* ['trænsplɑ:nt] (*Med*) transplantation *f*

**transport** *n* ['trænspɔ:t] transport *m* ▷ *vt* [træns'pɔ:t] transporter; **transportation** [trænspɔ:'teɪʃən] *n* (moyen *m* de) transport *m*

**transvestite** [trænz'vɛstaɪt] *n* travesti(e)

**trap** [træp] *n* (*snare, trick*) piège *m*; (*carriage*) cabriolet *m* ▷ *vt* prendre au piège; (*confine*) coincer

**trash** [træʃ] *n* (*pej: goods*) camelote *f*; (: *nonsense*) sottises *fpl*; (*US: rubbish*) ordures *fpl*; **trash can** *n* (*US*) poubelle *f*

**trauma** ['trɔ:mə] *n* traumatisme *m*; **traumatic** [trɔ:'mætɪk] *adj* traumatisant(e)

**travel** ['trævl] *n* voyage(s) *m(pl)* ▷ *vi* voyager; (*news, sound*) se propager ▷ *vt* (*distance*) parcourir; **travel agency** *n* agence *f* de voyages; **travel agent** *n* agent *m* de voyages; **travel insurance** *n* assurance-voyage *f*; **traveller** (*US* **traveler**) *n* voyageur(-euse); **traveller's cheque** (*US* **traveler's check**) *n* chèque *m* de voyage; **travelling** (*US* **traveling**) *n* voyage(s) *m(pl)*; **travel-sick** *adj*: **to get travel-sick** avoir le mal de la route (*or* de mer *or* de l'air); **travel sickness** *n* mal *m* de la route (*or* de mer *or* de l'air)

**tray** [treɪ] *n* (*for carrying*) plateau *m*; (*on desk*) corbeille *f*

**treacherous** ['trɛtʃərəs] *adj* traître(sse); (*ground, tide*) dont il faut se méfier

**treacle** ['tri:kl] *n* mélasse *f*

**tread** [trɛd] *n* (*step*) pas *m*; (*sound*) bruit *m* de pas; (*of tyre*) chape *f*, bande *f* de roulement ▷ *vi* (*pt* **trod**, *pp* **trodden**) marcher; **tread on** *vt fus* marcher sur

**treasure** ['trɛʒəʳ] *n* trésor *m* ▷ *vt* (*value*) tenir beaucoup à; **treasurer** *n* trésorier(-ière)

**treasury** ['trɛʒərɪ] *n*: **the T~**, (*US*) **the T~ Department** ≈ le ministère des Finances

**treat** [tri:t] *n* petit cadeau, petite surprise ▷ *vt* traiter; **to ~ sb to sth** offrir qch à qn; **treatment** *n* traitement *m*

**treaty** ['tri:tɪ] *n* traité *m*

**treble** ['trɛbl] *adj* triple ▷ *vt*, *vi* tripler

**tree** [tri:] *n* arbre *m*

**trek** [trɛk] *n* (*long walk*) randonnée *f*; (*tiring walk*) longue marche, trotte *f*

**tremble** ['trɛmbl] *vi* trembler

**tremendous** [trɪ'mɛndəs] *adj* (*enormous*) énorme; (*excellent*) formidable, fantastique

**trench** [trɛntʃ] *n* tranchée *f*

**trend** [trɛnd] *n* (*tendency*) tendance *f*; (*of events*) cours *m*; (*fashion*) mode *f*; **trendy** *adj* (*idea, person*) dans le vent; (*clothes*) dernier cri *inv*

**trespass** ['trɛspəs] *vi*: **to ~ on** s'introduire sans permission dans; **"no ~ing"** "propriété privée", "défense d'entrer"

**trial** ['traɪəl] *n* (*Law*) procès *m*, jugement *m*; (*test: of machine etc*) essai *m*; **trials** *npl* (*unpleasant experiences*) épreuves *fpl*; **trial period** *n* période *f* d'essai

**triangle** ['traɪæŋgl] *n* (*Math, Mus*) triangle *m*

**triangular** [traɪ'æŋgjuləʳ] *adj* triangulaire

**tribe** [traɪb] *n* tribu *f*

**tribunal** [traɪ'bju:nl] *n* tribunal *m*

**tribute** ['trɪbju:t] *n* tribut *m*, hommage

*m;* **to pay ~ to** rendre hommage à
**trick** [trɪk] *n (magic)* tour *m; (joke, prank)*
tour, farce *f; (skill, knack)* astuce *f; (Cards)*
levée *f* ▷ *vt* attraper, rouler; **to play a ~**
**on sb** jouer un tour à qn; **that should**
**do the ~** *(fam)* ça devrait faire l'affaire
**trickle** [ˈtrɪkl] *n (of water etc)* filet *m* ▷ *vi*
couler en un filet *or* goutte à goutte
**tricky** [ˈtrɪkɪ] *adj* difficile, délicat(e)
**tricycle** [ˈtraɪsɪkl] *n* tricycle *m*
**trifle** [ˈtraɪfl] *n* bagatelle *f; (Culin)*
≈ diplomate *m* ▷ *adv:* **a ~ long** un
peu long
**trigger** [ˈtrɪɡər] *n (of gun)* gâchette *f*
**trim** [trɪm] *adj (house, garden)* bien
tenu(e); *(figure)* svelte ▷ *n (haircut etc)*
légère coupe; *(on car)* garnitures *fpl*
▷ *vt (cut)* couper légèrement;
*(decorate):* **to ~ (with)** décorer (de);
*(Naut: a sail)* gréer
**trio** [ˈtriːəu] *n* trio *m*
**trip** [trɪp] *n (journey)* voyage *m; (excursion)*
excursion *f; (stumble)* faux pas ▷ *vi*
faire un faux pas, trébucher; **trip up** *vi*
trébucher ▷ *vt* faire un croc-en-jambe à
**triple** [ˈtrɪpl] *adj* triple
**triplets** [ˈtrɪplɪts] *npl* triplés(-ées)
**tripod** [ˈtraɪpɔd] *n* trépied *m*
**triumph** [ˈtraɪʌmf] *n* triomphe
*m* ▷ *vi:* **to ~ (over)** triompher (de);
**triumphant** [traɪˈʌmfənt] *adj*
triomphant(e)
**trivial** [ˈtrɪvɪəl] *adj* insignifiant(e);
*(commonplace)* banal(e)
**trod** [trɔd] *pt of* **tread**
**trodden** [ˈtrɔdn] *pp of* **tread**
**trolley** [ˈtrɔlɪ] *n* chariot *m*
**trombone** [trɔmˈbəun] *n* trombone *m*
**troop** [truːp] *n* bande *f*, groupe *m;*
**troops** *npl (Mil)* troupes *fpl; (: men)*
hommes *mpl*, soldats *mpl*
**trophy** [ˈtrəufɪ] *n* trophée *m*
**tropical** [ˈtrɔpɪkl] *adj* tropical(e)
**trot** [trɔt] *n* trot *m* ▷ *vi* trotter; **on the ~**
*(BRIT: fig)* d'affilée
**trouble** [ˈtrʌbl] *n* difficulté(s) *f(pl)*,
problème(s) *m(pl); (worry)* ennuis *mpl*,
soucis *mpl; (bother, effort)* peine *f; (Pol)*

conflit(s) *m(pl)*, troubles *mpl; (Med):*
**stomach** *etc* **~** troubles gastriques *etc*
▷ *vt (disturb)* déranger, gêner; *(worry)*
inquiéter ▷ *vi:* **to ~ to do** prendre la
peine de faire; **troubles** *npl (Pol etc)*
troubles; *(personal)* ennuis, soucis;
**to be in ~** avoir des ennuis; *(ship,*
*climber etc)* être en difficulté; **to have**
**~ doing sth** avoir du mal à faire qch;
**it's no ~!** je vous en prie!; **the ~ is ...**
le problème, c'est que ...; **what's the**
**~?** qu'est-ce qui ne va pas?; **troubled**
*adj (person)* inquiet(-ète); *(times, life)*
agité(e); **troublemaker** *n* élément
perturbateur, fauteur *m* de troubles;
**troublesome** *adj (child)* fatigant(e),
difficile; *(cough)* gênant(e)
**trough** [trɔf] *n (also:* **drinking ~)**
abreuvoir *m; (also:* **feeding ~)** auge *f;*
*(depression)* creux *m*
**trousers** [ˈtrauzəz] *npl* pantalon *m;*
**short ~** *(BRIT)* culottes courtes
**trout** [traut] *n (pl inv)* truite *f*
**trowel** [ˈtrauəl] *n* truelle *f; (garden tool)*
déplantoir *m*
**truant** [ˈtruənt] *n:* **to play ~** *(BRIT)* faire
l'école buissonnière
**truce** [truːs] *n* trêve *f*
**truck** [trʌk] *n* camion *m; (Rail)* wagon
*m* à plate-forme; **truck driver** *n*
camionneur *m*
**true** [truː] *adj* vrai(e); *(accurate)* exact(e);
*(genuine)* vrai, véritable; *(faithful)* fidèle;
**to come ~** se réaliser
**truly** [ˈtruːlɪ] *adv* vraiment, réellement;
*(truthfully)* sans mentir; **yours ~** *(in*
*letter)* je vous prie d'agréer, Monsieur
*(or* Madame *etc)*, l'expression de mes
sentiments respectueux
**trumpet** [ˈtrʌmpɪt] *n* trompette *f*
**trunk** [trʌŋk] *n (of tree, person)* tronc
*m; (of elephant)* trompe *f; (case)* malle
*f; (US Aut)* coffre *m;* **trunks** *npl (also:*
**swimming ~s)** maillot *m or* slip *m*
de bain
**trust** [trʌst] *n* confiance *f;*
*(responsibility):* **to place sth in sb's**
**~** confier la responsabilité de qch à

qn; (*Law*) fidéicommis *m* ▷ *vt* (*rely on*) avoir confiance en; (*entrust*): **to ~ sth to sb** confier qch à qn; (*hope*): **to ~ (that)** espérer (que); **to take sth on ~** accepter qch les yeux fermés; **trusted** *adj* en qui l'on a confiance; **trustworthy** *adj* digne de confiance

**truth** [truːθ, (*pl*) truːðz] *n* vérité *f*; **truthful** *adj* (*person*) qui dit la vérité; (*answer*) sincère

**try** [traɪ] *n* essai *m*, tentative *f*; (*Rugby*) essai ▷ *vt* (*attempt*) essayer, tenter; (*test: sth new: also: ~ out*) essayer, tester; (*Law: person*) juger; (*strain*) éprouver ▷ *vi* essayer; **to ~ to do** essayer de faire; (*seek*) chercher à faire; **try on** *vt* (*clothes*) essayer; **trying** *adj* pénible

**T-shirt** ['tiːʃəːt] *n* tee-shirt *m*

**tub** [tʌb] *n* cuve *f*; (*for washing clothes*) baquet *m*; (*bath*) baignoire *f*

**tube** [tjuːb] *n* tube *m*; (*BRIT: underground*) métro *m*; (*for tyre*) chambre *f* à air

**tuberculosis** [tjubəːkjuˈləusɪs] *n* tuberculose *f*

**tube station** *n* (*BRIT*) station *f* de métro

**tuck** [tʌk] *vt* (*put*) mettre; **tuck away** *vt* cacher, ranger; (*money*) mettre de côté; (*building*): **to be ~ed away** être caché(e); **tuck in** *vt* rentrer; (*child*) border ▷ *vi* (*eat*) manger de bon appétit; attaquer le repas; **tuck shop** *n* (*BRIT Scol*) boutique *f* à provisions

**Tue(s)** *abbr* (= *Tuesday*) ma

**Tuesday** ['tjuːzdɪ] *n* mardi *m*

**tug** [tʌg] *n* (*ship*) remorqueur *m* ▷ *vt* tirer (sur)

**tuition** [tjuːˈɪʃən] *n* (*BRIT: lessons*) leçons *fpl*; (*: private*) cours particuliers; (*US: fees*) frais *mpl* de scolarité

**tulip** ['tjuːlɪp] *n* tulipe *f*

**tumble** ['tʌmbl] *n* (*fall*) chute *f*, culbute *f* ▷ *vi* tomber, dégringoler; **to ~ to sth** (*inf*) réaliser qch; **tumble dryer** *n* (*BRIT*) séchoir *m* (à linge) à air chaud

**tumbler** ['tʌmblər] *n* verre (droit), gobelet *m*

**tummy** ['tʌmɪ] *n* (*inf*) ventre *m*

**tumour** (*US* **tumor**) ['tjuːmər] *n* tumeur *f*

**tuna** ['tjuːnə] *n* (*pl inv: also:* **~ fish**) thon *m*

**tune** [tjuːn] *n* (*melody*) air *m* ▷ *vt* (*Mus*) accorder; (*Radio, TV, Aut*) régler, mettre au point; **to be in/out of ~** (*instrument*) être accordé/désaccordé; (*singer*) chanter juste/faux; **tune in** *vi* (*Radio, TV*): **to ~ in (to)** se mettre à l'écoute (de); **tune up** *vi* (*musician*) accorder son instrument

**tunic** ['tjuːnɪk] *n* tunique *f*

**Tunis** ['tjuːnɪs] *n* Tunis

**Tunisia** [tjuːˈnɪzɪə] *n* Tunisie *f*

**Tunisian** [tjuːˈnɪzɪən] *adj* tunisien(ne) ▷ *n* Tunisien(ne)

**tunnel** ['tʌnl] *n* tunnel *m*; (*in mine*) galerie *f* ▷ *vi* creuser un tunnel (*or* une galerie)

**turbulence** ['təːbjuləns] *n* (*Aviat*) turbulence *f*

**turf** [təːf] *n* gazon *m*; (*clod*) motte *f* (de gazon) ▷ *vt* gazonner

**Turk** [təːk] *n* Turc (Turque)

**Turkey** ['təːkɪ] *n* Turquie *f*

**turkey** ['təːkɪ] *n* dindon *m*, dinde *f*

**Turkish** ['təːkɪʃ] *adj* turc (turque) ▷ *n* (*Ling*) turc *m*

**turmoil** ['təːmɔɪl] *n* trouble *m*, bouleversement *m*

**turn** [təːn] *n* tour *m*; (*in road*) tournant *m*; (*tendency: of mind, events*) tournure *f*; (*performance*) numéro *m*; (*Med*) crise *f*, attaque *f* ▷ *vt* tourner; (*collar, steak*) retourner; (*change*): **to ~ sth into** changer qch en; (*age*) atteindre ▷ *vi* (*object, wind, milk*) tourner; (*person: look back*) se (re)tourner; (*reverse direction*) faire demi-tour; (*become*) devenir; **to ~ into** se changer en, se transformer en; **a good ~** un service; **it gave me quite a ~** ça m'a fait un coup; **"no left ~"** (*Aut*) "défense de tourner à gauche"; **~ left/right at the next junction** tournez à gauche/ droite au prochain carrefour; **it's your ~** c'est (à) votre tour; **in ~** à son tour;

à tour de rôle; **to take ~s** se relayer;
**turn around** vi (person) se retourner
▷ vt (object) tourner; **turn away** vi se
détourner, tourner la tête ▷ vt (reject:
person) renvoyer; (: business) refuser;
**turn back** vi revenir, faire demi-tour;
**turn down** vt (refuse) rejeter, refuser;
(reduce) baisser; (fold) rabattre; **turn
in** vi (inf: go to bed) aller se coucher
▷ vt (fold) rentrer; **turn off** vi (from
road) tourner ▷ vt (light, radio etc)
éteindre; (tap) fermer; (engine) arrêter;
**I can't ~ the heating off** je n'arrive
pas à éteindre le chauffage; **turn on**
vt (light, radio etc) allumer; (tap) ouvrir;
(engine) mettre en marche; **I can't ~ the
heating on** je n'arrive pas à allumer
le chauffage; **turn out** vt (light, gas)
éteindre; (produce) produire ▷ vi (voters,
troops) se présenter; **to ~ out to be ...**
s'avérer ..., se révéler ...; **turn over**
vi (person) se retourner ▷ vt (object)
retourner; (page) tourner; **turn round**
vi faire demi-tour; (rotate) tourner;
**turn to** vt fus: **to ~ to sb** s'adresser à
qn; **turn up** vi (person) arriver,
se pointer (inf); (lost object) être
retrouvé(e) ▷ vt (collar) remonter;
(radio, heater) mettre plus fort;
**turning** n (in road) tournant m;
**turning point** n (fig) tournant m,
moment décisif
**turnip** ['tə:nɪp] n navet m
**turn**: **turnout** n (of voters) taux m de
participation; **turnover** n (Comm:
amount of money) chiffre m d'affaires;
(: of goods) roulement m; (of staff)
renouvellement m, changement m;
**turnstile** n tourniquet m (d'entrée);
**turn-up** n (BRIT: on trousers) revers m
**turquoise** ['tə:kwɔɪz] n (stone)
turquoise f ▷ adj turquoise inv
**turtle** ['tə:tl] n tortue marine;
**turtleneck (sweater)** n pullover m à
col montant
**tusk** [tʌsk] n défense f (d'éléphant)
**tutor** ['tju:tə*] n (BRIT Scol: in college)
directeur(-trice) d'études; (private

teacher) précepteur(-trice); **tutorial**
[tju:'tɔ:rɪəl] n (Scol) (séance f de)
travaux mpl pratiques
**tuxedo** [tʌk'si:dəu] n (US) smoking m
**TV** [ti:'vi:] n abbr (= television) télé f, TV f
**tweed** [twi:d] n tweed m
**tweezers** ['twi:zəz] npl pince f à épiler
**twelfth** [twelfθ] num douzième
**twelve** [twelv] num douze; **at ~
(o'clock)** à midi; (midnight) à minuit
**twentieth** ['twentɪɪθ] num vingtième
**twenty** ['twentɪ] num vingt
**twice** [twaɪs] adv deux fois; **~ as much**
deux fois plus
**twig** [twɪg] n brindille f ▷ vt, vi (inf)
piger
**twilight** ['twaɪlaɪt] n crépuscule m
**twin** [twɪn] adj, n jumeau(-elle) ▷ vt
jumeler; **twin(-bedded) room** n
chambre f à deux lits; **twin beds** npl lits
mpl jumeaux
**twinkle** ['twɪŋkl] vi scintiller; (eyes)
pétiller
**twist** [twɪst] n torsion f, tour m; (in
wire, flex) tortillon m; (bend: in road)
tournant m; (in story) coup m de théâtre
▷ vt tordre; (weave) entortiller; (roll
around) enrouler; (fig) déformer ▷ vi
(road, river) serpenter; **to ~ one's
ankle/wrist** (Med) se tordre la
cheville/le poignet
**twit** [twɪt] n (inf) crétin(e)
**twitch** [twɪtʃ] n (pull) coup sec, saccade
f; (nervous) tic m ▷ vi se convulser;
avoir un tic
**two** [tu:] num deux; **to put ~ and ~
together** (fig) faire le rapprochement
**type** [taɪp] n (category) genre m, espèce
f; (model) modèle m; (example) type m;
(Typ) type, caractère m ▷ vt (letter etc)
taper (à la machine); **typewriter** n
machine f à écrire
**typhoid** ['taɪfɔɪd] n typhoïde f
**typhoon** [taɪ'fu:n] n typhon m
**typical** ['tɪpɪkl] adj typique,
caractéristique; **typically** adv (as usual)
comme d'habitude; (characteristically)
typiquement

**typing** [ˈtaɪpɪŋ] n dactylo(graphie) f
**typist** [ˈtaɪpɪst] n dactylo m/f
**tyre** (US **tire**) [ˈtaɪə<sup>r</sup>] n pneu m; **I've got a flat ~** j'ai un pneu crevé; **tyre pressure** n (BRIT) pression f (de gonflage)

**UFO** [ˈjuːfəu] n abbr (= unidentified flying object) ovni m
**Uganda** [juːˈgændə] n Ouganda m
**ugly** [ˈʌglɪ] adj laid(e), vilain(e); (fig) répugnant(e)
**UHT** adj abbr = ultra-heat treated; **~ milk** lait m UHT or longue conservation
**UK** n abbr = **United Kingdom**
**ulcer** [ˈʌlsə<sup>r</sup>] n ulcère m; **mouth ~** aphte f
**ultimate** [ˈʌltɪmət] adj ultime, final(e); (authority) suprême; **ultimately** adv (at last) en fin de compte; (fundamentally) finalement; (eventually) par la suite
**ultimatum** (pl **~s** or **ultimata**) [ʌltɪˈmeɪtəm, -tə] n ultimatum m
**ultrasound** [ˈʌltrəsaund] n (Med) ultrason m
**ultraviolet** [ˈʌltrəˈvaɪəlɪt] adj ultraviolet(te)
**umbrella** [ʌmˈbrɛlə] n parapluie m; (for sun) parasol m
**umpire** [ˈʌmpaɪə<sup>r</sup>] n arbitre m; (Tennis) juge m de chaise

**UN** *n abbr* = **United Nations**

**unable** [ʌn'eɪbl] *adj*: **to be ~ to** ne (pas) pouvoir, être dans l'impossibilité de; (*not capable*) être incapable de

**unacceptable** [ʌnək'sɛptəbl] *adj* (*behaviour*) inadmissible; (*price, proposal*) inacceptable

**unanimous** [juː'nænɪməs] *adj* unanime

**unarmed** [ʌn'ɑːmd] *adj* (*person*) non armé(e); (*combat*) sans armes

**unattended** [ʌnə'tɛndɪd] *adj* (*car, child, luggage*) sans surveillance

**unattractive** [ʌnə'træktɪv] *adj* peu attrayant(e); (*character*) peu sympathique

**unavailable** [ʌnə'veɪləbl] *adj* (*article, room, book*) (qui n'est) pas disponible; (*person*) (qui n'est) pas libre

**unavoidable** [ʌnə'vɔɪdəbl] *adj* inévitable

**unaware** [ʌnə'wɛəʳ] *adj*: **to be ~ of** ignorer, ne pas savoir, être inconscient(e) de; **unawares** *adv* à l'improviste, au dépourvu

**unbearable** [ʌn'bɛərəbl] *adj* insupportable

**unbeatable** [ʌn'biːtəbl] *adj* imbattable

**unbelievable** [ʌnbɪ'liːvəbl] *adj* incroyable

**unborn** [ʌn'bɔːn] *adj* à naître

**unbutton** [ʌn'bʌtn] *vt* déboutonner

**uncalled-for** [ʌn'kɔːldfɔːʳ] *adj* déplacé(e), injustifié(e)

**uncanny** [ʌn'kænɪ] *adj* étrange, troublant(e)

**uncertain** [ʌn'səːtn] *adj* incertain(e); (*hesitant*) hésitant(e); **uncertainty** *n* incertitude *f*, doutes *mpl*

**unchanged** [ʌn'tʃeɪndʒd] *adj* inchangé(e)

**uncle** ['ʌŋkl] *n* oncle *m*

**unclear** [ʌn'klɪəʳ] *adj* (qui n'est) pas clair(e) or évident(e); **I'm still ~ about what I'm supposed to do** je ne sais pas encore exactement ce que je dois faire

**uncomfortable** [ʌn'kʌmfətəbl] *adj* inconfortable, peu confortable; (*uneasy*) mal à l'aise, gêné(e); (*situation*) désagréable

**uncommon** [ʌn'kɔmən] *adj* rare, singulier(-ière), peu commun(e)

**unconditional** [ʌnkən'dɪʃənl] *adj* sans conditions

**unconscious** [ʌn'kɔnʃəs] *adj* sans connaissance, évanoui(e); (*unaware*): **~ (of)** inconscient(e) (de) ▷ *n*: **the ~** l'inconscient *m*

**uncontrollable** [ʌnkən'trəuləbl] *adj* (*child, dog*) indiscipliné(e); (*temper, laughter*) irrépressible

**unconventional** [ʌnkən'vɛnʃənl] *adj* peu conventionnel(le)

**uncover** [ʌn'kʌvəʳ] *vt* découvrir

**undecided** [ʌndɪ'saɪdɪd] *adj* indécis(e), irrésolu(e)

**undeniable** [ʌndɪ'naɪəbl] *adj* indéniable, incontestable

**under** ['ʌndəʳ] *prep* sous; (*less than*) (de) moins de; au-dessous de; (*according to*) selon, en vertu de ▷ *adv* au-dessous; en dessous; **~ there** là-dessous; **~ the circumstances** étant donné les circonstances; **~ repair** en (cours de) réparation; **undercover** *adj* secret(-ète), clandestin(e); **underdone** *adj* (*Culin*) saignant(e); (: *pej*) pas assez cuit(e); **underestimate** *vt* sous-estimer, mésestimer; **undergo** *vt* (*irreg*: *like* **go**) subir; (*treatment*) suivre; **undergraduate** *n* étudiant(e) (qui prépare la licence); **underground** *adj* souterrain(e); (*fig*) clandestin(e) ▷ *n* (BRIT: *railway*) métro *m*; (*Pol*) clandestinité *f*; **undergrowth** *n* broussailles *fpl*, sous-bois *m*; **underline** *vt* souligner; **undermine** *vt* saper, miner; **underneath** [ʌndə'niːθ] *adv* (en) dessous ▷ *prep* sous, au-dessous de; **underpants** *npl* caleçon *m*, slip *m*; **underpass** *n* (BRIT: *for pedestrians*) passage souterrain; (: *for cars*) passage inférieur;

**underprivileged** adj défavorisé(e);
**underscore** vt souligner; **undershirt**
n (us) tricot m de corps; **underskirt** n
(BRIT) jupon m

**understand** [ʌndə'stænd] vt, vi (irreg:
like **stand**) comprendre; **I don't ~** je
ne comprends pas; **understandable**
adj compréhensible; **understanding**
adj compréhensif(-ive) ▷ n
compréhension f; (agreement) accord m

**understatement** ['ʌndəsteɪtmənt]
n: **that's an ~** c'est (bien) peu dire, le
terme est faible

**understood** [ʌndə'stud] pt, pp of
**understand** ▷ adj entendu(e); (implied)
sous-entendu(e)

**undertake** [ʌndə'teɪk] vt (irreg: like
**take**) (job, task) entreprendre; (duty)
se charger de; **to ~ to do sth** s'engager
à faire qch

**undertaker** ['ʌndəteɪkə'] n (BRIT)
entrepreneur m des pompes funèbres,
croque-mort m

**undertaking** ['ʌndəteɪkɪŋ] n
entreprise f; (promise) promesse f

**under**: **underwater** adv sous l'eau
▷ adj sous-marin(e); **underway**
adj: **to be underway** (meeting,
investigation) être en cours; **underwear**
n sous-vêtements mpl; (women's
only) dessous mpl; **underwent** pt of
**undergo**; **underworld** n (of crime)
milieu m, pègre f

**undesirable** [ʌndɪ'zaɪərəbl] adj peu
souhaitable; (person, effect) indésirable

**undisputed** ['ʌndɪs'pju:tɪd] adj
incontesté(e)

**undo** [ʌn'du:] vt (irreg: like **do**) défaire

**undone** [ʌn'dʌn] pp of **undo** ▷ adj: **to
come ~** se défaire

**undoubtedly** [ʌn'dautɪdlɪ] adv sans
aucun doute

**undress** [ʌn'drɛs] vi se déshabiller

**unearth** [ʌn'ə:θ] vt déterrer; (fig)
dénicher

**uneasy** [ʌn'i:zɪ] adj mal à l'aise,
gêné(e); (worried) inquiet(-ète); (feeling)
désagréable; (peace, truce) fragile

**unemployed** [ʌnɪm'plɔɪd] adj sans
travail, au chômage ▷ n: **the ~** les
chômeurs mpl

**unemployment** [ʌnɪm'plɔɪmənt] n
chômage m; **unemployment benefit**
(us **unemployment compensation**) n
allocation f de chômage

**unequal** [ʌn'i:kwəl] adj inégal(e)

**uneven** [ʌn'i:vn] adj inégal(e); (quality,
work) irrégulier(-ière)

**unexpected** [ʌnɪk'spɛktɪd]
adj inattendu(e), imprévu(e);
**unexpectedly** adv (succeed) contre
toute attente; (arrive) à l'improviste

**unfair** [ʌn'fɛə'] adj: **~ (to)** injuste
(envers)

**unfaithful** [ʌn'feɪθful] adj infidèle

**unfamiliar** [ʌnfə'mɪlɪə'] adj étrange,
inconnu(e); **to be ~ with sth** mal
connaître qch

**unfashionable** [ʌn'fæʃnəbl] adj
(clothes) démodé(e); (place) peu chic inv

**unfasten** [ʌn'fɑ:sn] vt défaire; (belt,
necklace) détacher; (open) ouvrir

**unfavourable** (us **unfavorable**)
[ʌn'feɪvrəbl] adj défavorable

**unfinished** [ʌn'fɪnɪʃt] adj inachevé(e)

**unfit** [ʌn'fɪt] adj (physically: ill) en
mauvaise santé; (: out of condition)
pas en forme; (incompetent): **~ (for)**
impropre (à); (work, service) inapte (à)

**unfold** [ʌn'fəuld] vt déplier ▷ vi se
dérouler

**unforgettable** [ʌnfə'gɛtəbl] adj
inoubliable

**unfortunate** [ʌn'fɔ:tʃnət] adj
malheureux(-euse); (event, remark)
malencontreux(-euse); **unfortunately**
adv malheureusement

**unfriendly** [ʌn'frɛndlɪ] adj peu
aimable, froid(e)

**unfurnished** [ʌn'fə:nɪʃt] adj non
meublé(e)

**unhappiness** [ʌn'hæpɪnɪs] n tristesse
f, peine f

**unhappy** [ʌn'hæpɪ] adj triste,
malheureux(-euse); (unfortunate:
remark etc) malheureux(-euse); (not

*pleased*): **~ with** mécontent(e) de, peu satisfait(e) de

**unhealthy** [ʌn'hɛlθɪ] *adj* (*gen*) malsain(e); (*person*) maladif(-ive)

**unheard-of** [ʌn'hə:dɔv] *adj* inouï(e), sans précédent

**unhelpful** [ʌn'hɛlpful] *adj* (*person*) peu serviable; (*advice*) peu utile

**unhurt** [ʌn'hə:t] *adj* indemne, sain(e) et sauf (sauve)

**unidentified** [ʌnaɪ'dɛntɪfaɪd] *adj* non identifié(e); *see also* **UFO**

**uniform** ['ju:nɪfɔ:m] *n* uniforme *m* ▷ *adj* uniforme

**unify** ['ju:nɪfaɪ] *vt* unifier

**unimportant** [ʌnɪm'pɔ:tənt] *adj* sans importance

**uninhabited** [ʌnɪn'hæbɪtɪd] *adj* inhabité(e)

**unintentional** [ʌnɪn'tɛnʃənəl] *adj* involontaire

**union** ['ju:njən] *n* union *f*; (*also*: **trade ~**) syndicat *m* ▷ *cpd* du syndicat, syndical(e); **Union Jack** *n* drapeau du Royaume-Uni

**unique** [ju:'ni:k] *adj* unique

**unisex** ['ju:nɪsɛks] *adj* unisexe

**unit** ['ju:nɪt] *n* unité *f*; (*section: of furniture etc*) élément *m*, bloc *m*; (*team, squad*) groupe *m*, service *m*; **kitchen ~** élément de cuisine

**unite** [ju:'naɪt] *vt* unir ▷ *vi* s'unir; **united** *adj* uni(e); (*country, party*) unifié(e); (*efforts*) conjugué(e); **United Kingdom** *n* Royaume-Uni *m* (R.U.); **United Nations (Organization)** *n* (Organisation *f* des) Nations unies (ONU); **United States (of America)** *n* États-Unis *mpl*

**unity** ['ju:nɪtɪ] *n* unité *f*

**universal** [ju:nɪ'və:sl] *adj* universel(le)

**universe** ['ju:nɪvə:s] *n* univers *m*

**university** [ju:nɪ'və:sɪtɪ] *n* université *f* ▷ *cpd* (*student, professor*) d'université; (*education, year, degree*) universitaire

**unjust** [ʌn'dʒʌst] *adj* injuste

**unkind** [ʌn'kaɪnd] *adj* peu gentil(le), méchant(e)

**unknown** [ʌn'nəun] *adj* inconnu(e)

**unlawful** [ʌn'lɔ:ful] *adj* illégal(e)

**unleaded** [ʌn'lɛdɪd] *n* (*also*: **~ petrol**) essence *f* sans plomb

**unleash** [ʌn'li:ʃ] *vt* (*fig*) déchaîner, déclencher

**unless** [ʌn'lɛs] *conj*: **~ he leaves** à moins qu'il (ne) parte; **~ otherwise stated** sauf indication contraire

**unlike** [ʌn'laɪk] *adj* dissemblable, différent(e) ▷ *prep* à la différence de, contrairement à

**unlikely** [ʌn'laɪklɪ] *adj* (*result, event*) improbable; (*explanation*) invraisemblable

**unlimited** [ʌn'lɪmɪtɪd] *adj* illimité(e)

**unlisted** ['ʌn'lɪstɪd] *adj* (*US Tel*) sur la liste rouge

**unload** [ʌn'ləud] *vt* décharger

**unlock** [ʌn'lɔk] *vt* ouvrir

**unlucky** [ʌn'lʌkɪ] *adj* (*person*) malchanceux(-euse); (*object, number*) qui porte malheur; **to be ~** (*person*) ne pas avoir de chance

**unmarried** [ʌn'mærɪd] *adj* célibataire

**unmistak(e)able** [ʌnmɪs'teɪkəbl] *adj* indubitable; qu'on ne peut ne pas reconnaître

**unnatural** [ʌn'nætʃrəl] *adj* non naturel(le); (*perversion*) contre nature

**unnecessary** [ʌn'nɛsəsərɪ] *adj* inutile, superflu(e)

**UNO** ['ju:nəu] *n abbr* = **United Nations Organization**

**unofficial** [ʌnə'fɪʃl] *adj* (*news*) officieux(-euse), non officiel(le); (*strike*) ≈ sauvage

**unpack** [ʌn'pæk] *vi* défaire sa valise ▷ *vt* (*suitcase*) défaire; (*belongings*) déballer

**unpaid** [ʌn'peɪd] *adj* (*bill*) impayé(e); (*holiday*) non-payé(e), sans salaire; (*work*) non rétribué(e)

**unpleasant** [ʌn'plɛznt] *adj* déplaisant(e), désagréable

**unplug** [ʌn'plʌg] *vt* débrancher

**unpopular** [ʌn'pɔpjulə*r*] *adj* impopulaire

**unprecedented** [ʌnˈprɛsɪdəntɪd] *adj* sans précédent

**unpredictable** [ʌnprɪˈdɪktəbl] *adj* imprévisible

**unprotected** [ˈʌnprəˈtɛktɪd] *adj* (*sex*) non protégé(e)

**unqualified** [ʌnˈkwɔlɪfaɪd] *adj* (*teacher*) non diplômé(e), sans titres; (*success*) sans réserve, total(e); (*disaster*) total(e)

**unravel** [ʌnˈrævl] *vt* démêler

**unreal** [ʌnˈrɪəl] *adj* irréel(le); (*extraordinary*) incroyable

**unrealistic** [ˈʌnrɪəˈlɪstɪk] *adj* (*idea*) irréaliste; (*estimate*) peu réaliste

**unreasonable** [ʌnˈriːznəbl] *adj* qui n'est pas raisonnable

**unrelated** [ʌnrɪˈleɪtɪd] *adj* sans rapport; (*people*) sans lien de parenté

**unreliable** [ʌnrɪˈlaɪəbl] *adj* sur qui (*or* quoi) on ne peut pas compter, peu fiable

**unrest** [ʌnˈrɛst] *n* agitation *f*, troubles *mpl*

**unroll** [ʌnˈrəul] *vt* dérouler

**unruly** [ʌnˈruːlɪ] *adj* indiscipliné(e)

**unsafe** [ʌnˈseɪf] *adj* (*in danger*) en danger; (*journey, car*) dangereux(-euse)

**unsatisfactory** [ˈʌnsætɪsˈfæktərɪ] *adj* peu satisfaisant(e)

**unscrew** [ʌnˈskruː] *vt* dévisser

**unsettled** [ʌnˈsɛtld] *adj* (*restless*) perturbé(e); (*unpredictable*) instable; incertain(e); (*not finalized*) non résolu(e)

**unsettling** [ʌnˈsɛtlɪŋ] *adj* qui a un effet perturbateur

**unsightly** [ʌnˈsaɪtlɪ] *adj* disgracieux(-euse), laid(e)

**unskilled** [ʌnˈskɪld] *adj*: **~ worker** manœuvre *m*

**unspoiled** [ˈʌnˈspɔɪld], **unspoilt** [ˈʌnˈspɔɪlt] *adj* (*place*) non dégradé(e)

**unstable** [ʌnˈsteɪbl] *adj* instable

**unsteady** [ʌnˈstɛdɪ] *adj* mal assuré(e), chancelant(e), instable

**unsuccessful** [ʌnsəkˈsɛsful] *adj* (*attempt*) infructueux(-euse); (*writer, proposal*) qui n'a pas de succès; **to be**

**~** (*in attempting sth*) ne pas réussir; ne pas avoir de succès; (*application*) ne pas être retenu(e)

**unsuitable** [ʌnˈsuːtəbl] *adj* qui ne convient pas, peu approprié(e); (*time*) inopportun(e)

**unsure** [ʌnˈʃuəʳ] *adj* pas sûr(e); **to be ~ of o.s.** ne pas être sûr de soi, manquer de confiance en soi

**untidy** [ʌnˈtaɪdɪ] *adj* (*room*) en désordre; (*appearance, person*) débraillé(e); (*person: in character*) sans ordre, désordonné; (*work*) peu soigné(e)

**untie** [ʌnˈtaɪ] *vt* (*knot, parcel*) défaire; (*prisoner, dog*) détacher

**until** [ənˈtɪl] *prep* jusqu'à; (*after negative*) avant ▷ *conj* jusqu'à ce que + *sub*; (*in past, after negative*) avant que + *sub*; **~ he comes** jusqu'à ce qu'il vienne, jusqu'à son arrivée; **~ now** jusqu'à présent, jusqu'ici; **~ then** jusque-là

**untrue** [ʌnˈtruː] *adj* (*statement*) faux (fausse)

**unused¹** [ʌnˈjuːzd] *adj* (*new*) neuf (neuve)

**unused²** [ʌnˈjuːst] *adj*: **to be ~ to sth/ to doing sth** ne pas avoir l'habitude de qch/de faire qch

**unusual** [ʌnˈjuːʒuəl] *adj* insolite, exceptionnel(le), rare; **unusually** *adv* exceptionnellement, particulièrement

**unveil** [ʌnˈveɪl] *vt* dévoiler

**unwanted** [ʌnˈwɔntɪd] *adj* (*child, pregnancy*) non désiré(e); (*clothes etc*) à donner

**unwell** [ʌnˈwɛl] *adj* souffrant(e); **to feel ~** ne pas se sentir bien

**unwilling** [ʌnˈwɪlɪŋ] *adj*: **to be ~ to do** ne pas vouloir faire

**unwind** [ʌnˈwaɪnd] *vb* (*irreg: like* **wind**) ▷ *vt* dérouler ▷ *vi* (*relax*) se détendre

**unwise** [ʌnˈwaɪz] *adj* imprudent(e), peu judicieux(-euse)

**unwittingly** [ʌnˈwɪtɪŋlɪ] *adv* involontairement

**unwrap** [ʌnˈræp] *vt* défaire; ouvrir

**unzip** [ʌnˈzɪp] *vt* ouvrir (la fermeture

éclair de); (*Comput*) dézipper

○ KEYWORD

**up** [ʌp] *prep*: **he went up the stairs/the hill** il a monté l'escalier/la colline; **the cat was up a tree** le chat était dans un arbre; **they live further up the street** ils habitent plus haut dans la rue; **go up that road and turn left** remontez la rue et tournez à gauche
▷ *adv* **1** en haut; en l'air; (*upwards, higher*): **up in the sky/the mountains** (là-haut) dans le ciel/les montagnes; **put it a bit higher up** mettez-le un peu plus haut; **to stand up** (*get up*) se lever, se mettre debout; (*be standing*) être debout; **up there** là-haut; **up above** au-dessus
**2**: **to be up** (*out of bed*) être levé(e); (*prices*) avoir augmenté *or* monté; (*finished*): **when the year was up** à la fin de l'année
**3**: **up to** (*as far as*) jusqu'à; **up to now** jusqu'à présent
**4**: **to be up to** (*depending on*): **it's up to you** c'est à vous de décider; (*equal to*): **he's not up to it** (*job, task etc*) il n'en est pas capable; (*inf: be doing*): **what is he up to?** qu'est-ce qu'il peut bien faire?
▷ *n*: **ups and downs** hauts et bas *mpl*

**up-and-coming** [ʌpənd'kʌmɪŋ] *adj* plein(e) d'avenir *or* de promesses
**upbringing** ['ʌpbrɪŋɪŋ] *n* éducation *f*
**update** [ʌp'deɪt] *vt* mettre à jour
**upfront** [ʌp'frʌnt] *adj* (*open*) franc (franche) ▷ *adv* (*pay*) d'avance; **to be ~ about sth** ne rien cacher de qch
**upgrade** [ʌp'greɪd] *vt* (*person*) promouvoir; (*job*) revaloriser; (*property, equipment*) moderniser
**upheaval** [ʌp'hiːvl] *n* bouleversement *m*; (*in room*) branle-bas *m*; (*event*) crise *f*
**uphill** [ʌp'hɪl] *adj* qui monte; (*fig: task*) difficile, pénible ▷ *adv* (*face, look*) en amont, vers l'amont; **to go ~** monter
**upholstery** [ʌp'həulstərɪ] *n*

rembourrage *m*; (*cover*) tissu *m* d'ameublement; (*of car*) garniture *f*
**upmarket** [ʌp'mɑːkɪt] *adj* (*product*) haut de gamme *inv*; (*area*) chic *inv*
**upon** [ə'pɔn] *prep* sur
**upper** ['ʌpəʳ] *adj* supérieur(e); du dessus ▷ *n* (*of shoe*) empeigne *f*; **upper-class** *adj* de la haute société, aristocratique; (*district*) élégant(e), huppé(e); (*accent, attitude*) caractéristique des classes supérieures
**upright** ['ʌpraɪt] *adj* droit(e); (*fig*) droit, honnête
**uprising** ['ʌpraɪzɪŋ] *n* soulèvement *m*, insurrection *f*
**uproar** ['ʌprɔːʳ] *n* tumulte *m*, vacarme *m*; (*protests*) protestations *fpl*
**upset** *n* ['ʌpset] dérangement *m* ▷ *vt* (*irreg: like* **set** [ʌp'sɛt]) (*glass etc*) renverser; (*plan*) déranger; (*person: offend*) contrarier; (: *grieve*) faire de la peine à; bouleverser ▷ *adj* [ʌp'sɛt] contrarié(e); peiné(e); **to have a stomach ~** (*BRIT*) avoir une indigestion
**upside down** ['ʌpsaɪd-] *adv* à l'envers; **to turn sth ~** (*fig: place*) mettre sens dessus dessous
**upstairs** [ʌp'stɛəz] *adv* en haut ▷ *adj* (*room*) du dessus, d'en haut ▷ *n*: **the ~** l'étage *m*
**up-to-date** ['ʌptə'deɪt] *adj* moderne; (*information*) très récent(e)
**uptown** ['ʌptaun] (*US*) *adv* (*live*) dans les quartiers chics; (*go*) vers les quartiers chics ▷ *adj* des quartiers chics
**upward** ['ʌpwəd] *adj* ascendant(e); vers le haut; **upward(s)** *adv* vers le haut; (*more than*): **upward(s) of** plus de
**uranium** [juə'reɪnɪəm] *n* uranium *m*
**Uranus** [juə'reɪnəs] *n* Uranus *f*
**urban** ['əːbən] *adj* urbain(e)
**urge** [əːdʒ] *n* besoin (impératif), envie (pressante) ▷ *vt* (*person*): **to ~ sb to do** exhorter qn à faire, pousser qn à faire, recommander vivement à qn de faire
**urgency** ['əːdʒənsɪ] *n* urgence *f*; (*of tone*) insistance *f*

**urgent** ['ə:dʒənt] *adj* urgent(e); (*plea, tone*) pressant(e)

**urinal** ['juərɪnl] *n* (*BRIT: place*) urinoir *m*

**urinate** ['juərɪneɪt] *vi* uriner

**urine** ['juərɪn] *n* urine *f*

**URL** *abbr* (= uniform resource locator) URL *f*

**US** *n abbr* = **United States**

**us** [ʌs] *pron* nous; *see also* **me**

**USA** *n abbr* = **United States of America**

**use** *n* [ju:s] emploi *m*, utilisation *f*; (*usefulness*) utilité *f* ▷ *vt* [ju:z] se servir de, utiliser, employer; **in ~** en usage; **out of ~** hors d'usage; **to be of ~** servir, être utile; **it's no ~** ça ne sert à rien; **to have the ~ of** avoir l'usage de; **she ~d to do it** elle le faisait (autrefois), elle avait coutume de le faire; **to be ~d to** avoir l'habitude de, être habitué(e) à; **use up** *vt* finir, épuiser; (*food*) consommer; **used** [ju:zd] *adj* (*car*) d'occasion; **useful** *adj* utile; **useless** *adj* inutile; (*inf: person*) nul(le); **user** *n* utilisateur(-trice), usager *m*; **user-friendly** *adj* convivial(e), facile d'emploi

**usual** ['ju:ʒuəl] *adj* habituel(le); **as ~** comme d'habitude; **usually** *adv* d'habitude, d'ordinaire

**utensil** [ju:'tɛnsl] *n* ustensile *m*; **kitchen ~s** batterie *f* de cuisine

**utility** [ju:'tɪlɪtɪ] *n* utilité *f*; (*also:* **public ~**) service public

**utilize** ['ju:tɪlaɪz] *vt* utiliser; (*make good use of*) exploiter

**utmost** ['ʌtməust] *adj* extrême, le (la) plus grand(e) ▷ *n*: **to do one's ~** faire tout son possible

**utter** ['ʌtəʳ] *adj* total(e), complet(-ète) ▷ *vt* prononcer, proférer; (*sounds*) émettre; **utterly** *adv* complètement, totalement

**U-turn** ['ju:'tə:n] *n* demi-tour *m*; (*fig*) volte-face *f inv*

**v.** *abbr* = **verse** (= *vide*) v.; (= *versus*) c.; (= *volt*) V

**vacancy** ['veɪkənsɪ] *n* (*BRIT: job*) poste vacant; (*room*) chambre *f* disponible; **"no vacancies"** "complet"

**vacant** ['veɪkənt] *adj* (*post*) vacant(e); (*seat etc*) libre, disponible; (*expression*) distrait(e)

**vacate** [və'keɪt] *vt* quitter

**vacation** [və'keɪʃən] *n* (*esp US*) vacances *fpl*; **on ~** en vacances; **vacationer** (*US* **vacationist**) *n* vacancier(-ière)

**vaccination** [væksɪ'neɪʃən] *n* vaccination *f*

**vaccine** ['væksi:n] *n* vaccin *m*

**vacuum** ['vækjum] *n* vide *m*; **vacuum cleaner** *n* aspirateur *m*

**vagina** [və'dʒaɪnə] *n* vagin *m*

**vague** [veɪg] *adj* vague, imprécis(e); (*blurred: photo, memory*) flou(e)

**vain** [veɪn] *adj* (*useless*) vain(e); (*conceited*) vaniteux(-euse); **in ~** en vain

**Valentine's Day** ['væləntaɪnz-] *n*

Saint-Valentin f

**valid** ['vælɪd] adj (document) valide, valable; (excuse) valable

**valley** ['vælɪ] n vallée f

**valuable** ['væljuəbl] adj (jewel) de grande valeur; (time, help) précieux(-euse); **valuables** npl objets mpl de valeur

**value** ['vælju:] n valeur f ▷ vt (fix price) évaluer, expertiser; (appreciate) apprécier; **values** npl (principles) valeurs fpl

**valve** [vælv] n (in machine) soupape f; (on tyre) valve f; (Med) valve, valvule f

**vampire** ['væmpaɪəʳ] n vampire m

**van** [væn] n (Aut) camionnette f

**vandal** ['vændl] n vandale m/f; **vandalism** n vandalisme m; **vandalize** vt saccager

**vanilla** [və'nɪlə] n vanille f

**vanish** ['vænɪʃ] vi disparaître

**vanity** ['vænɪtɪ] n vanité f

**vapour** (US **vapor**) ['veɪpəʳ] n vapeur f; (on window) buée f

**variable** ['vɛərɪəbl] adj variable; (mood) changeant(e)

**variant** ['vɛərɪənt] n variante f

**variation** [vɛərɪ'eɪʃən] n variation f; (in opinion) changement m

**varied** ['vɛərɪd] adj varié(e), divers(e)

**variety** [və'raɪətɪ] n variété f; (quantity) nombre m, quantité f

**various** ['vɛərɪəs] adj divers(e), différent(e); (several) divers, plusieurs

**varnish** ['vɑːnɪʃ] n vernis m ▷ vt vernir

**vary** ['vɛərɪ] vt, vi varier, changer

**vase** [vɑːz] n vase m

**Vaseline®** ['væsɪliːn] n vaseline f

**vast** [vɑːst] adj vaste, immense; (amount, success) énorme

**VAT** [væt] n abbr (BRIT: = value added tax) TVA f

**vault** [vɔːlt] n (of roof) voûte f; (tomb) caveau m; (in bank) salle f des coffres; chambre forte ▷ vt (also: ~ **over**) sauter (d'un bond)

**VCR** n abbr = **video cassette recorder**

**VDU** n abbr = **visual display unit**

**veal** [viːl] n veau m

**veer** [vɪəʳ] vi tourner; (car, ship) virer

**vegan** ['viːgən] n végétalien(ne)

**vegetable** ['vɛdʒtəbl] n légume m ▷ adj végétal(e)

**vegetarian** [vɛdʒɪ'tɛərɪən] adj, n végétarien(ne); **do you have any ~ dishes?** avez-vous des plats végétariens?

**vegetation** [vɛdʒɪ'teɪʃən] n végétation f

**vehicle** ['viːɪkl] n véhicule m

**veil** [veɪl] n voile m

**vein** [veɪn] n veine f; (on leaf) nervure f

**Velcro®** ['vɛlkrəu] n velcro® m

**velvet** ['vɛlvɪt] n velours m

**vending machine** ['vɛndɪŋ-] n distributeur m automatique

**vendor** ['vɛndəʳ] n vendeur(-euse); **street ~** marchand ambulant

**Venetian blind** [vɪ'niːʃən-] n store vénitien

**vengeance** ['vɛndʒəns] n vengeance f; **with a ~** (fig) vraiment, pour de bon

**venison** ['vɛnɪsn] n venaison f

**venom** ['vɛnəm] n venin m

**vent** [vɛnt] n conduit m d'aération; (in dress, jacket) fente f ▷ vt (fig: one's feelings) donner libre cours à

**ventilation** [vɛntɪ'leɪʃən] n ventilation f, aération f

**venture** ['vɛntʃəʳ] n entreprise f ▷ vt risquer, hasarder ▷ vi s'aventurer, se risquer; **a business ~** une entreprise commerciale

**venue** ['vɛnjuː] n lieu m

**Venus** ['viːnəs] n (planet) Vénus f

**verb** [vəːb] n verbe m; **verbal** adj verbal(e)

**verdict** ['vəːdɪkt] n verdict m

**verge** [vəːdʒ] n bord m; **"soft ~s"** (BRIT) "accotements non stabilisés"; **on the ~ of doing** sur le point de faire

**verify** ['vɛrɪfaɪ] vt vérifier

**versatile** ['vəːsətaɪl] adj polyvalent(e)

**verse** [vəːs] n vers mpl; (stanza) strophe f; (in Bible) verset m

**version** ['vəːʃən] n version f

**versus** ['vɜːsəs] prep contre
**vertical** ['vɜːtɪkl] adj vertical(e)
**very** ['vɛrɪ] adv très ▷ adj: **the ~ book which** le livre même que; **the ~ last** le tout dernier; **at the ~ least** au moins; **~ much** beaucoup
**vessel** ['vɛsl] n (Anat, Naut) vaisseau m; (container) récipient m; see also **blood**
**vest** [vɛst] n (BRIT: underwear) tricot m de corps; (US: waistcoat) gilet m
**vet** [vɛt] n abbr (BRIT: = veterinary surgeon) vétérinaire m/f; (US: = veteran) ancien(ne) combattant(e) ▷ vt examiner minutieusement
**veteran** ['vɛtərn] n vétéran m; (also: **war ~**) ancien combattant
**veterinary surgeon** ['vɛtrɪnərɪ-] (BRIT) (US **veterinarian** [vɛtrɪ'nɛərɪən]) n vétérinaire m/f
**veto** ['viːtəu] n (pl **-es**) veto m ▷ vt opposer son veto à
**via** ['vaɪə] prep par, via
**viable** ['vaɪəbl] adj viable
**vibrate** [vaɪ'breɪt] vi: **to ~ (with)** vibrer (de)
**vibration** [vaɪ'breɪʃən] n vibration f
**vicar** ['vɪkər] n pasteur m (de l'Église anglicane)
**vice** [vaɪs] n (evil) vice m; (Tech) étau m; **vice-chairman** n vice-président(e)
**vice versa** ['vaɪsɪ'vɜːsə] adv vice versa
**vicinity** [vɪ'sɪnɪtɪ] n environs mpl, alentours mpl
**vicious** ['vɪʃəs] adj (remark) cruel(le), méchant(e); (blow) brutal(e); (dog) méchant(e), dangereux(-euse); **a ~ circle** un cercle vicieux
**victim** ['vɪktɪm] n victime f
**victor** ['vɪktər] n vainqueur m
**Victorian** [vɪk'tɔːrɪən] adj victorien(ne)
**victorious** [vɪk'tɔːrɪəs] adj victorieux(-euse)
**victory** ['vɪktərɪ] n victoire f
**video** ['vɪdɪəu] n (video film) vidéo f; (also: **~ cassette**) vidéocassette f; (also: **~ cassette recorder**) magnétoscope m ▷ vt (with recorder) enregistrer;

(with camera) filmer; **video camera** n caméra f vidéo inv; **video (cassette) recorder** n magnétoscope m; **video game** n jeu m vidéo inv; **video shop** n vidéoclub m; **video tape** n bande f vidéo inv; (cassette) vidéocassette f
**vie** [vaɪ] vi: **to ~ with** lutter avec, rivaliser avec
**Vienna** [vɪ'ɛnə] n Vienne
**Vietnam, Viet Nam** ['vjɛt'næm] n Viêt-nam or Vietnam m; **Vietnamese** [vjɛtnə'miːz] adj vietnamien(ne) ▷ n (pl inv) Vietnamien(ne)
**view** [vjuː] n vue f; (opinion) avis m, vue ▷ vt voir, regarder; (situation) considérer; (house) visiter; **on ~** (in museum etc) exposé(e); **in full ~ of sb** sous les yeux de qn; **in my ~** à mon avis; **in ~ of the fact that** étant donné que; **viewer** n (TV) téléspectateur(-trice); **viewpoint** n point m de vue
**vigilant** ['vɪdʒɪlənt] adj vigilant(e)
**vigorous** ['vɪgərəs] adj vigoureux(-euse)
**vile** [vaɪl] adj (action) vil(e); (smell, food) abominable; (temper) massacrant(e)
**villa** ['vɪlə] n villa f
**village** ['vɪlɪdʒ] n village m; **villager** n villageois(e)
**villain** ['vɪlən] n (scoundrel) scélérat m; (BRIT: criminal) bandit m; (in novel etc) traître m
**vinaigrette** [vɪneɪ'grɛt] n vinaigrette f
**vine** [vaɪn] n vigne f
**vinegar** ['vɪnɪgər] n vinaigre m
**vineyard** ['vɪnjɑːd] n vignoble m
**vintage** ['vɪntɪdʒ] n (year) année f, millésime m ▷ cpd (car) d'époque; (wine) de grand cru
**vinyl** ['vaɪnl] n vinyle m
**viola** [vɪ'əulə] n alto m
**violate** ['vaɪəleɪt] vt violer
**violation** [vaɪə'leɪʃən] n violation f; **in ~ of** (rule, law) en infraction à, en violation de
**violence** ['vaɪələns] n violence f
**violent** ['vaɪələnt] adj violent(e)
**violet** ['vaɪələt] adj (colour) violet(te)

▷ *n* (*plant*) violette *f*
**violin** [vaɪə'lɪn] *n* violon *m*
**VIP** *n abbr* (= *very important person*) VIP *m*
**virgin** ['vəːdʒɪn] *n* vierge *f*
**Virgo** ['vəːgəu] *n* la Vierge
**virtual** ['vəːtjuəl] *adj* (*Comput, Physics*) virtuel(le); (*in effect*): **it's a ~ impossibility** c'est quasiment impossible; **virtually** *adv* (*almost*) pratiquement; **virtual reality** *n* (*Comput*) réalité virtuelle
**virtue** ['vəːtjuː] *n* vertu *f*; (*advantage*) mérite *m*, avantage *m*; **by ~ of** en vertu *or* raison de
**virus** ['vaɪərəs] *n* (*Med, Comput*) virus *m*
**visa** ['viːzə] *n* visa *m*
**vise** [vaɪs] *n* (*US Tech*) = **vice**
**visibility** [vɪzɪ'bɪlɪtɪ] *n* visibilité *f*
**visible** ['vɪzəbl] *adj* visible
**vision** ['vɪʒən] *n* (*sight*) vue *f*, vision *f*; (*foresight, in dream*) vision
**visit** ['vɪzɪt] *n* visite *f*; (*stay*) séjour *m* ▷ *vt* (*person: us: also:* **~ with**) rendre visite à; (*place*) visiter; **visiting hours** *npl* heures *fpl* de visite; **visitor** *n* visiteur(-euse); (*to one's house*) invité(e); **visitor centre** (*US* **visitor center**) *n* hall *m or* centre *m* d'accueil
**visual** ['vɪzjuəl] *adj* visuel(le); **visualize** *vt* se représenter
**vital** ['vaɪtl] *adj* vital(e); **of ~ importance (to sb/sth)** d'une importance capitale (pour qn/qch)
**vitality** [vaɪ'tælɪtɪ] *n* vitalité *f*
**vitamin** ['vɪtəmɪn] *n* vitamine *f*
**vivid** ['vɪvɪd] *adj* (*account*) frappant(e), vivant(e); (*light, imagination*) vif (vive)
**V-neck** ['viːnɛk] *n* décolleté *m* en V
**vocabulary** [vəu'kæbjulərɪ] *n* vocabulaire *m*
**vocal** ['vəukl] *adj* vocal(e); (*articulate*) qui n'hésite pas à s'exprimer, qui sait faire entendre ses opinions
**vocational** [vəu'keɪʃənl] *adj* professionnel(le)
**vodka** ['vɔdkə] *n* vodka *f*
**vogue** [vəug] *n*: **to be in ~** être en vogue *or* à la mode

**voice** [vɔɪs] *n* voix *f* ▷ *vt* (*opinion*) exprimer, formuler; **voice mail** *n* (*system*) messagerie *f* vocale; (*device*) boîte *f* vocale
**void** [vɔɪd] *n* vide *m* ▷ *adj* (*invalid*) nul(le); (*empty*): **~ of** vide de, dépourvu(e) de
**volatile** ['vɔlətaɪl] *adj* volatil(e); (*fig: person*) versatile; (*: situation*) explosif(-ive)
**volcano** (*pl* **-es**) [vɔl'keɪnəu] *n* volcan *m*
**volleyball** ['vɔlɪbɔːl] *n* volley(-ball) *m*
**volt** [vəult] *n* volt *m*; **voltage** *n* tension *f*, voltage *m*
**volume** ['vɔljuːm] *n* volume *m*; (*of tank*) capacité *f*
**voluntarily** ['vɔləntrɪlɪ] *adv* volontairement
**voluntary** ['vɔləntərɪ] *adj* volontaire; (*unpaid*) bénévole
**volunteer** [vɔlən'tɪə'] *n* volontaire *m/f* ▷ *vt* (*information*) donner spontanément ▷ *vi* (*Mil*) s'engager comme volontaire; **to ~ to do** se proposer pour faire
**vomit** ['vɔmɪt] *n* vomissure *f* ▷ *vt, vi* vomir
**vote** [vəut] *n* vote *m*, suffrage *m*; (*votes cast*) voix *f*, vote; (*franchise*) droit *m* de vote ▷ *vt* (*chairman*) élire; (*propose*): **to ~ that** proposer que + *sub* ▷ *vi* voter; **~ of thanks** discours *m* de remerciement; **voter** *n* électeur(-trice); **voting** *n* scrutin *m*, vote *m*
**voucher** ['vautʃə'] *n* (*for meal, petrol, gift*) bon *m*
**vow** [vau] *n* vœu *m*, serment *m* ▷ *vi* jurer
**vowel** ['vauəl] *n* voyelle *f*
**voyage** ['vɔɪɪdʒ] *n* voyage *m* par mer, traversée *f*
**vulgar** ['vʌlgə'] *adj* vulgaire
**vulnerable** ['vʌlnərəbl] *adj* vulnérable
**vulture** ['vʌltʃə'] *n* vautour *m*

# W

**waddle** ['wɒdl] *vi* se dandiner

**wade** [weɪd] *vi*: **to ~ through** marcher dans, patauger dans; (*fig: book*) venir à bout de

**wafer** ['weɪfəʳ] *n* (*Culin*) gaufrette *f*

**waffle** ['wɒfl] *n* (*Culin*) gaufre *f* ▷ *vi* parler pour ne rien dire; faire du remplissage

**wag** [wæg] *vt* agiter, remuer ▷ *vi* remuer

**wage** [weɪdʒ] *n* (*also*: **~s**) salaire *m*, paye *f* ▷ *vt*: **to ~ war** faire la guerre

**wag(g)on** ['wægən] *n* (*horse-drawn*) chariot *m*; (*BRIT Rail*) wagon *m* (de marchandises)

**wail** [weɪl] *n* gémissement *m*; (*of siren*) hurlement *m* ▷ *vi* gémir; (*siren*) hurler

**waist** [weɪst] *n* taille *f*, ceinture *f*; **waistcoat** *n* (*BRIT*) gilet *m*

**wait** [weɪt] *n* attente *f* ▷ *vi* attendre; **to ~ for sb/sth** attendre qn/qch; **to keep sb ~ing** faire attendre qn; **~ for me, please** attendez-moi, s'il vous plaît; **I can't ~ to ...** (*fig*) je meurs

d'envie de ...; **to lie in ~ for** guetter; **wait on** *vt fus* servir; **waiter** *n* garçon *m* (de café), serveur *m*; **waiting list** *n* liste *f* d'attente; **waiting room** *n* salle *f* d'attente; **waitress** ['weɪtrɪs] *n* serveuse *f*

**waive** [weɪv] *vt* renoncer à, abandonner

**wake** [weɪk] *vb* (*pt* **woke** *or* **~d**, *pp* **woken** *or* **~d**) ▷ *vt* (*also*: **~ up**) réveiller ▷ *vi* (*also*: **~ up**) se réveiller ▷ *n* (*for dead person*) veillée *f* mortuaire; (*Naut*) sillage *m*

**Wales** [weɪlz] *n* pays *m* de Galles; **the Prince of ~** le prince de Galles

**walk** [wɔːk] *n* promenade *f*; (*short*) petit tour; (*gait*) démarche *f*; (*path*) chemin *m*; (*in park etc*) allée *f* ▷ *vi* marcher; (*for pleasure, exercise*) se promener ▷ *vt* (*distance*) faire à pied; (*dog*) promener; **10 minutes' ~ from** à 10 minutes de marche de; **to go for a ~** se promener; faire un tour; **from all ~s of life** de toutes conditions sociales; **walk out** *vi* (*go out*) sortir; (*as protest*) partir (en signe de protestation); (*strike*) se mettre en grève; **to ~ out on sb** quitter qn; **walker** *n* (*person*) marcheur(-euse); **walkie-talkie** ['wɔːkɪ'tɔːkɪ] *n* talkie-walkie *m*; **walking** *n* marche *f* à pied; **walking shoes** *npl* chaussures *fpl* de marche; **walking stick** *n* canne *f*; **Walkman®** *n* Walkman® *m*; **walkway** *n* promenade *f*, cheminement piéton

**wall** [wɔːl] *n* mur *m*; (*of tunnel, cave*) paroi *f*

**wallet** ['wɒlɪt] *n* portefeuille *m*; **I can't find my ~** je ne retrouve plus mon portefeuille

**wallpaper** ['wɔːlpeɪpəʳ] *n* papier peint ▷ *vt* tapisser

**walnut** ['wɔːlnʌt] *n* noix *f*; (*tree, wood*) noyer *m*

**walrus** (*pl* ~ *or* **~es**) ['wɔːlrəs] *n* morse *m*

**waltz** [wɔːlts] *n* valse *f* ▷ *vi* valser

**wand** [wɒnd] *n* (*also*: **magic ~**) baguette *f* (magique)

**wander** ['wɒndəʳ] *vi* (*person*) errer, aller

sans but; (*thoughts*) vagabonder ▷ *vt* errer dans

**want** [wɔnt] *vt* vouloir; (*need*) avoir besoin de ▷ *n*: **for ~ of** par manque de, faute de; **to ~ to do** vouloir faire; **to ~ sb to do** vouloir que qn fasse; **wanted** *adj* (*criminal*) recherché(e) par la police; **"cook wanted"** "on recherche un cuisinier"

**war** [wɔːʳ] *n* guerre *f*; **to make ~ (on)** faire la guerre (à)

**ward** [wɔːd] *n* (*in hospital*) salle *f*; (*Pol*) section électorale; (*Law: child: also:* **~ of court**) pupille *m/f*

**warden** [wɔːdn] *n* (*BRIT: of institution*) directeur(-trice); (*of park, game reserve*) gardien(ne); (*BRIT: also:* **traffic ~**) contractuel(le)

**wardrobe** [ˈwɔːdrəub] *n* (*cupboard*) armoire *f*; (*clothes*) garde-robe *f*

**warehouse** [ˈwɛəhaus] *n* entrepôt *m*

**warfare** [ˈwɔːfɛəʳ] *n* guerre *f*

**warhead** [ˈwɔːhɛd] *n* (*Mil*) ogive *f*

**warm** [wɔːm] *adj* chaud(e); (*person, thanks, welcome, applause*) chaleureux(-euse); **it's ~** il fait chaud; **I'm ~** j'ai chaud; **warm up** *vi* (*person, room*) se réchauffer; (*athlete, discussion*) s'échauffer ▷ *vt* (*food*) (faire) réchauffer; (*water*) (faire) chauffer; (*engine*) faire chauffer; **warmly** *adv* (*dress*) chaudement; (*thank, welcome*) chaleureusement; **warmth** *n* chaleur *f*

**warn** [wɔːn] *vt* avertir, prévenir; **to ~ sb (not) to do** conseiller à qn de (ne pas) faire; **warning** *n* avertissement *m*; (*notice*) avis *m*; **warning light** *n* avertisseur lumineux

**warrant** [ˈwɔrnt] *n* (*guarantee*) garantie *f*; (*Law: to arrest*) mandat *m* d'arrêt; (*: to search*) mandat de perquisition ▷ *vt* (*justify, merit*) justifier

**warranty** [ˈwɔrənti] *n* garantie *f*

**warrior** [ˈwɔriəʳ] *n* guerrier(-ière)

**Warsaw** [ˈwɔːsɔː] *n* Varsovie *f*

**warship** [ˈwɔːʃɪp] *n* navire *m* de guerre

**wart** [wɔːt] *n* verrue *f*

**wartime** [ˈwɔːtaɪm] *n*: **in ~** en temps

de guerre

**wary** [ˈwɛəri] *adj* prudent(e)

**was** [wɔz] *pt of* **be**

**wash** [wɔʃ] *vt* laver ▷ *vi* se laver; (*sea*): **to ~ over/against sth** inonder/baigner qch ▷ *n* (*clothes*) lessive *f*; (*washing programme*) lavage *m*; (*of ship*) sillage *m*; **to have a ~** se laver, faire sa toilette; **wash up** *vi* (*BRIT*) faire la vaisselle; (*US: have a wash*) se débarbouiller; **washbasin** *n* lavabo *m*; **wash cloth** *n* (*US*) gant *m* de toilette; **washer** *n* (*Tech*) rondelle *f*, joint *m*; **washing** *n* (*BRIT: linen etc: dirty*) linge *m*; (*: clean*) lessive *f*; **washing line** *n* (*BRIT*) corde *f* à linge; **washing machine** *n* machine *f* à laver; **washing powder** *n* (*BRIT*) lessive *f* (en poudre)

**Washington** [ˈwɔʃɪŋtən] *n* Washington *m*

**wash**: **washing-up** *n* (*BRIT*) vaisselle *f*; **washing-up liquid** *n* (*BRIT*) produit *m* pour la vaisselle; **washroom** *n* (*US*) toilettes *fpl*

**wasn't** [ˈwɔznt] = **was not**

**wasp** [wɔsp] *n* guêpe *f*

**waste** [weɪst] *n* gaspillage *m*; (*of time*) perte *f*; (*rubbish*) déchets *mpl*; (*also:* **household ~**) ordures *fpl* ▷ *adj* (*land, ground: in city*) à l'abandon; (*leftover*): **~ material** déchets ▷ *vt* gaspiller; (*time, opportunity*) perdre; **waste ground** *n* (*BRIT*) terrain *m* vague; **wastepaper basket** *n* corbeille *f* à papier

**watch** [wɔtʃ] *n* montre *f*; (*act of watching*) surveillance *f*; (*guard: Mil*) sentinelle *f*; (*: Naut*) homme *m* de quart; (*Naut: spell of duty*) quart *m* ▷ *vt* (*look at*) observer; (*: match, programme*) regarder; (*spy on, guard*) surveiller; (*be careful of*) faire attention à ▷ *vi* regarder; (*keep guard*) monter la garde; **to keep ~** faire le guet; **watch out** *vi* faire attention; **watchdog** *n* chien *m* de garde; (*fig*) gardien(ne); **watch strap** *n* bracelet *m* de montre

**water** [ˈwɔːtəʳ] *n* eau *f* ▷ *vt* (*plant, garden*) arroser ▷ *vi* (*eyes*) larmoyer; **in**

**British ~s** dans les eaux territoriales Britanniques; **to make sb's mouth ~** mettre l'eau à la bouche de qn; **water down** vt (milk etc) couper avec de l'eau; (fig: story) édulcorer; **watercolour** (US **watercolor**) n aquarelle f; **watercress** n cresson m (de fontaine); **waterfall** n chute f d'eau; **watering can** n arrosoir m; **watermelon** n pastèque f; **waterproof** adj imperméable; **water-skiing** n ski m nautique

**watt** [wɔt] n watt m

**wave** [weɪv] n vague f; (of hand) geste m, signe m; (Radio) onde f; (in hair) ondulation f; (fig: of enthusiasm, strikes etc) vague f ▷ vi faire signe de la main; (flag) flotter au vent; (grass) ondoyer ▷ vt (handkerchief) agiter; (stick) brandir; **wavelength** n longueur f d'ondes

**waver** ['weɪvə'] vi vaciller; (voice) trembler; (person) hésiter

**wavy** ['weɪvɪ] adj (hair, surface) ondulé(e); (line) onduleux(-euse)

**wax** [wæks] n cire f; (for skis) fart m ▷ vt cirer; (car) lustrer; (skis) farter ▷ vi (moon) croître

**way** [weɪ] n chemin m, voie f; (distance) distance f; (direction) chemin, direction f; (manner) façon f, manière f; (habit) habitude f, façon; **which ~/that ~** par où or de quel côté? — par ici/par là; **to lose one's ~** perdre son chemin; **on the ~ (to)** en route (pour); **to be on one's ~** être en route; **to be in the ~** bloquer le passage; (fig) gêner; **it's a long ~ a~** c'est loin d'ici; **to go out of one's ~ to do** (fig) se donner beaucoup de mal pour faire; **to be under ~** (work, project) être en cours; **in a ~** dans un sens; **by the ~** à propos; **"~ in"** (BRIT) "entrée"; **"~ out"** (BRIT) "sortie"; **the ~ back** le chemin du retour; **"give ~"** (BRIT Aut) "cédez la priorité"; **no ~!** (inf) pas question!

**W.C.** n abbr (BRIT: = water closet) w.-c. mpl, waters mpl

**we** [wiː] pl pron nous

**weak** [wiːk] adj faible; (health) fragile; (beam etc) peu solide; (tea, coffee) léger(-ère); **weaken** vi faiblir ▷ vt affaiblir; **weakness** n faiblesse f; (fault) point m faible

**wealth** [wɛlθ] n (money, resources) richesse(s) f(pl); (of details) profusion f; **wealthy** adj riche

**weapon** ['wɛpən] n arme f; **~s of mass destruction** armes fpl de destruction massive

**wear** [wɛə'] n (use) usage m; (deterioration through use) usure f ▷ vb (pt **wore**, pp **worn**) ▷ vt (clothes) porter; (put on) mettre; (damage: through use) user ▷ vi (last) faire de l'usage; (rub etc through) s'user; **sports/baby~** vêtements mpl de sport/pour bébés; **evening ~** tenue f de soirée; **wear off** vi disparaître; **wear out** vt user; (person, strength) épuiser

**weary** ['wɪərɪ] adj (tired) épuisé(e); (dispirited) las (lasse); abattu(e) ▷ vi: **to ~ of** se lasser de

**weasel** ['wiːzl] n (Zool) belette f

**weather** ['wɛðə'] n temps m ▷ vt (storm: lit, fig) essuyer; (crisis) survivre à; **under the ~** (fig: ill) mal fichu(e); **weather forecast** n prévisions fpl météorologiques, météo f

**weave** (pt **wove**, pp **woven**) [wiːv, wəuv, 'wəuvn] vt (cloth) tisser; (basket) tresser

**web** [wɛb] n (of spider) toile f; (on duck's foot) palmure f; (fig) tissu m; (Comput): **the (World-Wide) W~** le Web; **web page** n (Comput) page f Web; **website** n (Comput) site m web

**wed** [wɛd] (pt, pp **~ded**) vt épouser ▷ vi se marier

**Wed** abbr (= Wednesday) me

**we'd** [wiːd] = **we had**; **we would**

**wedding** ['wɛdɪŋ] n mariage m; **wedding anniversary** n anniversaire m de mariage; **silver/golden wedding anniversary** noces fpl d'argent/d'or; **wedding day** n jour m du mariage; **wedding dress** n robe f de mariée;

**wedding ring** n alliance f
**wedge** [wɛdʒ] n (of wood etc) coin m; (under door etc) cale f; (of cake) part f ▷ vt (fix) caler; (push) enfoncer, coincer
**Wednesday** ['wɛdnzdɪ] n mercredi m
**wee** [wi:] adj (SCOTTISH) petit(e); tout(e) petit(e)
**weed** [wi:d] n mauvaise herbe ▷ vt désherber; **weedkiller** n désherbant m
**week** [wi:k] n semaine f; **a ~ today/on Tuesday** aujourd'hui/mardi en huit; **weekday** n jour m de semaine; (Comm) jour ouvrable; **weekend** n week-end m; **weekly** adv une fois par semaine, chaque semaine ▷ adj, n hebdomadaire (m)
**weep** [wi:p] (pt, pp **wept**) vi (person) pleurer
**weigh** [weɪ] vt, vi peser; **to ~ anchor** lever l'ancre; **weigh up** vt examiner
**weight** [weɪt] n poids m; **to put on/lose ~** grossir/maigrir; **weightlifting** n haltérophilie f
**weir** [wɪəʳ] n barrage m
**weird** [wɪəd] adj bizarre; (eerie) surnaturel(le)
**welcome** ['wɛlkəm] adj bienvenu(e) ▷ n accueil m ▷ vt accueillir; (also: **bid ~**) souhaiter la bienvenue à; (be glad of) se réjouir de; **you're ~!** (after thanks) de rien, il n'y a pas de quoi
**weld** [wɛld] vt souder
**welfare** ['wɛlfɛəʳ] n (wellbeing) bien-être m; (social aid) assistance sociale; **welfare state** n État-providence m
**well** [wɛl] n puits m ▷ adv bien ▷ adj: **to be ~** aller bien ▷ excl eh bien!; (relief also) bon!; (resignation) enfin!; **~ done!** bravo!; **get ~ soon!** remets-toi vite!; **to do ~** bien réussir; (business) prospérer; **as ~** (in addition) aussi, également; **as ~ as** aussi bien que or de; en plus de
**we'll** [wi:l] = **we will**; **we shall**
**well**: **well-behaved** adj sage, obéissant(e); **well-built** adj (person) bien bâti(e); **well-dressed** adj bien habillé(e), bien vêtu(e)
**well-groomed** [-'gru:md] adj très

soigné(e)
**wellies** ['wɛlɪz] (inf) npl (BRIT) = **wellingtons**
**wellingtons** ['wɛlɪŋtənz] npl (also: **wellington boots**) bottes fpl en caoutchouc
**well**: **well-known** adj (person) bien connu(e); **well-off** adj aisé(e), assez riche; **well-paid** [wɛl'peɪd] adj bien payé(e)
**Welsh** [wɛlʃ] adj gallois(e) ▷ n (Ling) gallois m; **the Welsh** npl (people) les Gallois; **Welshman** (irreg) n Gallois m; **Welshwoman** (irreg) n Galloise f
**went** [wɛnt] pt of **go**
**wept** [wɛpt] pt, pp of **weep**
**were** [wəːʳ] pt of **be**
**we're** [wɪəʳ] = **we are**
**weren't** [wəːnt] = **were not**
**west** [wɛst] n ouest m ▷ adj (wind) d'ouest; (side) ouest inv ▷ adv à or vers l'ouest; **the W~** l'Occident m, l'Ouest; **westbound** ['wɛstbaund] adj en direction de l'ouest; (carriageway) ouest inv; **western** adj occidental(e), de or à l'ouest ▷ n (Cine) western m; **West Indian** adj antillais(e) ▷ n Antillais(e)
**West Indies** [-'ɪndɪz] npl Antilles fpl
**wet** [wɛt] adj mouillé(e); (damp) humide; (soaked: also: **~ through**) trempé(e); (rainy) pluvieux(-euse); **to get ~** se mouiller; **"~ paint"** "attention peinture fraîche"; **wetsuit** n combinaison f de plongée
**we've** [wi:v] = **we have**
**whack** [wæk] vt donner un grand coup à
**whale** [weɪl] n (Zool) baleine f
**wharf** (pl **wharves**) [wɔːf, wɔːvz] n quai m

◯ **KEYWORD**

**what** [wɔt] adj **1** (in questions) quel(le); **what size is he?** quelle taille fait-il?; **what colour is it?** de quelle couleur est-ce?; **what books do you need?**

quels livres vous faut-il?
**2** (*in exclamations*): **what a mess!** quel
désordre!; **what a fool I am!** que je
suis bête!
▷ *pron* **1** (*interrogative*) que; de/à/en
*etc* quoi; **what are you doing?** que
faites-vous?, qu'est-ce que vous faites?;
**what is happening?** qu'est-ce qui se
passe?, que se passe-t-il?; **what are
you talking about?** de quoi parlez-
vous?; **what are you thinking about?**
à quoi pensez-vous?; **what is it called?**
comment est-ce que ça s'appelle?;
**what about me?** et moi?; **what about
doing ...?** et si on faisait ...?
**2** (*relative: subject*) ce qui; (: *direct object*)
ce que; (: *indirect object*) ce à quoi, ce
dont; **I saw what you did/was on the
table** j'ai vu ce que vous avez fait/ce
qui était sur la table; **tell me what
you remember** dites-moi ce dont
vous vous souvenez; **what I want is
a cup of tea** ce que je veux, c'est une
tasse de thé
▷ *excl* (*disbelieving*) quoi!, comment!

**whatever** [wɔt'ɛvəʳ] *adj*: **take ~ book
you prefer** prenez le livre que vous
préférez, peu importe lequel; **~ book
you take** quel que soit le livre que
vous preniez ▷ *pron*: **do ~ is
necessary** faites (tout) ce qui est
nécessaire; **~ happens** quoi qu'il
arrive; **no reason ~** *or* **whatsoever**
pas la moindre raison; **nothing ~** *or*
**whatsoever** rien du tout
**whatsoever** [wɔtsəu'ɛvəʳ] *adj see*
**whatever**
**wheat** [wiːt] *n* blé *m*, froment *m*
**wheel** [wiːl] *n* roue *f*; (*Aut: also:*
**steering ~**) volant *m*; (*Naut*)
gouvernail *m* ▷ *vt* (*pram etc*) pousser,
rouler ▷ *vi* (*birds*) tournoyer; (*also:*
**~ round**: *person*) se retourner, faire
volte-face; **wheelbarrow** *n* brouette *f*;
**wheelchair** *n* fauteuil roulant;
**wheel clamp** *n* (*Aut*) sabot *m* (de
Denver)

**wheeze** [wiːz] *vi* respirer bruyamment

**KEYWORD**

**when** [wen] *adv* quand; **when did he
go?** quand est-ce qu'il est parti?
▷ *conj* **1** (*at, during, after the time that*)
quand, lorsque; **she was reading
when I came in** elle lisait quand *or*
lorsque je suis entré
**2** (*on, at which*): **on the day when I met
him** le jour où je l'ai rencontré
**3** (*whereas*) alors que; **I thought I was
wrong when in fact I was right** j'ai
cru que j'avais tort alors qu'en fait
j'avais raison

**whenever** [wɛn'ɛvəʳ] *adv* quand donc
▷ *conj* quand; (*every time that*) chaque
fois que
**where** [wɛəʳ] *adv, conj* où; **this is ~**
c'est là que; **whereabouts** *adv* où
donc ▷ *n*: **nobody knows his
whereabouts** personne ne sait où
il se trouve; **whereas** *conj* alors que;
**whereby** *adv* (*formal*) par lequel (*or*
laquelle *etc*); **wherever** *adv* où donc
▷ *conj* où que + *sub*; **sit wherever
you like** asseyez-vous (là) où vous
voulez
**whether** ['wɛðəʳ] *conj* si; **I don't know
~ to accept or not** je ne sais pas si je
dois accepter ou non; **it's doubtful ~** il
est peu probable que + *sub*; **~ you go or
not** que vous y alliez ou non

**KEYWORD**

**which** [wɪtʃ] *adj* **1** (*interrogative: direct,
indirect*) quel(le); **which picture do
you want?** quel tableau voulez-vous?;
**which one?** lequel (laquelle)?
**2: in which case** auquel cas; **we got
there at 8pm, by which time the
cinema was full** quand nous
sommes arrivés à 20h, le cinéma
était complet
▷ *pron* **1** (*interrogative*) lequel (laquelle),

lesquels (lesquelles) *pl*; **I don't mind which** peu importe lequel; **which (of these) are yours?** lesquels sont à vous?; **tell me which you want** dites-moi lesquels *or* ceux que vous voulez

**2** (*relative: subject*) qui; (: *object*) que; sur/vers *etc* lequel (laquelle) (*NB: à + lequel* = **auquel**; *de + lequel* = **duquel**); **the apple which you ate/which is on the table** la pomme que vous avez mangée/qui est sur la table; **the chair on which you are sitting** la chaise sur laquelle vous êtes assis; **the book of which you spoke** le livre dont vous avez parlé; **he said he knew, which is true/I was afraid of** il a dit qu'il le savait, ce qui est vrai/ce que je craignais; **after which** après quoi

**whichever** [wɪtʃˈɛvəʳ] *adj*: **take ~ book you prefer** prenez le livre que vous préférez, peu importe lequel; **~ book you take** quel que soit le livre que vous preniez

**while** [waɪl] *n* moment *m* ▷ *conj* pendant que; (*as long as*) tant que; (*as, whereas*) alors que; (*though*) bien que + *sub*, quoique + *sub*; **for a ~** pendant quelque temps; **in a ~** dans un moment

**whilst** [waɪlst] *conj* = **while**

**whim** [wɪm] *n* caprice *m*

**whine** [waɪn] *n* gémissement *m*; (*of engine, siren*) plainte stridente ▷ *vi* gémir, geindre, pleurnicher; (*dog, engine, siren*) gémir

**whip** [wɪp] *n* fouet *m*; (*for riding*) cravache *f*; (*Pol: person*) chef *m* de file (*assurant la discipline dans son groupe parlementaire*) ▷ *vt* fouetter; (*snatch*) enlever (*or* sortir) brusquement; **whipped cream** *n* crème fouettée

**whirl** [wəːl] *vi* tourbillonner; (*dancers*) tournoyer ▷ *vt* faire tourbillonner; faire tournoyer

**whisk** [wɪsk] *n* (*Culin*) fouet *m* ▷ *vt*

(*eggs*) fouetter, battre; **to ~ sb away** *or* **off** emmener qn rapidement

**whiskers** [ˈwɪskəz] *npl* (*of animal*) moustaches *fpl*; (*of man*) favoris *mpl*

**whisky** (*IRISH, US* **whiskey**) [ˈwɪskɪ] *n* whisky *m*

**whisper** [ˈwɪspəʳ] *n* chuchotement *m* ▷ *vt, vi* chuchoter

**whistle** [ˈwɪsl] *n* (*sound*) sifflement *m*; (*object*) sifflet *m* ▷ *vi* siffler ▷ *vt* siffler, siffloter

**white** [waɪt] *adj* blanc (blanche); (*with fear*) blême ▷ *n* blanc *m*; (*person*) blanc (blanche); **White House** *n* (*US*): **the White House** la Maison-Blanche; **whitewash** *n* (*paint*) lait *m* de chaux ▷ *vt* blanchir à la chaux; (*fig*) blanchir

**whiting** [ˈwaɪtɪŋ] *n* (*pl inv*: *fish*) merlan *m*

**Whitsun** [ˈwɪtsn] *n* la Pentecôte

**whittle** [ˈwɪtl] *vt*: **to ~ away**, **to ~ down** (*costs*) réduire, rogner

**whizz** [wɪz] *vi* aller (*or* passer) à toute vitesse

**who** [huː] *pron* qui

**whoever** [huːˈɛvəʳ] *pron*: **~ finds it** celui (celle) qui le trouve (, qui que ce soit), quiconque le trouve; **ask ~ you like** demandez à qui vous voulez; **~ he marries** qui que ce soit *or* quelle que soit la personne qu'il épouse; **~ told you that?** qui a bien pu vous dire ça?, qui donc vous a dit ça?

**whole** [həʊl] *adj* (*complete*) entier(-ière), tout(e); (*not broken*) intact(e), complet(-ète) ▷ *n* (*all*): **the ~ of** la totalité de, tout(e) le (la); (*entire unit*) tout *m*; **the ~ of the town** la ville tout entière; **on the ~**, **as a ~** dans l'ensemble; **wholefood(s)** *n(pl)* aliments complets; **wholeheartedly** [həʊlˈhɑːtɪdlɪ] *adv* sans réserve; **to agree wholeheartedly** être entièrement d'accord; **wholemeal** *adj* (*BRIT: flour, bread*) complet(-ète); **wholesale** *n* (vente *f* en) gros *m* ▷ *adj* (*price*) de gros; (*destruction*) systématique; **wholewheat**

*adj* =**wholemeal**; **wholly** *adv*
entièrement, tout à fait

○ KEYWORD

**whom** [hu:m] *pron* **1** (*interrogative*) qui;
**whom did you see?** qui avez-vous vu?;
**to whom did you give it?** à qui l'avez-vous donné?
**2** (*relative*) que; à/de *etc* qui; **the man whom I saw/to whom I spoke** l'homme que j'ai vu/à qui j'ai parlé

**whore** [hɔːʳ] *n* (*inf: pej*) putain *f*

○ KEYWORD

**whose** [hu:z] *adj* **1** (*possessive: interrogative*): **whose book is this?**, **whose is this book?** à qui est ce livre?; **whose pencil have you taken?** à qui est le crayon que vous avez pris?, c'est le crayon de qui que vous avez pris?; **whose daughter are you?** de qui êtes-vous la fille?
**2** (*possessive: relative*): **the man whose son you rescued** l'homme dont or de qui vous avez sauvé le fils; **the girl whose sister you were speaking to** la fille à la sœur de qui or de laquelle vous parliez; **the woman whose car was stolen** la femme dont la voiture a été volée
▷ *pron* à qui; **whose is this?** à qui est ceci?; **I know whose it is** je sais à qui c'est

○ KEYWORD

**why** [waɪ] *adv* pourquoi; **why not?** pourquoi pas?
▷ *conj*: **I wonder why he said that** je me demande pourquoi il a dit ça; **that's not why I'm here** ce n'est pas pour ça que je suis là; **the reason why** la raison pour laquelle
▷ *excl* eh bien!, tiens!; **why, it's**

**you!** tiens, c'est vous!; **why, that's impossible!** voyons, c'est impossible!

**wicked** ['wɪkɪd] *adj* méchant(e); (*mischievous: grin, look*) espiègle, malicieux(-euse); (*crime*) pervers(e); (*inf: very good*) génial(e) (*inf*)

**wicket** ['wɪkɪt] *n* (*Cricket: stumps*) guichet *m*; (: *grass area*) espace compris entre les deux guichets

**wide** [waɪd] *adj* large; (*area, knowledge*) vaste, très étendu(e); (*choice*) grand(e)
▷ *adv*: **to open ~** ouvrir tout grand; **to shoot ~** tirer à côté; **it is 3 metres ~** cela fait 3 mètres de large; **widely** *adv* (*different*) radicalement; (*spaced*) sur une grande étendue; (*believed*) généralement; (*travel*) beaucoup; **widen** *vt* élargir ▷ *vi* s'élargir; **wide open** *adj* grand(e) ouvert(e); **widespread** *adj* (*belief etc*) très répandu(e)

**widow** ['wɪdəu] *n* veuve *f*; **widower** *n* veuf *m*

**width** [wɪdθ] *n* largeur *f*

**wield** [wi:ld] *vt* (*sword*) manier; (*power*) exercer

**wife** (*pl* **wives**) [waɪf, waɪvz] *n* femme *f*, épouse *f*

**wig** [wɪg] *n* perruque *f*

**wild** [waɪld] *adj* sauvage; (*sea*) déchaîné(e); (*idea, life*) fou (folle); (*behaviour*) déchaîné(e), extravagant(e); (*inf: angry*) hors de soi, furieux(-euse)
▷ *n*: **the ~** la nature; **wilderness** ['wɪldənɪs] *n* désert *m*, région *f* sauvage; **wildlife** *n* faune *f* (et flore *f*); **wildly** *adv* (*behave*) de manière déchaînée; (*applaud*) frénétiquement; (*hit, guess*) au hasard; (*happy*) follement

○ KEYWORD

**will** [wɪl] *aux vb* **1** (*forming future tense*): **I will finish it tomorrow** je le finirai demain; **I will have finished it by tomorrow** je l'aurai fini d'ici demain; **will you do it? - yes I will/no I won't** le

ferez-vous? - oui/non
**2** (in conjectures, predictions): **he will** or
**he'll be there by now** il doit être arrivé
à l'heure qu'il est; **that will be the
postman** ça doit être le facteur
**3** (in commands, requests, offers): **will
you be quiet!** voulez-vous bien vous
taire!; **will you help me?** est-ce que
vous pouvez m'aider?; **will you have a
cup of tea?** voulez-vous une tasse de
thé?; **I won't put up with it!** je ne le
tolérerai pas!
▷ vt (pt, pp **willed**): **to will sb to do**
souhaiter ardemment que qn fasse;
**he willed himself to go on** par un
suprême effort de volonté, il continua
▷ n volonté f; (document) testament m;
**against one's will** à contre-cœur

**willing** ['wɪlɪŋ] adj de bonne volonté,
serviable; **he's ~ to do it** il est disposé
à le faire, il veut bien le faire; **willingly**
adv volontiers
**willow** ['wɪləʊ] n saule m
**willpower** ['wɪl'paʊəʳ] n volonté f
**wilt** [wɪlt] vi dépérir
**win** [wɪn] n (in sports etc) victoire f ▷ vb
(pt, pp **won**) ▷ vt (battle, money) gagner;
(prize, contract) remporter; (popularity)
acquérir ▷ vi gagner; **win over** vt
convaincre
**wince** [wɪns] vi tressaillir
**wind¹** [wɪnd] n (also Med) vent m;
(breath) souffle m ▷ vt (take breath away)
couper le souffle à; **the ~(s)** (Mus) les
instruments mpl à vent
**wind²** (pt, pp **wound**) [waɪnd, waʊnd]
vt enrouler; (wrap) envelopper;
(clock, toy) remonter ▷ vi (road, river)
serpenter; **wind down** vt (car window)
baisser; (fig: production, business) réduire
progressivement; **wind up** vt (clock)
remonter; (debate) terminer, clôturer
**windfall** ['wɪndfɔːl] n coup m de
chance
**winding** ['waɪndɪŋ] adj (road)
sinueux(-euse); (staircase) tournant(e)
**windmill** ['wɪndmɪl] n moulin m à vent

**window** ['wɪndəʊ] n fenêtre f; (in
car, train: also: **~pane**) vitre f; (in
shop etc) vitrine f; **window box** n
jardinière f; **window cleaner** n (person)
laveur(-euse) de vitres; **window pane**
n vitre f, carreau m; **window seat** n (in
vehicle) place f côté fenêtre; **windowsill**
n (inside) appui m de la fenêtre; (outside)
rebord m de la fenêtre
**windscreen** ['wɪndskriːn] n pare-
brise m inv; **windscreen wiper** n
essuie-glace m inv
**windshield** ['wɪndʃiːld] (US) n
= **windscreen**
**windsurfing** ['wɪndsəːfɪŋ] n planche
f à voile
**windy** ['wɪndɪ] adj (day) de vent,
venteux(-euse); (place, weather)
venteux; **it's ~** il y a du vent
**wine** [waɪn] n vin m; **wine bar** n bar m
à vin; **wine glass** n verre m à vin; **wine
list** n carte f des vins; **wine tasting** n
dégustation f (de vins)
**wing** [wɪŋ] n aile f; **wings** npl (Theat)
coulisses fpl; **wing mirror** n (BRIT)
rétroviseur latéral
**wink** [wɪŋk] n clin m d'œil ▷ vi faire un
clin d'œil; (blink) cligner des yeux
**winner** ['wɪnəʳ] n gagnant(e)
**winning** ['wɪnɪŋ] adj (team)
gagnant(e); (goal) décisif(-ive);
(charming) charmeur(-euse)
**winter** ['wɪntəʳ] n hiver m ▷ vi
hiverner; **in ~** en hiver; **winter sports**
npl sports mpl d'hiver; **wintertime**
n hiver m
**wipe** [waɪp] n: **to give sth a ~** donner
un coup de torchon/de chiffon/
d'éponge à qch ▷ vt essuyer; (erase:
tape) effacer; **to ~ one's nose** se
moucher; **wipe out** vt (debt) éteindre,
amortir; (memory) effacer; (destroy)
anéantir; **wipe up** vt essuyer
**wire** ['waɪəʳ] n fil m (de fer); (Elec) fil
électrique; (Tel) télégramme m ▷ vt
(house) faire l'installation électrique
de; (also: **~ up**) brancher; (person: send
telegram to) télégraphier à

**wiring** ['waɪərɪŋ] n (Elec) installation f électrique

**wisdom** ['wɪzdəm] n sagesse f; (of action) prudence f; **wisdom tooth** n dent f de sagesse

**wise** [waɪz] adj sage, prudent(e); (remark) judicieux(-euse)

**wish** [wɪʃ] n (desire) désir m; (specific desire) souhait m, vœu m ▷ vt souhaiter, désirer, vouloir; **best ~es** (on birthday etc) meilleurs vœux; **with best ~es** (in letter) bien amicalement; **to ~ sb goodbye** dire au revoir à qn; **he ~ed me well** il m'a souhaité bonne chance; **to ~ to do/sb to do** désirer or vouloir faire/que qn fasse; **to ~ for** souhaiter

**wistful** ['wɪstful] adj mélancolique

**wit** [wɪt] n (also: **~s**: intelligence) intelligence f, esprit m; (presence of mind) présence f d'esprit; (wittiness) esprit; (person) homme/femme d'esprit

**witch** [wɪtʃ] n sorcière f

**⬤** KEYWORD

**with** [wɪð, wɪθ] prep **1** (in the company of) avec; (at the home of) chez; **we stayed with friends** nous avons logé chez des amis; **I'll be with you in a minute** je suis à vous dans un instant

**2** (descriptive): **a room with a view** une chambre avec vue; **the man with the grey hat/blue eyes** l'homme au chapeau gris/aux yeux bleus

**3** (indicating manner, means, cause): **with tears in her eyes** les larmes aux yeux; **to walk with a stick** marcher avec une canne; **red with anger** rouge de colère; **to shake with fear** trembler de peur; **to fill sth with water** remplir qch d'eau

**4** (in phrases): **I'm with you** (I understand) je vous suis; **to be with it** (inf: up-to-date) être dans le vent

**withdraw** [wɪθ'drɔː] vt (irreg: like **draw**) retirer ▷ vi se retirer; **withdrawal** n retrait m; (Med) état m de manque;

**withdrawn** pp of **withdraw** ▷ adj (person) renfermé(e)

**withdrew** [wɪθ'druː] pt of **withdraw**

**wither** ['wɪðəʳ] vi se faner

**withhold** [wɪθ'həʊld] vt (irreg: like **hold**) (money) retenir; (decision) remettre; (permission): **to ~ (from)** (permission) refuser (à); (information): **to ~ (from)** cacher (à)

**within** [wɪð'ɪn] prep à l'intérieur de ▷ adv à l'intérieur; **~ his reach** à sa portée; **~ sight of** en vue de; **~ a mile of** à moins d'un mille de; **~ the week** avant la fin de la semaine

**without** [wɪθ'aʊt] prep sans; **~ a coat** sans manteau; **~ speaking** sans parler; **to go** or **do ~ sth** se passer de qch

**withstand** [wɪθ'stænd] vt (irreg: like **stand**) résister à

**witness** ['wɪtnɪs] n (person) témoin m ▷ vt (event) être témoin de; (document) attester l'authenticité de; **to bear ~ to sth** témoigner de qch

**witty** ['wɪtɪ] adj spirituel(le), plein(e) d'esprit

**wives** [waɪvz] npl of **wife**

**wizard** ['wɪzəd] n magicien m

**wk** abbr = **week**

**wobble** ['wɔbl] vi trembler; (chair) branler

**woe** [wəʊ] n malheur m

**woke** [wəʊk] pt of **wake**

**woken** ['wəʊkn] pp of **wake**

**wolf** (pl **wolves**) [wʊlf, wʊlvz] n loup m

**woman** (pl **women**) ['wʊmən, 'wɪmɪn] n femme f ▷ cpd: **~ doctor** femme f médecin; **~ teacher** professeur m femme

**womb** [wuːm] n (Anat) utérus m

**women** ['wɪmɪn] npl of **woman**

**won** [wʌn] pt, pp of **win**

**wonder** ['wʌndəʳ] n merveille f, miracle m; (feeling) émerveillement m ▷ vi: **to ~ whether/why** se demander si/pourquoi; **to ~ at** (surprise) s'étonner de; (admiration) s'émerveiller de; **to ~ about** songer à; **it's no ~ that** il n'est pas étonnant que + sub; **wonderful** adj merveilleux(-euse)

**won't** [wəʊnt] = **will not**

**wood** [wʊd] n (timber, forest) bois m; **wooden** adj en bois; (fig: actor) raide; (: performance) qui manque de naturel; **woodwind** n: **the woodwind** (Mus) les bois mpl; **woodwork** n menuiserie f

**wool** [wʊl] n laine f; **to pull the ~ over sb's eyes** (fig) en faire accroire à qn; **woollen** (us **woolen**) adj de or en laine; **woolly** (us **wooly**) adj laineux(-euse); (fig: ideas) confus(e)

**word** [wɜːd] n mot m; (spoken) mot, parole f; (promise) parole; (news) nouvelles fpl ▷ vt rédiger, formuler; **in other ~ terms**, langage m; (of document) libellé m; **word processing** n traitement m de texte; **word processor** n machine f de traitement de texte

**wore** [wɔːʳ] pt of **wear**

**work** [wɜːk] n travail m; (Art, Literature) œuvre f ▷ vi travailler; (mechanism) marcher, fonctionner; (plan etc) marcher; (medicine) agir ▷ vt (clay, wood etc) travailler; (mine etc) exploiter; (machine) faire marcher or fonctionner; (miracles etc) faire; **works** n (BRIT: factory) usine f; **how does this ~?** comment est-ce que ça marche?; **the TV isn't ~ing** la télévision est en panne or ne marche pas; **to be out of ~** être au chômage or sans emploi; **to ~ loose** se défaire, se desserrer; **work out** vi (plans etc) marcher; (Sport) s'entraîner ▷ vt (problem) résoudre; (plan) élaborer; **it ~s out at £100** ça fait 100 livres; **worker** n travailleur(-euse), ouvrier(-ière); **work experience** n stage m; **workforce** n main-d'œuvre f; **working class** n classe ouvrière ▷ adj: **working-class** ouvrier(-ière), de la classe ouvrière; **working week** n semaine f de travail; **workman** (irreg) n ouvrier m; **work of art** n œuvre

f d'art; **workout** n (Sport) séance f d'entraînement; **work permit** n permis m de travail; **workplace** n lieu m de travail; **worksheet** n (Scol) feuille f d'exercices; **workshop** n atelier m; **work station** n poste m de travail; **work surface** n plan m de travail; **worktop** n plan m de travail

**world** [wɜːld] n monde m ▷ cpd (champion) du monde; (power, war) mondial(e); **to think the ~ of sb** (fig) ne jurer que par qn; **World Cup** n: **the World Cup** (Football) la Coupe du monde; **world-wide** adj universel(le); **World-Wide Web** n: **the World-Wide Web** le Web

**worm** [wɜːm] n (also: **earth~**) ver m

**worn** [wɔːn] pp of **wear** ▷ adj usé(e); **worn-out** adj (object) complètement usé(e); (person) épuisé(e)

**worried** ['wʌrɪd] adj inquiet(-ète); **to be ~ about sth** être inquiet au sujet de qch

**worry** ['wʌrɪ] n souci m ▷ vt inquiéter ▷ vi s'inquiéter, se faire du souci; **worrying** adj inquiétant(e)

**worse** [wɜːs] adj pire, plus mauvais(e) ▷ adv plus mal ▷ n pire m; **to get ~** (condition, situation) empirer, se dégrader; **a change for the ~** une détérioration; **worsen** vt, vi empirer; **worse off** adj moins à l'aise financièrement; (fig): **you'll be worse off this way** ça ira moins bien de cette façon

**worship** ['wɜːʃɪp] n culte m ▷ vt (God) rendre un culte à; (person) adorer

**worst** [wɜːst] adj le (la) pire, le (la) plus mauvais(e) ▷ adv le plus mal ▷ n pire m; **at ~** au pis aller

**worth** [wɜːθ] n valeur f ▷ adj: **to be ~** valoir; **it's ~ it** cela en vaut la peine, ça vaut la peine; **it is ~ one's while (to do)** ça vaut le coup (inf) (de faire); **worthless** adj qui ne vaut rien; **worthwhile** adj (activity) qui en vaut la peine; (cause) louable

**worthy** ['wɜːðɪ] adj (person) digne;

(*motive*) louable; **~ of** digne de

O **KEYWORD**

**would** [wud] *aux vb* **1** (*conditional tense*): **if you asked him he would do it** si vous le lui demandiez, il le ferait; **if you had asked him he would have done it** si vous lui aviez demandé, il l'aurait fait
**2** (*in offers, invitations, requests*): **would you like a biscuit?** voulez-vous un biscuit?; **would you close the door please?** voulez-vous fermer la porte, s'il vous plaît?
**3** (*in indirect speech*): **I said I would do it** j'ai dit que je le ferais
**4** (*emphatic*): **it WOULD have to snow today!** naturellement il neige aujourd'hui! *or* il fallait qu'il neige aujourd'hui!
**5** (*insistence*): **she wouldn't do it** elle n'a pas voulu *or* elle a refusé de le faire
**6** (*conjecture*): **it would have been midnight** il devait être minuit; **it would seem so** on dirait bien
**7** (*indicating habit*): **he would go there on Mondays** il y allait le lundi

**wouldn't** ['wudnt] = **would not**
**wound¹** [wu:nd] *n* blessure *f* ▷ *vt* blesser
**wound²** [waund] *pt, pp of* **wind**
**wove** [wəuv] *pt of* **weave**
**woven** ['wəuvn] *pp of* **weave**
**wrap** [ræp] *vt* (*also:* **~ up**) envelopper; (*parcel*) emballer; (*wind*) enrouler; **wrapper** *n* (*on chocolate etc*) papier *m*; (BRIT: *of book*) couverture *f*; **wrapping** *n* (*of sweet, chocolate*) papier *m*; (*of parcel*) emballage *m*; **wrapping paper** *n* papier *m* d'emballage; (*for gift*) papier cadeau
**wreath** [ri:θ, *pl* ri:ðz] *n* couronne *f*
**wreck** [rɛk] *n* (*sea disaster*) naufrage *m*; (*ship*) épave *f*; (*vehicle*) véhicule accidenté; (*pej: person*) loque (humaine) ▷ *vt* démolir; (*fig*) briser;

ruiner; **wreckage** *n* débris *mpl*; (*of building*) décombres *mpl*; (*of ship*) naufrage *m*
**wren** [rɛn] *n* (*Zool*) troglodyte *m*
**wrench** [rɛntʃ] *n* (*Tech*) clé *f* (à écrous); (*tug*) violent mouvement de torsion; (*fig*) déchirement *m* ▷ *vt* tirer violemment sur, tordre; **to ~ sth from** arracher qch (violemment) à *or* de
**wrestle** ['rɛsl] *vi*: **to ~ (with sb)** lutter (avec qn); **wrestler** *n* lutteur(-euse); **wrestling** *n* lutte *f*; (*also:* **all-in wrestling**: BRIT) catch *m*
**wretched** ['rɛtʃɪd] *adj* misérable
**wriggle** ['rɪgl] *vi* (*also:* **~ about**) se tortiller
**wring** (*pt, pp* **wrung**) [rɪŋ, rʌŋ] *vt* tordre; (*wet clothes*) essorer; (*fig*): **to ~ sth out of** arracher qch à
**wrinkle** ['rɪŋkl] *n* (*on skin*) ride *f*; (*on paper etc*) pli *m* ▷ *vt* rider, plisser ▷ *vi* se plisser
**wrist** [rɪst] *n* poignet *m*
**write** (*pt* **wrote**, *pp* **written**) [raɪt, rəut, 'rɪtn] *vt, vi* écrire; (*prescription*) rédiger; **write down** *vt* noter; (*put in writing*) mettre par écrit; **write off** *vt* (*debt*) passer aux profits et pertes; (*project*) mettre une croix sur; (*smash up: car etc*) démolir complètement; **write out** *vt* écrire; (*copy*) recopier; **write-off** *n* perte totale; **the car is a write-off** la voiture est bonne pour la casse; **writer** *n* auteur *m*, écrivain *m*
**writing** ['raɪtɪŋ] *n* écriture *f*; (*of author*) œuvres *fpl*; **in ~** par écrit; **writing paper** *n* papier *m* à lettres
**written** ['rɪtn] *pp of* **write**
**wrong** [rɔŋ] *adj* (*incorrect*) faux (fausse); (*incorrectly chosen: number, road etc*) mauvais(e); (*not suitable*) qui ne convient pas; (*wicked*) mal; (*unfair*) injuste ▷ *adv* mal ▷ *n* tort *m* ▷ *vt* faire du tort à, léser; **you are ~ to do it** tu as tort de le faire; **you are ~ about that, you've got it ~** tu te trompes; **what's ~?** qu'est-ce qui ne va pas?; **what's ~ with the car?** qu'est-ce qu'elle a, la

voiture?; **to go ~** (*person*) se tromper;
(*plan*) mal tourner; (*machine*) se
détraquer; **I took a ~ turning** je me suis
trompé de route; **wrongly** *adv* à tort;
(*answer, do, count*) mal, incorrectement;
**wrong number** *n* (*Tel*): **you have the
wrong number** vous vous êtes trompé
de numéro
**wrote** [rəut] *pt of* **write**
**wrung** [rʌŋ] *pt, pp of* **wring**
**WWW** *n abbr* = **World-Wide Web**; **the
~** le Web

**XL** *abbr* (= *extra large*) XL
**Xmas** [ˈɛksməs] *n abbr* = **Christmas**
**X-ray** [ˈɛksreɪ] *n* (*ray*) rayon *m* X;
(*photograph*) radio(graphie) *f* ▷ *vt*
radiographier
**xylophone** [ˈzaɪləfəun] *n* xylophone *m*

**yacht** [jɔt] *n* voilier *m*; (*motor, luxury yacht*) yacht *m*; **yachting** *n* yachting *m*, navigation *f* de plaisance

**yard** [jɑːd] *n* (*of house etc*) cour *f*; (*us: garden*) jardin *m*; (*measure*) yard *m* (= 914 *mm*; *3 feet*); **yard sale** *n* (*us*) brocante *f* (dans son propre jardin)

**yarn** [jɑːn] *n* fil *m*; (*tale*) longue histoire

**yawn** [jɔːn] *n* bâillement *m* ▷ *vi* bâiller

**yd.** *abbr* = **yard(s)**

**yeah** [jɛə] *adv* (*inf*) ouais

**year** [jɪəʳ] *n* an *m*, année *f*; (*Scol etc*) année; **to be 8 ~s old** avoir 8 ans; **an eight-~-old child** un enfant de huit ans; **yearly** *adj* annuel(le) ▷ *adv* annuellement; **twice yearly** deux fois par an

**yearn** [jəːn] *vi*: **to ~ for sth/to do** aspirer à qch/à faire

**yeast** [jiːst] *n* levure *f*

**yell** [jɛl] *n* hurlement *m*, cri *m* ▷ *vi* hurler

**yellow** ['jɛləu] *adj, n* jaune (*m*); **Yellow Pages®** *npl* (*Tel*) pages *fpl* jaunes

**yes** [jɛs] *adv* oui; (*answering negative question*) si ▷ *n* oui *m*; **to say ~ (to)** dire oui (à)

**yesterday** ['jɛstədɪ] *adv, n* hier (*m*); **~ morning/evening** hier matin/soir; **all day ~** toute la journée d'hier

**yet** [jɛt] *adv* encore; (*in questions*) déjà ▷ *conj* pourtant, néanmoins; **it is not finished ~** ce n'est pas encore fini *or* toujours pas fini; **have you eaten ~?** vous avez déjà mangé?; **the best ~** le meilleur jusqu'ici *or* jusque-là; **as ~** jusqu'ici, encore

**yew** [juː] *n* if *m*

**Yiddish** ['jɪdɪʃ] *n* yiddish *m*

**yield** [jiːld] *n* production *f*, rendement *m*; (*Finance*) rapport *m* ▷ *vt* produire, rendre, rapporter; (*surrender*) céder ▷ *vi* céder; (*us Aut*) céder la priorité

**yob(bo)** ['jɔb(əu)] *n* (*BRIT inf*) loubar(d) *m*

**yoga** ['jəugə] *n* yoga *m*

**yog(h)ourt** *n* = **yog(h)urt**

**yog(h)urt** ['jɔgət] *n* yaourt *m*

**yolk** [jəuk] *n* jaune *m* (d'œuf)

⭕ **KEYWORD**

**you** [juː] *pron* **1** (*subject*) tu; (*polite form*) vous; (*plural*) vous; **you are very kind** vous êtes très gentil; **you French enjoy your food** vous autres Français, vous aimez bien manger; **you and I will go** toi et moi *or* vous et moi, nous irons; **there you are!** vous voilà!

**2** (*object: direct, indirect*) te, t' + *vowel*; vous; **I know you** je te *or* vous connais; **I gave it to you** je te l'ai donné, je vous l'ai donné

**3** (*stressed*) toi; vous; **I told YOU to do it** c'est à toi *or* vous que j'ai dit de le faire

**4** (*after prep, in comparisons*) toi; vous; **it's for you** c'est pour toi *or* vous; **she's younger than you** elle est plus jeune que toi *or* vous

**5** (*impersonal: one*) on; **fresh air does you good** l'air frais fait du bien; **you**

**never know** on ne sait jamais; **you can't do that!** ça ne se fait pas!

**you'd** [juːd] = **you had**; **you would**

**you'll** [juːl] = **you will**; **you shall**

**young** [jʌŋ] adj jeune ▷ npl (of animal) petits mpl; (people®) **the ~** les jeunes, la jeunesse; **my ~er brother** mon frère cadet; **youngster** n jeune m/f; (child) enfant m/f

**your** [jɔːʳ] adj ton (ta), tes pl; (polite form, pl) votre, vos pl; see also **my**

**you're** [juəʳ] = **you are**

**yours** [jɔːz] pron le (la) tien(ne), les tiens (tiennes); (polite form, pl) le (la) vôtre, les vôtres; **is it ~?** c'est à toi (or à vous)?; **a friend of ~** un(e) de tes (or de vos) amis; see also **faithfully**; **mine¹**; **sincerely**

**yourself** [jɔːˈsɛlf] pron (reflexive) te; (: polite form) vous; (after prep) toi; vous; (emphatic) toi-même; vous-même; see also **oneself**; **yourselves** pl pron vous; (emphatic) vous-mêmes; see also **oneself**

**youth** [juːθ] n jeunesse f; (young man) (pl **~s**) jeune homme m; **youth club** n centre m de jeunes; **youthful** adj jeune; (enthusiasm etc) juvénile; **youth hostel** n auberge f de jeunesse

**you've** [juːv] = **you have**

**Yugoslav** [ˈjuːgəʊslɑːv] adj yougoslave ▷ n Yougoslave m/f

**Yugoslavia** [juːgəʊˈslɑːvɪə] n (Hist) Yougoslavie f

**zeal** [ziːl] n (revolutionary etc) ferveur f; (keenness) ardeur f, zèle m

**zebra** [ˈziːbrə] n zèbre m; **zebra crossing** n (BRIT) passage clouté or pour piétons

**zero** [ˈzɪərəʊ] n zéro m

**zest** [zɛst] n entrain m, élan m; (of lemon etc) zeste m

**zigzag** [ˈzɪgzæg] n zigzag m ▷ vi zigzaguer, faire des zigzags

**Zimbabwe** [zɪmˈbɑːbwɪ] n Zimbabwe m

**zinc** [zɪŋk] n zinc m

**zip** [zɪp] n (also: **~ fastener**) fermeture f éclair® or à glissière ▷ vt (file) zipper; (also: **~ up**) fermer (avec une fermeture éclair®); **zip code** n (US) code postal; **zip file** n (Comput) fichier m zip inv; **zipper** n (US) = **zip**

**zit** [zɪt] (inf) n bouton m

**zodiac** [ˈzəʊdɪæk] n zodiaque m

**zone** [zəʊn] n zone f

**zoo** [zuː] n zoo m

**zoology** [zuːˈɔlədʒɪ] n zoologie f

**zoom** [zu:m] *vi*: **to ~ past** passer en
trombe; **zoom lens** *n* zoom *m*
**zucchini** [zu:'ki:nɪ] *n(pl)* (*us*)
courgette(s) *f(pl)*

# VERB TABLES

## Introduction

The **Verb Tables** in the following section contain 29 tables of French verbs (some regular and some irregular) in alphabetical order. Each table shows you the following forms: **Present**, **Perfect**, **Future**, **Subjunctive**, **Imperfect**, **Conditional**, **Imperative** and the **Present** and **Past Participles**.

In order to help you use the verbs shown in Verb Tables correctly, there are also a number of example phrases at the bottom of each page to show the verb as it is used in context.

In French there are both **regular** verbs (their forms follow the normal rules) and **irregular** verbs (their forms do not follow the normal rules). The regular verbs in these tables are:

**donner** (regular -er verb, Verb Table 11)
**finir** (regular -ir verb, Verb Table 16)
**attendre** (regular -re verb, Verb Table 3)

The irregular verbs are shown in full.

For a further list of French irregular verb forms see pages xv–xvi.

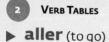

# ▶ aller (to go)

## PRESENT

|           |        |
|-----------|--------|
| je        | vais   |
| tu        | vas    |
| il/elle/on| va     |
| nous      | allons |
| vous      | allez  |
| ils/elles | vont   |

## PRESENT SUBJUNCTIVE

|           |         |
|-----------|---------|
| j'        | aille   |
| tu        | ailles  |
| il/elle/on| aille   |
| nous      | allions |
| vous      | alliez  |
| ils/elles | aillent |

## PERFECT

|           |                 |
|-----------|-----------------|
| je        | suis allé(e)    |
| tu        | es allé(e)      |
| il/elle/on| est allé(e)     |
| nous      | sommes allé(e)s |
| vous      | êtes allé(e)(s) |
| ils/elles | sont allé(e)s   |

## IMPERFECT

|           |          |
|-----------|----------|
| j'        | allais   |
| tu        | allais   |
| il/elle/on| allait   |
| nous      | allions  |
| vous      | alliez   |
| ils/elles | allaient |

## FUTURE

|           |       |
|-----------|-------|
| j'        | irai  |
| tu        | iras  |
| il/elle/on| ira   |
| nous      | irons |
| vous      | irez  |
| ils/elles | iront |

## CONDITIONAL

|           |         |
|-----------|---------|
| j'        | irais   |
| tu        | irais   |
| il/elle/on| irait   |
| nous      | irions  |
| vous      | iriez   |
| ils/elles | iraient |

## IMPERATIVE

va / allons / allez

## PAST PARTICIPLE

allé

## PRESENT PARTICIPLE

allant

---

## EXAMPLE PHRASES

*Vous **allez** au cinéma?* Are you going to the cinema?
*Je **suis allé** à Londres.* I went to London.
*Est-ce que tu **es** déjà **allé** en Allemagne?* Have you ever been to Germany?

---

**je/j'** = I   **tu** = you   **il** = he/it   **elle** = she/it   **on** = we/one   **nous** = we   **vous** = you   **ils/elles** = they

# ▶ **attendre** (to wait)

## PRESENT

| | |
|---|---|
| j' | attends |
| tu | attends |
| il/elle/on | attend |
| nous | attendons |
| vous | attendez |
| ils/elles | attendent |

## PRESENT SUBJUNCTIVE

| | |
|---|---|
| j' | attende |
| tu | attendes |
| il/elle/on | attende |
| nous | attendions |
| vous | attendiez |
| ils/elles | attendent |

## PERFECT

| | |
|---|---|
| j' | ai attendu |
| tu | as attendu |
| il/elle/on | a attendu |
| nous | avons attendu |
| vous | avez attendu |
| ils/elles | ont attendu |

## IMPERFECT

| | |
|---|---|
| j' | attendais |
| tu | attendais |
| il/elle/on | attendait |
| nous | attendions |
| vous | attendiez |
| ils/elles | attendaient |

## FUTURE

| | |
|---|---|
| j' | attendrai |
| tu | attendras |
| il/elle/on | attendra |
| nous | attendrons |
| vous | attendrez |
| ils/elles | attendront |

## CONDITIONAL

| | |
|---|---|
| j' | attendrais |
| tu | attendrais |
| il/elle/on | attendrait |
| nous | attendrions |
| vous | attendriez |
| ils/elles | attendraient |

## IMPERATIVE

attends / attendons / attendez

## PAST PARTICIPLE

attendu

## PRESENT PARTICIPLE

attendant

---

### EXAMPLE PHRASES

**Attends**-moi! Wait for me!
Tu **attends** depuis longtemps? Have you been waiting long?
Je l'**ai attendu** à la poste. I waited for him at the post office.
Je m'**attends** à ce qu'il soit en retard. I expect he'll be late.

**je/j'** = I  **tu** = you  **il** = he/it  **elle** = she/it  **on** = we/one  **nous** = we  **vous** = you  **ils/elles** = they

# ▶ **avoir** (to have)

| **PRESENT** | | **PRESENT SUBJUNCTIVE** | |
|---|---|---|---|
| j' | ai | j' | aie |
| tu | as | tu | aies |
| il/elle/on | a | il/elle/on | ait |
| nous | avons | nous | ayons |
| vous | avez | vous | ayez |
| ils/elles | ont | ils/elles | aient |

| **PERFECT** | | **IMPERFECT** | |
|---|---|---|---|
| j' | ai eu | j' | avais |
| tu | as eu | tu | avais |
| il/elle/on | a eu | il/elle/on | avait |
| nous | avons eu | nous | avions |
| vous | avez eu | vous | aviez |
| ils/elles | ont eu | ils/elles | avaient |

| **FUTURE** | | **CONDITIONAL** | |
|---|---|---|---|
| j' | aurai | j' | aurais |
| tu | auras | tu | aurais |
| il/elle/on | aura | il/elle/on | aurait |
| nous | aurons | nous | aurions |
| vous | aurez | vous | auriez |
| ils/elles | auront | ils/elles | auraient |

| **IMPERATIVE** | **PAST PARTICIPLE** |
|---|---|
| aie / ayons / ayez | eu |

**PRESENT PARTICIPLE**

ayant

---

*EXAMPLE PHRASES*

Il *a* les yeux bleus. He's got blue eyes.
Quel âge *as*-tu? How old are you?
Il *a eu* un accident. He's had an accident.
J'*avais* faim. I was hungry.
Il y *a* beaucoup de monde. There are lots of people.

---

**je/j'** = I   **tu** = you   **il** = he/it   **elle** = she/it   **on** = we/one   **nous** = we   **vous** = you   **ils/elles** = they

# ▶ **boire** (to drink)

## PRESENT

| | |
|---|---|
| je | bois |
| tu | bois |
| il/elle/on | boit |
| nous | buvons |
| vous | buvez |
| ils/elles | boivent |

## PRESENT SUBJUNCTIVE

| | |
|---|---|
| je | boive |
| tu | boives |
| il/elle/on | boive |
| nous | buvions |
| vous | buviez |
| ils/elles | boivent |

## PERFECT

| | |
|---|---|
| j' | ai bu |
| tu | as bu |
| il/elle/on | a bu |
| nous | avons bu |
| vous | avez bu |
| ils/elles | ont bu |

## IMPERFECT

| | |
|---|---|
| je | buvais |
| tu | buvais |
| il/elle/on | buvait |
| nous | buvions |
| vous | buviez |
| ils/elles | buvaient |

## FUTURE

| | |
|---|---|
| je | boirai |
| tu | boiras |
| il/elle/on | boira |
| nous | boirons |
| vous | boirez |
| ils/elles | boiront |

## CONDITIONAL

| | |
|---|---|
| je | boirais |
| tu | boirais |
| il/elle/on | boirait |
| nous | boirions |
| vous | boiriez |
| ils/elles | boiraient |

## IMPERATIVE

bois / buvons / buvez

## PAST PARTICIPLE

bu

## PRESENT PARTICIPLE

buvant

---

### EXAMPLE PHRASES

*Qu'est-ce que tu veux **boire**?* What would you like to drink?
*Il ne **boit** jamais d'alcool.* He never drinks alcohol.
*J'**ai bu** un litre d'eau.* I drank a litre of water.

---

**je/j'** = I  **tu** = you  **il** = he/it  **elle** = she/it  **on** = we/one  **nous** = we  **vous** = you  **ils/elles** = they

# ▶ connaître (to know)

## PRESENT

|   |   |
|---|---|
| je | connais |
| tu | connais |
| il/elle/on | connaît |
| nous | connaissons |
| vous | connaissez |
| ils/elles | connaissent |

## PRESENT SUBJUNCTIVE

|   |   |
|---|---|
| je | connaisse |
| tu | connaisses |
| il/elle/on | connaisse |
| nous | connaissions |
| vous | connaissiez |
| ils/elles | connaissent |

## PERFECT

|   |   |
|---|---|
| j' | ai connu |
| tu | as connu |
| il/elle/on | a connu |
| nous | avons connu |
| vous | avez connu |
| ils/elles | ont connu |

## IMPERFECT

|   |   |
|---|---|
| je | connaissais |
| tu | connaissais |
| il/elle/on | connaissait |
| nous | connaissions |
| vous | connaissiez |
| ils/elles | connaissaient |

## FUTURE

|   |   |
|---|---|
| je | connaîtrai |
| tu | connaîtras |
| il/elle/on | connaîtra |
| nous | connaîtrons |
| vous | connaîtrez |
| ils/elles | connaîtront |

## CONDITIONAL

|   |   |
|---|---|
| je | connaîtrais |
| tu | connaîtrais |
| il/elle/on | connaîtrait |
| nous | connaîtrions |
| vous | connaîtriez |
| ils/elles | connaîtraient |

## IMPERATIVE

connais / connaissons / connaissez

## PAST PARTICIPLE

connu

## PRESENT PARTICIPLE

connaissant

---

## EXAMPLE PHRASES

*Je ne **connais** pas du tout cette région.* I don't know the area at all.
*Vous **connaissez** M Amiot?* Do you know Mr Amiot?
*Il n'**a** pas **connu** son grand-père.* He never knew his granddad.
*Ils **se sont connus** à Rouen.* They first met in Rouen.

---

**je/j'** = I  **tu** = you  **il** = he/it  **elle** = she/it  **on** = we/one  **nous** = we  **vous** = you  **ils/elles** = they

# ▶ **courir** (to run)

| PRESENT | | PRESENT SUBJUNCTIVE | |
|---|---|---|---|
| je | cours | je | coure |
| tu | cours | tu | coures |
| il/elle/on | court | il/elle/on | coure |
| nous | courons | nous | courions |
| vous | courez | vous | couriez |
| ils/elles | courent | ils/elles | courent |

| PERFECT | | IMPERFECT | |
|---|---|---|---|
| j' | ai couru | je | courais |
| tu | as couru | tu | courais |
| il/elle/on | a couru | il/elle/on | courait |
| nous | avons couru | nous | courions |
| vous | avez couru | vous | couriez |
| ils/elles | ont couru | ils/elles | couraient |

| FUTURE | | CONDITIONAL | |
|---|---|---|---|
| je | courrai | je | courrais |
| tu | courras | tu | courrais |
| il/elle/on | courra | il/elle/on | courrait |
| nous | courrons | nous | courrions |
| vous | courrez | vous | courriez |
| ils/elles | courront | ils/elles | courraient |

**IMPERATIVE**

cours / courons / courez

**PAST PARTICIPLE**

couru

**PRESENT PARTICIPLE**

courant

---

*EXAMPLE PHRASES*

*Je ne **cours** pas très vite.* I can't run very fast.
*Elle est sortie en **courant**.* She ran out.
*Ne **courez** pas dans le couloir.* Don't run in the corridor.
*J'**ai couru** jusqu'à l'école.* I ran all the way to school.

---

**je/j'** = I  **tu** = you  **il** = he/it  **elle** = she/it  **on** = we/one  **nous** = we  **vous** = you  **ils/elles** = they

# ▶ **croire** (to believe)

**PRESENT**

| | |
|---|---|
| je | crois |
| tu | crois |
| il/elle/on | croit |
| nous | croyons |
| vous | croyez |
| ils/elles | croient |

**PRESENT SUBJUNCTIVE**

| | |
|---|---|
| je | croie |
| tu | croies |
| il/elle/on | croie |
| nous | croyions |
| vous | croyiez |
| ils/elles | croient |

**PERFECT**

| | |
|---|---|
| j' | ai cru |
| tu | as cru |
| il/elle/on | a cru |
| nous | avons cru |
| vous | avez cru |
| ils/elles | ont cru |

**IMPERFECT**

| | |
|---|---|
| je | croyais |
| tu | croyais |
| il/elle/on | croyait |
| nous | croyions |
| vous | croyiez |
| ils/elles | croyaient |

**FUTURE**

| | |
|---|---|
| je | croirai |
| tu | croiras |
| il/elle/on | croira |
| nous | croirons |
| vous | croirez |
| ils/elles | croiront |

**CONDITIONAL**

| | |
|---|---|
| je | croirais |
| tu | croirais |
| il/elle/on | croirait |
| nous | croirions |
| vous | croiriez |
| ils/elles | croiraient |

**IMPERATIVE**

crois / croyons / croyez

**PAST PARTICIPLE**

cru

**PRESENT PARTICIPLE**

croyant

---

*EXAMPLE PHRASES*

*Je ne te **crois** pas.* I don't believe you.
*J'**ai cru** que tu n'allais pas venir.* I thought you weren't going to come.
*Elle **croyait** encore au père Noël.* She still believed in Santa.

# ▶ devoir (to have to; to owe)

## PRESENT

| | |
|---|---|
| je | dois |
| tu | dois |
| il/elle/on | doit |
| nous | devons |
| vous | devez |
| ils/elles | doivent |

## PRESENT SUBJUNCTIVE

| | |
|---|---|
| je | doive |
| tu | doives |
| il/elle/on | doive |
| nous | devions |
| vous | deviez |
| ils/elles | doivent |

## PERFECT

| | |
|---|---|
| j' | ai dû |
| tu | as dû |
| il/elle/on | a dû |
| nous | avons dû |
| vous | avez dû |
| ils/elles | ont dû |

## IMPERFECT

| | |
|---|---|
| je | devais |
| tu | devais |
| il/elle/on | devait |
| nous | devions |
| vous | deviez |
| ils/elles | devaient |

## FUTURE

| | |
|---|---|
| je | devrai |
| tu | devras |
| il/elle/on | devra |
| nous | devrons |
| vous | devrez |
| ils/elles | devront |

## CONDITIONAL

| | |
|---|---|
| je | devrais |
| tu | devrais |
| il/elle/on | devrait |
| nous | devrions |
| vous | devriez |
| ils/elles | devraient |

## IMPERATIVE

dois / devons / devez

## PAST PARTICIPLE

dû (**NB**: due, dus, dues)

## PRESENT PARTICIPLE

devant

---

### EXAMPLE PHRASES

*Je **dois** aller faire les courses ce matin.* I have to do the shopping this morning.
*À quelle heure est-ce que tu **dois** partir?* What time do you have to leave?
*Il **a dû** faire ses devoirs hier soir.* He had to do his homework last night.
*Il **devait** prendre le train pour aller travailler.* He had to go to work by train.

---

**je/j'** = I   **tu** = you   **il** = he/it   **elle** = she/it   **on** = we/one   **nous** = we   **vous** = you   **ils/elles** = they

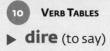
## ▶ **dire** (to say)

| PRESENT | | PRESENT SUBJUNCTIVE | |
|---|---|---|---|
| je | dis | je | dise |
| tu | dis | tu | dises |
| il/elle/on | dit | il/elle/on | dise |
| nous | disons | nous | disions |
| vous | dites | vous | disiez |
| ils/elles | disent | ils/elles | disent |

| PERFECT | | IMPERFECT | |
|---|---|---|---|
| j' | ai dit | je | disais |
| tu | as dit | tu | disais |
| il/elle/on | a dit | il/elle/on | disait |
| nous | avons dit | nous | disions |
| vous | avez dit | vous | disiez |
| ils/elles | ont dit | ils/elles | disaient |

| FUTURE | | CONDITIONAL | |
|---|---|---|---|
| je | dirai | je | dirais |
| tu | diras | tu | dirais |
| il/elle/on | dira | il/elle/on | dirait |
| nous | dirons | nous | dirions |
| vous | direz | vous | diriez |
| ils/elles | diront | ils/elles | diraient |

| IMPERATIVE | PAST PARTICIPLE |
|---|---|
| dis / disons / dites | dit |

**PRESENT PARTICIPLE**

disant

---

*EXAMPLE PHRASES*

*Qu'est-ce qu'elle **dit**?* What is she saying?
*"Bonjour!", **a-t-il dit**.* "Hello!" he said.
*Ils m'**ont dit** que le film était nul.* They told me that the film was rubbish.
*Comment ça **se dit** en anglais?* How do you say that in English?

---

**je/j'** = I   **tu** = you   **il** = he/it   **elle** = she/it   **on** = we/one   **nous** = we   **vous** = you   **ils/elles** = they

## ▶ **donner** (to give)

**PRESENT**

| | |
|---|---|
| je | donne |
| tu | donnes |
| il/elle/on | donne |
| nous | donnons |
| vous | donnez |
| ils/elles | donnent |

**PRESENT SUBJUNCTIVE**

| | |
|---|---|
| je | donne |
| tu | donnes |
| il/elle/on | donne |
| nous | donnions |
| vous | donniez |
| ils/elles | donnent |

**PERFECT**

| | |
|---|---|
| j' | ai donné |
| tu | as donné |
| il/elle/on | a donné |
| nous | avons donné |
| vous | avez donné |
| ils/elles | ont donné |

**IMPERFECT**

| | |
|---|---|
| je | donnais |
| tu | donnais |
| il/elle/on | donnait |
| nous | donnions |
| vous | donniez |
| ils/elles | donnaient |

**FUTURE**

| | |
|---|---|
| je | donnerai |
| tu | donneras |
| il/elle/on | donnera |
| nous | donnerons |
| vous | donnerez |
| ils/elles | donneront |

**CONDITIONAL**

| | |
|---|---|
| je | donnerais |
| tu | donnerais |
| il/elle/on | donnerait |
| nous | donnerions |
| vous | donneriez |
| ils/elles | donneraient |

**IMPERATIVE**

donne / donnons / donnez

**PAST PARTICIPLE**

donné

**PRESENT PARTICIPLE**

donnant

---

*EXAMPLE PHRASES*

**Donne**-moi la main. Give me your hand.
Est-ce que je t'**ai donné** mon adresse? Did I give you my address?
L'appartement **donne** sur la place. The flat overlooks the square.

---

je/j' = I  tu = you  il = he/it  elle = she/it  on = we/one  nous = we  vous = you  ils/elles = they

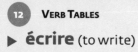

## ▶ **écrire** (to write)

### PRESENT

| | |
|---|---|
| j' | écris |
| tu | écris |
| il/elle/on | écrit |
| nous | écrivons |
| vous | écrivez |
| ils/elles | écrivent |

### PRESENT SUBJUNCTIVE

| | |
|---|---|
| j' | écrive |
| tu | écrives |
| il/elle/on | écrive |
| nous | écrivions |
| vous | écriviez |
| ils/elles | écrivent |

### PERFECT

| | |
|---|---|
| j' | ai écrit |
| tu | as écrit |
| il/elle/on | a écrit |
| nous | avons écrit |
| vous | avez écrit |
| ils/elles | ont écrit |

### IMPERFECT

| | |
|---|---|
| j' | écrivais |
| tu | écrivais |
| il/elle/on | écrivait |
| nous | écrivions |
| vous | écriviez |
| ils/elles | écrivaient |

### FUTURE

| | |
|---|---|
| j' | écrirai |
| tu | écriras |
| il/elle/on | écrira |
| nous | écrirons |
| vous | écrirez |
| ils/elles | écriront |

### CONDITIONAL

| | |
|---|---|
| j' | écrirais |
| tu | écrirais |
| il/elle/on | écrirait |
| nous | écririons |
| vous | écririez |
| ils/elles | écriraient |

### IMPERATIVE

écris / écrivons / écrivez

### PAST PARTICIPLE

écrit

### PRESENT PARTICIPLE

écrivant

---

### *EXAMPLE PHRASES*

*Tu **as écrit** à ta correspondante récemment?* Have you written to your penfriend lately?
*Elle **écrit** des romans.* She writes novels.
*Comment ça **s'écrit**, "brouillard"?* How do you spell "brouillard"?

---

**je/j'** = I   **tu** = you   **il** = he/it   **elle** = she/it   **on** = we/one   **nous** = we   **vous** = you   **ils/elles** = they

## ▶ **être** (to be)

**PRESENT**

| | |
|---|---|
| je | suis |
| tu | es |
| il/elle/on | est |
| nous | sommes |
| vous | êtes |
| ils/elles | sont |

**PRESENT SUBJUNCTIVE**

| | |
|---|---|
| je | sois |
| tu | sois |
| il/elle/on | soit |
| nous | soyons |
| vous | soyez |
| ils/elles | soient |

**PERFECT**

| | |
|---|---|
| j' | ai été |
| tu | as été |
| il/elle/on | a été |
| nous | avons été |
| vous | avez été |
| ils/elles | ont été |

**IMPERFECT**

| | |
|---|---|
| j' | étais |
| tu | étais |
| il/elle/on | était |
| nous | étions |
| vous | étiez |
| ils/elles | étaient |

**FUTURE**

| | |
|---|---|
| je | serai |
| tu | seras |
| il/elle/on | sera |
| nous | serons |
| vous | serez |
| ils/elles | seront |

**CONDITIONAL**

| | |
|---|---|
| je | serais |
| tu | serais |
| il/elle/on | serait |
| nous | serions |
| vous | seriez |
| ils/elles | seraient |

**IMPERATIVE**

sois / soyons / soyez

**PAST PARTICIPLE**

été

**PRESENT PARTICIPLE**

étant

---

*EXAMPLE PHRASES*

*Mon père est professeur.* My father's a teacher.
*Quelle heure est-il? – Il est dix heures.* What time is it? – It's 10 o'clock.
*Ils ne sont pas encore arrivés.* They haven't arrived yet.

---

**je/j'** = I  **tu** = you  **il** = he/it  **elle** = she/it  **on** = we/one  **nous** = we  **vous** = you  **ils/elles** = they

## ▶ faire (to do; to make)

| PRESENT | | PRESENT SUBJUNCTIVE | |
|---|---|---|---|
| je | fais | je | fasse |
| tu | fais | tu | fasses |
| il/elle/on | fait | il/elle/on | fasse |
| nous | faisons | nous | fassions |
| vous | faites | vous | fassiez |
| ils/elles | font | ils/elles | fassent |

| PERFECT | | IMPERFECT | |
|---|---|---|---|
| j' | ai fait | je | faisais |
| tu | as fait | tu | faisais |
| il/elle/on | a fait | il/elle/on | faisait |
| nous | avons fait | nous | faisions |
| vous | avez fait | vous | faisiez |
| ils/elles | ont fait | ils/elles | faisaient |

| FUTURE | | CONDITIONAL | |
|---|---|---|---|
| je | ferai | je | ferais |
| tu | feras | tu | ferais |
| il/elle/on | fera | il/elle/on | ferait |
| nous | ferons | nous | ferions |
| vous | ferez | vous | feriez |
| ils/elles | feront | ils/elles | feraient |

**IMPERATIVE**

fais / faisons / faites

**PAST PARTICIPLE**

fait

**PRESENT PARTICIPLE**

faisant

---

*EXAMPLE PHRASES*

*Qu'est-ce que tu **fais**?* What are you doing?
*Qu'est-ce qu'il a **fait**?* What has he done? *or* What did he do?
*J'**ai fait** un gâteau.* I've made a cake *or* I made a cake.
*Il **s'est fait** couper les cheveux.* He's had his hair cut.

---

**je/j'** = I  **tu** = you  **il** = he/it  **elle** = she/it  **on** = we/one  **nous** = we  **vous** = you  **ils/elles** = they

# ▶ **falloir** (to be necessary)

**PRESENT**

il faut

**PRESENT SUBJUNCTIVE**

il faille

**PERFECT**

il a fallu

**IMPERFECT**

il fallait

**FUTURE**

il faudra

**CONDITIONAL**

il faudrait

**IMPERATIVE**

*not used*

**PAST PARTICIPLE**

fallu

**PRESENT PARTICIPLE**

*not used*

---

*EXAMPLE PHRASES*

Il **faut** se dépêcher! We have to hurry up!
Il me **fallait** de l'argent. I needed money.
Il **faudra** que tu sois là à 8 heures. You'll have to be there at 8.

---

**je/j'**= I **tu** = you **il** = he/it **elle** = she/it **on** = we/one **nous** = we **vous** = you **ils/elles** = they

## ▶ **finir** (to finish)

**PRESENT**

| | |
|---|---|
| je | finis |
| tu | finis |
| il/elle/on | finit |
| nous | finissons |
| vous | finissez |
| ils/elles | finissent |

**PRESENT SUBJUNCTIVE**

| | |
|---|---|
| je | finisse |
| tu | finisses |
| il/elle/on | finisse |
| nous | finissions |
| vous | finissiez |
| ils/elles | finissent |

**PERFECT**

| | |
|---|---|
| j' | ai fini |
| tu | as fini |
| il/elle/on | a fini |
| nous | avons fini |
| vous | avez fini |
| ils/elles | ont fini |

**IMPERFECT**

| | |
|---|---|
| je | finissais |
| tu | finissais |
| il/elle/on | finissait |
| nous | finissions |
| vous | finissiez |
| ils/elles | finissaient |

**FUTURE**

| | |
|---|---|
| je | finirai |
| tu | finiras |
| il/elle/on | finira |
| nous | finirons |
| vous | finirez |
| ils/elles | finiront |

**CONDITIONAL**

| | |
|---|---|
| je | finirais |
| tu | finirais |
| il/elle/on | finirait |
| nous | finirions |
| vous | finiriez |
| ils/elles | finiraient |

**IMPERATIVE**

finis / finissons / finissez

**PAST PARTICIPLE**

fini

**PRESENT PARTICIPLE**

finissant

---

*EXAMPLE PHRASES*

*Finis ta soupe!* Finish your soup!
*J'ai fini!* I've finished!
*Je finirai mes devoirs demain.* I'll finish my homework tomorrow.

---

**je/j'** = I   **tu** = you   **il** = he/it   **elle** = she/it   **on** = we/one   **nous** = we   **vous** = you   **ils/elles** = they

# ▶ **se laver** (to wash oneself)

## PRESENT

|  |  |
|---|---|
| je | me lave |
| tu | te laves |
| il/elle/on | se lave |
| nous | nous lavons |
| vous | vous lavez |
| ils/elles | se lavent |

## PRESENT SUBJUNCTIVE

|  |  |
|---|---|
| je | me lave |
| tu | te laves |
| il/elle/on | se lave |
| nous | nous lavions |
| vous | vous laviez |
| ils/elles | se lavent |

## PERFECT

|  |  |
|---|---|
| je | me suis lavé(e) |
| tu | t'es lavé(e) |
| il/elle/on | s'est lavé(e) |
| nous | nous sommes lavé(e)s |
| vous | vous êtes lavé(e)(s) |
| ils/elles | se sont lavé(e)s |

## IMPERFECT

|  |  |
|---|---|
| je | me lavais |
| tu | te lavais |
| il/elle/on | se lavait |
| nous | nous lavions |
| vous | vous laviez |
| ils/elles | se lavient |

## FUTURE

|  |  |
|---|---|
| je | me laverai |
| tu | te laveras |
| il/elle/on | se lavera |
| nous | nous laverons |
| vous | vous laverez |
| ils/elles | se laveront |

## CONDITIONAL

|  |  |
|---|---|
| je | me laverais |
| tu | te laverais |
| il/elle/on | se laverait |
| nous | nous laverions |
| vous | vous laveriez |
| ils/elles | se laveraient |

## IMPERATIVE

lave-toi / lavons-nous / lavez-vous

## PAST PARTICIPLE

lavé(e)

## PRESENT PARTICIPLE

se lavant

---

### EXAMPLE PHRASES

***Lave-toi*** *vite, tu vas être en retard.* Have a quick wash, you're going to be late.
***Lavez-vous*** *les mains avant de vous mettre à table.* Wash your hands before you sit at the table.
*Nous nous sommes **lavé** les dents puis nous sommes allés nous coucher.* We cleaned our teeth and went to bed.

---

**je/j'** = I  **tu** = you  **il** = he/it  **elle** = she/it  **on** = we/one  **nous** = we  **vous** = you  **ils/elles** = they

# ▶ **mettre** (to put)

## PRESENT

| | |
|---|---|
| je | mets |
| tu | mets |
| il/elle/on | met |
| nous | mettons |
| vous | mettez |
| ils/elles | mettent |

## PRESENT SUBJUNCTIVE

| | |
|---|---|
| je | mette |
| tu | mettes |
| il/elle/on | mette |
| nous | mettions |
| vous | mettiez |
| ils/elles | mettent |

## PERFECT

| | |
|---|---|
| j' | ai mis |
| tu | as mis |
| il/elle/on | a mis |
| nous | avons mis |
| vous | avez mis |
| ils/elles | ont mis |

## IMPERFECT

| | |
|---|---|
| je | mettais |
| tu | mettais |
| il/elle/on | mettait |
| nous | mettions |
| vous | mettiez |
| ils/elles | mettaient |

## FUTURE

| | |
|---|---|
| je | mettrai |
| tu | mettras |
| il/elle/on | mettra |
| nous | mettrons |
| vous | mettrez |
| ils/elles | mettront |

## CONDITIONAL

| | |
|---|---|
| je | mettrais |
| tu | mettrais |
| il/elle/on | mettrait |
| nous | mettrions |
| vous | mettriez |
| ils/elles | mettraient |

## IMPERATIVE

mets / mettons / mettez

## PAST PARTICIPLE

mis

## PRESENT PARTICIPLE

mettant

---

### EXAMPLE PHRASES

*Mets* ton manteau! Put your coat on!
*Où est-ce que tu as mis les clés?* Where have you put the keys?
*J'ai mis le livre sur la table.* I put the book on the table.
*Elle s'est mise à pleurer.* She started crying.

---

**je/j'** = I   **tu** = you   **il** = he/it   **elle** = she/it   **on** = we/one   **nous** = we   **vous** = you   **ils/elles** = they

# ▶ mourir (to die)

## PRESENT

| | |
|---|---|
| je | meurs |
| tu | meurs |
| il/elle/on | meurt |
| nous | mourons |
| vous | mourez |
| ils/elles | meurent |

## PRESENT SUBJUNCTIVE

| | |
|---|---|
| je | meure |
| tu | meures |
| il/elle/on | meure |
| nous | mourions |
| vous | mouriez |
| ils/elles | meurent |

## PERFECT

| | |
|---|---|
| je | suis mort(e) |
| tu | es mort(e) |
| il/elle/on | est mort(e) |
| nous | sommes mort(e)s |
| vous | êtes mort(e)(s) |
| ils/elles | sont mort(e)s |

## IMPERFECT

| | |
|---|---|
| je | mourais |
| tu | mourais |
| il/elle/on | mourait |
| nous | mourions |
| vous | mouriez |
| ils/elles | mouraient |

## FUTURE

| | |
|---|---|
| je | mourrai |
| tu | mourras |
| il/elle/on | mourra |
| nous | mourrons |
| vous | mourrez |
| ils/elles | mourront |

## CONDITIONAL

| | |
|---|---|
| je | mourrais |
| tu | mourrais |
| il/elle/on | mourrait |
| nous | mourrions |
| vous | mourriez |
| ils/elles | mourraient |

## IMPERATIVE

meurs / mourons / mourez

## PAST PARTICIPLE

mort

## PRESENT PARTICIPLE

mourant

---

### EXAMPLE PHRASES

*Elle **est morte** en 1998.* She died in 1998.
*Ils **sont morts**.* They're dead.
*On **meurt** de froid ici!* We're freezing to death in here!

---

**je/j'** = I  **tu** = you  **il** = he/it  **elle** = she/it  **on** = we/one  **nous** = we  **vous** = you  **ils/elles** = they

# ▶ naître (to be born)

**PRESENT**

| | |
|---|---|
| je | nais |
| tu | nais |
| il/elle/on | naît |
| nous | naissons |
| vous | naissez |
| ils/elles | naissent |

**PRESENT SUBJUNCTIVE**

| | |
|---|---|
| je | naisse |
| tu | naisses |
| il/elle/on | naisse |
| nous | naissions |
| vous | naissiez |
| ils/elles | naissent |

**PERFECT**

| | |
|---|---|
| je | suis né(e) |
| tu | es né(e) |
| il/elle/on | est né(e) |
| nous | sommes né(e)s |
| vous | êtes né(e)(s) |
| ils/elles | sont né(e)s |

**IMPERFECT**

| | |
|---|---|
| je | naissais |
| tu | naissais |
| il/elle/on | naissait |
| nous | naissions |
| vous | naissiez |
| ils/elles | naissaient |

**FUTURE**

| | |
|---|---|
| je | naîtrai |
| tu | naîtras |
| il/elle/on | naîtra |
| nous | naîtrons |
| vous | naîtrez |
| ils/elles | naîtront |

**CONDITIONAL**

| | |
|---|---|
| je | naîtrais |
| tu | naîtrais |
| il/elle/on | naîtrait |
| nous | naîtrions |
| vous | naîtriez |
| ils/elles | naîtraient |

**IMPERATIVE**

nais / naissons / naissez

**PAST PARTICIPLE**

né

**PRESENT PARTICIPLE**

naissant

---

*EXAMPLE PHRASES*

Je **suis née** le 12 février. I was born on 12 February.
Le bébé de Delphine **naîtra** en mars. Delphine is going to have a baby in March.
Quand est-ce que tu **es né**? When were you born?

---

**je/j'** = I **tu** = you **il** = he/it **elle** = she/it **on** = we/one **nous** = we **vous** = you **ils/elles** = they

# ▶ ouvrir (to open)

| PRESENT | |
|---|---|
| j' | ouvre |
| tu | ouvres |
| il/elle/on | ouvre |
| nous | ouvrons |
| vous | ouvrez |
| ils/elles | ouvrent |

| PRESENT SUBJUNCTIVE | |
|---|---|
| j' | ouvre |
| tu | ouvres |
| il/elle/on | ouvre |
| nous | ouvrions |
| vous | ouvriez |
| ils/elles | ouvrent |

| PERFECT | |
|---|---|
| j' | ai ouvert |
| tu | as ouvert |
| il/elle/on | a ouvert |
| nous | avons ouvert |
| vous | avez ouvert |
| ils/elles | ont ouvert |

| IMPERFECT | |
|---|---|
| j' | ouvrais |
| tu | ouvrais |
| il/elle/on | ouvrait |
| nous | ouvrions |
| vous | ouvriez |
| ils/elles | ouvraient |

| FUTURE | |
|---|---|
| j' | ouvrirai |
| tu | ouvriras |
| il/elle/on | ouvrira |
| nous | ouvrirons |
| vous | ouvrirez |
| ils/elles | ouvriront |

| CONDITIONAL | |
|---|---|
| j' | ouvrirais |
| tu | ouvrirais |
| il/elle/on | ouvrirait |
| nous | ouvririons |
| vous | ouvririez |
| ils/elles | ouvriraient |

**IMPERATIVE**

ouvre / ouvrons / ouvrez

**PRESENT PARTICIPLE**

ouvrant

**PAST PARTICIPLE**

ouvert

---

### EXAMPLE PHRASES

Elle **a ouvert** la porte. She opened the door.
Est-ce que tu pourrais **ouvrir** la fenêtre? Could you open the window?
Je me suis coupé en **ouvrant** une boîte de conserve. I cut myself opening a tin.
La porte **s'est ouverte**. The door opened.

---

**je/j'** = I  **tu** = you  **il** = he/it  **elle** = she/it  **on** = we/one  **nous** = we  **vous** = you  **ils/elles** = they

# ▶ pouvoir (to be able)

**PRESENT**

|  |  |
|---|---|
| je | peux |
| tu | peux |
| il/elle/on | peut |
| nous | pouvons |
| vous | pouvez |
| ils/elles | peuvent |

**PRESENT SUBJUNCTIVE**

|  |  |
|---|---|
| je | puisse |
| tu | puisses |
| il/elle/on | puisse |
| nous | puissions |
| vous | puissiez |
| ils/elles | puissent |

**PERFECT**

|  |  |
|---|---|
| j' | ai pu |
| tu | as pu |
| il/elle/on | a pu |
| nous | avons pu |
| vous | avez pu |
| ils/elles | ont pu |

**IMPERFECT**

|  |  |
|---|---|
| je | pouvais |
| tu | pouvais |
| il/elle/on | pouvait |
| nous | pouvions |
| vous | pouviez |
| ils/elles | pouvaient |

**FUTURE**

|  |  |
|---|---|
| je | pourrai |
| tu | pourras |
| il/elle/on | pourra |
| nous | pourrons |
| vous | pourrez |
| ils/elles | pourront |

**CONDITIONAL**

|  |  |
|---|---|
| je | pourrais |
| tu | pourrais |
| il/elle/on | pourrait |
| nous | pourrions |
| vous | pourriez |
| ils/elles | pourraient |

**IMPERATIVE**

*not used*

**PAST PARTICIPLE**

pu

**PRESENT PARTICIPLE**

pouvant

---

**EXAMPLE PHRASES**

Je **peux** t'aider, si tu veux. I can help you if you like.
J'ai fait tout ce que j'**ai pu**. I did all I could.
Je ne **pourrai** pas venir samedi. I won't be able to come on Saturday.

---

**je/j'** = I   **tu** = you   **il** = he/it   **elle** = she/it   **on** = we/one   **nous** = we   **vous** = you   **ils/elles** = they

# ▶ **prendre** (to take)

## PRESENT

| | |
|---|---|
| je | prends |
| tu | prends |
| il/elle/on | prend |
| nous | prenons |
| vous | prenez |
| ils/elles | prennent |

## PRESENT SUBJUNCTIVE

| | |
|---|---|
| je | prenne |
| tu | prennes |
| il/elle/on | prenne |
| nous | prenions |
| vous | preniez |
| ils/elles | prennent |

## PERFECT

| | |
|---|---|
| j' | ai pris |
| tu | as pris |
| il/elle/on | a pris |
| nous | avons pris |
| vous | avez pris |
| ils/elles | ont pris |

## IMPERFECT

| | |
|---|---|
| je | prenais |
| tu | prenais |
| il/elle/on | prenait |
| nous | prenions |
| vous | preniez |
| ils/elles | prenaient |

## FUTURE

| | |
|---|---|
| je | prendrai |
| tu | prendras |
| il/elle/on | prendra |
| nous | prendrons |
| vous | prendrez |
| ils/elles | prendront |

## CONDITIONAL

| | |
|---|---|
| je | prendrais |
| tu | prendrais |
| il/elle/on | prendrait |
| nous | prendrions |
| vous | prendriez |
| ils/elles | prendraient |

## IMPERATIVE

prends / prenons / prenez

## PAST PARTICIPLE

pris

## PRESENT PARTICIPLE

prenant

---

### EXAMPLE PHRASES

*J'ai pris plein de photos.* I took lots of pictures.
*N'oublie pas de prendre ton passeport.* Don't forget to take your passport.
*Il prendra le train de 8h2o.* He'll take the 8.2o train.
*Pour qui est-ce qu'il se prend?* Who does he think he is?

**je/j'** = I   **tu** = you   **il** = he/it   **elle** = she/it   **on** = we/one   **nous** = we   **vous** = you   **ils/elles** = they

## ▶ **savoir** (to know)

### PRESENT

| | |
|---|---|
| je | sais |
| tu | sais |
| il/elle/on | sait |
| nous | savons |
| vous | savez |
| ils/elles | savent |

### PRESENT SUBJUNCTIVE

| | |
|---|---|
| je | sache |
| tu | saches |
| il/elle/on | sache |
| nous | sachions |
| vous | sachiez |
| ils/elles | sachent |

### PERFECT

| | |
|---|---|
| j' | ai su |
| tu | as su |
| il/elle/on | a su |
| nous | avons su |
| vous | avez su |
| ils/elles | ont su |

### IMPERFECT

| | |
|---|---|
| je | savais |
| tu | savais |
| il/elle/on | savait |
| nous | savions |
| vous | saviez |
| ils/elles | savaient |

### FUTURE

| | |
|---|---|
| je | saurai |
| tu | sauras |
| il/elle/on | saura |
| nous | saurons |
| vous | saurez |
| ils/elles | sauront |

### CONDITIONAL

| | |
|---|---|
| je | saurais |
| tu | saurais |
| il/elle/on | saurait |
| nous | saurions |
| vous | sauriez |
| ils/elles | sauraient |

### IMPERATIVE

sache / sachons / sachez

### PAST PARTICIPLE

su

### PRESENT PARTICIPLE

sachant

---

### EXAMPLE PHRASES

Tu **sais** ce que tu vas faire l'année prochaine? Do you know what you're doing next year?

Je ne **sais** pas. I don't know.

Elle ne **sait** pas nager. She can't swim.

Tu **savais** que son père était pakistanais? Did you know her father was Pakistani?

**je/j'** = I  **tu** = you  **il** = he/it  **elle** = she/it  **on** = we/one  **nous** = we  **vous** = you  **ils/elles** = they

# ▶ **sortir** (to go out)

**PRESENT**

| je | sors |
| tu | sors |
| il/elle/on | sort |
| nous | sortons |
| vous | sortez |
| ils/elles | sortent |

**PRESENT SUBJUNCTIVE**

| je | sorte |
| tu | sortes |
| il/elle/on | sorte |
| nous | sortions |
| vous | sortiez |
| ils/elles | sortent |

**PERFECT**

| je | suis sorti(e) |
| tu | es sorti(e) |
| il/elle/on | est sorti(e) |
| nous | sommes sorti(e)s |
| vous | êtes sorti(e)(s) |
| ils/elles | sont sorti(e)s |

**IMPERFECT**

| je | sortais |
| tu | sortais |
| il/elle/on | sortait |
| nous | sortions |
| vous | sortiez |
| ils/elles | sortaient |

**FUTURE**

| je | sortirai |
| tu | sortiras |
| il/elle/on | sortira |
| nous | sortirons |
| vous | sortirez |
| ils/elles | sortiront |

**CONDITIONAL**

| je | sortirais |
| tu | sortirais |
| il/elle/on | sortirait |
| nous | sortirions |
| vous | sortiriez |
| ils/elles | sortiraient |

**IMPERATIVE**

sors / sortons / sortez

**PAST PARTICIPLE**

sorti

**PRESENT PARTICIPLE**

sortant

---

*EXAMPLE PHRASES*

*Je ne **suis** pas **sortie** ce week-end.* I didn't go out this weekend.
*Aurélie **sort** avec Bruno.* Aurélie is going out with Bruno.
*Elle **est sortie** de l'hôpital hier.* She came out of hospital yesterday.
*Je n'**ai** pas **sorti** le chien parce qu'il pleuvait.* I didn't take the dog out for a walk because it was raining.

*i* Note that **sortir** takes **avoir** in the perfect tense when it is used with a

**je/j'** = I **tu** = you **il** = he/it **elle** = she/it **on** = we/one **nous** = we **vous** = you **ils/elles** = they

# ▶ **tenir** (to hold)

## PRESENT

| | |
|---|---|
| je | tiens |
| tu | tiens |
| il/elle/on | tient |
| nous | tenons |
| vous | tenez |
| ils/elles | tiennent |

## PRESENT SUBJUNCTIVE

| | |
|---|---|
| je | tienne |
| tu | tiennes |
| il/elle/on | tienne |
| nous | tenions |
| vous | teniez |
| ils/elles | tiennent |

## PERFECT

| | |
|---|---|
| j' | ai tenu |
| tu | as tenu |
| il/elle/on | a tenu |
| nous | avons tenu |
| vous | avez tenu |
| ils/elles | ont tenu |

## IMPERFECT

| | |
|---|---|
| je | tenais |
| tu | tenais |
| il/elle/on | tenait |
| nous | tenions |
| vous | teniez |
| ils/elles | tenaient |

## FUTURE

| | |
|---|---|
| je | tiendrai |
| tu | tiendras |
| il/elle/on | tiendra |
| nous | tiendrons |
| vous | tiendrez |
| ils/elles | tiendront |

## CONDITIONAL

| | |
|---|---|
| je | tiendrais |
| tu | tiendrais |
| il/elle/on | tiendrait |
| nous | tiendrions |
| vous | tiendriez |
| ils/elles | tiendraient |

## IMPERATIVE

tiens / tenons / tenez

## PAST PARTICIPLE

tenu

## PRESENT PARTICIPLE

tenant

---

## *EXAMPLE PHRASES*

**Tiens**-moi la main. Hold my hand.
Elle **tenait** beaucoup à son chat. She was really attached to her cat.
**Tiens**, prends mon stylo. Here, have my pen.
**Tiens-toi** droit! Sit up straight!

# ▶ **venir** (to come)

## PRESENT

| | |
|---|---|
| je | viens |
| tu | viens |
| il/elle/on | vient |
| nous | venons |
| vous | venez |
| ils/elles | viennent |

## PRESENT SUBJUNCTIVE

| | |
|---|---|
| je | vienne |
| tu | viennes |
| il/elle/on | vienne |
| nous | venions |
| vous | veniez |
| ils/elles | viennent |

## PERFECT

| | |
|---|---|
| je | suis venu(e) |
| tu | es venu(e) |
| il/elle/on | est venu(e) |
| nous | sommes venu(e)s |
| vous | êtes venu(e)(s) |
| ils/elles | sont venu(e)s |

## IMPERFECT

| | |
|---|---|
| je | venais |
| tu | venais |
| il/elle/on | venait |
| nous | venions |
| vous | veniez |
| ils/elles | venaient |

## FUTURE

| | |
|---|---|
| je | viendrai |
| tu | viendras |
| il/elle/on | viendra |
| nous | viendrons |
| vous | viendrez |
| ils/elles | viendront |

## CONDITIONAL

| | |
|---|---|
| je | viendrais |
| tu | viendrais |
| il/elle/on | viendrait |
| nous | viendrions |
| vous | viendriez |
| ils/elles | viendraient |

## IMPERATIVE

viens / venons / venez

## PAST PARTICIPLE

venu

## PRESENT PARTICIPLE

venant

---

### EXAMPLE PHRASES

*Elle ne **viendra** pas cette année.* She won't be coming this year.
*Fatou et Malik **viennent** du Sénégal.* Fatou and Malik come from Senegal.
*Je **viens** de manger.* I've just eaten.

---

**je/j'** = I  **tu** = you  **il** = he/it  **elle** = she/it  **on** = we/one  **nous** = we  **vous** = you  **ils/elles** = they

## ▶ **vivre** (to live)

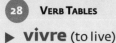

**PRESENT**

| | |
|---|---|
| je | vis |
| tu | vis |
| il/elle/on | vit |
| nous | vivons |
| vous | vivez |
| ils/elles | vivent |

**PRESENT SUBJUNCTIVE**

| | |
|---|---|
| je | vive |
| tu | vives |
| il/elle/on | vive |
| nous | vivions |
| vous | viviez |
| ils/elles | vivent |

**PERFECT**

| | |
|---|---|
| j' | ai vécu |
| tu | as vécu |
| il/elle/on | a vécu |
| nous | avons vécu |
| vous | avez vécu |
| ils/elles | ont vécu |

**IMPERFECT**

| | |
|---|---|
| je | vivais |
| tu | vivais |
| il/elle/on | vivait |
| nous | vivions |
| vous | viviez |
| ils/elles | vivaient |

**FUTURE**

| | |
|---|---|
| je | vivrai |
| tu | vivras |
| il/elle/on | vivra |
| nous | vivrons |
| vous | vivrez |
| ils/elles | vivront |

**CONDITIONAL**

| | |
|---|---|
| je | vivrais |
| tu | vivrais |
| il/elle/on | vivrait |
| nous | vivrions |
| vous | vivriez |
| ils/elles | vivraient |

**IMPERATIVE**

vis / vivons / vivez

**PAST PARTICIPLE**

vécu

**PRESENT PARTICIPLE**

vivant

---

### *EXAMPLE PHRASES*

*Ma sœur **vit** en Espagne.* My sister lives in Spain.
*Il **a vécu** dix ans à Lyon.* He lived in Lyons for 10 years.
*Les gorilles **vivent** surtout dans la forêt.* Gorillas mostly live in the forest.

---

**je/j'** = I  **tu** = you  **il** = he/it  **elle** = she/it  **on** = we/one  **nous** = we  **vous** = you  **ils/elles** = they

# ▶ **voir** (to see)

## PRESENT

| | |
|---|---|
| je | vois |
| tu | vois |
| il/elle/on | voit |
| nous | voyons |
| vous | voyez |
| ils/elles | voient |

## PRESENT SUBJUNCTIVE

| | |
|---|---|
| je | voie |
| tu | voies |
| il/elle/on | voie |
| nous | voyions |
| vous | voyiez |
| ils/elles | voient |

## PERFECT

| | |
|---|---|
| j' | ai vu |
| tu | as vu |
| il/elle/on | a vu |
| nous | avons vu |
| vous | avez vu |
| ils/elles | ont vu |

## IMPERFECT

| | |
|---|---|
| je | voyais |
| tu | voyais |
| il/elle/on | voyait |
| nous | voyions |
| vous | voyiez |
| ils/elles | voyaient |

## FUTURE

| | |
|---|---|
| je | verrai |
| tu | verras |
| il/elle/on | verra |
| nous | verrons |
| vous | verrez |
| ils/elles | verront |

## CONDITIONAL

| | |
|---|---|
| je | verrais |
| tu | verrais |
| il/elle/on | verrait |
| nous | verrions |
| vous | verriez |
| ils/elles | verraient |

## IMPERATIVE

vois / voyons / voyez

## PAST PARTICIPLE

vu

## PRESENT PARTICIPLE

voyant

---

## EXAMPLE PHRASES

*Venez me **voir** quand vous serez à Paris.* Come and see me when you're in Paris.
*Je ne **vois** rien sans mes lunettes.* I can't see anything without my glasses.
*Est-ce que tu l'**as vu**?* Did you see him? or Have you seen him?
*Est-ce que cette tache **se voit**?* Does that stain show?

**je/j'** = I  **tu** = you  **il** = he/it  **elle** = she/it  **on** = we/one  **nous** = we  **vous** = you  **ils/elles** = they

# ▶ **vouloir** (to want)

**PRESENT**

| | |
|---|---|
| je | veux |
| tu | veux |
| il/elle/on | veut |
| nous | voulons |
| vous | voulez |
| ils/elles | veulent |

**PRESENT SUBJUNCTIVE**

| | |
|---|---|
| je | veuille |
| tu | veuilles |
| il/elle/on | veuille |
| nous | voulions |
| vous | vouliez |
| ils/elles | veuillent |

**PERFECT**

| | |
|---|---|
| j' | ai voulu |
| tu | as voulu |
| il/elle/on | a voulu |
| nous | avons voulu |
| vous | avez voulu |
| ils/elles | ont voulu |

**IMPERFECT**

| | |
|---|---|
| je | voulais |
| tu | voulais |
| il/elle/on | voulait |
| nous | voulions |
| vous | vouliez |
| ils/elles | voulaient |

**FUTURE**

| | |
|---|---|
| je | voudrai |
| tu | voudras |
| il/elle/on | voudra |
| nous | voudrons |
| vous | voudrez |
| ils/elles | voudront |

**CONDITIONAL**

| | |
|---|---|
| je | voudrais |
| tu | voudrais |
| il/elle/on | voudrait |
| nous | voudrions |
| vous | voudriez |
| ils/elles | voudraient |

**IMPERATIVE**

veuille / veuillons / veuillez

**PAST PARTICIPLE**

voulu

**PRESENT PARTICIPLE**

voulant

---

**EXAMPLE PHRASES**

*Elle **veut** un vélo pour Noël.* She wants a bike for Christmas.
*Ils **voulaient** aller au cinéma.* They wanted to go to the cinema.
*Tu **voudrais** une tasse de thé?* Would you like a cup of tea?

---

je/j' = I **tu** = you **il** = he/it **elle** = she/it **on** = we/one **nous** = we **vous** = you **ils/elles** = they